EL DESMANTELAMIENTO DE LA DEMOCRACIA Y EL ESTADO TOTALITARIO
TRATADO DE DERECHO CONSTITUCIONAL - TOMO XV

Colección Tratado de Derecho Constitucional

I.   *Historia constitucional de Venezuela*, Caracas 2013, 1096 páginas.

II.   *Orígenes del constitucionalismo moderno en Hispanoamérica*, Caracas 2014, 980 páginas

III.   *Cambio político y consolidación del Estado de derecho (1958-1998)*, Caracas 2015, 1162 páginas

IV.   *Instituciones del Estado democrático de derecho. Constitución de 1961*, Caracas 2015, 1180 páginas

V.   *Derechos y garantías constitucionales en la Constitución de 1961 (La Justicia Constitucional)*, Caracas 2015, 1022 páginas

VI.   *Asamblea Constituyente y Proceso Constituyente (1999)*, Caracas 2013, 1198 páginas

VII.   *La Constitución de 1999: El Estado Democrático y Social de Derecho*, Caracas 2014, 1190 páginas

VIII.   *Golpe de Estado Constituyente, Estado Constitucional y Democracia*, Caracas 2015, 1018 páginas

IX.   *Concentración y centralización del poder y régimen autoritario*, Caracas 2015, 1198 páginas

X.   *Derechos y garantías constitucionales y la acción de amparo*, Caracas 2017, 1196 páginas.

XI.   *El derecho y la acción de amparo en el derecho constitucional comparado*, Caracas 2017, 1150 páginas.

XII.   *La justicia constitucional y Jurisdicción Constitucional*, Caracas 2017, 1198 páginas.

XIII.   *Práctica y distorsión de la justicia constitucional*, Caracas 2017, 954 páginas.

XIV.   *El juez legislador y la patología de la justicia constitucional*, Caracas 2017, 1060 páginas.

XV.   *El desmantelamiento de la democracia y el Estado Totalitario*, Caracas 2017, 1050 páginas.

XVI.   *La Destrucción del Estado de derecho, la ruina de la democracia y la dictadura judicial*, Caracas 2017, 1146 páginas

Allan R. Brewer-Carías

Profesor de la Universidad Central de Venezuela (desde 1963)
Simón Bolívar Professor, University of Cambridge (1985–1986)
Professeur Associé, Université de Paris II (1989–1990)
Adjunct Professor of Law, Columbia Law School, New York (2006–2008)

EL DESMANTELAMIENTO DE LA DEMOCRACIA Y EL ESTADO TOTALITARIO

COLECCIÓN

TRATADO DE DERECHO CONSTITUCIONAL
TOMO XV

Fundación de Derecho Público
Editorial Jurídica Venezolana

Caracas, 2017

Hecho el Depósito de Ley
ISBN: 978-980-365-302-6
Depósito Legal: lf5402015341076

Editado por: Editorial Jurídica Venezolana
Avda. Francisco Solano López, Torre Oasis, P.B., Local 4, Sabana Grande,
Apartado 17.598 – Caracas, 1015, Venezuela
Teléfono 762.25.53, 762.38.42. Fax. 763.5239
http://www.editorialjuridicavenezolana.com.ve
Email fejv@cantv.net

Impreso por: Lightning Source, an INGRAM Content company
para Editorial Jurídica Venezolana International Inc.
Panamá, República de Panamá.
Email: editorialjuridicainternational@gmail.com

Diagramación, composición y montaje
por: Francis Gil, en letra Times New Roman, 10,5
Interlineado 11, Mancha 19 x 12.5 cm

CONTENIDO GENERAL

PRESENTACIÓN 11

PRIMERA PARTE
MODELO POLÍTICO Y DERECHO DEL ESTADO

SEGUNDA PARTE
**EL DESMANTELAMIENTO DE LA DEMOCRACIA.
EL EXPERIMENTO AUTORITARIO DE CHÁVEZ**
*DISMANTLING DEMOCRACY.
THE CHÁVEZ AUTHORITARIAN EXPERIMENT*

INTRODUCTION: DEFRAUDING DEMOCRACY THROUGH NONCON-
SENSUAL CONSTITUENT ASSEMBLIES 47
PART ONE: THE POLITICAL ASSAULT ON STATE POWERS AND THE
FRAMEWORK FOR AUTHORITARIANISM 67
PART TWO: INSTITUTIONAL DEVELOPMENT TOWARD CONSOLI-
DAING AUTHORITARIANISM.. 168
PART THREE: CONSTITUTIONAL REFORMS DESIGNED TO CONSOLI-
DATE AUTHORITARIANISM 244
FINAL REFLECTIONS: THE RIGHT TO DEMOCRACY AND ITS VIOLA-
TION BY VENEZUELA'S AUTHORITARIAN GOVERNMENT: SOME
RELEVANT FACTS FROM THE PAST DECADE 322

TERCERA PARTE
**EL ESTADO TOTALITARIO Y LA DEMOLICIÓN DEL ESTADO
DEMOCRÁTICO Y SOCIAL DE DERECHO Y DE JUSTICIA,
DE ECONOMÍA MIXTA Y DESCENTRALIZADO**

INTRODUCCIÓN: EL ESTADO Y LA LEY (EL DERECHO ADMINISTRA-
TIVO Y EL ESTADO).. 364
SECCIÓN PRIMERA: LA AUSENCIA DE ESTADO DE DERECHO 375
SECCIÓN SEGUNDA: LA AUSENCIA DE ESTADO DEMOCRÁTICO 385
SECCIÓN TERCERA: LA AUSENCIA DE UN ESTADO SOCIAL Y DE ECO-
NOMÍA MIXTA.. 407

SECCIÓN CUARTA: LA AUSENCIA DE ESTADO DE JUSTICIA 439

SECCIÓN QUINTA: LA AUSENCIA DE ESTADO DESCENTRALIZADO 453

APRECIACIÓN FINAL: EL ESTADO TOTALITARIO Y LA DESCONSTITU-
CIONALIZACIÓN DEL ESTADO CONSTITUCIONAL 472

CUARTA PARTE
LA DESCONSTITUCIONALIZACIÓN Y DESJURIDIFICACIÓN DEL ESTADO CONSTITUCIONAL Y LA ESTRUCTURACIÓN PARALELA DEL ESTADO COMUNAL O DEL PODER POPULAR

SECCIÓN PRIMERA: LA DEMOCRACIA Y DE LA PARTICIPACIÓN POLÍ-
TICA Y POPULAR, Y EL AHOGAMIENTO DE LA DEMOCRACIA RE-
PRESENTATIVA EN NOMBRE DE UNA SUPUESTA "DEMOCRACIA
PARTICIPATIVA 482

SECCIÓN SEGUNDA: LOS ANTECEDENTES DEL NUEVO RÉGIMEN DEL
PODER POPULAR Y DEL ESTADO COMUNAL EN UNA LEY IN-
CONSTITUCIONAL DE 2006 Y EN EL INTENTO DE REFORMA
CONSTITUCIONAL EN 2007 486

SECCIÓN TERCERA: LA INSTITUCIONALIZACIÓN LEGAL DEL ESTADO
COMUNAL O DE CÓMO SE IMPUSO AL PAÍS UN MODELO DE ES-
TADO COMUNISTA, DE EJERCICIO DEL PODER POPULAR Y DE
SOCIEDAD SOCIALISTA POR LOS CUALES NADIE HA VOTADO. 500

SECCIÓN CUARTA: EL RÉGIMEN DE LOS CONSEJOS COMUNALES O LA
RESURRECCIÓN DE LOS SOVIETS EN EL CARIBE, CASI UN SIGLO
DESPUÉS 525

SECCIÓN QUINTA: EL RÉGIMEN DE LAS COMUNAS COMO SOPORTE
DEL ESTADO COMUNAL O LA DESMUNICIPALIZACIÓN EL ESTADO
CONSTITUCIONAL MEDIANTE UN SISTEMA DE "AUTOGOBIERNO"
NO REPRESENTATIVO MANEJADO POR EL PODER CENTRAL.............. 550

SECCIÓN SEXTA: EL RÉGIMEN DE LA CONTRALORÍA SOCIAL O LA
INSTITUCIONALIZACIÓN DE LA TÉCNICA DEL ESPIONAJE SO-
CIAL Y DE LA DENUNCIA POLÍTICA INDISCRIMINADA PARA IM-
PONER LA IDEOLOGÍA SOCIALISTA 570

SECCIÓN SÉPTIMA: EL RÉGIMEN DEL SISTEMA ECONÓMICO COMU-
NAL O DE CÓMO SE DEFINE E IMPONE LEGALMENTE UN SISTE-
MA ECONÓMICO COMUNISTA POR EL CUAL NADIE HA VOTADO. ... 576

QUINTA PARTE:
EL DESQUICIAMIENTO DE LA ADMINISTRACIÓN PÚBLICA

SECCIÓN PRIMERA: LA ADMINISTRACIÓN PÚBLICA Y LA CONCEP-
CIÓN DEL ESTADO: EL PASO DEL ESTADO DEMOCRÁTICO Y SO-
CIAL DE DERECHO Y DE JUSTICIA, Y DESCENTRALIZADO PRE-
VISTO EN LA CONSTITUCIÓN, AL ESTADO TOTALITARIO DE-
SARROLLADO AL MARGEN DE LA MISMA.. 602

SECCIÓN SEGUNDA: EL IMPACTO DEL ESTADO TOTALITARIO SOBRE LA ADMINISTRACIÓN PÚBLICA: LA INFLACIÓN DE LA ORGANI-ZACIÓN ADMINISTRATIVA Y LA CREACIÓN DE LAS "MISIONES" NO SOMETIDAS A LA LEY ORGÁNICA DE LA ADMINISTRACIÓN PÚBLICA 613

SECCIÓN TERCERA: LA FORMA FEDERAL DEL ESTADO, Y LA CEN-TRALIZACIÓN PROGRESIVA DE LA ADMINISTRACIÓN PÚBLICA 629

SECCIÓN CUARTA: LA CREACIÓN DEL ESTADO COMUNAL O DEL PO-DER POPULAR, EN PARALELO AL ESTADO CONSTITUCIONAL Y EL AHOGAMIENTO PROGRESIVO DE LA ADMINISTRACIÓN MU-NICIPAL 636

APRECIACIÓN GENERAL 653

SEXTA PARTE:
CONSTITUTIONAL LAW IN VENEZUELA (2015)
DERECHO CONSTITUCIONAL EN VENEZUELA (2015)

GENERAL INTRODUCTION 655

PART I. SOURCES OF CONSTITUTIONAL LAW 729

PART II. BASIC ELEMENTS OF THE REPRESENTATIVE AND PARTICIPATORY DEMOCRATIC POLITICAL SYSTEM............ 747

PART III. THE FEDERATION AND THE TERRITORIAL DISTRIBUTION OF STATE POWERS............ 762

PART IV. THE CONSTITUTIONAL SYSTEM OF SEPARATION OF POWERS 777

PART V. THE GOVERNMENT 807

PART VI. THE LEGISLATURE 830

PART VII. THE JUDICIARY............ 838

PART VIII. OTHER BRANCHES OF GOVERNMENT 860

PART IX. THE CONSTITUTIONAL SYSTEM OF HUMAN RIGHTS AND GUARANTEES............ 866

PART X. THE CONSTITUTIONAL REGIME OF THE ECONOMY 904

PART XI. RULE OF LAW AND JUDICIAL REVIEW............ 923

SÉPTIMA PARTE:
LA CONSTITUCIÓN COMO PROMESA INCUMPLIDA (2015)

ÍNDICE GENERAL............ 1021,

PRESENTACIÓN

Este Tomo XV de la *Colección Tratado de Derecho Constitucional*, sobre el tema del *Desmantelamiento de la democracia y Estado Totalitario* recoge, básicamente el texto de tres libros: el primero, titulado *Dismantling Democracy. The Chávez Authoritarian Experiment*, publicado por Cambridge University Press, New York, 2010; el segundo, titulado *Estado Totalitario y Desprecio a la Ley, La desconstitucionalización, desjuridificación, desjudicialización y desdemocratización de Venezuela*, publicado por Editorial Jurídica Venezolana, Caracas 2014; y el tercero, titulado *Constitutional Law. Venezuela*, publicado por Kluwer Law International, International Encyclopaedia of Laws, 2012, actualizado en febrero 2015. Además, se incluye otro texto sobre el proceso de desquiciamiento de la Administración Pública, como consecuencia de la progresiva implantación del Estado Totalitario.

El segundo de los libros citados estuvo precedido de la siguiente *Introducción*:

En Venezuela, después de quince años de régimen autoritario, el Estado democrático y social de derecho y de justicia, de economía mixta y descentralizado que reguló tan cuidadosamente la Constitución de 1999, ha sido totalmente desmantelado, habiéndose ensamblado en su lugar, sobre sus ruinas y escombros, pero sin dejar de usar algunos de sus despojos como parapeto y adorno, un Estado Totalitario[1] que se ha impuesto a los venezolanos sin que

---

1   Aun cuando no se trata ahora de entrar en la definición del Estado totalitario o el totalitarismo como sistema político de dominación total de la sociedad, basta ahora recordar lo expresado por Raymond Aron cuando caracterizó al totalitarismo, como un régimen político donde la concentración del poder es total; existe un partido único que se fusiona al Esta do y que posee el monopolio de la actividad política "legítima" y de la aplicación de la ideología del Estado, que se convierte en verdad oficial del Estado; donde el Estado asume el monopolio de los medios de persuasión y coacción, y de los medios de comunicación; donde la economía es totalmente controlada por el Estado y se convierte en parte del mismo; se produce la politización de toda actividad, originándose una confusión entre sociedad civil y Estado, de manera que las faltas cometidas por los individuos en el marco de la actividad política, económica o profesional se conforman simultáneamente como faltas ideológicas, originando un terror ideológico y policial. Véase Raymond Aron, *Democracia y totalitarismo*, Seix Barral, Madrid 1968. La diferencia con el autoritarismo, es que en éste la concentración del poder sin aceptación de oposición, no excluye la admisión de un cierto pluralismo en sus apoyos y la carencia de una intención o capacidad de homogeneización total de la sociedad. Véase por ejemplo, José Linz, *Totalitarian and Authoritarian Regimes*, Rienner, 2000.

nadie haya votado por su implementación, y que ha pasado a controlar todos los aspectos de la vida política, social y económica del país. [2]

Ese Estado Totalitario, que todos los venezolanos hemos ya resentido, se ha apoderado ya de todos los aspectos de la vida cotidiana, habiendo logrado que todos los ciudadanos, si todavía podemos llamarnos así, dependamos en una forma u otra de Estado, y de la burocracia cívico militar que lo controla, y frente al cual, por supuesto no hay ni derechos que reclamar, ni garantías que exigir, ni forma alguna de controlar, sino aceptación, asentimiento, sometimiento, sumisión, resignación o discriminación, desplazamiento, relegación o persecución.

Un Estado Totalitario en el cual el poder está totalmente concentrado y controlado por la burocracia que lo maneja, y que está imbricada a un partido político "único" que se ha fusionado al propio aparato estatal, y que en conjunto poseen el monopolio de la actividad política y económica del país, guiados por una ideología que se ha convertido legalmente en la única "legítima" y "legal" por ser ideología oficial del propio Estado, regulada en leyes, reglamentos, decretos y planes, y que aunque denominada en ellos como "socialista," no es más que un barato maquillaje de la doctrina "comunista," tal como incluso quedó plasmada en el artículo 6.12 de la Ley del llamado "Sistema Económico Comunal" (2010),[3] al definir el "modelo productivo socialista" montándolo sobre los tres pilares que conforme a Marx y Engels conforman la "sociedad comunista," que son: la apropiación por el Estado de todos los medios de producción ("propiedad social"); la "eliminación de la división social del trabajo, propio del modelo capitalista" y la "reinversión del excedente;" [4] con todo lo que de destructivo tiene la edificación de cada uno de ellos.

La consecuencia ha sido la persecución y proscripción de la iniciativa privada, pasando la ya marginal actividad económica que aún queda gerenciada por particulares, a una situación de dependencia total de lo que disponga y ordene una burocracia oficial que no puede ser controlada ni contestada, sobre todo lo que se pueda o no pueda hacerse, lo que se pueda o no importar o comprar para producir, y por supuesto, lo que se pueda calcular o no sobre costos de producción, ganancias y precios. Pero ello, en todo caso, es marginal, porque el grueso de la economía ya está en manos del Estado, no sólo por haber abusado de su condición de Estado petrolero, ya de antaño empresario exclusivo en de-

---

2   Incluso el *The New York Times*, en su Editorial del 17 de octubre de 2014, después de haber mostrado en el pasado, más de una vez, cierta simpatía por el régimen instaurado en Venezuela en 1999, ha calificado al Estado venezolano como "un Estado autocrático y despótico." Véase en "South America's New Caudillos," *The New York Times*, New York, 17 de octubre de 2010, p. A30.

3   Véase en *Gaceta Oficial* N° 6011 de 21 de diciembre de 2010. Véase los comentarios en Allan R. Brewer-Carías, "Sobre la Ley Orgánica del Sistema Económico Comunal o de cómo se implanta en Venezuela un sistema económico comunista sin reformar la Constitución," en *Revista de Derecho Público*, N° 124, (octubre-diciembre 2010), Editorial Jurídica Venezolana, Caracas 2010, pp. 102-109.

4   Véase en Karl Marx and Frederich Engels, "The German Ideology," en *Collective Works*, Vol. 5, International Publishers, New York 1976, p. 47. Véanse además los textos pertinentes en http://www.educa.madrid.org/cms_tools/files/0a24636f-764c-4e03-9c1d-6722e2ee60d7/Texto%20Marx%20y%20Engels.pdf

sarrollos industriales vinculados a la explotación de recursos naturales, que le ha asegurado históricamente el mayor ingreso fiscal jamás soñado por país alguno en tan corto tiempo, que se ha mal administrado y despilfarrado impunemente; sino por haber nacionalizado, depredado, confiscado, expropiado, ocupado y decomisado empresas y establecimientos industriales privados, sin estar sometido a control alguno y sin pagar la justa compensación de la que habla la Constitución.

En este Estado totalitario, todo depende del Estado, todos dependen en una forma u otra del Estado y de su burocracia, pero los que más dependencia tienen son las clases menos favorecidas, que han resultado siendo más pobres y miserables, sujetada su existencia a las dádivas del Estado, al cual ahora deben gratitud y sumisión, porque todo lo reciben del Estado, sin lo cual simplemente no pueden vivir, a través de las denominadas "Misiones" que son oscuros programas de dádivas que manejan, sin disciplina ni control fiscal alguno, ingentes recursos públicos, creados a partir de 2003, mal regulados en 2008 y que solo han sido objeto de una regulación legal en mediante la Ley de Misiones, Grandes Misiones y Micro-misiones de noviembre de 2014 . En ese Estado Totalitario, la generación de pobreza y miseria es una política de Estado, el cual vive de la pobreza y por ello la estimula, organiza y conforma hasta un ejército informal de grupos de agresión, y medio "formal" de milicias, para en todo caso asegurar la dependencia y sumisión.

Por otra parte, en ese esquema dadivoso, ninguna generación de empleo ni de riqueza es posible, y con la destrucción de la economía, que ha dejado poco margen de empleo, lo que hay es una enorme burocratización del Estado, que se ha convertido en un fin en sí mismo. Nada de lo que dice la Constitución se aplica, por ejemplo, que la Administración debe estar al servicio del ciudadano, pues al contrario, lo que se ha establecido es una Administración del Estado que antes que nada está al servicio de su propia burocracia, comandada por una casta de civiles y militares privilegiados, que son los nuevos ricos del país; siendo la atención al ciudadano totalmente marginal, salvo cuando se convierte en una fuente de ingresos paralelo derivada de la corrupción, en cuyo caso hay interés de servir, pero por razones estrictamente personales del funcionario.

Y en cuanto al resto de la población, lo que por ejemplo era la clase media, la misma quedó sometida a dicha burocracia a través de la política de escases, derivada de la ausencia de producción, la regulación de precios, y el control de la importación por el Estado al tener el control total de las divisas para ello. Con ellos, todas las personas, los de menos recursos y los de recursos de sobrevivencia, tienen que gastar sus horas, días y semanas buscando cómo atender sus necesidades más básicas en medicinas, y bienes de primera necesidad elementales, por los que tienen que materialmente pelear en colas interminables, mientras esos mismos bienes salen del país y se venden a precios no regulados al otro lado de la frontera. Es el contrabando de extracción que también se ha convertido en una política de Estado, sostenido por la burocracia que se beneficia de ello.

Ese Estado Totalitario, además, controla la casi totalidad de todos los medios de comunicación audio visual y escritos del país, por haber sido acaparados y confiscados progresivamente por la burocracia estatal, o por haber sido comprados por la misma a través de personas vinculadas o simplemente de testaferros, que después de la debida presión sobre sus antiguos dueños, pasaron a formar parte del coro que al unísono, bombardea todos los minutos, todas las horas, todos los días, al pueblo, con consignas buscando trastocar la inseguridad, escases, miseria y sumisión en la "mayor felicidad del mundo;" y convertir a las críticas, denuncias y disidencias en actos terroristas, y las protestas populares en actos de guerra o agresión, que son masacradas con un aparato represivo militar policial nunca antes visto en el país. Ese control total de los medios de comunicación, permiten a la propaganda oficial estar todos los minutos, horas, días y semanas en todas partes, en medio de un discurso de odio y exclusión permanente, creando falsos enemigos en todos los que puedan adversar o ser disidentes del gobierno. Ello, por supuesto ha originado lo que es propio de los Estados Totalitarios, y es la politización total de la vida social y política, entre la doctrina y política oficial del Estado y los que disienten, al punto de criminalizarse toda disidencia, de manera que lo que podrían ser faltas cometidas por los individuos en el marco de su actividad política, económica o profesional, se conforman simultáneamente como faltas ideológicas, originando un terror ideológico y policial.

El Estado Totalitario que existe en Venezuela, además, deriva de la concentración total del poder en manos de la burocracia estatal, comandada por el Jefe del Ejecutivo Nacional y los militares que asaltaron la Administración, todos miembros del partido de gobierno que preside el propio Presidente de la República, los cuales (burocracia y partido) controlan todos los Poderes del Estado. Controlan a la Asamblea Nacional, por la mayoría que se ha asegurado el partido oficial en la misma, aún sin haber sacado la mayoría de votos en las elecciones parlamentarias, y con ello, el control político sobre la Administración y el gobierno simplemente desapareció del marco institucional. El único control político que se puede ejercer sobre el gobierno es el que deriva de las directrices del propio partido oficial, pero sin estar a su vez sometido a control alguno por parte de los otros poderes del Estado Y como signo del Estado Totalitario, el control de la Asamblea Nacional ha conducido a la burocracia estatal y al partido oficial a simplemente desconocer a la oposición. Es decir, como en todo Estado Totalitario, se gobierna en un esquema de total concentración del poder sin aceptación de oposición.

El Estado Totalitario que existe en Venezuela, además, se caracteriza por el control que la burocracia estatal y el partido oficial ejercen sobre la totalidad del Poder Judicial, donde no hay jueces autónomos ni independientes, y los que pueda haber están totalmente neutralizados y acallados, razón por la cual no existe control judicial alguno que se pueda ejercer sobre el gobierno y la Administración, y más bien lo que ha ocurrido es que al Tribunal Supremo de Justicia se lo ha puesto al servicio del Estado Totalitario como un instrumento más para afianzar el autoritarismo. Ello ha llegado al punto de que dicho Tribunal ha sido el principal mecanismo del Estado para mutar y moldear la Constitución a favor de políticas autoritarismo, y el principal instrumento para inhabilitar políticamente a opositores o para revocarle el mandato a diputados y alcaldes, que solo podrían ser revocados por voto popular. En ese esquema, el resultado es que el Estado Totalitario que tenemos no está realmente sometido al derecho, cuyas normas se ignoran y desprecian; o se mutan o amoldan a discreción del gobierno; ni está sometido a control judicial alguno, por la sumisión del Poder Judicial al Poder Ejecutivo, de lo que deriva que en lugar de ser un Estado de justicia no es más que un "Estado de la injusticia."

En ese Estado Totalitario, además, el Poder Ciudadano también ha sido neutralizado y sometido, estando totalmente carente de autonomía e independencia y sujeto a la burocracia estatal y al partido de gobierno, de manera que el Ministerio Público no es más que el instrumento para la persecución de la disidencia, y paralelamente para garantizar la impunidad en los delitos comunes o de corrupción; el Defensor del Pueblo, totalmente sujeto a la burocracia oficial y al partido de gobierno, trastocó o confundió su rol, convirtiéndose en el principal defensor de las políticas totalitarias del Estado, habiéndose olvidado de la población y de los derechos colectivos; y la Contraloría General de la República, desde hace tres lustros no controla a la Administración, y mucho menos el mar de corrupción que se apoderó de la misma, habiéndose reducido sus ejecutorias conocidas, a dictar medidas de inhabilitación política contra funcionarios locales de oposición.

Por último, en cuanto al Poder Electoral, el mismo, secuestrado y sometido desde el inicio a los designios de la burocracia estatal y el partido oficial, con la complicidad de la Asamblea Nacional y del Tribunal Supremo de Justicia, no es garantía ni instrumento alguno de control y de aseguramiento de transparencia ni de imparcialidad en las elecciones o votaciones que se realizan, habiéndose convertido en un simple barniz, fachada o disfraz "electoral" del Estado Totalitario, trastocado el rol de imparcial que debería tener el Consejo Nacional Electoral, en el de ser un simple "agente" electoral del partido oficial.

El Estado Totalitario, además de tener el control de la totalidad del poder que se concentra en la Jefatura del Estado en combinación con el control de la Asamblea Nacional, además ha centralizado la totalidad del poder, ahogando y minimizando el rol de los Estados de la federación y de los Municipios, habiendo incluso montado en paralelo al Estado Constitucional, un Estado llamado "Estado Comunal" o Estado del "Poder Popular," para en nombre de una supuesta democracia participativa y protagónica, acabar con la democracia representativa, y con la propia estructura del Estado regulado en la Constitución; con el agravante, además, de que está controlado desde el exterior, sujeto a dictados de gobiernos extranjeros, con grave lesión a la soberanía a la cual ya ha renunciado quienes lo conducen. Estos, incluso, han llegado a admitir cláusulas arbitrales en contratos públicos suscritos con China, en los cuales se ha renunciado a la aplicación de ley venezolana, sujetos en cambio a la ley inglesa, y cuyos conflictos se deben someter a tribunales arbitrales con sede en Singapur; y en alguna emisión de bonos de deuda pública (2010), la República no solo se ha sometido a la jurisdicción de los tribunales en Londres y de Nueva York, sino que además de renunciar a la aplicación de la ley venezolana y sujetarse en cambio a la ley del Estado de Nueva York, ha incluso renunciado a todo tipo de inmunidad soberana.

Esa implantación de un Estado Totalitario en la estructura estatal que fue diseñada para otra cosa y que fue para consolidar un Estado irrevocablemente libre e independiente"(art. 1 de la Constitución), concebido en la Constitución como social y democrático de derecho y de justicia, descentralizado y de economía mixta (arts. 2 y 4), ha conducido a que en la actualidad el Estado no solo haya perdido su soberanía, sino que no sea un Estado democrático, ni un Estado Social, ni un Estado de derecho, ni un Estado de justicia, ni un Estado de economía mixta, ni un Estado descentralizado, y con ello, al desquiciamiento de todo el orden jurídico que rige al Estado, particularmente, del derecho público y del derecho administrativo, ramas sobre las cuales el proceso de totalitarismo ha tenido un extraordinario impacto que estamos en la necesidad de estudiar.

Y precisamente de todo eso se trata en las reflexiones que conforman este libro, producto de la redacción de diversas conferencias recientes que fui llamado a dictar en diversas instituciones académicas, en diversos lugares y tiempos, cuyos textos son los que aquí he recopilado. A tal efecto, guardado en general el contenido, sentido y forma de la exposición en cada caso, al material le he dado un sentido unitario derivado del motivo fundamental de reflexión que las orientó, y que fue el tema de los efectos de la implantación del Estado totalitario en el país. [...]

Como se puede observar de la descripción sobre el origen de cada una de las Partes y de las Secciones de este libro, el tema del desarrollo progresivo del Estado autoritario en Venezuela, en sus diversas manifestaciones particulares, no es un tema nuevo, y sobre ello me he venido ocupando desde hace varios años. Sin embargo, lo que si puede ahora ser algo nuevo, al menos para mí, es que de la visión de conjunto que resulta de la integración de todos los antes dispersos trabajos que conforman este libro, redactados en cada momento sobre la marcha, en torno a lo que fue aconteciendo con el Estado en el país, permite pasar del calificativo de Estado autoritario que siempre habíamos utilizado, al de Estado Totalitario como antes lo explicamos, producto de su progresiva desconstitucionalización, desjuridificación, desjudicialización y desdemocratización.

Ese Estado Totalitario, montado sobre el autoritarismo y militarismo progresivo, como todos los de su raza, y como puede apreciarse de los estudios aquí publicados, es el resultado directo de un proceso inducido de destrucción sistemática de todos los componentes del Estado democrático y social de derecho y de justicia, de economía mixta y descentralizado, del cual sólo quedan despojos. En su lugar, sobre sus escombros, se nos aparece ahora en la penumbra este Estado Totalitario, el cual, sin embargo, particularmente por la incompetencia de quienes lo manejan o tratan de amaestrar, no termina de adquirir una propia configuración definitiva. Es un amasijo de miembros y elementos que le dan cierta figura, terrible por cierto, pero que deambula sin rumbo fijo, destruyendo y ensuciando todo lo que encuentra a su paso; sin que estemos siquiera seguros de si realmente alguna vez tuvo rumbo, salvo en los delirios trasnochados y desfasados de algunos de sus creadores. [5]

---

5   Como lo ha resumido con toda crudeza Fortunato González Cruz, lo que se implantó en Venezuela fue un Estado donde: "El uso y abuso del poder, la apropiación del dinero público, el festín llevado a extremos pantagruélicos, el desprecio por las normas y la inmoralidad forman parte medular de un modelo que quizás alguna vez tuvo la pretensión de ser revolucionario y que ha degenerado en el mayor pillaje de nuestra historia. [...] // La historia venezolana muestra otras grandes estafas, como la Guerra Federal,

En todo caso, por sus ejecutorias y características auto destructivas, lo que parece ser cierto es que el animal ya quizás entró en un definitivo proceso de apoptosis,[6] condición que se da en los propios organismos como muerte programada de sus células; o de autodestrucción por parte de sus propios componentes, de manera que de la caricatura de *Leviathan* que se le pretendió dar, quizás veremos pronto a dicho Estado Totalitario transformado en un *Catoblepas* (del griego: Κατωβλεψ, *Katôobleps*), el terrible animal que al comienzo de nuestra era, las crónicas fantásticas decían que existía en Etiopía, con cabeza siempre inclinada, que tenía un aliento fatal y una mirada letal,[7] pero en la versión contemporánea que le dio Maurice Duverger, de no ser más que un animal tan estúpido, pero tan estúpido, que se comía sus propios miembros, sin darse cuenta.[8]

En todo caso, para los Estados y para los sistemas políticos, como sucede para cada célula, hay siempre un tiempo de vivir y un tiempo de morir. Lo importante es tener o tratar de tener conciencia histórica de cada tiempo

New York, enero 2014

En todo caso, para la comprensión global del proceso de implementación del Estado Totalitario en Venezuela, debe indicarse que los escritos contenidos en este volumen están precedidos por todos los trabajos ya publicados en los Tomos VIII y IX de esta *Colección sobre Tratado de Derecho Constitucional*, que tratan sobre el

---

pero ninguna ha sido tan demoledora habida cuenta de los inmensos recursos económicos y políticos dilapidados: el mayor capital de respaldo popular, una gigantesca y casi ilimitada cuenta petrolera, todas las instituciones en sus manos para terminar en esta grotesca tragedia. Siempre tuvo un tufo a charlatanería, un alarde de viveza y una impúdica exhibición de ignorancia. Hoy la degeneración tiene al país perplejo y al mundo sorprendido que no puede creer la situación venezolana, por absurda. // Así han sido y son los socialismos históricos, solo que en Venezuela adquiere dimensiones aterradoras. Una teoría económica (Marx) y una táctica política (Lenin) torcidas en sus interpretaciones, mezcladas con la doctrina de la seguridad nacional, el populismo y el estatismo. Cuando saborean el poder y los dólares se desata la corrupción y se generaliza a tal grado que elimina todo proceso limpio desde la selección de los magistrados hasta la asignación de contratos por pequeños que sean. En los últimos años el empeño es por corromper hasta el espacio íntimo con la creación de los compatriotas cooperantes, la institucionalización del delator vecinal, la forma más despiadada e inmoral del espionaje. // Al final es lo mismo de cualquier satrapía: el poder, su uso y abuso, sin limitaciones morales ni jurídicas, con todo lo que significa. [...]". Véase Fortunato González Cruz, "La niñera del compatriota," Mérida 1 de noviembre de 2014, en *Comunicación Continua*, en http://comunicacioncontinua.com/por-la-calle-real-la-ninera-del-compatriota/.

6   Fenómeno biológico que consiste en la muerte programada de las células (suicidio programado de las células), cuyo descubrimiento se atribuye a la neuróloga Rita Levi–Montalcini, Premio Nobel de Medicina, 2005.

7   El *catoblepas* (del griego "mirar hacia abajo") fue descrito por primera vez por Plinio el Viejo en su *Historia Natural*, 8, 77(siglo I), como teniendo cuerpo de búfalo y cabeza de cerdo, pesada, que miraba siempre hacia abajo. Se decía que su mirada o su respiración eran letales, y que podían convertir a la gente en piedra o matarlas.» Por su parte, Leonardo da Vinci lo describía así: "No es un animal muy grande, no es muy activo, y su cabeza es tan pesada que le cuesta mucho trabajo levantarla, por lo que siempre mira al suelo. De lo contrario sería una gran peste para la humanidad, ya que cualquiera que cruzara su mirada con sus ojos moriría inmediatamente. " Véase Leonardo da Vinci, *Cuaderno de notas*, Edimat Libros, ISBN: 84-9764-370-4.

8   Véase Maurice Duverger, *Las dos caras de Occidente*, Barcelona 1972, pp. 278–279.

Golpe de Estado Constituyente, Estado Constitucional y Democracia; y sobre *Concentración y centralización del poder y régimen autoritario*, editados en 2015, y en los cuales se analiza el proceso progresivo de desarrollo del autoritarismo, hasta desembocar en el Estado Totalitario.

New York, noviembre 2016

PRIMERA PARTE

MODELO POLÍTICO Y DERECHO DEL ESTADO

Esta Primera parte es el texto redactado para mi exposición sobre "Modelo político y derecho administrativo," en las XV Jornadas Internacionales de Derecho Administrativo organizadas por el Departamento de Derecho Administrativo de la Universidad Externado de Colombia, que versaron sobre el tema general de La Constitucionalización del Derecho Administrativo. Transformaciones del derecho administrativo. Desafíos y tareas pendientes en la constitucionalización. Dichas Jornadas se celebraron en Bogotá entre los días 3-5 de septiembre de 2014. Fue publicado en el libro *Estado Totalitario y desprecio a la Ley*, Editorial Jurídica Venezolana, Caracas 2014, pp. 21-43.

I

El derecho público y en particular el derecho administrativo un derecho estatal[9] o un derecho del Estado, lo que implica, ineludiblemente, que el mismo está necesariamente vinculado al modelo político en el cual opera el propio Estado conforme a la práctica política del gobierno, siendo ello históricamente hablando, uno de los más importantes elementos condicionantes del derecho administrativo.[10]

No hay que olvidar que éste, como tal derecho del Estado, comenzó realmente a manifestarse en tiempos del absolutismo, cuando el sistema político estaba basado en el principio del Poder absoluto del Monarca, quien era el único titular de la soberanía, y que concentraba en su persona todos los poderes del Estado, sin que existiese régimen alguno regulador o garantizador de derechos ciudadanos frente al Poder Público. Ese fue precisamente el tiempo durante el cual se concibieron todas las ideas políticas que luego contribuyeron a su superación, con las obras de Locke, Montesquieu y Rousseau a la cabeza. En esos inicios, el derecho administrativo era

---

9   Véase André Demichel, *Le droit administratif. Essai de réflexion théorique*, París 1978, p. 14.

10   Sobre el tema, bajo el ángulo de la Administración, nos ocupamos hace años en Allan R. Brewer-Carías, "Les conditionnements politiques de l'administration publique dans les pays d'Amérique Latine", en *Revue Internationale des Sciences Administratives*, Vol. XLV, N° 3, Institut International des Sciences Administratives, Bruselas 1979, pp. 213-233; y "Los condicionamientos políticos de la Administración Pública en los países latinoamericanos," en *Revista de la Escuela Empresarial Andina*, Convenio Andrés Bello, N° 8, Año 5, Lima 1980, pp. 239-258.

un derecho exclusivamente regulador de la propia acción de la Administración del Estado ante las personas, de sus poderes y de sus prerrogativas, y de los órganos públicos dispuestos para ejecutarlas. Fue el tiempo remoto de los antecedentes derecho administrativo situados en el derecho de la organización desarrollado por Consejos o Cámaras reales (*Cameralística*), o de la actividad de control del Estado sobre las personas en ejercicio de poderes y prerrogativas, configurado como *derecho de policía.*

Fue después del surgimiento del Estado de derecho como modelo político desde comienzos del siglo XIX como consecuencia de los aportes de la Revolución Norteamericana (1776) y de la Revolución francesa (1789) al constitucionalismo moderno, y más precisamente, con el agregado de los efectos liberales de la Constitución de Cádiz de 1812 en Europa y de los movimientos independentistas de Hispanoamérica (1811),[11] cuando puede decirse que el derecho administrativo comenzó a ser el derecho del Estado de derecho, caracterizado por el hecho político de que la soberanía efectivamente se trasladó del Monarca al pueblo, dando origen al desarrollo del principio de la representatividad democrática. En ese marco, el Estado se organizó conforme al principio de la separación de poderes, lo que permitió el control recíproco entre los diversos órganos del Estado, entre ellos, por parte el poder judicial; montado además, en la necesaria garantía de los derechos ciudadanos frente al propio Estado, que comenzaron a ser declarados constitucionalmente.

Fue en ese marco político cuando el derecho administrativo comenzó a ser un orden jurídico que además de regular a los órganos del Estado y su actividad, también comenzó a regular las relaciones jurídicas que en cierto plano igualitario se comenzaron a establecer entre el Estado y los ciudadanos, y que ya no sólo estaban basadas en la antigua ecuación entre prerrogativa del Estado y sujeción de las personas a la autoridad, sino entre poder del Estado y derecho de los ciudadanos.

Ese cambio, incluso, se reflejó en el propio contenido de las Constituciones que en su origen, particularmente en Europa hasta la mitad del siglo pasado, no habían sido más que cuerpos normativos destinados a regular solo la organización del Estado, sin que sus normas siquiera se aplicaran directamente a los ciudadanos ni tuvieran a éstos como sus destinatarios, y cuyo contenido se reducía a regular lo que históricamente se ha denominado su parte orgánica relativa a la organización y funcionamiento de los diversos poderes y órganos del Estado. El derecho administrativo en esa época, por tanto, en el marco de su constitucionalización, no era más que el derecho que regulaba a la Administración Pública, su organización en el ámbito del Poder Ejecutivo, sus poderes y prerrogativas, y su funcionamiento, habiéndose recogido en las Constituciones, en general, sólo normas sobre la organización administrativa.

A medida que se fue imponiendo el modelo político del Estado de derecho, las Constituciones comenzaron a desarrollar, además de su parte orgánica, una parte dogmática relativa al régimen político democrático representativo y a los derechos y

---

11   Véase Allan R. Brewer-Carías, *Reflexiones sobre la revolución norteamericana (1776), la revolución francesa (1789) y la revolución hispanoamericana (1810-1830) y sus aportes al constitucionalismo moderno*, 2ª Edición Ampliada, Serie Derecho Administrativo Nº 2, Universidad Externado de Colombia, Editorial Jurídica Venezolana, Bogotá 2008.

garantías constitucionales de los ciudadanos, como consecuencia de lo cual, la acción de Estado y de la propia Administración comenzó a encontrar límites formales, que también comenzaron a ser recogidas en normas constitucionales destinadas a regular las relaciones que se establecen entre el Estado y los ciudadanos o las personas, en muchos casos precisamente con ocasión de la actividad de la Administración. Ello implicó la incorporación en los textos constitucionales de normas de derecho administrativo, incluyendo las que se refieren a los medios jurídicos dispuestos para asegurar el control de la Administración, tanto político, como fiscal y jurisdiccional; y las Constituciones, como norma, comenzaron a tener a los ciudadanos como sus destinatarios inmediatos.[12]

La consecuencia de todo ello fue que progresivamente, el derecho administrativo y sus principios terminaron encontrando su fuente jurídica primaria y más importante en la propia Constitución, en la cual ahora se encuentran regulaciones sobre la organización, funcionamiento y actividad de la Administración Pública como complejo orgánico integrada en los órganos del Poder Ejecutivo; sobre el ejercicio de la función administrativa, realizada aún por otros órganos del Estado distintos a la Administración; sobre las relaciones jurídicas que se establecen cotidianamente entre las personas jurídicas estatales cuyos órganos son los que expresan la voluntad de la Administración, y los administrados; sobre los fines públicos y colectivos que estas persiguen, situados por encima de los intereses particulares; sobre los poderes y prerrogativas de los cuales disponen para hacer prevalecer los intereses generales y colectivos frente a los intereses individuales, y además, de los límites impuestos por normas garantizadoras de los derechos y garantías de los administrados, incluso frente a la propia Administración.

En el mundo contemporáneo, en consecuencia, ese derecho administrativo que se ha incrustado en la Constitución,[13] es sin duda el propio de un derecho del Estado de derecho, y su desarrollo y efectividad debería estar condicionado por los valores democráticos que están a la base del mismo.

II

Lo anterior implica, que a diferencia de otras ramas del derecho, por su vinculación con el Estado y el régimen político, el derecho administrativo no puede considerarse como una rama políticamente neutra, y menos aún como un orden jurídico que haya adquirido esa relativa rigidez o estabilidad como la que podría encontrarse en otras ramas.

---

12   Véase Eduardo García de Enterría, *La Constitución como norma y el Tribunal Constitucional*, Madrid 1985.

13   Sobre el proceso de constitucionalización del derecho administrativo en Colombia y en Venezuela, véase Allan R. Brewer-Carías, "El proceso de constitucionalización del Derecho Administrativo en Colombia" en Juan Carlos Cassagne (Director), *Derecho Administrativo. Obra Colectiva en Homenaje al Prof. Miguel S. Marienhoff*, Buenos Aires 1998, pp. 157-172, y en *Revista de Derecho Público*, Nº 55-56, Editorial Jurídica Venezolana, Caracas, julio-diciembre 1993, pp. 47-59; y "Algunos aspectos de proceso de constitucionalización del derecho administrativo en la Constitución de 1999," en *Los requisitos y vicios de los actos administrativos. V Jornadas Internacionales de Derecho Administrativo Allan Randolph Brewer-Carías, Caracas 1996*, Fundación Estudios de Derecho Administrativo (FUNEDA), Caracas 2000, pp. 23-37.

El derecho administrativo, aun conservando principios esenciales, inevitablemente tiene siempre un grado el dinamismo que lo hace estar en constantc cvolución, como consecuencia directa, precisamente, de la propia evolución del Estado, siempre necesitando adaptarse a los cambios que se operan en el ámbito social y político de cada sociedad. Como desde hace años lo constataba Alejandro Nieto, "las transformaciones sociales arrastran inevitablemente una alteración de la superestructura jurídica," y con ella, del derecho administrativo,[14] de manera que éste, en definitiva, siempre "refleja los condicionamientos políticos y sociales vigentes en un momento dado."[15] De allí aquella gráfica expresión de Prosper Weil en el sentido de que el derecho administrativo sufre permanentemente de una "crisis de crecimiento,"[16] que en definitiva, nunca concluye, pues las transformaciones económicas y sociales del mundo no cesan, y con ellas las del Estado y del rol que cumple.

Pero si nos atenemos solamente a la conformación del andamiaje constitucional del Estado en el mundo contemporáneo occidental, como Estado de derecho, hay una constante subyacente en el condicionamiento del derecho administrativo, que son los principios democráticos que ahora le son esenciales a mismo,[17] como quedó plasmado en una aislada sentencia de la Sala Político Administrativa del Tribunal Supremo de Justicia de Venezuela de 2000, olvidada muy rápidamente, en la cual se afirmó que:

> "el derecho administrativo es ante y por sobre todo un derecho democrático y de la democracia, y su manifestación está íntimamente vinculada a la voluntad general (soberanía) de la cual emana."[18]

Ello debería ser así, y es cierto si nos quedamos solo en la denominación y definición formal del Estado que se inserta en las Constituciones, como por ejemplo sucede precisamente en Colombia y en Venezuela. En Colombia, el artículo 1 de la Constitución precisa que: "Colombia es un Estado social de derecho, organizado en forma de República unitaria, descentralizada, con autonomía de sus entidades territoriales, democrática, participativa y pluralista, fundada en el respeto de la dignidad

---

14   Véase Alejandro Nieto "La vocación del derecho administrativo de nuestro tiempo", *Revista de Administración Pública*, Nº 76, Madrid, Centro de Estudios Constitucionales 1975; también en *34 artículos seleccionados de la Revista de Administración Pública con ocasión de su centenario*, Madrid, 1983, pp. 880 y 881.

15   Véase Martín Bassols, "Sobre los principios originarios del derecho administrativo y su evolución", en *Libro homenaje al profesor Juan Galván Escutia*, Valencia, 1980, p. 57.

16   Véase Prosper Weil, *El derecho administrativo*, Madrid, 1966, p. 31.

17   Véase Allan R. Brewer–Carías, "El Derecho a la democracia entre las nuevas tendencias del derecho administrativo como punto de equilibrio entre los poderes de la Administración y los derechos del Administrado," en *Revista Mexicana "Statum Rei Romanae" de Derecho Administrativo*. Homenaje al profesor Jorge Fernández Ruiz, Asociación Mexicana de Derecho Administrativo, Facultad de Derecho y Criminología de la Universidad Autónoma de Nuevo León, México, 2008, pp. 85–122; y "Prólogo: Sobre el derecho a la democracia y el control del poder", al libro de Asdrúbal Aguiar, *El derecho a la democracia. La democracia en el derecho y la jurisprudencia interamericanos. La libertad de expresión, piedra angular de la democracia*, Editorial Jurídica Venezolana, Caracas, 2008, pp. 19 ss.

18   Véase la sentencia Nº 1028 del 9 de mayo de 2000 en *Revista de Derecho Público*, Nº 82, Editorial Jurídica Venezolana, Caracas, 2000, p. 214. Véase también, sentencia de la misma Sala de 5 de octubre de 2006, Nº 2189 (Caso: *Seguros Altamira, C.A. vs. Ministro de Finanzas*), en *Revista de Derecho Público*, Nº 108, Editorial Jurídica Venezolana, Caracas, 2006, p 100.

humana, en el trabajo y la solidaridad de las personas que la integran y en la prevalencia del interés general." Igualmente en Venezuela, el artículo 2 de la Constitución indica que: "Venezuela se constituye en un Estado democrático y social de Derecho y de Justicia, que propugna como valores superiores de su ordenamiento jurídico y de su actuación, la vida, la libertad, la justicia, la igualdad, la solidaridad, la democracia, la responsabilidad social y, en general, la preeminencia de los derechos humanos, la ética y el pluralismo político."

Mejores definiciones formales del Estado democrático en el texto de una Constitución, ciertamente es imposible encontrar como marco general del ordenamiento jurídico que debería ser aplicable al Estado, y que debe moldear el derecho administrativo. Sin embargo, ante esas definiciones, lo que corresponde es determinar si realmente, en los respectivos países, la práctica política del gobierno responde a esos principios, o si son simples enunciados floridos, y nada más, de un Estado nada democrático, como es el caso de Venezuela.

Es decir, ante los enunciados constitucionales que proclaman la democracia como régimen político, la tarea central es determinar cuán efectiva ha sido la vigencia real de estas normas y cómo ello ha permeado efectivamente en el derecho administrativo. Si nos atenemos a los enunciados, sin duda, el derecho administrativo de nuestros dos países debería ser ese derecho precisamente de un Estado democrático sometido al derecho, lo que implicaría la ineludible existencia de un pleno control judicial de la actividad administrativa, teniendo a su cargo la Administración, además de la misión general de gestionar el interés general y la satisfacción de las necesidades colectivas, la de garantizar el ejercicio de los derechos de los administrados, todo dentro de un marco legal general que asegure pluralismo e igualdad.

III

Pero lamentablemente, ello no es necesariamente así en la actualidad, particularmente en Venezuela, ni lo fue en general desde que la figura del Estado de derecho surgió en la historia, hace doscientos años; período durante el cual fue cuando precisamente se desarrolló nuestra disciplina, sin que sin embargo pueda afirmarse que por ausencia de un régimen democrático, el derecho administrativo como rama del derecho no haya existido.

Al contrario, por ejemplo, y para sólo referirnos a un ejemplo que nos es muy cercano a los administrativistas latinoamericanos, allí está el ejemplo de desarrollo del derecho administrativo contemporáneo en España, que comenzó precisamente en ausencia de un régimen democrático, por el fenomenal impulso que le pudo dar el núcleo de profesores que se aglutinó en el viejo Instituto de Estudios Políticos que estaba inserto en la propia estructura del Estado autoritario, en torno a la *Revista de Administración Pública*, con Eduardo García de Enterría, Fernando Garrido Falla, José Luis Villar Palasí y Jesús González Pérez, entre otros. Y ello ocurrió en los años cincuenta del Siglo pasado, cuando España, lejos de la democracia, estaba en plena etapa del autoritarismo franquista, más de veinte años antes de la sanción de la Constitución de 1978. Fue incluso en aquélla época cuando se dictaron las muy importantes Leyes sobre el Régimen Jurídico de la Administración del Estado, y sobre Procedimientos Administrativos, que sin duda fueron, en el derecho positivo, la partida de nacimiento del derecho administrativo español contemporáneo para buscar garantizar el sometimiento del Estado al derecho.

No había democracia, pero sin duda, sí había derecho administrativo, porque a pesar del autoritarismo, el régimen permitía la existencia de cierto equilibrio entre los poderes del Estado y los derechos ciudadanos. Y para no irnos muy lejos, la raíz del derecho administrativo contemporáneo en Venezuela puede situarse en la rica jurisprudencia de la antigua Corte Federal que funcionó hasta 1961, contenida en múltiples sentencias que emanaron de dicho alto tribunal igualmente en la década de los cincuenta del siglo pasado, en plena dictadura militar que duró hasta 1958.[19] Tampoco había democracia, pero sin duda, en el marco de un régimen autoritario ya se estaban sentando las bases del derecho administrativo contemporáneo en Venezuela, como lo hemos conocido en las décadas pasadas, por la existencia al menos de principio del antes mencionado equilibrio.

Pero por supuesto, en aquél entonces no se trataba de un derecho administrativo de un Estado democrático de derecho, sino de un Estado autoritario con alguna sujeción al derecho. Es decir, en otros términos más generales, porque ejemplos como los indicados los podemos encontrar en la historia de nuestra disciplina de todos nuestros países, puede decirse que el sometimiento del Estado al derecho, que fue lo que originó el derecho administrativo desde comienzos del siglo XIX, no siempre tuvo el estrecho vínculo con la democracia, como régimen político, como hoy lo consideramos.

IV

En realidad, el elemento esencial que caracteriza al derecho administrativo de un Estado democrático de derecho se encuentra cuando el derecho administrativo deja de ser un derecho exclusivamente del Estado, llamado a regular sólo su organización, su funcionamiento, sus poderes y sus prerrogativas, y pasa a ser realmente un derecho administrativo encargado de garantizar el punto de equilibrio antes mencionado que en una sociedad democrática tiene que existir entre los poderes del Estado y los derechos de los administrados. En el marco de un régimen autoritario, ese equilibrio por esencia no existe, o es muy débil o maleable, y por ello es que en dicho régimen el derecho administrativo no es un derecho democrático, aun cuando pretenda someter el Estado al derecho.

Como lo señaló la Sala Político Administrativa del Tribunal Supremo de Justicia de Venezuela en la misma olvidada sentencia N° 1028 de 9 de mayo de 2000,

> "El derecho administrativo se presenta dentro de un estado social de derecho como el punto de equilibrio entre el poder (entendido éste como el conjunto de atribuciones y potestades que tienen las instituciones y autoridades públicas, dentro del marco de la legalidad), y la libertad (entendida ésta como los derechos y garantías que tiene el ciudadano para convivir en paz, justicia y democracia)."[20]

---

19 Véase Allan R. Brewer-Carías, *Las instituciones fundamentales del derecho administrativo y la jurisprudencia venezolanas*, Caracas 1964; y *Jurisprudencia de la Corte Suprema 1930-1974 y estudios de derecho administrativo*, Ediciones del Instituto de Derecho Público, Facultad de Derecho, Universidad Central de Venezuela, ocho volúmenes, Caracas 1975-1979.

20 Véase en *Revista de Derecho Público*, N° 82, Editorial Jurídica Venezolana, Caracas 2000, p. 214.

Ello es precisamente lo que caracteriza al derecho administrativo en un orden democrático, que no es otra cosa que ser el instrumento para asegurar la sumisión del Estado al derecho pero con a la misión de garantizar el respeto a los derechos ciudadanos, en medio de una persistente lucha histórica por controlar el poder y contra las "inmunidades del poder,"[21] que es lo que ha caracterizado el devenir de nuestra disciplina. Ese equilibrio entre el poder y el ciudadano, siempre latente, pero débil al inicio, efectivamente se comenzó consolidar bien entrado el Siglo XX, luego de la segunda guerra mundial, cuando el derecho administrativo comenzó a ser un derecho regulador no sólo del Estado, sino de los derechos ciudadanos en un marco democrático.

Con ello se consolidó la concepción del derecho administrativo de las sociedades democráticas como el instrumento por excelencia para, por una parte garantizar la eficiencia de la acción administrativa y la prevalencia de los intereses generales y colectivos, y por la otra, para asegurar la protección del administrado frente a la Administración; con lo cual se superó aquella caracterización del derecho administrativo que advertía hace años Fernando Garrido Fallo, cuando nos indicaba que se nos presentaba como "un hipócrita personaje de doble faz," que encerraba una "oposición aparentemente irreductible" entre el conjunto de prerrogativas que posee y que "sitúan a la Administración en un plano de desigualdad y favor en sus relaciones con los particulares"; y el conjunto de derechos y garantías de estos, que lo llevaban a regular lo que llamó "la más acabada instrumentación técnica del Estado liberal."[22]

Ese juego dialéctico entre esos dos puntos extremos contrapuestos: por una parte, los poderes y las prerrogativas administrativas de la Administración, y por la otra, los derechos y las garantías de los administrados, es lo que ha permitido, como lo apuntó Marcel Waline también hace unos buenos años, que por una parte se evite el inmovilismo y la impotencia de la Administración, y por la otra, se evite la tiranía.[23] La existencia o no del mencionado equilibrio, o la existencia de un acentuado desbalance o desequilibrio entre los dos extremos, es lo que resulta del modelo político en el cual se mueve y aplica el derecho administrativo. Y de allí que más democrático será el derecho administrativo solo si el equilibrio es acentuado; y menos democrático será si su regulación se limita sólo a satisfacer los requerimientos del Estado, ignorando o despreciando el otro extremo, es decir, el de las garantías y derechos ciudadanos.

El reto del derecho administrativo, como derecho del Estado, por tanto, está en lograr y asegurar el equilibrio mencionado para que el Estado esté configurado no sólo como un Estado de derecho sino como un Estado democrático, lo cual sólo es posible si el mismo asegura efectivamente el control del ejercicio del poder. Sin dicho control, el derecho administrativo no pasa de ser un derecho del Poder Ejecutivo o de la Administración Pública, montado sobre un desequilibrio o desbalance,

---

21   Véase Eduardo García de Enterría, *La lucha contra las inmunidades de poder en el derecho administrativo*, Madrid 1983.

22   Véase Fernando Garrido Falla, "Sobre el derecho administrativo", en *Revista de Administración Pública*, Nº 7, Instituto de Estudios Políticos, Madrid 1952, p. 223.

23   Véase Marcel Waline, *Droit administratif*, París, 1963, p. 4.

en el cual las prerrogativas y poderes de la Administración pudieran predominar en el contenido de su regulación.

V

Pero para que el equilibrio se logre y sea efectivo, es evidente que no bastan las declaraciones formales en las Constituciones, ni que el derecho administrativo se haya llegado a constitucionalizar efectivamente, como ha ocurrido por ejemplo en Colombia y Venezuela Las Constituciones de nuestros países son ejemplos de dicho proceso, estando incluso imbuidas del mencionado postulado del equilibrio en la relación Administración-administrados, dando cabida a un conjunto de previsiones para asegurarlo, regulando la actuación de la Administración y protegiendo en paralelo los derechos e intereses de las personas, pero sin el sacrificio o menosprecio de los intereses particulares, a pesar de la prevalencia de los intereses generales o colectivos.

En este campo se destaca, por ejemplo, la norma de la Constitución colombiana que regula la función administrativa, y que declara que la misma: "está al servicio de los intereses generales y se desarrolla con fundamento en los principios de igualdad, moralidad, eficacia, economía, celeridad, imparcialidad y publicidad, mediante la descentralización, la delegación y la desconcentración de funciones" (Art. 209); pero ello, a la vez, dentro del marco de una Constitución garantista de los individuos ante el Estado, que asegura, por ejemplo, la vigencia de la garantía del debido proceso no sólo a las actuaciones judiciales sino también en los procedimientos administrativos (Art. 29), y erige el principio de la buena fe como principio fundamental a cuyos postulados deben ceñirse "las actuaciones de los particulares y de las autoridades públicas," debiendo siempre presumírsela "en todas las gestiones que aquéllos adelanten ante éstas" (art. 83). Ello, sin duda, apunta hacia la protección de los administrados frente a la Administración, presumiéndose el principio de la libertad antes que la regulación, lo que se refuerza con normas como la del artículo 84, que establece como principio que: "Cuando un derecho o una actividad hayan sido reglamentados de manera general, las autoridades públicas no podrán establecer ni exigir permisos, licencias o requisitos adicionales para su ejercicio"; lo que se complementa con el artículo 333, que al regular la actividad económica y la iniciativa privada como "libres, dentro de los límites del bien común", agrega que "para su ejecución nadie podrá exigir permisos previos ni requisitos, sin autorización de ley."

La Constitución de Venezuela, por su lado, también está imbuida del mismo postulado del equilibrio en la relación Administración-administrado, destacándose, por ejemplo, la norma que al regular a la Administración Pública, declara que la misma "está al servicio de los ciudadanos, y se fundamenta en los principios de honestidad, participación, celeridad, eficacia, eficiencia, transparencia, rendición de cuenta y responsabilidad en el ejercicio de la función pública, con sometimiento pleno a la ley y al derecho" (art. 141); garantizándose igualmente a aquellos, el debido proceso, no sólo en las actuaciones judiciales sino en los procedimientos administrativos (art. 49). Pero la Constitución venezolana va más allá, y establece las regulaciones fundamentales relativas a la actuación del Estado como gestor del interés general en relación con los particulares o administrados, y en particular, en su actuación administrativa; constitucionalizando todo el régimen fundamental del derecho administrativo. Así, por ejemplo, la Constitución garantiza a los ciudadanos el derecho a ser informados oportuna y verazmente por la Administración Pública sobre el estado de las actuaciones en que estén directamente interesados, y a conocer las resoluciones definitivas que se adopten sobre el particular; e igualmente garantiza a los ciudadanos el acceso a los archivos y registros administrativos, sin perjuicio de los "límites aceptables dentro de una sociedad democrática" (Art. 143). La Constitución garantiza además, que los funcionarios públicos "están al servicio del Estado y no de parcialidad alguna", incluso disponiendo que "su nombramiento o remoción no podrán estar determinados por la afiliación u orientación política" (Art. 145).

VI

Pero es evidente que sea cual fuere la forma de redacción de la Constitución sobre la noción del Estado democrático de derecho y la extensión del proceso de constitucionalización del derecho administrativo, ello no es suficiente para que el equilibrio entre el poder del Estado y los derechos ciudadanos sea efectivo.

Es en realidad, la práctica política del gobierno la que pondrá de manifiesto si un Estado conformado constitucionalmente como un Estado de derecho, realmente se conduce como tal en su funcionamiento y actuación, y si el derecho administrativo aplicado al mismo obedece o no efectivamente a parámetros democráticos. Basta estudiar el caso venezolano para constatar que el "Estado democrático y social de derecho y de justicia" tal como lo define el artículo 2 de la Constitución, en la práctica política del gobierno autoritario que se apoderó de la República desde 1999,[24] no es tal, es decir, no es un Estado democrático, ni Social, ni de derecho ni de Justicia, y más bien es un Estado Totalitario, donde el poder está totalmente concentrado, tanto desde el punto de vista político y económico, el cual, además de haber empobrecido aún más al país, no está realmente sometido al derecho, cuyas normas se ignoran y desprecian; o se mutan o amoldan a discreción por los gobernantes; ni está sometido a control judicial alguno, por la sumisión del Poder Judicial al Poder Ejecutivo. Por todo ello, se lo puede caracterizar más bien como un "Estado de la injusticia" todo lo cual afecta tremendamente al derecho administrativo.

Y es que si algo es definitivo en esta perspectiva, es que el derecho administrativo no es, ni puede ser independiente de la actuación del gobierno, sea que del mismo resulte en un modelo político de Estado autoritario o de Estado democrático. Y para identificar dicho modelo por supuesto no podemos acudir a etiquetas o a definiciones constitucionales, sino a la práctica política del gobierno.

Un Estado autoritario será el resultado de la actuación de un gobierno autoritario, y en el mismo, lejos de haber un equilibrio entre los poderes de la Administración y los derechos de los particulares, lo que existe es más bien un marcado desequilibrio a favor del régimen de la Administración, con pocas posibilidades de garantía de los derechos de los particulares frente a su actividad.

En cambio, el equilibrio antes mencionado sólo tiene posibilidad de pleno desarrollo en Estados con gobiernos democráticos, donde la supremacía constitucional esté asegurada, donde la separación y distribución del Poder sea el principio medu-

---

24 Véase Allan R. Brewer-Carías, *Authoritarian Government vs. The Rule of Law, Lectures and Essays (1999-2014) on the Venezuelan Authoritarian Regime Established in Contempt of the Constitution*, Fundación de Derecho Público, Editorial Jurídica Venezolana, Caracas 2014.

lar de la organización del Estrado, donde el ejercicio del Poder Público pueda ser efectivamente controlado judicialmente y por los otros medios dispuestos en la Constitución, y donde los derechos de los ciudadanos sean garantizados por un Poder Judicial independiente y autónomo. Nada de ello se encuentra en los Estados con un régimen de gobierno autoritario, así sus gobernantes hayan podido haber sido electos, y se arropen con el lenguaje a veces florido de los textos constitucionales.

VII

En todo caso, en el devenir del derecho administrativo y como resultado del movimiento pendular que entre los extremos de su regulación se ha producido por la existencia de gobiernos más o menos democráticos, ha sido precisamente el desarrollo y consolidación de la democracia como régimen político el que ha condicionado más al derecho administrativo contemporáneo, asegurándole un desarrollo extraordinario, como precisamente ocurrió en las últimas décadas en muchos de nuestros países; y que además de haberse manifestado en su constitucionalización, dio origen a nuevas disposiciones legislativas como por ejemplo las contenidas en las leyes de procedimiento administrativo, las cuales además de regular y formalizar la actividad administrativa, establecen expresamente el contrapeso de la garantía de los derechos ciudadanos.[25]

Esas leyes, en efecto, se dictaron no sólo en interés de la Administración y del interés general que gestiona, sino además, en interés de los administrados, lo que incluso se declara en el propio texto de las propias leyes, como es el caso del Código Contencioso Administrativo de Colombia de 2011, en el cual se dispone que su finalidad es precisamente: "proteger y garantizar los derechos y libertades de las personas, la primacía de los intereses generales, la sujeción de las autoridades a la Constitución y demás preceptos del ordenamiento jurídico, el cumplimiento de los fines estatales, el funcionamiento eficiente y democrático de la administración, y la observancia de los deberes del Estado y de los particulares" (art. 1); y en el caso de la reciente Ley sobre Procedimiento Administrativo de República Dominicana de 2012 que también comienza señalando en su artículo 1º, que la misma "tiene por objeto regular los derechos y deberes de las personas en sus relaciones con la Administración Pública, los principios que sirven de sustento a esas relaciones y las normas de procedimiento administrativo que rigen a la actividad administrativa."

Mucho antes, incluso, la Ley General de la Administración Pública de Costa Rica, también precisó que el procedimiento administrativo se debe desarrollar "con respeto para los derechos subjetivos e intereses legítimos del administrado"(art. 10,1 y 214,1); y en la Ley de Procedimiento Administrativo de Honduras se indicó que el procedimiento se regula "como garantía de los derechos de los particulares frente a la actividad administrativa," lo que también se expresa en la Ley de Procedimientos Administrativos del Perú (art. III).

De todas esas normas resulta que un elemento central de la finalidad del procedimiento administrativo es precisamente, además de asegurar el adecuado funcio-

---

25   Véase Allan R. Brewer–Carías, *Principios del procedimiento administrativo en América Latina*, Universidad del Rosario, Colegio Mayor de Nuestra Señora del Rosario, Editorial Legis, Bogotá 2003.

namiento de la Administración, garantizar la satisfacción y protección de los derechos de los particulares. En Venezuela esos mismos principios sin duda orientaron la regulación del procedimiento administrativo durante la época democrática en la Ley Orgánica de Procedimientos Administrativos de 1982,[26] pero sin embargo, la práctica autoritaria del gobierno los ha hecho ilusorios, llegando el gobierno incluso al absurdo, hace unos años, de proponer en la rechazada reforma constitucional de 2007, la eliminación formal del postulado constitucional de que "la Administración Pública está al servicio de los ciudadanos" (art. 141).[27]

En todo caso, precisamente por la práctica política del gobierno autoritario, el régimen autoritario venezolano se ha dado el lujo de incluir a granel normas formalmente garantistas en leyes recientes, que en paralelo contienen el desprecio más absoluto a los derechos individuales. Basta hacer referencia, sobre esta contradicción, a los principios sobre el procedimiento administrativo formalmente incorporados en la legislación, pero en la práctica, totalmente olvidado por la Administración, y más si no se puede controlar la conducta de los funcionarios por la ausencia real de control judicial contencioso administrativo, dada la sujeción de los tribunales al poder.

En ese panorama, por ejemplo, ¿de qué sirve que las leyes declaren principios, si no tienen efectividad ni puede controlarse su ejecución? Basta un ejemplo, referido a una de las leyes que más ha atentado últimamente contra el derecho al ejercicio de la libertad económica y del trabajo, como es la Ley de Costos y Precios,[28] reguladora de una intervención extrema en la actividad económica, que asigna poderes draconianos a los funcionarios controladores, hasta permitirles decidir la intervención y clausura administrativa de establecimientos comerciales por sobrepasar un margen de ganancia arbitrariamente establecido; pero en la cual se declara que los procedimientos contemplados en la misma se rigen específicamente por los principios de "publicidad, dirección e impulsión de oficio (oficialidad), primacía de la realidad (verdad material), libertad probatoria, lealtad y probidad procesal, notificación única" (art. 49), a los que deben agregarse los principios declarados en la Constitución sobre la conducta general de la Administración que son los "principios de honestidad, participación, celeridad, eficacia, eficiencia, transparencia, rendición de cuentas y responsabilidad en el ejercicio de la función pública, con sometimiento pleno a la ley y al derecho" (art. 141); y en las leyes, como la Ley Orgánica de Procedimientos Administrativos, que son los principios de "celeridad, economía, sencillez, eficacia, e imparcialidad "(art. 30); la Ley de Simplificación de Trámites Administrativos de 1999, reformada en 2008, que son los principios de "simplicidad, transparencia, celeridad, eficacia, eficiencia, rendición de cuentas, solidaridad, presunción de bue-

---

26   Véase Allan R. Brewer–Carías, *El derecho administrativo y la Ley Orgánica de Procedimientos Administrativos. Principios del Procedimiento Administrativo*, Editorial Jurídica Venezolana, 6ª edición ampliada, Caracas 2002.

27   Véase Allan R. Brewer–Carías, *Hacia la consolidación de un Estado Socialista, Centralista, Policial y Militarista. Comentarios sobre el alcance y sentido de las propuestas de reforma constitucional 2007*, Editorial Jurídica Venezolana, Caracas 2007, pp. 31 ss.; *La Reforma Constitucional de 2007 (Inconstitucionalmente sancionada por la Asamblea nacional el 2 de noviembre de 2007)*, Editorial Jurídica Venezolana, Caracas 2007, pp. 50 ss.

28   Véase en *Gaceta Oficial* N° 39.715 del 18 de julio de 2011.

na fe del interesado o interesada, responsabilidad en el ejercicio de la función pública, desconcentración en la toma de decisiones por parte de los órganos de dirección y su actuación debe estar dirigida al servicio de las personas"; y la Ley Orgánica de la Administración Pública de 2001, reformada en 2008, que son "los principios de economía, celeridad, simplicidad, rendición de cuentas, eficacia, eficiencia, proporcionalidad, oportunidad, objetividad, imparcialidad, participación, honestidad, accesibilidad, uniformidad, modernidad, transparencia, buena fe, paralelismo de la forma y responsabilidad en el ejercicio de la misma, con sometimiento pleno a la ley y al derecho, y con supresión de las formalidades no esenciales" (art. 10).

A nivel de principios formalmente declarados en la legislación, por tanto, podría concluirse que no habría en el derecho comparado un derecho administrativo más "garantista y democrático" que el venezolano; lo que sin embargo lo desmiente la realidad de la acción de la Administración, caracterizada por la ausencia de control de cualquier tipo, lo que la hace el reino de la arbitrariedad.

VIII

De todo lo anterior resulta evidente que cuando se habla de Estado democrático de derecho, y en el mismo, del derecho administrativo como derecho de la democracia, ésta tiene que existir real y efectivamente y no sólo en el papel de las Constituciones y de las leyes, sino en la práctica de la acción del gobierno que origine un sistema político en el cual además de todos los derechos y garantías constitucionales generalmente conocidos (políticos, individuales, sociales, económicos, culturales, ambientales), se garantice efectivamente el derecho ciudadano a la Constitución y a su supremacía constitucional, es decir el derecho ciudadano a la propia democracia,[29] y el derecho de poder ejercer el control sobre las actividades gubernamentales, que hasta cierto punto son tan políticos como los clásicos derechos al sufragio, al desempeño de cargos públicos, a asociarse en partidos políticos y, más recientemente, el derecho a la participación política.

Estos derechos que son nuevos sólo en su enunciado, derivan de la comprensión cabal de lo que significa un régimen democrático, que sólo es aquél donde concurren una serie de *elementos esenciales* que por lo demás derivan de la *Carta Democrática Interamericana* de 2001, y que son los derechos: 1) al respeto a los derechos humanos y las libertades fundamentales; 2) al acceso al poder y su ejercicio con sujeción al Estado de derecho; 3) a la celebración de elecciones periódicas, libres, justas y basadas en el sufragio universal y secreto, como expresión de la soberanía del pueblo; 4) al régimen plural de partidos y organizaciones políticas y 5) a la separación e independencia de los poderes públicos (art. 3).

No hay ni puede haber democracia si el ciudadano no tiene garantizado su derecho político a la efectividad de esos elementos esenciales, que es lo que permite en definitiva distinguir un Estado democrático de derecho de un Estado de régimen autoritario. En este, a pesar de todas sus etiquetas constitucionales, esos derechos o

---

29   Véase Allan R. Brewer–Carías, "Prólogo: Sobre el derecho a la democracia y el control del poder", al libro de Asdrúbal Aguiar, *El derecho a la democracia. La democracia en el derecho y la jurisprudencia interamericanos. La libertad de expresión, piedra angular de la democracia*, Editorial Jurídica Venezolana, Caracas 2008, pp. 19 ss.

elementos esenciales no pueden ser garantizados, por la ausencia de controles al ejercicio del poder, aún cuando pueda tratarse de Estados en los cuales los gobiernos puedan haber tenido su origen en algún ejercicio electoral.

Entre todos esos derechos políticos a la democracia, está por supuesto, el derecho a la separación de poderes, que implica el derecho a ejercer el control del poder. Ello además, es lo que permite que se puedan materializar otros derechos políticos del ciudadano en una sociedad democrática, identificados en la misma Carta Democrática Interamericana como *componentes fundamentales* de la democracia, como son los derechos a: 1) la transparencia de las actividades gubernamentales; 2) la probidad y la responsabilidad de los gobiernos en la gestión pública; 3) el respeto de los derechos sociales; 4) el respeto de la libertad de expresión y de prensa; 5) la subordinación constitucional de todas las instituciones del Estado a la autoridad civil legalmente constituida y 6) el respeto al Estado de derecho de todas las entidades y sectores de la sociedad (art. 4).

IX

Entre esos derechos se destaca el derecho a la separación de poderes, materializado en el derecho al control del poder, que es el fundamento del propio derecho administrativo en una sociedad democrática, pues es precisamente el elemento fundamental para garantizar el necesario equilibro mencionado entre los poderes y prerrogativas de la Administración del Estado y los derechos ciudadanos. En definitiva, sólo controlando al Poder es que puede haber elecciones libres y justas; pluralismo político; efectiva participación democrática en la gestión de los asuntos públicos; transparencia administrativa en el ejercicio del gobierno; rendición de cuentas por parte de los gobernantes; sumisión efectiva del gobierno a la Constitución y las leyes; efectivo acceso a la justicia; y real y efectiva garantía de respeto a los derechos humanos. De lo anterior resulta, por tanto, que sólo cuando existe un sistema de control efectivo del poder es que puede haber democracia, y sólo en esta es que los ciudadanos pueden encontrar asegurados sus derechos debidamente equilibrados con los poderes Públicos, y sólo en ese marco es que es posible el desarrollo de un derecho administrativo de base democrática.

Ese derecho a la separación e independencia de los Poderes Públicos, que es lo que puede permitir el control del poder estatal por el poder estatal mismo, como pilar fundamental en la organización del Estado democrático constitucional, por supuesto exige no sólo que los Poderes del Estado tengan real independencia y autonomía, sino que la misma esté garantizada.

Para ello, de nuevo, no bastan las declaraciones constitucionales y ni siquiera la sola existencia de elecciones, siendo demasiadas las experiencias en el mundo contemporáneo de toda suerte de tiranos que usaron el voto popular para acceder al poder, y que luego, mediante su ejercicio incontrolado, desmantelar la democracia y desarrollar gobiernos autoritarios, contrarios al pueblo, que acabaron con la propia democracia y con todos sus elementos,[30] comenzando por el irrespeto a los derechos

---

30   Véase Allan R. Brewer-Carías, *Dismantling Democracy. The Chávez Authoritarian Experiment*, Cambridge University Press, New York 2010.

humanos. Situación que por lo demás ha sido la de Venezuela, donde se ha arraigado un gobierno autoritario partiendo de elementos que se insertaron en la misma Constitución de 1999.[31]

En ella, en efecto, a pesar de establecerse una peta división del poder público en Legislativo, Ejecutivo, Judicial, Ciudadano y Electoral, se dispuso el germen de la concentración del poder en manos de la Asamblea Nacional y, consecuencialmente, del Poder Ejecutivo que la controla políticamente, con lo cual, progresivamente, los otros Poderes Públicos, y particularmente el Poder Judicial[32], el Poder Ciudadano y el Poder Electoral[33] han quedado sometidos a la voluntad del Ejecutivo. Por ello en noviembre de 1999, aún antes de que la Constitución se sometiera a referendo aprobatorio, advertí que si la Constitución se aprobaba, ello iba a implicar la implantación en Venezuela, de:

"un esquema institucional concebido para el autoritarismo derivado de la combinación del centralismo del Estado, el presidencialismo exacerbado, la democracia de partidos, la concentración de poder en la Asamblea y el militarismo, que constituye el elemento central diseñado para la organización del poder del Estado."

En mi opinión –agregaba–, esto no era lo que en 1999 se requería para el perfeccionamiento de la democracia; la cual al contrario, se debió basar "en la descentralización del poder, en un presidencialismo controlado y moderado, en la participación

31   Véase los comentarios críticos a la semilla autoritaria en la Constitución de 1999, en Allan R. Brewer–Carías, *Debate Constituyente (Aportes a la Asamblea Nacional Constituyente), Tomo III (18 octubre–30 noviembre 1999),* Fundación de Derecho Público–Editorial Jurídica Venezolana, Caracas, 1999, pp. 311–340; "Reflexiones críticas sobre la Constitución de Venezuela de 1999," en el libro de Diego Valadés, Miguel Carbonell (Coordinadores), *Constitucionalismo Iberoamericano del Siglo XXI,* Cámara de Diputados. LVII Legislatura, Universidad Nacional Autónoma de México, México 2000, pp. 171–193; en *Revista de Derecho Público,* Nº 81, Editorial Jurídica Venezolana, Caracas, enero–marzo 2000, pp. 7–21; en *Revista Facultad de Derecho, Derechos y Valores,* Volumen III Nº 5, Universidad Militar Nueva Granada, Santafé de Bogotá, D.C., Colombia, Julio 2000, pp. 9–26; y en el libro *La Constitución de 1999,* Biblioteca de la Academia de Ciencias Políticas y Sociales, Serie Eventos 14, Caracas, 2000, pp. 63–88.

32   Véase Allan R. Brewer–Carías, "La progresiva y sistemática demolición de la autonomía en independencia del Poder Judicial en Venezuela (1999–2004)", en *XXX Jornadas J.M Domínguez Escovar, Estado de derecho, Administración de justicia y derechos humanos,* Instituto de Estudios Jurídicos del Estado Lara, Barquisimeto, 2005, pp. 33–174; y "La justicia sometida al poder [La ausencia de independencia y autonomía de los jueces en Venezuela por la interminable emergencia del Poder Judicial (1999–2006)]" en *Cuestiones Internacionales. Anuario Jurídico Villanueva 2007,* Centro Universitario Villanueva, Marcial Pons, Madrid, 2007, pp. 25–57.

33   Véase Allan R. Brewer–Carías, "El secuestro del Poder Electoral y la confiscación del derecho a la participación política mediante el referendo revocatorio presidencial: Venezuela 2000–2004,", en *Boletín Mexicano de Derecho Comparado,* Instituto de Investigaciones Jurídicas, Universidad Nacional Autónoma de México, Nº 112. México, enero–abril 2005 pp. 11–73; *La Sala Constitucional versus el Estado Democrático de Derecho. El secuestro del poder electoral y de la Sala Electoral del Tribunal Supremo y la confiscación del derecho a la participación política,* Los Libros de El Nacional, Colección Ares, Caracas, 2004, 172 pp.

política para balancear el poder del Estado y en la sujeción de la autoridad militar a la autoridad civil"[34].

La dependencia de todos los órganos de control respecto de la Asamblea Nacional, ha sido lo que originó la abstención total de los órganos de control de ejercer las potestades que le son atribuidas, y con ello, la práctica política de concentración total del poder en manos del Ejecutivo, dado el control político partidista que éste ejerce sobre la Asamblea Nacional, y por tanto la configuración de un modelo político autoritario. A consolidar ese sometimiento de todos los poderes al Ejecutivo, además, contribuyó la exacerbación del presidencialismo que la Constitución de 1999 impuso con la extensión del período presidencial a seis años; con la consagración de la reelección presidencial continua e indefinida en una Enmienda Constitucional aprobada en 2009,[35] y con la posibilidad de la delegación legislativa sin límites en manos del Ejecutivo, lo que efectivamente ha ocurrido en la práctica legislativa desde 2000, mediante sucesivas leyes habilitantes (Art. 203), de manera que toda la legislación básica del país durante los últimos quince años ha sido establecida por decretos leyes sin consulta popular alguna.

Ha sido todo este sistema de ausencia de autonomía y de independencia de los poderes del Estado respecto del Ejecutivo Nacional, lo que ha eliminado toda posibilidad real de asegurar un equilibrio entre el poder de la Administración del Estado y los derechos ciudadanos, siendo difícil por tanto poder identificar a la Administración Pública como entidad al servicio de estos, los cuales lamentablemente ahora sólo pueden entrar en relación con la misma en dos formas: por una parte, los que son privilegiados del poder, como consecuencia de la pertenencia política al régimen o a su partido único, con todas las prebendas y parcialidades de parte de los funcionarios; y por otra parte, los que como marginados del poder acuden a la Administración por necesidad ciudadana, a rogar las más elementales actuaciones públicas, como es por ejemplo solicitar autorizaciones, licencias, permisos o habilitaciones, las cuales no siempre son atendidas y más bien tratadas como si lo que se estuviera requiriendo fueran favores y no derechos o el cumplimiento de obligaciones públicas. En ambas situaciones, lamentablemente, el equilibrio entre poderes del Estado y derechos ciudadanos de los administrados ha desaparecido, sin que existan elementos de control para restablecerlo: se privilegia y se margina, como producto de una discriminación política antes nunca vista, sin posibilidad alguna de control.

En ese marco, el derecho administrativo formalmente concebido para la democracia, en la práctica pasó a ser un instrumento más del autoritarismo.

X

Bajo otro ángulo, y también como parte del derecho ciudadano a la separación de poderes y como parte del derecho a la democracia, que es lo que puede dar origen a

---

34 Documento de 30 de noviembre de 1999. *V.* en Allan R. Brewer–Carías, *Debate Constituyente (Aportes a la Asamblea Nacional Constituyente)*, Tomo III, Fundación de Derecho Público, Editorial Jurídica Venezolana, Caracas, 1999, p. 339.

35 Véase Allan R. Brewer-Carías, "El Juez Constitucional vs. La alternabilidad republicana (La reelección continua e indefinida), en *Revista de Derecho Público*, N° 117, (enero-marzo 2009), Caracas 2009, pp. 205-211.

un derecho administrativo democrático, está en particular el derecho ciudadano a la independencia y autonomía de los jueces que tienen que estar garantizadas en cualquier Estado democrático de derecho; siendo el control judicial del poder la piedra angular del equilibrio mencionado que debe asegurar el derecho administrativo en un Estado democrático de derecho.

Y de nuevo, en este campo, para calibrar su existencia, no podemos atenernos a las etiquetas constitucionales: Por ejemplo, el principio de la independencia y autonomía del Poder Judicial está declarado en el artículo 254 de la Constitución venezolana de 1999, pero como letra muerta pues la base fundamental para asegurarlas está en las normas relativas al ingreso de los jueces a la carrera judicial y a su permanencia y estabilidad en los cargos, que no se cumplen y nunca se han cumplido en los tres lustros de vigencia del texto fundamental. Pero el que lea las normas constitucionales, sin embargo, se maravillará de encontrar que el artículo 255 de la Constitución, en cuanto a la carrera judicial, que dice que el ingreso a la misma y el ascenso de los jueces solo se puede hacer mediante concursos públicos de oposición que aseguren la idoneidad y excelencia de los participantes, debiendo además la ley garantizar la participación ciudadana en el procedimiento de selección y designación de los jueces. Sin embargo, nunca, durante la vigencia de la Constitución, se han desarrollado esos concursos, en esa forma.

Pero además, en cuanto a la estabilidad de los jueces, dice la Constitución que los mismos sólo pueden ser removidos o suspendidos de sus cargos mediante juicios disciplinarios llevados a cabo por jueces disciplinarios (art. 255); pero tampoco en ese case ello jamás se ha implementado, y a partir de 1999,[36] más bien se regularizó, en una ilegítima transitoriedad constitucional, la existencia de una Comisión de Funcionamiento del Poder Judicial creada ad hoc para "depurar" el poder judicial.[37] Esa Comisión, durante más de 10 años destituyó materialmente a casi todos los jueces del país, discrecionalmente y sin garantía alguna del debido proceso,[38] los cuales fueron reemplazados por jueces provisorios o temporales,[39] por supuesto dependien-

---

36   Véase nuestro voto salvado a la intervención del Poder Judicial por la Asamblea Nacional Constituyente en Allan R. Brewer–Carías, *Debate Constituyente, (Aportes a la Asamblea Nacional Constituyente)*, Tomo I, (8 agosto–8 septiembre), Caracas 1999; y las críticas formuladas a ese proceso en Allan R. Brewer–Carías, *Golpe de Estado y proceso constituyente en Venezuela*, Universidad Nacional Autónoma de México, México, 2002.

37   Véase Allan R. Brewer–Carías, "La justicia sometida al poder y la interminable emergencia del poder judicial (1999–2006)", en *Derecho y democracia. Cuadernos Universitarios*, Órgano de Divulgación Académica, Vicerrectorado Académico, Universidad Metropolitana, Año II, Nº 11, Caracas, septiembre 2007, pp. 122–138.

38   La Comisión Interamericana de Derechos Humanos también lo registró en el Capítulo IV del *Informe* que rindió ante la Asamblea General de la OEA en 2006, que los "casos de destituciones, sustituciones y otro tipo de medidas que, en razón de la provisionalidad y los procesos de reforma, han generado dificultades para una plena vigencia de la independencia judicial en Venezuela" (párrafo 291); destacando aquellas "destituciones y sustituciones que son señaladas como represalias por la toma de decisiones contrarias al Gobierno" (párrafo 295 ss.); concluyendo que para 2005, según cifras oficiales, "el 18,30% de las juezas y jueces son titulares y 81,70% están en condiciones de provisionalidad" (párrafo 202).

39   En el *Informe Especial* de la Comisión sobre Venezuela correspondiente al año 2003, la misma también expresó, que "un aspecto vinculado a la autonomía e independencia del Poder Judicial es el relativo al carácter provisorio de los jueces en el sistema judicial de Venezuela. Actualmente, la información pro-

tes del poder y sin garantía alguna de estabilidad. Ello, por lo demás, ha continuado hasta el presente, demoliéndose sistemáticamente la autonomía judicial, sin que haya variado nada la creación en 2011 de unos tribunales de la llamada "Jurisdicción Disciplinaria Judicial" que quedó sujeta a la Asamblea Nacional, quien designa a los "jueces disciplinarios." [40]

Con todo ello, el derecho a la tutela judicial efectiva y al control judicial del poder del Estado ha quedado marginado, siendo imposible garantizar efectivamente equilibrio alguno entre el Estado y su Administración y los derechos de los ciudadanos–administrados; lo que se agrava con la configuración del Tribunal Supremo de Justicia de Venezuela como un poder altamente politizado[41], y lamentablemente sujeto a la voluntad del Presidente de la República, lo que en la práctica ha significado la eliminación de toda la autonomía del Poder Judicial.

Con todo esto, el Poder Judicial ha abandonado su función fundamental de servir de instrumento de control de las actividades de los otros órganos del Estado para asegurar su sometimiento a la ley, habiendo materialmente desaparecido el derecho ciudadano a la tutela judicial efectiva y al controlar del poder. En esa situación, por tanto, es difícil hablar siquiera de posibilidad alguna de equilibrio entre poderes y prerrogativas del Estado y derechos y garantías ciudadanas, lo que ha sido particularmente grave en el caso de los tribunales contencioso administrativos, precisamente por el hecho de que sus decisiones siempre implican enfrentar el poder, y particularmente, el Poder Ejecutivo. Si esta autonomía no está garantizada ni la independencia está blindada, el mejor sistema de justicia contencioso administrativa es letra muerta; y lamentablemente, esto es lo que también ha ocurrido en Venezuela en los últimos años durante el gobierno autoritario.

Ello ha afectado a la Jurisdicción Contencioso Administrativa, la cual en los últimos quince años dejó de ser un efectivo sistema para el control de las actuaciones administrativas, lo que se evidenció abiertamente desde 2003 con la lamentable destitución *in limine* de los magistrados de la Corte Primera de lo Contencioso Administrativa con ocasión de un proceso contencioso administrativo de nulidad y amparo iniciado el 17 de julio de 2003 a solicitud de la Federación Médica Venezolana en contra de los actos del Alcalde Metropolitano de Caracas, del Ministro de Salud y del Colegio de Médicos del Distrito Metropolitano de Caracas, por la contratación

---

porcionada por las distintas fuentes indica que más del 80% de los jueces venezolanos son "provisionales". *Informe sobre la Situación de los Derechos Humanos en Venezuela 2003, cit.* párr. 161

40   Véase Allan R. Brewer-Carías, "Sobre la ausencia de independencia y autonomía judicial en Venezuela, a los doce años de vigencia de la constitución de 1999 (O sobre la interminable transitoriedad que en fraude continuado a la voluntad popular y a las normas de la Constitución, ha impedido la vigencia de la garantía de la estabilidad de los jueces y el funcionamiento efectivo de una "jurisdicción disciplinaria judicial"), en *Independencia Judicial*, Colección Estado de Derecho, Tomo I, Academia de Ciencias Políticas y Sociales, Acceso a la Justicia org., Fundación de Estudios de Derecho Administrativo (Funeda), Universidad Metropolitana (Unimet), Caracas 2012, pp. 9-103.

41   Véase lo expresado por el magistrado Francisco Carrasqueño, en la apertura del año judicial en enero de 2008, al explicar que: "no es cierto que el ejercicio del poder político se limite al Legislativo, sino que tiene su continuación en los tribunales, en la misma medida que el Ejecutivo", dejando claro que la "aplicación del Derecho no es neutra y menos aun la actividad de los magistrados, porque según se dice en la doctrina, deben ser reflejo de la política, sin vulnerar la independencia de la actividad judicial". *V.* en *El Universal*, Caracas, 29–01–2008.

indiscriminada de médicos extranjeros no licenciados para ejercer la medicina en el país; todo en violación de la Ley de Ejercicio de la Medicina, para atender el desarrollo de un importante programa asistencial de salud en los barrios de Caracas.

La Federación Médica Venezolana consideró que la actuación pública era discriminatoria y violatoria de los derechos de los médicos venezolanos (derecho al trabajo, entre otros) a ejercer su profesión médica, al permitir a médicos extranjeros ejercerla sin cumplir con las condiciones establecidas en la Ley. Por ello la federación intentó la acción de nulidad y amparo, en representación de los derechos colectivos de los médicos venezolanos, solicitando su protección.[42] Un mes después, el 21 de agosto de 2003, la Corte Primera dictó una medida cautelar de amparo considerando que había suficientes elementos en el caso que hacían presumir la violación del derecho a la igualdad ante la ley de los médicos venezolanos, ordenando la suspensión temporal del programa de contratación de médicos cubanos, y ordenando al Colegio de Médicos del Distrito Metropolitano sustituir los médicos cubanos ya contratados sin licencia por médicos venezolanos o médicos extranjeros con licencia para ejercer la profesión en Venezuela.[43]

La respuesta gubernamental a esta decisión preliminar de carácter cautelar, que tocaba un programa social muy sensible para el gobierno, fue el anuncio público del Ministro de Salud, del Alcalde metropolitano y del propio Presidente de la República en el sentido de que la medida cautelar dictada no iba a ser acatada en forma alguna;[44] anuncios que fueron seguidos de varias decisiones gubernamentales:

La Sala Constitucional del Tribunal Supremo de Justicia, controlada por el Ejecutivo, adoptó la decisión de avocarse al caso decidido por la Corte Primera de lo Contencioso Administrativo, y usurpando competencias en la materia, declaró la nulidad del amparo cautelar decidido por esta. A ello siguió que un grupo de agentes de la policía política (DISIP) allanó la sede de la Corte Primera, después de detener a un escribiente o alguacil de la misma por motivos fútiles; el Presidente de la República, entre otras expresiones usadas, se refirió al Presidente de la Corte Primera como "un bandido;"[45] y unas semanas después, la Comisión Especial Judicial del Tribunal Supremo de Justicia, sin fundamento legal alguno, destituyó a los cinco magistrados de la Corte Primera, la cual fue intervenida.[46] A pesar de la protesta de los Colegios de Abogados del país e incluso de la Comisión Internacional de Juris-

---

42   Véase Claudia Nikken, "El caso "Barrio Adentro": La Corte Primera de lo Contencioso Administrativo ante la Sala Constitucional del Tribunal Supremo de Justicia o el avocamiento como medio de amparo de derechos e intereses colectivos y difusos," en *Revista de Derecho Público*, N° 93–96, Editorial Jurídica Venezolana, Caracas, 2003, pp. 5 ss.

43   Véase la decisión de 21 de agosto de 2003 en *Revista de Derecho Público*, N° 93–96, Editorial Jurídica Venezolana, Caracas, 2003, pp. 445 ss.

44   El Presidente de la República dijo: "*Váyanse con su decisión no sé para donde, la cumplirán ustedes en su casa si quieren…*", en el programa de TV *Aló Presidente*, N° 161, 24 de Agosto de 2003.

45   Discurso público, 20 septiembre de 2003.

46   Véase la información en *El Nacional*, Caracas, Noviembre 5, 2003, p. A2. En la misma página el Presidente destituido de la Corte Primera dijo: "*La justicia venezolana vive un momento tenebroso, pues el tribunal que constituye un último resquicio de esperanza ha sido clausurado*".

tas;[47] el hecho es que la Corte Primera permaneció cerrada sin jueces por más de diez meses,[48] tiempo durante el cual simplemente no hubo justicia contencioso administrativa en el país.

Esa fue la respuesta gubernamental a un amparo cautelar dictado por el juez contencioso administrativo competente respecto de un programa gubernamental sensible; respuesta que fue dada y ejecutada a través de órganos judiciales controlados políticamente. Ello, por supuesto, lamentablemente significó no sólo que los jueces que fueron luego nombrados para reemplazar a los destituidos comenzaron a entender cómo debían comportarse en el futuro frente al poder; sino que condujo a la abstención progresiva de todo control contencioso administrativa de las acciones gubernamentales. La Jurisdicción contencioso administrativa en Venezuela, de raigambre y jerarquía constitucional, simplemente hoy no existe en la práctica.

Y para que quedara claro, la demanda que intentaron los jueces contencioso administrativo destituidos ante la Comisión Interamericana de Derechos Humanos por violación a sus garantías constitucionales judiciales, a pesar de que fue decidida por la Corte Interamericana de Derechos Humanos, en 2008, condenando al Estado,[49] de nada sirvió sino para que la Sala Constitucional del Tribunal Supremo, en sentencia N° 1.939 de 12 de diciembre de 2008,[50] citando como precedente una sentencia del Tribunal Superior Militar del Perú de 2002, declarara la sentencia del tribunal internacional como "inejecutable" en Venezuela, solicitando al Ejecutivo que denunciara la Convención Americana de Derechos Humanos que supuestamente había usurpado los poderes del Tribunal Supremo, lo que el Ejecutivo cumplió cabalmente en 2011.

Este caso emblemático, por supuesto, contrasta con las previsiones de la Constitución de 1999, en la cual se encuentra una de las declaraciones de derechos más completas de América Latina, y sobre su protección por medio de la acción de amparo, así como previsiones expresas sobre la Jurisdicción Constitucional y la Jurisdicción Contencioso Administrativa difícilmente contenidas con tanto detalle en otros textos constitucionales.[51] Ello, por otra parte, lo que muestra es que para que exista control de la actuación del Estado no bastan declaraciones formales en la Constitución, sino que es indispensable que el Poder Judicial sea autónomo e independiente, y esté fuera del alcance del Poder Ejecutivo. Al contrario, cuando el Po-

---

47   Véase en *El Nacional*, Caracas, Octubre 12, 2003, p. A–5; y *El Nacional*, Caracas, Noviembre 18, 2004, p. A–6.

48   Véase en *El Nacional*, Caracas, Octubre 24, 2003, p. A–2; y *El Nacional*, Caracas, Julio 16, 2004, p. A–6.

49   Véase sentencia de la Corte Interamericana de 5 de agosto de 2008, Caso *Apitz Barbera y otros ("Corte Primera de lo Contencioso Administrativo") vs. Venezuela*, Excepción Preliminar, Fondo, Reparaciones y Costas, Serie C N° 182, en www.corteidh.or.cr.

50   Véase sentencia de la Sala Constitucional, sentencia N° 1.939 de 18 de diciembre de 2008 (Caso *Abogados Gustavo Álvarez Arias y otros*), en http://www.tsj.gov.ve/decisiones/scon/Diciembre/1939-181208-2008-08-1572.html.

51   Véase Allan R. Brewer-Carías, "Sobre la justicia constitucional y la justicia contencioso administrativo. A 35 años del inicio de la configuración de los procesos y procedimientos constitucionales y contencioso administrativos (1976-2011)," en *El contencioso administrativo y los procesos constitucionales* (Directores Allan R. Brewer Carías y Víctor Rafael Hernández Mendible), Colección Estudios Jurídicos N° 92, Editorial Jurídica Venezolana, Caracas, 2011, pp. 19-74.

der Judicial está controlado por el Poder Ejecutivo, como lo muestra el caso citado, las declaraciones constitucionales de derechos se convierten en letra muerta, y el derecho administrativo no puede servir para garantizar ningún equilibrio entre poderes del Estado y derechos ciudadanos, convirtiéndose solo en un instrumento más del autoritarismo.

XI

De todo lo anterior resulta, por tanto, que para que exista democracia como régimen político en un Estado constitucional y democrático de derecho, y para que exista un derecho administrativo que garantice el equilibrio antes referido, no son suficientes las declaraciones contenidas en los textos constitucionales que, por ejemplo, como es el caso de Venezuela, hablen y regulan el derecho al sufragio y a la participación política; la división o separación horizontal del Poder Público, y la distribución vertical o territorial del poder público, de manera que los diversos poderes del Estado puedan limitarse mutuamente; así como tampoco bastan las declaraciones que se refieran a la posibilidad de los ciudadanos de controlar el poder del Estado, mediante elecciones libres y justas que garanticen la alternabilidad republicana; mediante un sistema de partidos que permita el libre juego del pluralismo democrático; mediante la libre manifestación y expresión del pensamiento y de la información que movilice la opinión pública; o mediante el ejercicio de recursos judiciales ante jueces independientes que permitan asegurar la vigencia de los derechos humanos y el sometimiento del Estado al derecho. Tampoco bastan las declaraciones constitucionales sobre la "democracia participativa y protagónica" o la descentralización del Estado; así como tampoco la declaración extensa de derechos humanos. Tampoco es suficiente que se haya producido un completo proceso de constitucionalización del derecho administrativo, insertando en la Constitución todos sus principios más esenciales.

Además de todas esas declaraciones, es necesaria que haya un gobierno democrático y que la práctica política democrática asegure efectivamente la posibilidad de controlar el poder, como única forma de garantizar la vigencia del Estado de derecho, y el ejercicio real de los derechos humanos; y que el derecho administrativo pueda consolidarse como un régimen jurídico de la Administración que disponga el equilibrio entre los poderes del Estado y los derechos de los administrados.

Lamentablemente, en Venezuela, después de las cuatro décadas de práctica democrática que vivió el país entre 1959 y 1999, durante estos últimos tres lustros, a partir de 1999 hasta la fecha, en fraude continuo a la Constitución cometido por el Legislador y por el Tribunal Supremo de Justicia, guiados por el Poder Ejecutivo, a pesar de las excelentes normas constitucionales que están insertas en el Texto fundamental, y del proceso de constitucionalización del derecho administrativo, lo que se ha operado ha sido proceso de desmantelamiento de la democracia y de estructuración de un Estado autoritario en contra de las mismas,[52] que ha aniquilado toda

---

52   Véase Allan R. Brewer-Carías, "La demolición del Estado de derecho y la destrucción de la democracia en Venezuela (1999-2009)," en José Reynoso Núñez y Herminio Sánchez de la Barquera y Arroyo (Coordinadores), *La democracia en su contexto. Estudios en homenaje a Dieter Nohlen en su septuagésimo aniversario,* Instituto de Investigaciones Jurídicas, Universidad Nacional Autónoma de México, México 2009, pp. 477-517.

posibilidad real de control del ejercicio del poder y, en definitiva, el derecho mismo de los ciudadanos a la democracia. Y con ello, toda posibilidad de que el derecho administrativo sea ese derecho que asegure el equilibrio entre los poderes del Estado y los derechos ciudadanos que el Estado democrático de derecho exige, convirtiéndose en un derecho administrativo al servicio exclusivo de la Administración y de los funcionarios, donde no hay campo para reclamo o control, sino sólo para el acatamiento sin discusión.

En ese marco, por tanto, de nada vale el proceso de constitucionalización del derecho administrativo, que en la práctica es letra muerta, todo lo cual nos evidencia precisamente, la importancia del modelo político en la conformación de nuestra disciplina.

El problema, sin embargo, está en que los estudiosos de la materia, dado que a veces la práctica política del gobierno conforma un modelo político al margen de la Constitución, como un Estado autoritario o más aún totalitario; como ello constituye sin duda una anomalía respecto de sus previsiones formales del texto constitucional, la misma, precisamente por ser tal, tiende a ser marginada, para no decir ignorada, y con ello, igualmente no siempre se estudian las repercusiones que la anomalía estatal y política tiene sobre el derecho administrativo. Quizás ello incluso conduzca en el futuro, al desarrollo de alguna nueva sub rama del derecho administrativo para estudiar precisamente su patología.

SEGUNDA PARTE

EL DESMANTELAMIENTO DE LA DEMOCRACIA. EL EXPERIMENTO AUTORITARIO DE CHÁVEZ

DISMANTLING DEMOCRACY. THE CHÁVEZ AUTHORITARIAN EXPERIMENT

Esta Segunda parte de este Tomo XV de la Colección *Tratado de Dderecho Constitucional*, se conforma con el texto del libro: *Dismantling Democracy. The Chávez Authoritarian Experiment*, publicado por Cambridge University Press, New York, 2010. El libro estuvo precedido de la siguiente Nota del editor:

Since the election of Hugo Chávez Frías as president of the Republic of Venezuela in December 1998, and during the past decade, the country formerly envied for its democratic accomplishments over the second half of the twentieth century has suffered a tragic setback regarding democratic standards, suffering a continuous, persistent, and deliberate process of demolishing institutions and destroying democracy, which had never before experienced in the constitutional history of the country. The 1999 Constitution, although considered by some of its drafters as one of the best constitutional texts in contemporary Latin America, has been constantly violated by all branches of government, and more seriously by the Supreme Tribunal of Justice and its Constitutional Chamber. The chamber, completely controlled by the executive, has molded and accepted as legitimate all the constitutional violations that have occurred. Worse, the process has been conducted by defrauding the Constitution and the representative democratic regime in the name of a "participatory democracy" designed to be controlled by the central government. The result has been the complete lack of all essential elements of democracy, as defined by the 2001 Inter-American Democratic Charter: namely, access to power and its exercise subject to the rule of law; periodic, free, and fair elections based on the universal secret vote as an expression of the sovereignty of the people; a plural regime of political parties and organizations; separation and independence of branches of government; and respect for human rights and fundamental freedoms.

This book covers the Chávez Authoritarian Experiment on dismantling of democracy, which has influenced other countries as well, like Ecuador, Bolivia, and Honduras. It is based on a series of essays written as the facts were occurring during Venezuela's decade of authoritarian government (1999–2009).

Brewer-Carías has been Professor at the Central University of Venezuela since 1963. He also has been Simón Bolívar Professor at the Law Faculty of Cambridge University (1985–86), where he was Fellow of Trinity College; at the University of Paris II (1990); and at Columbia University, where he has been Visiting Scholar and Adjunct Professor of Law (2002–4, and 2006–7). He is Vice President of the International Academy of Comparative Law, and is a member of the Venezuelan National Academy of Political and Social Sciences, where he served as President (1997–99); he was also Senator for the Federal District, Minister for Decentralization, and an elected member of the 1999 National Constituent Assembly.

El libro, además, estuvo precedido de mi siguiente "Nota del Autor":

This book deals with the dismantling of Venezuelan democracy from within that the country's authoritarian government has accomplished during the past decade using some democratic tools defrauding the Constitution.[53] This process began after the election of Hugo Chávez Frías as president of the Republic of Venezuela in December 1998, the result of which was the tragic setback to democratic institutions and standards. Venezuela had been one of the most admired Latin American countries because of its stable democracy, which had consolidated during the second half of the twentieth century. During the past decade, the country has experienced a continuous, persistent, and deliberate demolishing of institutions and destruction of democracy, which has never before occurred in the constitutional history of the country.

The first step to subvert democratic principles and values materialized in 1999, with the forced convening of a constituent assembly –not established in the Constitution as a valid means for constitutional reform– through a consultative referendum to impose the "will of the people" over the Constitution itself (peoples' sovereignty over constitutional supremacy). The result was the interference and takeover of all recently elected branches of government by the newly elected Constituent Assembly, completely controlled by the president of the republic. For the election of the Assembly, an electoral system was adopted without any sort of agreements, the Constitution was sanctioned without any sort of consensus, and conditions were established for the imposition of an authoritarian and centralized government, which has since eliminated any checks and balances and, consequently, the rule of law.

The remote antecedent of the use of the constituent assembly procedure, not established in the constitution, to draft a new constitution without the interruption of the constitutional rule can be found in Colombia, during the transition between the governments of President Virgilio Barco and President César Gaviria in 1990, after the Supreme Court of Justice expressly accepted the constitutionality of the process. The Constituent Assembly was elected with a pluralistic composition, after the political actors had agreed on the electoral

---

53   See, in general, Allan R. Brewer-Carías, "La demolición del Estado de derecho y la destrucción de la democracia en Venezuela (1999-2009)," in *La democracia en su contexto. Estudios en homenaje a Dieter Nohlen en su septuagésimo aniversario*, coord. José Reynoso Núñez and Herminio Sánchez de la Barquera y Arroyo, Instituto de Investigaciones Jurídicas, Universidad Nacional Autónoma de México, Mexico City 2009, pp. 477-517

system. The assembly drafted the 1991 Constitution, also based on negotiations and consensus, thus contributing to the further development of democratic institutions in the country.

However, it was after the 1999 experience in Venezuela that a new formula was developed in which the general bylaws for the election of a Constituent Assembly, also not established in the 1961 Constitution as a constitutional review method, resulted not from consensus and agreements among political actors but from those who took the initiative to convene the referendum. The result in this case was the establishment and development not of a democratic government but of a framework for developing an authoritarian government through democratic tools. In Venezuela, a popular consultation or consultative referendum was convened to subvert the Constitution itself, as President Chávez unilaterally defined the assembly in a way that impeded the configuration of a plural political body. In 2007, Ecuador's president Rafael Correa also implemented this "formula" to depart from the Constitution then in force, and in 2009, Honduran President Manuel Zelaya tried to implement it, but the Supreme Court of Justice of Honduras declared it unconstitutional.[54] Unfortunately, in Honduras, instead of waiting for the results of the judicial process initiated against the president, indicted for violating the Constitution, the military eventually expelled him unconstitutionally from the country. His expulsion led to an international uproar from the less democratic leaders of Latin America, including Hugo Chávez and Raúl Castro, supposedly to defend democracy and to impose the 2001 Inter-American Democratic Charter.[55]

In Venezuela, contrary to the Colombia in 1991 and Honduras in 2009 cases, the Supreme Court of Justice, though requested to issue a decision on the interpretation of the constitutionality of the convening of the assembly, refused to rule in a clear way and instead issued an ambiguous decision that ultimately allowed the president to impose his own rules for the convening of the Constituent Assembly. In 1999, the executive unilaterally designed a constituent process that not only sanctioned a new Constitution in the name of the popular will but also proceeded with an aggressive takeover of the legislative and judicial branches.

Although many of its drafters consider it among the best constitutional texts in contemporary Latin America, to allow the intended institutional destruction, the 1999 Constitution has also been constantly violated under the watch of its own product, the Supreme Tribunal of Justice. The tribunal, particularly its Constitutional Chamber, is completely controlled by the government, and it has molded and accepted as legitimate all the subsequent constitutional violations.

Now in Venezuela there is a complete lack of the essential elements of democracy as defined by the 2001 Inter-American Democratic Charter: access to

---

54   The formula has been referred to as the Chávez franchise or the Chávez brand because of his ostensible involvement in the political processes of the countries that have previously applied it, such as Ecuador. See, e.g., "The Wages of Chavismo" (Opinion), *Wall Street Journal*, July 1, 2009, p. A12.

55   See, e.g., Moisés Naim, "Golpe en Honduras: Idiotas contra hipócritas," *El Pais*, Madrid July 5, 2009.

power and its exercise subject to the rule of law, the performing of periodic free and fair elections based on universal and secret vote as an expression of the sovereignty of the people, the plural regime of political parties and organizations, the separation and independence of all branches of government, and respect for human rights and fundamental freedoms.

I have been writing on the Venezuelan constitution-making process and its consequences over the past decade, since the process began in 1998, and have produced a series of essays that study the subversion of democracy from within and the violation of the Constitution.[56] This book is the result of those essays, mainly written from New York, where I have lived, able to continue my academic activities, since September 2005. My political opposition to Chávez's authoritarian government and the threats I received to my freedom unfortunately forced me to leave Venezuela in 2005.[57] I had begun such opposition in 1998, when Chávez became presidential candidate in the elections of that year after having led in 1992 a failed military coup against the democratic government. As president of the National Academy of Political and Social Sciences, I convened all the presidential candidates to explain their political projects for the state and the political system before the academy. When I introduced Chávez at an academy session on August 15, 1998, I stressed his "nondemocratic" way of entering the Venezuelan political arena and my opposition to his main electoral proposal of "convening the Constitutional Assembly without giving it constitutional basis by reforming the Constitution."[58] My opposition to

---

56   The text of all my academic works and papers and almost all my published books and articles can be downloaded from my website: http://allanbrewercarias.com/.

57   I was unjustly accused of "conspiring to change violently the Constitution" because I had given a legal opinion, as a lawyer, in the midst of the political crisis originated by Chávez's resignation on Apr. 11, 2002. I gave that opinion at the request of the head of the brief provisional government, established after such resignation was publicly announced. On those facts, see Allan R. Brewer-Carías, *La crisis de la democracia venezolana: La Carta Democrática Interamericana y los sucesos de abril de 2002*, Ediciones El Nacional, Caracas 2002 (full text available at http://allanbrewercarias.com/Content.aspx?id=449725d9-f1cb-474b-8ab2-41efb849fea5). Although my legal opinion defended the democratic principle and was contrary to what the provisional government eventually announced in its constitutive decree, the government immediately reacted against me and publicly condemned me, without trial, and accused me of having written the decree, which I did not. All this was in violation of my constitutional guarantees, particularly my right to defense and the presumption of innocence, and based on interested, malicious journalists' opinions. Thus, the government, using the public prosecutor as a tool for political persecution, as well as newspaper clippings as the sole evidence, accused me in a process that allowed the head of the Prosecutor General's Office to violate my rights. See the letter I sent to the prosecutor general on the eve of my departure from Venezuela, on Sept. 28, 2005, in Allan R. Brewer-Carías, *En mi propia defensa*, Editorial Jurídica Venezolana, Caracas 2006, 573-90 (full text available at http://allanbrewercarias.com/Content.aspx?id=449725d9-f1cb-474b-8ab2-41efb849fea5). I could not have possibly expected a fair trial from the Venezuelan Judiciary. Consequently, in Jan. 2007, I filed a complaint against the Venezuelan State before the Inter-American Commission on Human Rights based on the violation of my due process, defense, presumption of innocence, and free expression rights, as established in the American Convention on Human Rights. The Commission admitted my petition in Sept. 2009 (Case: 12.724: *Inter-American Commission on Human Rights, Allan Brewer Carías/Venezuela*). Available at http://www.cidh.oas.org/annualrep/2009eng/Venezuela84.07eng.htm.

58   It was my first and last personal encounter with Chávez. See my introduction to Allan R. Brewer-Carías, coord., *Los candidatos presidenciales ante la Academia: Ciclo de exposiciones 1998*, Academia de Ciencias Políticas y Sociales, Caracas 1998, pp. 23, 38, 92, 95, 137, 138, 320. See my foreword to the

that political project seeking the global take over of State power continued after his election as president, when in 1999 I personally went before the former Supreme Court of Justice to challenge his decree on the Constituent Assembly on the grounds of its unconstitutionality. After contributing to force the correction of the decree through judicial decisions, my opposition continued throughout the 1999 National Constituent Assembly, to which I was elected as an independent candidate. Myself and three other distinguished Venezuelan politicians and thinkers formed the very tiny but substantive minority opposition group of the assembly. I continued my opposition during the discussions on the draft 1999 Constitution because of the authoritarian trends it set forth to concentrate and centralize state powers. Since the approval of the Constitution, I have continued to denounce in books, essays, and speeches all the successive antidemocratic, centralistic, and militaristic decisions and measures taken by the government. This book and the essays that inspired it are part of that effort.

New York has been a formidable place to live, and being together with my wife, Beatriz, has helped us overcome the sadness of not having the always very important direct contact with our family and friends. Beatriz, as always during the almost five decades we have been married, with all her generous love, has helped me in an unimaginable way in allowing me to continue with my writings. As always, I am very grateful to her for all her love, understanding, support, and loyalty.

Since our arrival in New York, good friends gave us companionship, helping us continues with our daily lives; and, most important, after having been in the academic life for fifty years, I immediately received the hospitality of Columbia University. As adjunct professor of law at the Columbia Law School, I have been able to continue teaching, giving over various semesters the course Judicial Protection of Human Rights in Latin America: A Comparative Constitutional Law Study of the Latin American Injunction for the Protection of Constitutional Rights (*Amparo* Proceeding). The text I wrote for the course was published in 2009.[59]

Of course, also from an academic point of view, New York has been an extraordinary launching pad that has allowed me to get in touch with many other universities in the United States and to continue, increasingly, my already well-established, long relations with universities and law professors in Europe and Latin America. This has allowed me to continue with my work and writings.

---

same book: "A modo de presentación: Reflexiones sobre la crisis del sistema político, sus salidas democráticas y la convocatoria a una constituyente," in *id.*, pp. 9-66.

59   See Allan R. Brewer-Carías, *Constitutional Protection of Human Rights in Latin America: A Comparative Study of the Amparo Proceeding*, Cambridge University Press, New York 2009. The Appendix to the course, containing the text of all the *amparo* laws in force in Latin America, was also published in Mexico as *Leyes de amparo de America Latina*, 2 vols., Instituto de Administración Pública de Jalisco y sus Municipios, Instituto de Administración Pública del Estado de México, Poder Judicial del Estado de México, Academia de Derecho Constitucional de la Confederación de Colegios y Asociaciones de Abogados de México, Guadalajara 2009.

The truth is that if somebody in Venezuela at any moment considered that forcing me to leave the country would annihilate my academic work and life and press me to renounce my ideals and cease to diffuse them, they have noisily failed. It is enough to visit my Web site (http://www.allanbrewercarias.com) to appreciate the use I have made of my time in favor of freedom, of the rule of law and of democratic principles. In the end, they have allowed me to devote more time to continue analyzing the chaotic situation of Venezuela's constitutional and legal system that has resulted from the disorderly implementation of a supposedly "Bolivarian revolution," which, as Chávez confessed himself in January 2010, is no more than the phantasmagoric resurrection of the historically failed "Marxist revolution," but led by a president who has never even read Marx's writings.[60]

Nevertheless, on April 2010, the governmental United Socialist Party of Venezuela of which he presides, in its First Extraordinary Congress adopted a "Declaration of Principles" in which it officially declared itself as a "Marxist," "Anti-imperialist" and "Ant-capitalist" party. According to the same document, the party's actions are to be based on the "scientific socialism" and on the "inputs of Marxism as a philosophy of praxis," in order to substitute the "Capitalist Bourgeois State" by a "Socialist State" based on the Popular Power and the socialization of the means of production.[61]

With these declarations it can be said that, finally, the so called "Bolivarian Revolution" has been unveiled; a revolution for which nobody in Venezuela has voted except for its rejection in the December 2, 2007 referendum, in which the President's proposals for constitutional reforms in order to establish a Socialist, Centralized, Police and Militaristic state received a negative popular response.[62]

New York, August 4, 2010

---

60   In his annual speech before the National Assembly on Jan. 15, 2010, in which Chávez declared to have "assumed Marxism," he also confessed that he had never read Marx's works. See María Lilibeth Da Corte, "Por primera vez asumo el marxismo," in *El Universal*, Caracas Jan. 16, 2010, http://www.eluniversal.com/2010/01/16/pol_art_por-primera-vez-asu_1726209.shtml.

61   See "Declaración de Principios, I Congreso Extraordinario del Partido Socialista Unido de Venezuela," Apr. 23, 2010, at http://psuv.org.ve/files/tcdocumentos/Declaracion-de-principios-PSUV.pdf

62   See on the constitutional reforms proposals, Allan R. Brewer-Carías, *Hacia la consolidación de un Estado socialista, centralizado, policial y militarista. Comentarios sobre el sentido y alcance de las propuestas de reforma constitucional 2007*, Editorial Jurídica Venezolana, Caracas 2007; *La reforma constitucional de 2007 (Comentarios al proyecto inconstitucionalmente sancionado por la Asamblea Nacional el 2 de noviembre de 2007)*, Editorial Jurídica Venezolana, Caracas 2007.

INTRODUCTION

DEFRAUDING DEMOCRACY THROUGH NONCONSENSUAL CONSTITUENT ASSEMBLIES

I

Democracy is much more than voting. It is a political regime in which, in addition to the holding of periodic, free, and fair elections based on secret balloting and universal suffrage as an expression of the sovereignty of the people, the following other essential elements are all ensured: respect for human rights and fundamental freedoms, access to and exercise of power in accordance with the rule of law, a pluralistic system of political parties and organizations, and separation of powers and independence of the branches of government.

This is what is set forth in Article 3 of the Inter-American Democratic Charter (*Carta Democrática Interamericana*), which members of the Organization of American States signed in Lima, Peru, on September 11, 2001 (the same day of the terrorist attacks in the United States). After so many antidemocratic and militarist regimes that have existed in Latin American history, and so many authoritarian regimes disguised as democratic that still have been developed there, adoption of a continental doctrine about democracy was an imperious necessity. That is why, in addition to the foregoing essential elements, Article 4 of the same charter included the following essential components of the exercise of democracy: transparency in government activities, probity, responsible public administration on the part of governments, respect for social rights, freedom of expression and of the press, constitutional subordination of all state institutions to the legally constituted civilian authority, and respect for the rule of law by all institutions and sectors of society.

For the purpose of adopting this charter, the General Assembly of the Organization of American States assumed that representative democracy is indispensable for the stability, peace, and development of the region, its purposes being to promote and consolidate representative democracy with due respect for the principle of nonintervention; and considering that solidarity among and cooperation between American states requires that the political organization of those states be based on the effective exercise of representative democracy; and that democracy as well as economic growth and social development based on justice and equity are interdependent and mutually reinforcing. The General Assembly furthermore recognized the contributions of the organization and other regional and subregional mechanisms to the promotion and consolidation of democracy in the Americas, as well as the facts that a safe environment is essential to the integral development of the human being, which contributes to democracy and political stability; that the right of workers to associate themselves freely for the defense and promotion of their interests is fundamental for the fulfillment of democratic ideas; and that all the rights and obligations of member states under the organization's charter represent the foundation on which democratic principles in the Western Hemisphere are built.

Without doubt, the Inter-American Democratic Charter is the most important international instrument adopted in the contemporary world regarding democracy and democratic principles.[63] Article 1 recognizes and declares that the peoples of the Americas have a "right to democracy" and that their governments have an obligation to promote and defend that democracy, which is essential for the social, political, and economic development of the peoples of the Americas.[64]

Article 2 of the same charter states that the effective exercise of representative democracy is the basis for the rule of law and for the constitutional regimes of countries, which must be strengthened and deepened by the permanent, ethical, and responsible participation of the citizenry within a legal framework that conforms to a respective constitutional order. For such purposes, Article 5 of the charter considers that the strengthening of political parties and other political organizations is a priority for democracy; Article 6 declares that it is the right and responsibility of all citizens to participate in decisions relating to their own development because doing so is a necessary condition for the full and effective exercise of democracy; and Article 7 of the charter proclaims that democracy is indispensable for the effective exercise of fundamental freedoms and human rights in their universality, indivisibility, and interdependence, which is embodied in the respective constitutions of states and in inter-American and international human rights instruments.

Consequently, democracy is not only a matter of voting and elections; it is a political system in which elections must be held with a pluralistic system of political parties, the principles of the rule of law are ensured, the separation of powers is guaranteed, and human rights and freedoms are protected. In this context, any violation of a country's constitution is undemocratic, and any constitution-making process that contravenes or defrauds[65] an existing constitution is contrary to democracy.

II

Undemocratic constitution making is precisely what occurred in Venezuela in 1999. That year began the dismantling of democracy that Venezuela has suffered, with the convening of an illegitimate, unconstitutional constituent assembly for constitutional review; the imposition of new election rules adopted in a nonconsensual way and without the participation of the country's political forces; and the takeover of all branches of government by an exclusionist group aiming to destroy its opponents and impose its own political project.[66] In 2009, attempts aimed to impose

---

63   The Member States of the African Union in its Eight Ordinary Assembly held in Addis Abeba, Ethiopia, on Jan. 30, 2007, have also signed the "African Charter on Democracy, Elections and Governance." Available at http://www.un.org/democracyfund/Docs/AfricanCharterDemocracy.pdf.

64   See Asdrúbal Aguiar, *El derecho a la democracia: La democracia en el derecho y la jurisprudencia interamericanos: La libertad de expresión, piedra angular de la democracia*, Editorial Jurídica Venezolana, Caracas 2008. See also my foreword to that book "Sobre el derecho a la democracia y el control del poder" at pp. 17-37.

65   I have used the word *defraud* (to cause injury or loss by deceit) in general, as it is used in civil law systems, referred not only to persons but also to institutions, in the sense that you can defraud the Constitution, you can defraud a provision of a statute, and you can defraud democracy itself.

66   See, in general, Allan R. Brewer-Carías, "Constitution Making Process in Defraudation of the Constitution and Authoritarian Government in Defraudation of Democracy: The Recent Venezuelan Experien-

this method of assaulting power by using democratic tools but defrauding the Constitution, so successfully employed in Venezuela to destroy its democracy, were made
in Honduras.

In effect, in the first half of 2009, inspired by the constitutional formula that President Hugo Chávez had used in Venezuela a decade earlier (in 1999), Honduras's
President Manuel Zelaya decided to convene a consultative referendum to clear the
way for the convening of the National Constituent Assembly, which the Honduran
Constitution did not include as a valid way to reform the Constitution. The purpose
of such a proposal, which was conceived without any political consensus or agreements between political parties and political actors of the country, was to reshape
Honduras's constitutional principles, including the change of traditionally solid provisions, like the one establishing the absolute prohibition on presidential reelection.

The attorney general of the republic challenged Zelaya's attempt before the
courts, requesting judicial review of the administrative action. The courts did issue
preliminary judicial measures to suspend the presidential acts that had been challenged on grounds of unconstitutionality. The president ignored the judicial decisions
and publicly insisted on achieving his proposal through de facto means. After his
prosecution before the Supreme Court of Justice for contempt of court and for violating express provisions of the Constitution,[67] Zelaya's detention was ordered. In
Honduras, the president's actions provoked the functioning of the country's democratic checks-and-balances system (the Supreme Electoral Tribunal, the Supreme
Court, the attorney general, the human rights commissioner, and the Congress declared the president's intentions unlawful); unfortunately, the Supreme Court's decision was not enforced as ordered. Instead, the same military in charge of detaining
the president unconstitutionally expelled him from the country. With that action
began the well-known international political crisis in which even the general assemblies of the United Nations and the Organization of American States intervened.
Ironically, and suddenly, the crisis briefly converted the less democratic heads of
state of Latin America, like Hugo Chávez and Raúl Castro, into political leaders
defending democratic principles. That muddled many democratic leaders of the
world in a discussion to qualify the events in Honduras as a coup d'état and resulted
in the absurd dilemma of whether to impose international sanctions on a country in

---

ce," in *Lateinamerika Analysen* 19, German Institute of Global and Area Studies, Hamburg 2008, 119-
42; and "The 1999 Venezuelan Constitution-Making Process as an Instrument for Forming the Development of an Authoritarian Political Regime," in Laurel E. Miller, editor, *Framing the State in Times of
Transition: Case Studies in Constitution Making*, United States Institute of Peace, Washington 2010,
pp. 505-532.

67   In Honduras, the Constitution expressly prohibits any public official, including the president of the
republic, from proposing reforms to the Constitution to alter the principle of alternate government and to
change the prohibition established for presidential reelection, which is considered an unchangeable, solid principle. The Constitution even establishes that any public officials who propose such reforms will
immediately cease their public functions (art. 239). See, in general, Octavio Rubén Sánchez Barrientos,
*Los extravagantes y el Caudillo que se sacó a sí mismo de la Presidencia. Un ensayo sobre la historia
del Artículo 239 de la Constitución de la República de Honduras y del Principio de Alternabilidad en
el Ejercicio de la Presidencia de la República* (forthcoming book), Tegucigalpa, June 2010.

which the democratic institutions had worked – at least previous to the president's expulsion.[68]

The formula of forcing the convening of a constituent assembly not established in the Constitution by unilaterally imposing its bylaws without any consensual process or political agreement had been used a decade earlier, in 1999, in Venezuela. But in Venezuela, the Supreme Court, although requested to decide on the matter, abstained from adopting a clear interpretative decision on the constitutionality of such a proposal, thereby allowing the president to impose his rules for the election of the assembly. Something similar happened in Ecuador in 2007, where the president of the republic also convened a constituent assembly not established in the constitution by submitting to a popular referendum the rules for electing a constituent assembly, without any previous political agreement or consensual process. Nonetheless, in that case, no judicial decision on the matter was adopted by the Constitutional Tribunal and the constitution making continued without previous judicial review. All these cases and experiences are a contrast to the initial precedent developed in Colombia in 1991, where the convening of a constituent assembly not established by the Constitution was made only after political parties and political actors reached agreements to hold a consultative referendum on the matter, which only took place once the Supreme Court of Justice had ruled on the constitutionality of the procedure.

III

In any case, the convening of constituent assemblies for the purpose of reforming constitutions is not exceptional in Latin America. Latin American countries have a long history of constitution making by means of constituent assemblies, which have been convened and elected many times without indications for doing so in a constitution. Historically, such conventions have generally occurred after a de facto rupture of the legal constitutional order, produced by a coup d'état, a revolution, or a civil war. In such cases, those who have come to power have always convened the constituent assemblies, and according to the rules they unilaterally impose. Subsequently, a popular vote and the new leadership legitimized the newly sanctioned constitution. In such matters, Latin American countries have gained recognized expertise during their two hundred years of political turmoil.

Because of the rupture of the constitutional order, the elected constituent assemblies, according to the rules designed by the political winners, have usually exercised unlimited constitution-making power and have tried to represent the will of the people. However, they have not subjected themselves to provisions of the previous constitution, except regarding some solid or rocklike principles or traditionally preserved clauses imposed by the republican form of government.

---

68   See Allan R. Brewer-Carías, "Reforma constitucional, asamblea nacional constituyente y control judicial contencioso administrativo: El caso de Honduras (2009) y el precedente venezolano (1999)," *Revista Mexicana Statum Rei Romanae de Derecho Administrativo: Homenaje de Nuevo León a Jorge Fernández Ruiz,* No. 3, Asociación Mexicana de Derecho Administrativo, Facultad de Derecho y Criminología de la Universidad Autónoma de Nuevo León, Monterrey, México, 2009, pp. 11-77; *Reforma constitucional, asamblea constituyente, y control judicial: Honduras (2009), Ecuador (2007) y Venezuela (1999),* Universidad Externado de Colombia, Bogotá 2009.

It is in contrast with this traditional trend that, in the past decades, a new constitution-making process began to take shape in Latin America. This has occurred by means of electing unconstitutional constituent assemblies, particularly when there has been no previous rupture of the constitutional order. As a result, in many cases, the convening of a constituent assembly has occurred after issuing of a judicial interpretation of the constitution, which allows for the procedure to be applied without rupturing the constitutional order and through democratic elections, such that a plural entity can be figured to reshape the constitutional order. As already mentioned, this was the case in Colombia in 1991, where the rules and conditions for the election of the Constituent Assembly resulted from political agreements and consensus. In contrast, this was not the case in Venezuela in 1999, where the Supreme Court abstained from a clear and unambiguous decision on the constitutionality of the procedure, thereby allowing the president of the republic to impose his own rules and conditions for electing the Constituent Assembly. That process resulted in the election of a nonplural constituent assembly completely dominated by the president's followers. The assembly, far from just writing a new constitution, was the main tool of the newly elected president's assault on all branches of government to gain control, which violated the 1961 Constitution, whose supposed judicial interpretation helped to create the Assembly.[69] Consequently, the elected Constituent Assembly technically was a coup d'état,[70] unfortunately with the consent and complicity of the former Supreme Court of Justice. As always happens in cases of illegitimate institutional complicity, the Supreme Court was inexorably the first victim of the authoritarian government, which it helped to grab power. Just a few months later, that Supreme Court was eliminated from the institutional scene.[71] As a result, Venezuela has an authoritarian government created not by the classic Latin American military coup d'état but rather by a systematic process of destroying from within the state all the basic principles of democracy, its institutions, and the Constitution.

IV

The 1999 Constituent Assembly was, then, the instrument the president used to dissolve and interfere in all branches of government (particularly the judiciary) and to dismiss all public officials who had been elected just a few months earlier in November 1998: namely, the representatives to the national Congress, the state legislative assemblies, and the municipal councils, as well as the state governors and muni-

---

69   See Allan R. Brewer-Carías, *Debate constituyente (Aportes a la Asamblea Nacional Constituyente)*, Fundación de Derecho Público–Editorial Jurídica Venezolana, Caracas 1999, 1 (Aug. 8–Sept. 8), pp.17-122.

70   A coup d'état occurs, as affirmed by Diego Valadés, "when an elected constitutional organ ignores the Constitution." See Diego Valadés, *Constitución y democracia*, UNAM, México 2000, p. 35; and Allan R. Brewer-Carías, *Golpe de estado y proceso constituyente en Venezuela*, Universidad Nacional Autónoma de México, Mexico City 2002, pp. 194-195.

71   On Dec. 1999, after the popular approval of the new Constitution, the Constituent Assembly dismissed the members of the Supreme Court of Justice, created the Supreme Tribunal of Justice and appointed its members. See the study about the effects of the Dec. 1999 Transitory Regime established by the Constituent Assembly after the approval, by popular referendum, of the Constitution of 1999, in Allan R. Brewer-Carías, *La Constitución de 1999*, Editorial Arte, Caracas 2000; and *La Constitución de 1999: Derecho constitucional venezolano*, Editorial Jurídica Venezolana, Caracas 2004, Vol. 1, pp.150 ff.

cipal mayors. The sole exception to this interference was the president of the republic itself, precisely the author of the constitutional fraud, whose tenure was not affected. In addition, the Constituent Assembly interfered in all other branches of government, particularly in the judiciary, whose autonomy and independence was progressively and systematically demolished.[72] The result was tight executive control over the judiciary, particularly regarding the newly appointed Supreme Tribunal of Justice, whose Constitutional Chamber has been the most ominous instrument for consolidating authoritarianism in the country.[73]

The new constitution-making process established in Venezuela in 1999 can be characterized as a defrauding of the Constitution, which was deliberately used and interpreted without any consensus of the interested political parties and actors to elect a body with the final purpose of violating that same Constitution whose ambiguous judicial interpretation birthed the assembly. This assembly, which the president completely controlled, set forth the foundations for the enthroning of an authoritarian regime that has led the process of demolishing institutions in order to defraud democracy. That is, despite the relatively free but manipulated elections held for the purpose of allowing the president's supporters complete control of the assembly, the process began the destruction of democracy and the consolidation of an authoritarian government.

After defrauding the Constitution to gain power, once it controlled all the state branches of government, the government began another defrauding process, this time of democracy. It used processes of representative democracy to progressively eliminate the same and substitute it by a supposed "participative democracy" based on nonelected communal councils, which the president directly controls.

V

With different phrasing but the same sense and content of the 1999 Venezuelan convening of the constituent assembly to reshape the Constitution and the political system, in January 2007, the newly elected president of Ecuador, Rafael Correa Delgado, also convened a referendum to ask the people about the convening and election of a national constituent assembly not established by or regulated in the 1998 Constitution then in force, according to the rules and conditions Correa unilaterally established, again without previous political agreement or consensus. After three months of bitter political and institutional conflicts, particularly between Correa and the Congress, the referendum took place on April 15, 2007. Voters approved the president's proposal and the election of the assembly took place in September 2007, completely controlled by the president's supporters.

---

72 See Allan R. Brewer-Carías, "La progresiva y sistemática demolición de la autonomía e independencia del poder judicial en Venezuela (1999–2004)," in *XXX Jornadas J.M Domínguez Escovar, Estado de derecho, Administración de justicia y derechos humanos*, Instituto de Estudios Jurídicos del Estado Lara, Barquisimeto 2005, pp. 33-174.

73 See Allan R. Brewer-Carías, "*Quis Custodiet ipsos Custodes*: De la interpretación constitucional a la inconstitucionalidad de la interpretación," in *VIII Congreso Nacional de Derecho Constitucional*, Fondo Editorial and Colegio de Abogados de Arequipa, Arequipa, Perú, 2005, 463-89; and *Crónica de la "In"Justicia constitucional: La Sala constitucional y el autoritarismo en Venezuela*, Editorial Jurídica Venezolana, Caracas 2007, pp. 11-44, 47-79.

In modern constitutionalism, a constitution as a political pact sanctioned by the representatives of the people and their constitution-making process has always resulted from political conflicts, whether for their prevention or their solution, and consequently has tended to create democratic institutions to achieve political stability. This, of course, is the situation in democratic systems. In authoritarian systems, the Constitution, even with voter-approved veils of democracy, always remains the sole expression of a ruler's will. The question in democratic systems is the need to determine the extent to which constitutions can contribute to resolving conflict and creating stable democratic governments – in other words, how constitutions must be adopted to effectively prevent conflicts and build stable democratic institutions.

As constitutional history shows, those goals have not always been achieved. Constitutions are not the magical instrument that many think they are for guaranteeing the end of political conflicts or the founding of permanent stability. The real ability of a constitution to contribute to conflict resolution and prevention and to ensure stability depends on the way constitution-making processes are conceived of and developed and how constitutions are drafted and adopted.

During the past two hundred years, all kinds of constitutional review proceedings have occurred in the world, and the ideal path of constitution making so that a constitution contributes to conflict resolution and the creation of a stable democratic government has yet to be designed.[74] However, one thing is clear: No constitution-making process can endure in a given country when one political or social faction implements it to impose a way of life or a specific political and economic system to a given country. In such cases, conflicts are not resolved and constitution-making processes restart, sometimes over and over in an endless process.

In the events of Venezuela in 1999 and Ecuador in 2007, which have produced endless political conflicts, the commonality was that the constitution-making process began without any constitutional foundation and without agreement between political parties and actors but according to rules unilaterally imposed by the head of the executive branch. Moreover, they developed without any de facto rupture of the Constitution; that is, no coup d'état preceded the election of the Constituent Assembly, being the interpretation of the existing Constitution the fact that paved the way for it election. These same steps were found in the president of Honduras's failed attempt to establish a constituent assembly in 2009, which in that case was stopped by the judiciary.

In Venezuela, as mentioned earlier, it was the Constituent Assembly that resulted from the election in 1999, the one that gave the "constituent" coup d'état against the 1961 Constitution and against all existing elected constituted powers. In this case, the existing Constitution of 1961 and all democratic tools were fraudulently used to violate the Constitution, setting up the basis for the progressive undermining of the democratic form of government and allowing for authoritarian seizure of all state branches of government by the new political forces supporting the president – thereby crushing the traditional political parties.

---

74 See, in general, Laurel E. Miller, editor, *Framing the State in Times of Transition: Case Studies in Constitution Making*, United States Institute of Peace, Washington 2010.

The ultimate aims of the government regarding the Constituent Assembly were, of course, not previously announced, explained, or proposed to the people when the president convened it in February 1999. The publicly proposed aims of convening the assembly were to reform state institutions and to improve democracy, aims that hardly anybody could challenge and that nearly everybody was willing to support, particularly given the political crisis of the state institutions and the party system.

The Venezuelan people in January 1999, like the people of Ecuador in 2007, should have known before they voted what kind of institutions the president was proposing to conduct the constitution-making process. For example, in Honduran President Manuel Zelaya's failed attempt, the people knew some of the proposed constitutional reforms that the president was offering and could determine that they were contrary to the country's Constitution, which provoked challenges to his process.

In the case of Ecuador, the presidential decree of January 2007 proposed the election of the Constituent Assembly to draft not only the "new" Constitution but also one with full power to transform the institutional framework of the state. According to the assembly's bylaws, unilaterally drafted by the president, all decisions could take effect only after the new Constitution was approved through referendum. That provision, approved in the April 2007 referendum without clarification from the Constitutional Tribunal before the September elections, resulted (as in Venezuela in 1999) in the election of a nonplural constituent assembly with two different goals: first to transform the institutional framework of the state; second to write the draft of a new constitution. These were the goals assumed by a constituent assembly completely controlled by the president's followers, having full and unlimited powers to transform the institutional framework of the state and to interfere in all branches of government. With these powers, the assembly could, for example, remove or limit the government; dissolve the Congress and assume the legislative function itself; intervene in provincial and municipal powers; remove the magistrates of the Supreme Court, the Supreme Electoral Tribunal, and the Constitutional Tribunal, as well as the comptroller general of the state; and intervene in the judiciary and the Public Prosecutors' Office.

Thus, the main constitutional discussion that took place in Ecuador during the first month of 2007 was focused on limiting the full powers to be attributed to the Constituent Assembly to ensure that the recently elected (December 2006) branches would be respected. To realize the intensity of the bitter political conflicts that resulted from those discussions, it is enough to bear in mind the institutional decisions of the subsequent three months, from January to April 2007.[75] Once the Supreme Electoral Council received the presidential decree on January 16 convening the constituent assembly, the tribunal submitted the decree to Congress for its approval. Congress then issued a decision considering urgent the assembly's convening but mo-

---

75   See Allan R. Brewer-Carías, "El inicio del proceso constituyente en Ecuador en 2007 y las lecciones de la experiencia venezolana de 1999," in *Estudios sobre el Estado constitucional (2005-2006)*, Editorial Jurídica Venezolana, Caracas 2007, pp. 767-806. See also Allan R. Brewer-Carías, *Reforma constitucional, asamblea constituyente y control judicial: Honduras (2009), Ecuador (2007) y Venezuela (1999)*, Universidad Externado de Colombia, Bogotá 2009, pp. 13ff.

difying the original decree. The Supreme Electoral Tribunal ignored Congress's decision and, on March 1, it convened the referendum according to the original decree with some modifications proposed by the president himself. Congress, by a vote of fifty-seven members, dismissed the president of the Supreme Electoral Tribunal because he ignored Congress's decision, and Congress then challenged as unconstitutional the Supreme Electoral Tribunal's decision before the Constitutional Tribunal. In response to these actions, the Supreme Electoral Tribunal dismissed the congressional representatives who had adopted the decision for interfering with voting processes, even though the Constitution established only the possibility of a recall referendum for such purposes. Before the referendum took place on April 15, a few *amparo* actions were filed before the Constitutional Tribunal and before various lower courts, arguing that the representatives had been unconstitutionally dismissed. Some of the *amparo* judges granted constitutional protection to the dismissed representatives, ordering their reincorporation to Congress, a decision that the president of Congress accepted, even though he had sworn in their substitutes the previous week. Then, the Supreme Electoral Tribunal decided to dismiss the lower-court judges who had granted the *amparo* protection, ignoring the adjudication that protected the dismissed representatives, considering them invalid. The president also considered the *amparo* decisions invalid, even though the Constitutional Tribunal considered them as obligatory as any constitutional judicial decision. Members of the Supreme Electoral Tribunal threatened to dismiss the members of the Constitutional Tribunal because they admittedly considered some of the *amparo* actions filed against the convening of the referendum. Once the referendum took place on April 15, the Constitutional Tribunal, after reviewing one of the lower court's *amparo* decisions, ruled to constitutionally protect fifty of the dismissed representatives by ordering their reincorporation. Congress, this time with a different majority because of the recently sworn–in representatives, on April 23 considered exhausted the term of the magistrates of the Constitutional Tribunal from January 2007. That decision gave rise to endless discussions on the validity of all the constitutional decisions the tribunal had adopted since January 2007.

Thus, as can be deduced from this intense, three-month institutional quarrel, the constitutional discussion on the powers of the Constituent Assembly did not end. On the contrary, because the matter was not resolved before the election of the assembly in September 2007, the bitter political conflict was aggravated after the assembly's installment, which eventually assumed all political powers, prevailing over all the other branches of government.

VI

The case of the 1999 Constituent Assembly, although it was not the first convened in Venezuelan constitutional history,[76] in contrast with all the other previous assemblies, it did not result from a factual rupture of the constitutional order because of a revolution, a war, or a coup d'état, but rather from a process developed under a

---

76   For the text of previous Venezuelan constitutions (1811–1961), see Allan R. Brewer-Carías, *Las constituciones de Venezuela*, Biblioteca de la Academia de Ciencias Políticas y Sociales, Caracas 1997. On the constitutional history of those texts, see my "Estudio Preliminar" in *id.*, pp. 11-256.

democratic rule (as was the case of the 1991 Colombian process and the 2007 Ecuadorian one), though in the middle of the most severe political crisis of the country's democratic system.[77] In 1999, it was the same Constituent Assembly that carried out a coup d'état after its election in July 1999 and brushed aside the 1961 Constitution, whose ambiguous interpretation had served to allow its convening.

The Venezuelan process is important not only because it marks a new trend in Latin American constitution making (i.e., defrauding the Constitution) but also because of the lessons it offers to help avoid repeating it or to help understand it if something similar occurs again (i.e., fraudulent use of the Constitution and democratic tools to establish a system founded on violation of the former and demolition of the latter). In the Venezuelan case, the constitution–making process exploited the people's legitimate hopes and expectations regarding the state's political recomposition as a consequence of the decline of the party system.

The Venezuelan crisis of the politically centralized, democratic multiparty system that had functioned since 1958 imposed the need to redesign the system to ensure the democratic governance of the country. The situation required a search for new political instruments to ensure democratic conciliation between political forces by means of political pacts or consensus among all political actors and factions of society, which is why the convening of a constituent assembly could have been justified for those reasons.[78] Accordingly, in Chávez's presidential decree of February 1999, the issue submitted to popular vote was the election of a constituent assembly "with the purpose to transform the state and to create a new juridical order allowing the effective functioning of a social and participative democracy."[79] Such was the raison d'être of the 1999 process, a purpose that was difficult for anybody to contradict.

But, at that moment, the country expected a constitution-making process based on political conciliation with the participation of all sectors of society. That did not happen, and the convening actors never intended it to. Given the aggressive antiparty and anti-representative-democracy presidential campaign, the lack of effective popular participation, and the absence of any sort of political consensus, what resulted were accentuated differences among political sectors and reinforced factioning of the country. Far from being a mechanism for dialogue and peace, Venezuela's 1999 constitution-making process served to aggravate an existing political crisis.

VII

Eleven years after the 1999 constitution making, despite the political rhetoric and exuberant spending, which wasted the immense fiscal income of a rich state in a

77   See Allan R. Brewer-Carías, "La crisis de las instituciones: Responsables y salidas," in *Revista del Centro de Estudios Superiores de las Fuerzas Armadas de Cooperación*, 11, Caracas 1985, 57-83. See also Allan R. Brewer-Carías, *Instituciones políticas y constitucionales*, Universidad Católica del Táchira–Editorial Jurídica Venezolana, San Cristóbal–Caracas 1996, 1 (Evolución histórica del estado): pp. 523-541.

78   See Allan R. Brewer-Carías, "Reflexiones sobre la crisis del sistema político, sus salidas democráticas y la convocatoria a una Constituyente," in *Los candidatos presidenciales ante la academia*, Biblioteca de la Academia de Ciencias Políticas y Sociales, Caracas 1998, pp. 9-66.

79   Article 3, Decree N° 3 of Feb. 2, 1999, in *Gaceta Oficial* N° 36.634 of Feb. 2, 1999.

poor country, no effective reform of the state has been achieved. Instead of social and participatory democracy, the process resulted in the configuration of a centralized, militaristic, and concentrated authoritarian regime that seeks to impose a socialist model of society with a democratic veil – centralized populist programs and institutions that pretend to be participatory have almost completed the destruction of the direct representative democracy.

In this sense, from a democratic point of view, the 1999 constitution-making process was a failure. Any changes the country has experienced have accentuated the crisis of the democratic system by concentrating all power in the president's hands and centralizing all territorial and local governments, which have limited representation. There have been great changes among Venezuela's political actors, as new groups filled with extreme hate and resentment (fed by the president's well-orchestrated speeches and diffused by state media) have crushed traditional parties and accentuated differences among Venezuelans in a context of extreme political polarization, which makes conciliation even more difficult.[80]

From an authoritarian, antidemocratic point of view, the 1999 constitution-making process can be considered a success – it allowed one faction, person and party, to completely seize and take over political power, and subsequently use it to crush all others parties and opponents. That opened wounds and created social and political rivalries that had been unknown for decades in the country, thus reinforcing social and political conflicts and destroying the democratic institutions, including the Armed Forces that were created with so much effort during the second half of the twentieth century.

The 1999 crisis of the democratic and representative party system should have led Venezuela's leadership to seek transformation, not destruction. The democratic system needed to improve to give way to a more participative democracy, which, of course, can take place only at the level of autonomous local government. Such was the people's main objective in responding to the constitution-making process called for in 1999: to draft an effective decentralization framework of the federal state and to transform the country's decades' old centralized federation into a participatory, decentralized democracy.

In the modern world, consolidated democracies have always both resulted from and caused political decentralization; that is, decentralization has been a consequence of the democratization process and a condition for democracy's survival and improvement. Thus, decentralization is the political instrument designed into a democracy to articulate all intermediate political powers, thereby allowing for government accomplishments close to the regions, communities, and people. Decentralization is a matter of democracies; decentralized autocracies have never existed.

The convening of the Constituent Assembly in Venezuela in 1999, after more than forty years of democracy, was supposed to have accentuated the democratic principle by decentralizing power, not destroying it. However, in the past decade,

---

80   See Allan R. Brewer-Carías, "El proceso constituyente y la fallida reforma del Estado en Venezuela," in *Estrategias y propuestas para la reforma del estado,* Universidad Nacional Autónoma de México, Mexico City 2001, pp. 25-48.

the federal form of government has transformed into a simple constitutional rubber stamp to disguise a completely centralized state ruled by one person who is simultaneously head of the state, the executive, the public administration, the military, and the ruling United Socialist Party. He calls himself "the leader," to be "reelected" indefinitely.[81]

In 1999, other much-needed reforms included checks and balances among the branches of government. Achieving this, particularly reforming relations between the executive and legislative power, was why people accepted the constitution-making process of 1999. Paradoxically, the crisis of democratic governance in the 1990s was a result not of excess presidentialism but rather of excess party parliamentarianism, particularly given the tight political control that the traditional parties exercised over Congress. In particular, with respect to the exclusively partisan nomination and appointment of the nonelected public officials, like the magistrates of the Supreme Court, the head of the Comptroller General Office, the head of the Public Prosecutor's Office, and members of the Supreme Electoral Council, there were nasty criticisms given the excessive partisan character of those appointments, which were made without any possibility of civil–society participation. The reform of such matters aimed to ensure a better balance among independent powers and more effective checks among them, thus limiting their exclusive partisan conformation. Particularly, reform aimed to build a complete independent and autonomous judiciary. But none of these reforms was applied because of the absolute concentration of state powers that has developed during the past decade (1999-2010).

The fact is that the 1999 Venezuelan Constituent Assembly was not elected to govern the country or to substitute for all elected branches of government. According to the Supreme Court decision on the challenged bylaws, the assembly had neither full powers nor original constituent powers. In principle, it had the particular mission of drafting a new Constitution and was to function in parallel with the constituted branches of government that had been elected in November 1998: the national Congress, the states' legislatures and governors, and the municipal councils and mayors. Nonetheless, at its first session, through the vote of the overwhelming majority of its members and without any constitutional support, the assembly proclaimed itself as having original constituent power and, in particular, all the needed powers to "limit or to decide to cease the activities of the authorities conforming the branches of government." It set forth in its internal bylaws that "all the State entities are subordinated to the National Constituent Assembly and are obliged to execute and to provide for the execution of the public acts issued by the Assembly."[82]

---

81   In the "Declaration of Principles" of the United Socialist Party (Apr. 23, 2010), the proposal is to assure the leadership of Chávez during the "Bicentennial Era: 2010-2030." Available at http://psuv.org.ve/files/tcdocumentos/Declaracion-de-principios-PSUV.pdf

82   See *Gaceta Constituyente (Diario de Debates), Agosto-Septiembre 1999*, Aug. 3, 1999, N° 1, 4. See my dissenting vote in *Gaceta Constituyente (Diario de Debates), Agosto–Septiembre 1999*, Aug. 7, 1999, N° 4, pp. 6-13; Allan R. Brewer-Carías, *Debate constituyente (Aportes a la Asamblea Nacional Constituyente)*, Fundación de Derecho Público–Editorial Jurídica Venezolana, Caracas 1999, 1 (Aug. 8–Sept. 8): pp. 15-39.

VIII

Despite all those powers, the result of the constitution-making process, the 1999 Constitution, from a democratic point of view did not turn out to be the document promised to the people in the April 25 consultative referendum to transform the state and the democratic system. It did not conform to the new vision of consolidating democratic principles and politically reorganizing the country, substituting the centralized party and state system for a decentralized one.

On the contrary, the result was an authoritarian framework of centralized government based on state intervention in the economy – helped by uncontrolled public oil income – which reinforced a presidentialism that has concentrated and controlled all state powers with a sharp antiparty tendency and a military force never before incorporated in the Constitution. Today, a single-party system is embodied in the state.

It has been within this constitutional framework that, during the past decade, an authoritarian government has arisen in Venezuela, with a president who, after ten years in office, has succeeded in amending the Constitution to ensure his continued and indefinite reelection, which was eventually approved by referendum in 2009. Also, in defrauding the Constitution, the president has progressively erased the federation; has suffocated local governments through the creation, in 2006, of communal councils directly dependent on the president[83]; and has been building a socialist state contrary to the will of the people – who discarded it in rejecting the 2007 constitutional reform proposals – imposed upon them above the debris of the demolished democratic institutions.

All these trends found their origin in the exclusionist 1999 constitution-making process, which far from politically reconciling the country accentuated fundamental differences across social classes, multiplied and increased political division in the country, and provoked extreme polarization. The process also was the main instrument for ensuring that one and only one political group, in support of the president, could seize all state powers and take absolute control of all institutions – this was all fueled by the extraordinary increase in public funds that were dispensed without control. That is, the 1999 constitution-making process has been an instrument for excluding all political parties, especially those that dissent against the president's will, and for establishing hegemonic control.

IX

The assault, seizure, and takeover of power by the political group that controlled the Constituent Assembly did not finish with the drafting of the Constitution. It continued after the December 15 referendum. This time, the same assembly carried out a constitutional coup, this time against the new Constitution, to impose different

---

83 See Allan R. Brewer-Carías, "El inicio de la desmunicipalización en Venezuela: La organización del poder popular para eliminar la descentralización, la democracia representativa y la participación a nivel local," in *AIDA, Opera Prima de Derecho Administrativo. Revista de la Asociación Internacional de Derecho Administrativo*, Universidad Nacional Autónoma de México, Mexico City 2007, pp. 49-67.

constitutional provisions the people had never approved, which allowed for the complete seizure of all branches of government and the final assault on power.

On December 22, 1999, one week after the popular approval of the Constitution, paralleling the provisions of the Constitution but not submitted to popular approval, the assembly adopted the Decree for a Transitory Regime. Through the decree, as expected, only the president was ratified in his office; all other elected and nonelected state officials were definitively dismissed.[84]

To fill that institutional gap, the Assembly, again without following provisions of the new Constitution, appointed members of the Supreme Tribunal of Justice and of the National Electoral Council, the public prosecutor, the comptroller general, and the people's defender. In addition, also without any constitutional support, the Assembly created and appointed the members of the National Legislative Commission, not established in the Constitution, to act as a nonelected legislative body that would substitute for the dismissed Congress until a new National Assembly could be elected. The Constituent Assembly, again without constitutional authorization, directly assumed legislative functions and sanctioned some statutes – among them, the Electoral Law – to govern the first general elections that took place in August 2000.

All these unconstitutional decisions, unfortunately, were covered up and endorsed by the new Supreme Tribunal of Justice, particularly its Constitutional Chamber, whose members had been appointed by the same Constituent Assembly in the same unconstitutional transitory regime with the mandate of giving that Assembly judicial support in judicial proceedings. Consequently, the new tribunal appointed by the assembly recognized the supposedly "original character" of the Constituent Assembly and its "supraconstitutional" power, thereby justifying all transitory political decisions adopted, many of which have subsisted to the present and serve to justify and cover up the endless unconstitutional interventions of the judiciary.[85]

X

The result of the 1999 Venezuelan constitution–making process, despite any political changes that have since taken place, has been the complete takeover of all levels of power and branches of government by supporters of President Hugo Chávez. This has imposed on the Venezuelan people a centralized form of government and a political socialist project whose aim is found in the phrase "motherland, socialism, or death," repeatedly pronounced since Chávez took his second oath in

---

84   See the Decree of Dec. 22, 1999, "Transitory Constitutional Regime," in *Gaceta Oficial* N° 36.859 of Dec. 29, 1999. See also Allan R. Brewer-Carías, *Golpe de estado y proceso constituyente en Venezuela,* Universidad Nacional Autónoma de México, Mexico City 2002, 354ff.; and *La Constitución de 1999: Derecho constitucional venezolano,* Editorial Jurídica Venezolana, Caracas 2004.

85   See, e.g., the Jan. 26, 2000, Decision N° 4 (*Caso: Eduardo García*), and the Mar. 28, 2000, Decision N° 180 (Case: *Allan R. Brewer-Carías et al.*) in *Revista de Derecho Público* 81, Editorial Jurídica Venezolana, Caracas 2000, 93ff. and 86 ff. See also Allan R. Brewer-Carías, *Golpe de estado y proceso constituyente en Venezuela,* Universidad Nacional Autónoma de México, México City, 2002, pp. 354ff.

January 2007. That phrase is now the official military salute – though nobody voted on or approved it.[86]

In summary, the 1961 Constitution was fraudulently used to provoke the 1999 constitution making by means of the election of a constituent assembly not established in the Constitution. After the assembly was democratically elected according to bylaws that the president unilaterally imposed to gain complete control of the assembly, the assembly staged a coup d'état. Since 2000, under the authoritarian framework of the new Constitution, it has been the turn of representative democracy to be used to demolish democracy itself. That is, Venezuela's government moved from defrauding the Constitution to defrauding democracy. In the past decade, it has used representative democracy to eliminate democracy progressively and substitute for it a participatory democracy of popular power based on communal councils – a democracy that is participatory only in name.

In this way, a "state of the popular power" is progressively replacing the democratic rule of law, again through fraud. That substitute pretends to establish a supposedly "democratic" system based on a direct relationship between a leader and the people, basically through popular mobilization, populism, and organization of the aforementioned communal councils, whose members are not elected by the people but directly appointed by open citizens' assemblies, which are, of course, controlled by the government's single party, thus maintaining the populist system that has been developed from the uncontrolled distribution of oil wealth.[87]

The main identifier of such a system is that all power is concentrated in the head of state, who is surrounded by ministerial offices "of the popular power,"[88] not being discarded that, in the near future, he will pretend to be "president of the popular power." The system is not democratic, representative, or participatory, being completely controlled by the head of state through the United Socialist Party it has created.

---

86   See Alberto Muller Rojas (Military Presidential Chief of Staff), in Reuters, "Venezuelan military adopts Chavez socialism slogan" ("Venezuela's military has adopted President Hugo Chavez's 'Homeland, Socialism or Death' slogan as an official salute, a further sign of politicization of core institutions in the OPEC nation"), *El Universal*, Caracas May 13, 2007 ("Militares venezolanos adoptan lema socialista de Chávez), at http://www.reuters.com/article/idUSN1142580120070511; Vivian Castillo, "Chávez instó a la FAN a asumir el socialismo 'sin ambigüedades,'" in *El Universal* (Caracas), Apr. 13, 2007, at http://www.eluniversal.com/2007/04/13/pol_art_chavez-insto-a-la-fa_246899.shtml; Patricia Rivas, "Chávez: 'El 13 de Abril [2002] la revolución bolivariana se hizo antiimperialista y socialista,'" in Prensa Web YVKE Mundial, Caracas Apr. 13, 2009, at http://www.radiomundial.com.ve/yvke/noticia.php?22791. See in the "Declaration of Principles" of the United Socialist Party (Apr. 23, 2010), the proposal regarding the "Bolivarian Socialism" and the "Socialist State," all based on the slogan "Socialist Homeland or death." Available at http://psuv.org.ve/files/tcdocumentos/Declaracion-de-principios-PSUV.pdf.

87   See Allan R. Brewer-Carías, "El autoritarismo en Venezuela construido en fraude a la Constitución (De cómo en un país democrático se ha utilizado el sistema eleccionario para eliminar la democracia y establecer un régimen autoritario de supuesta "dictadura de la democracia")," Report to *VIII Jornadas de Derecho Constitucional y Administrativo* and to the *VI Foro Iberoamericano de Derecho Administrativo*, Universidad Externado de Colombia, Bogotá, July 25–27, 2007, available at http://www.allanbrewercarias.com.

88   See, e.g., the provisions of Decree N° 6670 of Apr. 22, 2009, on the Organization and Functioning of Public Administration, *Gaceta Oficial* N° 39163, Apr. 2, 2009.

All these proposals and reforms, officially announced in January 2007, tend toward what the then–vice president of the republic called the "the dictatorship of
democracy."[89] Nonetheless, in democracy, no dictatorship is acceptable, not even a
dictatorship of democracy. That harks back to a different context and time: the failed
dictatorship of the proletariat that emerged from the Russian Revolution in 1918,
based on the Soviets (Councils) of soldiers, workers, and peasants. With a ninety-
year delay, something similar has been designed and in process of being implemented in Venezuela, since the creation in 2006 of the aforementioned communal councils, directly dependent on the national executive,[90] to channel the popular power,
with the alleged participation of organized people, to install the "dictatorship of democracy."[91]

History has shown that popular dictatorships have always been fraudulent instruments that circumstantial leaders have used to gain power and then, in the name
of popular power, to demolish any trace of democracy and impose a socialist regime
on a country without a popular vote. Some countries have learned nothing from Boris Yeltsin. Yeltsin, the first elected president of the Russian Federation, on the occasion of the burial of the Romanov family's remains, in reaching closure on the
Russian Revolution, voiced one of the most bitter lessons of humanity: "The attempts to change life by means of violence are doomed to fail."[92]

Lesson learned or not, what is true is that any dictatorship, whatever its origin or
kind, being inevitably the result of the exercise of violence, physical or institutional,
is condemned to fail and collapse sooner or later.

XI

What has occurred in Venezuela since 1999 is a political lesson that must be
known about and learned, particularly because Chávez has sold the formula as a
magic one for resolving political crises in democratic regimes in Latin America. The
recent applications of the formula by Ecuador's President Rafael Correa and the
Honduras's former President Manuel Zelaya show the need for deep analysis, particularly of how leaders have defrauded the Constitution to demolish the rule of law
and to destroy democratic values and standards.

---

89   Vice President Jorge Rodríguez, in Jan. 2007: "Of course we want to install a dictatorship, the dictators-
     hip of the true democracy and the democracy is the dictatorship of everyone, you and us together, buil-
     ding a different country. Of course we want this dictatorship of democracy to be installed forever." *El
     Nacional*, Caracas Jan. 1, 2007, p. A-2.

90   See Allan R. Brewer-Carías, "El inicio de la desmunicipalización en Venezuela: La organización del
     poder popular para eliminar la descentralización, la democracia representativa y la participación a nivel
     local," in *AIDA, Opera Prima de Derecho Administrativo. Revista de la Asociación Internacional de
     Derecho Administrativo*, Universidad Nacional Autónoma de México, Mexico City, 2007, pp. 49-67.

91   That is why the political project of the Chávez's government has been identified as "communist." See
     Jesús Antonio Petit Da Costa, "La lucha en Venezuela es contra el comunismo," *La Razón*, Caracas Jan.
     10, 2010. On Jan. 15, 2010, in his annual speech before the National Assembly on the government's ac-
     complishments, President Chávez said: "For the first time, I assume Marxism." *El Universal*, Caracas
     Jan. 16, 2010, http://www.eluniversal.com/2010/01/16/pol_art_por-primera-vez-asu_1726209.shtml
     Dece16.

92   See *Daily Telegraph*, London Aug., 8, 1998, p. 1.

This book is devoted to analyzing in detail the Venezuelan experience that began in 1999, with all its subsequent political consequences, to show how the Constitution in force at the time was used to violate that same Constitution and how the use of the existing democratic tools destroyed democracy in that country. It is based on a series of essays I have written during the past decade, as the facts were occurring, in which I studied the unfortunate process of subverting democracy from within and of violating the Constitution to consolidate authoritarianism – all accompanied by a systematic process of demolishing institutions and destroying democracy.

I have reworked all those essays for this book, which is divided into three parts and fifteen chapters. Part I is devoted to in-depth analysis of the tools used to develop the exclusionist 1999 constitution–making process as a means to assault state powers and completely reshape the Constitution. Chapter 1 is based on the paper "The 1999 Venezuelan Constitution–Making Process as an Instrument for Framing the Development of an Authoritarian Political Regime," which I presented on October 11, 2002, at the U.S. Institute of Peace Conference Project on Constitution-Making, Peace Building and National Reconciliation, in Washington, DC.[93] Chapter 2 covers the endless transitory constitutional regime that the Constituent Assembly illegitimately sanctioned in 1999, after the Constitution had been approved by popular vote. The regime has prevented the complete enforcement of the 1999 Constitution. Chapter 2 is based on an essay I wrote between 2001 and 2002 that was first published as "Illegitimate Constitutional Transitory Regime Adopted by the National Constituent Assembly after the Popular Approval of the New Constitution" in a book by the Universidad Nacional Autónoma de México.[94] The transitory constitutional regime resulted in state entities adopting various arbitrary decisions in violation of the Constitution, but the Supreme Tribunal of Justice, consisting of magistrates appointed by that regime, obediently endorsed those decisions.[95] Chapters 3 and 4 are a critical reflection on the political and socioeconomic provisions of the 1999 Constitution, from its exclusionary process to later distortions in its implementation. The chapters are based on a few essays I wrote during the month following its approval, beginning with one for the Conference on Challenges to Fragile Democracies in the Americas: Legitimacy and Accountability, organized by the Faculty of Law of the University of Texas, in Austin on February 25, 2000,[96] and another, on

---

93   The paper was later published as "The 1999 Venezuelan Constitution-Making Process as an Instrument for Forming the Development of an Authoritarian Political Regime," in Laurel E. Miller, editor, *Framing the State in Times of Transition: Case Studies in Constitution Making*, United States Institute of Peace, Washington 2010, pp. 505-532.

94   See Allan R. Brewer-Carías, *Golpe de estado y proceso constituyente en Venezuela*, Universidad Nacional Autónoma de México, Mexico City 2002, pp. 343ff.

95   The initial version of these reflections was published in my book *Golpe de estado y proceso constituyente*, Universidad Nacional Autónoma de México, Mexico City, 2002, 341-405, and in my book *La Constitución de 1999. Derecho constitucional venezolano*, Caracas 2004, Vol 2, pp. 1.017-1115.

96   An abstract of my presentation was published in *Texas International Law Journal* 36, 2001, 333-38. See in addition my critical comments on the new Constitution immediately after its approval, in "Reflexiones críticas y visión general de la Constitución de 1999," Inaugural Lecture, Curso de Actualización en Derecho Constitucional, Universidad Católica Andrés Bello, Caracas Feb. 2, 2000; "La Constitución de 1999 y la reforma política, Colegio de Abogados del Distrito Federal, Caracas Feb. 9, 2000; "The Constitutional Reform in Venezuela and the 1999 Constitution," Seminar, Challenges to Fragile

"Global Values in the Venezuelan Constitution: Some Prioritizations and Several Incongruencies," in which I contrasted the formal constitutional provisions and the political reality written for a presentation at a National Constitutional Jurisprudence conference in Bellagio, Italy, on September 22–26, 2008.

Part II is devoted to analyzing the most important institutional developments deriving from the 1999 Constitution. It is divided into five chapters. Chapter 5 summarizes the previously described process of consolidating authoritarianism and is based on a paper on "Authoritarianism in Venezuela Built Defrauding the Constitution" that I initially wrote for the Ninth Ibero-American Congress on Constitutional Law and the Seventh National Symposium on Constitutional Law, organized by the Associação Brasileira dos Constitucionalistas Demócratas, Seção Brasileira do Instituto Ibero-Americano de Direito Constitucional, and Academia Brasileira de Direito Constitucional, held on November 11–15, 2006, in Curitiba, Brazil.[97] Chapter 6 covers the reinforcement of the centralization to which the state has been submitted. It is based on my paper, "Centralized Federation in Venezuela," presented at the seminar Federalism in the Americas and Beyond, at Duquesne School of Law in Pittsburgh, on November 13, 2004.[98] Chapter 7 discusses the concentration of power in the branches of government. It is based on an essay I wrote on the principle of separation of powers and authoritarian government in Venezuela, discussed in seminars at Fordham Law School in New York City (February 11, 2008), Duquesne University School of Law (November 7–8, 2008), and University of Pennsylvania Law School in Philadelphia (April 16, 2009).[99] Chapter 8 covers the catastrophic

---

Democracies in the Americas: Legitimacy and Accountability, organized by Faculty of Law, University of Texas, Austin, Feb. 25, 2000; "Reflexiones críticas sobre la Constitución de 1999," Seminar, *El constitucionalismo latinoamericano del siglo XXI en el marco del LXXXIII aniversario de la promulgación de la Constitución política de los Estados Unidos Mexicanos,* Cámara de Diputados e Instituto de Investigaciones Jurídicas UNAM, México City, Jan. 31, 2000; "La nueva Constitución de Venezuela del 2000," Centro Internationale per lo Studio del Diritto Comparato, Facoltà di Giurisprudenza, Facoltà di Scienze Politiche, Universita'degli Studi di Urbino, Urbino, Italia, Mar. 3, 2000; "Apreciación general sobre la Constitución de 1999," *Ciclo de conferencias sobre la Constitución de 1999, Academia de Ciencias Políticas y Sociales,* Caracas May 11, 2000. These papers were published in Diego Valadés and Miguel Carbonell, coords., *Constitucionalismo iberoamericano del siglo XXI,* Cámara de Diputados, LVII Legislatura, Universidad Nacional Autónoma de México, Mexico City 2000, pp. 171-93; in *Revista de Derecho Público* 81, Editorial Jurídica Venezolana, Caracas 2000, 7-21; in *Revista Facultad de Derecho, Derechos y Valores* 3, N° 5, Universidad Militar Nueva Granada, Santafé de Bogotá, D.C., Colombia, July 2000, pp. 9-26; *La Constitución de 1999,* Biblioteca de la Academia de Ciencias Políticas y Sociales, Caracas 2000, pp. 63-88.

97   The essay was rewritten in 2007 and published in *Temas constitucionales: Planteamientos ante una reforma,* Fundación de Estudios de Derecho Administrativo, Caracas 2007, pp. 13-74.

98   The essay was published in *Duquesne Law Review* 43, Duquesne University, Pittsburgh, PA, 2005, 629-43. I wrote some of the reflections for the paper "The Centralized Federation in Venezuela and Subnational Constitutions" for the conference Federalism and Subnational Constitutions, Design and Reform, organized by the Center for State Constitutional Studies, Rutgers University, New Jersey, held in Bellagio, Italy, May 23–26, 2004.

99   Published in *Duquesne Law Review* 47, Duquesne University, Pittsburgh, PA, 2009, pp. 813-38. I wrote a first version of the reflections, "Separation of Powers and Authoritarianism in Venezuela," for a lecture in Prof. Ruti G. Teitel's course Constitutional Comparative Law, at Fordham Law School, New York City, Feb. 11, 2008. I further developed the essay for the lecture "Venezuela under Chávez: Blurring between Democracy and Dictatorship?" at the University of Pennsylvania Law School, Philadelphia Apr. 16, 2009.

political subjection of the Supreme Tribunal and the illegitimate use of its jurisdictional powers to mutate the Constitution. The chapter is based on the essay I wrote for the Duquesne seminar Judicial Review in the Americas and Beyond in November 2006.[100] Chapter 9 deals with the state compulsory appropriation of economic activities, enterprises, and assets through expropriations and confiscations, with special reference to the oil industry. It is based on an essay on the state appropriation of Primary Hydrocarbons Joint Venture Exploitations established before 2001, their unilateral termination, and the confiscation of assets of their private parties, published in 2008.[101]

Part III deals with recent draft constitutional reforms that have been rejected (2007) or approved (2009) to consolidate the authoritarian, centralist, and militarist government that has been implemented during the past decade for the purpose of stringently controlling the state and all aspects of society. It also deals with the mutations (distortions) of the Constitution made by the Constitutional Chamber of the Supreme Tribunal. In Chapters 10, 11, and 12, I analyze the president's 2007 draft constitutional reforms, which fortunately the people rejected in the December referendum. The chapters are based on a 2007 essay published in Caracas by *Fundación Editorial Jurídica Venezolana*.[102] Chapter 13 deals with the irregular fraudulent implementation of the rejected constitutional reform through legislation, and mainly through decrees laws enacted in execution of the 2007 enabling law. Chapter 14 deals with the process of illegitimate mutation or distortion of the Constitution made by the Constitutional Chamber of the Supreme Tribunal of Justice, as Constitutional Jurisdiction, which via constitutional interpretation has modified the Constitution, even in order to implement the rejected constitutional reforms of 2007. The chapter is based on the essay "Judicial Review in Venezuela," which I wrote for the lecture "The Constitutional Judge and the Destruction of the Rule of Law" at the Administrative Law Seminar of Professor Eduardo García de Enterría, at the *Universidad Complutense de Madrid*, on April 1, 2009.[103] Finally, Chapter 15 discusses the 2009

100 Published in *Duquesne Law Review* 45, Duquesne University, Pittsburgh, PA. 2007, pp. 439-65.

101 Published as "The 'Statization' of the Pre-2001 Primary Hydrocarbons Joint Venture Exploitations: Their Unilateral Termination and the Assets' Confiscation of Some of the Former Private Parties," in *Oil, Gas & Energy Law Intelligence* 6 (http://www.gasandoil.com/ogel/); and as "La estatización de los convenios de asociación que permitían la participación del capital privado en las actividades primarias de hidrocarburos suscritos antes de 2002, mediante su terminación anticipada y unilateral y la confiscación de los bienes afectos a los mismos," in coord. Víctor Hernández Mendible, *Nacionalización, libertad de empresa y asociaciones mixtas*, Editorial Jurídica Venezolana, Caracas 2008, pp. 123-88.

102 See Allan R. Brewer-Carías, *Hacia la consolidación de un estado socialista, centralizado, policial y militarista: Comentarios sobre el sentido y alcance de las propuestas de reforma constitucional 2007*, Editorial Jurídica Venezolana, Caracas 2007, and *La reforma constitucional de 2007 (Comentarios al proyecto inconstitucionalmente sancionado por la asamblea nacional el 2 de noviembre de 2007)*, Editorial Jurídica Venezolana, Caracas 2007, p. 224. See also my essays "La reforma constitucional en Venezuela de 2007 y su rechazo por el poder constituyente originario," *Revista Peruana de Derecho Público* 8, 15, Lima, 2007, pp. 13-53; and as "La proyectada reforma constitucional de 2007, rechazada por el poder constituyente originario," in *Anuario de Derecho Público 2007* 1, Instituto de Estudios de Derecho Público de la Universidad Monteávila, Caracas 2008, pp. 17-65.

103 Published as "El juez constitucional al servicio del autoritarismo y la ilegítima mutación de la Constitución: El caso de la Sala Constitucional del Tribunal Supremo de Justicia de Venezuela (1999-2009)," in

Constitutional Amendment, approved by referendum on February 2009, which eliminates the alternating character of the government by establishing the possibility of
the continuous, indefinite reelection of the president, which has been always prohibited. I initially wrote the essay, "Venezuela 2009 Referendum on Continuous Reelection: Constitutional Implications," for the panel discussion Venezuela Referendum: Public Opinion, Economic Impact, and Constitutional Implications for the
Americas Society and Council of the Americas, held in New York on February 9,
2009.[104]

The entire process in Venezuela of institution demolishing and democracy destroying has gravely affected the country's democratic standards and accomplishments – democracy has been dismantled with democratic tools, and the Constitution
defrauded in the process. Therefore, "Final Reflections," I provide a general overview of the right to democracy and the violation of that right by Venezuela's authoritarian government from 1999 to 2010. The text of that final chapter generally
follows the lines of the essay on "The Inter-American Democratic Charter and the
Situation of the Venezuelan Democratic Regime," written between December 2001
and January 2002 to denounce all violations of democratic principles committed by
the Venezuelan government, a process that has continued to this date.[105]

A fact is definitive in these matters: All constitution–making processes developed in countries with durable democratic institutions, though generally resulting
from conflicts, have been the product of political agreements and consensus among
conflicting parties, with extended public participation and consultation. On the contrary, when those processes result from a political leader's, faction's, or party's own
particular concept of the state and society, without dialogue or political participation, eventually those processes implode.

When they result from agreement and consensus, in which parties effectively talk
to one another and where peace opens all doors to all, constitutions can be, at the
eve of a political conflict or of a civil war, the main tool to avoid them, providing
that they are the final product of a political pact of different forces of a society that
are in conflict. When irrational conduct prevents the possibility to achieve those
agreements and consensus before a conflict explodes, inevitably, at the end of a war,
constitutions can then be the result of a political armistice also between parties in
conflict. In both cases, when constitutions result from conflict, as political pacts,
they tend to create conditions for stability and democratic government. But constitutions also can be imposed by one political force on the rest of society, by controlling
power through institutional manipulations or through a revolution. In such cases,
they do not result from agreement of forces in conflict; they express the sole will of
the predominant faction of society, to be imposed on others. With such constitutions,

Revista de Administración Pública, 180, Centro de Estudios Políticos y Constitucionales, Madrid 2009,
pp. 383-418.

104 Published as "El juez constitucional vs. la alternabilidad republicana (la reelección continua e indefinida)," *Revista de Derecho Público*, 117, Editorial Jurídica Venezolana, Caracas 2009, pp. 205-214.

105 The text of the original essay, which was initially diffused through the Internet, was published as a
chapter of my book, *La crisis de la democracia en Venezuela: La Carta Democrática Interamericana y
los sucesos de abril de 2002*, Libros El Nacional, Caracas 2002, pp. 137-218.

no stability can be achieved in the post–conflict transition – and, of course, never the silence of the prisons or the graves could mean stability.

The fact is this: Forced imposition of a specific political system, a specific economic or social system, a territorial artificial organization, or the predominance of one ethnic group or religion over others has never attained long life. Eventually, the state and political institutions are demolished or implode. In other words, in any constitution-making processes, any attempt to impose a political system or a territorial division or integration on society, through violence, – including institutional violence – that is, the one exercise by means of using state power and institutions – will fail.

PART ONE

THE POLITICAL ASSAULT ON STATE POWERS AND THE FRAMEWORK FOR AUTHORITARIANISM

The main trend of the Venezuelan experience of dismantling democracy from within is that the process, aimed to replace representative democracy with "participatory democracy," used democratic tools but defrauded democracy itself, and using constitutional mechanisms it also defrauded the Constitution.[106] The result has been a political assault on state powers by a new resentful political group that was formed; nonetheless, profiting from the democratic rules during Venezuela's four decades of stable democracy. That group has destroyed the traditional parties, all democratic institutions, and any sort of pluralism seeking to implement a socialist model for which the people did not vote.

The process began in 1999 with the convening of the Constituent Assembly not authorized in the 1961 Constitution. That assembly allowed a resentful political class to take over all branches of government and completely reshape the Constitution (Chapter 1). In addition, to facilitate the dismantling of democracy, after popular approval of the Constitution and before its publication, without any authority to do so, the Constituent Assembly sanctioned the Transitory Constitutional Regime, which allowed many provisions of the Constitution not to be applied and split provisions into two categories: those approved by the people and others not submitted to popular approval (Chapter 2). The result of this constitution-making process was a new Constitution that formally reaffirmed all the democratic values constructed during the previous decades but sowed the seeds for the reinforcement of centralization (Chapter 3) and state intervention in the social and economic life (Chapter 4), allowing the dismantling and destruction of democracy by the elected governments.

---

106   In Dec. 2009, in a speech at an International Congress commemorating the tenth anniversary of the 1999 Constitution, the vice president of the Constitutional Chamber of the Supreme Tribunal of Justice (Francisco Carrasquero), considering that "it is impossible to construct socialism with the legal superstructure of representative democracy," proposed for the Parliament and the other branches of government together with the Executive to "start dismantling all that legal superstructure created by representative democracy elite," adding the role the Constitutional Chamber has "in order to dismantle all that megastructure of representative democracy statutes." Available at http://www.eluniversal.com/2009/12/09/pol_art_en-el-nuevo-constit_1687934.shtml.

CHAPTER 1:

THE 1999 EXCLUSIONIST CONSTITUTION-MAKING PROCESS

In December 1999, as a result of the constitution–making process developed during that year, a new Constitution was approved in Venezuela. A national constituent assembly elected that same year sanctioned the new Constitution, which was submitted to popular approval by referendum on December 15, 1999.

As a member of the National Constituent Assembly, participating in all its sessions and in all the constitutional discussions held, I opposed the Constitution and led the political campaign for a no vote in the referendum. This position was based on my multiple negative votes in the Constituent Assembly and on my publicly expressed fear that the new Constitution,[107] despite its advanced civil and political rights regulations,[108] was an instrument framed for the development of an authoritarian regime. This fear was due to the Constitution's provisions allowing for the possibility of the concentration of state power, state centralization, extreme presidentialism, extensive state participation in the economy, the general marginalization of civil society in public activities, exaggerated state social obligations reflecting state oil-income populism, and extreme militarism.[109]

Unfortunately, the warning signs of 1999–2000 have become reality, and the political system that resulted from the 1999 constitution making has turned out to be the current authoritarian regime, led by former Lieutenant-Colonel Hugo Chávez Frías, a leader of the failed 1992 military coup.[110] Chávez was elected president of the Republic of Venezuela in the general elections of December 1998,[111] elected in 2000 after the approval of the new 1999 Constitution, and reelected in December 2006.[112] After nine years of consolidating the existing authoritarian regime, in August 2007, he proposed before the National Assembly a radical reform to the Constitution to formally consolidate a socialist, centralized, militaristic and police state.[113]

---

107 See my dissenting votes in Allan R. Brewer-Carías, *Debate constituyente (Aportes a la Asamblea Nacional Constituyente)*, Fundación de Derecho Público–Editorial Jurídica Venezolana, Caracas 1999, 3 (Oct. 18–Nov. 30): pp. 107-308.

108 See my proposal on this matter in Brewer-Carías, *Debate constituyente, (Aportes a la Asamblea Nacional Constituyente)*, Fundación de Derecho Público–Editorial Jurídica Venezolana, Caracas 1999, 2 (Sept. 9–Oct. 17): pp. 76-155ff.

109 See "Razones para 'no' firmar el proyecto" and "Razones para el voto 'no' en el referéndum sobre la Constitución," in Brewer-Carías, *Debate constituyente, (Aportes a la Asamblea Nacional Constituyente)*, Fundación de Derecho Público–Editorial Jurídica Venezolana, Caracas 1999, 3 (Oct. 18–Nov. 30): pp. 311ff.

110 On the Feb. 4, 1992, coup d'état attempt, see H. Sonntag and T. Maingón, *Venezuela: 4F1992. Un análisis socio-político*, Caracas 1992; Gustavo Tarre Briceño, *4 de febrero. El espejo roto*, Caracas 1994.

111 In the 1998 presidential election, Hugo Chávez Frías obtained 56.20% of votes cast, followed by Henrique Salas Römer, with 39.99% of votes. Approximately 35% of eligible voters did not vote. See the references in *El Universal*, Caracas Dec. 11, 1998, p. 1-1.

112 In the 2006 presidential election, Hugo Chávez Frías obtained 62.84% of votes, and the opposition candidate, Manuel Rosales, obtained 36.9% of votes. Approximately 25.3% of eligible voters did not.

113 See *Proyecto de Reforma Constitucional. Elaborado por el ciudadano Presidente de la República Bolivariana de Venezuela, Hugo Chávez Frías,* Editorial Atenea, Caracas Aug. 2007, 58. See the com-

The Assembly sanctioned the reform on November 2, 2007, but the people rejected it in a referendum on December 2, 2007.[114] In any event, such fundamental transformations of the state could be sanctioned only by a National Constituent Assembly as expressly set forth in the 1999 Constitution (Article 347) and cannot be approved by a constitutional reform procedure (Article 342), as the president proposed in contravention of the Constitution.[115] Notwithstanding, even if the people did reject unconstitutional proposals, during 2008 and 2009, many of the rejected reforms were implemented by defrauding the Constitution, by means of legislation, decrees, laws, and even convenient judicial interpretations of the Constitution issued by the Constitutional Chamber of the Supreme Tribunal.

The 1999 Constitution replaced the previous 1961 Constitution,[116] becoming the twenty-sixth in the history of the country.[117] As mentioned, it was discussed and drafted by a national constituent assembly called and elected for that purpose, and it was approved by referendum on December 15, 1999.[118]

I. THE 1999 NATIONAL CONSTITUENT ASSEMBLY

The 1999 National Constituent Assembly was not the first of its kind in Venezuelan history. Originally, the independent and autonomous state of Venezuela was created through two constituent assemblies. The first took place in 1811, after the Declaration of Independence (July 5, 1811) by the former Spanish colonies, which had been integrated in 1777 in the General Captaincy of Venezuela, creating the Confederation of States of Venezuela (1811 Constitution). The second took place in

---

ments on the draft in Allan R. Brewer-Carías, *Hacia la consolidación de un estado socialista, centralizado, policial y militarista. Comentarios sobre el alcance y sentido de la Reforma Constitucional 2007*, Editorial Jurídica Venezolana, Caracas 2007; *La Reforma Constitucional de 2007 (sancionada inconstitucionalmente por la Asamblea Nacional el 2 de Noviembre de 2007)*, Editorial Jurídica Venezolana, Caracas 2007.

114 The reform was submitted to referendum on Dec. 2, 2007. A majority of the people rejected it. The no votes comprised 51% (4.5 million) of votes cast (9.2 million); approximately 44.11% of eligible voters did not vote.

115 See Allan R. Brewer-Carías, "El autoritarismo establecido en fraude a la Constitución y a la democracia y su formalización en Venezuela mediante la reforma constitucional. (De cómo en un país democrático se ha utilizado el sistema eleccionario para minar la democracia y establecer un régimen autoritario de supuesta 'dictadura de la democracia' que se pretende regularizar mediante la reforma constitucional)," in *Temas constitucionales. Planteamientos ante una Reforma*, Fundación de Estudios de Derecho Administrativo, Caracas 2007, 13-74; Allan R. Brewer-Carías, *Estudios sobre el estado constitucional 2005-2006*, Editorial Jurídica Venezolana, Caracas 2007, pp. 79ff.

116 See Allan R. Brewer-Carías, *La Constitución y sus enmiendas*, Editorial Jurídica Venezolana, Caracas 1991; and *Instituciones políticas y constitucionales*, Universidad Católica del Táchira–Editorial Jurídica Venezolana, San Cristóbal–Caracas 1996, 1 (Evolución histórica del estado): pp. 455ff.

117 See the text of all Constitutions (1811–1999) in Allan R. Brewer-Carías, *Las Constituciones de Venezuela*, Biblioteca de la Academia de Ciencias Políticas y Sociales, Caracas 2008. For the constitutional history behind those texts, see my "Estudio Preliminar" in the same book, Vol 1, pp. 23-526.

118 See Allan R. Brewer-Carías, *La Constitución de 1999*, Editorial Jurídica Venezolana, Caracas 2000; *La Constitución de 1999. Derecho Constitucional Venezolano*, Editorial Jurídica Venezolana, 2 vols., Caracas 2004. See also Hildegard Rondón de Sansó, *Análisis de la Constitución venezolana de 1999*, Editorial Ex Libris, Caracas 2001; Ricardo Combellas, *Derecho constitucional: Una introducción al estudio de la Constitución de la República Bolivariana de Venezuela*, McGraw-Hill, Caracas 2001; Alfonso Rivas Quintero, *Derecho constitucional*, Paredes Editores, Valencia, 2002.

1830, after the separation of the Provinces of Venezuela from the Republic of Colombia, which Simón Bolívar had created nine years earlier, in 1821, when he managed to integrate the former Spanish colonies of what is today Ecuador, Colombia,
and Venezuela (1830 Constitution).

After those two original constituent assemblies, seven other constitution-making
processes through similar elected institutions were carried out in 1858, 1863, 1893,
1901, 1914, 1946, and 1953. In each case, the constitution-making process through
constituent assemblies resulted from a de facto rejection of the existing constitution,
a coup d'état, a revolution, or a civil war.[119] In all these cases, the assemblies were
never elected peacefully under democracy, always serving as a political tool to reshape the political process of the country, in which they played a decisive role.

Thus, it is possible to define the basic political periods of Venezuelan constitutional history by those constituent assemblies: As mentioned, the first period began
in 1811 with the Constituent Congress that declared independence from Spain. After
the independence wars and the disappearance of Venezuela as an independent Republic because of being united with the former provinces of New Granada in the
Republic of Colombia, a new constitutional assembly was elected in 1830 to restore
the republic. This period of formation of the new state ended abruptly with the Federal Wars, which were preceded by the 1858 Constituent Assembly. At the end of the
wars, a constituent assembly was again elected in 1863 to establish the constitutional
basis of the federal state system.

This initiated the second political period, which once again ended abruptly after
the *Revolución Liberal Restauradora* in 1899, which provoked the election of the
Constituent Assembly of 1901. That assembly designed a radical change in the political system, giving birth to a centralized and autocratic state, which was consolidated by the Constituent Congress of 1914 and through other constitutional reforms
approved during the first half of the twentieth century.

This third political period of Venezuelan constitutional history ended abruptly
with the Revolution of October 1945. A new constituent assembly in 1946 assumed
the task of designating the democratic political system of a centralized state, which
prevailed for the second half of the twentieth century and was consolidated after a
military interregnum (1948–58) in which a constituent assembly was also convened
(1953). It was the system of state centralism and democracy of parties that at the end
of the 1990s demanded a radical change. That was the change that should have been
designed by the Constituent Assembly of 1999, which was to be convened, as never
before, within a democracy and without a previous de facto constitutional break.
That is why the Constituent Assembly and the constitution-making process of 1999
were different from all the previous ones in Venezuelan history and even from many
similar processes in other countries in the past decades. It did not result from a de
facto rejection of the 1961 Constitution or from a revolution, a war, or a coup. Rather, with some similarities to the 1991 Colombian and 2007 Ecuadorian Constituent

---

119 See Elena Plaza and Ricardo Combellas, coords., *Procesos constituyentes y reformas constitucionales
en la historia de Venezuela: 1811-1999*, Universidad central de Venezuela, Caracas 2005; Allan R.
Brewer-Carías, "Las asambleas constituyentes en la historia de Venezuela," *El Universal*, Caracas Sept.
8, 1998, p. 1-5.

Assemblies,[120] the Venezuelan Constituent Assembly of 1999 resulted from a formal democratic process that did not involve a rupture of the previous political regime.[121] Nonetheless, in Colombia, the Constituent Assembly resulted from political agreements and consensus between the political forces of the country. In Venezuela and Ecuador, the Constituent Assembly was unilaterally conceived and submitted to popular vote by the president, without any previous political agreements or participation by political parties.

In all cases, but particularly Venezuela, the constitution making of 1999 took place in the context of a severe political crisis,[122] which was affecting the democratic regime that had been established in 1958.[123] The crisis had arisen as a result of a lack of evolution from a system of overly centralized political parties,[124] which existed then and still exists today. In fact, the call for the referendum on establishing the Constituent National Assembly, made by the newly elected president, Hugo Chávez, on February 2, 1999, intended to ask the people their opinion on a constituent national assembly "aimed at transforming the State and creating a new legal order that allows the effective functioning of a social and participative democracy."[125] That was the formal raison d'être of the constitution making and is why, with few exceptions, it would have been difficult to find anyone in the country to disagree with those stated purposes: transforming the state and putting into practice a form of democracy that would be social, participatory, and effective. For that purpose, undoubtedly, a political conciliation and participative process was necessary.

Unfortunately, Chávez did not formally conceive of the constitutional process as an instrument for conciliation, aimed to reconstruct the democratic system and to ensure good governance. That would have required agreements and consensus to reach a political commitment from all components of society, as well as the partici-

---

120 See Allan R. Brewer-Carías, "El inicio del proceso constituyente en Ecuador en 2007 y las lecciones de la experiencia venezolana de 1999," in *Estudios sobre el estado constitucional 2005-2006*, Editorial Jurídica Venezolana, Caracas 2007, pp. 766 ff.

121 See Allan R. Brewer-Carías, "Reflexiones sobre la crisis del sistema político, sus salidas democráticas y la convocatoria a una constituyente," in *Los candidatos presidenciales ante la academia*, Aug. 10–18, 1998, Biblioteca de la Academia de Ciencias Políticas y Sociales, Caracas 1998, pp. 9-66.

122 See Allan R. Brewer-Carías, *La crisis de las instituciones: Responsables y salidas*, Cátedra Pío Tamayo, mimeo, Centro de Estudios de Historia Actual, Facultad de Economía y Ciencias Sociales, Universidad Central de Venezuela, Caracas 1985. Also see Allan R. Brewer-Carías, *Instituciones políticas y constitucionales*, Universidad Católica del Táchira–Editorial Jurídica Venezolana, San Cristóbal–Caracas 1996, 1 (Evolución histórica del estado): pp. 523-541.

123 On the democratic political process after 1958, see Allan R. Brewer-Carías. *Cambio político y reforma del estado en Venezuela. Contribución al estudio sobre el estado democrático y social de derecho*, Ed. Tecnos, Madrid 1975.

124 See Allan R. Brewer-Carías, *El estado: Crisis y reforma*, Academia de Ciencias Políticas y Sociales, Caracas 1982; and *Problemas del estado de partidos*, Editorial Jurídica Venezolana, Caracas 1988.

125 See the text of the decree at *Gaceta Oficial* N° 36.634, Feb. 2, 1999, and its modification in *Gaceta Oficial* N° 36.658, Mar. 10, 1999. See the criticisms of the decree as constitutional fraud, in Allan R. Brewer-Carías, *Asamblea constituyente y ordenamiento constitucional*, Biblioteca de la Academia de Ciencias Políticas y Sociales, Caracas 1999, pp. 229 ff.

pation of all sectors in the design of a new, functioning democracy – that did not occur.[126]

The Constituent Assembly of 1999, in fact, served to facilitate the total takeover of state powers by a new political group supporting the president, which crushed all the others, including existing political parties. As a result, almost all opportunities for inclusion and public participation were squandered. Moreover, the constitution-making process became an endless and continuous constituent coup d'état when the Constituent Assembly elected in July 1999, before changing the existing 1961 Constitution, began violating it by assuming powers it lacked under that text and under the terms of the April referendum that created it.[127] As an independent candidate, I was elected to the 1999 Constituent Assembly and thus able to participate in all its discussions. I dissented orally and in writing to all unconstitutional and undemocratic decisions.[128] I witnessed the seizure of power, beginning with the convening of the referendum on the Constituent Assembly in February 1999, then the April 1999 referendum to approve the convening of the Constituent Assembly, the election of the Constituent Assembly in July 1999, the exercise of "supraconstitutional" power by the Constituent Assembly from August 1999 to January 2000, the drafting and discussion of the draft constitution between October and November 1999, and the approval of the new constitution through referendum in December 1999.

The result of this brief but intensive process was that 1999 saw the failure of the constitution-making process as an instrument for political reconciliation and democratization, in that the stated democratic purposes of the process were not accomplished.[129] No effective democratic reform of the state occurred, just an authoritarian government; and no social and participatory democracy resulted, unless one can consider democratic the election of a populist government that concentrated all branches of government and crushed political pluralism. Thus, if it is true that there have been important political changes, then some of them have aggravated the factors that provoked the crisis in the first place.[130] New political actors have assumed power, but far from implementing a democratic conciliation policy, they have accentuated the differences among Venezuelans, thereby worsening political polarization and making conciliation increasingly difficult. The seizure of power has opened new wounds, making social and political rivalries difficult to reconcile. Despite Vene-

---

126 See the 1998 political discussion regarding the necessary inclusive character of the proposed constitution-making process in Allan R. Brewer-Carías, *Asamblea constituyente y ordenamiento constitucional*, Biblioteca de la Academia de Ciencias Políticas y Sociales, Caracas 1999, pp. 38 ff.

127 See Allan R. Brewer-Carías, *Golpe de estado y proceso constituyente en Venezuela*, Universidad Nacional Autónoma de México, Mexico City 2002, pp. 181 ff.

128 See my dissenting votes in Allan R. Brewer-Carías, *Debate constituyente, (Aportes a la Asamblea Nacional Constituyente)*, Fundación de Derecho Público–Editorial Jurídica Venezolana, Caracas 1999, 1 (Aug. 8–Sept. 8):17ff. and 3 (Oct. 18–Nov. 30): pp. 109 ff.

129 See Allan R. Brewer-Carías, "El proceso constituyente y la fallida reforma del estado en Venezuela," in *Estrategias y propuestas para la reforma del estado*, Universidad Nacional Autónoma de México, Mexico City 2001, pp. 25-48.

130 See, in general, A.C. Clark, *The Revolutionary Has No Clothes: Hugo Chávez's Bolivarian Farce*, Encounter Books, New York 2009.

zuela's extraordinary oil wealth gained during the first decade of the twenty-first century, the country's social problems have increased.

II. THE 1998 CRISIS OF THE POLITICAL SYSTEM AND THE NEED FOR DEMOCRATIC RECONSTRUCTION

To understand the failure of this constitution-making process as an instrument to reinforce democracy, it is essential to analyze its political background. As previously mentioned, the process began in the midst of a crisis facing Venezuela's political system, which had been established at the end of the 1950s. That system was established as a consequence of the democratic (civil-military) revolution of 1958, during which then–president General Marcos Pérez Jiménez, who had led a military government for almost a decade, fled the country.

Three main democratic political parties, whose consolidation began in the 1940s, mainly led the democratic revolution: the Social Democratic Party (Acción Democrática, AD), the Christian Democratic Party (COPEI), and the Liberal Party (Unión Republicana Democrática, URD) parties. The parties agreed to establish and consolidate democracy in Venezuela through a series of written agreements, the most important of which was the *Pacto de Punto Fijo* (1958).[131] That document is an exceptional example in Latin American political history of an agreement among political elites to ensure the democratic governance of a country,[132] and it went on to produce one of the most stable democracies of Latin America during the second half of the twentieth century.[133]

The democratic political system strengthened during the 1960s and 1970s, precisely under that extraordinary political agreement, and evolved into a democracy of

---

131 These parties compromised on the maintenance of a democratic regime obtained with more than 92% of votes in the 1958 general elections. The Communist Party, which obtained no more than 5% of votes, was left out of the pact because of its nondemocratic program and doctrine. It cannot be considered "a considerable force in Venezuela politics." See Daniel Hellinger, "Political Overview: The Breakdown of *Puntofijismo* and the Rise of Chavismo," in *Venezuelan Politics in the Chávez Era: Class, Polarization, and Conflicts*, eds. Steve Ellner and Daniel Hellinger, Lynne Rienner, London 2003, 29. See the Venezuelan election data up to 1975 in Allan R. Brewer-Carías, *Cambio político y reforma del estado en Venezuela*, Editorial Tecnos, Madrid 1975. Forty years after the first election of 1958, in the general elections of 1998, the Communist Party obtained only 1.25% of votes. See Richard Gott, *Hugo Chávez and the Bolivarian Revolution*, Verso, London 2005, p. 139.

132 On the Punto Fijo Pact, the origins of the 1961 Constitution, and the political-party system, see Juan Carlos Rey, "El sistema de partidos venezolano," in *Problemas socio políticos de América Latina*, Caracas 1980, 255-338; and Allan R. Brewer-Carías, *Instituciones políticas y constitucionales*, Universidad Católica del Táchira–Editorial Jurídica Venezolana, San Cristóbal–Caracas 1996, 1 (Evolución histórica del estado): pp. 394 ff.; *Las constituciones de Venezuela*, Caracas 1997, 201ff.; and *La Constitución y sus enmiendas*, 13 ff. The text of the pact was published in *El Nacional*, Caracas Jan. 27, 1998, D-2; Haydee Miranda Bastidas et al., *Documentos fundamentales de la historia de Venezuela 1777-1993*, Los Libros de El Nacional, Caracas 1999, 174ff.; *Documentos que hicieron historia*, Presidencia de la República, Caracas 1962, Vol 2, pp. 443ff.

133 See, e.g., Robert J. Alexander, *The Venezuelan Democratic Revolution: A Profile of the Régime of Rómulo Betancourt*, Rutgers University Press, New Brunswick, NJ, 1964; Daniel H. Levine, *Conflict and Political Change in Venezuela*, Princeton University Press, Princeton, NJ, 1973. For criticism of Venezuelan exceptionalism, see Steve Ellner and Miguel Tinker Salas, eds., *Venezuela, Hugo Chávez and the Decline of a "Venezuelan Democracy,"* Rowman & Littlefield, New York 2007, pp. 3ff.

parties that functioned in a centralized state and a system of presidential government subject to parliamentary control.

1. *Party Domination and Demand for Participation*

Political parties increasingly monopolized the political regime established in the 1960s as a representative and pluralist democracy. They had established the democratic regime, but they did not understand, after establishing it, that the effects of democratization would require the system of governance to become more representative and more participatory.[134]

Democratic representation ended up being an issue exclusively for parties themselves. The d'Hondt method of electing party representatives according to the system of proportional representation resulted in the elections of party representatives who felt they were more accountable to their own parties than to their constituents or community. In addition, political parties monopolized the possibility for people's participation and penetrated all of civil society, from trade unions to professional associations and neighborhood organizations.

It must be noted that the proportional representation system was established in the 1961 Constitution and applied to all representative elections at the national, state, and municipal levels, allowing for the statutory establishment of a different electoral method at the local level, which occurred in some places in the 1980s and 1990s.[135] The absolute dominance of Congress by representatives of two or three political parties who had no direct relationships to their constituencies provoked their rejection by the people and the rejection of Congress, which was viewed as an exclusive, partisan body, not as the House of Representatives of the people. As a consequence, electoral support for the two main parties (AD and COPEI) varied from 92.83% in 1988 to 45.9% in 1993, to 36.1% in November 1998, and to 11.3% in December 1998, when Chávez was elected president.[136]

Thus, at the beginning of the 1980s, the public began to make new and diverse demands for means of representation and political participation, but those demands were not met. Among other things, the public called for a reform of the electoral system. In general, they wanted to make democracy more participatory. There was thus an urgent need for local government reform, because it is the only effective way to ensure effective democratic participation. However, in general, this was not understood, particularly by the political parties and their leaders.

Municipalities in Venezuela were and still are so disconnected from the citizens that they are of sporadic benefit to them. They never managed to become the primary political unit, the center of political participation, or an effective instrument for

---

134 See Allan R. Brewer-Carías, *El estado: Crisis y reforma*, Academia de Ciencias Políticas y Sociales, Caracas 1982, 7-89; and *El estado incomprendido. Reflexiones sobre el sistema político y su reforma*, Editorial Jurídica Venezolana, Caracas 1985.

135 See Allan R. Brewer-Carías, "La reforma del sistema electoral," *Revista Venezolana de Ciencias Políticas* 1, CEPSAL-Postgrado en Ciencias Políticas, Universidad de Los Andes, Mérida, Dec. 1987, 55-75; and *Ley Orgánica del Sufragio*, Caracas 1993. See also J. G. Molina and C. Pérez Baralt, "Venezuela ¿un nuevo sistema de partidos? Las elecciones de 1993," *Cuestiones Políticas* 13, 1994, pp. 63-99.

136 See *El Universal*, Caracas Dec. 11, 1998, p. 1–1.

managing local interests. They were accountable to no one; no one was interested in them, except the political parties, and they became a mechanism of political partisan's use and unpunished corruption.[137]

Thus, without eliminating political representation, the proposed reforms tended to create mechanisms that would have allowed people to participate on a daily basis in local affairs. That should have been one purpose of the constitution–making process of 1999, or at least many people thought it would be.[138] In any case, the aim was to reform the democratic system, on the basis of the Pacto de Punto Fijo, not to destroy democracy through policies based on the demonization of the pact, the parties that subscribed to it, and representative democracy itself.[139]

2.   State Centralism and the Crisis of Decentralization

Democratic reforms were needed in relation to the organization of the state. Venezuela has been a federal state since the Constitution of the Confederation of the States of Venezuela, dated December 21, 1811. Just as federalism was the only constitutional force uniting the previously independent thirteen colonies of the United States in the eighteenth century, in 1811 in Venezuela, it was the only constitutional means of bringing together the dispersed and isolated seven provinces that constituted the General Captaincy of Venezuela. Subsequently, Venezuelan political history has been marked by the swing of the pendulum between centralization and decentralization.[140] In the early stages of the republic, despite the centralist orientations of Simón Bolívar (contained in the 1819 and 1821 Constitutions),[141] in 1830, regionalist pressure led to the formation of a mixed central-federal state, which definitively consolidated as a federal system in 1864, when the United States of Venezuela was established.

However, the federation as it existed in the nineteenth century was abandoned in 1901, and throughout the twentieth century, the country experienced political centra-

---

137   See Allan R. Brewer-Carías, "Municipio, democracia y participación. Aspectos de la crisis," *Revista Venezolana de Estudios Municipales* 11, Caracas 1988, 13-30; and "Democracia municipal, descentralización y desarrollo local, *Revista Iberoamericana de Administración Pública* 11, Ministerio de Administraciones Públicas, Madrid 2004, pp. 11-34.

138   On this, see my proposal to the 1999 Constituent Assembly in Allan R. Brewer-Carías, *Debate constituyente, (Aportes a la Asamblea Nacional Constituyente)*, Fundación de Derecho Público–Editorial Jurídica Venezolana, Caracas 1999, 1 (Aug. 8–Sept. 8): pp. 156ff.

139   This policy has characterized Chávez's actions to justify the takeover of all branches of government, including the attempted coup he led in 1992. On the justification of Chávez's demonization of the Punto Fijo Pact, see Nikolas Kozloff, *Hugo Chávez: Oil, Politics, and the Challenge to the United States*, Palgrave Macmillan, New York 2006, pp. 47, 61; Richard Gott, *In the Shadow of the Liberator: Hugo Chávez and the Transformation of Venezuela*, Verso, London 2000, 17; Julia Buxton, *The Failure of Political Reform in Venezuela*, Ashgate, Aldershot, UK 2001, p. 19.

140   On the evolution of the Venezuelan federation, see Allan R. Brewer-Carías, *Instituciones políticas y constitucionales*, Universidad Católica del Táchira–Editorial Jurídica Venezolana, San Cristóbal–Caracas 1996, Vol I (Evolución histórica del estado): pp. 351ff.; Vol II (El Régimen del Poder Público y su Distribución Vertical): pp. 394ff.

141   See Allan R. Brewer-Carías, "Ideas centrales sobre la organización del estado en la obra del libertador y sus proyecciones contemporáneas," in *Boletín de la Academia de Ciencias Políticas y Sociales* 95–96, Caracas 1984, pp. 137-51.

lization.[142] Centralized governance was autocratic in its first phase but, beginning in 1935, it started to evolve to the more democratic form of the second half of the twentieth century.

At the end of the twentieth century, Venezuela remained a centralized federation, with power concentrated at the national level and illusory delegations of power to the federal states. At the same time, the centralized state led to a centralized political system, as party leaders and party organizations that were governed from Caracas (the center) came to dominate the political parties.

Long after the regional and local leadership of caudillos in the nineteenth century and after the consolidation of the national state in the first decades of the twentieth century, the call for increased democratization and decentralization in the modern era faced formidable challenges. Not only was it difficult to enhance the autonomy of local authorities; there also was resistance to admit the need to devolve power even to intermediate levels of government.

This state of affairs impeded the complete democratization of the country. Decentralization is a consequence of democracy and, at the same time, a condition necessary to its survival and improvement. It is an instrument for the intermediate-level exercise of power in a territory, which should, in turn, link the activities of the center to communities and regions. There are no decentralized autocracies; decentralized power is possible only in a democracy.[143] Consequently, the public outcry of 1989 called for parties to accelerate state reforms to political decentralization that were based on provisions in the 1961 Constitution. As a result, in 1989, state governors were directly elected for the first time in one hundred years; at the local level, the introduction of direct election of mayors superseded exclusive government by council.[144]

Such democratic "remedies" without a doubt breathed life into the system and allowed democracy to survive in the 1990s. Nevertheless, the decentralizing advances as of 1993 were abandoned,[145] and the political system entered a terminal crisis

---

142   See Allan R. Brewer-Carías, "El desarrollo institucional del estado centralizado en Venezuela (1899-1935) y sus proyecciones contemporáneas," in *Revista de Estudios de la Vida Local y Autonómica* 227–228, Madrid 1985, pp. 487-514, 695-726; and *Instituciones políticas y constitucionales,* Universidad Católica del Táchira–Editorial Jurídica Venezolana, San Cristóbal–Caracas 1996, Vol I (Evolución histórica del estado): pp. 351ff.; "La reforma política del estado: La descentralización política," in *Estudios de derecho público (Labor en el Senado),* Ediciones del Congreso Nacional, Caracas 1983, 1 (1982): pp. 15-39.

143   See Allan R. Brewer-Carías, *Reflexiones sobre la organización territorial del estado en Venezuela y en la América colonial,* Editorial Jurídica Venezolana, Caracas 1997, pp. 108ff.

144   See Allan R. Brewer-Carías, "Los problemas de la federación centralizada en Venezuela," in *Revista Ius et Praxis* 12, Universidad de Lima, Lima 1988, 49-96; "Bases legislativas para la descentralización política de la federación centralizada (1990: El inicio de una reforma)," in Allan R. Brewer-Carías et al., *Leyes y reglamentos para la descentralización política de la federación,* Caracas 1994, 7-53. Also see Brewer-Carías, *Instituciones políticas y constitucionales,* Universidad Católica del Táchira–Editorial Jurídica Venezolana, San Cristóbal–Caracas 1996, Vol II (El régimen del poder Público y su Distribución Vertical): pp. 394ff.

145   See discussion of the 1993 efforts to reinforce the decentralization process in Venezuela in *Informe sobre la descentralización en Venezuela 1994. Memoria del Dr. Allan R. Brewer-Carías, Ministro de Estado para la Descentralización,* Presidencia de la República, Caracas 1994.

in the last years of that decade.[146] The crisis, as mentioned earlier, provoked the calling of a constituent assembly, whose main objectives should have been the realization of decentralized power and consolidated democracy, not the destruction of democracy.

3.   *The Demand for Reform*

Latin American constitutionalism in recent decades has experienced an expansion of the traditional horizontal concept of separation of powers beyond the classic legislative, executive, and judicial powers. Many Latin American states have introduced a series of constitutional and autonomous institutions outside of the three classical branches of government, such as general controllerships, defenders of the people or of human rights, judiciary councils, and public ministries (public prosecutors). In addition, to increase participation of citizens in the democratic order, they have introduced new remedies for the protection of rights. Such measures have included judicial review of the constitutionality of legislation and judicial guarantees of constitutional rights, together with improvement in citizens' ability to use the *amparo* action (a specific judicial remedy for the protection of constitutional rights),[147] all of which have required that the judiciary be more independent and autonomous. The reforms have brought about a significant transformation of the system of checks and balances that regulates the traditional powers in those states. There were demands to institute similar reforms in Venezuela in the late 1990s, which would have required a transformation of the balances among the traditional powers of the state. Without doubt, those reforms should have been accomplished through the constitution-making process of 1999.

There was a particular need for reform in Venezuela. Although the Venezuelan system, like other Latin American systems, has been characterized by presidentialism, it had been a moderate presidentialism because of a series of parliamentary controls on the executive. Paradoxically, the crisis of the Venezuelan system stem-

146   See Pedro Guevara, *Estado vs. democracia*, Universidad Central de Venezuela, Caracas 1997; Miriam Kornblith, *Venezuela en los 90. Crisis de la democracia*, Ediciones IESA, Caracas 1998. See also, Allan R. Brewer-Carías, *Cinco siglos de historia y un país en crisis*, Academia de Ciencias Políticas y Sociales y Comisión Presidencial del V Centenario de Venezuela, Caracas 1998, pp. 95-117; "La crisis terminal del sistema político," in *Una evaluación a estos cuarenta años de democracia*, El Globo, Caracas Nov. 24, 1997, pp. 12-13; "La crisis terminal del sistema político venezolano y el reto democrático de la descentralización," in *Instituciones políticas y constitucionales*, Universidad Católica del Táchira–Editorial Jurídica Venezolana, San Cristóbal–Caracas 1996, Vol III (La Distribución Horizontal del Poder Público): pp. 655-678; "Presentación," in *Los candidatos presidenciales ante la academia*, Academia de Ciencias Políticas y Sociales, Caracas 1998, 9-66; and *Asamblea constituyente y ordenamiento constitucional*, Academia de Ciencias Políticas y Sociales, Caracas 1999, pp. 15-85.

147   See Allan R. Brewer-Carías, *Constitutional Protection of Human Rights in Latin America: A Comparative Study of the Amparo Proceeding*, Cambridge University Press, New York, 2009; *El amparo a los derechos y garantías constitucionales (Una aproximación comparativa)*, Editorial Jurídica Venezolana, Caracas 1993; and *Instituciones Políticas y Constitucionales*, Universidad Católica del Táchira–Editorial Jurídica Venezolana, San Cristóbal–Caracas 1998, Vol V (Derecho y acción de amparo): pp. 111 ff.

med not from an excess of presidentialism but from an excess of parliamentarianism, which took the form of the political parties' monopoly on power.[148]

In the late 1990s, criticisms of that monopoly focused, in particular, on the appointment by Congress of the heads of the nonelected organs of public power (Supreme Court, Judicial Council, general controller of the republic, prosecutor general of the republic, Electoral Supreme Council). Serious criticism arose because of the excessive partisanship shown in those appointments and because of the lack of transparency and participation of civil society in them.[149]

Therefore, on the one hand, the demands for reform called for increased checks and balances to break the monopoly of the political parties and reduce partisanship and, on the other hand, for an increase in the judicial guarantees of constitutional rights to guarantee greater citizen participation in the democratic order.

Consequently, the 1999 Constituent Assembly should have been used as a vehicle for including and reconciling all political stakeholders beyond traditional political parties in the redesign of the democratic system.[150] The Constituent Assembly should have focused on establishing a system that would guarantee not only elections but also all the other essential elements of democracy, as were later set forth in the Inter-American Democratic Charter enacted by the General Assembly of the Organization of American States on September 11, 2001. Such elements include "the respect for human rights and fundamental freedoms, the access to power and its exercise subject to the rule of law, the making of periodic, free and fair elections based on universal and secret vote as an expression of the sovereignty of the people, the plural regime of parties and political organizations and the separation and independence of the public powers" (Article 3).

III. THE CONSTITUTION MAKING PROCESS AND ITS DEFORMATION

1. *The Choice of a National Constituent Assembly*

Although the call for a constituent assembly materialized in 1999, the demand for such a body as a vehicle of conciliation or political reconstruction had actually arisen earlier. It had been proposed before and in the aftermath of the two attempted military coups of 1992,[151] which had been carried out, among others, by then lieutenant–colonel Hugo Chávez Frías, later elected president of Venezuela in 1998.

The subject, in fact, was publicly discussed from 1992,[152] but the leaders of the main political parties failed to appreciate the magnitude of the political crisis. Inste-

---

148 See Allan R. Brewer-Carías, *Problemas del estado de partidos,* Editorial Jurídica Venezolana, Caracas 1988, 92 ff.

149 *Id.*

150 See my proposal regarding the convening of the 1999 Constituent Assembly in Allan R. Brewer-Carías, *Asamblea constituyente y ordenamiento constitucional*, Academia de Ciencias Políticas y Sociales, Caracas 1999, pp. 56-60.

151 See, e.g., Frente Patriótico, *Por una asamblea constituyente para una nueva Venezuela*, Caracas 1991.

152 On the initial 1992 proposals, see Elías García Navas, "La Constituyente es la única salida a la crisis política" (Interview, Allan R. Brewer-Carías), in *El Nacional*, Caracas Mar. 1, 1992, p. D-2; Consejo Consultivo de la Presidencia de la República, *Recomendaciones del Consejo Consultivo al Presidente*

ad of attempting to democratize institutions, they tried to maintain the status quo. This response served to discredit the leaders and their political parties, leading to a leadership vacuum in a regime that had been previously characterized by the hegemony of the political parties and their leaders.[153]

In the middle of this political crisis, in 1998, Chávez, as presidential candidate, raised the issue of calling a constituent assembly, only a few years after the removal of criminal charges against him stemming from his 1992 attempted military coup. Notwithstanding all the benefits of the proposal, some of the traditional political parties disputed the proposal and others rejected it; all politicà elements rejected the idea that the Congress elected in December 1998 could take the lead in the constitution-making process. That is, the political parties, although holding sufficient seats in Congress to shape the constituent process and assume the task of implementing the needed democratic political reforms declined to take on that role.[154] Their ignorance of the magnitude of the political crisis was pathetic; in the end, the Constituent Assembly turned out to be the exclusive political project of candidate Chávez,[155] and it remained such after he was elected president in December 1998 with an overwhelming majority of 60% of votes cast. Nonetheless, his proposal was not intended to reform the democratic system – he conceived of it as "revolutionary process which seeks to destroy this [democratic] system; unlike other project, ours does not seek to fix this system."[156] However, the call for a constituent assembly posed a seemingly insurmountable constitutional problem: The text of the 1961 Constitution did not provide for the institution of a constituent assembly as a mechanism of constitutional reform. That text set out only two procedures for the revision of the constitution, one that would apply in the case of a simple amendment and another that would apply in the case of a larger "general reform."[157] Both procedures required

---

de la República, Caracas 1992, p. 15; Oswaldo Álvarez Paz, *El camino constituyente*, Gobernación del Estado Zulia, Maracaibo, June 1992; Ricardo Combellas, "Asamblea constituyente. Estudio jurídico-político," and Ángel Álvarez, "Análisis de la naturaleza de la crisis actual y la viabilidad política de la Asamblea Constituyente," in COPRE, *Asamblea constituyente: Salida democrática a la crisis*, Folletos para la Discusión,No. 18, Caracas 1992; R. Escovar Salom, "Necesidad de una asamblea nacional constituyente," *Cuadernos Nuevo Sur* 2–3, Caracas 1992, pp. 156-160; Frente Amplio Proconstituyente *¿Qué es la Constituyente?*, *El Nacional*, Caracas June 30, 1994; Hermánn Escarrá Malavé, *Democracia, reforma constitucional y asamblea constituyente*, Caracas 1995.

153   The progressive implosion of the Venezuelan democratic regime, which Enrique Krauze considered "one of the great mysteries of contemporary Venezuela. A mystery and a tragedy," was provoked by the "blindness of the political parties' leadership that did not understand the people's cry out for reform." This blindness was also a main cause of what Krauze called democracy suicide. See Enrique Krauze, *El poder y el delirio*, Tusquests Editores, Mexico City 2009, pp. 47, 52.

154   See my comments from Nov. 1998, in Brewer-Carías, *Asamblea constituyente y ordenamiento constitucional*, 78-85. See also Daniel Hellinger, "Political Overview: The Breakdown of *Puntofijismo* and the Rise of Chavismo," in Ellner and Hellinger, *Venezuelan Politics in the Chávez Era*, p. 29.

155   See his "Propuestas para transformar Venezuela," in Hugo Chávez Frías, *Una revolución democrática*, Caracas 1998, p. 7.

156   See Agustín Blanco Muñoz (Entrevistas a Hugo Chávez Frías), *Habla el Comandante*, Universidad Central de Venezuela, Caracas 1998, p. 287. See also A. C. Clark, *The Revolutionary Has No Clothes: Hugo Chávez's Bolivarian Farce*, Encounter Books, New York 2009, p. 61.

157   See Allan R. Brewer-Carías, "Los procedimientos de revisión constitucional en Venezuela" in *I Procedimenti di revisione costituzionale nel Diritto Comparato*, Atti del Convegno Internazionale organizzato dalla Facoltà di Giurisprudenza di Urbino, Apr. 23–24, 1997, Università Degli Studi di Urbino, pub-

the vote of both houses of Congress, with additional approval by popular referendum or by the majority of the state assemblies, without any provision for the creation of a separate constituent assembly.

Consequently, the first fraudulent action committed against the then-in-force 1961 Constitution occurred in February 1999, when the then–newly elected President Hugo Chávez Frías, on the same day of his inauguration and after the Supreme Court of Justice had issued an ambiguous decision on the matter a few days before, convened a referendum without constitutional authorization and without any previous political agreement or consensual process, to ask for the opinion of the people on the convening and election of a Constituent Assembly not established in the Constitution to reshape the constitutional order of the country.[158]

2. *The Constitutional Debate Regarding the Election of the Constituent Assembly*

These constitutional impediments, the general claims of the people for political change, and the commitment of the elected President with the constituent assembly proposal, provoked that after the presidential elections, political discussion ceased to be about the need to convene a constituent assembly and turned to be about how to do it and, particularly, whether it was necessary to amend or reform the existing Constitution to create the institution.[159] Particularly regarding the question of whether the election of the Constituent Assembly required a previous constitutional amendment to establish such an institution, and if the concept of popular sovereignty could allow the election of a constituent assembly in the absence of preexisting constitutional authority. In short, it was a conflict between constitutional supremacy and popular sovereignty,[160] which has been a basic dilemma of all political crises, that is, constitutional review through either constitutional supremacy or popular sovereignty, and the weight that one or the other principle must have in modern constitutional states.

In hindsight, considerations of the rule of law should have resolved the debate. Viewed from that perspective, there is no doubt that a constitutional amendment was required. This was the only way the issue could have been resolved without violating the text of the existing Constitution.[161] On the contrary, the violation of the

---

blicazioni della Facoltà di Giurisprudenza e della Facoltá di Scienze Politiche, Urbino, Italy, 1999, pp. 137-181; and in *Boletín de la Academia de Ciencias Políticas y Sociales* 134, Caracas 1997, 169-222. See also Allan R. Brewer-Carías, *Asamblea constituyente y ordenamiento constitucional,* Academia de Ciencias Políticas y Sociales, Caracas 1999, pp. 84-149.

158 On the political discussion regarding the proposed constitution-making process, see Allan R. Brewer-Carías, *Asamblea constituyente y ordenamiento constitucional*, Biblioteca de la Academia de Ciencias Políticas y Sociales, Caracas 1999, pp. 38ff.

159 See my 1998 proposal in Brewer-Carías, *Asamblea nacional constituyente y ordenamiento constitucional,* 56–69; see the contrary position of Carlos M. Escarrá Malavé, *Proceso político y constituyente. Papeles constituyentes,* Maracaibo 1999, pp. 33ff.

160 See Allan R. Brewer-Carías, "El desequilibrio entre soberanía popular y supremacía constitucional y la salida constituyente en Venezuela en 1999," *Revista Anuario Iberoamericano de Justicia Constitucional* 3, 1999, Centro de Estudios Políticos y Constitucionales, Madrid 2000, 31-56; and *Asamblea constituyente y ordenamiento constitucional,* pp. 152ff.

161 See Allan R. Brewer-Carías, "Comentarios sobre la inconstitucional de la convocatoria a referéndum sobre una Asamblea Nacional Constituyente, efectuada por el Consejo Nacional Electoral en febrero de

Constitution to establish a new constitution–making process that would allegedly give preference to the will of the people (popular sovereignty) over the rule of law (constitutional supremacy) always leaves the indelible imprint of doubts of political legitimacy, which eventually can serve to revert the situation.[162]

Because the matter of constitutional reform was more political than legal, before the Supreme Court could issue any ruling on the matter, as civil society had requested, the elected president announced his intention to convene the Constituent Assembly as his first act of government, to be issued on Inauguration Day (February 2, 1999). Buoyed by his popularity at the moment, Chávez publicly pressured the Supreme Court to decide the question submitted to it in an interpretative recourse on consultative referendums filed by a nongovernmental organization, according to the statute governing the Supreme Court.

On January 19, 1999, almost two weeks before the president took office, the Court issued two ambiguous decisions that failed to expressly resolve the issue,[163] if there was a need to first reform the Constitution before the assembly could be convened; thus decreeing "the death of a Constitution."[164] The Court, in its decision, referred broadly to the traditional constitutional doctrine on constituent power, including quotations from the 1789 writings of Abate Sièyes, which those defending the possibility of convening the Assembly subsequently used to support their argument.[165] In this regard, the Court's ambiguous decision contrasted with the very clear and direct decision of the Supreme Court of Justice of Colombia in 1991, which allowed the Constituent Assembly to be convened, and with the clear deci-

---

1999," *Revista Política y Gobierno No. 1*, Fundación de Estudios de Derecho Administrativo, Caracas 1999, pp. 29 92. See also Brewer-Carías, *Asamblea constituyente y ordenamiento constitucional*, 229ff.

162   Among the authors who thought the convening of the Constituent Assembly needed a prior constitutional provision establishing it was Ricardo Combellas, who in 1998 was head of the Presidential Commission on State Reforms. See Ricardo Combellas, *¿Qué es la Constituyente?. Voz para el futuro de Venezuela*, COPRE, Caracas 1998, p. 38. The next year, after having been appointed by Chávez as member of the Presidential Commission for the Constitutional Reform, he changed his opinion, admitting the possibility of electing the assembly even without constitutional support. See Ricardo Combellas, *Poder constituyente*, Presentación, Hugo Chávez Frías, Caracas 1999, pp. 189ff. In 1999, Combellas was elected a member of the Constituent Assembly from the lists supported by Chávez, but a few years later, he withdrew his support for the president and became a critic of his antidemocratic government.

163   See the texts in *Revista de Derecho Público* 77–80, Editorial Jurídica Venezolana, Caracas 1999, 56-73; and Allan R. Brewer-Carías, *Poder constituyente originario y asamblea nacional constituyente*, Editorial Jurídica Venezolana, Caracas 1999, pp. 25ff.

164   See Alessandro Pace, "Morte di una Costituzione," *Giurisprudenza Costituzionale* XLIV, Fasc. 2-Giuffrè Editore, Milan 1999; "Muerte de una constitución," in *Revista Española de Derecho Constitucional* 57, Centro de Estudios Políticos y Constitucionales, Madrid 1999, pp. 271-283.

165   On the decisions, see Allan R. Brewer-Carías, "La configuración judicial del proceso constituyente o de cómo el guardián de la Constitución abrió el camino para su violación y para su propia extinción," *Revista de Derecho Público, No.* 77–80, Editorial Jurídica Venezolana, Caracas 1999, pp. 453-514; Allan R. Brewer-Carías, *Asamblea constituyente y ordenamiento constitucional*, Academia de Ciencias Políticas y Sociales, Caracas 1999, pp. 152-228; Allan R. Brewer-Carías, *Golpe de estado y proceso constituyente en Venezuela*, Universidad Nacional Autónoma de México, Mexico City 2002, pp. 65ff.; Lolymar Hernández Camargo, *La teoría del poder constituyente: Un caso de estudio: El proceso constituyente venezolano de 1999*, Universidad Católica del Táchira, San Cristóbal 2000, pp. 53ff.; Claudia Nikken, *La cour suprême de justice et la constitution vénézuélienne du 23 Janvier 1961*, Ph.D. diss., l'Université Panthéon Assas, Paris 2001, pp. 366ff.

sions of the contentious administrative jurisdiction courts in Honduras in 2009. This
is the main difference between the cases of Colombia in 1991 and Venezuela in
1999 – in the former, the Constituent Assembly was elected after the Supreme Court
expressly allowed it. In the case of Venezuela, the Supreme Court's decisions acknowledged the possibility of a consultative referendum to seek popular opinion on
the election of a constituent assembly and presented a theoretical summary of the
constitutional doctrine of constituent power. However, the Court said nothing about
the main issue of whether a previous constitutional amendment was required to elect
a constituent assembly to give constitutional rank to its status.[166]

The ambiguous Supreme Court decision emboldened the president who, without
constitutional authorization, issued his first official act on February 2, 1999: a decree
ordering a referendum to propose that the people authorize Chávez, and him alone,
to call the Constituent Assembly and to define its composition, procedure, mission,
and duration.[167] Thus, he purported to hold a referendum on a constituent assembly
in which people would vote blindly, without knowing the number of representatives
to be elected; the electoral system to be applied and the procedure for the assembly's
election, composition, or the nature or duration of its mission. That means that the
president began the process to convene a constituent assembly to transform the state
and the legal order, without any previous political consultation or consensus with the
political parties and forces of the country, thus disregarding any constitutional or
legal consideration.[168] In that way, he marked the process as one imposed by the
president on the basis of his own popularity, without the participation of the political
spectrum of the country. This was another main difference from Colombia's 1991
Constituent Assembly.

---

166   See comments on the decisions in Allan R. Brewer-Carías, "La configuración judicial del proceso cons-
tituyente o de cómo el guardián de la Constitución abrió el camino para su violación y para su propia
extinción," in *Revista de Derecho Público, No.* 77–80, Editorial Jurídica Venezolana, Caracas 1999,
V453-514; Allan R. Brewer-Carías, *Asamblea constituyente y ordenamiento constitucional,* 152-228;
Allan R. Brewer-Carías, *Golpe de estado y proceso constituyente en Venezuela,* Universidad Nacional
Autónoma de México, Mexico City 2002, pp. 65ff.; Lolymar Hernández Camargo, *La teoría del poder
constituyente. Un caso de estudio: el proceso constituyente venezolano de 1999,* Universidad Católica
del Táchira, San Cristóbal 2000, pp. 53ff.; Claudia Nikken, *La Cour Suprême de Justice et la Constitution vénézuélienne du 23 Janvier 1961,* Ph.D. diss., l'Université Panthéon Assas (Paris II), Paris 2001,
pp. 366ff.

167   See *Gaceta Oficial* N° 36.634, Feb. 2, 1999, and its modification in *Gaceta Oficial* N° 36.658, Mar. 10,
1999. See comments regarding the decree in Allan R. Brewer-Carías, *Golpe de estado y proceso constituyente en Venezuela,* Universidad Nacional Autónoma de México, Mexico City 2002, 113 ff.; Allan R.
Brewer-Carías, *Asamblea constituyente y ordenamiento constitucional,* Academia de Ciencias Políticas
y Sociales, Caracas 1998, pp. 229ff.

168   The same day, Feb. 2, 1999, in which he convened the Constituent Assembly, he said in a public rally:
"[Many think] that the Decree on the Constituent [Assembly] does not fulfill provisions, I don't know of
which law, or of which thing, or of which Constitution! Who cares that the Decree of the Constituent
[Assembly] does not fulfill with, I don't know what thing of a law, or of the Constitution, if it is the
people who is the one crying out for transformation; [the problem] is not legal, is political, and for those
in the Congress [beware]: there is no walk back; for those in the political parties [beware]: there is no
walk back." See Ana Teresa Torres, *La herencia de la tribu. Del mito de la independencia a la Revolución bolivariana,* Editorial Alfa, Caracas 2009, p. 224.

Because he tried to impose his exclusive and exclusionist proposal through the February decree, it is hardly surprising that the constitutionality of the decree was challenged before the Supreme Court,[169] which in a series of judicial review decisions ruled that the manner in which the president had acted in calling for the consultative referendum on the Constituent Assembly was unconstitutional. In one of the rulings, issued on March 18, 1999, the Supreme Court declared that the president could not exclusively formulate the composition, procedure, mission, and duration of the Constituent Assembly, and that those details would at least have to be submitted to popular vote.[170] Consequently, the National Electoral Council was required to submit to popular vote whether to convene the Constituent Assembly and the complete text of its bylaws, from the president, which were not the product of any sort of political agreement, compromise, or consensus among political forces of the country. In contrast, in Colombia, the Constituent Assembly was convened after political parties had reached agreements and consensus. But Ecuador followed the example of Venezuela in 2007. In both cases, even with some judicial corrections, the president unilaterally imposed the bylaws of the Constituent Assembly. On April 13, 1999, Venezuela's Supreme Court ruled that the Assembly had to be elected within the framework of the Court's interpretation of the 1961 Constitution and could not have "original constituent powers," as the president had proposed. The Court expressly ordered the National Electoral Council to eliminate those full and unlimited powers from the bylaws to be submitted to the April 25 referendum.[171]

The members of the Supreme Court had been elected years before by the party-controlled Congress, and it was that same Court that, under tremendous political pressure from President-Elect Chávez, issued the aforementioned decision of January 1999, by which it gave way, without express ruling, to the possibility of the election of a constituent assembly without previously reforming the Constitution. After having freed the political constituent forces of society as a means for participation, when the Supreme Court tried to control them by ruling that the Constituent Assem-

---

169 See the text of the challenge I brought before the Supreme Court in Brewer-Carías, *Asamblea constituyente y ordenación constitucional*, 255-321. On the other challenges brought before the Supreme Court, see Carlos M. Escarrá Malavé, *Proceso político y constituyente*, Caracas 1999.

170 See the text of Supreme Court decisions from Mar. 18, 1999; Mar. 23, 1999; Apr. 13, 1999; June 3, 1999; June 17, 1999; and July 21, 1999, in *Revista de Derecho Público* 77–80, Editorial Jurídica Venezolana, Caracas 1999, 73-110. See the comments in Allan R. Brewer-Carías, *Poder constituyente originario y asamblea nacional constituyente*, Editorial Jurídica Venezolana, Caracas 1999, 169-98, 223-51; "Comentarios sobre la inconstitucional convocatoria a referendo sobre una Asamblea Nacional Constituyente efectuada por el Consejo Nacional Electoral en febrero de 1999," *Revista Política y Gobierno* 1, Fundación de Estudios de Derecho Administrativo, Caracas 1999, 29-92; and *Golpe de estado y proceso constituyente en Venezuela*, Universidad Nacional Autónoma de México, Mexico City 2002, pp. 160 ff.

171 In particular, see Supreme Court decisions of Apr. 13, 1999; June 17, 1999; and July 21, 1999, in *Revista de Derecho Público* No. 77–80, Editorial Jurídica Venezolana, Caracas 1999, pp. 85 ff.; Brewer-Carías, *Poder constituyente originario y asamblea nacional constituyente*, pp. 169-198, 223-225. Venezuelan constitutional law distinguishes between "derivative" constituent authority and "original" constituent authority, the latter being the kind of nonlimited authority such an institution would have at the very moment of conception of a new state. The 1811 General Congress of the Confederation of the States of Venezuela as a constitutional convention would be an example of the kind of institution that would be considered original in this sense.

bly to be elected had to observe and act according to the 1961 Constitution, it was too late.[172] After the election in July 1999, the Constituent Assembly crushed all the constituted powers, including the Supreme Court itself, violating the in–force 1961 Constitution.[173]

3.   The Electoral Rule for the Election of the Assembly

Despite the Supreme Court's rulings and in the absence of any political negotiations, agreements, or consensus among various sectors of society, the president proceeded unilaterally with the consultative referendum to call a constituent assembly on April 25, 1999. In a voting process in which only 38.7% of eligible voters cast their ballots (62.2% of eligible voters did not turn out to vote), the yes votes obtained 81.9% and the no votes 18.1%.[174] The approved proposal provided for the election of a 131-member constituent assembly: 104 members to be elected in 24 regional constituencies corresponding to the political subdivisions of the territory (states and the federal district); 24 members to be elected in a national constituency, and 3 members representing the indigenous peoples, who constitute a small portion of Venezuela's population.

The referendum approved the electoral system that the president had proposed in which candidates were to run individually, allowing Chávez's supporters to easily dominate the Constituent Assembly.[175] The 104 regional constituency seats were allotted according to the population of each state and the federal district. A list of all the candidates in each regional constituency was placed on the ballot in each constituency, and the voters could vote for the number of candidates on their constituency's list that corresponded to the number of seats allotted to their constituency. The elected candidates were those who received the greatest number of votes. Voting proceeded in the same way on the national level for the twenty-four seats, except in that case, voters were allowed to choose only ten candidates from the list.

This electoral system was without any precedent in Venezuela. It amounted to a ruse by the president and his followers to ensure absolute control of the Constituent Assembly. In a campaign financed by Venezuelan insurance companies and foreign banks,[176] among others, the president appeared personally in every state of the country proposing his list of candidates for election in each constituency. On the national level, he proposed only twenty candidates for the twenty-four seats; dividing the country in two, he proposed a list of ten candidates to voters in the east and a separa-

---

172   In particular, see the Supreme Court decisions of Apr. 13, 1999; June 17, 1999; and July 21, 1999, in *Revista de Derecho Público* 77–80, Editorial Jurídica Venezolana, Caracas 1999, pp. 85ff.

173   See references to all those decisions in Brewer-Carías, *Debate constituyente, (Aportes a la Asamblea Nacional Constituyente)*, Fundación de Derecho Público–Editorial Jurídica Venezolana, Caracas 1999, 1 (Aug. 8–Sept. 8): pp. 11-124.

174   See José E. Molina and Carmen Pérez Baralt, "Procesos Electorales. Venezuela, abril, julio y diciembre de 1999," in *Boletín Electoral Latinoamericano* 22, CAPEL-IIDH, San José 2000, pp. 61ff.

175   See Gregory Wilpert, *Changing Venezuela by Taking Power: The History and Policies of the Chávez Government*, Verso, London 2007, p. 21.

176   For which a few high former officials of the Banco Bilbao Vizcaya of Spain were criminally indicted on Feb. 8, 2006, by the Juzgado Central de Instrucción N° 5, Audiencia Nacional, Madrid (Procedure N° 251/02-N).

te list of ten candidates to voters of the west. This was rather unusual in Venezuelan political tradition. After more than a hundred years of the constitutional rule of no reelection, Venezuelans were not used to having presidents directly involved in electoral campaigns, and any governmental involvement in elections had been considered illegitimate.

The election was carried out on July 25, 1999, without the participation of the traditional political parties; only 46.3% of eligible voters cast ballots (53.7% of eligible voters did not turn out to vote).[177] The candidates supported by the president obtained 65.8% of the votes cast, but the election resulted in his followers controlling 94% of the seats in the Constituent Assembly. All of the president's supported candidates except one were elected, for a total of 123 – of the 104 candidates elected at the state level, only one belonged to a traditional party (Acción Democrática); of the 24 candidates elected at the national level, only 4 independent candidates who opposed the president were elected without his support, mainly because the president had proposed only 20 candidates of 24 to be elected. Because the voters could vote for only ten candidates nationally, all those proposed by the president (ten each in the east and west) were elected. It can be deduced that if the president would have proposed three sets of eight candidates – instead of two sets of ten – all twenty-four candidates would have been elected. In addition, three indigenous representatives elected to the assembly were followers of the president and his party.

The result of this electoral scheme was that instead of contributing to democratic pluralism, the Constituent Assembly was totally controlled by the newly established government party and the president's followers, to the exclusion of all traditional political parties. As mentioned, only one member out of 131 belonged to the traditional parties (one regional member), and 4 others were elected independently, in opposition to the president.[178] Together, they became the opposition group in the assembly.

A constituent assembly formed by a majority of that nature was not a valid instrument for dialogue or for political conciliation and negotiation. It was a political instrument to impose the ideas of a dominant group on the rest of society and to totally exclude other groups.

4. The Seizure of the Constituted Powers

Meanwhile, and before the convening of the Constituent Assembly, President Chávez and all the representatives to the National Congress had been elected in November and December 1998, per the provisions of the 1961 Constitution. The governors of the 23 states, the representatives of the state legislative assemblies, and the mayors and members of the municipal councils of the 338 municipalities had also been elected in November 1998. That is, all the heads of the representative public entities set forth in the Constitution had been popularly elected before the constitution-making process of 1999 had begun. In addition, the nonelected heads of the

---

177   See José E. Molina and Carmen Pérez Baralt, "Procesos Electorales. Venezuela, abril, julio y diciembre de 1999," in *Boletín Electoral Latinoamericano* 22, CAPEL-IIDH, San José 2000, pp. 61ff.

178   Allan R. Brewer-Carías, Claudio Fermín, Alberto Franchesqui, and Jorge Olavarría.

organs of state, such as the judges of the Supreme Court of Justice, the prosecutor general of the republic, the general controller of the republic, and the members of the Supreme Electoral Council, had been appointed by the National Congress, again in accordance with the 1961 Constitution.

Therefore, by the time the Constituent Assembly was elected on July 25, 1999, the constituted public entities were functioning in parallel, with different missions. The Constituent Assembly was elected to design the reform of the state and to establish a new legal framework institutionalizing a social and participatory democracy, which was to be submitted for popular approval in a final referendum. It was not elected to govern, substitute, or interfere with the constituted powers. Moreover, as the Supreme Court of Justice declared in one of its decisions, it had no "original" constituent authority.[179]

However, in its first decision, which was the adoption of its own statute governing its functioning, the Constituent Assembly, in a contrary sense to what had ruled the Supreme Court a few months earlier, declared itself "an original constituent power," granted itself the authority to "limit or abolish the power of the organs of state," and set forth that "all the organs of the Public Power are subjected to the Constituent National Assembly" and "obliged to comply with its juridical acts."[180]

With that decision, the Constituent Assembly declared itself a state superpower and assumed powers that even the referendum had failed to grant. It was in that way that the Constituent Assembly, which functioned between July 1999 and January 2000, usurped public power, violated the Constitution of 1961, and accomplished a coup d'état.[181]

During the first months of it's functioning, from August to September 1999, the Assembly, instead of conciliating and forming a new political pact for society, usurped the role of the constituted powers elected in December 1998, which were functioning according to the 1961 Constitution. In August 1999, the Constituent Assembly decreed the reorganization of all branches of government:[182] It encroached on the judicial branch by creating the Commission of Judicial Emergency for the purpose of intervening in judicial matters to the detriment of the autonomy and inde-

179   See the decision of Apr. 13, 1999, in *Revista de Derecho Público* 77–80, Editorial Jurídica Venezolana, Caracas 1999, pp. 85ff.; Brewer-Carías, *Poder constituyente originario y asamblea nacional constituyente*, Editorial Jurídica Venezolana, Caracas 1999, *pp.* 169-198, pp. 223-251.

180   See *Gaceta Constituyente (Diario de Debates), Agosto-Septiembre 1999*, Aug. 3, 1999, N° 1, 4. See my dissenting vote in *Gaceta Constituyente (Diario de Debates), Agosto-Septiembre 1999*, Aug. 7, 1999, N° 4, pp. 6-13; and Allan R. Brewer-Carías, *Debate constituyente (Aportes a la Asamblea Nacional Constituyente)*, Fundación de Derecho Público–Editorial Jurídica Venezolana, Caracas 1999, 1 (Aug. 8–Sept. 8): pp. 15-39.

181   See Allan R. Brewer-Carías, *Golpe de estado y proceso constituyente en Venezuela*, Universidad Nacional Autónoma de México, Mexico City 2002, pp. 181 ff.

182   Decree of Aug. 12, 1999. See *Gaceta Constituyente (Diario de Debates), Agosto-Septiembre de 1999*, Aug. 12, N° 8, pp. 2-4, and *Gaceta Oficial* N° 36.764, Aug. 13, 2009. See my dissenting vote in Brewer-Carías, *Debate constituyente (Aportes a la Asamblea Nacional Constituyente)*, Fundación de Derecho Público–Editorial Jurídica Venezolana, Caracas 1999, 1 (Aug. 8–Sept. 8): pp. 43-56.

pendence of the existing judges,[183] it dissolved both the Senate and the Chamber of Representatives of the National Congress and the legislative assemblies of the states,[184] and it suspended municipal elections.[185]

All these actions were challenged before the Supreme Court, but the Court, in a decision of October 14, 1999, in contrast with its ruling in its earlier decisions, upheld their constitutionality, recognizing the Constitutional Assembly as a supraconstitutional power.[186] This implied the attribution to the assembly of sovereign power, which it did not have –the only sovereign power in a constitutional state is the people. It was the only way to justify the otherwise-unconstitutional intervention of the constituted branches of governments, a confusion that was expressly pointed out in various magistrates' dissenting votes.[187] In issuing the decision, the Court actually pronounced its own death sentence[188]; it disappeared two months later.

It must be noted that the Supreme Court did not rule consistently with its previous decisions on the Constituent Assembly, even with the ambiguous one. Political pressure on the Court provoked the change, and the Supreme Court not only adopted a ruling in support of the Constituent Assembly's intervention in the judiciary but also appointed one of its magistrates as a member of the Commission of Judicial Emergency. Only the president of the Supreme Court resigned.[189] The ot-

---

183   Decree of Aug. 19, 1999. See *Gaceta Constituyente (Diario de Debates), Agosto-Septiembre de 1999*, Aug. 18, 1999, N° 10, pp. 17-22, and *Gaceta Oficial* N° 36.782, Sept. 8, 1999. See my dissenting vote in Brewer-Carías, *Debate constituyente, (Aportes a la Asamblea Nacional Constituyente)*, Fundación de Derecho Público–Editorial Jurídica Venezolana, Caracas 1999, 1 (Aug. 8–Sept. 8):57-73. See comments in Brewer-Carías, *Golpe de estado y proceso constituyente en Venezuela*, 184ff. See Allan R. Brewer-Carías, "La progresiva y sistemática demolición institucional de la autonomía e independencia del Poder Judicial en Venezuela 1999-2004." *XXX Jornadas J.M. Domínguez Escovar, Estado de derecho, Administración de justicia y derechos humanos*, Instituto de Estudios Jurídicos del Estado Lara, Barquisimeto 2005, pp. 33-174.

184   Decree of Aug. 28, 1999. See the text in *Gaceta Constituyente (Diario de Debates), Agosto-Septiembre 1999*, Aug. 25, 1999, N° 13. See my dissenting vote in Brewer-Carías, *Debate constituyente (Aportes a la Asamblea Nacional Constituyente)*, Fundación de Derecho Público–Editorial Jurídica Venezolana, Caracas 1999, 1 (Aug. 8–Sept. 8), pp. 75-113.

185   Decree of Aug. 26, 1999. See *Gaceta Constituyente (Diario de Debates), Agosto-Septiembre 1999*, Aug. 26, 1999, N° 14, 7-8, 11, 13, and 14; and *Gaceta Oficial* N° 36.776, Aug. 31, 2009. See my dissenting vote in Brewer-Carías, *Debate constituyente, (Aportes a la Asamblea Nacional Constituyente)*, 1 (Aug. 8–Sept. 8), pp. 115-22.

186   See the decisión of Oct. 14, 1999, in *Revista de Derecho Público* 77–80, Editorial Jurídica Venezolana, Caracas 1999, 111-32. See comments in Allan R. Brewer-Carías, "La configuración judicial del proceso constituyente o de cómo el guardián de la Constitución abrió el camino para su violación y para su propia extinción," *Revista de Derecho Público* 77–80, Editorial Jurídica Venezolana, Caracas 1999, 453ff.

187   Particularly by Magistrate Humberto J. La Roche, who rendered the opinion of the Court in its initial decision of Jan. 19, 1999.

188   As predicted by the resigning president of the Supreme Court. See comments in Brewer-Carías, *Golpe de estado y proceso constituyente en Venezuela*, pp. 218 ff.

189   See the Decree of Judicial Emergency in *Gaceta Oficial* N° 36.772, Aug. 25, 1999, and in *Gaceta Oficial* N° 36.782, Sept. 9, 1999. The Supreme Court issued a formal act accepting the assembly's intervention in the judiciary, and later the new Supreme Tribunal upheld the decree on Mar. 24, 2000, Decisión N° 659 (Case: *Rosario Nouel*), in *Revista de Derecho Público* No. 81, Editorial Jurídica Venezolana, Caracas 2000, 102-5. See comments on the Supreme Court's submission to the assembly's will and its consequences in Brewer-Carías, *Debate constituyente (Aportes a la Asamblea Nacional Constituyente)*, 1 (Aug. 8–Sept. 8), pp. 141-52.

hers, by action or omission, submitted themselves to the new power, but only for two months, until the same Constituent Assembly sacked almost all of them using its supraconstitutional power to replace the Court.[190]

As a result, the initial period of the Constituent Assembly was a period of confrontation and political conflict between all branches of government and the various political sectors of the country. The constituent process, in that initial phase, was not a vehicle for dialogue and peace or an instrument for avoiding conflict. On the contrary, it was an elected political instrument for exclusion and confrontation, crushing all opposition or dissidence. The Constituent Assembly was thus subject to exclusive domination by one new political party (Movimiento V República [MVR]), that of the government, which answered to the president. It was in that way that the constitution-making process was used to abolish the political class and parties that had dominated the scene in former decades.

5. *The Drafting Phase: Haste and Exclusion*

After the constituted powers had been either encroached on or entirely usurped, the Constituent Assembly entered its second phase (September–October 1999), which involved elaborating the text of a draft constitution. The extreme brevity of the second phase did not allow for any real public discussion or popular participation. The Constituent Assembly rejected the traditional method adopted by other constitutional processes throughout the world whereby a broadly representative and plural constitutional commission elaborates a draft, through negotiations and consent, which is later presented in plenary session.[191]

It is true that the president of the republic, just before he took office, had informally created the Constitutional Commission, which though composed of independent political figures who all were at that time his supporters, actually devoted its time to the issues surrounding the drafting of the method of electing the Constituent Assembly. It never worked to develop a coherent constitutional draft, and its proceedings were not public or participatory. It held no public meetings and met with the president only during the weeks prior and subsequent to the installation of his government. Soon after, all of its members were already in the opposition.

Thus, the Constituent Assembly began to work collectively without an initial draft. The president did publish and submit to the Constituent Assembly a document prepared with the assistance of his appointed Constitutional Council. Its intention was to propose ideas for the new Constitution, but its contents were not completely coherent.[192] Even though the Constituent Assembly did not adopt the document as the draft constitution, the drafting commissions used parts of it, particularly because their members in general had no constitutional–studies expertise. Also, two draft

---

190   See the Decree of Dec. 22, 1999, on the transitory constitutional regime, in *Gaceta Oficial* N° 36.859, Dec. 29, 1999.

191   Such a method was used, for instance, to develop the 1947 Constitution. See *Anteproyecto de Constitución de 1947. Elección directa de gobernadores y eliminación de asambleas legislativas,* Papeles de Archivo N° 8, Ediciones Centauro, Caracas 1987.

192   See Hugo Chávez Frías, *Ideas fundamentales para la Constitución bolivariana de la V República,* Caracas Aug. 1999.

constitutions were submitted to the Constituent Assembly, one by a small-membership left-wing party and another by the nongovernmental organization Primero Justicia, which in 2002 became a center-right political party. Neither of these was adopted as drafts for discussions and, because of their origins, the parties had no particular influence in the drafting commissions.

After two months of dealing with the interference of all the constituted powers, the Constituent Assembly began to elaborate a draft by appointing twenty commissions to deal with the essential subjects of any constitution. Each commission was charged with coming up with a proposed draft for its subject area. This all occurred during only a few days, between September 2 and September 28, 1999. During that period, each commission acted alone and in isolation, consulting only briefly with groups the commission considered appropriate.[193]

The president, once the Constituent Assembly had usurped all public power, urged it to quickly complete drafting the constitution to end the political instability provoked by the constituent process and to use the new constitutional framework to relegitimate the branches of government through new elections. The timetable to finish the drafting of the constitution was established not by the referendum of April 1999 or the Constituent Assembly but by its board of directors in response to presidential pressure.

As of September 1999, the twenty commissions sent their drafts to an additional Constitutional Commission of the Constituent Assembly, in charge of integrating the texts received. Collectively, the commissions' submissions included more than eight hundred articles. The Constitutional Commission was charged with integrating the submissions to form a single draft. Unfortunately, the board of directors of the Constituent Assembly gave the Constitutional Commission just two weeks to integrate all those drafts. The hasty process of elaborating the draft left no room for public discussion or the participation of civil society, whose input could have been incorporated into the discussions in plenary session.[194]

The draft that the Constitutional Commission submitted to the Constituent Assembly on October 18, composed of 350 articles, was a very unsatisfactory text, sometimes contradictory, and full of good intentions.[195] The draft followed many of the provisions of the 1961 Constitution, with the addition of some portions of the president's proposed document. Some foreign constitutional provisions, particularly copied from the Colombian and Spanish constitutions,[196] were included in the draft

---

193 I was president of the Commission on Nationality and Citizenship. See the Report of the Commission in Allan R. Brewer-Carías, *Debate constituyente (Aportes a la Asamblea Nacional Constituyente)*, Fundación de Derecho Público–Editorial Jurídica Venezolana, Caracas 1999, 2 (Sept. 9–Oct. 17): Vol 2, pp.:45-74.

194 I was also a member of the Constitutional Commission of the Assembly. On the difficulties of participating in the drafting process, see Brewer-Carías, *Debate constituyente (Aportes a la Asamblea Nacional Constituyente)*, 2 (Sept. 9–Oct. 17): pp. 255-286.

195 See *Gaceta Constituyente (Diario de Debates)*, Oct.–Nov. 1999, N° 23, Oct. 19, 2009.

196 See, e.g., Allan R. Brewer-Carías, "La Constitución española de 1978 y la Constitución de la República Bolivariana de Venezuela de 1999: Algunas influencias y otras coincidencias," in *La Constitución de 1978 y el constitucionalismo iberoamericano*, coord. Francisco Fernández Segado, Ministerio de la Pre-

text, and part of the text of the American Convention on Human Rights enriched the draft as well. Nevertheless, it can be said that foreign experts or international or regional organizations played no specific publicly known role in the Constituent Assembly.[197] There was no time left for that possibility.

The government imposed an urgency to finish the constitutional draft, requiring the Constituent Assembly to discuss and approve the draft in just one month, from October 19 to November 17, 2000, to submit the constitution to referendum in December 1999. This schedule explains why only nineteen days were devoted to the first round of discussion sessions (October 20–November 9) and three days to the second round (November 12–14), for a total of twenty-two days. During that time, I proposed drafts and expressed my dissenting votes.[198] Together with the other opposition members, I participated in the political campaign for a no vote in the referendum on the Constitution because of its authoritarian content.[199]

After one month of campaigning, the Constitution was approved in the December 15, 1999, referendum. Turnout was low: only 44.3% of eligible voters cast votes (57.7% of eligible voters did not turn out), with 71.8% voting yes and 28.2% voting no.[200] This means that just 30% of Venezuelans with the right to vote approved the Constitution.

However, the approved text did not conform to the operational language of the consultative referendum of April 1999. It failed to provide the new democratic and pluralistic vision that society required, to define the fundamental principles required for reorganizing the country politically, and to create a decentralized state based on participatory democracy.

Despite some good intentions and brief attempts at public education, the hastiness of the process rendered any effective public and political participation impossible. It must be noted that one of the twenty commissions of the Constituent Assembly was the Participatory Commission, totally controlled by the president's followers, which did divulge some information, including to television programs, related to the drafting process and the content of the other commissions' drafts. The sessions of the Constituent Assembly were also directly broadcast on television, thus allowing the public to follow daily discussions. But the great debate that should

---

sidencia, Secretaría General Técnica, Centro de Estudios Políticos y Constitucionales, Madrid 2003, pp. 765-86.

197 All suggestions I made to the board of directors of the Constituent Assembly to invite the most distinguished constitutional lawyers of Latin America and Spain to advise in the constitution-making process were systematically denied. Nonetheless, after the Constitution was approved, it became known that some faculty of the University of Valencia, Spain, helped the vice president of the Assembly in the Technical Committee. See Roberto Viciano Pastor and Rubén Martínez Dalmau, *Cambio político y proceso constituyente en Venezuela (1998-2000)*, Valencia, 2001.

198 See the text of my 127 dissenting votes in Brewer-Carías, *Debate constituyente (Aportes a la Asamblea Nacional Constituyente)*, Fundación de Derecho Público–Editorial Jurídica Venezolana, Caracas 1999, 3 (Oct. 18–Nov. 30): pp. 107-308.

199 See arguments in Brewer-Carías, *Debate constituyente (Aportes a la Asamblea Nacional Constituyente)*, 3 (Oct. 18–Nov. 30): pp. 309-40.

200 See José E. Molina and Carmen Pérez Baralt, "Procesos Electorales. Venezuela, abril, julio y diciembre de 1999," in *Boletín Electoral Latinoamericano* 22, CAPEL-IIDH, San José 2000, pp. 67-68.

have taken place in the Constituent Assembly, on such issues as the monopoly of the political parties, decentralization and the power of local government, expansion of institutional protections of human rights, and the basic mission of the constitution, never took place. There was no public education to encourage the submission of proposals from civil–society groups and nongovernmental organizations. The only minority group that was offered an opportunity to participate was that of the indigenous peoples, who were allowed three seats in the assembly.

Those who controlled the work of the Constituent Assembly were conscious that participation required time; instead, they chose the fast track, working without participatory procedures. The result was that political participation was reduced just to the vote cast by the public, in which most eligible voters did not vote: first in the April 1999 consultative referendum on the convening of the Constituent Assembly, in which only 37% of potential voters participated; second, in the July 1999 election of members of the assembly, in which only 46% of voters participated; and third, in the December 1999 approval referendum of the new Constitution, in which only 44% of voters participated.

IV. THE PARALLEL TRANSITORY REGIME

The ramifications of the departure from the rule of law entailed in the deformation of the constitutional process can be perceived not only in the events that immediately followed but also in the crisis that continues to plague the political system.

In the week following the adoption of the new Constitution, the Constituent Assembly, without questioning the duration of its authority, on December 20, 1999, adopted a new decree establishing the Transitory Constitutional Regime,[201] which had not been approved by popular referendum and violated the newly adopted Constitution, including its transitional provisions.[202] According to it, the Constituent Assembly ratified the president in his post and, acting in violation of the new Constitution and in the absence of any participation by civil society, directly appointed the members of the new Supreme Tribunal of Justice, the new National Electoral Council, the prosecutor general, the people's defender, and the comptroller general, ending the tenure of those previously appointed. The Constituent Assembly, moreover, eliminated definitively Congress and created and appointed the new Legislative National Commission, which had not been provided for in the 1999 Constitution; the new commission assumed legislative power until the new National Assembly (supplanting the dissolved Congress) was elected. The unconstitutional transitional regime was challenged before the new Supreme Judicial Tribunal, created as part of the same regime. Deciding in its own cause, the tribunal upheld the transitional regime's constitutionality, justifying it on the basis of the Constituent Assembly's supraconstitutional powers.[203]

---

201 See *Gaceta Oficial* N° 36.859, Dec. 29, 1999.

202 See comments on this decree in Allan R. Brewer-Carías, *Golpe de estado y proceso constituyente en Venezuela*, 354 ff.; *La Constitución de 1999. Derecho constitucional venezolano*, Editorial Jurídica Venezolana, Caracas 2004, Vol II, p. 1.017.

203 See the Jan. 26, 2000, Decision N° 4 (Case: *Eduardo García*), and the Mar. 28, 2000, Decision N° 180 (Case: *Allan R. Brewer-Carías et al.*), in *Revista de Derecho Público* 81, Editorial Jurídica Venezolana,

The Transitional Constitutional Regime fixed the general framework for the subsequent concentration of powers and development of the current authoritarian political regime. This regime, which unfortunately has enjoyed the support of the Constitutional Chamber of the Supreme Judicial Tribunal, has taken shape in Venezuela as envisaged when President Chávez came to power in 1998 and is characterized by the president's complete control of all branches of government. In particular, the control of the Supreme Tribunal has lead to a judiciary composed of more than 90% provisional or temporary judges,[204] with no autonomy or independence whatsoever.[205]

V. THE DEMOCRATIC FAILURE OF THE CONSTITUTION-MAKING PROCESS

From all that has been stated herein, it is clear that the Venezuelan constitution-making process of 1999 failed to achieve its stated mission of political conciliation and improved democracy. Against a democratic principle, instead of offering the participation that so many sought, the process imposed the will of one political group on others and on the rest of the population.

Thus, as an instrument for the development of a constitutional authoritarian government, the Constitution can be considered a success. Undoubtedly, the democratically elected Constituent Assembly conducted a coup d'état against the 1961 constitutional regime, facilitated the complete takeover of all branches of government by one political group and crushed other political parties, and drafted and approved a constitution with an authoritarian framework that has allowed the installment of a government that has concentrated and centralized all state powers.

The durability of the new Constitution can be predicted to be the same as the durability of the power of those who imposed it and remain in control. That is why reforms of the political system, founded in the democratization and political decentralization of the country, remain pending tasks that the Constituent Assembly of 1999 was unable to accomplish.

Caracas 2000, pp. 93 ff. and 86 ff. See comments in Brewer-Carías, *Golpe de estado y proceso constituyente en Venezuela*, pp. 354ff.

204   Almost two years after the Constituent Assembly's intervention in the judiciary, some magistrates of the Supreme Tribunal acknowledged that more than the 90% of judges in Venezuela were provisional. See *El Universal*, Caracas Aug. 15, 2001. In May 2001, other magistrates recognized that the so-called judicial emergency was a failure. See *El Universal*, Caracas May 30, 2001, pp. 1-4. See also *Informe sobre la situación de los derechos humanos en Venezuela*; OAS/Ser.L/V/ II.118. d.C. 4rev. 2, Dec. 29, 2003, para. 11. It reads: "The Commission has been informed that only 250 judges have been appointed by opposition concurrence according to the constitutional text. From a total of 1.772 positions of judges in Venezuela, the Supreme Court of Justice reports that only 183 are holders, 1.331 are provisional and 258 are temporary." The same Commission also said that "an aspect linked to the autonomy and independence of the Judicial Power is that of the provisional character of the judges in the judicial system of Venezuela. Today, the information provided by the different sources indicates that more than 80% of Venezuelan judges are provisional"; in id., para. 161.

205   See Allan R. Brewer-Carías, "La progresiva y sistemática demolición institucional de la autonomía e independencia del poder judicial en Venezuela 1999-2004," pp. 33-174; Rogelio Pérez Perdomo, "Judicialization in Venezuela," in *The Judicialization of Politics in Latin America*, eds. Rachel Sieder, Line Schjolden, and Alan Angell, Palgrave Macmillan, 2005, pp. 145ff.

In the meantime, on August 15, 2007, the president submitted to the National Assembly a constitutional reform proposal intending to consolidate a socialist, centralized, and militaristic police state, minimizing democracy and limiting freedoms and liberties.[206] The main purpose of the proposals can be understood from the president's speech at the presentation of the draft constitutional reforms,[207] in which he said that the reforms' main objective is "the construction of a Bolivarian and Socialist Venezuela."[208] This is intended, as he explained, to sow "socialism in the political and economic realms."[209] This is something that the Constitution of 1999 did not do. When the Constitution of 1999 was sanctioned, said the president, "We were not projecting the road of socialism. Just as candidate Hugo Chávez repeated a million times in 1998, 'Let us go to a Constituent [Assembly],' so candidate President Hugo Chávez said [in 2006]: 'Let us go to Socialism' and, thus, everyone who voted for candidate Chávez then, voted to go to socialism."[210]

Although this assumption was false, because in the 2006 election nobody voted for a socialist program, the draft constitutional reforms presented by the president, according to what he said in his speech, proposed the construction of "Bolivarian Socialism, Venezuelan Socialism, our Socialism, and our socialist model."[211] It is a socialism whose "basic and indivisible nucleus" is "the community" (la comunidad), one "where common citizens shall have the power to construct their own geography and their own history."[212] This is all based on the premise that "real democracy is only possible in socialism."[213] However, the supposed democracy referred to is one that, as the president suggests in his proposed reform to Article 136, "is not born of suffrage or from any election, but rather is born from the condition of organized human groups as the base of the population." Of course, that is not democracy, as there can be no democracy without the election of representatives.

The president in his speech summarized all of the proposed reforms in this manner: "on the political ground, deepen popular Bolivarian democracy; on the economic ground, create better conditions to sow and construct a socialist productive economic model, our model; the same in the political field: socialist democracy; on the economic, the productive socialist model; in the field of Public Administration: incorporate new forms in order to lighten the load, to leave behind bureaucracy, co-

---

206 See *Proyecto de Reforma Constitucional. Elaborado por el ciudadano Presidente de la República Bolivariana de Venezuela, Hugo Chávez Frías,* 58. See comments on the draft in Brewer-Carías, *Hacia la consolidación de un estado socialista, centralizado, policial y militarista.*

207 "Discurso de Orden pronunciado por el ciudadano Comandante Hugo Chávez Frías, Presidente Constitucional de la República Bolivariana de Venezuela en la conmemoración del Ducentésimo Segundo Aniversario del Juramento del Libertador Simón Bolívar en el Monte Sacro y el Tercer Aniversario del Referendo Aprobatorio de su Mandato Constitucional," special session of Aug. 15, 2007, Asamblea Nacional, División de Servicio y Atención legislativa, Sección de Edición, Caracas 2007.

208 *Id.,* p. 4.

209 *Id.,* p. 33.

210 *Id.,* p. 4.

211 See "Discurso de Orden pronunciado por el ciudadano Comandante Hugo Chávez Frías...," p. 34.

212 *Id.,* p. 32.

213 *Id.,* p. 35.

rruption, and administrative inefficiency, which are heavy burdens of the past still upon us like weights, in the political, economic and social areas."[214]

All the 2007 constitutional reform proposals, although sanctioned by the National Assembly on November 2, 2007, were rejected by the people in the December 2, 2007, popular referendum, increasing the extreme polarization in the country that began in 1999.[215] In any case, and unfortunately for the constitutional process, the rejected reforms have been illegitimately implemented through legislation, through decree laws,[216] and by means of ex post facto judicial interpretations issued by the Constitutional Chamber of the Supreme Tribunal. In addition, in February 2009, after the Constitutional Chamber mutated the meaning of the Constitution, a constitutional amendment was submitted to popular vote to change the alternating form of government and allow the successive and continuous reelection of the president and all the elected representatives and officials, also one of the rejected constitutional reforms.[217]

During 2008 and in 2009 and 2010, all the reforms adopted by the National Assembly regarding statutes related to the functioning of the state have incorporated the figure of the communal council and of popular power, as an important piece, precisely implementing the 2007 rejected constitutional reform, aimed to transform the state into a popular state.[218]

CHAPTER 2

THE ENDLESS AND ILLEGITIMATE TRANSITORY CONSTITUTIONAL REGIME

The same Constituent Assembly that sanctioned the 1999 Constitution modified it one week after its popular approval through referendum, and more than one week before it began to be enforced through its publication in the *Official Gazette*.[219] The Constituent Assembly, evading any popular approval, issued a decree creating the Transitory Constitutional Regime preventing the effective enforcement of the Cons-

---

214 *Id.*, p. 74.

215 See the collective works on the 2007 draft constitutional reforms in *Revista de Derecho Público* 112 *(Estudios sobre la reforma constitucional)*, Editorial Jurídica Venezolana, Caracas 2007.

216 See the collective works on the 2008 delegate legislation implementing the rejected draft constitutional reforms in *Revista de Derecho Público* 115, *(Estudios sobre los Decretos Leyes)*, Editorial Jurídica Venezolana, Caracas 2008.

217 See comments in Allan R. Brewer-Carías, "El juez constitucional vs. la alternabilidad republicana (La reelección contínua e indefinida)," in *Revista de Derecho Público* 117, Caracas 2009, 205, p. 11.

218 See, for instance, on the communal councils and the "Popular Power," in Allan R. Brewer-Carías, *Ley de los Consejos Comunales,* Editorial Jurídica Venezolana, Caracas 2010. In June 2010, the National Assembly began the discusión of the *Ley de Comunas* and the *Ley Orgánica de Contraloría Social* in order to complete the dismantling of the federation and the consolidation of the Popular Power.

219 The Constituent Assembly sanctioned the 1999 Constitution on Nov. 15, 1999, and it was approved in the referendum on Dec. 15, 1999; formally proclaimed by the assembly on Dec. 20, 1999; and published in *Gaceta Oficial* N° 36.860 of Dec. 30, 1999. Nonetheless, in the interim, after popular approval and before publication, the Assembly on Dec. 22, 1999 modified the Constitution as to a transitional regime through a decree that was published in *Gaceta Oficial* N° 36.859 of Dec. 29, 1999.

titution, through which the country began to have two constitutions: one approved by the people and another without such approval.

I. FAILED EFFORTS TO CREATE A CONSTITUTIONAL FRAME-WORK TO TRANSITION PUBLIC POWERS THROUGH AN APPRO-BATORY REFERENDUM

The National Constituent Assembly, when sanctioning the new Constitution on November 15, 1999, included in its text just a few transitory provisions that were those approved by the people in the December 15, 1999, referendum. The Constitution does not contain any provision regarding the then-existing constituent powers or the situation of the head officials of branches of government elected in 1998, so the applicable principle was the continuation of the elected officials up to the election of new ones according to the provisions of the new Constitution.

Due to the fact that the draft constitution of November 15, 1999, did not contain any such provision regarding the tenure of those elected high officials, on November 19, 1999, the same day that the draft was signed for submission to approbatory referendum, the Constituent Assembly approved a decree seeking the convening of a parallel consultative referendum, which was to take place also on December 15, 1999 – that is, the same day fixed for the approbatory referendum of the new Constitution. The purpose of the proposed consultative referendum was for "the Venezuelan people to decide on the permanence (or not) of the President of the Republic, and of the governments of each of the 23 states, subject to popular election, in exercise of their functions."[220]

The underlying intention of the proposal was to convert the approbatory referendum of the Constitution into a plebiscite on the permanence of President Hugo Chávez Frías in power, thus distorting the significance of the popular approval of the Constitution. Nonetheless, in a very confusing way, a few days later, in its session of December 12, 1999, three days before the fixed approbatory referendum of the Constitution was to be held, the assembly revoked without any explanation the proposed consultative plebiscite, basing the decision only on a supposed prior one of revocation adopted in "plenary session," which actually never took place.[221] As a result, a first effort to change the transitory provisions of the 1999 draft constitution, which contained no clause that addressed the termination of terms of office of elected heads of branches of government, was frustrated. But this would be the case only for a short time.[222]

After the 1999 Constitution was approved by the people in the December 15 referendum, in the following ordinary session of the assembly, on December 20, 1999, the Constitution was formally proclaimed. That means that the assembly had ac-

---

220 *Gaceta Constituyente (Diario de Debates), Noviembre 1999–Enero 2000*, Sesión 19-11-99, N° 46, p. 3.

221 *Gaceta Constituyente (Diario de Debates), Noviembre 1999–Enero 2000*, Sesión 09-12-99, N° 48, p. 5.

222 It should be emphasized that the representative Hermán Escarrá Malavé, in the Assembly's session of Nov. 15, 1999, distinguished the transitory provisions (*disposiciones transitorias*) from a transitory regime (*régimen transitorio*), which ought to have been approved by referendum and about which he asked not to be questioned. See *Gaceta Constituyente (Diario de Debates), Noviembre 1999–Enero 2000*, Sesión de 15-11-1999, N° 45, p. 9.

complished its functions according to the basic rules (*bases comiciales*) adopted in the consultative referendum of April 25, 1999, that allowed the assembly to function for six months (from July to December 1999). But instead of ending its mission, the Constituent Assembly decided to self–extend its tenure and convened for its session of closure to be held on January 30, 2000.[223] With the decree, and despite the prior popular referendum approving the Constitution, the constituent assembly provided clear signs of its intention to continue exercising the "original" constituent power that it had bestowed on itself, well beyond the terms established for its existence in the consultative referendum of April 2009.[224] To set its session of closure on January 2000, the assembly considered that the powers given to it "had been recognized by the Supreme Court of Justice, in a formal decision, as original and supraconstitutional"[225] – that is, even above the new Constitution. It eventually concluded, ignoring the new Constitution, by announcing that it was "necessary to decree constitutional acts required for the transition to the new State foreseen in the Constitution approved by the people of Venezuela." The fact was that the latter was the only text that could establish a regime for a transition to the new state, but the transitional provisions that the same Constituent Assembly had drafted addressed nothing on this matter.

The assembly has, in a certain way, tricked the people: it sanctioned a constitution and submitted it to popular approval without any provision for the termination of the term of the 1998 elected officials, and after the Constitution was approved by the people and proclaimed, it decreed its violation, announcing that it would remain, thus exercising supraconstitutional powers to dictate constitutional acts that were not authorized by the transitional provisions of the new Constitution.

II. THE ILLEGITIMATE REGIME FOR THE TRANSITION OF PUBLIC POWERS

The first violation of the Constitution took place by the National Constituent Assembly itself in the days after the December 15, 1999, referendum, precisely during the nationwide commotion caused by massive flooding in the country's central coast, in the state of Vargas. The Assembly sanctioned on December 22, 1999, a decree containing the Regime for the Transition of Public Powers.[226] This occurred just two days after the proclamation of the new Constitution but before the Constitu-

---

223 *Gaceta Constituyente (Diario de Debates), Noviembre 1999–Enero 2000*, Sesión 20-12-99, N° 49, p. 6.

224 See Lolymar Hernández Camargo, *La teoría del poder constituyente. Un caso de estudio: El proceso constituyente venezolano de 1999*, Universidad Católica del Táchira, San Cristóbal 2000, p. 76.

225 Decision of Oct. 6, 1999, published Oct. 14, 1999 (Case: *Henrique Capriles, Decreto de regulación de funcionamiento del poder legislativo*), in which the Supreme Court of Justice ruled in an action filed by the president of the Representative Chamber of Congress, seeking to nullify the National Constituent Assembly Decree Regulating the Legislative Power, by attributing supraconstitutional rank to the provisions in the text approved in referendum on Apr. 25, 1999, for the election of the National Constituent Assembly but not to its acts.

226 See *Gaceta Oficial* N° 36.859, Dec. 29, 1999.

tion's entry into effect with its publication, which was deliberately delayed until December 30, 1999.[227]

In the context of political eagerness to name new officials without waiting for the election of the new National Assembly, on December 22, 1999, the Constituent Assembly, without any constitutional authority, sanctioned the aforementioned decree. In it, and to "make the process of transition to the regime established in the Constitution of 1999 effective" through the termination of the titular officers of the state, the Constituent Assembly once again relied on its supposed self-attributed powers as "original constituent," which it assumed in Article 1 of the Statute of Functioning, considering them as having supraconstitutional character.

The decree had the objective of establishing a "regime of transition" supposedly to "allow the immediate going into effect of the Constitution" (Article 1), which had not yet been published. In fact, nothing impeded the immediate effectiveness of the Constitution. Nonetheless, the Constituent Assembly decided to "develop and complement the Transitory Provisions of the new Constitution" (Article 2), but it had no authority to do so. This was not authorized in the new Constitution that it had drafted and sanctioned, that was approved in a referendum, and that was even formally proclaimed two days before, on December 20, 1999, by the same assembly.

Nonetheless, the new transitory regime decree, according to its text, was devoted to filling the vacuum that the Constituent Assembly had created in failing to incorporate into the transitory provisions of the draft constitution, such transitory regime for the transfer of power from the existing elected organs (1998) provided in the 1961 Constitution to the newly created organs in the new Constitution. In the absence of such provisions in it, the principle that then needed to be applied was one to ensure the continuity of government mentioned in Article 16 of the decree. Instead, the Constituent Assembly usurped the authority of the original constituent power (the people) and acted against what had been approved in referendum, violating, in addition, the basic text for its election approved by referendum on April 25, 1999 – this was another coup d'état, this time against the new 1999 Constitution.

1.   *Elimination of Congress and Creation of the National Legislative Commission*

The Constituent Assembly, in its transitory regime decree, first decided to definitively dissolve the former Congress (Article 4) and dismiss its elected (in 1989) senators and representatives. This decision, adopted after the popular approval of the new Constitution, violated the democratic principle and created a constitutional vacuum, in which, until the election of a new National Assembly, the republic would have been without a national legislative organ. For that reason, to fill the self-created vacuum, the Constituent Assembly made another decision, also without constitutional basis or authority, to create the "National Legislative Commission" (called *Congresillo*) not provided for in the new Constitution as approved by the people. By doing so, it illegitimately granted to the commission the exercise of the legislative power, "until the representatives to the new National Assembly are elected and in

---

227   See *Gaceta Constituyente (Diario de Debates), Noviembre 1999–Enero 2000*, Sesión de 22-12-9, N°
51, 2ff., Session of Dec. 22, 1999, N° 51, pp. 2 ff.; *Gaceta Oficial* N° 36.859, Dec. 29, 1999; *Gaceta Oficial* N° 36.860, Dec. 30, 1999.

office" (Article 5). The members of the commission were appointed by the Constituent Assembly (Article 5) from partisans of the new power and members of the political parties that supported the government.[228] The National Legislative Commission functioned "in a permanent form" from the date of its installation on February 1, 2000 (Article 7) until the date of the effective installment of the new elected National Assembly (August 2000) (Article 8), and it assumed all "the rights and obligations" of the former Congress (Article 9).

These decisions of the National Constituent Assembly violated the basic text adopted in the April 25 referendum for its election. The decision to terminate the popular mandates of elected representatives in democratic elections, to constitute a new legislative organ, even temporarily, and moreover to assign legislative functions to unelected persons, violated the principles of representative democracy and progressiveness of the political right to democratically participate and to have elections; it further violated international treaties requiring Venezuela to ensure the effective exercise of representative democracy.[229] The result of all these decisions was the installment of the National Legislative Commission, composed of unelected members and in open violation of the new Constitution.

A month later, on January 30, 2000, the Constituent Assembly issued another decree to amplify the powers of the National Legislative Commission,[230] assigning it a series of special powers to legislate on various matters. The assembly issued the decree, again "in the exercise of the sovereign original constituent power," which later the new Constitutional Chamber of the Supreme Tribunal of Justice considered as having "constitutional hierarchy."[231]

All these unconstitutional acts of the Constituent Assembly violated the new Constitution and were, successively and unfortunately, laundered by the new Supreme Tribunal, whose magistrates had also been appointed by the same Constituent Assembly precisely in the same transitory regime. On the occasion of deciding the judicial review actions challenging an act of the commission (Resolution Recommending the Reincorporation to Their Jobs of Labor Leaders and Workers Unjustly and Unconstitutionally Dismissed in Different Regions of the Country) of May 19, 2000,[232] in exercise of the powers conferred on it by the Constituent Assembly through the amplifying decree, the Constitutional Chamber of the Supreme Tribunal of Justice considered that such Resolution had constitutional rank.[233]

228 The assembly, on Jan. 28, 2000, again "in exercise of the original constituent power" that it had conferred on itself, named additional members of the National Legislative Commission. See *Gaceta Oficial* N° 36.903, Mar. 1, 2000.

229 Charter of the Organization of American States, and the American Convention on Human Rights, Art. 23. See Allan R. Brewer-Carías, *Debate Constituyente (Aportes a la Asamblea Nacional Constituyente)*, Fundación de Derecho Público–Editorial Jurídica Venezolana, Caracas 1999, 1 (Aug. 8–Sept. 8), pp. 76-81.

230 *Gaceta Oficial* N° 36.884, Feb. 3, 2000.

231 See Decision N° 1454 (Feb. 18, 2001) (Case: *C.A. Good Year de Venezuela*).

232 *Gaceta Oficial* N° 36.965, June 5, 2000.

233 The Constitutional Chamber ruled the following: "Because the then Supreme Court of Justice, in plenary session, on the 14th of Oct. of 1999, ruled that the basic text [*bases comiciales*] submitted to the Consultative Referendum on Apr. 25, of that year, were of *supraconstitutional rank* with respect to the

2. *Dissolution of State Legislative Assemblies and Creation of State Legislative Commissions*

The national Constituent Assembly, in its decree of December 22, 1999, also violated the new Constitution when it ordered the "dissolution of the Legislative Assemblies of the States" and the dismissal of the elected representatives (elected in 1998) who composed them (Article 11). The assembly had no constitutional authority to do so, as this was not provided for in the transitory provisions of the Constitution approved by the people.

At the state level, the Constituent Assembly created in each state the State Legislative Commission, empowering the Coordinating Commission of the National Constituent Assembly and not the assembly itself with the appointment of commission members (Article 12). This decision, not authorized in any constitutional or legal norm, also violated the previously mentioned democratic guarantee, one of the limits established on the Constituent Assembly.

On January 4, 2000, the Coordinating Commission of the Constituent Assembly, supposedly "in accordance with powers conferred to it by the Assembly in its session of December 22, 1999" (powers that were not identified), resolved to institute the Regime for the Creation of Legislative Commissions of the States,[234] for which purpose it created the National Nominating Commission to select candidates for the legislative commissions and conferred powers to those commissions. This was not even authorized by the Regime of Transition of the Public Powers, so the Coordinating Commission of the Constituent Assembly usurped the powers of constitutional regulation that the assembly had attributed to itself.

3. *Control over Municipalities*

With respect to municipalities, Article 15 of the decree on transition set forth that existing municipal councils were to exercise their functions "under the supervision and control of the National Constituent Assembly or the National Legislative Commission" until new popularly elected representatives were in office.[235] The decree further authorized the Coordinating Commission of the National Assembly or National Legislative Commission the power to partially or completely substitute members of the municipal councils and mayors in cases of serious administrative irregularities.

Constitution of 1961, it has been concluded that the normative and organizational acts of the National Constituent Assembly in execution of the *bases comiciales* have *constitutional rank*. Due to the fact that the National Constituent Assembly implicitly referred the *bases comiciales* in the 'Decree Amplifying the Powers of the National Legislative Commission' founding its authority on the '*referendum democratically approved on the twenty-fifth of April of nineteen hundred and ninety-nine*,' the Decree amplifying the powers of the Commission would also effectively have *constitutional rank*." See Decision N° 1454 (Feb. 18, 2001) (Case: *C.A. Good Year de Venezuela), in Revista de Derecho Público* 85–88, Editorial Jurídica Venezolana, Caracas 2001.

234   *Gaceta Oficial* N° 36.865, Jan. 7, 2000.

235   See *Gaceta Constituyente (Diario de Debates), Noviembre 1999–Enero 2000,* Sesión de 22-12-99, N° 51, p. 5.

The provisions were contrary to the new Constitution, which in a contrary sense guarantees municipal autonomy, and to the democratic principle with respect to municipal authorities, who needed to be popularly elected.

4.   *Intervention of the Judiciary*

Article 17 of the transitory regime decree also provided for the termination of the Supreme Court of Justice to give way to the Supreme Tribunal of Justice, even if the Constitution that created it was not still in force (it was published on December 30, 1999). For such purpose, the three chambers of the former Supreme Court of Justice (political-administrative, criminal, and civil cassation) were extinguished and its magistrates dismissed. In substitution, the Constituent Assembly, without any constitutional authority, created the new chambers of the Supreme Tribunal of Justice (constitutional, political-administrative, electoral, and social, civil, and criminal cassation), although the Constitution of 1999 was not yet in effect.

The Assembly also designated the new magistrates of the Supreme Tribunal of Justice (Article 19), but for such purpose did not hold itself to the conditions for those appointments established in the new Constitution (Article 263) or to the citizens' participation provisions established in Article 270 of the Constitution. Among the magistrates selected was the former president of the Supreme Court of Justice, who had occupied that position for the previous two months. His services to the new regime implementing, from the Supreme Curt, the unconstitutional framework used by the Constituent Assembly to usurp all branches of government, undoubtedly were acknowledged by the new political group that took over the control of the state.

In the text of the new Constitution, there was a glaring absence of transitory provisions regarding the functioning of the judicial power, with only one reference to the Commission on the Functioning and Restructuring of the Judicial System (fourth transitory provision) regarding the transitional system for public defense until relevant legislation had passed. Nothing more. Moreover, the referenced commission did not yet exist when the Constitution was drafted and submitted to referendum. It came into existence only later, through the aforementioned decree of transition (Article 27). In the new Constitution, however, this organ had competence only to develop a system for the public defense as stated in the fourth transitory provision.

The transitory regime decree, in any case, was completely incongruous. As mentioned, before the new Constitution came into effect (December 30, 1999), on December 22, 1999, the decree "created" the chambers of the Supreme Tribunal of Justice and appointed its judges (Articles 17 and 19), although provisionally (Article 20). In fact, those chambers had no constitutional existence, because the new Constitution did not provide for the number of its members and was not in effect. Thus, the assembly produced a constitutional act creating state organs (Article 17), something over which it had no constitutional authority.

The Assembly adopted a variety of transitory norms not provided for in the new 1999 Constitution to ensure the new Constitution's immediate effect, although as stated, the new Constitution was not yet operative. These included a provision that transformed the former Council for the Judiciary into the Executive Office of the Magistrature of the Supreme Tribunal of Justice, established in Article 267 of the new Constitution, not yet effective, and dismissed the members of the Council for the Judicature (Article 26).

Immediately following this, the Assembly provided for another transitional regime without any authority to do so, providing that until the Supreme Tribunal had organized the aforementioned executive office, the government, administration, inspection, and vigilance over the Courts, as well as all the powers that until that time had been legislatively lodged in the Council for Judicature, be exercised by the Commission on the Functioning and the Restructuring of the Judicial System (Article 21). The National Constituent Assembly thus confiscated from the Supreme Tribunal of Justice (whose members it had selected) one of the tribunal's new functions and attributed it to a commission whose members were appointed by the Constituent Assembly, not even by the Supreme Tribunal of Justice. The Supreme Tribunal accepted this situation even after the new Constitution went into effect, an irregular situation that the new Supreme Tribunal resignedly has accepted for the past decade (1999–2010).

Another unconstitutional provision adopted by the National Constituent Assembly in the decree was to attribute to the Commission on the Functioning and the Restructuring of the Judicial System the judicial disciplinary jurisdiction that Article 267 of the Constitution reserves to judicial courts or tribunals. This transitory provision was to be in effect "until the National Assembly approves legislation that determines the disciplinary procedures and tribunals," which through 2010 had never occurred.[236] In this way, during the past decade, no stability of judges had existed. In general, they are appointed temporarily and dismissed in a discretionary way by the aforementioned commission without any due process of law.[237]

According to the new Constitution, only judges can exercise judicial functions (Article 253), and it is totally illegitimate and contrary to the guarantee of due process (Article 49) to confer judicial functions to a commission, not a court. If the intention was to establish, even arbitrarily, a transitory regime of judicial discipline, the judicial diciplinary jurisdiction should have been vested in preexisting courts or judges, not in an ad hoc commission. The latter violated both the guarantee of due process and the right to a natural judge expressly regulated in the new Constitution (Article 49).

On January 18, 2000, also "in exercise of the sovereign original constituent power," the National Constituent Assembly issued two other decrees relating to the judicial power. These concerned the designation of the inspector of courts,[238] as well

---

236 In this regard, the Inter-American Commission on Human Rights in its *Annual Report 2009*, said that "even though the 1999 Constitution states that legislation governing the judicial system is to be enacted within the first year following the installation of the National Assembly, a decade later the Transitional Government Regime, created to allow the Constitution to come into immediate effect, remains in force. Under that transitional regime, the Commission for the Functioning and Restructuring of the Judicial System was created, and this body has ever since had the disciplinary authority to remove members of the judiciary." See Par. 481. Available at http://www.cidh.org/ annualrep/2009eng/Chap.IV.f.eng.htm.

237 The reorganization of the judiciary since 2000 has been a permanent situation. See the Resolution of the Supreme Tribunal of Justice N° 1009-0008 (Mar. 18, 2009), in which "all the Venezuelan Judicial Power" was declared in a process of "integral restructuring."

238 *Gaceta Oficial* N° 36.878, Jan. 26, 2000.

as the members of the Commission on the Functioning and the Restructuring of the Judicial System.[239]

5. Dismissal and Appointment of Officials of the Citizens' Power

The National Constituent Assembly, through the Decree on the Regime for the Transition of Public Powers,[240] also dismissed the comptroller general and the prosecutor general and appointed substitutes (Articles 35 and 36). It also appointed the people's defender (Article 34), which in fact was the only office that it was constitutionally authorized to designate under the transitory provisions of the 1999 Constitution. They were appointed until after the new National Assembly was elected and could name officials to those posts. Nonetheless, appointments were made without any sort of citizen participation as established in Article 279 of the Constitution.

In addition, the decree assigned powers to the comptroller general that were not authorized by any constitutional or legal provision, as was the power to intervene in the functions of the state and municipal comptrollers and to provisionally name officials of those entities (Article 37). This was in violation of state and municipal autonomy as guaranteed in the new Constitution.

6. Dismissal and Appointment of Members of the National Electoral Council

Finally, with respect to the electoral power, the National Constituent Assembly, being wholly without competence or authority, and in an illegitimate way, by means of the Decree on Transition Regime of December 22, 1999, conferred unto itself the power to appoint members of the new National Electoral Council (Article 40). Consequently, a few days later, it dismissed the members of the Supreme Electoral Council and provisionally appointed to the council persons all tied to the new power and to the political parties that supported the government, without any citizen participation. This act failed to guarantee electoral impartiality, thus violating Articles 295 and 296 of the new Constitution.

The Constituent Assembly also conferred on itself the power to set the dates for the first elections to fill representative offices established in the new Constitution (Article 39). It assigned to itself the power to issue the electoral statute (*estatuto electoral*) intended to govern the first elections for all representative legislative bodies and executive organs within the public powers.

III. JUDICIAL ACCEPTANCE OF A DOUBLE CONSTITUTIONAL TRANSITORY REGIME

The Decree on the Regime for the Transition of the Public Powers was challenged on the grounds of its unconstitutionality before the then-existing Supreme Court of Justice on December 29, 1999, with respect to its provisions for the appointments of the prosecutor general, the comptroller general, magistrates in the Supreme Tribunal of Justice, the people's defender, members of the National Electoral Council, and members of the National Legislative Commission.

---

239 *Id.*
240 See *Gaceta Oficial* N° 36.859, Dec. 29, 1999.

After January 1, 2000, the files of the action for judicial review were transferred to the new Constitutional Chamber of the Supreme Tribunal of Justice appointed in the same transitory regime decree, which decided the case in Decision N° 4 (January 26, 2000) (Case: Eduardo García), on the basis of the opinion by the same magistrate who was former president of the Supreme Court. The decision precisely recognized that the transition decree through which all the magistrates were appointed was "of constitutional rank and nature" and "of an organizational nature, producing the appointment of high officials in the National Public Powers, based upon the intent to re-organize the State, which purpose had been assigned to the National Constituent Assembly."[241]

On the basis of the latter, the Constitutional Chamber concluded its decision by determining "that given the original character of the power conferred by the people of Venezuela upon the National Constituent Assembly by means of Question No. 1 and the Eighth *Base Comicial* approved in the April 25, 1999, national consultative referendum, this power is not subject to the constitution then in effect [1961 Constitution], and the judicial challenge now proposed based on presumptive transgressions of the referenced constitution but not of the standards determined in the [April 25, 1999] referendum, is considered without merit to proceed."[242]

The Constitutional Chamber ruled similarly regarding the challenge on January 17, 2000, of the same decree. In Decision N° 6 (January 27, 2000), the action for judicial review unconstitutionally filed against the decree was also rejected on the basis of the following arguments:

[T]his Chamber understands that until the date of publication of the new Constitution [December 31, 1999], the Constitution that preceded it (of 1961) was in force. This derives from the Single Derogatory Clause [of the 1999 Constitution]; and as the acts of the National Constituent Assembly were not subject to the derogated Constitution (1961), those acts were subject to supra-constitutional norms only, as was ruled by the Plenary Supreme Court of Justice as quoted above. Thus, by obverse argument, only those acts issued by the National Constituent Assembly after the publication of the new Constitution were subject to it.

It arises from all the aforementioned that the act of the National Constituent Assembly that is challenged here, published in the Official Gazette on the 29th of December of 1999 [N° 36.859], before the Constitution of the Bolivarian Republic of Venezuela of 1999 entered into force, it is not subject to it, nor to the Constitution of 1961.[243]

The Supreme Tribunal of Justice, created by the challenged decree and the magistrates appointed for it, thus recognized the constitutional rank of the transitional regime invented by the National Constituent Assembly and contained in the decree, declaring that such decree was subject to neither the Constitution of 1961 nor to the

---

241   See *Revista de Derecho Público* 81, Editorial Jurídica Venezolana, Caracas 2000, pp. 91ff.
242   Id.
243   See *Revista de Derecho Público* 81, Editorial Jurídica Venezolana, Caracas 2000, pp. 81ff.

Constitution of 1999 but rather to supraconstitutional norms. Being an act on which all the magistrates had personal and direct interest, the least the magistrates could have done would have been to recuse themselves, but they did not. This and other decisions in which they judged the transition regime violated the most elemental principles of the rule of law: No one can be a judge in his own case.

The Supreme Tribunal of Justice ratified the criteria of the paraconstitutional character of the decree in Decision No. 186 (March 28, 2000) (Case: *Allan R. Brewer-Carías et al.*), issued to resolve the challenge for judicial review of the Electoral Statute of the Public Powers,[244] approved by the National Constituent Assembly in its last session on January 30, 2000. The Supreme Tribunal rejected the action of unconstitutionality filed by former members of the Constituent Assembly, basing its decision on the argument that the Constituent Assembly, according to the basic rules approved in the referendum of April 25, 1999 – to fulfill its mission of transforming the state, to create a new legal order, and to draft a new Constitution to replace that of 1961 – had several alternatives with respect to regulating a constitutional transition regime. First was to draft transitory provisions within the text of the Constitution approved by the people in the December 15, 1999, referendum; second was to pass separate constituent acts, giving origin to a parallel transitory regime of constitutional nature and rank, approved by the people. The Supreme Tribunal, in effect, ruled as follows:

> The National Constituent Assembly, with the purpose of fulfilling the mandate conferred to it by the people, had several alternatives: one to draft a constitution with a set of transitory provisions in order to regulate as possible the juridical implementation of the transition regime between the institutions provided for in the Constitution of the Republic of Venezuela of 1961, and those provided for in the Constitution of the Bolivarian Republic of Venezuela of 1999.
>
> Another alternative was not to include such implementation in the transitory provisions of the Constitution, and instead to effectuate it through a separate body of legislation [*sic*], complemented by acts aimed at filling the institutional vacuum that would be created when the new Constitution went into effect. This was the route chosen by the National Constituent Assembly, when it enacted the Decree on the Regime for the Transition of the Public Powers."[245]

This assertion had no constitutional or logical basis, and it violated the constitutional principle of the need for popular approval regarding the Constitution, set forth in the referendum of April 25, 1999, and particularly in its ninth basic rule (*base comicial*), which the former Supreme Court considered as having supraconstitutional rank. According to this provision, which the tribunal did not consider, any constitutional provision resulting from the constitution-making process of 1999 required popular approval through referendum. This was the will of the people as expressed on April 25, 1999: The National Constituent Assembly was not to place constitutional acts into force; only the people, by means of referendum, could place a new

---

244   *Gaceta Oficial* N° 36.884, Feb. 3, 2000.
245   See *Revista de Derecho Público* 81, Editorial Jurídica Venezolana, Caracas 2000, pp. 86 ff.

constitution into force. It was for that purpose that the Venezuelan people convened to vote in referendum on December 15, 1999 – to approve the new Constitution. In conformity with the people's will established on April 25, 1999, only the people themselves were authorized to approve the Constitution through an approbatory referendum. Thus, no other norm of constitutional rank could legitimately exist that the people had not approved.

Therefore, the Supreme Tribunal of Justice, by deciding that the electoral statute sanctioned by the National Constituent Assembly was of constitutional rank, enacted for the purpose of filling supposed gaps or vacuums in the transitory provisions of the 1999 Constitution – vacuums that had been both created and caused by the National Constituent Assembly itself, before publishing the 1999 Constitution – violated the people's sovereign will as expressed in referendum. The truth is that there was no point for Venezuelans to approve a constitution in the December 15 referendum if the National Constituent Assembly could pass other parallel constitutional texts not approved by the people.[246]

The most important feature of the Supreme Tribunal's decision is that it established the principle that the National Constituent Assembly could enact norms of constitutional hierarchy not approved through popular referendum. This, beyond a doubt, violated the ninth basic rule (*base comicial*) approved by referendum on April 25, 1999, which the former Supreme Court of Justice considered supraconstitutional in the decision of October 14, 1999 (Case: *Henrique Capriles Radonski vs. Decreto de Regulación de Funciones del Poder Legislativo*).

This *base comicial* approved by referendum, which, it must be emphasized, was considered as having supraconstitutional rank, established that the new Constitution would enter into force only if approved in another referendum. From this, it can be deduced that the popular will in Venezuela as expressed on April 25, 1999, was that the National Constituent Assembly could not give effect to the new constitution or to any constitutional provision of act not approved by the people through referendum.

However, that was not the criterion the Supreme Tribunal employed in its decision, opening the door to arbitrariness and to an endless transitory constitutional situation that, in some cases, has endured for a decade, as with intervention in the judicial power.

The Supreme Tribunal, in effect, deduced the constitutional absurdity that a constitutional transitional regime could exist even if not foreseen in the 1999 Constitution approved by the people but dictated by the National Constituent Assembly. It did so without mentioning the ninth *base comicial* (its decision referred only to the first and eighth basic rules) of the April 25 referendum that imposed with supraconstitutional status the requirement that every provision of constitutional rank produced by the National Constituent Assembly must be approved by the people in referendum to take effect. This was what took place regarding the transitory provisions of the 1999 Constitution approved in the December 15 referendum but that never occurred with the Regime for the Transition of the Public Powers issued a week later

---

246   See Allan R. Brewer-Carías, *La Constitución de 1999,* 3rd ed., Caracas 2001, pp. 270 ff.

(December 22, 1999). Nonetheless, the Supreme Tribunal, ignoring the will of the people, assigned to such a regime a "rank analogous to the Constitution" and a juridical status "parallel to the current [1999] Constitution."

From the aforementioned Decision N° 186 of the Supreme Tribunal (Case: *Allan R. Brewer-Carías et al.*),[247] the following irregular situation resulted:

1.   On November 17, 1999, the National Constituent Assembly approved a Constitution with a transition regime established in its transitory provisions that implied the permanence of the organs of the public powers until new officials were elected. In the expression of public will (in the referendum of December 15, 1999) and the will of the National Constituent Assembly that approved and proclaimed the Constitution, therefore, there was no legal vacuum whatsoever with respect to the constitutional transition.

2.   The Constitution of 1999, with the stated transitory provisions, was submitted to an approbatory referendum on December 15, 1999; was approved by the people; and was formally proclaimed by the National Constituent Assembly on December 20, 1999.

3.   Two days later, the National Constituent Assembly changed its opinion and resolved to alter the transitory provisions foreseen in the 1999 Constitution already approved by the people. Before publishing it in the *Official Gazette*, on December 22, 1999, the National Constituent Assembly enacted the Regime for the Transition of the Public Powers, which substituted all officials of government branches (except the president) and modified the structure of the state. This transition regime created, therefore, a "vacuum" that the Constituent Assembly sought to fill with provisions of constitutional rank not approved by the people.

4.   The Supreme Tribunal of Justice, in its decision of March 28, 2000, attributed constitutional rank and value to that transition regime enacted by the National Constituent Assembly without the approval of the people, in contravention of the ninth *base comicial* of the April 25 referendum, which allowed the election of the Constituent Assembly and had supraconstitutional rank, thus limiting the activity of the assembly.

5.   In Venezuela, then, and as a consequence of the Supreme Tribunal's decision, two parallel constitutional regimes existed at once: one contained in the transitory provisions of the 1999 Constitution, approved by the people; the other, passed after that approval, by the National Constituent Assembly, without constitutional support. The latter was not approved by the people and of imprecise duration – it was deemed to have legal effect until the passage of all implementing legislation foreseen by the Constitution of 1999, which could be a period of decades.

The Supreme Tribunal of Justice, unfortunately, instead of fulfilling its duty as guardian of the Constitution, wishing to resolve the supposed vacuum created by the same National Constituent Assembly after the popular approval of the 1999 Constitution, accepted the dual constitutional transitory regime in many aspects until 2009.

---

247   See *Revista de Derecho Público* 81, Editorial Jurídica Venezolana, Caracas 2000, pp. 86 ff.

For instance, it still prevails on judicial matters with the continuous interference of the Commission on the Functioning and the Restructuring of the Judicial Power.

IV. THE KIDNAPPING OF THE CONSTITUTION AND SUBJECTION OF THE JUDICIAL BRANCH TO THE GOVERNMENT

Transitory constitutional regimes defined by the Supreme Tribunal had different durations. The transitory provisions of the 1999 Constitution mainly devoted to define a legislative program that the new National Assembly was to develop had a "sunset clause" to take effect within a precise number of years. But the Decree of the Transition Regime was imprecise and, on that matter, the Constitutional Chamber issued contradictory rulings. For instance, in Decision N° 179 (March 28, 2000) (Case: *Gonzalo Pérez Hernández*), the tribunal decided that the constitutional transition regime created by the National Constituent Assembly was to last "until the constituted powers were designated or elected" (in 2000)[248]; however, in the aforementioned Decision N° 180 (Case: *Allan R. Brewer-Carías et al.*), also issued on March 28, 2000, the chamber stated: "The regime for the transition of the Public Powers projects into the future, not just until the National Assembly [Legislature] is formed, but even beyond that," until new legislation was approved. Consequently, "the norms and acts of the National Constituent Assembly remain in full effect, and will remain so until the legal regime that derogates the provisional regime is established in conformity with the Constitution, leaving without effects the norms and acts sanctioned by the Constituent Assembly."[249]

This situation implies that the 1999 Constitution has never been completely in force – in some respects, after a decade of application, the National Assembly has sanctioned no legislation; thus, an imprecise transition regime remains in effect, applied according to the variable interpretations of the government and the Supreme Tribunal. This has been particularly shocking regarding the judicial branch of government, particularly the constitutional provisions on the conditions and procedures for the appointment of magistrates of the Supreme Tribunal, and on the stability of judges, by means of implementing the judicial carrier and the disciplinary judicial Jurisdiction, which up to 2010 are still inapplicable. As the Inter-American Commission on Human Rights has said in its *Annual Report 2009*:

> Furthermore, even though the 1999 Constitution states that legislation governing the judicial system is to be enacted within the first year following the installation of the National Assembly, a decade later the Transitional Government Regime, created to allow the Constitution to come into immediate effect, remains in force.[250]

---

248   See *Revista de Derecho Público* 81, Editorial Jurídica Venezolana, Caracas 2000, p. 83.

249   See *Revista de Derecho Público* 81, Editorial Jurídica Venezolana, Caracas 2000, pp. 87-88.

250   See IACHR, *Annual Report 2009*, Chapter IV, "Human Rights Developments in the Region: Venezuela," Par. 481, available at http://www.cidh.org/annualrep/2009eng/Chap.IV.f.eng.htm.

CHAPTER 3

THE 1999 POLITICAL CONSTITUTION AND THE REINFORCEMENT OF CENTRALIZATION

The 1999 Constitution kept many provisions of the 1961 Constitution and mixed them with new principles and intents, in some cases confused with constitutional rights, including some important contradictions like the declaration of the State as a "decentralized federation," paralleling provisions that have further centralized the centralized federation the country had for more than one hundred years. Regarding the democratic character of the government, it emphasized participatory means but eroded the representative nature of democracy in an antiparty framework. Furthermore, the Constitution formally declares the rule of law but within a militaristic framework never before established by any previous constitution. The separation of powers was formally expressed, adding to the traditional ones (legislative, executive, and judicial) two new additional branches of government, the electoral and citizens' branches, but with a clear prevalence of the legislative power (National Assembly) over the others.

I began to analyze the 1999 Constitution and to make critical comments on its contents as a member of the National Constituent Assembly that drafted the Constitution. I strongly opposed its approval in the December 15, 1999 referendum, and began to write on the matter just a few weeks after the approval of the Constitution.[251] The comments on the Constitution have been developed in further works, in which I have studied the constitutional text in depth.[252] For the purpose of this book, I summarize in this and the following chapter the main aspects of the 1999 Constitution that can be considered as important reforms.

I.   **THE CONSTITUTION OF 1999: FRUSTRATION OF THE NECESSARY POLITICAL CHANGE**

According to the referendum of April 25, 1999, which created the National Constituent Assembly, the institution had as its mission the elaboration of a new constitution to transform the state and create a new legal order, which would permit the effective functioning of a social and participatory democracy. For that purpose, the members of the assembly were elected on July 25, 1999.

The creation of the assembly and the election of its members responded to the requirements of political change in the country, provoked by the crisis of the political system of centralized government and parties, which was based first on the state centralism and second on the democracy of parties, which exercised a monopoly over participation and representation.

---

251   See Allan R. Brewer-Carías, "Constitutional Reform in Venezuela and the 1999 Constitution," Symposium on Challenges to Fragile Democracies in the Americas: Legitimacy and Accountability, Faculty of Law, University of Texas, Austin, Feb. 25, 2000, in *Texas International Law Journal* 36, 2001, pp. 333-338.

252   See Allan R. Brewer-Carías, *La Constitución de 1999*, Editorial Jurídica Venezolana, Caracas 2000; *La Constitución de 1999. Derecho Constitucional Venezolano*, 2 vols., Editorial Jurídica Venezolana, Caracas 2004.

The democratic transformation to a decentralized and participatory state needed to be based on the political decentralization of the state's powers in the territory and local governments, and on people's participation. For this purpose, the assembly needed to introduce the following: to transform the state to make it more democratic, demolishing centralism and constructing a decentralized state within the federal framework, and to create a new legal order to allow the effective functioning of a social and participatory democracy, which would incorporate individuals and private institutions in the social, economic, and political process, and ensure political participation in the affairs of the state.

Nonetheless, the Constituent Assembly and the new Constitution it drafted did not respond to the demands of political transformation that were determined in the referendum of April 25, 1999: "transformation of the State" and "a new legal order," in order to strengthen democracy and the rule of law. It neither ensured nor established a basis for the transformation of the political system, and its content did not contribute to overcome the crisis of the system of centralized government of parties. That is, it did not structure a decentralized and participatory state that could have preserved democracy. On the contrary, it consolidated both the prevailing state centralism, even moving backward the decentralization process initiated in 1989, and partisanship, which has been aggravated by the distortion of the electoral system and the substitution of the traditional multiparty system with a one-party system integrated into the state. A unique historical opportunity to introduce those reforms was lost, and despite of the convening of a national constituent assembly without a previous constitutional rupture, the lack of any agreements or consensus, produced a constitution that did not solve the existing central problems and did not establish the basis of effective democratic political change.

Instead of the Constitution helping to overcome the crisis of centralism, it aggravated it by establishing the constitutional basis for the development of a political authoritarianism based on regulations that reinforce the centralism, presidentialism, "statism," state paternalism, partisanship, and militarism, thus endangering democracy itself.[253]

---

[253]   For instance, the Inter-American Commission on Human Rights, in its Preliminary Observations N° 23/02 of Oct. 5, 2002, produced on the occasion of the on-site visit to Venezuela after the facts of Apr. 2002, pointed out the following aspects of the new Constitution: "22. Notwithstanding these significant constitutional advances, the Commission notes that the Constitution also includes various parts that may hinder effective observance of the rule of law. These provisions include the requirement for a preliminary proceeding on the merits (*antejuicio de mérito*) for high-ranking officers of the Armed Forces prior to starting any investigation into a crime (Article 266(3)); the stipulation of the Office of the Comptroller General of the National Armed Forces without clarifying its relationship with the Office of the Comptroller General of the Republic (Article 291); and the participation of the National Electoral Council in trade union elections. Article 58, which stipulates the right to timely, accurate, and impartial information, has been criticized, among others by this Commission. Furthermore, Article 203 includes the concept of enabling statutes, and allows for the possibility of a delegation of legislative powers to the President of the Republic, without establishing limits on the content of this delegation. In so doing, new crimes may be established by Executive decrees – as has already happened – and not through statutes adopted by the National Assembly, in violation of the requirements of the American Convention on Human Rights. In addition, the Constitution has suppressed some constitutional provisions that are important for the rule of law, such as legislative review of military promotions, the provision that established the non-involvement of the Armed Forces in political decision-making, and the prohibition on the military aut-

In 2000, just a few months after the 1999 Constitution was approved and began to be enforced, the following were my initial thoughts regarding its provisions, as I considered it a constitution conceived of to promulgate authoritarianism:

From the aforementioned results, regarding the 1999 political Constitution that, when analyzed globally, highlights an institutional framework conceived for authoritarianism. It is derived from combining the State centralism, the exaggerated presidentialism, the democracy of parties, the concentration of power in the Assembly and the militarism that constitute the central elements designed for the organization of the Power of the State.

In my opinion, that is not the political Constitution required to improve democracy. On the contrary, it should be based on decentralization of power, a controlled presidentialism, politic participation to balance the powers of the state and the subjection of the military authority to the civil one.

Regarding the 1999 social constitution, when enumerating the human rights and guarantees and State obligations, the new Constitution, unfortunately, opens the door to their limitation by the Executive through delegated legislation. Moreover, analyzed globally, it shows a marginalization of society and private enterprises, falling on the State all the imaginable obligations, impossible to comply with. It is a Constitution conceived for paternalism, which leads to populism.

That is not the social Constitution needed to found a social and participating democracy. To that, it should re-value the participation of all private enterprises in educational, health and social security process, as activities in which a mutual responsibility between the state and Society must exist.

Finally, the new Constitution, in its component economic Constitution, completes the paternalist picture of social Constitution. It inclines the constitutional regime towards the state instead of the private enterprise, which originates an exaggerated statism. It creates the risk of increasing tax voracity that cannot be controlled, conceived to squash taxpayers, who aren't constitutionally protected.

That is not the economic Constitution needed to found the policy of economic development the country requires, which has to point to the creation of wealth and employment that the State is unable to accomplish without the decisive participation of private enterprises, which should be protected and stimulated.

Due to the aforementioned, in our opinion the Constitution of 1999 hasn't introduced the changes the country needed, on the occasion of the constituent moment that originated the crisis of the political model of Centralized State of Parties established from 1945 and restored in 1958. The country needed a radical change to improve the democracy, make it more representative and to structure a democratic decentralized and participating State. Nothing of this was ac-

hority and the civilian authority being exercised simultaneously." See the text of the Preliminary Observations in Allan R. Brewer-Carías, *La crisis de la democracia venezolana. La Carta Democrática Interamericana y los sucesos de abril de 2002*, Los Libros de El Nacional, Colección Ares, Caracas 2002.

complished, so only history will say if this Constitution is the last of the four politic historical periods of Venezuela or the first of the fifth.[254]

Unfortunately, the decade that has passed since the approval of the 1999 Constitution has proved the validity of these assertions: An authoritarian government has taken shape in Venezuela, using the Constitution and in many cases defrauding it, thereby undermining democracy from within.[255] This is the political frame of the new constitution, which I want to analyze referring to the three central elements that make up any constitution: first, the political constitution, which I comment on in this chapter; and second, the dogmatic constitution, referred to constitutional rights and guaranties, as well as the socioeconomic constitution, which I comment on in Chapter 4.

II. THE NEW "BOLIVARIAN" REPUBLIC AND ITS PARTISAN CHARACTER

The 1999 Constitution, in its first article, changed the name of Venezuela from the traditional *República de Venezuela* (Republic of Venezuela) to *República Bolivariana de Venezuela* (Bolivarian Republic of Venezuela). The motivation for the new name could be perceived as directed to refer to the ideas and actions of Simón Bolívar, who was not only the liberator of Venezuela but also of other "Bolivarian" republics in Latin America (Colombia, Ecuador, Bolivia an Peru). Although it has not been the first time in Venezuela's history that military and authoritarian rulers have evoked Simón Bolívar to attract followers and to give some doctrinal basis to their governments,[256] never before had adherence to a Bolivarian doctrine led to

---

254 Immediately after the approval of the Constitution, I expressed my critical comments in various lectures, which were published as "Reflexiones Críticas sobre la Constitución de 1999," in *Constitucionalismo Iberoamericano del Siglo XXI*, coords. Diego Valadés and Miguel Carbonell, Cámara de Diputados. LVII Legislatura, Universidad Nacional Autónoma de México, Mexico City 2000, pp. 171-93; *Revista de Derecho Público* 81, Editorial Jurídica Venezolana, Caracas 2000, 7-21; *Revista Facultad de Derecho, Derechos y Valores* 3, Universidad Militar Nueva Granada, Santafé de Bogotá, D.C., Colombia, 2000, pp. 9-26; and *La Constitución de 1999*, Biblioteca de la Academia de Ciencias Políticas y Sociales, Caracas 2000, pp. 63-88. See also "The constitutional reform in Venezuela and the 1999 Constitution," Symposium on *Challenges to Fragile Democracies in the Americas: Legitimacy and accountability*, Faculty of Law, University of Texas, Austin, February 25, 2000, in *Texas International Law Journal* 36, 2001, pp. 333-338.

255 See Allan R. Brewer-Carías, "La demolición del Estado de derecho y la destrucción de la democracia en Venezuela (1999-2009)," in *La democracia en su contexto. Estudios en homenaje a Dieter Nohlen en su septuagésimo aniversario,* coords. José Reynoso Núñez y Herminio Sánchez de la Barquera y Arroyo, Instituto de Investigaciones Jurídicas, Universidad Nacional Autónoma de México, Mexico City 2009, pp. 477-517.

256 It was the case of Antonio Guzmán Blanco in the nineteenth century and of Cipriano Castro, Juan Vicente Gómez, Eleazar López Contreras, and Marcos Pérez Jiménez in the twentieth century. John Lynch has pointed out: "The traditional cult of Bolívar has been used as a convenient ideology by military dictators, culminating with the regimes of Juan Vicente Gómez and Eleazar López Contreras; these had at least more or less respected the basic thought of the Liberator, even when they misrepresented its meaning." See John Lynch, *Simón Bolívar: A Life*, Yale University Press, New Haven, CT, 2007, p. 304. See also Germán Carrera Damas, *El culto a Bolívar, esbozo para un estudio de la historia de las ideas en Venezuela*, Universidad Central de Venezuela, Caracas 1969; Luis Castro Leiva, *De la patria boba a la teología bolivariana*, Monteávila, Caracas 1987; Elías Pino Iturrieta, *El divino Bolívar. Ensayo sobre una religión republicana*, Alfail, Caracas 2008; Ana Teresa Torres, *La herencia de la tribu. Del mito de*

changing a republic's name and to the invention of a Bolivarian doctrine to justify the government's policies, including the socialist character that Chávez wanted to impose.[257]

The country had been named the Republic of Venezuela through most of its constitutional political history since 1811, when after independence from Spain, the Confederation of States of Venezuela was constituted. The sole exception to this situation was from 1819 to 1830, the constitutional period that followed the Congress of Angostura in 1819 up to the reconstitution of the Republic of Venezuela by the 1830 Convention of Valencia. In 1819, Simón Bolívar proposed the Congress of the Republic of Venezuela to sanction the Law of the Union of the Peoples of Colombia, through which the Republic of Venezuela would disappear as an autonomous state. A new law similar to the former one was approved in 1821, and in that same year, the Constitution of Cucuta established the Republic of Colombia, comprising both the former Captaincy General of Venezuela (where the Republic of Venezuela had been established in 1811) and the former Viceroyalty of Nueva Granada. With the Constitution of 1821, part of Bolívar's dream for the union of the peoples of America came true.[258]

Thus, the idea of the "Bolivarian republic" from the point of view of Venezuela historically points to a political period and organization (1821-1830) in which Venezuela disappeared as an autonomous state, with its territory integrated in the Republic of Colombia. That is why the change of the republic's name in 1999 I considered was totally unacceptable being contrary to the idea of the country's sovereignty. But despite that approach, the renaming of the country in 1999 as a "Bolivarian republic" could also be explained as an intent to give the republic, in a certain way and ignoring two hundred years of history, a "definitive" national doctrine supposedly based on the thoughts of Bolívar. Nonetheless, what this approach can explain

---

la independencia a la Revolución bolivariana, Editorial Alfa, Caracas 2009. See also the historiography study on these books in Tomás Straka, La épica del desencanto, Editorial Alfa, Caracas 2009.

257   John Lynch has pointed out: "In 1998 Venezuelans were astonished to learn that their country had been renamed 'the Bolivarian Republic of Venezuela' by decree of President Hugo Chávez, who called himself a 'revolutionary Bolivarian.' Authoritarian populist, or neocaudillos, or Bolivarian militarists, whatever their designation, invoke Bolívar no less ardently that did previous rulers, though it is doubtful whether he would have responded to their calls...But the new heresy, far from maintaining continuity with the constitutional ideas of Bolívar, as was claimed, invented a new attribute, the populist Bolívar, and in the case of Cuba gave him a new identity, the socialist Bolívar. By exploiting the authoritarian tendency, which certainly existed in the thought and action of Bolívar, regimes in Cuba and Venezuela claim the Liberator as patron for their policies, distorting his ideas in the process." See John Lynch, Simón Bolívar: A Life, Yale University Press, New Haven, CT, 2007, 304. See also A.C. Clark, The Revolutionary Has No Clothes: Hugo Chávez's Bolivarian Farce, Encounter Books, New York 2009, pp. 5-14. The last attempt to completely appropriate Simón Bolívar for the "Bolivarian Revolution," was the televised exhumation of his remains that took place at the National Pantheon in Caracas on July 26, 2010, conducted by President Chávez himself and other high officials, including the Prosecutor General, among other things, for the purpose of determining if Bolivar died of arsenic poisoning in Santa Marta in 1830, instead of from tuberculosis. See Simon Romero, "Building a New History By Exhuming Bolívar," The New York Times, August 4, 2010, p. A7.

258   See the texts of all these Laws in Allan R. Brewer-Carías, Las Constituciones de Venezuela, Academia de Ciencias Políticas y Sociales, Caracas 2008, Vol. 1: pp. 643-46.

is that the real objective of the proposal was to give the new rulers the possibility to introduce their own socialist doctrine disguised as a Bolivarian one.

Conversely, another explanation of Venezuela's 1999 name change, other than evoking the ideas of Bolívar, who for instance rejected the federal form of government, can be found in exclusive political or partisan motivations. It must be remembered that the name of Chávez's initial political movement established in 1982 was the Bolivarian Revolutionary Movement 200 (MBR-200), which the president originally intended to transform into the Bolivarian Party. Nonetheless, because the Organic Law on Suffrage and Political Participation forbade using symbols of the motherland in parties' denominations, as a political movement its name needed to be changed in order to be converted into a political party. Thus, because it was impossible to use the Bolivarian denomination for the official party, the adherents of the president in the Constituent Assembly decided to use the name for the republic.[259] The party then became the Fifth Republic Movement (*Movimiento V República*, MVR) and later the United Socialist Party of Venezuela (PSUV), as a "Marxist" party.[260]

I was one of the few members of the Assembly who rejected the renaming proposal,[261] because I considered it not only as partisan motivated but also because a republic organized as "a federal decentralized State" was essentially anti-Bolivarian. Conversely, the last cry of Bolívar, on the eve of his death, was to abolish divisions and exclusions; and on the contrary, by adopting the new name of the republic in Article 1 of the Constitution, what the followers of the president were doing was to call for the bitter polarization of the country, between Bolivarian and those who are not and, consequently, between patriots and realists, good people and bad people, pure people and corrupt people, revolutionary and antirevolutionary or oligarchs; all that by manipulating history and popular feelings regarding the image of Bolivar.

The consequence of the constitutional reform on this matter has been that everything related to the new political regime has been called Bolivarian, beginning, for instance, with the "Bolivarian Circles" that were the first social or communal organizations promoted and supported by the government in order to react against any opposition to the government and to threaten anybody with views contrary to it.[262] In any event, after seven years of enforcing the Constitution, in the 2007 constitutional reform draft, it was proposed that the socialist "Bolivarian doctrine" be formally established as the fundamental doctrine of the state, defining the state's guiding doc-

---

259 *Mutatis mutandi*, in a certain way it happened with the use of the name of Augusto C. Sandino in the name of the *Frente Sandinista de Liberación* and of the Sandinista Republic of Nicaragua.

260 See "Declaration of Principles" of the United Socialist Party of Venezuela (Apr. 23, 2010), available at http://psuv.org.ve/files/tcdocumentos/Declaracion-de-principios-PSUV.pdf.

261 See Allan R. Brewer-Carías, *Debate constituyente (Aportes a la Asamblea Nacional Constituyente)* Fundación de Derecho Público–Editorial Jurídica Venezolana, Caracas 1999, 3 (Oct. 18–Nov. 30):237; pp. 251-252.

262 The general assembly of the Organization of American States, in its Report of Apr. 18, 2002, said about the Bolivarian Circles, that they "are groups of citizens or grassroots organizations who support the President's political platform. Many sectors consider them responsible for the human rights violations, acts of intimidation, and looting." See the reference in Allan R. Brewer-Carías, *La crisis de la democracia en Venezuela*, Libros El Nacional, Caracas 2002.

trine as "Bolivarian socialism" and also guiding international relations. It was to be the "twenty-first century socialism," all of which was rejected through popular vote in the December 2007 referendum.[263] Despite such rejection, in 2008 the armed forces formally became the Bolivarian Armed Forces, and a new military component was also created, the Bolivarian Popular Militia, established by the 2008 Organic Law on the Bolivarian Armed Forces,[264] organized to be at the service of the president. Also in April 2010, the official United Socialist Party of Venezuela, presided by the president of the "Bolivarian Republic," has adopted in its 'Declaration of Principles" as a "Marxist" party, the "Bolivarian socialism" doctrine, to be implemented through the "Bolivarian revolution."[265]

III. THE PROBLEM OF A POLITICAL CONSTITUTION DRAFTED FOR CENTRALISM AND AUTHORITARIANISM

The object of any political constitution is the organization of the state, and particularly of the constitutional branches of government and of the territorial distribution state power. That organization, in any constitution, can be determined differently. First, it can derive from the distribution of the state power, which creates either centralized (unitary) or decentralized states. Second, it can provoke distribution or division of powers, which results in either the concentration or the separation of powers. Last – the feature of democratic systems – organization is based on the separation, balance, and counterweight of powers of the state, which gives rise to the system of presidential or parliamentarian government. The political system, as laid out in the constitution, can also lead to autocracy or democracy, depending on whether sovereignty effectively lies in an autocrat or in the people through the electoral and party system.

With respect to Venezuela's Political Constitution of 1999, I want to highlight the most important substantive reforms that were introduced particularly in relation to the democratic system, bearing in mind that the Constitution, following the trends of the 1961 Constitution, contains all the provisions needed for the consolidation of the principles of the rule of law and justice (e.g., the excellent mechanisms of judicial review and of judicial reform established in the text).[266] Sadly, such mechanisms have been put out of action because of elements of authoritarianism set forth in the Constitution and the concentration of powers derived from other aspects of its text.

In effect, one of the great political changes that was to be made by the 1999 Constitution was to transform Venezuela's centralized federation of the past hundred years into an effectively decentralized federation, with distribution of power toward states and municipalities. The constitutional reform should have pointed in

---

263 See Allan R. Brewer-Carías, "Estudio sobre la propuesta de Reforma Constitucional para establecer un estado socialista, centralizado y militarista (Análisis del anteproyecto presidencial, Agosto de 2007)," *Cadernos da Escola de Direito e Relações Internacionais da UniBrasil* 7, Curitiba 2007, pp. 265-308.

264 Organic Law on the Bolivarian Armed Force, *Gaceta Oficial* N° 5.933, extra, Oct. 21, 2009.

265 See "Declaration of Principles" of the United Socialist Party of Venezuela (Apr. 23, 2010), available at http://psuv.org.ve/files/tcdocumentos/Declaracion-de-principios-PSUV.pdf.

266 See, for instance, Allan R. Brewer-Carías, "Judicial Review in Venezuela," in *Duquesne Law Review*, Volume 45, Number 3, Spring 2007, pp. 439-465.

that direction in order to effectively conceive the state as a decentralized federal state (Art. 4). For such a purpose, it should have foreseen the political decentralization of the federation as a national policy of strategic character as it is formally defined in the Constitution (Article 158).

However, the approved constitutional scheme of territorial distribution of power has not resulted in any substantial advance regarding the previous process of decentralization initiated in 1989 through the Organic Law of Decentralization and Transfer of Competencies of Public Power.[267] That process was abandoned in 1994, not being able to achieve the needed relegitimization of the political system, which progressively collapsed.[268] Moreover, in many aspects, the new Constitution has meant an institutional step backward. It being a "decentralized federal state" is only nominal, and decentralization continues to be a desideratum, as it was in the Constitution of 1961. Although Article 4 of the 1999 Constitution defines the state as a federal decentralized state, and Article 158 defines decentralization as a national policy, the fact is that other sections of the Constitution allow for an entirely different reality.[269] Those sections allow the centralization of powers at the national level, thus progressively drowning any real possibility of political participation by the states and municipalities of the federation (local governments).[270]

Some historical analysis will help underscore the incongruity. As noted previously, before the convening of the 1999 Constituent Assembly, there had been great public demand for reforms in order to bring about the decentralization of the federal state. The reforms were initiated in 1989, by introducing the direct election of state governors and establishing the framework for the transfer of national powers to the states. These reforms, once initiated, were quickly abandoned, and in the text of the new Constitution, in contrast to the same general declaration of decentralization policy contained in Article 158, other provisions have resulted in major setbacks to the prior reforms.

The Senate and the bicameral nature of the legislature, for instance, were eliminated in Article 159 of the Constitution, thus transforming Venezuela into the only federal state in the world with significant territory to function without a Senate. That has removed all possibility of equality among states that could be assured through equal number of votes in a senate or federal chamber and that are nonexistent in

---

267 Sanctioned according to Article 137 of the 1961 Constitution. See the last reform of such statute in *Gaceta Oficial* N° 39 140 of Mar. 17, 2009.

268 Ángel E. Álvarez, "State Reform before and after Chávez's Election," in *Venezuelan Politics in the Chávez Era: Class, Polarization & Conflicts*, eds. Steve Ellner and Daniel Hellinger, Lynne Rienner Publishers, London 2003, p. 147.

269 In the 2007 constitutional reform draft proposals, Article 158 of the Constitution and all the constitutional provisions referring to political decentralization were proposed to be eliminated and changed to consolidate a centralized state. See *Proyecto de Reforma Constitucional. Elaborado por el ciudadano Presidente de la República Bolivariana de Venezuela, Hugo Chávez Frías,* Editorial Atenea, Caracas Aug. 2007.

270 See Allan R. Brewer-Carías, *Federalismo y municipalismo en la Constitución de 1999 (Alcance de una reforma insuficiente y regresiva),* Editorial Jurídica Venezolana, Caracas-San Cristóbal 2001.

the new unicameral legislative chamber (National Assembly).[271] The unicameral organization of the National Assembly (Article 186) not only abandoned a tradition that goes back to 1811 but also contradicted the federal form of a state, which requires a legislative (federal) chamber with equal representation of states that serves as political counterweight to the chamber of people's representation (representation on which depends state populations). The elimination of the Senate was an attack on political decentralization, as it extinguished the instrument that made states equal in national affairs. It was also a step backward both in forming national laws and in exercising powers of parliamentary control over the executive branch.

With the new constitutional text, powers that previously had been designated as exclusive to the states were subjected to the regulations of national legislation (Article 164). Even the exercise of concurrent powers has become subject to the dictates of national law, thus contravening the autonomy of territorial entities. In particular, in the new Constitution, regulation of the functioning and organization of the state legislative councils is a competence of the National Assembly (Article 162), which contradicts the states' ability to dictate their own Constitution to organize their own branches of government. This regulation was an unacceptable interference of the national power into the regime of the states. The autonomy of the states was also seriously limited by constitutional provisions that allowed the National Assembly to regulate by means of a national statute the system of designation of the states' comptroller generals this being a competency of the states (Article 162).[272]

Conversely, regarding the distribution of powers between territorial entities, the decentralization process required, above all, the effective allocation of taxation powers to states, specifically sales tax, as in almost all federations. The advances from discussions of the draft Constitution on this matter were abandoned; in the second discussion, all taxation powers assigned to states were removed, which was a step backward even regarding provisions that existed in the 1961 Constitution. Accordingly, the national government has been given authority, as a residual competence, in all tax matters not expressly delegated to the states and municipalities (Article 156, Section 12); the states have no taxing power, and even their power over sales tax has been eliminated (Article 156, Section 12). Article 167, Section 5, provides that states have tax powers only in the matters expressly assigned by national law. In that way, states continue to completely depend on the national financial contribution (*situado constitutional*), to be established in the national budget with an amount not more that 20% of the national public income. That limit did not exist in the Constitution of 1961, which established only a minimum. And even though the new Consti-

---

271   See my dissenting vote in Allan R. Brewer-Carías, *Debate constituyente (Aportes a la Asamblea Nacional Constituyente)*, Fundación de Derecho Público, Caracas 1999, 3 (Oct. 18–Nov. 30): pp. 286 ff.

272   See Allan R. Brewer-Carías, "La 'federación descentralizada' en el marco de la centralización de la federación en Venezuela. Situación y perspectivas de una contradicción constitucional," in *Constitución, democracia y control el poder*, Centro Iberoamericano de Estudios Provinciales y Locales, Universidad de los Andes, Editorial Jurídica Venezolana, Mérida 2004, pp. 111-143. See my proposals to the Constituent Assembly on political decentralization of the federation in Allan R. Brewer-Carías, *Debate constituyente (Aportes a la Asamblea Nacional Constituyente)*, Fundación de Derecho Público–Editorial Jurídica Venezolana, Caracas 1999, 1 (Aug. 8–Sept. 8), pp. 155-170; 2 (Sept. 9–Oct. 17), pp. 227-233.

tution established the Federal Council of Government (Article 185) as an "intergo-vernmental" organ, the one that was organized by an organic law in February 2010[273] has been established as an instrument for central planning and for the development of the "communal or popular power," which is not provided in the Constitution, setting aside the formal federal organization of the state.

Regarding municipalities, their autonomy, traditionally guaranteed in the Constitution, was also interfered by subjecting it to the limits established not only in the Constitution but also those established in national laws (Article 168). Therefore, the basic decentralizing principle, autonomy, was minimized, and municipalities in practice continued to be organized very far from the citizens' reach, thus impeding any kind of real political participation.[274] In fact, what the 1999 Constitution created was a centralized, antiparticipatory democratic system that deliberately confuses the instruments of direct democracy with effective political participation. That is why the citizen's assemblies and the communal councils, which began to be established in 2006, have gradually replaced local governments, being in contrast, directed from the center, and without any general electoral representative origin. Nonetheless, they create the idea that the people are participating. With the new Organic Law on the Federal Council of Government (2010), new base organizations of the popular power have been created, like the "communes," formally implementing through legislation the 2007 constitutional reform that was rejected by the people.[275]

In any case, the result is that the scheme of centralized federation of the Constitution of 1961 has been strengthened and aggravated in the 1999 Constitution and through its unconstitutional developments, despite it identifying the federation formally as a "decentralized federation" (Article 4).

The great reform of the political system that was needed to improve democracy was definitively to change the centralism of the state and to distribute political power throughout the territory. That was the only way to effect true political participation and a motive that could justify the Constituent Assembly. Decentralization, however, was postponed, and a great opportunity lost.

The Constituent Assembly, to overcome the political crisis, should have transformed the state, decentralizing power and establishing the basis for local govern-

273   See *Official Gazette* N° 5.963 Extra. of Feb. 22, 2010.

274   See Allan R. Brewer-Carías et al., *Ley Orgánica del Poder Público Municipal*, Editorial Jurídica Venezolana, Caracas 2005; and "El inicio de la desmunicipalización en Venezuela: La organización del Poder Popular para eliminar la descentralización, la democracia representativa y la participación a nivel local," in *AIDA, Opera Prima de Derecho Administrativo. Revista de la Asociación Internacional de Derecho Administrativo*, Asociación Internacional de Derecho Administrativo, Universidad Nacional Autónoma de México, Mexico City, 2007, pp. 49-67.

275   In the 2007 constitutional reform draft proposals, a new branch of government was proposed to be created, the "popular power," and the "communes" seeking to consolidate the power of communal councils, with members who were not elected by popular vote and depended on the office of the head of state. See Allan R. Brewer-Carías, *Hacia la consolidación de un estado socialista, centralizado, policial y militarista. Comentarios sobre el alcance y sentido de la Reforma Constitucional 2007*, Editorial Jurídica Venezolana, Caracas 2007; and *La Reforma Constitucional de 2007 (Sancionada inconstitucionalmente por la Asamblea Nacional el 2 de Noviembre de 2007)*, Editorial Jurídica Venezolana, Caracas 2007.

ment organizations to effectively approach the exercise of state power to the citizen. The Constituent Assembly did not do that –it neither transformed the state nor arranged the elements for effective participation. To participate is to be part of, to appertain, or to be associated with, and that is possible for citizens only with decentralized and accessible political local governments. Thus, participative democracy, besides elections or voting in referenda, is possible only with effective decentralization of power through expanding local governments in the territory. Thus, only democracies can be decentralized.[276] Democracy can be part of everyday life only when local governments are established throughout a country.[277]

IV. THE DEMOCRATIC REGIME AND POLITICAL PARTICIPATION

One of the fundamental values established in the 1999 Constitution is democracy (preamble), not only as a political regime and condition of government but also as a way of life, founded in the ideas of political pluralism and equal participation of everyone in political processes. In that sense, the concept of the democratic state (*estado democrático*) is a constitutional principle that gives roots to the political organization of the nation, as it derives from the preamble ("democratic society") and from Articles 2, 3, 5, and 6 of the Constitution.

Democracy is also established in Article 6 of the Constitution as an immutable regime of the government of the republic and its political entities (states and municipalities), in the sense that such government must always be "democratic, participative, elective, decentralized, alternative, responsible, pluralist, and of revocable mandates." The Constitution also establishes provisions regarding accountability (*rendición de cuentas*) (Article 197), particularly for elected officers, and the possibility of them being subject to recall referenda (Articles 6, 70, 72 and 198).

Regarding these provisions, the Constitutional Chamber of the Supreme Tribunal of Justice, in Decision N° 23 (January 22, 2003), pointed out that the 1999 Constitution intended to "establish a democratic, participative and protagonist society, which implies that it is not just the State who has to adopt and submit its institutions to the ways and principles of democracy, but it is also the society (formed by the Venezuelan citizens) who must play a decisive and responsible role in the conduction of the Nation."[278]

To establish a democratic government with all such elements, defined in *cláusulas pétreas* (rock–like clauses), which must always exist, Article 5 of the Constitution, after setting forth that "sovereignty resides in an nontransferable way in the people," declares that sovereignty can be exercised in two ways: First, in a direct way by means of referenda and other instruments for direct democracy established

---

276   See Allan R. Brewer-Carías, "Democracia municipal, descentralización y desarrollo local," in *Revista Iberoamericana de Administración Pública* 11, Ministerio de Administraciones Públicas, Madrid 2004, pp. 11-34.

277   See Allan R. Brewer-Carías, "Democratización, descentralización política y reforma del estado" and "El municipio, la descentralización política y la democracia," in *Reflexiones sobre el constitucionalismo en América,* Editorial Jurídica Venezolana, Caracas 2001, 105-41 and pp. 243-253.

278   See Case: *Interpretación del artículo 71 de la Constitución,* in *Revista de Derecho Público*, 93-96, Editorial Jurídica Venezolana, Caracas 2003, pp. 530ff.

in the Constitution; second, and in an indirect way, "through suffrage, by the organs that exercise State Powers" (Article 5). The same enunciations are contained in Article 62 of the same Constitution, which sets forth citizens' political right to freely participate in all public affairs – that is, to participate in the formation, execution, and control of public activities to achieve their complete collective and individual development. It is the obligation of the state and society to facilitate and create the most favorable conditions for such participation. This political participation, an essential characteristic of any democracy, although not always accomplished, as already mentioned, is exercised in two ways according to the same provision of the Constitution: directly through instruments of direct democracy and indirectly through elected representatives, which is one of the essential elements of representative democracy (Article 62).

For the purpose of guaranteeing this right to political participation, Article 70 of the Constitution enumerates the following political means for citizens to exercise their sovereignty: by electing representatives to public office; by voting on referenda, including those to revoke mandates of elected officers; by participating in popular consultations; by assuming the initiative regarding legislative or constitutional reforms; and by participating in open town meetings and in citizens' assemblies (whose decisions are binding).

According to those constitutional provisions, the participatory democratic political system of Venezuela is characterized by the following elements: a representative democracy, assured by means of an electoral system that must guarantee free, universal, direct, and secret elections; a regime of plural political parties; an alternating system of government; and instruments of government accountability; and a direct democracy, assured by means of referenda, legislative initiatives, popular consultations, and the possibility of political participation in open town meetings and citizens' assemblies.

1. *Representative Democracy*

Representative democracy is a basic component of the participatory democratic system of Venezuela, through which citizens exercise sovereignty by electing representatives to state organs. This is an indirect means of exercising sovereignty, precisely "through suffrage, by the organs that exercise State Powers" (Article 5).

But suffrage and periodic fair and free elections, based on a universal, secret vote that expresses the will of the people, do not exhaust representative democracy. It has the following other essential elements: respect for human rights and fundamental liberties, access to power and its exercise with subjection to the rule of law, a regime of plural political parties and organizations, and separation and independence of public powers.

The exercise of sovereignty through representatives by means of elections not only is the most common element of representative democracy but also is irreplaceable. All head officials of the executive and legislative branches, in all levels of government, are elected by popular, direct, and secret vote. At the national level, the president is elected for a term of six years by popular, universal, direct, and secret vote by all citizens registered in the electoral registry by a simple majority of votes (Articles 228 and 230).

The representatives of the National Assembly are elected for a five-year term (Article 192) by citizens registered in the electoral registry by popular, universal, direct, and secret vote. In that case, the electoral system applied is mixed, combining a personal vote with proportional representation in a number fixed according to a population base of 1.1% of the country's total population (Article 186). In addition, three national representatives from each state must be elected. Also, the indigenous peoples have the right to elect three national representatives (Article 125). Each representative must have a substitute member, elected through the same process, who is called to act in cases of temporal or absolute absence of the principal (Article 186).

All other public officials of the branches of government (magistrates of the Supreme Tribunal of Justice, comptroller general, prosecutor general, peoples' defender, members of the National Electoral Council) are not elected in popular elections but appointed by the National Assembly (Articles 265, 279, and 296), in some cases, by a qualified majority of votes. That legislative election must be made with the participation of representatives of the various sectors of society that must integrate the nominating committees that must be established for such purposes.[279] Unfortunately, the latter provisions have been distorted by the National Assembly, reducing the participation scope of civil society by incorporating members of the National Assembly into such committees, controlling them.

At the state level, the governors of each state are elected, by a relative majority of votes, for a term of four years by popular, universal, direct, and secret vote of the citizens registered in the electoral registry from the constituency of the respective state (Article 160). The members of the legislative councils of each state are elected every four years, in a number of not more that fifteen or less than seven, also by the citizens registered in the electoral registry of each state. In this case, the same rules apply as for the election of the representatives to the National Assembly (Article 162). On the municipal level, mayors and members of municipal councils are elected every four years by popular, universal, direct, and secret vote of the majority of citizens registered in the electoral registry of the constituency of the respective municipality (Articles 174 and 175).

The 1999 Constitution initially established that the president, governors, and mayors could be reelected only once and in the immediately following constitutional term (Articles 160, 174, and 230) and that members of the National Assembly and the state legislative councils could be reelected for a maximum of two consecutive constitutional terms (Articles 162 and 192). Nonetheless, all the limits on the possible reelection of officials, which were a consequence of the principle of alternating government according to Article 6 of the Constitution, nonetheless were eliminated through a constitutional amendment approved by referendum on February 14, 2009.[280]

---

279   See Allan R. Brewer-Carías, "La participación ciudadana en la designación de los titulares de los órganos no electos de los poderes públicos en Venezuela y sus vicisitudes políticas," *Revista Iberoamericana de Derecho Público y Administrativo* 5-2005, San José, Costa Rica 2005, pp. 76-95.

280   See *Official Gazette* N° 5.908 Extra. of Feb. 19, 2009.

2. The Mixed Electoral System and Its Distortion

To guarantee representative democracy in the election of representatives and members of the National Assembly, legislative councils, and municipal councils, the Constitution has established an electoral system combining personalized and proportional representation ballots.[281] According to the 1961 Constitution, the election of representatives in general was governed by d'Hondt proportional representation system. In 1993, the Organic Law on Suffrage and Political Participation,[282] seeking to guarantee better representation in elections at the regional and local levels, introduced a combination of methods, mixing proportional representation with majority elections. That was finally constitutionalized in a general way in the 1999 Constitution as a "personalized proportional representation method" (Article 63). This mixed system required ensuring that in each state constituency a percentage of representatives is to be elected through majority ballot; and another percentage is to be elected in its subdivdsions, through lists ballot (proportional representation), through blocked and closed lists. Until 2009, the elections of representatives were governed by the already mentioned Organic Law on Suffrage and Political Participation of 1993, reformed in 1998, providing that for the definitive allocation of representatives, regarding elected by both methods in one constituency from candidates of the same party, a deduction was to be made in the corresponding list in order to allow the effective application of the proportional–representation principle allowing the election of candidates from the other parties.[283] Nonetheless, this method of deducting elected candidates was restricted by means of a constitutional interpretation of the Constitution made by the Constitutional Chamber of the Supreme Tribunal of Justice on January 25, 2006, [284] before the election of the members of the National Assembly that same year. That decision legitimized the defrauding method applied by the parties supporting the government,[285] allowing those parties that have entered into agreements, for some of them to file nominations only for majority ballots and for others only to file nominations for proportional–representation ballots. Thus, being formally different parties (though part of the same coalition), no deduction of the elected candidates was to be applied, as it happens when it is the same party the one that elects candidates through both methods, distorting in this way the application of the proportional–representation method.[286] Accordingly, the system became, in practice, a majority system that distorted proportional representation. In 2009, the

---

281 See Allan R. Brewer-Carías, "Reforma electoral en el sistema político de Venezuela," in *Reforma política y electoral en América Latina 1978-2007,* coords. Daniel Zovatto and J. Jesús Orozco Henríquez, Universidad Nacional Autónoma de México-IDEA internacional, Mexico City 2008, pp. 953-1019.

282 *Gaceta Oficial* Extra. N° 5.233, May 28, 1998.

283 Articles 12 ff. See *Gaceta Oficial.* N° 5.233 Extra of May 28, 1998.

284 Decision N° 74 (Case: *Acción Democrática vs. Consejo nacional Electoral y otras autoridades electorales*), in *Revista de Derecho Público* 105, Editorial Jurídica Venezolana, Caracas 2006, 122-44.

285 The method was named "The Twins" (*Las Morochas*) allowing the same group of parties to use and benefit from both electoral systems in uninominal and plurinominal constituencies, without the deduction attached to the mixed system.

286 See Allan R. Brewer-Carías, "El juez constitucional vs. el derecho al sufragio mediante la representación proporcional," in *Crónica sobre la "In"Justicia constitucional. La Sala Constitucional y el autoritarismo en Venezuela,* Caracas 2007, pp. 337 ff.

new Organic Law on Electoral Processes was sanctioned, legalizing this distorted electoral method,[287] which is the one that was to be applied in the legislative election in September 2010.

3.   *Principles of Participative Democracy and Their Distortion*

The 1999 Constitution, by establishing participation as a fundamental principle of democracy, also regulated it as a political constitutional right, "considering individuals as member of a determined political community, in order to take part in the formation of public decisions or of the will of the public institutions" – a right related to other political rights established in the Constitution, like the rights to vote (Article 63), to petition (Article 51), to have access to public offices (Article 62), to political association (Article 67), to demonstration (Article 68), and to be promptly informed by public administration offices on the course or result of petitions (Article 143). It also relates to social rights, like the right to health (Article 84); educational rights (Article 102); and environmental rights (Article 127).[288]

Participative democracy, besides representative (election) and direct democracy (referenda, citizens assembly whose decisions will be of binding force), also materializes in other constitutional instruments established for the direct intervention of citizens in public–affairs decision making such as the initiative for legislation, for constitutional reforms and for the constituent process, public consultations, and open town meetings (Article 70).

The Constitution also has directly regulated some mechanisms to guarantee direct participation of persons representing the different sectors of society in the adoption of some public decisions, particularly by integrating the nominating committees that are called to propose before the National Assembly the candidates to be appointed prosecutor general, comptroller general, people's defender, judges of the Supreme Court, and members of the Electoral National Council (Articles 270, 279, 295). With these provisions, the drafters of the Constitution were seeking to avoid the traditional agreements between political parties that characterized such appointment.[289] For such purpose, it was provided that the nominating committees were to be integrated exclusively by "representatives of the different sectors of the society," in order to select the candidates to be proposed before the National Assembly. That is, according to constitutional provisions, the National Assembly can appoint only candidates who have been nominated by such committees, representing the various sectors of society. This innovation in the Constitution was an attempt to reduce the discretional power of political parties in the National Assembly, which had been making nontransparent appointments based on patronage. Nonetheless, that participation has not occurred: The nominating committees have been regulated in the

---

287   *Gaceta Oficial* N° 5928, Extra., Aug. 12, 2009.

288   See Case: *Interpretación del artículo 71 de la Constitución* in *Revista de Derecho Público*, N° 93-96, Editorial Jurídica Venezolana, Caracas 2003, pp. 530ff.

289   See, e.g., Allan R. Brewer-Carías, *Los problemas del estado de partidos*, Editorial Jurídica Venezolana, Caracas 1988.

corresponding statutes[290] as simple parliamentary commissions and the National Assembly has kept the same discretional power that the old National Congress had.

In effect, once the new National Assembly was elected in August 2000, it adopted a "special statute,"[291] which granted to it almost the same appointment powers that the dissolved Congress had and that the Constituent Assembly had unconstitutionally exercised during the transitional period: the power to appoint the judges of the Supreme Tribunal of Justice, the prosecutor general, the general controller, the people's defender, and the National Electoral Council. Before the newly elected assembly had a chance to make appointments under that special statute, the people's defender brought an action challenging it before the transitional Supreme Tribunal. Several other judicial actions were brought before the Supreme Tribunal regarding other actions of the transitional authorities, but all were upheld as constitutional.[292]

Of all the decisions of the Supreme Tribunal of Justice, the one in response to the challenge of the people's defender against the 2000 Special Law providing for the appointments of high officials of the state, among them the judges of the Supreme Tribunal, was perhaps the most startling, as it called on the tribunal to be a judge and party in its own cause (as it was a ruling on the constitutionality of its own appointment). Even though the Supreme Tribunal did not finally decide the action regarding the constitutionality of the 2000 special statute, in a preliminary decision, it accepted that the newly elected National Assembly was exercising "transitional constitutional" authority.[293]

The subsequent statutes regulating the other branches of government also failed to respect the new Constitution. As mentioned, instead of forming the constitutionally required nominating committees integrating representatives of the various sectors of civil society, the National Assembly established only parliamentary commissions as vehicles for making appointments, and those commissions included the scattered participation of some members of civil society.[294]

---

290 See Organic Law on the Supreme Tribunal of Justice, in *Gaceta Oficial* N° 37.942, May 20, 2004 (the same provision exists in the new Law on the Supreme Tribunal of 2010); Orgánic Law on the Electoral Power, in *Gaceta Oficial* N° 37.573, Nov. 19, 2002; and Organic Law on the Citizen's Power, *Gaceta Oficial* N° 37.310, Oct. 19, 2001.

291 Special Statute for the Ratification or Appointment of the Public Officials of the Citizen Power and of the Magistrates of the Supreme Tribunal of Justice for the First Constitutional Term, Nov. 14, 2000, in *Gaceta Oficial* N° 37.077, Nov. 14, 2000.

292 See, e.g., Decision N° 179 (Mar. 28, 2000) (Case: *Gonzalo Pérez M.*), *Revista de Derecho Público* 81, Editorial Jurídica Venezolana, Caracas 2000, pp. 81 ff.

293 Decisión N° 84 (Dec. 12, 2000) (Case: *People's Defender*), in *Revista de Derecho Público* 84, Editorial Jurídica Venezolana, Caracas 2000, pp. 108 ff.

294 See Allan R. Brewer-Carías, "La progresiva y sistemática demolición institucional de la autonomía e independencia del poder judicial en Venezuela 1999-2004," in *XXX Jornadas J.M Domínguez Escovar, Estado de derecho, Administración de justicia y derechos humanos*, Instituto de Estudios Jurídicos del Estado Lara, Barquisimeto 2005, pp. 33-174; *La Sala Constitucional versus el estado democrático de derecho. El secuestro del poder electoral y de la estado Electoral del Tribunal Supremo y la confiscación del derecho a la participación política*, Los Libros de El Nacional, Colección Ares, Caracas 2004; "El secuestro del poder electoral y de la Sala Electoral del Tribunal Supremo y la confiscación del derecho a la participación política mediante el referendo revocatorio presidencial: Venezuela: 2000-2004," in *Revista Costarricense de Derecho Constitucional* 5, Instituto Costarricense de Derecho Constitucio-

In effect, regarding the judiciary, the Constitution conceives of the Judicial Nominating Committee (Article 270) as a counseling organization of the judiciary for the selection of candidates for magistrate of the Supreme Tribunal of Justice (Article 264), and the committee provides for the direct participation of the "diverse sectors of the society" in a public decision-making process. However, after enacting the 2000 special law without complying with the constitutional provision, in the 2004 Organic Law of the Supreme Tribunal of Justice of 2004,[295] the Judicial Nominating Committee, instead of being formed solely and exclusively by representatives of the diverse sectors of the society, was formed by "eleven (11) principal members, five (5) of them to be elected from within the representatives of the National Assembly, and the other six (6) members, from sectors of the society, elected by the Assembly in a public proceeding" (Article 13.2). The result has been the creation of an "amplified" parliamentary commission of the National Assembly (Article 13) of which National Assembly members are integrated, even though National Assembly representatives are not considered representatives of civil society.

Also, in the case of the electoral power, to guarantee the autonomy of the National Electoral Council, the Constitution limited the discretional power that the previous Congress had to appoint its members, establishing the Electoral Nominating Committee also integrated by representatives of different sectors of society. However, in the 2002 Organic Law of the Electoral Power,[296] regardless of the constitutional provisions, the integration of the Electoral Nominating Committee did not respect the Constitution. Instead, another "amplified" parliamentary commission was established as the nominating committee made up of "twenty-one (21) members, from which eleven (11) are representatives before the National Assembly, and ten (10) from sectors of society," all appointed by the same National Assembly. With that regulation, the right to political participation of different sectors of civil society, which had the exclusive right to conform the nominating committee, was confiscated.[297]

The same has occurred regarding the nomination and appointment of the high officials of the citizens' power (the branch of government comprising the prosecutor general, the comptroller general, and the peoples' defender), by means of the Orga-

nal, Editorial Investigaciones Jurídicas, San José, Costa Rica, 2004, 167-312; and in *Revista Jurídica del Perú* 55, Lima 2004, pp. 353-396.

295   See *Gaceta Oficial* N° 37.942, May 20, 2004. See comments in Allan R. Brewer-Carías, *Ley Orgánica del Tribunal Supremo de Justicia. Procesos y procedimientos constitucionales y contencioso-administrativos*, Editorial Jurídica Venezolana, Caracas 2004.

296   See *Gaceta Oficial* N° 37.573, Nov. 19, 2002.

297   See comments in Allan R. Brewer-Carías, *La Sala Constitucional versus el estado democrático de derecho. El secuestro del poder electoral y de la Sala Electoral del Tribunal Supremo y la confiscación del derecho a la participación política*, Los Libros de El Nacional, Colección Ares, Caracas 2004.

nic Law of the Citizens Power of 2004.[298] That also resulted in a parliamentary commission.[299]

The National Assembly completely distorted the constitutional mechanism created to guarantee the possibility of citizens' direct participation, through representatives from various sectors of society, in selecting and nominating nonelected public officers of the state.

With the distortion of the nominating committees, the diverse branches of government have become more dependent on political power, which has given way in the constitutional order to a concentrated system of powers that is contrary to the proclaimed principles of autonomy and independence of the different branches of government. Through legislative practice and the refusal of the Supreme Tribunal of Justice to exercise judicial review over such unconstitutional statutes, a very important constitutional innovation, unique in the world, has been neutralized. With this, unfortunately, the constitutionally guaranteed political participation of citizens has also been forgotten and has been manipulated by those who control power from the legislative branch.

Contrary to all the participative terminology it contains, the 1999 Constitution can be considered an interventionist and limiting text regarding the organizations of civil society. It establishes the jurisdiction of the National Electoral Council for "the organization of the elections of trade unions, professional associations and organizations with political objectives," in addition to its functions directed to guarantee "the equality, reliability, impartiality, transparency and efficiency of the electoral processes" (Article 293.6).

According to this provision, the internal elections that can take place within political parties, trade unions, and professional associations of any kind must be organized by the state, through one of the branches of government (electoral power). That openly contradicts the participatory feature attributed to the Constitution and its declared goal of promoting citizens' participation.

Consequently, all internal electoral processes in political parties in Venezuela, even those directed to select their candidates to general elections, from 2000 on must be organized by the National Electoral Council. That, in fact, has not always occurred because of the progressive configuration of the political arena in the country to one party.

With all those provisions, the state has actively intervened in civil–society organizations. For instance, even though trade unions are not considered "inside the structure of the Venezuelan public organization,"[300] the Electoral Chamber of the

---

298   According to the 1999 Constitution, the citizen power is composed by three state organs: the prosecutor general, comptroller general, and peoples' defender. See *Gaceta Oficial* N° 37.310, Oct. 19, 2001.

299   See Allan R. Brewer-Carías, "Sobre el nombramiento irregular por la Asamblea Nacional de los titulares de los órganos del poder ciudadano en 2007," *Revista de Derecho Público* 113, Editorial Jurídica Venezolana, Caracas 2008, pp. 85-88.

300   See *Revista de Derecho Público* 84, Editorial Jurídica Venezolana, Caracas 2000, pp. 132 ff.

Supreme Court, in Decision N° 46 (March 11, 2002), has justified such anomalous state intervention and supervision of those social organizations.[301]

With respect to other civil associations of individuals or corporations   –such as neighborhood associations;[302] social clubs or recreational associations;[303] and groups of a business, industrial, or commercial character[304]– on the basis of the same constitutional provision, the Electoral Chamber of the Supreme Tribunal of Justice has decided in many cases to participate in their internal functioning. In one emblematic case, the Electoral Chamber ruled on the obligatory intervention of the National Electoral Council in the electoral processes of civil associations, as occurred with the internal elections of the professors' association of Universidad Central de Venezuela.[305]

4. *Direct Democracy Institutions, Referenda, and the Distortion of the Recall Referendum*

Regarding direct democracy, the 1999 Constitution also established various mechanisms for its exercise to promote direct popular participation in conducting public affairs. In that context, Article 70 of the Constitution, referring to the need for prominent participation of the people, as aforementioned, enumerates as means for direct democracy: referenda; popular consultation; repeal of the public mandate; legislative, constitutional, and constituent initiatives; open town meetings (*cabildos abiertos*); and citizens' assemblies, "whose decisions shall have a binding character."

For referenda, the Constitution expressly established consultative referenda, recall referenda to revoke mandates, approbatory referenda of statutes and constitutional revisions, and referenda to abrogate statutes.[306]

Consultative referenda can be convened for questions of matters of preeminent national, state, or municipal importance. According to Article 71 of the Constitution, at the national level, they can be convened by the president in Council of Ministers;

---

301 See *Revista de Derecho Público* 89–92, Editorial Jurídica Venezolana, Caracas 2000, pp. 148-49.

302 See Constitutional Chamber Decision N° 61 (May 29, 2001), Exp. 000064 (Case: *Asociación de Residentes de la Urbanización La Trinidad*). See also Allan R. Brewer-Carías, *Derecho administrativo*, Universidad Externado de Colombia, Bogotá 2005, Vol I, pp. 413 ff.

303 See Electoral Chamber Decision of Nov. 1, 2000, Exp. 0115 (Case: *Asociación Civil Club Campestre Paracotos*). See also Allan R. Brewer-Carías, *Derecho administrativo*, Universidad Externado de Colombia, Bogotá 2005, Vol I, pp. 413 ff.

304 See Electoral Chamber Decision N° 18 (Feb. 15, 2001), Exp. 000017 (Case: *Cámara de Comercios e Industrias del Estado Aragua*). This jurisprudence was ratified by the same chamber, according to verdict N° 162, Exp. 2002-000077 (Oct. 17, 2002) (Case: *Cámara de Comercio e Industrias del Estado Bolívar*). See Allan R. Brewer-Carías, *Derecho administrativo*, Universidad Externado de Colombia, Bogotá 2005, Vol I, pp. 413 ff..

305 See Electoral Chamber Decision N° 51 (May 19, 2000) (Case: *Asociación de Profesores de la Universidad Central de Venezuela*), in *Revista de Derecho Público* 82, Editorial Jurídica Venezolana, Caracas 2000, pp. 92ff.

306 See Cosimina G. Pellegrino Pacera, "Una introducción al estudio del referendo como mecanismo de participación ciudadana en la Constitución de 1999," in *El derecho público a comienzos del siglo XXI. Estudios homenaje al Profesor Allan R. Brewer-Carías*, Instituto de Derecho Público, Universidad Central de Venezuela, Civitas Ediciones, Madrid 2003, Vol I, pp. 411-481.

the National Assembly, by means of a resolution approved by a majority of members; and citizens, by means of a petition signed by at least 10% of registered voters. At the local level (e.g., parish[307] [*parroquias*], municipal, state), consultative referenda can be convened by municipal councils or state legislative councils on the initiative of two-thirds of members; by the mayor or governor; or by the people, with a petition signed by no less than 10% of registered voters in the specific jurisdiction.

The Constitution also establishes approval referenda regarding draft statutes, which are debated before the National Assembly. According to Article 73 of the Constitution, that occurs when at least two-thirds of members of the assembly so decide. If the referendum results in the approval of a statute, provided that at least 25% of registered voters have concurred, the corresponding bill will become law. Approval referenda also can be proposed by popular initiative (Article 204.7) when the National Assembly fails to take up debate on bills that also were proposed by popular initiative (Article 205).

According to Article 73 of the Constitution, treaties, conventions, and other international agreements that can compromise national sovereignty or transfer national powers or competencies to supranational entities, as with treaties for regional economic integration, may be subject to approbatory referenda. In that case, the initiative corresponds to the president in Council of Ministers; to the National Assembly, when approved by a vote of at least two-thirds of members; or to popular initiative, with a petition signed by at least 15% of registered voters.

The Constitution also regulates referenda for the abrogation of statutes regarding laws other than budgetary, tax, public debt, amnesty, and human rights laws, and those laws approving international treaties (Article 74). Abrogation referenda can be convened on the initiative of at least 10% of registered voters or on the initiative of the president in Council of Ministers. Decrees laws issued by the president (Article 236.8) also may be subjected to abrogation referenda, in which case the convention initiative only can be popular, through a petition signed by at least 5% of registered voters. In all abrogation referenda, the concurrence of at least 40% of registered voters is necessary to abrogate a statute or decree law.

Revocation or recall referenda are the consequence of the principle established in the Constitution that all popular elected public officials are subject to revocation of their mandate (Article 6). Thus, Article 72 establishes recall referenda, which can take place only at the second half of the term in office. The popular revocation of mandates is one way that people have direct political participation in the exercise of their sovereignty (Article 70). Consequently, the corresponding petition for a recall referendum only can be of popular initiative and must be signed by at least 20% of registered voters in the corresponding jurisdiction.

For revocation of mandates, according to Article 72 of the Constitution, the following rules must be observed in the corresponding referendum. First, the recall referendum can be convened only once at the midpoint of the term of the elected officer. Second, the request to convene a recall referendum can be made only by popular initiative, signed by no less than 25% of registered voters in the correspon-

---

307   These are, of course, nonreligious territorial divisions of the municipalities.

ding constituency and filed before the National Electoral Council (Article 293.5). There cannot be more that one request for a recall referendum during the same constitutional term of the elected official. Third, in the convened recall referendum, a number greater than or equal to 25% of registered voters must concur as voting persons. Fourth, for approval of a mandate's recall, it is sufficient that a number of voters equal to or greater than that which elected the officer voted in the referendum to revoke the mandate. In that case, the official's mandate is considered revoked, and a new election must take place immediately to fill the absence (Articles 72 and 233).

Consequently, for a mandate to be recalled or revoked, the number of yes votes (to revoke) must be equal to or greater than the number of votes that originally elected the official, and voters must total at least 25% of registered voters in the corresponding jurisdiction. The Constitution says nothing about the fact that, in a recall referendum, voters who vote not to revoke the official's mandate could outnumber the votes to revoke. The provision is established for a recall referendum and not for a plebiscite; that is, it is established in order to decide the revocation of a mandate and not to decide on the confirmation or continuation of a mandate.

With respect to the president, because the revocation of his mandate has the effect of an absolute absence, in case a revocation occurs, replacement occurs as follows. If revocation takes place during the first four years of his mandate, there must be a new election of someone to complete the president's term. If the revocation takes place during the last two years of the presidential term, the executive vice president assumes the position of president until the end of the term (Article 233).

The Constitution also provides for revoking mandates of officials in the National Assembly. In that case, revoked representatives cannot seek a new election in the subsequent constitutional term (Article 198). This applies only to representatives in the National Assembly; the Constitution establishes nothing in this regard regarding the mandate revocation of other public elected officers.

On matters of recall referenda, Venezuela's only experience with them during the first decade of the 1999 Constitution is the recall referendum of the president (who was elected in 2000 by 3,757,774 votes), convened in 2004 by popular initiative signed by more than 3.5 million people.[308] That was distorted and illegitimately transformed, against the Constitution, into a sort of ratifying referendum of a plebiscite nature. In effect, in the 2004 referendum, 3,989,008 people voted to recall the

308   See Allan R. Brewer-Carías, "El secuestro del poder electoral y la confiscación del derecho a la participación política mediante el referendo revocatorio presidencial: Venezuela 2000-2004," *Revista Jurídica del Perú* 54, Lima 2004, pp. 353-96; "El secuestro del poder electoral y de la Sala Electoral del Tribunal Supremo y la confiscación del derecho a la participación política mediante el referendo revocatorio presidencial: Venezuela: 2000-2004," *Revista Costarricense de Derecho Constitucional* 5, Instituto Costarricense de Derecho Constitucional, Editorial Investigaciones Jurídicas, San José 2004, pp. 167-312; "El secuestro del poder electoral y la confiscación del derecho a la participación política mediante el referendo revocatorio presidencial: Venezuela 2000-2004," *Stvdi Vrbinati, Rivista tgrimestrale di Scienze Giuridiche, Politiche ed Economiche* 71, n.s., Università degli studi di Urbino, Urbino 2004, 379-436; "El secuestro del poder electoral y la confiscación del derecho a la participación política mediante el referendo revocatorio presidencial: Venezuela 2000-2004," *Boletín Mexicano de Derecho Comparado* 112, Instituto de Investigaciones Jurídicas, Universidad Nacional Autónoma de México, Mexico City 2005, pp. 11-73.

president's mandate, a number of votes greater than the ones that elected him in 2000. Nonetheless, the votes not to revoke were 5,800,629 votes – and so, according to express provision of the Constitution, the president's mandate was revoked and there should have been a new election. However, the National Electoral Council, following a phrase in a Constitutional Chamber of the Supreme Tribunal decision,[309] converted the recall referendum into a "ratification referendum,"[310] which does not exist in the Constitution, because a greater number of voters cast no. A recall referendum asks the people if the mandate of an elected official should be revoked; it does not ask whether the elected official must remain in office. In the 2004 recall referendum, the National Electoral Council, when giving the voting results, converted it into a plebiscite ratifying the president.[311]

In any event, participation cannot be achieved only by inserting instruments of direct democracy in a representative democratic framework, as has occurred in modern constitutionalism. Referenda can be useful instruments to perfect democracy but, by themselves, they cannot satisfy the aim of participation. The result of the implementation of the 1999 Constitution is that the Venezuelan democracy has transformed into a centralized plebiscite democracy, in which effectively all power is in one hand, that of the president, who is supported by the military and a one-party system. The plebiscite democracy has created the illusion of popular participation, particularly by means of the uncontrolled distribution of state oil income among the poor through governmental social programs that are not precisely tailored to promote investment or generate employment.

The plebiscite democracy, without doubt, is less representative and less participatory than traditional representative democracy, which, notwithstanding all the warnings that were raised,[312] traditional parties have failed to preserve. All this is unfortunately contributing to the disappearance in Venezuela of democracy as a political system (which is much more than elections and referenda, as made clear by the 2001 Inter-American Democratic Charter), a development that the November 2, 2007,

---

309   In Decision N° 2750 (Oct. 21, 2003) (Case: *Carlos E. Herrera Mendoza, Interpretación del artículo 72 de la Constitución*), the Chamber said: "It is a sort of relegitimizing [process] of the public official…so if in the referendum, more votes for the public official to remain in office are obtained, he must continue in it, even if enough number of persons votes for the revocation of his mandate." See in *Revista de Derecho Público*, N° 93-96, Editorial Jurídica Venezolana, Caracas 2003.

310   See Allan R. Brewer-Carías, "La Sala Constitucional vs. el derecho ciudadano a la revocatoria de mandatos populares: De cómo un referendo revocatorio fue inconstitucionalmente convertido en un 'referendo ratificatorio'," in *Crónica sobre la "in"justicia constitucional. La Sala Constitucional y el autoritarismo en Venezuela*, Colección Instituto de Derecho Público N° 2, Universidad Central de Venezuela, Caracas 2007, pp. 349-378.

311   That is why the 2004 recall referendum has been considered a "stunning victory" for Chávez that gave him an "overwhelming majority." See Richard Gott, *Hugo Chávez and the Bolivarian Revolution*, Verso, London 2005, 263. This is incorrect. The referendum was not a plebiscite, which does not exist in the Venezuelan Constitution. It was a referendum to revoke the mandate of the president. According to the Constitution, his mandate was revoked because more votes were cast to revoke than the president received in elections.

312   See Allan R. Brewer-Carías, *El estado. Crisis y reforma*, Academia de Ciencias Políticas y Sociales, Caracas 1982; and *Problemas del estado de partidos*, Editorial Jurídica Venezolana, Caracas 1988.

constitutional reforms sanctioned by the National Assembly intended to formalize, being rejected by popular vote in the December 2, 2007, referendum.

With respect to popular consultation, in addition to representatives of different sectors of society on nominating committees for appointment of high-ranking officials of the citizen, judicial, and electoral branches of government, Article 211 of the Constitution imposes on the National Assembly the obligation to always submit draft legislation to public consultation, asking the opinion of citizens and the organized society. Also, according to Article 206, the National Assembly before sanctioning statutes must consult states, through their legislative councils, when such statutes refer to matters concerning the states. Unfortunately, in practice, such consultations have not been made. Nonetheless, the wording of the general approach to participation has resulted in the fact that in all statutes that have been sanctioned under the 1999 Constitution, a chapter has always been included regarding popular participation in the matters regulated.

The Constitution also guarantees popular participation, not only for the introduction of draft legislation before the National Assembly by means of petitions signed by no less than 0.1% of registered voters (Article 204.7) but also for the purpose of convening consultative, approbatory, and abrogation referenda. In the case of the revocation or recall referendum, it is an exclusive right of the people, through popular initiative.

The Constitution conceives of municipalities as the primary political unit in the national organization (Article 168); thus, they were conceived to be the main institutional channel for political participation in matters belonging to local life, as ratified by Article 1 of the Organic Law on the Municipal Public Power.[313] That law sets forth that municipalities and other local entities, particularly the *parroquias* (parishes) to be established below municipalities, are the primary areas for citizens' participation in the planning, design, execution, control, and evaluation of public policies. For such purposes, municipal entities must create the needed mechanisms to guarantee participation of communities and social groups (Article 7), and they are obliged to promote them (Article 56). The law enumerates all the aspects of citizens' participatory rights (Articles 255 and 260), and for such purposes, it establishes that parishes *(parroquias)* must be the information, production, and promotion centers for participatory processes, for identifying budgetary priorities, and for promoting citizens' participation in public affairs (Article 37).

Article 70 of the Constitution specifically refers to town hall meetings, which are also regulated in the organic law, which can be convened by municipal councils, parish councils, and popular initiative according to what is established in municipal ordinances (Article 263). The decisions adopted in such meetings are valid if approved by the majority of persons present, provided that the decisions refer to matters concerning municipal life (Article 264).

The other direct democracy means established in the Constitution are the citizens' assemblies (Article 70), conceived in the municipal organic law as local enti-

---

313 *Gaceta Oficial* N° 38.421, Apr. 21, 2006. See Allan R. Brewer-Carías et al., *Ley Orgánica del Poder Público Municipal*, Editorial Jurídica Venezolana, Caracas 2006.

ties for participation, of deliberative character, established to enforce governance, drive planning, and decentralize services and resources, in which all citizens have the right to participate (Article 266). Their decisions have obligatory character (Article 70 of the Constitution), provided, as indicated in the municipal organic law, that they are not contrary to legislation or to the community and state interest. The law leaves regulation concerning citizens' assemblies to a special statute.

All these provisions regarding local governments (municipalities and parishes) have been set aside and have been progressively substituted by means of the organization of a so–called popular power not established in the Constitution and integrated by nonelected representative entities. Within these entities, the 2006 Communal Councils Law[314] has specifically regulated the citizens'assemblies an the communal councils that have been created at the communal level (subparish and submunicipal level) but without any relation whatsoever to the municipalities or parishes, except when the former transferred activities or services to them.

These communal councils are organized as nonrepresentative organs of the state, so their members are not elected by the people of the communities but rather appointed by the citizens' assemblies, which unfortunately are directly controlled by the official political party. In addition, these entities, from an institutional and financial point of view, depend directly on the president of the republic, initially through the Presidential Commission of the Popular Power and, since 2009, through a cabinet minister, minister of the popular power and for popular participation.[315]

5. *Plural Political Parties and the Move toward a Single-Party System*

A democratic regime cannot exist without political parties and pluralism. As has been mentioned, that is why, after a short experiment with a dominant-party system from 1945 to 1948, the democratic parties that in 1958 signed the *Pacto de Punto Fijo* after the democratic revolution initiated that same year against the military dictatorship, committed to establishing a competitive, plural multiparty democratic system. That system functioned until 1999.

That democratic period during the second half of the twentieth century was characterized, from the beginning, by the fact of the predominance of the political parties that dominated all aspects of political life, particularly participation and representation (party state).[316] It was their crisis and the crisis of their leadership – because of the lack of reforms and updating the democratic system – that eventually pro-

---

314 *Ley de los Consejos Comunales, Gaceta Oficial*, Extra N° 5.806, Apr. 10, 2006. This law was substituted in 2009 with the *Ley Orgánica de los Consejos Comunales, Gaceta Oficial* N° 39.335, Dec. 28, 2009. In June 2010, the National Assembly began the discussion of the Organic Law on the Communes (*Ley Orgánica de Comunas*).

315 See Allan R. Brewer-Carías, "El inicio de la desmunicipalización en Venezuela: La organización del poder popular para eliminar la descentralización, la democracia representativa y la participación a nivel local," in *AIDA, Opera Prima de Derecho Administrativo. Revista de la Asociación Internacional de Derecho Administrativo*, Universidad Nacional Autónoma de México, Mexico City 2007, pp. 49-67.

316 See Allan R. Brewer-Carías, *Problemas del estado de partidos*, Editorial Jurídica Venezolana, Caracas 1989. See the critics on this characterization of the political system up to 1999 as a party state, in Juan Carlos Rey, "El sistema de partidos falló," in *Revista Sic*, N° 772, Centro Gumilla, Caracas 2010, pp. 67-72.

voked the collapse of the democratic system after 1998. After forty years of controlling political power and having democratized the country, the parties underestimated the country's need for more means of representation and political participation,
failing to open the democratic system through, for instance, political decentralization
that would allow effective participation. In any case, at the end of the twentieth century, all the political ills of Venezuela were attributed, particularly by the new authoritarian military and populist leadership that took control of the state, to the political parties, to the 1958 *Pacto de Punto Fijo*, and, to the Constitution of 1961.

The fact is that the presidential election of that year (1998) and the election of
the Constituent Assembly in the following year (1999) were characterized by an
antiparty trend, which was reflected in the drafting of the 1999 Constitution, which
was conceived of as an antiparty instrument. Even the phrase "political party" was
eliminated from its text and substituted with the more general expression "organizations with political purposes" (Article 67).[317] Of course, what the drafters of the new
Constitution in 1999 tended to ignore, was the traditional political parties, which
until then, had been in power. For such purpose, the 1999 Constitution forbids public (state) financing of political organizations (a provision that the Supreme Tribunal of Justice has distorted through its interpretation),[318] as well as the existence of
party parliamentarian groups. It requires voting by the members of the National Assembly according to their own conscience, forbidding any kind of voting instructions; a provision that is not in force, particularly due to the strict control exercised
by the official party regarding its members in the National Assembly. Moreover, the
Constitution, in principle, limits the possibility of parties reaching agreement on the
appointment of nonelected public officials by requiring nominating committees to be
formed only on the basis of representation of various sectors of civil society; a provision that as has been distorted aforementioned.

As aforementioned, not one of those prescriptions is really in force: The president is the acting head of his own official party, which completely controls the National Assembly. He is, in fact, director of his party parliamentary group, in which
he has imposed rigid party discipline. Through such mechanisms, he has intervened
in the designation of magistrates of the Supreme Tribunal and members of the National Electoral Council, as well as the other nonelected officials, thus disregarding
the constitutional nominating committees. Those committees have effectively been
converted into extended parliamentary commissions firmly controlled by the government party.[319]

---

317   See Roberto V. Pastor and Rubén Martínez Dalmau, "La configuración de los partidos políticos en la
      Constitución venezolana," *Revista de Derecho Constitucional* 4, Editorial Sherwood, Caracas 2001,
      375-89; Allan R. Brewer-Carías, "Regulación jurídica de los partidos políticos en Venezuela," in *Regu-
      lación jurídica de los partidos políticos en América Latina*, coord. Daniel Zovatto, Universidad Nacio-
      nal Autónoma de México, International IDEA, Mexico City 2006, pp. 893-937.

318   See the Constitutional Chamber Decision N° 780 (May 8, 2008), in *Revista de Derecho Público* 114,
      Caracas 2008, pp. 127ff. See Allan R. Brewer-Carías, "El juez constitucional como constituyente: El ca-
      so del financiamiento de las campañas electorales de los partidos políticos en Venezuela," *Revista de
      Derecho Público* 117, Caracas 2009, pp. 195-203.

319   See Allan R. Brewer-Carías, "La progresiva y sistemática demolición institucional de la autonomía e
      independencia del poder judicial en Venezuela 1999-2004," in *XXX Jornadas J.M Domínguez Escovar,*

The constitution-making process of 1999 and the sanctioning of the new Constitution unfolded in this context and gave way to new political parties that were established mainly for electoral purposes and by the government. Those parties crushed and then marginalized the old political parties, which abstained from participating in the 1999 constitution-making process. During subsequent years, the new political parties continued to support the new government and its president, and they eventually became more centralized than the traditional parties, with internal governing structures linked to the president. The final result of this process was the presidential initiative, in 2006, to promote the single United Socialist Party, using state structures and services, over which President Hugo Chávez presides, which intends to unite all the various political parties that have supported his tenure. Nonetheless, complete unification has failed because, for instance, the Communist Party has refused to disappear, and other parties have left the official coalition.

The official United Socialist Party was in charge of supporting the presidential draft constitutional reforms submitted to referendum in 2007, which popular vote rejected, and was also the supporting instrument of government candidates in the regional and municipal elections of November 2008. The government's candidates lost elections in the most important and populated states and municipalities of the country, where opposition candidates to governors and mayors were elected. Nonetheless, their powers have been progressively eroded by the action of the national government privileging the communal councils organization.

The result of the first decade of political life under the 1999 Constitution, which seems to ignore political parties, has been an increase in partisanship and party autocracy, particularly regarding the official party that has been embodied in the state structures.

With respect to the constitutional provisions related to political organizations, the traditional lack of internal democracy in the parties, which traditionally elect leaders in perpetuity, led to a provision according to which not only members of governing boards must be elected by members of each party but also the choice of party candidates for elections to representative offices must be made through internal democratic elections (Article 67). To that end, the Constitution obligated the National Electoral Council to organize those internal elections (Article 293.6), which in practice, because of the lack of statutory development of the constitutional provisions, did not occur during the first decade of the Constitution's existence.

In addition, also as a reaction to the problems stemming from public funding of political parties, regulated under the 1998 Organic Law of Suffrage and Political Participation,[320] which led to a monopoly over those funds by the traditionally dominant parties, as aforementioned, the drafters of the 1999 Constitution simply

---

Estado de derecho, Administración de justicia y derechos humanos, Instituto de Estudios Jurídicos del Estado Lara, Barquisimeto 2005, pp. 33-174; La Sala Constitucional versus el estado democrático de derecho. El secuestro del poder electoral y de la Sala Electoral del Tribunal Supremo y la confiscación del derecho a la participación política, Los Libros de El Nacional, Colección Ares, Caracas 2004; and La crisis de la democracia en Venezuela (La Carta Democrática Interamericana y los sucesos de abril de 2002), Ediciones Libros El Nacional, Caracas 2002.

320   Gaceta Oficial Extra. N° 5.233, May 28, 1998.

prohibited public funding of organizations with political purposes and established new controls for their private financing (Article 67). This was a regression in addressing what is a constant problem in the democratic world: the possibility of public funding of political parties to avoid irregular and illegitimate funding, particularly of governing parties.[321] Nonetheless, in a 2008 decision of the Constitutional Chamber of the Supreme Tribunal interpreting such Article 67 of the Constitution, the Chamber mutated the Constitution, ruling that the article intended to prohibit public financing of only "internal activities" of parties, not of their electoral activities.[322]

Article 67 of the Constitution refers to a statute with the task of regulating the scope of private contributions to and finances of "organizations with political purposes," including mechanisms to oversee the origins and management of funds. The statute must regulate political and election campaigns, oversee their duration and spending limits, and encourage democratization. Until 2009, these matters were regulated by the 1998 Organic Law of Suffrage and Political Participation, but they are now subject to the Organic Law on Electoral Processes of 2009.[323]

In the same trend against political parties, the Constitution established the principle that members of the National Assembly are representatives of the whole of the people and "are not to be subject to mandates or instructions other than their own conscience" (Article 200), seeking to eliminate parliamentary party groups. Nonetheless, in practice, the parliamentary factions have changed only their names; since 2000, they have been called "opinion groups." In any case, and particularly regarding the governing party, its board presided over by the president itself, has had more centralized control over representatives to the National Assembly than did parties before 1999.

The result of all these provisions, constitutional distortions, and absence of legislation has been that, in practice, under the new Constitution, parties have greater presence than they ever had, to the point that since 1999, the president of the republic is also president of the governing party, and almost all ministers are also members of the party's National Coordination Board. As never before, the symbiosis between the governing political party and the state and its public administration has been completely established in Venezuela, opening lines of communication and financial channels as could not have been envisioned during the golden age of party autocracy in the 1980s. The same party state has continued, with the same vices of clientelism, and the same control by officials who have not been chosen in free and democratic internal elections on governing boards at the helm of parties.

---

321   See Allan R. Brewer-Carías, "Consideraciones sobre el financiamiento de los partidos políticos en Venezuela," in *Financiamiento y democratización interna de partidos políticos. Memora del IV Curso Anual Interamericano de Elecciones,* San José, Costa Rica, 1991, pp. 121-39.

322   Decision N° 780, Constitutional Chamber of the Supreme Tribunal of Justice (May 8, 2008) (Interpretaton of Article 67 of the Constitution), in *Revista de Derecho Público* 114, Editorial Jurídica Venezolana, Caracas 2008, pp. 126 ff. See the comments in Allan R. Brewer-Carías, "El juez constitucional como constituyente: el caso del financiamiento de las campañas electorales de los partidos políticos en Venezuela," in *Revista de Derecho Público,* N° 117, Editorial Jurídica Venezolana, Caracas 2009, pp. 195-203.

323   *Gaceta Oficial* Extra. N° 5.928, Aug. 12, 2009.

Finally, the Constitution conferred to one of the national braches of government, the public electoral power through the National Electoral Council, the duty not only to organize all electoral processes but also to "organize elections in the organizations with political purposes" (Article 293.6), thus establishing an intolerable principle of state intervention in the internal functioning of political parties.

6.   Institutions of Government Accountability and Liability

The 1999 Constitution establishes the general principle of state liability, incorporated expressly in Article 140, which sets forth that "the State is liable for the damages suffered by individuals in their goods and rights, provided that the injury be imputable to the "normal or abnormal functioning of Public Administration." Although doubts can result from the wording of the article as to the liability of the state caused by legislative actions that nonetheless derive from general principles of public law, express provisions of Articles 49.8 and 255 of the Constitution clarify liability caused by judicial acts, such as judicial errors or delay.

Article 139 of the Constitution establishes the general principle of liability of public officials in the exercise of public functions, based on the "abuse or deviation of powers or on the violation of the Constitution or of the law." In addition, Article 25, following a long constitutional tradition, expressly establishes the specific civil, criminal, and administrative liability of any public officials when issuing or executing acts violating human rights guarantees in the Constitution and statutes. No excuse can be alleged based on executing orders received from superiors.

From a political point of view, the Constitution provides for the accountability (rendición de cuentas) of elected public officials, specifically establishing the possibility that they are subject to recall referenda (Article 6).

With respect to transparency, Article 143 of the Constitution guarantees citizens' rights to be informed and have access to administrative information. First, it provides for the right of citizens to be promptly and truly informed by public administration regarding the procedures in which they have direct interest and to know about the definitive resolutions therein adopted, to be notified of administrative acts, and to be informed of the course of administrative procedures.

Article 143 also establishes the individual right to access administrative archives and registries, without prejudice of the acceptable limits imposed in a democratic society related to the national or foreign security, to criminal investigation, or to the intimacy of private life, all according to statutes regulating secret or confidential documents. The same article prohibits the possibility to establish any previous censorship on public officials regarding the information they have and could divulge when referred to matters under their responsibility.

Finally, some duties that Constitution imposes on the president must be mentioned, like to formulate before the National Assembly in its ordinary sessions each year during the first ten days of its installment, the State of the Republic address, which gives an account of the political, economic, social, and administrative aspects of the president's actions during the previous year (Article 237). State governors must give an account of their actions not before legislative councils but only before the comptroller general of each state, and they only have to present a report (Article 161). Representatives to the National Assembly have the duty to give an annual account of their actions to their electors because they are subject to recall referenda (Article 197).

V. THE SYSTEM OF GOVERNMENT AND THE SEPARATION OF POWERS

1. *Presidential System and Its Reinforcement*

In the horizontal organization of the sovereign power, in the new Constitution, the presidential system continues, even though with some parliamentary elements, already introduced in the Constitution of 1961.

However, the new Constitution has reinforced presidentialism because it combines the following factors, which reverse the tradition of checks and balances. First, the president continues to be elected by a relative majority, even though an absolute majority had long been recommended (Article 228).[324] Second, the president's term was increased from five years to six years (Article 230).[325] Third, for the first time in a century, the president could be elected for a consecutive additional term (Article 230),[326] a provision that was amended in February 2009 to allow the continuous and unlimited election of all elected officials, thus affecting the principle of alternating government. Fourth, although recall referenda are established, the complexity of their implementation (Article 72) makes them almost inapplicable. Fifth, the National Assembly may delegate lawmaking power to the president, and there is no limit on the powers of such a delegation (Articles 203 and 236.8).[327] Sixth, the president has the power to dissolve the National Assembly after three votes of censure against the vice president (Article 236, Section 21), who nonetheless is conceived of as an executive–branch official (appointed by the president) with no parliamentary role. The parliamentary censure vote has a long tradition in Venezuela for cabinet ministers, but the provision concerning the vice president was an invention of the 1999 Constitution.

With this presidential model, presidentialism has been reinforced, with no balance in a bicameral system due to the elimination of the Senate. Moreover, it was reinforced in other reforms, as the provisions of enabling laws or the legislative delegation to the president by the National Assembly to enact decrees-laws, not limited

324　See my dissenting vote in Allan R. Brewer-Carías, *Debate constituyente (Aportes a la Asamblea Nacional Constituyente)*, Fundación de Derecho Público, Editorial Jurídica Venezolana, Caracas 1999, Vol. 3 (Oct. 18–Nov. 30), pp.288 ff.

325　In the 2007 constitutional reform draft proposals, the term is extended to seven years. See *Proyecto de Reforma Constitucional. Elaborado por el ciudadano Presidente de la República Bolivariana de Venezuela, Hugo Chávez Frías,* Editorial Atenea, Caracas 2007.

326　See my dissenting vote in Allan R. Brewer-Carías, *Debate constituyente (Aportes a la Asamblea Nacional Constituyente),* Fundación de Derecho Público–Editorial Jurídica Venezolana, Caracas 1999, 3 (Oct. 18–Nov. 30), pp. 289ff. The 2007 constitutional reform draft proposals establish the indefinite possible reelection of the president. See *Proyecto de Reforma Constitucional. Elaborado por el ciudadano Presidente de la República Bolivariana de Venezuela, Hugo Chávez Frías*, Editorial Atenea, Caracas 2007.

327　See Allan R. Brewer-Carías, "Régimen constitucional de la delegación legislativa e inconstitucionalidad de los decretos leyes habilitados dictados en 2001," *Revista Primicia* (special issue), Caracas 2001.

only to economic and financial subjects (Article 203), as it was the case in the 1961 Constitution, but on any subject whatsoever.

2. *Unbalanced Powers Due to Concentrated Power in the National Assembly*

The Constitution adopts a separation-of-powers framework not only between the legislative and the executive but also between the judicial power, whose autonomy is repeatedly established, and two new powers of constitutional rank: the citizen power, which comprises the Public Ministry (prosecutor general of the republic), the people's defender, general controller of the republic, and the electoral power, exercised by the National Electoral Council.

The essence of the separation of powers in the Constitution is that each constitutionally established organ of the state exercises its respective function with independence and autonomy, in a system of checks and balances in which no branch of government is or can be subject to that of another, except on matters of judicial review, audit controls, and protection of human rights.[328] Nonetheless, the five-branched division of powers under the 1999 Constitution is deceiving because, in fact, it conceals that some of the principal branches of government are subject to the legislator, in a very dangerous system of democracy and rule of law that leaves an open door to the concentration of power in the state and to authoritarianism.

The Constitution, in fact, absurdly distorts separation of powers by giving to the National Assembly the authority not only to appoint but also to dismiss judges of the Supreme Tribunal of Justice, the prosecutor general, the comptroller general, the people's defender, and members of the National Electoral Council (Articles 265, 279, and 296); and, in some cases, they can do so even by simple majority.[329] The 2007 reform proposals suggested that the latter option be formally constitutionalized, and they sought to eliminate the guarantee of the qualified majority of members of the National Assembly for such dismissals and to establish a simple majority for that purpose.[330]

It is impossible to talk about separate powers or mutual control when the tenure of head officials of institutions depends on the political will of one branch of government.[331] The National Assembly's powers to dismiss alone make futile the formal consecration of the independence of powers – officials are aware that they can

---

328 See Allan R. Brewer-Carías, "La opción entre democracia y autoritarismo," in *Reflexiones sobre el constitucionalismo en América*, Editorial Jurídica Venezolana, Caracas 2001, 41-59; Allan R. Brewer-Carías, *Constitución, democracia y control del poder*, Centro Iberoamericano de Estudios Provinciales y Locales (CIEPROL), Universidad de Los Andes, Editorial Jurídica Venezolana, Mérida 2004.

329 This was also the case for the magistrates of the Supreme Tribunal that, according to Article 23.4 of the Supreme Tribunal Organic Law, provided that the administrative act of their appointment by the National Assembly could be decided by "simple majority," in the sense of more than 50% of those representatives present and voting. In the 2010 reform of this Organic Law, such provision was eliminated.

330 See Allan R. Brewer-Carías, *La reforma constitucional de 2007*, Editorial Jurídica Venezolana, Caracas 2007, pp. 108, 110, 112.

331 See Allan R. Brewer-Carías, "Democracia: sus elementos y componentes esenciales y el control del poder," in *Grandes temas para un observatorio electoral ciudadano, Tomo I, Democracia: retos y fundamentos*, comp. Nuria González Martín, Instituto Electoral del Distrito Federal, Mexico City 2007, pp. 171-220.

be removed at any time and precisely when they act effectively with independence.[332] In Venezuela, in practice, and together with the president, this has concentrated powers in the National Assembly and, because of the president's control over the assembly it has concentrated powers in the president. Consequently, the president has complete control regarding legislation, being the appropriation of the legislative framework a "key tool in the governmental practice to ensure its own perpetuity in power."[333] The other consequence has been the total absence of fiscal or audit control by the Comptroller General Office over the huge state income amount due to oil wealth; the total absence of protection from the people's defender, which is seen more as a defender of state power than of the people; the indiscriminate use by the public prosecutor of the judiciary and judicial procedures to persecute any political dissidence; and the absolute control exercised by the executive over the judiciary. In particular, the judiciary has lost its independence, which is confirmed by the fact that in 2009 at least 50% of judges were provisional or temporary judges and, thus, by definition, political dependents.[334] Unfortunately, the mastermind of this system of concentration of powers in the end has been the Supreme Tribunal itself, and particularly its Constitutional Chamber, which by means of successive constitutional interpretation has cleared all violations of the Constitution committed by other branches of government.[335] The Constitutional Chamber has become a most effective tool for the existing consolidation of power in the person of the president.[336]

All these facts create the antithesis of the independence and balance between powers of the state; it is a model of concentrated power in the National Assembly, which is totally incompatible with a democratic society. The model has allowed for the development of a centralized and plebiscitary system of government that is crushing democracy. This inconsistency within the Constitution is a direct consequence of successful efforts by the president and his followers to use the constitution-making process to consolidate their power while maintaining the appearance of adherence to democratic norms.

---

332 See Allan R. Brewer-Carías, *Constitución, democracia y control del poder,* CIEPROL, Universidad de Los Andes, Editorial Jurídica Venezolana, Mérida 2004.

333 See the *Report of the Socialist International Mission to Venezuela, 20-23 January 2010,* 3. Available at www.socialistinternational.org

334 The Inter-American Commission on Human Rights in its *2009 Annual Report* expressed that still in 2009, "more than 50% of judges in Venezuela do not enjoy tenure in their positions and can be easily removed when they make decisions that could affect government interests." IACHR Annual Report, 2009, para. 482. Available at http://www.cidh.org/annualrep/2009eng/Chap.IV.f.eng.htm.

335 See Allan R. Brewer-Carías, *Crónica sobre la "in"justicia constitucioal. La Sala Constitucional y el autoritarismo,* Editorial Jurídica Venezolana, Caracas 2007; in particular, *"Quis custodiet ipsos custodes: de la interpretación constitucional a la inconstitucionalidad de la interpretación,"* paper submitted to the *VIII Congreso Peruano de Derecho Constitucional.* Colegio de Abogados de Arequipa, Sept. 22–24, 2005, pp. 47 ff.

336 In 2001, when he approved more than forty-eight decree laws, via delegate legislation, the president said: "The law is me. The state is me" (*La ley soy yo. El estado soy yo.*). See Raquel Barreiro, "Chávez delega en la Asamblea Nacional cambios legales," in *El Universal,* Caracas Dec. 4, 2001, 1,1 and 2,1. Available at http://www.eluniversal.com/2001/12/04/eco_art_04201DD.shtml.

3. *The State of Justice and Its Incongruence*

The preamble of the Constitution refers to justice as a global and "fundamental value" that must contribute to "the construction of a just and peace–loving society resulting from the democratic exercise of popular will" (Article 3). For such purpose, the Constitutional Chamber has considered that the power to administer justice that must be exercised in the name of the Republic comes from the citizens (Article 253) and "must be executed with independence and impartiality" by judges "free from subordinations and inadequate pressures" (Articles 254 and 256). This has been considered "a new paradigm about values and constitutional principles connected to the justice," which has led to the state of justice, which considers the judiciary not just one more branch of government but rather "the integrating and stabilizing State power with authority to control and even dissolve the rest of the branches of government" (judicial state).[337]

This concept of the state of justice (*estado de justicia*) results not only from the provisions of the preamble and Article 1 that declare justice a constitutional value but also from constitutional provisions establishing "the prevalence of the notion of material justice over formalities and technicalities"[338] and providing for the "effective judicial protection" of human rights by means of a system of justice that must be "free, available, impartial, transparent, autonomous, independent, responsible, fair and expeditious, without improper delays, formalisms or useless repositions" (Article 26).[339] To that effect, procedural laws must establish the "simplification, uniformity and efficiency of the proceedings and adopt a brief, oral and public procedure, without sacrificing justice because omission of nonessential formalities" (Article 257).

Article 253 provides that the system of justice comprise not only the organs of the judicial branch (the Supreme Tribunal of Justice and all other courts established by law) but also the Public Ministry (public prosecutor), the people's defender, criminal investigatory organs, judicial staff and assistants, the penitentiary system, alternative means of adjudication, citizens who participate in the administration of justice, and attorneys authorized to practice law. Article 258 imposes on the legislator the duty to promote arbitration, conciliation, mediation, and other means of conflict resolution.

Article 254 of the Constitution declares the independence of the judicial branch and establishes that the Supreme Tribunal has "functional, financial, and administrative autonomy." To guarantee the independence and autonomy of courts and judges, Article 255 provides for a specific mechanism to ensure the independent appoint-

---

337   See Decision N° 659 of the Political-Administrative Chamber (Mar. 24, 2000) (Case: *Rosario Nouel vs. Consejo de la Judicatura y Comisión de Emergencia Judicial*), in *Revista de Derecho Público* 81, Editorial Jurídica Venezolana, Caracas 2000, pp. 103-104.

338   See Supreme Tribunal of Justice, in Decision N° 949 of the Political-Administrative Chamber (Apr. 26, 2000), in *Revista de Derecho Público* 82, Editorial Jurídica Venezolana, Caracas 2000, pp. 163ff.

339   The concept of the state of justice also has been analyzed by the Constitutional Chamber of the Supreme Tribunal of Justice, particularly in Decision N° 389 (Mar. 7, 2002), in which the principle of the informality of the process was repeated, also asserting *pro actione* as another principle of the state of justice. See *Revista de Derecho Público* No. 89–92, Editorial Jurídica Venezolana, Caracas 2002, pp. 175ff.

ment of judges and to guarantee their stability. In that regard, the judicial office is considered a career, in which the admission and promotion of judges within it must be the result of a public competition or examinations, to ensure that candidates are adequately qualified. The candidates are to be chosen by panels from the judicial circuits, and judges are to be designated by the Supreme Tribunal of Justice. The Constitution also creates the Judicial Nominations Committee (Article 270) to assist the judicial branch in selecting the magistrates for the Supreme Tribunal of Justice (Article 264) and to assist judicial colleges in selecting judges for the lower courts. The committee is to be composed of representatives from different sectors of society, as determined by law. The Constitution also guarantees the stability of all judges, prescribing that they can be removed or suspended from office only through judicial disciplinary procedures on trials led by judicial disciplinary judges (Article 255).

Unfortunately, those provisions have not been implemented and, in practice, the executive has completely controlled the judicial power. Contrary to the constitutional provisions regarding the appointment and stability of judges since 1999, the Venezuelan judiciary has been almost exclusively made up of temporary and provisional judges,[340] and no public competition processes for the appointment of judges with citizen participation has taken place. Consequently, in general, judges lack stability, and because the constitutional provisions creating the judicial disciplinary jurisdiction have not been implemented by legislation, matters of judicial discipline have been and are currently in the hands of the Functioning and Restructuring Commission of the judiciary[341] (not established in the Constitution but created by the National Constituent Assembly in 1999), which has the power to remove temporary judges without due–process guarantees.[342] The Judicial Commission of the Supreme Tribunal also has discretionary powers to remove all temporary judges.[343]

With respect to dismissal of judges of the Supreme Tribunal, although Article 265 provides that dismissal is possible only by the vote of a qualified majority of two-thirds of the National Assembly, following a hearing, in cases of "grave faults"

---

340   See *Informe sobre la situación de los derechos humanos en Venezuela*; OAS/Ser.L/V/II.118. d.C. 4 rev. 2, Dec. 29, 2003, para. 11, 161.

341   The Inter-American Commission on Human Rights, in its *2009 Annual Report,* has ratified that "Under that transitional regime, the Commission for the Functioning and Restructuring of the Judicial System was created, and this body has ever since had the disciplinary authority to remove members of the judiciary. This Commission, in addition to being a special, temporary entity, does not afford due guarantees for ensuring the independence of its decisions, since its members may also be appointed or removed at the sole discretion of the Constitutional Chamber of the Supreme Court of Justice, without previously establishing either the grounds or the procedure for such formalities." See IACHR, *Annual Report 2009*, Par. 481. Available at http://www.cidh.org/annualrep/2009eng/Chap.IV.f.eng.htm.

342   The Politico-Administrative Chamber of the Supreme Tribunal has ruled that the dismissal of temporary judges is a discretional power of the Functioning and Restructuring Commission of the Judiciary. This commission, created after 1999, adopts its decisions without administrative procedure. See Decision N° 00463-2007. The same doctrine has been established by the Constitutional Chamber in Decision N° 2414 (Dec. 20, 2007), Decision N° 280 (Feb. 23, 2007), and Decision N° 00673-2008. See Allan R. Brewer-Carías, "La justicia sometida al poder y la interminable emergencia del poder judicial (1999-2006)," in *Derecho y democracia. Cuadernos Universitarios* 2, Órgano de Divulgación Académica, Vicerrectorado Académico, Universidad Metropolitana, Caracas 2007, pp. 122-138.

343   See Decision N° 1.939 of the Constitutional Chamber of the Supreme Tribunal of Dec. 18, 2008 (Case: *Gustavo Álvarez Arias y otros*).

committed by the accused, based in a prior qualification by the citizens' power, the 2004 Organic Law of the Supreme Tribunal of Justice circumvented this requirement by authorizing the dismissal of magistrates by a simple majority vote, thus revoking the "administrative act of their appointment" (Article 23.4),[344] a power that the National Assembly has used to dismiss judges who have ruled on sensitive issues against the government's wishes. Nonetheless, this provision was abrogated in the 2010 reform of the Supreme Tribunal Organic Law.

The fact is that the constitutional principles that ensure the autonomy and independence of judges at all levels of the judiciary are yet to be applied, particularly the admission of candidates to a judicial career through public competition with citizens participation, and the prohibition on removing or suspending judges except through disciplinary trials before disciplinary courts and judges (Articles 254 and 267).

Since 1999, the Venezuelan judiciary has been dominated by politics, as commanded by the executive.[345] For example, in 2003, a contentious administrative court ruled[346] against the government in a politically charged case.[347] In response, the government intervened in (took over) the court and dismissed its judges.[348] After the Inter-American Court of Human Rights ruled in 2008 that the dismissal had violated the American Convention on Human Rights and Venezuela's international obligations,[349] the Constitutional Chamber upheld the government's argument that the decision of the Inter-American Court could not be enforced in Venezuela.[350] This is one of the leading cases that clearly show the subordination of the Venezuelan judiciary to the policies, wishes, and dictates of the president. In December 2009, another astonishing case was the detention of a criminal judge (María Lourdes Afiuni Mora) for having ordered the release from detention of a banker in order for him to face criminal trial while in freedom. The decision was based on a previous recommendation of the UN Working Group on Arbitrary Detention. The same day of

---

344   See comments on this reform in Allan R. Brewer-Carías, *Ley Orgánica del Tribunal Supremo de Justicia*, 3rd ed., Editorial Jurídica Venezolana, Caracas 2006, pp. 41ff.

345   See Inter-American Commission on Human Rights, *Informe sobre la situación de los derechos humanos en Venezuela*, OEA/Ser.L/V/II.118, d.C. 4 rev. 2, Dec. 29, 2003, para. 11, 3.

346   See First Contentious Administrative Court Decision of Aug. 21 2003, in *Revista de Derecho Público* 93–96, Editorial Jurídica Venezolana, Caracas 2003, pp. 445ff.

347   See Claudia Nikken, "El caso 'Barrio Adentro': La Corte Primera de lo Contencioso Administrativo ante la Sala Constitucional del Tribunal Supremo de Justicia o el avocamiento como medio de amparo de derechos e intereses colectivos y difusos," in *Revista de Derecho Público* 93–96, Editorial Jurídica Venezolana, Caracas 2003, pp. 5ff.

348   See Allan R. Brewer-Carías, "La progresiva y sistemática demolición institucional de la autonomía e independencia del Poder Judicial en Venezuela 1999–2004" in *XXX Jornadas J.M. Domínguez Escovar, Estado de derecho, Administración de justicia y derechos humanos,* Instituto de Estudios Jurídicos del Estado Lara, Barquisimeto 2005, pp. 33-174; "La justicia sometida al poder (La ausencia de independencia y autonomía de los jueces en Venezuela por la interminable emergencia del poder judicial (1999-2006)," in *Cuestiones internacionales. Anuario Jurídico Villanueva 2007,* Centro Universitario Villanueva, Marcial Pons, Madrid 2007, pp. 25-57.

349   See Decision of Aug. 5, 2008 (Case: *Apitz Barbera y otros ("Corte Primera de lo Contencioso Administrativo") vs. Venezuela*) at http://www.corteidh.or.cr. Excepción Preliminar, Fondo, Reparaciones y Costas, Serie C, N° 182.

350   See the Constitutional Chamber Decision N° 1939 (Dec. 12, 2008).

the decision, the president publicly asked for the judge to be incarcerated, asking to apply to the judge a 30–year prison term, which is the maximum punishment for horrendous or grave crimes. The judge has remained in detention without trial.[351]

4. The Constitutional Base for Militarism

The 1999 Constitution substantially departed from the provisions of the 1961 Constitution regarding the national security and defense system and the military. The 1961 Constitution contained three provisions on the subject: Article 131, prohibiting the simultaneous exercise of civilian and military authority by any public official other than the president as commander–in–chief of the armed forces; Article 132, referring to the general regulation of the armed forces subjected to civil government; and Article 133, establishing restrictions regarding the possession of arms.

The 1999 Constitution, on the contrary, gave a marked militarist shape to the state, with board provisions regarding not only the military but also the security and defense system – without precedent in Venezuelan constitutionalism.

Article 322 of the 1999 Constitution states that the security of the nation falls within the essential competence and responsibility of the state, founded on the state's "integral development." The defense of the state is the responsibility of Venezuelans and of all natural and legal persons, whether of public or private law, found within the geographic territory of the state.

In addition, Article 326 sets forth the general principles of national security, declaring that its preservation in "economic, social, political, cultural, geographic, environmental and military areas" mutually corresponds ("co-responsibility") to the state and to civil society, to fulfill the principles of "independence, democracy, equality, peace, liberty, justice, solidarity, promotion and conservation of the environment, the affirmation of human rights, and the progressive satisfaction of the individual and collective needs of Venezuelans on the basis of sustainable and productive development fully covering the national community." All those principles are also enumerated in Articles 1, 2, and 3 of the 1999 Constitution. To implement the principles of national security in the country's territorial border regions, Article 327 provides for the establishment of a special regime.

Also, the Constitution created a new council, the National Council of Defense (Article 323), the nation's highest authority for defense planning, advice, and consultation to the state (public powers) on all matters related to the defense and security of the nation's sovereignty, territorial integrity, and strategy. The president presides over the council, which also includes the executive vice president, the president of the National Assembly, the president of the Supreme Tribunal of Justice, the president of the Moral Republican Council (citizens' branch of government; Article

---

351 On Dec. 16, a panel of three independent UN human rights experts described the case as "a blow by President Hugo Chávez to the independence of judges and lawyers in the country," demanding the immediate freedom of the judge. Available at http://www.unog.ch/unog/website/news_media.nsf/%28httpNewsByYear_en%29/93687E8429BD53A1C125768E00529DB6?OpenDocument&cntxt=B35C3&cookielang=fr. In July 2010, the judge was still in detention without trial.

237), ministers of the defense sectors (interior security, foreign relations, and planning), and others whose participation is considered pertinent.

The Constitution integrated the traditional national armed forces (the army, the navy, the air force, and the national guard) into a single institution, the National Armed Force, called since the 2008 reform of the Organic Law on the Armed Force, the "Bolivarian Armed Force." Article 328 establishes that each unit works within its area of competence to fulfill its mission and with its own system of social security, as established by its respective organic legislation. The said 2008 reform of the Organic Law also created a new component of the Bolivarian Armed Force, the "Bolivarian Militia," which has been organized as a sort of personal guard of the president.

It must be mentioned that it was in the 2007 constitutional–reform project that the president proposed to change the name of the armed forces to the Bolivarian Armed Force, to create a Bolivarian military doctrine, to establish the Bolivarian Popular Militia as a new component of the armed forces, and to eliminate the character of the armed forces as an "essential professional institution, without political militancy," converting it into "an essentially patriotic, popular and anti-imperialist corp[s]." Despite the fact that those constitutional–reform proposals were rejected by popular referendum, the president approved all the proposed reforms, six months after the popular rejection, in the July 2008 Organic Law of the Bolivarian Armed Force issued through delegate legislation.[352]

According to Article 329 of the Constitution, the army, navy, air force, and national guard each has essential responsibilities for planning, executing, and controlling military operations necessary to ensure the defense of the nation. The national guard, however, has only a cooperative role in those functions and a basic responsibility to carry out operations necessary to maintain internal order in the country. The Constitution also establishes that the armed forces can carry out police administrative activities and criminal investigations as authorized by law.

As aforementioned, Article 328 of the Constitution defines the character of the armed forces as an essentially professional institution, without a militant political function, organized by the state to guarantee the independence and sovereignty of the nation and to ensure the integrity of the nation's geographic space by means of military defense and cooperation in the maintenance of internal order, as well as active participation in national development. According to the wording of Article 328, to fulfill those functions, the armed forces are at the exclusive service of the nation and in no case may be at the service of any particular person or political partiality. The foundations of the armed forces are discipline, obedience, and subordination.

The 1999 Constitution failed to provide for the "apolitical and non-deliberative" character of the armed forces established in Article 132 of the Constitution of 1961; it has no provision establishing the essential obligation of the armed forces to ensure "the stability of the democratic institutions" or "respect the Constitution and laws, the adherence which is above any other obligation," as was declared in Article 132

---

352   See Organic Law on the Bolivarian Armed Force, *Gaceta Oficial* N° 5.933, Extra. Oct. 21, 2009.

of the 1961 Constitution. Where the 1999 Constitution was innovative on these matters was in giving the military the right to vote (Article 325).

In addition, the Constitution established the general regime applicable to military promotions, providing that they are to be based on merit, seniority, and availability of vacancies and are the exclusive competence of the National Armed Force (Article 331). Consequently, the traditional intervention of the legislative branch in approving promotions of high-ranking military officials (Article 150.5, 1961 Constitution) was eliminated.

These constitutional provisions conform to a normative framework with clear marks of a militarist structure, thus "expanding the military's role in Venezuelan politics."[353] When combined with the tendency to centralize state power and concentrate power in the president, the result is a system that unfortunately has led to authoritarianism. In particular, in the 1999 Constitution's provisions on military matters, the idea of the subjection or subordination of military authority to civilian authority has disappeared; instead, what has been consecrated is a greater autonomy of the National Armed Force, whose four branches (and, since 2008, five branches) have been unified into one institution with the possibility of intervention in civilian functions. All these provisions paint a picture of militarism, unique in Venezuelan constitutional history, not even found in former military regimes, which has led to a global takeover of the civil administration of the state by the military, conducted by the president, himself as a retired officer. This has lead to the creation of the already mentioned Bolivarian militia (reserve force)[354] directly controlled by the president, tending toward the effective consolidation of a military party.

CHAPTER 4

THE 1999 SOCIAL AND ECONOMIC CONSTITUTION AND ITS PROBLEMS

The second part of every constitution in modern constitutionalism, as supreme law, is composed by the regulations referred to as constitutional rights and guarantees, including social rights, and to regulate from the economic and social point of view the relation between state and society.

The 1999 Constitution had signs of advances not only in the extensive enumeration of individual, social, economic, cultural, and environmental rights but also in the incorporation of international treaties on human rights, with preferential application when providing for a more favorable regime regarding internal law (Article 23). On economic matters, the Constitution has established a general framework for the development of a system of mixed economy, allowing important participation of the

---

353   See Deborah L. Norden, "Democracy in Uniform: Chávez and the Venezuelan Armed Forces," in *Venezuelan Politics in the Chávez Era: Class, Polarization & Conflicts*, eds. Steve Ellner and Daniel Hellinger, Lynne Rienner Publishers, London 2003, p. 99.

354   The 2007 draft constitutional reforms proposed a new component of the armed forces: the Popular Bolivarian Militia. See *Proyecto de Reforma Constitucional. Elaborado por el ciudadano Presidente de la República Bolivariana de Venezuela, Hugo Chávez Frías*, Editorial Atenea, Caracas 2007, p. 58. Although rejected by the people, the proposal was implemented through the reform of the Organic Law on the Bolivarian Armed Force, *Gaceta Oficial* 5.933, Extra. Oct. 21, 2009.

state, which has been used during the past decade in order to construct a capitalism of state system, through confiscation and expropriation of public property and enterprises. I refer in this chapter to this socioeconomic framework of the 1999 Constitution, as well as to the general values and principles on the matter declared in its text.

I. CONSTITUTIONAL VALUES AND DECLARATIVE PRINCIPLES

The 1999 Constitution formally establishes the general trends of a democratic regime and the rule of law, defining the country as a social democratic state of law and justice (*estado democrático y social de derecho y de justicia*) (Article 2) and declaring that the rule of law (*estado de derecho*) is the state submitted to the "empire of the Law." The Constitution also includes the principle of "supremacy of the Constitution" (Article 7), which submits all state entities to the Constitution and the laws (Article 137). It also establishes a complete judicial review system to ensure constitutionality (Articles 334 and 336) and legality of all state acts and actions (Article 259) (constitutional jurisdiction and administrative contentious jurisdiction).

On matters of principles and values, the 1999 Venezuelan Constitution is one of the recent Constitutions in the contemporary world containing not only an extensive amount of articles devoted to enumerating human rights (120) but also a rich text full of values, principles, and global declarations. It has, perhaps, one of the most florid constitutional wordings that can be found in constitutional texts,[355] establishing its axiological foundations, which in principle are set forth for the National Assembly and all branches of government, and particularly by the courts, to follow. For such purposes, the Constitutional Chamber of the Supreme Tribunal of Justice has said that the Constitution is "an instrument with legal spirit that connects, according to the nature of the applicable precept, both the bodies of the State and the individuals" and that imposes constitutional juridical situations "with reference to indispensable values for the assurance of the human freedom, equality and dignity" guaranteed by the judiciary.[356]

The global values that are declared in the Constitution are those "values generally share[d] by the society" as "declarations of intent" that "have an indubitable value, both for the bodies of the State that must be guided by them, and for the judges."[357] For such purposes, as ruled by the same Constitutional Chamber, "Constitutions are, among other things, texts in which 'legally organized societies regulate their structures and functioning, and determine the scope of the citizen rights and the public authorities' powers"; they also are texts "in which the wishes of this same society are exposed –sometimes difficult to satisfy– and the means that have been

---

355 See Allan R. Brewer-Carías, *La Constitución de 1999. Derecho Constitucional Venezolano*, 2 vols., Editorial Jurídica Venezolana, Caracas 2004; Hildegard Rondón de Sansó, *Análisis de la Constitución Venezolana de 1999*, Editorial Ex Libris, Caracas 2001; Ricardo Combellas, *Derecho constitucional: Una introducción al estudio de la Constitución de la República Bolivariana de Venezuela*, McGraw Hill, Caracas 2001; Alfonso Rivas Quintero, *Derecho constitucional*, Paredes Editores, Valencia 2002.

356 See Decision N° 963 (June 5, 2001). Case: *José A. Guía y otros vs. Ministerio de Infraestructura*, in *Revista de Derecho Público* No. 85–88, Editorial Jurídica Venezolana, Caracas 2001, p. 447.

357 See Constitutional Chamber Decision N° 1278 (June 17, 2005). Case: *Aclaratoria de la sentencia de interpretación de los artículos 156, 180 y 302 de la Constitución*, in *Revista de Derecho Público* 102, Editorial Jurídica Venezolana, Caracas 2005, pp. 56ff.

created to satisfy them...The diverse duties that the State assumes are orders that must be executed. A text lacking of compulsory character for its addressees (public authorities and individuals) would be of little use."[358]

Constitutional values in the Venezuelan Constitution are expressed not only in the preamble but also in many of its articles – where they are enumerated in a formal way – as goals to guide the state, the society, and individuals' general conduct.[359] Consequently, in Venezuela, global values and principles derive not only from the courts' interpretation and application of the Constitution but also from what is set forth expressly in the Constitution itself.[360]

The values expressed in the 1999 Constitution apply to the state (the republic, the nation), its organization (distribution of state powers and branches of government) and its functioning (government and public administration), and to the legal system. In that sense, the preamble of the Constitution begins by declaring that the representatives of the Venezuelan people adopted it aiming to achieve a series of goals "guided by social, economical, political and judicial values"[361] and to inspire the action of the state, "which must respond to equalitarian, international, democratic, moral and historical principles."

The state is defined as a "State of justice, federal and decentralized," that must enforce the values of "freedom, independence, peace, solidarity, common good, territorial integrity, cohabitation and the empire of the law, for these and all future generations," in a society that is "democratic, participatory, multiethnic and multicultural." The latter is confirmed, for instance, by the express recognition in the Constitution of the indigenous populations' status (Articles 119–126).

The goals constitute, without a doubt, the fundamental principles and constitutional values that inspire the constitutional text as a whole. As such, they have the same binding and constitutional rigidity as constitutional provisions and, consequently, are enforceable. As affirmed by the Constitutional Chamber of the Supreme Tribunal, "The statutes must have those values as their purpose, so those that do not follow them or that are contrary to those objectives, become unconstitutional."[362]

Besides the values guiding the configuration of the state declared in the preamble, the Constitution also enumerates the following as superior values of the legal system and of all state activity: "life, freedom, justice, equality, solidarity, democra-

358   See Case: *Aclaratoria de la sentencia de interpretación de los artículos 156, 180 y 302 de la Constitución*, Decision N° 1278 (June 17, 2005), in *Revista de Derecho Público* 102, Editorial Jurídica Venezolana, Caracas 2005, pp. 56ff.

359   See Allan R. Brewer-Carías, "La constitucionalización del derecho administrativo," in *Derecho administrativo*, Universidad Externado de Colombia, Bogotá 2005, Vol. 1, pp. 215ff.

360   See Allan R. Brewer-Carías, *Principios fundamentales del derecho público*, Editorial Jurídica Venezolana, Caracas 2005.

361   On the nature of the preamble and its constitutional value, see the decision of the former Supreme Court of Justice, Political-Administrative Chamber (Aug. 8, 1989), in *Revista de Derecho Público* 39, Editorial Jurídica Venezolana, Caracas 1989, p. 102.

362   See Case: *Deudores hipotecarios vs. Superintendencia de Bancos*, in *Revista de Derecho Público* 89–92, Editorial Jurídica Venezolana, Caracas 2002, pp. 94ff.

cy, social responsibility and, in general, the preeminence of the human rights, the ethics and the political pluralism" (Article 2).

Additionally, the Constitution identifies "the defense and the development of the individual and the respect of his or her dignity, the democratic exercise of the popular will, the construction of a fair and peace–loving society, the promotion of the prosperity and well-being of the people and the guaranty of the fulfillment of all principles, rights and duties recognized and enshrined in the Constitution" as essential goals of the state. It considers "education and work" fundamental processes to reach those ends (Article 3).

However, the "refoundation of the Republic" intended by the constitutional text responded to a series of social ends specified in the preamble, ensuring "the right to a life, work, culture, education, social justice and equality without discrimination nor subordination of any kind." Reference is also made to the social goals of society and of the state to achieve "social justice." Social justice is also mentioned as a fundamental social goal, the assurance of "equality without discrimination or subordination of any kind."

Referring to the republic, the Constitution expressly emphasizes a few fundamental values. In addition to the already-mentioned values of freedom, equality, justice, and international peace, there is the principle that the nation's rights ("independence, freedom, sovereignty, immunity, territorial integrity and the national self-determination"; Article 1) cannot be renounced or abandoned.

Regarding public administration, the Constitution provides that it must be "at the service of the people," enumerating the following principles and values on which it must be based: "honesty, participation, celerity, efficiency, effectiveness, transparency, the accounting and responsibility in the execution of the public function, with complete subjection to the statutes and to the Law" (Article 141).

As for the bodies of the electoral power, the Constitution enumerates the following principles that must be guaranteed in electoral processes: "equality, reliability, impartiality, transparency and efficiency," as well as "personalization of the vote and . . . proportional representation" (Article 293).

With respect to public services corresponding to the state, the Constitution enumerates a series of governing principles. For instance, the national public health system must be "inter-sectorial, decentralized and participative, and managed by the principles of gratuitousness, universality, integrality, impartiality, social integration and solidarity" (Article 84). Moreover, the social security system must be "universal, integral, of solidarity, unitary, [and] efficient and [have] participative financing, from direct or indirect contributions" (Article 86). The Constitution expresses that education must be "democratic, free and mandatory, based on the respect to all thought tendencies, in order to develop the creative potential of every human being and the complete exercise of his/her personality inside a democratic society based on the ethical valuation of the labor and the active, conscientious and solidarity participation in the processes of social transformation related with the values of the national identity and with a Latin American and universal vision" (Article 102).

With respect to socioeconomics, the Constitution enumerates the following principles on which the system must be based: "social justice, democracy, efficiency, free competition, environment protection, productivity and solidarity, in order to guarantee the integral human development, a dignified and prosperous existence for the collectivity, the generation of labor sources, high national added value, elevation of the standard of living of the people and to strengthen the economical supremacy of the country, guaranteeing juridical security, stability, dynamism, supportability, permanence and equity of the economy growth, in order to achieve a fair distribution of the wealth by means of a democratic, participative and of open consultation strategic planning" (Article 299). In particular, the Constitution states the principles that must rule fiscal management: "efficiency, solvency, transparency, responsibility and fiscal balance" (Article 311). Taxation must be ruled by the following principles: "progressiveness, protection of the national economy and the elevation of the standard of living of the population" (Article 316).

With respect to international relations, the preamble also mentions "peaceful cooperation between nations" as one of the goals of the state, which implies the commitment to look for peaceful solutions of controversies and the rejection of war. Peaceful cooperation must be executed in accordance with the principle of nonintervention in the affairs of other countries and with the principle of self-determination of the people. Also, it is said in the Preamble that international cooperation must be carried out "according to the universal and indivisible guarantee of human rights and the democratization of the international society."

The Preamble also refers to other values that must guide the international relations of the republic, like "nuclear disarmament, ecological balance and environment," which is considered as a "common and nonrenounceable patrimony of humanity." In particular, according to the Preamble, another fundamental goal that must guide the state's actions is "the impulse and consolidation of the Latin-American integration" also mentioned in Article 153.

But the fact has been that, despite all the constitutional values and principles, in political practice, they have been distorted. During the past decade, an authoritarian, militaristic, and centralized state has taken shape, based in populist policies of socialist trends. That state has demolished the principles of rule of law, separation of powers, and federation (decentralization). Thus, it has weakened the effectiveness of the protection of constitutional rights by subjecting the judicial review system and other checks and balances to the executive and by progressively destroying representative democracy itself in the name of participatory democracy.

In this sense, also, in Decision No. 23 (January 22, 2003) on the constitutional interpretation of Article 71 of the Constitution, the Constitutional Chamber of the Supreme Tribunal transformed the values incorporated in the Constitution into provisions subjected to the interpretation by the politically controlled constitutional judge. That is, the decision put aside the universal meaning of the values, considering that: "to interpret the legal system according to the Constitution, means to protect the Constitution itself from every diversion of principles and from every separation from the political project that it embodies by will of the people." [363] The Constitutional Chamber also said:

---

363   Case: *Interpretación del artículo 71 de la Constitución*, in *Revista de Derecho Público*, N° 93-96, Editorial Jurídica Venezolana, Caracas 2003, p. 107.

[A] system of principles, assumed to be absolute and supra historical, cannot be placed above the Constitution, nor that its interpretation could eventually contradict the political theory that supports it. From this perspective, any theory that proposes absolute rights or goals must be rejected and,…the interpretation or integration [of the Constitution] must be done according to the living culture tradition whose sense and scope depend on the specific and historical analysis of the values shared by the Venezuelan people. Part of the protection and guarantee of the Constitution is established then, in an *in fieri* politic perspective, reluctant to the ideological connection with theories that can limit, under pretext of universal validities, the supremacy and the national self-determination, as demanded in article 1° *eiusdem*.[364]

This doctrine of subjecting global constitutional values to a political project – as in the previous case – was ratified in Decision No. 1,939 (December 18, 2009) (Case *Gustavo Álvarez Arias y otros*).[365] In that case, the Constitutional Chamber declared a decision of the Inter-American Court of Human Rights to be unenforceable in Venezuela of August 5, 2008 (*Apitz Barbera et al. [Corte Primera de lo Contencioso Administrativo] vs. Venezuela*) condemning the republic for violating the rights of dismissed judges,[366] thus rejecting the existence of values superior to those of the Venezuelan government. The chamber argued that the legal order "is a normative theory at the service of politic defined in the axiological project of the Constitution"; that the standard for resolving conflicts between principles and provisions must be "compatible with the political project of the Constitution," and such provisions "cannot be affected with interpretations that could give prevalence to individual rights or that could give prevalence to the international order regarding the national one affecting the State sovereignty"; that no system of principles "supposedly absolute and supra-historic can be placed above the Constitution"; and that "theories based on universal values that pretend to limit the sovereignty and national auto-determination are unacceptable."[367]

II. THE GENERAL FRAMEWORK ON MATTERS OF HUMAN RIGHTS

1. *General Declarations*

One of the main values declared in the Constitution is "human dignity," considered by the courts "as inherent to the human condition" and existing "before the State"; all branches of government need to be "at the service of the human being."[368] This implies not only the existence of constitutional rights considered "inherent to human beings" but also the emergence of the "principle of progressiveness" in their

---

364 Case: *Interpretación del artículo 71 de la Constitución*, in *Revista de Derecho Público*, N° 93-96, Editorial Jurídica Venezolana, Caracas 2003, pp. 107-108 and 530-33.

365 See http://www.tsj.gov.ve/decisiones/scon/Diciembre/1939-181208-2008-08-1572.html.

366 Inter-American Court of Human Rights, *Apitz Barbera et al. (Corte Primera de lo Contencioso Administrativo) v. Venezuela* (Judgment of Aug. 5, 2008), *available at* www.corteidh.or.cr.

367 See http://www.tsj.gov.ve/decisiones/scon/Diciembre/1939-181208-2008-08-1572.html.

368 See decision of the First Court of the Administrative Jurisdiction (June 1, 2000) (Case: *Julio Rocco A.*), in *Revista de Derecho Público* 82, Editorial Jurídica Venezolana, Caracas 2000, pp. 287ff.

interpretation and enforcement expressly adopted in the constitutional text (Article 19). According to the criteria of the Constitutional Chamber of the Supreme Tribunal, in this regard, the courts have an obligation "to interpret the entire legal system in the light of the Right of the Constitution . . . which also means that they have to interpret the system congruently with the fundamental rights or human rights, that must be respected above all, making a progressive and complete interpretation."[369]

The Constitution refers to this value in many articles, when guaranteeing to anybody deprived of liberty the right to be "treated with respect due to the inherent dignity of the human being" (Article 46); when guaranteeing that the judicial seizure of a person's home be made "always respecting human dignity" (Article 47); when obligating the state's security offices to always "respect the human dignity and rights of all persons" (Article 55); when establishing the duty of the State to protect senior citizens and disabled persons always respecting their "human dignity" (Articles 80 and 81); and when guaranteeing that the salary of every worker be "sufficient to enable him or her to live with dignity" (Article 91).

In that regard, the Constitutional Chamber of the Supreme Tribunal of Justice has considered human dignity "one of the values on which the Social rule of law and Justice State is based, and around which all the legal system and all the actions of the branches of government [public powers] must turn." On the basis of that approach, the Constitutional Chamber has defined human dignity in Decision 2442 (September 1, 2003) as "the supremacy that persons have as an inherent attribute of its rational being, which imposes public authorities the duty to watch for the protection and safe-conduct of the life, freedom and autonomy of men and women for the sole fact of their existence, independently of any other consideration." That is why, "the sole existence of man grants him the right to exist and to obtain all the guarantees needed to assure him a dignified life, that is, his own existence, proportional and rational to the recognition of his essence as a rational being." This concept of human dignity according to the Tribunal ruling imposes "upon the State of the duty to adopt the necessary protective measures to safeguard the legal assets that define man as a person, that is, life, integrity, freedom, autonomy."[370]

In this same sense, the Political-Administrative Chamber of the same Supreme Tribunal of Justice has specially emphasized dignity, considering it the "axiological" element representing "the ideological base that supports the dogmatic order of the current Constitution," limiting the exercise of public power, and establishing an effective judicial guarantee system." That is why this "prevalent position of human dignity," considered a "superior value of the legal system," obligates "the State and of all its bodies to protect and guarantee human rights as the main purpose and objective of its public action." Consequently, the defense and development of human

---

369 *Id.*

370 See Decision N° 2442 (Sept. 1, 2003) (Case: *Alejandro Serrano López*) in *Revista de Derecho Público* 93–96, Editorial Jurídica Venezolana, Caracas 2003, 183ff. With this purpose, in the same Decision, the Tribunal said that Article 3 of the Constitution "establishes that the recognition of the human dignity constitutes a structural principle of the Social rule-of-law State and for that, it forbids, in its Title III, Chapter III, the forced disappearances, the degrading treatments, the tortures or cruel treatments that could harm the life as an inviolable right, the degrading punishments and all other inherent rights of the human person (Articles 43ff.)."

dignity is considered by the Supreme Tribunal "one of the superior values of the legal system," and its "defense and development [is] one of the essential objectives of the State" (Articles 2 and 3)."[371]

Human dignity, however, implies the idea of the "preeminence of human rights" (Preamble), which according to the "principle of progressiveness" (Article 19), means that statutes must be interpreted in the most favorable way for their enjoyment. In this regard, Article 19 of the 1999 Constitution begins "Duties, Rights and Constitutional Guarantees," setting forth that the state must guarantee every person, "according to the progressiveness principle and without discrimination whatsoever, the enjoyment and nonrenounceable, indivisible and interdependent exercise of human rights." The provision adds that "the respect and the guarantee of the rights are mandatory to all State bodies in accordance with the Constitution, the treaties on human rights signed and ratified by the Republic and the statutes."[372] That is, as affirmed by the courts, "the interpretation of the corresponding constitutional provisions and any future constitutional revision, must be performed in the most favorable way for the exercise and enjoyment of the rights." Courts have added that "this principle is so important that its application obliges the State to update legislation in favor of the defense of the human rights and in view to dignify the human condition, adapting the interpretation of the norms 'to the sensibility, thought and needs of the new times' in order to adapt them to the new established order and to reject any anachronisms that opposes to their effective force." [373]

To give human dignity its complete shape, Article 23 of the 1999 Constitution granted constitutional rank to international treaties on human rights signed and ratified by Venezuela, adding that they "prevail in the internal order, when containing more favorable provisions regarding their enjoyment than those contained in the Constitution and the laws of the Republic." This means that they have supraconstitutional rank when containing more favorable provisions regarding the exercise of rights. The same article provides for the immediate and direct application of treaties

---

371   See Decision N° 224 (Feb. 24, 2000) in *Revista de Derecho Público* No. 81, Editorial Jurídica Venezolana, Caracas 2000, pp. 131ff. See also Decision 3215 of the Constitutional Chamber of the Supreme Tribunal (June 15, 2004) in *Revista de Derecho Público* No. 97–98, Editorial Jurídica Venezolana, Caracas 2004, p. 428.

372   About this principle, the Constitutional Chamber of the Supreme Tribunal of Justice, quoting Article 2 of the American Convention on Human Rights, in Decision N° 1154 (June 29, 2001), based on the same principle, has ruled that it is necessary "to adapt the legal system in order to ensure the efficiency of said rights, being unacceptable the excuse of the inexistence or unsuitability of the means provided in the internal order for their protection and application." See *Revista de Derecho Público* 85–88, Editorial Jurídica Venezolana, Caracas 2001, pp. 111ff.

373   In this sense, the First Court of the Administrative Jurisdiction has considered its obligation "to interpret the entire legal system in the light of the Right of the Constitution, even more, when acting in exercise of the constitutional power for protection, which also means, that we have to interpret the system congruently with the fundamental rights or human rights, that must be respected above all, making a progressive and complete interpretation." See Decision from June 1, 2000 (Case: *Julio Rocco A.*), in *Revista de Derecho Público* 82, Editorial Jurídica Venezolana, Caracas 2000, pp. 287ff.

by the state bodies, particularly courts.[374] The inclusion of such provisions in the Constitution was a significant advancement in protecting human rights.

However, to reinforce the constitutional value of human dignity, the human rights that are guaranteed and protected are not only the ones enumerated in the Constitution but also those that, although not enumerated, are considered "inherent to the human person" (Article 22).[375] That is why the last phrase of Article 22 establishes that "the lack of regulatory statutes regarding human rights do not diminish their exercise"; that is, their application "cannot be conditioned by the existence of a statute developing it; and on the contrary, the lack of legal instruments regulating them, do not diminish their exercise, being such rights of immediate and direct application by the courts and all other bodies of the State" (Articles 22 and 23).[376]

But in light of these progressive provisions, in practice, the supraconstitutional rank that the Constitution has given to international instruments of human rights and to their direct and immediate and direct application by all courts has been curtailed. In effect, contrary to the provision of Article 23 of the Constitution, in judicial practice and particularly regarding the provisions of the American Convention on Human Rights, the doctrine of the Supreme Tribunal also has been progressively restrictive, eventually rejecting the supraconstitutional rank of international instruments of human rights. This restrictive approach by the Constitutional Chamber that has affected the role to be played on matters of international protection of human rights by the Inter-American institutions, began with a decision dated May 5, 2000, in which the Constitutional Chamber objected to the "quasi-jurisdictional" powers of the Inter-American Commission in issuing provisional protective measures regarding a state, qualifying them as "unacceptable." The Constitutional Chamber stated that they "impl[y] a gross intrusion in the country Judiciary, like the suspension of the judicial proceeding against the plaintiff, measures that can only be adopted by

---

374   The Constitutional Court of the Supreme Tribunal has, for instance, applied this provision regarding due process, applying preferentially Article 8 of the American Convention on Human Rights. See the Decision from Mar. 14, 2000 (Case: *C.A. Electricidad del Centro y C.A. Electricidad de los Andes*), in *Revista de Derecho Publico* No. 81, Editorial Jurídica Venezolana, Caracas 2000, pp. 157-58; quoted in Decision N° 328 (Mar. 9, 2001), of the same chamber, in *Revista de Derecho Publico* No. 85–88, Editorial Jurídica Venezolana, Caracas 2001, p. 108. The Political-Administrative Chamber of the Supreme Tribunal interpreted and developed the criteria established by the Constitutional Chamber regarding the lack of applications of Article 185 of the Organic Law of the Supreme Court of Justice in Decision N° 802 (Apr. 13, 2000) (Case: *Elecentro vs. Superintendencia Procompetencia*), in *Revista de Derecho Publico* 82, Editorial Jurídica Venezolana, Caracas 2000, 270. On a similar matter, see also Decision N° 449 (Mar. 27, 2001) (Case: *Dayco de Construcciones vs. INOS*) in *Revista de Derecho Publico* No. 85–88, Editorial Jurídica Venezolana, Caracas 2001. Nonetheless, the Political-Administrative Chamber has denied giving prevalence to Article 8 of the American Convention regarding requests by corporate persons, understanding that the convention refers only to the "human" rights of individuals. See Decision N° 278 (Mar. 1, 2001), in *Revista de Derecho Publico* No. 85–88, Editorial Jurídica Venezolana, Caracas 2001, p. 104.

375   This open clause is more extensive than the original wording of the U.S. Constitution (Amendment 9), in that it refers to rights and guarantees not enumerated in the Constitution and also in the international instruments on human rights, which creates a truly unlimited cast of unstated but protected rights inherent to the human person.

376   See Decision N° 723 (May 15, 2001) in *Revista de Derecho Público* 85–88, Editorial Jurídica Venezolana, Caracas 2001, p. 111.

the judges exercising their judicial attributions and independence, according to what is stated in the Constitution and the statutes of the Republic."[377]

This unfortunate ruling questioned the superior role of the international institutions on matters of human rights and can be considered contrary to Article 31 of the Constitution, which establishes the right of everybody to bring before international institutions on human rights, precisely the Inter-American Commission on Human Rights, petitions or complaints to seek protection (*amparo*) of their violated constitutional rights.

The restrictive approach regarding the role and value of international institutions for the protection of human rights was also applied in Decision N° 1942 (July 15, 2003) (Case: *Impugnación de artículos del Código Penal, Leyes de desacato*),[378] in which the Constitutional Chamber, in referring to international courts, stated that "in Venezuela, in general, in relation to Article 7 of the Constitution, no jurisdictional organ could exist above the Supreme Tribunal of Justice, and even in such case, its decisions when contradicting constitutional provisions are unapplicable in the country." The restrictive approach on the matter has finished with Decision No. 1939 of December 18, 2008 (Case *Abogados Gustavo Álvarez Arias y otros*), in which the Constitutional Chamber declared unenforceable a decision of the Inter-American Court of Human Rights. The decision of the Inter-American Court of August 5, 2008 (Case *Apitz Barbera y otros ["Corte Primera de lo Contencioso Administrativo"] vs. Venezuela*)[379] condemned the Venezuelan state for violating the judicial guarantees of three former judges of the First Contentious Administrative Court, who were dismissed by a special commission of the Supreme Tribunal. The Constitutional Chamber rejected the supraconstitutional character of the provisions of the American Convention on Human Rights, considering that in the case of contradiction of a provision of the Constitution and a provision of an international treaty, the judiciary will determine applicable provisions.[380]

The result has been that on the basis of sovereignty principles, the decisions adopted by international courts cannot be considered enforceable in Venezuela, except if they accord with what is stated in the Constitution as interpreted by the Constitutional Chamber. Thus, the Constitutional Chamber has eliminated the supraconstitutional rank of treaties that establish more favorable human rights regulations. The Constitutional Chamber has assumed an absolute monopoly over constitutional interpretation to determine when a treaty provision prevails in the internal order—power that, according to the Constitution, the Constitutional Chamber does not have.

This political-positivistic conception of the Constitution unfortunately leaves interpretation of the very rich constitutional values and principles extensively enumerated in the Constitution, and of the Constitution itself, to the mercy of the Constitu-

---

377   See Case: *Faitha M. Nahmens L. y Ben Ami Fihman Z. (Revista Exceso)*, Exp. N° 00-0216, Decision N° 386 (May 17, 2000). See Carlos Ayala Corao, "Recepción de la jurisprudencia internacional sobre derechos humanos por la jurisprudencia constitucional," *Revista del Tribunal Constitucional* 6, Sucre, Bolivia 2004, pp. 275ff.

378   See *Revista de Derecho Público* No. 93–96, Editorial Jurídica Venezolana, Caracas 2003, pp. 136ff.

379   See http://www.corteidh.or.cr. Excepción Preliminar, Fondo, Reparaciones y Costas, Serie C, N° 182.

380   See http://www.tsj.gov.ve/decisiones/scon/Diciembre/1939-181208-2008-08-1572.html.

tional Chamber. Because it unfortunately is controlled by the executive,[381] this implies the rejection of the power of all courts established in Article 23 of the Constitution to apply in a direct and immediate way to international instruments on human rights to resolve judicial cases. The Constitutional Chamber has established, contrary to the intention of the Constituent Assembly,[382] its own monopoly to interpret when a constitutional provision is of immediate application and, particularly, when its content is justiciable.[383] In Decision N° 1942 of July 7, 2003,[384] the Constitutional Chamber ruled that once the provisions of the international instruments have been incorporated to the constitutional hierarchy, "the maximum and last interpreter of them [including international instruments] regarding internal law, is the Constitutional Chamber, which must determine the content and scope of the constitutional norms and principles" (Article 335). From that proposition, the Constitutional Chamber concluded that "the Constitutional Chamber [is] the only one that determines which norms on human rights contained in treaties, covenants and conventions prevail in the internal legal order; as well as which human rights nonincorporated in such international instruments have effects in Venezuela." It concluded:

> This power of the Constitutional Chamber on the matter, derived from the Constitution, and cannot be diminished by adjective norms contained in the treaties or in other international texts on human rights subscribed by the country, which allows the States parties to ask international institutions for the interpretation of rights referred to in the Convention or covenant, as it is established in Article 64 of the Approbatory statute of the American Convention of Human Rights, San José Covenant, because otherwise, the situation would be of a constitutional amendment, without following the constitutional procedures, diminishing the powers of the Constitutional Chamber, transferring it to international or transnational bodies, with the power to dictate obligatory interpretations.[385]

---

381 See Allan R. Brewer-Carías, "El juez constitucional al servicio del autoritarismo y la ilegítima mutación de la constitución: El caso de la Sala Constitucional del Tribunal Supremo de Justicia de Venezuela (1999-2009)," in *Revista de Administración Pública No.* 180, Centro de Estudios Políticos y Constitucionales, Madrid 2009, pp. 383-418.

382 Allan R. Brewer-Carías, "Quis Custodiet ipsos Custodes: De la interpretación constitucional a la inconstitucionalidad de la interpretación," in *VIII Congreso Nacional de derecho Constitucional, Perú,* Fondo Editorial 2005, Colegio de Abogados de Arequipa, Arequipa, Sept. 2005, pp. 463-489.

383 See Case: *Aclaratoria de la sentencia de interpretación de los artículos 156, 180 y 302 de la Constitución,* Decision N° 1278 (June 17, 2005), in *Revista de Derecho Público* 102, Editorial Jurídica Venezolana, Caracas 2005, 56ff. The Constitutional Chamber ruled in Decision N° 332 (Mar. 14, 2001) that "it is the constitutional jurisdiction represented by this Constitutional Chamber, who will resolve the controversies that might arise as the result of the legislatively undeveloped constitutional provisions, until the laws that regulate the constitutional jurisdiction decide otherwise." See Case: *INSACA vs. Ministerio de Sanidad y Asistencia Social,* in *Revista de Derecho Público* 85–88, Editorial Jurídica Venezolana, Caracas 2001, p. 492.

384 See *Revista de Derecho Público* No. 93–96, Editorial Jurídica Venezolana, Caracas 2003, pp. 136ff.

385 See *Revista de Derecho PúblicoNo.* 93–96, Editorial Jurídica Venezolana, Caracas 2003, pp. 136ff.

2. *Social Rights and the Social State*

Article 2 of the 1999 Constitution defines the Venezuelan state as one of social-democratic rule of law, in which the principle of social responsibility (Preamble) prevails in public policies, thus configuring the state as a social state, with specific social duties to society. In particular, the Constitution refers to the social goal of society and the state to ensure "social justice," guaranteeing the equitable participation of all in the enjoyment of wealth, preventing its concentration only in a few hands, avoiding unfair income differences, and seeking the guarantee of a dignified and prosperous existence for the collectivity (Articles 112 and 299).

This idea of a social state (*estado social*) refers to a state with social obligations that strive for social justice as a welfare state, which allows for its intervention in social and economic activities. Such a social character mainly derives from the fundamental constitutional value of equality and nondiscrimination, in the Preamble and Article 1, but also from Article 21, which declares these as fundamental rights; Article 2, which establishes them as the benchmark of state performance; and Article 299, which establishes social justice as the basis of the economic system.

The Constitutional Chamber of the Supreme Court – in Decision No. 85 (January, 24 2002) – defined the social state as follows: "it searches for the harmony between classes, avoiding that the dominant class, having the economic, political or cultural power, abuses and subjugates the other classes or social groups, preventing their development and submitting them to poverty and ignorance; as natural exploited without the possibility to redeem their situation." The Constitutional Chamber continued:

> The Social State must protect people or groups that regarding others are in a situation of legal weakness, regardless of the principle of equality before the law, which in practice does not resolve anything, because unequal situations cannot be treated with similar solutions. In order to achieve the balance, the Social State not only intervenes in the labor and social security factor, protecting the salaried workers nonrelated to the economical or political power, but it also protects their health, housing, education and economical relations. That is why the Economic Constitution must be seen from an essentially social perspective.
> . . .
> The State is obligated to protect the weak, defend their interests protected by the Constitution, particularly through the courts; and regarding the strong, its duty is to watch that their freedom is not a load for everybody. As a juridical value, there cannot be constitutional protection at the expense of the fundamental rights of others. . . .
> The Social State tries to harmonize the antagonistic interests of society, without allowing unlimited actions from social forces, based on the silence of the statutes or their ambiguities, because otherwise that would lead to the establishment of an hegemony over the weak by those economically and socially stronger, in which the private power positions become an excessive diminution

of the real freedom of the weak, in a subjugation that constantly encourages the social crisis.[386]

Regarding solidarity as the social state's goal, it tends to reaffirm that people have social and community duties in addition to rights. Thus, the right of each individual necessarily finds its limits and boundaries in the right of others (Article 20). "Common good" ensures the satisfaction of all individual and collective needs, where the latter take priority over the former, which also implies that reasons of public and social order can always limit individual rights (Article 20).

On the basis of this conception of the social state, the Constitution contains very extensive declarations of social rights,[387] including family and social protection, health and social security, labor, education and culture, environment, and indigenous peoples' rights. However in many cases, the declarations are more aims or public policy regarding social welfare than specific justiciable rights. In effect, an essential principle of constitutional rank in the establishment of human rights is the altering principle, which implies that every right carries an obligation, and that everyone who is entitled to a right must have a relation with somebody who has a correlative obligation. Therefore, there are no rights without obligations. So, the establishment of rights that do not create obligations are no more than declarations of principles or intent.

This has happened with several social rights and guarantees as established in the Constitution whose satisfaction is simply impossible. Rather, they are indubitably teleological declarations of principles and intent, and they hardly can be considered constitutional rights: Nobody is or can be obliged to satisfy them. The right to health, for example, is established as a fundamental social right; the state is obligated by it and guarantees it as "part of the right to life" (Article 83). But, in fact, it is impossible that someone could guarantee somebody's health and that the right to health could be constitutionally established. The wording used in the article is incorrect because the Constitution, of course, cannot establish the right to not get sick, which is impossible. The right that, for instance, can be established and is in fact established is the constitutional right to health care, which is the one that could obligate the state to establish and provide public services of preventive and curative medicine that can be judicially claimed, including by means of amparo actions.

The same can be said of the right established in the Constitution in favor of "every person" "to an adequate, secure, comfortable, hygienic house with essential basic services that include a habitat that makes more human the familiar, neighboring and community relations" (Article 82). In the way it is established, this "right" is more a definition of public policy beautifully structured than a "right" that does not lead to anyone being obligated to satisfy. The wording that was used in the Constitution

---

386 See Case: *Deudores hipotecarios vs. Superintendencia de Bancos*, in *Revista de Derecho Público* 89–92, Editorial Jurídica Venezolana, Caracas 2002, pp. 94ff.

387 See Mercedes Pulido de Briceño, "La Constitución de 1999 y los derechos sociales," in *La cuestión social en la Constitución Bolivariana de Venezuela,* Editorial Torino, Caracas 2000, 15-28; Carlos Aponte Blank, "Los derechos sociales y la Constitución de 1999," in *id.*, 113-34; Emilio Spósito Contreras, "Aproximación a los derechos sociales en la Constitución de la República Bolivariana de Venezuela," in *Revista de derecho del Tribunal Supremo de Justicia* 9, Caracas 2003, pp. 381-98.

was also incorrect, for instance, regarding the case of the right to social security (Article 86), conceived more as a political aim than a justiciable right, except if it exists in a particular link based on legislation on social security between a person and a social public service, in order to claim some benefits. In this matter, in many cases, good intentions and social declarations were mistaken with constitutional rights and obligations that create other types of legal relations.

On the other hand, in regulating social rights, the Constitution puts in the state's hands excessive burdens, obligations, and guarantees in many cases of impossible compliance and execution; in parallel minimizing, and even excluding, private initiatives. In this way, public services, essentially and traditionally concurrent between the state and individuals, such as education, health care, and social security, are regulated with a marked state–exclusive accent, which in practice has curtailed private initiatives.

For example, regarding health, "to guarantee it, State will create, exercise the ruling and arrange a national public health system, . . . integrated to the social security system, ruled by principles of free health, universality, comprehensiveness, equity, social integration and solidarity" (Article 84). Therefore, this is really about a public health system, ruled as a free public service that is part of the social security system. Nothing is said in the article about private health services, even though another article indicates that the state "will regulate public and private health institutions" (Article 85).

Moreover, social security is declared a free public service. The state is obligated "to ensure the effectiveness of this right, creating a universal, comprehensive, unitary, efficient and participatory social security system of joint financing and of direct or indirect contributions." The obligatory contributions "can be administrated with social purposes under the ruling of the state" (Article 86). Thus, all private enterprise regarding social security is excluded, and private participation in the administration of pension funds is minimized.

Regarding education, the tendency is similar. Education is regulated, in general, as a human right and a fundamental social duty. It is declared "democratic, free and obligatory" and is defined as "a public service," which the state should assume as "a function that cannot be declined" (Article 102). Nothing is said of private education except that there is the people's right to "found and maintain private educational institutions under the strict inspection and surveillance of the State, previous its acceptance" (Article 106). The possibility of turning education into a state exclusive service does not have limits in the Constitution; and an article regarding the subject in the Constitution of 1961, which established that "the State will stimulate and protect private education given according to the principles established in this Constitution and laws" (Article 79), was eliminated.

3. *Limits to the Exercise of Constitutional Rights That Can Only Be Established through Statutes*

The progression characterizing the enumeration of constitutional rights has a general guarantee by establishing that any limit or restriction to their exercise can only be established by the legislator, through statutes. This means that the matter has been reserved for the National Assembly (*reserva legal*) implying the need for the sanctioning of formal statutes (laws), to limit or restrict human rights; statutes being defined in the Constitution as the acts issued by the legislative organ (National Assembly) (Article 103), which is the one integrated by representatives elected in a democratic way.

Nonetheless, this guarantee was diminished in the same 1999 Constitution, which provides for a system of delegated legislation through laws that can be decided by the National Assembly (Article 203) in a way that has no comparison with any other Latin American constitution. The system confers the possibility of the National Assembly to delegate authority on the ruling of any subject to the president, which in practice can signify the curtailment of the exhaustive list of rights established in the Constitution.

This possibility for legislative delegation by means of enabling laws in the extended way of referring to any matters is an innovation of the 1999 Constitution, without precedent in other constitutions. The 1999 Constitution substituted the provisions of the 1961 Constitution, which limited the authorization by enabling laws to the president to adopting extraordinary measures exclusively on economic and financial matters (Article 190.8). In contrast, the 1999 Constitution extends the possibility of legislative delegation, without limits regarding the matters that the executive can regulate, which contradicts the general constitutional guarantee of certain matters that must be reserved to the legislator (as a body composed of elected representatives), like establishing limits to the exercise of human rights, the approval of taxes (no taxation without representation), and the creation of criminal offenses.[388]

The fact is that according to this provision, the fundamental legislation of the country sanctioned from 1999 to 2009 has been contained in the decree laws issued by the president to execute those enabling laws, particularly in 2002 and 2008, which even were approved without ensuring the mandatory constitutional provision for public hearings, established in the Constitution (Article 211) to take place before the sanctioning of all statutes. That is contrary to the way the Constitution tends to ensure the exercise of the political participation right in the process of drafting legislation. This constitutional obligation, of course, also must be complied with by the president when a legislative delegation takes place. Nonetheless, in 2007 and 2008, the president, following the same steps he took in 2001,[389] extensively legislated without any public hearing or consultation. In this way, defrauding the Constitution by means of legislative delegation, President Chávez enacted decree laws without complying with the obligatory public hearings, thus violating citizens' right to political participation.

4. *Freedom of Expression and Its Limitations*

On matters of freedoms, the 1999 Constitution established a complete enunciation of all civil rights and freedoms, although in some cases it provided the basis for

---

388 See Pedro Nikken, "Constitución venezolana de 1999: La habilitación para dictar decretos ejecutivos con fuerza de ley restrictivos de los derechos humanos y su contradicción con el derecho internacional," *Revista de Derecho Público* 83, Editorial Jurídica Venezolana, Caracas 2000, pp. 5-19.

389 See Allan R. Brewer-Carías, "Apreciación general sobre los vicios de inconstitucionalidad que afectan los Decretos Leyes Habilitados," in *Ley Habilitante del 13-11-2000 y sus Decretos Leyes*, Academia de Ciencias Políticas y Sociales, Serie Eventos N° 17, Caracas 2002, pp. 63-103.

excessive state control. This has been the case particularly for the freedom of expression.

In this respect, Article 57 of the Constitution states that "everyone has the right to express freely his or her thoughts, ideas or opinions orally, in writing or by any other form of expression, and to use for such purpose any means of communication and diffusion, and no censorship shall be established." Anyone making use of this right assumes full responsibility for everything expressed. Anonymity, war propaganda, discriminatory messages, or those promoting religious intolerance are not permitted. Also, Article 57 provides that censorship restricting the ability of public officials (*funcionarios públicos*) to report on matters for which they are responsible is prohibited, a provision that is not applicable to judges.

For such purposes, Article 58 guarantees that communications are free and plural, and involve the duties and responsibilities indicated by law, thus providing citizens with the right to respond and to ask for rectification.[390] Additionally, the Constitution establishes everyone's right to information – that is, to be informed – by incorporating the adjectives "impartial, opportune and reliable" (Article 58). The problem with this enunciation is that it could originate a political or public control that can eventually lead to the possible definition of an "official" truth and, therefore, the rejection or persecution of any other possible truth. Following this in 2003, the Law on Social Responsibility of the Media was sanctioned, considerably expanding official control over radio and television.[391]

On the other hand, through judicial interpretations of the Constitution, the Supreme Tribunal of Justice has progressively been limiting freedom of information. In Decision N° 1155 (May 18, 2000), the Political-Administrative Chamber of the Supreme Tribunal (Case: *Tulio A. Álvarez et al. vs. Gobernación del Estado Apure*), in a decision ordering the media not to transmit certain information, developed a collective versus an individual aspect of freedom regarding impartiality, opportuneness, and the reliable nature of information to admit limits to be imposed to the media regardless of the general prohibition of censorship.[392]

The following year, in Decision N° 1013 (June 12, 2001) (Case: *Elías Santana y Asociación Civil Queremos Elegir vs. Presidente de la República y Radio Nacional de Venezuela*), the Constitutional Chamber of the Supreme Tribunal dismissed an

---

390   See, in general, Allan R. Brewer-Carías, "La libre expresión del pensamiento y el derecho a la información en la Constitución venezolana de 1999," in *Anuario de Derecho Constitucional Latinoamericano*, Konrad Adenauer Stiftung, Montevideo 2002, pp. 267-76; Héctor Faúndez Ledesma, "Las condiciones de las restricciones a la libertad de expresión," in *El derecho público a comienzos del siglo XXI. Estudios homenaje al Profesor Allan R. Brewer-Carías*, Instituto de Derecho Público, UCV, Civitas Ediciones, Madrid 2003, Vol 3, pp. 2598-2664; Rafael Ortiz-Ortiz, "Las implicaciones jurídico positivas del derecho a la información y a la libertad de expresión en el nuevo orden constitucional," *Revista de la Facultad de Derecho de la Universidad de Carabobo* 1, Valencia 2002, pp. 163-246.

391   See Ley de Responsabilidad Social en Radio y Televisión in *Gaceta Oficial* N° 38.333, Dec. 12, 2005. See comments on this statute in Allan R. Brewer-Carías, Asdrúbal Aguiar, José Ignacio Hernández, Margarita Escudero, Ana Cristina Núñez Machado, Juan José Raffalli, Carlos Urdaneta Sandoval and Juan Cristóbal Carmona Borjas, *Ley de Responsabilidad Social de Radio y Televisión*, Colección Textos Legislativos 35, Editorial Jurídica Venezolana, Caracas 2006.

392   See *Revista de Derecho Público* No. 82, Editorial Jurídica Venezolana, Caracas 2000, pp. 291ff.

amparo action against the president filed by a citizen and the nongovernmental organization he represented asking for the exercise of his right to response. Through an interpretation of Articles 57 and 58 of the Constitution, the scope of freedom of information was extremely reduced, and the right to response and rectification was eliminated regarding opinions in the media when they were expressed by the president in his weekly televised program (*Aló Presidente*). In addition, the tribunal excluded journalists and all those persons that have a regular program in the radio or a newspaper column from the right to rectification and response.[393]

In addition, the Constitutional Chamber, contrary to the doctrine of the Inter-American Commission on Human Rights,[394] in Decision N° 1942 (July 15, 2003) (Case: *Impugnación de los artículos 141, 148, 149, 150, 151, 152, 223, 224, 225, 226, 227, 444, 445, 446, 447 y 450 del Código Penal)*, dismissed an action on unconstitutionality of the articles of the penal code limiting the right to formulate criticism against public officials, considering that such provisions could not be considered as limiting the freedom of expression in a way contrary to the Constitution. The Constitutional Chamber ratified its doctrine contrary to the prohibition of censorship: admitting that through a statute, it was possible to prevent the diffusion of information when it could be considered contrary to other provisions of the Constitution.[395]

State intervention regarding freedom of information particularly through radio and television has been developed by means of the Telecommunications Law,[396] which empowers the state to administer and control the use of frequencies. By using the provision of this Law, the state has progressively revoked authorizations and permits given to radio and television stations that appertain to persons considered in opposition to the government and that are not government controlled. In application of the law, for instance, the government has repeatedly threatened to shut down the independent television station Globovisión and has effectively and arbitrarily shut down Radio Caracas Televisión, the oldest television station in the country – it confiscated its assets and equipment and assigned them to a state-owned enterprise through illegitimate Supreme Tribunal decisions.[397]

---

393   See *Revista de Derecho Público* 85–88, Editorial Jurídica Venezolana, Caracas 2001, 117ff. See comments on this decision in Allan R. Brewer-Carías, Héctor Faúndez Ledesma, Pedro Nikken, Carlos M. Ayala Corao, Rafael Chavero Gazdik, Gustavo Linares Benzo, and Jorge Olavarria, *La libertad de expresión amenazada. Sentencia 1013*, Instituto Interamericano de Derechos Humanos, Editorial Jurídica Venezolana, Caracas and San José 2001; Jesús A. Davila Ortega, "El derecho de la información y la libertad de expresión en Venezuela (Un estudio de la sentencia 1.013/2001 de la Sala Constitucional del Tribunal Supremo de Justicia)," *Revista de Derecho Constitucional No. 5*, Editorial Sherwood, Caracas 2002, pp. 305-25.

394   See Comisión Interamericana de Derechos Humanos, *Informe sobre la compatibilidad entre las leyes de desacato y la Convención Americana sobre derechos humanos* (Doc. 9, 88° período de sesiones, informe anual, Washington, 17-02-95, chap. 5).

395   See *Revista de Derecho Público* 93–94, Editorial Jurídica Venezolana, Caracas 2003, 136ff. and 164ff. See comments in Alberto Arteaga Sánchez et al., *Sentencia 1942 vs. Libertad de expresión*, Caracas 2004.

396   Ley Orgánica de Telecomunicaciones, in *Gaceta Oficial* N° 36.970, June 12, 2000.

397   See the Constitutional Chamber Decision N° 957 (May 25, 2007), in *Revista de Derecho Público* No. 110, Editorial Jurídica Venezolana, Caracas 2007, pp. 117ff. See comments on this decision and other

5. *The New Indigenous People's Collective Rights*

One novelty of the 1999 Constitution was the inclusion of a very important chapter on the rights of indigenous peoples, very rich as compared to the Constitution of 1961, which provided only for statutes to be enacted regarding the protection of the indigenous communities and "their progressive incorporation to Nation's life" (Article 77).

The chapter begins with a declaration that the state shall recognize the existence of indigenous peoples and communities; their social, political, and economic organization; their cultures, habits, and customs; their languages and religions; their habitat; and their original rights to the territories they ancestrally and historically occupy and that are necessary to develop and guarantee their ways of life. It is incumbent on the national executive, with the participation of the indigenous peoples, to mark the boundaries of and guarantee the collective property rights of their territories, considered to be inalienable, imprescriptibly, nonseizable, and nontransferable in accord with the Constitution and laws (Article 119).

The constitutional declaration recognizes the existence of political communities within the state, in the sense that it recognizes that there can be a people in the country with their own political organization and own geographic territory. Because those elements (people, government, and territory) are the essential components of every state, from the initial idea of special protection, the 1999 Constitution went to a global recognition of status and rights that could eventually signify the risk of attempts to establish some sort of a "state" within a state. That is, the important recognition of indigenous people's rights contained in the declaration of principles formulated as a constitutional right could undoubtedly result in serious risk of generating conflict affecting the territorial integrity of the nation. Nonetheless, to avoid problems with respect to the integrity of national territory, Article 126 of the Constitution states that the indigenous peoples, as cultures with ancestral roots, form part of the nation, the state, and the Venezuelan people, which is unique, sovereign, and indivisible. Consequently, the indigenous peoples have the duty to protect national integrity and sovereignty, and in no case will the term *people* be interpreted in the sense that it has in international law tending to the recognition of states.

In particular, Article 125 of the Constitution consecrates the right of indigenous peoples to political participation, which is established in Article 182, which guarantees "indigenous representation in the National Assembly and deliberating bodies of federal entities and of local entities where indigenous populations exist, in accordance with law."[398]

Supreme Tribunal decisions thorugh its Political-Administrative Chamber and Constitutional Chamber regarding the RCTV Case in Allan R. Brewer-Carías, "El juez constitucional en Venezuela como instrumento para aniquilar la libertad de expresión y para confiscar la propiedad privada: el caso RCTV" (I de III), in *Gaceta Judicial*, Santo Domingo, Dominican Republic 2007, pp. 24-27, and *Revista de Derecho Público* 110, Editorial Jurídica Venezolana, Caracas 2007, pp. 7-32.

398 See Ricardo Colmenares Olívar, "El derecho de participación y consulta de los pueblos indígenas en Venezuela," *Revista del Tribunal Supremo de Justicia* 8, Caracas 2003, pp. 21-48.

III. THE PROBLEM OF AN ECONOMIC CONSTITUTION CONCEIVED FOR STATE APPROPRIATION ("STATIZATION") OF THE ECONOMY

The third part of the Constitution, as in any contemporary constitution, is devoted to regulating the economics,[399] establishing the rules of the economic system of the country.

The 1999 Constitution established a mixed economy, recognizing private enterprise and the right of property and economic freedom; declaring the principles of social justice; and allowing the state to intervene in the economy, significantly in some cases.

1. *The Mixed Economic System*

Since the beginning of oil production in Venezuela, and particularly during the second half of the twentieth century, a mixed "social market economy"[400] has been developed that combines economic freedom, private initiative, and a free–market economic model (as opposed to a state-directed economy) with the possibility of state intervention in the economy to uphold principles of social justice. This has been possible particularly because of the special position of the state as owner of the subsoil and the oil industry, which has been nationalized since 1975.[401] This has made the state the most powerful economic entity in the nation, leading it to intervene in the country's economic activities in important ways.

It is precisely within this context that Article 299 of the 1999 Constitution sets forth that the social-economic regime of Venezuela shall be based on the principles of social justice, democratization, efficiency, free competition, environmental protection, productivity, and solidarity, with a view to ensuring overall human development and a dignified and useful existence for the community. Thus, Article 299 expressly establishes that the state must "jointly with private initiative" promote "the harmonious development of the national economy for the purpose of generating sources of employment, a high national level of added value, in order to elevate the standard of living of the population and strengthen the nation's economic sovereignty, guaranteeing legal certainty, solidity, dynamism, sustainability, permanence, and

399   See Allan R. Brewer-Carías, "Reflexiones sobre la Constitución Económica," in *Estudios sobre la Constitución Española. Homenaje al Profesor Eduardo García de Enterría,* Madrid 1991, pp. 3839-3853.

400   See Henrique Meier, "La Constitución económica," *Revista de Derecho Corporativo* 1, Caracas 2001, 9-74; Ana C. Núñez Machado, "Los principios económicos de la Constitución de 1999," *Revista de Derecho Constitucional No. 6,* Editorial Sherwood, Caracas 2002, pp. 129-140; Claudia Briceño Aranguren and Ana C. Núñez Machado, "Aspectos económicos de la nueva Constitución," in *Comentarios a la Constitución de la República Bolivariana de Venezuela,* Vadell Hermanos Editores, Caracas 2000, pp. 177ff.; Jesús Ollarves Irazábal, "La vigencia constitucional de los derechos económicos y sociales en Venezuela," in *Libro Homenaje a Enrique Tejera París, Temas sobre la Constitución de 1999,* Centro de Investigaciones Jurídicas (CEIN), Caracas 2001, pp. 159-192.

401   See Organic Law That Reserves to the State the Industry and Commerce of Hydrocarbons, *Gaceta Oficial* Extra, N° 1.769, Aug. 29, 1975. See Allan R. Brewer-Carías, "Introducción al régimen jurídico de las nacionalizaciones en Venezuela," *Archivo de Derecho Público y Ciencias de la Administración* 3, Instituto de Derecho Público, Facultad de Ciencias Jurídicas y Políticas, Universidad Central de Venezuela, Caracas 1981, pp. 23-44.

economic growth with equity, in order to guarantee a just distribution of wealth by means of strategic democratic, participative and open planning."

The economic system is therefore based on economic freedom, private initiative, and free competition in combination with the state as promoter of economic development, regulator of economic activity, and planner together with civil society. As the Constitutional Chamber of the Supreme Tribunal of Justice stated in Decision N° 117 (February 6, 2001),[402] this is "a socioeconomic system that is in between a free market (in which the state acts as a simple programmer [*programador*] for an economy that is dependent upon the supply and demand of goods and services) and an interventionist economy (in which the state actively intervenes as the 'primary entrepreneur')." The Constitution promotes "joint economic activity between the state and private initiative in the pursuit of, and in order to concretely realize the supreme values consecrated in the Constitution," and to pursue "the equilibrium of all the forces of the market, and joint activity between the State and private initiative." In accord with that system, the Supreme Tribunal ruled that the Constitution "advocates a series of superior normative values with respect to the economic regime, consecrating free enterprise within the framework of a market economy and, fundamentally, within the framework of the Social State under the Rule of Law (the *Welfare State*, the State of Well-being or the Social Democratic State). This is a social State that is opposed to authoritarianism."[403] Nonetheless, in practice, particularly during the past decade (1999–2009), this framework has been changed as a result of the authoritarian government that developed, inclining the balance toward state participation in the economy through a process of progressive state appropriation ("statization") of the economy, reduction of economic freedoms, and an increase in the country's dependency on oil production.[404]

2. Reduced Property Rights and Economic Freedoms

Title 3 of the 1999 Constitution also contains a declaration of economic rights (Chapter 7, Articles 112–118), including economic freedom and the right to private property.

Regarding economic freedom, Article 112 of the Constitution declares the right of all persons to develop the economic activity of their choice, without other limits than those established by statute for reasons of human development, security, sanitation, environmental protection, and other social interests. In any case, the state must promote private initiative, guaranteeing the creation of wealth and its just distribution, as well as the production of goods and services to satisfy the needs of the popu-

---

402 See *Revista de Derecho Público* 85–88, Editorial Jurídica Venezolana, Caracas 2001, pp. 212-218.

403 The values alluded to, according to the doctrine of the Constitutional Chamber, "are developed through the concept of free enterprise" (*libertad de empresa*), which encompasses both a subjective right "to dedicate oneself to the economic activity of one's choice" and a principle of economic regulation, "according to which the will of the business (*voluntad de la empresa*) to make its own decisions is manifest. The State fulfills its role of intervention in this context. Intervention can be direct (through businesses) or indirect (as an entity regulating the market)," id.

404 As reported by Simón Romero, "Chávez Reopens Oil Bids to West as Prices Plunge," *New York Times*, Jan. 12, 2009, p.1, in 2009, Venezuela was "reliant on oil for about 93 percent of its export revenue in 2008, up from 69 percent in 1998."

lation; freedom to work; and free enterprise, commerce, and industry – without pre-judice to the power of the state to promulgate measures to plan, rationalize, and regulate the economy and promote the overall development of the country.

In 2007, by means of the draft constitutional reforms (rejected by referendum held in December of that same year), the president proposed to eliminate this constitutional provision, substituting it with one defining as a matter of state policy the obligation to promote "the development of a Productive Economic Model, that is intermediate, diversified and independent . . . founded upon the humanistic values of cooperation and the preponderance of common interests over individual ones, guaranteeing the meeting of the people's social and material needs, the greatest possible political and social stability, and the greatest possible sum of happiness." The proposal added that the state, in the same way, "shall promote and develop different forms of businesses and economic units from social property, both directly or communally, as well as indirectly or through the state." According to that norm, the state was to promote "economic units of social production and/or distribution, that may be mixed properties held between the State, the private sector, and the communal power, so as to create the best conditions for the collective and cooperative construction of a Socialist Economy."[405]

Article 115 of the Constitution, although following the orientation of the previous 1961 Constitution in the sense of guaranteeing the right to property, did not establish private property as having a social function to be accomplished, as did the 1961 Constitution.[406] Nonetheless, it provides that property shall be subject to such contributions, restrictions, and obligations as may be established by law in the service of the public or general interest. However, Article 115 defines the attributes of the right to property that traditionally were enumerated only in the Civil Code (Article 545); that is, the right to use, enjoy, and dispose of property are now in the Constitution.

The 2007 constitutional reforms proposed radical changes to this constitutional regime regarding property rights. The president sought to eliminate private property as a constitutionally protected right and to substitute a recognition of private property as "assets for use and consumption or as means of production," together with other forms of properties and, in particular, public property. The proposed reform regarding Article 115 of the Constitution recognized and guaranteed "different forms of property" instead of guaranteeing the right to private property, enumerating them as follows: public property, which belongs to state entities; social property, which belongs to the people jointly and to future generations; collective property, which pertains to social groups or persons and is exploited for their common benefit, use, or enjoyment, and may be of social or private origin; mixed property, ownership of which is by the public, social, collective, and private sectors in different combina-

---

405 See Allan R. Brewer-Carías, *La Reforma Constitucional de 2007 (Sancionada inconstitucionalmente por la Asamblea Nacional el 2 de Noviembre de 2007)*, Editorial Jurídica Venezolana, Caracas 2007, pp. 127ff.

406 See Allan R. Brewer-Carías "El derecho de propiedad y libertad económica. Evolución y situación actual en Venezuela," in *Estudios sobre la Constitución. Libro Homenaje a Rafael Caldera*, Caracas 1979, vol. 2: pp. 1139-1246.

tions, for the exploitation of resources or the execution of activities, subject always to the absolute economic and social sovereignty of the nation; and private property, which is owned by "natural or legal persons, only regarding assets for use or consumption, or as means of production legitimately acquired."[407]

With respect to expropriation, Article 115 of the Constitution establishes that expropriation can be decreed for any kind of property only for reasons of public benefit or social interest, and then by means of a judicial process and payment of just compensation.[408] Consequently, the Constitution prohibits confiscation (expropriation without compensation), except in cases permitted by the Constitution itself, regarding property of persons responsible for crimes committed against public property or who have illicitly enriched themselves in exercising public office. Confiscations may also take place regarding property deriving from business, financial, or any other activities connected with illicit trafficking of psychotropic or narcotic substances (Articles 116 and 271).

Article 307 of the Constitution declares the regime of large private real estate holdings (*latifundio*) to be contrary to social interests, charging the legislator with taxing idle lands and establishing necessary measures to transform them into productive economic units, as well as to recover arable land. The same constitutional provision entitles peasants to own land, thus constitutionalizing the obligation of the state to protect and promote associative and private forms of property to guarantee agricultural production and to oversee sustainable arrangements on arable lands to guarantee their food-producing potential. In exceptional cases, the same article requires that the legislature use federal tax revenue to fund financing, research, technical assistance, transfer of technology, and other activities aimed to raise productivity and competitiveness of the agricultural sector.

3. The Almost-Unlimited Possibility of State Intervention in the Economy

In the economic arena, the Constitution is marked by statism, as it attributes to the state the fundamental responsibility in the arrangement and provision of basic public services in health, education, and social security areas and those pertaining to homes: distribution of water, gas, and electricity. It is also derived from the regulation of state power to control and plan economic activities.

Consequently, the articles of the Constitution regarding the economy are those destined for state intervention. Only succinct rules are devoted to regulating economic freedom (Article 112) and private property (Article 115); the necessary balance between public and private sectors is absent. In the latter, only activities not fundamental to generating wealth and employment are privileged, such as agricultural (Article 305), crafts (Article 309), small and medium enterprises (Article 308), and tourism (Article 310).

---

407   See Allan R. Brewer-Carías, *La Reforma Constitucional de 2007 (Sancionada inconstitucionalmente por la Asamblea Nacional el 2 de Noviembre de 2007)*, Editorial Jurídica Venezolana, Caracas 2007, pp. 122 ff.

408   See José L. Villegas Moreno, "El derecho de propiedad en la Constitución de 1999," in *Estudios de derecho administrativo: Libro homenaje a la Universidad Central de Venezuela*, Imprenta Nacional, Caracas 2001, Vol. II, pp. 565-582.

In effect, the Constitution also regulates various forms of state economic intervention that have developed in Venezuela in the past decades. The Constitution regulates the state as a promoter – that is, without substituting private initiatives – to foster and order the economy to ensure the development of private initiative. Article 112 sets forth that in any case, the state must promote private initiative, guaranteeing the creation of wealth and its just distribution, as well as the production of goods and services to satisfy needs of the population; freedom to work; and free enterprise, commerce, and industry – without prejudice to the power of the state to promulgate measures to plan, rationalize, and regulate the economy and promote the overall development of the country.

In this same regard, Article 299 sets forth that the state, jointly with private initiative, shall promote the harmonious development of the national economy to the end of generating sources of employment, a high rate of domestic added value, an increased standard of living for the population, and strengthened economic sovereignty of the country. It also guarantees the reliability of the law, as well as the solid, dynamic, sustainable, continuing, and equitable growth of the economy, to ensure just distribution of wealth through participatory democratic strategic planning with open consultation.

Specifically regarding agricultural activities, Article 305 of the Constitution establishes that the state shall promote sustainable agriculture as the strategic basis for overall rural development and, consequently, shall guarantee the population a secure food supply, defined as the sufficient and stable availability of food within the national sphere and timely and uninterrupted access to the same for consumers. A secure food supply must be achieved by developing and prioritizing internal agricultural and livestock production, understood as production deriving from the activities of agriculture, livestock, fishing, and aquaculture. Food production is in the national interest and is fundamental to the economic and social development of the nation. To that end, the state shall promulgate such financial, commercial, and technological transfer; land tenancy; infrastructure; training; and other measures as may be necessary to achieve strategic levels of self-sufficiency. In addition, it shall promote actions in the national and international economic context to compensate for the disadvantages inherent to agricultural activity. The state shall protect the settlement and communities of nonindustrialized fishermen, as well as their fishing banks in continental waters and those close to the coastline, as defined by law.

Regarding rural development, Article 306 imposes on the state the duty to promote conditions for overall rural development, for the purpose of generating employment and ensuring the rural population an adequate level of well-being, as well as their inclusion in national development. It shall likewise promote agricultural activity and optimum land use by providing infrastructure projects, supplies, loans, training services, and technical assistance.

Regarding industrial activities, Article 308 obligates the state to protect and promote small– and medium–sized manufacturers, cooperatives, savings funds, family-owned businesses, small businesses, and any other form of community association for purposes of work, savings, and consumption, under an arrangement of collective ownership, to strength the country's economic development based on the initiative of the people. Training, technical assistance, and appropriate financing are guaranteed. However, Article 309 provides that typical Venezuelan crafts and folk industries enjoy special protection of the state, to preserve their authenticity, and receive credit facilities to promote production and marketing.

On commercial matters, Article 301 reserves to the state the use of trade policy to protect the economic activities of public and private Venezuelan enterprises. In this regard, more advantageous status than that established for Venezuelan nationals will not be granted to foreign persons, enterprises, or entities. Foreign investment is subject to the same conditions as domestic investment.

Finally, Article 310 of the Constitution declares tourism an economic activity of national interest and of high priority in the country's strategy of diversification and sustainable development. As part of the foundation of the socioeconomic regime the Constitution contemplates, the state will promulgate measures to guarantee the development of tourism and will create and strengthen a national tourist industry.

Regarding economic planning, Article 112 empowers the state to promulgate measures to plan, rationalize, and regulate the economy and promote the overall development of the country. The president must formulate the National Plan of Development and, once approved by the National Assembly, direct its execution (Articles 187.8 and 236.18).

The Constitution establishes no provisions for the state to promote highly qualified or heavy industries, though it does establish that the state can reserve for its own exploitation, through an organic law and by reasons of national convenience, the petroleum industry (already nationalized since 1975) and other industries, operations, and goods and services that are in the public interest and of a strategic nature. The state shall promote the domestic manufacture of raw materials deriving from the exploitation of nonrenewable natural resources, with a view to assimilating, creating, and inventing technologies; generating employment and economic growth; and creating wealth and well-being for the people (Article 302).

As aforementioned, on the basis of a similar constitutional provision establishing the power of the state to reserve for its own exploitation services or resources (Article 97 of the 1961 Constitution), the oil industry was nationalized in 1975 and is managed by the state-owned enterprise Petróleos de Venezuela S.A. Article 303 of the 1999 Constitution set forth that for reasons of economic and political sovereignty and national strategy, the state shall retain all shares of that public enterprise, with the exception of its subsidiaries, strategic joint ventures, enterprises, and any other venture established or to be established as a consequence of carrying on the business of Petróleos de Venezuela. This last possibility has been considered a loosening of the strict nationalization process carried out through the 1975 organic law that reserves to the state the industry and commercialization of hydrocarbons.[409] The 2000 Organic Law on Hydrocarbons allowed for the establishment of mixed companies

---

409 See Allan R. Brewer-Carías, "El régimen de participación del capital privado en las industrias petrolera y minera: Desnacionalización y regulación a partir de la Constitución de 1999," in *VII Jornadas Internacionales de Derecho Administrativo Allan R. Brewer-Carías, El Principio de Legalidad y el Ordenamiento Jurídico-Administrativo de la Libertad Económica,* Fundación de Estudios de Derecho Administrativo FUNEDA, Caracas 2004, pp. 15-58.

for the exploitation of primary hydrocarbons activities, although with the state as majority shareholder[410] – that law was implemented in 2006–7.[411]

With respect to public enterprises in general, Article 300 of the Constitution refers to the statutes to determine the conditions for the creation of functionally decentralized entities to carry out social or entrepreneurial activities, with a view to ensuring the reasonable economic and social productivity of the public resources invested in such activities.

All the aforementioned provisions regarding the participation of the state in the economy were proposed to be radically changed in the 2007 draft constitutional reforms, which attempted to reduce the whole economic role of the state to promote and develop economic and social activities "under the principles of the socialist economy" (Article 300).

Thus, under the Constitution, the state is responsible for almost everything and is able to regulate everything. Private enterprise appears to be shunned. The 1999 Constitution did not assimilate the previous decades' experience of regulating, controlling, and planning an entrepreneurial state. The necessity of granting privileges to private enterprises and stimulating the generation of wealth and employment to society was not understood.

Globally, the result of the constitutional text regarding the economy is a Constitution created for state intervention in the economy, not for the development of the economy by private sectors under the principle of subsidiary state intervention.

PART TWO

INSTITUTIONAL DEVELOPMENT TOWARD CONSOLIDATING AUTHORITARIANISM

The 1999 Constitution established express provisions to construct a democratic rule-of-law state, based on the main following trends: first, the vertical distribution of state powers between territorial entities with self-government, according to the "federal decentralized" form of the state; second, the autonomy and independence of five different branches of government according to the principles of separation of powers; third, the attribution to an independent and autonomous Supreme Tribunal of Justice of the power to control the supremacy of the Constitution; and fourth, a mixed economic system that combines private initiative and economic freedom with state participation.

---

410   Ley Orgánica de Hidrocarburos, *Gaceta Oficial* N° 38.493, Aug. 4, 2006.

411   See Allan R. Brewer-Carías, "The 'Statization' of the Pre-2001 Primary Hydrocarbons Joint Venture Exploitations: Their Unilateral Termination and the Assets Confiscation of Some of the Former Private Parties," in *Oil, Gas & Energy Law Intelligence* 6. Available at http://www.gasandoil.com/ogel/; and "La estatización de los convenios de asociación que permitían la participación del capital privado en las actividades primarias de hidrocarburos suscritos antes de 2002, mediante su terminación anticipada y unilateral y la confiscación de los bienes afectos a los mismos," in *Nacionalización, libertad de empresa y asociaciones mixtas*, coord. Víctor Hernández Mendible, Editorial Jurídica Venezolana, Caracas 2008, pp. 123-88.

Nonetheless, and despite those express provisions, in practice, the institutions that have developed during the past decade – in many cases, manipulating constitutional provisions (Chapter 5) – have been used, first, to consolidate the centralized federation that the 1999 constitution-making process aimed to surpass, thus abandoning all the decentralization policies defined in the 1990s (Chapter 6); second, to concentrate power, blurring the principle of separation between the branches of government; third, to subject the Supreme Tribunal of Justice to the will of the executive (Chapter 7), converting its judicial review powers into an illegitimate means of distorting the Constitution (Chapter 8); and fourth, to establish a completely "statized" economy, by nationalizing, expropriating, and confiscating private assets and extinguishing private initiatives (Chapter 9), which has affected activities, enterprises, and assets in the oil, iron, steel, agriculture, electricity, telephone, and cement industries.

In addition, similar to what happened during the 1999 constitution-making process, in which the judicial interpretation of the Constitution was used to justify violation of the Constitution (constitutional fraud), and with the endless constitutional transitory regime established over the past decade, the political regime that began with fraud in 1999 has used representative democracy to progressively dismantle it and substitute a so-called participatory democracy of the popular power. This is participatory and democratic only in name – it is fraud.

Because of this fraud committed against the popular will by means of electoral means, the democratic rule of law has been and is being progressively substituted for with a "state of the popular power." In such a state, all power is concentrated in the head of state; thus, it is not democratic, representative, or participatory. On the contrary, it is severely controlled and directed from the summit of the political power that the president exercises as head of the executive and of the single governing party. He has proclaimed himself, de facto, as "president of the popular power" and has formally named the ministers of the executive cabinet as "Ministers of the Popular Power for...."[412] The final purpose of this policy, as announced by the vice president of the republic in January 2007 during the sanctioning of the legislative delegation law (Enabling Act) in favor of the president, is the installment of a "dictatorship of democracy,"[413] in which no other political group or party different from the one controlled by the president can govern or control political power.

In democracy, no dictatorship is acceptable, not even a "dictatorship of democracy." More than ninety years after the failed dictatorship of the proletariat in the Soviet Union, in Venezuela, communal councils have been created, which depend directly on the executive through a minister to channel the popular power, with the supposed participation of the people, and to install a dictatorship of democracy.

---

412   See Decree on the Organization of National Public Administration, N° 5246 of Mar. 20, 2007, *Gaceta Oficial* N° 38.654 of Mar. 28, 2007.

413   Vice President Jorge Rodríguez, in Jan. 2007, said: "Of course we want to install a dictatorship, the dictatorship of the true democracy and the democracy is the dictatorship of everyone, you and us together, building a different country. Of course we want this dictatorship of democracy to be installed forever," in Cecilia Caione, "Queremos instaurar la dictadura de la verdadera democracia," in *El Nacional*, Caracas Feb. 19, 2007, p. A-2.

Such popular dictatorships have been and are fraudulent instruments of power that in the name of the popular power, end every trace of democracy and impose, by force, a socialist regime in a country whose citizens have not voted for it.[414]

CHAPTER 5

CONSTITUTIONAL FRAUD AND DEFRAUDING DEMOCRACY

At the beginning of the twenty-first century, Latin America has witnessed in Venezuela the birth of a new model of authoritarian state that did not immediately originate in a military coup, as had occurred on many other occasions during the long decades of the previous century. In Venezuela, the authoritarian government has had its origin in popular elections, which despite its militaristic nature and its final goal of destroying representative democracy, have provided it the convenient camouflage of "constitutional" and "elective" marks.

We are talking about militarist authoritarianism with alleged popular support, like all fascist and communist authoritarianism regimes of the past century, in many cases with some electoral origin. Authoritarian political systems, no matter how constitutionally and electively disguised, cannot be democratic or considered to allow a state to be subject to the rule of law, particularly because they lack the essential components of democracy, which are much more than the sole popular or circumstantial election of governments.

I.   POPULAR AUTHORITARIANISM AND CONCENTRATED STATE POWERS

In particular, among all the essential elements and components of democracy, the one regarding the separation and independence of public powers is maybe the most fundamental pillar of the rule of law, because it can allow other factors of democracy to become political reality.[415] To be precise, democracy, as a political regime, can function only in a constitutional system of rule of law where control of power exists; that is, one that seriously considers the classic and clear advice, with all its political consequences, left as a legacy to the world by Charles Louis de Secondat, Baron of Montesquieu, decades before the French Revolution: "But constant experience shows us that every man invested with power is apt to abuse it, and to carry his authority as far as it will go.... To prevent this abuse, it is necessary from the very nature of things that power should be a check to power."[416]

---

414 On the contrary, in the Dec. 2007 referendum on constitutional reforms, the people voted rejecting the proposed reforms, including those that referred to the establishment of a socialist state.

415 On the Inter-American Democratic Charter and the crisis of Venezuelan democracy, see Allan R. Brewer-Carías, *La crisis de la democracia venezolana. La Carta Democrática Interamericana y los sucesos de abril de 2002*, Ediciones El Nacional, Caracas 2002, pp. 137ff.

416 Charles de Secondat, Baron of Montesquieu, *The Spirit of Laws*, Book XI, Chapter 4, translation by Thomas Nugent (1752), revised by J.V. Prichard. Based on a public-domain edition published in 1914 by G. Bell & Sons, Ltd., London. Available at http://www.constitution.org/cm/sol.txt.

Decades later, as a legacy of the North American and French revolutions,[417] this important political postulate about the separation of public powers began to be the inevitable premise of democracy as a political regime, such that democracy cannot exist without separation and power finds limits and can be stopped by power itself.

Consequently, for democracy to be a political system to ensure the government of the people, which is the legitimate holder of sovereignty, through the indirect means of representation and even through instruments for its direct exercise, it must be forged in a constitutionally political system that, above all, impedes the abuse of those who control any branches of government. This is the essence of the rule of law: For a democracy to effectively exist and function, a constitutional framework must exist that establishes and allows the control of power, both in its horizontal division regarding the branches of government and in its vertical or territorial distribution regarding regional and local government. Thus can the diverse powers of the state limit one another. This framework ensuring the separation of powers is the essential guarantee of all the values of democracy itself, among which are respect of popular will, enjoyment of freedoms and human rights, political pluralism, republican alternation, and submission to rule of law.

In Latin America, in one way or another, with all the ups and downs of the effectiveness of the rule of law, during the democratic periods of its countries, there have always been institutions aiming to ensure respect for human rights, subjection of power to the law, elections almost regular and free, and a plural regime of political parties. But if, as in many cases, democracy has not settled completely and the rule of law has not absolutely taken over political institutions, it is because those countries have failed to effectively establish the last of the essential elements of democracy: the implementation of effective separation and independence of powers. That is to say, the constitutional order that must exist in every democracy and that gives sense to the rule of law, devoted to controlling and limiting political power, is the one that can allow for effective political representation – a true possibility of citizens' political participation, a transparent and responsible government, and the effective force of the rule of law.

Without control of power, there is no true democracy – and one cannot exist – or effective rule of law. Moreover, without such control of power, none of the essential elements of democracy can be guaranteed because only by controlling power can absolutely free and fair elections take place, thus achieving efficient representation; only by controlling power can political pluralism be developed; only by controlling power can effective democratic participation be ensured; only by controlling power can effective transparency in the exercise of government be ensured with real government accountability; only by controlling power can a government submitted to the Constitution and the rule of law be structured; only by controlling power can there be effective access to justice, which functions with valuable autonomy and independence; and only by controlling power can there be a true and effective guarantee of human rights.

---

417   See Allan R. Brewer-Carías, *Reflexiones sobre la Revolución Americana (1776) y la Revolución Francesa (1789) y sus aportes al constitucionalismo moderno*, Editorial Jurídica Venezolana, Caracas 1992.

On the contrary, the excessive concentration and centralization of power, as occurs in any authoritarian government, despite its electoral origins, inevitably leads to tyranny if there are no efficient controls over governments – and, even worse, if those have or believe to have popular support. This is part of the history of humankind during the first half of the twentieth century: tyrants who used the vote of the majority to rise to power and apply, from there, authoritarian practices to eliminate democracy and all its elements, beginning with respect for human rights and alternating government.

It is useful to remember that since the beginnings of modern constitutionalism, in the French Declaration of the Rights of Man and of the Citizen (1789), the principle of the separation of powers was proclaimed, denying the existence of a constitution in "any society in which the guaranty of rights is not assured, nor the separation of powers is determined" (Article 16). That is why, during the two centuries that have passed and because of the progress experienced in implementing democracy, particularly during the past five decades, because both the principle of division or organic separation of powers as manifestation of the horizontal distribution of power and the principle of territorial or vertical distribution of power as a sign of political decentralization have been the strongest tools of contemporary constitutionalism. However, they are not necessarily the most developed in practice to ensure freedom, democratic government, and the rule of law. That is precisely why they have been progressively and systematically demolished and dismantled in Venezuela.

The authoritarian government that has taken root in Venezuela during the first decade of the twenty-first century finds its main support not only in how separation of powers was conceived of in the 1999 Constitution but also in how it has been deformed, allowing power to concentrate in the hands of the executive power because of its control over the National Assembly and, consequently, over all other branches of government. In a certain way, the 1999 Constitution, despite that it formally separates powers, had the germ of the concentration of powers that would lead to authoritarianism.

Along the same line, regarding the federal system of territorial distribution of power, despite the proclaimed "federal decentralized state" (Article 4 of the Constitution), what the Constitution continued to establish was a centralized federation, reinforced by the elimination of the Senate, an institution that had existed since 1811 as an instrument to ensure equal participation of the representatives of the states in national policies. After the 1999 Constitution, Venezuela became a rare example of a federation without a federal chamber, as is the case of a few existing federations in very small states. The authoritarian roots of the 1999 Constitution derived not only from its potential to concentrate powers but also from the centralized framework of the state it designed.

If interpreters limit themselves to the words of the 1999 Constitution, they can deduce that what the Constitution has established is a democratic government based on the participatory and protagonist role of citizens, based on the principles of organic separation of different branches of government and on territorial distribution of public power by means of a decentralized federation. However, in reality, the formal and sometimes misleading words designed the foundations of a government based on the concentration of public powers and on political centralization of the state.

The result has been the development of a new form of constitutional authoritarianism in Latin America that is based on the concentration and centralization of state powers, which impede any possibility of effective democratic participation. This is contrary to what a democratic rule-of-law state should be, built on the principles of separation of powers and political decentralization that could allow for effective democratic participation and representation.

II. THE PROCESS OF CONCENTRATING POWER SINCE 1999

The process of concentrating power in Venezuela in the hands of the executive was possible because of the majority votes the executive controlled for the 2000 elections of the National Assembly and the absolute and total control it obtained in the 2005 National Assembly. In the latter case, because of the decision of opposition parties not to participate in the 2005 legislative elections, given manipulation of the electoral rules in applying the mixed electoral system established in the Constitution, by a National Electoral Council that was completely controlled by the Executive, after its members were appointed by the Constitutional Chamber of the Supreme Tribunal, without complying with the constitutional provisions on the matter, kidnapping the citizen's rights to political participation.[418]

Once complete control of the National Assembly was obtained, authoritarianism took hold in Venezuela, given the concentration and centralization of powers allowed for in the 1999 Constitution. That is why when the Constitution was approved in the referendum on December 15, 1999, I warned – in a document to justify the reasons I advocated to vote no for the referendum – that, in Venezuela, the following would be established on approval of the Constitution:

> An institutional scheme conceived for the authoritarianism derived from the combination of centralism of State, aggravated presidential system, democracy of political parties, militarism and concentration of power in the Assembly that constitutes the central element intended for the organization of the State powers. In my opinion, this is not what was required in order to perfect democracy; which, on the contrary, should be based on the decentralization of power, a controlled and moderated presidential system, a political participation system to balance the power of the State and the subjection of the military authority to the civil authority.[419]

---

418   See decisions N° 2073 of Aug. 4, 2003 (Caso: *Hermánn Escarrá Malaver y oros*) and N° 2341 of Aug. 25, 2003 (Caso: *Hermánn Escarrá M. y otros*) in Allan R. Brewer-Carías, *La Sala Constitucional versus el Estado Democrático de Derecho. El secuestro del poder electoral y de la Sala Electoral del Tribunal Supremo y la confiscación del derecho a la participación política*, Los Libros de El Nacional, Colección Ares, Caracas 2004, p. 172; "El secuestro del Poder Electoral y la confiscación del derecho a la participación política mediante el referendo revocatorio presidencial: Venezuela 2000-2004," in *Boletín Mexicano de Derecho Comparado* No. 112, Instituto de Investigaciones Jurídicas, Universidad Nacional Autónoma de México, Mexico City 2005, pp. 11-73.

419   Document dated Nov. 30, 1999. See Allan R. Brewer-Carías, *Debate constituyente (Aportes a la Asamblea Nacional Constituyente)*, Fundación de Derecho Público–Editorial Jurídica Venezolana, Caracas 1999, 3 (Oct. 18–Nov. 30):p. 339.

Unfortunately, a decade later, my 1999 warnings had become a reality. The process began with the coup d'état given by the 1999 Constituent Assembly, which, without any authority whatsoever, assaulted and concentrated all power of the state under the in-effect 1961 Constitution. This had devastating results and produced unusual institutional sequels, like the endless and unfinished constitutional transitory regime of the country.[420] With this, the fundamental principles of democratic control over state power and the rule of law have been undermined.[421]

The Constitution framed by the 1999 Constituent Assembly contained an authoritarian institutional framework that has impeded the development of democracy and the consolidation of the rule of law. On the contrary, the Constitution that Venezuela needed in 1999 for its political development at the beginning of the twenty-first century was one that needed to ensure improved democracy by means of designing and effectively implementing organic separation of powers as an effective antidote to authoritarianism. Unfortunately, the formal progress from the establishment of the separation of powers beyond the three classical powers of the state (legislative, executive, and judicial), granting constitutional rank to the classic control institutions (e.g., comptroller general, prosecutor general, people's defender and electoral council) did not produce the desired results, particularly because of their factual dependence regarding the legislative power.

1. *The Germ of Concentrated Power: The National Assembly's Authority to Remove State Officials*

In effect, the 1999 Constitution (Article 136) established in Venezuela separation of powers defining five different branches of government: legislative, executive, judicial, citizen, and electoral. Nonetheless, for that separation to become effective, the independence and autonomy among those branches had to be consolidated to ensure the limitation and control of power by power. This, however, was not designed – the Constitution provided for an absurd distortion of separation by granting one branch of government, the National Assembly, the exercise of legislative power, as well as the power to appoint and remove judges of the Supreme Court of Justice, the prosecutor general, the comptroller general, the people's defender, and members of the National Electoral Council from their positions (Articles 265, 279, and 296). In some cases, they could do so by simple majority votes.

It is simply impossible to understand how the autonomy and independence of separate powers can function and exercise mutual control when the tenure of the officials of the branches of government (except the president) depends on the political will of one branch of government – that is, the National Assembly. The fact that the

---

420 See Allan R. Brewer-Carías, *Golpe de estado y proceso constituyente en Venezuela*, Universidad Nacional Autónoma de México, Mexico City 2003, pp. 179 ff.

421 See, e.g., Allan R. Brewer-Carías, *La Sala Constitucional versus el estado democrático de derecho. El secuestro del poder electoral y de la Sala Electoral del Tribunal Supremo y la confiscación del derecho a la participación política*, Los Libros de El Nacional, Colección Ares, Caracas 2004; "La progresiva y sistemática demolición institucional de la autonomía e independencia del poder judicial en Venezuela 1999-2004," in *XXX Jornadas J.M. Domínguez Escovar, Estado de derecho, Administración de justicia y derechos humanos*, Instituto de Estudios Jurídicos del Estado Lara, Barquisimeto 2005, pp. 33-174.

National Assembly can dismiss the heads of other branches makes futile the formal consecration of the autonomy and independence of powers, because the officials of the state are aware that they can be removed from office at any time, and especially if they act independently.[422]

Unfortunately, this has happened in Venezuela during the past decade. When there have been minimal signs of autonomy from some officials in state institutions who have dared to adopt their own decisions that distance them from the executive will, they have been dismissed. This occurred, for instance, in 2001 with the people's defender and the prosecutor general, originally appointed in 1999 by the Constituent Assembly, who were dismissed for failing to follow the dictates of the executive power.[423] This also happened with some judges of the Supreme Tribunal who dared to issue decisions questioning the executive action; they were immediately subjected to investigation, and some were removed or "retired" from their positions.[424]

The consequence of this factual "dependency" of state organs on the National Assembly has been the total absence of fiscal or audit control in all state entities. The Comptroller General Office has ignored the results of the massive, undisciplined expenditure of oil–wealth public income, not always in accordance with budgetary discipline rules, which has provoked the classification of Venezuela among the lowest ranks on government transparency in the world.[425] Nonetheless, the most important decisions of the comptroller general have been those directed at disqualifying many opposition candidates from the November 2008 regional and municipal elections, on the basis of "administrative irregularities," although the Constitution establishes that the right to run for office can be suspended only when a judicial criminal decision has been adopted (Articles 39 and 42).[426] Unfortunately, the Cons-

---

422   See "Democracia y control del poder," in Allan R. Brewer-Carías, *Constitución, democracia y control de poder*, Centro Iberoamericano de Estudios Provinciales y Locales, Universidad de Los Andes, Mérida 2004.

423   The prosecutor general, appointed in Dec. 1999, thought he could initiate criminal impeachment proceedings against the then-minister of the interior; and the people's defender also thought she could challenge the special law of the 2001 National Assembly on appointment of judges to the Supreme Tribunal without complying with constitutional requirements. They were both dismissed in 2001.

424   Franklin Arrieche, vice president of the Supreme Tribunal of Justice, delivered the decision of the Supreme Tribunal of Aug. 14, 2002, regarding the criminal process against the generals who acted on Apr. 12, 2002, declaring that there were no grounds on which to judge them given that, on that occasion, no military coup took place. The case of Alberto Martini Urdaneta, president of the Electoral Court, and Rafael Hernandez and Orlando Gravina, judges of the same court who undersigned Decision N° 24 (Mar. 15, 2004) (Case: *Julio Borges, César Pérez Vivas, Henry Ramos Allup, Jorge Sucre Castillo, Ramón José Medina y Gerardo Blyde vs. the National Electoral Council*), suspended the effects of Resolution N° 040302-131 (Mar. 2, 2004) of the National Electoral Council, which in that moment stopped the presidential-recall referendum.

425   See http://www.transparencia.org.ve.

426   In Oct. 2008, the European Parliament approved a resolution asking the Venezuelan government to end those practices (political incapacitation to make difficult the presence of opposition leaders in regional and local elections) and to promote a more global democracy with complete respect of the principles established in the 1999 Constitution. See http://venezuelanoticia.com/ archives/8298.

titutional Chamber of the Supreme Tribunal instead of declaring the unconstitutionality of such administrative decisions has upheld them, defrauding the Constitution.[427]

The people's defender has been perceived more as a defender of state powers
than of the peoples' rights, even if the Venezuelan state never before has been denounced so many times as in the past years before the Inter-American Commission
on Human Rights. Finally, the public prosecutor has been characterized as using its
powers to prosecute by using the controlled judiciary indiscriminately to persecute
any political dissidence.

The effects of this dependency, of course, have been catastrophic regarding the
judicial power, in which the Constituent Assembly intervened in 1999 by creating a
special commission for such purpose that in 2010 continues to exist, with the unfortunate consent and complicity of the Supreme Tribunal of Justice itself. This has
allowed for the judiciary reorganization commission, which has been legitimated, to
cohabit with it, with disciplinary powers contrary to those established in the Constitution. In addition, the National Assembly has taken over political control of the
magistrates of the Supreme Tribunal, who have the always-convenient warning that
they can be investigated or removed, even by absolute majority vote, as has been
unconstitutionally established in the 2004 Organic Law of the Supreme Court of
Justice.[428]

2.   *The Political Supremacy of the Executive and the Absence of Checks and
     Balances*

If the supremacy of the National Assembly over the judicial, citizen, and electoral powers is the most outstanding sign of the concentration of powers in the 1999
Constitution, the distortion of the separation of powers it declares also derives from
the supremacy that from a political partisan point of view, the executive power has
developed over the National Assembly.

In the 1999 Constitution, the presidential system was aggravated because of,
among other factors, the extension to six years of the presidential term and provisions for the immediate reelection of the president (Article 203), contrary to the previous tradition of no reelection, which violates the principle of alternating government. This provision allowed for a possible administration term of up to twelve years, particularly because of the complexity of the government recall referendum
(Article 72), which makes any referenda of that sort practically inapplicable. Nonet-

---

427   Teodoro Petkoff has pointed out that with this decision, "the authoritarian and autocratic government of
      Hugo Chávez has clearly shown its true colors in this episode," explaining, "The political right to run
      for office is only lost when a candidate has receive a judicial sentence that has been upheld in a higher
      court. The recent sentence by the Venezuelan Supreme Court, upholding the disqualifications, as well as
      the constitutionality of Article 105 [of the Organic Law of the Comptroller General Office], constitute a
      Constitution defrauding, and the way in which the decision was handed down was an obvious accom-
      modation to the president's desire to eliminate four significant opposition candidates from the electoral
      field." See Teodoro Petkoff, "Election and Political Power: Challenges for the Opposition," *ReVista:
      Harvard Review of Latin America*, David Rockefeller Center for Latin American Studies, Harvard Uni-
      versity, Cambridge, MA 2008, p. 11.

428   In the reform to the Organic Law of the Supreme Tribunal of Justice approved in 2010, this possibility
      was eliminated.

heless, in 2009, the provisions were radically changed through a constitutional amendment establishing continuous reelection for all public elected officials.

Another constitutional provision reinforcing the presidential system is the establishment of the possibility of an unlimited legislative delegation to the president by means of enabling laws, which authorize the president to issue decree laws on any matters, not only on economic and financial matters as established in the 1961 Constitution (Article 203). This constitutes an assault on the constitutional guarantee of the "legal reserve" (legislation that is always reserved to an elected representative body), particularly regarding the regulation of constitutional rights. The truth is that the fundamental legislation that has been sanctioned during the past decade (2002–9) is contained in these decree laws has been sanctioned without respect for the constitutionally imposed public hearing (Article 211).

In effect, the legislative power that can be delegated to the president has as one of its fundamental limits imposed by the Constitution the ensuring of political participation in the drafting of said legislation, which is not only a fundamental value of the constitutional text but also one of the most relevant constitutional rights foreseen in it. The Constitution established the right "of the people to participate in the formation, execution and control of the public policies," having the state, as one of its obligations, to "enable the generation of the most favorable conditions for its practice" (Article 62). Also, the Constitution ensures the right to participate in political matters, among other means, through "popular consult" (Article 70).

To define that constitutional right, the Constitution specifically obligates the National Assembly to submit draft legislation to public hearings, as follows. First, with a general character, Article 211 requires the National Assembly and permanent commissions to submit to public consultation during the approval proceedings of draft laws and to listen to the opinion of the organs of the state, the citizens, and civil society. Second, Article 206 requires the National Assembly to consult the states' legislative councils when legislating on matters related to them. In this way, the Constitution ensures the exercise of political participation in the management of public matters and in the formation of laws.

Of course, the president also must comply with the constitutional obligation to submit draft laws to public consultation when legislative delegation takes place. Any delegation transfers powers as well as duties – among them is the constitutional obligation to submit draft decrees to public consultation, in execution of the enabling law. That is, independently of the organ sanctioning the legislation (National Assembly or president in virtue of legislative authorization), submission to public consultation is a compulsory part of the constitutional procedure for drafting statutes. Nonetheless, in 2001 and 2007, the president, after requesting and obtaining the sanction of enabling laws with broad content to enact legislation on many important matters, issued dozens of decree laws without any transparency, without informing the nation as to the draft laws, without debating them, and without required public consultation (Articles 206 and 211).

In this way, in evident constitutional fraud, the National Assembly transferred to the president the authority to legislate on matters of national interest, even if parties in support of the president completely controlled the assembly; as such, he would not find opposition of any kind on legislation that affected other branches of government, particularly the judicial, citizens, and electoral branches, as well as the territorial distribution of state powers.

With all these provisions undermining the separation of powers, Venezuela, whose Constitution is filled with contradictions (e.g., a centralized federation without a senate; legislative power and unlimited legislative delegation; and five-branched state powers with unusual concentration in the representative political organ), has constitutionalized the road to authoritarianism. Thus, democracy and even less the rule of law can hardly be effective in this constitutional framework.

3.   *Continuous Interference and Subjection of the Judicial Power*

In Venezuela, after the National Assembly's unconstitutional intervention in the judicial power,[429] and despite the sanctioning of the 1999 Constitution, no effective independence and autonomy of the judicial branch has been ensured. On the contrary, there is a permanent and systematic process of demolishing independence and autonomy through submission to the political control of the president.[430]

In effect, according to the 1999 Constitution provision that eliminated the old Judicature Council, which since 1961 had administered the judiciary, the Supreme Tribunal has assumed the governance and management of the judiciary, controlling all the judicial system, particularly the appointment and removal of judges. The judges' instability, authorized and promoted by the same Supreme Tribunal, and their provisional appointment without the required public competition, is a main component of the Venezuelan courts' political subjection.

One of the basic principles concerning independence of the judiciary is stability of the judges,[431] considered by the Inter-American Court of Human Rights to be congruent with "the special nature and functions of the courts, because it guarantees the independence of the judges regarding all other branches of government and regarding the political-electoral changes."[432] Such stability is formally ensured in the 1999 Constitution by, first, the provision imposing the need for judges to be selected by public competition; and, second, the provision that to be removed, judges must be subjected to disciplinary trials carried out by disciplinary judges. Unfortunately,

---

429   See our reserved vote to the intervention of the judicial power by the Constituent Assembly in Allan R. Brewer-Carías, *Debate constituyente (Aportes a la Asamblea Nacional Constituyente)*, Fundación de Derecho Público–Editorial Jurídica Venezolana, Caracas 1999, 1 (Aug. 8–Sept. 8): 57-73. On the critiques of the process, see Allan R. Brewer-Carías, *Golpe de estado y proceso constituyente en Venezuela*, Universidad Nacional Autónoma de México, Mexico City 2002, pp. 213ff.

430   See Allan R. Brewer-Carías, "La progresiva y sistemática demolición de la autonomía e independencia del Poder Judicial en Venezuela (1999-2004)," in *XXX Jornadas J.M. Domínguez Escovar, Estado de derecho, Administración de justicia y derechos humanos*, Instituto de Estudios Jurídicos del Estado Lara, Barquisimeto 2005, pp. 33-174.

431   Basic Principles concerning the Independence of the Judicature adopted by the Seventh Congress of United Nations in Milan, Aug. 26–Sept. 6, 1985, confirmed by the General Assembly in its Resolutions 40/32 of Nov. 1985 and 40/146 of Dec. 1985.

432   Inter-American Court on Human Rights, *Carranza vs. Argentina*; Case 10.087. Report N° 30/97, Dec. 30, 1997, para. 41.

none of these provisions has been implemented, and with the complicity of the Supreme Tribunal, those provisions are dead letters.[433]

As a consequence, since 1999, the Venezuelan judiciary has been filled with provisional judges, a situation that since the 2003 Inter-American Commission on Human Rights has repeatedly noticed,[434] considering that provisional judges are susceptible to the political manipulation,[435] which alters the people's right to adequate administration of justice.[436] Since 2000, the Commission has also expressed worries that "the problem of the provisional status of the judges had deepened and increased since the current Government began a judicial re-organization process,"[437] a statement that has been repeated in all its subsequent annual reports on the human rights situation in Venezuela. The result has been, as mentioned by the Commission in its 2006 report filed before the General Assembly of the Organization of American States, the failure to guarantee judicial independence in Venezuela, where there are cases of dismissals and substitutions in retaliation for decisions contrary to the government's position.[438] Finally, in its 2008 report, the Commission verified the provisional character of the judiciary as an "endemic problem" because the appointment of judges was made without applying constitutional provisions on the matter[439] – thus exposing judges to discretionary dismissal – which highlights the "permanent state of urgency" in which those appointments have been made.[440] In its 2009 Annual Report, the same Inter-American Commission noted "with concern that in some cases, judges were removed almost immediately after adopting judicial decisions in cases with a major political impact," concluding by saying that "The lack of judicial independence and autonomy vis-à-vis political power is, in the IACHR's opinion, one of the weakest points in Venezuelan democracy."[441]

What has happened in Venezuela with intervention in the judiciary, as stated by the Constitutional Chamber of the Supreme Tribunal after deciding that the rulings

---

433   The Inter-American Commission on Human Rights, in its *2009 Annual Report*, reiterated "with concern the failure to organize public competitions for selecting judges and prosecutors, and so those judicial officials are still appointed in a discretionary fashion without being subject to competition. Since they are not appointed through public competitions, judges and prosecutors are freely appointed and removable, which seriously affects their independence in making decisions. The IACHR also observes that through the Special Program for the Regularization of Tenured Status, judges originally appointed on a provisional basis have been given tenured status, all without participating in a public competitive process," para. 479. Available at http://www.cidh.oas.org/annualrep/ 2009eng/Chap.IV.f.eng.htm.

434   *Informe sobre la situación de los derechos humanos en Venezuela*; OAS/Ser.L/V/II.118. d.C. 4 rev. 2; Dec. 29, 2003, para. 11.3. It reads: "The Commission has been informed that only 250 judges have been appointed by opposition concurrence according to the constitutional text. From a total of 1,772 positions of judges in Venezuela, the Supreme Court of Justice reports that only 183 are holders, 1,331 are provisional and 258 are temporary."

435   *Id.*, paras. 11-12.

436   *Id.*

437   *Id.*, para. 31.

438   *Id.*, paras. 295 ff.

439   *Annual Report 2008* (OEA/Ser.L/V/II.134. Doc. 5 rev. 1. 25 febrero 2009), para. 39

440   *Id.*

441   See this conclusión of the Commission in ICHR, *Annual Report 2009*, para. 483. Available at http://www.cidh.oas.org/annualrep/2009eng/Chap.IV.f.eng.htm.

of the Inter-American Court of Human Rights were not enforceable in the country, has been a process of "cleansing [*depuración*] of the Judiciary."[442]

As described earlier, the constitutional principles tending to ensure autonomy and independence of judges at all levels of the judiciary are yet to be applied, particularly regarding the appointment of candidates through public competition, with citizen participation in their selection and appointment, and regarding the prohibition on removing or suspending judges except through disciplinary trials before a disciplinary court and judges (Articles 254 and 267). Unfortunately, none of these provisions has been implemented; therefore, since 1999, the Venezuelan judiciary has been composed by temporal and provisional judges that are subjected to the political manipulation, with the possibility for their discretionary dismissal without due process of law for political reasons.[443]

The worst of this irregular situation is that in 2006, there were attempts to solve the problem of the provisional status of judges by means of the Special Program for the Regularization of Tenures, addressed at accidental, temporary, or provisional judges, bypassing the entrance system constitutionally established by means of public competitive exams (Article 255) and consolidating the effects of the provisional appointments and their consequent power dependency.

Disciplinary jurisdiction of judges has not yet been established, and with the authorization of the Supreme Tribunal, the "transitional" Reorganization Commission of the Judicial Power created in 1999 has continued to function, removing judges without due process.[444]

This reality amounts to political control of the judiciary, as demonstrated by the dismissal of judges who have adopted decisions contrary to the policies of the governing political authorities. An example can illustrate this point. When a contentious administrative court ruled against the government in a politically charged case, the government responded by intervening in the court and dismissing its judges. After the Inter-American Court of Human Rights ruled that the dismissal violated the American Convention on Human Rights and Venezuela's international obligations, the Constitutional Chamber upheld the government's argument that the decision of the Inter-American Court cannot be enforced in Venezuela.

The case developed as follows: On July 17, 2003, the Venezuelan National Federation of Doctors brought an *amparo* action in the First Court on Contentious Admi-

---

442 Decision N° 1.939 (Dec. 18, 2008) (Case: *Abogados Gustavo Álvarez Arias y otros*), in which the Constitutonal Chamber decided the nonenforceability of the decision of the Inter American Court of Human Rights of Aug. 5, 2008 (Case: *Apitz Barbera y otros ["Corte Primera de lo Contencioso Administrativo"] vs. Venezuela [Corte IDH]*, Case: *Apitz Barbera y otros ["Corte Primera de lo Contencioso Administrativo"] vs. Venezuela*, Sentencia de 5 de agosto de 2008, Serie C, N° 182.

443 This was reported by the Inter-American Commission on Human Rights in 2003; see *Report on the Situation of Human Rights in Venezuela*, OEA/Ser.L/V/II.118, doc. 4, rev. 2, Dec. 29, 2003, para. 174. Acailable at http://www.cidh.oas.org/country-rep/Venezuela2003eng/toc.htm.: and also in its *2009 Annual Report*, para. 479; at http://www.cidh.oas.org/annualrep/2009eng/Chap.IV.f.eng.htm.

444 See Allan R. Brewer-Carías, "La justicia sometida al poder y la interminable emergencia del poder judicial (1999-2006)," *in Derecho y democracia. Cuadernos universitarios* 2, Órgano de Divulgación Académica, Vicerrectorado Académico, Universidad Metropolitana, Caracas 2007, 122-38.

nistrative Matters in Caracas,[445] against the mayor of Caracas, the Ministry of Health, and the Caracas Metropolitan Board of Doctors (Colegio de Médicos). The petitioners asked for a declaration of the nullity of certain measures of the defendant officials, who had hired Cuban doctors for a much-publicized government health program in the Caracas slums but without complying with the legal requirements for foreign doctors to practice medicine in Venezuela. The National Federation of Doctors argued that by allowing foreign doctors to practice medicine without complying with applicable regulations, the program was discriminatory and violated the constitutional rights of Venezuelan doctors.[446] One month later, on August 21, 2003, the court issued a preliminary protective *amparo* measure, on the grounds that there were sufficient elements to consider that the constitutional guarantee of equality before the law was being violated. The court preliminarily ordered the suspension of the Cuban doctors' hiring program and ordered the Metropolitan Board of Doctors to replace the Cuban doctors already hired with Venezuelan or foreign doctors who had fulfilled the legal requirements to practice medicine.[447]

In response to that preliminary *amparo* decision, the minister of health, the mayor of Caracas, and President Chávez made public statements to the effect that the decision would not be respected or enforced.[448] Following those statements, the government-controlled Constitutional Chamber of the Supreme Tribunal of Justice adopted a decision, without any appeal filed, assuming jurisdiction over the case and annulling the preliminary *amparo* ordered by the first court; a group of officials of the Ministry of the Interior Intelligence Services seized the first court's premises; and the president publicly called the president of the first court a "bandit," among other things.[449] A few weeks later, in response to the court's decision in an unrelated case challenging a local registrar's refusal to record a land sale, the unconstitutional Special Commission for the Intervention of the Judiciary dismissed all five judges of the first court.[450] Despite nationwide protests from bar associations and the International Commission of Jurists,[451] the first court remained suspended and its premises

---

445 Contentious administrative courts have competence to review administrative decisions.

446 See Claudia Nikken, "El caso 'Barrio Adentro': La Corte Primera de lo Contencioso Administrativo ante la Sala Constitucional del Tribunal Supremo de Justicia o el avocamiento como medio de amparo de derechos e intereses colectivos y difusos," *Revista de Derecho Público* 93–96, Editorial Jurídica Venezolana, Caracas 2003, pp. 5ff.

447 See Decision of Aug. 21, 2003, in id., 445ff.

448 The president said: "Váyanse con su decisión no sé para donde, la cumplirán ustedes en su casa si quieren" (You can all go with your decision to I don't know where; you will enforce it in your house if you want). See *El Universal*, Caracas Aug. 25, 2003; *El Universal*, Caracas Aug. 28, 2003.

449 See Inter-American Court of Human Rights, *Apitz Barbera et al. (Corte Primera de lo Contencioso Administrativo) vs. Venezuela* (Decision of Aug. 5, 2008), available at http://www.corteidh.or.cr, para. 239. See also *El Universal*, Caracas Oct. 16, 2003; *El Universal*, Caracas Sept. 22, 2003.

450 See *El Nacional*, Caracas Nov. 5, 2003, A2. The dismissed president of the first court said: "La justicia venezolana vive un momento tenebroso, pues el tribunal que constituye un último resquicio de esperanza ha sido clausurado." (The Venezuelan judiciary is living a dark moment, because the court that was a last glimmer of hope has been shut down."). id. The Commission for the Intervention of the Judiciary had also dismissed almost all judges in the country without due process and had replaced them with provisionally appointed judges beholden to the ruling power.

451 See *El Nacional*, Caracas Oct. 10, 2003, A-6; *El Nacional*, Caracas Oct. 15, 2003, p. A-2; *El Nacional*, Caracas Sept. 24, 2003, p. A-4; *El Nacional*, Caracas Feb. 14, 2004, p. A-7.

closed for about nine months,[452] during which no judicial review of administrative action could be sought in the country.[453]

The dismissed judges of the first court brought a complaint to the Inter-American Commission on Human Rights for their unlawful removal by the government and for violations of their constitutional rights. The Commission, in turn, brought the case, *Apitz Barbera et al. (Corte Primera de lo Contencioso Administrativo vs. Venezuela)* before the Inter-American Court of Human Rights. On August 5, 2008, the Inter-American Court ruled that the Republic of Venezuela had violated the rights of the dismissed judges established in the American Convention on Human Rights and ordered the state to pay them due compensation, to reinstate them to a similar position in the judiciary, and to publish part of the decision in Venezuelan newspapers.[454] Nonetheless, on December 12, 2008, the Constitutional Chamber issued Decision N° 1.939, declaring that the August 5, 2008, decision of the Inter-American Court of Human Rights was unenforceable (*inejecutable*) in Venezuela. The Constitutional Chamber also accused the Inter-American Court of having usurped powers of the Supreme Tribunal of Justice, and it asked the executive branch to denounce the American Convention on Human Rights.[455]

The case just discussed, including in particular the ad hoc response of the Constitutional Chamber to the decision of the Inter-American Court of Human Rights, shows clearly the present subordination of the Venezuelan judiciary to the policies, wishes, and dictates of the president. The Constitutional Chamber has become a most effective tool for consolidating power in the person of President Chávez.

III. CENTRALIZING POWER AND THE ABSENCE OF EFFECTIVE POLITICAL PARTICIPATION

The authoritarian government that has taken root in Venezuela over the past decade has been possible thanks to the constitutionalization of elements contributing to the concentrated power of the state and to the reinforcement of the traditional centralized federation and the distortion of the exercise of democracy and popular participation – covered over by a false populist speech that pretends to replace representative democracy with participatory democracy and that has lead to the progressive dismantling of democracy.

---

452   See *El Nacional*, Caracas Oct. 24, 2003, p. A-2; *El Nacional*, Caracas July 16, 2004, p. A-6.

453   See, generally, Allan R. Brewer-Carías, "La progresiva y sistemática demolición institucional de la autonomía e independencia del poder judicial en Venezuela 1999–2004," in *XXX Jornadas J.M. Domínguez Escovar, Estado de derecho, Administración de justicia y derechos humanos*, Instituto de Estudios Jurídicos del Estado Lara, Barquisimeto 2005, pp. 33-174; Allan R. Brewer-Carías, "La justicia sometida al poder (La ausencia de independencia y autonomía de los jueces en Venezuela por la interminable emergencia del poder judicial [1999-2006])," in *Cuestiones internacionales. Anuario Jurídico Villanueva 2007*, Centro Universitario Villanueva, Marcial Pons, Madrid 2007, pp. 25-57, available at http://www.allanbrewercarias.com (N° 550, 2007).

454   Inter-American Court of Human Rights, *Apitz Barbera et al. (Corte Primera de lo Contencioso Administrativo) vs. Venezuela* (Decision of Aug. 5, 2008), available at http://www.corteidh.or.cr.

455   Supreme Tribunal of Justice, Constitutional Chamber, Decision N° 1.939 (Dec. 18, 2008) (Case: *Abogados Gustavo Álvarez Arias et al.*) (Exp. N° 08-1572).

1. *The Meaning of Democracy and the Illusion of Participatory Democracy*

Political participation – that is, the possibility for citizens to participate in political decision making – is possible only when power is available to the people in a decentralized power system based on the multiplication of self-governed local authorities.[456] On the contrary, in a centralized federation like the one reinforced in the 1999 Constitution, political participation turns into a rhetorical illusion, and the political system becomes an easy instrument of authoritarianism.[457]

For this reason, also on occasion of the referendum on the 1999 Constitution, I warned:

> The great reform of the political system necessary and essential to perfect democracy, was to dismantle the State centralism and to distribute the Public Power in the territory; the only way to make political participation a reality. The Constituent Assembly, in order to overcome the political crisis, had to design the transformation of the State, decentralizing power and setting the basis to make it more available to people. By not doing it, it neither transformed the State nor did it dispose of the necessary elements to make participation more effective.[458]

However, despite the centralized framework of state power clearly expressed in the Constitution, the word *participation* is used on multiple occasions. Moreover, it proclaims so-called participatory democracy as a global value but without allowing effective political participation of the people in public affairs through autonomous and decentralized political local entities. Thus, participation remains no more than the exercise of the right to vote in several mechanisms of direct democracy, like referenda, citizens' assemblies, and the communal councils. These, however, have no political autonomy; they are instruments established parallel to municipalities, conducted in a centralized way by a minister of the executive.

In fact, in authoritarian speech related to participatory democracy, expertly used as a response to the political failures of many representative democracies dominated by political parties, the term *participatory democracy* sometimes is confused with elements of direct democracy. It mainly is used as part of a misleading strategy to attack representative democracy as a political regime, aggravated by the popular distrust developed regarding the political parties and the state institutions, which are far too distant from citizens.

---

456 See proposals for the reinforcement of the decentralization of the federation and the dismantling of its centralization in Allan R. Brewer-Carías, *Debate constituyente (Aportes a la Asamblea Nacional Constituyente)*, Fundación de Derecho Público–Editorial Jurídica Venezolana, Caracas 1999, 1 (Aug. 8–Sept. 8): pp. 155ff.

457 See the studies "La opción entre democracia y autoritarismo (Julio 2001)," 41-59; "Democracia, descentralización política y reforma del Estado (Julio-Octubre 2001), 105-25; "El municipio, la descentralización política y la democracia (Octubre 2001), 127-41, in Allan R. Brewer-Carías, *Reflexiones sobre el constitucionalismo en América*, Editorial Jurídica Venezolana, Caracas 2001.

458 Document dated Nov. 30, 1999. See Allan R. Brewer-Carías, *Debate constituyente (Aporte a la Asamblea Nacional Constituyente)*, Fundación de Derecho Público–Editorial Jurídica Venezolana, Caracas 1999, 3 (Oct. 18–Nov. 30):p. 323.

The confusion produced by the clamor of participation in many Latin American countries, which is by essence contrary to authoritarianism, forces a reestablishing of the true concept of democracy to situate political participation where it belongs, precisely in the local ambit of political decentralization. Without a doubt, the two fundamental principles of democracy in the contemporary world continue to be representation and participation. Representation can be confronted with direct democracy; thus, the dichotomy in this case is between representative (or indirect) democracy and direct democracy.

Participation cannot be confronted with representation but rather with political exclusion, so the dichotomy in this case is between participatory democracy (democracy of inclusion) and exclusionary democracy (democracy of exclusion). This is precisely what is not clear in speeches on participatory democracy: In certain cases, it is used to refer to mechanisms of direct democracy; in others, the concepts are deliberately confused to eliminate or minimize representation and establish an alleged direct relation between a leader, generally a messianic one, and the people. In the case of Venezuela, this means nonelected institutional entities disposed to make the people believe that they are participating when in fact they are only being mobilized and submitted to control by centralized power.

Representative democracy will continue to be the essence of democracy.[459] Its substitution is essentially impossible in democracy, without detriment that it could be perfected, for instance, with the introduction of mechanisms of direct democracy in the political systems, like those included in the 1993 Organic Law on Suffrage and Political participation and in the 1999 Constitution, that complement it but will never replace it.

In the contemporary world, there can never be only direct democracy, based on plebiscites, referenda, or permanent open municipal or town hall councils. But this does not impede the fact that all contemporary constitutional systems have incorporated popular consultation mechanisms and citizens' assemblies to complement representation. In that sense, as in the case of the 1999 Venezuelan Constitution, all imaginable types of referenda have been regulated: consulting, approving, deciding, abrogating, authorizing, and recalling – as well as popular initiatives. Without doubt, this has contributed to popular mobilization and to the relative direct manifestation of the will of the people. But it is clear that those mechanisms cannot replace democracy driven by elected representatives. The challenge here, to contribute to the consolidation of the democratic rule of law, is to ensure that representatives truly regard the communities they represent and that they be elected by direct, universal, and secret–ballot systems, where political pluralism prevails, and by means of transparent electoral processes ensuring access to power with submission to the rule of law.

Without doubt, though, the second basic principle of democracy has more contemporary interest. Political participation, it has been said, is not more than a demo-

---

459   See the proposal on the regulation of the participatory and representative democratic principle in the 1999 Constitution in Allan R. Brewer-Carías, *Debate constituyente (Aportes a la Asamblea Nacional Constituyente)*, Fundación de Derecho Público–Editorial Jurídica Venezolana, Caracas 1999, Vol. 1 (Aug. 8–Sept. 8): pp. 183 ff.

cratic regime of political inclusion, where the citizen is part of its politically autonomous organized community and contributes to decision-making processes. To participate means to be included; for that reason, the opposite of political participation is political exclusion, which also can be of social and economic character. Unfortunately, however, in the democratic political doctrine, too often the concepts have been confused, and participatory democracy is often confused and reduced to mechanisms of direct democracy. But participatory democracy is much more than that.

To participate, in fact, in common language, is to be part of, to belong, to be incorporated, to contribute, to be associated or committed to; it is to have a role in, to have an active part in, to be involved in, or to lend a hand to; it is to be related, to share, or to have something to do with. Participation, then, in the political language, means nothing more than to be part of a political community, which, in essence, must have self-government with political autonomy in which individuals have a specific, active role according to which they contribute to decision making. This, consequently, cannot be exhausted by the sole exercise of the right to vote (which is undoubtedly a minimal form of participation); by being a member of intermediate societies, even those of political character, as political parties; by voting in referenda (another minimal form of participation); or by being part of citizens' assemblies controlled by the central power.[460]

Democratic political participation means, in reality, to be included in the political process and to be an active part of it, without interventions; it means, then, the ability to access the decision-making process in public matters to be decided by autonomous entities. This cannot be permanently accomplished in any democratic society solely with ballots in referenda or popular consultation. Nor is it accomplished with manifestations, even though they are multitudinous, and even less with those manifestations that are obedient and submissive to a leader. History, including the fascist authoritarianism of the previous century, has taken care to teach us this in all of its aspects; it should not be confused with political participation.

For democracy to be inclusive or of inclusion, it must allow citizens to be an effective part of political communities that, above all, are autonomous; it must allow them to develop their effective pertinence, that is, the sense of belonging in the political and social order, such as to a community, a place, a land, a field, a district, a town, a region, a city – in short, to a state – and to be elected for that purpose as a representative of the people.

Because of this, participatory democracy is not something new in political history. It has always been there, even since the revolutions of the nineteenth century, in the democratic political theories and practices. In all countries with a consolidated democracy, it exists imperceptibly, deeply rooted in the lowest level of the territories of the states, in the autonomous political entities, like municipalities or communes – in the base of the territorial distribution of power.

---

460   See Allan R. Brewer-Carías, "Democracia municipal, descentralización y desarrollo local" (Conferencia Inaugural del XXVI Congreso Iberoamericano de Municipios, Organización Iberoamericana de Cooperación Intermunicipal, Ayuntamiento de Valladolid; Valladolid, Oct. 13–15, 2004), *Revista Iberoamericana de Administración Pública* No. 11, INAP, Madrid 2003, pp. 11-34.

The great issue of political participation in democracies lacking participation is to determine where and how one can really participate. The answer points to the entities that result from the political decentralization of power and that are, above all, self-governed. Consequently, without replacing the vote and the instruments of direct democracy, political participation as democracy of inclusion, in which citizens can personally be part of a decision-making process regarding public activities of general interest, can exist only in the most politically reduced, decentralized, and autonomous territorial bodies – that is, at the local, community, or municipal level. Only in the lowest autonomous levels of self-government can a participatory organization be structured and allow incorporation of individual citizens, groups, or communities into the public life, particularly in the general public decision-making process or in administrative matters.

Thus, the central issue to be solved when talking properly about participatory democracy is that of determining the territorial level required for participation to be effective as a democratic routine. The classic answer is the municipality, as a self-governing political entity scattered throughout all parts of a state, in every village, town, and county, located very close to the citizen – not great urban or rural municipalities located far from the citizens.

Finally, in all of the democratically developed countries prevails many municipalities, and among them, small municipalities.[461] In contrast, in Latin America, municipalities are extremely distant from citizens.[462] In Europe and Latin America, municipalities were tributaries of the same basic principles derived from the French Revolution. The great difference is that since the beginning of the nineteenth century in Europe, municipalities were located in every borough, town, village, and city, very close to the citizen. In Latin America, municipalities that had their roots in colonialism have continued to have that same position after independence as metropolitan town councils, very far from citizens.

In Europe, and also in the United States, political participation is a daily life matter that many times passes by imperceptibly. In the second case, there is no participation of any kind because the territorial ambit is so distant from citizens that municipalities are useless in properly managing local interests or allowing for real political participation of the people in the management of their own communal affairs.

Therefore, participatory democracy is possible only when it is indissolubly linked not to direct democracy mechanisms, like referenda, popular consultation, popular

---

461 For instance, in approximate numbers: 2,350 municipalities in Austria, with an average population of 3,400; 589 municipalities in Belgium, with an average population of 17,000; 36,550 municipalities in France, with an average population of 1,600; 16,120 municipalities in Germany, with an average population of 5,000; 7,100 municipalities in Italy with an average population of 7,100; 8,050 municipalities in Spain, with an average population of 4,800; or 75,500 municipalities in the Unites States, with an average population of 3,880. See references in Allan R. Brewer-Carías, *Reflexiones sobre el constitucionalismo en América*, Editorial Jurídica Venezolana, Caracas 2001, pp. 139-41.

462 For instance, in approximate numbers: 1,617 municipalities in Argentina, with an average population of 22,000; 5,580 municipalities in Brazil, with an average population of 30,000; 1,068 municipalities in Colombia, with an average population of 39,000; 2,418 municipalities in México with an average population of 40,116; 1,800 municipalities in Peru, with an average population of 13,800; or 338 municipalities in Venezuela, with an average population of 71,006, in id.

initiatives, and citizens' assemblies, but rather to political decentralization, establishing local governments at the lowest level of the territory (municipalities). That is, participatory democracy cannot be mistaken for direct democracy, as often occurs when introducing means to perfect democracy.[463]

Political participation as a democratic routine or way of life can occur only at local levels of government. Consequently, political participation or participatory democracy is eventually related to localism and political decentralization, designed to limit the exercise of political power. That is why there cannot be and have never been decentralized authoritarianisms; the latter is always cemented in centralized government, not effectively allowing political participation. That is, centralized political power is essential to authoritarianism and opposite to democracy because it prevents real participation. The latter can occur only in a system of government where power is politically decentralized and close to citizens. There is no other instance in the state's organization for citizens to participate. The rest is falsehood and deceit, or direct democracy mechanisms. This is why political decentralization is not a noticeable political issue in the developed and consolidated European democracies, where participation is part of daily life in local questions that can be dealt with in small urban and rural municipalities.

Consequently, because political decentralization is the basis for participatory democracy and a means for controlling power, no political participation can exist without political or territorial decentralization, without the existence of a multiplicity of local and regional governments. Centralism, however, is the basis of political exclusion: It concentrates power in those few who are elected and it discredits representative democracy.[464]

Only authoritarianism fears and rejects both political decentralization and political participation. Thus, in Venezuela since 1999, the government has progressively dismantled the work of the 1990s to promote decentralization and, in the name of participatory democracy, has been centralizing all state power, dismantling what was left of the federal form of government – and, with it, representative democracy – but without allowing real and effective political participation.

2.   *The Reaction against the Federation as a Decentralized State*

In Venezuela, the great political transformation that should have taken place during the 1999 constitution-making process to improve democracy,[465] which should

---

463   See, e.g., in Venezuela, the set of studies published in *Participación ciudadana y democracia,* Comisión Presidencial para la Reforma del Estado, Caracas 1998.

464   See Allan R. Brewer-Carías, "El municipio, la descentralización política y la democracia," in *XXV Congreso Iberoamericano de Municipios, Guadalajara, Jalisco, México, Octubre 23-26, 2001,* Fundación Española de Municipios y Provincias, Madrid 2003, pp. 453 ff.

465   See the proposal during the discussion of the draft constitution in Allan R. Brewer-Carías, "Propuesta sobre la forma federal del estado en la nueva Constitución: Nuevo federalismo y nuevo municipalismo," in *Debate constituyente (Aportes a la Asamblea Nacional Constituyente),* Fundación de Derecho Público–Editorial Jurídica Venezolana, Caracas 1999, Vol. 1 (Aug. 8-Sept. 8): pp. 150-70; "El reforzamiento de la forma federal del estado venezolano en la nueva Constitución: Nuevo federalismo y nuevo municipalismo," Report to the International Conference on Federalism in an Era of Globalization, Quebec Oct. 1999, available at http://www.allanbrewercarias.com (N° 734, 1999).

have been its key motivation, was the effective substitution of the centralized federal system that had developed during the twentieth century with an effectively decentralized federation of two territorial levels: states and multiple autonomous municipalities.

In practice, though, decentralization was not achieved, even if Article 4 declares that "the Bolivarian Republic of Venezuela is a decentralized federal State." The fact is that it is so, of course, "in the terms established in this Constitution; which as occurred in the 1961 Constitution, organized a centralized State with just a federal veil, because of the absence of any real vertical distribution of State power.[466] The "decentralized federation" mentioned in Article 4 of the Constitution is no more than void words, with the power of the state organized in an even more centralized way.[467]

In the 1999 Constitution, as it has been said before, there was not much progress regarding the content of the previous 1961 Constitution, except for the provisions incorporated in 1999 partially following the content of some articles of the 1989 Organic Law of Decentralization, Delimitation, and Transfer of Competencies of the Public Power. Nonetheless, there was no progress or transformations to make decentralization of the federation a reality. Rather, there was an institutional backwardness on the matter. The Senate was eliminated and, for the first time in the constitutional history of Venezuela, the unicameral National Assembly was established, with the consequent formalization of a permanent institutional equality between the states (Article 186). Also, the Constitution provides for the possibility of establishing limits to the autonomy of the states (Article 162) and even the municipalities (Article 168) by means of national statutes. This fact denies, first, the idea of political decentralization, and second, of the territorial autonomy of local governments. The Constitution also established a precarious ambit of the state powers, whose exercise, additionally, was subject to the provisions of national legislation; and it centralized taxation, which increased states' financial dependency.

3. The Reaction against Local Governments and the Centralized Communal Councils

For local government (municipalities), the great democratic reform that should have been introduced with the 1999 Constitution was, essentially, to place municipal institutions closer to citizens by extending local governments in the territory, by increasing instead of reducing the number of municipalities. None of this was done;

---

466   See Allan R. Brewer-Carías, "Los problemas de la federación centralizada en Venezuela," *Revista Ius et Praxis* 12, Facultad de Derecho y Ciencias Políticas, Universidad de Lima, Perú 1988, 49-96; "Problemas de la federación centralizada (A propósito de la elección directa de gobernadores)," in *IV Congreso Iberoamericano de Derecho Constitucional*, Universidad Nacional Autónoma de México, Mexico City 1992, pp. 85-131.

467   See Allan R. Brewer-Carías, *Federalismo y municipalismo en la Constitución de 1999 (Alcance de una reforma insuficiente y regresiva)*, Cuadernos de la Cátedra Allan R. Brewer-Carías de Derecho Público 7, Universidad Católica del Táchira–Editorial Jurídica Venezolana, Caracas–San Cristóbal 2001, 187. See also Allan R. Brewer-Carías, "El 'estado federal descentralizado' y la centralización de la federación en Venezuela. Situación y perspectiva de una contradicción constitucional," *Revista de Estudios de la Administración Local (REAL)* No. 292–293, Madrid 2003, pp. 11-43.

no important reform on this matter was introduced. Instead, through the sanctioning of the Organic Law of the Municipal Public Power of 2005,[468] the expansion of local governments was prevented by establishing new limits for their creation. Instead of increasing municipalities or local governments, the Communal Councils Law of 2006, reformed in 2009, established communal councils as nonrepresentative institutions that function without elected members subject to the citizens' assemblies.[469] In June 2010, the National Assembly began the discussion of the new Law of the Communes, conceived as "the socialist local entity, from which the socialist society is to be edified" (Article 5), controlled by the central government. [470]

In effect, given the mechanisms of direct democracy established in the Constitution, like citizens' assemblies with binding decisions (Article 70), the Law on Communal Councils in 2006 established a centralized institutional system, parallel to the local government (municipalities), to replace it and to pretend to be ensuring popular participation. The result was to replace local governments in their constitutional task of being the basic instance for political participation. In the end, what has been established are the basic elements to construct a centralized state, without regional or local elected government, directed from the apex of the national executive through an organization called the "Popular Power," in which the citizens supposedly participate but according to the dictates of the central power diffused by the official party. The president announced this in January 2007, referring to "the revolutionary explosion of the communal power" by means of creating "some sort of regional, local and national Confederation of Communal Councils" to "march towards the conformation of a communal state," thus progressively dismantling the "old middle-class state that is still alive" and raising "the communal state, the socialist state, the Bolivarian state."[471] Two days later, on his second–term Inauguration Day, Chávez added that the objective was "to transit towards the road of a communal city, where no mayor's office or local government [municipal] boards are needed, only the communal power."[472] All these proposals, based on nondemocratic organizations, were incorporated in the constitutional reform draft he submitted to the National Assembly and that eventually was rejected by the people in the referendum of December 2, 2007.

The great difference between this communal entities is that and democratic local governments, is that in the latter, mayors and municipal councils are elected by popular universal and secret vote; on the contrary, in the framework of the so-called communal power, members of the communal councils are supposedly appointed

---

468 See *Gaceta Oficial* N° 38.204, June 8, 2005. The Organic Law was the subject of reform in Nov. 2005; *Gaceta Oficial* N° 38.327, Dec. 2, 2005, and then in Apr. 2006, *Gaceta Oficial* N° 5,806, Extra. Apr. 10, 2006, reprinted by material error in *Gaceta Oficial* N° 38.421, Apr. 21, 2006. See Allan R. Brewer-Carías et al., *Ley Orgánica del Poder Público Municipal*, Editorial Jurídica Venezolana, Caracas 2005.

469 See *Gaceta Oficial* N° 5.806, Extra., Apr. 10, 2006; *Gaceta Oficial* N° 39.335, Dec. 28, 2009.

470 See Eugenio G. Martínez, "Poca independencia tendrán comunas. Poder central debe aprobar todos los proyectos de las comunas," in *El Universal,* Caracas July, 5, 2010. Available at http://politica.eluniversal.com/2010/07/05/pol_art_poca-independencia-t_1961543.shtml

471 Speech of Hugo Chávez, 01-08-2007.

472 Speech of Hugo Chávez, *El Nacional*, Caracas Nov. 1, p. A2.

directly in citizens' assemblies, which the executive controls through ministers of the central government and the official party.

In this centralized system, communal councils do not have any political autonomy, so they are not part of the representative democratic system established in the Constitution. They supposedly result from the functioning of the "community" conceived outside local governments (municipalities), which, according to the Constitution, are the primary political unit in the national organization. Ignoring these provisions, the communal councils have been created as "instances for participation, articulation and integration between the different community organizations, social groups and the people," but without any autonomy –they are not even decentralized entities. The result of this process has been, with the establishment of nonautonomous parallel institutions, a process of dismantling representative democracy.

With the 2006 Law of Communal Councils, councils were established without any type of relation with local governments (municipalities) or any kind of democratic representation. They were initially organized through a pyramidal frame of regional and national presidential commissions that provided funds. In such councils, organized in a centralized way, the "organized people" supposedly "exercise directly the management of public politics and projects directed to respond to the needs and aspirations of the communities in the construction of a society of equality and social justice" (Article 2). In the 2009 reform of the Organic Law of Communal Councils, they also have been established without any sort of self-government or autonomy, and now they completely depend on the president.[473] In addition, in 2010 has been sanctioned the Organic Law on the Federal Council of Government,[474] in which the "organized society" is defined as constituted by "communal councils, communes and others base organizations of the Popular power" (Article 4). According to this new law, the "decentralization" process, bypassing states and municipalities, has been established for the purpose of transferring competencies to the "base organization of the popular power" (Article 2) and to newly created "Motor Districts for Development" (Article 7), in order "to achieve the integral development of the regions and the strengthening of the popular power for the purpose of facilitating the transition toward socialism" (Article 6). Finally, in June 2010, the National Assembly began the discussion of the Law of the Communes.

Within this centralist framework of the organization of popular power, what will ensure participation seems to be nothing less than the United Socialist Party that the head of state presides over himself, imbricate in the state bureaucracy as has never been seen in Venezuela, and that as a governmental political system was demolished in the world with the fall of the Berlin Wall.

---

473 *Gaceta Oficial* N° 39.335 of Dec. 28, 2009. See Allan R. Brewer-Carías, "Introducción general al régimen de los consejos comunales," in *Ley de los Consejos Comunales*, Editorial Jurídica Venezolana, Caracas 2010.

474 See in *Official Gazette* N° 5.963 Extra. of Feb. 22, 2010

IV. THE FORESEEABLE OUTCOME: THE DICTATORSHIP OF DEMOCRACY

For democratic rule of law to exist, the declarations contained in constitutional texts that speak of participatory and protagonist democracy or of the political decentralization of the state are not enough; neither is it enough to establish an elective system that allows the election of public officials through suffrage. The system must effectively ensure representation, political pluralism, and access to public offices according to rule of law and procedures.

Also, for a true democratic rule of law to exist, it is necessary and indispensable that the constitutional framework in which it is intended to function effectively allows for control of state power by power itself, in a checks-and-balances system, including the supreme power of the people. This is the only way to ensure rule of law, democratic principles, and full enjoyment of freedom and human rights.

Control of the state power under democratic rule of law can be achieved only by dividing, separating, and distributing public power, either horizontally among different branches of government or vertically among different territorial levels of government. Concentrations of power and its centralization are essentially antidemocratic state structures.

It is precisely within these principles where lie the problems of the formally declared rule of law in Venezuela – whose deformation rests in the proper constitutional text of 1999. Unfortunately, constitutional provisions encouraging authoritarianism were established, allowing neutralization of any form of power control and the centralization of power, thereby initiating the dismantling of federalism and municipalism. This has led to authoritarianism and, despite the direct democracy mechanisms established, has challenged the possibility of effective political participation. The result is constitutional authoritarianism that, although electoral in origin, negates the democratic rule of law.

On the basis of this framework of constitutional authoritarianism, in January 2007 at the beginning of his second term, President Chávez began to expose the steps to definitively dismantle democracy in Venezuela, by means of configuring a system of total concentration of state power – the popular power or communal power to construct a communal or socialist state) – totally concentrated and centralized, and politically conducted by the United Socialist Party directly connected with the head of state. Thus, both the popular power and the United Socialist Party instate a dictatorship of democracy, led by a single person.

As a result, the president began to refer to his ministries as "Ministries of the Popular Power for (Foreign Relations, Environment, etc.),", and he began to promote a general reform of the Constitution to transform a democratic, rule-of-law state into a centralized, socialist state.

Nonetheless, before drafting the constitutional-reform proposals and defrauding the Constitution, he began to implement some of the reforms by means of decree. He submitted to the National Assembly in January 2007 a draft of an enabling law to be authorized to enact statutes contrary to the Constitution "to update and transform the legal system that regulates State institutions" and to establish "the mechanisms of popular participation, by means of the social control, the social technical inspection and the practice of the voluntary enlistment of the organized community in the ap-

plication of the judicial system and the economical scope of the State; also, to adapt
the organization structure of the State institutions, to allow the direct exercise of the
popular supremacy." All these "constitutional" statutes were to be sanctioned by
means of decrees to advance the path toward constitutional reform and, after its approval, to further consolidate the socialist project.[475] That is, during another precise
process of defrauding the Constitution, the president asked the National Assembly to
enact an enabling law to prepare the way for implementation of a constitutional reform that was not yet approved or even drafted.

The general purpose of those reforms directed at the organization of the popular
power was the elimination of democracy as a plural and representative political regime that allows for election of public officials at all levels by means of the universal, direct, and secret ballot: mayors and councilors in the municipalities, governors
and legislators in the states, and representatives to the National Assembly.

Representative and indirect democracy was due to be substituted by alleged direct, participatory democracy in which there would be no popular election of any kind.
It would be based on citizens' assemblies and communal councils whose members
would not be elected but would be chosen in the community by citizens' assemblies,
of course, with the ideological direction of the United Socialist Party, the only one
with access to the state power organizations at all levels.

In the framework that could be foreseen from the presidential announcements,
the communal councils would appoint representatives to regional communal councils or to those of the federal cities ("regional and local confederation of communal
councils"); and the last step would be to appoint their representatives in the "National Assembly for the Popular Power" ("national confederation of communal councils"), which will eventually replace the National Assembly. In this way, every trace
of direct, universal, secret election of representatives to state and national legislative
organs would disappear. Finally, the National Assembly for the Popular Power, configured as such, would appoint the National Council (of government) for the Popular
Power, which, of course, would be presided over by the same person who would be
president of the Socialist Party.

All these political reforms eliminating representative democracy in the country
began to be implemented a few months before the presidential decrees, during 2006,
with the sanctioning of the Law of Communal Councils (Popular Power), substituted
in 2009 by the Organic Law of the Communal Councils, in a new and evident defrauding coup against the Constitution, establishing a parallel structure for existing

---

475   As it was written in the newspaper on Jan. 31, 2007: "The 18 month length period of force of the ena-
      bling Law, has the object of allowing Hugo Chávez, President of the Republic, to wait for the reform of
      the Constitution to be approved in order to write the norms that will base the socialist model of State he
      wants to instate." According to the opinions of members of parliament, during the first months the law
      decrees written by the Executive will be adapted to the 1999 Magna Charta, and in some of them, the
      omissions of the Legislative Power will be filled. . . . After the popular consult for the approval of the re-
      forms of the Constitution, several representatives have expressed that it could happen in Sept., the presi-
      dent would have time enough to adapt the legislation to the political model he proposes. Thus, represen-
      tatives assume that every legal instrument related to the State system will be announced by the end of
      2007 or the beginning of 2008." *El Nacional*, Caracas Jan. 31, 2007, p. A2.

municipalities, to definitively replace the local self-government framework of municipalities.

It is obvious that once the base structure of the "Popular Power" announced in the 2009 Organic Law of Communal Councils, in the 2010 Organic Law of the Federal Council of Government and in the 2010 Law of the Communes draft, finished to be completed, and provided enormous resources directly managed by the national Executive that are not given to municipalities, the following step that could be taken would be the elimination of the municipalities. In 2007, the president announced his intention to proceed simultaneously with the elimination of the states and any trace of direct election and political decentralization and, therefore, of the real possibility of political participation. What he announced was the elimination of all municipal and regional, representative, and elected bodies.[476] On a state level, only certain federal cities or regional confederations of communal councils would remain, whose leaders, again, would be appointed by the communal councils.

Following this framework of proposed reforms, what was next was the proposal to eliminate the National Assembly as a national representative organ and establish the National Assembly of the Popular Power (national confederation of communal councils) in its place, which would be the summit of the popular power, formed by persons appointed by the federal cities and communal councils; all of these, of course, are duly controlled, from the summit, by the United Socialist Party.

In the 2007 constitutional reforms, the president also referred to a proposal he initially expressed in 2006 on the possibility of his indefinite reelection. In the interim, after popular rejection of such a constitutional reform in 2007, the president managed to have approved in 2009 a constitutional amendment on the matter. Nonetheless, it was obvious that the purpose was to establish reelection in a system based on appointment by the National Confederation of the Popular Power, which would be the National Assembly of the Popular Power. That is, the continuous reelection of the president would be based not on his popular election but rather on his appointment.

These were in general terms the proposals announced to ensure the dictatorship of democracy, not different from the dictatorship of the proletariat that was supposed to be established by the Soviets in the Soviet Union since 1918, or from the popular power in Cuba since 1958, where the Popular Assembly appoints the council of state and, for many decades, always elected the same person to preside.

In conclusion, the main purpose of the reform proposals, many of which have already been implemented, is the complete elimination of representative democracy and its replacement by a supposed direct participatory democracy.

---

476   See the article on the president's statement in Laura Weffer Cifuentes, "Chávez: Empecemos a raspar a alcaldes y gobernadores," in *El Nacional*, Caracas Jan. 29, 2007, p. A2.

CHAPTER 6

THE REINFORCED CENTRALIZATION OF THE FEDERATION

As it is provided in the 1999 Constitution, federalism in Venezuela is a contradictory form of government.[477] Typically, a federation is a politically decentralized state organization based on the existence and functioning of autonomous states. The power of that decentralized state is distributed among the national state and the member states. In contrast, the federation in Venezuela is a centralized federation, which is a contradiction in itself.

Unfortunately, Venezuela is not a good example of the importance of federalism in Latin America because it is a federation based on a very centralized national government, with twenty-three formal autonomous states and one capital district. Each of these twenty-three formal autonomous states is without its own effective public policies and its own substantive subnational constitutions; and if it is true that they have elected authorities, those have been weakened by the central government. Regarding the capital district, against the provisions of the 1999 Constitution, it has been regulated in 2009 by a national law with the same trends as the former federal district; that is, without self-government, dependent of the national executive.[478]

But the federation in the country's history has not always been like it is now. The centralization of the federation occurred progressively during the twentieth century and has been particularly accentuated during the past decade.

Centralization began with the installment of the authoritarian government of the dictator Juan Vicente Gómez, who ruled for approximately three decades in the first half of the twentieth century. During those years, no democratic institutions were developed.

The transition from autocracy to democracy began in Venezuela between 1945 and 1958, when a democratic regime came into power and subsequently developed in accordance with the democratic Constitution of 1961. That Constitution was the longest Constitution in force in all of Venezuelan history (1961–99) and, as a product of the *Pacto de Punto Fijo* (1958), ensured the dominance of a centralized political–party system that due to its democratic centralized structure impeded the reinforcement of federal institutions.

---

477 See, in general, Allan R. Brewer Carías, *Federalismo y municipalismo en la Constitución de 1999 (Una reforma insuficiente y regresiva)*, Editorial Jurídica Venezolana, Caracas 2001; "El estado federal descentralizado y la centralización de la federación en Venezuela. Situación y perspectiva de una contradicción constitucional," *in Federalismo y regionalismo*, coord. Diego Valadés and José María Serna de la Garza, Tribunal Superior de Justicia del Estado de Puebla, Instituto de Investigaciones Jurídicas, Universidad Nacional Autónoma de México, Mexico City 2005, pp. 717-750; and *Constitución, democracia y control del poder*, Universidad de Los Andes, Mérida 2004, pp. 135-38.

478 See the Special Law on the Organization and Regime of the Capital District, *Gaceta Oficial* N° 39.156 of Apr. 13, 2009. See in general the comments in Allan R. Brewer-Carías et al, *Leyes sobre régimen de gobierno del Distrito Capital y del Área Metropolitana de Caracas*, Editorial Jurídica Venezolana, Caracas 2009.

Nonetheless, important efforts were made during the 1990s to politically decentralize the federation,[479] efforts that were later abandoned, mainly because of the crisis of the centralized party system and to the consequential political void in the country. That void was to be resolved with the constitution-making process of 1999, resulting in the approval of the 1999 Constitution of the Bolivarian Republic of Venezuela, which, under a democratic veil, has allowed the development of an authoritarian regime based on a centralized government that concentrates all powers of the state. The Constitution makes excellent declarations, including the definition of the state as a decentralized federal state, which other regulations in the same Constitution contradict and allow conduct to the contrary.

Nonetheless, as I already mentioned, the federation in Venezuela has not always been centralized. During the nineteenth century, notwithstanding the political turmoil of the institution-building process of the national state facing the regional caudillo powers, a federal system of government was established (1864). In it, as in many federations, development of the centrifugal and centripetal political forces took place, thus provoking the classical political pendulum between centralization and decentralization. In general terms, during the nineteenth century, federalism prevailed, particularly because of its historical roots.

I.   HISTORY AND DEVELOPMENT OF THE VENEZUELAN FEDERATION

It is important to bear in mind when studying federalism in Venezuela that the first constitution of an independent Latin American state was sanctioned in Venezuela two centuries ago, the Federal Constitution for the States of Venezuela, by an elected General Congress, on December 21, 1811, at the beginning of the independence wars. The Constitution declared the states or provinces as sovereign states, all of which in 1810–11 had declared independent from Spain and adopted their own provincial constitutions or form of government.

By means of the 1811 Constitution, the country adopted a federal form of government, following the influence of the U.S. Constitution. At that time, it must be remembered, a federation was the only new constitutional framework for the organization of states different from the centralized monarchical frame, which had been recently invented in the United States. The framers of the new Venezuelan state followed that invention to unite the seven former Spanish colonial provinces that formed the Venezuelan state and had never been previously united. In the territory of Venezuela, there were no viceroyalties or *audiencias* (until 1786), and a general captaincy for military purposes, to integrate the provinces was established only in 1777. Thus, Venezuela was the second country in constitutional history to adopt federalism, an important aspect of its constitutional history.[480]

---

479   I conducted that process as minister of state for decentralization (1993–94). See, in general, *Informe sobre la descentralización en Venezuela 1993, Memoria del Dr. Allan R. Brewer-Carías, Ministro de Estado para la Descentralización (junio 1993-febrero 1994)*, Presidencia de la República, Caracas 1994.

480   After U.S. independence (1776) and federation (1777), the first Latin American country to declare independence and adopt a constitution was Venezuela, in 1811; it adopted the federal form of state.

It was after the endless civil conflict that marked the history of Venezuela during the nineteenth century that the federal form of government began to be limited. The conflict stemmed from the permanent struggles between the regional caudillos and the weak central power that had formed. This was the consequence of centralizing tendencies, which derived from the consolidation of the national state, a process that was particularly reinforced during the first half of the twentieth century.

During those decades, the authoritarian regimes of the country, aided by income from the new exploitation of oil by the national state (oil and the subsoil always has been the public property of the state), contributed to the consolidation of the national state in all aspects. Contributions included the creation of a national army, a national public administration, national taxation, and national legislation.[481] These centralizing tendencies almost provoked the disappearance of the federation, the territorial distribution of power, and the effective autonomy of the states and the federal district, which compose the formal federal organization of the state.

The 1961 democratic Constitution, which kept the federal form of the state but with a highly centralized national organization, allowed for the possibility of state decentralization, a process that began in 1989, when the party–system crisis exploded with the transfer of powers and services from the national level of government to the state level and the provision for the election of governors, which until that year were public officials appointed by the president. The democratic pressure exercised against the political parties, all of which were in the middle of a severe leadership crisis, forced the process.

According to those reforms, in December 1989, for the first time since the nineteenth century, state governors were elected by universal, direct, and secret suffrage, and regional political life began to play an important role in the country, thereby increasing the appearance of regional and local political leaders, many of whom were from outside traditional political parties. During the 1990s, the transfer of public competencies from the national level to the states marked the political life of the country, giving life to the decentralization process.[482]

All these decentralizing policies were abandoned after the approval of the 1999 Constitution, which did not have the necessary provisions to undertake the most needed democratic changes in Venezuela – namely political decentralization of the federation and the reinforcement of state and local political powers. The Constitution of 1999, in fact, continued with the same centralizing foundation embodied in the previous Constitution and, in some cases, centralized even more aspects. If it is true that it defined the decentralization process as a "national policy devoted to strengthened democracy" (Article 158), then in contrast, the national public policy executed during the past decade can be characterized as progressive centralization of

481 See Allan R. Brewer-Carías, "El desarrollo institucional del Estado centralizado en Venezuela (1899-1935) y sus proyecciones contemporáneas," *Revista Paramillo* 7, Universidad Católica del Táchira, San Cristóbal 1988, pp. 439-80.

482 See Organic Law on Decentralization, Delimitation and Transfer of Competencies of Public Power, *Gaceta Oficial.* Extra. N° 4.153, Dec. 28, 1989. See the comments in Allan R. Brewer-Carías et al., *Leyes y Reglamentos para la descentralización política de la Federación,* Editorial Jurídica Venezolana, Caracas 1990.

government without any real development of local or regional authorities. Consequently, in Venezuela, federalism has been postponed and democracy has been progressively weakened.

II. FEDERALIST CONSTITUTIONAL PROVISIONS IN THE 1999 CONSTITUTION

A federation is, above all, a form of government in which public power is territorially distributed among various levels of government with autonomous political institutions. That is why, in principle, federalism and political decentralization are intimately related. Specifically, decentralization is the most effective instrument not only for guaranteeing civil and social rights but also for allowing effective participation of citizens in the political process. In this context, the relation between local government and the population is essential. That is why all consolidated democracies in the world today are embodied in clearly decentralized forms of governments, such as federations or the new "regional" states progressively established in countries like Spain, Italy, and France.[483] Thus, it can be said that the strong centralizing tendencies that have been developing in Venezuela in recent years are contrary to democratic governance and political participation.

According to Article 4 of the 1999 Constitution, the Republic of Venezuela is formally defined "as a decentralized Federal State under the terms set out in the Constitution," governed by the principles of "territorial integrity, solidarity, concurrence and co-responsibility." Nonetheless, "the terms set out in the Constitution" are without a doubt centralizing, and Venezuela continues to be a contradictory centralized federation.

Article 136 of the Constitution states that "public power is distributed among the municipal, state and national entities," thus establishing a federation with three levels of political governments and autonomy (similar to the Brazilian federation): a national level, exercised by the republic (federal level); the state level, exercised by the 23 states and a capital district; and the municipal level, exercised by the 338 existing municipalities or local governments. On each of the three levels, the Constitution requires that government always be "democratic, participatory, elected, decentralized, alternative, responsible, plural and with revocable mandates" (Article 6). The capital district substituted for the former federal district established in 1863, eliminating the traditional federal interventions that existed regarding the authorities of the capital city. Nonetheless, in 2009, by means of a statute contrary to the Constitution, the capital district was organized without any self-government and completely controlled by the national executive.[484]

According to the Constitution, the organization of the political institutions on each territorial level is formally guided by the principle of the organic separation of

---

483 Decentralized states based on political regions or autonomous communities.

484 See the Special Law on the Organization and Regime of the Capital District, *Gaceta Oficial* N° 39.156 of Apr. 13, 2009. See the comments in Allan R. Brewer-Carías, "La problemática del régimen jurídico del 'Distrito Capital' en la estructura federal del estado en Venezuela, y su inconstitucional regulación legal," *AIDA Opera Prima de Derecho Administrativo* No. 5, Universidad Nacional Autónoma de México, Mexico City 2009, pp. 81-119.

powers. On the national level, with a presidential system of government, the national public power is separated among five branches of government, including the "Legislative, Executive, Judicial, Citizen (which includes the Prosecutor General Office, the Comptroller General Office, and the People's Defender Office) and Electoral" (Article 136).

The new citizens and electoral branches, as well as the judiciary, only exist at the national or federal level of government. Therefore, Venezuela does not have a judiciary or an electoral power at the state level. Regarding the judicial branch, since 1945, it is reserved to the national level of government, basically because of the national character of all major legislation and codes (civil, commercial, criminal, labor, and procedural). Consequently, because all courts are national (federal), there is no room for state constitution regulations on those matters.

With respect to the legislative branch, it must be noted that the 1999 Constitution established the one-chamber National Assembly, thus ending the country's federalist tradition of bicameralism by eliminating the Senate. In the National Assembly, there are no state representatives, and members are global representatives of the citizens and of all states collectively. Theoretically, the global representatives are not subject to mandates or instructions, only to the "dictates of their conscience" (Article 201). This has effectively eliminated all vestiges of territorial representation.

Regarding the states, the 1999 Constitution established two branches of government: executive and legislative. Accordingly, each state has a governor who must be elected by a universal, direct, and secret vote (Article 160); and a legislative council, with elected representatives according to the principle of proportional representation (Article 162). According to the Constitution, it is the responsibility of each state's legislative council to enact its own Constitution "to organize their branches of government" along the guidelines of the national Constitution, which in principle guarantees the autonomy of the states (Article 159).

III. LIMITING THE CONTENTS OF SUBNATIONAL CONSTITUTIONS

Consequently, each state has constitutional power to enact its own subnational constitution to organize the state legislative and executive public branches of government and to regulate the states' own organ for audit control. Despite the regulations on the organization and functioning of the state branches of government, the 1999 Constitution has seriously limited the scope of state powers. Specifically, for the first time in federal history, the Constitution refers to a national legislation for the establishment of general regulation on this matter.

In effect, and in relation to the states' legislative branch of government, the 1999 Constitution states that the organization and functioning of the states' legislative councils must be regulated by a national statute (Article 162), which was a manifestation of centralism that had never before been envisioned. In any federation, it is inconceivable for the national (federal) congress to be able to enact legislation to determine the organization and functioning of all state legislatures.

In contrast, in Venezuela, according to the Constitution, the National Assembly sanctioned in 2002 the Organic Law for the State Legislative Councils, which established detailed regulations,[485] related not only to the organization and functioning of the state legislative councils (as the national Constitution allowed) but also the status and attributes of the council's members, as well as the general rules for the exercise of the legislative functions. With that national regulation, the effective contents of the state constitutions regarding their legislative branch have been voided and are limited to repeating what is established in the national organic law or statute.

Additionally, the possibility of organizing the executive branch of each state's government is also limited by the 1999 Constitution, which has established the basic rules concerning the governor as the head of the executive branch. The Constitution has additional regulations referring to the public administration (national, states, and municipal), public employees (civil service), and the administrative procedures and public contracts in all of the three levels of government. All of the pertinent rules were also developed in two 2001 national Organic Laws on Public Administration and on Civil Service.[486] Therefore, state constitutions have been voided of real content, and their norms tend to repeat what has been established in the national organic laws or statutes.

Finally, regarding other aspects of states' organizations, in 2001, the National Assembly also sanctioned a law on the appointment of the states controllers,[487] which limits the powers of the states' legislative councils without constitutional authorization.

On the other hand, it must be pointed out that the Constitutional Chamber of the Supreme Tribunal of Justice has intervened in the process of limiting the scope of the states autonomy, in particular, in decisions adopted between 2000 and 2004 annulling articles of three state constitutions that have created the Office of the State Citizens' Rights Defender, on the grounds that citizens' rights are a matter reserved to the national (federal) level of government.[488]

As mentioned, the national Constitution establishes three levels of territorial autonomy and regulates the distribution of state powers, directly and extensively regulating local or municipal government. Therefore, the state constitutions and legislation can regulate municipal or local government only according to what is established in the national Constitution and the national Organic Law on Municipal Government,[489] which leaves very little room for state regulation.

Thus, without any possibility for the state legislatures to regulate anything related to civil, economic, social, cultural, environmental, or political rights, and with limited powers to regulate their own branches of government and other state organiza-

---

485   See *Gaceta Oficial* N° 37.282, Sept. 13, 2001.

486   See *Gaceta Oficial* N° 37.522, Sept. 6, 2002.

487   See *Gaceta Oficial* N° 37.304, Oct. 16, 2001.

488   See Decisions N° 1182 (Oct. 11, 2000), N° 1395 (Aug. 7, 2001), and N° 111 (Feb. 12, 2004), in *Revista de Derecho Público*, N° 84, Editorial Jurídica Venezolana, Caracas 2000, pp. 177ff.; *Revista de Derecho Público*, N° 85-88, Editorial Jurídica Venezolana, Caracas 2001; 192ff. See the references in Allan R. Brewer-Carías, *La Constitución de 1999. Derecho constitucional venezolano*, Editorial Jurídica Venezolana, Caracas 2004, Vol. 1, pp. 363ff.

489   See *Gaceta Oficial* N° 38.421, Apr. 21, 2006. See the comments in Allan R. Brewer-Carías et al., *Ley Orgánica Del Poder Público Municipal*, Editorial Jurídica Venezolana, Caracas 2007.

tions, including the comptroller general and peoples' defenders, there is very little scope left to subnational constitutions.

IV. CONSTITUTIONAL DISTRIBUTION OF POWERS

Federalism is based on effective distribution of powers across the various levels of government, and in Venezuela's case, among the national, state, and municipal levels. Accordingly, the Constitution enumerates the competencies attributed exclusively to the national (Article 156), state (Article 154), and municipal (Article 178) levels of government. Those regulations, however, assigned most matters to the national level and an important portion of such matters to municipalities.[490] In contrast, few exclusive matters are attributed to the states.

According to Article 156, the national power has exclusive competencies in the following matters: international relations; security and defense; nationality and alien status; national police; economic regulations; mining and oil industries; national policies and regulations on education, health, the environment, land use, transportation, and industrial and agricultural production; the post; and telecommunications. The administration of justice, as mentioned, also falls under the exclusive jurisdiction of the national government (Article 156.31).

Article 178 assigned the municipalities competencies including urban land use, housing, urban roads and transport, advertising regulations, urban environment, urban utilities, electricity, water supply, garbage collection and disposal, basic health and education services, and municipal police. Some of the powers regarding these matters are exclusive, but most are concurrent with the national government. The autonomy of municipalities is set forth in the Constitution but without any constitutional guarantees, because national statute can limit municipal autonomy (Article 168).

The national Constitution fails to enumerate substantive matters of exclusive state jurisdiction and concentrates on formal and procedural ones. Furthermore, the competencies related to a limited number of matters are established in a concurrent way, common to all levels of government —only some aspects of the competencies are exclusive. This applies to municipal organizations, nonmetallic mineral exploitation, police, state roads, administration of national roads, and commercial airports and ports (Article 164). Nonetheless, regarding the latter matters, although defined as exclusive of the states, after the 2007 constitutional reform was rejected proposing to transform it into a national competency, the Constitutional Chamber of the Supreme Tribunal, at the request of the Attorney General of the Republic, interpreting Article 164.10 of the Constitution, mutated the Constitution and declared it as a concurrent competency subjected to the intervention of the national executive.[491]

---

490   Exclusive matters are matters attributed to only one state level.

491   See Decision N° 565 (Apr. 15, 2008) at http://www.tsj.gov.ve/decisiones/scon/Abril/565-150408-07-1108.htm. See the comments in Allan R. Brewer-Carías, "La Sala Constitucional como poder constituyente: la modificación de la forma federal del estado y del sistema constitucional de división territorial del poder público," in *Revista de Derecho Público*, N° 114, Editorial Jurídica Venezolana, Caracas 2008, pp. 247-62

On the other hand, the possibility of the state legislature regulating its own local government is also very limited, because it is subject to what is established in the national organic municipal law or statute.

According to the Constitution, state legislative councils can enact legislation on matters that are in the states' scope of powers (Article 162). However, those powers are referred to concurrent matters and, according to the Constitution, their exercise depends on the previous enactment of national statutes and regulations. As a result, the legislative powers of the States are very limited.

The concurrent matters formerly provided a broad scope for possible action by state bodies. However, now that their exercise is subject to what the National Assembly has previously established in "general statutes," the possibility for states to regulate is very small. The national Constitution also states that the legislation that refers to concurrent competencies must always adhere to the principles of "interdependence, coordination, cooperation, co-responsibility and subsidiarity," which theoretically allows for a broad possibility for judicial review (Article 165).

In terms of residual competencies, the principle of favoring the states as in all federations also is a constitutional tradition in Venezuela. Nonetheless, the 1999 Constitution limited that residual power of the states by expressly assigning the national government a parallel and prevalent residual taxation power in matters not expressly attributed to the states or municipalities (Article 156.12).

Also, the 1999 Constitution, following the provisions of the 1961 Constitution, established the possibility of decentralizing competencies by transfer from the national level to the states. This process was regulated in the 1989 Law on Decentralization and Transfer of Competencies.[492] Even though important efforts for decentralization were made between 1990 and 1994 to revert the centralizing tendencies, the process, unfortunately, was later abandoned. Since 2003, the transfers of competencies that occurred, including health services, started the reversion process; and, since 2006, according to the Communal Councils Law, reformed in 2009,[493] and to the 2010 Organic Law on the Federal Council of Government,[494] the process of transfer of competencies from the national level toward states and municipalities has been stopped and has been diverted toward new nondecentralized entities related to "organized society," particularly, the communal councils, and even new non–decentralized territorial bodies, like the development district, created within the centralized planning system.

V. THE FINANCING RULES OF THE FEDERATION

The constitutional rules regarding the financing of the federation should also be mentioned. Virtually everything in the 1999 Constitution concerning taxation is more centralized than in the previous 1961 Constitution, and the powers of the states in tax matters have essentially been eliminated.

---

492   See *Gaceta Oficial* N° 37.753, Aug. 14, 2003.

493   See *Gaceta Oficial* N° 5.806 Extra. Apr. 10, 2006.

494   See *Gaceta Oficial* N° 5.963 Extra. Feb 22, 2010.

The national Constitution lists the national government competencies with respect to basic taxes, including income tax; inheritance and donation taxes; taxes on capital, production, and value added; taxes on hydrocarbon resources and mines; taxes on the import and export of goods and services; and taxes on the consumption of liquor, alcohol, cigarettes, and tobacco (Article 156.12). The Constitution also expressly allocates local taxation powers to the municipalities, including property, commercial, and industrial activities taxes (Article 179). The Constitution gives the national government residual competencies in tax matters (Article 156.12).

In contrast, the Constitution does not grant the states competencies in matters of taxation, except with respect to official stationery and revenue stamps (Article 164.7). Thus, the states can collect taxes only when the National Assembly expressly transfers the power to them, by a statute that contains specific taxation powers (Article 167.5). No such statute has yet been approved and likely none will be approved in the near future.

Lacking their own resources from taxation, state financing is accomplished by the transfer of national financial resources through three different channels, which the national government controls. The first channel is the *situado constitucional* established as a constitutional contribution established to be incorporated in the national budget equivalent to a minimum of 15% and a maximum of 20% of the total estimated ordinary national income (Article 167.4), must be distributed among the states according to population. The second channel is a nationally established system of special economic allotments for the benefit of those states in which mining and hydrocarbon projects are being developed. The benefits that accompany this statute have also been extended to include other nonmining states (Article 156.16).[495] The third channel of financing for states and municipalities is national funds, such as the former Intergovernmental Fund for Decentralization (*Fondo Intergubrenamental para la Descentralización, [FIDES]*), created in 1993 as a consequence of the national regulation of value-added tax,[496] or the Interstate Compensation Fund, established in the Constitution (Article 167.6) and created in the 2010 Organic Law on the Federal Council of Government.[497]

Following a long tradition, the states and municipalities cannot borrow or have public debt because of the requirement of a special national statute to approve state borrowing.

VI. THE RECENTRALIZATION OF THE FEDERATION

As mentioned, the 1999 Constitution, in a very contradictory way, introduced elements to centralize power to the detriment of states, although it continued with the federal form of the government. All the centralizing elements have been used during the past decade to produce a very centralized government that has suffocated the regional and local autonomy of states and municipalities.

---

495   See the Law on the special contributions for the states derived from mines and hydrocarbons, *Gaceta Oficial,* N° 5.824, Oct. 13, 2006.

496   See *Gaceta Oficial,* Extra. N° 5.805, Mar. 22, 2006.

497   See *Gaceta Oficial,* N° 5.963 Extra. Feb. 22, 2010.

This process has been completed since 2008, when the government reverted to the centralization trend, abandoned the decentralization efforts of the 1990s, and recentralized competencies that had been transferred in areas like health and education.

Also in 2008, as mentioned, the Constitutional Chamber of the Supreme Tribunal interpreted the Constitution at the request of the attorney general and ruled in Decision N° 565 (April 15, 2008),[498] contrary to the provisions of the Constitution, that a very important exclusive attribution of the states to administer national highways, ports, and airports was not an exclusive attribution but only a concurrent one, subject to control of the national government, thus authorizing the central government to interfere in the exercise of that administration.

On the basis of that decision, which distorted the Constitution, and after opposition candidates won in the regional elections in December 2008, a few governorship and mayors in important states and cities (Maracaibo and Caracas), in a very quick way the National Assembly reformed the 1989 Decentralization Law[499] allowing a process of centralization that in fact was applied in such entities during 2009, completing the reversion of the decentralization process initiated in 1993.[500] In this regard, the Inter-American Commission on Human Rights in its 2009 Annual Report noted "how the State has taken action to limit some powers of popularly-elected authorities in order to reduce the scope of public functions in the hands of members of the opposition," noticing that "a series of legal reforms have left opposition authorities with limited powers, preventing them from legitimately exercising the mandates for which they were elected."[501]

Even the local government in Caracas has been almost extinguished by the unconstitutional re-creation of a nineteenth-century federal district as a capital district governed by an executive authority appointed by the president and with the National Assembly as its legislative authority.[502]

As can be deduced from the foregoing, the declaration of Article 4 of the 1999 Constitution regarding the "federal decentralized" form of the Venezuelan government is mere wording. It is a formula that is contradicted by all the other regulations regarding federalism contained in the Constitution, which, on the contrary, shows that the federation in Venezuela is a very centralized one, affecting the democratic regime and governance deeply.

---

498   Decision N° 565 of the Constitutional Chamber (Apr. 15, 2008) (Case: *Procuradora General de la República, Recurso de interpretación del artículo 164 de la Constitución*), http://www.tsj.gov.ve/decisiones/scon/Abril/565-150408-07-1108.htm. See comments in Allan R. Brewer-Carías, "La Sala Constitucional como poder constituyente: La modificación de la forma federal del estado y del sistema constitucional de división territorial del poder público," *Revista de Derecho Público* 114, Editorial Jurídica Venezolana, Caracas 2008, pp. 247-262.

499   *Gaceta Oficial* N° 39 140, Mar. 17, 2009.

500   For instance, it happened on matters of ports and airports. See General Port Law, *Gaceta Oficial* N° 39.140, Mar. 17, 2009; Civil Aviation Law, *Gaceta Oficial* N° 39.140, Mar. 2009.

501   See IACHR 2009 Annual report, at http://www.cidh.oas.org/annualrep/2009eng/Chap.IV.f.eng.htm.

502   Special Law on the Organization and Regime of the Capital District, *Gaceta Oficial* N° 39.156, Apr. 13, 2009.

Decentralization is the most effective instrument not only to guarantee civil and social rights but also to allow effective participation of citizens in the political process and to consolidate democracies. That is why decentralization in the contemporary world is a matter of democracies and is contrary to authoritarianism. That is, there have never been decentralized authoritarian governments; only democracies can be decentralized. And that is precisely why the authoritarian government developed in Venezuela has centralized all power at the national level of government, suffocating state and local governments and weakening democracy.

Although democracy is based on elections, it cannot be consolidated without real separation of powers and the real possibility of political participation. Because of an existing controlled judiciary and a judicial review organization controlled by the executive, instead of enforcing the democratic constitutional principles embodied in the Constitution, those bodies have acted as the main instrument of authoritarian government.

Over the past years, the most important democratic element of the Venezuelan political process was the weak federalist system, which in 2000 had allowed more than half of the municipal mayors and one-third of the elected state governors to be opposition leaders, thus ensuring some kind of political pluralism. Unfortunately, all of this was affected in the regional elections of 2004, in which almost all the candidates supported by the president were elected, except for two governors and with more than 75% of the electorate abstaining. In the 2008 regional elections, a few opposition governors and mayors were elected, provoking the already mentioned reaction from the central government to a point of politically suffocating the scope of action of states and municipalities.

Ultimately, this has resulted in a concentration of powers, which is almost complete. In addition to the horizontal concentration of powers caused by the predominance of the executive over the legislative, judicial, citizens', and electoral branches, the executive in Venezuela has also vertically concentrated powers through the centralized form of government. In that framework, it is very difficult to talk about federalism and democracy, in Venezuela.

CHAPTER 7

CONCENTRATION OF POWERS AND AUTHORITARIAN GOVERNMENT

I. THE SEPARATION OF POWERS IN MODERN CONSTITUTIONALISM AND THE VENEZUELAN CONSTITUTIONAL TRADITION

The principle of separation of powers in modern constitutionalism has its origin in the constitutions of the former colonies of North America. For example, the Constitution of Virginia of June 29, 1776, set forth the following:

SEC. 3. The legislative, executive, and judiciary department, shall be separate and distinct, so that neither exercise the powers properly belonging to the other: nor shall any person exercise the powers of more than one of them, at the same time.[503]

This provision and similar ones incorporated after 1776 in other constitutions of the former colonies of North America[504] have their theoretical backgrounds in the writings of Locke,[505] Montesquieu,[506] and Rousseau,[507] which were the most important weapons used during the eighteenth-century American and French revolutions in the battle against the absolute state – in North America to fight against the sovereignty of British Parliament, and in France to fight against the sovereignty of the monarch. The consequence of both revolutions was the replacement of the absolute state by a constitutional state, subject to the rule of law, based precisely on separation of powers as a guarantee of liberty, although with different trends of government: the presidential system of government in the United States resulting from the American Revolution and, decades after the French Revolution, the consolidation of the parliamentary system of government in Europe.

---

503 "The Constitution or Form of Government Agreed to and Resolved upon by the Delegates and Representatives of the Several Counties and Corporations of Virginia," June 29, 1776. This article has been considered "the most precise statement of the doctrine which had at that time appeared." M.J.C. Vile, *Constitutionalism and the Separation of Powers*, Oxford 1967, p. 118.

504 The Constitution of Massachusetts (1780) also contained the following categorical expression: "Article XXX: In the government of this Commonwealth, the legislative department shall not exercise the executive and judicial powers, or either one of them: The executive shall never exercise the legislative and judicial powers, or either one of them: The judicial shall never exercise the legislative and executive powers, or either one of them: to the end it may be a government of laws not of men."

505 See J. Locke, *Two Treatises of Government*, ed. Peter Laslett, Cambridge 1967, pp. 371, 383-85, 350.

506 It is always adequate to remember the famous proposition of Montesquieu: "But constant experience shows us that every man invested with power is apt to abuse it, and to carry his authority as far as it will go.... To prevent this abuse, it is necessary from the very nature of things that power should be a check to power.... In order to avoid the abuse of power, steps must be taken for power to limit power." That is why, in the well-known chapter 6, Book XI of his *De l'Ésprit of laws*, he formulated his theory of the separation of power into three categories: "the legislative; the executive in respect to things dependent on the law of nations; and the executive in regard to matters that depend on the civil law. By virtue of the first, the prince or magistrate enacts temporary or perpetual laws, and amends or abrogates those that have been already enacted. By the second, he makes peace or war, sends or receives embassies, establishes the public security, and provides against invasion. By the third, he punishes criminals, or determines the disputes that arise between individuals. The latter we shall call the judiciary power, and the other simply the executive power of the state." He added: "When legislative and executive powers are united in the same person, or in the same body of magistrates, there can be no liberty; because apprehensions arise, lest the same monarch or senate should enact tyrannical laws, to execute them in a tyrannical manner. Again, there is no liberty, if the judiciary be not separated from the legislative and the executive. Were it joined with the legislative, the life and liberty of the subject would be exposed to arbitrary control; for the judge would be then the legislator. Were it joined to the executive power, the judge might behave with violence and oppression. There would be an end of everything, were the same man or the same body, whether of the nobles or of the people, to exercise those three powers, that of enacting laws, that of executing the public resolutions, and of trying the causes of individuals." Charles de Secondat, Baron de Montesquieu, *The Spirit of Laws*, translation by Thomas Nugent (1752), revised by J.V. Prichard. Based on a public-domain edition published in 1914 by G. Bell & Sons, Ltd., London. Available at http://www.constitution.org/cm/sol.txt.

507 See J.J. Rousseau, *Du contrat social*, ed. Ronald Grimsley, Oxford 1972, bk. 1, chap. 4, p. 153.

Separation of powers thus became the most important and distinguishing principle of modern constitutionalism.[508] According to Madison:

> The accumulation of all powers, legislative, executive, and judiciary in the same hands, whether of one, a few, or many, and whether hereditary, self–appointed or elective, may justly be pronounced the very definition of Tyranny.[509]

That explains the provision of Article 16 of the French Declaration of Rights of Man and of the Citizen (1789), according to which: "every society in which the guarantee of rights is not assured or the separation of powers not determined has no Constitution."

All these principles inspired the first modern constitution adopted in Latin America, the Federal Constitution of the States of Venezuela, sanctioned on December 21, 1811, by an elected general Congress, even before the Constitution of the Spanish monarchy of Cádiz of 1812 was sanctioned.[510] The 1811 Constitution adopted the principle of separation of powers, setting forth in the preamble: "The exercise of authority conferred upon the Confederation never could be reunited in its respective functions. The Supreme Power must be divided in the Legislative, the Executive and the Judicial, and conferred to different bodies, independent between them and regarding their respective powers."

To that proposition, Article 189 of the same 1811 Constitution added: "The three essential Departments of government, that is, the Legislative, the Executive and the Judicial, must be always kept separated and independent one from the other according to the nature of a free government, which is convenient in the connexion chain that unite all the fabric of the Constitution in an indissoluble way of Friendship and Union."[511]

Consequently, since the beginning of modern constitutionalism, separation of constitutional powers also was adopted in Venezuela, in particular according to the trends of the presidential system of government with checks and balances and granting the judiciary specific powers of judicial review. The latter, according to the objective guarantee of the Constitution, was established in Article 227 of the 1811 Constitution: "The laws sanctioned against the Constitution will have no value except when fulfilling the conditions for a just and legitimate revision and sanction [of the Constitution]" and, in Article 199, in the sense that any law sanctioned by the

---

508　See Allan R. Brewer-Carías, *Reflexiones sobre la Revolución norteamericana (1776), la Revolución francesa (1789) y la Revolución hispanoamericana (1810-1830) y sus aportes al constitucionalismo moderno*, 2nd rev. ed., Serie Derecho Administrativo N° 2, Universidad Externado de Colombia, Editorial Jurídica Venezolana, Bogotá 2008.

509　See J. Madison, *The Federalist*, ed. B. F. Wright, Cambridge, MA, 1961, 336 (N° 47).

510　See Allan R. Brewer-Carías, "El paralelismo entre el constitucionalismo venezolano y el constitucionalismo de Cádiz (o de cómo el de Cádiz no influyó en el venezolano)," in *Libro Homenaje a Tomás Polanco Alcántara, Estudios de derecho público*, Universidad Central de Venezuela, Caracas 2005, pp. 101-89.

511　See the text of the 1811 Constitution and all other Venezuelan constitutions in Allan R. Brewer-Carías, *Las constituciones de Venezuela*, 2 vols., Academia de Ciencias Políticas y Sociales, Biblioteca de la Academia de Ciencias Políticas y Sociales, Caracas 2008.

federal legislature or by the provinces contrary to the fundamental rights enumerated in the Constitution "will be absolutely null and void."

Since 1811, all the constitutions in Venezuelan history have established and guaranteed the separation of powers, particularly among the three classic legislative, executive, and judicial branches of government (powers), in a system of checks and balances, and always giving the judiciary the judicial review power. For such purpose, the independence and autonomy of the branches of government have been the most important aspects regulated in the constitutions, particularly during the democratic regimes, because the separation of powers in contemporary constitutionalism has become one of the basic conditions for democracy and for the possibility of guaranteeing the enjoyment and protection of fundamental rights. On the contrary, without separation of powers and autonomy and independence between the branches of government, no democratic regime can develop and no guarantee of fundamental rights can exist.

II. SEPARATION OF POWERS AND DEMOCRACY

In effect, the essential components of democracy are much more than the sole popular or circumstantial election of government officials, as was formally recognized in the Inter-American Democratic Charter adopted by the Organization of American States in 2001,[512] in which the separation and independence of powers – that is, the possibility of controlling the different branches of government – is enumerated as one of the "essential elements of the representative democracy" (Article 3). The separation and independence of the branches of government is conceived of in such an important way; it allows for all the other "fundamental components of democracy" to be politically possible. To be precise, democracy, as a political regime, can function only in a system of constitutional rule of law where the control of power exists; that is, a system of checks and balances based on the separation of powers with their independence and autonomy guaranteed, so that power itself can stop power.

Consequently, without separation of powers, no free and fair elections and political pluralism can exist; no effective democratic participation can be possible; no effective transparency in the exercise of government can be ensured; no subjection of the government to the Constitution and the laws can be guaranteed; no effective access to justice with autonomy and independence can de expected; and no true and effective respect for human rights can be ensured.[513]

The constitutional situation in Venezuela since the constitution-making process of 1999, which resulted in the complete takeover of all powers of the state and the sanctioning of the current 1999 Constitution, unfortunately has been of a very weak

---

512 On the Inter-American Democratic Charter, see Allan R. Brewer-Carías, *La crisis de la democracia venezolana. La Carta Democrática Interamericana y los sucesos de abril de 2002*, Ediciones El Nacional, Caracas 2002, pp. 137ff.

513 See Allan R. Brewer-Carías, "Democracia: Sus elementos y componentes esenciales y el control del poder," in *Grandes temas para un observatorio electoral ciudadano, Tomo I, Democracia: retos y fundamentos,* comp. Nuria González Martín, Instituto Electoral del Distrito Federal, Mexico City 2007, pp. 171-220.

democracy, precisely because of the progressive demolishing of the separation of powers. In it, a process of concentrating powers has taken place, first with the 1999 constitution-making process, which intervened in all branches of government before sanctioning the new Constitution; second, because of the provisions of the 1999 Constitution, which do not guarantee the effective independence and autonomy of branches of government.

In effect, the 1999 Constitution, if read in a vacuum ignoring the political reality of the country, can be misleading. It is the only Constitution in the contemporary world that has established not only a tripartite separation of powers among the traditional legislative (*asamblea nacional*), executive (president and executive offices), and judicial (Supreme Tribunal of Justice and lower courts) branches of government but also a five-branched separation of powers adding to the traditional three two more branches of government: the electoral attributed to the National Electoral Council, in charge of the organization and conduction of the elections; and the citizens' power, attributed to three different state entities: the Prosecutor General Office (Public Ministry) (Fiscalía General de la República), the Comptroller General Office (Contraloría General de la República), and the Peoples' Defender (Defensor del Pueblo) (Article 136). The last two new branch of government was the culmination of a previous constitutional process and tendency initiated in 1961 with the consolidation in the Constitution of state organs with constitutional rank not subjected to the classical powers.[514]

But, as mentioned, despite the division of powers among five branches, the autonomy and independence of the branches of government is not completely and consistently ensured in the Constitution. Its application leads, on the contrary, to a concentration of state powers in the National Assembly and, through it, in the executive power.

In effect, in any system of separation of powers, even with five separate branches of government, for such separation to become effective, the independence and autonomy among them has to be ensured to allow for checks and balances – that is, the limitation and control of power by power itself. This was the aspect that was not designed as such in the 1999 Constitution, and an absurd distortion of the principle was introduced by giving the National Assembly the authority not only to appoint but also to dismiss judges of the Supreme Tribunal of Justice, the prosecutor general, the comptroller general, the people's defender, and members of the National Electoral Council (Articles 265, 279, and 296), and in some cases, even by a simple majority of votes. This latter solution was even proposed to be formally introduced in the rejected 2007 constitutional-reform proposals, which sought to eliminate the guarantee of the qualified majority of members of the National Assembly for such dismissals.[515]

---

514   See comments in Allan R. Brewer-Carías, *La Constitución de 1999*, Caracas 2000, pp. 106ff.

515   See Allan R. Brewer-Carías, *Hacia la consolidación de un estado socialista, centralizado y militarista. Comentarios sobre el alcance y sentido de las propuestas de reforma Constitucional 2007*, Editorial Jurídica Venezolana, Caracas 2007, 133ff.; *La reforma constitucional de 2007 (Comentarios al proyecto inconstitucionalmente sancionado por la Asamblea Nacional el 2 de noviembre de 2007)*, Colección Textos Legislativos N° 43, Editorial Jurídica Venezolana, Caracas 2007, pp. 108ff.

III. DEFRAUDING POLITICAL PARTICIPATION IN APPOINTING OFFICIALS

The process of concentrating powers that Venezuela has experienced during the past decade also has been the result of a process of defrauding the Constitution, particularly by ignoring the limits the Constitution established to reduce the discretional power of the National Assembly in the process of appointing the heads of the different branches of government.

In effect, independently of the constitutional provisions regarding the possible dismissal by the National Assembly of the heads of nonelected branches of government, and the distortions of that, one of the mechanisms established to ensure their independence was the provision in the Constitution of a system to ensure that their appointment by the National Assembly was to be limited by the necessary participation of special collective bodies, called nominating committees, that must be integrated with representatives from different sectors of society (Articles 264, 279, and 295). The nominating committees are in charge of selecting and nominating candidates, thus guaranteeing the political participation of citizens in the process.

Consequently, the appointment of the judges of the Supreme Tribunal, the members of the National Electoral Council, the prosecutor general, the people's defender, and the comptroller general can be made only among candidates proposed by the corresponding nominating committees, which are in charge of selecting and nominating candidates before the assembly. These constitutional provisions seek to limit the discretional power that the political-legislative organ traditionally had to appoint those officials through political–party agreements by ensuring political citizenship participation.[516]

Unfortunately, these exceptional constitutional provisions have not been applied because the National Assembly during the past years, also to defraud the Constitution, has deliberately transformed those committees into simple parliamentary commissions, thus reducing civil society's right to political participation. The assembly in all the statutes sanctioned regarding such committees and the appointment process has established the composition of all the nominating committees with a majority of parliamentary representatives (who, by definition, cannot be representatives of civil society), although providing, in addition, for the incorporation of some other members chosen by the National Assembly itself from strategically selected nongovernmental organizations.[517]

The result has been complete control of the nominating committees and the persistence of the discretional political and partisan way of appointing the head officials of the nonelected branches of government, which the provisions of the 1999 Consti-

---

516 See Allan R. Brewer-Carías, "La participación ciudadana en la designación de los titulares de los órganos no electos de los Poderes Públicos en Venezuela y sus vicisitudes políticas," *Revista Iberoamericana de Derecho Público y Administrativo* 5, San José, Costa Rica, 2005, pp. 76-95.

517 See Ley Orgánica del Poder Ciudadano, *Gaceta Oficial* N° 37.310 of Oct. 25, 2001; Ley Orgánica del Poder Electoral, *Gaceta Oficial* N° 37.573 of Nov. 19, 2002; Ley Orgánica del Tribunal Supremo de Justicia, *Gaceta Oficial* N° 37.942 of May 20, 2004.

tution intended to limit, by a National Assembly, which, since 2000, has been completely controlled by the executive.[518]

It was even attempted to constitutionalize this practice, with the proposal in the rejected constitutional reforms of 2007 to formally establish exclusive parliamentary nominating committees rather than have them comprise representatives from various sectors of civil society.[519]

IV. THE SUPREMACY OF THE EXECUTIVE AND THE ABSENCE OF CHECKS AND BALANCES

If the supremacy of the National Assembly over the judicial, citizen, and electoral powers is the most characteristic sign of the implementation of the Constitution of 1999 during the past decade, the distortion of separation of powers by a power concentration system also derives from the political – and, in this case, party – supremacy that the executive power has over the National Assembly.

The Constitution of 1999 reinforced the presidential system because, among other factors, it extended to six years the presidential term, it authorized the immediate reelection for an immediate period of the president (Article 203), and it maintained its election by simple majority (Article 228). In the rejected constitutional reforms of 2007, it was proposed that the term of the president be extended to seven years, and the indefinite reelection of the president was a main proposal.[520] The latter proposal eventually was the object of a constitutional amendment approved in the 2009 referendum establishing the possibility of the continuous and indefinite reelection of all elected positions.[521]

This presidential model that allows for the possibility of the president's dissolving of the National Assembly even in exceptional cases (Articles 236.22 and 240) has been reinforced by the weakening of checks and balances – for instance, with the elimination of the Senate in 1999.

Also, the presidential system has been reinforced with other reforms, like the provision for legislative delegation to authorize the president, through delegating statutes (enabling laws), to issue decree laws on any topic, not only on economic and financial matters (Article 203). According to this provision, the fact is that the fundamental legislation of the country sanctioned during the past decade is contai-

---

518 Regarding the appointment of the prosecutor general in 2007, see Allan R. Brewer-Carías, "Sobre el nombramiento irregular por la Asamblea Nacional de los titulares de los órganos del poder ciudadano en 2007," in *Revista de Derecho Público*, N° 113, Editorial Jurídica Venezolana, Caracas 2008, pp. 85-88.

519 See Allan R. Brewer-Carías, *Hacia la consolidación de un estado socialista, centralizado y militarista. Comentarios sobre el alcance y sentido de las propuestas de reforma Constitucional 2007*, Editorial Jurídica Venezolana, Caracas 2007, pp. 1337ff.; *La reforma constitucional de 2007 (Comentarios al proyecto inconstitucionalmente sancionado por la Asamblea Nacional el 2 de noviembre de 2007)*, Colección Textos Legislativos N° 43, Editorial Jurídica Venezolana, Caracas 2007, pp. 108ff.

520 See Allan R. Brewer-Carías, *Hacia la consolidación de un estado socialista, centralizado y militarista. Comentarios sobre el alcance y sentido de las propuestas de reforma Constitucional 2007*, Editorial Jurídica Venezolana, Caracas 2007, p. 136; *La reforma constitucional de 2007 (Comentarios al proyecto inconstitucionalmente sancionado por la Asamblea Nacional el 2 de noviembre de 2007)*, Colección Textos Legislativos N° 43, Editorial Jurídica Venezolana, Caracas 2007, p. 62.

521 See in *Gaceta Oficial* N° 5.908 of Feb. 19, 2009.

ned in those decree laws, which have been approved without ensuring the mandatory constitutional provision for public hearings, which should take place before the sanctioning of all statutes (Articles 206 and 211).

To enforce this constitutional right of citizens' participation, the Constitution has specifically set forth that the National Assembly must submit draft legislation to public consultation, thus asking the opinion of citizens and the organized society (Article 211). This is the concrete way the Constitution tends to ensure the exercise of the right of political participation in the process of drafting legislation. The president also must carry out this obligation with legislative delegation. But, nonetheless, in 2007 and 2008, the president, following the same steps he took in 2001, extensively legislated without any public hearing or consultation. In that way, defrauding the Constitution by means of legislative delegation, the president enacted decree laws without complying with the obligatory public hearings, thus violating citizens' right to political participation.[522]

V. THE RUPTURE OF THE RULE OF LAW AND THE REJECTED 2007 CONSTITUTIONAL REFORM

As it can be deduced, for a state of democratic rule of law to exist, declarations contained in constitutional texts on separation of powers are not enough; they are indispensable to effective checks and balances among state powers. This is the only way to ensure the enforcement of the rule of law, democracy, and the effective enjoyment of human rights.

Moreover, under democratic rule of law, checks and balances can be achieved only by dividing, separating, and distributing public power, either horizontally by means of the guarantee of the autonomy and independence of the different branches of government, to avoid the concentration of power; or vertically, by means of distributing it or spreading it in the territory, thus creating autonomous political decentralized entities with representatives elected by votes, to avoid its centralization. Concentrations of power and its centralization, then, are essentially antidemocratic state structures.

It is precisely there where lie the problems of the formally declared rule of law and democracy in Venezuela – whose deformation rests in the same constitutional text of 1999. Unfortunately, the institutional framework established in the Constitution encourages authoritarianism, thus affecting the possibility of controlling power. This has permitted the centralization of power, thereby provoking the dismantling of federalism and municipalism and distorting the possibility of the effective political participation, despite the direct democracy mechanisms established.

This centralization of powers was to be constitutionalized in 2007 by means of the rejected constitutional reform proposed by President Hugo Chávez and sanctioned by the National Assembly. In doing so, he aimed to transform the democratic rule-of-law and decentralized social state established in the 1999 Constitution into a

---

522 See comments in Allan R. Brewer-Carías, "Apreciación general sobre los vicios de inconstitucionalidad que afectan los decretos leyes habilitados" in *Ley Habilitante del 13-11-2000 y sus decretos leyes*, Academia de Ciencias Políticas y Sociales, Serie Eventos N° 17, Caracas 2002, pp. 63-103.

socialist, centralized, repressive, and militaristic state, grounded in a so-called Bolivarian doctrine, identified with twenty-first century socialism and an economic system of state capitalism, lead by a Marxist party. [523]

Despite its refusal by the people through referendum, it is important to stress that the president submitted it and the National Assembly sanctioned it, thus evading the procedure established in the 1999 Constitution for such fundamental changes. That is, the proposed reform also proposed defrauding the Constitution, to deceive the people. [524]

Article 347 of the 1999 Constitution required for those reforms to be approved at the convening and election of a national Constituent Assembly, which could not be undertaken by means of mere "constitutional reform" procedure, which is reserved exclusively for "a partial revision of the Constitution and a substitution of one or several of its norms without modifying the structure and fundamental principles of the Constitutional text." Consequently, following that procedure to achieve substantial constitutional changes, in 2007, the president and the National Assembly tried to repeat the political tactic that has become all too common in the authoritarian regime installed since 1999: acting fraudulently with respect to the Constitution.

As the Constitutional Chamber of the Supreme Tribunal of Justice ruled in another matter, in Decision No. 74 (January 25, 2006), defrauding of the Constitution (*fraude a la Constitución*) occurs when democratic principles are destroyed "through the process of making changes within existing institutions while appearing to respect constitutional procedures and forms." The Constitutional Chamber also ruled that a "falsification of the Constitution" (*falseamiento de la Constitución*) occurs when "constitutional norms are given an interpretation and a sense different from those that they actually possess: this is in reality an informal modification of the Constitution itself." The Constitutional Chamber concluded by affirming, "A Constitutional reform not subject to any type of limitations would constitute a defrauding of the constitution." [525] This is to say, a defrauding of the Constitution occurs when the existing institutions are used in a manner that appears to adhere to constitutional forms and procedures to proceed, as the Supreme Tribunal warned, "towards the creation of a new political regime, a new constitutional order, without altering the established legal system." [526]

---

523   See Allan R. Brewer-Carías, *Hacia la consolidación de un estado socialista, centralizado y militarista. Comentarios sobre el alcance y sentido de las propuestas de reforma Constitucional 2007*, Editorial Jurídica Venezolana, Caracas 2007, 11ff.; *La reforma constitucional de 2007 (Comentarios al proyecto inconstitucionalmente sancionado por la Asamblea Nacional el 2 de noviembre de 2007)*, Editorial Jurídica Venezolana, Caracas 2007, 19ff. See the "Declaration of Principles" of the United Socialist Party (Apr. 23, 2010), available at http://psuv.org.ve/files/ tcdocumentos/Declaracion-de-principios-PSUV.pdf.

524   See Allan R. Brewer-Carías, "Estudio sobre la propuesta de Reforma Constitucional para establecer un estado socialista, centralizado y militarista (Análisis del Anteproyecto Presidencial, Agosto de 2007)," *Cadernos da Escola de Direito e Relações Internacionais da UniBrasil* N° 07, Curitiba 2007; and "El sello socialista que se pretendía imponer al Estado," in *Revista de Derecho Público*, N° 112, Editorial Jurídica Venezolana, Caracas 2007, pp. 71-76.

525   See *Revista de Derecho Público* N° 105, Editorial Jurídica Venezolana, Caracas 2006, pp. 76ff.

526   Id.

As has been mentioned, this was precisely what occurred in February 1999 in the convening of a consultative referendum on whether to convene a constituent assembly when that institution was not prefigured in the Constitution of 1961; it occurred with the December 1999 Decree on the Transitory Regime of the Public Powers with respect to the Constitution of 1999, issued by the Constituent Assembly, which was never the subject of an approbatory referendum; and it continued to occur in the subsequent years with the progressive destruction of democracy through the exercise of power and the kidnapping of successive constitutional rights and liberties, all supposedly carried out on the basis of legal and constitutional provisions.[527]

In the case of the 2007 constitutional reforms, constitutional provisions were fraudulently used for ends other than those for which they were established – that is, to try to introduce a radical transformation of the state, disrupting the civil order of the social-democratic state under the rule of law and justice through the procedure for constitutional reform that is established for other purposes. The aim of the 2007 reform was the conversion of the rule-of-law constitutional state into a socialist, centralized, repressive, militarist state in which representative democracy, republican alternating of office, and the concept of decentralized power were to disappear, with all power concentrated in the decisions of the chief of state.[528] But despite the deliberate use of an erroneous constitutional review procedure, the Supreme Tribunal deliberately refused to adopt any decision on judicial review regarding the unconstitutional procedure followed by the president, the National Assembly, and the National Electoral Council regarding the 2007 constitutional-reform process.[529]

In any case, although the popular rejection of the 2007 constitutional reform constituted a very important step back to the authoritarian government of President Chávez, and although according to the Constitution itself, the proposed reform could not be formulated again in the same constitutional term of government, the president announced his intention to seek to impose the rejected constitutional reform, again,

---

527   See Allan R. Brewer-Carías, "Constitution Making in Defraudation of the Constitution and Authoritarian Government in Defraudation of Democracy: The Recent Venezuelan Experience," *Lateinamerika Analysen* 19, German Institute of Global and Area Studies, Institute of Latin American Studies, Hamburg 2008, pp. 119-142; "El autoritarismo establecido en fraude a la Constitución y a la democracia y su formalización en Venezuela mediante la reforma constitucional (De cómo en un país democrático se ha utilizado el sistema eleccionario para minar la democracia y establecer un régimen autoritario de supuesta 'dictadura de la democracia' que se pretende regularizar mediante la reforma constitucional)," in *Temas constitucionales. Planteamientos ante una reforma*, Fundación de Estudios de Derecho Administrativo, Caracas 2007, pp. 13-74.

528   See the comments on all the Constitutional Chamber decisions dissmising the cases in Allan R. Brewer-Carías, *Hacia la consolidación de un estado socialista, centralizado y militarista. Comentarios sobre el alcance y sentido de las propuestas de reforma Constitucional 2007*, Editorial Jurídica Venezolana, Caracas 2007; *La reforma constitucional de 2007 (Comentarios al proyecto inconstitucionalmente sancionado por la Asamblea Nacional el 2 de noviembre de 2007)*, Editorial Jurídica Venezolana, Caracas 2007.

529   See Allan R. Brewer-Carías, "El juez constitucional vs. la supremacía constitucional. O de cómo la jurisdicción constitucional en Venezuela renunció a controlar la constitucionalidad del procedimiento seguido para la 'reforma constitucional' sancionada por la Asamblea Nacional el 2 de noviembre de 2007, antes de que fuera rechazada por el pueblo en el referendo del 2 de diciembre de 2007," *Revista de Derecho Público* 112 (*Estudios sobre la Reforma Constitucional*), Editorial Jurídica Venezolana, Caracas 2007, pp. 661 ff.

thus defrauding the Constitution. In particular, for instance, he suggested that to ensure the possibility of his indefinite reelection, he could call himself for a recall referendum, seeking to convert the eventual rejection of such referendum into a plebiscite for his reelection.[530] Nonetheless, on this matter, it was the National Assembly that defrauding the Constitution proposed a "constitutional amendment" to achieve the same purpose, establishing the possibility of the continuous and indefinite reelection of all elected officials, which was eventually approved in the February 2009 referendum.[531]

In any case, during July and August of 2007, the president, defrauding the Constitution, proceeded to implement the rejected constitutional reforms using the powers to legislate by decree that were delegated to him by his completely controlled National Assembly in January 2007. He, in effect, sanctioned twenty-six very important new statutes[532] implementing – of course, fraudulently – many of the constitutional-reform proposals that the people rejected in the December 2007 referendum.[533]

Unfortunately, even though they all are unconstitutional, those decree laws were enacted and have been applied without any possibility of control or judicial review. The president was sure that no Constitutional Chamber judicial review decision would be adopted because the Constitutional Chamber is a wholly controlled entity that has proved his most effective tool to consolidate his authoritarian government.

This entire situation is the only explanation we can find to understand why a head of state of our times, as is the case of President Chávez in Venezuela, can say the following in challenging his opponents in a political rally held a few years ago, on August 28, 2008:

> I warn you, group of Stateless, putrid opposition.
>
> Whatever you do, the 26 Laws will go ahead! And the other 16 Laws . . . also. And if you go out in the streets, like on April 11 [2002]…we will sweep you

---

530 See *El Universal*, Caracas Jan. 27, 2008.

531 See *Gaceta Oficial* N° 5,908 of Feb. 19, 2009.

532 Regarding the 2008 decree laws, Teodoro Petkoff has pointed out: "In absolute contradiction to the results of the Dec. 2, 2007[,] referendum in which voters rejected constitutional reforms, in several of the laws promulgated the president presents several of the aspects of the rejected reforms almost in the same terms. The proposition of changing the name of the Venezuelan Armed Forces to create the Bolivarian National Militia was contained in the proposed reforms; the power given to the President to appoint national government officials over the governors and mayors to, obviously, weaken those offices and to eliminate the last vestiges of counterweight to the executive in general and the presidency in particular, was also contained in the reforms; the recentralization of the national executive branch of powers that today belong to the states and decentralized autonomous institutes was also part of the reforms: the enlargement of government powers to intervene in economic affairs was also contained in the reform. To ignore the popular decision about the 2007 proposal to reform the constitution in conformity with the will and designs of an autocrat, without heed to legal or constitutional norms, is, *stricto sensu*, a tyrannic act." See Teodoro Petkoff, "Election and Political Power: Challenges for the Opposition," *ReVista: Harvard Review of Latin America*, David Rockefeller Center for Latin American Studies, Harvard University, Cambridge, MA, 2008, p. 12.

533 See the comments to all the 2007–2008 decree laws in *Revista de Derecho Público* 115, *(Estudios sobre los Decretos Leyes 2008)*, Editorial Jurídica Venezolana, Caracas 2008.

in the streets, in the barracks, in the universities. I will close the *golpista* media; I will have no compassion whatsoever.... This Revolution came to stay, forever!

You can continue talking stupid thinks.... I am going to intervene all communications and I will close all the enterprises I consider that are of public usefulness or of social interest! Out [of the country] contractors and Fourth Republic corrupt people!

I am the Law.... I am the State !![534]

Nonetheless, this was not the first time that the president had declared himself to be the law and the State. In 2001, when he approved more than forty-eight decree laws, also via delegate legislation, he said in a different way: "The law is me. The State is me."[535]

This phrase – attributed to Louis XIV, although he never said it[536] – expressed now by a head of state in our times, is enough to understand the tragic institutional situation that Venezuela is currently facing: a complete absence of separation of powers and, consequently, of a democratic government.[537]

CHAPTER 8

THE CATASTROPHIC DEPENDENCE AND POLITICAL SUBJECTION OF THE SUPREME TRIBUNAL OF JUSTICE

The effects of the dependency of the branches of government subjected to the legislative power, and through it to the executive, have been particularly catastrophic for the judiciary. The Constituent Assembly initially intervened in the judiciary's

---

534 *"Yo soy la Ley..., Yo soy el Estado*!!" See references at the blog of Gustavo Coronel, *Las Armas de Coronel*, Oct. 15, 2008, http://las armasdecoronel.blogspot.com/2008/10/yo-soy-la-leyyo-soy-el-estado.html.

535 *"La ley soy yo. El Estado soy yo.".* See Raquel Barreiro, "Chávez delega en la Asamblea Nacional cambios legales," in *El Universal*, Caracas Dec. 4, 2001, 1,1 and 2,1. Available at http://www.eluniversal.com/2001/12/04/eco_art_04201DD.shtml.

536 This famous phrase was attributed to Louis XIV when, in 1661, he decided to govern alone after the death of Cardinal Mazarin, but he never actually uttered it. See Yves Giuchet, *Histoire constitutionnelle française (1789–1958)*, Ed. Erasme, Paris 1990, p. 8.

537 Teodoro Petkoff, editor and founder of *Tal Cual*, an important newspaper in Caracas, recently summarized this situation as follows: "Chávez controls all the political powers. More than 90% of the Parliament obey his commands; the Venezuelan Supreme Court, whose number were raised from 20 to 32 by the parliament to ensure an overwhelming official's majority, has become an extension of the legal office of the Presidency.... The Prosecutor General's Office, the Comptroller's Office and the Public Defender are all offices held by 'yes persons,' absolutely obedient to the orders of the autocrat. In the National Electoral Council, four of five members are identified with the government. The Venezuelan Armed Forces are tightly controlled by Chávez. Therefore, from a conceptual point of view, the Venezuelan political system is autocratic. All political power is concentrated in the hands of the President. There is no real separation of Powers." See Teodoro Petkoff, "Election and Political Power: Challenges for the Opposition," *Revista: Harvard Review of Latin America*, David Rockefeller Center for Latin American Studies, Harvard University, Cambridge, MA, 2008, p. 12.

powers in 1999,[538] and such intervention continued with the Supreme Tribunal of Justice's unfortunate consent and complicity. In the past decade, the country has witnessed permanent and systematic demolition of the autonomy and independence of the judicial power, aggravated by the fact that, according to the 1999 Constitution, the Supreme Tribunal, which is completely controlled by the executive, is in charge of administering the entire Venezuelan judicial system, particularly by appointing and dismissing judges.[539]

I.   THE SUBJECTION OF THE SUPREME TRIBUNAL OF JUSTICE

The process began with the appointment, in 1999, of new Magistrates of the Supreme Tribunal of Justice without complying with the constitutional conditions, made by the Constituent Assembly itself, by means of a constitutional transitory regime sanctioned after the Constitution was approved by referendum.[540] From that point, intervention in the judiciary has continued, including the fact that the president has politically controlled the Supreme Tribunal of Justice and, through it, the complete Venezuelan judicial system.

1.   *The Confiscation of Civil Society's Right to Participate in the Appointment of the Magistrates of the Supreme Tribunal in 2000*

As mentioned, one of the principal purposes of the constitution-making process of 1999 was to reform the procedure for the appointment of the nonelected officials of the state, in a way out of the reach of the political parties' control and with citizens' participation in such appointments, thus removing the absolute discretion that the former Congress had on the matter. Consequently, the 1999 Constitution regulated a precise system of active participation of society in those appointments by creating various nominating committees, composed of representatives from different sectors of society, with the exclusive authority to nominate candidates before the National Assembly. In a Constitution with more that fifty articles referring to citizens' participation, the only means for such participation that the Constitution provides for directly is to ensure the participation of "different sectors of society" in the nominating committees. In this case, the provision is not established as a means for consultation, much less for dialogue, but rather as a mechanism for active participation. The consequence of this system is that under the Constitution, the National Assembly cannot directly nominate nonelected officials; the committees must bring

---

538   See Allan R. Brewer-Carías, *Debate constituyente (Aportes a la Asamblea Nacional Constituyente)*, Fundación de Derecho Público–Editorial Jurídica Venezolana, Caracas 1999, 1 (Aug. 8–Sept. 8): pp. 57ff.

539   See Allan R. Brewer-Carías, "La progresiva y sistemática demolición de la autonomía e independencia del Poder Judicial en Venezuela (1999-2004)," in *XXX Jornadas J.M. Domínguez Escovar, Estado de derecho, Administración de justicia y derechos humanos*, Instituto de Estudios Jurídicos del Estado Lara, Barquisimeto 2005, pp. 33-174; "La justicia sometida al poder (La ausencia de independencia y autonomía de los jueces en Venezuela por la interminable emergencia del Poder Judicial (1999-2006)," in *Cuestiones internacionales. Anuario Jurídico Villanueva 2007*, Centro Universitario Villanueva, Marcial Pons, Madrid 2007, pp. 25-57.

540   On this transition regime, see Allan R. Brewer-Carías, *Golpe de estado y proceso constituyente en Venezuela*, Universidad Nacional Autónoma de México, Mexico City 2002, 345ff.

those nominations beforehand. The National Assembly has no constitutional authority to appoint persons not presented by the committees.

Following those principles, regarding the judicial branch Article 270 of the Constitution of 1999 provides that only the Judicial Nominating Committee may nominate candidates for Magistrates to the Supreme Tribunal of Justice. Candidates may file their proposals before the committee on their own initiative or through organizations with activities in legal and judicial matters. To propose candidates before the National Assembly, the committee must follow a very complex procedure of selection, with citizens' participation, and the participation of the citizen power branch of government.

Nonetheless, the Constituent Assembly, when issuing the Decree on the Transition Regime of December 22, 1999, provisionally appointed Magistrates to the Supreme Tribunal who were to remain in office until the new National Assembly could make permanent appointments "according to the requirements of the Constitution" (Article 20), without following the strict constitutional procedure or guaranteeing the citizens' right to participation. Thus, the new National Assembly elected on August 2000 had a constitutional obligation to make permanent the Magistrates' appointments in accord with constitutional procedure. The same was to be done regarding appointments by the National Assembly of the prosecutor general, the comptroller general, the people's defender, and members of the National Electoral Council (Articles 279 and 295). However, this was never done.

In effect, to create the nominating committees according to the provisions of the Constitution, the National Assembly elected in August 2000 was obligated to enact the respective organic laws of the different entities, and particularly the organic law of the Supreme Tribunal of Justice. The assembly could not "legislate in order to not legislate," which it did when sanctioning on November 14, 2000, the Special Law for the Ratification or Appointment of Officials of the Citizens' Power and Magistrates to the Supreme Tribunal of Justice,[541] thus providing for the appointments of nonelected state officials without following the constitutional provisions, and thus violating Articles 264, 270, and 279 of the Constitution, as well as Articles 20 and 33 of the National Constituent Assembly's Decree on the Transitory Regime. The special law, in effect, organized the nominating committees as a parliamentary commission of fifteen representatives and six other persons elected by the assembly (Articles 3 and 4), not as provided in the Constitution. The special law thus extended rather than ended the transitional regime, thereby confiscating the right to political participation guaranteed in express form in the Constitution.[542]

This motivated the people's defender to file an action presenting the unconstitutionality of the special law and to seek its judicial review and annulment by the Su-

---

541   *Gaceta Oficial* N° 37.077, Nov. 14, 2000.

542   *Gaceta Oficial,* N° 37.105, Dec. 22, 2000. That is why the Inter-American Commission on Human Rights, in its *2003 Report on the Situation of Human Rights in Venezuela*, noted that "the constitutional amendments introduced for the election of these authorities as guarantees of their independence and impartiality were not put into practice in this instance," para. 186. Available at http://www.cidh.oas.org/countryrep/Venezuela2003eng/chapter1.htm#B.

preme Tribunal.[543] Even though the Supreme Tribunal never decided the case, in preliminary Decision No. 1.562 (December 12, 2000) (asking the people's defender to clarify the *amparo* petition filed together with the nullity action), the Tribunal recognized that "the full normalization of new institutions such as the Citizens' Power and the Supreme Tribunal of Justice requires Organic Laws developed in the constitutional context" and affirmed that, "as long as these are not enacted, these institutions are governed by two co-existent formative bodies of law, the Decree for the Transition of the Public Powers and the Constitution of the Bolivarian Republic of Venezuela," which form a single "constitutional block" – the Constitutional Chamber decided similarly in its decisions of March 14 and 28, 2000.[544] The consequence was that the transitory provisions of the Constitution and the transitional regime enacted by the Constituent Assembly were to remain in effect until the National Assembly enacted those organic laws. But instead of exhorting the National Assembly to enact the needed organic laws, by annulling the special law that failed to apply the Constitution, the Constitutional Chamber legitimized the contents of the previously mentioned special law.[545]

Is important to point out that the Justification Report of the Special Law Draft referred to the "absence of express provisions regulating the appointment of the members of the Citizens' Power and of the Magistrates to the Supreme Tribunal" (which only the National Assembly could enact), and to the fact that the nominating committees for the appointments "[did] not yet exist" (only the National Assembly could regulate their existence); instead of enacting the required organic law, the special law was a draft for the "the National Assembly to fill the legal vacuum," without ending the provisional regime or forfeiting its obligation to legislate.

2.   *The Appointment of the Magistrates of the Supreme Tribunal of Justice*

The systematic violation of the 1999 Constitution on this matter of appointment of Magistrates of the Supreme Tribunal in 2000 reached its zenith when the Constitutional Chamber of the Supreme Tribunal of Justice held that eligibility require-

---

543   See Clodovaldo Hernández, "Designaciones de la Asamblea bajo juicio de nulidad," in *El Universal,* Caracas Dec. 13, 2000, pp. 1–2.

544   See *Revista de Derecho Público* 84, Editorial Jurídica Venezolana, Caracas 2000, 108ff.

545   The director general of the Office of the People's Defender, Juan Navarrete, characterized the decision of the Supreme Tribunal of Justice as an abuse of power. See *El Universal,* Caracas Dec. 14, 2000, 1–2. In its *2003 Report on the Situation of Human Rights in Venezuela*, the Inter-American Commission on Human Rights, noted "with concern that the Supreme Court of Justice itself justified the mechanism imposed by this law, by upholding the legality of the transition process," para. 187; and reiterated its concern regarding what has been called the "Transitional Regime," which, in its opinion, undermines the full currency of the Constitution. The aforesaid Transitional Government Regime was enacted by the National Assembly as a mechanism intended to ensure the survival of provisions that would have been tacitly repealed under the new constitution until such time as the corresponding legislation could be enacted. The implementation of this regime, as explained previously, led to the failure to implement mechanisms enshrined in the constitution for the appointment of Supreme Court magistrates, the People's Defender, the Prosecutor General, and Comptroller General of the Republic. This is all because the Supreme Court of Justice has maintained that the full currency of the Constitution requires the adoption of a set of specific laws that, to date, have not yet been enacted. See para. 188. OEA/ser.L/V/II.118 doc.4 rev 2. Available at http://www.cidh.oas.org/countryrep/ Venezuela2003eng/chapter1.htm#B.

ments for Magistrates of the tribunal, set forth very precisely in Article 263 of the Constitution, were inapplicable to the Magistrates sitting on the Supreme Tribunal in 2000 who were issuing the provisional ruling in the aforementioned case filed by the people's defender.

The Magistrates decided that they could be "ratified" in their positions by the National Assembly, without complying with the conditions set forth in the Constitution for appointment. The Constitution, as supreme norm, was deemed to be mandatory for all people and institutions (Article 7), except for the Magistrates of the Supreme Tribunal of Justice, whose signatures appeared at the foot of the decision. For such purpose, the Constitutional Chamber created the argument that ratification was a concept not foreseen in the Constitution; therefore, Article 263 applied only to *ex novo* appointments of Magistrates, not to the tenure of those provisionally appointed. This concept of ratification, instead, was incorporated in the Decree for the Transition Regime enacted by the Constituent Assembly, only applicable to the Magistrates of the Supreme Tribunal. Because the decree only provided the need to appoint new Magistrates "according to the Constitution," the Tribunal concluded that ratification of the Magistrates did not need to respect the Constitution.

Accordingly, with a single stroke, the Constitutional Chamber – the institution established to guarantee the supremacy of the Constitution – decided that it was inapplicable precisely to its own Magistrates, who were the deciding judges in this case. Those who stood to benefit from the decision handed down "justice."[546]

The result was that the Magistrates of the Constitutional Chamber created and defined a special regime concerning the conditions of eligibility for their own offices, applicable only to them. They found that to require conditions other than the effective accomplishment of their functions would be to discriminate against those whose positions were to be ratified and favor those who have not been Magistrates but aspire to sit on the Supreme Tribunal of Justice.

The consequence of this decision was the decision of the National Assembly in December 2000 ratifying or appointing the Magistrates of the Supreme Tribunal of Justice, many of whom did not fill the conditions set forth in the Constitution to be Magistrates,[547] and almost all were close allies of the government. With this, the political control of the Supreme Tribunal was consolidated and, consequently, began the endless intervention of the judiciary by the Commission on the Functioning and Restructuring of the Judicial System, established during the 1999 constitution-making process.

---

546 Because of this situation, the People's Defender (Dilia Parra) asked the Judges to recuse themselves, because being in the case "judges and party" (*Ellos son juez y parte*). See in Taynem Hernández, "Solicitan inhibición del TSJ," in *El Nacional,* Caracas Dec. 16, 2000, pp. 1–4.

547 The Inter-American Commission on Human Rights, in its *2003 Report on the Situation of Human Rights in Venezuela,* mentioned as another issue of concern with respect to the guarantees of judicial independence and impartiality in Venezuela "the failure to follow the mechanisms set forth in the new Constitution for the election of its top authorities. The Commission believes that this failure to apply the procedures established by the Constitution as the guarantees of domestic law for ensuring the independence of the members of the judiciary means that the institutional legitimacy of that branch of government is undermined and the rule of law is weakened," para. 178. Available at http://www.cidh.oas.org/countryrep/Venezuela2003eng/chapter1.htm#B.

3. *The Consolidation of the Commission on the Functioning and Restructuring of the Judicial System and the Complete Political Control of the Judiciary*

Since 2001–2, the Commission on the Functioning and Restructuring of the Judicial System has continued to exist parallel to the Supreme Tribunal of Justice and with its recognition. This has consolidated the political intervention of the judiciary, making inapplicable the 1999 constitutional provisions that guarantee the independence and autonomy of judges.

In effect, according to the 1999 Constitution, judges can enter the judicial career only by means of public competition with citizens' participation (Article 255) in order to choose the most competent persons. Unfortunately, this provision a decade later had not been enforced. That is why the Inter-American Commission on Human Rights in 2010 noted:

> with concern the failure to organize public competitions for selecting judges and prosecutors, and so those judicial officials are still appointed in a discretionary fashion without being subject to competition. Since they are not appointed through public competitions, judges and prosecutors are freely appointed and removable, which seriously affects their independence in making decisions.[548]

On the other hand, also in order to guarantee the independence of the Judiciary, according to the Constitution, judges can be dismissed from the their tenure only through disciplinary processes, conducted by disciplinary courts and judges conforming to a disciplinary judicial jurisdiction (Article 253). Consequently, according to the constitutional provisions it is completely illegitimate and contrary to the due-process guarantee (Article 49) to assign disciplinary judicial functions regarding judges to an ad hoc commission, as the aforementioned one. If the original purpose was to provisionally assign the disciplinary jurisdiction to specific entities before the formal creation of the disciplinary jurisdiction, then that function must have been attributed to preexisting courts or judges, not to an ad hoc commission not integrated by judges. Doing so violated the due process guaranteed and the right of everybody to be judged by their "natural judge" (Article 49).

The fact is that the ad hoc commission has continued to exist, to the extent that the Inter-American Commission, in its *2009 Annual Report*, pointed out that:

> even though the 1999 Constitution states that legislation governing the judicial system is to be enacted within the first year following the installation of the National Assembly, a decade later the Transitional Government Regime, created to allow the Constitution to come into immediate effect, remains in force. Under that transitional regime, the Commission for the Functioning and Restructuring of the Judicial System was created, and this body has ever since had the disciplinary authority to remove members of the judiciary. This Commission, in addition to being a special, temporary entity, does not afford due guarantees for ensuring the independence of its decisions, since its members may also be appointed or removed at the sole discretion of the Constitutional Cham-

---

548 See IACHR, *2009 Annual Report*, para. 479. Available at http://www.cidh.oas.org/annualrep/
    2009eng/Chap.IV.f.eng.htm.

ber of the Supreme Court of Justice, without previously establishing either the grounds or the procedure for such formalities.[549]

In effect, after its creation in the December 22, 1999, Transitory Regime Decree of the Constituent Assembly, it enacted two more decrees on the matter on January 18, 2000, also in exercise of a supposedly "original constituent power." It appointed a tribunal inspector and members of the Commission on the Functioning and Restructuring of the Judicial System.[550]

The situation of the lack of complete inapplicability of the Constitution due to the transitory regime has been indefinitely prolonged because the omission of the legislature and the Supreme Tribunal as head of the judiciary, despite the regulations the same Supreme Tribunal enacted on August 2, 2000 – the Rules on the Direction, Government and Administration of the Judiciary, by which supposedly the provision of Article 267 would by satisfied to "end the effects of the transitory regime issued by the Constituent Assembly," a fact that did not occur.

In effect, Article 1 of the rules issued by the Supreme Tribunal had the purpose of creating the Executive Office of the judiciary to exercise by delegation the functions of direction, government, and administration of the judiciary assigned to the Supreme Tribunal. Nonetheless, in matters of disciplinary jurisdiction, through Article 30 of the rules, the Supreme Tribunal without any authority, and defrauding the Constitution, extended the existence of the Commission on the Functioning and Restructuring of the Judicial System, which was to continue in its transitional functions according to the rules to be established by the Supreme Tribunal, assigning it "disciplinary functions while the corresponding legislation is enacted and the Disciplinary Judicial Courts are created."

With those rules, the Supreme Tribunal declined to exercise its own normative attributions on judicial-organization matters, and it was the Commission on the Functioning and Restructuring of the Judicial System that enacted, without any constitutional or legal basis, the new rules to punish and dismiss judges.[551]

It has been according to those new rules that the Commission has "cleansed"[552] the judiciary of judges not in line with the new political authoritarian regime. The extraordinary thing about the rules is that they were not even issued by the Supreme Tribunal, which, according to the Constitution, is the branch of government precisely in charge of the government and of administering the judiciary. It also is extraordinary that the Supreme Tribunal accepted them, thus endorsing the functioning of an unconstitutional entity and allowing that it could enact not only its own functio-

---

549   See IACHR, *2009 Annual Report*, para. 481. Available at http://www.cidh.oas.org/annualrep/ 2009eng/Chap.IV.f.eng.htm.

550   See *Gaceta Oficial* N° 36.878, Jan. 26, 2000.

551   See *Gaceta Oficial* N° 37.080, Nov. 17, 2000.

552   The word used by the Constitutional Chamber to describe the commission's functions is *depurar*, which means "to cleanse." See Decision N° 1.939 (Dec. 18, 2008) (Case: *Abogados Gustavo Álvarez Arias et al.*) on the unenforceability in Venezuela of the Aug. 8, 2008, decision of the Inter-American Court of Human Rights in the case of former Judges of the First Court of Contentious Administrative Matters (Case: *Apitz Barbera y otros ["Corte Primera de lo Contencioso Administrativo"] vs. Venezuela*). See *Revista de Derecho Público* No. 116, Editorial Jurídica Venezolana, Caracas 2008.

ning rules but also the disciplinary regime for judges; that is, it established the rules and reasons for judges' dismissal.

Accordingly, the ad hoc commission continued to exist with the endorsement of the Supreme Tribunal; and its existence was again extended, this time by the legislature in the Organic Law of the Supreme Tribunal of May 2004,[553] which included a transitory disposition (Paragraph 2.e) setting forth that the following:

> (e) The Commission on the Functioning and Restructuring of the Judicial System will only have disciplinary functions while legislation is enacted, and the disciplinary jurisdiction and the corresponding disciplinary courts are created.

Consequently, during all the years of enforcing the 1999 Constitution, the constitutional provision requiring that "the disciplinary jurisdiction will be in charge of disciplinary courts determined by law" (Article 267) has never been applied; and, until 2010, judges have not had any guarantee of their stability – their permanence in the judiciary has been at the mercy of a nonjudicial, ad hoc commission that has cleansed the judiciary, particularly removing judges in a discretionary way, particularly when they have issued decisions not within the complacency of the government. As it was observed by the Inter-American Commission on Human Rights in its *2009 Annual Report*:

> in Venezuela, judges and prosecutors do not enjoy the guaranteed tenure necessary to ensure their independence following changes in policies or government. Also, in addition to being freely appointed and removable, a series of provisions have been enacted that allow a high level of subjectivity in judging judicial officials' actions during disciplinary proceedings. Even the Code of Ethics of Venezuelan Judges, adopted in August 2009, contains provisions that, by reason of their breadth or vagueness, allow disciplinary agencies broad discretion in judging the actions of judges.[554]

Unfortunately, on those judicial matters, the judicial activism of the Constitutional Chamber was deployed in other fields. For instance, it has decided ex officio cases of unconstitutional legislative omissions like the one referred to in the Organic Municipal Power Law.[555] On the contrary, the Political-Administrative Chamber of the Supreme Tribunal affirmed in Decision No. 673 (2008) that "the exercise of disciplinary functions in all its extension, that is, regarding titular judges that have attained stability by means of public competition, and regarding provisional judges, is today attributed in an exclusive way to the Commission on the Functioning and Restructuring of the Judicial System, as an organ created with transitory character while the disciplinary jurisdiction is created."[556]

---

553 See *Gaceta Oficial* N° 37942, May 20, 2004.

554 See IACHR, *2009 Annual Report*, para. 480. Available at http://www.cidh.oas.org/annualrep/2009eng/Chap.IV.f.eng.htm.

555 See Decision N° 3118 (Oct. 6, 2003), in *Revista de Derecho Público* 93-96, Editorial Jurídica Venezolana, Caracas 2003. See Allan R. Brewer-Carías, *La Constitución de 1999. Derecho constitucional venezolano*, Editorial Jurídica Venezolana, Caracas 2004, Vol. 2, pp. 970ff.

556 Quoted in Decision N° 1.939 (Dec. 18, 2008) (Case: *Abogados Gustavo Álvarez Arias et al.*), in *Revista de Derecho Público* 116, Editorial Jurídica Venezolana, Caracas 2008, pp. 89ff.

The same Constitutional Chamber of the Supreme Tribunal of Justice summarized this situation in Decision No. 1.939 (December 18, 2008), issued to declare and justify that an August 2008 decision of the Inter-American Court of Human Rights, condemning Venezuela for violating the due-process rights of the judges of the First Court on Administrative Contentious Matters, was not enforceable in Venezuela. The tribunal, in addition to recognizing the powers on disciplinary matters of the Commission on the Functioning and Restructuring of the Judicial System, confirmed that the Supreme Tribunal itself through its Judicial Commission has the power to dismiss, in any case, in a discretionary way, without due process, any provisionally appointed judge. Therefore, the Constitutional Chamber rejected the Inter-American Court's decision, considering it contrary to the sovereignty of the Republic of Venezuela and not enforceable, because such a court cannot impose its decisions on the Venezuelan judicial power.[557]

The fact is that the absence of stability of judges has led, in practice, to the dismissal of judges when adopting decisions contrary to the will or intterest of the executive branch. This was also pointed out by the Inter-American Commission on Human Rights, in its *2009 Annual Report*, noting:

> with concern that in some cases, judges were removed almost immediately after adopting judicial decisions in cases with a major political impact. The lack of judicial independence and autonomy vis-à-vis political power is, in the IACHR's opinion, one of the weakest points in Venezuelan democracy.[558]

4. *The 2004 Reform of the Supreme Tribunal Organic Law and the Reinforcement of Executive Control over the Judiciary*

After the National Assembly sanctioned the special law to provisionally appoint the Magistrates of the Supreme Tribunal without complying with the Constitution, the transitory situation continued in 2004, led again by the National Assembly with its sanctioning of the Organic Law of the Supreme Tribunal of Justice, which increased the number of magistrates from twenty to thirty-two and distorted the constitutional conditions for their appointment and dismissal.[559] The sanctioning of such a law allowed the government to assume absolute control of the Supreme Tribunal, particularly of its Constitutional Chamber.[560] The reform, as the Inter-American

---

557   *Id.*

558   See IACHR, *2009 Annual Report*, para. 483. Available a http://www.cidh.oas.org/annualrep/2009eng/Chap.IV.f.eng.htm.

559   The Inter-American Commission on Human Rights, in its *2003 Report on the Situation of Human Rights in Venezuela*, raised "its concern regarding certain provisions set forth in the draft Organic Law of the Supreme Court of Justice; these, were they to become positive law, could have a negative impact on the independence of the Venezuelan judiciary. These provisions entail several innovations: the increase in the number of Supreme Court magistrates; the granting of powers to the National Assembly whereby it can increase or decrease, by an absolute majority vote, the number of judges in the different chambers of the Supreme Court; and the empowerment of the Assembly to decree, by a simple majority vote, the revocation of Supreme Court magistrates' appointments," para. 158. OEA/ser.L/V/II.118 doc.4 rev 2. Available at http://www.cidh.oas.org/ countryrep/Venezuela2003eng/ chapter1.htm#B.

560   See comments on this statute in Allan R. Brewer-Carías, *Ley del Tribunal Supremo de Justicia*, Editorial Jurídica Venezolana, Caracas 2004.

Commission emphasized in 2004, "takes no account of the concerns expressed by the IACHR in its report over possible threats to the independence of the judiciary."[561] In its *2009 Annual Report*, the same Inter-American Commission "reiterates what it has said on previous occasions: that the rules for the appointment, removal, and suspension of magistrates set out in the Organic Law of the Supreme Court of Justice lack the safeguards necessary to prevent other branches of government from undermining the Supreme Court's independence and to keep narrow or temporary majorities from determining its composition."[562]

After the reform of 2004, the final process for selecting new judges, although being an exclusive competency of the National Assembly to be exercised without intervention of the executive, was submitted to the president, and on the eve of appointments, the president of the parliamentary commission declared:

> Although we, the representatives, have the authority for this selection, the President of the Republic was consulted and his opinion was very much taken into consideration…. Let's be clear, we are not going to score auto-goals. In the list, there were people from the opposition who comply with all the requirements. The opposition could have used them in order to reach an agreement during the last sessions, but they did not want to. We are not going to do it for them. There is now one in the group of postulates that could act against us. [563]

With good reason, the Inter-American Commission on Human Rights suggested in its *2004 Annual Report* that "These provisions of the Organic Law of the Supreme Court of Justice also appear to have helped the executive manipulate the election of judges during 2004."[564]

This configuration of the Supreme Tribunal, as highly politicized and subjected to the will of the president, has eliminated all autonomy of the judicial power and even the basic principle of the separation of powers.

---

561 See IACHR, *2004 Annual Report* (Follow-Up Report on Compliance by the State of Venezuela with the Recommendations made by the IACHR in its Report on the Situation of Human Rights in Venezuela [2003]), para. 174. Available at http://www.cidh.oas.org/annualrep/2004eng/chap.5b.htm

562 See IACHR *2009 Annual Report*, para. 478. Available at http://www.cidh.oas.org/annualrep/2009eng/Chap.IV.f.eng.htm.

563 See declaration of Pedro Carreño in *El Nacional*, Caracas Dec. 13, 2004. That is why the Inter-American Commission suggested in its report to the General Assembly of the Organization of American States in 2004 that "these regulations of the Organic Law of the Supreme Court of Justice would have made possible the manipulation, by the Executive Power, of the election process of judges that took place during 2004." See Inter-American Commission on Human Rights, *2004 Report on Venezuela*, para. 180.

564 The IACHR added: "The IACHR learned of complaints filed from various quarters, including law faculties, international observers and opposition forces, to the effect that a simple majority of the National Assembly, composed of government supporters, had arranged for the election of judges to *pack* the Supreme Court with a clear government majority. As a result, the 49 judges (17 full judges and 32 alternates) elected were politically sympathetic to the government, and they included among their number two judges who are sitting parliamentary members for the government majority," para. 180. See IACHR, *2004 Annual Report* (Follow-Up Report on Compliance by the State of Venezuela with the Recommendations made by the IACHR in its Report on the Situation of Human Rights in Venezuela [2003]). Available at http://www.cidh.oas.org/annualrep/2004eng/chap.5b.htm.

The president admitted his own influence on the Supreme Tribunal when he publicly complained that the Supreme Tribunal had issued an important ruling in which it "modified" the Income Tax Law without previously consulting the "leader of the Revolution"; he also warned courts against decisions that would be "treason to the People" and "the Revolution." That was a very controversial case, decided by the Constitutional Chamber in Decision No. 301 (February 27, 2007).[565] The president said:

> Many times they come, the National Revolutionary Government comes and wants to make a decision against something that, for instance, deals with or has to pass through judicial decisions, and then they begin to move against it in the shadows, and many times they succeed in neutralizing decisions of the Revolution through a judge, or a court, and even through the very same Supreme Tribunal of Justice, behind the backs of the Leader of the Revolution, acting from within against the Revolution. This is, I insist, treason to the people, treason to the Revolution.[566]

To ensure the control of the Supreme Tribunal, another important provision of the new Organic Law of the Supreme Tribunal of Justice concerned dismissal of Judges. According to Article 265 of the 1999 Constitution, a judge can be dismissed in cases of "grave faults" (*faltas graves*) committed by the accused, only by the vote of a qualified majority of two-thirds of the National Assembly, following a hearing and prior qualification by the citizens' power. The Organic Law of the Supreme Tribunal of Justice defines "grave faults" broadly, leaving open the possibility of dismissal based exclusively on political motives.[567] Furthermore, the Constitution required the qualified two-thirds majority to avoid leaving the tenure of Judges in the hands of a simple majority of legislators. Unfortunately, this provision was distorted by the 2004 Organic Law of the Supreme Tribunal of Justice, which established that Judges could be dismissed by simple majority when the "administrative act of their appointment" is revoked (Article 23.4).[568] This distortion, contrary to the independence of the judiciary, was attempted to be constitutionalized in the rejected 2007 constitutional reforms, which proposed that Magistrates of the Supreme Tribu-

---

565 Supreme Tribunal of Justice, Constitutional Chamber, Decision N° 301 (Feb. 27, 2007) (Case: *Adriana Vigilanza y Carlos A. Vecchio*) (Exp. N° 01-2862), in *Gaceta Oficial* N° 38.635, Mar. 1, 2007. See Allan R. Brewer-Carías, "El juez constitucional en Venezuela como legislador positivo de oficio en materia tributaria," in *Revista de Derecho Público* 109, Editorial Jurídica Venezolana, Caracas 2007, pp. 193-212; and "De cómo la jurisdicción constitucional en Venezuela, no sólo legisla de oficio, sino subrepticiamente modifica las reformas legales que 'sanciona,' a espaldas de las partes en el proceso: El caso de la aclaratoria de la sentencia de Reforma de la Ley de Impuesto sobre la Renta de 2007," *Revista de Derecho Público* 114, Editorial Jurídica Venezolana, Caracas 2008, pp. 267-76.

566 *Discurso en el Primer Encuentro con Propulsores del Partido Socialista Unido de Venezuela desde el teatro Teresa Carreño* (Speech in the First Event with Supporters of the Venezuela United Socialist Party at the Teresa Carreño Theater), Mar. 24, 2007, available at http://www.minci.gob.ve/alocuciones/4/13788/primerencuentrocon.html, 45.

567 See Allan R. Brewer-Carías, *Ley Orgánica del Tribunal Supremo de Justicia*, Editorial Jurídica Venezolana, Caracas 2004, p. 41.

568 Id., 39-41. The provision was abrogated in the 2010 reform of the Organic Law of the Supreme Tribunal of Justice.

nal could be dismissed in case of grave faults but only by the vote of the majority of members of the National Assembly.[569] The National Assembly used this power to dismiss Judges who have ruled against the government's wishes on sensitive issues.

All of this has allowed the government to assume absolute control of the Supreme Tribunal of Justice in general, and of every one of its chambers, especially the Constitutional Chamber.

II. THE SUPREME TRIBUNAL AS A TOOL TO DISTORT THE CONSTITUTION AND RECOURSE FOR CONSTITUTIONAL INTERPRETATION

If Constitutions are superior laws that support the validity of a legal order, then the institutional solution to ensure their enforcement is the existence of a supreme court that can act as guardian of the Constitution, with powers to annul unconstitutional state acts or declare their unconstitutionality. In democracies, such courts have always been the main institutional guarantee of freedom and the rule of law. Nonetheless, the same courts in authoritarian governments, far from ensuring the rule of law, have been used to demolish the foundations of the democracy. Unfortunately, the latter has been the case in Venezuela over the past decade (1999–2010), notwithstanding the formal provisions on judicial review in the Constitution.

The 1999 Constitution, in effect, expressly established constitutional supremacy (Article 7), according to which the Constitution must prevail above the will of all the constituted bodies of the state, including, of course, the Supreme Tribunal of Justice itself. This supremacy is ensured by means of two provisions: those regarding the absolute, rigid character of the Constitution implying that its modification can take place only with the necessary and indispensable popular intervention, and those concerning the constitutional judicial review system to guarantee said supremacy.

As for the institutional system of constitutional reform, three different procedures have been established in the Constitution: constitutional reform, constitutional amendment, and constituent assembly – the last is needed in cases of transforming the state to establish a new legal order and to fully reform the Constitution (Article 347). In the other two cases, constitutional review procedures are designed to introduce reforms without changing or modifying the structure or fundamental principles of the Constitution (Articles 340 and 342). The common trend in all cases is the intervention of the people through referendum by convening the Constituent Assembly or to approve the constitutional reforms or the amendments. Any modification of the Constitution carried out differently from those three procedures is considered unconstitutional and illegitimate.

The constitutional judicial review system,[570] as a result of the principles of constitutional supremacy and rigidity, has been established with a mixed or integral cha-

---

569   See Allan R. Brewer-Carías, *La reforma constitucional de 2007 (Comentarios al proyecto inconstitu- cionalmente sancionado por la Asamblea Nacional el 2 de noviembre de 2007)*, Editorial Jurídica Venezolana, Caracas 2007, p. 108.

570   See Mauro Cappelletti, *Judicial Review in the Contemporary World*, Bobbs-Merrill, Indianapolis 1971; Allan R. Brewer-Carías, *Judicial Review in Comparative Law*, Cambridge University Press, Cambridge 1989; *Instituciones políticas y constitucionales*, Universidad Católica del Táchira–Editorial Jurídica

racter that combines diffused and concentrated methods of judicial review.[571] That is, the guarantee for constitutional supremacy is ensured, first, by assigning all judges of the republic the obligation to "guarantee the integrity of the Constitution" (Article 334); and second, by assigning the Supreme Court of Justice, as "the higher and last interpreter of the Constitution," the task of ensuring "the supremacy and effectiveness of constitutional provisions and principles" and their "uniform interpretation and application" (Article 335). The Constitution also assigns constitutional jurisdiction to the Constitutional Chamber of the Supreme Tribunal (Articles 266.1 and 336), through which it has the power to annul unconstitutional statutes and other state acts of statutory character exercising the concentrated method of judicial review.

In accordance with these provisions, the Constitutional Chamber is, without a doubt, the most powerful instrument for ensuring the supremacy of the Constitution and the rule of law. As a guardian of the Constitution, it is of course subject to it, a matter that is in any rule-of-law system, is absolutely understood and is not subject to discussion. It would be inconceivable that a constitutional court can violate the Constitution it is called on to apply and interpret. As a matter of principle, other state bodies might violate it, but not its guardian. For such purpose and to ensure that this does not occur, the constitutional court must have absolute independence and autonomy. On the contrary, a constitutional court submitted to the will of the political power, instead of being the guardian of the Constitution, becomes the most atrocious instrument of authoritarianism. Thus, the best constitutional justice system, in the hands of judges subjected to political power, is a dead letter for individuals and is an instrument to defraud the Constitution.

Unfortunately, the latter has been occurring in Venezuela since 2000. The Constitutional Chamber of the Supreme Tribunal, as constitutional judge, far from acting within the expressed constitutional attributions, has been adopting decisions that, in some cases, contain unconstitutional constitutional interpretations,[572] not only of its own powers of judicial review but also of substantive matters. It changed or modified constitutional provisions, in many cases to legitimize and support the progressi-

Venezolana, San Cristóbal–Caracas 1996, 6 (La justicia constitucional): pp. 131 ff.; *El control concentrado de la constitucionalidad de las leyes (Estudio de derecho comparado),* Editorial Jurídica Venezolana, Caracas 1994.

571   See Manuel Arona Cruz, "El control de la constitucionalidad de los actos jurídicos en Colombia ante el derecho comparado," in *Archivo de Derecho Público y Ciencias de la Administración, Derecho público en Venezuela y Colombia,* Instituto de Derecho Público, UCV, Caracas 1986, 7:39-114; Allan R. Brewer-Carías, *El sistema mixto o integral de control de la constitucionalidad en Colombia y Venezuela,* Universidad Externado de Colombia, Pontificia Universidad Javeriana, Bogotá 1995; *El sistema de justicia constitucional en la Constitución de 1999,* Editorial Jurídica Venezolana, Caracas 2000; *La justicia constitucional. Procesos y procedimientos constitucionales,* Universidad Nacional Autónoma de México, Mexico City 2007; "La justicia constitucional en la nueva Constitución," *Revista de Derecho Constitucional* No. 1, Editorial Sherwood, Caracas 1999, pp. 35-44.

572   See Allan R. Brewer-Carías, *"Quis Custodiet Ipsos Custodes*: De la interpretación constitucional a la inconstitucionalidad de la interpretación," in *VIII Congreso Nacional de derecho Constitucional, Perú,* Fondo Editorial 2005, Colegio de Abogados de Arequipa, Arequipa 2005, pp. 463-89; and *Revista de Derecho Público* 105, Editorial Jurídica Venezolana, Caracas 2006, pp. 7-27. See also Allan R. Brewer-Carías, *Crónica sobre la "in" justicia constitucional. La Sala Constitucional y el autoritarismo en Venezuela,* Editorial Jurídica Venezolana, Caracas 2007.

ve building of the authoritarian state. That is, it has distorted the Constitution through illegitimate and fraudulent "constitutional mutations" (*mutaciones constitucionales*)."[573] These illegitimate modifications, of course, have been made by the Constitution's supreme guardian, exercising a sort of derived constituent power that does not belong to it and is not regulated in the Constitution. The eternal question arising from the uncontrolled powe – *Quis custodiet ipsos custodes* – is particularly relevant.

One of the most important instruments for distorting the Constitution that has been used in Venezuela is the abstract recourses of interpretation of the Constitution, created by the Constitutional Chamber of the Supreme Tribunal from the interpretation of Article 335 of the Constitution, which grants the Supreme Tribunal the character of "maximum and final interpreter of the Constitution." In other words, this autonomous recourse for the abstract interpretation of the Constitution, which is not established in the Constitution or in any statute, has served as the main tool for adopting some of the most distinguishable and illegitimate distortions (*mutaciones*) of the Constitution. Many of the latter have their origin in the decision on autonomous requests for the abstract interpretation of the Constitution, in many cases filed by the national executive through the attorney general.

The 1999 Constitution grants the Supreme Tribunal of Justice only the power to "decide the recourses of interpretation on the content and scope of the legal texts" (statutes) (Article 266.6), a faculty that is to be exercised "by all the Chambers [of the Tribunal] pursuant to the provisions of this Constitution and the law" (Article 266). No reference is made in the Constitution to a recourse for the abstract interpretation of the Constitution itself.

Nonetheless, before the Supreme Tribunal of Justice's organic law was sanctioned in 2004, and without any constitutional or legal support, in 2000 the Constitutional Chamber created an autonomous "recourse of interpretation of the Constitution."[574] The court's ruling was founded on Article 26 of the Constitution, which established the right to access justice, considering that, although the action was not set forth in any statute, it was not forbidden, either. Therefore, the Constitutional Chamber decided that "citizens do not require statutes establishing the recourse for constitutional interpretation, in particular, to raise it."[575]

573 A "constitutional mutation" (distortion) occurs when the content of a constitutional provision is modified in such a way that even when the provision maintains its content, it receives a different meaning. See Néstor Pedro Sagüés, *La interpretación judicial de la Constitución*, Abeledo-Perrot, Buenos Aires 2006, 56-59, 80-81, pp. 165 ff.; Salvador O. Nava Gomar, "Interpretación, mutación y reforma de la Constitución. Tres extractos," in *Interpretación constitucional*, coord. Eduardo Ferrer Mac-Gregor, Ed. Porrúa, Universidad Nacional Autónoma de México, Mexico City 2005, 2:804 ff.; Konrad Hesse, "Límites a la mutación constitucional," in *Escritos de derecho constitucional*, Centro de Estudios Constitucionales, Madrid 1992.

574 Decision N° 1077 of the Constitutional Chamber (Sept. 22, 2000), Case: *Servio Tulio León Briceño;* see in *Revista de Derecho Público*, N° 83, Editorial Jurídica Venezolana, Caracas 2000, pp. 247ff.

575 This criterion was ratified later in Decision N° 1347 (Sept. 11, 2000), in *Revista de Derecho Público* 84, Editorial Jurídica Venezolana, Caracas 2000, 264 ff.

To raise this recourse for constitutional interpretation, the Constitutional Chamber has considered that a particular interest shall exist in the plaintiff. The court ruled:

> a public or private person shall have a current legitimate legal interest, grounded in a concrete and specific legal situation, which necessarily requires the interpretation of constitutional rules applicable to the case, in order to cease the uncertainty impeding the development and effects of said legal situation.[576]

Regarding the purpose of the recourse for constitutional interpretation, in Decision No. 1077 (August 22, 2001), the Constitutional Chamber considered that it is "a declaration of certainty on the scope and content of a constitutional provision," seeking for a constitutional interpretation in order to "clear doubts and ambiguities about the supposed collision." The Constitutional Chamber added that the petition for interpretation might be inadmissible "if it does not specify which is the obscurity, ambiguity or contradiction between the provisions of the constitutional text."[577] The petition, if applicable, also must specify "the nature and scope of the applicable principles" or "the contradictory or ambiguous situations aroused between the Constitution and the rules of its transitory regime."[578] The interpretation of the Constitution by the Constitutional Chamber in these cases is binding.[579]

This extraordinary interpretive power, although theoretically an excellent judicial means for interpreting the Constitution, unfortunately has been extensively abused by the Constitutional Chamber to distort important constitutional provisions, to interpret them contrary to the text, and to justify constitutional solutions according to the will of the executive.[580] That is, this instrument for abstract interpretation of the Constitution, without a doubt, has distorted the Constitution and has amplified the constitutional powers of the Constitutional Chamber. This autonomous recourse for abstract interpretation of the Constitution has no precedent in comparative law.[581]

---

576   Id.

577   Case: *Servio Tulio León Briceño*, in *Revista de Derecho Público* No. 83, Editorial Jurídica Venezolana, Caracas 2000, pp. 247ff.

578   *Id.*

579   Decision N° 1347 of the Constitutional Chamber (Nov. 9, 2000), in *Revista de Derecho Público* 84, Editorial Jurídica Venezolana, Caracas 2000, pp. 264ff.

580   See Decision N° 1139 (June 5, 2002) (Case: *Sergio Omar Calderón Duque y William Dávila Barrios*); N° 137 (Feb. 13, 2003) (Case: *Freddy Lepage y otros*); N° 2750 (Oct. 21, 2003) (Case: *Carlos E. Herrera Mendoza*); N° 2432 (Aug. 29, 2003) (Case: *Luis Franceschi y otros*); and N° 2404 (Aug. 28, 2003) (Case: *Exsel Alí Betancourt Orozco, Interpretación del artículo 72 de la Constitución*), in Allan R. Brewer-Carías, *La Sala Constitucional versus el estado democrático de derecho. El secuestro del poder electoral y de la Sala Electoral del Tribunal Supremo y la confiscación del derecho a la participación política*, Los Libros de El Nacional, Colección Ares, Caracas 2004, p. 172; "El secuestro del Poder Electoral y la confiscación del derecho a la participación política mediante el referendo revocatorio presidencial: Venezuela 2000-2004," *Boletín Mexicano de Derecho Comparado* 112, Instituto de Investigaciones Jurídicas, Universidad Nacional Autónoma de México, Mexico City 2005, pp. 11-73.

581   See Allan R. Brewer-Carías, "Le recours d'interprétation abstrait de la Constitution au Vénézuéla," in *Le renouveau du droit constitutionnel, Mélanges en l'honneur de Louis Favoreu*, Dalloz, Paris 2007, 61-70; "La ilegítima mutación de la Constitución por el juez constitucional: la inconstitucional ampliación y modificación de su propia competencia en materia de control de constitucionalidad," in *Libro*

As I have mentioned, an autonomous recourse for abstract interpretation of the Constitution, in the hands of an autonomous and independent constitutional judge, can be an efficient instrument for adapting the norms of the Constitution to the changes in the constitutional order of a country at a point in time. However, a recourse of that nature in the hands of a constitutional judge who is absolutely dependant on the executive power, in an authoritarian regime like the one in Venezuela during the past decade, is an instrument for the illegitimate distortion (*mutación*) of the Constitution. That is, through a series of judicial-review decisions interpreting the Constitution, many of which issued at the request of executive through the attorney general filing recourses for the abstract interpretation of the Constitution, the Constitutional Chamber eventually has "reformed" the Constitution. It is what has been called a process of *mutación ilegítima* of the Constitution – in many cases, even enforcing proposals for constitutional reforms that were formulated in 2007 and were rejected by the people in the December 2007 referendum.[582]

CHAPTER 9

STATE APPROPRIATION, NATIONALIZATION, EXPROPRIATION, AND CONFISCATION OF PRIVATE ASSETS

A general trend of the economic policy of the authoritarian government that has taken shape in Venezuela, following the framework established in the 1999 Constitution, has been the progressive appropriation by the state of private industries and services; a public policy that has been fueled during the past decade because of the state's uncontrolled expenditure of outstanding fiscal revenues derived from increased oil prices in the nationalized oil industry.

This process of state appropriation of the economy has occurred through the consensual acquisition of industries and services by means of private law contracts and agreements, as was the case with the main electricity (Electricidad de Caracas C.A.) and telephone (C.A. Teléfonos de Venezuela) companies. It also has occurred through public law instruments allowed for in the Constitution, like the nationalization of economic sectors, which always implies expropriation of private assets. But, in many cases, the forced appropriation of private assets occurred through unconstitutional confiscations.[583]

I. THE COMPULSORY ACQUISITION OF PRIVATE ASSETS

In the Venezuelan legal system, the term *nationalization* refers to the public law institution through which the state, by means of a statute, reserves for itself an economic sector or activity, followed by the acquisition, normally through expropria-

---

Homenaje a Josefina Calcaño de Temeltas, Fundación de Estudios de Derecho Administrativo (FUNEDA), Caracas 2009, pp. 319-62.

582 See Allan R. Brewer-Carías, *Reforma constitucional y fraude a la Constitución (1999-2009)*, Academia de Ciencias Políticas y Sociales, Caracas 2009, pp. 217ff;

583 See, in general, Antonio Canova González, Luis Alfonso Herrera Orellana, and Karina Anzola Spadaro, *¿Expropiaciones o vías de hecho? (La degradación continuada del derecho fundamental de propiedad en la Venezuela actual,"* Funeda, Universidad Católica Andrés Bello, Caracas 2009.

tion, of the private assets used in that sector or activity. The institution of nationalization was established in the 1961 Constitution (Article 97) and was first applied in the 1970s, through processes in which always was combined a legislative decision to reserve to the state the economic sector or activity and the administrative process of expropriation of the needed private assets, in order to make the reservation effective."[584]

In effect, Article 97 of the 1961 Constitution established the possibility of the state, through organic law and based on motives of national convenience or interest, reserving for itself some industries and services. That article was initially used to nationalize the natural gas industry in 1971 and the iron mineral exploitation industry in 1974.[585]

The oil industry and commerce were nationalized in 1975 by means of the 1975 Organic Law Reserving to the State the Industry and Commerce of Hydrocarbons,[586] which reserved that activity to the state; terminated foreign enterprises' existing concessions for the exploration and exploitation of oil; and established a procedure to expropriate private assets used for that activity, including payment to private industry participants.

The state's reservation institution was maintained in Article 302 of the 1999 Constitution, which establishes that "the State reserves for itself, by means of the corresponding organic law and for reasons of national convenience, the oil activity and other industries, exploitations, services and assets of public interest and strategic character." Regarding the reservation of the oil industry to the state, which, as mentioned, was decided in 1975, was ratified in the 2001 Organic Hydrocarbons Law, providing in Article 9 that:

> activities relating to the exploration in search of hydrocarbon reservoirs encompassed in this Decree-Law, to their extraction in natural state, to their initial production, transport and storage, are denominated as primary activities for purposes of this Decree-Law. In accordance with what is provided in Article 302 of the Constitution of the Bolivarian Republic of Venezuela, the primary activities indicated, as well as those relating to works required by their mana-

---

584 See Allan R. Brewer-Carías, "Introducción al Régimen Jurídico de las Nacionalizaciones en Venezuela", in *Archivo de Derecho Público y Ciencias de la Administración*, III (1972-1979), Instituto de Derecho Público, Universidad Central de Venezuela, Caracas 1981, Vol. 2: pp. 23-44.

585 *Ley que Reserva al Estado la Industria del Gas Natural*, in *Gaceta Oficial* N° 29.594, Aug. 26, 1971; Decree Law N° 580, Nov. 26, 1974 (*Decreto Ley que Reserva al Estado la Industria de la Explotación del Mineral de Hierro*), in *Gaceta Oficial* N° 30.577, Dec. 16, 1974.

586 *Gaceta Oficial*, Extra. N° 1.769, Aug. 29, 1975. The 1975 Organic Nationalization Law reserved to the state all matters "related to the exploration of the national territory in search for petroleum, asphalt and any other hydrocarbons; to the exploitation of reservoirs thereof, the manufacturing or upgrading, transportation by special means and storage; internal and external trade of the exploited and upgraded substances, and the works required for their handling" (Article 1). Article 5 ordered that the activities be exercised directly by the national executive or entities owned by it, and it authorized private participation through operating agreements or association agreements in certain circumstances. See Allan R. Brewer-Carías, "Comentarios en torno a la nacionalización petrolera," in *Revista Resumen* 5, Caracas 1974, 22; Román J. Duque Corredor, *El derecho de la nacionalización petrolera*, Editorial Jurídica Venezolana, Caracas 1975, p. 22.

gement, remain reserved to the State in the terms established in this Decree-Law.[587]

Other constitutional mean for compulsory acquisition of private rights and property is expropriation, defined in Article 115 of the Constitution as the compulsory acquisition by the state of any privately owned assets, rights, or property through a specific procedure (due process) and with payment of just compensation; which applies regardless of whether the economic sector or activity affected has been or not reserved to the state, and of whether the decision is taken regarding a specific private asset or assets affected to an economic activity. According to the constitutional provision, the 2002 Expropriation Law defines expropriation in Article 2 as:

> an institution of Public Law, by which the State acts for the benefit of a cause of public utility or social interest, with the purpose of obtaining the compulsory transfer of the right to property or any other right of private individuals to its [the state's] patrimony, through a final judicial decision and timely payment of just compensation.[588]

Expropriation can be made through an act of general effects, like a special statute. This was the case, for instance, with the 1970 expropriations in connection with the iron and oil industries. In those cases, the statutes implementing nationalization declared the reservation and ordered expropriation of the interests of the former concessionaries following specific rules of procedure.

The 2002 Expropriation Law establishes the general procedure for expropriation and contemplates the possibility of an expropriation decree applying to more than one asset of more than one individual or entity (Articles 5 and 6). The Expropriation Law also contemplates that through special laws it is possible to provide for other procedures and rules to be applied to specific expropriation cases, including expropriation of multiple assets of multiple subjects (Article 4).

The former Supreme Court of Justice held that "the institution of expropriation applies not only when the State resorts to it, through the organisms authorized to do so, in compliance with the Law that governs it, but also within its conceptual amplitude, its principles are applied by extension to all the cases of deprivation of private property, or of patrimonial diminution, for reasons of public utility or public interest."[589]

Consequently, in Venezuela, all property, rights, and assets are subject to lawful expropriation and protected from unlawful expropriation, being an important change introduced in the 1999 Constitution and the 2002 Expropriation Law the clarification that expropriation, as the compulsory acquisition of assets by the state, can refer to the right to property (*derecho de propiedad*) and to any other right of private par-

---

587 2001 Organic Law of Hydrocarbons in *Gaceta Oficial* N° 37.323, Nov. 13, 2001.

588 *Gaceta Oficial* N° 37.475, July 1, 2002. See the comments to this Law in Allan R. Brewer-Carías et al., *Ley de Expropiación por causa de utilidad pública o social*, Editorial Jurídica Venezolana, Caracas 2002, pp. 7-100.

589 See Supreme Court of Justice, Politico-Administrative Chamber, Decision of Oct. 3, 1990 (Case: *Inmobiliaria Cumboto, C.A.*), in *Jurisprudencia Ramírez & Garay* 114, Caracas 1990, pp. 551-552.

ties (*algún otro derecho de los particulares*) (Article 2) or assets of any nature (*bienes de cualquier naturaleza*) (Article 7). Accordingly, expropriation is conceived in Article 115 of the Constitution as a constitutional guarantee of the right to property, any other rights or assets of any nature, which cannot be taken by the state except through a judicial procedure (juridical guarantee) and with just compensation (patrimonial or economic guarantee). The consequence of these provisions is that any appropriation of private rights by the state without compensation is a confiscation, and it is unconstitutional except as a criminal sanction imposed by judges in cases of corruption or drug trafficking (Article 116). That is, any taking of private property, rights, or assets by the state, or any termination of private individual rights by the state without following expropriation procedures or other means for acquiring property (e.g., requisition, seizure, reversion, criminal sanction) is considered confiscation, which is prohibited in the Constitution.

Consequently, any limitations, contributions, restrictions, or obligations imposed on property, rights, or assets implying deprivation of the essence of the right or asset or when such regulations annihilate the property, right, or asset in question, must be considered as an expropriation. As it was ruled by the Constitutional Chamber of the Supreme Tribunal with respect to Articles 115 and 116 of the Constitution, the limits that can be established regarding private rights and property "must be established on the basis of a legal text, as long as said restrictions do not constitute an absolute or irrational impairment of such property right. That is, impeding the patrimonial capacity of the individuals in such a way that it eventually extinguishes it."[590] In the same sense, the former Supreme Court explained:

> Article 99 of the Constitution establishes the guarantee of the right to property.... [T]he limitation imposed on that right cannot represent an impairment that implies absorption of its attributions to the extent that it eliminates it.... This is, the right to property may be limited, restricted with respect to most of its content, attributions and scope, but this cannot exceed the limit – it is emphasized – by virtue of which such right is left completely empty, there is a central core of that right that is not susceptible of being impaired by the legislator, since if this were so, we would find ourselves before another legal institution (for example, expropriation).[591]

With regard to the prohibition on confiscation, the Court also explained:

> The prohibition of confiscation is related to the principle of reasonability that must guide the adjustment between the actions of the State and the impact on the legal sphere of those subject to the law, for which care must be taken that the activity does not formally or substantially reach the confiscation of the

---

590   Supreme Tribunal of Justice, Constitutional Chamber, Decision N° 3003 of Oct. 14, 2005 (Exp. 04-2538).

591   See Supreme Court of Justice, Decision of Apr. 29, 1997, in *Revista de Derecho Público No. 69–70*, Editorial Jurídica Venezolana, Caracas 1997, pp. 391-92.

assets of the person, which occurs with the total dispossession of the assets or their equivalent.[592]

The aforementioned, in general terms, the constitutional and legal framework established in Venezuela in order for the state to acquire private assets and rights, whether or not the state has reserved for itself an economic sector or activity, except in cases of confiscation imposed as a criminal judicial sanction, always implies the right of the affected individual or enterprise to be compensated. Nonetheless, during the past decade and as a state unconstitutional policy, in numerous cases the state has appropriated private rights and assets without compensation.

II. THE 2006–2007 STATE APPROPRIATION OF PRIVATE ENTERPRISES IN THE NATIONALIZED OIL INDUSTRY

The 1975 Nationalization Organic Law, notwithstanding the decision it contained to reserve the oil industry to the state, provided for private enterprises to participate in primary hydrocarbons activities (Article 5) in two ways: operating agreements and association agreements, including exploration-at-risk and profit-sharing agreements.[593] Consequently, according to the state policy named "oil opening" (*Apertura petrolera*) defined during the 1990s through Congress resolutions (Acuerdos), [594] the state-owned oil nationalized enterprises entered into agreements with private foreign and national enterprises. Consequently, pursuant to such public policy, private oil companies did in fact participate in primary hydrocarbon activities in Venezuela through Operating Agreements, Association Agreements for the Exploration at Shared-Risk-and-Profit, and Association Agreements for the development of the Orinoco Oil Belt (*Faja Petrolífera del Orinoco*).

Although the 2001 Organic Hydrocarbons Law changed the legal framework for the participation of private enterprises in the oil industry, reshaping such participation to only mixed companies –thus repealing the 1975 Nationalization Organic Law– in light of the nonretroactive nature of laws (Article 24 of the 1999 Constitution), the association agreements signed in the 1990s and also those signed in 2001,[595] remained as valid compromise executed by the state that continued to be in force.

592 Supreme Tribunal of Justice, Constitutional Chamber, Decision N° 2152 of Nov. 14, 2007, in *Revista de Derecho Público* 112 (*Estudios sobre la refroma constitucional*), Editorial Jurídica Venezolana, Caracas 2007, pp. 519ff.

593 Regarding the interpretation of Article 5 of the 1975 Organic Nationalization Law and the participation of private companies in the oil industry activities, see Isabel Boscán de Ruesta et al., *La Apertura Petrolera, I Jornadas de Derecho de Oriente*, Fundación Estudios de Derecho administrativo, Caracas 1997.

594 On these legislative decisions, see Allan R. Brewer-Carías, "El régimen nacional de los hidrocarburos aplicable al proceso de la apertura petrolera en el marco de la reserva al Estado de la Industria Petrolera," in *La apertura petrolera, I Jornadas de Derecho de Oriente*, Fundación de Estudios de Derecho Administrativo FUNEDA, Caracas 1997, pp. 2-3.

595 Still in 2001, after the sanctioning of the new Hydrocarbons Law (*Gaceta Oficial* N° 37.323 Nov. 13, 2001), the "Oil Opening" policy was applied by the government according to Article 5 of the 1975 Organic Nationalization Law. For such purpose, legislative authorization was sough for the signing of an association agreement with the China National Oil and Gas Exploration and Development Corporation, a subsidiary of China National Petroleum Corporation, for the production of bitumen and the design,

Starting in 2006, Venezuela initiated a state appropriation policy of the oil industry through the gradual elimination or reduction, by law, of private capital in oil industry activities. This was not a process of nationalization, which, as aforementioned, in Venezuela combines the decision to reserve to the state certain activities followed by expropriation (with compensation) of the affected assets. The oil industry and commerce, as aforementioned, was nationalized in 1975, so in the process developed in 2006–7, based on the 2001 Hydrocarbon Law, no reserve of activities to the state was decided because the reserve of the oil industry to the state already existed. The new policy produced what was the termination of the agreements entered with private companies but without compensation.[596]

This elimination or sharp reduction of private capital in the industry was achieved through three legislative instruments.

First, the Law Regulating Private Participation in Primary Activities, of April 18, 2006, declared the early and unilateral termination of existing operating agreements,[597] considering that they have denaturalized the oil industry "as a result of the so-called Oil Opening, to a point where it violated the higher interests of the State and the basic elements of sovereignty" (Article 1). Hence, Article 2 of that law declared that the content of the operating agreements that arose as a result of the oil "opening" was "incompatible with the rules set forth in the oil nationalization regime." Moreover, "they will be extinguished and the execution of their precepts will no longer be possible as of the publication of this Law in the *Official Gazette*" (Article 2). The termination constitutes an expropriation of rights, even if done through legislative act.[598] Article 3 of the Decree Law ratified the principle set forth in the 2001 Hydrocarbons Organic Law, whereby private capital could participate in primary hydrocarbons activities only by incorporating as mixed companies, which was exactly what had been proposed in the draft constitutional reforms that were rejected

---

construction, and operation of a unit for production and emulsification of natural bitumen for the elaboration of *orimulsión* (BITOR Agreement). The agreement was authorized by the National Assembly on Dec. 17, 2001 (*Gaceta Oficial* N° 37.347 of Dec. 17, 2001), just days before the entry into force of the new 2001 Hydrocarbons Organic Law (Jan. 1, 2002). The approval of the BITOR Agreement was possible because when enacting the 2001 Organic Hydrocarbons Law thorugh a Decree Law, the National Executive included a provision postponing its entry into force until Jan. 1, 2002, that is, after the BITOR agreement was already authorized and signed. See the comments in Allan R. Brewer-Carías, "La estatización de los convenios de asociación que permitían la participación del capital privado en las actividades primarias de hidrocarburos sucritos antes de 2002, mediante su terminación anticipada y unilateral y la confiscación de los bienes afectos a los mismos," in *Nacionalización, Libertad de Empresa y Asociaciones Mixtas*, coord.. Víctor Hernández Mendible, Editorial Jurídica Venezolana, Caracas 2008, pp. 123-88.

596   On the concept of nationalization in Venezuela, see Allan R. Brewer-Carías, "Introducción al régimen jurídico de las nacionalizaciones en Venezuela," in *Archivo de derecho público y ciencias de la administración*, Instituto de Derecho Público, Facultad de Ciencias Jurídicas y Políticas, Universidad Central de Venezuela, Caracas 1981, Vol 1, pp. 23-44.

597   *Gaceta Oficial* N° 38.419, Apr. 18, 2006.

598   See Allan R. Brewer-Carías, "Algunas reflexiones sobre el equilibrio financiero en los contratos administrativos y la aplicabilidad en Venezuela de la concepción amplia de la Teoría del Hecho del Príncipe," in *Revista Control Fiscal y Tecnificación Administrativa* No. 13, Contraloría General de la República, Caracas 1972, pp. 86-93.

in a 2007 referendum.[599] To such end, the National Assembly adopted in March 2006 the Accord Approving the Terms and Conditions for the Creation and Operation of Mixed Companies.[600]

Second, Decree-Law No. 5200 Concerning the Migration of the Association Agreements of the Orinoco Belt and of the Exploration-at-Risk and Profit-Sharing Agreements into Mixed Companies, of February 2007, started the early and unilateral termination of the existing association agreements entered into between 1993 and 2001, establishing the possibility for their transformation (migration) into new mixed companies with a minimum of 50% state equity participation (2001 Organic Hydrocarbon Law, Articles 22 and 27–32). The law required that if the private investors in associations did opt for a mixed company arrangement, they could only be shareholders of those companies with maximum equity participation of 40%. The state shareholder Corporación Venezolana de Petróleo, S.A., or an affiliate of PDVSA would have a 60% maximum equity share (Article 2). For those companies that could not reach an agreement with the state to transform the joint ventures into mixed enterprises, the Decree Law 5200 implied the expropriation of the contractual rights, and the right to be fairly compensated for the damages caused by the execution of such law.

On the other hand, the legislative decision to begin the unilaterally and prematurely end of the association contracts implied the need to ensure the state's immediate assumption of actual industrial operations of each association agreement. Nonetheless, Article 4 of the law gave the private-sector companies that had been party to terminated agreements four months from the date the law was published (February 26, 2007) – that is, until June 26, 2007 – to "agree on the terms and conditions of their possible participation in the new mixed companies" with the ministry of Energy and Mines. It also provided that in such a case they would be conceded two extra months "to submit the aforementioned terms and conditions to the National Assembly for the corresponding authorization, pursuant to the Organic Hydrocarbons Law." Once the four months had elapsed, "without having reached an agreement on the incorporation and operation of the mixed companies," then the republic, through Petróleos de Venezuela, S.A., or its affiliates, was to directly take over the activities exercised by the associations to ensure their continuity, by reason of their character of public use and social interest (Article 5), as it occurred in many cases. Nonetheless, the law mentioned nothing about indemnifying the private companies that did not agree to continue as mixed companies.

Regarding these two laws, by beginning the process of termination of existing public contracts, it can be said that according to the Constitution, they initiated an expropriation process of the contractual rights of private companies, and they did so directly by statute without following the general procedure set forth in the 2001 Expropriations Law. Pursuant to Article 115 of the Constitution, those two laws generated inalienable rights for the contracting companies to be fairly compensated for

---

599   See Allan R. Brewer-Carías, *La Reforma Constitucional de 2007 (Comentarios al proyecto inconstitucionalmente sancionado por la Asamblea Nacional el 2 de Noviembre de 2007)*, Editorial Jurídica Venezolana, Caracas 2007, pp. 129ff.

600   *Gaceta Oficial*, N° 38.410, Mar. 31, 2006.

damages (expropriation of contractual rights) arising from the take over of assets derived from public contracts they validly entered into with the state.

Third, the Law on the Effects of the Migration Process to Mixed Companies of the Orinoco Belt Association Agreements and the Exploration-at-Risk and Profit-Sharing Exploration Agreements, of October 2007,[601] "confiscated" the interests, shares, participation, and rights of companies that had participated in such agreements and associations but had not complied with the requirement to migrate to mixed companies. That is, according to this law, what might have been expropriation initially became, by unilateral and early termination of contracts, a confiscation of rights – in this case, the rights of those companies that did not reach an agreement with the state to continue operating as mixed companies.

In effect, according to this Law on the Effects of the Migration Process, the associations referred to in the Law of the Migration "were extinguished" as of the publication date of such Law or of the "decree that ordered the transfer of the right to exercise primary activities to the mixed companies incorporated pursuant to such Law" in the *Gaceta Oficial* (Article 1).

Decree Law N° 5200 made no mention of the rights to compensation of the private companies that had not agreed to continue as partners of the new mixed companies. However, instead of proceeding to do this in the Law on the Effects of the Migration Process, the state definitively confiscated such rights by declaring the agreements "extinguished" in the dates established in the said Law on the Effects, of October 5, 2007.

For purposes of executing such confiscation, Article 2 of the Law on the Effects of the Migration Process expressly provided that "the interests, shares and participations" in the associations referred to in Article 1 of the migration law, in the companies incorporated to develop the corresponding projects, and in "the assets used to conduct the activities of such associations, including property rights, contractual and other rights," which, until June 26, 2007 (pursuant to the term established in Article 4 of the migration law), "belonged to the private sector companies with whom agreement was not reached for migrating to a mixed company, are hereby transferred, based on the principle of reversion, without the need for any additional action or instrument, to the new mixed companies incorporated as a result of the migration of the respective associations, except for the provisions of Article 2 herein." This provision, according to the Venezuelan constitutional regime constitutes a confiscation of such assets, which Article 116 of the Constitution prohibits.

In other words, the state, by law, ordered the forced transfer of privately owned assets to newly incorporated mixed companies without compensation or due process; constituting an unconstitutional confiscation. In these cases, in no way could the takeover be justified by the principle of reversion, which is essentially associated with the figure of administrative concessions, which do not exist in hydrocarbons

601   *Gaceta Oficial* N° 38.785, Oct. 8, 2007.

matters, and is applicable only when the corresponding contract arrives to its term, once assets are duly amortized.[602]

III. THE 2008–2009 NATIONALIZATION AND STATE APPROPRIATION

1. *The Nationalization of the Iron and Steel Industry*

On April 30, 2008, in Decree Law N° 6,058[603] issued by the national executive according to the legislative delegation contained in the 2007 enabling law,[604] the iron and steel exploitation and transformation industry located in the Guayana region was nationalized. The motives for nationalization were strategic, as Guayana has the highest iron mineral reserves of the country, and those reserves have been nationalized since 1975[605] (Article 1). As a direct consequence of the reservation to the state of this industry, and to complete the nationalization process by means of expropriation, all business activities of the company SIDOR, C.A., and those of any of its subsidiaries and affiliates were declared of "public utility and social interest" (Article 3).

Therefore, the iron and steel industry was reserved to the state as a consequence of the order to transform SIDOR, C.A., its subsidiaries, and it affiliates to state-owned companies, with state shareholder participation of at least 60%, according to Article 100 of the Organic Law of Public Administration (Article 3).

With regard to the managerial transformation, Article 4 of the decree law establishes that the republic, through the Popular Power Ministry for Basic and Mining Industries or any of its decentralized organizations, would be the legal stockowner of the percentage belonging to the public sector in the newly created state-owned companies. To ensure the proper transfer of all activities resulting from this transformation, and in accordance with Article 5 of the law, the Popular Power Ministry for Basic and Mining Industries or any of its decentralized organizations, within seven days of publication of the law, was to establish a transitional commission for each company that would be incorporated in SIDOR's executive board. For nationalized private companies, Article 5 mandated that they fully cooperate with the nationalization process to guarantee a successful and safe transition, which ended on June 30, 2008. Article 10 of the law exempted from any direct or indirect tax contribution all business agreements, title transfers, and negotiations, as well as any operation that could result in economic gains, needed to transfer the private companies to state-owned companies.

---

602   As has been said by Eduardo García de Enterría and Tomás R. Fernández, the reversion has lost "its old character of being an essential element of every concession and comes to be regarded as an accidental element of the business, that is, it is admissible only in the case of an express accord, like one more piece, when conceived in this way, of the economic formula that all concessions consist in," in their *Curso de derecho administrativo*, 13th ed., Thomson-Civitas, Madrid 2006, Vol 1, pp.763.

603   *Gaceta Oficial* N° 38.928, May 12, 2008.

604   *Gaceta Oficial* N° 38.617, Feb. 1, 2007.

605   Decree Law N° 580, Nov. 26, 1974 (*Decreto Ley que Reserva al Estado la Industria de la Explotación del Mineral de Hierro*), in *Gaceta Oficial* N° 30.577, Dec. 16, 1974.

To ensure the transfer of property and compensation to private companies being nationalized, Article 6 provided for sixty continuous days, beginning on the publication date of the organic decree law – that is, until August 12, 2008 – to agree on the terms and conditions of their possible participation in the state-owned companies. A technical committee with state and private representation was formed in order to determine a fair value to base the appropriate compensation owned to the nationalized companies (Article 7). On March 25, 2009, it was announced that the state and the Argentine enterprise Techint, which previously held majority ownership of SIDOR shares, reached an agreement to fix compensation and establish a schedule for payment.

The decree law established that if no agreement for the transformation of the private companies into state-owned companies had been reached by August 12, 2008, as in fact occurred, then the republic, through the Popular Power Ministry for Basic and Mining Industries or any of its decentralized organizations, would assume total control and management of the private companies to ensure the continuous operation of the nationalized industry. Articles 9 and 11 provided that all layoffs were to be frozen from the time of the publication of the organic law until the transformation process was over, and that all employees of the iron and steel industry would be covered under their respective collective contracts.

Additionally, in case no agreement was reached for transformation, Article 8 provided an expropriation clause for the shares of such companies based on the Expropriation Law. However, Article 8 also provided that to estimate the "compensation or fair value" of the assets being expropriated, no lost profit or indirect damages would be taken into account.

2.   The Nationalization of the Cement Industry

Following the same trend used to nationalize the iron and steel industry, on May 27, 2008, in Decree Law N° 6091, as part of the 2007 enabling law, the cement industry was nationalized. The motive for nationalization was strategic (Article 1), and as a direct consequence of the reservation to the state of this industry, and to complete the nationalization process by means of expropriation, the activities developed by the main existing cement companies[606] – as well as any of their subsidiaries and affiliates – were declared of public utility and social interest (Article 3).

Therefore, the cement industry was reserved to the state and transformed, in accordance with Article 100 of the Organic Law of Public Administration, into state-owned companies, with state shareholder participation of at least 60% (Article 3).

With regard to the managerial transformation, Article 4 of the decree law established that the republic, through the Popular Power Ministry for Basic and Mining Industries or any of its decentralized organizations, would be the legal stockowner of the percentage belonging to the public sector in the newly created state-owned companies. To ensure the proper transfer of all activities resulting from the trans-

---

606   Cemex Venezuela, S.A.C.A.; Holcim Venezuela, C.A.; and C.A. Fábrica Nacional de Cementos, S.A.C.A. (Grupo Lafarge de Venezuela).

formation, and in accordance with Article 5 of the law, the Popular Power Ministry for Basic and Mining Industries or any of its decentralized organizations, within seven days of publishing the law would establish a transitional commission for each company to be incorporated into the executive board of the nationalized companies. In fact, no such committee was established, and public officials occupied the enterprises. In any case, Article 5 mandated that private shareholders fully cooperate with nationalization to guarantee a successful and safe transition, to be completed by December 31, 2008 (Article 6). Article 10 of the law exempted from any direct or indirect tax contribution, all business agreements, title transfers, and negotiations needed to conclude the transformation and any operation that could result in economic gains.

Because the takeover of the cement industry was formally a nationalization, to ensure the transfer of property and the compensation due to the private companies being nationalized, Article 6 of the decree law gave them sixty continuous days, beginning on the publication date of the organic decree law – that is, until September 18, 2008 – to agree on terms and conditions of possible participation in the new state-owned companies. A technical committee with the participation of state and private representation was formed to determine the fair value to base the appropriate compensation owned to the nationalized companies (Article 7).

The government signed a memorandum of understanding with two of the shareholders of the nationalized enterprises (Holcim and Lafarge), in which they agreed on the compensation price and payment conditions. The agreements were not effective, and at least one of the enterprises initiated international arbitration. The third enterprise (Cemex) did not reach an agreement with the state and submitted to international arbitration. In that latter case, however, the state signed an agreement for technical assistance with the company, with limited duration, that allowed the nationalized industry to continue operations but with the systems of the private company.

In this case of the cement industry, in similar terms to the provisions regarding the nationalization of the iron and steel industry, the decree law established that if no agreement for the transformation was reached by December 31, 2008, as in fact occurred, then the republic, through the Popular Power Ministry for Basic and Mining Industries or any of its decentralized organizations, would assume total control and management of the private companies to ensure continuous operations of the nationalized industry.

3.   *The State Appropriation of Assets and Services Related to Primary Hydrocarbon Activities*

In May 2009, the National Assembly, also on the basis of strategy, sanctioned the organic law reserving for the state the assets and services related to the primary activities of the oil industry[607] established in the Hydrocarbon Law (Article 1), which were formerly conducted by Petróleos de Venezuela, S.A. (PDVSA) and its subsidiaries, and later assumed by private companies, being activities essential to the industry (Article 2). The consequence of the nationalization was according to Article

---

607   See *Gaceta Oficial* N° 39.173, May 7, 2009.

1 of the law, that activities were to be "directly executed by the Republic, by Petró-leos de Venezuela, S.A. (PDVSA), or any of its designed subsidiaries, or by mixed companies under Petróleos de Venezuela, S.A. (PDVSA) control."

Article 7 of the law assigned "public order" character to its provisions, meaning that provisions "shall have preference over any other legal dispositions related to the matter." However, Article 5 established that all the aforementioned assets and servi-ces provided or required were to be considered "public services and of public and social interest." Such assets and services are enumerated in Article 2 of the law as follows: water, steam, or gas injections aimed to increase the oilfield's energy and improve the recovery factor; gas compression; and all goods and services connected to activities in the Lago de Maracaibo (boats for personnel transport, divers, and maintenance); cargo ships (including diesel, industrial waters, and any other sup-plies), crane ships, tug boats, buoys, padding and filling cranes, pipe and wire lines, ship maintenance, workshops, docks, floating docks, and ports of any nature.

To carry out the state appropriation, Article 3 of the Law empowered the Popular Power Ministry for Energy and Oil to define by unilateral administrative acts (reso-lutions) the assets and services listed in the provisions of Articles 1 and 2. In the case that such resolutions are issued, according to Article 3 of the organic law, all previous contracts and agreements regarding the reserved activities and signed bet-ween private companies and state-owned companies will be considered *ipso jure* extinguished by virtue of the law. The law recognized the contracts, for the purpose of their early termination, as "administrative contracts" (Article 3).

The reservation to the state of the assets and services related to primary hydro-carbon activities –different from previous nationalization processes– provided that as of the date of the law's publication (May 7, 2009), "Petróleos de Venezuela, S.A., (PDVSA) or any of its subsidiaries will take possession of any assets and control of all operations related to the reserved activities," which effectively occurred. That is, according to the law, an "expedite mechanism" was provided according to the needs of the oil industry, "allowing Petróleos de Venezuela, S.A. (PDVSA) or any of its subsidiaries, to take over assets and control the operations of related the reserved activities, as a previous step to complete the expropriation process."

To that effect, the law authorized the Popular Power Ministry for Energy and Oil to take all available measures to ensure the continuous operation of the reserved activities, with authorization to ask for support from any state organ or entity. In this case, the National Guard was chosen to achieve this goal. Additionally, the law compelled all actors in the process to fully and peacefully collaborate in the transfer of operations, facilities, documents, and property affected by the law provisions; otherwise, they could be subject to administrative or criminal sanctions (Article 4).

To ensure the transfer to the state of all assets and services, Article 8 provided that any permits, certifications, authorizations, and valid registries belonging to the private operating companies, or pertaining to any of the reserved activities, would *ipso jure* be transferred to Petróleos de Venezuela or a designated subsidiary.

Additionally, to facilitate the transfer, Article 9 establishes that any act, business, or agreement related to the transfer of assets and operations enshrined under the organic law would be exempt from any national taxes.

Also, Article 10 of the organic law, as part of the transfer process, gives power to the Popular Power Ministry for Energy and Oil to make any decisions regarding the transfer of all working personnel from the statized companies to Petróleos de Venezuela or any of its subsidiaries. The state appropriation and immediate takeover of all goods, services, and assets obligated the state to fairly compensate shareholders of the private companies that the state took over. Nonetheless, for such purpose, the law only referred to the expropriation process as a mere possibility, providing that the state could (*podrá*) decree total or partial expropriation of all shares and assets belonging to any company doing business or conducting any of the reserved, in accordance with the Expropriation Law. In such cases, Petróleos de Venezuela, S.A., or any of its subsidiaries would be the expropriating entity (Article 6).

In the case of the state appropriation of the oil industry assets and services, the law established restricted criteria regarding the just and fair compensation provided for in Article 115 of the Constitution. To estimate the fair value of the assets being expropriated, Article 6 provided that in no case could lost profits or indirect damages be taken into account and that valuation would be based on "book value less all wages, payroll and environmental passives determined by the proper authorities." Article 6 adds that the time to effectively take possession would be taken into account to establish fair value. Additionally, payments could be through cash, bonds, or obligations issued by public entities (Article 6).

In any event, the day after the publication of the organic law, on May 8, 2009, the Popular Power Ministry for Energy and Oil passed Resolution N° 051,[608] listing all services, sectors, goods, and companies "affected by the takeover measures" (Article 1), and instructing Petróleos de Venezuela, S.A., or any of its subsidiaries, "to take control over operations and immediate possession of the mentioned facilities, documents, capital assets and equipment" (Article 2).

To ensure immediate takeover, the law provided that to register all information related to all affected goods, services, and assets, within the following fifteen days an inventory must be made to be signed by Petróleos de Venezuela, S.A., or any of its subsidiaries and the private companies, or be made through a judicial inspection or notarized act (Article 2). In that same resolution, the Popular Power Ministry for Energy and Oil reserved to itself the right to apply any necessary measures to guarantee the continuous operation of the affected business, as well as the right to identify other assets, services, companies, or sectors that follow under the provisions of the organic law (Article 3).

A few days later, on May 13, 2009,[609] the Popular Power Ministry for Energy and Oil passed Resolution N° 54, naming an additional list of companies conducting business and in possession of essential capital assets (gas compression) connected with primary hydrocarbon activities in accordance with the Hydrocarbon Organic Law, the list being considered as a declarative not compelling one (Article 1).

The fact of all the provisions and actions was the immediate takeover of all the assets and services unilaterally enumerated by the state, without any compensation

---

608   See *Gaceta Oficial* N° 39.174, May 8, 2009.
609   See *Gaceta Oficial* N° 39.177, May 13, 2009.

paid or expropriation process initiated. It simply was another confiscation of private property, prohibited in the Constitution.

4. *The Reservation to the State of Petrochemical Activities*

On June 2009, the Law for the Development of the Petrochemical Activities was sanctioned,[610] reserving to the state the basic and intermediate petrochemical industry, as well as the works, assets, and installations required for its accomplishment (Article 5). "Basic petrochemical" includes the industrial processes related to physical transformation of the basic components of hydrocarbons, understood as products obtained from hydrocarbons with a very specific chemical formula (Article 4.2). "Intermediate petrochemical" includes industrial processes related to the chemical or physical transformation obtained from the basic petrochemical (Article 4.3).

The reservation to the state of petrochemical activities means that only the state, enterprises it exclusively owns, or mixed enterprises it controls can undertake such activities. Mixed enterprises are subject to prior authorization from the National Assembly, once informed by the Ministry of Energy and Oil about the specific circumstances and conditions in each case (Article 5).

The same law declared that because of economic and political sovereignty and for reasons of national strategy, the state shall remain as the owner of all shares of Petroquímica de Venezuela, S.A., or of any other entity that in its substitution could be established to manage the petrochemical industry (Article 6).

IV. THE STATE APPROPRIATIONS OF RURAL LAND AND ALIMENTARY INDUSTRIES

Since the enactment of the Land and Farming Law,[611] not only the possibility for the state to occupy and expropriate private land was extended, leading to the massive appropriation of private land by the state, without compensation, but also the possibility for the state to take over rural land simply ignoring its condition of private own property supported in the due registered titles, imposing in many cases to the owner, without legal support, the impossible burden to proof a property tradition for almost two hundred years.[612]

On the other hand, sine 2007, a massive process of expropriation, in many cases without due compensation, and of forced occupation of assets and industries by public authorities, with the support of the national guard, have taken place, based on "strategic" or "alimentary sovereignty" motives. In the latter case, the process has been based on the provisions of the Organic Law on Farming and Alimentary Secu-

---

610   See *Gaceta Oficial* N° 39.203, June 18, 2009.

611   See Ley de Tierras y Desarrollo Agrario in *Gaceta Oficial* N° 5.771 Extra. of May 18, 2005.

612   See Antonio Canova González, Luis Alfonso Herrera Orellana and "Karina Anzola Spadaro, *¿Expropiaciones o Vías de hecho? (La degradación continuada del derecho fundamental de propiedad en la Venezuela actual)*, FUNEDA, Caracas 2009, pp. 115 ff. See also Allan R. Brewer-Carías, "El régimen de las tierras baldías y la adquisición del derecho de propiedad privada sobre tierras rurales en Venezuela," in *Estudios de derecho administrativo* 2005-2007, Editorial Jurídica Venezolana, Caracas 2007, pp. 327-374.

rity and Sovereignty,[613] which assigns expropriation powers to the executive without the need of a previous declaration of a specific public interest or public utility, and allowing the State to occupy private industries without compensation.[614] Also, the Law for the defense of persons in their access to goods and services [615] has allowed indiscriminate occupations of private property and industries, supporting its take over by public authorities, in many cases *sine die* and without compensation. [616]

PART THREE

CONSTITUTIONAL REFORMS DESIGNED TO CONSOLIDATE AUTHORITARIANISM

The 1999 Constitution, after being applied for one decade by an authoritarian government, during the years 2007 and 2009 was the object of two reform projects, one that has failed and the other that has succeeded – both marked by authoritarian trends. The president announced the first one in January 2007 and, at his initiative, submitted the proposed reforms to the National Assembly in August 2007. Once approved by the National Assembly as draft constitutional reforms, they were submitted to approval referendum in December 2007, where they were rejected by popular vote. The intent of this constitutional reform was to consolidate the authoritarian government that had taken shape in the country, by formalizing a constitutional framework for a socialist, centralist, military, and police state (Chapters 10, 11, and 12). Nonetheless, despite its popular rejection and contrary to the Constitution, many of the proposals have been unconstitutionally implemented through statutes and decree laws (Chapter 13) and through decisions adopted by the Constitutional Chamber of the Supreme Tribunal (Chapter 14). The president announced the second constitutional reform in 2008, after the first one had been rejected. That reform

---

613 See Ley Orgánica de soberanía y seguridad alimentaria, *Gaceta Oficial* N° 5.889, Extra., July 31, 2008. See the comments in José Ignacio Hernández G., "Planificación y soberanía alimentaria," in *Revista de Derecho Público (Estudios sobre los Decretos Leyes)* 115, Editorial Jurídica Venezolana, Caracas 2008, pp. 389-394.

614 See Carlos García Soto, "Notas sobre la expansión del ámbito de la declaratoria de utilidad pública o interés social en la expropiación," in *Revista de Derecho Público*, N° 115 (Estudios sobre los Decretos Leyes), Editorial Jurídica Venezolana, Caracas 2008, 149-151; Antonio Canova González, Luis Alfonso Herrera Orellana and Karina Anzola Spadaro, *¿Expropiaciones o Vías de hecho? (La degradación continuada del derecho fundamental de propiedad en la Venezuela actual)*, FUNEDA, Caracas 2009, pp. 143ff.

615 See Decreto Ley N° 6,092 para la defensa de las personas en el acceso a los bienes y servicios, *Gaceta Oficial* N° 5,889 Extra. of July 31, 2008,

616 See Juan Domingo Alfonzo Paradisi, "Comentarios en cuanto a los procedimientos administrativos establecidos en el decreto N° 6.092 con rango valor y fuerza de Ley para la defensa de las personas en el acceso a los bienes y servicios," in *Revista de Derecho Público No.* 115, *(Estudios sobre los Decretos Leyes)*, Editorial Jurídica Venezolana, Caracas 2008, pp. 246ff.; Karina Anzola Spadaro, "El carácter autónomo de las 'medidas preventivas' contempladas en el artículo 111 del Decreto Ley para la defensa de las personas en el acceso a los bienes y servicios," in id., 271-79; Antonio Canova González, Luis Alfonso Herrera Orellana and Karina Anzola Spadaro, *¿Expropiaciones o Vías de hecho? (La degradación continuada del derecho fundamental de propiedad en la Venezuela actual)*, FUNEDA, Caracas 2009, pp. 163ff.

referred precisely to one of the rejected constitutional reform proposals, the one to substitute the constitutional limits on reelection of public officials –in particular, the president– with the possibility of continuous, unlimited reelection of public officials. This reform was conceived of as a constitutional amendment and elaborated as an initiative of the National Assembly. It was submitted to approval referendum in February 2009 and was approved by popular vote (Chapter 15).

CHAPTER 10
THE FAILED ATTEMPT TO CONSOLIDATE AN AUTHORITARIAN AND ANTIDEMOCRATIC POLITICAL SYSTEM IN THE CONSTITUTION

I.   A NEW FRAUD ON THE CONSTITUTION

On November 2, 2007, the National Assembly of Venezuela, following President Chávez's proposals, sanctioned a major constitutional reform to transform the democratic rule-of-law and decentralized social state established in the 1999 Constitution into a socialist, centralized, repressive, and militaristic state.[617] In the referendum for the approval of the constitutional reform on December 2, 2007, the people rejected the proposed reform.[618]

The constitutional reform was intended to transform the most essential and fundamental aspects of the state, making it one of the most important reforms in all of Venezuelan constitutional history. With it, the decentralized, democratic, pluralistic, and social state built and consolidated since the Second World War would have been radically changed to create a socialist, centralized, repressive, and militaristic state grounded in a so-called Bolivarian doctrine, which has been identified with twenty-first-century socialism and an economic system of state capitalism.[619] This reform was sanctioned following the president's proposal, which evaded the procedure established in the Constitution for such fundamental change. Thus, the reform defrauded the Constitution, being sanctioned through a procedure established for other purposes, to deceive the people.[620] That is why it has been qualified as one more step of the "permanent coup d'état" that has occurred in Venezuela.[621]

---

617 See Allan R. Brewer-Carías, *La reforma constitucional de 2007 (Comentarios al proyecto inconstitucionalmente sancionado por la Asamblea Nacional el 2 de noviembre de 2007)*, Editorial Jurídica Venezolana, Caracas 2007.

618 According to information from the National Electoral Council on Dec. 2, 2007, of 16,109,664 registered voters, only 9,002,439 voted (44.11% abstention); of voters, 4,504,354 rejected the proposal (50.70%). This means that there were only 4,379,392 votes to approve the proposal (49.29%), so only 28% of registered voters voted for the approval.

619 See *Proyecto de exposición de motivos para la reforma constitucional, Presidencia de la República, Proyecto Reforma Constitucional. Propuesta del Presidente Hugo Chávez*, Caracas Agosto 2007, p. 19.

620 See Rogelio Pérez Perdomo, "La Constitución de papel y su reforma," in *Revista de Derecho Público No. 112 (Estudios sobre la reforma constitucional)*, Editorial Jurídica Venezolana, Caracas 2007, p. 14; Gerardo Fernández, "Aspectos esenciales de la modificación constitucional propuesta por el Presidente de la república. La modificación constitucional en fraude a la democracia," in id., pp. 21-25; Fortunato González, "Constitución histórica y poder constituyente," in id., pp. 33-36; Lolymar Hernández Camargo, "Los límites del cambio constitucional como garantía de pervivencia del Estado de derecho," in id.,

The most important consequence of this draft reform from citizens' perspective was that, with it, an official state ideology and doctrine was to be formally establis-hed in Venezuela. That ideology was socialist and supposedly Bolivarian, which as a state doctrine (despite its imprecision –therein lies the danger) would allow for no dissidence. It must not be forgotten that the citizens have a constitutional duty to ensure the enforcement of the Constitution (Article 131); thus, if this reform had been approved, all citizens would have had the duty to actively contribute to the implementation of the state's official doctrine. Even a neutral position would not have been admissible. Thus, any thought, expression of thought, action, or omission that could have been considered contrary to the official socialist and Bolivarian doc-trine, or that the authorities might have considered as not contributing to the deve-lopment of socialism, could have been determined a violation of constitutional duty, subject to possible criminalization and criminal sanctions. It was a unique and offi-cial way of thinking.

The rejected reforms were the conclusion of a process that the president began in January 2007, when he announced that he would propose a series of reforms to the Constitution of 1999.[622] For such purpose, he designated the Presidential Council for the Reform of the Constitution.[623] The council was presided over by the president of the National Assembly and composed of officials from each branch of government, including the second vice president of the National Assembly and four additional deputies, the president of the Supreme Tribunal of Justice, the people's defender, the minister of labor, the attorney general, and the prosecutor general. The president instructed the council by decree to "work according to the Chief of State's guideli-nes in strict confidentiality" (Article 2),[624] contrary to the principles of any form of constitutional reform in a democratic country.

Guidelines for the proposed reforms emerged from various discussions and spee-ches of the president. These pointed to, on the one hand, the formation of a state of popular power or of communal power, or a communal state (*estado del poder popu-lar o del poder communal, o estado comunal*), built on the communal councils (*con-sejos comunales*) as primary political units or social organizations. The communal councils, whose members are not elected by means of universal, direct, and secret suffrage, had already been created by statute in 2006,[625] parallel to the municipal

---

pp. 37-45; Claudia Nikken, "La soberanía popular y el trámite de la reforma constitucional promovida por iniciativa presidencial el 15 de agosto de 2007," in id., pp. 51-58.

621 See José Amando Mejía Betancourt, "La ruptura del hilo constitucional," in id., 47. The term was first used by Francois Mitterand, *Le coup d'État permanent*, Éditions 10/18, Paris 1993.

622 See the 1999 Constitution in *Gaceta Oficial* N° 36.860, Dec. 30, 1999, republished in *Gaceta Oficial* N° 5452, Extra. Mar. 24, 2000. For commentary on the Constitution, see Allan R. Brewer-Carías, *La Constitución de 1999. Derecho constitucional venezolano,* 2 vols., Editorial Jurídica Venezolano, Cara-cas 2004.

623 Decree N° 5138 (Jan. 17, 2007), in *Gaceta Oficial* N° 38.607, Jan. 18, 2007, establishing the Consejo Presidencial para la Reforma de la Constitución.

624 Id., Art. 2. This was also declared publicly by the president of the National Assembly when she took her seat as part of the council. *El Universal*, Caracas Feb. 20, 2007.

625 Ley de Consejos Comunales, *Gaceta Oficial, Extra.* 5.806, Apr. 10, 2006. This statute was replaced by Ley Orgánica de los Consejos Comunales. See *Gaceta Oficial* N° 39.335, Dec. 28, 2009.

entities, supposedly to channel citizen participation in public affairs. However, they operate within a system of centralized management by the national executive power and without any territorial autonomy.[626] On the other hand, the guidelines for reform also referred to the structuring of a socialist state and the substitution of the existing system of economic freedom and mixed economy with a state and collectivist economic system subject to centralized planning, which minimizes the role of individuals and eliminates any vestige of economic liberties or private property as constitutional rights.

In accordance with these orientations, the 2007 rejected reform intended to radically transform the state by creating a completely new juridical order. A change of that nature, according to Article 347 of the 1999 Constitution, required the convening and election of a Constituent Assembly and could not be undertaken by means of mere constitutional reform. The procedure for constitutional reform is applicable only to "a partial revision of the Constitution and a substitution of one or several of its norms without modifying the structure and fundamental principles of the Constitutional text." This limited constitutional change is obtained through debate and sanctioning in the National Assembly, followed by approval in popular referendum.[627]

Nonetheless, despite these constitutional provisions, with the rejected reforms, a political tactic that has been a common denominator in the actions of the authoritarian regime was repeated: acting fraudulently with respect to the Constitution. That is, existing institutions were used in a manner that appeared to adhere to constitutional form and procedure to proceed, as the Supreme Tribunal has warned, "towards the creation of a new political regime, a new constitutional order, without altering the established legal system."[628] This occurred in February 1999, in the convening of a consultative referendum on whether to convene a constituent assembly when that institution was not prefigured in the then-existing Constitution of 1961.[629] It occurred with the December 1999 Decree on the Transitory Regime of the Public Powers, with respect to the 1999 Constitution, which was never the subject of an approbatory referendum.[630] It has continued to occur in subsequent years with the progressive destruction of democracy through the exercise of power and the sequeste-

626   See Allan R. Brewer-Carías, "El inicio de la desmunicipalización en Venezuela: La organización del poder popular para eliminar la descentralización, la democracia representativa y la participación a nivel local," in *AIDA, Revista de la Asociación Internacional de Derecho Administrativo,* Universidad Nacional Autónoma de México, Asociación Internacional de Derecho Administrativo, Mexico City 2007, pp. 49-67.

627   See Allan R. Brewer-Carías, *Hacia la consolidación de un estado socialista, centralizado y militarista. Comentarios sobre el alcance y sentido de las propuestas de reforma Constitucional 2007*, Editorial Jurídica Venezolana, Caracas 2007.

628   See the decision of the Constitutional Chamber of the Supreme Tribunal of Justice N° 74 (Jan. 25, 2006), in *Revista de Derecho Público* 105, Editorial Jurídica Venezolana, Caracas 2006, pp. 76ff.

629   See Allan R. Brewer-Carías, *Asamblea constituyente y ordenamiento constitucional*, Academia de Ciencias Políticas y Sociales, Caracas 1999.

630   See Allan R. Brewer-Carías, *Golpe de estado y proceso constituyente en Venezuela,* Universidad Nacional Autónoma de México, Mexico City 2002.

ring of successive public rights and liberties, all supposedly based on legal and constitutional provisions.[631]

In this instance, once again, constitutional provisions were fraudulently used for ends other than those for which they were established; they were used to radically transform the state, thus disrupting the civil order of the social-democratic state to convert the state into a socialist, centralized, repressive, and militarist state in which representative democracy, republican alternation in office, and the concept of decentralized power would have disappeared, with all power instead concentrated in the decisions of the head of state. As is constitutionally proscribed, and as the Constitutional Chamber of the Supreme Tribunal of Justice summarized in Decision No. 74 (January 25, 2006), a symbolic case, it occurred "with the fraudulent use of powers conferred by martial law in Germany under the *Weimar* Constitution, forcing the Parliament to concede to the fascist leaders, on the basis of terms of doubtful legitimacy, plenary constituent powers by conferring an unlimited legislative power."[632] In the case of the 2007 reforms, the various acts adopted (the presidential initiative, the sanction by the National Assembly, the convening of referendum by the National Electoral Council) were all challenged through judicial review through actions of unconstitutionality and *amparo* and, in all cases, the Supreme Tribunal diligently declared all as inadmissible.[633]

Nonetheless, the fraud on the Constitution was initially evidenced in the proposals elaborated by the president's Council for Constitutional Reform that began to circulate in June 2007, despite the president's ordered "pact of confidentiality,"[634] thus demonstrating the intent of the highest government and state officials who sat on the council. The proposals were later given concrete form in the first draft constitutional reforms, which the president presented to the National Assembly on August

---

631 See Allan R. Brewer-Carías, "Constitution-Making Process in Defraudation of the Constitution and Authoritarian Government in Defraudation of Democracy: The Recent Venezuelan Experience," paper presented at the VII International Congress of Constitutional Law, Athens, June 2007. See also Allan R. Brewer-Carías, "El autoritarismo establecido en fraude a la Constitución y a la democracia y su formalización en Venezuela mediante la reforma constitucional. (De cómo en un país democrático se ha utilizado el sistema eleccionario para minar la democracia y establecer un régimen autoritario de supuesta 'dictadura de la democracia' que se pretende regularizar mediante la reforma constitucional)," in *Temas constitucionales. Planteamientos ante una reforma,* Fundación de Estudios de Derecho Administrativo, Caracas 2007, pp. 13-74.

632 See the Constitutional Chamber of the Supreme Tribunal of Justice, Decision N° 74 (Jan. 25, 2006) in *Revista de Derecho Público* No. 105, Editorial Jurídica Venezolana, Caracas 2006, pp. 76ff.

633 On these decisions, see Allan R. Brewer-Carías, "El juez constitucional vs. la supremacía constitucional. O de cómo la jurisdicción constitucional en Venezuela renunció a controlar la constitucionalidad del procedimiento seguido para la 'reforma constitucional' sancionada por la Asamblea Nacional el 2 de noviembre de 2007, antes de que fuera rechazada por el pueblo en el referendo del 2 de diciembre de 2007," in *Revista de Derecho Público* 112 *(Estudios sobre la reforma constitucional)*, Editorial Jurídica Venezolana, Caracas 2007, pp. 661-694.

634 The document circulated in June 2007 under the title *Consejo Presidencial para la Reforma de la Constitución de la República Bolivariana de Venezuela, "Modificaciones propuestas".* The complete text was published as *Proyecto de reforma constitucional. Versión atribuida al Consejo Presidencial para la reforma de la Constitución de la República Bolivariana de Venezuela,* Editorial Atenea, Caracas 2007, p. 146.

15, 2007,[635] proposing a radical transformation of the state to create a new juridical order.[636] Finally, the defrauding of the Constitution was consummated in November 2007 with the National Assembly's sanctioning of the reform.

First, the state was to be converted into a centralized state of concentrated power under the illusory guise of a popular power, implying definitive elimination of the federal form of the state, rendering political participation impossible, and degrading representative democracy. All of this was to be done by means of the organization of the population to participate in the Councils of the Popular Power (Consejos del Poder Popular), such as the communal councils. These institutions wholly lacked autonomy, and their members are not directly elected; they are controlled by the head of the national government; in their functioning, they were to be controlled by the United Socialist Party, an instrument the government created in 2007.

Second, in addition, the state was to be converted into a socialist state, with a political official doctrine of socialist character – Bolivarian doctrine – by means of which any thoughts different from the official one were rejected, as the official political doctrine was incorporated into the Constitution itself, which established a constitutional duty for all citizens to ensure its compliance. As a consequence, the basis for criminalizing all dissidence has been formally established.

Third, the economic system was to be converted into a state-owned, socialist, centralized economy by means of eliminating economic liberty and private initiative as constitutional rights, as well as the constitutional right to private property; conferring the means of production to the state, to be centrally managed; and configuring the state as an institution on which all economic activity depended and to whose bureaucracy the totality of the population is subject. All the reforms collided with the ideas of liberty and solidarity proclaimed in the 1999 Constitution and established a state that substitutes for society itself and private economic initiative.

Fourth, the state was to be converted into a repressive (police) state, given the regressive character of the regulations established in the reform regarding human rights, particularly civil rights, and the expansion of the president's emergency powers, under which he was authorized to indefinitely suspend constitutional rights.

---

635 The full text was published as *Proyecto de Reforma Constitucional. Elaborado por el ciudadano Presidente de la República Bolivariana de Venezuela, Hugo Chávez Frías,* Editorial Atenea, Caracas 2007.

636 In this sense, the director of the National Electoral Council, Vicente Díaz, stated on July 16, 2007, "The presidential proposal to reform the constitutional text modifies fundamental provisions and for that reason it would be necessary to convene a National Assembly to approve them." This council member was consulted on this matter on Unión Radio, Aug. 16, 2007, at http://www.unionradio.com.ve/Noticias/Noticia.aspx?noticiaid=212503. The initiation of the reform process in the National Assembly could have been challenged before the Constitutional Chamber of the Supreme Tribunal on the basis of unconstitutionality. Nonetheless, the president of the Constitutional Chamber – who was also a member of the Presidential Council for the Reform of the Constitution – made clear that "no legal action related to modifications of the constitutional text would be heard until such modifications had been approved by citizens in referendum," adding that "any action must be presented after a referendum, when the constitutional reform has become a norm, since we cannot interpret an attempted norm. Once a draft reform has become a norm we can enter into interpretations of it and hear nullification actions." See Juan Francisco Alonso, *El Universal,* Caracas Aug. 18, 2007.

Fifth, and finally, the state was to be converted into a militarist state, on the basis of the role assigned to the Bolivarian Armed Force (*Fuerza Armada Bolivariana*), which was configured to function wholly under the president, and the creation of the new Bolivarian National Militia (*Milicia Nacional Bolivariana*).

All the reforms implied the radical transformation of the Venezuelan political system; sought to establish a centralized socialist, repressive, and militaristic state of popular power; and departed fundamentally from the concept of a civil social-democratic state under the rule of law and justice based on a mixed economy.

Moreover, under the sanctioned reforms, representative democracy at the local level and territorial political autonomy would have materially disappeared, substituted with a supposed participatory and protagonist democracy that would, in fact, be controlled by the president and that proscribed any form of political decentralization and territorial autonomy.

In this way, eight years after the sanctioning of the 1999 Constitution by a Constituent Assembly that was totally controlled by the president, in 2007, further constitutional reforms were proposed, this time through the National Assembly.

As aforementioned, according to Article 344 of the Constitution, the reform sanctioned by the National Assembly on November 2, 2007,[637] was submitted to referendum on December 2, 2007, and the popular vote, expressing the will of the original constituent power, rejected it.

According to the Constitution, the consequence of the will expressed by the people was that no new constitutional reforms on the same matters could be again proposed during the constitutional term (2006–2012). Even though the people rejected the 2007 reform, it is important to analyze its contents, which clearly show the shape of the authoritarian government in Venezuela over the past decade (1999–2010). For such purpose, I analyze the meaning and scope of the reform, as sanctioned by the National Assembly, comparing in each case the proposed changes with the corresponding provision of the 1999 Constitution.

II. PROPOSED CHANGES TO THE FUNDAMENTAL PRINCIPLES OF THE POLITICAL SYSTEM

Throughout 2007, particularly in a speech at the presentation of the draft reforms before the National Assembly, the president said that the reforms' main objective was "the construction of a Bolivarian and socialist Venezuela" – that is, to sow "socialism in the political and economic realms." [638] This is something that the 1999

---

637   On the reform proposals, see Allan R. Brewer-Carías, *Hacia la consolidación de un estado socialista, centralizado, policial y militarista. Comentarios sobre el sentido y alcance de las propuestas de reforma constitucional 2007,* Colección Textos Legislativos N° 42, Editorial Jurídica Venezolana, Caracas 2007; *La reforma constitucional de 2007 (Comentarios al proyecto inconstitucionalmente sancionado por la Asamblea Nacional el 2 de noviembre de 2007),* Colección Textos Legislativos N° 43, Editorial Jurídica Venezolana, Caracas 2007. See also all the articles published in *Revista de Derecho Público* 112 *(Estudios sobre la reforma constitucional),* Editorial Jurídica Venezolana, Caracas 2007.

638   See *Discurso de orden pronunciado por el ciudadano Comandante Hugo Chávez Frías, Presidente Constitucional de la República Bolivariana de Venezuela en la conmemoración del ducentécimo segundo aniversario del juramento del Libertador Simón Bolívar en el Monte Sacro y el tercer aniversa-*

Constitution did not do, and in 1998 and 1999, when the President proposed and convened the National Constitutent Assembly, he did not propose it for the purpose of "projecting the road of socialism." He just offered the convening of a Constituent Assembly. In contrast, in 2006, as candidate for reelection, he said: "Let us go to Socialism" and, consequently, he deducted that "everyone who voted for candidate Chávez then, voted to go to socialism."[639]

Thus, the draft constitutional reforms presented, according to the president's speech aimed to construct "Bolivarian Socialism, Venezuelan Socialism, our Socialism, and our socialist model," having "the community" (*la comunidad*), a "basic and indivisible nucleus," and considering that "real democracy is only possible in socialism." However, the democracy referred to was not a democracy because it was a nonrepresentative one, that was "not born of suffrage or from any election, but rather is born from the condition of organized human groups as the base of the population."[640]

The president in that speech summarized the aims of his reform proposals explaining that on the political ground, the purpose was to "deepen popular Bolivarian democracy"; on the economic ground, to "create better conditions to sow and construct a socialist productive economic model," which he considered "our model." That is, "in the political field: socialist democracy; on the economic, the productive socialist model; in the field of public administration, incorporate new forms in order to lighten the load, to leave behind bureaucracy, corruption, and administrative inefficiency, which are heavy burdens of the past still upon us like weights, in the political, economic and social areas."[641]

All his proposals to construct socialism were linked by the president to Simón Bolívar's 1819 Constitution of Angostura, which he considered "perfectly applicable to a socialist project" in the sense of considering that it was possible to "take the original Bolivarian ideology as a basic element of a socialist project."[642] Of course, this assertion has no serious foundations: it is enough to read Bolívar's 1819 Angos-

---

rio del referendo aprobatorio de su mandato constitucional, special session, Aug. 15, 2007, Asamblea Nacional, División de Servicio y Atención legislativa, Sección de Edición, Caracas 2007, No. 4, p. 33.

639   Id., 4. That is, it sought to impose the wishes of only 46% of registered voters who voted to reelect the president on the remaining 56% of registered voters who did not vote for presidential reelection. According to official statistics from the National Electoral Council, of 15,784,777 registered voters, only 7,309,080 voted to reelect the president.

640   See Discurso de orden pronunciado por el ciudadano Comandante Hugo Chávez Frías, op cit., pp. 32, 34, 35.

641   Id., 74.

642   Id., 42. Only one month before the president's speech on the proposed constitutional reforms, the former minister of defense, General in Chief Raúl Baduel, who was in office until July 18, 2007, stated on leaving the Ministry of Popular Power for the Defense that the president's call to "construct socialism for the twenty-first century, implied a necessary, pressing and urgent need to formalize a model of Socialism that is theoretically its own, autochthonous, in accord with our historical, social, political and cultural context." He added, "Until this moment, this theoretical model does not exist and has not been formulated." It is hard to imagine that it could have been formulated just one month later.

tura discourse on presenting the draft constitution to realize that it has nothing to do with a "socialist project" of any kind.[643]

The rejected constitutional reform, without doubt, would have altered the basic foundations of the state.[644] This is true particularly with respect to the proposals on the constitutional amplification of the Bolivarian doctrine; the substitution of the democratic, social state with the socialist state; the elimination of decentralization as a policy of the state designed to develop public political participation; the dismantling of the public administration; and the elimination of budgetary discipline and the unity of the treasury.

1. *Bolivarian Doctrine*

An innovation of the 1999 Constitution was the change in the name of the Republic of Venezuela to Bolivarian Republic of Venezuela (Article 1). This substituted the name the republic had had since 1811, with the sole exception of the period between 1821 and 1830, when that denomination disappeared because Venezuela itself had disappeared as an autonomous state, integrated into the Republic of Colombia, precisely on the proposal of Simón Bolívar. This latter political organization can then be considered the Bolivarian conception of the state: one in which Venezuela, as such, simply does not exist as a sovereign state.

That is why the name change, in principle, had nothing to do with Bolívar and his thought or with the construction of socialism – just as the president stated in his August 15 speech, in 1999, socialism had not been proposed. The name change had a partisan political motivation, as the name derived from the political group established by the president, which could not legally use the word *Bolívar* in its name. In this manner, it was the Bolivarian party that gave the republic its name[645] and the teaching of the "*ideario bolivariano*" (Bolivarian ideology) became obligatory in schools (Article 170).

But, in 2007, the president, with his proposed reforms, and the National Assembly, through its sanctioning of the 2007 reform, identified the Bolivarian doctrine with the socialist political and economic model of the state and, thus, with the republic itself. It is in this sense, then, that the word *bolivariano* must be understood. The proposed reform to Article 100 of the 1999 Constitution declared the Bolivarian Republic "the historical product of a confluence of various cultures." It was in the same sense of the complete identification between socialism and Bolivarianism that the 2007 constitutional reform identified the Armed Force as the Bolivarian Armed

---

643   See Simón Bolívar, *Escritos fundamentales*, Caracas 1982. See also Pedro Grases ed., *El Libertador y la Constitución de Angostura de 1819*, Caracas 1969; José Rodríguez Iturbe, ed., *Actas del Congreso de Angostura*, Caracas 1969.

644   See Eugenio Hernández Bretón, "Cuando no hay miedo (ante la Reforma Constitucional)," in *Revista de Derecho Público* 112 *(Estudios sobre la reforma constitucional)*, Editorial Jurídica Venezolana, Caracas 2007, 17-20; Manuel Rachadell, "El personalismo político en el Siglo XXI," in id., pp. 65-70.

645   According to the Political Parties Law, *Gaceta Oficial* N° 27.725, Apr. 30, 1965, political parties cannot use the name of the founders of the country or homeland symbols. The political organization the president formed before campaigning for the 1998 election was Movimiento Bolivariano 200. That name could not be used to identify the political party he founded, which became Movimiento V República.

Forces (Articles 156.8, 236.6, 328, and 329) and the components of the armed forces as the Bolivarian National Army, the Bolivarian National Navy, the Bolivarian National Air Force, the Bolivarian National Guard, and the Bolivarian National Militia (Article 329).

Moreover, the proposed reform to Article 328 of the Constitution stated that the functioning of the Bolivarian Armed Forces was to be realized "by means of the study, planning and execution of Bolivarian military doctrine" – that is, according to socialist doctrine, that they be enabled to guarantee the independence and sovereignty of the nation, to preserve it from external or internal attack, and ensure the integrity of the national geography.

In addition, the proposed reform of Article 103 of the Constitution attempted to seal the relationship between Bolivarianism and socialism by stating that the priority investment of the state in education must be done "according to the humanistic principles of the Bolivarian socialism."

2.   The Substitution of the Social-Democratic State for a Socialist State

Article 2 of the 1999 Constitution, following the tradition of contemporary constitutionalism, defines Venezuela as a "social democratic state under the rule of law and justice." This phrase (*estado democrático y social de derecho y de justicia*) was constructed precisely to design a nonsocialist state, just as it was adopted in postwar contemporary constitutions like the Constitution of the Federal Republic of Germany of 1949 (Article 20.1), the Spanish Constitution of 1978 (Article 1), and the Constitution of Colombia of 1991 (Article 1).

This corresponds to a conception of a liberal, nonsocialist state in a mixed economy, which follows the contemporary trends of the social state, one with obligations to resolve problems of social justice. This leads the state to intervene in economic and social activity, as a provider of benefits, assistance, and services (*estado prestacional*). This social character of the state derives principally from the fundamental values of equality and nondiscrimination (Articles 2 and 21) and from the declaration of social justice as a foundation of the economic system (Article 299). The democratic state is the concept on which the whole of the political organization of the nation rests, which derives from the Preamble of the 1999 Constitution (with the phrase "democratic society"), and is present in Articles 2, 3, 5, and 6, which identify the fundamental value of constitutionalism as democracy exercised through representatives (elective democracy) and through instruments of direct democracy. The rule-of-law state (*estado de derecho*) is the concept of a state under the rule of law, or legality, as provided in the Preamble to the 1999 Constitution. This implies that all acts of the state and the public administration must adhere to the principle of legality (Article 141) and are subject to independent judicial control (Articles 7, 137, 258, 334, and 336). The state is also defined, for this reason, as a state of justice, in which justice, beyond the mere affording of formal procedure, is guaranteed (Article 26).

Even though the 2007 reform makes no mention of Article 2 of the 1999 Constitution, it is evident that its sense is radically altered by the creation of a socialist state[646] in place of the traditional social-democratic state under the rule of law and justice. This is so because the model of a socialist state is absolutely incompatible with that of the social-democratic state, with the rule of law and justice. This confirms, again, the deception of reforming the Constitution to establish a socialist state without changing its Article 2 and justifying the claims that reforms have left untouched fundamental aspects of the state and, thus, the convening of the Constituent Assembly was unnecessary to approve them.[647] The 2007 reform was the result of one more fraud on the Constitution.

Many articles of the reform contain references to the socialist state. Article 16 of the Constitution creates "the communes and communities" (*comunas y comunidades*) as "the basic and indivisible spatial nuclei of the Venezuelan Socialist State." Article 70 added to the definition of the "means of political participation and protagonist of the people in the direct exercise of their sovereignty" the only objective to be directed "for the construction of socialism"; the same article added a stipulation to various forms of citizens' political associations, requiring that they be "constituted to develop the values of mutual cooperation and socialist solidarity." Article 112 established that the economic model created, achieve "the best conditions for the collective and cooperative construction of a Socialist Economy" and Article 113 stated the need to constitute "mixed corporations and/or socialist units of production."

In the rejected reform, Article 158 read: "the State must promote people's participation as a national policy, devolving its power and creating the best conditions for the construction of a Socialist democracy." Article 168 referred to socialist means of production; Articles 184 and 300 mentioned the socialist economy; Article 299 mentioned the socialist principles of the socioeconomic system; and Articles 318 and 320 referred to the socialist state and the socialist development of the nation.

3. *The Elimination of Decentralization as a State Policy*

Article 4 of the 1999 Constitution states, "The Bolivarian Republic of Venezuela is a federal decentralized state in the terms consecrated by this Constitution." The Constitution incorporated some elements of the Organic Law of Decentralization, Delimitation, and Transfer of Competencies of the Public Powers of 1989,[648] which

---

646   See Rogelio Pérez Perdomo, "La Constitución de papel y su reforma," in *Revista de Derecho Público* 112 *(Estudios sobre la reforma constitucional)*, Editorial Jurídica Venezolana, Caracas 2007, p. 14; G. Fernández, "Aspectos esenciales de la modificación constitucional propuesta por el Presidente de la República. La modificación constitucional como un fraude a la democracia," *Id*, p. 22; Alfredo Arismendi, "Utopía Constitucional," in id., p. 31; Manuel Rachadell, "El personalismo político en el Siglo XXI," in *id.*, 66; Allan R. Brewer-Carías, "El sello socialista que se pretendía imponer al Estado," in *id.*, pp. 71-75; Alfredo Morles Hernández, "El nuevo modelo económico para el Socialismo del Siglo XXI," in *id.*, pp. 233-236.

647   The president of the National Assembly stated this on Aug. 23, 2007, on approval of the draft reforms, as a whole, in the first debate. See *El Universal*, Caracas Aug. 24, 2007.

648   Ley Orgánica de Descentralización, Delimitación y Transferencia de Competencias del Poder Público de 1989, *Gaceta Oficial* N° 4.153, Dec. 28, 1989. This law was reformed in 2003, *Gaceta Oficial* N° 37.753, Aug. 14, 2003; and again in 2009, *Gaceta Oficial*, N° 39.140, Mar. 17, 2009.

promoted the transfer of certain competencies of the national public power to the state powers. As a policy of the state, decentralization was also reflected in various other norms in the 1999 Constitution. Article 6 defines the government as "decentralized," and Article 16 refers to "municipal autonomy and political administrative decentralization"; Article 84, to a decentralized national public health system; Articles 269 and 272, to decentralized administration of justice and the penitentiary system; Article 285, to decentralized electoral administration; and Article 300, to the functional decentralization of the economic administrative organization of the state.

In addition, Article 158 defined decentralization as a general national policy to be implemented to "deepen democracy, to bring power closer to the population, creating the best conditions for the exercise of democracy and for the effective and efficient meeting of state commitments" with respect to all public activities.

Following the political practice of recent years, the 2007 reform, contrary to the 1999 Constitution, definitively centralized the state and eliminated any vestige of decentralization in public policy and organization in territorial autonomy and representative democracy at the local level, or the primary political units of the land. Without a doubt, this changed a fundamental characteristic of the state, which could not be achieved through constitutional reform.

The 2007 reform eliminated all vestiges of political decentralization beginning with the fundamental principle of territorial decentralization and autonomy established in Article 16 of the Constitution.[649] Autonomy and decentralization are basic elements of participatory democracy, and Article 16 of the 1999 Constitution requires the territorial political division of the republic to guarantee "municipal autonomy and public administrative decentralization." The reform, however, sought to create a new territorial division that guaranteed only "participation of the popular power," with no reference to political autonomy or decentralization.

The 2007 reform also tended to derogate Article 158 of the Constitution, which defined the national policy of decentralization to "deepen democracy"; establishing in its place only that "the State shall promote, as a national policy, the protagonist participation of the people, transferring power to them, and creating the best conditions for the construction of a Social Democracy." This fundamental change, as the president stated on August 15, constituted "the development of what we understand by decentralization, because the Fourth Republic concept of decentralization is very different from the concept we must work with. For this reason, we have here stated 'the protagonist participation of the people, transferring power to them, and creating the best conditions for the construction of social democracy.'"[650]

In addition, *decentralization* was to be eliminated, with the proposed reform of Articles 272 (decentralization of prisons), 295 (decentralized electoral administration), and 300 (decentralized public enterprises).

---

649   See Manuel Rachadell, "El personalismo político en el Siglo XXI," in *Revista de Derecho Público* 112 *(Estudios sobre la reforma constitucional)*, Editorial Jurídica Venezolana, Caracas 2007, 67; Ana Elvira Araujo, "Proyecto de reforma constitucional (agosto a noviembre 2007). Principios fundamentales y descentralización política," in id., pp. 77-81; José Luis Villegas, "Impacto de la reforma constitucional sobre las entidades locales," in id., pp. 119-123.

650   See *Discurso de orden pronunciado por el ciudadano Comandante Hugo Chávez Frías, op. cit.*, p. 50.

4. *Fragmentation of Public Administration*

One of the most important innovations in the 1999 Constitution is that it incorporated a normative framework of fundamental principles specifically designed to regulate and rationalize the public administration of the state. First, Article 141 provided that the public administration was to operate at the service of citizens; second, it was to be based on principles of honesty, public participation, speediness, effectiveness, efficiency, transparency, accountability, and responsibility in the exercise of public functions; and third, it was to fully operate under the law, thus implicating the constitutional formulation of the principle of legality.

The 2007 reform eliminated the requirement that the public administrative apparatus, as a single universe, exist at the service of citizens and replaced it with another –the public administration exists solely at the service of the state– which terminated the right of citizens to have the administration operate in their service. In this sense, it was further proposed to establish in Article 141 that "the public administrations are organizational structures destined to serve as instruments of the public powers, for the exercise of their functions and for the provision of services."

The new language proposed for Article 141 would have signified the fragmentation of public administration and departure from a universal regulation of one apparatus to a regulation of various public administrations.[651] These, contrary to any proper legislative technique, were classified in a way that was more suited to an academic "paper" than to a constitution. In the text of the proposed reform, public administrations were classified into two categories: "the bureaucratic or traditional public administrations," which were those that attend to structures established and regulated under the 1999 Constitution and the laws, and the "missions" (*misiones*), which were "organizations of a variety of natures, created to meet the most deeply felt and urgent needs of the population." Their provision of services would require the use of exceptional systems, including experimental systems, which were to be "established by the Executive Power by means of organizational and functional regulations."

Thus, the 2007 reform –instead of seeking to correct the almost decade-old administrative disaster produced by a lack of budgetary and administrative discipline from the creation of funds assigned to missions that existed outside of the general organization of the state– would constitutionalize administrative disorder by characterizing the administrative structures of the state as "bureaucratic or traditional." It would not convert the institutions into the proper instruments for meeting the most deeply felt, urgent needs of the population. Moreover, all this left the public administration subject to the sole volition of the president, to be exercised by means of regulations.

---

651 See José Antonio Muci Borjas, "El trastocamiento de la Administración Pública en la reforma Constitucional de 2007," in *Revista de Derecho Público No.* 112 *(Estudios sobre la reforma constitucional)*, Editorial Jurídica Venezolana, Caracas 2007, pp. 163-67; José Araujo Juárez, "Consideraciones sobre el cambio institucional de la Administración Pública en la reforma constitucional," in id., pp. 169-73; José Ignacio Hernández, "La administración paralela como instrumento del Poder Público," in id., 175-78; Ninoska Rodríguez Laverde, "Las Administraciones Públicas: potestad sancionadora y ámbitos competenciales en el proyecto de reforma constitucional," in *id.*, pp. 183-89.

5.   *The Abandonment of Budgetary Discipline and the Unity of the Treasury*

Even though the 2007 reform did not contain express changes to Articles 313 and 314 of the Constitution – the principal articles establishing the general principle of budgetary discipline – it sought to eliminate the fundamental principle of state economic and financial administration through changes to Article 321.[652]

In effect, under Articles 313 and 314, the economic and financial administration of the entire national public administration must be governed by a budget approved annually through legislation of the National Assembly, which provides an estimate of public revenues and authorized public spending. Thus, Article 314 declares that "there shall be no form of spending that has not been provided for in the annual Budget law," the only exceptions being those provided by additional budget credits for unforeseen expenses and underfunded items, which also require approval of the National Assembly. That system is designed to guarantee that ordinary revenues are sufficient to cover ordinary expenses and that "the income generated from the exploitation of the wealth derived from the subsoil and minerals, in general, will tend to be used to finance real productive investments, education and health" (Article 311).

The rejected 2007 reform of Article 321 was intended to bring the whole system of budgetary discipline into complete chaos, through constitutional provisions. In that sense, it eliminated the constitutional provision requiring the creation of "a fund for macroeconomic stabilization destined to guarantee the expenses of the State at the municipal, regional and national levels, in the event of fluctuations in ordinary revenues" and declared that such funds must function under "basic principles of efficiency, equity, and nondiscrimination between the public entities that bring resources to it." Instead, it established that "at the end of each year, the Chief of State shall establish, in coordination with the Central Bank of Venezuela, the level of reserves needed for the national economy, as well as the amount of surplus reserves. The surplus reserves shall be destined to funds established by the National Executive for productive investments, development and infrastructure, financing of the Missions, and, definitively, to the integral, endogenous, humanist and socialist development of the nation." By means of the reform, the president was charged with administering international reserves (Article 318).

In this way, the definitive rupture of the unity of the treasury was to be constitutionalized, establishing a financial mechanism parallel to the budget of funds created solely by the national executive destined for the missions. As has been said, the missions are also under the charge of the national executive and exist as public administrative organizations parallel to the "bureaucratic and traditional Public Administration."

---

652   See Enrique Sánchez Falcón, "La propuesta de modificación constitucional y el régimen de la Administración Financiera Pública," in *Revista de Derecho Público* No. 112 *(Estudios sobre la reforma constitucional)*, Editorial Jurídica Venezolana, Caracas 2007, pp. 191-93.

III. PROPOSED CHANGES IN THE POLITICAL SYSTEM: FROM REPRESENTATIVE DEMOCRACY TO PARTICIPATORY DEMOCRACY

1. *The Elimination of Representative Democracy at the Local Level*

Article 5 of the 1999 Constitution establishes that "sovereignty resides untransferrable in the people, who exercise it directly in the manner provided in this Constitution and the Law, and indirectly, by means of suffrage through the organs that exercise the Public Power." This norm followed Venezuela's republican tradition that began with the Constitution of 1811[653] by providing for the exercise of popular sovereignty through political representation (indirect democracy) and the direct exercise of democracy as complementary. The 1999 Constitution also establishes mechanisms for popular participation in Article 62, which consecrates the right of all citizens to "freely participate in public affairs, directly or through their representatives," as well as through the "means of participation" set forth in Article 70.

For democracy to exist as such, it must be representative, although it may contain mechanisms of direct democracy. For this reason, the 1999 Constitution requires that representative democracy always have its source in elections that are popular, universal, direct, and secret (Article 70) and that such elections are to select the titular heads of almost all organs of the different branches of government, established in the Constitution according to the principles of the separation and distribution of powers (Article 136). In the 2007 reform, the right to vote was extended to all citizens over the age of sixteen years (Article 64).

This form of representative democracy is, of course, not contradictory to participative democracy, and both are different from mechanisms of direct democracy such as referenda (consultative, approbatory, abrogating, and recall) (Articles 71–74) that serve to perfect democracy and from the various forms of political participation regulated in the Constitution. The latter include popular consultations, legislative, constitutional and constituent initiatives, *cabildos abiertos* (open town hall meetings), and citizens' assemblies (Article 70).

In any case, participatory democracy cannot substitute for representative democracy, especially if participation is conducted from above. For democracy to be participatory, in addition to being essentially representative, it must allow citizens the possibility of participating in public affairs, which is possible only when they have access to power. This is possible only when power is near to citizens, which necessarily implies the presence of a well-established, well-developed autonomous local government in every locality and urban or rural settlement. This means that political participation can be founded only on political decentralization, through the creation of autonomous political entities that permit local self-government. It is possible to participate politically only when, through decentralized government, local authorities are established by means of elections through suffrage at the smallest territorial

---

653   On the presence of this principle in all of Venezuela's constitutions, see Allan R. Brewer-Carías, *Las constituciones de Venezuela,* Academia de Ciencias Políticas y Sociales, Caracas 2008, Vol 1, pp. 109-322.

level. As a whole, this implies the spreading of public power throughout the territory of the state.

This is, of course, contrary to the concentration of power and centralization that the rejected reform of 2007 attempted to consolidate. The reform, as stated, attempted to eliminate from the Constitution all references to political decentralization and to definitively substitute representative democracy at the local level with a supposed participatory democracy. This would have finished off democracy itself as a political regime, substituting it with an authoritarian one that centralizes and concentrates power and impedes political participation because of the nonexistence of autonomous local entities.

This was to be achieved through proposals to eliminate all vestiges of local territorial autonomy and political decentralization, thereby precluding the possibility of participatory democracy. As mentioned, democratic participation requires the existence of autonomous territorial political entities; without them, the central power can develop simple and controlled mobilization of the population. But popular mobilization cannot be confounded with the democratic participation, as in that of the communal councils.[654] Members of the communal councils are not elected by means of direct suffrage (Article 136) but are appointed by citizens' assemblies under the control of the national executive power. The proposal to reform Article 16 of the Constitution sought to constitutionally consolidate this system through its reference to new territorial divisions that would guarantee "the participation of the popular power."

According to the rejected 2007 reform of Article 16 of the 1999 Constitution, a new "popular power" (*poder popular*) –a proposed new level of state power (in addition to the national, state, and municipal levels)– was to be created from the bottom up. This was to begin with communities (*comunidades*), each of which "shall constitute a basic and indivisible spatial nucleus of the Venezuelan Socialist State, where ordinary citizens will have the power to construct their own geography and their own history." The communities were to be grouped into communes (*comunas*) that were "geographic areas or extensions" and "geo-human cells of the territory."[655] The communes, in turn, were to be grouped into cities (*ciudades*), "the primary political unit in the organization of the national territory." The latter were to be understood as "all of the popular settlements within the municipality" (*municipio*). In this

654 *Ley de los Consejos Comunales*, *Gaceta Oficial* N° 5806, Extra., Apr. 4, 2006. See Giancarlo Henríquez Maionica, "Los Consejos Comunales (una breve aproximación a su realidad y a su proyección ante la propuesta presidencial de reforma constitucional)," in *Revista de Derecho Público* 112 *(Estudios sobre la reforma constitucional)*, Editorial Jurídica Venezolana, Caracas 2007, 89-99; Allan R. Brewer-Carías, "El inicio de la desmunicipalización en Venezuela: La organización del poder popular para eliminar la descentralización, la democracia representativa y la participación a nivel local," in *AIDA, Opera Prima de Derecho Administrativo. Revista de la Asociación Internacional de Derecho Administrativo*, Universidad Nacional Autónoma de México, Asociación Internacional de Derecho Administrativo, Mexico City 2007, pp. 49-67. The 2006 law was replaced by *Ley Orgánica de los Consejos Comunales*, *Gaceta Oficial* N° 39.335, Dec. 28, 2009. See the comments on this Law in Allan R. Brewer-Carías, *Ley de los Consejos Comunales*, Editorial Jurídica Venezolana, Caracas 2010.

655 The communes have been created in the statute on the Federal Council of Government. See *Ley Orgánica del Consejo Federal de Gobierno*, *Gaceta Oficial* N° 5.963 Extra. of Feb. 22, 2010). In June 2010, the National Assembly began the discusión of the Law on the Communes.

manner, from the community and the commune, "the Popular Power shall develop forms of political-territorial communal aggregation that are to be regulated by Law and shall constitute forms of Self-government and any other expression of direct democracy."

The rejected reform of Article 136 of the Constitution was precise in its reference to the popular power. It provided that the popular power "is expressed through the constitution of communities, communes, and the self-government of the cities, by means of the communal councils, workers' councils, peasant councils, student councils, and other entities established by law." However, although "the people" (*el pueblo*) were designated as the "depositary of sovereignty," to be "exercised directly through the popular power," it was stated that the popular power "does not arise from suffrage or from any election, but arises from the condition of the organized human groups that form the base of the population."

What was sought, then, in that reform was to put an end to representative democracy at the local level, and with that, to put an end to any vestige of political territorial autonomy, which is necessary to public political participation. For such purpose, the reforms were proposed as creating participatory democracy, substituting representation with the supposed direct democracy of participation in citizens' assemblies, communities, communes, and cities that were not autonomous political territorial entities but rather controlled from the central power.

2. *Elimination of Republican Alternation in Office by Establishing the Possibility of Indefinite Reelection of the President*

According to Article 4 of the 1999 Constitution, the republic's government and all the political entities that constitute it are required to be democratic and alternating (*democrático* and *alternativo*). On the basis of this principle, the Constitution established term limits governing reelection of all officers.

With respect to the president, Article 230 of the Constitution, in a radical departure from the previous constitutional tradition forbidding immediate presidential election, allowed the immediate reelection of the president, but for only one more term. Regarding members (*diputados*) of the National Assembly, Article 192 provides that they may be reelected for no more than "two consecutive terms." Article 160 provides that state governors "may be immediately reelected for a new term, but only once," and Article 162 provides that members of the states' legislative councils may be reelected for only "two consecutive terms." Finally, Article 174 provides that mayors "may be immediately reelected for a new term, but only once."

Regarding these matters, the 2007 constitutional reform of Article 230 not only would have increased the length of the presidential term from six to seven years but also was designed to establish the possibility of the president being reelected. This would have signified the inclusion in the Constitution of the principle of indefinite reelection of the president, thus contradicting the democratic principle of alternation in office and perpetuating the president's power.[656]

656   See Carlos Ayala Corao, "Reforma constitucional 2007. El presidencialismo y la reelección," in *Revista de Derecho Público* No. 112 *(Estudios sobre la reforma constitucional)*, Editorial Jurídica Venezolana,

Nonetheless, and despite that the reforms were rejected, in the following year, the National Assembly approved a constitutional amendment with the same purpose and extended the reelection principle to all elected officials, thereby defrauding the Constitution.[657]

3. The Contradictory Restrictions on Citizens' Right to Political Participation

Regarding the principle of political participation, the 1999 Constitution directly establishes regulations ensuring the participation of civil society in public affairs. This was the case with the mechanism created to ensure civil-society participation in the appointment of nonelected state officials (judiciary, citizens' power, and electoral power), with political participation by means of referenda, and with citizens' political participation in matters of constitutional review.

A. The Elimination of the Civil Society's Participation in Nominating State Officials

The rejected 2007 reform proposed to eliminate civil society's direct participation in public affairs (established in the 1999 Constitution as an institutional novelty) in nominating the magistrates of the Supreme Tribunal, members of the National Electoral Council, the people's defender, the comptroller general, and the prosecutor general. The nomination is to be made before the National Assembly by various nomination committees, required to comprise only "representatives of the various sectors of society" (Articles 264, 279, and 295).

The provisions of the 1999 Constitution were distorted through political praxis and subsequent legislation by the Constituent Assembly (1999), followed by the National Assembly (2000). This transformed the nominating committees into amplified parliamentary commissions (2002–4), thus limiting civil society's right to political participation.[658] This trend was intended to be constitutionalized in the 2007 reform, which sought to establish that the nominating committees, instead of comprising representatives from various sectors of civil society, comprise almost entirely state officials.

With respect to Article 270 on the Judicial Nominating Committee, the proposed reform established a parliamentary commission that was similar to that regulated in the 2004 Organic Law of the Supreme Tribunal of Justice.[659] The reform provided that the National Assembly would convene the Judicial Nominating Committee, to comprise "members of the Assembly, representatives of the Popular Power and representatives related to juridical activities," adding that the "Popular Power Coun-

Caracas 2007, pp. 137-143; Carlos Luis Carrillo, "La desnaturalización del sistema presidencial en Venezuela. Del presidencialismo exacerbado consagrado en la Constitución de 1999 al ultrapresidencialismo pretendido en la reforma constitucional de 2007," in id., pp. 145-49.

657   See Gaceta Oficial N° 5.908 Extra. of Feb. 19, 2009.

658   See Allan R. Brewer-Carías, "La participación ciudadana en la designación de los titulares de los órganos no electos de los poderes públicos en Venezuela y sus vicisitudes políticas," in Revista Iberoamericana de Derecho Público y Administrativo 5, San José, Costa Rica, 2005, pp. 76-95.

659   See Allan R. Brewer-Carías, Ley Orgánica del Tribunal Supremo de Justicia, Editorial Jurídica Venezolana, Caracas 2006, pp. 32ff.

cils, social sectors and organizations related to juridical activities can nominate candidates."

With respect to the Electoral Nominating Committee for the National Electoral Council, the rejected 2007 reform to Article 295 also established a parliamentary commission similar to that regulated in the 2002 Organic Law of the Electoral Power. The reform provided that the National Assembly would convene the committee, to comprise "members of the Assembly, and of representatives of the Popular Power, of social organizations and of sectors." Thus, it would be composed basically of representatives of state organs, thereby abandoning the principle of exclusive participation of civil society. The provision in the 1999 Constitution that provides that law faculties around the country are to propose candidates was to be eliminated by reform, whereby popular power representatives and representatives from the educational and social sectors would nominate candidates.

Finally, regarding the citizens' power nominating committee to appoint the people's defender, the comptroller general, and the prosecutor general, the rejected proposed reform to Article 279 also established that the National Assembly would convene a committee "of members of the Assembly, and of representatives of the different sectors of the Popular Power," and it eliminated any reference to civil society.

B. *Limits to Political Participation by Means of Referenda and Restrictions on Direct Democracy*

Articles 5 and 62 of the 1999 Constitution establish that the right to political participation can be exercised indirectly by the election of representatives and directly through the means regulated in the Constitution. Political participation is exercised directly through those means provided for in Article 70 and by means of referenda, enumerated in Articles 71–74 as consultative, recall, approbatory, and abrogating referenda.

The important aspect of these provisions is the establishment of the popular initiative to convene the referendum, attributing to 10% of registered voters the right to call for convening consultative referenda (Article 71); to 20%, the right to call for convening recall referenda (Article 72); to 15%, the right to call for convening approbatory referenda of certain international treaties (Article 73); to 10%, the right to call for convening referenda to abrogate statutes (Article 74); and to 5%, the right to call for convening referenda to abrogate executive decree laws (Article 74).

The rejected reform sought to limit the political right to participate by increasing the percentage of registered voters required to file such popular initiatives as follows: 20% for consultative referenda (Article 71), 30% for recall referenda (Article 72), 30% for approbatory referenda (Article 73), 30% for convening approbatory referenda on certain international treaties (Article 73), 30% for referenda to abrogate statutes (Article 74), and 30% for referenda to abrogate executive decree laws (Article 74).[660]

---

660 See Alberto Blanco Uribe Quintero, "Menoscabo al derecho humano a la participación, por la reforma constitucional," in *Revista de Derecho Público No.* 112 *(Estudios sobre la reforma constitucional)*, Editorial Jurídica Venezolana, Caracas 2007, pp. 191-202.

The 2007 reform regarding Article 72 sought to change the system to make it less participatory and more difficult to initiate recall elections. The reform establis- hed, first, that instead of not less than 20% of registered voters directly convening a recall referendum, a petition was to be filed before the National Electoral Council to activate a proceeding through which no fewer than 30% of registered voters could petition for a recall referendum. Second, instead of fixing electoral participation in recall votes to at least 25% of registered voters, the reform would require participa- tion of 40% of registered voters. Third, to achieve a recall, in addition to requiring that the number of votes for the recall be equal to or greater than the number of vo- tes through which the official in question was originally elected (as is provided in the 1999 Constitution), the reform would add the new requirement that the final vote in favor of a recall must be greater than the total number of votes against it, even though the number of votes for the recall would be greater than the number of votes that elected the official to begin with. Thus, the recall referendum was to be conver- ted into a ratification referendum, which had already occurred de facto in 2004.[661]

C. Limits on the Right to Political Participation in Constitutional Review Procedures

The 1999 Constitution provides for three means or procedures for constitutional review according to the importance of the reforms to be implemented: amendment, constitutional reform, and constituent assembly.

Amendments can apply only in matters of adding or modifying one or various ar- ticles, without altering the fundamental structure of the Constitution (Article 340). The amendment process initiates with a popular initiative of at least 15% of registe- red voters. The 2007 reform sought to augment the requirement to 20% of registered voters (Article 341.1), making the process more difficult to initiate. In addition, the reform proposed that the National Assembly, distorting the character of the popular initiative, was to approve amendments.

Amendments must be approved by referendum in which at least 25% of registe- red voters participate. The rejected 2007 reform sought to raise that percentage to 30% of registered voters.[662]

The constitutional reform procedure, according to Article 342 of the 1999 Cons- titution, is intended to partially review the Constitution and to substitute one or va- rious articles but without modifying the structure and fundamental principles of the constitutional text. The initiative for the constitutional reform procedure is popular initiative of at least 15% of registered voters. The rejected reform sought to augment the requirement to 25% of registered voters (Article 342).

---

661 See Allan R. Brewer-Carías, "La Sala Constitucional vs. el derecho ciudadano a la revocatoria de man- datos populares: De cómo un referendo revocatorio fue inconstitucionalmente convertido en un 'refe- rendo ratificatorio,'" in *Crónica sobre la "in" justicia constitucional. La Sala Constitucional y el auto- ritarismo en Venezuela*, Colección Instituto de Derecho Público, Universidad Central de Venezuela– Editorial Jurídica Venezolana, Caracas 2007, pp. 349-78.

662 See Alberto Blanco Uribe Quintero, "Menoscabo al derecho humano a la participación, por la reforma constitucional," in *Revista de Derecho Público* 112, *(Estudios sobre la reforma constitucional*, Edito- rial Jurídica Venezolana, Caracas 2007, pp. 191-202.

Finally, constituent assembly, under Article 347 of the 1999 Constitution, can occur to "transform the state, create a new legal order and write a new Constitution." The initiative for the convening of a constituent assembly is popular initiative of at least 15% of registered voters. The rejected 2007 reform sought to augment the requirement to 30% of registered voters (Article 342), making it much more difficult to initiate.

4.   *Reducing the Right to Political Participation to Implementing Socialist Ideology*

Article 62 of the 1999 Constitution declares it to be a political right of citizens "to freely participate in public affairs, directly or through their elected representatives," and it refers to "the people's participation in the conception, execution and control of public management [as a] necessary means to be protagonist in order to guarantee complete individual and collective development." For this purpose, the article establishes the "obligation of the state and duty of society to provide for the generation of more favorable conditions for its practice."

Article 62 is complemented by Article 70 of the 1999 Constitution, which provides for the following means for people's participation and the exercise of popular sovereignty: From the political point of view, the election of public officials, referenda, popular hearings, mandate recalls, legislative and constitutional review initiatives, open town hall meetings, and citizens' assemblies whose decisions are of an obligatory nature. From the social and economic point of view, citizens' attention, self-management, cooperatives in all their forms, including those of a financial character, savings institutions, community enterprises, and other associative means guided by mutual cooperation and solidarity.

The end result of the rejected 2007 reform was that it restricted political participation. On the one hand, the enumeration of means of participation in Article 70 was expanded to include "the councils of popular power, the communal councils, the workers' councils, the students' councils, the peasants councils, the artisans' councils, the fishermen's councils, the sporting councils, the youth councils, the senior citizens' councils, the women's councils, and the disabled people's councils." On the other hand, all of them restricted citizens' right to freely participate in public affairs because the means of political participation were reduced to one purpose: "the construction of socialism." Consequently, those who do not want to construct socialism would be excluded from the right to political participation, which was reserved for developing "socialist solidarity" and was not free, as is provided in Article 62 of the Constitution.

5.   *Political Parties, Political Association, and Public Financing of Electoral Activities*

In a marked reaction against political parties, the 1999 Constitution omitted express reference to "political parties," and instead it established a set of provisions regulating "associations for political purpose," guaranteeing citizens "the right to associate for political ends by means of democratic methods, organization, functioning and leadership" (Article 67).

A traditional problem associated with political parties is the financing of their activities through public funds, established in the former Organic Law of Suffrage and Political Participation of 1998,[663] which led to inequitable concentrations of funds in hands of official (governmental) parties. The drafters of the 1999 Constitution reacted to this problem in Article 67 by inconveniently prohibiting public financing of all "associations for political purposes." This was considered a regression in the context of contemporary democratic trends regarding public (state) financing of political activity because it could open the door to irregular and illegitimate public financing of political parties supporting the government.

The 2007 rejected reform sought to modify the prohibition on state funding of political parties, instead proposing that "the state may finance electoral activities" without indicating whether that referred to political parties in general or also to self-nominated candidates. The proposal provided for the enactment of a law to establish "means for the financing, for the use of public space, and for access to social communications media in elections campaigns." In any event, if an official state ideology were to be established, the financing of electoral activities other than those tending to consolidate socialism would have been considered contrary to the Constitution. Nonetheless, this reform was carried out in an illegitimate way through constitutional interpretation by the Constitutional Chamber of the Supreme Tribunal in 2008.[664]

The 2007 rejected reform attempted to eliminate from Article 67 the general prohibition directed to "the directors of associations with political ends" to "contract with public sector entities." In a system in which the proposal was to consolidate the United Socialist Party, such elimination could have completely intertwined the party and the state. The reform proposal also established in Article 67 a general prohibition against "the financing of associations with political ends or of persons participating in electoral processes by any foreign public or private entity."

CHAPTER 11

THE FAILED ATTEMPT TO CONSOLIDATE A CENTRALIZED STATE IN THE CONSTITUTION

In addition to consolidating an authoritarian and nondemocratic state in the Constitution, the rejected 2007 constitutional reform sanctioned by the National Assembly, also sought to consolidate a centralized state in the Constitution in complete substitution of the federation.

---

663   Ley Orgánica del Sufragio y Participación Política, *Gaceta Oficial* N° 5.233, Extra., May 28, 1998.

664   See the comments in Allan R. Brewer-Carías, "El juez constitucional como constituyente: El caso del financiamiento de las campañas electorales de los partidos políticos en Venezuela," in *Revista de Derecho Público* No. 117, Editorial Jurídica Venezolana, Caracas 2009, pp. 195ff.

I. PROPOSED CHANGES IN THE STATE FORM: FROM CENTRALI-ZED FEDERATION TO CENTRALIZED STATE

From the time the Republic of Venezuela was established in 1811, and from when it was subsequently reconstituted in 1830, the Venezuelan state, in formal terms, has always been that of a federation – a state whose public powers are distributed between autonomous political-territorial entities on three levels: national (republic), state (individual states), and municipal (municipalities). The respective autonomies of each level have been constitutionally guaranteed.

Despite its vicissitudes and a tendency toward centralization, the Venezuelan federation has implied a vertical distribution of the public powers. Although it is not expressly eliminated in formal terms, the 2007 reform was to result in the disappearance of the federation. This was to perpetrate fraud on the Constitution.

1.   *The Destruction of the Federation*

A.   *Taking Away Territoriality from the Federation*

Although the 2007 reform did not expressly propose eliminating the federal form, its content was designed to eliminate the federation.[665] With respect to the states and municipalities (Article 16 of the Constitution of 1999), on which the concept of federalism is built, the 2007 reform sought to eliminate the constitutional guarantee of municipal autonomy and political-administrative decentralization, thus laying the groundwork to remove any jurisdictional competencies and power from those territorial entities. The reforms also proposed stripping municipalities of their traditional constitutional characterization as primary political units of the republic (Article 168). They proposed instead that "the primary political unit of the national territory shall be the city, by which is understood all of the populated settlements within the municipality, which are composed of geographic areas or extensions called communes."

According to the proposed reform to Article 15 of the Constitution, the communes forming the popular power (a new vertical level of government) were conceived to be the basic human cells of the territory "composed of communities, each of which shall constitute an indivisible spatial nucleus of the Venezuelan Socialist State, in which the citizens shall have the power to construct their own geography and their own history." It concluded: "from the community and the commune, the popular power shall develop forms of political-territorial communal aggregation that are to be regulated by law, and which shall constitute forms of self-government and any other expression of direct democracy."

The reform of Article 16 added that "the communal city [*ciudad comunal*] shall be constituted when, within the totality of its perimeter, the organized communities,

---

665   See Manuel Rachadell, "El personalismo político en el Siglo XXI," in *Revista de Derecho Público* No. 112 *(Estudios sobre la reforma constitucional)*, Editorial Jurídica Venezolana, Caracas 2007, 67; Ana Elvira Araujo, "Proyecto de reforma constitucional (agosto a noviembre 2007). Principios fundamentales y descentralización política," in *id.*, pp. 77-81; José Luis Villegas, "Impacto de la reforma constitucional sobre las entidades locales," in *id.*, pp. 119-23.

the communes, and communal self-government have been established," and once approved by popular referendum to be convened by the president.

Furthermore, the proposed reform to Article 136, which addressed the popular power, sets forth that

> the popular power is expressed through the constitution of communities, communes, and the self-government of the cities, by means of the communal councils, workers' councils, peasant councils, student councils, and other entities established by law....[The popular power] does not arise from suffrage or from any election, but arises from the condition of the organized human groups that form the base of the population.

This definitively sought to eliminate representative democracy and local political autonomy and to eliminate political decentralization as a condition of political participation. What the reform sought to achieve was to cease democratic election of local public powers, contrary to the constitutional principle of representative democracy.

B. *A Territorial Division of the Republic Tied to the Central Power*

The territorial scheme proposed in the 2007 reform had the purpose of dismembering the federation – that is, to eliminate any sort of organization of the territory into political entities enjoying political territorial autonomy with elective governments as it is provided in Article 6 of the Constitution.

Instead of the political organization of the republic based on division of the national territory into states, the capital district, and municipalities with democratically elected governments, as laid out in the Constitution of 1999, the 2007 rejected reform of Article 16 provided for the establishment of a new division of the national territory, according to a "new geometry of power,"[666] composed "by a federal district in which the capital of the republic shall have its seat, by the states, by the maritime regions, by the federal territories, by the federal municipalities and by the island districts."

Rather than organizing the national territory in municipalities, as set forth in the 1999 Constitution, the 2007 reform stated that "the states are organized in municipalities" (Article 16), which would have disappeared when the new entities engulfed their territories. Thus, in the reform, the municipality was to disappear as the primary political unit.

The proposed reforms to Article 16 sought to authorize the president to decide with the intervention of the National Assembly, the creation of "maritime regions [*regiones marítimas*], federal territories [*territorios federales*], federal municipalities [*municipios federales*], insular districts [*distritos insulares*], federal provinces [*provincias federales*], federal cities [*ciudades federales*], and functional districts [*distritos funcionales*], and any other entity established by law." Under the reform, therefore, the territorial political division of the republic would have ceased to have cons-

---

666   See Gustavo Tarre Briceño, "La nueva geometría del poder," in *Revista de Derecho Público* 112 *(Estudios sobre la reforma constitucional)*, Editorial Jurídica Venezolana, Caracas 2007, pp. 115-18.

titutional rank, as it always has been, or even to be regulated by legislation; it would become solely the subject of executive regulation. It would be difficult to centralize power more than that.

All the territorial entities, according to the proposed reforms, were not conceived of as political entities with autonomy. They were to be subject to the central national power, which would designate their respective authorities.

C.   *The Capital City: No Political Autonomy or Democratic Government*

An important reform introduced in the 1999 Constitution was to definitively ensure decentralized, democratic local government in Caracas, the capital and federal city, guaranteeing municipal autonomy and political participation of the diverse entities in the urban area. To that end, a two-tiered metropolitan government structure was created to ensure a general (metropolitan) government for the city as well as the existence of a democratically elected local government with political autonomy. The 1999 Constitution thus eliminated the federal district, which was a vestige of the traditional nineteenth-century federation, in which the capital city had no self-government.

On the contrary, the rejected 2007 constitutional reform sought to return to the nineteenth-century model in which local government in the capital city was absent, a model that all federations of the world have abandoned. For such purpose, the proposed reform of Article 18 of the Constitution sought to eliminate the capital district and its municipal organization, substituting for it a revived federal district with no constitutional guarantee of municipal or territorial autonomy and no guarantee of a "democratic and participative character of government," as is established in the 1999 Constitution. The intent was to pass the city to control by the national power, so that in the capital of the republic (and the seat of the national power), only national government organs, not local ones, could act.

This reform, nonetheless, and despite its popular rejection, was carried out unconstitutionally in 2009, by means of the Law on the Government Regime of the capital District and the metropolitan Area of Caracas.[667] In it, violating Article 18 of the Constitution, Caracas as the capital of the republic and the seat of the organs of the national branches of government was regulated as a "political territorial unit," wholly dependent on the central power, without any local political autonomy whatsoever. The proposed norm added that "the National Power, through the Executive Power, and with the collaboration and participation of all of the entities of the national, state and municipal public powers, in addition to those of the popular power, its communities, communes, and communal councils and other social organizations, shall provide for all that is necessary for urban reorganization, the restructuring of roadways, environmental recuperation, optimal results in public and personal security, the comprehensive strengthening of neighborhoods, urban development, the provision of systems for health, education, sports, culture and entertainment, the total restoration of the historic city center and historical sites, the construction of a system

---

667   See *Gaceta Oficial* N° 39.156 of Apr. 13, 2009. See the comments on this Law in Allan R. Brewer-Carías et al., *Leyes sobre el Distrito Capital y el Área metropolitana de Caracas*, Editorial Jurídica Venezolana, Caracas 2009.

of small and midsized satellite cities along the territorial axes." That is, the reform sought to nationalize and centralize the entire government in Caracas.

In addition, Article 18 included a provision regarding the establishment of a national system of cities and declared the right to a city (*derecho a la ciudad*) to be understood as "the equitable benefit that each of the inhabitants receives, in conformity with the strategic role that the city formulates regrading both the urban regional context and the national system of cities."

2. *Abandoning Vertical Distribution of the Public Powers*

In the history of Venezuela's constitutions, the federation has always materialized through a vertical system of distribution of the public powers among the municipal, state, an national levels of government, as it is stated in Article 136 of the 1999 Constitution.

The rejected 2007 reform of Article 136 proposed a radical change to this traditional distribution of powers adding to it a new territorial level, that of the popular power, which was to express itself through the already mentioned councils of popular power.[668] It was supposed that through the councils, people, as the depository of sovereignty, would exercise that sovereignty directly, with the particularity that the communal councils were not representatives. On the contrary, it was expressly provided in the reform proposal that the popular power arises not "from suffrage or from any election, but arises from the condition of the organized human groups that form the base of the population."

In addition, popular power was incorporated in the rejected constitutional reform as to the composition of the nominating committees to appoint various offices of the government.

3. *Nationalizing Federated States' Competencies*

Article 136 of the 1999 Constitution, in organizing the federal state, distributes and assigns various competencies among three levels of government –national, state, and municipal– which are to be exercised autonomously and according to vertical distribution of power. Nonetheless, in political practice, the tendency has been to centralize almost all competencies in the national power, which has left very few competencies to the states and municipalities.

In this same tendency, the 2007 rejected reform sought to materially centralize all competencies of the public powers at the national level by assigning new competencies to the national powers, centralizing the states' competencies under the 1999 Constitution, and obligating states and municipalities to transfer their competencies to communal councils. The reforms would have left the states as voided entelechies.

The reject reform sought to attribute to the national level of government various competencies to organize the state. The first sought to confer competency to the

---

668   See Gustavo Linares Benzo, "Sólo un Poder Público más. El Poder Popular en la reforma del 2007," in *Revista de Derecho Público No. 112 (Estudios sobre la reforma constitucional)*, Editorial Jurídica Venezolana, Caracas 2007, pp. 102-105; Arturo Peraza, "Reforma, Democracia participativa y Poder Popular," in *id.*, pp. 107-13.

central national government in order to regulate and administer the territory, and in particular to establish the regime "of the territorial regime of the federal district, of the states, of the municipalities, of the federal dependencies and of other regional entities" (Article 156.10). The second sought to confer competency to the national power with respect to "the creation, regulation and administration of federal provinces, federal and communal territories, and federal and communal cities" (Article 156.11). Under the reforms, states and municipalities would have become totally dependent on the national-level government, as organs without autonomy of any kind, peripheral administrations of the central power, subject to the regulation and administration of the national power.

The reform also proposed attributing to the national power competency for administrative legislation (Article 156.32), which was to imply the total centralization of all legislation governing public administration, whether national, state, or municipal.

The reform also sought to reassign several competencies that the 1999 Constitution attributed to states and municipalities to the national power. In particular, proposed changes to Article 156.27 sought to nationalize, or attribute to the national power, the competency that Article 164.10 assigned to states regarding the "conservation, administration, and use of national roads and highways." Approval would also have implied modifications to Sections 9 and 10 of Article 164 of the Constitution, which assigns states the competency for the "conservation, administration, and use of national roads and highways, and of ports and airports of commercial use, in coordination with the national executive." Nonetheless, and despite the popular rejection of these reforms proposal, they were illegitimately carried out in 2008 through a judicial constitutional interpretation of the provision of the Constitution issued by the Constitutional Chamber of the Supreme Tribunal of Justice.[669]

Finally, in the area of shared national and municipal competencies, Article 156.14 of the 1999 Constitution assigns to the national power the creation and organization of land taxes on rural lands and real property transactions, whereas their "collection and control corresponds to the municipalities, in accord with this Constitution." The 2007 reform proposed to eliminate all references to the municipal role and added "collection of land taxes on rural lands" to the competencies of the national power.

Following this centralizing orientation, the 2007 reform proposed to eliminate the competency of the states in the exploitation of nonmetallic minerals, salt deposits, and oyster beds (Article 164.5), which was to be transferred to the national level and could only be delegated to states (Article 157.17).

In a definitive coup de grace, the rejected 2007 reform proposed to eliminate the residual competency of the states, something inherent in every federation and established in Article 164.11 of the Constitution of 1999, regarding "all those that do not correspond to the national or municipal competency, according to this Constitution." The rejected reform sought to substitute the provision with one that established the rule inversely and attributed residual competency to the national power. This change was proposed in the reform to Article 156 that states that the competency of the national public power embraces all other subject matters "that by their kind or nature correspond to it, or that are not expressly attributed to state or municipal competencies."

4. *Obligating States and Municipalities to Transfer Their Competencies to the Organs of the Popular Power*

In Article 184, the 1999 Constitution establishes that the law must create open and flexible mechanisms through which states and municipalities can decentralize and transfer the rendering of their respective public services to communities and organized neighborhood organizations, once those have demonstrated the ability to provide those services. The article intends to promote the provision of services in the areas of health, education, housing, sports, culture, social programs, the environment, the maintenance of industrial areas, the maintenance and conservation of urban areas, neighborhood prevention and protection, works in construction, and other public services. The policy intends to promote the participation of communities and citizens through neighborhood associations and nongovernmental organizations; to have state and municipal authorities formulate investment proposals; and to participate in the implementation, evaluation, and monitoring of public works, social programs, and public services provided in their jurisdictions. In addition, the policy is intended to promote the creation of new subjects of decentralization at the submunicipal level of the *parroquias* ("parishes"), communities, neighborhoods, and localities. This needs to be done to guarantee the principle of coresponsibility (*corresponsabilidad*) in public business in local and state government and to develop self-management and comanagement in the administration and control of state and municipal services.

The rejected 2007 constitutional reform, seeking to redefine the federal decentralized democratic state and to convert it into a communal, centralized, nondemocratic state, proposed to establish that the "decentralization and transferring" required by the Constitution was to be done in "the organized communities, the communal councils, the communes, and other entities of the popular power" (Article 184). This implied "the assumption of the activity of municipal and/or state public enterprises by the communal organizations" (Article 184.2) and "the transference of the administration and control of state and municipal public services to the Communal organizations, on the basis of the principle of coresponsibility in public business" (Article 184.7).

The rejected 2007 reform defined the structure of "the organized community" (*la comunidad organizada*), which "shall have as its maximum authority the assembly of citizens [*asamblea de ciudadanos*] of the popular power, which, in that capacity, was to designate and revoke the organs of the communal power [*poder comunal*] in the communities, communes, and other political-territorial entities constituting the city, as the primary political unit of the territory." It also stated that "the communal council constitutes the executive organ for the decisions of the citizen's assemblies, formulating and composing the diverse communal organizations and social groups." The proposed reform to Article 184 also added that the communal council "shall assume the role of the justice of the peace and the provision of neighborhood prevention and protection services," which traditionally were competencies of municipalities. Finally, it was proposed that "a fund for the financing of the projects of the communal councils shall be created through legislation." This institutional framework must, of course, be adequately linked to what the rejected reform proposed with respect to Article 136 of the Constitution relative to the popular power and elimination of any vestige of representative democracy.[670]

5. Eliminating the Constitutional Guarantee of Municipal Autonomy

Under Article 168 of the 1999 Constitution, municipalities constitute the primary political unit (*unidad política primaria*) of national organization. They have juridical personality and enjoy autonomy. This status includes the election of their authorities; the management and administration of matters within their competencies; the creation, collection, and investment of revenues; and the constitutional protection that provides that municipal acts "may not be challenged except before the competent courts, according with the Constitution and the laws." Thus, municipal acts are not subject to any form of review –other than judicial– by the organs of the national level of government or of the states.

The rejected 2007 reform attempted to eliminate this final element of the legal and institutional autonomy of municipalities. The reform would have left open the possibility of establishing by law that the acts of municipalities be challenged and reviewed by organs of the executive powers of the states or of the national power, and would eliminate the guarantee that municipal acts can be reviewed only by judicial authorities.[671]

II. PROPOSED CHANGES IN THE ORGANIZATION OF THE NATIONAL LEVEL OF GOVERNMENT

1. Proposed Reforms Regarding the International Activities of the Republic

The rejected 2007 constitutional reform sought to substantially modify Articles 152 and 153 of the Constitution, which define the basis for the international activities of the republic, as well as the participation of Venezuela in regional Latin American economic-integration processes.

The proposed reform to Article 152 redefined the guidelines for international activity of the state adding to all those established in the 1999 Constitution, that the external policy must be oriented "in an active way toward the configuration of a multipolar world, free from the hegemony of any center of imperial, colonial, and neocolonial power."

---

670 See Arturo Peraza, "Reforma, Democracia participativa y Poder Popular," in *Revista de Derecho Público* No. 112 *(Estudios sobre la reforma constitucional)*, Editorial Jurídica Venezolana, Caracas 2007, p. 113.

671 See José Luis Villegas Moreno, "Impacto de la Reforma Constitucional sobre las entidades locales," in *Revista de Derecho Público* No. 112, *(Estudios sobre la reforma constitucional)*, Editorial Jurídica Venezolana, Caracas 2007, pp. 119-123.

The reform proposed completely eliminating the republic's participation in Latin American economic integration processes.[672] Instead, it established few principles of foreign affairs: "The republic must promote the integration, the confederation and the union of Latin America and the Caribbean in order to configure a political, economic and social great regional block." The provision added that "to attain that objective, the state will privilege the structure of new models of integration and union on our continent, allowing the creation of geopolitical spaces, within which peoples and governments of our America could construct a single great national [*gran nacional*] project, which Simón Bolívar called 'A Nation of Republics.'" Thus, the reform would have allowed Venezuela "to subscribe to international treaties and covenants based on the most ample political, social, economic, cultural, great national, productive, complementarily, solidarity and just trade cooperation."[673]

2. *Proposed Reforms to the Executive Power and Reinforcing the Presidential System*

With the rejected 2007 reform, the presidential system was sought to be reinforced, particularly through the extension of the president's term of office, the possibility of indefinite reelection of the president, the establishment in addition to the existent position of executive vice president, of new position of vice presidents, and the expansion of presidential powers and attributions.

A. *The Extension of the President's Term and Unlimited Reelection*

The 2007 reform, in addition to ensuring the possibility of the president's indefinite reelection, sought to extend the presidential term from six to seven years (Article 230).[674] Never has there been such a lengthy presidential term in the whole of the country's constitutional history. Never in the whole of Venezuela's political history has a president exercised the executive power continuously for as many years as the

---

672   See Jorge Luis Suárez, "La reforma del artículo 153 de la Constitución de 1999: un severo retroceso luego de un gran avance," in id., pp. 125-30; Maria Auxiliadora Andrade, "la integración económica latinoamericana en la Constitución de 1999 y en la reforma Constitucional de 2007," in *id.*, pp. 131-35.

673   See for instance, regarding the tight international relations that have been established with Cuba, Fernando Olivares Méndez (Interview), "Agustín Blanco Muñoz/ Fidel es el presidente de Venecuba" (July 5, 2010), available at http://www.enfoques365.net/N6902-agustn-blanco-muoz---fidel-es-el-presidente-de-venecuba.html. See also the discussion organized the same Agustín Blanco Muñoz, in the Cátedra Pío Tamayo, Central University of Venezuela, on the subject "¡Aqui manda Fidel! Venecuba, ¿un proyecto montado por y para la traición a la patria?," May 2010. Available at http://www.vlinea.com/index.php?option=com_content&view=article&id=9182:iaqui-manda-fidel-venecuba-iun-proyecto-montado-por-y-para-la-traicion-a-la-patria&catid=1:nacionales&Itemid=64; and http://www.gentiuno.com/articulo.asp?articulo=8934. In contrast, on July 22, 2010, the president broke off all diplomatic relations with Colombia, after the Colombian ambassador before the Organization of American States presented at a meeting of the organization evidence of Colombian rebel camps and bases inside Venezuela, asking for independent observers to visit the country. See "Chávez Cuts Ties with Colombia," *The New York Times*, July 23, 2010, p. A7.

674   See Carlos Ayala Corao, "Reforma constitucional 2007: El presidencialismo y la reelección," in *Revista de Derecho Público* No. 112, *(Estudios sobre la reforma constitucional)*, Editorial Jurídica Venezolana, Caracas 2007., 137-43; Carlos Luis Carrillo Artiles, "La desnaturalización del sistema presidencial en Venezuela. Del presidencialismo exacerbado consagrado en la Constitución de 1999 al ultrapresidencialismo pretendido en la reforma constitucional de 2007," in *id.*, pp. 145-49.

current president has governed the country. Nonetheless, after the popular rejection of the 2007 constitutional reform, the president managed to succeed in his objective of establishing the possibility for his continuous and indefinite reelection, by means of the constitutional amendment approved in February 2009.[675]

B. *The New Executive Organs: Vice Presidents*

An innovation of the 1999 Constitution was the creation of the office of the executive vice president (*vicepresidente ejecutivo*), as a nonelected officer freely named and removed by the president, thus rendering the office completely subject to the political will of the president (Article 225).

The rejected 2007 reform of Article 225 sought to increase the number of vice presidents by changing the title from executive vice president to first vice president (*primer vicepresidente*) and by enabling the president to designate the number of vice presidents he "deems necessary." The new vice presidents also would have exercised the executive power and, as was publicly announced, would have been assigned to determined territories, sectors, or subject matters, in particular to conduct what the president and the reform proposal called the "new geometry of power."[676] Consequently, these public officials would have reinforced the direct action of the president in the territory or determined subject areas, independently of the vertical distribution of the public powers that could exist.

C. *Extending the Powers of the President*

Article 236 of the Constitution of 1999 enumerates the competencies of the president, which the 2007 constitutional reform sought to expand and amplify[677] as follows.

First, in addition to the power to direct the government, as is provided in Article 236.2, the reform sought to give him the power to direct the state and to coordinate relations between the other national public powers while acting in his capacity as head of state. This reform sought to assign to the president the power to direct the actions of the state, which implied that the president was to direct not only the actions of the national executive power but also those of all organs of the national power (including the other branches of government) and of all the state and municipal powers. This implies complete centralization of the state.

Second, a new power was proposed to be conferred to the president in Article 236.3 regarding not only matters of territorial organization and land use planning but also the "regime of the federal district, the states, the municipalities, the federal de-

---

675 See *Gaceta Oficial* N° 5,908 of Feb. 19, 2009. See the comments in Allan R. Brewer-Carías, "El juez constitucional vs. la alternabilidad republicana," in *Revista de Derecho Público* 117, Caracas 2009, pp. 205ff.

676 See Gustavo Tarre Briceño, "La nueva geometría del poder," in *Revista de Derecho Público* No. 112 *(Estudios sobre la reforma constitucional)*, Editorial Jurídica Venezolana, Caracas 2007, pp. 115-18.

677 See Margarita Escudero León, "La concentración de poderes en el Presidente de la república de acuerdo con la propuesta de reforma constitucional sancionada por la Asamblea Nacional el 2 de noviembre de 2007," in id., pp. 151-55; Aurilivi Linares Martínez, "La ampliación de los poderes presidenciales en la práctica y en el proyecto de reforma constitucional de 2007," in id., pp. 157-61.

pendencies and other regional entities." With these powers, all vestiges of autonomy and territorial division would have disappeared, granted exclusively to the executive.

Third, the reform of Article 236.4 sought to assign the president the power to create "the federal provinces, federal territories, federal cities, functional districts, federal municipalities, maritime regions and insular districts, as provided in the Constitution, and to designate their authorities as established by law." This implied the creation of territorial entities that would have been totally dependent on the national executive and would be superimposed upon states and municipalities.

Fourth, Article 236.19 sought to attribute to the president the competence to "formulate a national plan for development and direct its execution," eliminating the requirement of the assembly's approval of the plan (Article 236.18).[678] This change would have eliminated all participation in the planning process of the popular representation (in the National Assembly).

Fifth, the reforms of Articles 236.5 and 236.6 sought to reinforce the role of the president in "command[ing] the Bolivarian Armed Forces as commander in chief, exercising supreme hierarchical authority in all of its corps, components and units, determining its contingent," Article 236.7 added the power to "promote officials in all [of the armed force's] ranks and hierarchies and designate their corresponding positions." Under the reforms, the whole of the Bolivarian Armed Forces would have become directly subject to the will of the president and, of course, his political project.

Sixth, the proposed reform to Article 236.9 sought to empower the president to "decree the suspension and restriction of constitutional guaranties" when declaring state of exception, in contrast to the 1999 Constitution, which authorizes the president only to "restrict" guarantees, not to suspend them. This attribution was also ratified in the proposed reform to Article 337, which expanded the president's powers in cases of states of exception (Articles 338 and 339).[679]

Finally, in addition to the classical attribution to the president to "administer the national treasury," the constitutional reform also proposed assigning the president the power to administer "the international reserves, as well as to establish and regulate the monetary policy, in coordination with the central bank."

The proposed reforms also attributed entirely new and broad competencies to the president. First, the reform to Article 11 of the Constitution established a new competency for the president to create by "decree special military regions in order to guarantee the sovereignty, the security and the defense in any part of the territory and geographic spaces of the republic," as well as to create by "decree special authorities in the event of contingencies, disasters, or any other requiring immediate and strategic intervention of the state."

Second, the reform to Article 16 sought to assign the president the power to create, by decree, communal cities within organized communities, communes, and communal self-governments. The reforms also sought to confer to the president the

---

678   See Juan M. Raffalli A., "El Consejo de Estado y el Plan nacional de Desarrollo," in id., p. 182.

679   See Jesús María Casal, "Los estados de excepción en la reforma constitucional," in id., pp. 325-329.

competency to "create by decree maritime regions, federal territories, federal municipalities, insular districts, federal provinces, federal cities and functional districts, as well as any other entity established in the Constitution or in statute."

Third, the reforms to Article 16 also assigned to the national government (directed by the president) the power to develop and activate a district mission with the corresponding functional-strategic plan to create a functional district.

Fourth, the reform to Article 16 also assigned the national executive power competency to designate and dismiss authorities of the maritime regions, federal territories, federal district, federal municipalities, insular districts, federal provinces, federal cities, and functional districts, as well as any other entity established in the Constitution or by statute.

Fifth, the reform to Article 13 sought to attribute competency to the executive power – with the collaboration and participation of all entities of the national, state, and municipal public powers, as well as of the popular power, its communities, communes, councils, and other social organizations – to provide for "all that is necessary for urban reorganization; the restructuring of roadways; environmental recuperation; the achievement of optimal results in public and personal security; the comprehensive strengthening of neighborhoods; urban development; the provision of systems for health, education, sports, culture and entertainment; the total restoration of the historic city center; and, the construction of a system of small and midsized satellite cities along its territorial axes of expansion." Under the provisions, the legislative power would have been left materially void of competency in all of these areas.

Sixth, the reform of Article 141 sought to confer competencies to the executive power to establish missions as "public administrations" by means of organizational and functional regulations. Missions were understood to be "organizations of varied of natures, created to meet the most deeply felt and urgent needs of the population, requiring the use of exceptional systems, including experimental systems." The consequence of this reform was that organization and regulation concerning all the public administration would have been the exclusive competency of the national executive, beyond the reach of the legislature. These rejected constitutional reforms, nonetheless, were illegitimately carried out through a decree law on the Organic Law on Public Administration in 2008.[680]

Seventh, the reform to Article 318 proposed conferring competency to the president or executive power to establish "monetary policies and exercise the monetary competencies of the national power" in coordination with the Central Bank of Venezuela. This power was conferred so that the president or the executive power could jointly, with the Central Bank of Venezuela, "achieve stability in prices and preserve the internal and external value of the currency," and share with the Central Bank of Venezuela the functions "of participating in the formulation and execution of monetary policy, the design and execution of exchange policy, the regulation of

---

680 See *Gaceta Oficial* N° 5,890 of July 31, 2008. See the comments in Allan R. Brewer-Carías, "El sentido de la reforma de la Ley Orgánica de la Administración Pública," in *Revista de Derecho Público* 115, *(Estudios sobre los Decretos Leyes)*, Caracas 2008, pp. 155-62.

money and credit, and the fixing of interest rates." As administrator of the National Public Treasury (Hacienda Pública Nacional), competency was proposed to be passed to the president to administer and direct the republic's international reserves, which are to be managed by the Central Bank of Venezuela. Nonetheless, and despite the popular rejection of the 2007 constitutional reform, many of these reforms have been implemented by means of successive reforms of the Law on the Central Bank of Venezuela.[681]

Last, the reform to Article 321 assigned competency to the chief of state, within the framework of his administration of international reserves, to establish, in coordination with the Central Bank of Venezuela, at the end of each year, the level of reserves necessary for the national economy, as well as the amount of surplus reserves, which were to be directed to funds "established by the national executive for productive investments, development and infrastructure, financing of the missions, and, definitively, to the integral, endogenous, humanist and socialist development of the nation." That is, under the proposed reforms, all competencies in the area of monetary and fiscal policy would have been in the hands of the president.

3. *Proposed Reforms Regarding the Legislative Power and Political Permeability*

The 1999 Constitution, following the principle of separation of powers, to ensure separation between the executive and the legislative powers, established that members of the National Assembly could not be appointed to executive positions without losing their legislative tenure (Article 191). This means that once appointed to an executive post, a former member of the legislative body cannot return to the assembly.

The proposed reform diluted this separation by seeking to establish that members of the National Assembly could accept executive positions without losing legislative tenure. It was proposed that, when named to a position by the president, they could return to the assembly once finished with the executive appointment, to finish the period of the legislative tenure for which they were elected (Article 191). This provision, of course, is inconceivable in presidential systems of government. It is normal in parliamentary systems, where parliament is in charge of forming the government with its members.

4. *Proposed Reforms Regarding the Appointing and Dismissing of the Head Officers of the Nonelected Branches of Government*

As aforementioned, one of the important reforms introduced in the 1999 Constitution in order to ensure the independence and autonomy of the different branches of government was to establish limits on the National Assembly powers to appoint the head officers of the nonelected branches of government – that is, the magistrates of the Supreme Tribunal of Justice, the prosecutor general, the comptroller general, the peoples' defender and the members of the National Electoral Council. For such purpose, the Constitution created different nominating committees integrated by repre-

---

681   See *Gaceta Oficial* 39.300, Nov. 5, 2009. In Mar. 2010, a new reform of the Central Bank of Venezuela Law was sanctioned by the Nacional Assembly.

sentatives of the different sectors of society, in charge of selecting and proposing the candidates before the National Assembly.

The 2007 constitutional reform sought to change the composition of the committees, transforming it into a parliamentary commission of members of the National Assembly, other public officials (e.g., the representative of the popular power), and representatives of social organizations (Article 279).

In addition, regarding the appointment of the officials, the reform sought to eliminate the guarantee of the qualified majority of members of the National Assembly for such appointments (Article 279), seeking to establish a simple majority for that purpose as well.

In the same sense as the proposed changes to nominations of members of the National Electoral Council, the proposed reforms aimed to change the requirement that the Electoral Nominating Committee comprise representatives from various sectors of society (Article 292). The reform provided that the National Assembly, to make appointments, must itself convene a nominating committee composed of members of the assembly, representatives of the popular power, and representatives of other social organizations (Article 295). That is, the nominating committee was to be composed of a majority of public officials. The reform also sought to eliminate the requirement that candidates be nominated by civil society and law faculties of the country; instead, it is established that such nominations are to be made by the councils of popular power and other educational and social sectors (Article 296). The proposed reforms follow the trend established in the 2002 Organic Law of the Electoral Power, which unconstitutionally converted the nominating committee into a parliamentary commission.

The reform was also to eliminate the provision of the 1999 Constitution imposing the need for a majority of two-thirds of assembly members to appoint members of the National Electoral Council (Article 296); instead, it established that a simple majority vote was sufficient (Article 295). The reform also established that a majority of votes of members of the National Assembly was sufficient to dismiss members of the electoral power (Article 296).

III. PROPOSED CHANGES IN THE ARMED FORCES: FROM A CIVIL MANAGED STATE TO A MILITARIST STATE

Another area of innovation in the 1999 Constitution was the regime of the National Armed Forces, established under the regime of security and defense. The changes in 1999 reinforced militarism.

The 2007 reforms proposed radical changes in the military institution. The proposed reforms for Articles 328 and 329 sought to transform the military from a professional, apolitical institution that does not deliberate and that operates at the service of the republic into a militia that operates at the service of the chief of state and at the service of his political party.

In effect, the rejected 2007 reform regarding Article 328 sought, first, to eliminate the constitutional clause that states that the armed forces "is an institution that is essentially professional, without political affiliation." In its place, it was proposed that the Constitution state that the armed forces is "a corps that is essentially patriotic, popular, and anti-imperialist." Under the reform, the military as a professional institution would have disappeared, as would the prohibition on the military's politi-cal partisanship. The definition of the institution as "patriotic, popular, and anti-imperialist" would have opened an avenue to integrate the armed forces into the political party of the commander in chief, who would, under the proposed reforms for Article 236.6, exercise supreme hierarchical authority in each of its corps, com-ponents, and units. Unfortunately, this was implemented in an unconstitutional way by means of the Organic Law of the Bolivarian Armed Forces.[682]

Second, although Article 328 sets forth the objectives of the armed forces "to guarantee the independence and sovereignty of the nation, and assure the integrity of its geographic space," the reform proposed to add "to reserve [the nation] from any internal or external attack."

Third, instead of stating that the objectives of the armed forces are to be achieved "through military defense, through cooperation in the maintenance of internal order, and through active participation in national development," the reform established that the objectives be obtained "by means of study, planning and execution of Boli-varian military doctrine, by means of the application of principles of comprehensive military defense and the popular war of resistance [*guerra popular de resistencia*], by means of permanent participation in the tasks of maintaining citizen security and the conservation of internal order, and in the same sense, by means of actively parti-cipating in the plans for the economic, social, scientific and technical development of the nation." In this way, the Bolivarian military doctrine would be incorporated into the Constitution as an essential element of the armed forces, even though the exact content of the doctrine remains unknown. Guerrilla elements were proposed to be incorporated as "popular war of resistance", and the armed forces was to be con-verted into a national police organization, charged with citizen security and conser-vation of internal order. In addition, providing that the armed force is to, among other functions, "actively participate in the plans for the economic, social, scientific and technical development of the nation," the reform sought to constitutionalize the militarization of the state and the public administration.

Fourth, instead of providing, as the Constitution of 1999 does, that in fulfilling its function the armed forces operates "exclusively at the service of the nation, and not of any person or political partiality," the 2007 reform proposed that the armed forces, "in the fulfillment of its function, shall always be at the service of the Vene-zuelan people in defense of their sacred interests, and in no case shall be at the ser-vice of any oligarchy or foreign imperial power." The consequence of this change would have been to eliminate the constitutional prohibition on the armed forces from operating in the service of any person or political preference. This proposal, again, sought to open a path to the integration of the armed forces into the political party of the commander in chief, who could place the armed forces at his service or at the service of the government's party.

It should be remembered, also, that the reform for Article 236.7 sought to attribu-te to the president, acting in his or her capacity as commander in chief, the power to "promote officials in all [of the armed forces'] ranks and hierarchies and to assign

---

682   See *Gaceta Oficial* N° 5.891 of July 31, 2008.

them to their corresponding positions." This power would have constituted an instrument for securing a political hold on such officials.

Fifth, where Article 328 asserts that the fundamental pillars of the armed forces are the Constitution and the laws, discipline, obedience, and subordination, the reform proposed adding: "its historic pillars stand in the mandate of Bolívar: 'Liberate the homeland, take up the sword in defense of the social guarantees and be deserving of the people's blessings.'"

Article 329 of the Constitution of 1999 states that "the army, the navy and the air force have, as an essential responsibility, the duty to plan, execute and oversee those military operations that are required to assure the defense of the nation." The national guard is to "cooperate in the development of those operations and shall have as a basic responsibility, the duty to carry out operations necessary for maintaining the internal order of the country." The provision adds that "the armed forces may exercise those administrative police and criminal investigative activities that are assigned by law."

The reform proposed to change Article 329. It proposed increasing the number of military components of the Bolivarian Armed Forces to five, including land, air, and sea corps, and to administratively organize these into the Bolivarian National Army, the Bolivarian National Navy, the Bolivarian National Air Force, the Bolivarian National Guard, and the Bolivarian National Militia. The reform also established that the Bolivarian Armed Forces "could accomplish police activities attributed by law."

All the reforms sought to reinforce the political character of the armed forces and the militarism of the state that began with the Constitution of 1999. The provision asserting the "apolitical and nondeliberating character" of the armed forces established in Article 132 of the 1961 Constitution had already disappeared from the 1999 constitutional text, as had the essential obligation of the armed forces to ensure "the stability of the democratic institutions and respect of the Constitution and the laws, whose obedience is always above any other obligation," in the same article. The traditional prohibition against the simultaneous exercise of military and civil authority contained in Article 131 of the Constitution of 1961, and the control held by the former Senate over military promotions in the upper levels under Article 331 of the Constitution of 1961, had already disappeared in the Constitution of 1999.

Notwithstanding the popular rejection of all these reforms in 2007, they were all implemented fraudulently and illegitimately by means of a decree law enacted by the president in 2008 to reform the Organic Law of the Bolivarian Armed Forces,[683] in which the National Bolivarian Militia was created without any constitutional support.[684] This National Bolivarian Militia, directly dependent on the president, is composed of a Military Reserve and a Territorial Militia, the latter integrated not

683 See Jesús María Alvarado Andrade, "La nueva Fuerza Armada Bolivariana (comentarios a raíz del Decreto N° 6.239, con rango, valor y fuerza de Ley Orgánica de la Fuerza Armada Nacional Bolivariana)," in *Revista de Derecho Público* No. 115, *(Estudios sobre los Decretos Leyes 2008)*, Editorial Jurídica Venezolana, Caracas 2008, pp. 205 ff.

684 See *Gaceta Oficial* N° 5.891 Extra. of July 31, 2008.

only by Venezuelan citizens but also by non-Venezuelans, resulting in a new military component structured in parallel to the army.

CHAPTER 12

THE FAILED ATTEMPT TO CONSOLIDATE A SOCIALIST CENTRALIZED ECONOMIC SYSTEM IN THE CONSTITUTION

In addition to the aforementioned reform proposals sanctioned by the National Assembly in 2007 regarding the organization of the State, the rejected 2007 constitutional reform also sought to transform the socio-political foundations of the state's order of mixed economy, establishing instead a Socialist system.

According to the trends in constitutionalism developed since the middle of the past century, the economic constitution of Venezuela has been established on the model of the mixed economy, which is based on the principle of liberty as opposed to the directed economy – this is similar to the economic models of all Western nations.[685] This economic system, then, is founded on economic liberty, private initiative, and free competition, without excluding the participation of the state as a promoter of economic development, regulator of economic activity, and planner together with the civil society.

Following this orientation, the 1999 Constitution establishes a mixed economic system, a social market economy. This is an economic system that is based on economic liberty but must be developed according to principles of social justice – therefore, it requires the intervention of the state.[686] This socioeconomic regime, in accord with Article 299 of the Constitution, rests on the following principles: social justice, democratization, efficiency, free competition, environmental protection, productivity, and solidarity. These aim to ensure comprehensive human development, existence with dignity, and the maximum benefit for the collective. For these purposes, Article 299 expressly sets forth that the state must, "jointly with private initiative," promote "the harmonious development of the national economy for the purpose of generating sources of employment and a high national level of added value to elevate the standard of living of the population and strengthen the nation's economic sovereignty, thus guaranteeing legal certainty, solidity, dynamism, sustainability, permanence, and economic growth with equity, to guarantee a just distribution of wealth by means of strategic democratic, participative, and open planning."

As the Constitutional Chamber of the Supreme Tribunal of Justice stated in Decision N° 117 (February 6, 2001),[687] this is "a socioeconomic system that is intermediate between a free market (in which the State acts as a simple programmer [*programador*] for an economy that is dependent upon the supply and demand of goods

---

685 See Allan R. Brewer-Carías, "Reflexiones sobre la Constitución económica," in *Estudios sobre la Constitución Española. Homenaje al Profesor Eduardo García de Enterría*, Editorial Civitas, Madrid 1991, Vol. 5, pp.:3.839-3.853.

686 On the economic constitution in the 1999 Constitution see Allan R. Brewer-Carías, *La Constitución de 1999. Derecho Constitucional Venezolano*, Editorial Jurídica Venezolana, Caracas 2004, Vol 1, pp.:818-82.

687 See *Revista de Derecho Público No. 85–88*, Editorial Jurídica Venezolana, Caracas 2001, pp. 212-18.

and services) and an interventionist economy (in which the State actively intervenes as the 'primary entrepreneur')." The Constitution promotes "joint economic activity between the State and private initiative in the pursuit of, and in order to concretely realize the supreme values consecrated in the Constitution," and to pursue "the equilibrium of all the forces of the market, and, joint activity between the State and private initiative." In accord with that system, the Tribunal ruled, the Constitution "advocates a series of superior normative values with respect to the economic regime, consecrating free enterprise within the framework of a market economy and, fundamentally, within the framework of the Social State under the Rule of Law (the Welfare State, the State of Well-being or the Social Democratic State). This is a social State that is opposed to authoritarianism."[688]

The practical application of this constitutional model brought about the development of an economy based on economic freedom and private initiative but subject to important and necessary intervention by the state to ensure the constitutionally required orientation of social justice. State intervention has increased because the state owns title, within the public domain, to the petroleum-rich subsoil, as it always has in Venezuela's legal history.

In 2007, the rejected constitutional reform proposed to radically alter this model in order to accentuate the existing disequilibrium between the public and private sectors and to transform the system into a state economy based on central planning within a socialist state and socialist economy.[689]

I. PROPOSED CHANGES ON MATTERS OF ECONOMIC FREEDOM AND PRIVATE PROPERTY

1. *Eliminating Economic Freedom as a Constitutionally Protected Right*

As a fundamental principle of the constitutional system, Article 112 of the 1999 Constitution establishes the right of every person to freely dedicate him- or herself to the economic activity of choice, without limitations beyond those established in the Constitution and the laws based on reasons related to human development, security, public health, the protection of the environment, or other social interests. Thus, under the 1999 Constitution, the state is obligated to promote "private initiative, in order to guarantee the creation and just distribution of wealth, the production of

---

688 The values alluded to, according to the doctrine of the Constitutional Chamber, "are developed through the concept of free enterprise" (*libertad de empresa*), which encompasses both the notion of a subjective right "to dedicate oneself to the economic activity of one's choice" and a principle of economic regulation according to which the will of the business (*voluntad de la empresa*) to make its own decisions is manifest. The state fulfills its role of intervention in this context. Intervention can be direct (through businesses) or indirect (as an entity regulating the market)." Id.

689 See Rogelio Pérez Perdomo, "La Constitución de papel y su reforma," in *Revista de Derecho Público* 112 *(Estudios sobre la reforma constitucional)*, Editorial Jurídica Venezolana, Caracas 2007, p. 14; Alfredo Arismendi, "Utopía Constitucional," in id., p. 31; Gerardo Fernández, "Aspectos esenciales de la modificación constitucional propuesta por el Presidente de la República. La modificación constitucional como un fraude a la democracia," in id., p. 22; Manuel Rachadell, "Personalismo político en el Siglo XXI," p. 65; Allan R. Brewer-Carías, "El sello socialista que se pretendía imponer al Estado," in id., pp. 71-75; Alfredo Morles Hernández, "El nuevo modelo económico para erl Socialismo del Siglo XXI," in id., pp. 233-236.

goods and services meeting the needs of the population, the freedom to work, free enterprise, and commercial and industrial liberty, while not diminishing [the state's] power to take measures in order to plan, rationalize, and regulate the economy to promote comprehensive development within the nation."

The reform proposed to eliminate both the constitutional right to develop economic activities and economic freedom by seeking to substitute such provision by one reduced to define, as only a matter of state policy, the obligation to promote "the development of a productive economic model, that is intermediate, diversified and independent." Moreover, the proposed model was to be "founded upon the humanistic values of cooperation and the preponderance of common interests over individual ones, guaranteeing the meeting of the people's social and material needs, the greatest possible political and social stability, and the greatest possible sum of happiness." The proposal added that the state, in the same way, "shall promote and develop different forms of businesses and economic units from social property, both directly or communally, as well as indirectly or through the state." According to that norm, the state was to promote "economic units of social production and/or distribution, that may be mixed properties held between the State, the private sector, and the communal power, so as to create the best conditions for the collective and cooperative construction of a socialist economy."

The reforms sought simply to derogate and eliminate the right to the free exercise of economic activities as a constitutional right and economic freedom itself. [690] This would, of course, have been contrary to the principle of progressivism in human and constitutional rights that Article 19 of the 1999 Constitution guarantees. It also would have fundamentally transformed the state, which cannot be accomplished through the constitutional-reform procedures.

The 1999 Constitution confers a set of attributes to the state for it to regulate the exercise of economic rights. In particular, the Constitution prohibits monopolies, declaring activities that tend to establish them or that can lead to their existence as contrary to the fundamental principles of the Constitution (Article 113). The abuse of a position of market dominance, independent of the cause of such dominance, is also declared as contrary to the fundamental principles of the Constitution. In each case, the norm affords the state the power to take measures necessary to avoid the harmful and restrictive effects of monopoly, the abuse of market dominance, and the concentration of demand for the purpose of protecting consumers and producers and to protect effective conditions for competition in the economy.

The rejected constitutional reform on these matters also proposed to radically alter the regime of economic activity. The reform for Article 113 provided for a series

---

690 See Gerardo Fernández, "Aspectos esenciales de la modificación constitucional propuesta por el Presidente de la República. La modificación constitucional como un fraude a la democracia," in *Revista de Derecho Público* No. 112 *(Estudios sobre la reforma constitucional)*, Editorial Jurídica Venezolana, Caracas 2007, p. 24; Alfredo Arismendi, "Utopía Constitucional," in *id.*, 31; José Antonio Muci Borjas, "La suerte de la libertad económica en el proyecto de Reforma de la Constitución de 2007," in id., pp. 203-208; Tamara Adrián, "Actividad económica y sistemas alternativos de producción," in id., p. 209-14; Víctor Hernández Mendible, "Réquiem por la libertad de empresa y derecho de propiedad," in id., pp. 215-218; Alfredo Morles Hernández, "El nuevo modelo económico para el Socialismo del Siglo XXI," in id., pp. 233-236.

of limitations that far exceeded restrictions on monopoly and abuse of market dominance; it moved to establish a privileged public or state economy and privileged socialist means of production.

In this context, the reform included a norm that prohibited activities, agreements, practices, conduct, and omissions by individuals that could damage the methods and systems of social and collective production and affect social and collective property. This norm was also to prohibit acts by individuals that prevent or make difficult the just and equitable confluence of goods and services. This norm would therefore have rendered all the private economic activity the subject of the absolute discretion of public authorities.

The reform also added that in cases involving the exploitation of natural resources or other assets within national domain that are of a strategic character or that involve the provision of essential services, the state may reserve the exploitation of resources or the provision of services to itself, either directly or through state-owned corporations. This was to be made, however, "without prejudice to the establishment of corporations were to be direct social property, of mixed corporations, and/or socialist units of production that ensure social and economic sovereignty, that respect the oversight of the state, and meet their imputed social responsibilities in accordance with the terms of legislation corresponding to their respective sector of the economy."

2. *Eliminating Property as a Constitutionally Protected Right*

In addition to economic liberty, another fundamental pillar of the Constitution of 1999 is the guarantee of the right to private property – that is, the right of every person "to the use, enjoyment, benefit, and disposition of his or her assets" (Article 115). The right to an asset is subject to "those contributions, restrictions, and obligations established by law for the purposes of public utility or general interest," and it is "only for the cause of public utility or social interest, and on the basis of a final judicial decision and timely payment of just indemnification," that any asset may be expropriated.

The constitutional reforms sought to alter radically the regime of the right to private property by eliminating private property as a constitutionally protected right[691] and by "recognizing" private property (*propiedad privada*) as one sort of property among many. The supposed "right" to property was reduced only regarding "assets for use and consumption or as means of production," which minimized the protections of private property in comparison with other properties recognized, particularly public property.

With respect to Article 115 of the Constitution, the proposed reform, in effect, recognized and guaranteed "different forms of property" as follows:

---

691 See Román José Duque Corredor, "La reforma constitucional y la desnaturalización del derecho de propiedad y su transformación en una simple relación de hecho permitida por el Estado," in *Revista de Derecho Público* No. 112 *(Estudios sobre la reforma constitucional)*, Editorial Jurídica Venezolana, Caracas 2007, pp. 241-48; Gustavo A. Grau Fortoul, "Aproximación preliminar al tratamiento de la propiedad privada en la primera propuesta de modificación de la Constitución de 1999," in id., pp. 249-55; Uxúa Ojer, "La propiedad en la propuesta de cambio constitucional," in id., pp. 257-60.

1. "Public property [*propiedad pública*] is that which belongs to the entities of the state; social property [*propiedad social*] is that which belongs to the people jointly and to future generations, and can be of two kinds: (a) indirect social property [*propiedad social indirecta*] when exercised by the state in the name of the community, and (b) direct social property [*propiedad social directa*], when the state assigns property, in its different forms, and within the ambit of demarcated territories, to one or several communities, or to one or several communes, so that it constitutes communal property [*propiedad comunal*]; or the property is assigned to one or several cities, so that it constitutes citizens' property [*propiedad ciudadana*]."

2. "Collective property [*propiedad colectiva*] is property pertaining to social groups or persons, exploited for their common benefit, use, or enjoyment, that may be of social or private origin."

3. "Mixed property [*propiedad mixta*] is property that is constituted between the public sector, the social sector, the collective sector and the private sector, in different combinations, for the exploitation of resources or the execution of activities, subject always to the absolute economic and social sovereignty of the nation."

4. "Private property [*propiedad privada*] is that which is owned by natural or legal persons, is recognized as assets for use or consumption, or as means of production legitimately acquired."

The reforms aimed to reduce private property to assets for use or consumption or means of production. What is to be understood by assets for consumption remained to be defined but, in common parlance, they are those assets not used to produce others goods; they are used to meet the specific needs of the consumers who acquire them. "Means of production" refers to a set of work objects used in production to create material assets.

With respect to the guarantee of private property being taken only by expropriation, the proposed reform to Article 115 sought to add express "authority to organs of the State to previously occupy assets that are the object of expropriation during judicial proceedings," and thus constitutionalized a mechanism for prior occupation. Nonetheless, and despite the popular rejection to the 2007 constitutional reform, many of the Decree Laws subsequently enacted have implemented these means of affecting private property, allowing takeover and occupations, in many cases *sine die*, of industries and private assets, as it was provided in Law for the defense of persons in their access to goods and services.[692]

---

692 See Decreto Ley N° 6,092 para la defensa de las personas en el acceso a los bienes y servicios, *Gaceta Oficial* N° 5,889 Extra. of July 31, 2008. See Juan Domingo Alfonzo Paradisi, "Comentarios en cuanto a los procedimientos administrativos establecidos en el decreto N° 6.092 con rango valor y fuerza de Ley para la defensa de las personas en el acceso a los bienes y servicios," in *Revista de Derecho Público* No. 115, *(Estudios sobre los Decretos Leyes 2008)*, Editorial Jurídica Venezolana, Caracas 2008, pp. 246ff.; Karina Anzola Spadaro, "El carácter autónomo de las 'medidas preventivas' contempladas en el artículo 111 del Decreto Ley para la defensa de las personas en el acceso a los bienes y servicios," in *id.*, pp. 271-279.

3. *The Elimination of the Latifundio*

Article 307 of the 1999 Constitution declares the latifundio as contrary to social interests. In common usage, *latifundio* refers to large tracts of privately owned rural land subject to agricultural exploitation on a large scale but that make inefficient use of the available resources. To correct the situation, the Constitution indicates that the legislature must pass legislation "in the area of taxation, in order to levy taxes on idle lands and to establish the measures necessary to transform these into productive economic units, and, equally, recover lands with agricultural potential."

The norm contained in Article 307 also establishes property rights for rural workers (*campesinos*) and other agricultural and livestock producers working the land according to the forms established in respective legislation. However, the article places an obligation on the state to protect and promote associational and private forms of property to guarantee agricultural production and to safeguard the sustainable organization of arable lands with the objective of ensuring their agricultural and alimentary potential. The same article states that the legislature shall on an exceptional basis create non-tax-based contributions for the purpose of facilitating the funding of financing, research, technical assistance, technical transfers, and other activities aimed to promote the competitiveness and productivity of the agricultural sector.

The rejected reforms regarding Article 307 sought to eliminate any concept of the public policy of promoting the disappearance of the *latifundio* through tax measures by taxing idle lands, and to eliminate the policy of transforming the *latifundios* into productive economic units while recovering lands with agricultural potential. Instead, the reform established that "the republic shall determine by law the form in which the latifundios will be transferred into the property of the state, or into that of public entities or public corporations, cooperatives, communities, or social organizations that are capable of administering them and of making the lands productive." Consequently, the reform was not a matter of making any privately own *latifundio* productive but rather of transferring the property to the state.[693]

The reform also added to this norm that for purposes of guaranteeing agricultural production, the state shall protect and promote social property, and legislation shall be enacted to tax productive lands that are not devoted to agriculture or livestock.

Finally, it was proposed that a clause be added stating that "farms whose owners execute irreparable actions of environmental destruction, or dedicate farms to the production of psychotropic substances or narcotics, or trade in persons, or use the farms, or permit the farms to be used as areas for the commission of crimes against the security and defense of the nation, shall be confiscated."

---

693 In the Land and Farming Law, the possibility for the state to occupy and take over private land was extended. See Ley de Tierras y Desarrollo Agrario in *Gaceta Oficial* N° 5.771 Extra. of May 18, 2005.

II. PROPOSED CHANGES ON MATTERS OF PUBLIC ECONOMY MANAGEMENT

1. *The Regime Governing State Intervention in the Economy*

One of the classic forms of active state intervention in the economy is through the constitution of public corporations or public enterprises. Regarding the regulation of such corporations, Article 300 of the 1999 Constitution refers only to national legislation for the establishment of conditions for the creation of public corporations as "entities that are functionally decentralized." The purpose of the public enterprises, under Article 300, is to realize social or entrepreneurial activities aimed to ensure the reasonable economic and social productivity of the public resources invested.

The rejected 2007 reform sought to alter this regulation by eliminating any reference to decentralization and by reducing the scope of possible purposes serving as the basis for creating public enterprises or entities to the single purpose of promoting and realizing the ends of the socialist economy. In particular, the reform proposed that Article 300 referred only to the creation of "regional corporations or entities for the promotion and realization of economic and social activities under the principles of the socialist economy," and that these established "mechanisms for oversight and accounting that ensure transparency in the management of the public resources invested in them and their reasonable economic and social productivity."

Article 301 of the 1999 Constitution requires the state to defend the economic activity of national public and private enterprises and establishes that foreign investments are subject to the same regulatory conditions as national investments. The rejected reform, however, not only placed the defense of the economic activities of public and private enterprises within the scope of the state's trade policy but also added the defense of the communal, mixed, collective, and social enterprises. The proposed reform also eliminated all reference to foreign investment.

With respect to economic activities to be reserved to the state, Article 302 of the 1999 Constitution sets forth that "by means of the respective organic legislation and for reasons of national interest, the state shall reserve to itself the oil industry and activity," adding that activities in other "industries, forms of exploitation, and areas of goods and services that are in the public interest and are of a strategic character" also may be reserved to the state. In this way, the state's reservation of the oil industry that had already been effectuated through the organic law of the nationalization of the oil industry in 1975 acquired constitutional rank. However, the constitutional text tied the terms of the reservation to what was established in the organic law, which could be changed legislatively, as in fact occurred in 2000.[694] The reservation of the petroleum industry to the state was thus neither rigid nor absolute but rather flexible, in accord with what was established in the corresponding organic law.

The rejected reform sought to radically change the conception of this regulation by establishing the reservation in the Constitution itself, for reasons of national in-

---

694   See Organic Law on Hydrocarbons, in *Gaceta Oficial* N° 37.323 of Nov. 13, 2001. Reformed in 2006. See in *Gaceta Oficial* N° 38.493 of Aug. 4, 2006.

terest, with respect to "the exploitation of liquid, solid and gaseous hydrocarbons, as well as to the initial recollection, transport and manufacturing and the works required for it." The reform added that "the state shall promote national manufacture to process the raw material, assimilating, creating or innovating national technology, in particular referred to the Orinoco Oil Belt [Faja Petrolífera del Orinoco], gas belts in land and offshore and the petrochemical corridors, in order to develop productive forces, to drive economic growth and achieve social justice." In addition, "the state by means of organic legislation can reserve for itself any other activity related to hydrocarbons."

Reforms of the same article sought to add that the activities reserved to the state were to be accomplished "directly by the national executive, or through entities or enterprises of its exclusive property, or by means of mixed enterprises in which the state have the control and majority of shares," therefore constitutionalizing the mixed-enterprise regime established in 2006 and 2007.[695]

In addition, the proposed reform to Article 113 provided that the state could also reserve for itself, directly or by means of enterprises of its property, the exploitation or execution of natural resources or any other public of the domain of the nation (*dominio de la nación*) considered by the Constitution or by the law of a strategic character, as well as the rendering of vital public services (public utilities) considered as such in the Constitution or in the law.

Finally, regarding reserved activities, the proposed reform of Article 303 sought to establish the absolute prohibition on privatization of any of those resources and activities.

Another important innovation of the 1999 Constitution was the regulation of principles and policies in the area of sustainable agricultural production and nutritional security in Article 305. The reform proposed to add to this article that "if necessary to guarantee nutritional security, the republic may assume indispensable sectors of agricultural, livestock, fishing and aquatic production, and transfer their operation to autonomous entities, public corporations and social, cooperative, or communal organizations." Further, the proposal added that the republic might "fully utilize its powers of expropriation, encumbrance, and occupation according to the terms established by this Constitution and the law."

2.   *Proposed Changes in the State's Fiscal and Economic Regime*

In the area of the fiscal regime, for the first time in Venezuelan constitutionalism, the 1999 Constitution incorporated a set of norms relating to the Central Bank of Venezuela and the macroeconomic policy of the state (Articles 318–21). In particular, the Constitution attributes the national power's competencies relating monetary policy to the Central Bank of Venezuela, requiring exercise exclusively and obligatorily for the fundamental objectives of achieving stability in prices and preserving

---

695   See the comments in Allan R. Brewer-Carías, "The 'Statization' of the Pre 2001 Primary Hydrocarbons Joint Venture Exploitations: Their Unilateral Termination and the Assets' Confiscation of Some of the Former Private Parties" in *Oil, Gas & Energy Law Intelligence*, available at www.gasandoil.com/ogel/ ISSN: 1875-418X, Vol. 6, Issue 2 (OGEL/TDM Special Issue on Venezuela: The Battle of Contract Sanctity vs. Resource Sovereignty, Elizabeth Eljuri ed.), Apr. 2008.

the internal and external values of the currency. The Constitution guarantees the bank's autonomy in formulating policies within its competency. In addition, so that the Bank could adequately meet its objectives, the Constitution assigns to it competencies to formulate and execute monetary policy, to participate in the design and execution of exchange policy, to regulate money and credit, to set interests rates, to administer international reserves, and to assume all of those attributes established by law.

A. Eliminating the Autonomy of the Central Bank of Venezuela

Contrary to the provisions of the 1999 Constitution, the constitutional reforms sought to change the regime governing monetary policy and the Central Bank of Venezuela by seeking to eliminate the Bank's competencies and autonomy, thus rendering the bank totally and directly dependent on the national executive.[696]

To this end, the following reforms were proposed regarding Article 318 of the Constitution. First is the requirement that "the national monetary system be directed toward the achievement of the essential ends of the socialist state and the well-being of the people, above any other consideration." Second, the competencies to fix monetary policies would be attributed to the national executive and the Central Bank "in strict and obligatory coordination." Third, the autonomy of the bank was formally eliminated through language stating that the bank "is a person in public law without autonomy in the formulation and execution of the corresponding policies." The Bank's functions were to be subordinated to general economic policy and the national development plan to achieve the superior objectives of the socialist state and the greatest possible sum of happiness for the whole of the people. Fourth, it was established that the functions of the Central Bank were to be "shared with the executive power," and that for the adequate fulfillment of its specific objectives, the bank "shall have, among its functions, shared with the national executive power," only the power to "participate in the formulation and execution of monetary policy, in the design and execution of exchange policy, in the regulation of money and credit, and the fixing of interest rates."

Last, competency to "administer international reserves" was entirely removed from the bank, so the norm stated instead that "the international reserves of the republic shall be managed by the Central Bank of Venezuela, under the administration and direction of the president of the republic, as administrator of the National Public Treasury."

Nonetheless, through successive reforms of the Central Bank Law, many of the rejected proposed reforms affecting the autonomy of the institution have been implemented.[697]

---

696 See Manuel Rachadell, "Personalismo político en el Siglo XXI," in *Revista de Derecho Público* No 112 *(Estudios sobre la reforma constitucional)*, Editorial Jurídica Venezolana, Caracas 2007, p. 67; Enrique J. Sánchez Falcón, "La propuesta de modificación constitucional y el régimen de la Administración Financiera Pública," in *id.*, p. 192.

697 See *Gaceta Oficial* 39.300, Nov. 5, 2009. In Mar. 2010, a new reform of the Central Bank of Venezuela Law was sanctioned by the National Assembly.

B. *Macroeconomic Policy at the Mercy of the National Executive*

Article 320 of the 1999 Constitution establishes detailed regulation in relation to the coordination of macroeconomic policy, first relating to economic stability and second to the Macroeconomic Stabilization Fund (Fondo de Estabilización Macroe-conómica). The rejected reform sought radically to change both regulations.[698]

Article 320 sets forth that "the state must promote and defend economic stability, avoid economic vulnerability and safeguard the price stability in order to ensure social well-being." The provision establishes the obligation "of the ministry responsible for the finances and of the Central Bank of Venezuela" to contribute "to the harmonization of fiscal policy with monetary policy, facilitating the achievement of the macroeconomic objectives." The Constitution further states that, "in the exercise of its functions, the Central Bank of Venezuela shall not be subordinated to the directives of the executive power and shall not validate or finance deficit fiscal policies."

In addition, the constitutional norm requires that the coordinated action of the executive power and the bank be realized "through an annual policy agreement," which must include the "final growth objectives and their social repercussions, the foreign exchange balance, inflation, fiscal, exchange and monetary policy, as well as the levels of intermediate and instrumental variables necessary for the achievement of the indicated final objectives." Article 320 sets forth the formal procedures required for the approval of the agreement, which included the signature of the president of the bank, the signature of the head of the Ministry of Finances, and the presentation of the agreement to the National Assembly at the time of the assembly's approval of the budget. The Constitution provides that the institutions signatory to the agreement are responsible for ensuring that its "policy actions are consistent with its objectives" and that it specifies "the anticipated results, and the policies and actions directed towards reaching those results."

The rejected 2007 reform sought to eliminate the entire detailed regulatory framework designed to guarantee economic stability and coordination between the national executive and the bank, proposing instead that Article 320 contain the following language: "the state must promote and defend economic stability, avoid economic vulnerability and safeguard the monetary and price stability, in order to assure social well being. Equally, the state shall safeguard the harmonization of fiscal and monetary policies to achieve the macro-economic objectives." The changes would have eliminated any principle of coordination between the national executive and the Central Bank. Under the reforms, the Central Bank would have remained without autonomy as an executing arm of the executive's disposal.

With respect to the regime governing the Fund for Macroeconomic Stabilization, Article 321 of the 1999 Constitution refers to it as "destined to guarantee the expenditures of the state at the municipal, regional and national levels in the event of fluctuations in ordinary revenues." The article requires that the functioning of the fund

---

698   See Enrique J. Sánchez Falcón, "La propuesta de modificación constitucional y el régimen de la Administración Financiera Pública," in *Revista de Derecho Público* No. 112 (*Estudios sobre la reforma constitucional)*, Editorial Jurídica Venezolana, Caracas 2007, p. 193.

be tied to "basic principles of efficiency, equity, and nondiscrimination among the public entities that bring resources to it." The rejected reform totally eliminated the Fund for Macroeconomic Stabilization and instead proposed that Article 321 attribute the "administration of international reserves . . . to the Head of State" and authorize the head of state "in coordination with the Central Bank of Venezuela, to establish the level of reserves needed for the national economy, at the end of each year, as well as the amount of surplus reserves." The express indication was added that the surplus reserves shall be destined to funds established by the national executive for productive investments, development, and infrastructure; financing of the missions; and, definitively, to the integral, endogenous, humanist, and socialist development of the nation.

III. PROPOSED CHANGES IN MATTERS OF HUMAN RIGHTS

With respect to human rights, the 1999 Constitution introduced very important and notable reforms, marked by progressiveness, which was expressly included in Article 19. Unfortunately, a few important and radical changes were incorporated into the reforms, like restrictive changes in matters of political rights and political participation, in matters of economic freedom and property rights, and in matters of right to education, in particular the right to university autonomy. In addition, in matters of emergency or states of exception, the reforms were notably regressive, and the state was configured as a repressive (police) state.[699] Other reforms in matters of human rights referred to the right of nondiscrimination and labor rights. Reforms in the latter category do not require a constitutional reform because they can be achieved through legislation.

1. The Extension of the Principle of Equality

Article 21 of the 1999 Constitution extensively regulated equality and nondiscrimination, with very rich content. The proposed reform extended those principles by enumerating forms of forbidden discrimination. Where the 1999 Constitution referred to discriminatory motives based on "race, sex, religion and social condition," the reform proposed adding discrimination based on "ethnic, gender, age, sex, health, creed, political orientation, sexual orientation, social, and religious conditions."[700]

---

699   See Manuel Rachadell, "Personalismo político en el Siglo XXI," in *Revista de Derecho Público* No. 112 *(Estudios sobre la reforma constitucional)*, Editorial Jurídica Venezolana, Caracas 2007, 67; in id., p. 68; Verónica Espina Molina, "El principio de progresividad de los derechos humanos," in *id.*, pp. 261-266; Víctor Hernández Mendible, "La regresión constitucional en materia de derechos humanos," in id., pp. 267-286; Alberto Blanco Uribe Quintero, "Menoscabo al derecho humano a la participación, por la reforma constitucional," in *id.*, p. 199; Ana Cristina Núñez Machado, "La eliminación del derecho a la información del artículo 337 de la Constitución: Violación del 'principio de progresividad' de los derechos humanos," in *id.*, pp. 331-335.

700   See Carlos Urdaneta Sandoval, "El principio de igualdad en el proyecto de reforma constitucional de 2007," in *id.*, 275-93; Tamara Adrián, "Protección constitucional de la mujer y de la diversidad sexual" in *id.*, pp. 295-300.

2. Proposed Changes in the States of Exception

Chapter 2 of Title 8 of the 1999 Constitution ("Protection of the Constitution") aims to establish the regime governing exceptional circumstances that could originate states of exception or emergency that could gravely affect the security of the nation, its institutions, and persons, and impose the need to adopt exceptional measures (Article 337).

The proposed reform would radically change the protective regulations established in the 1999 Constitution regarding human rights, including revocation of the Organic Law on the States of Exception of 2001 in the only derogatory disposition of the reform.[701]

A. The Expansion of States of Exception

According to Article 338 of the 1999 Constitution, a "state of alarm" can be decreed "when catastrophes, public calamities and other similar situations could constitute a serious peril for the security of the nation or its citizens."

The proposed reform extended states of alarm, establishing two sorts: first, one that established hypothetical situations that could originate the new form of a state of alarm, in cases where "a certain and imminent possibility exists for the occurrence of situations capable of originating catastrophes, public calamities and other similar situations, in order to adopt the necessary measures to protect the nation and its citizens"; and second, the previous "state of alarm" became "state of emergency."

B. The Elimination of the Duration of a State of Emergency

The 1999 Constitution establishes that the states of exception (alarm, emergency, or commotion) must necessarily be limited to a duration that varies from thirty to ninety days, with the possibility of an extension. The reforms sought to eliminate from Article 338 the terms of duration from the various states of exception (thirty days for state of alarm; sixty days for state of economic emergency; and ninety days for states of interior or exterior commotion). It proposed converting them to situations without temporal limits whose enforcement was subject to the sole will and discretion of the president.

The consequence of this reform was that the National Assembly would lose its power according to the 1999 Constitution to approve or deny extensions of states of emergency.

C. The Possibility of Suspending Constitutional Guarantees

The 1999 Constitution expressly eliminated the possibility of the president to "suspend" the constitutional guarantees of human rights, as had been authorized in the 1961 Constitution and had in the past led to unacceptable institutional abuses.[702]

---

701 See Jesús María Casal, "Los estados de excepción en la reforma constitucional," in id., Editorial Jurídica Venezolana, Caracas 2007, pp. 325-329.

702 See, e.g., Allan R. Brewer-Carías, "Consideración sobre la suspensión o restricción de las garantías constitucionales," in *Revista de Derecho Público* 37, Editorial Jurídica Venezolana, Caracas 1989, pp. 5-25.

In states of exception, the president's power was reduced to only temporarily "restrict" (Article 236.7) those constitutional guarantees.

The reform proposed, regressively, reestablishing that the President could suspend constitutional guarantees, which is inadmissible in a democratic society.

D.   Changes Regarding the Constitutional Guarantees of Human Rights That Can Be Suspended or Restricted in Situations of Exception

Within the constitutional guarantees that, according to the 1999 Constitution, could not be affected in states of exception are the right to life, the prohibition on incommunicado detentions, the prohibition on torture, the right to due process of law, the right to be informed, and all the other intangible human rights. The latter includes the guarantees that, according to the International Covenant of Civil and Political Rights and to the American Convention on Human Rights, cannot be suspended, such as the guarantee of equality and nondiscrimination, the guarantee to not be condemned to prison on the basis of contractual obligations, the guarantee against ex post facto laws, the right to personality, the right to religious liberty, the principle of legality, the protection of the family, the rights of the child, the guarantee against being arbitrarily deprived of nationality, the exercise of political rights, and the right to access public functions.

The proposed reforms aimed to eliminate from Article 337 the prohibition on suspending or restricting due process of law, the right to be informed,[703] and all the other intangible human rights. Nonetheless, in a contradictory way, the reform added to the reduced list of unsuspended rights, a few specific rights conforming the due process, as are the prohibition on the disappearance of persons, the right to self-defense, the right to personal integrity, the right to be judged by a competent natural court, and the right not be condemned to punishment in excess of thirty years.

E.   The Elimination of the Control Mechanisms of States of Exception

The 1999 Constitution, in its provisions on states of exception, establishes three mechanisms for controlling the executive powers: the National Assembly, the Constitutional Chamber of the Supreme Tribunal, and international organizations. The constitutional reforms proposed eliminating all of these mechanisms.

First, the reform eliminated the possibility of the National Assembly to control and revoke the executive decree declaring states of exception (including the possibility to extend their term) and established that only the president could end the decree "when their motivating cause ceases" (Article 339). The decree declaring the state of exception was to be presented to the assembly, but the assembly would retain no power to revoke it, as established in the 1999 Constitution.

Second, the reform also eliminated from Article 339 the obligatory constitutional control attributed to the Constitutional Chamber of the Supreme Tribunal regarding

---

703   See Ana Cristina Núñez Machado, "La eliminación del derecho a la información del artículo 337 de la Constitución: Violación del 'principio de progresividad' de los derechos humanos," in *Revista de Derecho Público* No. 112 *(Estudios sobre la reforma constitucional)*, Editorial Jurídica Venezolana, Caracas 2007, pp. 331-335.

decrees on states of exception. Nonetheless, the competency of the Supreme Tribunal remained in Article 336.6, which attributed to the Constitutional Chamber the power to review the constitutionality of the decrees, even ex officio, on the basis of its own initiative.

Third, the reforms also proposed eliminating the constitutional provision established in Article 339 that requires that executive decrees of states of exception comply with "the conditions, principles and guarantees established in the International Covenant on Civil and Political Rights and in the American Convention on Human Rights."

3. *Proposed Changes in Education Rights: The Limits to University Autonomy*

On matters of social rights, the 2007 constitutional reforms also proposed changed in Article 109 of the 1999 Constitution in which the autonomy of universities is guaranteed. The proposed reform sought to incorporate workers within the university academic community with full rights, including those in order to elect the authorities of the universities. Also, the reform pretended to give equal electing votes to students and professors and extended the right to vote to all teachers even without permanent tenure.[704] The purpose was to eliminate the autonomy of the Universities, for which purpose, in 2010, proposals were made to initiate a "university constituent" process.[705]

4. *Proposed Changes in Labor Rights: A Useless Constitutional "Reform"*

The constitutional reforms also proposed changes to two articles from the chapter of the 1999 Constitution on labor rights. First, Article 87 referred to social security for nondependent workers; second, Article 90 concerned the maximum length of the workday. The content of the proposed reforms, however, was not a matter for constitutional review and required no constitutional modification for their implementation, which could be achieved through legislation.[706]

---

704   See Juan Domingo Alfonzo Paradisi, "La autonomía universitaria y el proyecto de reforma constitucional de 2007," in *Revista de Derecho Público No. 112 (Estudios sobre la reforma constitucional)*, Editorial Jurídica Venezolana, Caracas 2007, pp. 301-311. See also Eugenio Hernández Bretón, ""Cuando no hay miedo (ante la reforma Constitucional)," in *id.*, 18; Manuel Rachadell, "Personalismo político en el Siglo XXI," in *id.*, p. 67.

705   See regarding the threats against the national autonomous Universities, Gustavo Méndez, "Universidades bajo amenaza de constituyente e intervención. Ejecutivo y Asamblea Nacional enfilan sus baterías contra las instituciones," in *El Universal*, Caracas July 4, 2010. Available at http://politica.eluniversal.com:80/2010/07/04/pol_art_universidades-bajo-a_1961598.shtml.

706   See, on this matter of labor rights in the reform proposal, Juan Carlos Pro Rísquez, "Las reformas laborales," in *Revista de Derecho Público No. 112 (Estudios sobre la reforma constitucional)*, Editorial Jurídica Venezolana, Caracas 2007, pp. 313-318.

CHAPTER 13

THE IRREGULAR FRAUDULENT IMPLEMENTATION OF THE REJECTED CONSTITUTIONAL REFORM THROUGH LEGISLATION

Once the 2007 constitutional reforms were rejected by popular vote, the president and main officials of the National Assembly publicly announced that, despite such rejection, they would implement the reforms by means of statutes and decree laws, contrary to the Constitution.

Consequently, many of the rejected constitutional reforms were illegitimately and fraudulently implemented by means of decree laws issued by the president in execution of the February 1999 enabling law.[707] This legislative delegation was sanctioned by the National Assembly parallel to the announcement by the president at the beginning of the 2007 constitutional reform process. Nonetheless, and assuming that the presidential constitutional-reform proposal was to be approved by the people, the president began implementing it before even being sanctioned by the National Assembly and, of course, without popular approval, by means of the execution of the enabling law (delegate legislation) sanctioned in 2007 that was then used fraudulently to implement the rejected reforms,[708] particularly in economic and social matters, to structure a socialist centralized state.[709] This process, on the other hand, was developed in absolute secrecy with any public consultation and participation, in violation of Article 210 of the Constitution.[710]

The process began even before the draft reforms were even submitted to the National Assembly, when Decree Law N° 5,841 was enacted on June 12, 2007,[711] containing the organic law creating the Central Planning Commission. This was the first formal state act devoted to building the socialist state.[712] Once this reform was rejec-

---

707   *Gaceta Oficial,* 38.617, Feb. 1, 2007.

708   See Lolymar Hernández Camargo, "Límites del poder ejecutivo en el ejercicio de la habilitación legislativa: Imposibilidad de establecer el contenido de la reforma constitucional rechazada vía habilitación legislativa," in *Revista de Derecho Público* No. 115 *(Estudios sobre los Decretos Leyes),* Editorial Jurídica Venezolana, Caracas 2008, pp. 51ff.; Jorge Kiriakidis, "Breves reflexiones en torno a los 26 Decretos-Ley de julio-agosto de 2008, y la consulta popular refrendaría de diciembre de 2007," in *id.,* pp. 57ff.; José Vicente Haro García, "Los recientes intentos de reforma constitucional o de cómo se está tratando de establecer una dictadura socialista con apariencia de legalidad (A propósito del proyecto de reforma constitucional de 2007 y los 26 decretos leyes del 31 de julio de 2008 que tratan de imponerla)," in *id.,* pp. 63ff.

709   See Ana Cristina Nuñez Machado, "Los 26 nuevos Decretos-Leyes y los principios que regulan la intervención del Estado en la actividad económica de los particulares," in id., pp. 215-220.

710   See Aurilivi Linares Martínez, "Notas sobre el uso del poder de legislar por decreto por parte del Presidente venezolano," in id., pp. 79-89; Carlos Luis Carrillo Artiles, "La paradójica situación de los Decretos Leyes Orgánicos frente a la Ingeniería Constitucional de 1999," in id., 93-100; Freddy J. Orlando S., "El "paquetazo," un conjunto de leyes que conculcan derechos y amparan injusticias," in id., pp. 101-104.

711   *Gaceta Oficial* N° 5.841, Extra., June 22, 2007.

712   See Allan R. Brewer-Carías, "Comentarios sobre la inconstitucional creación de la Comisión Central de Planificación, centralizada y obligatoria," in *Revista de Derecho Público* No. 110, Editorial Jurídica Venezolana, Caracas 2007, pp. 79-89; Luis A. Herrera Orellana, "Los Decretos-Leyes de 30 de julio de 2008 y la Comisión Central de Planificación: Instrumentos para la progresiva abolición del sistema polí-

ted in referendum, on December 13, 2007, the National Assembly approved the 2007–13 Economic and Social Development National Plan, established in Article 32 of the Decree Law enacting the Planning Organic Law,[713] in which the basis of the "planning, production and distribution system oriented towards socialism" is established, providing that "the relevant matter is the progressive development of social property of the production means." For such purpose, the proposed 2007 rejected constitutional reforms to assign the state all powers over farming, livestock, fishing, and aquaculture, and in particular the production of food, materialized in the decree law Organic Law on Farming and Food Security and Sovereignty.[714] That law assigned to the state power not only to authorize food imports but also to prioritize production and directly assume distribution and commercialization. The law also expanded expropriation powers of the executive violating the constitutional guarantee of the previous declaration of a specific public interest or public utility involved, and allowing the State occupation of industries without compensation.[715]

Decree Law N° 6,130 of June 3, 2008, enacted the Popular Economy Promotion and Development Law, establishing a "socio-productive communal model," with different socio-productive organizations following the "socialist model."[716] In the same openly socialist orientation, Decree Law N° 6,092 was issued enacting the Access to Goods and Services Persons Defense Law,[717] which derogated the previous Consumer and Users Protection Law,[718] with the purpose of regulating all commercialization and different economic aspects of goods and services, extending the state powers of control to the point of establishing the possibility of confiscating

tico y del sistema económico previstos en la Constitución de 1999," in *Revista de Derecho Público* No. 115, *(Estudios sobre los Decretos Leyes)*, Editorial Jurídica Venezolana, Caracas 2008, pp. 221-232.

713   *Gaceta Oficial* N° 5.554 of Nov. 13, 2001.

714   *Gaceta Oficial* N° 5.889, Extra., July 31, 2008. See José Ignacio Hernández G., "Planificación y soberanía alimentaria," in *Revista de Derecho Público* No. 115, *(Estudios sobre los Decretos Leyes)*, Editorial Jurídica Venezolana, Caracas 2008, pp. 389-94; Juan Domingo Alfonso Paradisi, "La constitución económica establecida en la Constitución de 1999, el sistema de economía social de mercado y el decreto 6.071 con rango, valor y fuerza de Ley Orgánica de seguridad y soberanía agroalimentaria," in id., 395-415; Gustavo A. Grau Fortoul, "La participación del sector privado en la producción de alimentos, como elemento esencial para poder alcanzar la seguridad alimentaria (Aproximación al tratamiento de la cuestión, tanto en la Constitución de 1999 como en la novísima Ley Orgánica de soberanía y seguridad alimentaria)," in id., pp. 417-424.

715   See Carlos García Soto, "Notas sobre la expansión del ámbito de la declaratoria de utilidad pública o interés social en la expropiación," in id., pp. 149-151.

716   *Gaceta Oficial* N° 5.890, Extra., July 31, 2008. See Jesús María Alvarado Andrade, "La desaparición del bolívar como moneda de curso legal (Notas críticas al inconstitucional Decreto N° 6.130, con rango, valor y fuerza de la ley para el fomento y desarrollo de la economía comunal, de fecha 3 de junio de 2008," in *Revista de Derecho Público* No. 115, *(Estudios sobre los Decretos Leyes)*, Editorial Jurídica Venezolana, Caracas 2008, pp. 313-320.

717   *Gaceta Oficial* N° 5,889 Extra of July 31, 2008; José Gregorio Silva, "Disposiciones sobre el Decreto-Ley para la defensa de las personas en el acceso a bienes y servicios," in id., pp. 277-279; Carlos Simón Bello Rengifo, "Decreto N° 6.092 con rango, valor y fuerza de la ley para la defensa de las personas en el acceso a los bienes y servicios (Referencias a problemas de imputación)," in id., pp. 281-305; Alfredo Morles Hernández, "El nuevo modelo económico del socialismo del siglo XXI y su reflejo en el contrato de adhesión," in id., pp. 229-232.

718   *Gaceta Oficial* N° 37.930, May 4, 2004.

goods and services, by means of their takeover and occupation through administrative decisions.[719]

Regarding the 2007 reforms related to eliminating local-level representative democracy, the same began to be implemented in 2006 with the sanctioning of the Communal Councils Law,[720] which created them as social units and organizations not directed by popularly elected officials, without any sort of territorial autonomy, supposedly devoted to channeling citizens' participation but in a centralized conducted system from the apex of the national executive.[721]

A primary purpose of the 2007 constitutional reforms was to complete the dismantling of the federal form of the state by centralizing power attributions of the states, creating administrative entities to be established and directed by the national executive, attributing powers to the president to interfere in regional and local affairs, and voiding state and municipal competency by means of compulsory transfer of that competency to communal councils.[722] The implementation of the rejected constitutional reforms regarding the organization of the "Public Power" based on the strengthening of the communes and communal councils has been completed with the approval in 2010 of the Law on the Federal Council of Government.[723]

To implement these reforms, not only the last mentioned aspect has been achieved forcing the states and municipalities to transfer its attributions to local institutions controlled by the central power (communal councils) but also by means of Decree Law N° 6217 of July 15, 2008, on the Organic Law of Public Administration[724] that is now directly applicable to the States' and Municipalities' Public Ad-

---

719 See Juan Domingo Alfonso Paradisi, "Comentarios en cuanto a los procedimientos administrativos establecidos en el Decreto N° 6.092 con rango, valor y fuerza de Ley para la defensa de las personas en el acceso a los bienes y servicios," in *Revista de Derecho Público* No. 115, *(Estudios sobre los Decretos Leyes)*, Editorial Jurídica Venezolana, Caracas 2008, pp. 245-260; Karina Anzola Spadaro, "El carácter autónomo de las 'medidas preventivas' contempladas en el artículo 111 del Decreto-Ley para la defensa de las personas en el acceso a los bienes y servicios," in id., pp. 271-76.

720 Ley de Consejos Comunales, *Gazeta Oficial* N° 5806, Extra., Apr. 10, 2006. See Allan R. Brewer-Carías, "El inicio de la desmunicipalización en Venezuela: La organización del poder popular para eliminar la descentralización, la democracia representativa y la participación a nivel local," in *AIDA, Opera Prima de Derecho Administrativo. Revista de la Asociación Internacional de Derecho Administrativo*, Universidad Nacional Autónoma de México, México City, 2007, pp. 49-67.

721 Ley Orgánica de los Consejos Comunales, *Gazeta Oficial* N° 39.335, Dec. 28, 2009. See Juan M. Raffalli A., "Límites constitucionales de la Contraloría Social Popular," in *Revista de Derecho Público*, No. p. 115, *(Estudios sobre los Decretos Leyes)*, Editorial Jurídica Venezolana, Caracas 2008, in *id.*, pp. 133-147.

722 See Manuel Rachadell, *"La centralización del poder en el Estado federal descentralizado,"* in *id.*, pp. 111-131.

723 See *Ley Orgánica del Consejo Federal de Gobierno*, *Gaceta Oficial* N° 5.963 Extra. of Feb. 22, 2010.

724 *Gaceta Oficial* N° 5.890, Extra., July 31, 2008. See Allan R. Brewer-Carías, "El sentido de la reforma de la Ley Orgánica de la Administración Pública," in *Revista de Derecho Público* No. 115, *(Estudios sobre los Decretos Leyes)*, Editorial Jurídica Venezolana, Caracas 2008, pp. 155-161; Cosimina G. Pellegrino Pacera, "La reedición de la propuesta constitucional de 2007 en el Decreto N° 6.217, con Rango, Valor y Fuerza de Ley Orgánica de la Administración Pública," in id., pp. 163-168; Jesús Caballero Ortíz, "Algunos comentarios sobre la descentralización funcional en la nueva Ley Orgánica de la Administración Pública," in *id.* pp. 169-174; Alberto Blanco-Uribe Quintero. "Afrenta a la Debida Dignidad frente a la Administración Pública. Los Decretos 6.217 y 6.265," in *id.*, pp. 175-79.

ministrations, the national executive has implemented the principle of centralized planning, subjection regional and local authorities to the Central Planning Commission. This Organic Law also assigns to the president, as proposed in the 2007 reforms, the power to appoint regional authorities with powers to plan, execute, follow up on, and control land use and territorial development policies, thus subjecting all programs and projects to central planning approval.

Regarding the vertical distribution of state attributions between the national level and the states, the proposed and rejected constitutional reforms sought to eliminate the exclusive attribution assigned to the states in Article 164.10 of the Constitution to "maintain, administrate and profited use of national roads and highways, as well as ports and airports of commercial use, in coordination with the national power." In this case, the fraudulent implementation of the rejected constitutional reform was made by the Constitutional Chamber of the Supreme Tribunal of Justice, when deciding recourse for constitutional interpretation filed by the attorney general representing the national executive. In Decision N° 565 of April 15, 2008,[725] the Supreme Tribunal through an obligatory interpretation simply "modified" the content of the mentioned constitutional provision, urging the National Assembly to approve legislation in accordance with the judicial made constitutional reform. This was effectively accomplished in May 2009 by reforming the Organic Law on Decentralization, Delimitation, and Transfer of Public Attributions,[726] eliminating the exclusive attributions of the states established in its Articles 11.3 and 11.5, and adding two new provisions authorizing the national executive to revert the transfer of competencies already made to the states (Article 8) and to decree the intervention of transferred assets and public services (Article 9). With the reforms, the fraud on the Constitution was completed, and the federation disrupted.[727]

The rejected 2007 constitutional reforms also sought to eliminate the capital district, created in the federal framework of the Constitution as one political entity in the territory. Notwithstanding popular rejection of the 2007 reform proposals, in April 2009, the reform was unconstitutionally implemented by the National Assembly, defrauding once more the Constitution by sanctioning the Special Law on the Organization and Regime of the Capital District.[728] In it, instead of creating a democratic entity to govern the capital district, the law established an organization completely dependent on the national level of government in the same territorial jurisdiction that "used to be one of the extinct federal district" equivalent to one of the cu-

---

725   See Constitutional Chamber Decision N° 565 (Apr. 15, 2008) (Case: *Procuradora General de la República*), interpretation recourse of Article 164.10 of the 1999 Constitution, at http://www.tsj.gov.ve/decisiones/scon/Abril/565-150408-07-1108.htm.

726   *Gaceta Oficial* N° 39.140, Mar. 17, 2009.

727   See Allan R. Brewer-Carías, "La Sala Constitucional como poder constituyente: La modificación de la forma federal del estado y del sistema constitucional de división territorial del poder público," in *Revista de Derecho Público* 114, Editorial Jurídica Venezolana, Caracas 2008, 247-62; Manuel Rachadell, "*La centralización del poder en el Estado federal descentralizado,*" in *Revista de Derecho Público*, N° 115 (Estudios sobre los Decretos Leyes), Editorial Jurídica Venezolana, Caracas 2008, p. 120.

728   *Gaceta Oficial* N° 39.156, Apr. 13, 2009. See the comments on this Law in Allan R. Brewer-Carías et al., *Leyes sobre el Distrito Capital y el Área Metropolitana de Caracas*, Editorial Jurídica Venezolana, Caracas 2009.

rrent Libertador municipality in Caracas. According to this law, the capital district, contrary to what is provided for in the Constitution, has no elected authorities of government and is governed by the national level by means of a "special regime" consisting of the exercise of the legislative function by the National Assembly itself and a chief of government in charge of the executive branch (Article 3) and appointed by the president. This means that through a national statute, in the same territory of Libertador, a new national structure has been unconstitutionally imposed.

Finally, although the 2007 constitutional reforms proposed regarding the military and the Armed Force, seeking to transform them into the Bolivarian Armed Force organized for the purpose of reinforcing socialism, were rejected in the December 2007 referendum, the radical changes it contained have been implemented by the president, usurping the constituent power, by means of a decree law reforming the Organic Law on the Armed Force,[729] creating the Bolivarian National Armed Force subjected to a "military Bolivarian Doctrine," and creating in it the "National Bolivarian Militia" – all of this according to what was proposed and rejected by the people in the 2007 Constitutional Reform.[730]

CHAPTER 14

THE ILLEGITIMATE MUTATION OF THE CONSTITUTION THROUGH JUDICIAL CONSTITUTIONAL INTERPRETATION

According to the 1999 Constitution, its provisions can be reviewed and modified only through the specific means established for such purpose, that is, the convening of a National Constituent National Assembly; the proposing, sanctioning, and popular approving of a "constitutional reform"; or the proposing and popular approving of a "constitutional amendment" (Articles 340-349). The common trend of all these constitutional review procedures is that the intervention of the people through referenda is always required for the Constitution to be modified,[731] so no constitutional review is possible without the vote of the people. Any other modification, reform, or amendment to the Constitution adopted through any other means is to be considered illegitimate.

That is why, in 2007, in order to modify the Constitution for the purpose of reinforcing the authoritarian, socialist, centralized, and militaristic state that has been built during the past decade, the president proposed an extensive "constitutional reform" that after being sanctioned by the National Assembly was rejected by the people in the December 2007 referendum. After this defeat, the following year, the

---

729   Decree Law N° 6.239, on the Organic Law of the National Bolivarian Armed Force, in *Gaceta Oficial* N° 5.933, Extra., Oct. 21, 2009.

730   See Alfredo Arismendi A., "Fuerza Armada Nacional: Antecedentes, evolución y régimen actual," in *Revista de Derecho Público*, N° 115 (Estudios sobre los Decretos Leyes), Editorial Jurídica Venezolana, Caracas 2008, pp. 187-206; Jesús María Alvarado Andrade, "La nueva Fuerza Armada Bolivariana (Comentarios a raíz del Decreto N° 6.239, con rango, valor y fuerza de Ley Orgánica de la Fuerza Armada Nacional Bolivariana)," in id., pp. 207-214.

731   See Allan R. Brewer-Carías, "La intervención del pueblo en la revisión constitucional en América latina," en *El derecho público a los 100 números de la Revista de Derecho Público 1980-2005*, Editorial Jurídica Venezolana, Caracas 2006, pp. 41-52.

National Assembly sanctioned a "constitutional amendment" draft in order to implement one aspect of the 2007 reforms proposals rejected by the people, referred to the continuous and indefinite possibility for reelection of the president and other elected officials, which eventually was approved in the referendum that took place in February 2009.

Notwithstanding the limits imposed in the rigid constitution for their review, it is accepted that without any formal review of the Constitution, the sense of one of its provisions can be changed, particularly in the case of old constitutions, when its meaning is judicially interpreted particularly by constitutional judges, in order to adapt its content to the current social development of a society, applying democratic principles and values that derive from the same Constitution. In these cases of constitutional interpretation, the result can be what has been called a "constitutional mutation" (*mutación constitucional*) that may occur when the content of the constitutional-provision is modified in such a way that even if the provision maintains its textual content, it receives a different meaning, which is generally accepted according to the democratic values of society.[732]

The problem with these "constitutional mutations" is that they can be illegitimate when the judicial constitutional interpretation is the result of a deliberate process directed to distort the Constitution, in order to force the modification of the meaning of its provisions without altering its text, for the purpose of reinforcing authoritarianism and defrauding democracy, as it has occurred, for instance, in Venezuela when via judicial constitutional interpretation issued by the Constitutional Chamber of the Supreme Tribunal of Justice, the government succeeded in implementing many of the constitutional-reform proposals that were rejected by the people through the 2007 referendum.

This process of illegitimate distortion of the Constitution began in Venezuela in 2000, when the Constitutional Chamber, deciding on the unconstitutionality of the challenged Decree of Transitory Regime issued in December 1999 by the National Constituent Assembly after the popular approval of the Constitution, admitted the existence of constitutional provisions that were not included in the text of the 1999 Constitution as it was approved by the people. The process has continued during the past decade through multiple decisions of the Constitutional Chamber through which the Constitution has been illegitimately distorted or "mutated." Following are a few examples of this process that could only be explained due to the tragic subjection of the Supreme Tribunal of Justice to the executive.[733]

---

732 See Néstor Pedro Sagües, *La interpretación judicial de la Constitución*, Abeledo-Perrot, Buenos Aires 2006, pp. 56-59, 80-81, 165 ff.; Salvador O. Nava Gomar, "Interpretación, mutación y reforma de la Constitución. Tres extractos," in *Interpretación constitucional*, coord. Eduardo Ferrer Mac-Gregor, Ed. Porrúa, Universidad Nacional Autónoma de México, Mexico City 2005, Vol 2, pp. 804ff.; Konrad Hesse, "Límites a la mutación constitucional," in *Escritos de derecho constitucional*, Centro de Estudios Constitucionales, Madrid 1992.

733 On this process of illegitimate mutations of the constitution see, in general, the comments in Allan R. Brewer-Carías, *Reforma constitucional y fraude a la Constitución (1999-2009)*, Academia de Ciencias Políticas y Sociales, Caracas 2009, pp. 217ff.; "El juez constitucional al servicio del autoritarismo y la ilegítima mutación de la Constitución: el caso de la Sala Constitucional del Tribunal Supremo de Justicia de Venezuela (1999-2009)," in *Revista de Administración Pública*, N° 180, Madrid 2009, pp. 383-

I. THE ACCEPTANCE OF A TRANSITORY CONSTITUTIONAL RE-GIME NOT APPROVED BY THE PEOPLE

The first constitutional mutation (distortion) regarding the 1999 Constitution was decided by the Constitutional Chamber of the Supreme Tribunal of Justice a few weeks after approval of the Constitution. It admitted the existence of constitutional transitory provisions different from those approved by popular vote and embodied in the text of the Constitution. The 1999 Constitution was approved by referendum on December 15, 1999, with a text that included transitory provisions. The popular approval of the Constitution, in principle, concluded the mission of the Constituent Assembly.

However, one week after the approval of the Constitution, on December 22, 1999, the Constituent Assembly sanctioned the Decree of the Regime of Transition of the Public Power,[734] "to give effect to the transition process towards the regime established in the Constitution of 1999." In that decree, it decided, without any attribution foreseen in the new Constitution, to eliminate the prior Congress, along with its senators and deputies, and to assign legislative power to the National Legislative Commission, not established in the Constitution; to dissolve the states' legislative assemblies; to assign legal attributions in their place to state legislative commissions, which were not provided for in the Constitution; to take control of the mayor's offices and municipal councils; to eliminate the former Supreme Court of Justice, create new chambers of the Supreme Tribunal and assign them a fixed number of judges –not established in the Constitution– and to appoint them without complying with what the Constitution demanded; to create the Commission for the Reorganization and Functioning of the Judiciary to take it over, removing judges from office without due process; to appoint the officials of the different branches of government; and to dictate an electoral statute without any constitutional provision supporting it.

None of these reforms was constitutional – they were not approved by the people. Consequently, the transition regime decree was challenged before the Constitutional Chamber on the basis of the violation of the Constitution that the people had recently approved. The result was that the same Constitutional Chamber decided in its own cause, holding that the Constituent Assembly had supraconstitutional power to create constitutional provisions without popular approval and that, as a consequence, in Venezuela there were two transitional constitutional regimes: that contained in the transitory provisions approved by the people and that approved by the Constituent Assembly without popular approval.

In Decision N° 6 (January 27, 2000), the Constitutional Chamber decided that because the transition regime of December 22, 1999, was adopted by the Constituent

---

418; "La fraudulenta mutación de la Constitución en Venezuela, o de cómo el juez constitucional usurpa el poder constituyente originario," in *Anuario de Derecho Público*, Centro de Estudios de Derecho Público de la Universidad Monteávila, Año 2, Caracas 2009, pp. 23-65; "La ilegítima mutación de la Constitución por el juez constitucional y la demolición del Estado de derecho en Venezuela," in *Revista de Derecho Político*, N° 75-76, Homenaje a Manuel García Pelayo, Universidad Nacional de Educación a Distancia, Madrid 2009, pp. 289-325.

734   *Gaceta Oficial* N° 36.859, Dec. 29, 1999.

Assembly prior to publication of the Constitution on December 31, 1999, it was not subject to that Constitution or to the previous Constitution of 1961 still in force.[735] Later, in Decision N° 186 (March 28, 2000) (Case: *Allan R. Brewer-Carías et al.*), when deciding the constitutionality of the electoral statute of the public power adopted by the Constituent Assembly on January 30, 2000,[736] the Constitutional Chamber ratified that to create a new legal order and adopt a new Constitution, the Constituent Assembly had several alternatives for regulating the transitory constitutional regime. First was to incorporate transitory dispositions that would be part of the Constitution to be approved by the people via referendum. Second was to dictate separate acts, of constitutional scope and value, which would create a parallel constitutional transitory regime not approved by the people.[737]

With those decisions, the constitutional judge proceeded to illegitimately interpret and distort the Constitution, violating popular sovereignty, by holding that the Constituent Assembly could dictate constitutional provisions not approved by the people through referendum. This began a long period of constitutional instability that, ten years later, has not ended; it is evidenced, for instance, in the survival of judiciary interference. Thus, Venezuela has been under a constitutional transitory regime not approved by the people, by the grace of a constitutional judge who legitimized the usurpation of the popular will.

II. FROM REVOCATION REFERENDA TO RATIFYING REFERENDA

In Venezuela, Article 72 of the Constitution established, as a political right of the people, the revocation of mandates of all popularly elected offices. The recall is required after the midterm for which the official was elected, by popular initiative of no less than 20% of voters registered in the corresponding constituency. The Constitution determined that when equal to or greater than 25% of registered voters vote in the referendum and "a number of electors equal or higher than that of those who elected the official, vote in favor of the revocation," the official's mandate is considered revoked and that void must be covered immediately through a new election.

That is, the necessary votes to revoke a mandate must be equal to or greater than the votes that elected the officer, independent of the number of votes cast against the revocation – the Constitutional Chamber ratified this in several decisions.[738] The Constitution provides for a revocation referendum of popular election mandates, not a ratifying referendum (plebiscite) of mandates. Precisely for that reason, there is nothing in the Constitution regarding the case when a number of electors, greater than the number of votes obtained by the official at the time of election, could vote

---

735 See *Revista de Derecho Público* No 81, Editorial Jurídica Venezolana, Caracas 2000, pp. 81ff.

736 See *Gaceta Oficial* N° 36,884, Feb. 3, 2000.

737 On the illegitimate transitory regime created outside the Constitution, see in Allan R. Brewer-Carías, *Golpe de Estado y Proceso Constituyente en Venezuela*, Universidad Nacional Autónoma de México, México 2002, pp. 345 ff.

738 See Decision N° 2750 (Oct. 21, 2003) (Case: *Carlos Enrique Herrera Mendoza, Interpretación del artículo 72 de la Constitución*), Exp. 03-1989; Decision N° 1139 (June 5, 2002) (Case: *Sergio Omar Calderón Duque and William Dávila Barrios*). See *Revista de Derecho Público No. 89–92*, Editorial Jurídica Venezolana, Caracas 2002, p. 171. The same criterion was followed in Decision N° 137 (Feb. 13, 2003) (Case: *Freddy Lepage Scribani et al.*) (Exp. 03-0287).

for no revocation. This could occur but, according to the constitutional text, it would have no effect at all, because the regulation establishes the revocation referendum. To be revoked, it is enough for the votes to revoke to be equal to or greater than those obtained by the official at the time of election.

Nevertheless, clearly in an unconstitutional way, in 2003, when a recall referendum was first called by popular initiative to revoke the president's mandate, the National Electoral Council issued a regulation on the matter.[739] That regulation held that even though a mandate is considered revoked, "if the number of votes in favor of the revocation is equal or higher to the number of the electors that vote for the officer," but added a phrase providing that: "the number must not be lower than the number of electors that voted against the revocation" (Article 60), changing the constitutional provisions on the matter. With that addition – in a regulation of sublegal scope – the right of the people to politically participate by revoking popular mandates was restricted, thus disrupting the nature of the referendum regulated by Article 72 of the Constitution and, in evident fraud to the Constitution, turning it into a ratifying referendum of mandates of popular election.

What was without precedent in this constitutional fraud was that the illegitimate constitutional "reform" was endorsed by the Constitutional Chamber of the Supreme Court when it decided a recourse on the abstract interpretation of the Constitution in Decision N° 2750 (October 21, 2003) (Case: *Carlos E. Herrera Mendoza, Interpretación del artículo 72 de la Constitución*) stating:

> It has to do with some kind of re-legitimating the officer and, even, in this democratic process of majorities, *if the option of his permanence obtains more votes in the referendum, he should remain in office,* even if a sufficient number of people vote against him to revoke his mandate.[740]

In this way, the constitutional judge illegitimately distorted the Constitution.[741] Actually, in a revocation referendum, there cannot be votes in favor of the permanence of the official. There can be votes to revoke the mandate and votes not to revoke. The vote not to revoke cannot be turned into a vote to ratify the official. With this distortion, the Constitutional Chamber changed the nature of the revocation referendum, turning it into a vote to relegitimate or ratify mandates of popular election, when that was not the intention of the Constitution. The only issue regulated in Article 72 of the Constitution is the revocation of mandates, and for that, the only thing it demands in regard to the voting process is that "a number of electors equal or higher than that of those who elected the official, vote in favor of the revocation."

This illegitimate distortion of the Constitution, nonetheless, had a precise objective: to avoid the revocation of President Hugo Chávez's mandate in 2004. He was

---

739 See *Normas para regular los procesos de referendos revocatorios de mandatos de elección popular,* Res. N° 030925-465, Sept. 25, 2003.

740 Exp. 03-1989.

741 See Allan R. Brewer-Carías, "La Sala Constitucional vs. el derecho ciudadano a la revocatoria de mandatos populares: de cómo un referendo revocatorio fue inconstitucionalmente convertido en un "referendo ratificatorio," in *Crónica sobre la "In" Justicia Constitucional. La Sala Constitucional y el autoritarismo en Venezuela,* Editorial Jurídica Venezolana, Caracas 2007, pp. 349-78.

elected in August 2000 with 3,757,744 votes – the number of votes to revoke had to surpass that number to revoke his mandate. As the National Electoral Council announced on August 27, 2004, the number of votes to revoke the president's mandate, casted in the referendum of August 15, 2004, was 3,989,008, and so his mandate was constitutionally revoked.

However, the Constitution had already been illegitimately distorted, and regardless of fraud accusations, the National Electoral Council (on August 27, 2004), because more people (5,800,629) voted not to revoke his mandate, decided to ratify the president in his position until the culmination of the constitutional term in January 2007.[742]

III. THE ELIMINATION OF THE CONSTITUTIONAL PRINCIPLE OF ALTERNATE GOVERNMENT AND THE LIMITS TO CONTINUOUS REELECTION

Article 6 of the Constitution establishes the fundamental principles of republican government:

> The government of the Bolivarian Republic of Venezuela and its political entities is and will always be democratic, participative, elective, decentralized, alternate, responsible, pluralist and of revocable mandates.

Consequently, among the fundamental principles of the constitutional system that cannot be modified either by means of constitutional reform or amendment are those principles of government, and with them the principle that the government must be not only democratic but also elective and alternate.

This latter principle was incorporated for the first time in Venezuela's constitutional history as a reaction to the continuation in the exercise of political power, and was based on the very "doctrine of Simón Bolívar," on which the republic is based according to Article 1 of the Constitution:

> There is nothing as dangerous as to allow the long term permanence in office of a single citizen. The people gets used to obeying him and he gets used to

---

742 In fact, on the Web page of the National Electoral Council, the following appeared on Aug. 27, 2004: "Francisco Carrasquero Lopez, President of the National Electoral Council, addressed the country in national broadcast, to announce the definite and official results of the electoral act that took place on Aug. 15th, which ratified Hugo Rafael Chávez Frías, as President of the Republic with a total of 5 million 800 thousand 629 votes in favor of the option 'NO.' 9 million 815 thousand 631 electors participated in the election, of which 3,989,008 voted in favor of the option 'YES' to revoke the mandate of President Chávez. The total showed that the option 'NO' represented 59.25% of the ballot, while the option 'YES' achieved 40.74% of the grand total, with a 30.02% of non-participation. It must be said that for these elections, the Electoral Registry increased significantly, reaching a universe of 14,027,607 electors with the right to vote in the Revocation Referendum. On this Friday, Aug. 27, based on the expression of the popular will, the National Electoral Council will ratify Hugo Chávez Frías in the Presidency of the Bolivarian Republic of Venezuela, whose constitutional term will culminate in the year 2006." In fact, during a solemn act that took place the same day, the National Electoral Council agreed to ratify the president in his position, despite the fact that a number of electors greater than that which had elected him had voted in favor of revoking his mandate. See *El Nacional*, Caracas Aug. 28, 2004, pp. A-1 and A-2.

rule over them.... [O]ur citizens must fear, with abundant justice, that the same Judge who has ruled them for a long time, rules them forever.[743]

According to this doctrine, which as Bolivarian must be considered part of the values of the constitution itself (Article 1), in Venezuelan constitutionalism, the alternating of government has always meant that people take turns in certain positions or that positions are carried out in terms. As stated by the Electoral Chamber of the Supreme Tribunal of Justice in Decision No. 51 (March 18, 2002), the alternate principle means "the successive exercise of a position by different persons, belonging or not to the same party."[744]

This principle of alternating government was historically conceived to face the desires to remain in power – that is, continuation – and also to avoid the advantages in electoral processes that those occupying positions when being candidates to occupy the same positions could have. The principle of alternating government, thus, is not equivalent to that of elective government. Election is one thing, but the need for people to take turns in office is another. Thus, the principle has always been reflected in the establishment of limits on the reelection of officials, which is common in presidential systems. This is what happened in the Constitutions of 1830, 1858, 1864, 1874, 1881, 1891, 1893, 1901, 1904, 1909, 1936, 1845, and 1947 – they prohibited the reelection of the president of the republic for the immediate constitutional term.[745]

This prohibition regarding the president, during the democratic period that began in 1958, was extended in the Constitution of 1961 for the two subsequent terms (ten years). The 1999 Constitution softened that principle to allow for the possibility of immediate presidential reelection, only once, for a new term. That is why President Chávez, after being elected in 1998, and again in 2000 under the new constitutional regime, and being "ratified" in 2004, was reelected in 2006.

The alternation of government, thus, is a principle of constitutionalism that contests continuation or permanence in power by the same person; for that reason, any provision that would allow for permanence or continuation is contrary to it. Thus, the principle cannot be confused with the elective principle of government or the most general democratic principle established by Article 6 of the Constitution. It is one thing to elect government officials, different to the principle of alternation tending to impede the successive election of the same government official.

Thus, it is contrary to the Constitution to interpret – as the Constitutional Chamber did in Decision N° 53 of February 3, 2009[746] – that the principle of alternation "demands that the people, as the holder of sovereignty, have the periodical possibili-

---

743   See Simón Bolívar, "Discurso de Angostura" (1819), in *Escritos fundamentales*, Monteávila Ediciones, Caracas 1982.

744   Case *Francisco Caracciolo vs. Consejo Nacional Electoral*. Available at http://www.tsj.gov.ve/decisiones/selec/ Marzo/51-180302-000207.htm.

745   Actually, in the constitutional history of the country, the prohibition on immediate presidential reelection was eliminated in the constitutions of authoritarian governments: the Constitution of 1857; the Constitutions of Juan Vicente Gómez of 1914, 1922, 1925, 1928, 1929, and 1931; and the Constitution of Marcos Pérez Jiménez of 1953.

746   See *Revista de Derecho Público* No. 117, Editorial Jurídica venezolana, Caracas 2009, pp. 205-211.

ty to choose their government officials or representatives," thus confusing alternate government with elective government. What the Constitutional Chamber stated was wrong in deciding that the principle of alternating "would only be violated" if the possibility of election is impeded. With its decision, once more, the Constitutional Chamber illegitimately distorted the constitutional text. Contrary to what has been said, the elimination of the ineligibility clause derived from the fact of a citizen being currently in the exercise of a public position misrepresents the alternation principle in the exercise of power.[747]

What the Constitutional Chamber decided allowing the possibility of continuous reelection alters the fundamental principle of alternate government, a democratic value that informs Venezuelan juridical order. Because the formula used in Article 6 of the Constitution ("is and always will be"), alternating government cannot be the object of any constitutional reform, and in the event that it could be modified, it could not be modified through constitutional amendment or reform but only through the convening of a Constituent Assembly.

With its decision, the Constitutional Chamber smoothed the road for the referendum that took place a few days later, on February 15, 2009, in which people approved a constitutional amendment project proposed by the National Assembly regarding Articles 160, 162, 174, 192, and 230 of the Constitution. Even though the same proposal was rejected in the 2007 "constitutional reform" referendum, this time, using the procedure for a "constitutional amendment," a modification of the Constitution was approved (2009) in order to establish in Venezuela the possibility of continuous reelection of elective positions, which antagonizes the constitutional republican alternating principle (Article 6), which consequently in this regard resulted as void and ineffective.

IV. LIFTING THE PROHIBITION ON REPEATING REFERENDA FOR CONSTITUTIONAL REVIEW

In the aforementioned Decision No. 53 of February 3, 2009,[748] of the Constitutional Chamber regarding the illegitimate change of alternate government, the chamber also adopted another illegitimate distortion of the Constitution. It loosened the constitutional prohibition on calling for a popular referendum on constitutional reforms that the people had already rejected in the same constitutional term (Article 345).

Article 345 of the Constitution, regarding constitutional reforms, expressly prohibits the submission to the National Assembly during the same constitutional term any initiative for constitutional reform that has already been rejected in referendum. Notwithstanding, the Constitution establishes nothing regarding the effects of the rejection of a "constitutional reform" proposal on the possibility to proceed to submit the same matter again to referendum but through the "constitutional amendment" procedure.

---

747   See Allan R. Brewer-Carías, "El Juez Constitucional vs. La alternabilidad republicana (La reelección continua e indefinida)," in *id.*, 2009, pp. 205-211.

748   See *Revista de Derecho Público* 117, Editorial Jurídica Venezolana, Caracas 2009, 205-211. Also available at http://www.tsj.gov.ve/decisiones/scon/Febrero/53-3209-2009-08-1610.html.

In December 2007, a constitutional-reform proposal sanctioned by the National Assembly – including a provision to allow for the continuous reelection of the president – was rejected by popular vote. Thus, as the populace had already expressed its will on the matter, according to the teleological interpretation of Article 345 of the Constitution, it was not possible to submit the same matter to popular vote again during the same constitutional term. Nonetheless, and notwithstanding popular rejection, in January 2009, the National Assembly took the initiative and approved a constitutional amendment to modify Article 230 of the Constitution regarding limits to presidential reelection and to modify Articles 160, 162, 174, and 192 regarding reelection of other elective officials. It eliminated all established limits.

Instead of looking at the intent of the constitutional provision establishing the rules for not repeating referenda on the same constitutional issues (Article 345), the Constitutional Chamber, in the aforementioned Decision N° 53 of February 3, 2009,[749] confusing the sense of the prohibition, sustained that the provision established was not directed to fix limits to successive popular votes on the same matter, only to provide limits for the National Assembly to consider reforms initiatives. In that way, they reasoned, the National Assembly could not be asked to twice discuss the same constitutional modifications it had already rejected. Nonetheless, the Constitutional Chamber "forgot" that the constitutional principle aimed to regulate popular expression of will in matters modifying the Constitution and their effects, and not to regulate the debates in the National Assembly, being its purpose to avoid for the people asked, again and again in the same constitutional term about the same constitutional modification once it has already been rejected.

Any way, by admitting the possibility to modify the Constitution in the same constitutional period through an amendment procedure when the matter has been rejected through a reform procedure, as was resolved in Decision N° 53 can be considered another defrauding of the Constitution. The fact is that, in 2007, the National Assembly sanctioned a "constitutional reform" to establish the continuous and indefinite reelection of the president, which the people rejected. In the same constitutional term, in 2009, the same National Assembly sanctioned a proposal for reforming the Constitution for the same purpose, this time through the "constitutional amendment" procedure; it only added to the original proposal – perhaps to try to differentiate both – all the other elected representatives.

The result, then, was that, although the people had rejected the proposal for the continuous and indefinite reelection of the president, the same proposal was submitted to referendum in 2009, again, and was approved. For such purpose, the Constitutional Chamber issued a constitutional interpretation of Article 345 that ignored that citizens cannot be summoned during the same constitutional term, consecutively and without limits, to express their will on the same matter.[750]

---

749   See *Revista de Derecho Público* 117, Editorial Jurídica Venezolana, Caracas 2009, pp. 205-211.

750   See the comments on the Constitutional Chamber decision in Allan R. Brewer-Carías, "El Juez Constitucional vs. La alternabilidad republicana (La reelección continua e indefinida), en *Revista de Derecho Público* 117, Editorial Jurídica Venezolana, Caracas 2009, pp. 205-211.

V.   ILLEGITIMATE TRANSFORMATION OF THE FEDERAL SYSTEM

Article 4 of the 1999 Constitution establishes that the republic "is a decentralized federal State in the terms expressed in this Constitution," wording that as it has been analyzed contradicts the real sense of the constitutional provisions that qualify the state as a "centralized federation."[751] But, despite those limits, and notwithstanding any contradiction, the Constitution expressly distributed some state powers to various public and territorial levels of government – that is, the municipalities, the states, and the national government. Those powers cannot be changed except by means of constitutional reform (Articles 136, 156, 164, 178, and 179).[752]

Specifically, the Constitution provides that the conservation, administration, and use of roads and national highways, as well as of national ports and airports of commercial use, correspond exclusively to the states, which they must exercise in "coordination with the National Power" (Article 164.10).

A general purpose of the rejected 2007 constitutional reform was to change the federal form of the state and the territorial distribution of the competencies established in Articles 156 and 164 of the Constitution, thus centralizing the state even more by concentrating almost all competencies of the public power at the national level. Particularly, one purpose of the reform was to "nationalize" the competency set forth in Article 164.10 of the Constitution, which attributes to the states jurisdiction on the conservation, administration, and use of national highways, roads, ports, and airports.[753]

Because the people rejected the constitutional reforms in a December 2007 referendum, Article 164.10 did not change. However, the Constitutional Chamber, in Decision No. 565 (April 15, 2008),[754] deciding an autonomous recourse for abstract constitutional interpretation filed by the attorney general of the republic, ruled to modify the content of that constitutional provision. It held that the exclusive attribution was not exclusive but concurrent – meaning that the national government could

---

751   See Allan R. Brewer-Carías, *Federalismo y municipalismo en la Constitución de 1999 (Alcance de una reforma insuficiente y regresiva),* Universidad Católica del Táchira–Editorial Jurídica Venezolana, Caracas–San Cristóbal 2001; "El estado federal descentralizado y la centralización de la federación en Venezuela. Situación y perspectiva de una contradicción constitucional," in *Federalismo y regionalismo,* coord. Diego Valadés and José María Serna de la Garza, Universidad Nacional Autónoma de México, Supreme Court of Justice of the State of Puebla, Instituto de Investigaciones Jurídicas, Mexico City 2005, pp. 717-750.

752   See Allan R. Brewer-Carías, "Consideraciones sobre el régimen de distribución de competencias del poder público en la Constitución de 1999," in *Estudios de derecho administrativo. Libro homenaje a la Universidad Central de Venezuela, Facultad de Ciencias Jurídicas y Políticas, con ocasión del vigésimo aniversario del Curso de Especialización en Derecho Administrativo,* eds. Fernando Parra Aranguren and Armando Rodríguez García, Tribunal Supremo de Justicia, Caracas 2001, Vol. 1, pp. 107-36.

753   See Allan R. Brewer-Carías, *Hacia la consolidación de un estado socialista, centralizado, policial y militarista. Comentarios sobre el sentido y alcance de las propuestas de reforma constitucional 2007,* Editorial Jurídica Venezolana, Caracas 2007, pp. 41 ff.; and *La Reforma Constitucional de 2007 (Comentarios al proyecto inconstitucionalmente sancionado por la Asamblea Nacional el 2 de noviembre de 2007),* Editorial Jurídica Venezolana, Caracas 2007, pp. 72 ff.

754   See Decision N° 565 of the Constitutional Chamber (Apr. 15, 2008) (Case: *Procurador General de la república, Interpretación del artículo 164.10 de la Constitución),* available at http://www.tsj.gov.ve/decisiones/scon/Abril/565-150408-07-1108.htm.

also exercise that competency interfering with the states' powers. The attorney general said the provision "was not clear enough to establish, in an efficient and precise way, the scope and performance of the National Executive, regarding the coordination with the States about the administration, conservation and use of national roads and highways, as well as ports and airports of commercial use." The Constitutional Chamber decided, accordingly, that the National Public Administration, "in exercise of its coordination authority, can directly assume the conservation, administration and use of the national roads and highways, as well as all ports and airports of commercial use" and that it corresponds to the national executive (the president and cabinet ministers) to decree such intervention and assume the rendering of services and assets when considered deficient or inexistent.

With that interpretation, the chamber illegitimately modified the Constitution usurping popular sovereignty and changed the federal form of the state by misrepresenting the territorial distribution system of powers between the national power and the states. Particularly, it nationalized what the Constitution expressly established as attributions that are exclusive to the states. As a result, the Constitutional Chamber "reformed" the Constitution and eliminated the exclusive competency of the states in that matter. By turning the competency into a concurrent one, being subjected to possible decentralization, it also can be reverted to the national government.[755] The chamber held: "it corresponds to the National Executive, to decree the intervention in order to assume the rendering of services and assets of national roads and highways, as well as ports and airports of commercial use, in those cases where, even though said competencies had been transferred, the rendering of the service, either by the States, is deficient or inexistent."[756]

This judicial made illegitimate constitutional modification, as warned by the same Constitutional Chamber, generated the need for a "revision and modification of great scope and magnitude of the current legal system," leading the Chamber to warn the National Assembly to "proceed to the revision and corresponding modification of the legal provisions related to the obligatory interpretation established in this decision, and to sanction statutes congruent with the constitutional principles derived from the interpretation established by this Chamber in exercise of its competencies."[757] That is, the chamber forced the legislator to issue legislation against the provisions of the 1999 Constitution and in line with the illegitimate constitutional modification imposed. So, after the electoral triumph of opposition governors and mayors in key states and municipalities in the elections of December 2008, the National Assembly, in March 2009, diligently reformed the Organic Law for Decentra-

---

755 See the comments on the Constitutional Chamber decision in Allan R. Brewer-Carías, "La ilegítima mutación de la Constitución y la legitimidad de la jurisdicción constitucional: la "reforma" de la forma federal del Estado en Venezuela mediante interpretación constitucional," in *Memoria del X Congreso Iberoamericano de Derecho Constitucional*, Instituto Iberoamericano de Derecho Constitucional, Asociación Peruana de Derecho Constitucional, Instituto de Investigaciones Jurídicas-UNAM y Maestría en Derecho Constitucional-PUCP, IDEMSA, Lima 2009, Vol 1 pp.29-51

756 See Decision N° 565 of the Constitutional Chamber (Apr. 15, 2008) (Case: *Procurador General de la República, Interpretación del artículo 164.10 de la Constitución*), available at http://www.tsj.gov.ve/decisio-nes/scon/Abril/565-150408-07-1108.htm.

757 Id.

lization,[758] to eliminate the exclusive attribution to the states of those powers established in Articles 11.3 and 11.5 of said Law. It added, according to the illegitimate Constitutional Chamber Decision, two new provisions allowing the national executive to "revert, for strategic reasons, of merit, opportunity or convenience, the transfer of attributions to the States, for the conservation, administration and use of assets and services considered to be of general public interest" (Article 8); and to decree the intervention of the said assets and rendering of public services transferred to ensure users and consumers quality service (Article 9). With this, the National Assembly completed the defrauding of the Constitution that the Constitutional Chamber had started – a constitutionally assigned exclusive attribution became a concurrent one.

VI. THE LIFTING OF THE PROHIBITION ON GOVERNMENT FINANCING OF ELECTORAL ACTIVITIES

Article 67 of the Constitution of 1999 expressly established that "the financing of political associations with Government funds will not be allowed," a provision that was an emphatic, radical change from the previous regime of public financing of political parties, established in Article 230 of the Organic Law of Suffrage and Political Participation of 1998. That law sought to establish greater balance and impartiality for parties' participation in democratic life and, especially, in electoral campaigns, in an attempt to mitigate any imbalances or perversions resulting from only private financing (e.g., possible drug financing) and the possible indirect, irregular, corrupt public financing.[759] The constitutional prohibition, by derogating such article of the organic law, eliminated any public funding of political parties, abandoning the technique that predominates in comparative law.[760]

This express constitutional prohibition regarding public financing of political parties was also one of the matters referred to in the 2007 constitutional reform,[761] which proposed modification of Article 67 by providing that "the State.... be able to finance electoral activities." As already mentioned, the constitutional reform was rejected by popular vote in referendum on December 2, 2007, with which the governmental financing of political parties regarding their electoral activities continued to be prohibited in the Constitution.

However, despite those constitutional prohibitions and the popular rejection of its modification, the Constitutional Chamber of the Supreme Court of Justice, in

---

758 *Gaceta Oficial* N° 39 140, Mar. 17, 2009.

759 See Allan R. Brewer-Carías, "Consideraciones sobre el financiamiento de los partidos políticos en Venezuela," in *Financiamiento y democratización interna de partidos políticos. Memoria del IV Curso Anual Interamericano de Elecciones,* San José, Costa Rica, 1991, pp. 121-39.

760 See Allan R. Brewer-Carías, "Regulación jurídica de los partidos políticos en Venezuela," in *Estudios sobre el estado constitucional (2005-2006)*, Cuadernos de la Cátedra Fundacional Allan R. Brewer Carías de Derecho Público N° 9, Universidad Católica del Táchira, Editorial Jurídica Venezolana, Caracas 2007, pp. 655-686.

761 See *Proyecto de Exposición de Motivos para la Reforma Constitucional, Presidencia de la República, Proyecto Reforma Constitucional. Propuesta del presidente Hugo Chávez Agosto 2007,* Editorial Atenea, Caracas 2007, p. 19.

Decision No. 780 (May 8, 2008)[762] by means of constitutional interpretation, has illegitimately distorted the Constitution. It has substituted itself for the popular will and the original constitutional power in holding that, "regarding the scope of the prohibition of public financing of political associations," the norm only "limits the possibility to provide resources for the internal expenses of the different forms of political associations, but…said limitation, is not extensive to the electoral campaign, as a fundamental stage of the electoral process."

That is, the Constitutional Chamber, facing a clear though censurable constitutional provision in Article 67 of the Constitution, usurped the constituent power, substituting itself for the people. It ruled to reform the provision in the same way that of the constitutional-reform draft that was rejected by the people in the December 2007 referendum, expressly allowing governmental financing of the electoral activities of the political parties and associations – the opposite of what is provided for in the Constitution.[763]

Therefore, the constitutional judge decided simply that the Constitution does not say what it actually says but the opposite. That when the Constitution says that "the financing of political associations with Government funds will not be allowed," the Constitution actually means to prohibit only "financing of current and internal expenses of the political associations with resources coming from the State"; thus, expenses of electoral campaigns can be financed with funds from the state.

The absurd conclusion, against any democratic logic, derives from the false premise that, supposedly, in democratic systems, the state can finance current and internal expenses of the parties. This is not conceived of in democracies, and so it does not require any prohibition. In democracies, the operations of parties are financed but always with a view to electoral campaigns. That financing is withdrawn if parties do not obtain a certain percentage of votes in the elections.

The result of this Supreme Tribunal Decision is that through it, the constitutional judge has reformed the Constitution, usurped the original constituent power of the people, and went against the people's express wish in the December 2007 referendum rejecting state electoral financing.

VII. THE ILLEGITIMATE ELIMINATION OF THE SUPRACONSTITUTIONAL RANK OF INTERNATIONAL HUMAN RIGHTS TREATIES

A contemporary universal trend has allowed constitutional courts to directly apply international treaties for the protection of human rights, thus progressively widening the scope for their protection. For such purpose, contemporary constitutions have progressively recognized the normative scope of those treaties, assigning them,

---

762   File N° 06-0785. See *Revista de Derecho Público No.* 114, Editorial Jurídica Venezolana, Caracas 2008, pp. 127ff.

763   See the comments on the Constitutional Chamber decision in Allan R. Brewer-Carías, "El juez constitucional como constituyente: el caso del financiamiento de las campañas electorales de los partidos políticos en Venezuela," in *Revista de Derecho Público* No. 117, Editorial Jurídica Venezolana, Caracas 2009, pp. 195-203.

regarding internal law, supraconstitutional, constitutional, supralegal, and legal rank.[764]

Article 23 of Venezuela's 1999 Constitution expressly sets forth the following:

> Treaties, pacts and conventions regarding human rights, subscribed and rati-
> fied by Venezuela, have constitutional rank and prevail in the internal order, as
> long as they contain norms about their enjoyment and exercise, more favorable
> than those established in this Constitution and in the laws of the Republic, and
> are to be direct and immediately applicable, by the courts and other bodies of
> the State.

Without a doubt, this article and the norms it expresses are among the most important in matters of human rights in the country. The formulation is unique in Latin
America because it grants international human rights treaties, not only constitutional
rank but also supraconstitutional rank; that is, they rank superior to the Constitution
itself in the case that they contain more favorable regulations. The article also establishes the direct and immediate application of treaties by the courts and other authorities of the country. This provision of the Constitution was, without a doubt, a
significant advance in constructing the human rights protection framework, which
the courts have applied, for instance, in declaring that the American Convention on
Human Rights prevails over certain legal and constitutional provisions.

For example, the right to appeal before a second judicial instance invoked before
the contentious administrative jurisdiction was been excluded in the former 1976
Organic Law of the Supreme Court of Justice. The Constitution of 1999 establishes
a constitutional right to appeal only in matters of criminal procedures in favor of the
person declared guilty (Article 40.1). So, in contentious administrative suit, there
was no express constitutional guarantee of appeal and, therefore, the decisions of the
First Court of Contentious Administrative matters were not appealable. Nonetheless,
the content of Article 23 of the Constitution finally led the Constitutional Chamber
of the Supreme Tribunal to rule in 2000 on the prevailing application of the American Convention on Human Rights, considering:

> That article 8.1 and 8.2.h of the American Convention on Human Rights,
> are part of the Venezuelan constitutional order; that its dispositions, containing
> the right to appeal judicial decision, are more favorable, concerning the benefit
> and exercise of said right, than that foreseen in article 49,1 of said Constitution;

---

764   On this general classification, see Rodolfo E. Piza R., *Derecho internacional de los derechos humanos:
       La Convención Americana*, San José, Costa Rica, 1989; Carlos Ayala Corao, "La jerarquía de los ins-
       trumentos internacionales sobre derechos humanos," in *El nuevo derecho constitucional latinoamerica-
       no*, vol. 2, IV Congreso Venezolano de Derecho Constitucional, Caracas 1996; *La jerarquía constitu-
       cional de los tratados sobre derechos humanos y sus consecuencias*, Ed. Porrúa, México City, 2003;
       Humberto Henderson, "Los tratados internacionales de derechos humanos en el orden interno: La impor-
       tancia del principio pro homine," in *Revista IIDH* 39, Instituto Interamericano de Derechos Humanos,
       San José, Costa Rica, 2004, pp. 71 ff. See also Allan R. Brewer-Carías, *Mecanismos nacionales de pro-
       tección de los derechos humanos*, Instituto Internacional de Derechos Humanos, San José, Costa Rica,
       2004, pp. 62 ff.

and that are of immediate and direct application by the courts and other State bodies.[765]

However, in Decision N° 1,939 (December 18, 2008) (Case: *Gustavo Álvarez Arias et al.*),[766] by declaring unenforceable a decision of the Inter-American Court of Human Rights of August 5, 2008 – the case of former judges of the First Court on Contentious Administrative matters (*Apitz Barbera et al. vs. Venezuela, First Court on Contentious Administrative*),[767] the Constitutional Chamber definitely resolved that Article 23:

> does not grant supraconstitutional rank to international treaties on human rights, thus, in case of antinomy or contradiction between one disposition of the Constitution and a provision of an international pact, it would correspond to the Judicial Power to determine which would be applicable, considering both what is established in the referred provision, and in the jurisprudence of this Constitutional Chamber of the Supreme Court of Justice, paying attention to the content of articles 7, 266.6, 334, 335, 336.11 *ejusdem* and to Decision N° 1.077/2000 of this Chamber.[768]

To base this Decision rejecting superior values that could not be modifiable by any political project, the chamber clarified, "that law is a normative theory at the service of politics that underlines behind the axiological project of the Constitution," adding that "the standards to resolve the conflict between the principles and the provisions have to be compatible with the political project of the Constitution (Democratic and Social State of Law and Justice) and cannot affect the force of said project with ideological interpretative elections that privilege individual rights decisively, or that welcome the supremacy of the international judicial order over national law at the sacrifice of the sovereignty of the State."[769]

The Constitutional Chamber concluded in its Decision N° 1,939 (December 18, 2008) by declaring that "a system of principles, supposedly absolute and suprahistoric, cannot be above the Constitution" and that the theories that pretend to limit "under the pretext of universal legalities, the sovereignty and the national autodetermination" are unacceptable;[770] quoting in support another of its decisions (Decision N° 1265/2008) in which the Chamber considered "that when a contradiction is evidenced between the Constitution and an international convention or treaty, "the constitutional provision that privilege the general interest and the common well-

---

765 Decision N° 87 (Mar. 13, 2000) (Case: *C.A. Electricidad del Centro (Elecentro) y otra vs. Superintendencia para la Promoción y Protección de la Libre Competencia (Procompetencia)*, in *Revista de Derecho Público* No. 81, Editorial Jurídica Venezolana, Caracas 2000, pp. 157ff.

766 See http://www.tsj.gov.ve/decisiones/scon/Diciembre/1939-181208-2008-08-1572.html.

767 See www.corteidh.or.cr. Excepción Preliminar, Fondo, Reparaciones y Costas, Serie C, N° 182.

768 See at http://www.tsj.gov.ve/decisiones/scon/Diciembre/1939-181208-2008-08-1572.html.

769 Id.

770 See http://www.tsj.gov.ve/decisiones/scon/Diciembre/1939-181208-2008-08-1572.html.

being must prevail, applying the dispositions that privilege the collective interests . . . over particular interests."[771]

With this decision, the Constitutional Chamber illegitimately distorted the Constitution, reforming Article 23 of the Constitution by eliminating the supraconstitutional rank of the American Convention on Human Rights in cases where that document contains more favorable provisions for the benefit and exercise of human rights than the Constitution.[772]

Moreover, the matter decided by the Constitutional Chamber also was one of the express reform proposals made in 2007 by the Presidential Council for the Constitutional Reform.[773] Regarding Article 23, the intention of the proposal was to completely eliminate the constitutional hierarchy of the provisions of international human rights treaties, and their prevalence over the internal order, by reformulating Article 23 as follows: "treaties, pacts and conventions related to human rights, subscribed and ratified by Venezuela, as long as they remain current, are part of the internal order, and are of immediate and direct application by the bodies of the public power."

This proposal for constitutional reform formulated by the presidential commission in 2007 was a hard blow to the progressiveness in protecting the rights established in Article 19 of the Constitution, which does not allow for regressions in their protection. However, what the authoritarian regime was not able to accomplish through constitutional reform, the Constitutional Chamber of the Supreme Court carried out through constitutional interpretation.

VIII. THE ELIMINATION OF JUDGES' POWER TO IMMEDIATELY AND DIRECTLY APPLY INTERNATIONAL HUMAN RIGHTS TREATIES

In matters of human rights, Article 23 of the Constitution, after granting supraconstitutional rank to the provisions of international treaties, pacts, and conventions on human rights, "as long as they contain provisions more favorable to their enjoyment and exercise," it also expressly declares that those instruments are "of direct and immediate application by the courts and other bodies of the State."

Regarding that provision, the Constitutional Chamber, reaffirming its role as maximum and ultimate interpreter of the Constitution and treaties on human rights, established in Decision N° 1492 (July 15, 2003) (Case: *Impugnación de diversos artículos del Código Penal*) that, because those treaties have constitutional rank, the Constitutional Chamber itself is the only body capable of interpreting them, deter-

---

771   Quoted in http://www.tsj.gov.ve/decisiones/scon/Diciembre/1939-181208-2008-08-1572.html.

772   See the comments on the Constitutional Chamber Decision N° 1,939/2008 in Allan R. Brewer-Carías, "La interrelación entre los Tribunales Constitucionales de América Latina y la Corte Interamericana de Derechos Humanos, y la cuestión de la inejecutabilidad de sus decisiones en Venezuela," in *Gaceta Constitucional*. Análisis multidisciplinario de la jurisprudencia del Tribunal Constitucional, Gaceta Jurídica, Tomo 16 Año 2009, Lima 2009, pp. 17-48.

773   See the comments on the draft in Allan R. Brewer-Carías, *Hacia la consolidación de un estado socialista, centralizado, policial y militarista. Comentarios sobre el sentido y alcance de las propuestas de reforma constitucional 2007*, Editorial Jurídica Venezolana, Caracas 2007, pp. 122 ff.

mining which of their provisions prevail in the internal legal order, and deciding which human rights not contemplated in those international instruments have force in Venezuela.[774] With this unconstitutional decision, the Constitutional Chamber again illegitimately distorted the Constitution. According to Article 23, not only the Constitutional Chamber but also all courts of the republic, have those powers when acting as constitutional judges, for instance, when declaring the unconstitutionality of a statute (diffused judicial review) or when deciding *amparo* cases proceeding. The intent of the Constitutional Chamber to concentrate all constitutional justice procedures is not in accordance with the Constitution or the system of judicial review established there.[775]

IX. THE DENIAL OF THE PEOPLE'S RIGHT TO INTERNATIONAL HUMAN RIGHTS PROTECTION

The Venezuelan Constitution expressly contains the right to access international protections in matters of human rights, obligating the state to carry out the decisions adopted by the competent international bodies. To that effect, Article 31 of the Constitution establishes the following:

> Every person has the right, within the terms established by the treaties, pacts and conventions on human rights ratified by the Republic, to file petitions or complaints before the international bodies established for such purposes, in order to ask for the protection of their human rights.

> The State shall adopt, in accordance with the proceedings established in this Constitution and statutes, the necessary measures for the enforcement of the decisions issued by the international bodies indicated in this article.

Nonetheless, the Constitutional Chamber, in the same Decision N° 1.939 (December 18, 2008) (Case: *Gustavo Álvarez Arias et al.*) issued at the request of the Attorney General seeking for a "constitutional interpretation" by the Chamber of the aforementioned Inter-American Court of Human Rights decision of August 5, 2008, adopted in the case *Apitz Barbera et al. vs. Venezuela, First Court on Contentious Administrative*,[776] ignored the effects of the decisions of the Inter-American Court of Human Rights, declaring them unenforceable in Venezuela, thus contradicting the international regime of the treaties.[777]

With that decision, issued in a proceedings initiated by the attorney general as a dependant organ of the executive branch, the Constitutional Chamber declared that the August 5, 2008, decision of the Inter-American Court of Human Rights in the case of former judges of the First Court of Contentious Administrative – who were

---

774   See *Revista de Derecho Público* No. 93–96, Editorial Jurídica Venezolana, Caracas 2003, pp. 135 ff.

775   See the comments on Decision N° 1,492/2003 in Allan R. Brewer-Carías, *El sistema de justicia constitucional en la Constitución de 1999 (Comentarios sobre su desarrollo jurisprudencial y su explicación, a veces errada, en la Exposición de Motivos),* Editorial Jurídica Venezolana, Caracas 2000.

776   See www.corteidh.or.cr. Excepción Preliminar, Fondo, Reparaciones y Costas, Serie C, N° 182.

777   See the comments on these aspects of Decision N° 1,939/2008 in Allan R. Brewer-Carías, "El juez constitucional vs. La justicia internacional en materia de derechos humanos," in *Revista de Derecho Público* No. 116, Editorial Jurídica Venezolana, Caracas 2008, pp. 249-260.

illegitimately dismissed without due process – was not enforceable in Venezuela. The Inter-American Court had decided that the Republic of Venezuela had violated the judicial guarantees of those judges established in the American Convention on Human Rights by removing them from office without due process. The court condemned Venezuela to compensate the judges, reinstate them to their former positions or a similar one, and to publish the verdict in Venezuelan newspapers.[778]

In the case of the American Convention on Human Rights, once member states recognize the jurisdiction of the Inter-American Court of Human Rights, according to Article 68.1 of the Convention, they must "commit themselves to comply[ing] with the decisions of the Court in every case in which they are a part of."[779] Nonetheless, in some cases, countries have resisted the decisions of the Inter-American Court and have tried to avoid being responsible for their enforcement. An example is the decision of the Inter-American Court in the *Castillo Petruzzi* case (May 30, 1999).[780] After the Inter-American Court declaring that Peru, under the authoritarian leadership of President Fujimori, had violated various articles of the Convention (Articles 1.1 and 2; 5; 7.5; 7.6; 8.1; 8.2.b,c,d, and f; 8.2.h; 8.5; 9; 20; 25),[781] the Plenary Chamber of the Supreme Council of Military Justice of Peru refused to enforce the verdict,[782] holding that it ignored the Constitution of Peru, by arguing that the

---

778   See http://www.corteidh.or.cr. Excepción Preliminar, Fondo, Reparaciones y Costas, Serie C, N° 182.

779   As stated by the Inter-American Court on Human Rights in *Castillo Petruzzi*, on the "enforcement decision" of Nov. 17, 1999 (Series C, *N°* 59), "the conventional obligations of the State party entail all the powers and bodies of the State" (para. 3), adding "this obligation corresponds to a basic principle of international responsibility right of the State, endorsed by the international jurisprudence, according to which the States must comply with their conventional duties in good faith (*pacta sunt servanda*) and, as it has been mentioned by this Court, cannot, due to reasons of internal order, stop complying with the established international responsibility" (para. 4). See Sergio García Ramírez, coord., *La jurisprudencia de la Corte Interamericana de Derechos Humanos*, Universidad Nacional Autónoma de México, Corte Interamericana de Derechos Humanos, Mexico City 2001, 628-29.

780   Series C, N° 52. in *id.*

781   Consequently, the Inter-American Court declared "the nullity, of the process against Mr. Jaime Francisco Sebastián Castillo Petruzzi and others, for being incompatible with the Convention," ordering "the guaranty of a new trial with the complete observance of the legal due process," and "the State to adopt the necessary measures in order to reform the provisions that had been declared to be against the American Convention of Human Rights in the present decision, and to ensure the benefit of the rights established in the American Convention on Human Rights to all the people under its jurisdiction, without any exception." See http://www.tsj.gov.ve/ decisiones/scon/Diciembre/1939-181208-2008-08-1572.html.

782   It is precisely because of this decision of the Plenary Chamber of the Supreme Council of Military Justice of Peru that the Inter-American Court ruled on Nov. 7, 1999, that "the State has the duty to promptly fulfill the decision of May 30, 1999[,] ruled by the Inter-American Court in the case of Castillo Petruzzi and others." See Sergio García Ramírez, coord., *La jurisprudencia de la Corte Interamericana de Derechos Humanos*, Universidad Nacional Autónoma de México, Corte Interamericana de Derechos Humanos, Mexico City 2001, p. 629. This occurred during the authoritarian regime in Peru, under President Fujimori, which, two months after the decision of the Inter-American Court, drove the Congress of Peru to approve the withdrawal of the recognition of the contentious competency of the court. The Inter-American Court declared the withdrawal inadmissible in its decision in *Ivcher Bronstein* (Sept. 24, 1999): "a State party can only remove itself to the competency of the Court through the formal complaint of the complete treaty," in id., pp. 769-771. In any case, in 2001, Peru derogated the resolution of July 1999, completely reestablishing for the state the competency of the Inter-American Court.

decision subjected "the American Convention on Human Rights to the interpretation that the judges of said Court can carry out *ad libitum*."

In the case of Venezuela, the Constitutional Chamber, quoting its previous Decision N° 1.942 (July 15, 2003)[783] – also issued deciding about an interpretation request formulated by the republic – ruled that the Inter-American Court of Human Rights could not "intend to exclude or ignore the internal constitutional order" and that its "guidelines on the government and administration of the Judiciary" affected matters that it considered being "of exclusive and excluding attributions of the Supreme Tribunal of Justice." The Constitutional Chamber also considered that the rules directed to the Legislature in the Inter-American Court Decision on matters of judicial liability of the judges were inadmissible considering contrary to the sovereignty of the Venezuelan State. The Constitutional Chamber even accused the Inter-American Court of having used its decision "to intervene, unacceptably, in the judicial government and administration, which exclusively corresponds to the Supreme Tribunal," arguing that the Inter-American Court intended to "ignore the strength and force of judicial and administrative decisions that have acquired *res judicata*, by demanding the reincorporation of the judges that have been removed from office." To make those assertions, the Venezuelan Constitutional Chamber turned, precisely, as precedent, to the aforementioned 1999 decision of the Peruvian Plenary Chamber of the Supreme Council of Military Justice, which considered unenforceable in Peru the decisions of the Inter-American Court.

The Constitutional Chamber did not stop there. In an evident usurpation of power – international relations are a matter of exclusive attribution to the executive – the chamber requested "the National Executive to proceed to denounce the Convention, in view of the evident usurpation of functions in which the Inter-American Court of Human Rights has incurred into with the ruling object of this decision." With that, Venezuela continued in the process of announcing possible separation from the American Convention on Human Rights and the jurisdiction of the Inter-American Court of Human Rights, using it own Supreme Tribunal of Justice for such purpose.

However, in doing so, the Constitutional Chamber again illegitimately distorted the Constitution by reforming Article 23 by changing its text to say that it "corresponds to the courts of the Republic to decide upon the violations on matters established in said treaties," in the same way it was proposed in the constitutional reform draft prepared by the presidential commission in 2007, which was not even approved by the National Assembly or submitted to popular vote.[784] Once again, what the authoritarian regime could not do by means of constitutional reform was

---

783 In this Decision, the Constitutional Chamber, referring to international courts, stated that in Venezuela, "above the Supreme Court of Justice and according to Article 7 of the Constitution, there is no jurisdictional body, unless stated otherwise by the Constitution or the law, and even in this last possible case, any decision contradicting the Venezuelan constitutional order, lacks of application in the country." See Case: *Impugnación de artículos del Código Penal, Leyes de desacato,* in *Revista de Derecho Público* No. 93–96, Editorial Jurídica Venezolana, Caracas 2003, pp. 136 ff.

784 See Allan R. Brewer-Carías, *Hacia la consolidación de un estado socialista, centralizado, policial y militarista. Comentarios sobre el sentido y alcance de las propuestas de reforma constitucional 2007,* Editorial Jurídica Venezolana, Caracas 2007, p. 122.

done by the Constitutional Chamber of the Supreme Court through constitutional interpretation.

CHAPTER 15

THE ALTERNATE PRINCIPLE OF GOVERNMENT AND THE 2009 CONSTITUTIONAL AMENDMENT ON CONTINUOUS REELECTION

One of the main reform proposals contained in the 2007 rejected constitutional reform was the one seeking to establish the continuous and indefinite reelection of the president of the republic, eliminating the restrictions established in the 1999 Constitution.

Nonetheless, and despite the popular rejection of the reform, the matter continued to be proposed and eventually was the object of a constitutional amendment approved by the National Assembly, submitted to a referendum held on February 15, 2009. The result was the popular approval of the constitutional amendment, which changed the traditional principle of the alternate character of the democratic government of Venezuelan constitutionalism, allowing the continuous and indefinite reelection not only of the president but also of all elected public officials. This constitutional amendment defrauded the prohibition established in the Constitution to submit to popular vote the same constitutional reform proposal during the same constitutional term and, in addition, violated the Constitution by eliminating one of the unchangeable constitutional principles as it was the alternation in government.[785]

I. THE REPUBLICAN PRINCIPLE OF ALTERNATE GOVERNMENT AND THE VENEZUELAN TRADITION OF NO REELECTION

In effect, the general restriction on elected officials' continuous reelection has been a tradition of Venezuela's constitutional history – since Venezuela adopted the presidential system of government in 1811, as occurred in all Latin America countries.[786]

The restriction on presidential reelection was first established in the 1830 Constitution as a reaction to continuity in office (*continuismo*), precisely to confront individuals' desire to perpetuate themselves in power and to avoid the advantages that public officials might have in electoral processes.

Simón Bolívar clearly expressed his thoughts against continuity in power in his famous Angostura speech (1819):

---

785 The president considered this constitutional amendment "vital for the Revolution" (in his weekly program *Aló President*, Jan. 11, 2009), but in reality, it modified a vital principle for the future of democracy.

786 Restrictions to presidential reelection are traditional in the presidential system of government, not in the parliamentary system of government mainly followed in Europe. See Allan R. Brewer-Carías, *Reflexiones sobre la Revolución norteamericana (1776), la Revolución francesa (1789) y la Revolución hispanoamericana (1810-1830) y sus aportes al constitucionalismo moderno*, Universidad Externado de Colombia, Bogotá 2008, pp. 106ff.

The continuation of the authority in the same individual has frequently been the end of democratic governments. Repeated elections are essentials in popular systems, because nothing is more dangerous than to leave for a long term the same citizen in power. The people get used to obey him, and he gets used to command them; from where usurpation and tyranny is originated.... Our citizens must fear with more than enough justice that the same Official, who has governed them for a long time, could perpetually command them.[787]

In Venezuela, this principle of limiting the term of elected officials imposing the need for changing the head of elected public offices is called the principle of *alternabilidad*, from the Latin word *alternatium*, which means "interchangeably" or "by turns." This principle of alternate government refers to the idea that elected public offices must be occupied by turns, not continuously by the same elected person. It is in that sense that the Electoral Chamber of the Supreme Tribunal of Justice of Venezuela, in Decision N° 51 (March 18, 2002) ruled that *alternabilidad* means "the successive exercise of public offices by different persons."[788] The principle is not the same as the "elective" principle or election to public office. To be elected is one thing; it is another to occupy public offices by turns.

The principle has always been established as an immutable constitutional clause (*cláusula pétrea*) that must never be changed. Article 6 of the Constitution establishes that the government of the Republic and of its political entities "*is and will always be*" alternate, as well as "democratic, participatory, elective, decentralized, responsible, plural and of recall mandates" (Article 5), which means that the principle cannot be changed.

Regarding the president of the republic, the principle has been included in almost all the Venezuelan constitutions since 1830 (1830, 1858, 1864, 1874, 1881, 1891, 1893, 1901, 1904, 1909, 1936, 1845, and 1947),[789] by establishing a general prohibition for the immediate reelection of the president for the subsequent term. In the 1961 Constitution, the prohibition on reelection was extended up to two terms (ten years), and in the 1999 Constitution, that provision was made more flexible by establishing for the first time in more than a century the possibility for the immediate reelection of the president, but only once and in the subsequent term (Article 230).

In Venezuelan history, the only constitutions not prohibiting presidential reelection were the short-lived 1857 Constitution, the authoritarian constitutions of the period of Juan Vicente Gómez (1914–33), and the 1953 Constitution of Marcos

---

787 "La continuación de la autoridad en un mismo individuo frecuentemente ha sido el término de los gobiernos democráticos. Las repetidas elecciones son esenciales en los sistemas populares, porque nada es tan peligroso como dejar permanecer largo tiempo en un mismo ciudadano el poder. El pueblo se acostumbra a obedecerle y él se acostumbra a mandarlo; de donde se origina la usurpación y la tiranía...nuestros ciudadanos deben temer con sobrada justicia que el mismo Magistrado, que los ha mandado mucho tiempo, los mande perpetuamente." See Simón Bolívar, *Escritos fundamentales*, Monteávila Ed., Caracas 1982.

788 Quoted in the dissenting vote to the Constitutional Chamber of the Supreme Tribunal of Justice, Decision N° 53 (Feb. 2, 2009) (Case: *Interpretation of Articles 340.6 and 345 of the Constitution*), http:/www.tsj.gov.ve/decisions/scon/Febrero/53-3209-2009-08-1610.html.

789 For text of all the Constitutions, see Allan R. Brewer-Carías, *Las Constituciones de Venezuela*, Academia de Ciencias Políticas y Sociales, Caracas 2008, pp. 709-1341.

Pérez Jiménez – both military dictators of the previous century. Now, in the twenty-first century, Hugo Chávez Frías proposed the same, having been the object of the amendment to the 1999 Constitution approved by referendum in February 2009.

On the other hand, Venezuelan history shows that each time the principle of no reelection has been changed through disputed constitutional reforms, the outcome has been a political crisis ending in overthrow of the government. It occurred in 1858 with the continuation attempt of President José Tadeo Monagas, who after reforming the Constitution in 1857, was ousted a few months later by the Julián Castro March Revolution. It happened in 1891, when President Raimundo Andueza Palacios reformed the Constitution to allow for his reelection – he was overthrown the following year by the Joaquin Crespo Legalist Revolution. It also occurred, although in another context, in 1945, with the constitutional reform promoted by President Isaías Medina Angarita that failed to establish direct presidential election, thus allowing for the continuation of indirect presidential election of government candidates by Congress, a fact that contributed to the 1945 October Revolution. Finally, it occurred in 1957, when Marcos Pérez Jiménez convened a referendum (plebiscite) to approve his own reelection, which led in the next year to the Democratic Revolution of 1958.[790] This shows that countries do not always follow the lessons of history, and frequently the result is the unwanted repetition of similar facts.

In any case, the restriction established in the 1999 Constitution for the reelection of the president (Article 230) and similar provisions establishing reelection restrictions for governors, mayors, and representatives to the National Assembly and state legislative councils (Articles 160, 162, 174, 192) were proposed by the National Assembly to be changed through constitutional amendment, which the Venezuelan people approved in the February 2009 referendum.

II. THE LIMITS IMPOSED BY THE CONSTITUTION ON CONSTITUTIONAL REVIEW

The 1999 Constitution establishes three institutional mechanisms for constitutional review, distinguishable according to the importance and magnitude of the changes proposed: constitutional amendment, constitutional reform, and constituent assembly. The constitutional amendment procedure is established to add or modify one or more provisions to the Constitution without altering its fundamental structure (Article 340); constitutional reforms are designed for partial revisions of the Constitution and for the substitution of one or several provisions, but without modifying its structure and fundamental principles (Article 342). Both procedures need to be approved by referendum and cannot be used to change fundamental constitutional principles or the structure of the Constitution. Only through a national constituent assembly can the Constitution be reviewed to "transform the State, to create a new legal order, and to write a new Constitution" (Articles 347).

---

790   See Allan R. Brewer-Carías, *Historia constitucional de Venezuela*, Editorial Alfa, Caracas 2008, Vol 2, pp. 9-31.

The Constitution establishes the effects of popular rejection of a constitutional reform, in the sense that a similar proposal cannot be filed again as another "constitutional reform" before the National Assembly in the remainder of the constitutional term (Article 345). Nothing is expressly established in the Constitution on the effects of the rejection of constitutional amendments, and nothing is established on the possibility to file the same rejected constitutional reform proposal through constitutional amendment, as occurred in 2009.

This provision needed to be interpreted in order to determine the intent of the constituent assembly for the inclusion of the constitutional limit to the possibility of repeatedly asking for the direct expression of the will of the people by referenda. That is, once the people have expressed their popular will in referendum, it is not possible to ask the people, again and again, without limits, on the same matters in the same constitutional term.

The matter of the continuous presidential reelection, as aforementioned, had been already proposed through the draft constitutional reform formulated by the president in 2007 and rejected by the people in the referendum on December 2007.[791] Nonetheless, at the suggestion of the president one year later, the National Assembly voted on January 15, 2009, to modify the Constitution, this time through constitutional amendment, initially intended to establish the possibility of indefinite and continuous reelection of the president, which was later extended to all elected public offices.[792]

III. THE BINDING CONSTITUTIONAL INTERPRETATION

Two questions with constitutional implication result from the amendment proposal and were the object of endless constitutional discussions and legal contention in the country. First is the possibility of using a constitutional amendment procedure through which no fundamental constitutional principle can be changed, to alter and change the principle of *alternabilidad* of the government, a fundamental republican

---

791 See Allan R. Brewer-Carías, *La reforma constitucional de 2007 (Comentarios al proyecto inconstitucionalmente sancionado por la Asamblea Nacional el 2 de noviembre de 2007)*, Editorial Jurídica Venezolana, Caracas 2007, pp. 62ff.

792 One constitutional implication of the Feb. 15 referendum remained unsolved. The question approved in referendum, in fact, was "Do you approve of the amendment of Articles 160, 162, 174, 192, and 230 of the Constitution of the Republic prepared by initiative of the National Assembly, which extends the political rights of the people to allow any citizen in exercise of a public office by popular election to become a candidate to the same office for the constitutionally established term, his or her election depending exclusively from the popular vote?" As the amendment aimed to eliminate restrictions on reelection of all elected public officials and representatives, it is is not clear why the question submitted to referendum did not clearly state this or use the words *reelection, indefinite*, or *continuous reelection*. However, according to the Constitution, any approved constitutional amendment must be published as a continuation of the Constitution without altering the original text – amended articles carry a footnote referring to the number and date of their amendment. With the question as formulated, the result was to eliminate the limits imposed in Articles 162 and 192 of the Constitution on representatives to the state legislative councils and the National Assembly (reelection only for up to two terms) and in Articles 160, 174, and 230 on the president, the governors, and municipal mayors (reelection only once for an immediate new term). In the publication of the Constitution, after the constitutional amendment was approved, the text of the articles was changed, including in all of them the expression that the officer "can be reelected." See *Gaceta Oficial* N° 5,908 Extra. of Feb. 19, 2009.

principle formulated in Article 6 of the Constitution. Second is the possibility of using the constitutional amendment to effect the continuous election of the president, thus changing the limits imposed in the Constitution (reelection only once and in the subsequent period), a proposal already submitted to referendum in December 2007 and rejected by the people.

It was on these matters that the Constitutional Chamber of the Supreme Tribunal of Justice issued on February 3, 2009, two decisions (Decisions Nos. 46 and 53),[793] which established a binding interpretation of the Constitution.

First, on the possibility of submitting to popular vote a modification of the Constitution via constitutional amendment on the same matter already rejected by referendum, the Constitutional Chamber argued that the limit imposed in the Constitution was directed only to the National Assembly to discuss again a constitutional reform on the same subject once rejected by the people, without considering the substantive aspect of the prohibition regarding the limits to ask the people to express again, and endlessly, their will through referenda.

Second, on the possibility of using the constitutional amendment to change the fundamental principle of *alternabilidad* in government, the Constitutional Chamber said that the principle of *alternabilidad* imposes "for the people as sovereign to have the possibility to periodically elect their representatives," confusing alternate government (*gobierno alternativo*) with elective government (*gobierno electivo*). According to the Chamber decision, confusing the terms, the principle of alternate government (*gobierno alternative)* can be infringed only if the possibility of having elections (*gobierno electivo*) is impeded.

With those decisions, the Supreme Tribunal resolved the constitutional challenges to the February referendum and, through constitutional interpretation, modified the text of the Constitution.

FINAL REFLECTIONS

*THE RIGHT TO DEMOCRACY AND ITS VIOLATION BY VENEZUELA'S
AUTHORITARIAN GOVERNMENT: SOME RELEVANT FACTS FROM THE
PAST DECADE*

I.   REPRESENTATIVE DEMOCRACY AND THE VENEZUELAN AUTHORITARIAN GOVERNMENT

The Inter-American Democratic Charter of September 11, 2001,[794] recognized democracy as a right of the peoples of the Americas, with the consequent

---

793 See the Constitutional Chamber of the Supreme Tribunal of Justice, Decision N° 53 (Feb. 3, 2009) (Case: *Interpretación de los artículos 340,6 y 345 de la Constitución* Case), http:/www.tsj.gov.ve/decisions/scon/Febrero/53-3209-2009-08-1610.html. On that decision, see Allan R. Brewer-Carías, "El Juez Constitucional vs. La alternabilidad republicana (La reelección continua e indefinida), in *Revista de Derecho Público* 117, Editorial Jurídica Venezolana, Caracas 2009, pp. 205-211

794 See http://www.oas.org/charter/docs/resolution1_en_p4.htm.

obligations of Latin American governments to promote and defend it as essential to their social, political, and economic development. Democracy, in this context, is indispensable to the effective exercise of fundamental freedoms and human rights in their universality, indivisibility, and interdependence, embodied in the national constitutions and in international human rights instruments (Article 7).

The charter considered the effective exercise of representative democracy as the basis for the rule of law, enumerating its essential elements as follows: respect for human rights and fundamental freedoms; access to and the exercise of power in accordance with the rule of law; the holding of periodic, free, and fair elections based on secret balloting and universal suffrage as an expression of the sovereignty of the people; a pluralistic system of political parties and organizations; and separation of powers and independence of the branches of government (Article 3). In addition, Article 4 of the charter enumerated the following essential components of the exercise of democracy: transparency in government activities, probity and responsible public administration, respect for social rights, and freedom of expression and of the press (Article 4). Furthermore, the charter considered equally essential to democracy the constitutional subordination of all state institutions to the legally constituted civilian authority and respect for the rule of law on the part of all institutions and sectors of society.

Regarding political parties and other political organizations, their strengthening is considered a priority for democracy (Article 5), which highlights the special attention that must be paid to the problems associated with the high cost of electoral campaigns and the establishment of a balanced and transparent system for their financing.

Finally, regarding participation, Article 6 of the charter declared it a right and responsibility of all citizens to participate in decisions relating to their own development in order to promote and foster diverse forms of participation, a necessary condition for the full and effective exercise of democracy.

The general importance of these provisions of the Inter-American Democratic Charter is that they impose a standard of conduct on all Latin American states to preserve democracy, understanding democracy as a system not only in which elections are held but also in which all the aforementioned essential elements and components of democracy are enforced. Consequently, the violation of the charter occurs when a coup d'état is carried out against the constituted organs of a state and when the constituted organs of the state violate the essential elements and components of representative democracy, as when they use them fraudulently. This is what has been happening with the progressive configuration of a new model of an authoritarian state in Venezuela of a supposed "popular power." Despite the elective origin of its government and its camouflage of "constitutional" forms, the model has been designed precisely to destroy representative democracy itself.[795]

---

795   See Allan R. Brewer-Carías, "Constitution Making in Defraudation of the Constitution and Authoritarian Government in Defraudation of Democracy: The Recent Venezuelan Experience," in *Lateinamerika Analysen* No. 19, German Institute of Global and Area Studies, Institute of Latin American Studies, Hamburg 2008, pp. 119-142; "El autoritarismo establecido en fraude a la Constitución y a la democracia y su formalización en Venezuela mediante la reforma constitucional (De cómo en un país democráti-

All the aforementioned essential elements and components of democracy have been ignored or fractured in Venezuela, thereby dismantling representative democracy in the name of a participatory democracy. The result is that in the past decade, there have been more violations of human rights than ever before, as confirmed by the numerous petitions that have been filed before the Inter-American Commission on Human Rights and the numerous decisions of the Inter-American Court of Human Rights condemning the Republic of Venezuela.[796] The access to power in many instances has been achieved contrary to the provisions established in the Constitution, as that for appointing heads of the judicial, citizens', and electoral branches of government.[797]

The basic rule of representative democracy by means of elections has also been violated through the creation of communal councils, which substitute electoral representation with citizens' assemblies and councils whose members are not elected but rather appointed by citizens' assemblies that are controlled by the national executive.[798] The plural regime of parties has been destroyed, and the government has created the official "Marxist" *Partido Socialista Unido de Venezuela* (PSUV) (United Socialist Party of Venezuela),[799] using public funds, directly controlled by the president, which functions in a completely imbricate way with the state apparatus. In such a party, public employees are forced to be registered as members. Consequently, because everything depends on the oil income of the resource-rich

co se ha utilizado el sistema eleccionario para minar la democracia y establecer un régimen autoritario de supuesta 'dictadura de la democracia' que se pretende regularizar mediante la reforma constitucional)," in *Temas constitucionales. Planteamientos ante una reforma,* Fundación de Estudios de Derecho Administrativo, Caracas 2007, pp. 13-74.

796 See http://www.corteidh.or.cr/buscar.cfm?clave=casos%20venezuela.

797 See Allan R. Brewer-Carías, "El secuestro del poder electoral y la confiscación del derecho a la participación política mediante el referendo revocatorio presidencial: Venezuela 2000-2004," *Revista Jurídica del Perú* No. 54, Lima 2004, pp. 353-396; "El secuestro del poder electoral y de la Sala Electoral del Tribunal Supremo y la confiscación del derecho a la participación política mediante el referendo revocatorio presidencial: Venezuela: 2000-2004," *Revista Costarricense de Derecho Constitucional* No. 5, Instituto Costarricense de Derecho Constitucional, Editorial Investigaciones Jurídicas S.A., San José 2004, pp. 167-312; "El secuestro de la Sala Electoral por la Sala Constitucional del Tribunal Supremo de Justicia, in *La Guerra de las Salas del TSJ frente al Referendum Revocatorio*," Editorial Aequitas, Caracas 2004, pp. 13-58; "El secuestro del poder electoral y la confiscación del derecho a la participación política mediante el referendo revocatorio presidencial: Venezuela 2000-2004," *Stvdi Vrbinati, Rivista Trimestrale di Scienze Giuridiche, Politiche ed Economiche* 71, n.s., Università degli Studi di Urbino, Urbino 2004, pp. 379-436; "El secuestro del poder electoral y la confiscación del derecho a la participación política mediante el referendo revocatorio presidencial: Venezuela 2000-2004," *Boletín Mexicano de Derecho Comparado No.* 112, Instituto de Investigaciones Jurídicas, Universidad Nacional Autónoma de México, Mexico City 2005, pp. 11-73.

798 See Allan R. Brewer-Carías, "El inicio de la desmunicipalización en Venezuela: La organización del poder popular para eliminar la descentralización, la democracia representativa y la participación a nivel local," *AIDA, Opera Prima de Derecho Administrativo. Revista de la Asociación Internacional de Derecho Administrativo*, Universidad Nacional Autónoma de México, Facultad de Estudios Superiores de Acatlán, Coordinación de Postgrado, Instituto Internacional de Derecho Administrativo "Agustín Gordillo," Asociación Internacional de Derecho Administrativo, Mexico City 2007, pp. 49-67.

799 See the "Declaration of Principles" of the United Socialist Party (Apr. 23, 2010). Available at http://psuv.org.ve/files/tcdocumentos/Declaracion-de-principios-PSUV.pdf.

state, only those who are part of the United Socialist Party and its entities can have effective access to political and administrative life.

This entire institutional democratic distortion has been established without real separation or independence of the different branches of government, not only in their horizontal division but also in their vertical distribution. What was left of the federation has been progressively dismantled. Consequently, the powers of the federated states and municipalities have been minimized by means of eliminating every trace of political decentralization of the autonomous entities in the territory, thereby preventing any real possibility of democratic participation.

Moreover, the governmental activity of the rich and wealthy oil state has ceased to be transparent – there are no checks and balances, and so it is not possible to demand any kind of accountability or responsibility from the government. The consequence is rampant governmental corruption developed in a way never seen before and promoted by the different agencies of the state, as the 2009-10 financial and banking crisis has shown. In addition, freedom of speech and the press has been systematically threatened as has been evidenced in the case of *Globovisión*,[800] and the state has closed or appropriated media outlets as has happened with *Radio Caracas Televisión.*[801] In other cases, self-censorship has been imposed by journalists and dissidents who fear systematic persecution.

So it is that, during the past years, all essential elements and fundamental components of representative democracy have been progressively dismantled in Venezuela, particularly the principle of separation of powers, to the point that the Inter-American Commission on Human Rights has said in its *2009 Annual Report* that the conditions analyzed in it "indicates the absence of due separation and independence between the branches of government in Venezuela."[802] In December 2009, the president of the Supreme Tribunal of Justice considered such separation an element designed to "debilitate the State."[803]

---

800   In June 2010, the main shareholders of Globovisión were persecuted by the government, using for such purpose criminal judicial accusations "motivated" on supposed commerce or financial offences. See Juan Francisco Alonso, "Ministerio Público solicitó extradición de Zuloaga, El Universal, June 30, 2010. Available al http://www.eluniversal.com/2010/06/30/pol_art_ministerio-publicos_1956783.shtml; and "Mezerhane: No regresará hasta que haya seguridad jurídica," (En entrevista con CNN en Español), in El Universal, June 14, 2010. Available at http://www.eluniversal.com/2010/06/14/pol_ava_mezerhane:-no-regres_14A4022131.shtml.

801   See, e.g., the case of the shutdown of Radio Caracas Televisión, in Allan R. Brewer-Carías, "El juez constitucional en Venezuela como instrumento para aniquilar la libertad de expresión y para confiscar la propiedad privada: El *caso RCTV*" (I de III), *Gaceta Judicial*, Santo Domingo, República Dominicana, 2007, pp. 24-27.

802   See IACHR, *2009 Annual Report*, para. 472. See http://www.cidh.oas.org/annualrep/2009-eng/Chap.IV.f.eng.htm. The President of the Commission, Felipe González, said in Apr. 2010: "Venezuela is a democracy that have grave limitations, because democracy implies the functioning of the principle of separation of powers, and a Judiciary free of political factors." See Juan Francisco Alonso, "Últimas medidas judiciales certifican informe de la CIDH," in *El Universal*, Apr. 4, 2010. Available at http://universo.eluniversal.com/2010/04/04/pol_art_ultimas-medidas-jud_1815569.shtml.

803   See Juan Francisco Alonso, "La división de poderes debilita al estado. La presidenta del TSJ [Luisa Estela Morales] afirma que la Constitución hay que reformarla," *El Universal*, Caracas Dec. 15, 2009, http://www.eluniversal.com/2009/12/05/pol_art_morales:-la-divisio_1683109.shtml.

Consequently, the country has faced an excess of concentrated and centralized power, as occurs in any authoritarian government, despite their electoral origin. In such cases, as history has shown, and in the current case of Venezuela, an inevitable tendency toward tyranny develops, particularly when there are no efficient means of control over those who govern – it is even worse when those who govern have or believe to have popular support. In Venezuela, the authoritarian government that has taken root during the past decade has concentrated all power in the hands of the executive, President Chávez, who at once controls the National Assembly and all other branches of government.

This situation is in contrast to the democratic system that, with all its defects, had consolidated in Venezuela during the second half of the twentieth century, and democracy still was among the most important historical, political, and cultural heritages of Venezuela's population at the beginning of the twenty-first century. At the end of the twentieth century, after forty years of democratic rule, Venezuela had Latin America's oldest, most tested stable contemporary democracy. Since 1999, that legacy has been systematically destroyed against the people's will.[804]

II. REPRESENTATIVE DEMOCRACY AND ITS DEFORMATIONS

The Inter-American Democratic Charter began by stating that the effective exercise of representative democracy is the basis for the rule of law and for constitutional regimes (Article 2), revaluating representative democracy as a political system that is the antithesis of a regime based on the popularity of a populist leader supported by the armed forces.[805] Representative democracy is contrary to the well-known nonelective relationship of leader, people, and military that created the fascist and national-socialist praxis of the first half of the twentieth century and was used to confiscate democracy in the second half.

In the Venezuela of 1999, representative democracy as basis of the rule of law and the constitutional regime, without doubt needed to be improved to make it more representative of the people, regarding their organizations, regions, communities, and neighborhoods, and not only of the political parties that monopolized it. That was the great political change that Venezuelans called for, and that call provoked the electoral process of 1998. In those elections, a vast majority did not vote for traditional parties and many voted against them. But instead of perfecting representative democracy, during the past decade, representative democracy has been distorted, particularly through the systematic manipulation of the electoral system and the progressive destruction of pluralism. The result has been the adoption of a political system with reduced representation. Instead of allowing

---

804 Still in Dec. 2009, according to a Latinobarómetro poll of eighteen Latin American countries, Venezuela and Uruguay were the countries with the highest number of people expressing that "democracy is preferable to any other type of government," and with the lowest percentage of people expressing that "in certain circumstances an authoritarian government can be preferable to a democratic one." See *Economist* 393, Dec. 12, 2009, p. 42.

805 The express inclusion of the reference to representative democracy in the charter was despite suggestions to replace it with "participatory democracy," as in the meeting of heads of state and governments of the Americas (3rd Summit of the Americas), Quebec City, 2001, and in the General Assembly of the Organization of American States, in San José, Costa Rica, in 2001.

representation of various political parties, representation has been reduced to only one governmental party, with no other representation. That is why, even in 2000, the organization secretary of the government party, facing the possibility of losing the majority in the National Assembly, expressed that if the majority were lost, "it would be the end of the democratic way of the process due to the fact that through parliament it is possible to abrogate statutes, to censure ministries, to indict the president."[806] Eight years later, President Chavez, facing a possible setback for the government in the regional elections of 2008 said that if the opposition groups would eventually win important positions of governorships and mayors in Caracas and states like Miranda, Carabobo, Táchira or Anzoategui, "the next step will be war."[807] The following year, in 2009, it was also President Chávez, who in referring to the September 2010 elections of new members of the National Assembly, said:

> The vital objective in order to maintain the stability of the country, to maintain peace in the country, is for the Revolution to obtain next year a resonant triumph in the Assembly, obtaining a majority of representatives. Just imagine for a minute, on the possibility for the counterrevolution, due to any factor, to obtain a majority in the National Assembly. They will begin to reverse the statutes, this law would be quickly abrogated, and as the people will not keep quiet, and then the country would take the violent way. The same happens with the government: just suppose for an instant that a recall referendum could take place next year. Suppose that my mandate would be revoked. The country would enter into an earthquake, violence, destabilization, which is their objective. The government is their objective, and again to control the State as they did so for a long time.[808]

That is, for Chávez and his followers, a "democratic" system in Venezuela is conceivable only if it exclusively represents his supporters. It is simply inconceivable if it represents any in the opposition. In fact, the political system in Venezuela has progressively moved toward a supposed "democracy" representing only one party, which has declare itself as a "Marxist" party, monopolizing most of the representative bodies, manipulating election rules, and taken control of the electoral branch of government. The fact is, in Venezuela, during the last four decades of the past century, there was never a party autocracy as the one now seen that admits no dissidence.

That is why since the beginning of his government, Chávez and his followers have not admitted that the composition of the National Assembly could be democratically changed. This was true even in January 2001, when threatened by the possible defection of some representatives supporting the government, the majority in the National Assembly could be changed. As aforementioned, in 2009, Chávez himself considered such change the beginning of violence.

---

806   See *El Universal,* Caracas Dec. 28, 2001, 1–2.

807   See report of Chavez's speech, "Al ganar la oposición vendrá la Guerra," *El Universal,* Caracas Jan. 21, 2008, available at http://noticias.eluniversal.com/2008/01/21/pol_art_al-ganar-la-oposici_680614.shtml.

808   See Joaquin Chaffardet, "Amenaza presidencial y pasividad opositora," Nov. 1, 2009, at http://webarticulista.net.

For the government to arrive at this political monopoly on representation, it has changed the electoral system. Members of the National Assembly were traditionally elected by the method of d'Hondt proportional representation introduced in 1946 and reformed by the 1993 Organic Law on Suffrage and Political Participation.[809] Following the reforms introduced in the law, the 1999 Constitution provided for a combination of methods, adding to the proportional representation a parallel majority method to be applied in the constituency: the "personalized proportional representation method" (Article 63).[810] This mixed system requires ensuring the election in each constituency of a percentage of representatives elected in uninominal ballot and another percentage in plurinominal ballot through blocked and closed lists. This was the method applied in the elections of representatives to the National Assembly in 2000, but it was distorted in 2005 regarding the election of the same members of the National Assembly when the parties supporting the government applied the fraudulent "*Las Morochas*" method. This distortion was later legitimized through a constitutional interpretation of the Constitutional Chamber of the Supreme Tribunal of Justice on January 25, 2006.[811] The method allowed the various parties supporting official candidates to enter into agreements for some of them to file nominations only for the uninominal election and others only for the plurinominal one in the respective constituencies. As they formally were different parties (although part of the same government coalition) no deduction of the elected candidates would be applied.[812] In that way, the system in practice became one of a preponderant majority, thus distorting proportional representation. In 2009, the Organic Law on the Electoral Processes was sanctioned, "regularizing" the method.[813] In addition to the distortion of the mixed system, the complete lack of independence and autonomy of the National Electoral Council must be mentioned because it has prevented any possible guarantee of impartiality. All these facts forced opposition parties not to participate in the legislative elections of 2005, with catastrophic consequences for democracy.

Another important distortion of the electoral system has been the deliberate use of the comptroller general's office, illegitimately controlled by the executive, to disqualify many opposition candidates' participation in electoral process through supposed administrative "irregularities" that they committed while in public positions. This is notwithstanding the provision of the Constitution guaranteeing that the political right to run for office can be suspended only by a criminal judicial decision (Articles 39 and 42).[814] On this matter, the Inter-American Commission on

---

809   *Gaceta Oficial* Extra. N° 5.233, May 28, 1998.

810   See Decision N° 74 (Jan. 25, 2006) of the Constitutional Chamber of the Supreme Tribunal of Justice, in *Revista de Derecho Público No.* 105, Editorial Jurídica Venezolana, Caracas 2006, pp. 122-144.

811   Decision N° 74 (Case: *Acción Democrática vs. National Electoral Council and other electoral authorities*), in *Revista de Derecho Público* No. 105, Editorial Jurídica Venezolana, Caracas 2006, pp. 122-44.

812   See Allan R. Brewer-Carías, "El juez constitucional vs. el derecho al sufragio mediante la representación proporcional," in *Crónica sobre la "in" justicia constitucional. La Sala Constitucional y el autoritarismo en Venezuela,* Caracas 2007, pp. 337ff.

813   *Gaceta Oficial* N° 5.928 Extra. of Aug. 12, 2009.

814   In Oct. 2008, the European Parliament approved a resolution asking the Venezuelan government to end these practices (political disqualification to prevent election of opposition leaders in regional and local

Human Rights, in its *2009 Annual Report*, has highlighted this mechanism restricting "the possibilities of candidates opposed to the government for securing access to power," emphasizing that "through administrative resolutions of the Office of the Comptroller General of the Republic, whereby 260 individuals, mostly opposed to the government, were disqualified from standing for election," and pointing out that "these disqualifications from holding public office were not the result of criminal convictions and were ordered in the absence of prior proceedings, in contravention of the American Convention's standards."[815]

Unfortunately, the Constitutional Chamber of the Supreme Tribunal legitimized these unconstitutional administrative measures limiting this right, defrauding the Constitution.[816] The result was the elimination of many possible opposition candidates from the November 2008 regional and municipal elections. The same sort of decision was publicly announced in November 2009, when many possible opposition candidates for the National Assembly in 2010 were disqualified from participating in such elections.[817]

But one of the biggest distortions of the electoral system occurred in 2004, before the recall presidential referendum that year. First, the date of the referendum was delayed without justification to allow the sudden and indiscriminate incorporation to the electoral list of almost 2 million new voters, many of whom were formerly illegal immigrants whose status had been regularized.[818] Second, more that 1 million voters were illegally moved to voting centers in other cities. Third, more that eighteen thousand members of the electoral centers were dismissed for having signed the petition to convene the 2004 recall referendum. Fourth, in general, the names of all 3.5 million persons who signed that petition were incorporated in a public list (*"Lista Tascón"*) that was published for political purposes by one member of the National Assembly, who and thus were massively discriminated against in their relations with the public administration. Fifth, public servants who signed the same petition were openly dismissed from their positions.

Of all these distortions that have affected the implementation of free and fair elections, the most serious one has been the complete absence of independence and autonomy of the National Electoral Council, which according to the Constitution was to comprise five members with no ties to political organizations and appointed

elections) and to promote a more global democracy with complete respect for the principles established in the 1999 Constitution. See http://venezuelanoticia.com/ archives/8298.

815 See IACHR, *2009 Annual Report*, para. 473. See http://www.cidh.oas.org/annualrep/2009eng/Chap.IV.f.eng.htm.

816 See Teodoro Petkoff, "Election and Political Power: Challenges for the Opposition," in *ReVista: Harvard Review of Latin America*, David Rockefeller Center for Latin American Studies, Cambridge, MA, Harvard University, 2008, p. 11.

817 On May 25, 2010, the disqualification of two former governors (from the states of Zulia and Sucre) opposing Chávez as candidates for the Sept. 2010 legislative elections was announced. See http://www.globovision.com/news.php?nid=150031.

818 See Decree N° 2,823 of Feb. 3, 2004, *Gaceta Oficial* N° 37,871 of Feb. 2, 2004, reformed by Decree N° 3,041 of Aug. 3, 2004, *Gaceta Oficial* N° 38,002 of Aug. 17, 2004. See the comments on this process in Allan R. Brewer-Carías, *Régimen de la nacionalidad, Ciudadanía y Extranjería*, Editorial Jurídica Venezolana, Caracas 2005, pp. 57ff.

by the National Assembly, following the nominations of an electoral nominating committee exclusively composed of representatives from different sectors of society. That nominating committee was to receive nominations from the law and political science faculties of national universities, the citizens' branch of government, and civil society organizations.

In any event, since 2000, the configuration of the Committee for Electoral Nominations and those of all other nominating committees has been distorted. The committees were never structured as provided for in the Constitution with representatives from various sectors of civil society. They have mainly included elected members of the National Assembly and members of the official party. This began in 2002, after the Organic Law of the Electoral Power[819] was sanctioned and the National Assembly was due to appoint new members of the National Electoral Council. Because representatives supporting the government did not have the qualified majority to approve such appointments and did not want to agree on the matter with the opposition, the National Assembly failed to appoint members of the National Electoral Council. The consequence of this omission was that the Constitutional Chamber of the Supreme Tribunal of Justice, controlled by the executive, decided an action filed against such unconstitutional legislative omission and directly appointed members of the Electoral Council, without complying with the conditions established in the Constitution. That move ensured the government's complete control of the state electoral organ.[820]

The provisions of the Organic Law of the Electoral Power tending to guarantee political participation of civil society converted the nominating committee into a parliamentary commission, with some additional members appointed by the same assembly. The result is that members of the Electoral Council have been, in their great majority, supporters of the government or members of the United Socialist Party, which has been confirmed in the appointment of new members of the council in November 2009, a decision that opposition parties formally challenged before the Supreme Tribunal.

Consequently, the elections held in Venezuela during the past decade have been organized by a politically dependent branch of government without any guarantee of independence or impartiality. This is the only explanation, for instance, of the complete lack of official information on the final voting results of the December 2007 referendum, in which the people rejected the president's draft constitutional reforms. The country, in June 2010, still ignored the number of votes that effectively

---

819   See *Gaceta Oficial* N° 37.573, Nov. 19, 2002.

820   See Decisions N° 2073 (Aug. 4, 2003) (Case: *Hermánn Escarrá Malaver y otros*) and N° 2341 (Aug. 25, 2003) (Case: *Hermánn Escarrá M. y otros*) in Allan R. Brewer-Carías, *La Sala Constitucional versus el estado democrático de derecho. El secuestro del poder electoral y de la Sala Electoral del Tribunal Supremo y la confiscación del derecho a la participación política*, Los Libros de El Nacional, Colección Ares, Caracas 2004, p. 172; "El secuestro del poder electoral y la confiscación del derecho a la participación política mediante el referendo revocatorio presidencial: Venezuela 2000-2004," *Boletín Mexicano de Derecho Comparado No.* 112, Instituto de Investigaciones Jurídicas, Universidad Nacional Autónoma de México, Mexico City 2005, pp. 11-73; Rafael Chavero G. et al., *La guerra de las salas del TSJ frente al referéndum revocatorio*, Editorial Aequitas, Caracas 2004, pp. 13-58.

rejected the proposed reform for the establishment in Venezuela of a socialist, centralized, militaristic, and police state, as proposed by President Chávez.

The constitutional regime of political parties was designed in the 1999 Constitution, following the antiparty trends resulting from the political crisis of the 1990s, which was reflected in the drafting of the new Constitution. That text eliminated the phrase "political party" from its text and substituted the more general "organizations with political purposes" (Article 67).[821] Of course, what in 1998 and 1999 were ignored were the traditional political parties that, until then, had been in control of power. Those parties were completely crushed and marginalized, with weak possibilities of participating in the political process. In the subsequent years, new political parties controlled by the government developed, with more centralized organizations than the traditional ones, directly controlled by the president. The final result was the presidential initiative, in 2006, to promote the founding of the United Socialist Party of Venezuela, using for such purposes the state structures and services, which in its first Congress in April 2010 declared to be a "Marxist" party. This official party is, of course, led by the president himself, with the intention of uniting all the various political parties that have supported his government. Only the tiny Communist Party initially refused to disappear, and others have abandoned their support to the government.[822]

The United Socialist Party was in charge of supporting the presidential draft constitutional reforms submitted to referendum in 2007, which was rejected by popular vote. The party was also the supporting instrument of government candidates in regional and municipal elections of November 2008 – the government's candidates lost elections in the most important and populated states and municipalities of the country, where some opposition candidates were elected as governors and mayors. This latter fact provoked the reaction of the government affecting the constitutional right to hold elected positions. This has been highlighted by the Inter-American Commission on Human Rights in its *2009 Annual Report*, in which it noticed "how the State has taken action to limit some powers of popularly-elected authorities in order to reduce the scope of public functions in the hands of members of the opposition," particularly through "a series of legal reforms [that] have left opposition authorities with limited powers, preventing them from legitimately exercising the mandates for which they were elected."[823]

In any case, the result of the first decade of political life under the 1999 Constitution, which seems to ignore political parties in its regulations, has been to increase partisanship and party autocracy, particularly regarding the official party, in

---

821   See Roberto V. Pastor and Rubén Martínez Dalmau, "La configuración de los partidos políticos en la Constitución venezolana," *Revista de Derecho Constitucional No. 4*, Editorial Sherwood, Caracas 2001, pp. 375-389; Allan R. Brewer-Carías, "Regulación jurídica de los partidos políticos en Venezuela," in *Regulación jurídica de los partidos políticos en América Latina*, coord. Daniel Zovatto, Universidad Nacional Autónoma de México, International IDEA, Mexico City 2006, pp. 893-937.

822   The case of the party *Patria para Todos* PPT, which after supporting the government until 2010, Chávez sentenced: "The PPT is finished, that party does not exist." See http://elobservador.rctv.net/Noticias/VerNoticia.aspx?NoticiaId=283197&Tipo=14.

823   See IACHR, *2009 Annual Report*, para. 474. See http://www.cidh.oas.org/annualrep/2009-eng/Chap.IV.f.eng.htm.

a way never before seen. The traditional multiparty government of the second half of the twentieth century has been substituted with a single-party government that is completely imbricate with the state.

The traditional lack of internal democratic rules of parties, with their traditional pattern of leaders in perpetuity, led to a provision in the 1999 Constitution according to which not only the members of governing boards must elect the members of each party, but also the party candidates for elections to representative offices must be selected through democratic internal elections (Article 67). To that end, the Constitution required that the National Electoral Council organize such internal elections (Article 293.6). In practice, because of the lack of statutory development of the constitutional provisions, that has not occurred.

Also as a reaction against problems stemming from the public funding of political parties that was established in the 1998 Organic Law of Suffrage and Political Participation,[824] the application of which led the traditionally dominant parties to monopolize those funds, the drafters of the 1999 Constitution simply prohibited public funding of organizations with political purposes and established new controls for their private financing (Article 67). This was a regression in addressing what is a constant problem in the democratic world: the possibility for public funding of political parties to avoid irregular and illegitimate funding, particularly of governing parties.[825] Nonetheless, in a 2008 decision of the Constitutional Chamber of the Supreme Tribunal interpreting such Article 67 of the Constitution, the chamber distorted the Constitution, concluding contrary to the constitutional provision that the article intended to prohibit only public financing regarding internal activities of parties, not their electoral activities.[826] Of course, because of the monopoly of the United Socialist Party over the electoral branch of government, it is easy to understand that public funding will eventually end up in the official party's budget.

Also as a reaction against political parties, the Constitution established that members of the National Assembly are representatives of the people as a whole and "are not to be subject to mandates or instructions other than their own conscience" (Article 200), thus seeking to eliminate parliamentary party groups and blind voting. Nonetheless, in practice, parliamentary factions have only changed their names – since 2000, they have been called "opinion groups." On the vote of members of the National Assembly, particularly those elected by the official party, the president of the National Assembly was emphatic in 2002 that they "are not independent at all,

---

824 *Gaceta Oficial* Extra. N° 5.233, May 28, 1998.

825 See Allan R. Brewer-Carías, "Consideraciones sobre el financiamiento de los partidos políticos en Venezuela," in *Financiamiento y democratización interna de partidos políticos. Memora del IV Curso Anual Interamericano de Elecciones,* Instituto Interamericano de Derechos Humanos, San José, Costa Rica, 1991, pp. 121-39.

826 Decision N° 780 (May 8, 2008),of the Constitutional Chamber of the Supreme Tribunal of Justice (Ca-se: *Interpretación del artículo 67 de la Constitución*), in *Revista de Derecho Público* No. 114, Editorial Jurídica Venezolana, Caracas 2008, pp. 126ff. See the comments in "El juez constitucional como cons-tituyente: el caso del financiamiento de las campañas electorales de los partidos políticos en Venezuela," in *Revista de Derecho Público* 117, Editorial Jurídica Venezolana, Caracas 2009, pp. 195-203.

but are subject to discipline. The one who pretend[s] to act as an independent must resign, and just be an independent candidate."[827]

In any case, the governing party has had more centralized control over members of the National Assembly than had parties before 1999. As a result, the constitutional provision aimed to guarantee the internal renovation of the political directors of the parties is a dead letter – the president of the republic presides over the official party, and the board of directors is made up of state officers appointed by the president.

The result of all these provisions, constitutional distortions, and the absence of legislation is that after the enactment of the 1999 Constitution, the political parties have greater presence than they ever had. In addition, the symbiosis between the governing political party and the state and its public administration that has been established in the past years confirms that a party state has continued to exist, with the same vices of clientelism and the same control by officials sitting permanently on the governing boards. The consequence has been that the constitutional provision establishing the prohibition on public officers serving any party (Article 145) has been forgotten. As never before, the country has a president who has continued acting more like the chief of a political party than a head of government and state. This has been the situation in the country since 2000.[828]

In Venezuela, representative democracy has not been based on pluralism, tolerance, dissidence, discussion, dialogue, and consensus. It is a system in which only the government parties and the supporters of the president are "represented"; the opposition parties and organizations are completely excluded or marginalized from political life.

III. PARTICIPATORY DEMOCRACY AND THE VIOLATION OF THE CITIZENS' RIGHT TO PARTICIPATION

The Inter-American Democratic Charter not only reaffirms the need for an effective exercise of representative democracy as basis for the rule of law and of the constitutional regime but also states that such representative democracy shall be strengthened and deepened by permanent, ethical, and responsible participation of the citizenry within a legal and constitutional order (Article 2). Furthermore, the charter adds that citizens' participation in decisions relating to their own development is a right, a responsibility, and a necessary condition for the full and effective exercise of democracy. Therefore, it affirms that promoting and fostering diverse forms of participation strengthens democracy (Article 6).

It can be said that the 1999 Constitution is marked by the concept of participation, not only by declaring the government of the republic and all political entities as participatory (Article 6) but also by formally establishing the right to

---

827   See *El Nacional,* Caracas Dec. 27, 2001, D-2.

828   On May 25, 2010, for instance, it was Chávez who officially announced the Party candidates for the Sept. 2010 legislative elections. See Alejandra M. Hernández F., "Chávez anuncia candidatos que enca-bezan lista para la AN," in *El Universal,* May 25, 2010. See http://politica.eluniver-sal.com/2010/05/25/pol_art_chavez-anuncia-candi_25A3904931.shtml.

political participation (Article 62), for which purpose the Constitution lists, beyond the election of public representatives, the diverse ways to participate in political matters: election, referenda, popular consultation; revocation of mandates; legislative, constitutional, and constituent initiatives; open town hall meetings; and citizens' assemblies of binding character (Article 70).

In addition to all these participatory political means that must be developed through legislation for their complete exercise, the Constitution has established through self-executing provisions two specific ways to participate in public management. First is the exercise of the legislative function by obligating the National Assembly to consult state organs, citizens, and the organized society to hear their opinions on draft statutes (Article 211) and obligating it to consult the states' legislative councils on draft laws on matters regarding the states (Article 206). This obligation of the National Assembly, without doubt, applies to the president when, through enabling laws, the assembly authorizes the president to issue decree laws (Article 203). The converse would be to defraud the Constitution.

Second is the process of appointing the head officers of the organs of the citizens' power (attorney general, comptroller general, and human rights ombudsman), the electoral power (National Electoral Council), and the judicial power (magistrates of the Supreme Tribunal of Justice) by imposing limits to the former discretional power of the former Congress to make those appointments. According to provisions of the Constitution, in all those cases, the National Assembly can make those appointments only from candidates proposed by the corresponding nominating committees integrated by "representatives of the diverse sectors of society" (Articles 270, 279, and 295).

Nonetheless, these two direct means for political participation have been completely ignored and distorted over the past decade. On the need for public consultation on matters of legislation, the violation of the constitutional provisions was made in all cases of decree laws approved by the president in execution of the 2001 and 2007 Enabling Laws authorizing the President of the Republic to enact them, through which the main legislation of the country has been enacted. It occurred in November 2001, when the president issued forty-eight decree laws regulating matters of primary importance in the country without submitting drafts to public consultation, as required by the Constitution and as established in the Organic Law of Public Administration of October 2001, which punishes with absolute nullity (Article 137) any statute approved without following the procedure of public consultation set forth.[829] It also happened in 2007–8, also through the approval of more that fifty decree laws, many of which were to implement the rejected 2007

---

829 See Allan R. Brewer-Carías, "Apreciación general sobre los vicios de inconstitucionalidad que afectan los decretos leyes habilitados," in *Ley Habilitante del 13-11-2000 y Sus Decretos Leyes*, No. 17, Academia de Ciencias Políticas y Sociales, Caracas 2002, pp. 63-103. See also *El Universal*, Caracas Nov. 25, 2001, pp. 1-1 and 1-2; *Revista Primicia* 206, Caracas Dec. 11, 2001, special report; *La Nación*, San Cristóbal, Nov. 23, 2001, p. 1-C.

constitutional reforms of the president that were not submitted to popular consultation.[830]

Constitutional provisions regarding citizens' rights to participate in the appointment of officials of the judicial, citizens', and electoral powers has also been systematically violated during the past decade. The text of the Constitution was ignored by the National Assembly when it issued the transitional Special Law for the Ratification or Designation of Officers of the Citizen Power and Magistrates of the Supreme Court of Justice for the first constitutional period of November 2000,[831] and when it approved laws regulating the electoral power, the citizens' power and the Supreme Tribunal of Justice.[832]

Because of the unconstitutionality of the 2000 special law, even the people's defender challenged it before the Supreme Tribunal.[833] The tribunal never ruled on the claim, but in a preliminary decision of December 12, 2000, it decided that the Constitution was not to be applied to the magistrates deciding the case who were expecting to be "ratified,"[834] in violation of the most elemental principle of the rule of law: no one shall be judge and a party in the same process. The Tribunal justified its ruling on the basis of the 1999 Transitory Constitutional Regime.[835]

The Inter-American Commission on Human Rights highlighted these violations in its Preliminary Observations of May 10, 2002, issued after its last visit to Venezuela, noting that at that time members of the Supreme Court of Justice, as well as the Peoples' Defender, the Prosecutor General, and the Comptroller General, "were not nominated by such committees as required by the Constitution," whose provisions "were aimed precisely at limiting undue interference, ensuring greater independence and impartiality, and allowing various voices of society to be heard in the selection of such high-level authorities." The commission concluded by urging the state "to adopt the organic laws so as to establish the mechanisms provided for in the Constitution for the selection of the members of the Supreme Court of Justice, as

---

830   For essays on the 2008 decree laws, see *Revista de Derecho Público* 115 *(Estudios sobre los Decretos Leyes 2008)*, Editorial Jurídica Venezolana, Caracas 2008.

831   See Allan R. Brewer-Carías, *Golpe de estado y proceso constituyente en Venezuela,* Universidad Autónoma de México, Mexico City 2002, pp. 389 ff.

832   See Ley Orgánica del Poder Ciudadano, *Gaceta Oficial* No. 37.310, Oct. 25, 2001; Ley Orgánica del Poder Electoral, *Gaceta Oficial* N° 37.573, Nov. 19, 2002; Ley Orgánica del Tribunal Supremo de Justicia, *Gaceta Oficial* N° 37.942, May 20, 2004. On the 2007 appointment of the prosecutor general, see Allan R. Brewer-Carías, "Sobre el nombramiento irregular por la Asamblea Nacional de los titulares de los órganos del poder ciudadano en 2007," in *Revista de Derecho Público* No. 113, Editorial Jurídica Venezolana, Caracas 2008, pp. 85-88.

833   The people's defender considered that the statute "was a fault against the democratic system, and the kidnapping of the right to citizen right, excluding the possibility to be plural." See *El Universal,* Caracas Nov. 21, 2000, pp. 1-4.

834   The general director of the People's Defender Office stated that this was because "many of the magistrates do not fulfill the necessary conditions to be ratified." See *El Universal,* Caracas Dec. 14, 2000, 1-2.

835   On this, see the statements by one of the magistrates of the Supreme Tribunal (Delgado Ocando) in *El Universal,* Caracas Jan. 12, 2001, pp. 1-4.

well as the Peoples' Defender, the Prosecutor General, and the Comptroller General."[836]

After 2002, the corresponding statutes regarding all those public offices were sanctioned, but in all of them, instead of being integrated by representatives of diverse sectors of civil society, as mandated in the Constitution, they are appointed by simple parliamentary commission of a majority of National Assembly representatives.[837] Civil society was discriminated against, and the heads of the citizens', electoral, and judicial powers were appointed by the National Assembly and directly controlled by the executive – sometimes without observing the strict conditions established in the Constitution. This was also the case regarding the appointment of members of the National Electoral Council in 2009. Although the Constitution expressly prohibits them to be members of any political party, some were formally registered members of the United Socialist Party.[838]

Participatory democracy, in all cases provided for directly in the Constitution by means of self-executing provisions, has been postponed by state organs. The same has occurred with the statutory development and application of other constitutional provisions regarding participatory democracy. As aforementioned, on matters of referenda, one of the most important ones established in the Constitution is the recall referendum that must be convened by popular initiative to revoke the mandate of elected officials. The only referendum of this type convened during the past decade – after a petition signed by more than 3.5 million people – was the recall or recall referendum regarding the mandate of President Chávez. In violation of the constitutional right to political participation, the National Electoral Council, following a ruling of the Constitutional Chamber of the Supreme Tribunal of Justice,[839] illegitimately converted the recall referendum of the president into a ratifying referendum[840] which does not exist in the Constitution.

Prior to the 2004 recall referendum, attempts to convene a consultative referendum, also by popular initiative, to ask the people about the permanence or resignation of the president in his position, were systematically frustrated. First, in 2003, more than 3 million signatures supporting the petition were openly ignored

---

836 Paras. 26-29. See the reference in Allan R. Brewer-Carías, *La crisis de la democracia venezolana. La Carta Democrática Interamericana y los sucesos de abril de 2002,* Los Libros de El Nacional, Colección Ares, Caracas 2002, p. 154.

837 See Ley Orgánica del Poder Ciudadano, *Gaceta Oficial* N° 37.310 of Oct. 25, 2001; Ley Orgánica del Poder Electoral, *Gaceta Oficial* N° 37.573 of Nov. 19, 2002; Ley Orgánica del Tribunal Supremo de Justicia, *Gaceta Oficial* N° 37.942 of May 20, 2004.

838 Juan M. Raffalli A. "Rectores del partido. Se ha consumado otro fraude a la Constitución y quedó al descubierto," in *El Universal,* Caracas May 7, 2010. See http://guarenasguatire. eluniver-sal.com/2010/05/07/opi_art_rectores-del-partido_1884615.shtml.

839 See Decision N° 2750 (Oct. 21, 2003) (Case: *Carlos E. Herrera Mendoza, Interpretación del artículo 72 de la Constitución*), in *Revista de Derecho Público No.* 93-96, Editorial Jurídica Venezolana, Caracas 2003, pp. 229 ff.

840 See Allan R. Brewer-Carías, "La Sala Constitucional vs. el derecho ciudadano a la revocatoria de mandatos populares: De cómo un referendo revocatorio fue inconstitucionalmente convertido en un "referendo ratificatorio," in *Crónica sobre la "in"justicia constitucional. La Sala Constitucional y el autoritarismo en Venezuela,* Universidad Central de Venezuela–Editorial Jurídica Venezolana, Caracas 2007, pp. 349-378.

and rejected by the National Electoral Council, a process that ended with a decision by the Electoral Chamber of the Supreme Tribunal to annul the convening of the referendum. In the interim, police seized copies of the signatures. Second, regarding the 2004 recall referendum, prior to carrying it out, the National Electoral Council annulled more that half of the 3 million signatures in support of the petition. Third, in the same process, the National Electoral Council converted the process of signing for a petition of this kind from an open process to an administrative procedure subject to strict public control. Fourth, the decision of the National Electoral Council annulling the signatures was challenged before the Electoral Chamber of the Supreme Tribunal, which issued a preliminary ruling suspending the National Electoral Council decision, thus allowing the referendum to be held. The Constitutional Chamber, without any power to do so, annulled the electoral chamber decision, ratifying the annulment of signatures decided by the National Electoral Council. In the end, after it had been tactically *ex profeso* postponed, the referendum took place in 2004, but after all the legal battles developed before entities completely controlled by the executive, it was eventually converted into a ratifying referendum.[841]

Another distortion that has occurred during the past decade regarding political participation is the progressive interference of the state in civil society organizations. First, in 2000, the Constitutional Chamber of the Supreme Tribunal denied citizens' right to participate through organizations of civil society that had any sort of financing from transnational or foreign institutions or foundations, improperly limiting the freedom of the people.[842] Second, in 2003, the Supreme Electoral Council suspended internal elections of all professional boards in the country, improperly limiting the rights of professionals to choose their boards of directors. Third, in particular, regarding the elections of the capital district's Colegio de

---

841   See Allan R. Brewer-Carías, "El secuestro del poder electoral y la confiscación del derecho a la partici-pación política mediante el referendo revocatorio presidencial: Venezuela 2000-2004," *Revista Jurídica del Perú* 54, Lima 2004, pp. 353-396; "El secuestro del poder electoral y de la Sala Electoral del Tribu-nal Supremo y la confiscación del derecho a la participación política mediante el referendo revocatorio presidencial: Venezuela: 2000-2004," *Revista Costarricense de Derecho Constitucional* 5, Instituto Costarricense de Derecho Constitucional, Editorial Investigaciones Jurídicas, San José 2004, pp. 167-312; "El secuestro del poder electoral y la confiscación del derecho a la participación política mediante el referendo revocatorio presidencial: Venezuela 2000-2004," *Stvdi Vrbinati* 71, n.s., Università degli Studi di Urbino, Urbino 2004, pp. 379-436; "El secuestro del poder electoral y la confiscación del dere-cho a la participación política mediante el referendo revocatorio presidencial: Venezuela 2000-2004," *Boletín Mexicano de Derecho Comparado No.* 112, Instituto de Investigaciones Jurídicas, Universidad Nacional Autónoma de México, Mexico City, pp. 11-73.

842   In its *2009 Annual Report*, the Inter-American Commission on Human Rights has express its concern about the provisions included in an "International Cooperation Bill." And the vague language used in it giving a broad margin of discretion to the authorities responsible for regulating it, which could result in the violation of rights including freedom of association, freedom of expression, political participation, and equality, affecting the functioning of nongovernmental organizations. Regarding the limits on NGO funding, the Commission noted that it "could hamper freedom of association in a way that is incompati-ble with the American Convention's standards," para. 498. See http://www.cidh.oas.org/annual-rep/2009eng/Chap.IV.f.eng.htm.

Abogados (Lawyers' Board), in 2008, the Constitutional Chamber ignored the lawyers' election and appointed new members to that board.[843]

Finally, mention must be made of the communal councils, established since 2006 as the supposed means for citizens participation, substituting for municipalities, which were, according to Article 168 of the Constitution, the "primary political unit of the national organization" and the basis for political participation. In lieu of developing these local government structures with elected members (mayors and councilors), the authoritarian regime preferred to create a parallel structure of centrally controlled communal councils,[844] whose members are not elected by the people but designated by local "assemblies of the citizens" (Article 70), controlled by the central government through the president and channels of the United Socialist Party. The citizens' assemblies according to the 2009 reform of the Law are the "highest deliberation and decision instance for the exercise of the communal power" (Article 20), but being directly controlled by a Ministry for the Popular Power on Political Participation, in fact they are the instrument of the official party and the central government in politically interfering in all social and economic activities, through control of the Ministry (Article 56).[845]

IV. DISRESPECTING HUMAN RIGHTS

Among the essential elements of representative democracy listed in the Inter-American Charter is respect for human rights and fundamental freedoms (Article 3). The relation between democracy and constitutional rights and freedoms is so important that the charter specifies that democracy is indispensable to the effective exercise of fundamental freedoms and human rights, in their universality, indivisibility, and interdependence, which are embodied in the Constitution and in inter-American and international human rights instruments.

However, in the past decade, in Venezuela, human rights have suffered in a way never seen before in the country.[846] This critical situation has been systematically denounced during the past decade by organizations dealing with their protection, including the Inter-American Commission on Human Rights. It is enough to analyze the annual reports from the commission on the situation of human rights in Venezuela, and the many decisions adopted by the Inter-American Court of Human Rights condemning Venezuela, for a complete panorama of the situation. Never before has the Inter-American Commission on Human Rights received so many petitions to protect human rights from the state, including violations of the freedom

---

843   See Decision N° 11 of Feb. 14, 2008 (Case, *Juan Carlos Velásquez Abreu y otro*), N° Expediente: 04-1263.

844   *Gaceta Oficial* N° 5.806, Extra., Apr. 10, 2006. See Allan R. Brewer-Carías, "El inicio de la desmunici-palización en Venezuela: La organización del poder popular para eliminar la descentralización, la democracia representativa y la participación a nivel local," in *Revista de la Asociación Internacional de Derecho Administrativo*, Mexico City 2007, pp. 49-67.

845   The 2006 law was substituted with the 2009 Organic Law on Communal Councils. See *Gaceta Oficial* N° 39.335, Dec. 28, 2009.

846   See, in general, Human Right Watch, *A Decade under Chávez: Political Intolerance and Lost Opportunities for Advancing Human Rights in Venezuela*, Sept. 2008, http://www.hrw.org/ reports/2008/venezuela0908/.

to form and join trade unions; attacks on freedom of association; violations of judicial guarantees and due process; interference of the executive branch in other branches of government, including submission of the judicial branch to the executive; disrespect of the right to life – as denounced in 2002, over extrajudicial executions and death squads of local police units[847]; and attacks on the freedom of expression and violations of the right to privacy of communications. On the matter of death squads, the Inter-American Commission on Human Rights, since 2002, expressed its concerns regarding various extrajudicial executions perpetrated by those groups, pointing out that, in many cases, they operate within the state's police force.[848]

Violent actions by social groups have also transferred to the political arena and, during the past decade, the country has witnessed open harassment, intimidation, and significant acts of vandalism and looting, exercised by groups connected with the government or with the official government party, against institutions, demonstrators, media, and even the freedoms of opposition members of the National Assembly and legislative councils. All this recalls fascist practices of harassment, threats, and destruction.[849]

The situation of human rights after the decade of authoritarian government can be summarized as follows. First, the constitutional rank of human rights declared and contained in international treaties of human rights recognized in Article 23 of the Constitution has been distorted by the Constitutional Chamber of the Supreme Tribunal of Justice in various decisions (N° 1.013 of 2001, N° 1.492 of 2003, and N° 1.939 of 2008) that have denied the direct applicability of such international provisions.[850] Also, the state has denied enforcement in the country of provisional protective measures adopted by the Inter-American Commission on Human Rights and the Inter-American Court of Human Rights, as in the case of the television station Globovisión, where the president publicly declared in 2003 that the government would not respect those bodies. The state has also formally declared the decision of the Inter-American Court of Human Rights of August 5, 2008 (*Apitz Barbera et al. (Corte Primera de lo Contencioso Administrativo) vs. Venezuela*)[851]

---

847   See, e.g., the statement of Human Rights Watch representative on death squads; impunity surrounding their activities; and indifference of the government, judges, and state police. See *El Universal*, Caracas Jan. 18, 2002, p. 1-5.

848   See the Preliminary Observation of May 10, 2002.

849   In its *2009 Annual Report*, the Inter-American Commission on Human Rights noted "extreme concern that in Venezuela, violent groups such as the *Movimiento Tupamaro, Colectivo La Piedrita, Colectivo Alexis Vive, Unidad Popular Venezolana, and Grupo Carapaica* are perpetrating acts of violence with the involvement or acquiescence of state agents. These groups have similar training to that of the police or the military, and they have taken control of underprivileged urban areas. The IACHR has received alarming information indicating that these violent groups maintain close relations with police forces and, on occasion, make use of police resources." Para. 509. See http://www.cidh.oas.org/annual-rep/2009eng/Chap.IV.f.eng.htm.

850   See the comments on these decisions in Allan R. Brewer-Carías, "El juez constitucional vs. La justicia internacional en materia de derechos humanos," in *Revista de Derecho Público No.* 116, Editorial Jurídica Venezolana, Caracas 2008, pp. 249-260

851   Inter-American Court of Human Rights, *Apitz Barbera et al. (Corte Primera de lo Contencioso Administrativo) v. Venezuela* (Judgment of Aug. 5, 2008), available at www.corteidh.or.cr.

condemning the republic for violating the rights of dismissed judges, as unenforceable in Venezuela (2008).[852]

Neither has the right to life and personal security been guaranteed. To understand this tragic situation, during the past decade, the annual toll of homicides in the country rose from 5,968 to 14,800, an average of more than 10,000 homicides per year.[853] In 2008, according to the information made available to the Inter-American Commission, "there were a total of 13,780 homicides in Venezuela, which averages out to 1,148 murders a month and 38 every day."[854] Caracas was considered the murder capital of the world.[855]

The right to equality and nondiscrimination has also been massively violated, particularly on political matters. As a consequence of the exercise in 2003 and 2004 of the right to petition for a presidential recall referendum, all those who signed the petition (more than 3.5 million people) were included in a list used to openly discriminate them. In this respect, in general, in its *2009 Annual Report*, the Inter-American Commission on Human Rights found that "in Venezuela, not all persons are ensured full enjoyment of their rights irrespective of the positions they hold vis-à-vis the government's policies," highlighting "that the State's punitive power is being used to intimidate or punish people on account of their political opinions."[856]

Moreover, the right to privacy in correspondence has been openly violated. In 2000–1, the National Assembly tapped telephone conversations of individuals without any judicial order, and transcripts were later published in state-owned media. The same sort of privacy rights were violated in 2002, when the Bank Supervision Agency ordered banks to inform the state's secret police of the accounts of opposition leaders, also without any judicial order.

Against expressions of tolerance in the Constitution, during the past decade, the country has witnessed the most bitter attacks by the president himself against the

---

852 See Decision N° 1,939 (Dec. 18, 2009) (Case *Gustavo Álvarez Arias y otros*), available at http://www.tsj.gov.ve/decisiones/scon/Diciembre/1939-181208-2008-08-1572.html.

853 In contrast, in New York City, only 461 homicides occurred in 2009, and about 500 per year over the past decade. In the past fifty years, the highest rate of homicides in New York was 2,245 in 1990. See Al Baker, "Homicides Near Record Low in New York City," *New York Times*, Dec. 29, 2009, pp. A1 and A3.

854 Inter-American Commission on Human Rights, *2009 Annual Report*, para. 505, available at http://www.cidh.oas.org/annualrep/ 2009eng/Chap.IV.f.eng.htm.

855 See "The List: Murder Capitals of the World," *Foreign Policy*, Sept. 2008, http://www.foreign-policy.com/story/cms.php?story_id=4480; David Paulin, "Caracas: Murder Capital of the World," Oct. 1, 2008, *American Thinker*, http://www.americanthinker.com/ 2008/10/ caracas_murder_capi-tal_of_the.html.

856 Inter-American Commission on Human Rights, *2009 Annual Report*, para. 472. In para. 475 of this *Report*, the Commission also noted "a troubling trend of punishments, intimidation, and attacks on individuals in reprisal for expressing their dissent with official policy. This trend affects both opposition authorities and citizens exercising their right to express their disagreement with the policies pursued by the government. These reprisals are carried out through both state actions, including harassment, and acts of violence perpetrated by civilians acting outside the law as violent groups. The Commission notes with concern that in some extreme cases, criminal proceedings have been brought against dissidents, accusing them of common crimes in order to deny them their freedom on account of their political positions." Available at http://www.cidh.oas.org/annualrep/2009eng/Chap.IV.f.eng.htm.

Catholic Church, the Cardinal and clerics[857]; in 2003, the foreign minister, at a meeting of the Organization of American States in Chile, promoted religious discrimination, denigrated the Catholic faith, and disqualified opposition; and then there were raids on Jewish schools and synagogues in 2008–9. The president himself promoted divisions in the Catholic Church in Venezuela,[858] and in July 2010, again he publicily insulted the Venezuelan Cardinal.[859]

With respect to labor rights, particularly the freedom to organize and manage trade unions has been violated since 2000. Trade unions have been subjected to administrative control. This is why, the Inter-American Commission on Human Rights, in its *2009 Annual Report*, noted "that Venezuela is still characterized by constant intervention in the functioning of its trade unions, through actions of the State that hinder the activities of union leaders and that point to political control over the organized labor movement, as well as through rules that allow government agencies to interfere in the election of union leaders," observing "with concern that in Venezuela, trade-union membership is subject to pressure related to the political position or ideology of the particular union."[860]

A massive violation of the right to work occurred in 2003, with the dismissal of more than nineteen thousand workers of the state-owned Petróleos de Venezuela, S.A., after a general strike that took place in 2003, paralyzing the oil industry. The dismissals were compulsory, without any recognition of accumulated labor rights. The workers also saw their right to dwelling openly violated when they were violently evicted by the government from their homes in oilfield settlements by the national guard, with riot equipment.

Since 2002, exercise of the right to demonstrate has been severely reduced given continuous, systematic armored attacks of public police and military forces against any opposition demonstrations. In this regard, in its *2009 Annual Report*, the Inter-American Commission on Human Rights noted "that exercising the right of peaceful demonstration in Venezuela frequently leads to violations of the rights to life and humane treatment, which in many cases are the consequence of excessive use of state force or the actions of violent groups." In addition, the Commission noted the tendency "toward the use of criminal charges to punish people exercising their right to demonstrate or protest against government policies" (e.g., "blocking public highways, resisting the authorities, damage to public property, active obstruction of

---

857 The open attacks against the Catholic Church began in 2002, when the president qualified it as "one of the tumors the country has," rejecting the right of Cardinal Velasco to censure the use of churches for political purposes "without consulting anybody." See *El Nacional,* Caracas Jan. 25, 2002, p. D-4; *El Nacional,* Caracas Jan. 27, 2002, p. D-2; *El Universal,* Caracas Jan. 28, 2002, p. 1-4.

858 That is why the rector of the Catholic University Andrés Bello (Luis Ugalde, S.J.) expressed his contrary opinion, affirming that "Chávez could not divide the Church." See *El Universal,* Caracas Jan. 31, 2002, 1-1. Another Jesuit (Jesús Gazo, S.J.) dissented. See *El Universal,* Caracas Oct. 16, 2000, p. 1-12.

859 The Cardinal responded from Rome to the insults, insisting that "the president and his government wants to take the country through the road of Marxist socialism that fill all spaces, is totalitarian and lead to dictatorship." See "Cardenal Urosa Savino rechazó acusaciones del presidente Chávez," Rome, July 7, 2010, available at http://www.globovision.com/news.php?nid=154155.

860 Inter-American Commission on Human Rights, *2009 Annual Report,* para. 477, available at http://www.cidh.oas.org/annualrep/ 2009eng/Chap.IV.f.eng.htm.

legally-established institutions, offenses to public officials, criminal instigation and criminal association, public incitement to lawbreaking, conspiracy, restricting freedom of employment, and breaches of the special secure zones regime, among others"), stressing that "this practice constitutes a restriction of the rights of assembly and freedom of expression guaranteed in the American Convention, the free exercise of which is necessary for the correct functioning of a democratic system that includes all sectors of society."[861] In addition, since 2002, the president has declared extensive urban areas to be military and security zones, completely excluding demonstrations in key areas of Caracas and other important cities.

In the realm of economic rights, property rights in particular have been systematically violated by means of the continuous seizure of rural land through the application of a land law and through confiscation (expropriation without compensation) of industrial assets, rights, and enterprises in the oil, iron, steel, and cement industries (2006–9). There was the case of the confiscation of the rights and assets of Radio Caracas Televisión, considered to be opposition, after the government arbitrarily decided not to renew its concession. In that case, the Supreme Tribunal of Justice supported the confiscation of private property and assigned private rights to a state-owned entity without trial or compensation.[862]

For judicial guarantees of human rights, the general trend of the past decade has been systematic violation of due process. In some cases, by allowing impunity, like the massacre of peaceful demonstrators on April 11, 2002, that led to the resignation of the president,[863] and by transforming its authors into "heroes of the revolution" (Case: *Pistoleros de Puente Llaguno*). In that case, the police who were protecting demonstrators became criminals, condemned to a maximum prison term without due-process guarantees.[864]

Due process has been systematically violated in all cases regarding the dismissal of judges.[865] In other cases, the government has ignored judicial decisions, as was the case in 2003 with a decision of the First Court on Contentious Administrative, matters provisionally suspending the process of hiring foreign physicians not licensed to practice medicine. The president ignored the decision and ordered the

---

861   Inter-American Commission on Human Rights, *2009 Annual Report*, para. 476, available at http://www.cidh.oas.org/annualrep/ 2009eng/Chap.IV.f.eng.htm.

862   See, in general, Antonio Canova González, Luis Alfonso Herrera Orellana, and Karina Anzola Spadaro, *Expropiaciones o vías de hecho? (La degradación continuada del derecho fundamental de propiedad en la Venezuela actual)*, Funeda, Universidad Católica Andrés Bello, Caracas 2009.

863   On the facts surrounding the resignation of the president Chávez on Apr. 11, 2002, see Allan R. Brewer-Carías, *La crisis de la democracia venezolana. La Carta Democrática Interamericana y los sucesos de abril de 2002*, Los Libros de El Nacional, Colección Ares, Caracas 2002, pp. 63ff.

864   See "Ex comisarios Simonovis, Forero y Vivas sentenciados a 30 años de prisión," Apr. 3, 2009. See http://www.globovision.com/news.php?nid=113766 and http://www.vtv.gov.ve/ noticias-nacionales/16500.

865   The Inter-American Commission on Human Rights, in its *2009 Annual Report*, observed "that in Venezuela judges and prosecutors do not enjoy the guaranteed tenure necessary to ensure their independence following changes in policies or government. Also, in addition to being freely appointed and removable, a series of provisions have been enacted that allow a high level of subjectivity in judging judicial officials' actions during disciplinary proceedings," para 480. See http://www.cidh.oas.org/annualrep/2009eng/Chap.IV.f.eng.htm.

dismissal of those judges without due process. After a decision of the Inter-American Court of Human Rights was issued in 2008 condemning the state for violating the dismissed judges' judicial guarantees, in 2008, the state considered the decisions of that court unenforceable in Venezuela.[866]

But the violation of due process also has occurred in past years through a systematic process of criminalizing dissidence, in which the government uses criminal prosecution and processes to persecute persons in opposition to the government.[867] In this regard, the Inter-American Court has already condemned the state for such violations, as in the 2009 case of a former minister of finance of Chávez's government who defected from government ranks once the president resigned in April 2002.[868] Afterward, he was condemned for insulting the armed forces when he explained on television how a flamethrower functions; a fact for which the Venezuelan state was condemned in 2009 by the Inter-American Court of Human Rights, for violation of his rights.[869]

In all cases in which judicial processes have been used to criminalize dissidence, the government has used the tools of the Public Prosecutor's Office to persecute elected opposition leaders, governors and mayors, opposition presidential candidates, and even former ministers and supporters of the government – in many cases, they have been detained and condemned (Case: *Baduel* – Former Minister of Defense-) or forced to leave the country (Case: *Peña* – Former Mayor of Caracas; Case: *Rosales* – Former Governor of Zulia state; Case: *Lapi* – Former Governor of Yaracuy state). In other cases, the docile and manageable public prosecutor has been used by the government to persecute entrepreneurial leaders not aligned with official policies (Case: *Anderson*). The most outrageous and scandalous case was that of a criminal judge (Case: *María Lourdes Afiuni Mora*) who, in 2009, and after recommendations by an independent panel of the United Nations on arbitrary detention, ordered the release from preventive prison (after more than two years without trial) of a businessman accused of financial crimes, to be prosecuted in freedom. The president ordered the judge to be imprisoned, violating all of his constitutional guarantees.[870]

---

866   See Decision N° 1.939 (Dec. 18, 2009) (Case *Gustavo Álvarez Arias y otros*), in http://www.tsj.gov.ve/decisiones/scon/Diciembre/1939-181208-2008-08-1572.html.

867   See Inter-American Commission on Human Rights, *2009 Annual Report*, para. 475. See http://www.cidh.oas.org/annualrep/ 2009eng/Chap.IV.f.eng.htm.

868   On the resignation of president Chávez on Apr. 11, 2002, see Allan R. Brewer-Carías, *La crisis de la democracia venezolana. La Carta Democrática Interamericana y los sucesos de abril de 2002,* Los Libros de El Nacional, Colección Aries, Caracas 2002, 63ff; Humberto de la Calle, *El día que Chávez renunció. El golpe en la intimidad de la OEA*, Ediciones B, Bogotá 2008.

869   Decision of Nov. 20, 2009, Case *Usón Ramírez vs. Venezuela*, available at http://www.corteidh.or.cr/ docs/casos/articulos/seriec_207_esp.pdf.

870   See http://www.unog.ch/unog/website/news_media.nsf/%28httpNewsByYear_en%29/ 93687E8429-BD53A1C125768E00529DB6?OpenDocument&cntxt=B35C3&cookielang=fr. Also http://www.union-radio.net/ Actualidad/#&&NewsId=35473.

V. ACCESS TO POWER AND ITS EXERCISE CONTRARY TO THE RULE OF LAW

The second essential element of democracy according to the Inter-American Democratic Charter is access to and exercises of power in accordance with the rule of law. This implies that for democracy to exist, access to power must be in line with prescribed constitutional rules; furthermore, power must be exercised in accordance with the rule of law. There is no democracy without respect for the Constitution.

The first violation to the rule of law in the past decade was in 1999, by means of convening the Constituent Assembly in violation of the provisions of the 1961 Constitution. That process was completely controlled by Chávez's supporters, which excluded all other political actors from participating, leading to a constituent coup d'état. The Constituent Assembly assumed all state powers without any authority from the people and even issued transitional constitutional provisions without power to do so. Ex post facto, the same Supreme Tribunal of Justice appointed in the transitory constitutional regime, and challenged on the grounds of its unconstitutionality, ruled in 2000 that the Constituent Assembly had supraconstitutional powers and accepted two constitutional provisions: one approved by the people and the other not. It thus prolonged *sine die* the existence of the transitory and malleable constitutional regime. The fact is that, as mentioned by the Inter-American Commission on Human Rights in its *2009 Annual Report*, for instance, "even though the 1999 Constitution states that legislation governing the judicial system is to be enacted within the first year following the installation of the National Assembly, a decade later the Transitional Government Regime, created to allow the Constitution to come into immediate effect, remains in force."[871]

This regime was also the main tool that allowed the access to power in violation of the Constitution and the rule of law. In effect, in December 1999, the Constituent Assembly dismissed elected and unelected officials of the state and appointed, transitionally, new public servants, without complying with the Constitution. The Supreme Tribunal of Justice in 2001 extended the constitutional term of the president to allow "reelection" according to the provisions of the new Constitution[872]; and the transitory National Legislative Commission, exercising legislative powers without any constitutional authorization, appointed members of the National Electoral Council without following constitutional procedure. In 2000, the newly elected National Assembly, to nominate and appoint head officials, sanctioned a "special law" to regulate appointment for the first constitutional term, without complying with the constitutional provisions. The people's defender challenged the special law before the Supreme Tribunal. The judicial action was never decided; the people's defender and transitional magistrates were ratified in their positions. Later in 2002, members of the National Electoral Council were appointed by the Constitutional Chamber of the Supreme Tribunal, thus bypassing

---

871 See Inter-American Commission on Human Rights, *2009 Annual Report*, para. 481. See http://www.cidh.oas.org/annualrep/ 2009eng/Chap.IV.f.eng.htm.

872 The decision was adopted according to the public request formulated by the president. On Decision N° 457 (Apr. 5, 2001), see Allan R. Brewer-Carías, "Formas constitucionales de terminación del mandato del Presidente de la República," *Revista Primicia* No. 199, Caracas 2001, p. 2.

some constitutional provisions and violating others. In the same year, the Constitutional Chamber appointed the deputy prosecutor general, an appointment that corresponded to the National Assembly.

The result of all this is that, yes, many electoral processes have taken place to elect the president; governors; mayors; and members of the National Assembly, regional councils, and municipal councils. Nonetheless, access to power in accordance with the rule of law has been openly violated in other cases, particularly those of the organs of the citizens' power, electoral power, and judicial power. There, the provisions of the Constitution were set aside, and so it is that the executive completely controls all branches of government.

This situation, together with others facts observed by the Inter-American Commission on Human Rights in 2002, led it to point out the necessity of strengthening the rule of law in the country in its Preliminary Observations:

> 17.   The IACHR considers that the lack of independence of the Judiciary, the limitations on freedom of expression, the proclivity of the Armed Forces to engage in politics, the extreme polarization of society, the action of the death squads, the scant credibility of the oversight institutions due to the uncertainty surrounding the constitutionality of their designation and the partiality of their actions, and the lack of coordination among the security forces, represent a clear weakness of the basic elements of the rule of law in a democracy, in the terms of the American Convention and the Inter-American Democratic Charter. Accordingly, the Commission calls for the rule of law to be strengthened in Venezuela as soon as possible.[873]

But the second essential element of democracy defined in the Inter-American Democratic Charter not only imposes the need for a political system to ensure the access to power in accordance with the rule of law but also expressly prescribes the need for its exercise to be in accordance with the rule of law. When government violates the Constitution and legal order, or defrauds the Constitution, it violates the rule of law and it violates democracy. During the past decade, this has been the pattern of conduct of the authoritarian government of Venezuela.

In the legislative branch, during the past decade, particularly when representatives backing the government did not control a majority of votes, the interior regulations of the assembly were openly manipulated and reformed in 2003 and 2004 to allow the incorporation of deputies without formal requirements and to allow the assembly to annul its own previous decisions by simple majority. Sessions of the assembly were held outside the parliament official headquarters, in public spaces, to prevent the participation of opposition representatives because of violent threats from so-called Bolivarian circles. The provision of the Constitution guaranteeing representatives their right to vote according to their conscience has never been enforced, and never during the past decade have representatives been accountable to their constituency, as provided for in the Constitution.

---

873   See Allan R. Brewer-Carías, *La crisis de la democracia venezolana. La Carta Democrática Interamericana y los sucesos de abril de 2002,* Los Libros de El Nacional, Colección Ares, Caracas 2002.

Many Organic Laws were sanctioned by the National Assembly without complying with the need for a qualified majority to begin discussions, a procedure that the Constitutional Chamber of the Supreme Tribunal supported in 2004. That same year, it sanctioned the Organic Law of the Supreme Tribunal, which allowed the National Assembly to dismiss the tribunal's magistrates by simple majority vote. That is why in its *2009 Annual Report*, the Inter-American Commission on Human Rights has reiterated that "the rules for the appointment, removal, and suspension of magistrates set out in the Organic Law of the Supreme Court of Justice lack the safeguards necessary to prevent other branches of government from undermining the Supreme Court's independence and to keep narrow or temporary majorities from determining its composition."[874]

The National Assembly has renounced its basic function of legislating. In 2001, by sanctioning an enabling law, it delegated the legislative function to the president, who has since enacted all basic statutes through decree laws. The same occurred in 2007. Through such legislative delegations, the executive has violated the principle of the legislative reserve – that the Constitution place in the National Assembly certain legislative power that cannot be delegated, such as human rights, taxation, and criminal provisions. The 2007 delegation was the worst – it authorized the executive to legislate on matters that needed the approval of constitutional reform. The people rejected the 2007 draft constitutional reforms; nonetheless, the president issued decree laws implementing the reforms, thereby defrauding the will of the people.[875]

Also, special reference must be made to the role of the Constitutional Chamber as "positive legislator" by means of constitutional interpretation. In many cases, the Constitutional Chamber has openly issued legislation, as when reforming the procedural rules regarding *amparo*[876]; when it decided an action of unconstitutionality of various articles of the Income Law, it reformed ex officio one article that was not even challenged.[877] By means of a recourse for the abstract interpretation of the Constitution, the Constitutional Chamber has illegitimately reformed the Constitution, changing the meaning of its provisions and, in some cases, even implementing through judicial means the rejected constitutional reforms.[878]

---

874   See Inter-American Commission on Human Rights, *2009 Annual Report*, para. 478. See http://www.cidh.oas.org/annualrep/ 2009eng/Chap.IV.f.eng.htm.

875   On these decree laws, see the articles published in *Revista de Derecho Público* 115 *(Estudios sobre los decretos leyes 2008)*, Editorial Jurídica Venezolana, Caracas 2008.

876   See Allan R. Brewer-Carías, "El juez constitucional como legislador positivo y la inconstitucional reforma de la Ley Orgánica de Amparo mediante sentencias interpretativas," in *La ciencia del derecho procesal constitucional. Estudios en homenaje a Héctor Fix-Zamudio en sus cincuenta años como investigador del derecho*, coords. Eduardo Ferrer Mac-Gregor and Arturo Zaldívar Lelo de Larrea, Instituto de Investigaciones Jurídicas, Universidad Nacional Autónoma de México, Mexico City 2008, Vol. 5: pp. 63-80.

877   See Allan R. Brewer-Carías, "El juez constitucional en Venezuela como legislador positivo de oficio en materia tributaria," in *Revista de Derecho Público* No. 109, Editorial Jurídica Venezolana, Caracas 2007, pp. 193-212.

878   See Allan R. Brewer-Carías, "La fraudulenta mutación de la Constitución en Venezuela, o de cómo el juez constitucional usurpa el poder constituyente originario," *Anuario de Derecho Público No. 2*, Cen-

VI. BROKEN REPRESENTATIVE DEMOCRACY

Another essential element of democracy according to the Inter-American Democratic Charter is periodic, free, and fair elections based on secret balloting and universal suffrage as an expression of the sovereignty of the people. Therefore, elections are essential in representative democracy, and the impartiality and independence of the organ of electoral control are essential to its effectiveness and the fair character of the elections.

The 1999 Constitution makes the electoral power one of the branches of government with due autonomy and independence, in which no political party can have any sort of participation – also, citizens' participation must be guaranteed. This electoral body must function according to the principles of decentralized electoral administration, transparency, speed of balloting, and scrutiny (Article 294).

Nonetheless, in 1999–2000, members of the National Electoral Council were appointed transitionally, first by the National Constituent Assembly and later by the National Legislative Commission, in violation of Article 295 of the Constitution. This regime violated the Constitution by infringing on the autonomy of the electoral branch.

In 2002, after the sanctioning of the Organic Law of the Electoral Power, the National Assembly was due to appoint members of the National Electoral Council, but the Assembly failed to do so because representatives supporting the government could not achieve the two-thirds majority required for appointments and did not want to agree on the matter with the opposition. The consequence of this legislative omission was that the Constitutional Chamber of the Supreme Tribunal of Justice, when deciding an action filed against it, directly appointed members of the Electoral Council, without complying with conditions in the Constitution. Again in 2009, appointments did not respect the constitutional prohibition on electing members with party affiliation.[879]

---

tro de Estudios de Derecho Público de la Universidad e Monteávila, Caracas 2009, pp. 23-65; "El juez constitucional al servicio del autoritarismo y la ilegítima mutación de la Constitución: El caso de la Sala Constitucional del Tribunal Supremo de Justicia de Venezuela (1999-2009)," *IUSTEL, Revista General de Derecho Administrativo* No. 21, Madrid 2009; "La ilegitima mutación de la Constitución y la legitimidad de la jurisdicción constitucional: La 'reforma' de la forma federal del estado en Venezuela mediante interpretación constitucional," in *Memoria del X Congreso Iberoamericano de Derecho Constitucional,* Instituto Iberoamericano de Derecho Constitucional, Asociación Peruana de Derecho Constitucional, Instituto de Investigaciones Jurídicas-UNAM y Maestría en Derecho Constitucional-PUCP, IDEMSA, Lima 2009, Vol 1, pp. 29-51; "El juez constitucional como constituyente: el caso del financiamiento de las campañas electorales de los partidos políticos en Venezuela," *Revista de Derecho Público* 117, Caracas 2009, pp. 195-203.

879   See Decisions N° 2073 (Aug. 4, 2003) (Caso: *Hermánn Escarrá Malaver y oros*) and N° 2341 (Aug. 25, 2003) (Caso: *Hermánn Escarrá M. y otros*), in Allan R. Brewer-Carías, *La Sala Constitucional versus el estado democrático de derecho. El secuestro del poder electoral y de la Sala Electoral del Tribunal Supremo y la confiscación del derecho a la participación política,* Los Libros de El Nacional, Colección Ares, Caracas 2004, p. 172; "El secuestro del poder electoral y la confiscación del derecho a la participación política mediante el referendo revocatorio presidencial: Venezuela 2000-2004," *Boletín Mexicano de Derecho Comparado* No. 112, Instituto de Investigaciones Jurídicas, Universidad Nacional Autónoma de México, Mexico City 2005, pp. 11-73; Rafael Chavero G. et al., *La guerra de las salas del TSJ frente al referéndum revocatorio,* Editorial Aequitas, Caracas 2004, pp. 13-58.

The foregoing has served to weaken progressively representative democracy in Venezuela – the elections are directed by an organ in which civil society and most political parties have no confidence. In 2002, again, the Inter-American Commission on Human Rights, on its last visit to the country, pointed out the following regarding the composition of the National Electoral Council:

> 51.   The organs of public power with jurisdiction to settle claims regarding the transparency and legality of elections should be endowed with the utmost impartiality, and should resolve such matters fairly and promptly, as the best way to ensure the effective exercise of the right to elect and be elected established in Article 23 of the American Convention. Accordingly, the Commission recommends that the full and definitive composition of the National Electoral Council proceed as regulated in the Constitution.[880]

VII. WEAKENED DEMOCRACY DUE TO THE ABSENCE OF PLURALISM

The fourth essential element of representative democracy is a pluralistic system of political parties and organizations, for which the strengthening of political parties and other political organizations is a priority (Article 5). Political pluralism is opposed to all ideas of concentrated power and political organization of society promoted by the state or from the state.

Thus, a plural democratic regime is always opposed to state power. In it, parties and political organizations try to be outside the sphere of the state and its influence so individuals and social groups can freely develop. Pluralism, furthermore, ought to ensure free elections, government alternation, political participation, and power decentralization. A plural regime of parties and political organizations is the antidote to authoritarianism.

Political pluralism, therefore, implies the need for the democratic existence of a multiplicity of political groups, parties, and organizations, outside the reach of the state. The Constitution in several provisions refers to associations or organizations with political purposes (Article 67), to organizations of civil society (Articles 293.6 and 296), and to organized society (Article 211). In contrast, the Constitution grants the electoral power interference in the organizations of civil society through the power to organize the internal elections not only of trade unions and professional groups but also of organizations with political purposes (Article 293.6). This, in itself, is a step back for political pluralism and an inconvenient transformation of social organizations into part of the state.

Social groups outside the ambit of state power guarantee political pluralism as an essential element of democracy. Thus, the Constitution bestows on public officers the obligation to be "at the service of the state and not at the service of any party" (Article 145), to clearly separate the political organization of the society (the state) from the organized groups of society (parties and organizations of civil society),

---

880   See Allan R. Brewer-Carías, *La crisis de la democracia venezolana. La Carta Democrática Interamericana y los sucesos de abril de 2002,* Los Libros de El Nacional, Colección Ares, Caracas 2002, p. 164.

preventing in the Constitution, even though inconvenient and contrary to the provisions of the Democratic Charter (Article 5), the financing of the associations with political purposes with funds from the state (Article 67). This constitutional prohibition was "reformed" in 2008 by the Constitutional Chamber, which allowed public financing of electoral activities.[881]

In Venezuela, political pluralism has been severely harmed by the integration of the government party into the state in a way never known before in Venezuelan political history. The United Socialist Party has been created from within the state, and with public funds, and its authorities are the officials of the state. The president has been president of the government party and the ministers have been directors of the same.[882] The state, therefore, is at the service of the official government party, and the latter is at the service of the state. Other political organizations and parties different from that of the government have been discriminated against – and now the official party could receive all the public financing.

The integration of the government party into the state has provoked the complete inapplicability of all constitutional rules regarding civil service, for instance, appointment of officers only by means of public competition and their stability. In the imbricate grid between state and party, the appointments of public servants are discretionary, as is their dismissal. Public Administration, having been cleansed, is the exclusive "booty" of the government party.[883] Consequently, the new public service comprises exclusively members of the government party or those who support its policies.

During the past decade, the state has tried to politically organize society. At the beginning, this was carried out through so-called Bolivarian circles, groups that were the antithesis of pluralism because of their full dependence of the organs of power. They were used for political purposes, threatening and violently attacking institutions, organizations, or persons not supporting the government. They have acted as shock troops to verbally and physically assault those identified as enemies of the political process, particularly leaders of the opposition, including members of the National Assembly and municipal authorities, journalists and communicators, and social leaders, especially in the trade union and university movements. In his report to the general assembly of the Organization of American States, the secretary-general of that organization said: "The Bolivarian Circles are groups of citizens or grassroots organizations who support the President's political platform. Many sectors consider them responsible for the human rights violations, acts of

---

881 See the Constitutional Chamber Decision N° 780 (May 8, 2008), in *Revista de Derecho Público No.* 114, Caracas 2008, pp. 127ff. See Allan R. Brewer-Carías, "El juez constitucional como constituyente: El caso del financiamiento de las campañas electorales de los partidos políticos en Venezuela," in *Revista de Derecho Público* N° 117, Caracas 2009, pp. 195-203.

882 Since the beginning of the Chávez government, the "political command of the revolution" was establis-hed by the president with officials of the state. See *El Nacional,* Caracas Nov. 11, 2001, D-4, and Jan. 20, 2002, D-6. See Angela Zago, Felipe Mújica, and Pablo Medina, *El Nacional,* Caracas Jan. 20, 2002, p. H-1.

883 In 2002, the head of the "political command of the revolution," Guillermo García Ponce, announced the definitive cleansing of public administration to sack all civil servants "not identified politically with the process." See *El Nacional,* Caracas Jan. 22, 2002, p. D-1.

intimidation, and looting." The secretary-general added: "The state, and let there be no doubt about this, must retain a monopoly on the legitimate use of force. The accusations that certain sectors are jeopardizing the legitimate use of force must be investigated. In all cases, any use of force must occur under authorization and within the normative framework to which the military adheres."[884]

The Inter-American Commission on Human Rights asserted also in 2002: "The international responsibility of the State is triggered if groups of civilians act freely violating rights, with the support or acquiescence of the Government. Accordingly, the Commission called on the Government to investigate seriously the acts of violence attributed to some 'Bolivarian Circles,' and to take, as urgently as possible, all measures necessary to prevent these acts from recurring. In particular, it is essential that the monopoly of force be maintained exclusively by the public security forces; complete disarmament of any group of civilians should immediately be guaranteed."[885]

These Bolivarian circles, informally created by the government to attack any opposition institution, have lost their protagonist role – many have remained "institutionalized" in certain urban sectors as instruments for political control of the population; many of them are armed by the government and remain at its disposal.

The interference of the state in trade unions must be highlighted, as well, and even the interference of the president himself in their elections, such as by ignoring their results or promoting a government candidate to the Venezuelan Confederation of Workers.[886]

The Inter-American Commission on Human Rights in 2002 gave a particular treatment to the subject of the right to form and join trade unions in the country as well. In a May 2002 press release, stressing that it was informed "that once the elections were held, in keeping with the rules of the National Electoral Council, the elected directors of the union federation (*Confederación de Trabajadores de Venezuela CTV*) were not recognized by the national authorities," urging "Venezuelan State to resolve as soon as possible, and in keeping with Venezuela's international obligations, the conflict that came about due to the failure of the authorities to recognize the freely elected authorities of the CTV.[887]

Sadly, since 2000, the Supreme Tribunal of Justice has been in charge of regimenting and distorting the organizations of civil society, as when it denied that members of the Catholic Church be "representatives" of society[888]; when it excluded

---

884   See Allan R. Brewer-Carías, *La crisis de la democracia en Venezuela*, Libros El Nacional, Caracas 2002, p. 168.

885   Paras. 57-58. See Allan R. Brewer-Carías, *La crisis de la democracia venezolana. La Carta Democrática Interamericana y los sucesos de abril de 2002*, Los Libros de El Nacional, Colección Ares, Caracas 2002, p. 170.

886   See *El Nacional*, Caracas Jan. 8, 2002, p. D-1; *El Nacional*, Caracas Sept. 3, 2001, p. p. D-1.

887   See Allan R. Brewer-Carías, *La crisis de la democracia venezolana. La Carta Democrática Interamericana y los sucesos de abril de 2002*, Los Libros de El Nacional, Colección Ares, Caracas 2002, pp. 171-172.

888   See *El Nacional*, Caracas Nov. 24, 2000, p. D-1; *El Universal*, Caracas Sept. 18, 2000, 1-4. See Liliana Ortega, *El Nacional*, Caracas Nov. 27, 2000, p. D-4; and references to the tribunal decisions in Pedro

from the concept of civil society the associations, groups, and institutions that receive foreign financial help (as from international solidarity); and has said that whoever acts on behalf of a social organization shall do so "elected by someone to fulfill such representation."[889] Political pluralism, as an essential element of democracy, has been seriously threatened in Venezuela by the State power.

VIII. VANISHING DEMOCRACY AND ABSENT SEPARATION OF POWERS

The fifth essential element of representative democracy according to the Inter-American Democratic Charter is separation and independence of branches of government: checks and balances.

With no institutional control of power, democracy could not exist: only by controlling state power can respect for human rights and fundamental freedoms exist; only by controlling state power can the rule of law be achieved; only by controlling state power can periodic, free, and fair elections be held; and only by controlling state power can a plural regime of parties and political organizations exist. Without separation and independence of all branches of government, vertically and horizontal, there is no effective democracy.

The 1999 Constitution provides a double distribution (separation and independence) of branches of government and state powers. The vertical distribution establishes that the public power is distributed among municipalities, states, and the national government, each with political autonomy. The horizontal distribution is made across five branches – legislative, executive, judicial, citizen, and electoral – each with independence and autonomy (Article 136).

From the horizontal point of view, as has been highlighted throughout this book, separation of powers has progressively vanished as a fundamental principle of the constitutional state, to the point that in December 2009, the president of the Supreme Tribunal of Justice proposed a final reform of the 1999 Constitution to definitively eliminate the principle of separation of powers that she considered "debilitates the State" and one of the aspects of the Constitution that contradicts the implementation of "the regime."[890] Unfortunately, it has been precisely because of this, that control on the exercise of state power has disappeared[891] and, in particular, that the Judiciary has been progressively subjected to the executive for the purpose of assuring the support of the "regime." That is why, for instance, in 2010 the

Nikken, "El Tribunal Supremo de Justicia ¿Juez o parte?," in Allan R. Brewer-Carías et al., *La libertad de expresión amenazada. Sentencia 1.013*, Instituto Interamericano de Derechos Humanos, Editorial Jurídica Venezolana, Caracas 2001, pp. 130 ff.

889   See the comments on the Supreme Tribunal decisions in Allan R. Brewer-Carías, *Derecho Administrativo*, Universidad Externado de Colombia, Bogotá 2005, Vol 1, pp. 413ff.

890   See Juan Francisco Alonso on the statement of Luisa Estela Morales, "Morales: 'La división de poderes debilita al estado.' La presidenta del TSJ afirma que la Constitución hay que reformarla," *El Universal*, Caracas Dec. 5, 2009. See the entire text of the statement of the president of the Supreme Tribunal at http://www.tsj.gov.ve/informacion/notasde prensa/notasdeprensa.asp?codigo=7342.

891   See Allan R. Brewer-Carías, *Constitución, democracia y control del poder*, Centro Iberoamericano de Estudios Provinciales y Locales, Universidad de Los Andes/Editorial Jurídica Venezolana. Mérida, octubre 2004.

constitutional provision establishing disciplinary jurisdiction for judges (Article 267) is not in force. The provisional status of judges has been the common trend of the judiciary and with it, unfortunately, the break in their autonomy and independence. In this regard, the Inter-American Commission on Human Rights in its *2009 Annual Report* noted "with concern the failure to organize public competitions for selecting judges and prosecutors, and so those judicial officials are still appointed in a discretionary fashion without being subject to competition. Since they are not appointed through public competitions, judges and prosecutors are freely appointed and removable, which seriously affects their independence in making decisions"; observing, in addition, that "in Venezuela judges and prosecutors do not enjoy the guaranteed tenure necessary to ensure their independence following changes in policies or government."[892]

This situation has led during the past decade to the long-standing problem of a Judiciary mainly composed by provisional judges, a situation that has a negative impact on the stability, independence, and autonomy that should govern the Judiciary. This situation has been raised with concern since 2002 by the Inter-American Commission on Human Rights in all its *Annual Reports* on the situation of human rights in Venezuela,[893] having expressed in its Preliminary Observations issued in its last visit to the country that "the problem of provisional judges has become more severe and more widespread since the current administration began the process of restructuring the Judiciary."[894]

Unfortunately, none of those recommendations have been implemented, and the commission continued to make those observations through 2009. The procedure established in the Constitution to appoint judges through public competition has not yet been implemented, and the disciplinary jurisdiction to guarantee judges' stability did not yet exist in 2010. The Supreme Tribunal has continued to accept their discretionary dismissal.

The final expression of the absolute lack of judges' autonomy and stability occurred in December 2009, when a criminal judge (María Lourdes Afiuni Mora) ordered the conditional release pending trial of a detainee whose detention was declared arbitrary by the UN Working Group on Arbitrary Detention. That same day, the judge was incarcerated together with the court clerks, without any disciplinary procedure or intervention of the Judicial Commission of the Supreme Tribunal. The president publicly asked to apply a thirty-year prison term to the judge, the maximum punishment established in the Constitution for horrendous or grave crimes.[895] In Venezuela, no judge can adopt any decision that could affect the

---

892 See IACHR, *2009 Annual Report*, para. 479-480. See http://www.cidh.oas.org/annualrep/
2009eng/Chap.IV.f.eng.htm.

893 See Allan R. Brewer-Carías, *La crisis de la democracia venezolana. La Carta Democrática Interamericana y los sucesos de abril de 2002*, Los Libros de El Nacional, Colección Ares, Caracas 2002, p. 180.

894 *Id.*

895 On Dec. 16, 2009 a panel of three independent UN human rights experts (chair-rapporteur of the Working Group on Arbitrary Detention, El Hadji Malick Sow; special rapporteur on the independence of
judges and lawyers, Gabriela Carina Knaul de Albuquerque e Silva; and special rapporteur on the situation of human rights defenders, Margaret Sekaggya) said they were deeply disturbed about a controversial detention of Judge Maria Lourdes Afiuni in Venezuela and the court clerks, which they described as

president's wishes, the state's interest, or public servants' will without previous authorization. That is why the Inter-American Commission on Human Rights, after describing in its *2009 Annual Report* "how large numbers of judges have been removed or their appointments voided without the applicable administrative proceedings," it noted "with concern that in some cases, judges were removed almost immediately after adopting judicial decisions in cases with a major political impact," concluding that "The lack of judicial independence and autonomy vis-à-vis political power is, in the IACHR's opinion, one of the weakest points in Venezuelan democracy."[896]

In this situation, there is no way for the judiciary to effectively control actions of the executive or for any separation of power principle.

In the citizens' branch of government, the situation has been not less dramatic. The comptroller general has not acted as a comptroller; unfortunately, Venezuela has ranked one of the most corrupt governments in the contemporary world.[897] In a whole decade, there has been no administrative procedure to persecute government corruption. The only procedures that have been decided are minor cases related to former public servants, now in the opposition, to disqualify them as candidates in elections.[898]

As for the people's defender, since 2000, the position has been occupied by persons attached to the executive, so the worst cases of constitutional rights violations have received little attention from that office: police death squads, rights violations, discrimination, attacks on freedoms. The international control organs needed to act because of the absence of action by the office, despite the wide range of faculties it has in the Constitution (Article 281).

Vertical distribution is a consequence of the theoretically decentralized state as federation (Article 4, Constitution), in which to deepen democracy, power is close to

---

"a blow by President Hugo Chávez to the independence of judges and lawyers in the country," demanding the immediate freedom of the judge. In a television and radio program, Chávez openly instructed the attorney general and the president of the Supreme Court to punish Afiuni as severely as possible to prevent similar actions by other judges. He also suggested that defense attorneys in the case had engaged in criminal conduct in requesting the release of the detained person, and the attorney general gave interviews to the press slandering the judge. The experts concluded that "reprisals for exercising their constitutionally guaranteed functions and creating a climate of fear among the judiciary and lawyers' profession serve no purpose except to undermine the rule of law and obstruct justice." Available at http://www.unog.ch/unog/website/
news_media.nsf/%28httpNewsByYear_en%29/93687E8429BD53A1C125768E00529DB6?OpenDocu ment&cntxt=B35C3&cookielang=fr.   Also   available   at   http://www.unionradio.net/Actuali-dad/#&&NewsId=35473.

896   See Inter-American Commission on Human Rights, *2009 Annual Report*, para. 483. See http://www.cidh.oas.org/annualrep/ 2009eng/Chap.IV.f.eng.htm. The same problem was highlighted by the Commission in its Preliminary Observations of 2002, Paras. 30-33. See Allan R. Brewer-Carías, *La crisis de la democracia venezolana. La Carta Democrática Interamericana y los sucesos de abril de 2002*, Los Libros de El Nacional, Colección Ares, Caracas 2002, 181.

897   See Transparency International, *2009 Global Corruption Barometer*, http://www.trans-parency.org/policy_research/surveys_indices/gcb/2009.

898   See Inter-American Commission on Human Rights, *2009 Annual Report*, para. 473. See http://www.cidh.oas.org/annualrep/ 2009eng/Chap.IV.f.eng.htm.

citizens and there are conditions both to exercise democracy and to render effectively states' purposes (Article 158, Constitution). Political decentralization is essential to participatory democracy; participation in managing public affairs is possible only when power is close to citizens, which in democratized societies, manifes in primary political organizations like the municipalities.

Unfortunately, Venezuela has suffered a process of centralization and concentration of resources and public competencies at the national level to the detriment of the autonomy of states and municipalities, the latter being conceived as political instances organized very far from the citizenship. The 1999 Constitution, in this regard, is contradictory – at the same time it exalted decentralization and define municipalities as the primary unit in the state organizatrion, it reduced autonomy of states and municipalities and even nationalized the regulation and the organization of the legislative councils. Moreover, centralization doomed the states financially, and national organs now manage funds related to all taxes, including consumers tax. In this regard, democracy as political regime has moved backward.

One of the last events of centralization was in 2008: the illegitimate distortion of the Constitution by the Constitutional Chamber of the Supreme Tribunal, which nationalized administration of national highways, ports, and airports – an exclusive attribution to states in the Constitution.[899] This provoked, in 2009, reform by the National Assembly of the Organic Law of Decentralization to revert competencies transferred to the states since 1989. The National Assembly also sanctioned the Law on the Special Regime of the Capital District, contrary to the express provisions of the Constitution and to the will expressed by the people in the 2007 referendum.[900]

IX. DEMOCRACY AND PROBLEMS OF TRANSPARENCY

The Inter-American Democratic Charter also establishes as a fundamental component of democracy transparency in government activities, probity, responsible public administration, respect for social rights, and freedom of expression and of the press (Article 4). Unfortunately, all of these components have a negative balance in Venezuela.

Among components of the exercise of democracy, transparency in government activities is fundamental – the government must act in an open, frank, and confident way, subject to scrutiny. Hidden government activities are contrary to transparency.

During the past decade, the government has not been transparent, and access to public information has not been guaranteed. On the contrary, openness and transparency has been substituted with secrecy and hidden work, as with decree laws whose text was known only after publication in the *Gaceta Oficial*. Political and

---

899 See Allan R. Brewer-Carías, "La ilegitima mutación de la Constitución y la legitimidad de la jurisdicción constitucional: La 'reforma' de la forma federal del estado en Venezuela mediante interpretación constitucional," in *Memoria del X Congreso Iberoamericano de Derecho Constitucional,* Instituto Iberoamericano de Derecho Constitucional, Asociación Peruana de Derecho Constitucional, Instituto de Investigaciones Jurídicas-UNAM y Maestría en Derecho Constitucional-PUCP, IDEMSA, Lima 2009, vol. 1, pp. 29-51.

900 See comments on this law in Allan R. Brewer-Carías et al., *Ley Orgánica del Distrito Capital,* Editorial Jurídica Venezolana, Caracas 2009.

civil society organizations were greatly discriminated against in this process, which has not respected the constitutional requirement of public consultation.

Additionally, signs of severe corruption have appeared in the public administration, and Venezuela has been classified as one of the most corrupt governments in the world.[901] With almost unlimited access to state oil revenue, in an economic system of state capitalism, public officers have been creating, promoting, and participating in a new "oligarchy," members of which have amassed extraordinary fortunes in just a few years. This began in 2000 with the uncontrolled execution of government social programs, initially attributed to the military like *Plan Bolívar 2000*, which implied management of great budget resources by the regiments of the armed forces, without control or accountability.[902] Subsequently, for instance, the import and distribution of goods programs developed as a State function, particularly food and consuming goods as a consequence of the reduction of internal production because State intervention or confiscation of industries. This process originated immense fortunes for persons benefiting from favors from the state and its officials. All of these events have been openly occurring during the past years. The result was the explosion in November 2009 of the most outstanding framework of government-related corruption ever seen in the history of Venezuela, which resulted in the dismissal of a minister close to the president.[903] It must be mentioned, in addition, that due to the assumption by the state of the import and distribution of food, during the first months of 2010, more that 120,000 tons of rotten food have been found in ports and official deposits, but nobody has been found responsible.[904]

In a centralized system like the one that has developed under Chávez, in which he claims to know what is going on everywhere, it is hard to believe that he, himself, has not been aware of the situation. The fact is that a new group of oligarchs have developed, called *boliburgeses* or *boligarcas* due to their relation with the Bolivarian revolution[905]; others call them *chaviburgueses* or *chavigarcas*.[906]

---

901   See, on these matters, Mercedes De Freitas, executive director of *Transparencia Venezuela*, http://www.transparency.org/news_room/latest_news/press_releases_nc/2010/2010_05_27_oae_venezu ela_es.

902   On the military intelligence documents regarding Plan Bolívar 2000, see *El Universal*, Caracas Feb. 6, 2002, p. 1-6, and Feb. 7, 2002, p. 1-8; *El Universal*, Caracas Jan. 31, 2002, p. 1-8; *Tal Cual*, Caracas Jan. 31, 2002, p. 5.

903   On Dec. 16, 2009, an opposition member of the National Assembly, former supporter of President Chávez, asked the National Assembly to initiate an investigation related to the possible relation of public officials to the buying and selling and final intervention in ten banks, referring to a "four mafia war" within the government lead by ministers and high officials, indicating that President Chávez "knew all about it." See http://www.reporte360.com/detalle.php?id=19229&c=1.

904   See Maria Teresa Luengo, "Pablo Pérez: Diputados son cómplices de la comida podrida" (Inteview to the Governor of Zulia State), in *El Universal*, Caracas June 22, 2010. Available at http://www.eluniversal.com/2010/06/22/pol_ava_pablo-perez:-diputad_22A4068777.shtml.

905   See "Fall of the Boligarchs," *Economist* 393, Dec. 12, 2009, p. 40.

906   See Teodoro Petkoff, "Chaviburguesía" (editorial), *Tal Cual*, Caracas Dec. 14, 2009.

X. FEEBLE DEMOCRACY AND RESTRICTIONS ON FREEDOMS OF EXPRESSION AND THE PRESS

The other essential component of democracy enumerated in the Inter-American Democratic Charter is freedom of expression and of the press, which in Venezuela has suffered severe attacks from government and in particular from the president.[907] Even the Supreme Tribunal has limited those freedoms, contrary to the Constitution.[908]

There also have been governmental threats and harassment of the media and media directors, particularly after sanctioning of the Telecommunications Law and of the Law on the Social Responsibility of Media.[909] Regarding the provisions of this law dealing with accusations of incitement, the Inter-American Commission on Human Rights in its 2009 Annual Report has stated "that because of their extreme vagueness, the severity of the associated punishments, and the fact that their enforcement is the responsibility of a body that depends directly on the executive branch...may lead to arbitrary decisions that censor or impose a subsequent disproportionate penalty on citizens or the media for simply expressing criticisms or dissent that may be disturbing to public officials temporarily holding office in the enforcement agency."[910] In this regard, the case of the former state governor and opposition leader Oswaldo Álvarez Paz, who was detained in February 2010 for expressing criticisms against government policies, is pathetic. After arbitrarily being detained for a few weeks, he was submitted to prosecution for crimes such as "diffusion of false information" and "hate public instigation."[911]

Regarding freedom of information violations, the Inter-American Court of Human Rights since 2002 has condemned the actions of the state and of groups related to it and has issued protective preliminary measures for television stations

---

907   Since 2002, the president has openly attacked editors and media directors: Andrés Mata, *El Universal*; Alberto Federico Ravell, *Globovisión;* and Miguel Enrique Otero, *El Nacional.* See *El Universal*, Feb. 10, 2002, 1-4. The threats against Globovisión began in Oct. 2001. See the statement by the president of the station, Guillermo Zuloaga, in *El Universal*, Caracas Oct. 29, 2001, p. 1-6. See my comment in *El Nacional*, Caracas Oct. 6, 2001, pp. A-1 and D-2; *El Impulso*, Barquisimeto, Oct. 6, 2001, pp. A-1 and D-6.

908   See *El Nacional*, Caracas June 29, 2001, p. D-2, and Jan. 2, 2002, p. D-1; *El Universal*, Caracas July 23, 2001, 1-4. On Decision No. 1.013 (June 12, 2001), see *El Universal*, Caracas June 15, 2001, p. 1-4; *El Nacional*, Caracas June 15, 2001, p. D-1; June 16, 2001, p. D-4; June 24, 2001, p. H-1; June 23, 2001, p. D-1. On this decision, see Allan R. Brewer-Carías, Héctor Faúndez Ledesma, Pedro Nikken, Carlos M. Ayala Corao, Rafael Chavero Gazdik, Gustavo Linares Benzo, and Jorge Olavarría, *La libertad de expresión amenazada. Sentencia 1.013*, Instituto Interamericano de Derechos Humanos, Editorial Jurídica Venezolana, Caracas 2001.

909   See Allan R. Brewer-Carías et al., *Ley de Responsabilidad Social de Radio y Televisión*, Editorial Jurídica Venezolana, Caracas 2006.

910   See Inter-American Commission on Human Rights, *2009 Annual Report*, para. 489. See http://www.cidh.oas.org/annualrep/ 2009eng/Chap.IV.f.eng.htm.

911   See Rafael Rodríguez, "Tribunal ordena juicio contra Oswaldo Álvarez Paz, (Interview)," in El Universal June 27, 2010. See http://politica.eluniversal.com/2010/05/28/pol_ava_tribunal-ordena-juic_28A-3924891.shtml.

and journalists, which the government has refused to enforce.[912] In general terms, as expressed by the executive secretary of the Inter-American Commission, "the harassment acts against journalist[s] and media have a very grave multiplied effect on the violations against human rights regarding all the people of Venezuela."[913] In its *2009 Annual Report*, the Inter-American Commission noted "that recent months have seen an increase in administrative proceedings sanctioning media that criticize the government," expressing concern that "in several of these cases, the investigations and administrative procedures began after the highest authorities of the State called on public agencies to take action against *Globovisión* and other media outlets that are independent and critical of the government."[914]

One tool for limiting freedom of information that the government, particularly that the president has used, is the systematic, compulsory, and abrupt interruption of programming on private radio and television signals, with long blanket broadcast of statements and political messages from the president.[915] The Inter-American Commission, in its *2009 Annual Report,* has referred to the use by the president of this powers "to broadcast his speeches simultaneously across the media, with no time constraints," expressing that "the duration and frequency of these presidential blanket broadcasts could be considered abusive on account of the information they contain, which might not always be serving the public interest."[916]

---

912   See Carlos Ayala Corao, *El Nacional*, Caracas Jan. 11, 2002, p. D-2; Pedro Nikken, *El Universal*, Caracas Jan. 15, 2002, p. 1-5; Lileana Ortega, *El Nacional*, Caracas Jan. 18, 2002, p. D-1. See also *El Nacional*, Jan. 22, 2002; *El Nacional*, Caracas Jan. 22, 2002, p. D-4. The secretary-general of the Inter-American Commission, Santiago Cantón, compelled the government to execute preliminary measures. See *El Universal*, Feb. 8, 2002, p. 1-4. In Jan. 2002, the Inter-American Commission issued protective measures for the director of *El Universal*, Andrés Mata. See *El Universal*, Caracas Jan. 25, 2002, p. 1-8; *El Nacional*, Caracas Jan. 25, 2002, p. D-6. The premises of *El Universal* were also "visited" by groups supporting the government. See *El Universal*, Caracas Jan. 14, 2002, p. 1-9.

913   See *El Universal*, Caracas Feb. 9, 2002, p. 1-6.

914   See Inter-American Commission on Human Rights, *2009 Annual Report*, para. 486. See http://www.cidh.oas.org/annualrep/ 2009eng/Chap.IV.f.eng.htm.

915   Opposition members of the National Assembly challenged before the Supreme Tribunal Article 209 of the Telecommunications Law that authorizes such blanket broadcasts "considering unconstitutional because "contrary to the right to information." See *El Nacional*, Caracas Feb. 8, 2002, D-6. The executive secretary of the Inter-American Commission on Human Rights considered the use of such blanket broadcast as acceptable only in cases of "extreme necessity to inform public interest matters" and that the president "has used it in an unreasonable way." See *El Nacional*, Caracas Feb. 9, 2002, p. D-4; *El Universal*, Caracas Feb. 10, 2002, p. 1-4.

916   See Inter-American Commission on Human Rights, *2009 Annual Report*, para. 492. See http://www.cidh.oas.org/annualrep/ 2009eng/Chap.IV.f.eng.htm. As reported by Luís Carías, "From 1999 up to Jan. 2010, the president has transmitted 1995 *cadenas* [blanket broadcasts] through radio and TV, which is equal to 1,310 hours, 36 minutes and three seconds, which means almost two months of broadcasts." See Luis Carías, "Mil 995 cadenas ha transmitido Chávez desde que asumió el poder," in *Diario El Carabobeno*, Jan. 28, 2010. Available at http://www.el-carabobeno.com/p_pag_hnot.aspx?art=a280110 e04&id=t280110-e04.

XI. DEMOCRACY AND SUBMISSION OF THE MILITARY TO CIVIL POWER

The Inter-American Democratic Charter states furthermore that the constitutional subordination of all state institutions to civil authority legally constituted is a fundamental component of democracy (Article 4). That points to the subordination of the military to the civilian authority. However, in contrast, in Venezuela, the progressive militarization of the state as a governmental policy has broken that subordination, and the danger of a military party at the service of the president has arisen. This situation, denounced since 2001,[917] has worsened during the past decade, with the military and retired military occupying all high positions in the public administration; and with the military participating in administrative and police functions, or in upholding law and order, considered by the Inter-American Commission on Human Rights as "incompatible with a democratic approach to the defense and security of the State"; considering that "a democratic society demands a clear and precise separation between domestic security, as a function of the police, and national defense, as a function of the armed forces, since the two agencies have substantial differences in the purposes for which they were created and in their training and skills."[918]

The militaristic process of the state peaked in 2008 with the transformation of the armed forces, against the will expressed by the people in the 2007 constitutional reform referendum, into the Bolivarian Armed Force and the Bolivarian Militia at the service of the president.[919] That was the beginning of the consolidation of the "military party"[920] – since 2009, the president has been "president commander" (*comandante presidente*) of the republic.

Also since 2001, the president has encouraged politics within the armed forces, as when justifying the elimination from the Constitution of the prohibition on them being deliberative. That has justified public expressions of generals supporting the president as party chief, not as commander in chief of the armed forces. In addition, a formal compulsory military salute was imposed for use on any occasion by the military: *patria, socialismo o muerte* ("patriotism, socialism, or death").[921]

---

917 See the criticisms by Pablo Medina, as secretary-general of the party Patria para Todos, which used to be part of the coalition of parties supporting the government, saying that what the president wanted was to impose an "authoritarian militarism," in *El Universal,* Caracas Mar. 23, 2000, 1-7; *El Nacional,* Caracas Jan. 12, 2002, D-3; *El Nacional,* Caracas Jan. 15, 2002, p. D-6. See the report *Consultores 21* for *Veneconomía* on the "Militarization of Government," *El Universal,* Caracas Dec. 23, 2001, p. 1-10.

918 See IACHR, *2009 Annual Report,* para. 501. See http://www.cidh.oas.org/annualrep/2009-eng/Chap.IV.f.eng.htm.

919 See Organic Law on the Bolivarian Armed Force, *Gaceta Oficial* No. 5,891 of July 31, 2008; reformed in 2009, *Gaceta Oficial* N° 5.933, Extra., of Oct. 21, 2009.

920 The first signs of the idea of a military party were expressed in 2001, when high officers of the Armed Forces made public a communiqué of adherence to the head of state and his revolution. See *El Nacional* (Caracas), Nov. 8, 2001, D-1, Nov. 9, 2001, D-1; Norberto Ceresole, foreign adviser to the president, considered the communiqué a "legitimate" expression of the "military party." *El Nacional* (Caracas), Nov. 11, 2001, p. D-4.

921 See Alberto Muller Rojas (Military Presidential Chief of Staff), in Reuters, "Venezuelan military adopts Chavez   socialism   slogan,"   *El   Universal,*   Caracas   May   13,   2007,   in

The Inter-American Commission on Human Rights since 2002 expressed its concerns on the "undue influence of the Armed Forces in the political life of the country, and the existence of excessive involvement by the Armed Forces in political decisions" that could be "traced back to the fact that the 1999 Venezuelan Constitution removed a rule traditionally included in the constitutions that preceded it, according to which the Armed Forces are an *'apolitical and non-deliberating'* body." The Commission in its Preliminary Observations issued after its last visit to Venezuela in 2002 remained that "the reality in the region shows that the involvement of the armed forces in politics generally precedes departures from the constitution, which in almost all cases leads to serious human rights violations."[922]

All the aforementioned problems affecting democracy in Venezuela have been provoked by a government that does not believe in representative democracy and that conceives of participatory democracy as a tool to concentrate and centralize power – thus confusing mobilization with participation. This situation has provoked an extreme polarization and has caused bitter, apparently irreconcilable intolerance between the government and the opposition. Much hate has been spread by the president for what is now a long decade in his attempts to impose his so-called Bolivarian revolution and a socialist system, which in 2010 has been officially identified as a Marxist revolution and system, for which nobody has voted – and was indeed rejected by the people in the 2007 constitutional reform referendum – and the majority rejects.[923] That is, most Venezuelans want democracy as a political system with all its fundamental elements and essential components, as defined in the Inter-American Democratic Charter – precisely those that the government has systematically violated and demolished.

Unfortunately, the hate that has been spread by the president has led to the consolidation of irreconcilable extremes and, regrettably, there is only a short pace from hate to violence, particularly with devastating destruction of institutions, worsening economic and social conditions, and increasing poverty.[924]

---

http://www.reuters.com/article/idUSN1142580120070511. On the official slogan of the United Socialist Party of Venezuela: *"Patria socilaista o muerte,"* see its "Declaration of Principles" (Apr. 23, 2010), Available at http://psuv.org.ve/files/tcdocumentos/Declaracion-de-principios-PSUV.pdf

922 See para. 65 in Allan R. Brewer-Carías, *La crisis de la democracia venezolana: La Carta Democrática Interamericana y los sucesos de abril de 2002,* Los Libros de El Nacional, Colección Ares, Caracas 2002, p. 195.

923 According to the results of a poll made by Alfredo Keller y Asociados, Consultoría en Asuntos Públicos, 74% is against elimination of private property; 74% is against expropriation of all private enterprises; 66% is against substitute private property by a social property; 58% is against transforming Venezuela into a socialist country, and 83% is against converting Venezuela into a communist country like Cuba. See *Estudio de Opinión Pública*, 2d, Semester 2010, May 2010, 14.

924 See Francisco Rodríguez, "An Empty Revolution: The Unfulfilled Promises of Hugo Chávez," *Foreign Affairs* 87, http://www.foreignaffairs.com/articles/63220/francisco-rodr%C3%83%C2% ADguez/an-empty-revolution.

The government has made every imaginable effort to provoke a political and social definitive confrontation and to complete its total destruction of the country, its institutions, and what remains of democracy after being progressively dismantled.[925]

---

925 In the 2008 report of Human Rights Watch, the following was the conclusion of its executive summary: "A country's citizens cannot participate fully and equally in its politics when their rights to freedom of expression and association are at risk. Ensuring these essential rights requires more than constitutional guarantees and political rhetoric. It requires institutions that are capable of countering and curbing abusive state practices. Above all, it requires a judiciary that is independent, competent, and credible. It is also critical that non-state institutions – such as the media, organized labor, and civil society – are free from government reprisals and political discrimination. President Chávez has actively sought to project himself as a champion of democracy, not only in Venezuela, but throughout Latin America. Yet his professed commitment to this cause is belied by his government's willful disregard for the institutional guarantees and fundamental rights that make democratic participation possible. Venezuela will not achieve real and sustained progress toward strengthening its democracy – nor will it serve as a useful model for other countries in the region – so long as its government continues to flout the human rights principles enshrined in its own constitution." See Human Rights Watch, *A Decade under Chávez: Political Intolerance and Lost Opportunities for Advancing Human Rights in Venezuela*, Sept. 2008, http://www.hrw.org/reports/2008/venezuela0908/.

TERCERA PARTE

EL ESTADO TOTALITARIO Y LA DEMOLICIÓN DEL ESTADO DEMOCRÁTICO Y SOCIAL DE DERECHO Y DE JUSTICIA, DE ECONOMÍA MIXTA Y DESCENTRALIZADO

Esta Tercera Parte de este Tomo XV de la Colección *Tratado de Derecho Constitucional* es el texto de la Segunda parte del libro *El Estado Totalitariuo y el deprecio a la ley. La desconstitucionalización, desjuridificación, desjudicialización y desdemocratización de Venezuela*, Editorial Jurídica Venezolana, Caracas 2014, pp. 45-165. El texto completo de esta segunda parte fue elaborado con ocasión de la preparación de mi presentación ante *Congreso Internacional Conmemorativo del Acto Legislativo del 10 de septiembre de 1914 por el cual se estableció el Consejo de Estado*, celebrado en Bogotá en la Biblioteca Luis Ángel Arango, los días 8 al 10 de septiembre de 2014, al cual no pude asistir, y fue además presentado a las *XVII Jornadas Centenarias Internacionales. Constitución, Derecho Administrativo y Proceso: Vigencia, reforma e innovación,"* organizadas por el Colegio de Abogados del Estado Carabobo, Instituto de Estudios Jurídicos "Dr. José Ángel Castillo Moreno," Valencia, 6 al 8 de noviembre de 2014.

En la situación actual del Estado venezolano, después de tres lustros de desjuridificación, desjudicialización, desdemocratización y desconstituionalización del Estado Constitucional, lo que tenemos es un Estado Totalitario, que es precisamente la negación del Estado democrático y social de derecho y de justicia, descentralizado y de economía mixta que es el que regula la Constitución de 1999.

Al estudio de ese fenómeno de destrucción de las previsiones constitucionales y en su lugar apuntalar un Estado totalitario es que se dedican las diversas reflexiones que conforman esta parte, formuladas en diversos foros académicos, que se agrupan en las siguientes seis partes, en las que he analizado sucesivamente, luego de una introducción sobre la relación entre el Estado y la Ley (el derecho administrativo y el Estado), el impacto de la conformación de ese Estado totalitario sobre el derecho administrativo que ha conducido paralelamente a: (i) la ausencia de Estado de derecho; (ii) la ausencia de Estado democrático; (iii) la ausencia de Estado Social y de Economía Mixta; (iv) la ausencia de Estado de Justicia; (v) y la ausencia de Estado descentralizado.

Ese marco general de anomia, que se analiza en esas diversas partes y que se enfoca particularmente en los problemas que afectan al derecho administrativo, en todo caso, no hay que olvidarlo, a la vez se enmarca en el cuadro más general del derecho constitucional del Estado, que también ha sido desquiciado es sus componentes más elementales, que son los que conforman su soberanía, y que han afectado a los cuatro componentes esenciales de la misma, que son el territorio, la población, la ley o el derecho y el gobierno.

En cuanto al territorio, durante los últimos quince el gobierno materialmente abandonó en forma total la reclamación frente a Guyana, por el territorio de la Guayana Esequiba, que había sido sometida hace décadas a uno de los mecanismos de solución de controversias de Naciones Unidas.[926]

En cuanto a la población, desde 2004[927] el gobierno ha desarrollado una política irracional o criminal de entrega de la soberanía mediante la concesión sin límites e incontrolada de la nacionalidad venezolana a todo tipo de extranjeros, sin vínculo alguno con el país,[928] e incluso, de los propios sistemas de control del régimen de la identificación de los venezolanos, que se manejan desde el exterior.[929]

En cuanto al derecho aplicable a los asuntos del Estado, en los últimos años, en materia de resolución de conflictos derivados de contratos de interés público, el gobierno ha llegado incluso a renunciar a la cláusula de inmunidad de jurisdicción soberana del Estado, estableciendo en contratos suscritos con empresas chinas, por ejemplo, la renuncia a la aplicación de la propia ley venezolana, sometiendo la solu-

---

926 Sobre el tema, véase entre lo más reciente, el Comunicado del Instituto de Estudios Fronterizos, "Ante la grave situación imperante, en detrimento de la justa reclamación de Venezuela de su territorio Esequibo, birlado por el colonialismo imperial en el nulo e írrito Laudo de París de 1899," Caracas, 5 de julio de 2014, en http://institutodeestudiosfronterizos1.blogspot.com/

927 Sobre el régimen de excepción y el proceso de naturalización indiscriminada en 2004, provocado por motivos electorales en la víspera del referendo revocatorio presidencial, en Allan R. Brewer-Carías, *Régimen legal de la nacionalidad, ciudadanía y extranjería*, Editorial Jurídica Venezolana, Caracas 2005, pp. 24-16.

928 Sobre el tema, la información resumida en 2014 por Moisés Naím: "Las autoridades canadienses han detectado que un importante número de ciudadanos iraníes y de otras nacionalidades vinculados a grupos radicales islámicos han entrado a ese país utilizando pasaportes venezolanos. La organización Centro para una Sociedad Libre Segura –SFS-, estima que entre 2008 y 2012 al menos 173 pasaportes venezolanos fueron entregados a miembros de estos grupos radicales para entrar a América del Norte. De hecho, personas involucradas en varios atentados terroristas en Bulgaria y Líbano, por ejemplo- portaban pasaportes emitidos en Venezuela, donde los servicios de identificación son controlados por Cuba." En "Venezuela: Pasaportes para el terrorismo, en efecto Naím, 2014, en http://efectonaim.net/venezuela-pasaportes-para-el-terrorismo/. Véase igualmente la información: "El gobierno de Venezuela emitió visas fraudulentas a terroristas de Hezbollah," en *Infobae.América*, 4 de junio de 2014, en http://www.infobae.com/2014/06/04/1570258-el-gobierno-venezuelaemitio-visas-fraudulentas-terroristas-hezbollah. Véase igualmente el reportaje: "Informe revela que presuntos terroristas ingresan a EE.UU. con pasaportes legítimos venezolanos," en *NTN24*, 14 de septiembre de 2014, en http://www.ntn24.com/video/informe-revela-que-presuntos-terroristas-ingresan-a-eeuu-con-pasaportes-legitimos-venezolanos-25523

929 Véase el texto del Convenio suscrito al efecto entre Venezuela y Cuba en 2007, en http://www.elnuevoherald.com/incoming/article1553516.ece/binary/EXCLUSIVO:%20Contrato%20confiden-cial%20entre%20Cuba%20y%20Venezuela%20para%20transformaci%C3%B3n%20del%20sistema%20de%20identificaci%C3%B3n. Véase el reportaje de Joaquim Ibarz, "Los cubanos ya controlan sectores claves de Venezuela," en *La vanguardia.com internacional*, 7 de febrero de 2010, en http://www.lavanguardia.com/internacional/20100207/538851106-93/los-cubanos-controlan-ya-sectores-claves-de-venezuela.html

ción de las mismas a la ley inglesa y a la decisión de tribunales arbitrales con sede en Singapore, y en idioma inglés, es decir, renunciando incluso totalmente al uso del idioma oficial de Venezuela.[930] En otros casos como la emisión de Bonos de la deuda pública de 2010 (US$ 3.000,000,000), para cualquier controversia la República no sólo acordó someterse a la jurisdicción de los tribunales de Londres y de Manhattan, Nueva York, sino que además de renunciar a la aplicación de la ley venezolana y sujetarse en cambio a la ley del Estado de Nueva York, ha incluso renunciado a todo tipo de inmunidad soberana incluso conforme a las previsiones de la *Foreign Sovereign Immunities Act* de 1976 de los Estados Unidos y de la *State Immunity Act* de 1978 del Reino Unido. En el "Memorandum Informativo" de dicha emisión de Bonos, la República incluso llegó a afirmar contra el principio establecido en la Constitución de 1999 (art. 150), que: "bajo la ley venezolana, ni Venezuela ni sus propiedades gozan de inmunidad de jurisdicción" ante tribunal extranjero alguno o respecto de cualquier procedimiento legal, excepto la inmunidad que Venezuela y sus propiedades situadas en Venezuela, tengan en Venezuela respecto de procesos que se desarrollen en el país.[931]

Y en cuanto al gobierno, la injerencia de gobiernos extranjeros, particularmente Cuba, en la conducción política venezolana, consolidada a través de innumerables acuerdos y convenios internacionales,[932] ha hecho ya dudar de su propia autonomía.

---

930   Sobre el tema, véase la información en Gustavo Coronel, "La soberanía nacional en la basura cuando contratamos con China," en Las Armas de Coronel, 19 de octubre de 2014, en http://lasarmasdecoronel.blogspot.com/2014/10/la-soberania-nacional-en-la-basura.html

931   El texto dice: "Under Venezuelan law, neither Venezuela nor any of Venezuela's property have any immunity from the jurisdiction of any court or from set-off or any legal process (whether through service or notice, attachment prior to judgment, attachment in aid of execution of judgment, execution or otherwise), except that Venezuela, as well as Venezuela's properties located in Venezuela, have immunity from set-off, attachment prior to judgment, attachment in aid of execution of judgment and execution of a judgment in actions and proceedings in Venezuela." Ello contradice el espíritu de lo dispuesto en el artículo 1de la Constitución de 1999 que dispone: Véase el texto del "Listing Memorandum, U.S.$ 3,000,000,000 12.75% Amortizing Bonds due 2022 (the "Bonds") de 23 de Agosto de 2010 en http://www.100octa-nos.com/pdf/4ce8231cf06617db1bc921a0868de9ab.pdf. Dicha declaración sin duda, es contraria al espíritu del artículo 151 de la Constitución de 1999, que establece: "*Artículo 151.* En los contratos de interés público, si no fuere improcedente de acuerdo con la naturaleza de los mismos, se considerará incorporada, aun cuando no estuviere expresa, una cláusula según la cual las dudas y controversias que puedan suscitarse sobre dichos contratos y que no llegaren a ser resueltas amigablemente por las partes contratantes, serán decididas por los tribunales competentes de la República, de conformidad con sus leyes, sin que por ningún motivo ni causa puedan dar origen a reclamaciones extranjeras."

932   Sobre el tema, para sólo referirnos a un autor, se destaca lo expresado por Moisés Naím, al preguntarse "¿Cómo conquistó Cuba a Venezuela," diciendo que "La respuesta es Hugo Chávez. Dejar entrar a los cubanos fue la expresión de su poder absoluto." Naím explica en efecto, que "La enorme influencia que Cuba ha logrado ejercer en Venezuela es uno de los acontecimientos geopolíticos más sorprendentes y menos comprendidos del siglo XXI. Venezuela es nueve veces más grande que Cuba, tiene el triple de población y su economía es cuatro veces mayor. El país alberga las principales reservas de petróleo del mundo. Sin embargo, algunas funciones cruciales del Estado o han sido delegadas a funcionarios cubanos o son directamente controladas por La Habana. Y esto, el régimen cubano lo conquistó sin un solo disparo." Véase en Moisés Naím, "¿Cómo conquistó Cuba a Venezuela," en el Observador Global. Blog de Moisés Naím, 20 de abril de 2014, en http://voces.latercera.com/2014/04/20/moises-naim/como-conquisto-cuba-a-venezuela/ Igualmente, Moisés Naím, "Cuba fed a president's fears and took over Venezuela," en *Financial Times*, 15 de abril de 2014, en http://www.ft.com/cms/s/0/b7141b78-c497-11e3-b2fb-00144feabdc0.html.

Todo ello ha afectado la soberanía nacional, que se encuentra, en la práctica, extremadamente comprometida.

INTRODUCCIÓN:

EL ESTADO Y LA LEY (EL DERECHO ADMINISTRATIVO Y EL ESTADO)

Esta Introducción es básicamente el texto del documento elaborado para mi intervención oral en el *Congreso Internacional Conmemorativo del Acto Legislativo del 10 de septiembre de 1914 por el cual se estableció el Consejo de Estado,* sobre *Tendencias actuales del derecho público,* organizado por la Universidad del Rosario y el Consejo de Estrado, Biblioteca Luis Ángel Arango, Bogotá 8 al 10 de septiembre de 2014.

I.   EL DERECHO ADMINISTRATIVO ENTRE EL DEBER SER Y LA REALIDAD QUE RESULTA DE LA PRÁCTICA POLÍTICA

En relación con la relación entre el Estado y la Ley y determinar en ese marco hacia dónde va el derecho público o en particular el derecho administrativo con el desarrollo de un Estado Totalitario en Venezuela, una primera aproximación al tema sería que nos dedicáramos a argumentar en el plano del deber ser, es decir, determinar *hacia dónde nosotros pensamos que debería ir el derecho público* como derecho del Estado. En ese caso, esa perspectiva nos llevaría a esbozar, desde un punto de vista principista y optimista, lo que también pensamos que deberían ser las nuevas tendencias del derecho administrativo hacia el futuro, en el marco de ese derecho público y del Estado que quisiéramos, conforme a todo lo que hemos estudiado y enseñado durante tantos años.

Pero la segunda aproximación al tema es la que nos impone buscar o determinar *hacia dónde es que efectivamente se está dirigiendo el derecho público y el Estado en la actualidad,* lo que implica entonces esbozar, partiendo de la realidad contemporánea, las nuevas tendencias que ese derecho público y el propio Estado le están imponiendo al derecho administrativo, que como bien sabemos, siempre está condicionado por el entorno político.

La primera aproximación, nos llevaría sólo a expresar buenos deseos, o buenas intenciones, argumentando sobre lo que quisiéramos que fuera el derecho administrativo y sus nuevas tendencias en una sociedad democrática, como por ejemplo sería el aseguramiento del sometimiento efectivo de la Administración al derecho, y el necesario reforzamiento y perfeccionamiento del control contencioso administrativo sobre la actividad de la Administración; el control ciudadano sobre el funcionamiento de la Administración mediante mecanismos efectivos de participación; la garantía de que la Administración realmente funcione basada en los principios de seguridad jurídica, trasparencia e igualdad; el aseguramiento de que los recursos públicos sean inviertan conforme a los principios de buena administración, con la erradicación o persecución de la corrupción administrativa; el desarrollo efectivo de la meritocracia en la Administración Pública de manera que haya un servicio civil que esté al servicio exclusivo del Estado y no de una determinada parcialidad política; en fin, el que se materialicen todos los principios del derecho administrativo que tanto hemos analizado.

Esta aproximación, sin duda, es la que todos hemos seguido en la enseñanza cotidiana de nuestra disciplina, la que todos hemos oído, sobre la cual todos hemos escrito, muchas veces aislándonos de la realidad A esa no es precisamente a la cual quiero referirme en esta Ponencia.

Me preocupa ahora la otra perspectiva, la de tratar de entender hacia dónde va realmente el derecho público en algunos de nuestros países, y cuáles son las nuevas perspectivas que el derecho administrativo está experimentando en ellos, y me refiero a aquellos países de nuestra América Latina que han venido siendo sometidos durante los últimos lustros a gobiernos totalitarios y populistas, con todas las consecuencias desastrosas que ello ha tenido para nuestra disciplina, construida con tanto esfuerzo, con arreglo a otros paradigmas estatales. Y lo cierto es que muchas veces, en general, tendemos a obviar estas realidades en nuestros estudios de derecho, considerándolos como anomalías que no requieren de nuestra atención. Sin embargo, allí están, y no muy lejos, incluso en muchos casos del otro lado de las fronteras.

Al exponer sobre el tema del "Modelo político y derecho administrativo," en la Primera Parte, explicaba que nuestra disciplina, como parte del derecho público, es ante todo, un derecho del Estado; y que como tal, gústenos o no nos guste, está ineludible y necesariamente vinculado al modelo político en el cual el mismo opera, conforme a la práctica política del gobierno actuante, siendo los condicionamientos políticos uno de los más importantes elementos que moldean a nuestra disciplina.[933]

Superado desde hace siglos el marco del Estado Absoluto con el surgimiento, a partir de las revoluciones francesa y norteamericana de finales del siglo XVIII, del Estado de derecho, basado en los principios de la supremacía constitucional, soberanía popular, republicanismo, separación de poderes y declaración de derechos; y el desarrollo posterior de la democracia como régimen político, particularmente después de la segunda guerra mundial; el marco político del derecho administrativo comenzó a ser un orden jurídico que además de regular a los órganos del Estado y a su actividad, también comenzó a regular las relaciones jurídicas que en plano igualitario se comenzaron a establecer entre el Estado y los ciudadanos, basadas no ya en la antigua ecuación entre prerrogativas del Estado y sujeción de las personas a la autoridad, sino entre poder del Estado y derechos de los ciudadanos, los cuales además pasaron a ser declarados en las Constituciones. Se estableció, así, el famoso equilibrio entre uno y otro aspecto: prerrogativas estatales y derechos ciudadanos, el cual ha sido el que ha conformado la columna vertebral de nuestra disciplina.[934]

---

933 Sobre el tema, bajo el ángulo de la Administración, nos ocupamos hace años en Allan R. Brewer-Carías, "Les conditionnements politiques de l'administration publique dans les pays d'Amérique Latine", en *Revue Internationale des Sciences Administratives*, Vol. XLV, N° 3, Institut International des Sciences Administratives, Bruselas 1979, pp. 213-233; y "Los condicionamientos políticos de la Administración Pública en los países latinoamericanos" en *Revista de la Escuela Empresarial Andina*, Convenio Andrés Bello, N° 8, Año 5, Lima 1980, pp. 239-258

934 Véase Allan R. Brewer-Carías, "El derecho a la democracia entre las nuevas tendencias del Derecho Administrativo como punto de equilibrio entre los Poderes de la Administración y los derecho del administrado," en Víctor Hernández Mendible (Coordinador), *Desafíos del Derecho Administrativo Contem-*

En ese marco fue que se consolidó el modelo político del Estado de derecho, funcionando montado sobre un régimen político de democracia representativa, basado en el principio del sometimiento del Estado al derecho y a la justicia, y en la primacía de los derechos y garantías constitucionales de los ciudadanos. En dicho marco, la acción de Estado y de la propia Administración comenzó a encontrar límites formales, los cuales también comenzaron a ser recogidos en normas constitucionales, produciéndose así la muy conocida y progresiva constitucionalización del propio derecho administrativo.[935]

Ello ha implicado incluso, que en la actualidad, la Constitución sea la fuente jurídica primaria y más importante en nuestra disciplina, regulando directamente aspectos de la organización, del funcionamiento y de la actividad de la Administración Pública; del ejercicio de la función administrativa; de las relaciones jurídicas que se establecen entre la Administración y los administrados; de los poderes y prerrogativas de los cuales aquella dispone para hacer prevalecer los intereses generales y colectivos frente a los intereses individuales; y de los medios de control de la Administración por los administrados, para asegurar su sometimiento al derecho.

II. EL DERECHO ADMINISTRATIVO Y EL PARADIGMA DEMOCRÁTICO EN LAS FORMULACIONES CONSTITUCIONALES

Esos han sido los grandes avances jurídico formales de nuestra disciplina, todo lo cual nos confirma lo que es una realidad incontestable, y es que el derecho administrativo no es ni puede ser una rama políticamente neutra, y menos aún, un orden jurídico que haya encontrado la relativa rigidez o estabilidad de la que gozan otras ramas del derecho.

El derecho administrativo, aun cuando conservando principios esenciales, en realidad, tiene un inevitable grado el dinamismo que lo hace estar en constante evolución, como consecuencia directa, precisamente, de la propia evolución del Estado; lo que impone a ambos, al Estado y a su derecho administrativo, la necesidad de adaptarse a los cambios que se operan en el ámbito social y político de cada sociedad, de manera que siempre "refleja los condicionamientos políticos y sociales vigentes en un momento dado."[936]

Por ello, podemos responder a la pregunta de ¿hacia dónde va el derecho público?, afirmando que el mismo, en definitiva, va hacia donde vaya el Estado; y las

---

poráneo (*Conmemoración Internacional del Centenario de la Cátedra de Derecho Administrativo en Venezuela*, Tomo II, Ediciones Paredes, Caracas 2009, pp. 1417-1439.

935   Sobre el proceso de constitucionalización del derecho administrativo en Colombia y en Venezuela, véase Allan R. Brewer-Carías, "El proceso de constitucionalización del Derecho Administrativo en Colombia" en Juan Carlos Cassagne (Director), *Derecho Administrativo. Obra Colectiva en Homenaje al Prof. Miguel S. Marienhoff*, Buenos Aires 1998, pp. 157-172, y en *Revista de Derecho Público*, N° 55-56, Editorial Jurídica Venezolana, Caracas, julio-diciembre 1993, pp. 47-59; y "Algunos aspectos de proceso de constitucionalización del derecho administrativo en la Constitución de 1999" en *Los requisitos y vicios de los actos administrativos. V Jornadas Internacionales de Derecho Administrativo Allan Randolph Brewer-Carías, Caracas 1996*, Fundación Estudios de Derecho Administrativo (FUNEDA), Caracas 2000, pp. 23-37.

936   Véase Martín Bassols, "Sobre los principios originarios del derecho administrativo y su evolución", en *Libro homenaje al profesor Juan Galván Escutia*, Valencia, 1980, p. 57.

nuevas tendencias del derecho administrativo serán las que resulten o se deriven de regular a la Administración de ese Estado.

Hemos dicho que en los últimas décadas, particularmente en la segunda mitad del siglo pasado, el condicionamiento político básico del derecho administrativo se lo suministró la conformación del Estado de derecho como Estado constitucional montado sobre un régimen político democrático,[937] lo que por ejemplo en 2000 le permitió afirmar a la Sala Político Administrativa del Tribunal Supremo de Justicia de Venezuela (que es el órgano equivalente en cuanto a sus competencias, y *mutatis mutandi*, al Consejo de Estado de Colombia), antes de que pasara a ser presa definitiva del Estado Totalitario que hoy tenemos,[938] en una frase que por supuesto ahora ha sido completamente olvidada e incluso, quizás considerada obsoleta; –afirmó la Sala– que:

"el derecho administrativo es ante y por sobre todo un derecho democrático y de la democracia, y su manifestación está íntimamente vinculada a la voluntad general (soberanía) de la cual emana."[939]

Ello, sin duda, debería ser así, y quizás así lo creyó entonces el Tribunal Supremo. Pero con esa afirmación en realidad en lo que caemos es en el deber ser, en lo que quisiéramos que fuera la tendencia del derecho administrativo, por supuesto, si el Estado fuera realmente, siempre, un Estado democrático.[940]

Pero ya a estas alturas del conocimiento de nuestra disciplina, no creo equivocarme al afirmar que ninguno de los estudiosos del derecho público, para analizar un régimen político y la estructura de un Estado, puede basarse sólo en expresiones como esa, ni incluso, en las solas denominaciones y definiciones oficiales de los Estado insertas en las Constituciones. Tomen ustedes por ejemplo el caso de Co-

---

937   Véase Allan R. Brewer–Carías, "El Derecho a la democracia entre las nuevas tendencias del derecho administrativo como punto de equilibrio entre los poderes de la Administración y los derechos del Administrado," en *Revista Mexicana "Statum Rei Romanae" de Derecho Administrativo*. Homenaje al profesor Jorge Fernández Ruiz, Asociación Mexicana de Derecho Administrativo, Facultad de Derecho y Criminología de la Universidad Autónoma de Nuevo León, México, 2008, pp. 85–122; y "Prólogo: Sobre el derecho a la democracia y el control del poder", al libro de Asdrúbal Aguiar, *El derecho a la democracia. La democracia en el derecho y la jurisprudencia interamericanos. La libertad de expresión, piedra angular de la democracia*, Editorial Jurídica Venezolana, Caracas, 2008, pp. 19 ss.

938   Por ejemplo, la Conferencia Episcopal de Venezuela ha advertido la grave situación el panorama político actual de Venezuela, destacando "la pretensión de imponer un modelo político totalitario y un sistema educativo fuertemente ideologizado y centralizado," así como "la criminalización de las protestas y la politización del poder judicial, que se manifiesta, entre otras cosas, en la existencia de presos políticos y en la situación de tantos jóvenes privados de libertad por haber participado en manifestaciones" Véase reportaje de Sergio Mora: "Los obispos de Venezuela: Pretenden imponer un modelo totalitario," en *Zenit. El mundo visto desde Roma*, Roma, 12 julio 2014, en http://www.zenit.org/es/articles/los-obispos-de-venezuela-pretenden-imponer-un-modelo-totalitario

939   Véase la sentencia N° 1028 del 9 de mayo de 2000 en *Revista de Derecho Público*, N° 82, Editorial Jurídica Venezolana, Caracas, 2000, p. 214. Véase también, sentencia de la misma Sala de 5 de octubre de 2006, N° 2189 (Caso: *Seguros Altamira, C.A. vs. Ministro de Finanzas*), en *Revista de Derecho Público*, N° 108, Editorial Jurídica Venezolana, Caracas, 2006, p 100

940   Véase por ejemplo, Jesús María Alvarado Andrade, "Aproximación a la tensión Constitución y libertad en Venezuela," en *Revista de Derecho Público* N° 123, Editorial Jurídica Venezolana, Caracas, 2010, pp. 17-43

lombia, cuya Constitución la proclama como "un Estado social de derecho, organizado en forma de República unitaria, descentralizada, con autonomía de sus entidades territoriales, democrática, participativa y pluralista, fundada en el respeto de la dignidad humana, en el trabajo y la solidaridad de las personas que la integran y en la prevalencia del interés general" (art. 1). No voy yo por supuesto a analizar aquí ni hacer ejercicio de validación alguna sobre esa declaración, como sé que los profesores colombianos lo habrán hecho tantas veces.

Pero en cambio, sí me voy a referir a la norma similar que se encuentra en la Constitución de Venezuela, y que declara, también, que: "se constituye en un Estado democrático y social de derecho y de justicia, que propugna como valores superiores de su ordenamiento jurídico y de su actuación, la vida, la libertad, la justicia, la igualdad, la solidaridad, la democracia, la responsabilidad social y, en general, la preeminencia de los derechos humanos, la ética y el pluralismo político" (art. 2), agregando el texto constitucional, además, que el Estado es "un Estado Federal descentralizado"(art. 4).

Mejor y más completa definición formal del Estado democrático en el texto de una Constitución, ciertamente es casi imposible encontrar para que sirva de marco general del ordenamiento jurídico que debería ser aplicable al Estado, y que debería ser el que habría de moldear al derecho administrativo. Sin embargo, ante esa definición, lo que corresponde es determinar si realmente, en la práctica política del gobierno del Estado de Venezuela, el mismo responde a esos principios, o si son simples enunciados floridos, y nada más, de un Estado que no es nada de derecho, ni democrático, ni social, ni de economía mixta, ni de justicia, ni descentralizado, tal como efectiva y trágicamente es nuestro caso.

Si esa definición se ajustara a la realidad, aquí nada tendríamos que agregar más que decir que ante un Estado Constitucional de derecho, y además, democrático, descentralizado, social, de economía mixta y de justicia, la tendencia del derecho administrativo sería precisamente la que debería resultar de regular a la Administración de ese Estado, donde el pluralismo y la alternabilidad republicana tendrían que estar garantizada; donde la Administración y todos los órganos del Estado deberían estar sometidos al derecho, a través de un riguroso sistema de control judicial de la actividad administrativa; donde la Administración debería ejercer con imparcialidad y respetando la igualdad de todos, su tarea de gestionar el interés general y asegurar la satisfacción de las necesidades colectivas; dando con ello, plena garantía a los derechos de los administrados, en un marco de transparencia gubernamental y de pulcro manejo de los recursos financieros sometidos a escrupulosos controles fiscales. ¡Qué más quisiéramos…! Realmente, ¡qué más quisiéramos tener en Venezuela!

III. EL DERECHO ADMINISTRATIVO Y LOS AUTORITARISMOS

Pero lamentablemente, ello no es así. Como dije, en la realidad, en Venezuela, contra lo que dice la Constitución, no hay ni un Estado de derecho, ni un Estado democrático, ni un Estado Social, ni un Estado de Economía Mixta, ni un Estado de Justicia, y además, no hay un Estado descentralizado. Lo que dice la Constitución simplemente no existe en la realidad, y ni siquiera su implementación fue la intención de los exmilitares que como grupo de destrucción[941] asaltaron el poder en el país 1999, como bien resulta de los documentos que fundamentaron el intento de golpe militar que ellos mismos ejecutaron en 1992, en el cual afortunadamente fracasaron, donde exponían lo que querían establecer, que no era otra cosa que un Estado totalitario y comunista en el país,[942] lo que sin embargo han logrado, pero esta vez usando o abusando de los instrumentos democráticos, que a la vez han desmantelado,[943] para someter al país a sus designios totalitarios.[944]

En efecto, ante el deterioro de los partidos políticos tradicionales; con la ceguera suicida de buena parte de la dirigencia civil y de la sociedad que como siempre pretendió que un mesías o un "Melquiades" como el de Macondo, le solucionaría todos sus problemas y frustraciones, y además, con la complicidad ingenua, pero no menos suicida, de otra parte de la población; en el segundo intento de asalto al poder en 1999, los mismos exmilitares del fallido golpe de 1992, esta vez acompañados de civiles resentidos que pronto abandonaron desilusionados y equivocados la empresa en la cual creyeron; esa vez efectivamente lograron asaltar el poder pero mediante una votación y elección para una inconstitucional Asamblea Constituyente. Ello lo lograron, además, con la abstención de muchos y el voto de pocos, todos obnubilados por el afán y las promesas de cambio; por supuesto, sin darse cuenta de que estaban votando por el establecimiento de un Estado autoritario,[945] que pronto derivó

---

941 Que como lo expresó el psiquiatra Franzel Delgado Senior, refiriéndose al grupo que asaltó el poder en 1999, el mismo opera como una "secta destructiva," definiendo ésta como "Un grupo organizado que emerge en el seno de una sociedad con las intenciones de destruir las instituciones y valores y obligarles a asumir los de la secta". Véase en "Franzel Delgado Sénior: "El chavismo opera como una secta destructiva," entrevista realizada por Gloria Bastidas, en *El Nacional*, 24 octubre de 2011, en: http://www.lapatilla.com/site/2011/10/26/franzel-delgado-senior-el-chavismo-opera-como-una-secta-destructiva/ Véase igualmente, Carlos Vílchez Navamuel, "El chavismo es una secta destructiva," 5 de octubre de 2014, en http://www.carlosvil-cheznavamuel.com/el-chavismo-es-una-secta-destructiva/

942 Así se puede apreciar de los papeles del golpe de Estado de 1992, publicados en: Kléber Ramírez Rojas, *Historial documental de 4 de febrero*, Colección Alfredo Maneiro, Ministerio de la Cultura, Fundación Editorial El Perro y la Rana, Caracas 2006.

943 Véase Allan R. Brewer-Carías, *Dismantling Democracy. The Chávez Authoritarian Experiment*, New York, 2010; y "La demolición del Estado de derecho y la destrucción de la democracia en Venezuela (1999-2009)," en José Reynoso Núñez y Herminio Sánchez de la Barquera y Arroyo (Coordinadores), *La democracia en su contexto. Estudios en homenaje a Dieter Nohlen en su septuagésimo aniversario*, Instituto de Investigaciones Jurídicas, Universidad Nacional Autónoma de México, México 2009, pp. 477-517.

944 Por eso Nelson Castellanos con razón anotó recientemente sobre "la gran mentira bolivariana, esa que prometió un proyecto social y terminó instalando el sistema comunista de los Castro. La que ofreció trabajar para los pobres, cuando su intención era seguir manteniéndolos abajo, para poder manipularlos.// Una banda que se preocupó por enriquecerse rápidamente y por tomar el control de todos los poderes del Estado, afín de no tener que irse nunca. Aunque para ello violara leyes y derechos, reprimiera o persiguiera a los ciudadanos que pretendieron oponerse a sus planes de perennidad." En "La mentira Bolivariana", en Noticiero Digital.com, julio 13, 2014, en http://www.noticierodi-gital.com/2014/07/la-mentira-bolivariana/.

945 En 1999, al propugnar el voto NO por la Constitución de 1999 elaborada por la Asamblea Constituyente y sometida a aprobación popular, advertí que si la Constitución se aprobaba, ello iba a implicar la implantación en Venezuela, de "un esquema institucional concebido para el autoritarismo derivado de la combinación del centralismo del Estado, el presidencialismo exacerbado, la democracia de partidos, la concentración de poder en la Asamblea y el militarismo, que constituye el elemento central diseñado para la organización del poder del Estado." En mi opinión esto no era lo que en 1999 se requería para el

en totalitario y populista, que ha violado y moldeado el orden jurídico como sus líderes han querido, que ha desmantelado la democracia como régimen político, que ha empobrecido y hecho miserable a un país otrora próspero, y donde simplemente han eliminado la justicia.

Y en el marco de esta conferencia, es precisamente ese Estado, y la Administración Pública desarrollada por el mismo, lo que hay que analizar para poder responder a la pregunta de *¿Hacia dónde va el derecho púbico?* en un país como Venezuela, tan cerca de ustedes; y precisar algo sobre cuáles son *las nuevas tendencias del derecho administrativo* que se han venido mostrando en el funcionamiento de la Administración de ese Estado.

Pero por favor, no nos alarmemos. La historia de nuestra disciplina está llena de casos de desarrollo del derecho administrativo en el marco de regímenes autoritarios, en los cuales incluso se dictaron leyes fundamentales para nuestra materia, aun cuando en el momento, por supuesto, con aplicación en la medida de las circunstancias. Allí está el caso de España en los años cincuenta, lejos de la democracia, en plena etapa del autoritarismo franquista, casi treinta años antes de la sanción de la Constitución de 1978, pero donde se sancionaron leyes tan importantes como las relativas al Régimen Jurídico de la Administración del Estado, y sobre Procedimientos Administrativos, las cuales sin duda, en el derecho positivo, fueron el punto de partida del derecho administrativo español y de buena parte del derecho administrativo latinoamericano contemporáneos, para buscar asegurar el sometimiento del Estado al derecho.

Allí, en ese momento, no había democracia, pero sin duda, sí había derecho administrativo, pues el Estado, sometido parcialmente al derecho y controlado también parcialmente por la jurisdicción contencioso administrativa, en el marco de un régimen en el cual, a pesar de que no había ni siquiera consagración efectiva de derechos y garantías constitucionales, no llegó a tener una conformación totalitaria, manteniendo el derecho administrativo cierto equilibrio entre los poderes del Estado y los derechos o situaciones de los administrados.

Y para no irnos muy lejos, la raíz del derecho administrativo contemporáneo en Venezuela puede situarse en la rica jurisprudencia de la antigua Corte Federal que funcionó en los años cincuenta, y que está contenida en múltiples sentencias que emanaron de dicho alto tribunal igualmente en la década precisamente de la dictadura militar que duró hasta 1958.[946] Tampoco allí había democracia, pero sin duda, aun en el marco de un régimen autoritario, aun cuando no totalitario, ya se habían sentado las bases del derecho administrativo contemporáneo en Venezuela, tal como se

---

perfeccionamiento de la democracia; la cual al contrario, se debió basar "en la descentralización del poder, en un presidencialismo controlado y moderado, en la participación política para balancear el poder del Estado y en la sujeción de la autoridad militar a la autoridad civil" Documento de 30 de noviembre de 1999. *V.* en Allan R. Brewer–Carías, *Debate Constituyente (Aportes a la Asamblea Nacional Constituyente)*, Tomo III, Fundación de Derecho Público, Editorial Jurídica Venezolana, Caracas, 1999, p. 339.

946   Véase Allan R. Brewer-Carías, *Las instituciones fundamentales del derecho administrativo y la jurisprudencia venezolanas*, Caracas 1964; y *Jurisprudencia de la Corte Suprema 1930-1974 y estudios de derecho administrativo*, Ediciones del Instituto de Derecho Público, Facultad de Derecho, Universidad Central de Venezuela, ocho volúmenes, Caracas 1975-1979.

desarrolló en las décadas sucesivas, montadas sobre un cierto equilibrio entre poderes del Estado y derechos ciudadanos.

Es decir, en otros términos más generales, porque ejemplos como los indicados los podemos encontrar en la historia de nuestra disciplina de todos nuestros países, puede decirse que el sometimiento del Estado al derecho, que fue lo que originó el derecho administrativo desde comienzos del siglo XIX, no siempre tuvo el estrecho vínculo con la democracia como régimen político, como hay tanto consideramos; y el mismo pudo desarrollarse porque a pesar de la carencia democrática, el Estado estaba montado sobre un sistema que respetaba cierto equilibrio entre los poderes del Estado y los derechos ciudadanos, y en un sistema económico liberal, no llegándose a consolidarse como un Estado totalitario.

Otra realidad fue la de los Estados totalitarios, en los cuales la totalidad del Poder estuvo en manos de un partido o de una nomenklatura que asaltó al poder y lo puso a su servicio, sin control de naturaleza alguna, salvo las depuraciones sucesivas del liderazgo, apoderándose de todo, de propiedades, medios de producción, medios de comunicación, vidas y bienes, volviendo el ciudadano a ser siervo del Estado. En esos estados totalitarios, el derecho, si es que le podemos darle ese nombre, solo fue un amasijo de reglas maleables por el poder para asegurar el control total de la sociedad. Fue el caso de la Unión Soviética, y antes, del Estado Nazista o del Estado Fascista, y desde hace cinco décadas el Estado cubano. En realidad, todos fueron y son fascistas, donde el derecho administrativo, como nosotros lo hemos conocido, simplemente no existió, ni existe. En ese grupo, lamentablemente, ya entró el Estado venezolano.

IV. EL DERECHO ADMINISTRATIVO Y EL DESEQUILIBRIO ENTRE PODERES ESTATALES Y DERECHOS CIUDADANOS

En efecto, no olvidemos que el elemento esencial que caracteriza al derecho administrativo de un Estado democrático de derecho, se da cuando el dicho derecho deja de ser un derecho exclusivamente del Estado, llamado a sólo regular su organización, su funcionamiento, sus poderes y sus prerrogativas, y pasa a ser realmente un derecho administrativo encargado de garantizar el punto de equilibrio que en una sociedad democrática tiene que existir entre los poderes del Estado y los derechos de los administrados. En el marco de un régimen totalitario, ese equilibrio por esencia no existe, y por ello es que en dicho régimen, el derecho administrativo no es un derecho democrático, aun cuando pretenda regular al Estado.

Como también lo señaló la Sala Político Administrativa del Tribunal Supremo de Justicia de Venezuela en la misma hoy olvidada sentencia N° 1028 de 9 de mayo de 2000,

> "El derecho administrativo se presenta dentro de un estado social de derecho como el punto de equilibrio entre el poder (entendido éste como el conjunto de atribuciones y potestades que tienen las instituciones y autoridades públicas, dentro del marco de la legalidad), y la libertad (entendida ésta como los dere-

chos y garantías que tiene el ciudadano para convivir en paz, justicia y democracia)."[947]

Lo que caracteriza al derecho administrativo en un orden democrático, por tanto, no es otra cosa que ser el instrumento para asegurar la sumisión del Estado al derecho pero con a la misión de garantizar el respeto a los derechos ciudadanos, en medio de una persistente lucha histórica por controlar el poder y como nos lo insistió Eduardo García de Enterría, contra las "inmunidades del poder,"[948] que es lo que ha caracterizado el devenir de nuestra disciplina. De manera que más democrático será el derecho administrativo si dicho equilibrio es acentuado; y menos democrático será, si su regulación se limita sólo a satisfacer los requerimientos del Estado, ignorando o despreciando el otro extremo, es decir, el de las garantías y derechos ciudadanos.

En todo caso, con el mencionado equilibrio se superó aquella visión del Estado como el "hipócrita personaje de doble faz" del que nos habló hace décadas Fernando Garrido Falla, que encerraba una "oposición aparentemente irreductible" entre, por una parte, el conjunto de prerrogativas que posee y que "sitúan a la Administración en un plano de desigualdad y favor en sus relaciones con los particulares"; y por la otra, y el conjunto de derechos y garantías de estos, que lo llevaban a regular lo que Garrido llamó "la más acabada instrumentación técnica del Estado liberal."[949]

En un Estado Totalitario, en cambio, definitivamente, esa doble faz queda eliminada, pero volcando el desequilibrio a favor del Estado, reduciéndose el derecho administrativo a ser, sola y exclusivamente, el conjunto de reglas destinadas a regular el funcionamiento de la Administración del mismo, y nada más.

Es en este marco, en el cual, entonces, quisiera tratar de responder en relación con Venezuela a la pregunta fundamental de *¿Hacia dónde va el derecho público?*, por supuesto, como derecho del Estado; y conforme a ello, tratar de identificar cuáles son las *nuevas tendencias del derecho administrativo* que se han venido manifestando.

Dije anteriormente que a pesar de que la Constitución venezolana diga que Venezuela se constituye en un Estado democrático y social de derecho y de justicia, y además, Federal descentralizado, después de tres lustros de gobierno autoritario, y de destrucción masiva de las instituciones del Estado Constitucional, el Estado venezolano se ha estructurado como un Estado totalitario, que no es ni democrático, ni social, ni de derecho, ni de justicia, ni descentralizado.

Ello implica por tanto que el derecho público que tenemos, no es el de la fórmula constitucional, sino el propio de un Estado Totalitario, que ha sido progresivamente desconstitucionalizado,[950] lo que implica que las nuevas tendencias del derecho ad-

947 Véase en *Revista de Derecho Público*, Nº 82, Editorial Jurídica Venezolana, Caracas 2000, p. 214.

948 Véase Eduardo García de Enterría, *La lucha contra las inmunidades de poder en el derecho administrativo,* Madrid 1983.

949 Véase Fernando Garrido Falla, "Sobre el derecho administrativo", en *Revista de Administración Pública,* Nº 7, Instituto de Estudios Políticos, Madrid, 1952, p. 223.

950 Véase Jesús María Alvarado Andrade, "Sobre Constitución y Administración Pública ¿Es realmente el Derecho Administrativo en Venezuela un Derecho Constitucional Concretizado?" en José Ignacio

ministrativo que hemos estado experimentando son las que rigen en un Estado en el cual, siguiendo a Raymond Aron,[951] la concentración del poder ha sido total; donde existe un partido político estatal y militar único fusionado al propio Estado, que rechaza la democracia representativa y el parlamentarismo; un partido que posee el monopolio de la actividad política "legítima" y el monopolio de la aplicación de la ideología "socialista" "oficial" del Estado, que en realidad es la ideología comunista, la cual se ha convertido en verdad oficial del Estado y de la sociedad conforme a un Plan impuesto obligatoriamente denominado "Plan de la patria;" un Estado donde se niegan los derechos individuales y la libertad como valor máximo del liberalismo, siendo sustituidos por unos supuestos derechos colectivos de los cuales es presuntamente depositario, desconociéndose además la dignidad de la persona humana; un Estado que si bien desde 1975 controlaba en exclusiva la producción del petróleo, ahora ha asumido el monopolio total de todos los medios de producción, de manera que la economía es ahora totalmente controlada por el Estado y se convierte en parte del mismo; que ha asumido el control total de los medios de persuasión y coacción, incluso las policías locales; que ha asumido el monopolio de los medios de comunicación; en el cual se ha producido la politización de toda actividad, originándose una confusión entre sociedad civil y Estado, de manera que las faltas cometidas por los individuos en el marco de la actividad política, económica o profesional se conforman simultáneamente como faltas ideológicas. Ello, acompañado de una campaña cotidiana contra los "enemigos" inventados o imaginarios como la "burguesía," basada en expresiones llenas de odio, resentimiento, agresividad, belicosidad, y de mentiras repetidas una y mil veces, ha originado un terror ideológico generalizado.[952] Además, para mantenerse en el poder, el gobierno y su partido militar emplean el terror sobre la población, eliminando cualquier tipo de opinión disidente a la oficial, sirviéndose para ello de la policía y de los militares.

E incluso, el ingrediente clásico del totalitarismo del culto a la personalidad basado en la exaltación de un líder, también la hemos sufrido, aunque ahora sea un fantasma con el cual la dirigencia se comunica por medio de un "pajarito," y que a pesar de haber fallecido, sin embargo en los medios, todos controlados por el Estado, "habla" todos los días y a toda hora, en televisión y radio, repitiéndose grabacio-

---

Hernández (Coord.), *100 Años de Enseñanza del Derecho Administrativo en Venezuela 1909-2009*, Centro de Estudios de Derecho Público de la Universidad Monteávila, Fundación de Estudios de Derecho Administrativo (FUNEDA), Caracas, 2011, pp. 165-263.

951 Véase Raymond Aron, *Democracia y totalitarismo*, Seix Barral, Madrid 1968

952 Como lo ha observado Leandro Area, como una de las características de lo que acertadamente califica como el "Estado misional," no menos importante, es la de que los gobernantes "al sentirse dueños de la verdad, poseedores del fuego originario, desarrollan una actividad de expansión del modelo de creencias y valores que conformando actitudes desencadenen en comportamientos. Adopta entonces la forma de Estado misionero. De allí que tantos catecismos, predicadores, fórmulas, catequesis rumiante. De allí que tantos micrófonos, antenas repetidoras, multiplicadores de consignas, milagreros, organizadores de resentidos, gerentes de la miseria humana no para salir de ella, superándola, sino para multiplicarla en epidemia. Y esta cruzada no se limita a la esfera de lo nacional, sino que siguiendo con los principios de la "revolución permanente" y el "internacionalismo proletario" entre otros, tiene la obligación y cobra fuerza, el establecimiento de aliados complementarios, ya no por condicionantes económicas de existencia simplemente, sino como socios ideológicos y militares si fuera el caso." Véase Leandro Area, "El 'Estado Misional' en Venezuela," en *Analítica.com*, 14 de febrero de 2014, en http://analitica.com/opinion/opinion-nacional/el-estado-misional-en-venezuela/

nes de lo que dijo tanto y tantas veces; y al cual además, por fallecido, se le reza una "plegaria" como si fuera una deidad.[953] Lo cierto es que en el autoritarismo que habíamos tenido hasta hace poco tiempo, la concentración del poder que existió, aun cuando rechazaba a la oposición, sin embargo no excluía la admisión de cierto pluralismo en algunos medios y en los apoyos que el gobierno recibía, y no había la clara intención de homogeneización total de la sociedad, que ahora en cambio se ha manifestado brutalmente.[954]

Lo cierto, en todo caso, es que en Venezuela, el Estado que tenemos es un Estado Totalitario, que es la negación del Estado democrático y social de derecho, de economía mixta, de justicia y descentralizado, y las tendencias del derecho administrativo son las que resultan de el mismo, muy alejadas de aquél derecho vinculado a la democracia del cual nos hablaba el Tribunal Supremo hace casi tres lustros, y que tenía por misión garantizar los derechos de las personas, además de asegurar la gestión de los intereses públicos. Ahora sólo atiende a velar por la imposición a la población inerme, políticas autoritarias comunistas, incluso violando la Constitución y las leyes.

Para demostrar nuestra afirmación, analizaremos a continuación cómo en la práctica constitucional legislativa y gubernamental, el Estado en Venezuela ha deja-

---

953 Véase sobre la plegaria "Chávez nuestro de cada día," lo expresado por la Conferencia Episcopal de Venezuela en el reportaje "Iglesia Católica de Venezuela rechaza el "Chávez nuestro", diario *El Tiempo*, Bogotá, 4 de septiembre de 2014, en http://www.eltiempo.com/mundo/latino-america/padrenuestro-en-honor-a-hugo-chavez-rechazado-por-la-iglesia-venezolana/14483977. Véase sobre ello lo expresado por Monseñor Baltazar Porras en "El Chávez nuestro es una burla," en http://www.lapatilla.com/site/2014/09/06/monsenor-baltazar-porras-el-chavez-nuestro-es-una-burla/. Véase igualmente el Editorial del diario *El Tiempo*, "Chávez nuestro que estás en el cielo...," Bogotá, 5 de septiembre de 2014, en http://www.eltiempo.com/opinion/edito-rial/editorial-chavez-nuestro-que-estas-en-los-cielos-editorial-el-tiempo-/14492815. Quien ejerce la Presidencia de la República, Nicolás Maduro, sin embargo defiende la oración. Véase en "Venezuela: Maduro defiende oración "Chávez nuestro" y la compara con poema de Neruda," en *emol.com*, 4 de septiembre de 2014http://www.emol.com/noticias/internacional/2014/09/04/678653/venezuela-maduro-defiende-oracion-chavez-nuestro-y-pide-respeto-al-pueblo-creador.html. Sobre el tema, Tulio Hernández, después de analizar el desafuero, explicó que si en lugar de haberse modificado el Padre Nuestro se hubiese modificado "un versículo del Corán, y lo hubiese leído públicamente no en Venezuela sino en algún país donde opere el Estado Islámico, para el momento de escribir estas líneas hace rato que debería haberse quedado sin cabeza. Con transmisión en vivo y a manos de alguno de los fanáticos yihadistas que se han especializado en degollamientos globales de herejes. [...]. La perversión mayor de "la oración del delegado" y la de todas las oraciones de culto a la personalidad, es atribuir a una persona humana cualidad o acciones propias de Dios. [...] "Como no solo quieren el poder, también poseer el corazón, las creencias y la fe de los ciudadanos, los modelos totalitarios hacen cualquier cosa para lograrlo, incluyendo el culto al Jefe Único. En América Latina ya conocíamos el de Fidel y, un poco más un poco menos, los de Perón y Evita. Pero ninguno de ellos había llegado a los desafueros mística y grotescamente manipuladores del chavismo," concluyendo que terminó "de comprender por qué hay quienes creen que Venezuela ya no es una república sino un sanatorio mental donde los pacientes tomaron el control y aseguran que los médicos están locos." Véase Tulio Hernández, "Dios nació en Sabaneta," en *El Nacional*, 7 de septiembre de 2014, en http://www.el-nacional.com/tulio_hernandez/Dios-nacio-Sabaneta_0_478152190.html.

954 Véase lo expresado por Diosdado Cabello, Presidente de la Asamblea Nacional, al declarar que la oposición "no va a gobernar más nunca. Ni por las buenas ni por las malas," en *La Nación*, 1 de septiembre de 2014, en http://www.lanacion.com.ve/politica/diosdado-cabello-no-van-a-gobernar-este-pais-nunca-mas-ni-por-las-buenas-ni-por-las-malas/. Véase el comentario de Antonio Sánchez García, "Oposición y Resistencia," en *El Nacional*, Caracas 7 de septiembre de 2014, en *El Universal*, http://www.el-nacional.com/antonio_sanchez_garcia/Oposicion-resistencia_0_476352527.html.

do de ser un Estado de derecho, un Estado democrático, un Estado Social, un Estado de economía mixta, un Estado de justicia y un Estado descentralizado, con la advertencia de que si bien el análisis lo haremos separadamente por razones metodológicas, refiriéndonos a cada una de esas facetas constitucionales del Estado, la Constitución, al regular su específica concepción del Estado, lo hizo interrelacionando e imbricando todas ellas, sin que ninguna tenga ni pueda tener prevalencia sobre las otras. En consecuencia, el *Estado de derecho* no puede llegar a ser tal sin ser, a la vez, en Estado democrático, social, de economía mixta, de justicia y descentralizado; *el Estado democrático* no puede llegar a ser tal sin ser, a la vez, un Estado de derecho, social, de economía mixta, de justicia y descentralizado; *el Estado social* no puede llegar a ser tal sin ser, a la vez, un Estado de derecho, democrático, de economía mixta, de justicia y descentralizado; *el Estado de economía mixta* no puede llegar a ser tal sin ser, a la vez, un Estado de derecho, democrático, social, de justicia y descentralizado; *el Estado de justicia* no puede llegar a ser tal sin ser, a la vez, un Estado de derecho, democrático, social, de economía mixta y descentralizado; y en fin *el Estado descentralizado* no puede llegar a ser tal sin ser, a la vez, un Estado de derecho, democrático, social, de economía mixta y de justicia.

Es la integración de todos sus componentes o facetas, en plano de igual valor constitucional, lo que caracteriza precisamente al Estado en la Constitución. Y es precisamente la ausencia de realización de todos sus componentes lo que hace que el Estado en Venezuela sea hoy un Estado Totalitario, y el derecho administrativo se encuentre desquiciado.

SECCIÓN PRIMERA:

LA AUSENCIA DE ESTADO DE DERECHO

El texto de esta Sección primera, lo constituye buena parte de la ponencia sobre "El Estado de derecho como fundamento constitucional del derecho administrativo. Problemas en el Estado autoritario," redactada para el *XIII Congreso Iberoamericano de Derecho Administrativo*, sobre el tema general del Derecho Fundamental a la Buena Administración" (tema 1: "Fundamentos constitucionales del Derecho Administrativo"), organizado por el Foro Iberoamericano de Derecho Administrativo y la Universidad Panamericana, en ciudad de México, entre el 13 y el 16 Octubre de 2014

Ante todo, cuando afirmamos que el Estado en Venezuela está configurado como un Estado Totalitario, es porque a pesar de lo que establece y declara la Constitución, el mismo no es un Estado de derecho, con lo que se ha quebrado uno de los pilares esenciales del derecho administrativo, que es el sometimiento pleno de la Administración a la ley y al derecho, en un régimen democrático.

Un Estado de derecho, para ser tal, en efecto, necesariamente tiene que estar estructurado conforme a una serie de elementos esenciales de la democracia, todos los cuales están totalmente imbricados y que, por tanto, conforman una unidad,[955] teniendo como el primero de todos ellos, la necesaria existencia de un orden constitucional que como ley suprema rija efectivamente a los órganos del Estado y a los ciudadanos, tal como se establece en el artículo 7 de la Constitución de 1999.

Lamentablemente, ese elemento no está asegurado en la Venezuela actual, ya que la Constitución dejó de ser la norma suprema obligatoria, como lo declara la propia Constitución (art 7), pasando a ser en el marco de un derecho público completamente desconstitucionalizado, un texto violable y violado, maleable, mutable y reformable, sin formalidad alguna, a discreción del gobierno. Hacia esa situación de ausencia de supremacía y rigidez constitucional es hacia la cual ha ido encaminándose el derecho público en el país de América Latina donde precisamente fue que por primera vez se sancionó una Constitución moderna en diciembre de 1811. De ello lo que nos resulta un derecho administrativo sin estabilidad, ya que su fuente primaria carece de rigidez.

I.   LA CONSTITUCIÓN VIOLADA

En efecto, en la situación actual, *primero*, puede decirse que la Constitución se ha violado tantas veces cuanto los gobernantes la han blandido mostrando el famoso "librito azul" que la contiene, generalmente para tratar de justificar algún desafuero.[956] Se violó cuando se convocó una Asamblea Constituyente al margen de la Constitución en 1999;[957] se violó al intervenir la Asamblea Constituyente a todos los poderes constituidos en 1999;[958] se violó, al suspenderse *sine die* la vigencia de la Constitución, al sancionarse, al margen de la voluntad popular, una transitoriedad constitucional sin límites a partir de 2000;[959] se violó al designarse en 2000, y luego sucesivamente, a los altos funcionarios del Estado, sin garantizarse la participación ciudadana que impone su texto;[960] se violó a partir de 2000, en 2001, 2008 y 2014

---

955   Véase sobre los elementos y componentes esenciales de la democracia como régimen político tal como se regularon en la Carta Democrática Interamericana, en Allan R. Brewer-Carías, "Algo sobre las nuevas tendencias del derecho constitucional: el reconocimiento del derecho a la constitución y del derecho a la democracia," en Sergio J. Cuarezma Terán y Rafael Luciano Pichardo (Directores), *Nuevas tendencias del derecho constitucional y el derecho procesal constitucional*, Instituto de Estudios e Investigación Jurídica (INEJ), Managua 2011, pp. 73-94.

956   Véase en general, Asdrúbal Aguiar, *Historia Inconstitucional de Venezuela*, Editorial Jurídica Venezolana, Caracas 2014. Véase nuestro Prólogo a dicha obra "Sobre cómo, desde sus inicios, el gobierno de H. Chávez se caracterizó por su política hostil contra la democracia," al libro de Asdrúbal Aguiar sobre *Historia Inconstitucional de Venezuela, 1999-2012*, Editorial Jurídica Venezolana, Caracas 2012, pp. 23-76.

957   Véase Allan R. Brewer-Carías, "Comentarios sobre la inconstitucional de la convocatoria a Referéndum sobre una Asamblea Nacional Constituyente, efectuada por el Consejo Nacional Electoral en febrero de 1999" en *Revista Política y Gobierno*, Vol. 1, Nº 1, enero-junio 1999, Caracas 1999, pp. 29-92.

958   Véase Allan R. Brewer-Carías, *Debate Constituyente (Aportes a la Asamblea Nacional Constituyente)*, Tomo I, Fundación de Derecho Público, Editorial Jurídica Venezolana, Caracas 1999.

959   Véase Allan R. Brewer-Carías, *Golpe de Estado y Proceso Constituyente en Venezuela*, Universidad Nacional Autónoma de México, México 2002

960   Véase Allan R. Brewer-Carías, "La participación ciudadana en la designación de los titulares de los órganos no electos de los Poderes Públicos en Venezuela y sus vicisitudes políticas", en *Revista Iberoamericana de Derecho Público y Administrativo*, Año 5, Nº 5-2005, San José, Costa Rica 2005, pp. 76-95

con la sanción de legislación delegada sin efectuarse la consulta popular que impone la Constitución para las leyes.[961] Y casi todos esos casos, las violaciones recibieron el aval de la Sala Constitucional, en algunos casos absteniéndose de decidir impugnaciones, y en otros casos, mutando el texto constitucional,[962] como se verá más adelante.

II. LA CONSTITUCIÓN MALEABLE

Segundo, la Constitución ha sido un texto maleable según las circunstancias, para lo cual el gobierno ha contado igualmente, como artífice máximo para la inconstitucional operación, con la Sala Constitucional del Tribunal Supremo (equivalente, también *mutatis mutandi* a la Corte Constitucional de Colombia). Se maleó, por ejemplo, cuando el Poder Ejecutivo y el Poder Legislativo, en 2007, propusieron y sancionaron una sustancial modificación de la Constitución siguiendo sin embargo el procedimiento de la "reforma constitucional," que no era el aplicable, pues por su contenido, dichas reformas sólo las podía efectuar una Asamblea Constituyente que debía convocarse al efecto.[963]

Sin embargo, la Sala Constitucional simplemente se negó a controlar la evidente inconstitucionalidad, para lo cual sin duda tenía competencia,[964] y declaró "improponibles" las demandas de nulidad por inconstitucionalidad que se intentaron contra el procedimiento de reforma,[965] la cual sin embargo fue el pueblo el que se encargó de rechazarla mediante referendo realizado en diciembre de 2007.[966]

Pero a pesar del rechazo popular, se moldeó de nuevo la Constitución por parte de la Asamblea Nacional, al utilizar, dos años después, el procedimiento de "en-

---

961   Véase Allan R. Brewer-Carías, "Apreciación general sobre los vicios de inconstitucionalidad que afectan los Decretos Leyes Habilitados" en *Ley Habilitante del 13-11-2000 y sus Decretos Leyes*, Academia de Ciencias Políticas y Sociales, Serie Eventos N° 17, Caracas 2002, pp. 63-103; "El derecho ciudadano a la participación popular y la inconstitucionalidad generalizada de los decretos leyes 2010-2012, por su carácter inconsulto," en *Revista de Derecho Público*, N° 130, (abril-junio 2012), Editorial Jurídica Venezolana, Caracas 2012, pp. 85-88.

962   Véase Allan R. Brewer-Carías, *Reforma constitucional y fraude a la Constitución (1999-2009)*, Academia de Ciencias Políticas y Sociales, Caracas 2009.

963   Véase Allan R. Brewer-Carías, "Hacia la creación de un Estado Socialista, Centralizado y Militarista en Venezuela. Análisis de la propuesta presidencial de reforma constitucional," en *Estudios Jurídicos*, Volumen XIII, Enero 2004-Diciembre 2007, Asociación Hipólito Herrera Billini, Santo Domingo, República Dominica 2008, pp. 17-66.

964   Véase Allan R. Brewer-Carías, "La reforma constitucional en América Latina y el control de constitucionalidad", en *Reforma de la Constitución y control de constitucionalidad. Congreso Internacional*, Pontificia Universidad Javeriana, Bogotá Colombia, junio 14 al 17 de 2005, Bogotá, 2005, pp. 108-159.

965   Véase Allan R. Brewer-Carías, "El juez constitucional vs. la supremacía constitucional O de cómo la jurisdicción constitucional en Venezuela renunció a controlar la constitucionalidad del procedimiento seguido para la 'reforma constitucional' sancionada por la Asamblea Nacional el 2 de noviembre de 2007, antes de que fuera rechazada por el pueblo en el referendo del 2 de diciembre de 2007," en Eduardo Ferrer Mac Gregor y César de Jesús Molina Suárez (Coordinadores), *El juez constitucional en el Siglo XXI*, Universidad nacional Autónoma de México, Suprema Corte de Justicia de la Nación, México 2009, Tomo I, pp. 385-435.

966   Véase Allan R. Brewer-Carías,, "La proyectada reforma constitucional de 2007, rechazada por el poder constituyente originario", en *Anuario de Derecho Público 2007*, Año 1, Instituto de Estudios de Derecho Público de la Universidad Monteávila, Caracas 2008, pp. 17-65.

mienda constitucional" que menos aún era aplicable para implementar una de las reformas rechazadas, que era la modificación del principio sustancial de la alternabilidad republicana; previéndose en cambio y en sustitución al mismo, el principio de la reelección presidencial indefinida. Ese cambio, además, menos se podía hacer en el mismo período constitucional en el cual ya esa "reforma" se había rechazada por el pueblo en el referendo de 2007. En este último caso, sin embargo, fue la Sala Constitucional la que moldeó la Constitución[967] para permitir la mencionada enmienda que fue luego aprobada por el pueblo en referendo de 2009.[968]

III. LA CONSTITUCIÓN MUTABLE

Tercero, la Constitución ha sido un texto mutable y mutado en múltiples ocasiones por parte de la Sala Constitucional, de manera que sin modificarse formalmente la letra de su texto, el juez constitucional le ha dado otro significado acorde con lo que le ha solicitado del gobierno, y para, en fraude a la voluntad popular, implementar la reforma constitucional que fue rechazada en 2007. Es decir, a pesar de la votación popular en contra de que se insertara en la Constitución un esquema de Estado Socialista, Centralizado, Militarista y Policial como el que se quería incorporar al Texto en 2007, el gobierno se negó a aceptarlo,[969] y en fraude a la voluntad popular y a la propia Constitución, la reforma se comenzó a implementar de inmediato mediante mutaciones constitucionales y legislación delegada.[970]

Y así fue que, por ejemplo, se mutó la Constitución en 2007, cuando una "competencia exclusiva" de los Estados en el régimen federal para administrar y mantener los puertos y aeropuertos nacionales situados en su territorio, fue transformada en una "competencia concurrente," permitiendo la indebida intervención del Poder Nacional en la materia;[971] se mutó la Constitución en 2009, cuando la prohibición de

---

967 Véase Allan R. Brewer-Carías, "El Juez Constitucional vs. La alternabilidad republicana (La reelección continua e indefinida), en *Revista de Derecho Público*, Nº 117, (enero-marzo 2009), Caracas 2009, pp. 205-211.

968 Véase la Enmienda Constitucional en *Gaceta Oficial* Nº 5908 de 19 de febrero de 2009.

969 Muestra de ello es que siete años después, el Vicepresidente de la República, expresó que al contrario, la Constitución de 1999 supuestamente es una "Constitución socialista" llegando a afirmar lo siguiente: "Si a uno le preguntan: ¿qué es un Estado socialista?, uno tranquilamente pudiera definirlo, es un Estado democrático Social de Derecho y de Justicia pero uno no puede definir así el capitalismo. El Estado liberal, el Estado burgués, el Estado capitalista, ésta es – y sacó el librito azul del paltó – una Constitución socialista, ésta es una Constitución que nos brinda todas las herramientas, para que a partir de la organización del pueblo, para que a partir de la producción nacional podamos distribuir la riqueza equitativamente entre el pueblo, democratizar el acceso a la educación, a la salud, a la vivienda a la alimentación: la mayor suma de la felicidad posible de la cual nos habló El Libertador y el Comandante nos repitió con tanta insistencia." Véase el reportaje: "Arreaza: La Constitución es Socialista," en *Noticiero Digital.com*, 20 de julio de 2014, en http://www.noticierodigi-tal.com/2014/07/arreaza-la-constitucion-es-socialista/.

970 Véase Allan R Brewer-Carías, *Reforma constitucional y fraude a la Constitución (1999-2009)*, Academia de Ciencias Políticas y Sociales, Caracas 2009.

971 Véase Allan R. Brewer-Carías, "La Ilegítima mutación de la Constitución y la Legitimidad de la Jurisdicción Constitucional: La "Reforma" de la forma federal del Estado en Venezuela mediante interpretación constitucional," en *Anuario Nº 4, Diciembre 2010,* Instituto de Investigación Jurídicas, Facultad de Jurisprudencia y Ciencias Sociales, Universidad Dr. José Matías Delgado de El Salvador, El Salvador 2010, pp. 111-143.

financiamiento público a los partidos políticos, se cambió para admitir el financiamiento público de las campañas electorales, en beneficio por supuesto del partido oficial, argumentándose que lo único que impedía la Constitución supuestamente era el financiamiento del funcionamiento interno de los mismos;[972] se mutó la Constitución en 2004, al transformarse el "referendo revocatorio" presidencial en un referendo "ratificatorio" para permitir a un Presidente cuyo mandato fue revocado por el pueblo en 2004, continuar ejerciendo el cargo;[973] se mutó la Constitución en 2009, al confundirse el principio de la "alternabilidad" republicana con el principio "electivo," de manera que, eliminándose el primero, la prohibición de la reelección presidencial se convirtió en reelección indefinida, luego incorporada en una ilegítima enmienda constitucional; [974] se mutó la Constitución desde 2008, al eliminarse la jerarquía constitucional de los tratados de derechos humanos y el principio de su aplicación inmediata por los jueces, estableciéndose en su lugar un régimen de monopolio de la Sala Constitucional para decidir en la materia, no previsto en la Constitución.[975]

Además, se mutó la Constitución en 2014, al trastocarse la prohibición de que la Fuerza Armada pueda realizar proselitismo político, interpretándose al contrario, que los militares si pueden realizar actividad política, conforme a las órdenes que reciban de la superioridad, partiendo del supuesto de que el Presidente-Comandante en Jefe, es el Presidente del partido de gobierno;[976] se mutó la Constitución al eliminarse el derecho a la participación política mediante consulta popular en materia de leyes, cuando se emitan por el Poder Ejecutivo;[977] y en fin, se mutó la Constitución al asumir la propia Sala Constitucional competencias en materia de justicia constitucional no previstas en la Constitución, como la de conocer el recurso autónomo de

---

972   Véase Allan R. Brewer-Carías, "El juez constitucional como constituyente: el caso del financiamiento de las campañas electorales de los partidos políticos en Venezuela," en *Revista de Derecho Público*, N° 117, (enero-marzo 2009), Caracas 2009, pp. 195-203.

973   Véase Allan R. Brewer-Carías, La Sala Constitucional vs. el derecho ciudadano a la revocatoria de mandatos populares: de cómo un referendo revocatorio fue inconstitucionalmente convertido en un "referendo ratificatorio," en el libro *Crónica sobre la "In" Justicia Constitucional. La Sala Constitucional y el autoritarismo en Venezuela*, Colección Instituto de Derecho Público, Universidad Central de Venezuela, N° 2, Caracas 2007, pp. 349-378.

974   Véase Allan R. Brewer-Carías, "El Juez Constitucional vs. La alternabilidad republicana (La reelección continua e indefinida), en *Revista de Derecho Público*, N° 117, (enero-marzo 2009), Caracas 2009, pp. 205-211.

975   Véase Allan R. Brewer-Carías, "El juez constitucional vs. La justicia internacional en materia de derechos humanos," en *Revista de Derecho Público*, N° 116, (julio-septiembre 2008), Editorial Jurídica Venezolana, Caracas 2008, pp. 249-260.

976   Véase el reportaje: "Maduro nombrado presidente del PSUV y Chávez líder eterno," en *El Universal*, Caracas 27-7-2014, en http://www.eluniversal.com/nacional-y-politica/140727/ma-duro-nombrado-presidente-del-psuv-y-chavez-lider-eterno.

977   Véase la sentencia N° 203 de 25 de marzo de 2014 (Caso *Síndica Procuradora Municipal del Municipio Chacao del Estado Miranda, impugnación del Decreto Ley de Ley Orgánica de la Administración Pública de 2008*), en http://www.tsj.gov.ve/decisiones/scon/marzo/162349-203-25314-2014-09-0456.HTML. Véase el comentario en Allan R. Brewer-Carías, "El fin de la llamada "democracia participativa y protagónica" dispuesto por la Sala Constitucional en fraude a la Constitución, al justificar la emisión de legislación inconsulta en violación al derecho a la participación política," en Allan R. Brewer-Carías, *El golpe a la democracia dado por la Sala Constitucional*, Colección Estudios Políticos N° 8, Editorial Jurídica venezolana, Caracas 2014, pp. 325-339.

interpretación abstracta de la misma que ha servido para que los órganos del Estado obtengan de la Sala Constitucional, a la carta,[978] interpretaciones ajustadas a sus políticas, pero contrarias a los principios constitucionales.[979] Tal fue el caso en 2014 de la sentencia de la Sala Constitucional mediante la cual, a petición del gobierno, la misma al supuestamente interpretar el artículo 68 de la Constitución procedió a "reformar" el artículo 43 de la Ley de Partidos Políticos que en materia de manifestación públicas sólo requiere de "participación previa" ante la autoridad civil para su realización, estableciendo como *obligatorio* que las organizaciones políticas requieran de una autorización de la primera autoridad civil de la jurisdicción correspondiente, para cualquier manifestación pública. [980]

IV   EL ABANDONO DE LA RIGIDEZ CONSTITUCIONAL

Cuarto, la Constitución además dejó de ser un texto rígido como lo exige su supremacía, lo que impone la necesidad de que su reforma se realice exclusivamente mediante los mecanismos previstos en su propio texto, que son: la convocatoria de una "Asamblea Constituyente," la "reforma constitucional" y la "enmienda constitucional," según lo sustancial de las modificaciones; y ha pasado a ser un texto reformable por medio de legislación ordinaria e incluso mediante decretos leyes, evidentemente en violación abierta a su texto. Esto ha ocurrido en Venezuela, sistemáticamente a partir de 2008, como respuesta de los Poderes Ejecutivo y Legislativo al rechazó popular al proyecto de reforma constitucional de 2007,[981] de manera que en abierto fraude a la propia Constitución y más grave aún, a la soberanía popular expresada en dicho referendo, el contenido de la reforma se ha ido implementando progresiva y sucesivamente mediante leyes y decretos leyes, ante la mirada cómplice de la Sala Constitucional que se ha abstenido de ejercer el control de constitucionalidad sobre dichos actos.

---

978   Véase Allan R. Brewer-Carías, *"Quis Custodiet Ipsos Custodes*: De la interpretación constitucional a la inconstitucionalidad de la interpretación", en *Revista de Derecho Público*, N° 105, Editorial Jurídica Venezolana, Caracas 2006, pp. 7-27. Publicado en *Crónica sobre la "In" Justicia Constitucional. La Sala Constitucional y el autoritarismo en Venezuela*, Colección Instituto de Derecho Público. Universidad Central de Venezuela, N° 2, Editorial Jurídica Venezolana, Caracas 2007, pp. 47-79.

979   Véase Allan R. Brewer-Carías, "El juez constitucional al servicio del autoritarismo y la ilegítima mutación de la Constitución: el caso de la Sala Constitucional del Tribunal Supremo de Justicia de Venezuela (1999-2009)", en *Revista de Administración Pública*, N° 180, Madrid 2009, pp. 383-418.

980   Véase sentencia N° 276 de 23 de abril de 2014, en http://www.tsj.gov.ve/deci-siones/scon/abril/163222-276-24414-2014-14-0277.HTML. Véase el comentario en Allan R. Brewer-Carías, "Un nuevo atentado contra la democracia: el secuestro del derecho político a manifestar mediante una ilegítima "reforma" legal efectuada por la Sala Constitucional del Tribunal Supremo," en Allan R. Brewer-Carías, *El golpe a la democracia dado por la Sala Constitucional*, Colección Estudios Políticos N° 8, Editorial Jurídica venezolana, Caracas 2014, pp. 305-324.

981   Véase en general sobre el contenido del Proyecto de Reforma Constitucional de 2007 los trabajos publicados en *Revista de Derecho Público*, N° 112 (Estudios sobre la Reforma Constitucional) (octubre-diciembre 2007), Editorial Jurídica Venezolana, Caracas 2007; y sobre los Decretos Leyes de 2008 los trabajos publicados en *Revista de Derecho Público*, N° 115, (julio septiembre 2008) (Estudios sobre los decretos leyes), Editorial Jurídica Venezolana, Caracas 2008.

Así, todos los aspectos fundamentales de la rechazada reforma constitucional de 2007[982] puede decirse que han sido puestos en vigencia mediante leyes y decretos leyes, en abierta violación de la Constitución, entre ellos están: la creación del Distrito Capital dependiente del Poder Nacional como lo era el viejo Distrito Federal eliminado en 1999;[983] la eliminación de la garantía de derecho de propiedad que impone la expropiación sólo después de pagada la justa compensación, habiéndose regulado en multitud de leyes una "expropiación administrativa" que permite el despojo de propiedades privadas sin pago previo de justa compensación, lo que se ha convertido en una confiscación, prohibida por lo demás en la propia Constitución;[984] la sustitución de la Fuerza Armada Nacional, por una Fuerza Armada Bolivariana, con nuevos componentes no establecidos en la Constitución;[985] y además, la pérdida de autonomía del Banco Central de Venezuela, convirtiéndolo en un instrumento más del manejo discrecional de las finanzas del Estado.[986]

Pero en el marco de la violación del principio de la rigidez constitucional, entre los aspectos de mayor importancia que deben destacarse es el proceso de desconstitucionalización del Estado, que se ha producido mediante la implementación, a través de leyes, del contenido de la rechazada reforma constitucional de 2007, con lo que se ha trastocado completamente el derecho público en Venezuela, surgiendo un "derecho administrativo" paralelo al del Estado Constitucional, que no tiene su fuente primaria en la Constitución de 1999, sino en leyes dictadas al margen de la misma.

Con ello, la Constitución perdió su carácter integral y auto comprehensivo como instrumento de organización de la totalidad del Estado y de protección de los derechos ciudadanos, y fuente de todo el derecho, especialmente del derecho administrativo, creándose en paralelo al Estado Constitucional que ejerce el Poder Público, un "nuevo" Estado que es el llamado "Estado Comunal" o "Estado del Poder Popular,"

---

982 Véase Allan R. Brewer-Carías, "El autoritarismo establecido en fraude a la Constitución y a la democracia, y su formalización en Venezuela mediante la reforma constitucional," en el libro *Estudios sobre el Estado Constitucional (2005-2006)*, Cuadernos de la Cátedra Fundacional Allan R. Brewer Carías de Derecho Público, Universidad Católica del Táchira, N° 9, Editorial Jurídica Venezolana, Caracas, 2007, pp. 78-113.

983 Véase Allan R. Brewer-Carías, "La problemática del régimen jurídico del "Distrito Capital" en la estructura federal del Estado en Venezuela, y su inconstitucional regulación legal", *AIDA Opera Prima de Derecho Administrativo*, N° 5, Universidad Nacional Autónoma de México, enero-junio 2009, México 2009, pp. 81-119

984 Véase Antonio Canova González, Luis Alfonso Herrera Orellana, and Karina Anzola Spadaro, *¿Expropiaciones o vías de hecho? (La degradación continuada del derecho fundamental de propiedad en la Venezuela actual,"* Funeda, Universidad Católica Andrés Bello, Caracas 2009.

985 Véase Jesús María Alvarado Andrade, "La nueva Fuerza Armada Bolivariana (comentarios a raíz del Decreto N° 6.239, con rango, valor y fuerza de Ley Orgánica de la Fuerza Armada Nacional Bolivariana), en *Revista de Derecho Público*, N° 115 (Estudios sobre los decretos leyes 2008), Editorial Jurídica venezolana, Caracas 2008, pp. 197 ss. La Ley se reformó nuevamente en 2014: véase en *Gaceta Oficial* N° 6.156 Extra de 19-11-2014.

986 Véase la Ley Orgánica del Banco Central de Venezuela en *Gaceta Oficial* N° 39419 de 7-5-2010. Véase Domingo Maza Zavala, "Maza Zavala: Reforma de la ley del BCV anula su autonomía,", en La Cl@se.info, 28-10-2009, en http://www.laclase.info/nacionales/maza-zavala-reforma-de-la-ley-del-bcv-anula-su-autonomia. La Ley se reformó nuevamente en 2014: véase en *Gaceta Oficial* N° 6.155 Extra de 19-11-2014.

por supuesto no previsto en la Constitución,[987] pero establecido legalmente para destruir al propio Estado Constitucional.

Puede decirse, en efecto, que esa fue la médula de lo que se buscaba establecer con la reforma constitucional de 2007 y que fue rechazada por el pueblo, que era sustituir el Estado Constitucional por el Estado Comunal o del Poder Popular, que es un Estado realmente configurado como Estado comunista. Como ello no se logró al rechazar el pueblo la reforma n 2007, la Asamblea Nacional, en abierta violación a la Constitución, impuso la misma en 2010, a través de la sanción de un conjunto de Leyes Orgánicas sobre el Poder Popular, las Comunas, los Consejos Comunales, la Economía Popular, y la Contraloría Social,[988] confirmando con ello el proceso de desconstitucionalización del Estado Constitucional y del derecho público, estableciéndose una estructura estatal paralela al Estado Constitucional que tiene por objeto final desmantelarlo y absorberlo, sustituyéndolo de hecho, mediante su ahogamiento. Y eso es lo que ha venido ocurriendo en los últimos años.[989]

En la Administración Pública Central, que es uno de los objetos fundamentales del derecho administrativo, ello se ha evidenciado por ejemplo, en la sustitución de los anteriores Ministerios del Ejecutivo Nacional que ejercen el Poder Ejecutivo, como uno de los poderes públicos del Estado Constitucional,[990] por unos "Ministerios del Poder Popular," y en la creación de unos "Vicepresidentes del Consejo de Ministros" (como si se tratara de un órgano diferenciado del gobierno, cuando en realidad es una de las formas de actuación del Presidente de la República) que violan abiertamente las previsiones constitucionales,[991] de manera que entre las nuevas tendencias del derecho administrativo está el desarrollo de estas formas de organización administrativa fuera del marco constitucional, que sin embargo han encontrado cabida en 2014 en la reforma de la Ley Orgánica de la Administración Pública. [992]

---

987   Véase Allan R. Brewer-Carías, "Las leyes del Poder Popular dictadas en Venezuela en diciembre de 2010, para transformar el Estado Democrático y Social de Derecho en un Estado Comunal Socialista, sin reformar la Constitución," en *Cuadernos Manuel Giménez Abad,* Fundación Manuel Giménez Abad de Estudios Parlamentarios y del Estado Autonómico, N° 1, Madrid, Junio 2011, pp. 127-131

988   Véase Allan R. Brewer-Carías, "Introducción General al Régimen del Poder Popular y del Estado Comunal (O de cómo en el siglo XXI, en Venezuela se decreta, al margen de la Constitución, un Estado de Comunas y de Consejos Comunales, y se establece una sociedad socialista y un sistema económico comunista, por los cuales nadie ha votado)," en Allan R. Brewer-Carías, Claudia Nikken, Luis A. Herrera Orellana, Jesús María Alvarado Andrade, José Ignacio Hernández y Adriana Vigilanza, *Leyes Orgánicas sobre el Poder Popular y el Estado Comunal (Los consejos comunales, las comunas, la sociedad socialista y el sistema económico comunal)* Colección Textos Legislativos N° 50, Editorial Jurídica Venezolana, Caracas 2011, pp. 9-182.

989   Véase Allan R. Brewer-Carías, "La Ley Orgánica del Poder Popular y la desconstitucionalización del Estado de derecho en Venezuela," en *Revista de Derecho Público*, N° 124, (octubre-diciembre 2010), Editorial Jurídica Venezolana, Caracas 2010, pp. 81-101.

990   Véase los Decretos N° 1.226, N° 1.227 y N° 1.228, publicados en *Gaceta Oficial* N° 40.489 de 4 de septiembre de 2014.

991   Véase sobre el régimen ministerial en la Constitución y la Ley Orgánica de la Administración Pública en "Introducción general al régimen jurídico de la Administración Pública", en Allan R. Brewer-Carías (Coordinador y Editor), Rafael Chavero Gazdik y Jesús María Alvarado Andrade, *Ley Orgánica de la Administración Pública, Decreto Ley N° 4317 de 15-07-2008,* Colección Textos Legislativos, N° 24, 4ª edición actualizada, Editorial Jurídica Venezolana, Caracas 2009.

992   Véase en *Gaceta Oficial* N° 6.147 Extra. de 17-11-2014.

A ellas se suman las nuevas formas de organización de la Administración Pública creadas también fuera del orden ministerial, y del propio régimen de la Ley Orgánica de la Administración Pública, que no se les aplica, como son las denominadas "Misiones" con formas organizativas de las más variada naturaleza, a cargo de programas de subsidios sociales,[993] que sólo han sido reguladas recientemente en la Ley Orgánica de Misiones, Grandes Misiones y Micro-Misiones de 2014;[994] y las derivadas de la ceración de los Consejos Comunales, hacia los cuales se han ido desviando muchas funciones otrora de la Administración Central, pero que formalmente no están regidas por la Ley Orgánica de la Administración Pública sino por su propia Ley Orgánica de los Consejos Comunales.[995]

Estas nuevas instancias del Poder Popular, por otra parte, además de no estar regidas por la Ley Orgánica de la Administración Pública, tampoco están regidas por la Ley Orgánica del Poder Público Municipal, habiendo suplantado dichos Consejos Comunales y las Comunas, el carácter constitucional del Municipio de ser la unidad política primaria y autónoma de la organización nacional (art. 168). Con ello, además se ha producido una desmunicipalización de la vida local,[996] al buscarse estructurar a los Consejos Comunales como el centro de realización de una supuesta "democracia participativa" que nada tiene ni de democracia ni de participación,[997] pues no pasan de ser sino unos mecanismos institucionales comandados por personas no electas, controladas directamente por el partido de gobierno y uno de los "Ministerios del Poder Popular" del Ejecutivo Nacional, el ´Ministerio del Poder Popular para las Comunas y Movimientos Sociales," que en septiembre de 2014 se ha integrado a un "Vicepresidente del Consejo de Ministros para Desarrollo del Socialismo Territorial."[998] De dicho Ministerio incluso dependen, en su propia existencia, las Comunas y los Consejos Comunales; que para poder existir tienen que ser previamente autorizados y registrados por el Ejecutivo Nacional, para lo cual la condición mínima es su afiliación a la ideología oficial, el socialismo, y al partido oficial.

---

993 Véase Allan R. Brewer-Carías, "Una nueva tendencia en la organización administrativa venezolana: las "misiones" y las instancias y organizaciones del "poder popular" establecidas en paralelo a la administración pública," en *Retos de la Organización Administrativa Contemporánea, X Foro Iberoamericano de Derecho Administrativo* (26-27 de septiembre de 2011), Corte Suprema de Justicia, Universidad de El Salvador, Universidad Doctor José Matías Delgado, El Salvador, El Salvador, 2011, pp. 927-978.

994 Véase en *Gaceta Oficial* N° 6.154 Extra. de 19-11-2014.

995 Véase Allan R. Brewer-Carías, *Ley Orgánica de Consejos Comunales,* Colección Textos Legislativos, N° 46, Editorial Jurídica Venezolana, Caracas 2010.

996 Véase Allan R. Brewer-Carías, "El inicio de la desmunicipalización en Venezuela: La organización del Poder Popular para eliminar la descentralización, la democracia representativa y la participación a nivel local", en *AIDA, Opera Prima de Derecho Administrativo. Revista de la Asociación Internacional de Derecho Administrativo,* Universidad Nacional Autónoma de México, Facultad de Estudios Superiores de Acatlán, Coordinación de Postgrado, Instituto Internacional de Derecho Administrativo "Agustín Gordillo", Asociación Internacional de Derecho Administrativo, México, 2007, pp. 49 a 67.

997 Véase Allan R. Brewer-Carías, "La necesaria revalorización de la democracia representativa ante los peligros del discurso autoritario sobre una supuesta "democracia participativa" sin representación," en *Derecho Electoral de Latinoamérica. Memoria del II Congreso Iberoamericano de Derecho,* Bogotá, 31 agosto-1 septiembre 2011, Consejo Superior de la Judicatura, ISBN 978-958-8331-93-5, Bogotá 2013, pp. 425-449.

998 Véase en *Gaceta Oficial* N° 40.489 de 4 de septiembre de 2014.

A estos Consejos Comunales se ha referido, a partir de 2008, toda la legislación especial posterior reguladora de cualesquiera que sean las relaciones entre la Administración y los administrados, asignándoseles sistemáticamente el derecho de intervenir en las más variadas formas, pero sin embargo, estableciéndose que a los mismos no se le aplican las normas relativas a Administración Pública Nacional ni las relativas al Poder Público Municipal, es decir, el derecho administrativo del Estado Constitucional, dando así origen a una nueva tendencia del derecho administrativo, que es su propia desregulación, en cuanto a estas nuevas formas de organización administrativa, lo que ha implicado a la vez, su desconstitucionalización, desjuridificación, desadministrativización y desmunicipalización.

V. LA DESINSTITUCIONALIZACIÓN GENERAL DEL PAÍS

Todo este proceso de desmantelamiento del orden constitucional ha tenido sus repercusiones directas en el orden institucional. El hecho de que la Constitución sea impunemente violable, maleable, mutable y desrigidizada, y que la estructura del Estado sea desconstitucionalizada y desjuridificada, ha tenido un efecto catastrófico sobre las instituciones y sobre el orden del derecho administrativo, agravado por el desapego sistemático y absoluto que han demostrado quienes conducen al Estado respecto de la ley y de las instituciones.

Respecto de las leyes, las mismas, insólitamente, dejaron de ser obligatorias para el gobierno, por la falta de control de legalidad, de manera que no es anormal que el gobierno actúe al margen de las mismas, convirtiéndose su acatamiento en la excepción y no en la regla.[999]

Y ese desprecio a la ley se ha reflejado también respecto de instituciones, y el valor social e histórico que tienen, sobre todo aquellas que precisamente tienen historia. Por ello, estas últimas han sido en efecto las más sistemáticamente golpeadas y desmanteladas, y en todo caso, cambiadas o reformadas, sólo para tratar de reescribir la historia, conducta por lo demás típica de los regímenes Totalitarios y Populistas, para tratar de borrar el pasado, en el caso de Venezuela, lo que se ha llamado impropiamente la "Cuarta República," por ejemplo, para tratar de demostrar que la Nación materialmente ha "nacido" con el régimen autoritario iniciado en 1999, en la llamada también erradamente, desde el punto de vista histórico, como la "Quinta República." Esto ha ocurrido, por ejemplo, con los nombres y denominaciones de materialmente todos los órganos de la Administración, y con las leyes, todas las cuales han sido reformadas, en gran parte sin embargo conservando su mismo contenido, pero cambiándoles de nombre, como para que su partida de nacimiento esté en el siglo XXI y no en el siglo pasado. Ciertamente, se pueden cambiar hasta los nombres de las avenidas, puentes y autopistas, pero lo que es cierto es que la historia no se puede borrar.

---

999 Por eso Francisco Mieres, al referirse en particular a la tema de la criminalidad expresa que "en los países anómicos los criminales no viven al margen [de la ley] pues en ellos cumplir la ley es la excepción y su no acatamiento es la regla. El caso de Venezuela es aún más grave. Allí las leyes son órdenes que emanan desde el gobierno, es decir, la anomia ya alcanzó al, y viene desde el, gobierno. Es un caso único en América Latina." En Fernando Mieres, "Venezuela Anómica," en *prodavinci*, 7 de octubre de 2014, en http://prodavinci.com/blogs/venezuela-anomica-por-fernando-mires/.

En todo caso, todo este proceso de resquebrajamiento institucional de la estructura del Estado de derecho, ha dado origen a un cuadro progresivo de inseguridad jurídica que se agrava, abandonándose incluso toda idea de razonabilidad, predictibilidad, claridad y estabilidad de las reglas aplicables, todo lo cual hace cada vez más difícil el poder identificar con claridad y precisión los componentes íntegros del ordenamiento que es aplicable en determinadas áreas de actividad administrativa, es decir, las fuentes mismas del propio derecho administrativo. Por ello es que hemos dicho que la tendencia global que surge de esta realidad en cuanto al derecho administrativo, es su alteración y desquiciamiento.

En el marco anterior de carecer el Estado de una Constitución como norma suprema y rígida, sino de una Constitución sucesivamente violada, sin control, y además, de una Constitución maleable y mutable, conforme a los requerimientos del Gobierno, con el abandono total del principio de su rigidez, han originado un proceso de desinstitucionalización general del país y ausencia de garantías, que son los que lamentablemente están marcando las nuevas tendencias del derecho administrativo como rama del derecho desconstitucionalizada y desjuridificada.

SECCIÓN SEGUNDA:

LA AUSENCIA DE ESTADO DEMOCRÁTICO

El texto de esta Sección segunda, recoge parte de las reflexiones elaboradas con ocasión de la preparación de la conferencia que conforma la Sección primera, sobre el tema "¿Hacia dónde va el derecho público?: Estado Totalitario y nuevas tendencias del derecho administrativo," redactada para el mencionado 2014 *Congreso Internacional Conmemorativo del Acto Legislativo del 10 de septiembre de 1914 por el cual se estableció el Consejo de Estado,* **sobre** *Tendencias actuales del derecho público,* **organizado por la Universidad del Rosario y el Consejo de Estrado, Biblioteca Luis Ángel Arango, Bogotá 8 al 10 de septiembre de 2014.**

Además de por la ausencia de Estado de derecho, el Estado en Venezuela también ha quedado configurado como un Estado Totalitario, porque a pesar de que lo establece y declara la Constitución, el mismo, en la realidad, tampoco es un Estado democrático, lo que ha implicado que al derecho administrativo se le haya sustraído su base democrática, como garantía del ciudadano, y haya quedado efectivamente sólo como un marco regulador del ejercicio del Poder por los funcionarios del Estado.

Un Estado democrático, en efecto, es aquél en el cual, además de estar asegurada la supremacía constitucional y la sumisión del Estado al derecho, concepto con el cual está esencialmente imbricado, exista *primero*, un régimen político de democracia representativa que permita y aliente la participación ciudadana, mediante la celebración de elecciones periódicas, libres, justas y basadas en el sufragio universal y secreto, como expresión de la soberanía del pueblo; *segundo*, un régimen plural de partidos y organizaciones políticas con libre actuación en plano de igualdad; *tercero*, un efectivo sistema de separación horizontal entre los poderes del Estado, que sirva para que el Poder controle al poder, de manera que el ejercicio del Poder Público pueda ser efectivamente controlado tanto judicialmente como por los otros medios dispuestos en la Constitución,[1000] que aseguren la probidad y la responsabilidad de los gobiernos en la gestión pública; *cuarto*, un sistema de distribución vertical del Poder Público como principio medular de la organización del Estrado, para permitir, a través de la descentralización política del poder, la participación ciudadana; y *quinto*, una declaración de derechos humanos y libertades fundamentales, entre ellos, los derechos individuales, sociales, económicos y ambientales, en particular, la libertad de expresión, que estén todos garantizados constitucionalmente y sean asegurados y justiciables por un Poder Judicial independiente y autónomo.[1001]

Para que exista un Estado democrático, por tanto, tampoco bastan las declaraciones constitucionales, y ni siquiera, la sola existencia de elecciones. Ya el mundo contemporáneo ha conocido demasiadas experiencias de toda suerte de tiranos que usaron el voto popular para acceder al poder, y que luego, mediante su ejercicio incontrolado, desmantelaron la propia democracia y desarrollaron gobiernos autoritarios, contrarios al pueblo, que acabaron con la democracia y con todos sus elementos,[1002] comenzando por el irrespeto a los derechos humanos. Esta es la lamentable situación que se ha dado en Venezuela, donde se ha arraigado un gobierno autoritario y un Estado Totalitario, partiendo de elementos que se insertaron en la misma Constitución de 1999,[1003] lo que permite afirmar que no tenemos un Estado democrático.

Más bien, lo que tenemos es un Estado donde no hay efectiva democracia representativa; donde no existe democracia participativa, no pasando, la "democracia participativa y protagónica" que se pregona, de ser un esquema si acaso de movilización popular pero controlada por el gobierno central; donde no hay separación de poderes; donde no sólo los militares no están sometidos a la autoridad civil, sino que los mismos controlan el poder y a la Administración; y donde no hay libertad de

---

1000   Véase Allan R. Brewer–Carías, "Prólogo: Sobre el derecho a la democracia y el control del poder", al libro de Asdrúbal Aguiar, *El derecho a la democracia. La democracia en el derecho y la jurisprudencia interamericanos. La libertad de expresión, piedra angular de la democracia*, Editorial Jurídica Venezolana, Caracas 2008, pp. 19 ss.

1001   Véase Allan R. Brewer-Carías, "Algo sobre las nuevas tendencias del derecho constitucional: el reconocimiento del derecho a la constitución y del derecho a la democracia," en Sergio J. Cuarezma Terán y Rafael Luciano Pichardo (Directores), *Nuevas tendencias del derecho constitucional y el derecho procesal constitucional*, Instituto de Estudios e Investigación Jurídica (INEJ), Managua 2011, pp. 73-94.

1002   Véase en relación con el caso de Venezuela: Allan R. Brewer-Carías, *Dismantling Democracy. The Chávez Authoritarian Experiment*, Cambridge University Press, New York 2010.

1003   Véase los comentarios críticos a la semilla autoritaria en la Constitución de 1999, en Allan R. Brewer–Carías, *Debate Constituyente (Aportes a la Asamblea Nacional Constituyente), Tomo III (18 octubre–30 noviembre 1999)*, Fundación de Derecho Público–Editorial Jurídica Venezolana, Caracas, 1999, pp. 311–340; "Reflexiones críticas sobre la Constitución de Venezuela de 1999," en el libro de Diego Valadés, Miguel Carbonell (Coordinadores), *Constitucionalismo Iberoamericano del Siglo XXI*, Cámara de Diputados. LVII Legislatura, Universidad Nacional Autónoma de México, México 2000, pp. 171–193; en *Revista de Derecho Público*, N° 81, Editorial Jurídica Venezolana, Caracas, enero–marzo 2000, pp. 7–21; en *Revista Facultad de Derecho, Derechos y Valores*, Volumen III N° 5, Universidad Militar Nueva Granada, Santafé de Bogotá, D.C., Colombia, Julio 2000, pp. 9–26; y en el libro *La Constitución de 1999*, Biblioteca de la Academia de Ciencias Políticas y Sociales, Serie Eventos 14, Caracas, 2000, pp. 63–88.

expresión, habiendo quedado en su mínima expresión, entre otros factores, por el acaparamiento de los medios de comunicación por parte del Estado.

I. LAS FALLAS DE LA REPRESENTATIVIDAD DEMOCRÁTICA

En efecto, en la situación actual, *primero*, en Venezuela no hay un sistema efectivo y real de democracia representativa, entre otros aspectos, por las previsiones contenidas en la reforma de la Ley Orgánica de Procesos Electorales,[1004] la cual al regular la representación proporcional y la personificación del sufragio, lo que logró fue permitirle al partido de gobierno que con minoría del voto popular haya asegurado controlar la mayoría de los escaños en la Asamblea Nacional.[1005] Además, el sistema se caracteriza por el abuso que deriva de la imbricación total entre el partido oficial y el aparato del Estado, el cual ha sido íntegramente puesto al servicio de los candidatos oficiales; por la recepción consecuente por parte del partido oficial que preside el propio Presidente de la República, de un ingente financiamiento directo e indirecto del Estado, sin que nunca se haya rendido cuentas de ello; por el control obsceno de todos los medios de comunicación por parte del Estado, y por el abuso de los candidatos oficiales en la utilización limitada de los mismos de comunicación, en las campañas electorales.

El sistema electoral y de escrutinio, además, ha estado controlado por un conjunto de órganos, como son los que conforman el Poder Electoral, que al contrario del carácter independiente, autónomo, despartidizado, imparcial y con participación ciudadana que prevé la Constitución (art. 294), ha estado comandado, desde 2004, por un Consejo Nacional Electoral totalmente dependiente del Poder Ejecutivo, sin autonomía, completamente partidizado, integrado en su mayoría por miembros del partido oficial y controlado por el mismo, totalmente parcializado a favor de éste último, y en cuya gestión se niega toda forma de participación ciudadana, salvo la que deriva de las cargas ciudadanas para el cumplimiento temporal de funciones electorales. Ese órgano no ha podido, por tanto, garantizar ni la igualdad, ni la imparcialidad, ni la transparencia, ni la eficiencia de los procesos electorales que exige la Constitución (art. 293), particularmente desde cuándo a partir de 2004 fue doblemente secuestrado por la Sala Constitucional del Tribunal Supremo de Justicia, y puesto al servicio de los intereses electorales del partido oficial.[1006]

1004   Véase sobre la Ley Orgánica de los Procesos Electorales en *Gaceta Oficial* N° 5928 Extra. de 12 de agosto de 2009. Sobre el sistema electoral antes de esta Ley véase Allan R. Brewer-Carías, "Reforma electoral en el sistema político de Venezuela", en Daniel Zovatto y J. Jesús Orozco Henríquez (Coordinadores), *Reforma Política y Electoral en América Latina 1978-2007,* Universidad Nacional Autónoma de México-IDEA internacional, México 2008, pp. 953-1019.

1005   Véase Allan R. Brewer-Carías, "Reforma electoral en el sistema político de Venezuela", en Daniel Zovatto y J. Jesús Orozco Henríquez (Coordinadores), *Reforma Política y Electoral en América Latina 1978-2007,* Universidad Nacional Autónoma de México-IDEA internacional, México 2008, pp. 953-1019.

1006   Véase Allan R. Brewer-Carías, "El Poder Electoral y la confiscación del derecho a la participación política mediante el referendo revocatorio presidencial: Venezuela 2000-2004", en Juan Pérez Royo, Joaquín Pablo Urías Martínez, Manuel Carrasco Durán, Editores), *Derecho Constitucional para el Siglo XXI. Actas del Congreso Iberoamericano de Derecho Constitucional,* Tomo I, Thomson-Aranzadi, Madrid 2006, pp. 1081-1126; y "La autonomía e independencia del Poder Electoral y de la Jurisdicción Electoral en Venezuela, y su secuestro y sometimiento por la jurisdicción Constitucio-

El resultado de todo ello ha sido que lejos de ser el régimen político venezolano el de una democracia, donde la conjunción de intereses y posiciones contrapuestas es indispensable para poder gobernar, mediante el diálogo, acuerdos y compromisos; se trata, de hecho, de un régimen de partido único que controla todos los poderes, y que incluso no reconoce a la oposición; lo que se ha manifestado en más de una ocasión, con los anuncios públicos y sucesivos de que la mayoría oficialista en la Asamblea Nacional de no dialogarán siquiera con la oposición. Ello ocurrió, por ejemplo, en 2010, cuando la mayoría oficialista perdió la mayoría calificada que tenía en la Asamblea Nacional, y ha ocurrido de nuevo recientemente.[1007] Este desconocimiento de la oposición ha conducido, de hecho, a que el sistema político sea en la práctica uno de partido único, al punto de que el nombramiento de los altos funcionarios del Estado que desde hace años tienen sus períodos vencidos, como el Contralor General de la República y los miembros del Consejo Nacional Electoral, no puede tener lugar porque el partido de gobierno se niega a entrar siquiera en conversaciones con los diputados representantes de la oposición, sin cuyos votos no pueden efectuarse tales nombramientos.

II. LAS FALLAS DE LA LLAMADA DEMOCRACIA PARTICIPATIVA

Segundo, en la situación actual, en Venezuela tampoco hay un sistema real y efectivo de democracia participativa, y aún menos "protagónica." En la actualidad, la participación del pueblo en política, como en la más típica de las democracias formales, se ha reducido a la participación mediante voto en las elecciones. Los mecanismos de democracia directa, como los referendos, se han hecho de imposible ejercicio por las condiciones y requisitos legales impuestos para que por iniciativa popular puedan convocarse como lo exige la Constitución;[1008] y los mecanismos de participación ciudadana directamente previstos en la Constitución han sido arrebatados al pueblo, al distorsionarse en la legislación la integración de los Comités de Postulaciones Judiciales, Electorales y del Poder Ciudadano, que quedaron bajo el control político de la mayoría oficialista de la Asamblea Nacional sin que el ciudadano y sus organizaciones pueda participar;[1009] y al haberse vaciado, por la Sala

---

nal," Documento preparado para el *III Congreso Iberoamericano de Derecho Electoral*, Facultad de Estudios Superiores de Aragón de la Universidad Nacional Autónoma de México, Estado de México, 27-29 Septiembre de 2012.

1007   Véase por ejemplo lo declarado por el Presidente de la Asamblea Nacional en *El Universal*, Caracas 17 de julio de 2014, en http://www.eluniversal.com/nacional-y-politica/140717/ca-bello-descarta-cualquier-reunion-con-partidos-de-la-oposicion.

1008   Véase Allan R. Brewer-Carías, *La Sala Constitucional versus el Estado democrático de derecho. El secuestro del Poder Electoral y de la Sala Electoral del Tribunal Supremo y la confiscación del derecho a la participación política*, Los Libros de El Nacional, Colección Ares, Caracas 2004; "El secuestro del Poder Electoral y la confiscación del derecho a la participación política mediante el referendo revocatorio presidencial: Venezuela 2000-2004", en *Boletín Mexicano de Derecho Comparado*, Instituto de Investigaciones Jurídicas, Universidad Nacional Autónoma de México, N° 112. México, enero-abril 2005 pp. 11-73.

1009   Véase Allan R. Brewer-Carías, "La participación ciudadana en la designación de los titulares de los órganos no electos de los Poderes Públicos en Venezuela y sus vicisitudes políticas", en *Revista Iberoamericana de Derecho Público y Administrativo*, Año 5, N° 5-2005, San José, Costa Rica 2005, pp. 76-95; y "Sobre el nombramiento irregular por la Asamblea Nacional de los titulares de los órga-

Constitucional, la norma constitucional que prevé la consulta popular necesaria e indispensable antes de la sanción de las leyes, al haber dispuesto, en fraude a la Constitución, que ello no se aplica a la legislación delegada, dictada mediante decretos leyes, que en definitiva se ha convertido en la forma normal de legislación en el país.[1010]

Pero la ausencia de participación política también queda evidenciada en la forma cómo se ha estructurado el denominado Poder Popular o Estado Comunal, sobre la base de Consejos Comunales comandados por voceros que no son electos, sino impuestos por el partido de gobierno que los controla, y sin cuyo manejo ni siquiera pueden obtener reconocimiento por el Ministerio de la Participación.[1011]

En realidad, la "democracia participativa" que se ha vendido supuestamente consolidando a través de la creación de estas organizaciones del llamado "Poder Popular," no es más que una falacia de participación,[1012] pues se trata de instituciones propias del populismo de Estado, que maneja el Poder Central, para repartir recursos fuera de los canales regulares del Estado y particularmente fuera de los gobiernos locales, vaciando en paralelo a los Municipios de competencias, pero que dependen totalmente, incluso en su propia existencia, de una decisión del Ejecutivo Nacional. En esos Consejos, en realidad, el único que "participa" es el partido de gobierno y los derivados de su clientelismo, y si alguna participación se le da a la población local en el proceso de inversión de los recursos repartidos, por supuesto es sólo parcial, solo para los sectores que se identifican con el socialismo como doctrina oficial. De resto, lo que hay es exclusión y marginamiento.

III. LA AUSENCIA DE SEPARACIÓN DE PODERES

Tercero, la ausencia de Estado democrático en Venezuela, deriva de la ausencia de aplicación del principio de la separación de poderes, el cual en un Estado de derecho, es el fundamento de la democracia, y el elemento fundamental para garantizar el necesario equilibrio que debe haber entre los poderes y prerrogativas de la Admi-

---

nos del poder ciudadano en 2007", en *Revista de Derecho Público*, N° 113, Editorial Jurídica Venezolana, Caracas 2008, pp. 85-88.

1010   Véase Allan R. Brewer-Carías, "Apreciación general sobre los vicios de inconstitucionalidad que afectan los Decretos Leyes Habilitados" en *Ley Habilitante del 13-11-2000 y sus Decretos Leyes,* Academia de Ciencias Políticas y Sociales, Serie Eventos N° 17, Caracas 2002, pp. 63-103; y "El derecho ciudadano a la participación popular y la inconstitucionalidad generalizada de los decretos leyes 2010-2012, por su carácter inconsulto," en *Revista de Derecho Público,* N° 130, (abril-junio 2012), Editorial Jurídica Venezolana, Caracas 2012, pp. 85-88.

1011   Véase Allan R. Brewer-Carías, *Ley Orgánica de Consejos Comunales,* Colección Textos Legislativos, N° 46, Editorial Jurídica Venezolana, Caracas 2010.

1012   Véase Allan R. Brewer-Carías, "La necesaria revalorización de la democracia representativa ante los peligros del discurso autoritario sobre una supuesta "democracia participativa" sin representación," en *Derecho Electoral de Latinoamérica. Memoria del II Congreso Iberoamericano de Derecho,* Bogotá, 31 agosto-1 septiembre 2011, Consejo Superior de la Judicatura, ISBN 978-958-8331-93-5, Bogotá 2013, pp. 425-449. Véase además, el texto de la Ponencia: "La democracia representativa y la falacia de la llamada "democracia participativa," *Congreso Iberoamericano de Derecho Electoral,* Universidad de Nuevo León, Monterrey, 27 de noviembre 2010.

nistración del Estado y los derechos ciudadanos.[1013] Su importancia es de tal naturaleza que solo controlando al Poder es que puede haber democracia, es decir, elecciones libres y justas; pluralismo político; efectiva participación en la gestión de los asuntos públicos; transparencia administrativa en el ejercicio del gobierno; rendición de cuentas por parte de los gobernantes; sumisión efectiva del gobierno a la Constitución y las leyes; efectivo acceso a la justicia; y real y efectiva garantía de respeto a los derechos humanos. [1014]

En cambio, nada de ello se logra en un Estado Totalitario, como el que se ha configurado en Venezuela, donde al contrario, la totalidad del Poder está concentrada, y los poderes son manejados por el binomio establecido entre Poder Legislativo y Poder Ejecutivo. A pesar de que la Constitución establece, no tres sino cinco poderes públicos separados, que son los poderes Legislativo, Ejecutivo, Judicial, Ciudadano y Electoral, la realidad es que en el propio texto constitucional se dispuso el germen de la concentración del poder en manos de la Asamblea Nacional y, consecuencialmente, del Poder Ejecutivo, que la controla políticamente.[1015] Con ello, progresivamente, los otros Poderes Públicos, y particularmente el Poder Judicial, el Poder Ciudadano y el Poder Electoral han quedado sometidos a la voluntad del Ejecutivo.[1016]

Esta dependencia de todos los órganos de los poderes del Estado respecto del Ejecutivo y del Legislativo, y en especial en lo que se refiere a los órganos de control, ha sido lo que ha originado la abstención total de los mismos de ejercer las potestades que le son atribuidas, y con ello, la práctica política de concentración total del poder en manos del Ejecutivo, dado el control político partidista que éste ejerce sobre la Asamblea Nacional, y por con ello, la configuración de un modelo político autoritario. Además, la designación de los jefes de dichas instituciones de control ha quedado a la merced de la Asamblea Nacional, por la violación sistemática de la previsión garantizadora del derecho a la participación política en la designación de los mismos, mediante unos Comités de postulaciones que debían estar integrados exclusivamente por representantes de los diversos sectores de la sociedad. Desde

---

1013   Véase sobre el tema Gustavo Tarre Briceño, *Solo el poder detiene al poder, La teoría de la separación de los poderes y su aplicación en Venezuela*, Colección Estudios Jurídicos Nº 102, Editorial Jurídica Venezolana, Caracas 2014; y Jesús María Alvarado Andrade, "División del Poder y Principio de Subsidiariedad. El Ideal Político del Estado de Derecho como base para la Libertad y prosperidad material" en Luis Alfonso herrera Orellana (Coord.), *Enfoques Actuales sobre Derecho y Libertad en Venezuela*, Academia de Ciencias Políticas y Sociales, Caracas, 2013, pp. 131-185.

1014   Véase Allan R. Brewer-Carías, "Prólogo" al libro de Gustavo Tarre Briceño, *Solo el poder detiene al poder, La teoría de la separación de los poderes y su aplicación en Venezuela*, Colección Estudios Jurídicos Nº 102, Editorial Jurídica Venezolana, Caracas 2014, pp. 13-49.

1015   Véase Allan R. Brewer-Carías, El sistema presidencial de gobierno en la Constitución de Venezuela de 1999 (Bogotá, junio 2005), *Estudios sobre el Estado Constitucional (2005-2006)*, Cuadernos de la Cátedra Fundacional Allan R. Brewer Carías de Derecho Público, Universidad Católica del Táchira, Nº 9, Editorial Jurídica Venezolana, Caracas, 2007, pp. 475-624.

1016   Véase Allan R. Brewer-Carías, El sistema presidencial de gobierno en la Constitución de Venezuela de 1999 (Bogotá, junio 2005), *Estudios sobre el Estado Constitucional (2005-2006)*, Cuadernos de la Cátedra Fundacional Allan R. Brewer Carías de Derecho Público, Universidad Católica del Táchira, Nº 9, Editorial Jurídica Venezolana, Caracas, 2007, pp. 475-624.

2000, dichos Comités, se sustituyeron por simples "comisiones parlamentarias ampliadas" controladas completamente por el partido de gobierno.[1017]

En ese contexto, entonces, a pesar de que hay un Poder Ciudadano supuestamente autónomo e independiente, dentro del mismo, la Contraloría General de la República dejó de ejercer control fiscal alguno de la Administración Pública, y ello a pesar de la inflación de las prácticas de corrupción que impiden que en el país siquiera se pueda obtener el más simple de los servicios administrativos sin pago previo, lo que ha ubicado al país en el primer lugar del índice de corrupción en el mundo, según las cifras difundidas por Transparencia Internacional.[1018]

Por su parte, el Defensor del Pueblo, desde cuando la primera persona designada para ocupar el cargo en 2000 fue removida por haber ejercido recursos judiciales contra políticas en defensa del derecho colectivo a la participación en la designación de las altas autoridades de los Poderes Públicos,[1019] dicho órgano perdió completamente la orientación, y sin brújula alguna, se convirtió en el órgano oficial para avalar la violación por parte de las autoridades administrativas de los derechos humanos.[1020]

Y la Fiscalía General de la República, el otro órgano del Poder Ciudadano que ejerce el Ministerio Público, en lugar de ser la parte de buena fe del proceso penal y de la vindicta pública, es el principal instrumento para la prevalencia de la impuni-

---

1017   Véase Allan R. Brewer-Carías, "La participación ciudadana en la designación de los titulares de los órganos no electos de los Poderes Públicos en Venezuela y sus vicisitudes políticas", en *Revista Iberoamericana de Derecho Público y Administrativo*, Año 5, Nº 5-2005, San José, Costa Rica 2005, pp. 76-95.

1018   Véase el Informe de la ONG alemana, Transparencia Internacional de 2013, en el reportaje: "Aseguran que Venezuela es el país más corrupto de Latinoamérica," en *El Universal*, Caracas 3 de diciembre de 2013, en http://www.eluniversal.com/nacional-y-politica/131203/aseguran-que-venezuela-es-el-pais-mas-corrupto-de-latinoamerica. Igualmente véase el reportaje en BBC Mundo, "Transparencia Internacional: Venezuela y Haití, los que se ven más corruptos de A. Latina," 3 de diciembre de 2013, en
http://www.bbc.co.uk/mundo/ultimas_noticias/2013/12/131203_ultnot_transparencia_corrupcion_lp. shtml. Véase al respecto, Román José Duque Corredor, "Corrupción y democracia en América Latina. Casos emblemáticos de corrupción en Venezuela," en *Revista Electrónica de Derecho Administrativo*, Universidad Monteávila, 2014.

1019   Véase los comentarios en Allan R. Brewer-Carías, "La participación ciudadana en la designación de los titulares de los órganos no electos de los Poderes Públicos en Venezuela y sus vicisitudes políticas", en *Revista Iberoamericana de Derecho Público y Administrativo*, Año 5, Nº 5-2005, San José, Costa Rica 2005, pp. 76-95.

1020   Por ejemplo, ante la crisis de la salud denunciada por la Academia Nacional de Medicina en agosto de 2014, reclamando la declaratoria de emergencia del sector, la respuesta de la Defensora del Pueblo fue simplemente que en Venezuela no había tal crisis. Véase el reportaje: "Defensora del Pueblo Gabriela Ramírez afirma que en Venezuela no existe ninguna crisis en el sector salud," en *Noticias Venezuela*, 20 agosto de 2014, en http://noticiasvene-zuela.info/2014/08/defensora-del-pueblo-gabriela-ramirez-afirma-que-en-venezuela-no-existe-ninguna-crisis-en-el-sector-salud/; y el reportaje: "Gabriela Ramírez, Defensora del Pueblo: Es desproporcionada petición de emergencia humanitaria en el sector salud," en El Universal, Caracas 20 de agosto de 2014, en http://m.eluniversal.com/nacional-y-politica/140820/es-desproporcionada-peticion-de-emergencia-humanitaria-en-el-sector-sa. Por ello, con razón, el Editorial del diario *El Nacional* del 22 de agosto de 2014, se tituló: "A quien defiende la defensora?" Véase en http://www.el-nacional.com/opinion/editorial/defiende-defensora_19_46-8743123.html.

dad en el país, y para asegurar la persecución política y la extorsión gubernamental. Como se destacó en el Informe sobre *Fortalecimiento del Estado de Derecho en Venezuela*, publicado en Ginebra en marzo de 2014, "El incumplimiento con la propia normativa interna ha configurado un Ministerio Público sin garantías de independencia e imparcialidad de los demás poderes públicos y de los actores políticos, con el agravante de que los fiscales en casi su totalidad son de libre nombramiento y remoción, y por tanto vulnerables a presiones externas y sujetos órdenes superiores."[1021]

Por su lado, el Consejo Nacional Electoral, configurado en la Constitución como el quinto de los Poderes Públicos, como se ha dicho, en lugar de ser el árbitro independiente en las elecciones, después de haber sido secuestrado por el Poder Ejecutivo a partir de 2004,[1022] utilizando para ello como instrumento del plagio a la Sala Constitucional, ignorándose la norma constitucional que exige que esté integrado por personas no vinculadas a organizaciones políticas; ha sido integrado por agentes del partido de gobierno, de manera que, controlado por el Ejecutivo, ha actuado más bien como su agente político electoral oficial, minando la credibilidad en la posibilidad efectiva de que en el país se puedan realizar elecciones libres.

IV. LA AUSENCIA DE AUTONOMÍA E INDEPENDENCIA DEL PODER JUDICIAL

Cuarto, también en relación con la carencia de democracia por la ausencia de régimen alguno de separación de poderes, el más grave atentado al Estado de derecho, al derecho público y al derecho administrativo que se ha hecho en Venezuela, ha sido el sometimiento del Poder Judicial, en su conjunto, a los designios y control político por parte del Poder Ejecutivo.[1023] Ello comenzó con la inconstitucional intervención del Poder Judicial por parte de la Asamblea Nacional Constituyente en 1999, con lo que se procedió a la destitución masiva de Magistrados y jueces sin

---

1021   Véase en http://icj.wpengine.netdna-cdn.com/wp-content/uploads/2014/06/VENEZUELA-Informe-A4-elec.pdf

1022   Véase Allan R. Brewer–Carías, "El secuestro del Poder Electoral y la confiscación del derecho a la participación política mediante el referendo revocatorio presidencial: Venezuela 2000–2004,", en *Boletín Mexicano de Derecho Comparado*, Instituto de Investigaciones Jurídicas, Universidad Nacional Autónoma de México, N° 112. México, enero–abril 2005 pp. 11–73; *La Sala Constitucional versus el Estado Democrático de Derecho. El secuestro del poder electoral y de la Sala Electoral del Tribunal Supremo y la confiscación del derecho a la participación política*, Los Libros de El Nacional, Colección Ares, Caracas, 2004, 172 pp.

1023   Véase Allan R. Brewer–Carías, "La progresiva y sistemática demolición de la autonomía en independencia del Poder Judicial en Venezuela (1999–2004)", en *XXX Jornadas J.M Domínguez Escovar, Estado de derecho, Administración de justicia y derechos humanos*, Instituto de Estudios Jurídicos del Estado Lara, Barquisimeto, 2005, pp. 33–174; y "La justicia sometida al poder [La ausencia de independencia y autonomía de los jueces en Venezuela por la interminable emergencia del Poder Judicial (1999–2006)]" en *Cuestiones Internacionales. Anuario Jurídico Villanueva 2007*, Centro Universitario Villanueva, Marcial Pons, Madrid, 2007, pp. 25–57; "La demolición de las instituciones judiciales y la destrucción de la democracia: La experiencia venezolana," en *Instituciones Judiciales y Democracia. Reflexiones con ocasión del Bicentenario de la Independencia y del Centenario del Acto Legislativo 3 de 1910*, Consejo de Estado, Sala de Consulta y Servicio Civil, Bogotá 2012, pp. 230-254..

garantías judiciales;[1024] y siguió con el apoderamiento por parte del partido de gobierno, desde 2000, a través de la Asamblea Nacional, del proceso de designación de los Magistrados del Tribunal Supremo, sacrificándose la previsión que exigía la participación en ello de representantes de la sociedad civil. Ello se consolidó en 2004, con el aumento del número de Magistrados del Tribunal Supremo en la Ley Orgánica del Tribunal Supremo de Justicia, los cuales además quedaron con posibilidad de ser removidos por simple mayoría de votos de los diputados en la Asamblea Nacional, que entonces alcanzaba la bancada oficialista;[1025] y en 2010, con la irregular "reforma" de la Ley Orgánica del Tribunal Supremo de Justicia mediante la "re-publicación" de la Ley,[1026] para impedir que en la designación pudieran participar con su voto los diputados de oposición, llenándose el Tribunal Supremo de jueces incluso con militancia abierta del partido de gobernó.[1027] Y mediante el control y asalto al Tribunal Supremo de Justicia, que es el órgano que en Venezuela tiene a su cargo todo el gobierno y administración del sistema de Justicia, la totalidad del Poder Judicial quedó controlado políticamente.

En este campo, por supuesto, para calibrar la situación del Poder Judicial, es imposible atenerse a las etiquetas constitucionales. Por ejemplo, el principio de la independencia y autonomía del Poder Judicial está declarado en el artículo 254 de la Constitución de 1999, previendo el ingreso de los jueces a la carrera judicial y a su permanencia y estabilidad en los cargos, primero, mediante la realización de concursos públicos de oposición que aseguren la idoneidad y excelencia de los participantes, debiendo además garantizarse la participación ciudadana en el procedimiento de selección y designación de los jueces (art. 255). Estas previsiones, que cualquiera se maravillaría de encontrar en el texto de una Constitución, sin embargo, son letra muerta, no se cumplen y nunca se han cumplido en los tres lustros de vigencia del texto fundamental; es decir, nunca, durante la vigencia de la Constitución, se han desarrollado esos concursos, en esa forma.

Pero segundo, además, en cuanto a la estabilidad de los jueces, la Constitución dispone que los mismos sólo pueden ser removidos o suspendidos de sus cargos mediante juicios disciplinarios, llevados a cabo por jueces disciplinarios mediante un proceso disciplinario judicial con las debidas garantías (art. 255). Sin embargo,

1024   Véase nuestro voto salvado a la intervención del Poder Judicial por la Asamblea Nacional Constituyente en Allan R. Brewer–Carías, *Debate Constituyente, (Aportes a la Asamblea Nacional Constituyente)*, Tomo I, (8 agosto–8 septiembre), Caracas 1999; y las críticas formuladas a ese proceso en Allan R. Brewer–Carías, *Golpe de Estado y proceso constituyente en Venezuela*, Universidad Nacional Autónoma de México, México, 2002

1025   Véase en *Gaceta Oficial* N° 37942 de 20 de mayo de 2004. Sobre dicha Ley y las reformas introducidas véase, Véase Allan R. Brewer-Carías *Ley Orgánica del Tribunal Supremo de Justicia*, Caracas 2010.

1026   Véase en *Gaceta Oficial* N° 39483 de 9-8-2010. Véase Allan R. Brewer-Carías y Víctor Hernández Mendible, *Ley Orgánica del Tribunal Supremo de Justicia*, Caracas 2010. Sobre la reforma efectuada mediante la re-publicación de la Ley Orgánica, véase Víctor Hernández Mendible, "Sobre la nueva reimpresión por "supuestos errores" materiales de la Ley Orgánica del Tribunal Supremo, octubre de 2010," y Antonio Silva Aranguren, "Tras el rastro del engaño en la web de la Asamblea Nacional," en *Revista de Derecho Público*, N° 124, Editorial Jurídica Venezolana, Caracas 2010, pp. 110-114.

1027   Véase los comentarios de Hildegard Rondón de Sansó, "*Obiter Dicta*. En torno a una elección," en *La Voce d'Italia*, Caracas 14-12-2010.

en ese caso, ello tampoco jamás se ha implementado, y a partir de 1999, [1028] más bien se regularizó, en una ilegítima transitoriedad constitucional, la existencia de una Comisión de Funcionamiento del Poder Judicial creada ad hoc para "depurar" el poder judicial, removiéndolos sin garantías judiciales.[1029]

Esa Comisión, por tanto, durante más de 10 años destituyó materialmente a casi todos los jueces del país, discrecionalmente y sin garantía alguna del debido proceso,[1030] los cuales fueron reemplazados por jueces provisorios o temporales,[1031] por supuesto dependientes del Poder y sin garantía alguna de estabilidad. Ello, por lo demás, ha continuado hasta el presente, demoliéndose sistemáticamente la autonomía judicial, sin que haya variado nada la creación en 2011, de unos tribunales de la llamada "Jurisdicción Disciplinaria Judicial" que quedó sujeta a la Asamblea Nacional, que como órgano político, es la que designa a los "jueces disciplinarios."[1032]

La consecuencia de todo este proceso de quince años es que Venezuela carece completamente de un Poder Judicial autónomo e independiente, estando, el que existe, completamente al servicio del gobierno del Estado y de su política autoritaria, como lo han incluso declarado expresamente sus Magistrados.[1033] El resultado es

---

1028   Véase nuestro voto salvado a la intervención del Poder Judicial por la Asamblea Nacional Constituyente en Allan R. Brewer–Carías, *Debate Constituyente, (Aportes a la Asamblea Nacional Constituyente)*, Tomo I, (8 agosto–8 septiembre), Caracas 1999; y las críticas formuladas a ese proceso en Allan R. Brewer–Carías, *Golpe de Estado y proceso constituyente en Venezuela*, Universidad Nacional Autónoma de México, México, 2002.

1029   Véase Allan R. Brewer–Carías, "La justicia sometida al poder y la interminable emergencia del poder judicial (1999–2006)", en *Derecho y democracia. Cuadernos Universitarios*, Órgano de Divulgación Académica, Vicerrectorado Académico, Universidad Metropolitana, Año II, Nº 11, Caracas, septiembre 2007, pp. 122–138.

1030   La Comisión Interamericana de Derechos Humanos también lo registró en el Capítulo IV del *Informe* que rindió ante la Asamblea General de la OEA en 2006, que los "casos de destituciones, sustituciones y otro tipo de medidas que, en razón de la provisionalidad y los procesos de reforma, han generado dificultades para una plena vigencia de la independencia judicial en Venezuela" (párrafo 291); destacando aquellas "destituciones y sustituciones que son señaladas como represalias por la toma de decisiones contrarias al Gobierno" (párrafo 295 ss.); concluyendo que para 2005, según cifras oficiales, el "el 18,30% de las juezas y jueces son titulares y 81,70% están en condiciones de provisionalidad" (párrafo 202).

1031   En el *Informe Especial* de la Comisión sobre Venezuela correspondiente al año 2003, la misma también expresó, que "un aspecto vinculado a la autonomía e independencia del Poder Judicial es el relativo al carácter provisorio de los jueces en el sistema judicial de Venezuela. Actualmente, la información proporcionada por las distintas fuentes indica que más del 80% de los jueces venezolanos son "provisionales". *Informe sobre la Situación de los Derechos Humanos en Venezuela 2003, cit.* párr. 161

1032   Véase Allan R. Brewer–Carías, "Sobre la ausencia de independencia y autonomía judicial en Venezuela, a los doce años de vigencia de la constitución de 1999 (O sobre la interminable transitoriedad que en fraude continuado a la voluntad popular y a las normas de la Constitución, ha impedido la vigencia de la garantía de la estabilidad de los jueces y el funcionamiento efectivo de una "jurisdicción disciplinaria judicial"), en *Independencia Judicial*, Colección Estado de Derecho, Tomo I, Academia de Ciencias Políticas y Sociales, Acceso a la Justicia org., Fundación de Estudios de Derecho Administrativo (Funeda), Universidad Metropolitana (Unimet), Caracas 2012, pp. 9-103.

1033   Véase por ejemplo lo expresado por el magistrado Francisco Carrasqueño, en la apertura del año judicial en enero de 2008, al explicar que : "no es cierto que el ejercicio del poder político se limite al Legislativo, sino que tiene su continuación en los tribunales, en la misma medida que el Ejecutivo", dejando claro que la "aplicación del Derecho no es neutra y menos aun la actividad de los magistra-

que, como lo destacó la Comisión Internacional de Juristas, en el *Informe* antes mencionado de marzo de 2014, que resume todo lo que en el país se ha venido denunciando en la materia, al dar "cuenta de la falta de independencia de la justicia en Venezuela," se destaca que *"el Poder Judicial ha sido integrado desde el Tribunal Supremo de Justicia (TSJ) con criterios predominantemente políticos en su designación. La mayoría de los jueces son "provisionales" y vulnerables a presiones políticas externas, ya que son de libre nombramiento y de remoción discrecional por una Comisión Judicial del propio Tribunal Supremo, la cual, a su vez, tiene una marcada tendencia partidista;"* concluyendo sin ambages afirmando que:

> "Un sistema de justicia que carece de independencia, como lo es el venezolano, es comprobadamente ineficiente para cumplir con sus funciones propias. En este sentido en Venezuela, un país con una de las más altas tasas de homicidio en Latinoamérica y en el de familiares sin justicia, esta cifra es cercana al 98% en los casos de violaciones a los derechos humanos. Al mismo tiempo, el poder judicial, precisamente por estar sujeto a presiones externas, no cumple su función de proteger a las personas frente a los abusos del poder sino que por el contrario, en no pocos casos es utilizado como mecanismo de persecución contra opositores y disidentes o simples críticos del proceso político, incluidos dirigentes de partidos, defensores de derechos humanos, dirigentes campesinos y sindicales, y estudiantes."[1034]

Con todo esto, el Poder Judicial ha abandonado su función fundamental de servir de instrumento de control de las actividades de los otros órganos del Estado para asegurar su sometimiento a la ley, habiendo materialmente desaparecido el derecho ciudadano a la tutela judicial efectiva y a controlar el poder, produciéndose una desjusticiabilidad, al disiparse la posibilidad de que el Poder Judicial pueda ser utilizado para enjuiciar la conducta de la Administración y frente a ella, garantizar los derechos ciudadanos. En esa situación, por tanto, es difícil hablar siquiera de lo que es la piedra angular de nuestra disciplina, que es el equilibrio entre poderes y prerrogativas del Estado y derechos y garantías ciudadanas, lo que ha sido particularmente grave en el caso de los tribunales contencioso administrativos, precisamente por el hecho de que sus decisiones siempre implican enfrentar el poder, y particularmente, el Poder Ejecutivo. Si la autonomía de los jueces contencioso administrativos no está garantizada ni la independencia está blindada, el mejor sistema de justicia contencioso administrativa es letra muerta; y lamentablemente, esto es lo que también ha ocurrido en Venezuela en los últimos años durante el gobierno autoritario, con el consecuente desquiciamiento del derecho administrativo.

Todo este panorama nos confirma, en conclusión, la trágica realidad de que en Venezuela todos los órganos de los Poderes Públicos han sido y están controlados por el Poder Ejecutivo, y el parido de gobierno que preside el propio Jefe de Estado. A ese sometimiento de los Poderes estatales al Ejecutivo, además, ha contribuido, la

---

dos, porque según se dice en la doctrina, deben ser reflejo de la política, sin vulnerar la independencia de la actividad judicial". *V.* en *El Universal*, Caracas, 29–01–2008

1034   Véase en http://icj.wpengine.netdna-cdn.com/wp-content/uploads/2014/06/VENEZUELA-Informe-A4-elec.pdf

exacerbación del presidencialismo gubernamental que la propia Constitución de 1999 impuso con la extensión del período presidencial a seis años (art. 230); lo que se ha reafirmado con la consagración de la reelección presidencial continua e indefinida en la Enmienda Constitucional aprobada en 2009,[1035] con la cual se abandonó el bicentenario principio del gobierno alternativo (art. 6); y se ha agravado con la previsión constitucional de la posibilidad de la delegación legislativa, sin límites, a favor del Ejecutivo (art. 203), que ha conducido a que toda la legislación fundamental del país, básicamente se haya aprobado mediante decretos leyes.

Su uso a discreción, además, ha provocado que en la práctica legislativa, desde 2001, toda la legislación básica del país ha sido sancionada sin consulta popular alguna, violándose una de las dos previsiones constitucionales que establecieron mecanismos directos de participación ciudadana, como la de la consulta popular de las leyes (art. 211), que la Sala Constitucional ha mutado en 2014, al interpretar el artículo 211 de la Constitución en el sentido de la práctica inconstitucional, excluyendo la consulta popular de las leyes cuando se dictan mediante decretos leyes.[1036]

V. LA ADMINISTRACIÓN DEJÓ DE ESTAR AL SERVICIO DEL CIUDADANO

Quinto, con la ausencia de autonomía y de independencia de los poderes del Estado respecto del Ejecutivo Nacional, por supuesto, quedó eliminado en Venezuela, no sólo el principio de que el poder controle al poder, sino toda posibilidad real de asegurar un equilibrio entre el poder de la Administración del Estado y los derechos ciudadanos, siendo difícil, por tanto, poder identificar a la Administración Pública como entidad que conforme a la Constitución debería estar "al servicio del ciudadano" (art. 141). Al contrario lo que ha ocurrido es que se ha convertido en una estructura burocrática discriminadora, sin garantía alguna de imparcialidad, con la cual los ciudadanos ahora sólo pueden entrar en relación en dos formas: por una parte, los que son privilegiados del poder, como consecuencia de la pertenencia política al régimen o a su partido único, con todas las prebendas y parcialidades de parte de los funcionarios; y por otra parte, los que como marginados del poder acuden a la Administración por necesidad ciudadana, a rogar las más elementales actuaciones públicas, como es por ejemplo solicitar autorizaciones, licencias, permisos o habilitaciones, las cuales no siempre son atendidas y más bien tratadas como si lo que se estuviera requiriendo fueran favores y no derechos o el cumplimiento de obligaciones públicas, con el consecuente "pago" por los servicios recibidos, y no precisamente a través de timbres fiscales que es lo propio de las tasas legalmente estableci-

---

1035   Véase Allan R. Brewer-Carías, "El Juez Constitucional vs. La alternabilidad republicana (La reelección continua e indefinida), en *Revista de Derecho Público*, N° 117, (enero-marzo 2009), Caracas 2009, pp. 205-211.

1036   Véase la sentencia N° 203 de 25 de marzo de 2014 (Caso *Síndica Procuradora Municipal del Municipio Chacao del Estado Miranda, impugnación del Decreto Ley de Ley Orgánica de la Administración Pública de 2008)*, en http://www.tsj.gov.ve/decisiones/scon/marzo/162349-203-25314-2014-09-0456.HTML.Véase el comentario en Allan R. Brewer-Carías, "La revocación del mandato popular de una diputada a la Asamblea Nacional por la Sala Constitucional del Tribunal Supremo, de oficio, sin juicio ni proceso alguno (*El caso de la diputada María Corina Machado*), en revista de Derecho Público, N° 137, Editorial Jurídica Venezolana, Caracas 2014.

das. En ambas situaciones, lamentablemente, el equilibrio entre poderes del Estado y derechos ciudadanos de los administrados ha desaparecido, sin que existan elementos de control para restablecerlo, de manera que se privilegia y se margina, sin posibilidad alguna de control.

En ese marco, el derecho administrativo formalmente concebido para la democracia y para asegurar el equilibro mencionado entre el Poder del Estado y los derechos ciudadanos, en la práctica pasó a ser un instrumento más del autoritarismo, regulador de una Administración Pública al servicio del propio Estado del cual es parte y de su propia burocracia.

VI. LA NEGACIÓN DEL DERECHO DE ACCESO A LA INFORMACIÓN ADMINISTRATIVA

La burocratización del Estado ha sido tal, que incluso a pesar de que la Constitución, basado en el principio de la transparencia que debe guiar la actividad de la Administración (art. 141), expresamente garantiza a los ciudadanos el derecho a tener acceso a la información administrativa, es decir, "a los archivos y registros administrativos," sujeta sólo a "los límites aceptables dentro de una sociedad democrática en materias relativas a seguridad interior y exterior, a investigación criminal y a la intimidad de la vida privada" que permita considerar ciertos documentos como confidenciales o secretos (art. 143);[1037] sin embargo la Sala Constitucional lo ha negado, incluso con el argumento de que cuando para cumplir con el deber de informar sea necesario que los funcionarios tengan que trabajar para recabar la información, dicho derecho se niega. Ello confirma el carácter burocrático del Estado en la más clásica apreciación que sobre el mismo hizo Max Weber cuando caracterizó al "Estado Burocrático," como la organización que trata "de incrementar la superioridad del conocimiento profesional de las autoridades públicas, precisamente a través del secretismo y de la confidencialidad de sus intenciones," de todo lo cual concluía indicando que los gobiernos burocráticos, debido a sus tendencias, son siempre "gobiernos que excluyen la publicidad,"[1038] como precisamente es el caso en Venezuela

En efecto, después de que la Sala Constitucional negó, en 2010, en general, dicho derecho de acceso a la información administrativa cuando una ONG solicitó información sobre los niveles de sueldos de los altos funcionarios públicos, particularmente de la Contraloría General de la república, y que la Sala materialmente consideró casi ultra secretos y sujetos al derecho a la intimidad del funcionario;[1039] más

---

1037   Véase en general sobre este derecho Allan R. Brewer-Carías, "Algunos aspectos del derecho en acceso a la información pública y la transparencia en la administración pública contemporánea. Una perspectiva comparada partiendo de la experiencia mexicana," en *Revista de Derecho Público*, N° 121, (enero-marzo 2010), Editorial Jurídica Venezolana, Caracas 2010, pp. 67-78.

1038   Véase Max Weber, *Economía y Sociedad*, Vol. II, Fondo de Cultura Económica, México 1969, p. 744.

1039   Véase la sentencia de la Sala Constitucional del Tribunal Supremo de Justicia N° 745 de 15 de julio de 2010 (Caso: *Asociación Civil Espacio Público*), en http://www.tsj.gov.ve/decisiones/scon/Julio/745-15710-2010-09-1003.html. Véase los comentarios en: Allan R. Brewer-Carías. "De la Casa de Cristal a la Barraca de Hierro: el Juez Constitucional Vs. El derecho de acceso a la in-

recientemente, la misma Sala Constitucional negó el derecho de otras ONG's de obtener oportuna respuesta a la petición que formularon ante Ministerio de Salud sobre información relativa a adquisiciones de medicamentos vencidos a la República de Cuba, que incluso habían sido ya detectadas por la Contraloría General de la República; considerando que ese tipo de peticiones donde "se pretende recabar información sobre la actividad que ejecuta o va a ejecutar el Estado para el logro de uno de sus fines, esto es, la obtención de medicinas en pro de garantizar la salud de la población, atenta contra la eficacia y eficiencia que debe imperar en el ejercicio de la Administración Pública, y del Poder Público en general, debido a que si bien toda persona tiene derecho a dirigir peticiones a cualquier organismo público y a recibir respuesta en tiempo oportuno, no obstante el ejercicio de ese derecho no puede ser abusivo de tal manera que entorpezca el normal funcionamiento de la actividad administrativa la cual, en atención a ese tipo de solicitudes genéricas, tendría que dedicar tiempo y recurso humano a los fines de dar explicación acerca de la amplia gama de actividades que debe realizar en beneficio del colectivo, situación que obstaculizaría y recargaría además innecesariamente el sistema de administración de justicia ante los planteamientos de esas abstenciones."[1040]

Con base en ello, simplemente y de un plumazo, se eliminó el derecho ciudadano de acceso a la información en una muestra directa más de que la Administración no está al servicio de los ciudadanos sino al servicio del propio Estado y de su burocracia, y no responde al principio de la "transparencia" que el artículo 141 de la Constitución establece. En ese marco, el derecho administrativo está perdido.

VII. EL MILITARISMO PREVALENTE Y AVASALLANTE AL MARGEN DE LA AUTORIDAD CIVIL

Sexto, otro aspecto que muestra la ausencia de un Estado democrático en Venezuela, ha sido el desarrollo del militarismo en el país, que comenzó con el asalto al poder que se dio con la elección a la Asamblea Nacional Constituyente de un grueso número de los militares que habían intentado, junto con Hugo Chávez, los dos fracasados golpes de Estado de 1992. Ese asalto a la Asamblea Constituyente originó el diseño de una Constitución militarista, como lo advertimos en 1999, de la cual se eliminó toda idea de sujeción o subordinación de la autoridad militar a la autoridad civil, consagrándose, al contrario, una gran autonomía de la autoridad militar y de la Fuerza Armada, con la posibilidad de intervenir en funciones civiles. El desarrollo del militarismo se efectuó, así, en los últimos lustros, por la eliminación de la tradicional prohibición de que la autoridad militar y la civil no podían ejercerse simultáneamente, como se estableció en las Constituciones anteriores; la eliminación del control por parte de la Asamblea Nacional respecto de los ascensos de los militares

formación administrativa," en *Revista de Derecho Público*, N° 123, (julio-septiembre 2010), Editorial Jurídica Venezolana, Caracas 2010, pp. 197-206.

1040   Véase sentencia N° 1177 de 6-8-2014 de la Sala Constitucional (Caso: Asociación Civil Espacio Público, Asociación Civil Acción Solidaria, Asociación Civil Transparencia Venezuela, y Asociación Civil Programa Venezolano de Educación-Acción en Derechos Humanos (PROVEA) vs. Ministerio para la Salud, en http://www.tsj.gov.ve/decisiones/spa/agosto/167892-01177-6814-2014-2013-0869.HTML.

de alta graduación, como se había regulado en el constitucionalismo histórico, siendo ahora un asunto exclusivo de la Fuerza Armada (art. 331); la eliminación de la obligación de la Fuerza Armada de velar por la estabilidad de las instituciones democráticas que preveía el artículo 132 de la Constitución de 1961, con lo cual el respeto a la democracia dejó de ser obligación constitucional de la Fuerza Armada; la eliminación de la otra obligación de la Fuerza Armada de respetar la Constitución y las leyes, "cuyo acatamiento - como lo decía el artículo 132 de la Constitución de 1961 - estará siempre por encima de cualquier otra obligación." Y entre otros factores más, la adopción en la Constitución de 1999 del concepto de la doctrina de la seguridad nacional, como globalizante, totalizante y omnicomprensiva, conforme a la cual todo lo que acaece en el Estado y la Nación, concierne a la seguridad del Estado, incluso el desarrollo económico y social (art. 326)"; y la eliminación del principio del carácter no deliberante y apolítico de la institución militar, como lo establecía el artículo 132 de la Constitución de 1961.[1041]

Todo ello abrió la vía para que la Fuerza Armada, como institución militar, y para que los militares, comenzar a deliberar políticamente, configurándose a la Fuerza Armada como un partido militar "chavista,"[1042] luego de un proceso sostenido y continuo de destrucción del profesionalismo militar.[1043] El proselitismo político de los militares, además, ha sido formalmente regularizado recientemente por la Sala

1041   Véase lo que expusimos sobre el marco militarista de la Constitución en 1999, en Allan R. Brewer-Carías, *Debate Constituyente (Aportes a la Asamblea Nacional Constituyente)*, Fundación de Derecho Público, Editorial Jurídica Venezolana, Caracas 1999; y en *Asamblea Constituyente y Poder Constituyente 1999*, Colección Tratado de Derecho Constitucional, Tomo VI, Fundación de Derecho Público, Editorial Jurídica Venezolana, Caracas 2014, pp. 1049-1050.

1042   El general Vladimir Padrino, Jefe del Comando Estratégico Operacional de la Fuerza Armada en el discurso de orden que pronunció en la Asamblea nacional el día de la Independencia, el 5 de julio de 2014, expresó: "Lo voy a decir con mucha responsabilidad atendiendo a la ética y a la gran política: esta FANB es chavista." Véase en http://www.diariolasamericas.com/america-latina/jefe-militar-venezolano-asegura-que-fuerzas-armadas-chavistas.html . Tres meses después, el 23 de octubre de 2014 apareció publicado el decreto mediante el cual se lo designó Ministro del Poder Popular para la defensa. Véase Decreto N° 1346 en *Gaceta Oficial* N° 40.526, de 25 de octubre de 2014.

1043   Fernando Ochoa Antich ha resumido este proceso expresado que: "Hugo Chávez, decidido a destruir el profesionalismo militar, aprobó casi de manera continua tres leyes orgánicas: la de los años 2005, 2008 y 2010. La ley orgánica del año 2005 tuvo un aspecto positivo al eliminar las funciones de mando del ministerio de la Defensa, pero al centralizar la conducción de la Fuerza Armada en el presidente de la República y crear inconstitucionalmente el Comando General de la Milicia comprometió la autonomía de las tradicionales Fuerzas y su capacidad de mando sobre las unidades operativas. No satisfecho con esta reforma aprobó la ley orgánica del año 2008. Esta ley mantuvo la tendencia centralizadora de la concepción militar chavista, fortaleció a la Milicia Bolivariana como respuesta a su objetivo de consolidar el régimen mediante una vanguardia revolucionaria y transformó a los suboficiales profesionales de carrera en oficiales técnicos sin considerar los grados militares y la antigüedad. De manera sorprendente, aprobó en el año 2010 una nueva ley orgánica, que tuvo por finalidad concederle al presidente de la República el grado militar de comandante en jefe y mando efectivo sobre las unidades operativas; crear al oficial de milicias, con posibilidad de optar a cualquier grado, permitiendo que ciudadanos sin formación militar pudieran formar parte de sus cuadros; y permitir a los suboficiales de tropa ascender a oficiales efectivos. Estas reformas legales tenían un solo objetivo: destruir los tradicionales valores militares y permitir ideologizar a la Fuerza Armada Nacional." Véase Fernando Ochoa Antich, "Destruir el profesionalismo militar," en *El Nacional*, Caracas 28 de septiembre de 2014, en http://www.el-nacional.com/fernando_ochoa_antich/Destruir-profesionalismo-militar_0_490151147.html

Constitucional, mutando la Constitución,[1044] y en todo caso, los militares forman parte ya de un grupo privilegiado en la sociedad, con seguro acceso a bienes y servicios a los cuales los ciudadanos comunes no llegan. [1045]

Ese esquema militarista, puesto en práctica durante tres lustros, con el nombramiento, además, de militares y exmilitares para la mayoría de los altos cargos públicos, y su elección también, para los gobiernos locales, ha conducido al apoderamiento casi total de la Administración civil del Estado por parte de los militares y por la Fuerza Armada, a la cual, incluso se le atribuye en la Constitución "la participación activa en el desarrollo nacional" (art. 328). En esa línea, en septiembre de 2014, quien ejerce la Presidencia de la República entregó a los militares el control total de la economía al designar a militares para dirigir todos los órganos de la Administración Pública del sector económico. [1046]

Pero el militarismo no sólo se ha manifestado en la organización de la Administración, sino en el extraordinario gasto militar en que ha ocurrido Venezuela en los últimos años, no superado por ningún país de la región; [1047] así como por la militarización progresiva de funciones otrora administrativas, como las de policía, lo que se ha visto en particular, con extrema gravedad en 2014, en la militarización de la represión a las protestas y no sólo estudiantiles, sino vecinales y sindicales, como aca-

1044 Véase la sentencia de la Sala Constitucional N° 651 de 11 de junio de 2014 (Caso *Rafael Huizi Clavier y otros*) en http://www.tsj.gov.ve/decisiones/scon/junio/165491-651-11614-2014-14-0313.HTML. Véase el comentario en Allan R. Brewer-Carías, "Una nueva mutación constitucional: el fin de la prohibición de la militancia política de la Fuerza Armada Nacional, y el reconocimiento del derecho de los militares activos de participar en la actividad política, incluso en cumplimiento de las órdenes de la superioridad jerárquica," en *Revista de Derecho Público*, N° 138, Editorial Jurídica Venezolana, Caracas 2014.

1045 Véase por ejemplo el reportaje publicado en *Bloomberg News*: "New Cars for the Army as Venezuelans Line Up for Food," 19 de septiembre de 2014, en http://www.bloomberg.com/news/2014-09-29/venezuelan-army-enjoys-meat-to-cars-denied-most-citizens.html.

1046 Véase el comentario sobre los cambios ministeriales de septiembre de 2014 por Francisco Mayoirga, "Gustavo Azócar Alcalá, Los militares y la economía," en *ACN, Agencia Carabobeña de Noticias*, 10 de septiembre de 2014, en http://acn.com.ve/opinion/los-militares-y-la-economia/. Sin embargo, la entrega de la conducción de la economía a los militares no es nueva. Véase por ejemplo lo escrito meses antes por: Patricia Claremboux, AFP, "Bajo el ala de Maduro, los militares toman control del poder económico de Venezuela. En sus primeros 9 meses de gobierno, el mandatario ya nombró a 368 uniformados en puestos políticos. Ahora, con la designación de un general del Ejército al frente del Ministerio de Finanzas, la militarización se extiende a la economía," 20 enero de 2014, en http://www.infobae.com/2014/01/20/1538269-bajo-el-ala-maduro-los-militares-toman-control-del-poder-economico-venezuela. Véase además el reportaje: "Maduro dejó en manos de un militar los problemas económicos de Venezuela. El presidente venezolano puso a Hebert García Plaza al frente del Órgano Superior de la Economía, creado para enfrentar la emergencia," 13 de septiembre de 2013, en http://elcomer-cio.pe/mundo/actualidad/maduro-dejo-manos-militar-problemas-economicos-venezuela-noticia-1630919; y el reportaje: "Militares comandan economía en Venezuela," en *Agencia France Press*, 20 de enero de 2014, en http://www.em.com.br/app/noticia/internacional/2014/01/20/interna_internacional,489796/militares-comandam-economia-na-venezuela-afirmam-analistas.shtml. Véase además, Peter Wilson, "A Revolution in Green. The Rise of Venezuela's Military," en *Foreign Affairs*, 2014, disponible en http://www.foreignaffairs.com/arti-cles/142133/peter-wilson/a-revolution-in-green.

1047 Véase Carlos E. Hernández, Venezuela tuvo el mayor crecimiento en gasto militar de Latinoamérica," en *Notitarde.com*, 6 de febrero de 2014, en http://www.notitarde.com/Pais/Vene-zuela-tuvo-el-mayor-crecimiento-en-gasto-militar-de-Latinoamerica/2014/02/06/303181.

ba de suceder en Guayana, contra trabajadores precisamente de las empresas del Estado, que han sido quebradas por sus gerentes.[1048]

Uno de esos graves signos de militarización de la represión, ha sido la creación, en junio de 2014, cumpliendo un supuesto "deber del Estado de lograr la irrupción definitiva del Nuevo Estado Democrático y Social, de Derecho y de Justicia [...] conforme al Plan de la Patria y Segundo Plan Socialista de Desarrollo Económico y Social de la Nación 2013-2019," de un nuevo órgano del Estado, la "Brigada Especial contra las Actuaciones de los Grupos Generadores de Violencia" (BEGV), con nombre y estructura militar, a cargo de un "Comandante General de la Brigada," como órgano desconcentrado con capacidad de gestión presupuestaria, administrativa, financiera y autonomía funcional dependiente jerárquicamente – parece una ironía - del Ministerio del "Interior, Justicia y Paz," con la tarea de coordinar, analizar, evaluar, organizar, dirigir, ejecutar y recabar las informaciones y acciones provenientes de todos los órganos de seguridad del Estado "para neutralizar y controlar las actividades que pudieran llevarse a cabo relacionas con las actuaciones de grupos generadores de violencia," o sea, simplemente "neutralizar" y reprimir a los "enemigos de la patria" conforme lo defina su Comandante, y eventualmente hacer iniciar la persecución penal.[1049] Para ello se obliga a todos los órganos de seguridad e instituciones públicas a aportar información a dicha Brigada; obligación que también se impone a todas las instituciones privadas. Algún parecido con la Gestapo, no pasa de ser mera coincidencia.[1050] A lo anterior se suma la creación y activación, en el Ministerio de la Defensa, de una unidad denominada "La Fuerza Choque," sin indi-

---

1048   Como lo destacó recientemente la destacada dirigente política, Paulina Gamus:"Con Chávez se inaugura no solo la militarización del gobierno, sino también la politización del mundo militar." "La inspiración para ese modelo" agregó, está en "el culto a la personalidad, la transformación de los hombres de armas en la guardia pretoriana del gobernante y la presencia atropellante de militares en cargos públicos, con licencia para robar." Véase en el artículo "Mamá, yo quiero un cadete. El apoyo de partidos de izquierda a los gobiernos militarizados de Chávez y Maduro en Venezuela es oprobioso," en *El País, Internacional*, 14 de julio de 2014, en http://internacional.elpais.com/internacional/2014/07/14/actualidad/1405349965_980938.html

1049   Véase en decreto 1014 de 30-5-2014 en *Gaceta Oficial* N° 40440 de 26-6-2014

1050   Por ello ha observado Adolfo Taylhardat, en su artículo "Gestapove," que se trata de "un gigantesco instrumento de espionaje y represión", de manera que "si hasta ahora se han cometido los atropellos y agresiones más bestiales contra la disidencia, con este nuevo mecanismo el régimen podrá seguir actuando libremente y hasta más violentamente, escudado tras una estructura que gozará de total autonomía como la que tuvo la Gestapo [...]Evidentemente, la ambigüedad del lenguaje, la ausencia de precisión en las atribuciones y la inmunidad ante la justicia que tendrá ese organismo lo convierte en instrumento de persecución y represión sólo comparable con la nefasta Gestapo". En dicho artículo, el embajador Taylhardat hace referencia a lo expresado por el Coordinador de la ONG Provea, Marino Alvarado, al rechazar la creación de este servicio "por considerar que este tipo de organismos, con poco control por parte de las instituciones del Estado, pueden distorsionar su función y poner en riesgo los derechos humanos de la disidencia; más aun tomando en cuenta el concepto genérico que se utiliza para definir a los grupos que pueden desestabilizar." Agregó Alvarado que "El gobierno se afianza cada día más en la doctrina de la seguridad nacional que prioriza la seguridad del Estado por encima de los derechos de los ciudadanos y que parte de identificar que en Venezuela hay un enemigo interno que hay que derrotar y contra ese enemigo interno hay que desplegar toda la capacidad del Estado. Ese enemigo es la disidencia, sea de la oposición o del propio chavismo." Véase en *El republicano Liberal*, 10-8-2014, en http://elrepublicanoliberal.blogspot.com/2014/08/adolfo-r-taylhardat-gestapoven.html?spref=bl.

cación alguna de cuál es su misión y propósito (salvo el que deriva de su propia denominación).[1051] El futuro lo dirá.

A todo ello, para completar el signo de la militarización general de todas las actividades ciudadanas, debe agregarse la sanción, también en 2014, de la Ley de Registro y Alistamiento Militar para la Defensa Integral de la Nación, publicada en la misma *Gaceta Oficial* en la cual se publicó el decreto de la Brigada Especial, que ahora impone a todos, como en los tiempos superados de las dictaduras militares, la obligación de inscribirse y tener credencial militar, como requisito indispensable, por ejemplo, hasta para obtener grado en alguna Universidad, obtener la licencia de conducir o la solvencia laboral, inscribirse en el registro de contratistas del Estado o ser contratado por empresas públicas y privadas.[1052]

Sin embargo, en forma absolutamente contradictoria con el militarismo avasallante, de hecho, y como política de gobierno, la Fuerza Armada, durante estos últimos lustros, perdió el monopolio de las armas y de la fuerza, no sólo por la creación de la llamada Milicia, fuera de los componentes tradicionales de la misma, sino por la proliferación de armas en manos de toda suerte de delincuentes y la dotación de armas a grupos civiles urbanos, con vínculos criminales, fuera del control de los militares e incluso de las policías.[1053]

1051   Véase Resolución N° 6574 de 17 de septiembre de 2014, en *Gaceta Oficial* N° 40502 de 22 de septiembre de 2014. En la Resolución lo único que se dispuso fue la "estructura organizativa," de la unidad (5 unidades), y su adscripción al Comando Estratégico Operacional del Ministerio.

1052   Véase en *Gaceta Oficial* N° 40440 de 26-6-2014. Por ello, recientemente Douglas Bravo, exguerrillero que fue quien reclutó a Chávez en el proyecto de su Partido de la Revolución Venezolana, denunció con toda desilusión que en Venezuela "Vivimos una dictadura militar. Un capitalismo de Estado." Véase la entrevista de Ailyn Hidalgo Araujo, publicada el 17-7-2014, en http://www.frentepatriotico.com/inicio/2014/07/17/douglas-bravo-vivimos-una-dictadura-militar-un-capitalismo-de-estado/ . En la misma línea, Alberto Barrera Tyszka, uno de los biógrafos de Chávez, con razón expresaba en un reciente artículo titulado "¿Quién manda aquí?," "Que aquí gobiernan los militares," recordando la expresión de Chávez, cuando dijo: "Yo no creo en ningún partido, ni siquiera en el mío. Yo creo en los militares, que es dónde me formé," y luego de analizar el creciente militarismo del país y la "militarización de cualquier experiencia ciudadana." Véase en *Grupo La Colina AC*, Caracas 17 de agosto de 2014, en http://grupolacolina.blogspot.com/2014/08/quien-manda-quien-alberto-barrera.html?spref=tw&m=1

1053   Fernando Ochoa Antich ha comentado que la desconfianza de Chávez en la lealtad de laFuerza Armada lo llevó a "debilitar sus principales valores profesionales, buscando crear, al mismo tiempo, dos organizaciones armadas que sirvieran de equilibrio a una posible acción militar: la Milicia Bolivariana y los Colectivos Revolucionarios. Esta acción, no sólo fue inconstitucional sino totalmente irresponsable al repartir armamento de guerra sin ningún control. Esa ha sido la causa fundamental del incremento de la violencia. Para colmo, se ha perdido el control de los Colectivos representando un verdadero riesgo para la estabilidad nacional."Agregó Ochoa que contrariamente al "principio fundamental de la seguridad del Estado [de que] el monopolio de las armas de guerra lo debe tener exclusivamente la Fuerza Armada Nacional y los organismos de seguridad, ha sido tal la falta de control y la irresponsabilidad del régimen chavista que permanentemente los delincuentes se encuentran mejor armados que los organismos policiales y de seguridad, equiparándose en muchas oportunidades con el equipamiento de las unidades militares: Véase "Violencia y más violencia," en El nacional, 12 de octubre de 2014, en http://www.el-nacional.com/fernando_ochoa_antich/Violencia-violencia_0_499150202.html

VIII. LA ELIMINACIÓN DE LA LIBERTAD DE EXPRESIÓN Y COMU-NICACIÓN

Séptimo, el Estado venezolano también dejó de ser un Estado democrático, adquiriendo en cambio todos los contornos de un Estado totalitario, desde el momento en el cual materialmente todos los medios de comunicación audiovisual, y casi todos los medios escritos de comunicación, han sido apoderados por el propio Estado o adquiridos por grupos de personas vinculadas al poder o enriquecidos al amparo del poder. A lo cual se agrega el inevitable cierre que se ha producido en varios importantes diarios por falta de papel, porque el Estado que todo lo acapara, no permite la importación de papel al negar el suministro de las divisas necesarias para ello. [1054]

Lo anterior, aunado al proceso de restricción a la libertad de expresión diseñado por la Sala Constitucional desde 2001;[1055] seguido de la intervención y limitación impuesta a los medios de comunicación, desde 2005, con la sanción de la Ley de Responsabilidad Social de la Radio y Televisión;[1056] y de la negativa de la propia Sala Constitucional, en 2003, de ejercer el control de constitucionalidad y de convencionalidad en relación con las normas sancionatorias de los delitos de opinión en relación con los funcionarios públicos y las instituciones del Estado (leyes de desacato) establecidas en el Código Penal.[1057]

Todo ello ha abierto un extraordinario campo a la criminalización de la opinión que ha llevado a juicio penal incluso hasta a articulistas y a directores de medios,[1058]

1054 En 2014, según la información de Leonardo Pizani, "el Instituto Prensa y Sociedad contabilizó el cierre de 10 medios impresos, 6 definitivos y 4 temporales, por falta de papel." Véase en Leonardo Pizani, "El modus operandi de la censura venezolana," en *Opinión.infobae.com*, 8 de octubre de 2014, en http://opinion.infobae.com/leonardo-pizani/2014/10/08/el-modus-operandi-de-la-censura-venezolana/

1055 Véase entre otras, la sentencia N° 1013/2001 y los comentaros a la misma, en el libro: Allan R. Brewer-Carías (Coordinador y editor), Héctor Faúndez Ledesma, Pedro Nikken, Carlos M. Ayala Corao, Rafael Chavero Gazdik, Gustavo Linares Benzo y Jorge Olavarría, (con Pórticos: Roberto Cuellar M. y Santiago Cantón y Prólogo: Alberto Quiroz Corradi), *La libertad de expresión amenazada. (Sentencia 1013)*, Edición Conjunta Instituto Interamericano de Derechos Humanos y Editorial Jurídica Venezolana, Caracas-San José 2001.

1056 Véase los comentarios sobre esta Ley, en el libro: Allan R. Brewer-Carías (Coordinador y Editor), Asdrúbal Aguiar, José Ignacio Hernández, Margarita Escudero, Ana Cristina Núñez Machado, Juan José Raffalli A., Carlos Urdaneta Sandoval, Juan Cristóbal Carmona Borjas, *Ley de Responsabilidad Social de Radio y Televisión (Ley Resorte)*, Colección Textos Legislativos N° 35, Editorial Jurídica Venezolana. Caracas 2006.

1057 Véase sentencia N° 1.942 de 15 de julio de 2003 (Caso: *Impugnación de artículos del Código Penal, Leyes de desacato*), en *Revista de Derecho Público*, N° 93-96, Editorial Jurídica Venezolana, Caracas 2003, pp. 136 ss.

1058 El más reciente ha sido el nuevo proceso penal iniciado por denuncia de un militar, Presidente de la Asamblea Nacional, contra un articulista (Sr. Genatios, ex ministro del régimen, 1999) y contra los Directores (Teodoro Petkoff) y Junta Directiva, del Diario *Tal Cual* de Caracas. Véase sobre esta denuncia las informaciones en: http://www.talcualdigital.com/Te-mas.aspx?Tag=Demanda+contra+TalCual. So esta persecución contra *Tal Cual*, Leonardo Pizani ha señalado que por el problema político que "la libertad de pensamiento y de expresión" representa para el gobierno, y "que se da en la lógica comunicacional de *Tal Cual*," a este diario "lo han atacado personalmente los hombres más fuertes del régimen como son el Tte. Cnel. Chávez y el Capitán Cabello, porque no pueden soportar la idea de la desobediencia civil que representa, que no es la desobediencia a una medida coyuntural, es la desobediencia a la disciplina de la obediencia militar, es el ejercicio de la libertad." Véase, Leonar-

conduciendo a la censura y a la autocensura, incompatible con los principios más elementales de una sociedad democrática. En esas circunstancias, por tanto, cualquier crítica o denuncia de las fallas de las políticas gubernamentales, el gobierno las considera como parte de una conspiración contra el mismo, y amenaza con perseguir a los autores.[1059]

Por todo lo anterior, Catalina Botero, hasta octubre de 2014 Relatora Especial para Libertad de Expresión de la Organización de Estados Americanos se refirió al estado crítico de la prensa en Venezuela, expresando:

"Hay un sistema muy articulado de control que va desde la estigmatización pública mediante un poderoso conglomerado de medios controlados hasta la aplicación de normas penales a quienes tienen un pensamiento crítico. Por ejemplo, los directivos del diario *Tal Cual* están siendo procesados penalmente porque Diosdado Cabello consideró inexacta una frase de un artículo. Hoy tienen prohibido salir del país y pueden terminar en cualquier momento en la cárcel. Esto sin contar los innumerables procesos civiles y administrativos por presentar noticias incómodas al gobierno, la dramática ausencia de papel periódico, la no renovación de licencias por razones por razones políticas, el cierre de medios como NTN 24, la absoluta oscuridad sobre lo que sucede en el Estado y más recientemente las denuncias por posibles bloqueos de Internet por parte de la empresa estatal que controla la prestación de este servicio a una parte importante de la población. Todo esto sin garantías legales suficientes ni jueces

---

do Pizani, "El modus operandi de la censura venezolana," en *Opinión.infobae.com*, 8 de octubre de 2014, en http://opinion.infobae.com/leonardo-pizani/2014/10/08/el-modus-operandi-de-la-censura-venezolana/

1059   Véase por ejemplo lo escrito en el Editorial "Venezuela's Crachdopwn on Opposition," *The New York Times*: New York, September 21, 2014, p. 10. El caso más reciente fue el de los profesores Ricardo Haussmann y Miguel Ángel Santos, de la Universidad de Harvard, quienes publicaron un trabajo analizando las catastróficas consecuencias de la errada política económica del gobierno, titulado: "Should Venezuela Default?", en *Project Syndicate. The World's Opinion Page*, September 4, 2014, en http://www.project-syndicate.org/commentary/ricardo-hausmann-and-miguel-angel-santos-pillory-the-maduro-government-for-defaulting-on-30-million-citizens--but-not-on-wall-street. La reacción de quien ejerce la Presidencia, además de calificar al profesor Haussmann como un "bandido," fue considerar que con su trabajo perseguía desestabilizar al gobierno, ordenando a la Fiscalía General de la República iniciar una investigación y acciones judiciales en su contra. Véase la noticia en José Orozco y Sebastian Boyd, "Venezuela Threatens Harvard professor for Default Comment," Bloomber, Septmber 12, 2014, en http://www.bloomberg.com/news/2014-09-12/venezuela-threatens-harvard-professor-for-default-comment.html ; Andrew Cawthorne, "Venezuela's Maduro vows legal action against Harvard professor," September 14, 2014, en http://www.reuters.com/article/2014/09/12/us-venezuela-hausmann-idUSKBN0H71MN20140912; y en Simon Tegel, *The Global Post*: "Maduro Calls Harvard Professor a "Bandit" for Critizising Venezuela's Economy," en http://www.nbcnews.com/news/latino/maduro-calls-harvard-prof-bandit-criticizing-venezuelan-economy-n206166. Véase la respuesta del profesor Haussman "Venezuela's president is crafting a disaster," en *The Boston Globe*. Opinion, September 18, 2014 en http://www.bostonglobe.com/opinion/2014/09/18/amid-venezuela-economic-woes-president-attacks-harvard-academic/j6H2tUj4vGLuKaf0yStfQL/story.html.

independientes. Hoy se sabe más de lo que sucede en Venezuela afuera que adentro del país." [1060]

IX. LA VIOLACIÓN Y ELIMINACIÓN DEL PRINCIPIO DEMOCRÁTICO

Y *octavo*, entre los últimos atentados contra el principio democrático mismo, y por tanto, contra el Estado de derecho, que han hecho desaparecer todo vestigio del Estado democrático, están los que han distorsionado tanto el derecho de los electores a revocar, conforme a la Constitución, el mandato popular de los representantes electos; como el derecho de los representantes electos a ejercer sus cargos con la seguridad de que sólo podrían ser revocados por voluntad popular, mediante referendo revocatorio. Ambos derechos han sido mutados y violados, en contra de lo dispuesto en la Constitución.

En cuanto al derecho ciudadano a decidir mediante voto popular expresado en referendo, la revocación del mandato de los funcionarios electos, el mismo, por una parte, ha sido limitado in extremis, al regularse de tal manera la forma de manifestarse la iniciativa popular para convocar el referendo revocatorio (firmas) que materialmente es imposible hacerlo;[1061] y por la otra, particularmente en relación con el referendo revocatorio presidencial, el mismo, para proteger el mandato de Hugo Chávez, fue ilegítimamente mutado por la Sala Constitucional del Tribunal Supremo en 2004, y convertido en un referendo ratificatorio.

En efecto, el artículo 72 de la Constitución, establece que cuando en un referendo revocatorio voten a favor de la revocación un número de votantes "*igual o mayor número de electores* que los que eligieron al funcionario," se considerará revocado su mandato, independientemente del número de votantes que hubiesen votado por la no revocación. Sin embargo, ello fue cambiado en forma evidentemente inconstitucional, en las *Normas para regular los procesos de Referendos Revocatorios de mandatos de Elección Popular* dictadas por el Consejo Nacional Electoral en 25 de septiembre de 2003[1062], en las cuales luego de reconocer que se considera revocado el mandato "si el número de votos a favor de la revocatoria es igual o superior al número de los electores que eligieron al funcionario," se agregó la frase: "y no resulte inferior al número de electores que votaron en contra de la revocatoria" (Art. 60).

Con este agregado, en una norma de rango sublegal, se restringió el derecho ciudadano a la participación política mediante la revocación de mandatos populares, trastocándose la naturaleza "revocatoria" del referendo que regula el artículo 72 de la Constitución, y en evidente fraude a la Constitución, se lo convirtió en un referendo "ratificatorio" de mandatos de elección popular; lo cual, además, ya había

---

1060   Véase Gaspar Ramírez, "Catalina Botero: En Venezuela las consecuencias por criticar al gobierno pueden ser muy graves," El Mercurio Chile 18 de octubre de 2014, en *El Nacional*, Caracas 22 de octubre de 2014, en http://www.el-nacional.com/gda/Catalina-Botero-Venezuela-consecuencias-criticar_0_502749892.html.

1061   Véase Allan R. Brewer-Carías, "El secuestro del Poder Electoral y la confiscación del derecho a la participación política mediante el referendo revocatorio presidencial: Venezuela 2000-2004", en *Boletín Mexicano de Derecho Comparado*, Instituto de Investigaciones Jurídicas, Universidad Nacional Autónoma de México, N° 112. México, enero-abril 2005 pp. 11-73.

1062   Resolución Consejo Nacional Electoral N° 030925-465 de 25-09-2003.

sido avalado por la Sala Constitucional del Tribunal Supremo al decidir un recurso de interpretación abstracta de la norma constitucional en 2003, y concluir, en contra de la Constitución, que la misma supuestamente regularía "una especie de relegitimación del funcionario y en ese proceso democrático de mayorías, incluso, si en el referendo obtuviese más votos la opción de su permanencia, debería seguir en él, aunque voten en su contra el número suficiente de personas para revocarle el mandato."[1063] Y todo ello, con el único objeto de evitar que en 2004, el mandato del Presidente de República, Hugo Chávez, fuera revocado,[1064] como en estricto derecho constitucional así ocurrió, siendo al contrario "ratificado" en su cargo.[1065]

Pero la afectación del principio democrático también ha ocurrido como consecuencia de las decisiones adoptadas por órganos del Estado para revocarle el mandato a funcionarios y representantes electos, violentándose la voluntad popular y la propia Constitución. Ese fue el insólito caso en el cual la Sala Constitucional del Tribunal Supremo en marzo de 2014 sin que hubiese juicio penal alguno, inventó un supuesto desacato de un mandamiento de amparo dirigido a unos Alcaldes de cumplir en forma genérica con sus obligaciones legales de velar por la seguridad ciudadana y la circulación por las vías públicas, todo bien orquestado, desde la solicitud de amparo contra la supuesta omisión de los Alcaldes de cumplir con dicha obligación, hasta la revocación del mandato popular de los mismos, asumiendo además para ello la Sala Constitucional, en forma totalmente inconstitucional, las competencias propias de los jueces penales.[1066]

1063   Véase sentencia N° 2750 de 21 de octubre de 2003 (Caso: *Carlos E. Herrera Mendoza, Interpretación del artículo 72 de la Constitución*), Exp. 03-1989.

1064   Hugo Chávez había sido electo en agosto de 2000 con 3.757.774 votos, por lo que bastaba para que su mandato fuese revocado, que el voto a favor de la revocación superara esa cifra. Como lo anunció el Consejo Nacional Electoral el 27 de agosto de 2004, el voto a favor de la revocación del mandato del Presidente de la República en el referendo efectuado ese mismo mes y año, fue de 3.989.008, por lo que constitucionalmente el mandato de Chávez había quedado revocado.

1065   En efecto, en la *página web* del Consejo Nacional Electoral del día 27 de agosto de 2004, apareció la siguiente nota: "El presidente del Consejo Nacional Electoral, Francisco Carrasquero López, se dirigió al país en cadena nacional para anunciar las cifras definitivas y oficiales del evento electoral celebrado el pasado 15 de agosto, *las cuales dan como ratificado en su cargo al Presidente de la República*, Hugo Rafael Chávez Frías, con un total de 5 millones 800 mil 629 votos a favor de la opción "No". En la contienda electoral participaron 9 millones 815 mil 631 electores, de los cuales 3.989.008 se inclinaron por la opción "Sí" para revocar el mandato del Presidente Chávez. La totalización arrojó que la opción "No" alcanzó el 59,25% de los votos, mientras el "Sí" logró el 40,74% del total general, y la abstención fue del 30,02%. Vale destacar que para estos comicios el Registro Electoral se incrementó significativamente, alcanzando un universo de 14. 027.607 de electores con derecho a sufragar en el RR. Con base en la expresión de la voluntad popular, el Consejo Nacional Electoral, este viernes 27 de agosto, *ratificará en la Presidencia de la República* Bolivariana de Venezuela a Hugo Chávez Frías, quien culminará su período constitucional en el año 2006. Y en efecto, en acto solemne efectuado ese día, el Consejo Nacional Electoral acordó "ratificar" al Presidente de la República en su cargo, a pesar de que un número de electores mayor que los que lo eligieron hubieran votado a favor de la revocación de su mandato. Otro tanto haría la Asamblea Nacional, sin que esa figura de la ratificación estuviese prevista en norma constitucional alguna." Véase además, *El Nacional*, Caracas, 28-08-2004, pp. A-1 y A-2.

1066   Véase sentencias de la Sala Constitucional del Tribunal Supremo de Justicia, N° 138 de 17 de marzo de 2014, en http://www.tsj.gov.ve/decisiones/scon/marzo/162025-138-17314-2014-14-0205.HTML; N° 137 de 17 de marzo de 2014 en http://www.tsj.gov.ve/decisio-nes/scon/marzo/162286-150-20314-

El otro insólito caso de violación del principio democrático fue el también realizado por la Sala Constitucional igualmente en marzo de 2014 al conocer de una petición de amparo para proteger el mandato popular de una diputada frente a las amenazas verbales formuladas por el Presidente de la Asamblea Nacional de impedirle el cumplir sus funciones y sacarla del parlamento. Al decidir la acción propuesta, en forma por demás insólita, la Sala la declaró inadmisible, pero sin embargo, en evidente abuso de poder, de oficio pasó a decidir en un *obiter dictum*, todo contrario de lo peticionado, es decir, procedió a revocarle el mandato popular de la diputada por el hecho de haber ésta hablado en una sesión del Consejo de la Organización de Estados Americanos, en su condición de diputada a la Asamblea Nacional venezolana, sobre la situación de Venezuela, pero desde el puesto de la delegación de Panamá atendiendo a la invitación que le formuló el representante de ese país.[1067]

El derecho administrativo que resulta de todo lo anterior, es un derecho administrativo muy lejos de ser un derecho de la democracia, que más bien está condicionado por un sistema político que se caracteriza tener graves fallas de representatividad democrática y de funcionamiento de la llamada democracia participativa; por no tener como base un sistema de separación de poderes, con la consecuente ausencia de autonomía e independencia del Poder Judicial; por regir una Administración que dejó de estar al servicio del ciudadano, y estar sólo al servicio de su propia burocracia, y en la cual se niega incluso el derecho de acceso a la información administrativa, habiéndose impuesto un sistema de secretud y reserva en el funcionamiento de la Administración nunca antes visto; por la implantación de un militarismo prevalente y avasallante al margen de la autoridad civil; por la eliminación de la libertad de expresión y de comunicación; y por la violación y eliminación del principio democrático, al revocarse el mandato de funcionarios electos al margen de la voluntad popular.

SECCIÓN TERCERA:

LA AUSENCIA DE UN ESTADO SOCIAL Y DE ECONOMÍA MIXTA

Pero el Estado en Venezuela, además de haber dejado de ser un Estado democrático e derecho, como antes se ha dicho, habiéndose configurado como un Estado Totalitario, también, a pesar de lo que está inscrito en la Constitución, tampoco es realmente un Estado Social de Economía Mixta, en el cual la iniciativa privada debería tener un rol tan importante como la del propio Estado, razón por la cual al

2014-14-0194.HTML; y sentencia de N° 245 el día 9 de abril de 2014, en http://www.tsj.gov.ve/decisiones/scon/abril/162860-245-9414-2014-14-0205.HTML Véase también en *Gaceta Oficial* N° 40.391 de 10 de abril de 2014. Véase sobre estas sentencias los comentarios en Allan R. Brewer-Carías, *Golpe a la democracia dado por la Sala Constitucional*, Editorial Jurídica Venezolana, Caracas 2014, pp. 117 ss.

1067   Véase la sentencia de la Sala Constitucional del Tribunal Supremo de Justicia, N° 207 de 31 de marzo de 2014, en http://www.tsj.gov.ve/decisiones/scon/marzo/162546-207-31314-2014-14-0286.HTML Véase además en *Gaceta Oficial* N° 40385 de 2 de abril de 2014. Véase sobre estas sentencias los comentarios en Allan R. Brewer-Carías, *Golpe a la democracia dado por la Sala Constitucional*, Editorial Jurídica Venezolana, Caracas 2014, pp. 167 ss.

derecho administrativo se le ha sustraído su rol de ser el marco del equilibrio y garantía de las relaciones entre el Estado y los particulares, habiendo quedado sólo para limitar y perseguir a las iniciativas privadas, y proteger a la burocracia estatal. En ese marco, al Estado se lo ha convertido en un Estado Burocrático, Comunista y Populista, que ha sido montado sobre un sistema económico de capitalismo de Estado, destructor de las iniciativas individuales. Y en ese marco es que se está desarrollando el derecho administrativo.

I. EL ESTADO SOCIAL Y SU IMBRICACIÓN CON EL ESTADO DE ECONOMÍA MIXTA

Un Estado Social , tal como se deriva de lo expresado en el artículo 299 de la Constitución, es el que tiene como misión fundamental velar por la satisfacción de las necesidades colectivas de la población, en conjunción con las iniciativas privadas, mediante el fortalecimiento de los servicios públicos, para garantizar a todos el goce y efectividad de los derechos sociales, como son los derechos a la salud, a la educación, a la vivienda, al trabajo, a la seguridad social, a la cultura, a la asistencia social y a la protección del ambiente, de manera de asegurar la justicia social.

En términos de la jurisprudencia de la Sala Constitucional del Tribunal Supremo de Justicia expresada en 2004,

"el Estado Social de Derecho es el Estado de la *procura existencial*, su meta es satisfacer las necesidades básicas de los individuos distribuyendo bienes y servicios que permitan el logro de un *standard* de vida elevado, colocando en permanente realización y perfeccionamiento el desenvolvimiento económico y social de sus ciudadanos."[1068]

El objetivo de este modelo de Estado social, como lo expresa la Constitución, es asegurar el "desarrollo humano integral y una existencia digna y provechosa para la colectividad;" teniendo el Estado, con tal propósito, sin duda, deberes de actuación que debe realizar como lo impone la Constitución, "conjuntamente con la iniciativa privada," lo que implica garantizar los derechos y libertades económicos de las personas; y todo ello, con el objeto de "promover el desarrollo armónico de la economía nacional con el fin de generar fuentes de trabajo, alto valor agregado nacional, elevar el nivel de vida de la población y fortalecer la soberanía económica del país," para lograr una justa distribución de la riqueza" (art. 299).[1069] Lo anterior, además,

---

1068   Véase sentencia N° 1002 de 26 de mayo de 2004 (caso: Federación Médica Venezolana vs. Ministra de Salud y Desarrollo Social y el Presidente del Instituto Venezolano de los Seguros Sociales), en *Revista de Derecho Público*, N° 97-98, Editorial Jurídica Venezolana, Caracas 2004, pp. 143 ss.

1069   La Sala Constitucional del Tribunal Supremo en sentencia N° 85 del 24 de enero de 2002 (Caso *Asociación Civil Deudores Hipotecarios de Vivienda Principal (Asodeviprilara)*, precisó en cuanto a "la protección que brinda el Estado Social de Derecho," no sólo que la misma está vinculada al "interés social" que se declara como "un valor que persigue equilibrar en sus relaciones a personas o grupos que son, en alguna forma, reconocidos por la propia ley como débiles jurídicos, o que se encuentran en una situación de inferioridad con otros grupos o personas, que por la naturaleza de sus relaciones, están en una posición dominante con relación a ellas;" sino que dicha protección "varía desde la defensa de intereses económicos de las clases o grupos que la ley considera se encuentran en una situación de desequilibrio que los perjudica, hasta la defensa de valores espirituales de esas personas o grupos, tales como la educación (que es deber social fundamental conforme al artículo 102

mediante un sistema tributario que debe procurar "la justa distribución de las cargas públicas atendiendo al principio de la progresividad, así como la protección de la economía nacional y la elevación del nivel de vida de la población" (art. 316).[1070]

La consecuencia de lo anterior es que la noción de Estado Social está imbricada con las otras nociones que resultan de la configuración del Estado en la Constitución, en el sentido de que además de tratarse de un Estado Social, también es un Estado de derecho, un Estado democrático, un Estado de Justicia, un Estado descentralizado y, en especial, un Estado con un sistema de Economía Mixta,[1071] en el cual se debe desenvolver.

Por tanto, para captar adecuadamente el sentido de esta precisión constitucional del Estado Social, ésta no puede interpretarse aisladamente ni puede dársele un sentido interpretativo global, único y superior ignorando los otros componentes que en la Constitución deben configurar al Estado, ni dársele un sentido prevalente sobre los otros, al punto de aniquilarlos.

Todos los componentes del Estado en la Constitución, y no sólo el del Estado Social, al contrario de lo que ha pretendido la Sala Constitucional en reciente sentencia, son los que comportan "verdaderos efectos normativos y por ende, de necesaria y vinculante observación, con la significación y trascendencia que las normas constitucionales implican para el Estado, en todos y cada uno de sus componentes."[1072] Es decir, no sólo el Estado Social es un "parámetro constitucional" para la hermenéutica, sino también los son las otras nociones que identifican al Estado en la Constitución, como el de ser de economía mixta, democrático, de derecho, descentralizado y de justicia, sin que pueda dársele, se insiste, prevalencia a ningún concepto sobre otro, y aniquilar alguno de los condicionamientos del Estado en beneficio de otro.

Ello implica que en la Constitución hay parámetros de libertad para los ciudadanos que sin duda implican normas permisivas, cuando se garantiza la iniciativa privada y la libre empresa con ámbitos negativos o abstencionistas para el Estado, en

---

constitucional), o la salud (derecho social fundamental según el artículo 83 constitucional), o la protección del trabajo, la seguridad social y el derecho a la vivienda (artículos 82, 86 y 87 constitucionales), por lo que el interés social gravita sobre actividades tanto del Estado como de los particulares, porque con él se trata de evitar un desequilibrio que atente contra el orden público, la dignidad humana y la justicia social.". Véase en http://www.tsj.gov.ve/decisiones/scon/enero/85-240102-01-1274%20.htm.

1070 Véase Leonardo Palacios Márquez, "Medidas fiscales para el desarrollo económico," en *Revista de Derecho Tributario*, N° 97, Asociación Venezolana de Derecho Tributario, Legislec Editores, Caracas 2002, pp. 179-224.

1071 Véase Allan R. Brewer-Carías, "Reflexiones sobre la Constitución económica" en *Estudios sobre la Constitución Española. Homenaje al Profesor Eduardo García de Enterría*, Editorial Civitas, Madrid, 1991, Tomo V, pp. 3.839-3.853; y lo expuesto en relación con la Constitución de 1999 en Alan R. Brewer-Carías, "Sobre el régimen constitucional del sistema económico," en *Debate Constituyente (Aportes a la Asamblea Nacional Constituyente), Tomo III (18 octubre-30 noviembre 1999)*, Fundación de Derecho Público-Editorial Jurídica Venezolana, Caracas 1999, pp. 15-52.

1072 Véase la sentencia N° 1158 de 18 de agosto de 2014 (Caso: amparo en protección de intereses difusos, Rómulo Plata, contra el Ministro del Poder Popular para el Comercio y Superintendente Nacional para la Defensa de los Derechos Socio Económicos), en http://www.tsj.gov.ve/decisiones/scon/agosto/168705-1158-18814-2014-14-0599.HTML.

paralelo a una regulación de la actuación activa del mismo, que implica prestaciones positivas estatales; parámetros que en el Estado Social deben necesariamente articularse para lograr una coexistencia armónica entre ambos extremos, estando los dos y no sólo uno de ellos, sujetos a ser regulados y canalizados por normas, precisamente de derecho administrativo, sin que ninguno de ellos, ni los derechos de libertad ni los derechos sociales puedan tornarse en instrumentos para el atropello y el abuso, que signifiquen desconocimiento y cercenamiento de derechos y libertades o generación de asimetrías sociales en la población. Todo ello implica, que la interpretación de los derechos sociales no puede conducir a vaciar totalmente de valor y contenido a los derechos de libertad de los ciudadanos.

Por ello, el Estado Social, en la Constitución, no se puede desligar del Estado de Economía Mixta que la misma Constitución establece en el artículo 299, al prescribir que el régimen socioeconómico de la República se fundamenta en los principios de justicia social, democratización, eficiencia, libre competencia, protección del ambiente, productividad y solidaridad, a los fines de asegurar el desarrollo humano integral y una existencia digna y provechosa para la colectividad; todo lo cual configura un sistema económico que se fundamenta en la libertad económica, la iniciativa privada y la libre competencia, por una arte, y por la otra, con la participación del Estado como promotor del desarrollo económico, regulador de la actividad económica, y planificador con la participación de la sociedad civil.

De ello deriva que la Constitución, al regular al Estado Social en el marco de un Estado de economía mixta,[1073] lo ha hecho, como lo destacó la Sala Constitucional

---

1073   Véase en general, sobre el tema del Estado Social y el sistema de economía mixta: José Ignacio Hernández G. "Estado Social y Libertad de Empresa en Venezuela: Consecuencias Prácticas de un Debate Teórico" en *Seminario de Profesores de Derecho Público*, Caracas, 2010, en http://www.uma.edu.ve/admini/ckfinder/userfiles/files/Libertad_economica_seminario.pdf ; y "Estado social y ordenación constitucional del sistema económico venezolano," Biblioteca Jurídica Virtual del Instituto de Investigaciones Jurídicas de la UNAM, en http://www.juridi-cas.unam.mx/publica/librev/rev/dconstla/cont/2006.1/pr/pr14.pdf; Tomás A. Arias Castillo, "Vendiendo Utopías. Una respuesta al profesor José Ignacio Hernández" en *Seminario de Profesores de Derecho Público*, Caracas, 2010, en http://www.uma.edu.ve/admini/ckfinder/user-files/files/VENDIENDO%20UTO-PIAS.pdf; José Ignacio Hernández G. "La Constitución Fabulada. Breve contra réplica a la respuesta del profesor Tomás Arias Castillo" en *Seminario de Profesores de Derecho Público*, Caracas, 2010, en http://www.uma.edu.ve/admini/ck-finder/userfiles/files/Contra%20r%C3%A9plica%20Arias.pdf; Tomás A. Arias Castillo "Una Réplica no es una Contrarréplica Contrarréplica al Profesor José Ignacio Hernández" en *Seminario de Profesores de Derecho Público*, Caracas, 2010 en http://www.uma.edu.ve/admini/ck-finder/userfiles/files/Contrarr%C3%A9plica%20para%20el%20Blog%2029%2012%2010_.pdf ; Luis A. Herrera Orellana "A propósito de la polémica entre los profesores Hernández y Arias en torno al Estado social y la libertad económica en la Constitución de 1999" en *Seminario de Profesores de Derecho Público*, Caracas, 2010 en http://www.uma.edu.ve/admini/ckfinder/user-files/files/Comentarios%20a%20pol%C3%A9mica%20JIHG-TAAC.pdf; Oscar Ghersi Rassi, "Comentarios al debate Hernández – Arias. Estado Social y Libertad de Empresa en Venezuela: Consecuencias Prácticas de un Debate Teórico" en *Seminario de Profesores de Derecho Público*, Caracas, 2011, en http://www.uma.edu.ve/admini/ckfinder/userfiles/files/Comentarios%20al%20debate%20Hern%C3%A1ndez%20-%20Arias.pdf ; José Valentín González P, "Las Tendencias Totalitarias del Estado Social y Democrático de Derecho y el carácter iliberal del Derecho Administrativo", CEDICE-Libertad, 2012. http://cedice.org.ve/wp-content/uploads/2012/12/Tendencias-Totalitarias-del-Edo-Social-y-Democr%C3%A1tico-de-Derecho-Administrativo.pdf; y José Valentín González P, "Nuevo Enfoque sobre la Constitución Económica de 1999," en el libro *Enfo-*

del Tribunal Supremo en sentencia N° 117 de 6 de febrero de 2001, reiterando expresamente un fallo anterior de la antigua Corte Suprema de 15 de diciembre de 1998, estableciendo un conjunto de normas constitucionales:

> "destinadas a proporcionar el marco jurídico fundamental para la estructura y funcionamiento de la actividad económica, [que] no está destinada -salvo el caso de las constituciones socialistas de modelo soviético- a garantizar la existencia de un determinado orden económico, sino que actúan como garantes de una economía social de mercado, inspiradas en principios básicos de justicia social y con una "base neutral" que deja abiertas distintas posibilidades al legislador, del cual sólo se pretende que observe los límites constitucionales."[1074]

La Sala Constitucional además, consideró en dicha sentencia, que la Constitución de 1999, al igual que sucedía en la Constitución de 1961:

> "propugna una serie de valores normativos superiores del régimen económico, consagrando como tales la libertad de empresa en el marco de una economía de mercado y fundamentalmente el del Estado Social de Derecho (Welfare State, Estado de Bienestar o Estado Socialdemócrata), *esto es un Estado social opuesto al autoritarismo*. Los valores aludidos se desarrollan mediante el concepto de libertad de empresa, que encierra, tanto la noción de un derecho subjetivo "a dedicarse libremente a la actividad económica de su preferencia", como un principio de ordenación económica dentro del cual se manifiesta la voluntad de la empresa de decidir sobre sus objetivos. En este contexto, los Poderes Públicos, cumplen un rol de intervención, la cual puede ser directa (a través de empresas) o indirecta (como ente regulador del mercado) [...]

A la luz de todos los principios de ordenación económica contenidos en la Constitución de la República Bolivariana de Venezuela, se patentiza el carácter mixto de la economía venezolana, esto es, un sistema socioeconómico intermedio entre la economía de libre mercado (en el que el Estado funge como simple programador de la economía, dependiendo ésta de la oferta y la demanda de bienes y servicios) y la economía interventora (en la que el Estado interviene activamente como el "empresario mayor"). Efectivamente, la anterior afirmación se desprende del propio texto de la Constitución, promoviendo, expresamente, la actividad económica conjunta del Estado y de la iniciativa privada en la persecución y concreción de los valores supremos consagrados en la Constitución."[1075]

---

ques sobre Derecho y Libertad, Academia de Ciencias Políticas y Sociales, Serie Eventos, Caracas 2013.

1074   Véase en *Revista de Derecho Público*, N° 85-88, Editorial Jurídica Venezolana, Caracas, 2001. Véase José Ignacio Hernández, "Constitución económica y privatización (Comentarios a la sentencia de la Sala Constitucional del 6 de febrero de 2001)", en *Revista de Derecho Constitucional*, N° 5, julio-diciembre-2001, Editorial Sherwood, Caracas, 2002, pp. 327 a 342.

1075   Véase en *Revista de Derecho Público*, N° 85-88, Editorial Jurídica Venezolana, Caracas, 2001. Véase José Ignacio Hernández, "Constitución económica y privatización (Comentarios a la sentencia de la Sala Constitucional del 6 de febrero de 2001)", en *Revista de Derecho Constitucional*, N° 5, julio-diciembre-2001, Editorial Sherwood, Caracas, 2002, pp. 327 a 342.

El carácter mixto del sistema socioeconómico de Venezuela, por tanto, concluyó la Sala Constitucional en esa sentencia, "persigue el equilibrio de todas las fuerzas del mercado y la actividad conjunta del Estado e iniciativa privada," lo que impide por supuesto, el sacrificio de ésta última en beneficio del Estado, y menos esgrimiendo la noción de Estado Social.

En ese sistema de economía mixta, la Constitución, en efecto, regula los derechos económicos, en particular, siguiendo la tradición del constitucionalismo venezolano, la libertad económica como el derecho de todos de dedicarse libremente a la actividad económica de su preferencia, sin más limitaciones que las previstas en la Constitución y las que establezcan las leyes, por razones de desarrollo humano, seguridad, sanidad, protección del ambiente u otras de interés social (art. 112), y el derecho de propiedad; y la garantía de la expropiación (art. 115) y prohibición de la confiscación (art. 116). La Constitución, además, regula el derecho de todas las personas a disponer de bienes y servicios de calidad, así como a una información adecuada y no engañosa sobre el contenido y características de los productos y servicios que consumen, a la libertad de elección y a un trato equitativo y digno. (art. 117). Por la otra, en el texto constitucional se regulan las diferentes facetas de la intervención del Estado en la economía, como Estado promotor, es decir, que no sustituye a la iniciativa privada, sino que fomenta y ordena la economía para asegurar su desarrollo, en materia de promoción del desarrollo económico (art. 299); de promoción de la iniciativa privada (art. 112); de promoción de la agricultura para la seguridad alimentaria (art. 305); de promoción de la industria (art. 302); de promoción del desarrollo rural integrado (art. 306); de promoción de la pequeña y mediana industria (art. 308); de promoción de la artesanía popular (art. 309); y de promoción del turismo (art. 310).Además, se establecen normas sobre el Estado Regulador, por ejemplo en materia de prohibición de los monopolios (art. 113), y de restricción del abuso de las posiciones de dominio en la economía con la finalidad de proteger al público consumidor y los productores y asegurar condiciones efectivas de competencia en la economía. Además, en materia de concesiones estatales (art. 113); protección a los consumidores o usuarios (art. 117); política comercial (art. 301); y persecución de los ilícitos económicos (art. 114).Igualmente la Constitución prevé normas sobre la intervención del Estado en la economía, como Estado empresario, (art. 300); con especial previsión del régimen de la nacionalización petrolera y el régimen de la reserva de actividades económicas al Estado (art. 302 y 303).

Este modelo de Estado Social y de Economía Mixta previsto en la Constitución era el llamado a permitir el desenvolvimiento de una economía basada en la libertad económica y la iniciativa privada, pero con una intervención importante y necesaria del Estado para asegurar los principios de justicia social que constitucionalmente deben orientar el régimen económico; lo que en el caso de Venezuela, sin duda, siempre se acrecentó por el hecho de ser el Estado el titular del dominio público sobre el subsuelo.

Pero como antes dijimos, nada de ello en la realidad existe en el Estado contemporáneo, donde el Estado dejó de ser un Estado Social de Economía Mixta, pasando a ser un Estado totalitario donde la iniciativa privada está totalmente marginada, siendo una de las piezas fundamentales para ese logro la Ley Orgánica de Precios Justos de 2014.[1076]

II. LA LEY ORGÁNICA DE PRECIOS JUSTOS Y EL FIN DE LA LIBERTAD ECONÓMICA

Dicha Ley, en efecto, supuestamente tiene por objeto, siguiendo a la letra lo que dice la Constitución, "asegurar el desarrollo armónico, justo, equitativo, productivo y soberano de la economía nacional," pero mediante una medida extremadamente restrictiva de la iniciativa privada como es "la determinación de precios justos de bienes y servicios" por parte de la burocracia estatal, "mediante el análisis de las estructuras de costos, la fijación del porcentaje máximo de ganancia y la fiscalización efectiva de la actividad económica y comercial;" todo ello, supuestamente, con el "fin de proteger los ingresos de todos los ciudadanos, y muy especialmente el salario de los trabajadores; el acceso de las personas a los bienes y servicios para la satisfacción de sus necesidades;" y además establecer un marco de criminalización a la iniciativa privada, mediante la previsión de "ilícitos administrativos, sus procedimientos y sanciones, los delitos económicos, su penalización y el resarcimiento de los daños sufridos;" y todo lo anterior, no para asegurar un Estado social de economía mixta, sino para lograr la "consolidación de un orden económico socialista productivo," que el artículo 3 precisa que es el consagrado en el "Plan de la patria," y que está totalmente alejado del Estado Social en el marco de una economía mixta del cual nos habla la Constitución.

Con ese último propósito, y salvo haber logrado la destrucción de la economía mixta como sistema político económico, ninguno de los supuestos "fines" de la ley se han logrado ni se pueden lograr, de manera que en la práctica, no se ha podido incrementar el nivel de vida del pueblo venezolano, salvo por la ilusión de dádivas y subsidios no productivos, y mucho menos se ha logrado "alcanzar la mayor suma de felicidad posible;" no se ha logrado "el desarrollo armónico y estable de la economía," y la determinación de supuestos "precios justos" de los bienes y servicios, lo que ha hecho es conspirar contra la protección del salario y demás ingresos de las personas; no se han logrado "fijar criterios justos de intercambio," y la normativa adoptada que ha incidido negativamente en los costos, y en la determinación de porcentajes de supuestas "ganancia razonables," han conspirado contra la iniciativa privada y la productividad. En ese esquema, de destrucción de la producción, no se ha garantizado "el acceso de las personas a los bienes y servicios para la satisfacción de sus necesidades" ni por supuesto, se ha privilegiado "la producción nacional de bienes y servicios," dependiendo, resultado que no se ha podido proteger a al pueblo contra las prácticas que puedan afectar el acceso a los bienes o servicios.

La Ley, en realidad ha decretado el fin de la libertad económica y de la iniciativa privada, haciendo depender todo de la burocracia estatal, al sujetar a su normativa a absolutamente todas las personas naturales y jurídicas de derecho público o privado, nacionales o extranjeras, que desarrollen actividades económicas en el país, "incluidas las que se realizan a través de medios electrónicos" (Art. 2), imponiéndole a

---

1076   Véase en *Gaceta Oficial* N° 5156 Extra de 19-11-2014.

todas dichas personas la necesidad de "inscribirse y mantener sus datos actualizados en el Registro Único de Personas que Desarrollan Actividades Económicas," estableciendo que dicha "inscripción es requisito indispensable, a los fines de poder realizar actividades económicas y comerciales en el país" (art. 22). En el pasado, y en el olvido quedó, por tanto, la norma constitucional que garantiza a todas las personas el derecho a "dedicarse libremente a la actividad lucrativa de su preferencia" y la obligación del Estado de "promover la iniciativa privada" (art. 112).

Al contrario lo que existe en la práctica es un esquema legal de persecución contra la iniciativa privada, que incluso se aprecia por la atribución a la burocracia estatal de establecer "el margen máximo de ganancia" "de cada actor de la cadena de comercialización" estableciendo un límite máximo de "treinta (30) puntos porcentuales de la estructura de costos del bien o servicio" (art. 32); persecución que se materializa con el conjunto de "medidas preventivas" que se regulan en la Ley y que la burocracia estatal puede imponer durante las inspecciones o fiscalizaciones que realicen los funcionarios, cuando detecten "indicios de incumplimiento de las obligaciones" previstas en la Ley, y a su juicio existan "elementos que permitan presumir que se puedan causar lesiones graves o de difícil reparación a la colectividad," estando facultados para "adoptar y ejecutar en el mismo acto, medidas preventivas destinadas a impedir que se continúen quebrantando las normas que regulan la materia, entre las cuales, el artículo 39 de la Ley enumera el comiso; la ocupación temporal de los establecimientos o bienes indispensables para el desarrollo de la actividad, o para el transporte o almacenamiento de los bienes comisados; el cierre temporal del establecimiento; la suspensión temporal de las licencias, permisos o autorizaciones emitidas por la burocracia; el ajuste inmediato de los precios de bienes destinados a comercializar o servicios a prestar; y en general "todas aquellas que sean necesarias para impedir la vulneración de los derechos de las ciudadanas protegidos" por la Ley. En definitiva, lo que resulta es un régimen de terror económico que pone a las empresas a la merced de la burocracia y lamentablemente, en manos de la corrupción que tal poder genera, al permitir, por ejemplo, que "la ocupación temporal" se pueda materializar "mediante la posesión inmediata, la puesta en operatividad y el aprovechamiento del establecimiento, local, vehículo, nave o aeronave, por parte del órgano o ente competente; y el uso inmediato de los bienes necesarios para la continuidad de las actividades de producción o comercialización de bienes, o la prestación de los servicios, garantizando el abastecimiento y la disponibilidad de éstos durante el curso del procedimiento" (art. 39). Esto, sólo, respecto de las medidas preventivas, porque por lo que se refiere a las sanciones que regula el artículo 45, mediante las mismas, se puede proceder a la "suspensión temporal en el Registro" lo que implica la prohibición pura y simple de poder realizar actividad económica; la "ocupación temporal con intervención," el cierre temporal" o la "clausura" de "almacenes, depósitos, industrias, comercios, transporte de bienes," lo que implica el despojo de la propiedad privada;" la "revocatoria de licencias, permisos o autorizaciones, y de manera especial, los relacionados con el acceso a las divisas," y finalmente, la "confiscación de bienes," a pesar de que ello está prohibido en la Constitución.

Esta normativa, como se dijo, es la negación más paladina de los principios más elementales de la Constitución sobre libertad económica y derecho de propiedad, y por tanto, del modelo de Estado Social de economía mixta, y la implementación, vía legislación, de lo que se pretendió establecer mediante el; proyecto de reforma constitucional de 2007, que fue rechazado por el pueblo.

III. EL INTENTO Y RECHAZADO PROYECTO DE REFORMA CONSTITUCIONAL DE 2007 PARA SUSTITUIR EL ESTADO SOCIAL Y DE ECONOMÍA MIXTA

En efecto, el esquema constitucional de Estado Social y de Economía Mixta en Venezuela puede decirse que comenzó a distorsionarse por la progresiva construcción de un desbalance a favor de la participación del Estrado en la economía, del desarrollo de poderes reguladores de todo orden en reacción con las iniciativas privadas, que comenzaron a frenar la producción, y la subsiguiente implementación de una política desenfrenada de estatización generalizada de la economía, que se agudizó después de la reelección del Presidente Hugo Chávez a finales de 2006.

Basado en el hecho de que durante su campaña electoral había abogado por la implementación de una política socialista, a partir de enero de 2007 el mismo Chávez comenzó a diseñar la propuesta de plasmar en la Constitución un modelo de Estado, diametralmente distinto al Estado social de economía mixta previsto en la misma, denominado Estado Comunal o del Poder Popular, pero en paralelo al Estado Constitucional, lo que fue presentado en el proyecto de reforma constitucional de 2007,[1077] el cual tenía como supuesto que el Estado todo lo podía, aún en sacrificio de las iniciativas privadas, es decir, que podía ser a vez, investigador, productor, agricultor, empleador, exportador, importador, prestador de servicios, constructor, distribuidor, almacenador, educador; transportista, y que para todo ello tendría siempre recursos ilimitados.

Inmerso en esa desenfrenada ilusión, en el proyecto de reforma constitucional que Chávez presentó a la Asamblea Nacional en 2007, y esta sancionó, al contrario de lo dispuesto en la Constitución, en lugar del sistema de Estado de economía mixta, se propuso establecer un sistema de economía totalmente estatal, de planificación centralizada, de propiedad de todos los medios de producción por el Estado, y de proscripción de la propiedad privada y de libertad económica; esquema propio de un Estado y economía comunista, donde desaparecía la iniciativa privada, la libertad económica y el derecho de propiedad como derechos constitucional.[1078]

Por tanto, por ejemplo, en lugar de regularse la libertad económica y la iniciativa privada, y su compaginación con el rol del Estado en procura conjunta de la justicia social, en la reforma de 2007 lo que se establecía era una norma en la cual sólo se definía una política estatal para promover "el desarrollo de un modelo económico

---

1077   Véase los comentarios al proyecto de reforma constitucional presentado por el Presidente de la república a la Asamblea Nacional en Allan R. Brewer-Carías, *Hacia la consolidación de un Estado socialista, centralizado, policial y militarista. Comentarios sobre el sentido y alcance de las propuestas de reforma constitucional 2007*, Colección Textos Legislativos, N° 42, Editorial Jurídica Venezolana, Caracas 2007.

1078   Véase los comentarios a la reforma constitucional de 2007 aprobada por la Asamblea Nacional en Allan R. Brewer-Carías, *La reforma constitucional de 2007 (Comentarios al proyecto inconstitucionalmente sancionado por la Asamblea Nacional el 2 de noviembre de 2007)*, Colección Textos Legislativos, N° 43, Editorial Jurídica Venezolana, Caracas 2007.

productivo, intermedio, diversificado e independiente," agregándose que el Estado, debía, "fomentar y desarrollar distintas formas de empresas y unidades económicas de propiedad social, tanto directa o comunal como indirecta o estatal, así como empresas y unidades económicas de producción o distribución social, pudiendo ser estas de propiedad mixta entre el Estado, el sector privado y el poder comunal, creando las mejores condiciones para la construcción colectiva y cooperativa de una economía socialista." La consecuencia de ello fue que también se buscó eliminar de la Constitución, los principios del sistema económico que están en el artículo 299, y que son la justicia social, la libre competencia, la democracia y la , y al contrario, lo que buscaba establecer en su lugar, eran los principios "socialistas, antiimperialistas, humanistas".

Y en cuanto a la propiedad privada, en el proyecto rechazado de reforma constitucional de 2007, lo que se buscaba simplemente era eliminarla como derecho constitucional, quedando materialmente reducida a la que pudiera existir solo respecto de "los bienes de uso, consumo y medios de producción legítimamente adquiridos," quedando por tanto minimizada y marginalizada en relación con la propiedad pública. Y en cuanto a la garantía de la expropiación, la misma quedaba ilusoria, al buscarse establecer en la Constitución, "la facultad de los órganos del Estado de ocupar previamente, durante el proceso judicial, los bienes objeto de expropiación" sin pago o consignación previa alguna de la justa indemnización. Todo ello, sin duda, conducía a una "transformación de la estructura del Estado" que fue rechazado por el pueblo.[1079]

Ahora bien, ateniéndonos a los principios que conforman la noción de Estado Social de economía mixta en la Constitución, a pesar de que no se lograron barrer con la rechazada reforma de 2007, sin embargo, los mismos en la realidad del Estado venezolano de la actualidad, han sido pospuestos, es decir, no se aplican, y al contrario, el Estado, después de tres lustros de aplicación del llamado "socialismo del siglo XIX" obedeciendo a todos los principios que se quisieron incorporar en la Constitución con la rechazada reforma constitucional, dejó de ser ese Estado Social de economía mixta, trastocándose en un Estado Totalitario,[1080] Comunista, Burocrá-

---

1079   Véase por ejemplo lo expresado en el Voto Salvado del Magistrado Jesús Eduardo Cabrera a la sentencia N° 2042 de la Sala Constitucional del Tribunal Supremo de 2 de noviembre de 2007, en el cual expresó sobre el proyecto de reforma constitucional de 2007 sobre el régimen de la propiedad, que: "El artículo 113 del Proyecto, plantea un concepto de propiedad, que se adapta a la propiedad socialista, y que es válido, incluso dentro del Estado Social; pero al limitar la propiedad privada solo sobre bienes de uso, es decir aquellos que una persona utiliza (sin especificarse en cual forma); o de consumo, que no es otra cosa que los fungibles, surge un cambio en la estructura de este derecho que dada su importancia, conduce a una transformación de la estructura del Estado. Los alcances del Derecho de propiedad dentro del Estado Social, ya fueron reconocidos en fallo de esta Sala de 20 de noviembre de 2002, con ponencia del Magistrado Antonio García García."

1080   Pompeyo Márquez, conocido dirigente de la izquierda venezolana ha expresado lo siguiente al contestar a una pregunta de un periodista sobre si "¿Existe "el socialismo bolivariano", tal como se define el Partido Socialista Unido de Venezuela (Psuv) en su declaración doctrinaria?" Dijo: "-No existe. Esto no tiene nada que ver con el socialismo. Después del XX Congreso del Partido Comunista de la Unión Soviética, donde Nikita Jrouschov denunció los crímenes de Stalin, se produjo un gran debate a escala internacional sobre las características del socialismo, y las definiciones, que se han esgrimido: Felipe González, Norberto Bobbio, para mencionar a un español y a un italiano son contestatarias a lo que se está haciendo aquí. // -Esto es una dictadura militar, que desconoce la Constitución, y la

tico y Populista; para lo cual incluso, se han implementado las reformas rechazadas en 2007, pero mediante leyes, en forma contraria a la Constitución y en fraude a la voluntad popular, como ha sido precisamente la Ley Orgánica de Precios Justos de 2014.[1081]

IV. IMPLANTACIÓN DE UN ESTADO COMUNISTA

Con todo ello, en primer lugar, el Estado en Venezuela se ha configurado como un Estado totalitario, al haber sido legalmente regulado a partir de 2010, como un Estado Comunista, disponiéndose el aplastamiento progresivo de toda iniciativa privada, y su sustitución por parte del aparato Estado, por el apoderamiento público de casi todos los medios de producción, pretendiendo con ello acaparar la producción de bienes y servicios en casi todos los aspectos y actividades, así como la exportación e importación de bienes, [1082] con el resultado de la configuración de un sistema de capitalismo de Estado altamente ineficiente, burocratizado y corrupto.[1083]

La denominación en este caso del Estado como "Estado comunista" no es una simple calificación literaria, sino que resulta del texto mismo de una Ley, la Ley Orgánica del Sistema Económico Comunal de 2010,[1084] que define el "modelo pro-

---

que reza en su artículo 6: "Venezuela es y será siempre una República democrática". Además, en el artículo 4 habla de un estado de derecho social. Habla del pluralismo y de una serie de valores, que han sido desconocidos por completo durante este régimen chavomadurista, que no es otra cosa que una dictadura. // -Esto se ve plasmado en la tendencia totalitaria, todos los poderes en manos del Ejecutivo. No hay independencia de poderes. No hay justicia. Aquí no hay donde acudir, porque no hay justicia. Cada vez más se acentúa la hegemonía comunicacional." Véase en *La Razón*, 31 julio, 2014, en http://www.larazon.net/2014/07/31/pompeyo-marquez-no podemos-esperar-hasta-el-2019/

1081   Véase en *Gaceta Oficial* N° 5156 Extra de 19-11-2014.

1082   Leandro Area al referirse al "Estado Misional" y Estado invasor" que se ha venido imponiendo en el país, se refiere a las "características del intento de la implantación del comunismo en Venezuela" considerando que "persigue destruir al Estado burgués, extinguirlo, creando uno nuevo en consonancia con el modelaje comunista de larga y sangrienta trayectoria teórica y de fracaso reiterado. Marxismo de libreto acompasado a los nuevos tiempos y circunstancias de salón. La forma es importante aunque nada tenga que ver con el fondo." Véase Leandro Area, "El 'Estado Misional' en Venezuela," en *Analítica.com*, 14 de febrero de 2014, en http://analitica.com/opi-nion/opinion-nacional/el-estado-misional-en-venezuela/

1083   Tal ha sido la devastación económica provocada por el Estado, que uno de los artífices de esta política económica, quien fue Ministro de Economía y Presidente de PDVSA, ha tenido que afirmar, tres lustros después, en 2014, "Está demostrado que el Estado no puede asumir todas las actividades económicas." Véase "Ali Rodríguez Araque: El Estado no puede asumirlo todo.", en *Reporte Confidencial*, 10 de agosto de 2014, en http://www.reporteconfi-dencial.info/noticia/3223366/ali-rodriguez-araque-el-estado-no-puede-asumirlo-todo/

1084   Véase en *Gaceta Oficial* N° 6.011 Extraordinario del 21 de diciembre de 2010. Véase mis comentarios sobre esta Ley Orgánica, en Allan R. Brewer-Carías, "Sobre la Ley Orgánica del Sistema Económico Comunal o de cómo se implanta en Venezuela un sistema económico comunista sin reformar la Constitución," en *Revista de Derecho Público*, N° 124, (octubre-diciembre 2010), Editorial Jurídica Venezolana, Caracas 2010, pp. 102-109. Véase además el libro Allan R. Brewer-Carías et al., *Leyes Orgánicas sobre el Poder Popular y el Estado Comunal (Los Consejos Comunales, Las Comunas, La Sociedad Socialista y el Sistema Económico Comunal),* Colección Textos Legislativos N° 50, Editorial Jurídica Venezolana, Caracas 2011. Véase igualmente, Allan R. Brewer-Carías, "La reforma de la Constitución económica para implantar un sistema económico comunista (o de cómo se reforma la Constitución pisoteando el principio de la rigidez constitucional), en Jesús María Casal y María Gabriela Cuevas (Coordinadores), *Homenaje al Dr. José Guillermo Andueza. Desafíos de la*

ductivo socialista" que se ha dispuesto para el país, como el "modelo de producción basado en la *propiedad social* [de los medios de producción], orientado hacia la *eliminación de la división social del trabajo* propio del modelo capitalista," y "dirigido a la satisfacción de necesidades crecientes de la población, a través de nuevas formas de generación y apropiación así como de la *reinversión social del excedente*" (art. 6.12).

En todo caso, para cualquiera que haya leído algo de marxismo, este texto no es más que un parafraseo de lo que Marx y Engels escribieron hace más de 150 años, en 1845 y 1846, en su conocido libro *La Ideología Alemana* sobre la definición de lo que es la "sociedad comunista," aun cuando refiriéndose a la sociedad primitiva de la época, en muchas partes aún esclavista y en todas, preindustrial; pero basándose en los mismos tres principios de la sociedad comunista incluidos en la ley venezolana, que son: la *"propiedad social de los medios de producción,"* la *"eliminación de la división social del trabajo"* y la *"reinversión social del excedente."*[1085]

Ese es el Estado que una Ley Orgánica, por supuesto, al margen de la Constitución, le ha impuesto a los venezolanos a pesar de que votaron contra el mismo en el referendo de diciembre de 2007, y cuya implementación legal a simplemente eliminado o minimizado a la casi inexistencia al sector privado, mediante ocupaciones y confiscaciones masivas de empresas, fincas y medios de producción, sin garantía de justa indemnización, y que luego han sido abandonadas o desmanteladas, acabando con el aparato productivo del país y eliminando la libertad de empresa y la principal

---

República en la Venezuela de hoy. Memoria del XI Congreso Venezolano de Derecho Constitucional, Universidad Católica Andrés Bello, Caracas 2013, Tomo I, pp. 247-296.

1085 Por ejemplo, Marx y Engels, después de afirmar que la propiedad es "el derecho de suponer de la fuerza de trabajo de otros" y declarar que la "división del trabajo y la propiedad privada" eran "términos idénticos: uno de ellos, referido a la esclavitud, lo mismo que el otro, referido al producto de ésta," escribieron que: "la división del trabajo nos brinda ya el primer ejemplo de cómo, mientras los hombres viven en una sociedad natural, mientras se da, por tanto, una separación entre el interés particular y el interés común, mientras las actividades, por consiguientes no aparecen divididas voluntariamente, sino por modo natural [que se daba según Marx y Engels "en atención a las dotes físicas, por ejemplo, la fuerza corporal, a las necesidades, las coincidencias fortuitas, etc.] los actos propios del hombres se erigen ante él en un poder hostil y ajeno, que lo sojuzga, en vez de ser él quien los domine. En efecto, a partir del momento en que comienza a dividirse el trabajo, cada cual se mueve en un determinado circulo exclusivo de actividad, que le es impuesto y del cual no puede salirse; el hombre es cazador, pescador, pastor o crítico, y no tiene más remedio que seguirlo siendo, si no quiere verse privado de los medios de vida; al paso que en la sociedad comunista, donde cada individuo no tiene acotado un círculo exclusivo de actividades, sino que puede desarrollar sus aptitudes en la rama que mejor le parezca, la sociedad se encarga de regular la producción general, con lo que hace cabalmente posible que yo pueda por la mañana cazar, por la tarde pescar y por la noche apacentar ganado, y después de comer, si me place, dedicarme a criticar, sin necesidad de ser exclusivamente cazador, pescador, pastor o crítico, según los casos." Véase en Karl Marx and Frederich Engels, "The German Ideology," en *Collective Works,* Vol. 5, International Publishers, New York 1976, p. 47. Véanse además los textos pertinentes en http://www.educa.madrid.org/cmstools/files/0a24636f-764c-4e03-9c1d-6722e2ee60d7/Texto%20Marx%20y%20Engels.pdf. Véase sobre el tema Jesús María Alvarado Andrade, "La 'Constitución económica' y el sistema económico comunal *(*Reflexiones Críticas a propósito de la Ley Orgánica del Sistema Económico Comunal)," en Allan R. Brewer-Carías (Coordinador), Claudia Nikken, Luis A. Herrera Orellana, Jesús María Alvarado Andrade, José Ignacio Hernández y Adriana Vigilanza, *Leyes Orgánicas sobre el Poder Popular y el Estado Comunal (Los Consejos Comunales, las Comunas, la Sociedad Socialista y el Sistema Económico Comunal),* Editorial Jurídica Venezolana, Caracas 2011, pp. 377-456.

fuente de ingreso que puede tener un país.[1086] La consecuencia de todo ello, ha sido el surgimiento de una nueva realidad a la cual estaría ahora dirigida la regulación propia del derecho administrativo, reducido a normar, por ejemplo, la sola actividad del Estado, el empleo público, los servicios públicos y las empresas del Estado.

Ello nos obliga a que debemos olvidarnos entonces, ya, de ese esquema del derecho administrativo que estaba destinado, por ejemplo, a regular las actividades desarrolladas por empresas privadas y particulares en sus relaciones con la Administración, las cuales ahora materialmente han desaparecido, y que debamos comenzar a pensar en un derecho administrativo que sólo regula al aparato estatal y a la burocracia, y que, por tanto, desprecia el orden jurídico que se había establecido para asegurar calidad de vida por las empresas privadas, y se rebela a someterse al mismo. Eso ha pasado, por ejemplo, con el derecho ambiental, el derecho urbanístico y el derecho sanitario, de los grandes pilares de nuestro derecho administrativo, que el Estado comunista, que todo lo ha acaparado, menosprecia, con lo que hoy, con la excusa de desarrollo de proyectos sociales, el principal depredador urbanístico y del ambiente es el propio Estado, sin que nadie lo controle;[1087] y el primer violador de las normas, por ejemplo, sobre medicamentos es el propio Estado.[1088]

1086   El que fue Ministro de Economía del país, Alí Rodríguez Araque, y artífice de la política económica en los últimos lustros ha explicado la situación así: "Hay que hacer ciertas definiciones estratégicas que no están claras. ¿Qué es lo que va a desarrollar el Estado?, porque la revolución venezolana no es la soviética, donde los trabajadores armados en medio de una enorme crisis asaltan el poder, destruyen el viejo Estado y construyen uno nuevo. Ni es la revolución cubana, donde un proceso armado asalta el poder y construye uno nuevo. Aquí se llegó al Gobierno a través del proceso electoral. La estructura del Estado es básicamente la misma Yo viví la experiencia de la pesadez de la democracia. Una revolución difícilmente puede avanzar exitosamente con un Estado de esas características. Eso va a implicar un proceso tan largo como el desarrollo de las comunas. Un nuevo Estado tiene que basarse en el poder del pueblo. Mientras, durante un muy largo periodo, se van a combinar las acciones del Estado con las del sector privado. Tiene que haber una definición en ese orden, los roles que va a cumplir ese sector privado, estableciendo las regulaciones para evitar la formación de monopolios. Está demostrado que el Estado no puede asumir todas las actividades económicas. ¿Qué vamos a hacer con la siderúrgica? Yo no estoy proponiendo que se privatice, pero ¿vamos a continuar pasando más actividades al Estado cuando su eficacia es muy limitada?. ¿Qué vamos a hacer con un conjunto de actividades en las cuales se ha venido metiendo el Estado y que están francamente mal y no lo podemos ocultar? Esto no es problema del proceso revolucionario, su raíz es histórica". Véase "Ali Rodríguez Araque: El Estado no puede asumirlo todo.", en *Reporte Confidencial*, 10 de agosto de 2014, en http://www.reporteconfidencial.info/noticia/3223366/ali-rodriguez-araque-el-estado-no-puede-asumirlo-todo/ Véase igualmente lo expuesto por quien fue el ideólogo del régimen, y a quien se le debe la denominación de "socialismo del siglo XXI", que ha expresado: que "El modelo del socialismo impulsado por Chávez fracasó:, siendo "El gran error del gobierno de Maduro es seguir con la idea de Chávez, insostenible, de que el gobierno puede sustituir a la empresa privada. El gobierno usará su monopolio de importaciones y exportaciones para repartir las atribuciones en las empresas," en *El Nacional*, Caracas 19 de abril de 2014, en http://www.el-nacional.com/politica/Heinz-Dieterich-Venezuela-surgimiento-republica_0_394160741.html.

1087   En 2014, incluso, en un retroceso de décadas, en la reestructuración ministerial decretada, simplemente se eliminó el Ministerio del Ambiente y de los recursos Naturales renovables, habiendo sido sus competencias trasladadas a un Ministerio del Poder Popular para Vivienda, Hábitat y Ecosocialismo." Véase en *Gaceta Oficial* N° 40489 de 3 de septiembre de 2014.

1088   Véase por ejemplo lo expresado por Freddy Ceballos, Presidente de la Federación Farmacéutica Venezolana, al expresar que el Poder Ejecutivo "está violando la Ley de Medicamentos, al traer desde Cuba medicinas que no tienen registro sanitario ni señalan sus componentes" agregando que "El Estado es el primer violador" de dicha Ley, no pudiendo garantizar la calidad de los productos.. Véase

En materia urbanística, por ejemplo, basta ver lo que ha ocurrido con la construcción de viviendas de interés social desarrolladas por el Estado, por ejemplo en Caracas y el Litoral Central, hechas incluso con la más clásica arquitectura que desarrollaron los invasores soviéticos en la Europa del Este, carentes de todos los principios del urbanismo contemporáneo, destrozando la calidad de vida urbana en forma irreparable, y haciendo a los ocupadores de vivienda, a quienes además se le niega la propiedad de las mismas, aún más miserables.

De resultas, lo que indudablemente aún tenemos es un derecho administrativo "formal" porque está en los libros y en las leyes, que ha sido el que hemos estudiado y explicado en las últimas décadas, pero que en la realidad está en desuso, porque incluso ya no hay ni siquiera empresas privadas a las cuales se le pueda aplicar, ni hay tribunales contencioso administrativos donde se pueda controlar a la Administración; y en paralelo, lo que tenemos es un contra derecho administrativo fáctico, que es el que regula la acción del Estado, pero desjuridificándolo.

Y lo mismo ocurre en todas las áreas tradicionales de nuestra disciplina, como el derecho minero, el derecho de la competencia, el derecho bancario, el derecho de seguros, el derecho aguas, el derecho agrario, el derecho forestal, cuyas normas se aplican a los pocos y pobres particulares o empresas privadas que subsisten, pero por supuesto no se aplican al Estado, sus empresas y su burocracia, cuando realiza actividades bancarias, explotan bienes y servicios, realizan actividad agrícola, explotan la los bosques o la minería, incluso entregándola a "nuevos" consorcios extranjeros soviéticos o chinos, que sí son verdaderamente imperialistas, acaparando la casi totalidad de la actividad económica.

V. DESARROLLO DE UN ESTADO BUROCRÁTICO, ACAPARADOR DE TODA LA ACTIVIDAD ECONÓMICA

En *segundo lugar*, el Estado totalitario, además de originar un Estado Comunista, se ha convertido en un Estado burocrático, como consecuencia de la desaparición, persecución y estigmatización de la iniciativa privada, a pesar de lo que dice y garantiza la Constitución; y con ello, de toda posibilidad de efectiva generación de riqueza y de empleo en el país, el cual sólo la iniciativa privada puede asegurar; con la lamentable generación de altas tasas de desempleo o de empleo informal. El más claro ejemplo de ello, como se ha dicho, es la normativa contenida en la Ley Orgánica de Precios Justos, de persecución y terror contra la iniciativa privada.

El resultado ha sido que al perseguirse al sector privado y destruirse el aparato productivo, la política social, como solución al desempleo, lamentablemente no ha sido otra que la burocratización mediante el aumento del empleo público a niveles nunca antes vistos, por supuesto bien lejos de la meritocracia que prescribe la Constitución, conforme a la cual el ingreso a la función pública debería ser sólo mediante concurso público (art. 146). La consecuencia de esta política está en que Venezuela, después de quince años de estatizaciones, hoy tiene casi el mismo número de em-

---

el reportaje de Stephanie Méndez, "Presidente Fefarven: El estado venezolano es el primer violador de la Ley de Medicamentos," en *noticierodigital,com*, 10 de octubre de 2014, en http://www.noticierodigital.com/forum/viewtopic.php?t=1056029.

pleados públicos civiles que los que por ejemplo existen en toda la Administración Federal de los Estados Unidos.[1089]

En ésta última, por ejemplo, en 2012 existían aproximadamente 2.700.000 de empleados públicos civiles que sirven a 316 millones de personas, y Venezuela, que tiene una población de 30 millones de personas, en 2012 contaba con cerca de 2.470.000 (comparado con los 90.000 que había en 1998).[1090] Ello implica que cerca del 20% de las personas laboran para el Estado, comparado por ejemplo, con el 3,9% en Colombia. Lo cierto en todo caso, es que durante los últimos 10 años el número de empleados públicos aumentó en un 156%, pero con una disminución lamentablemente, quizás en proporción mayor, respecto de la eficiencia de la Administración en la prestación de los servicios sociales.[1091]

Además, en esa burocracia estatal, quedó en el papel la norma constitucional que prescribe que "los funcionarios públicos están al servicio del Estado y no de parcialidad política alguna," y de que su "nombramiento o remoción no pueden estar determinados por la afiliación u orientación política" (art. 145), pues en la práctica gubernamental actual sucede todo lo contrario, pues para ingresar a la función pública el interesado tiene que haber demostrado lealtad al gobierno, y a los funcionarios se los hace estar al servicio del partido de gobierno, de manera que quien no se adapte a ese principio, es simplemente removido de su cargo, sin contemplación.

El "nuevo" derecho administrativo de la función pública que surge de esa situación, es la antítesis de lo que antes conocíamos como el estatuto de la función pública, teniendo sin embargo una Ley que la regula, que incluso establece concursos para ingresar a la carrera administrativa, y causales de destitución, la cual en realidad, cayó en desuso. ,

En todo caso, para poder uno darse cuenta del efecto que ha tenido esta burocratización en la Administración del Estado, basta constatar que la misma hasta 2014 tenía una dimensión monstruosa, formada en su cúspide por 36 Ministerios del despacho Ejecutivo (en 1999 eran 16), con 107 Viceministros designados.[1092] El número de Ministerios fue reducido en septiembre de 2014 a 27 Ministerios, mediante la

---

1089   Véase la información de la Office of Personal Management, en http://www.opm.gov/policy-data-oversight/data-analysis-documentation/federal-employment-reports/historical-tables/total-government-employment-since-1962/

1090   Véase Víctor Salmerón, "A ritmo de 310 por día crecen los empleados públicos," en *El Nacional*, Caracas 2 de diciembre de 2012, en http://www.eluniversal.com/economia/121202/a-ritmo-de-310-por-dia-crecen-los-empleados-publicos.

1091   Véase Jairo Márquez Lugo, "Venezuela tiene más empleados que Estados Unidos," en http://entresocios.net/ciudadanos/venezuela-tiene-mas-empleados-publicos-que-estados-unidos. Véanse también los datos en: "1999 versus 2013: Gestión del Desgobierno en números", en https://twitter.com/sushidavid/status/451006280061046784.

1092   Véanse el reportaje "Venezuela rompió récord mundial con la mayor cantidad de ministerios," en *Notitarde.com*, 3 de julio de 2014, en http://www.notitarde.com/Pais/Venezuela-rompio-record-mundial-con-la-mayor-cantidad-de-ministerios-2189733/2014/07/03/336113. Véase además, los datos en "1999 versus 2013: Gestión del Desgobierno en números," en https://twitter.com/sushidavid/status/451006280061046784. Véase también la información en Nelson Bocaranda, "Runrunes del jueves 21 de agosto de 2014," en http://www.lapa-tilla.com/site/2014/08/21/runrunes-del-jueves-21-de-agosto-de-2014/.

fusión entre varios, cuando se crearon seis Vicepresidentes sectoriales, [1093] para "coordinar" los Ministerios de los "sectores" las cuales luego se han regulado en la reforma de la Ley Orgánica de la Administración Pública de noviembre de 2014. [1094]
Además, existen cientos de empresas del Estado, sin control ni coordinación alguna,
todo lo cual complica en demasía el aparato burocrático del Estado. Por todo eso,
con toda razón, *The Economist* en septiembre de 2014 estimaba que Venezuela era
"probablemente la economía peor gerenciada del mundo" donde "el precio de la
sobrevivencia de la revolución parece ser la muerte lenta del país;" [1095] gerencia que
durante más de una década estuvo a cargo de un ingeniero mecánico, y que en 2014,
se ha entregado a un militar general del ejército, [1096] teniendo ambos, en común, la
formación que deriva de haber sido sólo burócratas durante los tres últimos lustros.

Para calibrar la situación de las mismas, por otra parte, basta analizar solo una
empresa del Estado, la del sector económico más importante del país, que es la que
maneja la industria petrolera, y de la cual depende el 97% de las divisas que recibe
el país. [1097] Allí, de los 42.000 empleados que Petróleos de Venezuela S.A. (PDVSA)
tenía en 1998, después de que se despidieron en 2002 en la forma más inicua posible
a más de 20.000 empleados calificados como consecuencia de una huelga petrolera,
sin reconocimiento de derechos sociales algunos derivados de la legislación laboral;
la industria pasó a tener 120.000 empleados. La antigüedad promedio de los empleados despedidos era de quince años, y con ellos se perdieron 280.000 años de
experiencia, con un entrenamiento formal que tenían de 21 millones de horas. De
este daño irreversible derivado de la masiva pérdida de conocimiento, talento y experiencia, las consecuencias han sido desastrosas para el país, de lo cual nunca se ha
podido recuperar la industria, siendo una de sus manifestaciones, por ejemplo, que
de 3.5Mbd que la industria producía en 1998 se ha pasado a producir 2.6Mbd en
2013, y de un costo de producción de US$ 4bd en 1998 se ha pasado a un costo de
US% 24bd. Y en cuanto a la productividad, medida en barriles por día por trabaja-
dor, de los 83pb en 1998, se pasó a 23 en 2013, es decir, una caída del 72%. [1098] La
empresa, además, se ha endeudado en cifras astronómicas, con un total de pasivos
de 142,596.000.000 US$ en 2012 y una deuda externa de 40.026.000.000 US$; cifra
ahora impagable por la imposibilidad de aumentar la producción. [1099]

Y lo más insólito de este desastre venezolano, es que el país con las más grandes
reservas de petróleo de América, que antes de la creación de la OPEP era todavía el

---

1093   Véanse los Decretos en *Gaceta Oficial* N° 40489 de 3 de septiembre de 2014.

1094   Véanse en *Gaceta Oficial* No. 6147 Extra. de 17 de noviembre de 2014.

1095   Véanse "Venezuela's Economy. Of oil and coconut wáter. Probably the world's managed economy,"
        en *The Economist*, N° 8905, September 20th. 2014, pp. 31-32.

1096   Véanse "Venezuela's Economy. Of oil and coconut wáter. Probably the world's managed economy,"
        en *The Economist*, N°8905, September 20th. 2014, pp. 31-32.

1097   *Idem.*

1098   Véase Ramón Espinasa, El Sector Petrolero quince años después", 2014, en http://elreca-
        dero.blogspot.com/2014/07/ramon-espinasa-el-sector-petrolero.html.

1099   Véase Diego González Cruz, "Pdvsa colapsó. Pdvsa llegó al colapso. Su deuda externa es impagable
        en el corto y en el mediano plazo," en *El Universal*, 23-12-2013, en http://www.eluni-versal.com/opi-
        nion/131223/pdvsa-colapso.

primer país exportador de petróleo del mundo, y que en toda su historia era un exportador nato de gasolina terminada y semi-terminada, ahora, teniendo el centro refinador más grande de América Latina, no es capaz de cubrir el consumo interno de gasolina, e importa desde los Estados Unidos más de 3.3 millones de litros diarios de gasolina (unos 150.000bd). Los mismos se venden al detal a menos de un centavo de dólar por litro, perdiendo la empresa aproximadamente 107 US$ por cada barril.[1100] Además, en octubre de 2014 se anunciaba que el país estaba iniciando la importación de petróleo crudo desde Argelia.[1101] Adicionalmente, en 2014, el gobierno estaba inmerso en un proceso de decidir la venta de la empresa Citgo, ubicada en los Estados Unidos, que es refinadora y distribuidora de gasolina, que fue desarrollada exitosamente desde los tiempos de la internacionalización de la industria petrolera en los años noventa,[1102] proceso que en los Estados Unidos de América, se comenzaba a calificar como una operación penosa.[1103]

A toda esta catástrofe, sin duda, además de las fallas gerenciales y la errada política de Estado, contribuyó el mencionado despido de más de 20.000 profesionales formados durante décadas en las mejores Universidades del mundo, además fueron desplazados, pues incluso se les impidió trabajar en el país, en lo que ha sido la más

---

1100   Véase el reportaje de Carolina Pezoa A.: "El mundo militar se consolida en el aparato estatal de Venezuela. Reciente cambio de gabinete del Presidente Nicolás Maduro apuntaló a uniformados en áreas productivas y financieras clave," en *La Tercera.com*, 6 de septiembre de 2014, en http://www.latercera.com/noticia/mundo/2014/09/678-594664-9-el-mundo-militar-se-consolida-en-el-aparato-estatal-de-venezuela.shtml.

1101   Véase el reportaje "Primer buque de importación petrolera parte para Venezuela," donde se informa que: "Lo que será la primera importación de crudo en la historia del país partió desde el norte de África, en una operación que busca reducir los costos de Pdvsa para diluir el crudo pesado de la Faja Petrolífera Hugo Chávez en la región del Orinoco," en El Nacional, caracas 15 de octubre de 2014, en http://www.el-nacional.com/economia/Primer-buque-importacion-petrolera-Venezuela_0_501549924.html. Por ello, Diego Arria con razón señaló, que "La revolución bolivariana se puede atribuir el triunfo de haber convertido a Venezuela, el país con las mayores reservas petroleras mundiales, en un importador de petróleo de Argelia y de Rusia, después que destruyó a Pdvsa como empresa modelo." En Alfredo Fermín, "El gran triunfo de Maduro, convertirnos en importadores de petróleo," en *El Carabobeño*, Lectura Dominical, Valencia 26 de octubre de 2014.

1102   Como lo advirtió José Toro Hardy: "Ahora la vorágine revolucionaria, hundida en el fango de una ideología obsoleta, una incompetencia abismal y una corrupción inenarrable, está a punto de cometer un último e insuperable acto de destrucción: la entrega de Citgo." Véase José Toro Hardy, "J'accuse': Le entrega de Citgo," en *lapatilla.com*. 29 de julio de 2014, en http://www.lapati-lla.com/si-te/2014/07/29/jose-toro-hardy-jaccuse-la-entrega-de-citgo/.

1103   En el *The New York Times* del 14 de agosto de 2014, se informaba que Venezuela estaba con dicha venta configurándose como un 'vendedor angustiado," indicando: "The country wants to offload Citgo, its American refinery and pipelines unit. It may be worth up to $15 billion, money that's sorely needed because of President Nicolás Maduro's foolish economic policies. And the drop in value of heavy-oil assets like Citgo owns makes it a bad time to sell." Véase "Venezuela as a distressed seller," en *The New York Times*, New York, 14 de Agosto de 2014. Alberto Quirós Corradi, uno de los más destacados expertos petroleros, al analizar la venta de Citgo, simplemente concluyó afirmando: "Citgo no se puede vender porque lo que se obtenga de esto irá, otra vez, a destinos improductivos." Véase Alberto Quirós Corradi, "Citgo", *El Nacional*, Caracas 21 de agosto de 2014, en http://www.el-nacional.com/alberto_quiros_corra-di/Citgo_0_4679-53295.html después de preguntarse." Finalmente, por ahora, a fines de octubre de 2014 se anunció por el gobierno, de la decisión de abstenerse de la venta de Citgo. Véase Kejar Vyas, "Venezuela Says it Won't Sell Citgo," en *The Wall Street Journal*, New York, 27 de Octubre de 2014, p. B3.

grande y masiva persecución laboral y política que América Latina haya conocido jamás. Pero como sucede en la vida con harta frecuencia, las pérdidas para unos siempre son las ganancias para otros, como ha sido precisamente el caso de los aportes que dichos profesionales venezolanos han dado fuera de Venezuela, en la producción petrolera de tantos otros países que necesitaban de tecnología de punta, siendo precisamente una muestra de ello el caso de Colombia, donde han sido los petroleros venezolanos desplazados de su país, quienes han contribuido significativamente al despegue de la industria petrolera colombiana, en una forma que era difícil de imaginar hace unos lustros.[1104]

Y si todo esto ha ocurrido en la industria más importante del país, lo que tenemos en el resto de la industria pesada estatificada es desolador, como se aprecia de la industria siderúrgica, del aluminio, e incluso de la industria eléctrica que han hecho del país con uno de los mayores potenciales energéticos de América latina, un país asolado por apagones y racionamiento de luz eléctrica. Y por supuesto, mejor es no hablar de la desolación en el campo, luego de las ocupaciones y confiscaciones indiscriminadas de fincas productivas, que hoy están totalmente abandonadas, teniendo que importarse en el país casi todo de la cesta alimentaria. La llamada soberanía alimentaria, por tanto, tristemente quedó en el papel, materializándose sólo en la existencia de un monopolio del Estado para importar alimentos, ya que él sólo puede obtener divisas, las cuales por otra parte, son cada vez más escasas, por el pago de la deuda que agobia al Estado.

En efecto, dicha soberanía agroalimentaria proclamada en la Constitución, fue enterrada por la burocracia oficial recurriendo al expediente que creía más fácil, que era importarlo todo, para distribuirlo por medio de canales comercializadores del propio Estado, sustituyendo a la iniciativa privada, porque en un momento dado había dólares fáciles que el Estado podía destinar a tal fin. Pero con un país con menos ingresos petroleros, por la reducción de la producción y por haber comprometido la misma a futuro, por la descomunal deuda externa que tiene, ya no hay dólares para poder destinar a las importaciones, ni siquiera racionalmente diseñadas.

Venezuela en efecto, en 2014 tiene hoy una deuda pública externa de US$ 104.481.000.000,[1105] de la cual sólo adeuda con China es de US$ 55.000.000.000; y una deuda no financiera con el sector privado por las importaciones, repatriación de dividendos, expropiaciones y los servicios prestados de US$ 56.215.000.000 US$. [1106] En cuanto a la deuda interna la misma aumentó en los tres últimos lustros en 8.424% situándose en la astronómica suma de US$ 216.000.000.000.000.[1107]

1104 Véase por ejemplo, el reportaje sobre "Venezuela's oil diáspora. Brain haemorrhage. Venezuela's loss of thousands of oil workers has been other countries' gain," en *The Economist*, July 19, 2014, Vol. 412, N° 8896, pp. 31-32; y en http://www.economist.com/news/americas/21607824-venezuelas-loss-thousands-oil-workers-has-been-other-countries-gain-brain-haemorrhage.

1105 Véase en Antonio de la Cruz, "La ruta de Maduro hacia el hambre en 7 gráficos," en file:///C:/Users/Alan%20Brewer/Downloads/LA%20RUTA%20DE%20MADURO%20HACIA%20EL%20HAMBRE%207...%20(4).pdf.

1106 *Idem.*

1107 Véase los datos en "1999 versus 2013: Gestión del Desgobierno en números," en https://twitter.com/sushidavid/status/451006280061046784.

El resultado de todo lo anterior ha estado trágicamente a la vista: la escases de todos los productos básicos, y la consecuente disminución de la calidad de vida, que además afecta a los que tienen menos recursos, pues sus ingresos son cada vez menores por la galopante inflación que Venezuela padece (60% en 2014) que es la mayor de toda América Latina.[1108] Y nada vale en el país lo poco que se produce; estando además la venta de los productos, nacionales o importados, sometida a supuestos "precios justos" regulados, precisamente en la Ley Orgánica de Precios Justos de 2014[1109] que afectan los ingresos de las empresas, dejando a muchas operando a pérdida, disminuyendo la producción, todo lo cual además ha generado escases generalizada, llegándose comenzar a implementar a partir de septiembre de 2014, sistemas de racionamientos para los bienes de consumo, sólo vistos en Cuba,.[1110] Y en Corea del Norte.[1111] Todo ello ha originado un descomunal y cotidiano contrabando de extracción, que todos quienes viven en la muy extensa frontera entre Venezuela y Colombia conocen; de manera que es sabido que lo que escasea en Venezuela a precios regulados irrisorios, con seguridad se encuentra fácilmente en Cúcu-

---

1108   Véase la información en http://www.infobae.com/2014/04/24/1559615-en-un-ano-la-inflacion-oficial-venezuela-llego-al-60-ciento.

1109   En la cual, a pesar de que en la reforma de 2013 se le eliminó del nombre la regulación de los "costos" además de los precios, sigue siendo una pieza esencial del régimen de la misma. Antes era "Ley de Costos y Precios Justos," cuya última reforma es precisamente de 2013. Véase Decreto Ley N° 600 de 21 de noviembre de 2013 en *Gaceta Oficial*, N° 40.340 de 23 de enero de 2014.

1110   El 23 de agosto de 2014: "El Superintendente de Precios en Venezuela, Andrés Eloy Méndez, informó que todo establecimiento comercial estará controlado por las máquinas captahuellas. El control será extendido más allá de los alimentos y las medicinas. Méndez dijo que antes del 30 de noviembre deberá estar instalado en todo el país el sistema que contempla máquinas captahuellas para registrar el control de las compras que hacen los consumidores. Adelantó cuáles serán algunos de los rubros que serán controlados." Véase el reportaje "Gobierno de Venezuela impone racionamiento de productos," en *Queen's Latino*, 23 de agosto de 2014, en http://www.queenslatino.com/racionamiento-de-todo-en-venezuela/." Información ratificada por el Presidente de la República. Véase la información: "Captahuellas' para hacer mercado en Venezuela comenzaría en 2015," en El Tiempo, Bogotá, 23 de agosto de 2014, en http://www.eltiempo.com/mundo/latinoamerica/captahuellas-para-hacer-mercado-en-venezuela-comenzaria-en-2015/14419076. Sobre esto, la Nota de Opinión del diario *Tal Cual* del 22 de agosto de 2014, con el título "Racionamiento," expresa : "Si se entiende bien lo que nos ha avisado el superintendente de precios justos, por ahí viene rodando el establecimiento de cupos para la adquisición de artículos de primera necesidad, alimentos en particular.[...] Es, pues, un sistema de racionamiento, pero en lugar de una cartilla, como en Cuba, los avances tecnológicos (y los dólares) permiten apelar a mecanismos tan sofisticados como el del sistema biométrico." Véase en *Tal Cual*, 22-8-2014, en http://www.talcualdigital.com/Movil/visor.aspx?id=106710. La propuesta ya se había anunciado desde junio de 2013, "Venezuela instaurará en Venezuela la cartilla de razonamiento al mejor estilo cubano," en ABC.es Internacional, 4 de junio de 2013, en http://www.abc.es/internacional/20130603/abci-maduro-cartilla-racionamiento-201306032115.html.

1111   Por ello, en el *The Wall Street Jornal* del 23 de octubre de 2014, se indicaba que "Entre el agravamiento de la escases, Venezuela recientemente recibió una extraordinaria y dudosa distinción, y es que alcanzó el rango de Corea del Norte y de Cuba en el racionamiento de comida para sus ciudadanos," refiriéndose a la imposición del sistema de "capta-huellas" digitales en ciertos establecimientos, para el control de la venta de productos. Véase el reportaje de Sara Schaffer Muñoz, "Despite Riches, Venezuela Starts Food rations," en *The Wall Street Journal*, New York, 23 de octubre de 2014, p. A15.

ta, pero a precios de mercado. [1112] Y lo que no escasea pero es muy barato, también se encuentra, como ocurre precisamente con la gasolina.

Con la destrucción del aparato productivo y la material eliminación de las exportaciones, ya que lo poco que se produce no alcanza para el mercado interno, y lo que en buena parte sale del país es mediante contrabando, el único que puede obtener divisas es el propio Estado, para lo cual depende en un 94% de PDVSA. [1113]

En todo caso, para controlar la adquisición de divisas, el Estado ha montado todo tipo de sistemas de control de cambios, constituyéndose en una de las principales fuentes de corrupción administrativa, y de tráfico de influencias, quedando incluso la posibilidad real de importación de bienes sólo a cargo del propio Estado. [1114]

Como lo resumió Fernando Londoño en el diario *El Tiempo* de Bogotá, reproducido por el Jefe de Redacción (Elides Rojas) del diario *El Universal* de Caracas el 24 de mayo de 2014:

"Lo que pasa en Venezuela tenía que llegar y llegó, así sea que toda-vía falte lo peor. Por desgracia. El castrochavismo será recordado como autor de un milagro económico a la inversa, de los que se registran tan pocos en el devenir de los pueblos. Convertir en país miserable el más rico de América no es hazaña de todos los días. Habiendo tanta pobreza en tantas partes, en pocas tiene que pelear la gente, a dentelladas, por una bolsa de leche, por una libra de harina o por un pedazo de carne. Convertir en despojos una de las más organizadas, pujantes y serias empresas petroleras del mundo no es cualquier tontería. Llevar a la insolvencia una nación ante las líneas aéreas, los proveedores comerciales y los que suministran material quirúrgico y hospitalario no es cosa que se vea cualquier día. Y arruinar al tiempo el campo y la industria, el comercio y los servicios, la generación eléctrica, la ingeniería, la banca y las comunicaciones es tarea muy dura, cuando se recuerda que la sufre el país que tiene las mayores reservas petroleras del mundo. En esa frenética carrera hacia el desastre, el gobierno castrochavista tuvo que proceder a la eliminación paulatina de todas las

---

1112   El Presidente del Colegio de Profesores del Estado Táchira, declaraba el 21 de agosto de 2014, que el 72% de los jóvenes en edad escolar, abandonan la escuela para contrabandear," Véase en El Universal, 21 de agosto de 2014, en http://www.eluniversal.com/nacional-y-politica/140821/denuncian-que-72-de-los-jovenes-abandona-la-escuela-para-contrabandear

1113   Véase los datos en "1999 versus 2013: Gestión del Desgobierno en números," en https://twitter.com/sushidavid/status/451006280061046784

1114   El Ministro de Planificación y Economía durante los últimos años, Jorge Gordani, al renunciar a su cargo en 2014 calificó esas entidades como "focos de corrupción," pero sin que durante su gestión se hubiese hecho nada para extirparlo. Véase el texto de la Carta Pública, "Testimonio y responsabilidad ante la historia," 17-8-2014, en http://www.lapatilla.com/site/2014/06/18/gior-dani-da-la-version-de-su-salida-y-arremete-contra-maduro/. Según esas denuncias, "a través de los mecanismos de cambio de divisas "desaparecieron alrededor de 20.000.000.000 de dólares." Véase César Miguel Rondón, "Cada vez menos país," en *Confirmado*, 16-8-2014, en http://confirmado.com.ve/opinan/cada-vez-menos-pais/. Por todo ello, con razón en un editorial del diario *Le Monde* de París, titulado "Los venezolanos en el callejón sin salida del chavismo", se afirmaba que con todo eso *"Se ha creado una economía paralela, un mercado de tráfico interno y externo que beneficia a una pequeña nomenklatura sin escrúpulos."* Véase Editorial de *Le Monde*, 30- marzo 2014, en http://www.eluniversal.com/nacional-y-politica/140330/le-monde-dedico-un-editorial-a-venezuela.

libertades, al sacrificio del pensamiento y la conciencia, a la ruina de las instituciones, del periodismo, de los partidos, de la universidad, de los gremios, de los
sindicatos."[1115]

VI. IMPLANTACIÓN DEL ESTADO POPULISTA

En tercer lugar, el Estado totalitario, comunista y burocrático que se ha desarrollado, sostenido por una cada vez menor producción petrolera, en lugar de haberse
desarrollado como un Estado Social en el marco un sistema económico de economía
mixta, que propicia con la participación activa de la iniciativa privada la generación
de riqueza, el ahorro y la inversión, que a la vez es la que genera el empleo; en realidad se ha configurado como un Estado Populista, que se ha montado casi exclusivamente sobre una política económica basada en el control de precios, que ha aniquilado la producción y perseguido la iniciativa privada; y sobre una política social
basada fundamentalmente en el reparto directo de subsidios[1116] –aparte del más
común y general que es el del precio de la gasolina– , que se distribuyen en efectivo
o en bienes de consumo a la población de menos recursos.

En cuanto a la política social de regulación de precios, supuestamente "precios
justos," como los que se ha pretendido establecer con base en la Ley de Precios Justos de 2014, basta citar lo que escribió Heinz Dieterich, quién fue el ideólogo del
"Socialismo del Siglo XXI" del Presidente Chávez, sobre el antecedente inmediato
de dicha Ley dictada en 2011:

> "1. *Miraflores: el Vaticano económico.* El gobierno venezolano acaba de
> hacer un milagro económico legislativo: en el Decreto 8.331 reglamentó con
> ochenta y ocho artículos algo que no existe: el *precio justo* de la economía de
> mercado. Las alucinaciones de la mente humana son generalmente asuntos de
> psiquiatras o negocios de teólogos; pero la nueva "Ley de Costos y Precios Jus-
> tos" demuestra que en Venezuela forman parte de la cartera del gabinete
> económico."[1117]

1115   Véase "Fernando Londoño en *El Tiempo*: Venezuela en llamas. Santos calla," en *El Universal*, Cara-
        cas 24 de mayo de 2014, en http://www.eluniversal.com/blogs/sobre-la-mar-cha/140524/fernando-
        londono-en-el-tiempo-venezuela-en-llamas-santos-calla.

1116   Una de las notas esenciales del populismo, tal como la describe Jorge Reinaldo Vanossi, es en efecto
        el "Reparto "*ad infinitum*"; con despreocupación por el simultáneo y equivalente esfuerzo en la crea-
        ción de riqueza. Sin la cooperación del capital y el trabajo no hay ahorro; sin ahorro no hay inversio-
        nes; sin inversión no hay más y nuevos emprendimientos; y sin ellos no se crean fuentes de trabajo,
        que sólo con ellas bajan los índices de la desocupación y, al propio tiempo, elevan el nivel y la cali-
        dad de vida. Únicamente con todo ello, sube la oferta y, consecuentemente, aumenta la demanda en
        forma genuina. Si no se respeta esa ecuación se desciende al triple infierno de la gestación del efecto
        "espejista" del consumismo *in crescendo*, de la inflación desmedida, y de la "estanflación" (cuando
        no del estallido de la "híper-inflación"), todas ellas, plagas que acentúan una crisis del crecimiento y
        desarrollo, desembocando en un "achicamiento" de la Nación en todos sus órdenes.". Véase en Jorge
        Reinaldo Vanossi, *Razones y Alcances del Descaecimiento Constitucional. Violencia con anomia
        más anarquía con autoritarismo*, Academia Nacional de Ciencias Morales y Políticas, Buenos Aires,
        2014.

1117   Supuestamente "precios justos," como los que se pretenden regular con la Ley de Costos y Precios
        Justos, cuya última reforma es de 2013. Véase Decreto Ley N° 600 de 21 de noviembre de 2013 en

Lo cierto de la política de fijación de costos y precios justos, en todo caso, ha sido la destrucción de la industria privada de producción de bienes y servicios, la sentencia de muerte de la productividad y de la competencia, y todo para generar escases e inflación; en fin, lo contrario de lo que se pensó se lograría con la implantación de la Ley.

En cuanto a la política social de basada en subsidios, la misma se ha realizado a través de programas públicos denominados "Misiones," que han encontrado incluso cabida en la Ley Orgánica de la Administración Pública de 2008, pero para estar excluida de sus regulaciones;[1118] y paralelamente, la exclusión y persecución de la iniciativa privada.

La consecuencia ha sido entonces, que además de la existencia de entes y de los órganos en la organización de la Administración, ahora se han insertado en la misma a las "Misiones" –que en realidad no son nada distinto, en su forma jurídica de los tradicionales entes y órganos administrativos, pero con la diferencia de que se los denomina "Misiones,"– pero con la absurda nota de que las mismas quedan fuera de la regulación de dicha Ley Orgánica de la Administración Pública, lo que se ha ratificado en la reforma de la Ley de noviembre de 2014.[1119]

La consecuencia de este signo del Estado populista en relación con el derecho administrativo, por tanto, es ostensible, pues implica que el mismo, cuyo objeto es regular a la Administración Pública, simplemente no la regula totalmente pues no se aplica a estas "Misiones" que por tanto pueden actuar al margen del derecho de la organización administrativa, y que son las que manejan fuera de la disciplina fiscal y presupuestaria, ingentes recursos del Estado, con el consecuente desquiciamiento de la Administración Pública y del derecho administrativo.

Pero desde el punto de vista social, si bien la tarea de las "Misiones" de "administrar" el sistema extendido de subsidios directos a las personas de menos recursos contribuyó efímeramente y con una carga electoral conocida, a aumentar el ingreso de una parte importante de la población, éste sin embargo, con el fomento del consumismo exagerado que eliminó espacio para el ahorro, y con la inflación galopante que, como se dijo, en mayo de 2014 alcanzó al 60%,[1120] dicho incremento se ha disipado, dejando como secuela el deterioro de los valores fundamentales de toda socie-

---

Gaceta Oficial, Nº 40.340 de 23 de enero de 2014. Sobre esta Ley Véase Heinz Dieterich, "Un simulacro de combate a las "ganancias excesivas" del capital. Milagro económico en Venezuela: La Ley de Costos y Precios Justos," 26 de julio de 2011, en http://www.apo-rrea.org/ideologia/a127333.html

1118   Véase Allan R. Brewer-Carías, "Una nueva tendencia en la organización administrativa venezolana: las "misiones" y las instancias y organizaciones del "poder popular" establecidas en paralelo a la administración pública," en Retos de la Organización Administrativa Contemporánea, X Foro Iberoamericano de Derecho Administrativo (26-27 de septiembre de 2011), Corte Suprema de Justicia, Universidad de El Salvador, Universidad Doctor José Matías Delgado, San Salvador, El Salvador, 2011.

1119   Véanse en Gaceta Oficial Nº 6147 Extra. de 17 de noviembre de 2014. En paralelo a la emisión de esta Ley, sin embargo, en la Gaceta Oficial Nº 6154 de 19 de enero de 2014, se publicó el Decreto Ley No. 1.394, de mediante el cual se dictó la Ley Orgánica de Misiones, Grandes Misiones y Micro-Misiones, en la cual las mismas encontraron su regulación.

1120   Véase César Miguel Rondón, "Cada vez menos país," en Confirmado, 16-8-2014, en http://confirmado.com.ve/opinan/cada-vez-menos-pais/

dad, como consecuencia de recibir beneficios sin enfrentar sacrificios o esfuerzos, como por ejemplo, el valor del trabajo productivo como fuente de ingreso, que materialmente se ha eliminado, sustituido por el que encuentra que es preferible recibir sin trabajar.

Este Estado Populista es lo Leandro Area ha calificado acertadamente como "Estado Misional," por estar montado sobre dichas Misiones "como actores colectivos no formales de política pública, que manejan un oscuro e inmenso mar de recursos," resultando ser un "espécimen no incluido aún en las tipologías de la Ciencia Política," entendiendo por tal:

> "aquel Estado que haciendo uso de sus recursos materiales y simbólicos le impone, por fuerza u operación de compra-venta o combinación de ambas a la sociedad, un esquema de disminución, de minusvalía consentida, en sus capacidades y potencialidades de crecimiento a cambio de sumisión. Se lanza sobre ella también amparado en la institucionalidad cómplice. Se encarama sobre ella en su ayer, hoy y mañana, amaestrándola con la dieta diaria cuyo menú depende del gusto del gobernante. Confisca, privatiza, invade, expropia, conculca, controla, asfixia, acoquina hasta decir basta, poniendo en evidencia lo frágil del concepto de propiedad privada creando así miedo, emigración, desinversión, fuga de capitales. Y aunque usted no lo crea esas son metas o simples desplantes o locura u obscura necesidad de auto bloqueo como forma de amurallarse para obtener inmunidad e impunidad para sus tropelías, frente a la mirada de una época que no los reconoce sino como entes del pasado, objeto de museo o de laboratorio, insectos atrapados en el ámbar del tiempo; fracaso, derrota." [1121]

A lo anterior agrega el mismo Leandro Area, que dicho Estado Misional en definitiva es un tipo de Estado Socialista, que nada tiene que ver con el Estado Social del cual habla la Constitución, concebido en paralelo al Estado Constitucional, "con la intención de acabarlo o mejor, de extinguirlo." Para ello, indica Area:

> "El gobierno crea misiones a su antojo que son estructuras burocráticas y funcionales "sui generis" y permanentes, con un control jurisdiccional inexistente y que actúa con base a los intereses de dominio. Además si el gobernante se encuentra por encima del bien y del mal, como es el caso venezolano, nadie es capaz de controlar sus veleidades y apetitos. En ese sentido el Estado es un apéndice del gobernante que es el repartidor interesado de los bienes de toda la sociedad y que invierte a su gusto, entre otras bagatelas, en compra de conciencias y voluntades de acólitos y novicios aspirantes. Por su naturaleza, todo Estado misional es un Estado depredador sin comillas. Vive de la pobreza, la estimula, la paga, organiza, la convierte en ejercito informal y también paralelo. El gobierno y su partido los tiene censados, chequeados, uniformados de banderas, consignas y miedos. Localizados, inscritos, con carnet, lo que quiere decir que fotografiados, listos para la dádiva, la culpa, castigos y perdones." [1122]

1121   Véase Leandro Area, "El 'Estado Misional' en Venezuela," en *Analítica.com*, 14 de febrero de 2014, en http://analitica.com/opinion/opinion-nacional/el-estado-misional-en-venezuela/

1122   *Idem*

Todo ello, por tanto, las misiones, sujetas, como lo observa Heinz Sonntag a un "patrón de organización destinado a darles dadivas a los sectores pobres y garantizar así su adhesión a la Revolución Bolivariana," [1123] además de haber provocado más miseria y control de conciencia sobre una población de menos recursos totalmente dependiente de la burocracia estatal y sus dádivas, en las cuales creyó encontrar la solución definitiva para su existencia, también provocó el deterioro de otra parte de la población, particularmente la clase media, que junto con todos los demás componentes de la misma ha visto desaparecer su calidad de vida, y sufren en conjunto los embates de la inflación y de la escases. [1124] Y todo ello, con un deterioro ostensible y trágico de los servicios públicos más elementales como los servicios de salud y atención médica. Por ello se ha considerado, por ejemplo, que Venezuela durante estos tres últimos lustros, ha retrocedido entre 50 y 60 años en medicina, [1125] lo que llevó incluso a la Academia Nacional de Medicina a proponer el 19 de agosto de 2014, "ante la catastrófica crisis humanitaria en salud," que se declarase "la emergencia sanitaria" a fin de que el Estado tomase las decisiones "que permitan la fluidez de las divisas, la reanudación de los créditos y la reaparición de los insumos y materiales quirúrgicos, y que asigne recursos económicos suficientes, con prioridad hacia el área de salud," estimando que era:

"inadmisible desde el punto de vista ético y moral que la red hospitalaria y la red primaria de salud se encuentren en precarias condiciones de funcionamiento sin que se haya hecho nada en concreto para remediarla; como consecuencia del proceso de abandono, se ha profundizado la crisis que ha alcanzado también a la red asistencial privada. En razón de la falta de medicamentos e insumos para la salud, del deterioro de las condiciones laborales y de seguridad en los ambientes de trabajo, de la carencia de personal médico calificado y de otros profesionales de la salud que han emigrado, buscando mayor seguridad personal y trabajo digno. Ni en los peores momentos de la historia republicana se había presenciado el efecto de la indiferencia e incompetencia gubernamental sobre la población toda, sin distingos de capacidad económica."[1126]

1123   Véase Heinz Sonntag "¿Cuántas Revoluciones más? "en El *Nacional*, Caracas 7 de octubre de 2014, en http://www.el-nacional.com/heinz_sonntag/Cuantas-Revoluciones_0_496150483.html

1124   Como el mismo Area lo ha descrito en lenguaje común y gráfico, pero tremendamente trágico: "Vivimos pues "boqueando" y de paso corrompiéndonos por las condiciones impuestas por y desde el poder que nos obligan a vivir como "lateros", "balseros", "abasteros" mejor dicho, que al estar "pelando" por lo que buscamos y no encontramos, tenemos que andar en gerundio, ladrando, mamando, haciendo cola, bajándonos de la mula, haciéndonos los bolsas o locos, llevándonos de caleta algo, caribeando o de chupa medias, pagando peaje, tracaleando, empujándonos los unos contra los otros, en suma, degradándonos, envileciéndonos, para satisfacer nuestras necesidades básicas de consumo. Es asfixia gradual y calculada, material y moral. Desde el papel toilette hasta la honestidad. ¡Pero tenemos Patria! Falta el orgullo, la dignidad, el respeto, el amor a uno mismo." Véase en "El 'Estado Misional' en Venezuela," en *Analítica.com*, 14 de febrero de 2014, en http://analitica.com/opinion/opinion-nacional/el-estado-misional-en-venezuela/

1125   Véase César Miguel Rondón, "Cada vez menos país," en *Confirmado*, 16-8-2014, en http://confirmado.com.ve/opinan/cada-vez-menos-pais/

1126   Véase la información enhttp://www.el-nacional.com/economia/Piden-decretar-emergencia-humanitaria-sector_0_467353465.html; y en http://www.noticierodigital.com/2014/08/no-titarde-emergencia-humanitaria-piden-clinicas-y-hospitales-del-pais/ El planteamiento ha sido respaldado

Esta crisis de la salud, sin duda, ha contribuido a hacer más miserable la totalidad de la población, sin distingos.

Y otro tanto ha ocurrido, por ejemplo, en los servicios de educación, pudiendo afirmarse que en Venezuela la educación también está en crisis, a pesar de que la educación debía considerarse como el medio fundamental para reducir la pobreza. La realidad, sin embargo, es que en un Estado totalitario y populista como el que tenemos en Venezuela, la misión de educar con criterios de excelencia no es del interés real del Estado ni del gobierno, y menos que la misma sea libre y que por tanto, pueda significar formar a los jóvenes que puedan adversar el régimen, razón por la cual lo que ha hecho el régimen autoritario ha sido "reorientar" la educación para, eliminando toda idea de excelencia, hacerla un instrumento más del autoritarismo. Para ello, como lo ha resumido Mariana Suárez de Mendoza,

"En Venezuela han tratado de cambiar varias veces el pensum académico de los colegios, han tratado de incluir a los consejos comunales como parte de la comunidad educativa, se han propuesto eliminar la autonomía universitaria y se han empeñado en deslegitimar a todo estudiante o profesor que vaya en contra de las propuestas socialistas del gobierno. Las protestas en las calles hicieron dar un paso atrás al gobierno, por temor a incendiarse en el país una ola de protestas que luego serían indetenibles. El gobierno tomó el camino de crear una educación paralela con amplio contenido ideológico en escuelas, institutos y universidades, ignorando en las mesas de trabajo a la verdadera comunidad educativa, establecida en la Constitución, y utilización en medios de comunicación a los estudiantes universitarios afectos al oficialismo. Hoy, la educación universitaria está paralizada por falta de presupuesto, discusión de contrataciones colectivas y normas de homologación."[1127]

En particular, y específicamente sobre la Universidad, la misma también está en absoluta crisis en Venezuela, y lo único que ha hecho el gobierno autoritario para remediarla, además de ahogar a las Universidades privadas y a las Universidades autónomas,[1128] pretendiéndolas sustituir por un ideologizado parasistema[1129] ha sido

por la Red de Sociedades Científicas del país, Caracas 21 de agosto de 2014, que han expresado que: "La grave situación de salud que atraviesa Venezuela y que se ha reagudizado durante el presente año, *no tiene precedentes en la historia de la medicina de nuestro país*, estamos indudablemente padeciendo una grave crisis económica que ha repercutido en la salud de la población, que ha afectado de manera contundente la atención médica en nuestras emergencias médicas y quirúrgicas colocando en riesgo la vida de nuestros pacientes, más aun no escapan de esta crisis los pacientes crónicos de nuestras consultas: oncológicos, nefropatas, diabéticos, cardiópatas, pacientes con VIH entre otros." Véase en http://www.reporte24.com/index.php?target=l33r3sungust03star1nf0rmad03sm1d3r3ch0&id=10569

1127 Véase Mariana Suárez de Mendoza, "Crisis de la educación venezolana," *El Universal*, Caracas 29 de junio de 2013, en http://www.eluniversal.com/opinion/130629/crisis-en-la-educacion-venezolana

1128 Por ejemplo, el ex Rector Luis Ugalde s.j., ha expresado ante la absurda regulación de las tarifas de la Universidad privada que: "A la universidad no le conviene encarecer la mensualidad estudiantil, pero si no lo hace no puede pagar y entra en deterioro hacia la quiebra. Eso sin contar el aumento inflacionario (con frecuencia de más del 100%) en los insumos (tinta, papel, computadoras…) y en los inevitables gastos de mantenimiento e inversiones. Si el ministro no entiende esto, debería renunciar; pero seguramente sí lo entiende y lo celebra, porque arruina las universidades privadas, cuya extinción se propone el régimen, junto con la muerte de las universidades autónomas y plurales." Véase Luis

empobrecer a los docentes al punto de que "un profesor de la UCV en términos reales gana menos de la tercera parte de lo que ganaba hace unas décadas y en esa proporción es el empobrecimiento de todos los educadores en primaria y secundaria, pagados por el presupuesto oficial." [1130] Es decir, un profesor de derecho a tiempo convencional, por ejemplo, no gana más del equivalente de US$ 8,00 mensuales al cambio oficial (y a tiempo integral no más del equivalente de US$ 60.00 mensuales), pero frente a ello, la política del gobierno ha sido más bien multiplicar supuestas universidades e institutos de "formación superior" que gradúan en forma exprés a "profesionales," que no estudian ni pueden estudiar una carrera profesional por el corto tiempo de las carreras y sus programas distorsionados, que ni siquiera la propia Administración y las propias empresas del Estado quieren contratar. [1131]

VII. ESTRUCTURACIÓN PARALELA DEL ESTADO COMUNAL Y DEL PODER POPULAR

A todo lo anterior se suma, en cuarto lugar, que el Estado Comunista, Burocrático y Populista se ha estructurado, además, como producto del deliberado proceso de desconstitucionalización del Estado Constitucional, como el llamado "Estado Comunal," que ha sido creado al margen y en contra de las instituciones previstas en la Constitución, configurando órganos como si fueran las "unidades primarias en la

---

Ugalde s.j., "Educación en ruina", en *El Universal*, Caracas, 29 de septiembre de 2014, en http://www.eluniversal.com/opinion/140928/educacion-en-ruina.

1129   Como lo ha expresado Isabel Pereira Pizani, "Uno de los procesos más dolorosos y tristes que vivimos los venezolanos es la guerra a muerte contra nuestras universidades nacionales decretada por Cuba y ejecutada por la revolución chavista Es una de las grandes metas para imponer el Estado Comunal totalitario, con un solo partido y un pensamiento único. [''] La construcción del Estado Comunal totalitario exige la desaparición de nuestras universidades. Su defensa tiene que ser asumida por toda la sociedad: gremios profesionales, sindicatos, partidos y, sobre todo, las familias responsables de las nuevas generaciones. Si no detenemos el decreto de guerra a muerte contra las casas que vencen la sombra, la obscuridad totalitaria se apoderara de ellas y de nuestras vidas. Se trata esencialmente de una lucha por nuestra libertad como seres humanos." Véase Isabel Pereira Pizani, "Guerra contra la Universidad," octubre 2014, en *cedice@cedice.org.ve*

1130   *Idem.* Véase además, Véase Rafael Díaz Casanova, "Asfixiar a las Universidades," en opiniónynoticias.com, 8 octubre de 2014, en http://www.opinionynoticias.com/opinionedu-cacion/20738-asfixiar-a-las-universidades

1131   Por ejemplo, como lo ha resumido Sabino J. Manolesina, al referirse a lo que está ocurriendo con los profesionales egresados de algunas Universidades oficiales recientemente constituidas: "¿Por qué será que las empresas del estado no quieren contratar a los egresados de esas Universidades? En el caso de PDVSA los ponen a realizar cursos para nivelar conocimientos porque sin ellos no podrían trabajar eficientemente en esa industria.// ¿Por qué será que en los hospitales se tienen problemas con los profesionales egresados en medicina comunitaria? Será porque algunos graduados en medicina comunitaria se esconden en las emergencias para no tener que enfrentarse al paciente y explicarles que no saben lo que le está pasando.//¿Por qué será que ni los directivos de algunas zonas educativas quieren contratar a los Licenciados en Educación Integral egresados de estas Universidades? Será que saben que en esta carrera, un solo profesor dicta hasta ocho o diez asignaturas diferentes, ya que no se cuenta con la cantidad de profesores especialista necesarios para atender esa gran masa estudiantil ávida de querer realizar estudios universitarios y que estuvieron marginados por los gobiernos anteriores." Véase Sabino J. Manolasina, "Crisis en el sistema educativo como consecuencia de la situación salarial del docente venezolano," en *Aporrea*, 23 de mayo de 2011, en http://www.aporrea.org/educacion/a123858.html.

organización nacional" para supuestamente garantizar la participación de los ciudadanos en la acción pública, pero suplantando a los Estados y Municipios como entes descentralizados del Estado federal. Esta estructuración del Estado Comunal, además, se ha hecho negándole recursos financieros a los propios del Estado Constitucional (Estados y Municipios), montando un sistema de entidades denominadas del Poder Popular, creadas al margen de la Constitución y en paralelo a los órganos del Poder Público.

Estas son básicamente los antes mencionadas Comunas y Consejos Comunales, creadas como instrumentos para la recepción de subsidios directos y reparto de recursos presupuestarios públicos, pero con un grado extremo de exclusión, lo que deriva de su propia existencia que sólo se puede materializar con el registro de las mismas ante el "Ministerio del Poder Popular para las Comunas y Movimientos Sociales" que además depende del "Vicepresidente del Consejo de Ministros para Desarrollo del Socialismo Territorial," por supuesto, siempre que estén controlados y manejados por el partido de gobierno, sean socialistas y comprometidas con la política socialista del Estado; condición indispensable para poder ser aceptados como instrumentos de supuesta "participación protagónica," y de recepción de subsidios dinerarios directos, que por lo demás se están sometidos a control fiscal alguno.

En efecto, la práctica legislativa y gubernamental desarrollada después del rechazo popular a la reforma constitucional de 2007 que pretendía consolidar un Estado totalmente centralizado, y además, crear en paralelo al Estado Constitucional, a una estructura denominada como "Estado del Poder Popular" o "Estado Comunal," ha originado que el mismo haya sido efectivamente crearlo al margen de la Constitución con el propósito de desmantelar el Estado Constitucional federal, centralizando hacia el nivel nacional competencias estadales, y transfiriendo competencias estadales y municipales hacia los Consejos Comunales, que a su vez como se ha dicho, dependen del Ejecutivo Nacional.[1132]

En ese esquema, el proceso de desconstitucionalización, centralismo y desmunicipalización en Venezuela, en los últimos años se ha llevado a cabo, en *primer lugar*, mediante el establecimiento como obligación legal para los órganos, entes e instancias del Poder Público, es decir del Estado Constitucional, de promover, apoyar y acompañar las iniciativas populares para la constitución, desarrollo y consoli-

1132   Véase en general sobre este proceso de desconstitucionalización del Estado, Allan R. Brewer-Carías, "La desconstitucionalización del Estado de derecho en Venezuela: del Estado Democrático y Social de derecho al Estado Comunal Socialista, sin reformar la Constitución," *en Libro Homenaje al profesor Alfredo Morles Hernández, Diversas Disciplinas Jurídicas,* (Coordinación y Compilación Astrid Uzcátegui Angulo y Julio Rodríguez Berrizbeitia), Universidad Católica Andrés Bello, Universidad de Los Andes, Universidad Monteávila, Universidad Central de Venezuela, Academia de Ciencias Políticas y Sociales, Vol. V, Caracas 2012, pp. 51-82; en Carlos Tablante y Mariela Morales Antonorzzi (Coord.), *Descentralización, autonomía e inclusión social. El desafío actual de la democracia,* Anuario 2010-2012, Observatorio Internacional para la democracia y descentralización, En Cambio, Caracas 2011, pp. 37-84; y en *Estado Constitucional,* Año 1, Nº 2, Editorial Adrus, Lima, junio 2011, pp. 217-236.

dación de las diversas formas organizativas y de autogobierno del pueblo, es decir, del llamado Estado Comunal (art. 23).[1133]

En *segundo lugar*, la desconstitucionalización del Estado se ha impuesto mediante la sujeción de todos los órganos del Estado Constitucional que ejercen el Poder Público, a los mandatos de las organizaciones del Poder Popular, al instituirse un nuevo principio de gobierno, consistente en "gobernar obedeciendo" (artículo 24).[1134] Como las organizaciones del Poder Popular no tienen autonomía política pues sus "voceros" no son electos democráticamente mediante sufragio universal, directo y secreto, sino designados por asambleas de ciudadanos controladas e intervenidas por el partido oficial y el Ejecutivo Nacional que controla y guía todo el proceso organizativo del Estado Comunal, en el ámbito exclusivo de la ideología socialista, sin que tenga cabida vocero alguno que no sea socialista; en definitiva, esto de "gobernar obedeciendo" es una limitación a la autonomía política de los órganos del Estado Constitucional electos, como la Asamblea Nacional, los Gobernadores y Consejos Legislativos de los Estados y los Alcaldes y Concejos Municipales, a quienes se le impone en definitiva la obligación de obedecer lo que disponga el Ejecutivo Nacional y el partido oficial enmarcado en el ámbito exclusivo del socialismo como doctrina política, con la máscara del Poder Popular. La voluntad popular expresada en la elección de representantes del Estado Constitucional, por tanto, en este esquema del Estado Comunal no tiene valor alguno, y al pueblo se le confisca su soberanía trasladándola de hecho a unas asambleas que no lo representan.

En *tercer lugar*, la desconstitucionalización del Estado Constitucional se ha reforzado con el establecimiento de la obligación para los órganos y entes del Poder Público en sus relaciones con el Poder Popular, de dar "preferencia a las comunidades organizadas, a las comunas y a los sistemas de agregación y articulación que surjan entre ellas, en atención a los requerimientos que las mismas formulen para la satisfacción de sus necesidades y el ejercicio de sus derechos, en los términos y lapsos que establece la ley" (art. 29). Igualmente se ha previsto que los órganos, entes e instancias del Poder Público, es decir, del Estado Constitucional, en sus diferentes niveles político-territoriales, deben adoptar "medidas para que las organizaciones socio-productivas de propiedad social comunal, gocen de prioridad y preferencia en los procesos de contrataciones públicas para la adquisición de bienes, prestación de servicios y ejecución de obras" (art. 30).[1135]

1133   Una norma similar está en el artículo 62 de la Ley Orgánica de las Comunas, a los efectos de "la constitución, desarrollo y consolidación de las comunas como forma de autogobierno."

1134   El artículo 24 de la Ley Orgánica del Poder Popular, en efecto, sobre dispone sobre las "Actuaciones de los órganos y entes del Poder Público" que "Todos los órganos, entes e instancias del Poder Público guiarán sus actuaciones por el principio de gobernar obedeciendo, en relación con los mandatos de los ciudadanos, ciudadanas y de las organizaciones del Poder Popular, de acuerdo a lo establecido en la Constitución de la República y las leyes."

1135   En particular, conforme al artículo 61 de la Ley Orgánica de las Comunas, se dispone que "todos los órganos y entes del Poder Público comprometidos con el financiamiento de proyectos de las comunas y sus sistemas de agregación, priorizarán aquéllos que impulsen la atención a las comunidades de menor desarrollo relativo, a fin de garantizar el desarrollo territorial equilibrado.

En *cuarto lugar*, la desconstitucionalización del Estado también ha derivado de la previsión de la obligación para la República, los Estados y Municipios, de acuerdo con la ley que rige el proceso de transferencia y descentralización de competencias y atribuciones, de trasferir "a las comunidades organizadas, a las comunas y a los sistemas de agregación que de éstas surjan; funciones de gestión, administración, control de servicios y ejecución de obras atribuidos a aquéllos por la Constitución de la República, para mejorar la eficiencia y los resultados en beneficio del colectivo" (art. 27).[1136] Con ello, se dispuso legalmente el vaciamiento de competencias de los Estados y Municipios, de manera que queden como estructuras vacías, con gobiernos representativos electos por el pueblo pero que no tienen materias sobre las cuales gobernar.

A tal efecto, la Ley Orgánica del Poder Público Municipal[1137] dispone, en su artículo 281 que "la transferencia de competencias y servicios de los Estados a los Municipios, y de éstos a las instancias del Poder Popular, se realizará de acuerdo a lo establecido en la Ley Orgánica del Consejo Federal de Gobierno," que como se ha dicho, está controlado por el Poder Central, siendo los lineamientos que establezca dicho Consejo de carácter "vinculante para las entidades territoriales (art. 2).

VIII. DESARROLLO DEL ESTADO CLIENTELAR

En quinto lugar, como consecuencia de todo lo antes expuesto sobre la configuración del Estado en Venezuela, en lugar del Estado Social y de Economía Mixta que es el descrito y regulado en la Constitución, además de haberse desarrollado como un Estado Comunista, Burocrático, Populista y Comunal, lo que ha resultado, como consecuencia de todo ello, es la estructuración de un Estado Clientelar, que ha dado origen a una nueva "clase social" totalmente dependiente del Estado, que es la que subsiste con la recepción de los múltiples y a veces paralelos subsidios directos provenientes de las "Misiones," o de los repartidos a través de Consejos Comunales y Comunas, que el Estado aprovecha para comprometer; y otra que ha surgido de la multiplicación sin límites del empleo público, que también está sujeta a chantaje comprometedor.

Esas nuevas clases sociales, "privilegiadas" en cierta forma por el reparto del ingreso público, es por lo demás, la principal fuente de soporte "popular" cuando el Gobierno y el partido oficial lo reclamen o necesiten. Ello es tan cierto que nunca, en cualquiera que hubiese sido la elección o votación desarrollada o acaecida en los últimos tres lustros, ni el fallecido Presidente Chávez ni su partido de gobierno ni los candidatos montados en su imagen, han sacado jamás, más votos de los que suman los privilegiados por los subsidios de las misiones y del empleo público.

Esa nueva "clase media," en buena parte profesional subsidiada y funcionarial, además, se ha desarrollado en paralelo a otra nueva clase, muy "alta" por cierto, llamada "boliburguesía," con diferencia mucho más pronunciada en relación con las

---

1136   Esta misma norma se repite en la Ley Orgánica de las Comunas (art. 64). El 31 de diciembre de 2010, aún estaba pendiente en la Asamblea Nacional la segunda discusión del proyecto de Ley Orgánica del Sistema de Transferencia de Competencias y atribuciones de los Estados y Municipios a las organizaciones del Poder Popular.

1137   Véase en *Gaceta Oficial* Nº 6015 Extra. De 28-10-2010.

clases medias y bajas, la cual se desarrolló al amparo de la corrupción o con la complicidad del Estado y su burocracia.[1138] En realidad, más propiamente, se trata de una clase formada mediante el saqueo impune de las arcas públicas de un Estado inerme y no controlado, [1139] que ha arrasado con buena parte de la ingente riqueza que éste recibió en los últimos lustros por los altos precios del petróleo, y que por supuesto no se invirtió ni en servicios sociales ni en infraestructura.

Las antiguas clases medias profesionales, ante tanta riqueza súbita sin justificación, pasaron a ser clases disminuidas sin perspectiva de progreso, salvo entrando en el esquema de valores de una revolución corrupta.

En todo caso, ese Estado Clientelar del cual medran esos nuevos ricos, ha resultado ser un Estado altamente discriminatorio y excluyente de todo aquél que no sea "socialista" o beneficiado del gobierno, al punto de quien no tenga y exprese lealtad al mismo, queda marginado política y administrativamente hablando.

La consecuencia de todo este esquema de ausencia de Estado Social y de Estado de economía mixta, y el establecimiento en su lugar del Estado comunista, burocratizado, populista y clientelar, ha sido que en nombre del "socialismo," Venezuela hoy tiene el record de ser el país que ocupa el primer lugar en el índice de miseria del mundo,[1140] y la sociedad con el más alto riesgo de América Latina.[1141] Esa es la

---

1138   Por ello, Alvaro R. Barrios ha destacado por ejemplo que "la corrupción es uno de los males que se ha enraizado en las entrañas del proyecto del Socialismo del Siglo XXI. Cientos de casos han explotado en el transcurrir de estos tres lustros en la cara de los dos gobiernos revolucionarios (Chávez y Maduro). Peor aún, la nomenclatura roja ni condena ni ha juzgado a casi ninguno de los funcionarios de la revolución involucrados en este mal que carcome a la revolución.// La corrupción es un delito que se aúna a una visión obsoleta y fracasada de país que, soportada en una generalizada incompetencia gerencial y administrativa, hace abortar cualquier plan de mejora o cualquier esfuerzo para dar resultados positivos en toda área o sector de la vida nacional.// Cuando estos dos flagelos se unen, forman un binomio explosivo que aniquila todo derecho humano y constitucional –entre ellos el del acceso a la atención médica de los ciudadanos–.'" Véase en "Un binomio criminal," en *Veneconomía*, July 18, 2014, en https://www.face-book.com/alvaror.barrios/posts/10204410616371128.

1139   Es lo que Moisés Naím, ha calificado como un "Estado mafioso" indicando que "No son solo países donde impera la corrupción o donde el crimen organizado controla importantes actividades económicas y hasta regiones completas. Se trata de países en los que el Estado controla y usa grupos criminales para promover y defender sus intereses nacionales y los intereses particulares de una élite de gobernantes.[...] En los Estados mafiosos, no son los criminales quienes han capturado al Estado a través del soborno y la extorsión de funcionarios, sino el Estado el que ha tomado el control de las redes criminales. Y no para erradicarlas, sino para ponerlas a su servicio y, más concretamente, al servicio de los intereses económicos de los gobernantes, sus familiares y socios. [...] "Agregó además, Naim, el hecho de que en Venezuela, un "exmagistrado del Tribunal Supremo Eladio Aponte ha ofrecido amplias evidencias que confirmarían que altos funcionarios del Estado venezolano son los principales jefes de importantes bandas criminales transnacionales." Véase Moisés Naím, "Estados Mafiosos," en *El País*, 5-5-2012, en http://internacional.elpais.com/internacional/2012/05/05/actualidad/1336245036_975620.html

1140   Venezuela tiene el "ignominioso" primer lugar en el Índice de miseria del mundo. Véase el Informe de Steve H. Hanke, "Measury Misery arround the World," publicado en mayo 2104, en *Global Asia*, en http://www.cato.org/publications/commentary/measuring-misery-around-world Véase igualmente *Índice Mundial de Miseria*, 2014, en http://www.razon.com.mx/spip.php?article215150; y en http://vallartaopina.net/2014/05/23/en-indice-mundial-de-miseria-venezuela-ocupa-primer-lugar/

1141   Véase   en   http://www.elmundo.com.ve/noticias/actualidad/noticias/infografia-riesgo-pais-de-venezuela-cerro-el-201.aspx

hazaña o el milagro de la política económica del gobierno durante los pasados quince años, que tanto va a costar superar en el futuro,[1142] lo que se suma el indicado primer lugar en criminalidad, falta de transparencia e inflación.

Todo lo cual, sin duda, ha sido uno de los objetivos del gobierno durante los últimos quince años de manera que como lo ha expresó Pedro Palma, la explicación de lo incomprensible, es decir, del "milagro económico" de destrucción a mansalva de la economía y de la creación de miseria, está en que para el gobierno lo importante es mantener la condición de pobreza:

> "pues ella crea dependencia del Estado y abona el terreno para el clientelismo político, asegurándose el apoyo incondicional de una amplia masa poblacional a través de la manipulación informativa y de la explotación descarada de su ignorancia y buena fe. Eso, a su vez, facilita el logro e uno de los objetivos buscados, cual es la eliminación de la vieja oligarquía del anterior sistema, para sustituirlo por otra, pero revolucionaria."[1143]

Por eso se ha hablado, con razón, de que la política de Estado en Venezuela es la de una "una fábrica de pobres,"[1144] o como lo ha resumido Leandro Area, al insistir en su idea del "Estado Misional":

> "El consumo, por su parte, en un país que no produce nada, viene determinado por la oferta restringida de quien monopoliza, petroliza, en todos los sentidos, los productos de la cesta de las mercancías de consumo social entre los que destacan el trabajo, la salud, la educación, la vivienda, etc. Populismo, demagogia, asistencialismo, plebeyismo, "peronismo", cultura de la sumisión, degradación de la civilidad, desesperanza aprehendida, envilecimiento, etc., son expresiones, realidades, cercanas a la idea del Estado misional." [1145]

Este Estado Misional, Comunista, Burocrático, Populista, Comunal y del Poder Popular y Clientelar, acaparador de toda la actividad económica, en definitiva, es el

---

1142   Pedro Carmona Estanga ha resumido la hazaña económica del régimen explicando que: "Por desgracia para el país, a lo largo de estos 16 años se han dilapidado unos US$ 1,5 billones que no volverán, de los cuales no quedan sino la destrucción del aparato productivo, el deterioro de la calidad de vida, de la infraestructura, de la institucionalidad, y distorsiones macroeconómicas y actitudinales en la población de una profundidad tal, que costará sudor y sangre superar a las generaciones venideras. Esa es la hazaña histórica lograda y cacareada por el régimen." Véase Pedro Carmona Estanga, "La destrucción de Venezuela: hazaña histórica," 19 de octubre de 2014, en http://pcarmonae.blogspot.com/2014/10/la-destruccion-de-venezuela-hazana.html

1143   Véase Pedro Palma, "Las Revoluciones fatídicas,", en *El Nacional*, Caracas, 8 de septiembre de 2014, en http://www.el-nacional.com/pedro_palma/Revoluciones-fatidicas_0_478752208.html

1144   En tal sentido, Brian Fincheltub, ha destacado que "Las misiones se convirtieron en fábrica de personas dependientes, sin ninguna estabilidad, que confiaban su subsistencia exclusivamente al Estado. Nunca hubo interés de sacar a la gente de la pobreza porque como reconoció el propio ministro Héctor Rodríguez, se "volverían escuálidos". Es decir, se volverían independientes y eso es peligrosísimo para un sistema cuya principal estrategia es el control." Véase Brian Fincheltub, "Fabrica de pobres," en *El Nacional*, Caracas, 5 de junio de 2014, en http://www.el-nacional.com/opinion/Fabrica-pobres_0_421757946.html

1145   Véase Leandro Area, "El 'Estado Misional' en Venezuela," en *Analítica.com*, 14 de febrero de 2014, en http://analitica.com/opinion/opinion-nacional/el-estado-misional-en-venezuela/

que ha sustituido al Estado Social y de Economía Mixta que está en la Constitución, conduciendo a su negación total, pues se ha convertido como observa Isaac Villamizar, es un "Estado inepto, secuestrado por la élite de la burguesía corrupta gubernamental, que niega todos los derechos sociales y económicos constitucionales, y que manipula la ignorancia y pobreza de las clases sociales menos favorecidas," argumentando al contrario, que:

"Si Venezuela fuera un Estado Social, no habría neonatos fallecidos por condiciones infecciosas en hospitales públicos. Si Venezuela fuera un Estado Social, toda persona tendría un empleo asegurado o se ejercería plenamente la libertad de empresa y de comercio. Si Venezuela fuera un Estado Social no exhibiríamos deshonrosamente las tasas de homicidios más altas del mundo. Si Venezuela fuera un Estado Social no estaría desaparecida la cabilla y el cemento y las cementeras intervenidas estarían produciendo al máximo de su capacidad instalada. Si Venezuela fuera un Estado Social todos los establecimientos de víveres y artículos de primera necesidad estarían abarrotados en sus anaqueles. Si Venezuela fuera un Estado Social las escuelas no tendrían los techos llenos de filtraciones, estarían dotadas de materiales suficientes para la enseñanza-aprendizaje y los maestros y profesores serían el mejor personal pagado del país. Si Venezuela fuera un Estado Social no habría discriminación por razones políticas e ideológicas para tener acceso a cualquier servicio, beneficios y auxilios públicos y bienes de primera necesidad. Si Venezuela fuera un Estado Social el problema de la basura permanente en las grandes ciudades ya estaría resuelto con los métodos más modernos, actualizados y pertinentes a la protección ambiental."[1146]

En ese contexto, por supuesto, el panorama del derecho público y el derecho administrativo ha cambiado radicalmente, habiendo cesado de ser el régimen jurídico llamado a garantizar el equilibrio entre los poderes y prerrogativas del Estado y los derechos y garantías de los ciudadanos, convirtiéndose sólo en un régimen regulador de los poderes y prerrogativas del Estado para imponer su voluntad y sus políticas discriminatorias, sin que los ciudadanos tengan posibilidad alguna de garantías de sus derechos, habiendo pasado buena parte de los mismos a ser simples dependientes del Estado, de su burocracia y de los subsidios y repartos que reciben, y la otra parte, mayoritaria por cierto, con estatus de marginados y excluidos, es decir, en cierta forma exiliados dentro de su propio país.

Un ejemplo de ello, es precisamente la Ley Orgánica de Precios Justos de 2014,[1147] que materialmente eliminó la garantía constitucional de la libertad económica, e hizo depender de la burocracia estatal la posibilidad misma que cualquier persona pueda realizar alguna "actividad económica," cualquiera que ella sea, sujetándolas a las medidas más draconianas imaginables, todas sujetas a la valoración y aplicación por parte de una burocracia poco confiable.

1146   Véase Isaac Villamizar, "Cuál Estado Social?," en *La Nación*, San Cristóbal, 7 de octubre de 2014, en http://www.lanacion.com.ve/columnas/opinion/cual-estado-social/

1147   Véase en *Gaceta Oficial* N° 6.156 Extra de 19-11-2014.

SECCIÓN CUARTA:

LA AUSENCIA DE ESTADO DE JUSTICIA

Pero además de que el Estado Totalitario en Venezuela, en una forma radicalmente distinta a lo expresado en la Constitución, no es un Estado de derecho, ni un Estado democrático, ni un Estado social, ni un Estado de economía mixta, y por tanto, donde no está asegurada realmente la justicia social, tampoco es un Estado de Justicia, donde ésta, como valor social, ha sido preterida. Como Estado totalitario que es, en el mismo, en realidad, la justicia perdió todo su valor social, y más bien, para los ciudadanos lo que perciben es una situación generalizada de injusticia y de impunidad.

En efecto, entre los valores más importantes expresados en la Constitución de 1999 está la concepción del Estado como "Estado de Justicia" (artículo 1), respecto de lo cual la Sala Político Administrativa del Tribunal Supremo de Justicia, señaló en 2000 que esa "nueva concepción de Estado de Justicia trae consigo no tan solo una transformación orgánica del sistema judicial (Artículos 253 y 254 de la Constitución)," sino también un cambio en la concepción del Poder Judicial como "el poder integrado y estabilizador del Estado, ya que es el único que tiene competencia para controlar y aún disolver al resto de los Poderes Públicos," lo que a juicio del Tribunal Supremo "nos hace un Estado Judicialista."[1148] En definitiva, como lo observó la misma Sala Político Administrativa del Tribunal Supremo de Justicia, en otra sentencia de 2000, cuando la Constitución califica al Estado "como de Derecho y de Justicia y establece como valor superior de su ordenamiento jurídico a la Justicia y la preeminencia de los derechos fundamentales, no está haciendo más que resaltar que los órganos del Poder Público -y en especial el sistema judicial- deben inexorablemente hacer prelar una noción de justicia material por sobre las formas y tecnicismos, propios de una legalidad formal que ciertamente ha tenido que ceder frente a la nueva concepción de Estado."[1149]

Un Estado de Justicia, por tanto, en los términos de la Constitución,[1150] es un Estado que por sobre todo está sujeto al valor superior de la Justicia, lo que implica, por una parte, en cuanto a la regulación del orden social y político que la misma se garantice mediante leyes que sean justas, que aseguren a cada quien lo que le pertenece, y además, revestidas de seguridad jurídica, en las cuales se establezcan las reglas conforme a las cuales se asegure para todos sin distinción, bienestar general y calidad de vida, el respeto a la dignidad humana, el libre desarrollo de la personalidad, y el goce irrestricto de los derechos humanos.

1148   Véase sentencia N° 659 de 24 de marzo de 2000 (Caso: *Rosario Nouel vs. Consejo de la Judicatura y Comisión de Emergencia Judicial*), en *Revista de Derecho Público*, N° 81 (enero-marzo), Editorial Jurídica Venezolana, Caracas, 2000, p. 103 y 104.

1149   Véase sentencia N° 949 de la Sala Político Administrativa de 26 de abril de 2000, en *Revista de Derecho Público*, N° 82, Editorial Jurídica Venezolana, Caracas, 2000, pp. 163 y ss.

1150   Véase sobre este concepto, la decisión de la sala Constitucional del Tribunal Supremo N° 389 de 7 de marzo de 2002, en *Revista de Derecho Público*, N° 89-92, Editorial Jurídica Venezolana, Caracas, 2002, 175ff.

Por la otra, en cuanto a la misión de impartir y administrar justicia a los ciudadanos, el Estado de Justicia exige que la misma se imparta por órganos independientes, autónomos e imparciales, a los cuales todos tengan derecho de acceder en forma gratuita y sin discriminación, y que aseguren el derecho de todos a lograr la tutela efectiva de sus derechos, y la condena y castigo a quienes violen las leyes, debiendo prevalecer, en todo caso, la justicia material sobre las formalidades. [1151] Lamentablemente, nada de lo anterior se encuentra efectivamente asegurado en Venezuela.

I.   AUSENCIA DE LEYES JUSTAS Y MULTIPLICACIÓN DE LEYES INCONSULTAS

En *primer lugar*, Venezuela carece de un sistema de leyes justas que respondan a la voluntad popular y en cuya formación quede asegurada la participación del pueblo a través de las organizaciones como lo prescribe la Constitución. La práctica del sistema de formación de las leyes en Venezuela no asegura que las mismas resulten ser leyes justas, en el sentido de que permitan efectivamente dar a cada quien lo que le corresponda, mediante su elaboración por una representación popular plural.

Las leyes, en realidad, son elaboradas por una Asamblea Nacional unicameral dominada por un solo partido político, que es el partido del gobierno, que preside el propio jefe de Estado, en la cual se ha negado el debate parlamentario, y menos aún se han tenido en cuenta las opiniones y propuestas de la oposición sobre los proyectos de ley; y menos aún, la participación popular mediante la consulta popular de las leyes que impone la Constitución en el proceso de su formación y discusión (art. 211), ni la consulta obligatoria a los Estados sobre las leyes que os afecten (art. 206).

Además, en esta materia, lo más grave es que la misma Asamblea Nacional ha renunciado a su tarea legislativa, al haberse impuesto, desde 2001, la renuncia a esa función con la práctica parlamentaria de delegar la función legislativa en el Poder Ejecutivo, siendo el resultado de ello que la casi totalidad de las leyes importantes en Venezuela en los últimos 15 años han sido dictadas mediante decretos leyes,[1152] sin que haya habido posibilidad alguna de debate sobre su contenido por parte de los representantes del pueblo, y mucho menos realización de consulta popular alguna para conocer la opinión de los diversos sectores de la población. Esto sucedió en 2001, en 2008 y más recientemente en noviembre de 2014, cuando, el último día de vigencia de la habilitación legislativa el Presidente de la República dictó casi cincuenta leyes, reformando las más importantes del país, sin que se hubiese asegurado el derecho a la participación; e incluso, varios días después de anunciadas en la *Gaceta Oficial*, [1153] las leyes ni siquiera se habían publicado. En esta forma, mediante la delegación legislativa, los órganos del Estado lo que han hecho es burlarse de la

---

1151   Véase sentencia de la Sala Política Administrativa del Tribunal Supremo N° 949 de 26 de abril de 2000, en *Revista de Derecho Público*, N° 82, Editorial Jurídica Venezolana, Caracas, 2000, pp. 163 ss.

1152   Véase Tomás Aníbal Arias Castillo, "Las cuatro delegaciones legislativas hechas al Presidente de la república (1999-2012)," en *Revista de Derecho Público*, N° 130, Editorial Jurídica Venezolana, Caracas 2012, pp. 393-399.

1153   Véase *Gacetas Oficiales* N° 40.543 y 40. 544 de 18 y 19 de noviembre de 2014.

Constitución, al violar el derecho que la misma garantiza a los ciudadanos de poder participar políticamente en el proceso de formación de las leyes, mediante una consulta popular que en cada caso la Asamblea Nacional está obligada a realizar antes de la sanción de las mismas.

En todo caso, el derecho ciudadano a la participación política que consagra el artículo 211 de la Constitución para que se conozca la opinión de las organizaciones de la sociedad sobre los proyectos de ley, y la obligación constitucional del Estado de consultar, así como el derecho de los Estados de la federación que establece el artículo 206 de la misma Constitución, de ser consultados en los casos de proyectos de leyes que los afecten o interesen, por supuesto, por su base constitucional, no debería entenderse que queda eliminado por el hecho de que se cambie la forma de sanción de las leyes y se haga mediante delegación legislativa. Sin embargo, lo contrario es lo que precisamente ha ocurrido en los últimos tres lustros, pues en la práctica política, el Ejecutivo Nacional, al emitir decretos leyes, nunca ha efectuado consulta popular alguna; y además, tampoco ha consultado a los Estados como lo exige la Constitución cuando las leyes los afecten. Y lo grave de esta situación inconstitucional, es que la misma fue regularizada en 2014 mediante una sentencia de la Sala Constitucional mediante la cual se mutó la Constitución y se eliminó el derecho a la participación política de los ciudadanos mediante la consulta pública de las leyes, precisamente cuando las mismas se aprueban mediante legislación delegada, que son la mayoría, en cuyo caso el Tribunal Supremo simplemente consideró que no existe derecho alguno a la participación política.[1154]

II. INFLACIÓN DE LA INSEGURIDAD JURÍDICA

En segundo lugar, en Venezuela también se puede afirmar que no hay un sistema de leyes justas, porque las mismas no están revestidas de seguridad jurídica alguna y más bien, lo que caracteriza a la legislación sancionada en el país durante los últimos lustros, ha sido una situación de inseguridad jurídica permanente respecto de su vigencia, lo que provoca que los ciudadanos a veces no llegan a saber con certeza qué ley está vigente, desde cuándo lo está, y cómo y cuándo es que se reforman.

Al contrario, para que puedan existir leyes justas para los ciudadanos, en efecto, lo primero que es necesario es que las mismas no sólo tengan validez general, sino además, que tengan garantía de estabilidad y seguridad jurídica, de manera que una vez sancionadas por la Asamblea Nacional se respete la voluntad de los diputados representantes del pueblo que la aprobaron, y se publique el texto sancionado; y que luego de promulgadas las leyes con su publicación, las mismas sólo se modifiquen por otras leyes como lo prescribe la Constitución y el Código Civil, mediante el procedimiento prescrito para su formación y modificación.

Pero al contrario, las leyes en Venezuela, en el proceso de su elaboración y promulgación, ha estado signadas por una inseguridad jurídica permanente, que impide

---

1154   Véase la sentencia N° 203 de 25 de marzo de 2014 (Caso *Síndica Procuradora Municipal del Municipio Chacao del Estado Miranda, impugnación del Decreto Ley de Ley Orgánica de la Administración Pública de 2008*), en http://www.tsj.gov.ve/decisiones/scon/marzo/162349-203-25314-2014-09-0456.HTML Véase los comentarios en Allan R. Brewer-Carías, *Golpe a la democracia dado por la Sala Constitucional*, Editorial Jurídica Venezolana, Caracas 2014, pp. 319 ss.

al ciudadano saber con exactitud cuál es la ley vigente, no garantizándose a los ciudadanos seguridad jurídica en relación con la vigencia de las mismas, siendo reformadas y modificadas indiscriminadamente por otras vías irregulares, distintas al procedimiento constitucional para de su formación y sanción.

Esto ha ocurrido, primero, con la práctica ilegal de reformar las leyes, pero obviando dictar una "ley de reforma" como lo prescribe la Ley de Publicaciones Oficiales, sino publicando íntegramente la Ley, de manera que se haga difícil, si no imposible, para el ciudadano común saber qué fue lo que se modificó;[1155] y segundo, con la práctica generalizada de reformar las leyes, una vez sancionadas y promulgadas, mediante el irregular procedimiento de "re-publicación" del texto en la *Gaceta Oficial*, con cambios y reformas no aprobadas por la representación popular.

Esto último, incluso comenzó a ocurrir, desde el inicio del régimen autoritario en el año 1999 con el texto de la propia Constitución de 1999, pues incluso, el que fue publicado en la *Gaceta Oficial* del 30 de diciembre de 1999, no sólo no fue el texto sancionado por la Asamblea Nacional el 30 de noviembre de 1999, sino que tampoco fue el que se sometió al referendo popular aprobatorio el 15 de diciembre de 1999, habiendo aparecido en la publicación oficial de la *Gaceta*, modificaciones a los textos originales, como por ejemplo, el agregado con la excusa de ser modificaciones de estilo, del uso indiscriminado del género femenino, tema que ni siquiera se discutió en la Asamblea Nacional Constituyente, además de otras reformas sustanciales.[1156]

Luego, el texto constitucional fue de nuevo modificado en marzo de 2000, cuando se "re-publicó" la Constitución, introduciéndose a su texto nuevos y numerosos cambios de palabras y frases por supuestos errores de copia y de "estilo," que no eran tales, sino que fueron modificaciones sustanciales, y además, se le agregó una "Exposición de Motivos," clandestina hasta entonces, redactada *ex post facto*, que nadie conocía y que nunca fue debatida en la Asamblea Constituyente.[1157]

O sea, los venezolanos, en ciertas materias, desde el inicio no han tenido seguridad de cuál es el texto constitucional realmente vigente, al punto de que el Fiscal General de la República llegó a intentar en 2000, una acción de interpretación constitucional específicamente sobre seis artículos que habían sido objeto de las "re-publicaciones" mencionadas, para saber cuál es el texto constitucional vigente, que la Sala Constitucional nunca resolvió.

Una situación igualmente irregular y grave, pero multiplicada con exceso, ha ocurrido también con las leyes, y para constatarlo basta revisar la *Gaceta Oficial* y

---

1155   Véase *Gacetas Oficiales* N° 40.543 y 40. 544 de 18 y 19 de noviembre de 2014.

1156   Fue precisamente lo que ocurrió con los 48 decretos leyes contentivos de leyes y leyes orgánicas dictados el último día de vigencia de la Ley habilitante dictada en 2013, pues la mayoría se publicaron íntegras como si se tratase de leyes nuevas, siendo que fueron todas reformas de leyes anteriores, pero sin que el intérprete pueda saber en qué consistió la reforma en cada caso. Véase en *Gacetas Oficiales* Extraordinarias N° 6.150; 6.151; 6.152; y 6153 de 18-11-2014; y N° 6.154; 6.155; y 6.156 de 19-11-2014.

1157   Véase el texto en *Gaceta Oficial* N° 5453 extra de 24-3-200. Véanse los cambios sobre las "reformas" en Allan R. Brewer-Carías, *La Constitución de 1999*, 2ª edición, Editorial Jurídica Venezolana, Caracas 2000.

captar la práctica cotidiana de los órganos del Estado de re-publicar el texto de las leyes después de promulgadas y publicadas en la *Gaceta Oficial*, incluso varias veces, por supuestos errores materiales de copia, siguiendo un procedimiento previsto en la vieja Ley de Publicaciones Oficiales de 1946, que quizás se justificaba, dicho sea de paso, cuando los textos se transcribían a mano o a máquina, y se imprimían con textos compuestos en linotipo, riesgo que no existe cuando se trata de archivos electrónicos, que ahora se copian escaneados y exactos en las páginas de la *Gaceta Oficial*, de manera que no hay riesgo alguno de errores de transcripción.

El procedimiento irregular es, sin duda, una manipulación inaceptable del proceso de publicación de las leyes y de los actos estatales de efectos generales, primero por parte del Poder Ejecutivo, y más recientemente, por parte de la propia Asamblea Nacional, siendo lo más grave el carácter discrecional y arbitrario de las republicaciones de los textos, con las cuales además se han introducido auténticas "reformas" a leyes sin haberse pasado por el procedimiento de formación de las mismas.[1158]

Con esta práctica, por tanto, las leyes, luego de publicadas, se han reimpreso una y otra vez en la *Gaceta,* y con ello lo que se ha hecho es reformarlas clandestina y subrepticiamente mediante "Avisos" que publica el Secretario de la Asamblea Nacional, acrecentándose la inseguridad jurídica. Casos recientes de esta práctica están, por ejemplo, en la reimpresión por supuestos errores materiales, en 2010, de la Ley Orgánica de la Jurisdicción Contencioso Administrativa[1159] y de la Ley Orgánica del Tribunal Supremo de Justicia.

En este último caso, en efecto, en 2010, después de la elección de los nuevos diputados a la Asamblea Nacional en septiembre de ese año, elección en la cual los diputados oficialistas perdieron la mayoría calificada que tenían y que les había permitido designar libremente hasta entonces, sin la participación de los diputados de la oposición, a los magistrados del Tribunal Supremo, los diputados oficialistas acometieron una "reforma" burda de la Ley Orgánica, mediante su reimpresión por supuesto error de copia ordenada por el Secretario de la Asamblea, cambiando la palabra de calificación del lapso para la designación de los Magistrados, de ser un lapso "máximo" pasando a ser un lapso "mínimo." [1160] Ese cambio de palabras de máximo por mínimo, fue suficiente para permitir a los viejos diputados, antes de la toma de posesión de los nuevos, designar los nuevos magistrados del Tribunal Su-

---

1158   Véase Allan R. Brewer-Carías, "Autoritarismo e inseguridad jurídica en Venezuela. O sobre la irregular forma utilizada para "reformar" la Constitución y las leyes," en Rafael Valim, José Roberto Pimenta Oliveira, e Augusto Neves Dal Pozzo (Coordinadores), *Tratado sobre o princípio da segurança jurídica no Direito Administrativo*, Editora Fórum, Sao Paulo, 2013.

1159   Véase Allan R. Brewer-Carías y Víctor Hernández Mendible, *Ley Orgánica de la Jurisdicción Contencioso Administrativa*, Editorial Jurídica Venezolana, Caracas 2010.

1160   Véase el texto de la Ley en *Gaceta Oficial* N° 39.483 de 9-8-2010, en Allan R. Brewer-Carías y Víctor Hernández Mendible, *Ley Orgánica del Tribunal Supremo de Justicia*, Editorial Jurídica Venezolana, Caracas 2010, pp. 225-226. Véase sobre los cambios efectuados al texto de la Ley con su re-publicación en Víctor Hernández Mendible, "Sobre la nueva reimpresión por "supuestos errores" materiales de la Ley Orgánica del Tribunal Supremo, octubre de 2010," y Antonio Silva Aranguren, "Tras el rastro del engaño en la web de la Asamblea Nacional," en *Revista de Derecho Público*, N° 124, Editorial Jurídica Venezolana, Caracas 2010, pp. 110-114.

premo, llenando el Tribunal de miembros del partido oficial e incluso de exdiputados que no habían sido reelectos.[1161]

Así se reforman las leyes en Venezuela, sin debate ni discusión parlamentaria, simplemente mediante un "Aviso" que publica el Secretario de la Asamblea, en ausencia absoluta de seguridad jurídica, lo que es la antítesis de un Estado de Justicia.

III. EL SOMETIMIENTO POLÍTICO DEL PODER JUDICIAL

En *tercer lugar*, la ausencia de Estado de Justicia en Venezuela, deriva del ya comentado sometimiento del Poder Judicial en su conjunto, al Poder Ejecutivo y al Poder Legislativo. A este último, específicamente, mediante el control político que ha venido ejerciendo la Asamblea en forma progresiva, desde 2000 hasta 2010, sobre el Tribunal Supremo, mediante el nombramiento como Magistrados a personas totalmente comprometidas con el partido oficial, que han expresado además públicamente que su misión, antes que impartir justicia, es contribuir a la ejecución de la política socialista del gobierno.[1162]

Además, como se ha indicado, la Asamblea Nacional se ha atribuido inconstitucionalmente la potestad de nombrar a los jueces de la corte y tribunal de la Jurisdicción Disciplinaria del Poder Judicial, que es la que ejecuta la remoción de los jueces del país, para lo cual, por supuesto, siguen la pauta dictada por el partido de gobierno en la Asamblea, de la cual dependen.

Además, como se dijo, en Venezuela, los jueces los designa el propio Tribunal Supremo de Justicia, sin que se cumpla la Constitución en cuanto a la exigencia de concurso público con participación ciudadana. El nombramiento ha sido libre, con el resultado de que la gran mayoría de los jueces son provisionales y temporales, y por tanto, totalmente dependientes y controlados políticamente.

Por ello, los jueces en Venezuela, en general, no son capaces ni pueden realmente impartir justicia justa, particularmente, si con ello afectan en alguna forma alguna política gubernamental o a algún funcionario público, sabiendo, como lo saben, que una decisión de ese tipo significa destitución inmediata, como tantas veces ha ocu-

---

1161 Ante la designación de los nuevos magistrados luego de la ilegal reforma de la Ley la ex Magistrada de la antigua Corte Suprema de Justicia, Hildegard Rondón de Sansó, advirtió que "El mayor de los riesgos que plantea para el Estado la desacertada actuación de la Asamblea Nacional en la reciente designación de los Magistrados del Tribunal Supremo de Justicia, no está solo en la carencia, en la mayoría de los designados de los requisitos constitucionales, sino el haber llevado a la cúspide del Poder Judicial la decisiva influencia de un sector d. Véase el Poder Legislativo, ya que para diferentes Salas, fueron elegidos cinco parlamentarios." Agregó que con ello: "todo un sector fundamental del poder del Estado, va a estar en manos de un pequeño grupo de sujetos que no son juristas, sino políticos de profesión, y a quienes corresponderá, entre otras funciones el control de los actos normativos;" agregando que "Lo más grave es que los designantes, ni un solo momento se percataron de que estaban nombrando a los jueces máximos del sistema jurídico venezolano que, como tales, tenían que ser los más aptos, y de reconocido prestigio como lo exige la Constitución." Véase en Hildegard Rondón de Sansó, *"Obiter Dicta.* En torno a una elección," en *La Voce d'Italia,* Caracas 14-12-2010.

1162 Véase el Discurso de Orden de la Magistrada Deyanira Nieves Bastidas, Apertura del Año Judicial 2014, en http://www.tsj.gov.ve/informacion/miscelaneas/DiscursodeOrdenApertura2014DeyaniraNie-ves.pdf.

rrido en los últimos años. En algunos casos, incluso con encarcelamiento de los jueces que osaron dictar una sentencia que no complació al gobierno.

Allí está como muestra, el caso de la Juez Afiuni, destituida por haber seguido la recomendación del Grupo de Expertos de la ONU sobre detenciones arbitrarias, y cambiarle la detención a un procesado por un régimen libertad con presentación ante el Tribunal, que no le gustó al Presidente de la República. Por orden personal pública de éste último, la juez fue encarcelada de inmediato, con trato brutal, incluso sin desarrollo del proceso penal por algunos años, lo que llevó al mismo Grupo de Expertos de la ONU a considerar estos hechos como "un golpe del Presidente Hugo Chávez contra la independencia de los jueces y abogados" solicitando la "inmediata liberación de la juez," concluyendo que "las represalias ejercidas sobre jueces y abogados por el ejercicio de sus funciones garantizadas constitucionalmente creando un clima de temor, solo sirve para minar el Estado de derecho y obstruir la justicia."[1163].

Con un Poder Judicial sometido políticamente, es evidente que no puede existir un Estado de Justicia, y menos aún si el mismo es utilizado como instrumento para la persecución política de la disidencia. En este sentido, los tribunales llenos están de causas abiertas por razones políticas para la persecución, con el objeto de apresar disidentes sin que exista voluntad efectiva de someterlos a juicio, porque ni motivos ni pruebas habría para ello. Ese fue, por ejemplo, el resultado de las detenciones de estudiantes realizadas con ocasión de la manifestaciones estudiantiles de febrero de 2014, quienes en su mayoría luego fueron liberados, pero sin gozar de libertad plena, después de sufrir brutal escarmiento. Otro ejemplo ha sido la detención del dirigente político de oposición Leopoldo López, a quien se ha sometido a juicio penal por los más graves delitos políticos, sin prueba alguna, sólo para encerrarlo en prisión con un juicio cuya audiencia preliminar ni siquiera se ha realizado y quizás, seguramente; no se realizará jamás. También hay que referirse al caso de la amenaza de detención, para que acudieran a declarar como testigos, proferida contra otro grupo de reconocidos dirigentes políticos, por un supuesto e imaginario delito de magnicidio, sólo basado en supuestos emails falsos,[1164] sólo para amedrentarlos y buscar alejarlos el país.

IV. EL ESTADO IRRESPONSABLE, ESCAPADO DE LA JUSTICIA INTERNA

En cuarto lugar, en Venezuela tampoco existe Estado de Justicia, desde el momento en que el propio Estado, sus organizaciones y sus funcionarios se han escapado de la justicia, es decir, de hecho no están ni pueden ser sometidos a la Justicia.

1163   Véase   en   at   http://www.unog.ch/unog/website/news_media.nsf/%28httpNewsByYear_en %29/93687E8429BD53A1C125768E00529DB6?OpenDocument&cntxt=B35C3&cookielang=fr. El 14-10-2010, el mismo Grupo de Trabajo de la ONU solicitó formalmente al Gobierno venezolano que la Juez fuse "sometida a un juicio apegado al debido proceso y bajo el derecho de la libertad provisional". Véase en *El Universal*, 14-10-2010, en http://www.eluniversal.com/2010/10/14/pol_ava_instancia-de-la-onu_14A4608051.shtml

1164   Véase la información en http://www.venezuelaaldia.com/2014/07/gobierno-falsifico-correos-sobre-magnicidio-dice-pedro-burelli/

De ello ha resultado, que en Venezuela tenemos un Estado totalmente incontrolado e irresponsable, al cual no se lo puede someter a juicio, pues los tribunales garantizan que no responda ante los mismos de sus acciones inconstitucionales o ilegales, o que causan daños a las personas.

Basta analizar las sentencias del Tribunal Supremo de Justicia en los últimos tres lustros, para constar que en materia de control de constitucionalidad de las leyes y otros actos estatales, a pesar de que contamos con la acción popular y un completísimo sistema mixto de control de constitucionalidad de las leyes, las acciones intentadas por los particulares contra las leyes jamás son decididas, y por tanto, difícilmente se encuentra alguna sentencia anulatoria, salvo que haya sido intentada por los abogados del propio Estado, en interés del mismo

Ello ha afectado también a la Jurisdicción Contencioso Administrativa, la cual en los últimos quince años dejó de ser un efectivo sistema para el control judicial de las actuaciones administrativas, lo que se evidenció abiertamente desde 2003 con la lamentable destitución *in limine* de los Magistrados de la Corte Primera de lo Contencioso Administrativa. Todo se inició con ocasión de un proceso contencioso administrativo de nulidad y amparo formulado el 17 de julio de 2003 por la Federación Médica Venezolana en contra los actos del Alcalde Metropolitano de Caracas, del Ministro de Salud y del Colegio de Médicos del Distrito Metropolitano de Caracas, por la contratación indiscriminada de médicos extranjeros no licenciados para ejercer la medicina en el país, para atender el desarrollo de un importante programa asistencial de salud en los barrios de Caracas; todo en violación de la Ley de Ejercicio de la Medicina.

La Federación Médica Venezolana consideró que la actuación pública era discriminatoria y violatoria de los derechos de los médicos venezolanos (derecho al trabajo, entre otros) a ejercer su profesión médica, al permitir a médicos extranjeros ejercerla sin cumplir con las condiciones establecidas en la Ley. Por ello la Federación intentó la acción de nulidad y amparo, en representación de los derechos colectivos de los médicos venezolanos, solicitando su protección.[1165] Un mes después, el 21 de agosto de 2003, la Corte Primera dictó una medida cautelar de amparo considerando que había suficientes elementos en el caso que hacían presumir la violación del derecho a la igualdad ante la ley de los médicos venezolanos, ordenando la suspensión temporal del programa de contratación de médicos cubanos, y ordenando al Colegio de Médicos del Distrito metropolitano sustituir los médicos cubanos ya contratados sin licencia por médicos venezolanos o médicos extranjeros con licencia para ejercer la profesión en Venezuela.[1166]

La respuesta gubernamental a esta decisión preliminar de carácter cautelar, que tocaba un programa social muy sensible para el gobierno, fue el anuncio público del Ministro de Salud, del Alcalde Metropolitano y del propio Presidente de la Repúbli-

---

1165   Véase Claudia Nikken, "El caso "Barrio Adentro": La Corte Primera de lo Contencioso Administrativo ante la Sala Constitucional del Tribunal Supremo de Justicia o el avocamiento como medio de amparo de derechos e intereses colectivos y difusos," en *Revista de Derecho Público*, Nº 93–96, Editorial Jurídica Venezolana, Caracas, 2003, pp. 5 ss.

1166   Véase la decisión de 21 de agosto de 2003 en *Revista de Derecho Público*, Nº 93–96, Editorial Jurídica Venezolana, Caracas, 2003, pp. 445 ss.

ca en el sentido de que la medida cautelar dictada no sería acatada en forma alguna;[1167] anuncios que fueron seguidos de varias decisiones gubernamentales:

La Sala Constitucional del Tribunal Supremo de Justicia, controlada por el Ejecutivo, adoptó la decisión de avocarse al conocimiento del caso decidido por la Corte Primera de lo Contencioso Administrativo, y usurpando competencias en la materia, declaró la nulidad del amparo cautelar decidido por esta. A ello siguió que un grupo de agentes de la policía política allanó la sede de la Corte Primera, después de detener a un escribiente o alguacil de la misma por motivos fútiles; el Presidente de la República, entre otras expresiones usadas, se refirió al Presidente de la Corte Primera como "un bandido;"[1168] y unas semanas después, la Comisión Especial Judicial del Tribunal Supremo de Justicia, sin fundamento legal alguno, destituyó a los cinco magistrados de la Corte Primera, la cual fue intervenida.[1169] A pesar de la protesta de los Colegios de Abogados del país e, incluso, de la Comisión Internacional de Juristas;[1170] el hecho es que la Corte Primera permaneció cerrada, sin jueces, por más de diez meses,[1171] tiempo durante el cual simplemente no hubo justicia contencioso administrativa en el país.

Esa fue la respuesta gubernamental a un amparo cautelar dictado por el juez contencioso administrativo competente respecto de un programa gubernamental sensible; respuesta que fue dada y ejecutada a través de órganos judiciales controlados políticamente. Todo ello, por supuesto, lamentablemente significó, no sólo que los jueces que fueron luego nombrados para reemplazar a los destituidos comenzaron a entender cómo debían comportarse en el futuro frente al poder; sino que condujo a la abstención progresiva de todo control contencioso administrativa respecto de las acciones gubernamentales. La Jurisdicción contencioso administrativa en Venezuela, de larga tradición y de raigambre y jerarquía constitucional, simplemente hoy no existe en la práctica; y con ello, el derecho administrativo ya no es un parámetro legal para controlar a la Administración y sus funcionarios

Y para que quedara clara la situación catastrófica de estas actuaciones sobre el Poder Judicial, la demanda que intentaron los jueces contencioso administrativo destituidos ante el Sistema Interamericano de protección de los Derechos Humanos por violación a sus garantías constitucionales judiciales, a pesar de que fue decidida por la Corte Interamericana de Derechos Humanos, en 2008, condenando al Estado,[1172] de nada sirvió sino para

1167   El Presidente de la República dijo: "*Váyanse con su decisión no sé para donde, la cumplirán ustedes en su casa si quieren...*", en el programa de TV *Aló Presidente*, N° 161, 24 de Agosto de 2003.

1168   Discurso público, 20 septiembre de 2003.

1169   Véase la información en *El Nacional*, Caracas, Noviembre 5, 2003, p. A2. En la misma página el Presidente destituido de la Corte Primera dijo: "*La justicia venezolana vive un momento tenebroso, pues el tribunal que constituye un último resquicio de esperanza ha sido clausurado*".

1170   Véase en *El Nacional*, Caracas, Octubre 12, 2003, p. A–5; y *El Nacional*, Caracas, Noviembre 18,2004, p. A–6.

1171   Véase en *El Nacional*, Caracas, Octubre 24, 2003, p. A–2; y *El Nacional*, Caracas, Julio 16, 2004, p. A–6.

1172   Véase sentencia de la Corte Interamericana de 5 de agosto de 2008, Caso *Apitz Barbera y otros ("Corte Primera de lo Contencioso Administrativo") vs. Venezuela*, Excepción Preliminar, Fondo, Reparaciones y Costas, Serie C N° 182, en www.corteidh.or.cr

que la Sala Constitucional del Tribunal Supremo, en sentencia N° 1.939 de 12 de diciembre de 2008,[1173] citando como precedente una sentencia del Tribunal Superior Militar del Perú de 2002, declarara que la sentencia del tribunal internacional era "inejecutable" en Venezuela. La Sala además, solicitó al Ejecutivo que denunciara la Convención Americana de Derechos Humanos porque la Corte Interamericana supuestamente había usurpado los poderes del Tribunal Supremo, lo que el Ejecutivo cumplió cabalmente en 2011.

La consecuencia de todo ello es que la Jurisdicción contencioso administrativa, cayó en desuso, de manera que no más del uno por ciento de la totalidad de las sentencias dictadas por dichos tribunales son anulatorias de actos administrativos o de responsabilidad administrativa,[1174] habiendo quedado reducida a resolver cuestiones laborales de la función pública o tributarias.

Siendo el Estado venezolano uno no sometido al derecho, por no poder ser controlado ni respecto del cual los ciudadanos pueden exigir responsabilidad, sin duda, no puede haber Estado de Justicia, lo que conduce a consolidar la existencia de un derecho público al sólo servicio exclusivo del Estado, y al derecho administrativo como un orden desequilibrado, donde sólo encuentra protección el propio Estado sin que los particulares sean objeto de protección y menos de garantía.

V. EL ESTADO ESCAPADO DE LA JUSTICIA INTERNACIONAL

La irresponsabilidad del Estado y la decisión de escaparse de la justicia y negarse a someterse a la misma ha llegado a tal nivel, que no sólo se ha desligado y desentendido de poder ser juzgado por los tribunales nacionales, sino que como antes se dijo se ha desligado de la justicia internacional. Ello ocurrió, primero, al denunciar en 2006 el Tratado de la Comunidad Andina de Naciones, escapándose de la jurisdicción del Tribunal Andino de Justicia,[1175] y segundo, al denunciar en 2012 la Convención Americana sobre Derechos Humanos, para escaparse de la jurisdicción de la Corte Interamericana de Derechos Humanos,[1176] incluso, en este último caso, después de haber declarado como "inejecutables" en Venezuela varias sentencias con-

---

1173   Véase sentencia de la Sala Constitucional, sentencia N° 1.939 de 18 de diciembre de 2008 (Caso *Abogados Gustavo Álvarez Arias y otros*), en http://www.tsj.gov.ve/decisiones/scon/Diciembre/1939-181208-2008-08-1572.html

1174   Véase Antonio Canova González, *La realidad del contencioso administrativo venezolano (Un llamado de atención frente a las desoladoras estadísticas de la Sala Político Administrativa en 2007 y primer semestre de 2008)*, Funeda, Caracas 2008.

1175   Comunicación oficial del Ministro de Relaciones Exteriores de 22-4-2006 enviada a la CAN. Véase el texto en http://www10.iadb.org/intal/cartamensual/cartas/Articulo.aspx?Id=2e424fd3-30ec-46e9-8c92-fcce18b3e128. Véase así mismo la información en http://www10.iadb.org/intal/cartamensual/car-tas/Articulo.aspx?Id=2e424fd3-30ec-46e9-8c92-fcce18b3e128. Véase los comentarios en "El largo camino para la consolidación de las bases constitucionales de la Integración Regional Andina y su abandono por el régimen autoritario de Venezuela", en André Saddy (Coord.), *Direito Público Econômico Supranacional*, Rio de Janeiro: Lumen Juris Editora, 2009, pp. 319-351.

1176   Comunicación del Ministro de Relaciones Exteriores al Secretario General de la OEA de 6-9-2012. Véase la Nota de Prensa de la OEA lamentando la decisión en http://www.oas.org/es/cidh/prensa/comunicados/2012/117.asp

denatorias contra el Estado venezolano pronunciadas por la Corte por responsabilidad derivada de la violación de derechos humanos.[1177]

Además, incluso, la decisión del Estado de escaparse a toda costa de la justicia internacional, llevó al gobierno hasta a denunciar el Convenio sobre Arreglo de Diferencias Relativas a Inversiones entre Estados y Nacionales de Otros Estados, con base en el cual funciona el Centro Internacional de Arreglo de Diferencias Relativas a Inversiones (CIADI), que regula los medios de arbitraje internacional para la protección de inversiones.[1178]

VI. LA JUSTICIA AL SERVICIO DEL AUTORITARISMO

En quinto lugar, en Venezuela tampoco tenemos un Estado de Justicia, porque la justicia impartida, particularmente en materia constitucional, en lugar de ser el supremo valor de dar a cada quien lo que le corresponde en plano de igualdad, se ha convertido en un instrumento utilizado por el propio Estado, que es utilizado "a la carta," para moldear la justicia de acuerdo con lo que sus órganos necesiten para la ejecución de las propias políticas estatales, así sean contrarias a la Constitución, y particularmente cuando se ha necesitado de una "interpretación" de la misma o de leyes para torcerlas, en forma acorde, no con la Constitución, sino con la decisión política del Ejecutivo de que se trate.

En esta forma, la Constitución, vía interpretación constitucional vinculante, como antes se ha dicho, por ejemplo, ha sido objeto de mutaciones decididas por la Sala Constitucional, por ejemplo, para centralizar competencias que eran exclusivas de los Estados de la Federación; para eliminar el principio de la alternabilidad republicana dando paso a la reelección indefinida; para asegurar el financiamiento de las actividades electorales del partido oficial; para impedir la revocación popular del

1177   Véase en particular la sentencia N° 1.939 de la Sala Constitucional del Tribunal Supremo de Venezuela de 18 de diciembre de 2008 (Caso *Abogados Gustavo Álvarez Arias y otros*), que declaró inejecutable una sentencia de la Corte Interamericana de Derechos Humanos (de 5 de agosto de 2008, caso *Apitz Barbera y otros ("Corte Primera de lo Contencioso Administrativo") vs. Venezuela*, Excepción Preliminar, Fondo, Reparaciones y Costas, Serie C N° 182). Véase en http://www.tsj.gov.ve/decisiones/scon/Diciembre/1939-181208-2008-08-1572.html. Igualmente la sentencia N° 1547 de 17 de octubre de 2011 (Caso *Estado Venezolano vs. Corte Interamericana de Derechos Humanos*) que declaró inejecutable otra sentencia de la Corte Interamericana (de 1° de septiembre de 2011, caso *Leopoldo López vs. Estado de Venezuela*), en http://www.tsj.gov.ve/decisiones/scon/Octubre/1547-171011-2011-11-1130.html. Véase los comentarios sobre estas sentencias en Allan R. Brewer-Carías, "La interrelación entre los Tribunales Constitucionales de América Latina y la Corte Interamericana de Derechos Humanos, y la cuestión de la inejecutabilidad de sus decisiones en Venezuela," en Armin von Bogdandy, Flavia Piovesan y Mariela Morales Antonorzi (Coordinadores), *Direitos Humanos, Democracia e Integraçao Jurídica na América do Sul*, Lumen Juris Editora, Rio de Janeiro 2010, pp. 661-70; y en *Anuario Iberoamericano de Justicia Constitucional*, Centro de Estudios Políticos y Constitucionales, N° 13, Madrid 2009, pp. 99-136; y "El ilegítimo "control de constitucionalidad" de las sentencias de la Corte Interamericana de Derechos Humanos por parte la Sala Constitucional del Tribunal Supremo de Justicia de Venezuela: el caso de la sentencia *Leopoldo López vs. Venezuela, 2011*," en *Constitución y democracia: ayer y hoy. Libro homenaje a Antonio Torres del Moral*. Editorial Universitas, Vol. I, Madrid, 2013, pp. 1.095-1124.

1178   Comunicación oficial del Estado enviada al CIADI el 24-1-2012. Véase la información del CIADI en https://icsid.worldbank.org/ICSID/FrontServlet?requestType=CasesRH&actionVal=OpenPage&PageType=AnnouncementsFrame&FromPage=Announcements&pageName=Announcement100

mandato del Presidente de la República; para ampliar las competencias de la Juris-dicción Constitucional, como por ejemplo ocurrió en materia de interpretación abs-tracta de la Constitución[1179] e incluso para asegurar el absurdo e improcedente "con-trol de la constitucionalidad" de las sentencias de la Corte Interamericana de Dere-chos Humanos, que condujo a declararlas "inejecutables" en Venezuela. La interpre-tación constitucional a la carta, además, ha servido para que por la vía de interpreta-ción inconstitucional, la Sala Constitucional ha procedido a reformar leyes, como por ejemplo sucedió, en materia del procedimiento de amparo[1180] o para establecer normas tributarias nuevas en materia de impuesto sobre la renta;[1181] y todo ello, casi siempre a iniciativa de los propios abogados del Estado.

Con una Constitución maleable en esa forma, es difícil imaginar un Estado de justicia, salvo que sea de justicia sólo impartida a la medida del propio Estado.

VII. LA AUSENCIA DE JUSTICIA

En sexto lugar, tampoco puede hablarse en Venezuela de Estado de Justicia, cuando hay áreas de la misma que el Estado ha eliminado, como es el caso de la justicia de paz, que la Constitución reguló para ser organizada en las comunidades y ser impartida por jueces electos mediante sufragio universal directo y secreto (art 258).

A tal efecto, desde la Ley Orgánica de la Justicia de Paz de 1994[1182] se reguló la materia en el ámbito municipal y parroquial, debiendo los jueces ser electos en la forma prescrita en la Constitución. Sin embargo, todo ello se eliminó con la Ley Orgánica de la Jurisdicción de la Justicia de Paz Comunal de 2012,[1183] al transfor-marse la justicia de paz en una supuesta "justicia de paz comunal," pero para sim-plemente eliminar la justicia de paz, o nombrase unos escasos jueces provisionales, por supuesto, no electos, violándose así la Constitución.[1184]

1179   Véase Luis A. Herrera Orellana, "El recurso de interpretación de la Constitución: reflexiones críticas desde la argumentación jurídica y la teoría del discurso," en *Revista de Derecho Público*, N° 113, Editorial Jurídica Venezolana, Caracas 2008, pp. 7-29.

1180   Véase Allan R. Brewer-Carías, "El juez constitucional como legislador positivo y la inconstitucional reforma de la Ley Orgánica de Amparo mediante sentencias interpretativas," en Eduardo Ferrer Mac-Gregor y Arturo Zaldívar Lelo de Larrea (Coordinadores), *La ciencia del derecho procesal constitu-cional. Estudios en homenaje a Héctor Fix-Zamudio en sus cincuenta años como investigador del derecho*, Instituto de Investigaciones Jurídicas, Universidad Nacional Autónoma de México, México 2008, Tomo V, pp. 63-80. Publicado en *Crónica sobre la "In" Justicia Constitucional. La Sala Constitucional y el autoritarismo en Venezuela*, Colección Instituto de Derecho Público. Universidad Central de Venezuela, N° 2, Editorial Jurídica Venezolana, Caracas 2007, pp. 545-563.

1181   Véase Allan R. Brewer-Carías, "De cómo la Jurisdicción constitucional en Venezuela, no sólo legisla de oficio, sino subrepticiamente modifica las reformas legales que "sanciona", a espaldas de las par-tes en el proceso: el caso de la aclaratoria de la sentencia de Reforma de la Ley de Impuesto sobre la Renta de 2007, *Revista de Derecho Público*, N° 114, Editorial Jurídica Venezolana, Caracas 2008, pp. 267-276.

1182   Véase en *Gaceta Oficial* N° 4.817 Extra. de 21-12-1994.

1183   Véase en *Gaceta Oficial* N° 39.913 del 2-5-2012

1184   Tan es así, que en agosto de 2014, el Tribunal Supremo anunciaba en su página web, que en un universo de 328 Municipios en el país, "la Comisión Judicial del Alto Tribunal, ha nombrado un total

VIII. LA INJUSTICIA DE LA IMPUNIDAD

En séptimo lugar, en Venezuela tampoco existe un Estado de Justicia, teniendo más bien un Estado de injusticia, por el hecho de que simplemente, la justicia no funciona para juzgar y castigar a quienes violan la ley. Así, la impunidad campea y es absoluta respecto de los depredadores del patrimonio público, es decir, a los funcionarios corruptos y a sus cómplices particulares, incluyendo a los que a la vista de todos incurren en peculado de uso, al tener a su servicio el uso bienes públicos, sin título alguno para ello, comenzando por el uso indebido de inmuebles oficiales. A esos, ni se los investiga y menos se los sanciona. Y los casos de investigaciones administrativas resueltos por la Contraloría General de la República por supuestos motivos de irregularidades administrativas, en general, sólo han concluido con medidas de inhabilitaciones políticas impuestas exclusivamente a funcionarios de oposición.[1185]

La impunidad también es el signo de la injusticia en materia de delitos comunes, en un país como Venezuela, que tiene el récord mundial de violencia, secuestros y crímenes callejeros,[1186] que en 2013 alcanzó la cifra de 24.773 personas asesinadas,[1187] siendo considerado en 2014, como el país más inseguro del mundo,[1188] y Caracas, la capital, como la segunda ciudad más peligrosa del Planeta;[1189] pero donde dichos crímenes no se persiguen y quedan impunes.[1190]

---

de 18 juezas y jueces de paz provisorios y suplentes.". Véase en http://www.tsj.gov.ve/informacion/notasdeprensa/notasdeprensa.asp?codigo=11987.

1185   Véase por ejemplo, Allan R. Brewer-Carías, "La incompetencia de la Administración Contralora para dictar actos administrativos de inhabilitación política restrictiva del derecho a ser electo y ocupar cargos públicos (La protección del derecho a ser electo por la Corte Interamericana de Derechos Humanos en 2012, y su violación por la Sala Constitucional del Tribunal Supremo al declarar la sentencia de la Corte Interamericana como "inejecutable"), en Alejandro Canónico Sarabia (Coord.), *El Control y la responsabilidad en la Administración Pública, IV Congreso Internacional de Derecho Administrativo, Margarita 2012*, Centro de Adiestramiento Jurídico, Editorial Jurídica Venezolana, Caracas 2012, pp. 293-371

1186   Por ello, con razón en un editorial del diario *Le Monde* de París, titulado "Los venezolanos en el callejón sin salida del chavismo", se afirmaba que "Al derrumbamiento de la economía se agrega una inseguridad galopante: 25 mil homicidios por año, sin contar los robos, agresiones de todo tipo y secuestros. Caracas es la capital más peligrosa del planeta. Se necesita toda la atracción del "exotismo latino" para que ciertos intelectuales franceses le encuentren algún encanto al "chavismo". Sobre todo porque este, ya sea bajo Maduro o bajo Chávez, cercena las libertades públicas, silencia a una parte de la prensa y maltrata a toda la oposición. En la realidad, el chavismo se ha convertido en una pesadilla." Véase Editorial de *Le Monde*, 30- marzo 2014, en http://www.eluniversal.com/nacional-y-politica/140330/le-monde-dedico-un-editorial-a-venezuela.

1187   Véase César Miguel Rondón, "Cada vez menos país," en *Confirmado*, 16-8-2014, en http://confirmado.com.ve/opinan/cada-vez-menos-pais/

1188   Véase el reportaje de la Encuesta Gallup, "Venezuela fue considerado como el país más inseguro del mundo," en *Notitarde.com*, Caracas 21 de agosto de 2014, en http://www.noti-tarde.com/Pais/Venezuela-fue-seleccionado-como-el-pais-mas-inseguro-del-mundo/2014/08/21/347656.

1189   Después de San Pedro Sula, Caracas es considerada la segunda ciudad más peligrosa del mundo. Véase la información en *Sala de Información, Agencia de Comunicaciones Integradas. Información, opinión y análisis*, 16-1-2914, en http://saladeinfo.wordpress.com/2014/01/16/ca-racas-es-la-segunda-ciudad-mas-peligrosa-del-planeta-2/. Véase igualmente la información en El País Interna-

Tenemos lamentablemente un país lleno de asaltantes de caminos, como los había en la Venezuela del siglo XIX, pero no en el campo, sino ahora en las calles de nuestras ciudades, y más grave aún, en los barrios de las mismas, afectando a la población de menores recursos. Y frente a todo ello, lo que hay es una justicia totalmente ausente, siendo Venezuela el reino de la impunidad, donde al delincuente no se lo castiga, el que roba es protegido, al honrado se lo investiga, a la libertad no se la protege, a la propiedad se la depreda, y al trabajo honesto se desprecia, de lo cual resulta no sólo que no siempre tenemos leyes justas y seguras, sino que no siempre tenemos jueces justos y definitivamente, carecemos de un gobierno justo.

Por todo ello, el Estado venezolano no es un Estado de justicia, pues la práctica política del gobierno autoritario que se apoderó de la República desde 1999,[1191] lo que ha originado es un Estado totalitario que además de haber empobrecido aún más al país, no está realmente sometido al derecho, cuyas normas no siempre son justas y la mayor de las veces se ignoran y desprecian; o se mutan o amoldan a discreción por los gobernantes; y que además, no está sometido a control judicial alguno, por la sumisión del Poder Judicial al Poder Ejecutivo y legislativo.

De todo lo anterior resulta entonces que en lugar de un Estado de Justicia, el Estado venezolano más bien puede considerarse como un "Estado de la injusticia," donde no hay garantía de la existencia de leyes justas, habiéndose sancionado las existentes sin que se haya respetado siquiera el derecho a la participación ciudadano mediante consulta popular de los proyectos de ley, habiéndose multiplicado las leyes inconsultas; donde además ha ocurrido una inflación ilimitada de la inseguridad jurídica, basada en la reforma irregular de leyes sin cumplirse el procedimiento de formación de las mismas; donde el Poder Judicial, como antes se ha dicho está controlado por el poder político y puesto a su servicio; lo que ha originado, de hecho, que el Estado sea un Estado irresponsable y ajusticiable, que se ha escapado de la justicia tanto interna como internacional, donde en su globalidad el Poder Judicial ha sido puesto al servicio del autoritarismo; y donde campea la impunidad particularmente en materia penal.

Ese es el Estado al cual sirve ahora el derecho público, y su funcionamiento es el que ahora permite fijar las tendencias del derecho administrativo como derecho al

---

cional, 20 de agosto de 2014, en http://internacional.elpais.com/interna-cional/2014/08/20/actualidad/1408490113_417749.html

1190   Sobre el tema de la "actividad hamponil" y la impunidad, Leandro Area ha observado que :"se ha convertido en el pan y plan nuestro y maestro de cada día, sea por el éxito malandro que se ve apenas reflejado en muerte y desolación en la prensa que queda y que está en vías de extinción o bien por el semblante que se enseña en el rostro de todo aquel que sigue vivo y que debe enfrentar la penuria de existir secuestrado por una realidad impuesta. Pero el asunto va más allá. El concubinato legitimado entre poder político, hampa común, poder judicial, policía, fuerzas armadas y demás, no es misterio ni secreto a voces. Es un plan convertido en acción permanente." Véase Leandro Area, "El 'Estado Misional' en Venezuela," en *Analítica.com*, 14 de febrero de 2014, en http://analitica.com/opinion/opinion-nacional/el-estado-misional-en-venezuela/.

1191   Véase Allan R. Brewer-Carías, *Authoritarian Government vs. The Rule of Law, Lectures and Essays (1999-2014) on the Venezuelan Authoritarian Regime Established in Contempt of the Constitution*, Fundación de Derecho Público, Editorial Jurídica Venezolana, Caracas 2014.

servicio del autoritarismo, que responde a esa realidad, no siendo en forma alguna independiente de la actuación del gobierno.

SECCIÓN QUINTA:

LA AUSENCIA DE ESTADO DESCENTRALIZADO

Esta Sección quinta, es el texto de la Ponencia sobre la "La destrucción de la Institución municipal en Venezuela, en nombre de una supuesta democracia "participativa y protagónica," redactada para el *XXX Congreso Ordinario de la Organización Iberoamericano de Cooperación Intermunicipal*, Estado de Jalisco, Ciudad de Guadalajara, Guadalajara 5-8 de noviembre de 2014

Pero además de no ser, el Estado venezolano, un Estado de derecho, ni un Estado democrático, ni un Estado social, ni un Estado de economía mixta, ni un Estado de justicia, tampoco puede hoy considerarse como un Estado descentralizado, así sea precariamente en el marco de la Federación Centralizada que reguló la Constitución de 1999, siendo al contrario, un Estado centralizado.

En efecto, un Estado democrático es aquél en el cual además de estar asegurada la supremacía constitucional y la sumisión del Estado al derecho, concepto con el cual está esencialmente imbricado, existe, *primero*, un régimen político de democracia representativa que permita y aliente la participación política, entre otros medios, mediante la celebración de elecciones periódicas, libres, justas y basadas en el sufragio universal y secreto, como expresión de la soberanía del pueblo; *segundo*, un régimen plural de partidos y organizaciones políticas con libre actuación en plano de igualdad; *tercero*, un efectivo sistema de separación horizontal entre los poderes del Estado, que sirva para que el Poder controle al poder, de manera que el ejercicio del Poder Público pueda ser efectivamente controlado tanto judicialmente como por los otros medios dispuestos en la Constitución,[1192] que aseguren la probidad y la responsabilidad de los gobiernos en la gestión pública; *cuarto*, un sistema de distribución vertical del Poder Público como principio medular de la organización del Estrado, para permitir, a través de la descentralización política del poder, la participación ciudadana; y *quinto*, una declaración de derechos humanos y libertades fundamentales, entre ellos, los derechos individuales, sociales, económicos y ambientales, en particular, la libertad de expresión, que estén todos garantizados constitucionalmente y sean asegurados y justiciables por un Poder Judicial independiente y autónomo.[1193]

1192   Véase Allan R. Brewer–Carías, "Prólogo: Sobre el derecho a la democracia y el control del poder", al libro de Asdrúbal Aguiar, *El derecho a la democracia. La democracia en el derecho y la jurisprudencia interamericanos. La libertad de expresión, piedra angular de la democracia*, Editorial Jurídica Venezolana, Caracas 2008, pp. 19 ss.

1193   Véase Allan R. Brewer–Carías, "Algo sobre las nuevas tendencias del derecho constitucional: el reconocimiento del derecho a la constitución y del derecho a la democracia," en Sergio J. Cuarezma Terán y Rafael Luciano Pichardo (Directores), *Nuevas tendencias del derecho constitucional y el derecho procesal constitucional*, Instituto de Estudios e Investigación Jurídica (INEJ), Managua 2011, pp. 73-94.

Para que exista un Estado democrático, por tanto, no bastan las declaraciones constitucionales, y ni siquiera, la sola existencia de elecciones. Ya el mundo contemporáneo ha conocido demasiadas experiencias de toda suerte de tiranos que usaron el voto popular para acceder al poder, y que luego, mediante su ejercicio incontrolado, desmantelaron la propia democracia y desarrollaron gobiernos autoritarios, contrarios al pueblo, que acabaron con la democracia y con todos sus elementos,[1194] comenzando por el irrespeto a los derechos humanos. Esta es la lamentable situación que se ha dado en Venezuela, donde se ha arraigado un gobierno autoritario y un Estado Totalitario, partiendo de elementos que se insertaron en la misma Constitución de 1999,[1195] lo que permite afirmar que hoy lamentablemente no tenemos un Estado democrático.

Más bien, lo que tenemos es un Estado donde no hay efectiva democracia representativa; donde no existe democracia participativa, no pasando, la "democracia participativa y protagónica" que se pregona, de ser un esquema, si acaso, de movilización popular pero controlada por el gobierno central; donde no hay separación de poderes; donde no sólo los militares no están sometidos a la autoridad civil, sino que los mismos controlan el poder y a la Administración; donde no hay libertad de expresión, habiendo quedado en su mínima expresión, entre otros factores, por el acaparamiento de los medios de comunicación por parte del Estado; y donde se ha venido destruyendo la institución municipal, precisamente, bajo la excusa de promover una supuesta "participación protagónica" del pueblo..

I. LAS FALLAS DE LA DEMOCRÁTICA REPRESENTATIVA

Todo lo anterior ha llevado a la situación de que en Venezuela, las fallas de la democracia afectan tanto a la democracia representativa como a la democracia participativa.

En efecto, en cuanto a la democracia representativa, en la situación actual, en la Venezuela actual carecemos de un sistema efectivo y real que la asegure, entre otros aspectos, por las previsiones contenidas en la reforma de la Ley Orgánica de Procesos Electorales,[1196] la cual al regular la representación proporcional y la personifica-

---

1194   Véase en relación con el caso de Venezuela: Allan R. Brewer-Carías, *Dismantling Democracy. The Chávez Authoritarian Experiment*, Cambridge University Press, New York 2010.

1195   Véase los comentarios críticos a la semilla autoritaria en la Constitución de 1999, en Allan R. Brewer–Carías, *Debate Constituyente (Aportes a la Asamblea Nacional Constituyente), Tomo III (18 octubre–30 noviembre 1999)*, Fundación de Derecho Público–Editorial Jurídica Venezolana, Caracas, 1999, pp. 311–340; "Reflexiones críticas sobre la Constitución de Venezuela de 1999," en el libro de Diego Valadés, Miguel Carbonell (Coordinadores), *Constitucionalismo Iberoamericano del Siglo XXI*, Cámara de Diputados. LVII Legislatura, Universidad Nacional Autónoma de México, México 2000, pp. 171–193; en *Revista de Derecho Público*, N° 81, Editorial Jurídica Venezolana, Caracas, enero–marzo 2000, pp. 7–21; en *Revista Facultad de Derecho, Derechos y Valores*, Volumen III N° 5, Universidad Militar Nueva Granada, Santafé de Bogotá, D.C., Colombia, Julio 2000, pp. 9–26; y en el libro *La Constitución de 1999*, Biblioteca de la Academia de Ciencias Políticas y Sociales, Serie Eventos 14, Caracas, 2000, pp. 63–88.

1196   Véase sobre la Ley Orgánica de los Procesos Electorales en *Gaceta Oficial* No. 5928 Extra. de 12 de agosto de 2009. Sobre el sistema electoral antes de esta Ley véase Allan R. Brewer-Carías, "Reforma electoral en el sistema político de Venezuela", en Daniel Zovatto y J. Jesús Orozco Henríquez (Coor-

ción del sufragio, lo que logró fue permitirle al partido de gobierno, que con minoría del voto popular haya asegurado controlar la mayoría de los escaños en la Asamblea Nacional.[1197] Además, el sistema se caracteriza por el abuso que deriva de la imbricación total entre el partido oficial y el aparato del Estado, el cual ha sido íntegramente puesto al servicio de los candidatos oficiales; por la recepción consecuente por parte del partido oficial que preside el propio Presidente de la República, de un ingente financiamiento directo e indirecto del Estado, sin que nunca se haya rendido cuentas de ello; por el control obsceno de todos los medios de comunicación por parte del Estado, y por el abuso de los candidatos oficiales en la utilización limitada de los mismos de comunicación, en las campañas electorales.

El sistema electoral y de escrutinio, además, ha estado controlado por un conjunto de órganos, como son los que conforman el Poder Electoral, que al contrario del carácter independiente, autónomo, despartidizado, imparcial y con participación ciudadana que prevé la Constitución (art. 294), ha estado comandado, desde 2004, por un Consejo Nacional Electoral totalmente dependiente del Poder Ejecutivo, sin autonomía, completamente partidizado, integrado en su mayoría por miembros del partido oficial y controlado por el mismo, totalmente parcializado a favor de éste último, y en cuya gestión se niega toda forma de participación ciudadana, salvo la que deriva de las cargas ciudadanas para el cumplimiento temporal de funciones electorales. Ese órgano no ha podido, por tanto, garantizar ni la igualdad, ni la imparcialidad, ni la transparencia, ni la eficiencia de los procesos electorales que exige la Constitución (art. 293), particularmente desde cuándo a partir de 2004 fue doblemente secuestrado por la Sala Constitucional del Tribunal Supremo de Justicia, y puesto al servicio de los intereses electorales del partido oficial.[1198]

El resultado de todo ello ha sido que lejos de ser el régimen político venezolano el de una democracia, donde la conjunción de intereses y posiciones contrapuestas es indispensable para poder gobernar, mediante el diálogo, acuerdos y compromisos; se trata, de hecho, de un régimen de partido único que controla todos los poderes, y que incluso no reconoce a la oposición; lo que se ha manifestado en más de una ocasión, con los anuncios públicos y sucesivos de que la mayoría oficialista en la Asamblea Nacional de no dialogarán siquiera con la oposición. Ello ocurrió, por ejemplo, en 2010, cuando la mayoría oficialista perdió la mayoría calificada que

---

dinadores), *Reforma Política y Electoral en América Latina 1978-2007,* Universidad Nacional Autónoma de México-IDEA internacional, México 2008, pp. 953-1019.

1197   Véase Allan R. Brewer-Carías, "Reforma electoral en el sistema político de Venezuela", en Daniel Zovatto y J. Jesús Orozco Henríquez (Coordinadores), *Reforma Política y Electoral en América Latina 1978-2007,* Universidad Nacional Autónoma de México-IDEA internacional, México 2008, pp. 953-1019.

1198   Véase Allan R. Brewer-Carías, "El Poder Electoral y la confiscación del derecho a la participación política mediante el referendo revocatorio presidencial: Venezuela 2000-2004", en Juan Pérez Royo, Joaquín Pablo Urías Martínez, Manuel Carrasco Durán, Editores), *Derecho Constitucional para el Siglo XXI. Actas del Congreso Iberoamericano de Derecho Constitucional,* Tomo I, Thomson-Aranzadi, Madrid 2006, pp. 1081-1126; y "La autonomía e independencia del Poder Electoral y de la Jurisdicción Electoral en Venezuela, y su secuestro y sometimiento por la jurisdicción Constitucional," Documento preparado para el *III Congreso Iberoamericano de Derecho Electoral,* Facultad de Estudios Superiores de Aragón de la Universidad Nacional Autónoma de México, Estado de México, 27-29 Septiembre de 2012

tenía en la Asamblea Nacional, y ha ocurrido de nuevo recientemente.[1199] Este desconocimiento de la oposición ha conducido, de hecho, a que el sistema político sea en la práctica uno de partido único, al punto de que el nombramiento de los altos funcionarios del Estado que desde hace años tienen sus períodos vencidos, como el Contralor General de la República y los miembros del Consejo Nacional Electoral, no puede tener lugar porque el partido de gobierno se niega a entrar siquiera en conversaciones con los diputados representantes de la oposición, sin cuyos votos no pueden efectuarse tales nombramientos.

II LAS FALLAS DE LA DEMOCRÁTICA PARTICIPATIVA

Pero además, en la situación actual, en Venezuela tampoco hay un sistema real y efectivo de democracia participativa, y aún menos "protagónica." En la actualidad, en realidad, la participación del pueblo en política, como en la más típica de las democracias formales, se ha reducido a la participación mediante voto en las elecciones; y ello, primero, porque los mecanismos de democracia directa, como las asambleas de ciudadanos han sido secuestrados por el Poder Ejecutivo nacional y el partido de gobierno, habiendo sido convertidas en instrumentos de políticas populistas como parte de la estructura del denominado Estado Comunal o del Poder Popular, creado en 2010 mediante leyes orgánicas, al margen de la Constitución y en paralelo al Estado Constitucional;[1200] segundo, porque los mecanismos de democracia semidirecta, como los referendos, se han hecho de imposible ejercicio por las condiciones y requisitos legales impuestos para que puedan convocarse por iniciativa popular como lo exige la Constitución;[1201] y tercero, porque los mecanismos de participación ciudadana directamente previstos en la Constitución han sido arrebatados al pueblo, al distorsionarse en la legislación la integración de los Comités de Postulaciones Judiciales, Electorales y del Poder Ciudadano, donde debía haber representantes de los diversos sectores de la sociedad, pero que quedaron bajo el control político de la mayoría oficialista de la Asamblea Nacional sin que el ciudadano y sus organizaciones pueda participar;[1202] y al haberse además vaciado, por la Sala Constitucional, la

---

1199　Véase por ejemplo lo declarado por el Presidente de la Asamblea Nacional en *El Universal*, Caracas 17 de julio de 2014, en http://www.eluniversal.com/nacional-y-politica/140717/cabello-descarta-cualquier-reunion-con-partidos-de-la-oposicion.

1200　Véase las Leyes Orgánicas del Poder Popular en *Gaceta Oficial* Nº 6011 de 21 de diciembre de 2010. Véanse los comentarios en Allan R. Brewer-Carías et al., *Leyes Orgánicas del Poder Popular (Los Consejos Comunales, las Comunas, la Sociedad socialista y el Sistema Económico Comunal)*, Editorial Jurídica Venezolana, Caracas 2011.

1201　Véase Allan R. Brewer-Carías, *La Sala Constitucional versus el Estado democrático de derecho. El secuestro del Poder Electoral y de la Sala Electoral del Tribunal Supremo y la confiscación del derecho a la participación política*, Los Libros de El Nacional, Colección Ares, Caracas 2004; "El secuestro del Poder Electoral y la confiscación del derecho a la participación política mediante el referendo revocatorio presidencial: Venezuela 2000-2004," en *Boletín Mexicano de Derecho Comparado*, Instituto de Investigaciones Jurídicas, Universidad Nacional Autónoma de México, Nº 112. México, enero-abril 2005 pp. 11-73.

1202　Véase Allan R. Brewer-Carías, "La participación ciudadana en la designación de los titulares de los órganos no electos de los Poderes Públicos en Venezuela y sus vicisitudes políticas", en *Revista Iberoamericana de Derecho Público y Administrativo*, Año 5, Nº 5-2005, San José, Costa Rica 2005, pp. 76-95; y "Sobre el nombramiento irregular por la Asamblea Nacional de los titulares de los órga-

norma constitucional que prevé la consulta popular necesaria e indispensable antes de la sanción de las leyes, al haber dispuesto, en fraude a la Constitución, que ello no se aplica a la legislación delegada, dictada mediante decretos leyes, que en definitiva en los últimos quince años se ha convertido en la forma normal de legislación en el país.[1203]

Pero la ausencia de participación política también queda evidenciada en la forma cómo se ha estructurado el antes mencionado Estado del Poder Popular o Estado Comunal, sobre la base de Consejos Comunales comandados por denominados "voceros" que no son electos, sino impuestos en asambleas de ciudadanos por el partido de gobierno que las controla, y sin cuyo manejo ni siquiera pueden obtener reconocimiento por el Ministerio de la Participación.[1204]

En realidad, la "democracia participativa" que se ha vendido supuestamente consolidando a través de la creación de estas organizaciones del llamado "Poder Popular," no es más que una falacia de participación,[1205] pues se trata de instituciones propias del populismo de Estado, que maneja el Poder Central, para repartir recursos fuera de los canales regulares del Estado y particularmente fuera de los gobiernos locales, vaciando en paralelo a los Municipios de competencias, pero dependiendo totalmente, incluso en su propia existencia, de una decisión del Ejecutivo Nacional. En esos Consejos, en realidad, el único que "participa" es el partido de gobierno y los derivados de su clientelismo, y si alguna participación se le da a la población local en el proceso de inversión de los recursos repartidos, por supuesto es sólo parcial, solo para los sectores que se identifican con el socialismo como doctrina oficial. De resto, lo que hay es exclusión y marginamiento.

Ese proceso de creación de un Estado Comunal o del Poder Popular, por otra parte, contradice la esencia del Estado democrático, que es la descentralización política, así sea en la forma precaria cómo se estableció en el marco de la Federación Centralizada que reguló la Constitución de 1999.

En efecto, uno de los grandes cambios políticos que debió consolidar la Constitución de 1999, tenía que haber sido la transformación definitiva de la "Federación

---

nos del poder ciudadano en 2007", en *Revista de Derecho Público*, N° 113, Editorial Jurídica Venezolana, Caracas 2008, pp. 85-88.

1203   Véase Allan R. Brewer-Carías, "Apreciación general sobre los vicios de inconstitucionalidad que afectan los Decretos Leyes Habilitados" en *Ley Habilitante del 13-11-2000 y sus Decretos Leyes*, Academia de Ciencias Políticas y Sociales, Serie Eventos N° 17, Caracas 2002, pp. 63-103; y "El derecho ciudadano a la participación popular y la inconstitucionalidad generalizada de los decretos leyes 2010-2012, por su carácter inconsulto," en *Revista de Derecho Público*, No. 130, (abril-junio 2012), Editorial Jurídica Venezolana, Caracas 2012, pp. 85-88.

1204   Véase Allan R. Brewer-Carías, *Ley Orgánica de Consejos Comunales*, Colección Textos Legislativos, N° 46, Editorial Jurídica Venezolana, Caracas 2010.

1205   Véase Allan R. Brewer-Carías, "La necesaria revalorización de la democracia representativa ante los peligros del discurso autoritario sobre una supuesta "democracia participativa" sin representación," en *Derecho Electoral de Latinoamérica. Memoria del II Congreso Iberoamericano de Derecho*, Bogotá, 31 agosto-1 septiembre 2011, Consejo Superior de la Judicatura, ISBN 978-958-8331-93-5, Bogotá 2013, pp. 425-449. Véase además, el texto de la Ponencia: "La democracia representativa y la falacia de la llamada "democracia participativa," *Congreso Iberoamericano de Derecho Electoral*, Universidad de Nuevo León, Monterrey, 27 de noviembre 2010.

Centralizada" que existió en Venezuela durante todo el siglo XX, por una efectiva "Federación Descentralizada," montada en un real sistema de distribución territorial del poder entre los tres niveles de gobierno: nacional, estadal y municipal. En tal sentido es que debió apuntar la reforma constitucional, y que no se hizo, quedando el tema en sólo un enunciado nominal al definirse al Estado en la Constitución, como un "Estado Federal Descentralizado" (art. 4) que no lo es, pues está concebido en un marco centralista, en ausencia de una efectiva descentralización política de la Federación.

Es decir, la normativa sancionada en 1999 no significó ni siquiera avance sustancial alguno respecto del proceso de descentralización que se había venido desarrollando durante la última década del siglo pasado en el país, al amparo de la Constitución de 1961 y de las previsiones de la Ley Orgánica de Descentralización, Delimitación y Transferencia de competencias del Poder Público de 1989[1206]; y más bien, en muchos aspectos, lo que significó fue un retroceso institucional,[1207] que se ha consolidado con la práctica legislativa y gubernamental de los últimos quince años.

Retroceso que por ejemplo quedó plasmado al lesionar incluso la igualdad de los Estados, al eliminarse el Senado y preverse una Asamblea Nacional uninominal (art. 186) y, con ello, impedirse la posibilidad de la participación política igualitaria de los Estados en la conducción de las políticas nacionales. Se rompió, así, con una tradición que se remonta a 1811, estableciendo una institución legislativa contradictoria con la forma federal del Estado, y un caso único de Estado federal con territorio extenso.

III LA CONCEPCIÓN CENTRALISTA DE LA "FEDERACIÓN DESCENTRALIZADA"

Para facilitar el retroceso en materia de descentralización política, la Constitución comenzó por establecer un régimen "centralista" del Estado, aun cuando calificándolo contradictoriamente como "descentralizado," siendo esa contradicción el signo más característico de la Constitución al regular el régimen de las entidades territoriales,[1208] pues en paralelo a regular la autonomía política, normativa y admi-

---

1206   Véase, en general, Allan R. Brewer-Carías, *Informe sobre la Descentralización en Venezuela 1993*, Memoria del Ministro de Estado para la Descentralización, Caracas 1993.

1207   Véase Allan R. Brewer-Carías, "Reflexiones Críticas sobre la Constitución de Venezuela de 1999" en el libro de la Academia de Ciencias Políticas y Sociales, *La Constitución de 1999*, Caracas 2000, págs. 63 a 88.

1208   Ello lo advertimos apenas se sancionó la Constitución en Allan R. Brewer-Carías, *Federalismo y municipalismo en la Constitución de 1999 (Alcance de una reforma insuficiente y regresiva)*, Cuadernos de la Cátedra Allan R. Brewer-Carías de Derecho Público, N° 7, Universidad Católica del Táchira, Editorial Jurídica Venezolana, Caracas-San Cristóbal 2001; y "El Estado federal descentralizado y la centralización de la federación en Venezuela. Situación y perspectiva de una contradicción constitucional" en *Federalismo y regionalismo*, Coordinadores Diego Valadés y José María Serna de la Garza, Universidad Nacional Autónoma de México, Tribunal Superior de Justicia del Estado de Puebla, Instituto de Investigaciones Jurídicas, Serie Doctrina Jurídica N° 229, México 2005, pp. 717-750.

nistrativa de los Estados y Municipios, el texto la niega al remitir a la Ley para su regulación, con lo que la garantía constitucional de la misma desapareció.

En efecto, la autonomía de los entes territoriales, es decir, de los Estados y de los Municipios, ante todo, como sucede en toda federación o Estado descentralizado, exigía la previsión de su garantía constitucional, en el sentido de que los límites a la misma sólo podían estar en la propia Constitución, y no podía ser remitida su regulación por ley nacional posterior. La Constitución de 1999, sin embargo, al regular el funcionamiento y la organización de los Consejos Legislativos Estadales remitió su regulación a la ley nacional (art. 162), que se dictó en 2001, como Ley Orgánica de los Consejos Legislativos de los Estados,[1209] lo cual, además de contradictorio con la atribución a los mismos de dictarse su propia Constitución para organizar sus poderes públicos (art. 164.1), se configuró como una intromisión inaceptable del Poder Nacional en el régimen de los Estados.

En cuanto a los Municipios, la autonomía municipal tradicionalmente garantizada en la propia Constitución, también se interfirió en la Constitución, al señalarse que los Municipios gozan de la misma, no sólo "dentro de los límites" establecidos en la Constitución, sino de los establecidos en la ley nacional (art. 168), con lo cual el principio descentralizador básico, que es la autonomía, quedó minimizado.

IV. EL DESBALANCE HACIA EL NIVEL NACIONAL EN LA DISTRIBUCIÓN TERRITORIAL DEL PODER

En cuanto a la distribución de competencias del Poder Público entre los entes político territoriales, que es lo que origina la descentralización política, el texto constitucional está concebido también bajo un signo centralista, de manera que casi todas las competencias quedaron en el Poder Nacional. Los Estados, en la Constitución materialmente carecen de materias sobre las cuales actuar como competencia exclusiva de los mismos, a pesar de que el artículo 164 hable, precisamente, de "competencias exclusivas."[1210] Las pocas indicadas en dicha norma, en realidad, son en su mayoría materias de competencia parcial de los Estados, en algunos casos concurrentes con el Poder Nacional o con el Poder Municipal, y en cuanto a las competencias que se habían descentralizado y convertido en "exclusiva" de los Estados, como la de la administración y manejo de los aeropuertos y puertos nacionales ubicados en cada Estado, como se dijo, fue centralizada o nacionalizada por la Sala Constitucional del Tribunal Supremo de Justicia en 2008, mutándose a tal efecto la Constitución.[1211]

1209   *Gaceta Oficial* N° 37.282 del 13 de septiembre de 2001.

1210   Véase Allan R. Brewer-Carías, "La distribución territorial de competencias en la Federación venezolana" en *Revista de Estudios de Administración Local. Homenaje a Sebastián Martín Retortillo*, N° 291, enero-abril 2003, Instituto Nacional de Administración Pública, Madrid 2003, pp. 163-200.

1211   Véase sentencia de la Sala Constitucional, N° 565 de 15 de abril de 2008 (*caso Procuradora General de la República, recurso de interpretación del artículo 164.10 de la Constitución de 1999*) en http://www.tsj.gov.ve/decisiones/scon/Abril/565-150408-07-1108.htm . Véase los comentarios sobre esta sentencia, en Allan R. Brewer-Carías, "La Sala Constitucional como poder constituyente: la modificación de la forma federal del estado y del sistema constitucional de división territorial del poder público, en *Revista de Derecho Público*, N° 114, (abril-junio 2008), Editorial Jurídica Venezolana, Caracas 2008, pp. 247-262.

En materia de competencias concurrentes, que los Estados hubieran podido haber asumido mediante ley estadal, las mismas, en la Constitución, quedaron sujetas a lo dispuesto en unas leyes nacionales denominadas "de base," con lo que pueden quedar condicionadas (art. 165), quedando en todo caso sujetas a lo dispuesto en la ley nacional. Y si bien en la Constitución se estableció la garantía de participación previa de los Estados en el proceso de elaboración de leyes nacionales que los puedan afectar (art. 206), que podía permitir a los Estados expresar su opinión sobre leyes que los afecten, ello nunca se ha garantizado en la práctica legislativa.

Y así las leyes nacionales dictadas en relación con materias de competencias concurrentes, en todo caso, lo que han producido es más bien una acentuada centralización, casi total, de las mismas, como ha ocurrido en materia de policía, respecto de la cual, los Estados y Municipios han sido vaciados casi completamente.[1212]

Por otra parte, en cuanto a la distribución de competencias entre los entes territoriales, el proceso de descentralización exigía, además, la asignación efectiva de competencias tributarias a los Estados, sobre todo en materia de impuestos al consumo, como sucede en casi todas las Federaciones. Los avances que se discutieron incluso en la Asamblea Constituyente en esta materia, sin embargo, se abandonaron, quitándosele a los Estados todas las competencias tributarias que se le habían asignado, con lo que incluso se retrocedió aún más respecto del esquema que existía en la Constitución de 1961.

Por tanto, en realidad, la Constitución de 1999 terminó de vaciar totalmente a los Estados de competencias tributarias, estableciéndose incluso en la Constitución una competencia residual, no a favor de los Estados como ocurre en las federaciones, sino en forma contraria al principio federal, a favor del Poder Nacional, en materia de impuestos, tasas y rentas no atribuidas a los Estados y Municipios por la Constitución o por la ley (art. 156,12). En consecuencia, a los Estados sólo les quedaron las competencias en materia de papel sellado, timbres y estampillas como se había establecido en la Ley Orgánica de Descentralización, Delimitación y Transferencia de Competencias del Poder Público de 1989,[1213] y nada más, pues incluso las materias que se les había transferido como las relativas a la atención de la salud, han sido progresivamente centralizadas.[1214]

1212   Lo que comenzó a realizarse con la Ley de Coordinación de Seguridad Ciudadana, en *Gaceta Oficial* N° 37.318 del 6 de noviembre de 2001. Véase además, la Ley Orgánica del Servicio de Policía y del Cuerpo de Policía Nacional, y la Ley Orgánica de la Función Policial en *Gaceta Oficial* N° 5940 de 7 de diciembre de 2009.

1213   Véase Allan R. Brewer-Carías, "Bases legislativas para la descentralización política de la federación centralizada (1990: El inicio de una reforma", en Allan R. Brewer-Carías (Coordinador y editor), Carlos Ayala Corao, Jorge Sánchez Meleán, Gustavo Linares y Humberto Romero Muci, *Leyes para la Descentralización Política de la Federación,* Colección Textos Legislativos, N° 11, Editorial Jurídica Venezolana, Caracas 1990, pp. 7-53; y "La descentralización política en Venezuela: 1990. El inicio de una reforma" en Dieter Nohlen (editor), *Descentralización Política y Consolidación Democrática Europa-América del Sur,* Madrid-Caracas 1991, pp. 131-160.

1214   Véase por ejemplo el Decreto N° 6.543, "mediante el cual se decreta la transferencia al Ministerio del Poder Popular para la Salud, de los Establecimientos y las Unidades Móviles de Atención Médica adscrito a la Gobernación del estado Bolivariano de Miranda," en *Gaceta Oficial* N° 39.072 de 3-12-2008.

La consecuencia de todo ese proceso de centralización es que los Estados han seguido siendo totalmente dependientes de los aportes provenientes del Presupuesto Nacional (Situado Constitucional), habiéndose atribuido la coordinación de la inversión de sus ingresos a un Consejo Federal de Gobierno (art. 185), que conforme a la Ley que lo reguló, lo que ha hecho es reforzar el control de los mismos por parte de los órganos nacionales. En efecto, en dicha la Ley Orgánica que regula el Consejo Federal de Gobierno de 2010,[1215] además de preverse su organización y funcionamiento, se establecen "los lineamientos de la planificación y coordinación de las políticas y acciones necesarias para el adecuado desarrollo regional," e igualmente, "el régimen para la transferencia de las competencias entre los entes territoriales, y a las organizaciones detentadoras de la soberanía originaria del Estado" (art. 1). En este último caso, además, haciendo referencia, sin duda, a los órganos del llamado Poder Popular o Estado Comunal, lo que significa que además del centralismo por asunción de poderes de intervención por parte del Poder Central, se ha previsto otro mecanismo de centralización pero por "vaciamiento" de competencias hacia las entidades del llamado Poder Popular que están controlados precisamente por el Poder Nacional.

Conforme a dicha Ley Orgánica, en efecto, dicho Consejo Federal es el órgano encargado de la planificación y coordinación de las políticas y acciones para el desarrollo del proceso de descentralización y transferencia de competencias del Poder Nacional a los Estados y Municipios, teniendo los lineamientos que dicte en materia de transferencia de competencias, carácter "vinculantes para las entidades territoriales" (art. 2). La Ley Orgánica estableció, además, que dicha transferencia de competencias "es la vía para lograr el fortalecimiento de las organizaciones de base del Poder Popular y el desarrollo armónico de los Distritos Motores de Desarrollo y regiones del país," (art. 7), órganos todos que por lo demás, como se ha dicho, son dependientes del Ejecutivo Nacional.

V. EL MUNICIPIO QUE NO SE QUISO REGULAR EFECTIVAMENTE COMO LA UNIDAD PRIMARIA EN LA ORGANIZACIÓN NACIONAL

Por otra parte, en la Constitución de 1999, siguiendo la tradición formal anterior, se reguló al Municipio como la unidad política primaria de la organización nacional, gozando de personalidad jurídica y de gobierno democrático y, más importante, de autonomía (art. 169). Sin embargo, particularmente en cuanto a ésta última, como se dijo, se la previó en la Constitución no sólo dentro de los límites establecidos en la misma, como antes se disponía, y que era su garantía constitucional, sino también dentro de los límites establecidos por "la ley," con lo que se abrió el camino definitivo para la propia destrucción del régimen municipal. Para ello, la Sala Constitucional "interpretó" que la "libre gestión de las materias de su competencia" que garantiza la Constitución a los Municipios conforme a dicha autonomía, no es más que "una *libertad condicionada*, no sólo por las limitaciones que directamente impone el Constituyente sino por todas aquellas que pueda imponer el Legislador Nacional, y

---

1215   Véase en *Gaceta Oficial* N° 5.963 Extra. de 22-2-2010.

los legisladores estadales al ejercicio de la autonomía municipal, de acuerdo con las normas de la propia Constitución y dentro de los límites por ella indicados"[1216].

Ello, precisamente, es lo que ha permitido que se haya venido implementando mediante ley, en paralelo al régimen municipal, para destruirlo, el denominado Poder Popular, con el que se dio inicio más bien al proceso de desmunicipalización del país. [1217]

En efecto, para que el Municipio pudiera haber llegado a ser la unidad política primaria en la organización nacional, debió haberse regulado en la Constitución en una forma que estuviese bien descentralizado en el sentido de bien cerca del ciudadano, lo que debió haber implicado la efectiva municipalización del territorio, ubicando Municipios allí donde hubiera una comunidad con vínculos permanentes de vecindad. Pero lamentablemente ello no se logró prever en la Constitución, y el Municipio, tal como se lo había regulado en la ley nacional, se lo concibió bien lejos de los ciudadanos. Ello además, lo avaló la Sala Constitucional del Tribunal Supremo al interpretar que para que pueda existir un Municipio, conforme a los artículos 164 y 165 de la Constitución, el mismo debía poseer "como elementos esenciales de su existencia, los siguientes: un territorio claramente delimitado, una cantidad poblacional que amerite su existencia, un centro de población que funja de asiento permanente del gobierno local, un gobierno elegido democráticamente y una capacidad racional para autosatisfacer las necesidades del colectivo que se desarrolla bajo su jurisdicción, es decir, en términos de finanzas públicas, suficiencia presupuestaria (una relación coherente entre los ingresos y gastos que fomente el desarrollo de la entidad, atendiendo a sus propias necesidades)"[1218].

Con esos "elementos esenciales" por supuesto, el Municipio perdió todo su carácter de unidad política primaria, quedando al contrario como una entidad territoriales ubicada territorialmente bien lejos de los ciudadanos y sus comunidades, lo que se evidencia de sólo tener en cuenta que en un territorio de casi un millón de kilómetros cuadrados, en Venezuela solo haya 338 Municipios, con promedio de casi 100.000 habitantes por autoridad local.

Y la lejanía respecto del ciudadano, que ha impedido la efectiva municipalización del territorio que debió haber conducido a multiplicar todos los centros urbanos con entidades locales con gobiernos propios electos democráticamente por vía del sufragio; lo que ha provocado, al contrario, es la desmunicipalización del territorio, lo que se ha consolidado con la creación de las Comunas y los Consejos Comunales, como integrantes del Estado Comunal que se ha venido implementando al margen de la Constitución y en fraude a la voluntad popular que lo rechazó en 2007. Con todo ello, lo que se ha buscado, como lo advirtió José Luis Villegas, ha sido "con-

---

1216 Véase sentencia N° 2257 de 13 de noviembre de 2001, en *Revista de Derecho Público*, N° 85-88, Editorial Jurídica Venezolana, Caracas, 2001, pp. 202 y ss.

1217 Véase nuestras propuestas para la reforma hacia un Nuevo Municipalismo en Allan R. Brewer-Carías, *Debate Constituyente*, Tomo I, Fundación de Derecho Público, Editorial Jurídica Venezolana, Caracas 1999, pp. 164 a 169; y los comentarios críticos al proyecto constitucional en Tomo II, *op. cit.*, pp. 230 ss.

1218 Véase sentencia N° 618 de 2 de mayo de 2001 (Caso: *Municipio Simón Bolívar, Estado Zulia*), en *Revista de Derecho Público*, N° 85-88, Editorial Jurídica Venezolana, Caracas, 2001, pp. 199 ss.

centrar el poder, destruyendo el federalismo, la descentralización y el municipio, e imponer un nebuloso Estado comunal como expresión de tránsito hacia el socialismo."[1219]

Y además, ello, mediante entidades que no son democrático-represen-tativas, sino integradas con "voceros" nombrados a mano alzada, y dependientes del Ejecutivo Nacional a través del partido oficial, mediante los cuales no sólo se ha buscado despojar a los Municipios de su carácter de unidad política primaria en la organización nacional, sino que se han regulado para vaciarlos de competencias mediante su transferencia a los mismos.[1220]

Para lograrlo, además, en lugar de haberse multiplicado las Juntas Parroquiales representativas previstas en la Constitución que era lo que correspondía, con miembros electos mediante sufragio; al contrario, en la reforma de la Ley Orgánica del Poder Público Municipal de 2010,[1221] las mismas fueron inconstitucionalmente eliminadas como entidades locales representativas de gobierno democráticamente electos, pasando a ser entes "consultivos" de los referidos Consejos Comunales a los cuales se asignó el carácter de representantes de las Comunas como entidades locales (art. 19), totalmente desligadas de los Municipios y sin que sus miembros sean electos mediante sufragio.

VI. LAS COMUNAS VERSUS LOS MUNICIPIOS

Las Comunas, que no existen en la Constitución, en efecto, y a pesar de que su creación fue una propuesta de la rechazada reforma constitucional de 2007, fueron creadas en fraude a la voluntad popular, y reguladas en la Ley Orgánica de las Comunas de 2010. Las mismas fueron además concebidas en la Ley Orgánica del Poder Popular, para suplantar al Municipio constitucional, como la "célula fundamental" del Estado Comunal.[1222]

Para ese efecto, a la Comuna se la definió en el artículo 15.2 de esta Ley Orgánica del Poder Popular, como el "espacio socialista que como entidad local es definida

---

1219   Véase lo expresado por José Luis Villegas M., "Hacia la instauración del Estado Comunal en Venezuela: Comentario al Decreto Ley Orgánica de la Gestión Comunitaria de Competencia, Servicios y otras Atribuciones, en el contexto del Primer Plan Socialista-Proyecto Nacional Simón Bolívar 2007-2013," en *Revista de Derecho Público*, N° 130, Editorial Jurídica Venezolana, Caracas 2012, pp. 127 ss.

1220   Véase *Ley Orgánica de los Consejos Comunales*, Editorial Jurídica Venezolana, Caracas 2010; y Armando Rodríguez García, "Participación ciudadana, institucionalidad local y consejos comunales en Venezuela," en *Revista de la Facultad de Ciencias Jurídicas y Políticas de la Universidad Central de Venezuela*, N° 129, Universidad Central de Venezuela, Caracas, 2007, pp. 125-164.

1221   Véase en *Gaceta Oficial* N° 6.015 Extraordinario del 28 de diciembre de 2010.

1222   Véase en *Gaceta Oficial* N° 6.011 Extra. de 21-12-2010. Véase sobre esta Ley el libro de Allan R. Brewer-Carías (Coordinador), Claudia Nikken, Luis A. Herrera Orellana, Jesús María Alvarado Andrade, José Ignacio Hernández y Adriana Vigilanza, *Leyes Orgánicas sobre el Poder Popular y el Estado Comunal (Los Consejos Comunales, las Comunas, la Sociedad Socialista y el Sistema Económico Comunal)*, Colección Textos Legislativos N° 50, Editorial Jurídica Venezolana, Caracas 2011. Véase además, Allan R. Brewer-Carías, "La Ley Orgánica del Poder Popular y la desconstitucionalización del Estado de derecho en Venezuela," en *Revista de Derecho Público*, N° 124, (octubre-diciembre 2010), Editorial Jurídica Venezolana, Caracas 2010, pp. 81-101.

por la integración de comunidades vecinas con una memoria histórica compartida, rasgos culturales, usos y costumbres que se reconocen en el territorio que ocupan y en las actividades productivas que le sirven de sustento y sobre el cual ejercen los principios de soberanía y participación protagónica como expresión del Poder Popular, en concordancia con un régimen de producción social y el modelo de desarrollo endógeno y sustentable contemplado en el Plan de Desarrollo, Económico y Social de la Nación." Esta misma definición de la Comuna como "espacio socialista," está también en el artículo 5 de la Ley Orgánica de las Comunas; noción que implica que la misma está vedada a todo aquél que no sea socialista o que no crea en el socialismo, o que no comulgue con el socialismo como doctrina política. La concepción legal de la Comuna, por tanto, es contraria al pluralismo democrático que garantiza la Constitución (art. 6), siendo abiertamente discriminatoria y contraria a la igualdad que también garantiza el artículo 21 de la Constitución.

Pero para consolidar la institución, aún en forma contraria al pluralismo, en la Ley Orgánica del Poder Popular se define a la Comuna como una "entidad local," y la misma calificación se encuentra en el artículo 1 de la Ley Orgánica de las Comunas, que la define "como entidad local donde los ciudadanos y ciudadanas en el ejercicio del Poder Popular, ejercen el pleno derecho de la soberanía y desarrollan la participación protagónica mediante formas de autogobierno para la edificación del estado comunal, en el marco del Estado democrático y social de derecho y de justicia" (art. 1). También en la reforma de la Ley Orgánica del Poder Público Municipal de diciembre de 2010, se incluyó a las comunas en el listado de las "entidades locales territoriales" (art. 19) disponiéndose que las mismas, al estar reguladas por una legislación diferente como es la relativa al Poder Popular, y al poder constituirse "entre varios municipios," quedan exceptuadas de las disposiciones de la Ley Orgánica del Poder Público Municipal.

Ahora bien, en cuanto a calificar a las Comunas como "entidades locales," el Legislador olvidó que conforme a la Constitución (arts. 169, 173), esta expresión de "entidad local" sólo se puede aplicar a las "entidades políticas" del Estado en las cuales necesariamente tiene que haber gobiernos integrados por representantes electos mediante sufragio universal, directo y secreto (arts. 63, 169), ceñidos a los principios establecidos en el artículo 6 de la Constitución, es decir, que ser "siempre democrático, participativo, electivo, descentralizado, alternativo, responsable, pluralista y de mandatos revocables."

Conforme a la Constitución, por tanto, no puede haber "entidades locales" con gobiernos que no sean democráticos representativos en los términos mencionados, y menos "gobernadas" por "voceros" designados por otros órganos públicos. Y esto es precisamente lo que ocurre con los llamados "gobiernos de las comunas," que conforme a esta legislación sobre el Poder Popular y sus organizaciones, no se garantiza su origen democrático mediante elección por sufragio universal, directo y secreto, siendo en consecuencia inconstitucional su concepción. Por ello, con razón, Silva Michelena se ha referido al Estado Comunal como un "Estado de siervos," indicando que:

"El establecimiento de las comunas es la demolición de la República porque la República está asentada sobre el municipio que es su célula primaria. Las gobernaciones, consejos municipales, asambleas legislativas, alcaldes son la base de una República democrática. En esta estructura el voto es universal, directo y secreto. En las leyes aprobadas para las comunas se deja ese tema abierto sin mayor precisión, solo se menciona que habrá una elección popular, pero es a mano alzada, consulté con constitucionalistas y personas que han estado en consejos comunales en varios estados del país y es así. Después no hay más elecciones, la votación es de segundo o tercer grado.

Este es un sistema que sirve para que el chavismo continúe en el poder, la idea es que los voceros elegidos a mano alzada sean representantes del partido."[1223]

VII.   EL AHOGAMIENTO DE LA INSTITUCIÓN MUNICIPAL

En este esquema de establecimiento del Poder Popular y el Estado Comunal, a los efectos de ahogar y estrangular progresivamente el Estado Constitucional, la primera de las instituciones territoriales afectadas, por supuesto, ha sido el Municipio, el cual, siendo la unidad política primaria dentro la organización de la República, ha quedado desvinculado totalmente del proceso de desarrollo comunal y de la llamada participación popular. A tal efecto, entre las diversas reformas se introdujeron en diciembre de 2010 a la Ley Orgánica del Poder Público Municipal (LOPP),[1224] se destacan las siguientes:

En primer lugar, la previsión, como objetivo de la Ley, además de la regulación de los Municipios y su gobierno, del proceso denominado de comunas en su condición especial de entidad local, como a otras organizaciones del Poder Popular" (Art. 1). Se entiende que se trata de un proceso de transferencia de "competencias," aun cuando la misma no puede calificarse como "descentralización," pues ésta, en el marco territorial y político, exige que las entidades receptoras de las competencias a ser transferidas, sean entidades locales como entidades políticas con gobiernos electos democráticamente. No puede haber conceptualmente descentralización política mediante transferencia de competencias a órganos dependientes del Poder Central; y las Comunas, las cuales se denominan como "entidades locales especiales," no son gobernadas por órganos cuyos integrantes sean electos por votación universal directa y secreta, y por tanto, no tienen autonomía política ni pueden formar parte del esquema de descentralización territorial del Estado, sino que son conducidas por "voceros" designados a mano alzada por asambleas controladas por el partido oficial, sujetas al gobierno nacional.

En segundo lugar, el artículo 2 de la Ley Orgánica del Poder Municipal, a pesar de que repite el principio constitucional de que el Municipio "constituye la unidad política primaria de la organización nacional de la República," ya no habla de que "gozan de autonomía" como lo garantiza el artículo 168 de la Constitución, sino de que "ejerce sus competencias de manera autónoma." Ello, sin embargo, es contradicho con lo que la propia Ley establece en el sentido de que "el municipio se regirá por el Sistema Nacional de Planificación establecido en la ley que regula la mate-

---

1223   Véase en Víctor Salmerón, "La comuna es una sociedad de súbditos," Entrevista a Héctor Silva Michelena, en *Prodavinci*, 25 de septiembre de 2014, en http://prodavinci.com/2014/09/25/actualidad/la-comuna-es-una-sociedad-de-subditos-entrevista-a-hector-silva-michelena-por-victor-salmeron/1nm. Véase además, Héctor Silva Michelena, *Estado de Siervos. Desnudando al Estado Comunal*, bid & co., Caracas 2014.

1224   Véase en *Gaceta Oficial* N° 6.015 Extraordinario del 28 de diciembre de 2010.

ria," (art. 110) que como se sabe, es una planificación centralizada regulada en la Ley que creó la Comisión Central de Planificación,[1225] y desarrollada en la Ley Orgánica de Planificación Pública y Popular de 2010, reformada en 2014.[1226]

A tal efecto, en la Ley Orgánica del Poder Público Municipal, además, se eliminó la iniciativa ejecutiva de la planificación local que se asignaba al Alcalde, quien debía presentar al Consejo Local de Planificación las líneas maestras de su plan de gobierno, y se establece, en cambio, que el Consejo Local de Planificación Pública es "el órgano encargado de diseñar el Plan Municipal de Desarrollo y los demás planes municipales, en concordancia con los lineamientos que establezca el Plan de Desarrollo Económico y Social de la Nación y los demás planes nacionales y estadales, garantizando la participación protagónica del pueblo en su formulación, ejecución, seguimiento, evaluación y control, en articulación con el Sistema Nacional de Planificación" (art. 111).

Ese Consejo, además, en la Ley Orgánica, quedó encargado de "diseñar el Plan de Desarrollo Comunal, en concordancia con los planes de desarrollo comunitario propuestos por los Consejos Comunales y los demás planes de interés colectivo, articulados con el Sistema Nacional de Planificación, de conformidad con lo establecido en la legislaciones que regula a las Comunas y los Consejos Comunales;" contando para ello con el apoyo de los órganos y entes de la Administración Pública. A tales efectos, agrega la norma, "es deber de las instancias que conforman la organización del municipio, atender los requerimientos de los diversos consejos de planificación existentes en cada una de las comunas para el logro de sus objetivos y metas" (art. 112)

En tercer lugar, en la reforma de la Ley Orgánica del Poder Púbico Municipal se encasilló y limitó el rol del Municipio como promotor de la participación del pueblo sólo "a través de las comunidades organizadas," que son las que se regulan en las Leyes Orgánicas del Poder Popular identificadas con el socialismo, en contra de la previsión del artículo 62 de la Constitución que garantiza el carácter libre de la participación. La desvinculación de las comunidades organizadas respecto del Municipio, se aseguró además, en la propia Ley, al excluirse su registro ante los órganos competentes "del Municipio" como decía la Ley Orgánica anterior que se reformó, previéndose ahora su registro sólo ante "los órganos competentes" (art. 33.3) que en las Leyes Orgánica del Poder Popular es uno de los Ministerios del Ejecutivo Nacional, el Ministerio del Poder Popular para las Comunas y Movimientos Sociales.

Es decir, con la reforma de la Ley Orgánica del Poder Municipal se produjo la total desmunicipalización de las entidades locales, y su total control por el Poder central. Se recuerda, además, que de acuerdo con la Ley Orgánica del Poder Popular (art. 32), los Consejos Comunales y las Comunas adquieren personalidad jurídica mediante el registro ante el Ministerio del Poder Popular de las Comunas y Movimientos Sociales, con lo que, en definitiva, se deja en manos del Ejecutivo Nacional

1225   Véase Allan R. Brewer-Carías, "Comentarios sobre la inconstitucional creación de la Comisión Central de Planificación, centralizada y obligatoria", en *Revista de Derecho Público*, Nº 110, (abril-junio 2007), Editorial Jurídica Venezolana, Caracas 2007, pp. 79-89.

1226   Véase en *Gaceta Oficial* Nº 6.011 Extraordinario del 21 de diciembre de 2010; y en *Gaceta Oficial* Nº 6.148 de 18 de noviembre de 2014.

la decisión de registrar o no un Consejo Comunal, una Comuna o una Ciudad comunal, y ello debe hacerse, por supuesto, aplicando la letra de la Ley, lo que significa que si está dominada por "voceros" que no sean socialistas, no cabe su registro ni, por tanto, su reconocimiento como persona jurídica, así sea producto genuino de una iniciativa popular.

En cuarto lugar, como parte de ese proceso de desmunicipalización de la vida local, a las Comunas, como se dijo, se las incorporó en el régimen del Poder Público Municipal como "entidad local territorial" (art. 19) aun cuando de "carácter especial," pues conforme al artículo 19, "se rige por su ley de creación," y pueden constituirse "dentro del territorio del Municipio o entre los límites político administrativo de dos o más municipios, sin que ello afecte la integridad territorial de los municipios donde se constituya." Como tales "entidades locales" de carácter especial, sin embargo, se las excluyó completamente del régimen de la Ley Orgánica del Poder Municipal quedando "reguladas por la legislación que norma su constitución, conformación, organización y funcionamiento" (art. 5). Ello se reafirmó en el artículo 33 de la Ley, al disponer que "los requisitos para la creación de la comuna, en el marco de su régimen especial como entidad local," son los establecidos en la propia Ley Orgánica de las Comunas."

Es precisamente hacia las Comunas, hacia las cuales se prevé que se deben vaciar a los Municipios de sus competencias, al dictarse la Ley Orgánica para la Gestión Comunitaria de Competencias, Servicios y Otras Atribuciones (Decreto Ley N° 9.043),[1227] con el objeto de implementar la "transferencia de la gestión y administración de servicios, actividades, bienes y recursos del Poder Público Nacional y de las entidades político territoriales, al pueblo organizado." La motivación de dicha transferencia, por otra parte, en esa ley fue la peregrina idea de que las entidades político territoriales que están gobernadas por representantes electos mediante sufragio, supuestamente, supuestamente "usurparon lo que es del pueblo soberano," y por tanto, supuestamente "restituyen al Pueblo Soberano, a través de las comunidades organizadas y las organizaciones de base del poder popular, aquellos servicios, actividades, bienes y recursos que pueden ser asumidas, gestionadas y administradas por el pueblo organizado" (art. 5.3).

Dicha Ley se ha sustituido en 2014, por la Ley Orgánica para la Transferencia al Poder Popular de la Gestión y Administración Comunitaria de Servicios,[1228] precisamente con el objeto de implementar la "transferencia de la gestión y administración de servicios, actividades, bienes y recursos del Poder Público a las Comunidades, Comunas, Consejos Comunales, Empresas de propiedad Social Directas o Indirectas y otras organizaciones de base del Poder Popular legítimamente registradas" (art. 1) o reconocidas, por supuesto, por el gobierno central; de la cual sin embargo se eliminó la noción de "usurpación" como motivación de la transferencia y limitándose la idea de "restitución al pueblo soberano" sólo al supuesto de que una entidad territorial por cuenta propia, decida hacer la transferencia pero conforme al Plan Regional de Desarrollo y autorización del Consejo Federal de Gobierno (art. 5.3).

1227   Véase en *Gaceta Oficial* N° 6.097 Extra. de 15 de junio de 2012.
1228   Véase en *Gaceta Oficial* N° 40.540 de 13 de noviembre de 2014.

Además, se destaca que la transferencia para "restituir" las mencionadas competencias a las organizaciones del Poder Popular conforme por los lineamientos que a tal efecto dicte el Consejo Federal de Gobierno (art. 20), que es un órgano controlado por el Poder Central, abarca materialmente todas las competencia imaginables de las entidades de gobierno local, relativas a la salud, educación, vivienda, deporte, cultura, programas sociales, protección del ambiente, recolección de desechos sólidos, áreas industriales, mantenimiento y conservación de áreas urbanas, prevención y protección comunal, construcción de obras comunitarias, servicios públicos, además de prestación de servicios financieros y producción y distribución de alimentos y de bienes de primera necesidad, entre otras" (art. 27),[1229] es decir, materialmente de todo lo imaginable como acción de gobierno local. Con ello, como se dijo, se busca vaciar de competencias a los entes políticos territoriales, especialmente los Municipios,[1230] y ahogarlos financieramente, para lo cual, como lo afirmó la Sala Constitucional en la sentencia que analizó el carácter orgánico de la Ley, la misma "incide de forma evidente en la estructura orgánica o institucional de un Poder Público como es el Poder Ejecutivo, y a su vez los distintos entes político-territoriales quienes *están sujetos* a los planes de transferencia planteados en sus normas."[1231]

Por supuesto, este proceso de transferencia no es, en absoluto, un proceso de descentralización. Más bien como lo destacó José Ignacio Hernández, "la descentralización no se concibe aquí como la transferencia de competencias a favor de Estados y Municipios para democratizar el Poder acercándolo al ciudadano," pues "la transferencia de competencias del Poder Nacional, Estadal y Municipal –así como por parte de los Distritos– a favor de las instancias del Poder Popular, [...] desnatu-

---

1229   Véase sobre esta Ley los comentarios de: José Luis Villegas Moreno, "Hacia la instauración del Estado Comunal en Venezuela: Comentario al Decreto Ley Orgánica de la Gestión Comunitaria de Competencia, Servicios y otras Atribuciones, en el contexto del Primer Plan Socialista-Proyecto Nacional Simón Bolívar 2007-2013"; de Juan Cristóbal Carmona Borjas, "Decreto con rango, valor y fuerza de Ley Orgánica para la Gestión Comunitaria de Competencias, Servicios y otras atribuciones;" Cecilia Sosa G., "El carácter orgánico de un Decreto con fuerza de Ley (no habilitado) para la gestión comunitaria que arrasa lentamente con los Poderes estadales y municipales de la Constitución;" José Ignacio Hernández, "Reflexiones sobre el nuevo régimen para la Gestión Comunitaria de Competencias, Servicios y otras Atribuciones;" Alfredo Romero Mendoza, "Comentarios sobre el Decreto con rango, valor y fuerza de Ley Orgánica para la Gestión Comunitaria de Competencias, Servicios y otras Atribuciones;," Enrique J. Sánchez Falcón, "El Decreto con Rango, Valor y Fuerza de Ley Orgánica para la Gestión Comunitaria de Competencias, Servicios y otras Atribuciones o la negación del federalismo cooperativo y descentralizado," en *Revista de Derecho Público*, N° 130, Editorial Jurídica Venezolana, Caracas 2012, pp. 127 ss.

1230   Como observó Cecilia Sosa Gómez, para entender esta normativa hay que "aceptar la desaparición de las instancias representativas, estadales y municipales, y su existencia se justifica en la medida que año a año transfiera sus competencias hasta que desaparezcan de hecho, aunque sigan sus nombres (Poderes Públicos Estadal y Municipal) apareciendo en la Constitución. El control de estas empresas, las tiene el Poder Público Nacional, específicamente el Poder Ejecutivo, en la cabeza de un Ministerio." Véase Cecilia Sosa G "El carácter orgánico de un Decreto con fuerza de Ley (no habilitado) para la gestión comunitaria que arrasa lentamente con los Poderes estadales y municipales de la Constitución;" *cit.* en *Revista de Derecho Público*, N° 130, Editorial Jurídica Venezolana, Caracas 2012, p. 152.

1231   Véase sentencia N° 821 de la Sala Constitucional (Exp. N° AA50–T–2012–0702) de 18 de junio de 2012, en http://www.tsj.gov.ve/decisiones/scon/junio/821-18612-2012-12-0704.HTML.

raliza el concepto constitucional de descentralización, pues el Poder Popular, como quedó regulado en las Leyes del Poder Popular, es en realidad el conjunto de instancias reguladas y controladas por el Poder Ejecutivo Nacional cuyo objetivo único, exclusivo y excluyente es el socialismo, que pasa a ser así a ser doctrina de Estado." [1232]

En quinto lugar, también debe observarse, como antes se indicó, que se eliminó el carácter de entidad local que en la Constitución tienen las parroquias, y por tanto, se eliminó su carácter democrático representativo. Es más, en la Disposición Transitoria segunda de la Ley Orgánica se dispuso que unos días después de la promulgación de la Ley, los miembros principales y suplentes, así como los secretarios de las actuales juntas parroquiales, cesaron en sus funciones. En esta forma, eliminadas las Juntas parroquiales, las cuales en el artículo 35 de la Ley Orgánica pasaron a denominarse "juntas parroquiales comunales," las mismas se regularon sólo como entidades con "facultades consultivas, de evaluación y articulación entre el poder popular y los órganos del Poder Público Municipal," con las funciones enumeradas en el artículo 37 de la Ley Orgánica, de la cual se eliminó todo vestigio de gobierno local.

En esta forma, cada una de dichas juntas parroquiales comunales debe ser "coordinada por una junta parroquial comunal integrada por cinco miembros y sus respectivos suplentes cuando corresponda a un área urbana y tres miembros y sus respectivos suplentes cuando sea no urbana, elegidos o elegidas para un período de dos años," pero no por el pueblo mediante sufragio universal, directo y secreto, sino "por los voceros de los consejos comunales de la parroquia respectiva," quienes "en dicha elección deberán ser fiel expresión del mandato de sus respectivas asambleas de ciudadanos." La norma prevé que dicha designación, debe ser "validada por la asamblea de ciudadanos," quedando eliminado, en esta forma, toda suerte de sufragio universal, directo y secreto y con ello, la democracia representativa.

Al desmunicipalizarse las juntas parroquiales comunales, y eliminarse su carácter de entidad política local de orden democrático representativo, el artículo 36 previó que sus miembros, que deben ser avalados por la asamblea de ciudadanos, incluso pueden ser menores de edad, aun cuando mayores de quince años, e incluso extranjeros.

VIII. EL AHOGAMIENTO Y NEUTRALIZACIÓN DE LAS ENTIDADES TERRITORIALES POR PARTE DEL PODER NACIONAL

Pero el proceso de centralización del Estado no sólo se ha producido por la creación paralela de los órganos del Estado Comunal en relación con el Estado Constitucional, para vaciarlo y ahogarlo, sino por la acción de los propios órganos del Poder Nacional, que han venido, a la vez, ahogando directamente a las entidades territoriales.

Ello comenzó a ocurrir mediante el establecimiento de una estructura organizativa de la Administración Pública nacional, dependiente del Vicepresidente Ejecutivo

---

[1232]   Véase José Ignacio Hernández, "Reflexiones sobre el nuevo régimen para la Gestión Comunitaria de Competencias, Servicios y otras Atribuciones," cit., en Revista de Derecho Público, Nº 130, Editorial Jurídica Venezolana, Caracas 2012, pp. 157.

de la República, en forma paralela y superpuesta a la Administración de los Estados, denominada como "Órganos Desconcentrados de las Regiones Estratégicas de Desarrollo Integral (REDI),"[1233] a cargo de funcionarios denominados "Autoridades Regionales," las cuales además, tienen "Dependencias" en cada Estado de la República, que están a cargo de Delegaciones Estadales, todos del libre nombramiento del Vicepresidente de la República. Dichos funcionarios se regularon en la reforma de la Ley Orgánica de la Administración Pública de 2014 con el nombre de "jefes de gobierno" (arts. 34, 41, 44).

Estos Delegados o jefes de gobierno, que ejercen sus funciones "dentro del territorio del Estado que le ha sido asignado" (art. 19), se los ha concebido como los canales de comunicación de los Gobernadores de Estado con el Poder Nacional y viceversa, del Poder Nacional con los Estados, teniendo además como misión "realizar las acciones tendentes a impulsar la integración y operación de las comunidades organizadas, instancias del poder popular, organizaciones del poder popular, los consejos de economía y contraloría comunal bajo su demarcación, en términos de la normatividad aplicable, cumpliendo con los criterios establecidos por la Autoridad Regional de las Regiones Estratégicas de Desarrollo Integral (REDI)"(art. 20). En definitiva, estas Autoridades nacionales Regionales y los Delegados Estadales, son los órganos administrativos del Poder Nacional montados en paralelo a las autoridades estadales, con el objeto de asegurar el vaciamiento de sus competencias y la neutralización del poder de los Gobernadores de Estado, particularmente si no son miembros del partido oficial. Dichas autoridades, en todo caso, también han encontrado regulación en noviembre de 2014, en la Ley de Regionalización Integral para el Desarrollo Socioproductivo de la Patria. [1234]

Ese proceso de ahogamiento y neutralización de las entidades territoriales de la República, se había comenzado particularmente respecto de las existentes en la Región Capital, en 2008, con la creación de autoridades en el Distrito Capital totalmente dependientes del Poder Ejecutivo, violándose la Constitución. En efecto, en la Constitución de 1999 se había buscado cambiar radicalmente la concepción del viejo Distrito Federal creado desde 1863 como entidad dependiente del Poder Nacional, estableciéndose el Distrito Capital como una entidad política más de la República (art. 16), con sus propios órganos legislativo y ejecutivo de gobierno democrático, es decir, integrado por funcionarios electos popularmente, que debía ser regulado por el Poder Nacional (art. 156,10). Debe mencionarse que ese esquema de autonomía territorial también se pretendió reformar en la rechazada Reforma Constitucional de 2007, en la cual se buscaba eliminar el Distrito Capital y recrear la desaparecida figura del Distrito Federal como entidad totalmente dependiente del Poder Nacional, en particular del Presidente de la República, sin gobierno propio.

1233   Véase Resolución N° 031 de la Vicepresidencia de la República, mediante la cual se establece la Estructura y Normas de Funcionamiento de los órganos Desconcentrados de las Regiones Estratégicas de Desarrollo Integral (REDI), en *Gaceta Oficial* N° 40.193 de 20-6-2013. Todo esto se ha regulado en noviembre de 2014 en la Ley de regionalización Integral para el desarrollo Socioproductivo de la Patria, publicada en *Gaceta Oficial* N° 6.151 Extra. De 18-11-2014.

1234   Véase .Decreto Ley N° 1.425, en *Gaceta Oficial* N° 6.151 Extra. de 18 de noviembre de 2014.

Después del rechazo popular a dicha reforma constitucional, sin embargo, esta reforma se ha implementado en fraude a la Constitución, y por supuesto a la voluntad popular, mediante la Ley Especial Sobre la Organización y Régimen del Distrito Capital,[1235] en la cual se lo ha regulado como una dependencia del Poder Nacional, con el mismo ámbito territorial del extinto Distrito Federal; y con un supuesto "régimen especial de gobierno," conforme al cual, la función legislativa en el Distrito está a cargo de la Asamblea Nacional, y el órgano ejecutivo es ejercido por un Jefe de Gobierno (art. 3), que de acuerdo con el artículo 7 de la Ley Especial, es "de libre nombramiento y remoción" por parte del Presidente de la República; es decir, un "régimen especial de gobierno" dependiente del Poder Central.

Con ello, en el mismo territorio del Municipio Libertador y de parte del territorio del Distrito metropolitano a cargo de un Alcalde y un Consejo Metropolitanos de Caracas, se le ha superpuesto una estructura nacional, como entidad dependiente funcionalmente del Ejecutivo nacional, sin gobierno democrático ni autonomía político territorial, ignorando además la existencia del régimen municipal metropolitano a dos niveles previsto en la Constitución, duplicando las funciones del mismo, dispuesto para ahogarlo y controlarlo.

Como consecuencia de todo lo anteriormente expuesto, puede decirse entonces que la Federación que se plasmó en la Constitución de 1999 no sólo siguió siendo, más acentuadamente, la misma Federación centralizada desarrollada en las décadas anteriores, sino que los pocos elementos que podían contribuir a su descentralización política, fueron desmontados progresivamente en los últimos tres lustros.

En esta perspectiva, el Estado venezolano que nunca ha sido ni ha tenido realmente las características de un " Federal descentralizado," expresión que sólo fue una etiqueta contradictoria e ilusa inserta en una Constitución centralista, progresivamente se ha centralizado aún más, ubicándose todo el poder público en el Estado nacional, que ahora está configurado como un Estado Totalitario y centralizado. Esa centralización ha sido el resultado de un progresivo desbalance hacia el nivel nacional en la distribución territorial del Poder, en el cual se ha vaciado a los Estados de toda competencia sustantiva, y a los Municipios se les ha quitado su carácter de unidad primaria en la organización nacional, montándose en paralelo y en contra de la Constitución, una organización del llamado Poder Popular Estado Comunal, integrada por Comunas y Consejos Comunales, que han venido neutralizando y ahogando a los Municipios, como instrumentos realmente del Poder nacional. Con ese esquema estatal, sin duda, el derecho público y administrativo que se ha desarrollado es un derecho propio de un Estado centralizado.

1235   Véase en *Gaceta Oficial* N° 39.156 de 13 de abril de 2009.

APRECIACIÓN FINAL:

*EL ESTADO TOTALITARIO Y LA DESCONSTITUCIONALIZACIÓN DEL ESTA-
DO CONSTITUCIONAL*

**Estas Reflexiones finales también formaron parte del texto redactado para
la conferencia sobre "¿Hacia dónde va el derecho público?** : **Estado Totalitario
y nuevas tendencias del derecho administrativo," prevista para ser dictada en
el** *Congreso Internacional Conmemorativo del Acto Legislativo del 10 de septiembre de 1914 por el cual se estableció el Consejo de Estado***, sobre el tema general
de las** *Tendencias actuales del derecho público,* **organizado por la Universidad
del Rosario y el Consejo de Estado, y celebrado en Bogotá en la Biblioteca Luis
Ángel Arango, los días 8 al 10 de septiembre de 2014**

Todo lo que anteriormente hemos expuesto, nos confirma que en Venezuela, durante los últimos tres lustros, lo que se ha desarrollado en relación con el estado ha
sido un proceso sistemático y permanente de demolición de las instituciones públicas y privadas que antes existían, particularmente las desarrolladas en el marco del
Estado Constitucional, mediante su desconstitucionalización, desinstitucionalización, desjuridificación, desjusticiabilidad, desadministraivización y desdemocratización, que han configurado progresivamente al Estado como un Estado totalitario, que terminó sustituyendo al Estado democrático, social, de derecho, descentralizado y de justicia del que habla la Constitución, pero sin que la misma se haya
reformado conforme a los procedimientos de revisión constitucional.

Y decimos que lo que ha resultado es un Estado Totalitario, pues, limitándonos
incluso a la caracterización de Raymond Aron, el Estado venezolano está efectivamente montado sobre un régimen político fundamentado en un sistema de concentración total del poder, en el cual todos los órganos del Estado actúan en el mismo
sentido que ordene el Poder Ejecutivo, para lo cual como instrumento facilitador, se
ha configurado un partido único ayudado por un partido militar, que se encuentra
fusionados al propio Estado y que posee el monopolio de la actividad política "legítima," que es la que define al Estado, y que es la doctrina "socialista." Dicho partido
es el que garantiza la aplicación de la ideología del Estado, que en definitiva es la
verdad oficial.

Ese Estado Totalitario, además, de haber asumido el monopolio de la conducción
del Estado, también ha asumido el monopolio de los medios de persuasión y coacción, para imponer su voluntad a los ciudadanos; y además, ha asumido el monopolio de los medios de comunicación. Adicionalmente, el Estado Totalitario ha concentrado la casi totalidad de la economía, la cual ha quedado totalmente controlada
por el mismo, configurándose un extraordinario Capitalismo de Estado, lo que ha
sido facilitado por control total de la industria petrolera por parte del Estado. El monopolio por parte del Estado de la actividad política y económica, ha producido
además, la total politización de cualquier actividad que pueda realizarse en la vida
social, económica y política, lo que ha originado una confusión entre sociedad y
Estado, de manera que las faltas cometidas por los individuos en el marco de la actividad política, económica o profesional se conforman simultáneamente como faltas
"ideológicas," o políticas, originando un terror ideológico y policial.

Ese Estado configurado como Estado Totalitario, en primer lugar, ha hecho desaparecer todo vestigio de Estado de derecho que prevé la Constitución, lo que ha resultado de la violación sistemática de la Constitución que ha perdido su carácter de ley suprema, lo que ha sido acompañado de un proceso sistemático de maleabilidad, mutabilidad y desrigidización constitucional, todo lo cual ha producido una completa desinstitucionalización y además, una desconstitucionalización del Estado por la creación fuera de la Constitución de un Estado Comunal en paralelo al Estado Constitucional. [1236]

En segundo lugar, el Estado totalitario ha hecho desaparecer, igualmente, todo vestigio del Estado democrático que regula la Constitución, lo que ha resultado de la distorsión de la representatividad política en la legislación electoral; de las fallas en la implementación de la democracia participativa; de la ausencia de separación de poderes en la organización del Estado, y en particular, de la ausencia de autonomía e independencia del Poder Judicial; de la distorsión de la Administración Pública que dejó de estar al servicio del ciudadano; de la militarización avasallante de la sociedad y el Estado; de la eliminación de la libertad de expresión y comunicación; y de la eliminación y violación del principio democrático.

En tercer lugar, el Estado totalitario también ha hecho desaparecer todo vestigio del Estado Social y de Economía Mixta que regula la Constitución, y con ello, se ha logrado la material eliminación de la libertad económica y de la garantía del derecho de propiedad, resultando la configuración de un Estado Comunista, Burocrático acaparador de la totalidad de la actividad económica, basado en sistema de Capitalismo de Estado, de un Estado Populista, de un Estado Comunal y del Poder Popular, y de un Estado Clientelar.

En cuarto lugar, el Estado totalitario adicionalmente ha hecho desaparecer todo vestigio del Estado de Justicia que regula la Constitución, lo que ha resultado de la ausencia de leyes justas y la multiplicación de leyes inconsultas; de una extrema inflación de la inseguridad jurídica; del sometimiento político del Poder Judicial al Poder Ejecutivo; del hecho del Estado haberse escapado de la justicia interna y de la justicia internacional, tornándose en un Estado irresponsable; de haberse puesto la Justicia al servicio del autoritarismo; de haber áreas con carencia de justicia; y haberse desarrollado la injusticia de la impunidad.

Y por último, el Estado totalitario también ha hecho desaparecer todo vestigio del Estado descentralizado que bajo una concepción centralista de la "federación descentralizada" regula la Constitución, habiéndose consolidado un desbalance hacia el nivel nacional en la distribución territorial del poder; un Municipio que no

---

1236   Véase lo expuesto en Allan R. Brewer-Carías, "La desconstitucionalización del Estado de derecho en Venezuela: del Estado Democrático y Social de derecho al Estado Comunal Socialista, sin reformar la Constitución," *en Libro Homenaje al profesor Alfredo Morles Hernández, Diversas Disciplinas Jurídicas,* (Coordinación y Compilación Astrid Uzcátegui Angulo y Julio Rodríguez Berrizbeitia), Universidad Católica Andrés Bello, Universidad de Los Andes, Universidad Monteávila, Universidad Central de Venezuela, Academia de Ciencias Políticas y Sociales, Vol. V, Caracas 2012, pp. 51-82; en Carlos Tablante y Mariela Morales Antonorzzi (Coord.), *Descentralización, autonomía e inclusión social. El desafío actual de la democracia,* Anuario 2010-2012, Observatorio Internacional para la democracia y descentralización, En Cambio, Caracas 2011, pp. 37-84; y en *Estado Constitucional,* Año 1, Nº 2, Editorial Adrus, Lima, junio 2011, pp. 217-236.

se configuró efectivamente como la unidad primaria de la organización nacional; la creación, en paralelo a las entidades políticas territoriales previstas en la Constitución, del Estado Comunal y de las Comunas para acabar con los Municipios, los cuales han sido vaciados de competencia a favor de las mismas; y por último, el ahogamiento y neutralización de las mismas entidades políticas territoriales por parte del Poder Nacional.

Todo ello ha originado una desconstitucionalización del Estado Constitucional la cual incluso se ha pretendido realizar mediante el uso ilegítimo del texto del artículo 5 de la Constitución que dispone que "La soberanía reside intransferiblemente en el pueblo, quien la ejerce directamente en la forma prevista en esta Constitución y en la ley, e indirectamente, mediante el sufragio, por los órganos que ejercen el Poder Público." Con base en ello, fue que precisamente se estructuró en la propia Constitución el Estado Constitucional, basado en el concepto de democracia representativa o indirecta que se ejerce mediante el sufragio por los órganos del Poder Público. Y ha sido igualmente con base en la primera parte de la norma, la que se refiere al ejercicio directo de la soberanía, que se ha pretendido estructurar otro Estado, el Estado Comunal, con la Comuna como su célula fundamental, pero carente de base democrática.

Ese Estado Comunal, producto del supuesto ejercicio de una democracia directa, sin sufragio ni representación, se ha concebido para ir vaciando progresivamente de competencias al Estado Constitucional; y en su organización formal, si bien se proclama como la negación de la representatividad democrática, en la práctica actúa mediante "representantes," pero sin que los mismos sean electos mediante sufragio, sino que son "nombrados" como "voceros" a mano alzada en "asambleas de ciudadanos" controladas por el partido de gobierno, para ejercer el Poder Popular, con la participación directa del partido oficial de gobierno y el propio Poder Ejecutivo.

Por ello, lo cierto es que el "Estado Comunal" que se ha buscado establecer en fraude a la Constitución y a la voluntad popular, nada democrático, en definitiva, está controlado todo por un Ministerio del Ejecutivo Nacional, el "Ministerio del Poder Popular para las Comunas y Movimientos Sociales" cuyo titular además es un "Vicepresidente del Consejo de Ministros para Desarrollo del Socialismo Territorial,"[1237] por lo que lejos de ser un instrumento de descentralización –concepto que está indisolublemente unido a la autonomía política– es un sistema de centralización y control férreo de las comunidades por el Poder Central. Por ello la aversión al sufragio universal, directo y secreto que se aprecia en su implementación.

1237   Véase en *Gaceta Oficial* N° 40.489 de 4 de septiembre de 2014. Sobre este Ministerio y Vicepresidencia, por ejemplo, el equipo de Redacción Internacional del Diario El Tiempo, expresó que tiene por objeto retomar la idea "de crear el "estado comunal", en el que el poder ya no se distribuye entre alcaldías y gobernaciones sino en miles de "comunas" creadas en todo el país pero coordinadas directamente por la Presidencia de la República." Se trata de un esquema para "redistribuir el poder entre las comunidades pero controlando directamente su fuente de ingresos y su funcionamiento, lo que en el fondo implica una mayor concentración en el Poder Ejecutivo." Véase en el reportaje "Qué hay detrás del 'revolcón' en el gabinete del Gobierno venezolano," en El Tiempo, Bogotá, 3 de septiembre de 2014, en http://www.eltiempo.com/mun-do/latinoamerica/analisis-de-las-principales-reformas-en-el-gabinete-de-nicolas-maduro/14478895.

En realidad, si se tratase efectivamente de mecanismos de participación, los miembros de los Consejos Comunales, las comunas y todas las organizaciones e instancias del Poder Popular tendrían que ser electas por sufragio universal, directo y secreto, y no designadas a mano alzada por asambleas controladas por el partido oficial y el Ejecutivo Nacional, en contravención al modelo de Estado democrático, social, de derecho, de justicia y descentralizado establecido en la Constitución.

Es decir, la supuesta democracia participativa no es más que una falacia, pues en definitiva en el "edificio" del Estado Comunal se le niega al pueblo el derecho de elegir libremente, mediante sufragio universal, directo y secreto a quienes van a representarlo en todos esos ámbitos. Se trata más bien de un "edificio" de organizaciones para evitar que el pueblo realmente ejerza la soberanía e imponerle mediante férreo control central, políticas por las cuales nunca tendrá la ocasión de votar.

Por otra parte, el principio esencial del régimen político democrático, basado en la igualdad, la no discriminación y el pluralismo se ha roto desde que el sistema de Estado Comunal, establecido en paralelo al Estado Constitucional, se monta sobre una concepción única, que es el Socialismo, de manera que quien no sea socialista está automáticamente discriminado e impedido de participar. [1238]

No es posible, por tanto, en el marco de estas Leyes del Poder Popular, poder conciliar el pluralismo que garantiza la Constitución y el principio de la no discriminación por razón de "opinión política," con sus disposiciones que persiguen todo lo contrario, es decir, el establecimiento de un Estado Comunal, cuyas instancias sólo pueden actuar en función del Socialismo y en las cuales todo ciudadano que tenga otra opinión queda excluido.

En fin, la concepción misma del Estado Comunal para desarrollar y consolidar el Poder Popular, se ha formulado ignorando los valores y principios constitucionales básicos que tienen que tener todas las instancias de gobierno en Venezuela que deben ser los principios del "electivo, descentralizado, alternativo, responsable, pluralista y de mandatos revocables" (Artículo 6 de la Constitución). Al contrario, las "formas de autogobierno comunitarias y comunales, para el ejercicio directo del poder" que se regulan en la Ley Orgánica del Poder Popular (art. 1), son contrarias a la concepción de un Estado descentralizado, siendo carentes de autonomía política, y más bien son instrumentos para asegurar el centralismo de Estado que es lo que caracteriza al Estado Totalitario.

En esta forma, al fraude a la Constitución, que ha sido la técnica constantemente aplicada por el gobierno autoritario en Venezuela desde 1999 para imponer sus de-

---

1238   Véase el reportaje: "El Estado Comunal excluye a la mitad de la población," donde se cita lo expuesto por Maria Pilar García-Guadilla, en *Aporrea*: "El modelo reproduce un modelo de inclusión excluyente porque ignora a quienes difieren de la ideología socialista, es decir, la mitad de la población, si se revisan los últimos resultados electorales.[…] El financiamiento de los proyectos productivos pasa por el aparato político-ideológico (el PSUV), correa transmisora de las prebendas, Y en las Asambleas solo serán reconocidos como interlocutores del Estado las comunas socialistas." Véase en *El Nacional*, Caracas 7 de septiembre de 2014, en http://www.el-nacional.com/politica/comunal-excluye-mitad-poblacion_0_477552461.html

cisiones a los venezolanos al margen de la Constitución,[1239] se ha sumado el fraude a la voluntad popular, al imponerle a los venezolanos mediante leyes orgánicas, un modelo de Estado totalitario, comunista y centralizado por el cual nadie ha votado, con lo que se ha cambiado radical e inconstitucionalmente el texto de la Constitución de 1999, que no ha sido reformado conforme a sus previsiones, en abierta contradicción y desprecio al rechazo popular mayoritario que se expresó en diciembre de 2007 a la reforma constitucional que entonces se intentó realizar incluso violando la propia Constitución.

Es ese marco de Estado totalitario y de desconstitucionalización del Estado Constitucional, el cual en la actualidad está condicionando al derecho público en Venezuela, y es lo que está originando unas "nuevas tendencias al derecho administrativo," que nos lo muestran como una rama del derecho que dejó de ser el punto de equilibrio entre los poderes y prerrogativas del Estado y las garantías de derechos de los particulares, y en un marco de desquiciamiento, sólo sirve ahora, sin seguridad jurídica alguna, para regular exclusivamente al Estado, a sus poderes y prerrogativas, pero en la medida en la cual los gobernantes decidan, sin control judicial de naturaleza alguna; siendo su misión el servir de medio de imposición de la voluntad del Estado y los funcionarios a los ciudadanos

---

1239   Véase Allan R. Brewer-Carías, *Reforma constitucional y fraude a la Constitución (1999-2009)*, Academia de Ciencias Políticas y Sociales, Caracas 2009; *Dismantling Democracy. The Chávez Authoritarian Experiment*, Cambridge University Press, New York 2010.

CUARTA PARTE

LA DESCONSTITUCIONALIZACIÓN Y DESJURIDIFICACIÓN DEL ESTADO CONSTITUCIONAL Y LA ESTRUCTURACIÓN PARALELA DEL ESTADO COMUNAL O DEL PODER POPULAR

El texto de esta Cuarta parte del Tomo XV de la Colección Tratado de Derecho Constitucional, es el de la "Introducción General al régimen del Poder Popular y del Estado Comunal," escrita para al libro Allan R. Brewer-Carías et al., *Leyes Orgánicas del Poder Popular*, Editorial Jurídica Venezolana, Caracas 2011, pp. 9-182. Este texto recoge y refunde las reflexiones hechas en diversas conferencias y documentos, y entre ellos, los siguientes publicados: "La Ley Orgánica del Poder Popular y la desconstitucionalización del Estado de derecho en Venezuela," en *Revista de Derecho Público*, Nº 124, (octubre-diciembre 2010), Editorial Jurídica Venezolana, Caracas 2010, pp. 81-101; y "La desconstitucionalización del Estado de derecho en Venezuela: del Estado Democrático y Social de derecho al Estado Comunal Socialista, sin reformar la Constitución," que fue publicado en *Estado Constitucional*, Año 1, Nº 2, Editorial Adrus, Lima, junio 2011, pp. 217-236; en Revista *Aequitas*, Facultad de Ciencias Jurídicas, Universidad de El Salvador, Tercera Etapa, Año V, Número 5, Buenos Aires 2011, pp. 105-138; y en *Revista Aequitas Virtual*, Número 15, Año V, Facultad de Ciencias Jurídicas, Universidad de El Salvador, Buenos Aires, Mayo 2011; en *El Cronista del Estado Social y Democrático de Derecho*, Nº 19, Editorial Iustel, Madrid 2011, pp. 26-39; en Carlos Tablante y Mariela Morales Antonorzzi (Coord.), *Descentralización, autonomía e inclusión social. El desafío actual de la democracia*, Anuario 2010-2012, Observatorio Internacional para la democracia y descentralización, En Cambio, Caracas 2011, pp. 37-84; y en *Libro Homenaje al profesor Alfredo Morles Hernández, Diversas Disciplinas Jurídicas*, (Coordinación y Compilación Astrid Uzcátegui Angulo y Julio Rodríguez Berrizbeitia), Universidad Católica Andrés Bello, Universidad de Los Andes, Universidad Monteávila, Universidad Central de Venezuela, Academia de Ciencias Políticas y Sociales, Vol. V, Caracas 2012, pp. 51-82.

La Constitución de 1999 de Venezuela, actualmente vigente, constituyó al país como un *Estado Democrático y Social de Derecho y de Justicia*, "que propugna como valores superiores de su ordenamiento jurídico y de su actuación, la vida, la libertad, la justicia, la igualdad, la solidaridad, la democracia, la responsabilidad social y, en general, la preeminencia de los derechos humanos, la ética y el pluralismo político" (art. 2), organizando a la República como "un *Estado federal descentralizado*" que "se rige por los principios de integridad territorial, cooperación, solidaridad, concurrencia y corresponsabilidad" (art. 4).

Ese es el Estado Constitucional en Venezuela: un Estado Federal descentralizado, Democrático y Social de Derecho y de Justicia,[1240] que está montado sobre un sistema de distribución vertical del Poder Público en tres niveles territoriales de entidades políticas: el Poder Nacional que ejercen los órganos de la República; el Poder de los Estados que ejercen los Estados de la Federación, y el Poder Municipal (art. 136) que ejercen los Municipios, cada uno debiendo tener siempre un gobierno de carácter "electivo, descentralizado, alternativo, responsable, pluralista y de mandatos revocables," tal como lo manda el artículo 6 de la Constitución.[1241]

No es posible, por tanto, constitucionalmente hablando, crear por ley instancias políticas que vacíen de competencias a los órganos del Estado (la República, los Estados, los Municipios y demás entidades locales) y menos aún establecerlos con funciones políticas sin que se asegure su carácter electivo-representativo mediante la elección de representantes del pueblo a través de sufragio universal, directo y secreto; sin que se asegure su autonomía política, propia del carácter descentralizado del Estado y del gobierno; y sin que se garantice su carácter pluralista, en el sentido de que no pueden estar vinculados a una ideología determinada como es el Socialismo.

Ese modelo de Estado Constitucional desarrollado a partir de la Constitución de 1961 y que se consolidó formalmente en la Constitución de 1999, se intentó cambiar radicalmente mediante una Reforma Constitucional que fue sancionada por la Asamblea Nacional en noviembre de 2007 con el objeto de establecer un Estado Socialista, Centralizado, Militarista y Policial[1242] denominado Estado del Poder Po-

---

1240   Véase el estudio de la Constitución en cuanto a la regulación de este modelo de Estado Constitucional en Allan R. Brewer-Carías, *La Constitución de 1999. Derecho Constitucional venezolano*, 2 tomos, Caracas 2004.

1241   En el Reglamento de la Ley Orgánica del Consejo Federal de Gobierno, sin embargo, se ha definido el "federalismo" en forma totalmente contraria al esquema de división política territorial que consagra la Constitución, indicándose que ahora es un: "Sistema de organización política de la República Bolivariana de Venezuela, regido por los principios de integridad territorial, económica y política de la Nación venezolana, cooperación, solidaridad, concurrencia y corresponsabilidad entre las instituciones del Estado y el pueblo soberano, para la construcción de la sociedad socialista y del Estado Democrático y Social de Derecho y de Justicia, mediante la participación protagónica del pueblo organizado en las funciones de gobierno y en la administración de los factores y medios de producción de bienes y servicios de propiedad social, como garantía del ejercicio pleno de la soberanía popular frente a cualquier intento de las oligarquías nacionales y regionales de concentrar, centralizar y monopolizar el poder político y económico de la Nación y de las regiones"(art. 3). Véase en *Gaceta Oficial* N° 39.382 del 9 de marzo de 2010.

1242   Véase Allan R. Brewer-Carías, *Hacia la Consolidación de un Estado Socialista, Centralizado, Policial y Militarista. Comentarios sobre el sentido y alcance de las propuestas de reforma constitucional 2007*, Colección Textos Legislativos, N° 42, Editorial Jurídica Venezolana, Caracas 2007.

pular o Estado Comunal,[1243] la cual sin embargo, una vez sometida a consulta popular, fue rechazada por el pueblo en el referendo de 7 de diciembre de 2007.[1244]

Sin embargo, en burla a la voluntad popular y en fraude a la Constitución, desde antes de que se efectuara dicho referendo, la Asamblea Nacional, en abierta violación a la Constitución, comenzó a desmantelar el Estado Constitucional para sustituirlo por un Estado Socialista, imponiendo a la fuerza como ideología única la socialista, mediante la estructuración *paralela* de un Estado del Poder Popular o Estado Comunal, a través de la sanción de la Ley de los Consejos Comunales de 2006,[1245] reformada posteriormente y elevada al rango de ley orgánica en 2009.[1246]

Posteriormente, el empeño por implantar en Venezuela ese Estado Socialista y borrando todo vestigio de pluralismo, fue indirectamente rechazado de nuevo con ocasión de las elecciones legislativas efectuadas el 26 de septiembre de 2010, las cuales fueron planteadas por el Presidente de la República y la mayoría oficialista de la propia Asamblea Nacional, quienes hicieron una masiva campaña a favor de sus candidatos como un "plebiscito" respecto al propio Presidente, y de su actuación y sus políticas socialistas ya previamente rechazadas por el pueblo en 2007; "plebiscito" que el Presidente de la República y su partido perdieron abrumadoramente pues la mayoría del país votó en contra de las mismas.

Sin embargo, al haber perdido en dichas elecciones parlamentarias, el Presidente y su partido, teniendo aún el control absoluto sobre la Asamblea Nacional y sabiendo que luego de las elecciones legislativas de diciembre de 2010 ya no podrían imponer a su antojo la legislación que quisieran, antes de que los nuevos diputados electos a la Asamblea pudieran tomar posesión de sus cargos en enero de 2011, en diciembre de 2010, atropelladamente y de nuevo en fraude a la voluntad popular y a la Constitución, utilizaron la deslegitimada Asamblea Nacional precedente para proceder a la sanción de un conjunto de Leyes Orgánicas mediante las cuales se ha terminado de definir, al margen de la Constitución y en violación a la misma,[1247] el marco normativo de un nuevo Estado Socialista, *paralelo al Estado Constitucional*, que se denomina "Estado Comunal" y que si nos atenemos a las experiencias histó-

1243   Véase Allan R. Brewer-Carías, *La reforma constitucional de 2007 (Comentarios al Proyecto inconstitucionalmente sancionado por la Asamblea Nacional el 2 de noviembre de 2007)*, Colección Textos Legislativos, N° 43, Editorial Jurídica Venezolana, Caracas 2007.

1244   Véase Allan R. Brewer-Carías, "La proyectada reforma constitucional de 2007, rechazada por el poder constituyente originario", en *Anuario de Derecho Público 2007*, Año 1, Instituto de Estudios de Derecho Público de la Universidad Monteávila, Caracas 2008, pp. 17-65.

1245   Véase en *Gaceta Oficial* N° 5.806 Extra. de 10-04-2006

1246   Véase en *Gaceta Oficial* N° 39.335 de 28-12-2009. Véase la sentencia N° 1.676 de 03-12-2009 de la Sala Constitucional del Tribunal Supremo de Justicia sobre la constitucionalidad del carácter orgánico de esta Ley Orgánica de los Consejos Comunales. Véase en http://www.tsj.gov.ve/decisiones/scon/diciembre/1676-31209-2009-09-1369.html

1247   Véase el estudio de José Ignacio Hernández, Jesús María Alvarado Andrade y Luis A. Herrera Orellana, "Sobre los vicios de inconstitucionalidad de la Ley Orgánica del Poder Popular," en Allan R. Brewer-Carías (Coordinador), Claudia Nikken, Luis A. Herrera Orellana, Jesús María Alvarado Andrade, José Ignacio Hernández y Adriana Vigilanza, *Leyes Orgánicas sobre el Poder Popular y el Estado Comunal (Los Consejos Comunales, las Comunas, la Sociedad Socialista y el Sistema Económico Comunal)* pp. 509 ss.

ricas precedentes, todas fracasadas, unas desaparecidas como el de la Unión Soviética, y otros en vías de extinción como el de Cuba, no es otra cosa que un Estado Comunista, para el cual se adopta al Socialismo como doctrina oficial pública impuesta
a los ciudadanos para poder participar, montado en un sistema Centralizado, Militarista y Policial para el ejercicio del poder; y se adoptan expresa y textualmente los
postulados marxistas más tradicionales sobre el comunismo, como son la propiedad
social de los medios de producción; eliminación de la división social del trabajo; y
reinversión social del excedente productivo tal como ha quedado plasmado en la Ley
Orgánica del Sistema Económico Comunal de 2010[1248] (arts. 2; 3.2; 3.3;. 3.8; 5;
6.12; 6.15 y 9).

Las Leyes Orgánicas dictadas en diciembre de 2010, en efecto fueron las Leyes
Orgánicas del Poder Popular,[1249] de las Comunas,[1250] del Sistema Económico Co-
munal,[1251] de Planificación Pública y Comunal[1252] y de Contraloría Social.[1253]
Además, en el mismo marco de estructuración del Estado Comunal montado sobre
el Poder Popular se destaca la sanción de la Ley Orgánica del Consejo Federal de
Gobierno,[1254] y la reforma de la Ley Orgánica del Poder Público Municipal,[1255] y de
las Leyes de los Consejos Estadales de Planificación y Coordinación de Políticas
Públicas,[1256] y de los Consejos Locales de Planificación Pública.[1257]

La deslegitimada Asamblea Nacional, además, sancionó una Ley habilitante au-
torizando al Presidente de la República para, por vía de legislación delegada, dictar
leyes en todas las materias imaginables, incluso de carácter orgánico, vaciando así
por un período de 18 meses, hasta 2012, a la nueva Asamblea Nacional de materias
sobre las cuales poder legislar;[1258] y la propia Asamblea Nacional en diciembre de
2010, en la víspera de cesar su mandato, reformó el Reglamento Interior y de Deba-

---

1248   Véase en *Gaceta Oficial* N° 6.011 Extra. de 21-12-2010. La Sala Constitucional mediante sentencia
        N° 1329 de 16-12-2010 declaró la constitucionalidad del carácter orgánico de esta Ley. Véase en
        http://www.tsj.gov.ve/decisiones/scon/Diciembre/1329-161210-2010-10-1434.html.

1249   Véase en *Gaceta Oficial* N° 6.011 Extra. de 21-12-2010. La Sala Constitucional mediante sentencia
        N° 1329 de 16-12-2009 declaró la constitucionalidad del carácter orgánico de esta Ley.

1250   Véase en *Gaceta Oficial* N° 6.011 Extra. de 21-12-2010. La Sala Constitucional mediante sentencia
        N° 1330 de 17-12-2010 declaró la constitucionalidad del carácter orgánico de esta Ley. Véase en
        http://www.tsj.gov.ve/decisiones/scon/Diciembre/1330-171210-2010-10-1436.html.

1251   Véase en *Gaceta Oficial* N° 6.011 Extra. de 21-12-2010. La Sala Constitucional mediante sentencia
        N° 1329 de 16-12-2010 declaró la constitucionalidad del carácter orgánico de esta Ley. Véase en
        http://www.tsj.gov.ve/decisiones/scon/Diciembre/1329-161210-2010-10-1434.html.

1252   Véase en *Gaceta Oficial* N° 6.011 Extra. de 21-12-2010. La Sala Constitucional mediante sentencia
        N° 1326 de 16-12-2009 declaró la constitucionalidad del carácter orgánico de esta Ley.

1253   Véase en *Gaceta Oficial* N° 6.011 Extra. de 21-12-2010. La Sala Constitucional mediante sentencia
        N° 1329 de 16-12-2010 declaró la constitucionalidad del carácter orgánico de esta Ley. Véase en
        http://www.tsj.gov.ve/decisiones/scon/Diciembre/%201328-161210-2010-10-1437.html.

1254   Véase en *Gaceta Oficial* N° 5.963 Extra. de 22-02-2010.

1255   Véase en *Gaceta Oficial* N° 6.015 Extra. de 28-12-2010.

1256   Véase en *Gaceta Oficial* N° 6.017 Extra. de 30-12-2010.

1257   Véase en *Gaceta Oficial* N° 6.017 Extra. de 30-12-2010.

1258   Véase en *Gaceta Oficial* N° 6.009 Extra. de fecha 17 de diciembre de 2010.

tes[1259] para materialmente impedir que la nueva Asamblea Nacional que tomó posesión en enero de 2011, pueda funcionar.[1260]

Ahora bien, el marco definitorio general del Estado Comunista con una ideología única Socialista que se quiere imponer a los venezolanos, y por el cual nadie ha votado; montado sobre el supuesto ejercicio de la soberanía por el pueblo exclusivamente en forma directa a través del ejercicio del "Poder Popular" y el establecimiento de un "Estado Comunal," está contenido básicamente en la Ley Orgánica del Poder Popular (LOPP), en la Ley Orgánica de los Consejos Comunales, en la Ley Orgánica de las Comunas y en la Ley Orgánica de Contraloría Social, cuyas disposiciones, conforme al artículo 6 de la LOPP, "son aplicables a todas las organizaciones, expresiones y ámbitos del Poder Popular, ejercidas directa o indirectamente por las personas, las comunidades, los sectores sociales, la sociedad en general y las situaciones que afecten el interés colectivo, acatando el principio de legalidad en la formación, ejecución y control de la gestión pública."

Es decir, las disposiciones de la LOPP y de las otras leyes son omnicomprensivas, aplicándose a todos, y a todo, como piezas esenciales de un nuevo y paralelo Estado regido por un principio de legalidad "socialista" que se impone a todos para la formación, ejecución y control de la gestión pública.

Nuestro objetivo en estas líneas, es estudiar el sentido de las regulaciones establecidas en estas Leyes en torno al Estado Comunal o Comunista. Antes sin embargo, analizaremos el marco constitucional de la democracia y de la participación política con cuya distorsión se quiere acabar con la primera; los intentos de reformar la Constitución para institucionalizar el Estado Socialista en 2007; y el logro de dicha institucionalización violando la Constitución y en fraude a la voluntad popular impuesta en diciembre de 2010 mediante las referidas Leyes relativas al Poder Popular, los Consejos Comunales, las Comunas y el Estado Comunal; y las relativas a la Contraloría Social y al Sistema Económico Comunal, que no es otro que un sistema comunista concebido dentro de la más clara ortodoxia marxista.

Con estas leyes orgánicas, no cabe duda de la decisión política adoptada en diciembre de 2010 por la completamente deslegitimada Asamblea Nacional que había sido electa en 2005, y que ya no representaba a la mayoría de la voluntad popular que se expresó el 26 de septiembre de 2010 en contra del Presidente de la República, de la propia Asamblea Nacional y de la política socialista que han adelantado; de imponerle a los venezolanos en contra de la voluntad popular y en fraude a la Constitución, un modelo de Estado Comunista montado sobre el Socialismo como doctrina de Estado y como dogma político impuesto a la Sociedad, denominado "Estado Comunal," basado en el ejercicio del Poder Popular por el pueblo, como supuesta forma de ejercicio de la soberanía en forma directa (lo que no es cierto pues se ejerce mediante "voceros" que lo "representan" y que no son electos en votaciones universales, directas y secretas).

1259   Véase en *Gaceta Oficial* N° 6.014 Extra. de 23 de diciembre de 2010.

1260   Se redujeron las sesiones de la Asamblea a sólo cuatro por semana y se limitó el tiempo durante el cual los diputados podrían intervenir.

Ese modelo de Estado Comunal o Comunista, se ha establecido en forma parale-la al Estado Constitucional como Estado federal descentralizado, democrático y social, de derecho, y de justicia previsto en la Constitución de 1999, establecido para el ejercicio del Poder Público por el pueblo tanto en forma indirecta mediante repre-sentantes electos en votaciones universales, directas y secretas, como en forma dire-cta mediante los mecanismos autorizados en la Constitución, donde se incluye a las Asambleas de Ciudadanos.

Esta regulación, en paralelo, de dos Estados y dos formas de ejercicio de la sobe-ranía, uno, el Estado Constitucional regulado en la Constitución y el otro, el Estado Comunal o Estado Comunista basado en el Socialismo exclusionista regulado en leyes orgánicas inconstitucionales, se ha dispuesto en forma tal que el segundo irá actuando como el árbol *Ficus benjamina L.*, es decir, como "estranguladora," rode-ando al primero hasta formar un tronco hueco, destruyéndolo.

En esta forma, al fraude a la Constitución, que ha sido la técnica constantemente aplicada por el gobierno autoritario en Venezuela desde 1999 para imponer sus de-cisiones a los venezolanos al margen de la Constitución,[1261] se suma ahora el fraude a la voluntad popular, al imponerle a los venezolanos mediante leyes orgánicas, un modelo de Estado por el cual nadie ha votado y que cambia radical e inconstitucio-nalmente el texto de la Constitución de 1999, que no ha sido reformada conforme a sus previsiones, en abierta contradicción al rechazo popular mayoritario que se ex-presó en diciembre de 2007 respecto de la reforma constitucional que se intentó aprobar, incluso violando la propia Constitución, y al rechazo popular mayoritario del pueblo expresado respecto de la política del Presidente de la República y de su Asamblea Nacional con ocasión de las elecciones parlamentarias del 26 de septiem-bre de 2010.

Lo que está claro de todo esto, es que ya no hay máscaras que puedan engañar a alguien, o con motivo de las cuales, alguien pretenda ser engañado o dejarse enga-ñar.

SECCIÓN PRIMERA:

LA DEMOCRACIA Y LA PARTICIPACIÓN POLÍTICA Y POPULAR, Y EL AHO-GAMIENTO DE LA DEMOCRACIA REPRESENTATIVA EN NOMBRE DE UNA SUPUESTA "DEMOCRACIA PARTICIPATIVA"

Una de las más importantes innovaciones contenidas en la Constitución de 1999, fue sin duda, la inclusión del principio y del derecho a la participación política de las personas en los asuntos públicos, materializados en dos ámbitos diferenciados:

Por una parte, la participación política o participación ciudadana, concebida co-mo derecho político que se otorga únicamente a los ciudadanos, quienes además tienen el deber de participar solidariamente en la vida política del país (art. 132); y por la otra, la participación individual y comunitaria en los asuntos públicos, conce-

---

1261   Véase Allan R. Brewer-Carías, *Reforma constitucional y fraude a la Constitución (1999-2009)*, Academia de Ciencias Políticas y Sociales, Caracas 2009; *Dismantling Democracy. The Chávez Aut-horitarian Experiment*, Cambridge University Press, New York 2010.

bida como un derecho de toda persona individualmente considerada o como derecho colectivo, concebido, incluso, como un deber general de participar solidariamente en la vida civil y comunitaria del país (art. 132).

En relación con la participación política o participación ciudadana, se trata del derecho constitucional de todos los ciudadanos "de participar libremente en los asuntos públicos, directamente o por medio de sus representantes elegidos" (art. 62), a los efectos de la conformación de un gobierno democrático y participativo (arts. 6, 18, 171), regulándose a tal efecto diversas manifestaciones concretas de su ejercicio (arts. 55, 62, 70, 125, 168, 173, 178, 187, 253, 255, 294.

En relación con la participación en la vida civil y comunitaria, responde al principio general de organización de la sociedad que la Constitución de 1999 ha previsto como "una sociedad democrática, participativa y protagónica, multiétnica y pluricultural" (Preámbulo), declarando que "la participación del pueblo en la formación, ejecución y control de la gestión pública es el medio necesario para lograr el protagonismo que garantice su completo desarrollo, tanto individual como colectivo" (art. 62). Ello, en particular, se materializa en el ejercicio de diversos derechos sociales (arts. 79, 80, 81, 83, 84, 86, 91, 102, 118, 119, 122) y ambientales (art. 127, 128) o en mecanismos de participación de las comunidades en los asuntos públicos (art. 184, 299).

En el régimen constitucional sobre la participación, por tanto, la participación ciudadana como derecho político, es distinto al derecho que tiene todo habitante de una comunidad de participar en los asuntos relativos con dicha comunidad. En este último caso, no se trata de un "derecho político" que en la Constitución se reserva a los venezolanos-ciudadanos (por ejemplo, el participar en elecciones, en referendos o en las asambleas de ciudadanos), sino que se trata de un derecho de toda persona de participar en los asuntos públicos que es consecuencia del derecho esencial al libre desenvolvimiento de la personalidad que toda persona tiene (art. 20).

Es importante hacer esta distinción entre "participación ciudadana" como derecho político y "participación general" como derecho individual y comunitario, pues conforme a la Constitución, los titulares para su ejercicio son distintos: en cuanto al derecho político a la participación ciudadana el mismo sólo corresponde a los venezolanos-ciudadanos; en cambio, el derecho individual y social a la participación comunitaria, corresponde a todo habitante de la comunidad, incluyendo a los extranjeros y a los menores.

Por otra parte, y ahora concentrándonos en la previsión del artículo 62 de la Constitución que consagra el derecho político de los ciudadanos "de participar libremente en los asuntos públicos, directamente o por medio de sus representantes elegidos," en el mismo, al regularse el derecho a la participación política en los asuntos públicos, se establece un derecho esencial de la democracia que siempre tiene que poder ejercerse *libremente*, o sea, con entera libertad, en las dos formas precisas que establece la norma: por una parte, *directamente*, conforme a los mecanismos establecidos en el artículo 70 de la misma Constitución, mediante referendos, consultas populares, revocación de mandatos, iniciativas legislativas, cabildos abiertos y asamblea de ciudadanos; y por la otra, *indirectamente*, conforme al artículo 63 de la Constitución, mediante sufragio para la elección de representantes elegidos a través de votaciones libres, universales, directas y secretas, en las cuales se garantice el principio de la personalización del sufragio y la representación proporcional.

El derecho a la participación política ejercido *indirectamente* se materializa en la democracia representativa, a cuyo efecto la Constitución ha establecido como sistema de gobierno de todas las entidades políticas, un sistema electivo, garantizándose el derecho de los ciudadanos al sufragio y a ser electos, conforme a un sistema electoral que garantice votaciones libres, universales, directas y secretas, y el principio de la personalización del sufragio y la representación proporcional (art. 63).

En cuanto al derecho a la participación política ejercido *directamente*, el mismo se materializa en la democracia participativa, a cuyo efecto la Constitución ha previsto su ejercicio a través de diversos mecanismos, todos vinculados a la organización descentralizada del Poder Público entre el Poder Nacional, el Poder Estadal y el Poder Municipal, como los referendos (en materias de índole nacional, estadal y municipal), las consultas populares (sobre asuntos nacionales, estadales o municipales), la revocación de mandatos (de los funcionarios electos en el ámbito nacional, estadal y municipal), las iniciativas legislativas (ante la Asamblea Nacional, los Consejos Legislativos de los Estados y los Concejos Municipales), los cabildos abiertos (en los Concejos Municipales) y las asambleas de ciudadanos (en los ámbitos de la unidad primaria de la organización nacional que son los Municipios).[1262]

Ahora bien, partiendo de lo anteriormente señalado y teniendo en cuenta el marco constitucional sobre la democracia y la participación, incluyendo la mencionada distinción entre la participación ciudadana como derecho político, y la participación popular como derecho individual y colectivo de todo habitante de una comunidad de hacerse parte en los asuntos relativos a dicha comunidad, es que debe analizarse el régimen establecido en las Leyes sobre el Poder Popular y el Estado Comunal, y en particular, la Ley Orgánica de los Consejos Comunales de 2009. En todas las referidas leyes se ha establecido una mezcolanza en el ejercicio de ambos derechos, y por ejemplo en la Ley Orgánica del Poder Popular, de los Consejos Comunales y de las Comunas, se ha otorgado un derecho político que es exclusivo de los ciudadanos, como es el de la participación *en las Asambleas de Ciudadanos* consagrado en los artículos 62 y 70 de la Constitución, a quienes no son ciudadanos, como son los extranjeros y los menores de 18 años. Con ello, la base de toda la regulación establecida en estas leyes, simplemente, fue mal concebida.

Sin duda es posible y deseable que los extranjeros y menores participen en asambleas de la comunidad, vecinales o en cualquier otra instancia comunitaria como

1262   Véase sobre el tema Allan R. Brewer-Carías,. "La necesaria revalorización de la democracia representativa ante los peligros del discurso autoritario sobre una supuesta "democracia participativa" sin representación," en *Derecho Electoral de Latinoamérica. Memoria del II Congreso Iberoamericano de Derecho*, Bogotá, 31 agosto-1 septiembre 2011, Consejo Superior de la Judicatura, ISBN 978-958-8331-93-5, Bogotá 2013, pp. 425-449; "Democracia participativa, descentralización política y régimen municipal", en Miguel Alejandro López Olvera y Luis Gerardo Rodríguez Lozano (Coordinadores), *Tendencias actuales del derecho público en Iberoamérica*, Editorial Porrúa, México 2006, pp. 1-23; y 'Democracia participativa, descentralización política y régimen municipal", en *Urbana*, No. 36, Revista editada por el Instituto de Urbanismo, Facultad de Arquitectura y Urbanismo, , Universidad Central de Venezuela y por el Instituto de Investigaciones de la Facultad de Arquitectura y Diseño, Universidad del Zulia, 2005, pp. 33-48.

manifestación del derecho a la participación social y comunitaria que corresponde a toda persona habitante de la República, pero no es posible constitucionalmente que se les otorgue el derecho de participar en las Asamblea de "ciudadanos," o de votar en referendos que son específicos mecanismos de participación "política" que, como se dijo, de acuerdo con la Constitución, son una manifestación esencial de un derecho político que se ha reservado a los ciudadanos.

Ahora bien, refiriéndonos ahora en concreto al derecho a la participación política en forma *directa* (democracia participativa) en la Constitución de 1999, como se ha dicho, el mismo está concebido, primero, como un derecho *político* (distinto a los civiles, sociales, educativos, culturales, ambientales, etc.), el cual, por tanto corresponde sólo a los *ciudadanos*, es decir, a los venezolanos que no estén sujetos a inhabilitación política ni a interdicción civil y conforme a la edad que se determine en la ley (art. 30); segundo, se lo concibe como un derecho político que tiene que poder ejercerse *libremente*, es decir, sin limitaciones o condicionamientos algunos salvo los que puedan derivarse "del derecho de las demás y del orden público y social" (art. 20), razón por la cual no pueden estar encasillados en una ideología única compulsiva como el socialismo; tercero, se lo concibe como tal derecho político que debe ejercerse en el marco de la organización descentralizada del Poder Público (Nacional, Estadal y Municipal) que responde a su distribución en el territorio conforme a la forma federal del Estado (arts. 4 y 136); y cuarto, se lo concibe como un derecho político que por su naturaleza (la necesidad de que el Poder esté cerca del ciudadano), ha de ejercerse particularmente en la unidad política primaria y autónoma de la organización nacional que conforme a la Constitución es el Municipio, concebido como una entidad política con gobierno propio electo mediante sufragio universal directo y secreto (democracia representativa). Es en las actuaciones de esta unidad política, conforme al artículo 168 de la Constitución, que fundamentalmente se debe incorporar "la participación ciudadana al proceso de definición y ejecución de la gestión pública y al control y evaluación de sus resultados, en forma efectiva, suficiente y oportuna."

Es contrario a la Constitución, por tanto, que el derecho político a la participación se extienda a quienes no son ciudadanos, como son los extranjeros o los menores; que se lo conciba en forma restringida, es decir, sin poder ejercerse libremente, al reducírselo en su ejercicio sólo para la ejecución de una orientación política exclusionista como es el socialismo, eliminando cualquier otra; que su ejercicio se organice en forma centralizada, sometido a la sola conducción por parte del Poder Nacional y en particular del Ejecutivo Nacional, excluyéndose de su ámbito a los Estados y Municipios; y en particular, que se excluya a este último (el Municipio) como unidad política primaria que es en la organización nacional, del ámbito de su ejercicio, desmunicipalizándoselo, al concebirse otra entidad no autónoma políticamente para materializarlo como es el caso de los Concejos Comunales creados sin autonomía política y fuera del gobierno local.

En otras palabras, sólo mediante una reforma constitucional del artículo 30 de la Constitución es que podría extenderse la ciudadanía a los extranjeros, a los efectos de que puedan ejercer el derecho político a la participación; sólo mediante una reforma constitucional del artículo 62 de la Constitución es que podría eliminarse el carácter libre del ejercicio del derecho a la participación ciudadana y restringírselo sólo para la consecución del socialismo; sólo mediante una reforma constitucional de los artículos 4 y 136 de la Constitución, es que se podría eliminar la forma descentralizada del ejercicio de la participación ciudadana en el sistema de distribución vertical del Poder Público, y concebir su ejercicio sólo sometido a la sola conducción por parte del Poder Nacional y, en particular, del Ejecutivo Nacional; y sólo mediante una reforma constitucional del artículo 168 de la Constitución es que se podría excluir al Municipio del ámbito de ejercicio del derecho político a la participación ciudadana, desmunicipalizándoselo, y concebirse una unidad primaria no autónoma políticamente, como los Concejos Comunales creados sin autonomía política y fuera del gobierno local, para canalizar su ejercicio.

Y esto es precisamente lo que se ha establecido en las Leyes Orgánicas del Poder Popular, de los Consejos Comunales y de las Comunas, al regularse el régimen del derecho a la participación ciudadana, y crearse a dichos Concejos Comunales, como "una instancia de participación para el ejercicio directo de la soberanía popular" (art. 1) "en la construcción del nuevo modelo de sociedad socialista"(art. 2), "con el fin de establecer la base sociopolítica del socialismo que consolide un nuevo modelo político, social, cultural y económico" (art. 3); en una forma completamente distinta a la establecida en la Constitución, cuyo texto se viola abiertamente. Con estas Leyes Orgánicas, en realidad, y en forma completamente inconstitucional, lo que se ha pretendido es implementar las reformas constitucionales sobre el "Poder Popular" que se habían pretendido introducir con la Reforma Constitucional sancionada de 2007,[1263] la cual, sin embargo, fue rechazada mayoritariamente por el pueblo.

Ahora bien, para entender adecuadamente el contenido y sentido de estas nuevas regulaciones relativas al Poder Popular y al Estado Comunal, montado sobre las Comunas y los Consejos Comunales, consideramos necesario referirnos a sus antecedentes inmediatos: primero, al contenido de la rechazada reforma constitucional de 2007, en lo que se refería a la estructuración del Poder Popular en paralelo al Poder Público, y que, como se dijo, fue rechazado mayoritariamente por el pueblo en el referendo de diciembre de 2007; y segundo, a la institucionalización efectuada en 2006 de los Consejos Comunales como pieza del Estado Socialista.

SECCIÓN SEGUNDA:

LOS ANTECEDENTES DEL NUEVO RÉGIMEN DEL PODER POPULAR Y DEL ESTADO COMUNAL EN UNA LEY INCONSTITUCIONAL DE 2006 Y EN EL INTENTO DE REFORMA CONSTITUCIONAL EN 2007

Como se dijo, los antecedentes inmediatos de las leyes del Poder Popular y del Estado Comunal en Venezuela, es decir, para el establecimiento del Estado Comunista, fueron: primero, la sanción en 2006 y sin soporte alguno en la Constitución, de la Ley de los Consejos Comunales[1264] con la que se inició el proceso de desmuni-

---

1263   Véase Sobre dicha reforma Allan R. Brewer-Carías, *La Reforma Constitucional de 2007*, Editorial Jurídica Venezolana, Caracas 2007.

1264   Véase *Gaceta Oficial* N° 5806 Extra. de 10 de abril de 2006. Véase sobre esta Ley de 2006, lo expuesto en el estudio de Claudia Nikken, "La Ley Orgánica de los Consejos Comunales y el derecho a la participación ciudadana en los asuntos públicos," en Allan R. Brewer-Carías (Coordinador), Claudia Nikken, Luis A. Herrera Orellana, Jesús María Alvarado Andrade, José Ignacio Hernández y

cipalización en el país; y segundo, la formulación del proyecto de reforma constitucional por el Presidente de la República en 2007, para la institucionalización de un Estado centralista Socialista y Militarista, el cual a pesar de haber sido sancionado por la Asamblea Nacional en noviembre de 2007, fue rechazada por el pueblo en el referendo de diciembre de 2007.

I   LA "DESMUNICIPALIZACIÓN" DE LA PARTICIPACIÓN CIUDADANA Y LOS CONSEJOS COMUNALES CREADOS EN 2006

1.   *Los Municipios y los Consejos Comunales*

En efecto, desde 2006, con la sanción de la Ley de los Consejos Comunales y la progresiva creación de los mismos, el gobierno autoritario había venido tratando de regular y confinar la participación ciudadana con un doble propósito: por una parte, para eliminar la democracia representativa; y por la otra, para desmunicipalizar su ámbito de ejercicio.[1265]

Como se ha dicho, conforme a la Constitución, el Municipio es la unidad política primaria dentro de la organización pública nacional (art. 168) que, como parte del sistema constitucional de distribución vertical del Poder Público (art. 136), en el nivel territorial inferior es la entidad política llamada a hacer efectiva la participación ciudadana. Por ello, el artículo 2° de la Ley Orgánica del Poder Público Municipal de 2005[1266] conforme a lo dispuesto en el artículo 168 de la Constitución dispuso que las actuaciones del municipio deberían incorporar "la participación ciudadana de manera efectiva, suficiente y oportuna, en la definición y ejecución de la gestión pública y en el control y evaluación de sus resultados."

Para ello, en todo caso, lo que resultaba necesario era acercar el poder municipal al ciudadano, municipalizándose el territorio, lo que la propia Ley Orgánica impidió. Pero en lugar de reformar dicha Ley Orgánica y establecer entidades municipales o del municipio más cerca de las comunidades, lo que se buscó establecer con la Ley de los Consejos Comunales de 2006 fue un sistema institucional centralizado para la supuesta participación popular, denominado "del Poder Popular", en paralelo e ignorando la propia existencia del régimen municipal, concibiéndose a la "comunidad" fuera del mismo Municipio, organizada en Consejos Comunales, "en el marco

Adriana Vigilanza, *Leyes Orgánicas sobre el Poder Popular y el Estado Comunal (Los Consejos Comunales, las Comunas, la Sociedad Socialista y el Sistema Económico Comunal),*Editorial Jurídica Venezolana, Caracas 2011, pp. 183 ss.

1265   Véase lo que hemos expuesto en Allan R. Brewer-Carías, "El inicio de la desmunicipalización en Venezuela: La organización del Poder Popular para eliminar la descentralización, la democracia representativa y la participación a nivel local", en *AIDA, Opera Prima de Derecho Administrativo. Revista de la Asociación Internacional de Derecho Administrativo*, Universidad Nacional Autónoma de México, Facultad de Estudios Superiores de Acatlán, Coordinación de Postgrado, Instituto Internacional de Derecho Administrativo "Agustín Gordillo", Asociación Internacional de Derecho Administrativo, México, 2007, pp. 49 a 67.

1266   Véase la Ley de Reforma Parcial de la Ley Orgánica del Poder Público Municipal, *Gaceta Oficial* N° 38.327 de 02-12-2005. Véanse los comentarios a esta Ley en el libro: *Ley Orgánica del Poder Público Municipal*, Editorial Jurídica Venezolana, Caracas 2007. La Ley ha sido reformada en 2010, *Gaceta Oficial* N° 6.015 Extra. de 28 de diciembre de 2010.

constitucional de la democracia participativa y protagónica", como "instancias de participación, articulación e integración entre las diversas organizaciones comunitarias, grupos sociales y los ciudadanos." Fue en estos Consejos Comunales, conforme a la Ley de 2006, establecidos sin relación alguna con los Municipios, en los que se ubicaron las Asambleas de Ciudadanos como la instancia primaria para el ejercicio del poder, la participación y el protagonismo popular, cuyas decisiones se concibieron como de carácter vinculante para el consejo comunal respectivo (art. 4,5).

Con esta Ley de los Consejos Comunales de 2006, puede decirse que se comenzó el inconstitucional proceso de desmunicipalización de la participación ciudadana, sustituyéndose al Municipio como la unidad política primaria en la organización nacional que exige la Constitución conforme a un sistema de descentralización política (distribución vertical) del poder, por un sistema de entidades sin autonomía política alguna que se denominaron del "Poder Popular" (Consejos Comunales), directamente vinculadas y dependientes en un esquema centralizado del poder, dirigido desde el más alto nivel del Poder Ejecutivo Nacional, por el Presidente de la República mediante una Comisión Presidencial del Poder Popular.[1267]

La Ley, además, supuestamente abogando por una participación popular, en un esquema completamente antidemocrático, sustituyó la representación que origina el sufragio en entidades políticas como los Municipales, por la organización de entidades denominadas del "Poder Popular" que no tienen origen representativo electoral, en las cuales se pretendió ubicar la participación ciudadana, pero sometida al control del vértice del poder central, y sin que los titulares rindan cuentas al pueblo.

En efecto, en abril de 2006, en lugar de reformarse nuevamente la Ley Orgánica del Poder Público Municipal para municipalizar el país y hacer efectiva la participación ciudadana en un esquema de descentralización política del poder público, se optó por sancionarse la Ley de los Consejos Comunales con el objeto de crear, desarrollar y regular la conformación de dichas supuestas instancias de participación, totalmente desvinculadas de Municipios, parroquias y organizaciones vecinales, estableciéndose su integración, organización y funcionamiento, así como su relación con los órganos del Estado, para la formulación, ejecución, control y evaluación de las políticas públicas (art. 1).

Estos Consejos Comunales, supuestamente "en el marco constitucional de la democracia participativa y protagónica", se regularon como se dijo, sin relación alguna con la organización municipal, para en paralelo, supuestamente permitir "al pueblo organizado ejercer directamente la gestión de las políticas públicas y proyectos orientados a responder a las necesidades y aspiraciones de las comunidades en la construcción de una sociedad de equidad y justicia social" (art. 2). Se trata, como se dijo, de un esquema organizacional completamente paralelo y desvinculado con la

---

1267   Sobre esto, por ejemplo, María Pilar García-Guadilla ha señalado al referirse al "solapamiento y usurpación de competencias entre los Concejos Comunales y el concejo municipal," que los primeros "debilitan la idea de un gobierno municipal autónomo con propiedad sobre el espacio geográfico en donde tiene jurisdicción y no promueven la descentralización," en "La praxis de los consejos comunales en Venezuela: ¿Poder popular o instancia clientelar?," en *Revista Venezolana de Economía y Ciencias Sociales*, abr. 2008, Vol. 14, N° 1, p. 125-151. Véase en http://www.scielo.org.ve/scielo.php?pid=S1315-6411200-8000100009&script=sci_arttext.

descentralización política o la distribución vertical del poder público; es decir, completamente desvinculado de la organización territorial del Estado que establece la Constitución, es decir, desvinculado de los Estados, Municipios y Parroquias.

Por ello, los Consejos Comunales se integraron conforme a un esquema estatal centralizado, que tenía en su cúspide una Comisión Nacional Presidencial del Poder Popular designada y presidida por el Presidente de la República, la cual, a su vez, designaba en cada Estado a las Comisiones Regionales Presidenciales del Poder Popular, previa aprobación del Presidente de la República (art. 31); y designaba además, en cada municipio, las Comisiones Locales Presidencial del Poder Popular, también previa aprobación del Presidente de la República (art. 32); sin participación alguna de los Gobernadores de Estado ni de los Alcaldes municipales.

En todo caso, la Ley dispuso que la organización, funcionamiento y acción de dichos consejos comunales "se rige conforme a los principios de corresponsabilidad, cooperación, solidaridad, transparencia, rendición de cuentas, honestidad, eficacia, eficiencia, responsabilidad social, control social, equidad, justicia e igualdad social y de género"(art. 3). La práctica, sin embargo, no evidencia que no se logró desarrollar los concejos comunales conforme al discurso gubernamental y a las previsiones teóricas de la Ley, de manera que como lo ha observado María Pilar García-Guadilla, "Mientras que los objetivos y el discurso presidencial hablan de empoderamiento, transformación y democratización, las praxis observadas apuntan hacia el clientelismo, la cooptación, la centralización y la exclusión por razones de polarización política."[1268]

2. La "comunidad" como la unidad básica de organización del pueblo

La Ley de 2006 estableció como unidad social básica para el funcionamiento de los Consejos Comunales a la "comunidad" la cual se definió como "el conglomerado social de familias, ciudadanos y ciudadanas que habitan en un área geográfica determinada, que comparten una historia e intereses comunes, se conocen y relacionan entre sí, usan los mismos servicios públicos y comparten necesidades y potencialidades similares: económicas, sociales, urbanísticas y de otra índole (art. 4,1). Ella, en realidad, debió haber sido el nuevo municipio que debió haberse creado en otra concepción democrática y participativa del mismo.

La Ley de 2006 definió además, a las Comunidades Indígenas como "grupos humanos formados por familias indígenas asociadas entre sí, pertenecientes a uno o más pueblos indígenas, que están ubicados en un determinado espacio geográfico y organizados según las pautas culturales propias de cada pueblo, con o sin modificaciones provenientes de otras culturas (art. 4,2).

La Ley de 2006 estableció tres elementos claves para identificar a la "comunidad" como organización social, que fueron un territorio, una población y una organización.

1268   Véase en María Pilar García-Guadilla "La praxis de los consejos comunales en Venezuela: ¿Poder popular o instancia clientelar?," en *Revista Venezolana de Economía y Ciencias Sociales*, abr. 2008, Vol. 14, N° 1, p. 125-151. Véase en http://www.scielo.org.ve/scielo.php?pid=S1315-641120080001-00009&script =sci_arttext

En cuanto al territorio, el de las comunidades debía estar formado por el área geográfica atribuida a la misma, conformado por el Territorio que ocupan sus habitantes, cuyos límites geográficos se debían establecer en Asamblea de Ciudadanos dentro de los cuales debía funcionar el Consejo Comunal. El área geográfica debía ser decidida por la Asamblea de Ciudadanos de acuerdo con las particularidades de cada comunidad (art. 4,3).

En cuanto a la población, a los efectos de "la participación protagónica, la planificación y la gobernabilidad de los consejos comunales", la misma se debía determinar conforme a una "base poblacional de la comunidad" haciendo la Ley referencia a los criterios técnicos y sociológicos que señalaban –en cierto sentido similar a los que se utilizaron en la vieja Ley Orgánica de Régimen Municipal para las asociaciones de vecinos- que las comunidades se agrupaban en familias, entre 200 y 400 en el área urbana, a partir de 20 familias en el área rural y a partir de 10 familias en las comunidades indígenas. La base poblacional debía ser decidida por la Asamblea de Ciudadanos de acuerdo con las particularidades de cada comunidad, tomando en cuenta las comunidades aledañas. (art. 4,4).

En cuanto a la organización política de las Comunidades, la Ley estableció las siguientes estructuras básicas de la comunidad, sin ningún elemento de democracia representativa o de gobierno electivo: la Asamblea de Ciudadanos, el Consejo Comunal y sus órganos ejecutivo, financiero y de control, y las demás organizaciones comunitarias. Estas últimas eran las que "existen o pueden existir en las comunidades y que agrupan a un conjunto de ciudadanos y ciudadanas con base en objetivos e intereses comunes, tales como: comités de tierras, comités de salud, mesas técnicas de agua, grupos culturales, clubes deportivos, puntos de encuentro y organizaciones de mujeres, sindicatos y organizaciones de trabajadores y trabajadoras, organizaciones juveniles o estudiantiles, asociaciones civiles, cooperativas, entre otras" (art. 4,8).

3. *Las asambleas de ciudadanos*

La Ley de 2006, en paralelo al Municipio como la unidad primaria para la participación, concibió a la Asamblea de Ciudadanos como la instancia primaria para el ejercicio del poder, la participación y el protagonismo popular, cuyas decisiones son de carácter vinculante para el consejo comunal respectivo.(art. 4,5). Esta Asamblea de Ciudadanos se la reguló como "la máxima instancia de decisión del Consejo Comunal", integrada por los habitantes de la comunidad, mayores de 15 años. En esta forma, como se dijo, se violó la Constitución (arts. 62 y 70) que reserva el derecho de participar en las "Asambleas de ciudadanos," como lo indica su nombre, solo a los "ciudadanos," lo que excluye a los extranjeros y a los menores de 18 años. El legislador, quizás, lo que quiso fue regular Asambleas de la comunidad o de vecinos, pero las denominó erróneamente como Asambleas de ciudadanos, violando la Constitución.

La Ley reguló todo el proceso de constitución inicial (por primera vez) de las Asambleas de Ciudadanos (Asamblea Constituyente Comunal o Comunitaria) con la asistencia de al menos el 20% de los miembros de la comunidad, mayores de 15 años (art. 19), convocada, conducida y organizada por una comisión promotora integrada por el número variable de miembros de la comunidad que asumieran esta iniciativa, con la participación de un representante designado por la Comisión Presidencial del Poder Popular respectivo. (arts. 15, 16). Esta Comisión promotora debía, conforme al artículo 17 de la Ley de 2006, entre otras funciones, difundir entre los habitantes de la comunidad el alcance, objeto y fines de los Consejos Comunales; elaborar un croquis del área geográfica de la comunidad; recabar la información de su historia; organizar y coordinar la realización del censo demográfico y socioeconómico comunitario; y convocar a la Asamblea Constituyente Comunitaria. La Comisión Promotora cesaba en sus funciones al momento de la conformación del Consejo Comunal.

La Asamblea de Ciudadanos conforme al artículo 6 de la Ley de 2006, tenía entre sus atribuciones, el aprobar las normas de convivencia de la comunidad; aprobar los estatutos y el acta constitutiva del Consejo Comunal con la indicación de su nombre, el área geográfica, el número de familias que lo integraban, el listado de asistentes y el lugar, fecha y hora de reunión; la aprobación del Plan de Desarrollo de la Comunidad y los proyectos presentados al Consejo Comunal en beneficio de la comunidad; el ejercicio de la contraloría social; y la adopción de las decisiones esenciales de la vida comunitaria, y entre ellas, elegir a los integrantes de los diversos voceros e integrantes de los órganos comunitarios, y revocarles el mandato. La Asamblea de Ciudadanos también debía determinar y elegir el número de voceros de los diversos comités de trabajo, de acuerdo a la cantidad que se conformasen en la comunidad (art. 9), en áreas como salud, educación, tierra urbana o rural, vivienda, protección e igualdad social, economía popular, cultura, seguridad integral, medios de comunicación, recreación y deportes, alimentación, agua, energía y gas, y servicios (art. 9).

Todos los voceros de los comités de trabajo, conforme al artículo 12 de la Ley de 2006 debían ser electos en "votaciones directas y secretas por la Asamblea de Ciudadanos," para lo cual el artículo 13 de la Ley exigía ser habitante de la comunidad, con al menos 6 meses de residencia en la misma; mayor de 15 años, y no ocupar cargos de elección popular. Iguales condiciones se establecieron para los integrantes de las diversas unidades del Consejo Comunal. Se eliminaba así el sufragio universal, y se otorgaba la "ciudadanía" a quien no podía tenerla constitucionalmente.

La Asamblea de Ciudadanos debía nombrar una Comisión Electoral (art. 18) con el fin de organizar y conducir el proceso de elección de los voceros y demás integrantes de los órganos del Consejo Comunal, debiendo a tal efecto, entre otras funciones, elaborar un registro electoral y conducir el proceso de designación los mismos.

4. La organización de los Consejos Comunales

El Consejo Comunal organizado por la Asamblea de Ciudadanos, conforme a lo dispuesto en el artículo 7 de la Ley de 2006, debía estar integrado por un órgano ejecutivo, integrado por los voceros de cada comité de trabajo; una Unidad de Gestión Financiera, como órgano económico-financiero; y una Unidad de Contraloría Social, como órgano de control. Los ciudadanos integrantes de los consejos comunales debían responder a los principios de corresponsabilidad social, rendición de cuentas, y manejo transparente, oportuno y eficaz de los recursos que dispusieran (art. 5).

A los efectos de una adecuada articulación de su trabajo, el artículo 24 de la Ley disponía que los órganos ejecutivo, de control y económico financiero del Consejo Comunal, debían realizar reuniones de coordinación y seguimiento, y los gastos que se generasen por concepto de la actividad de los voceros y demás integrantes de los órganos del Consejo Comunal, debían ser compensados por el fondo de gastos de funcionamiento del Consejo Comunal.

Los consejos comunales debían ser registrados ante la Comisión Local Presidencial del Poder Popular, para lo cual debían hacer entrega de los estatutos y acta constitutiva aprobados por la Asamblea de Ciudadanos (art. 20). Este registro ante la Comisión Presidencial del Poder Popular respectiva, era lo que revestía a los Consejos de personalidad jurídica para todos los efectos relacionados con la Ley. Las tareas de procesamiento de este registro, sin embargo, fueron delegadas en la Fundación estatal FUNDACOMÚN, de larga tradición en materia de desarrollo de la comunidad, desde los años sesenta.[1269]

El órgano ejecutivo del Consejo Comunal, integrado por los voceros de cada comité de trabajo (art. 7), se lo concibió en la Ley de 2006 como la instancia encargada de promover y articular la participación organizada de los integrantes de la comunidad, los grupos sociales y organizaciones comunitarias en los diferentes comités de trabajo, y tenía como funciones básicas, conforme al artículo 21 de la Ley de 2006, ejecutar las decisiones de la Asamblea de Ciudadanos; promover la creación de nuevas organizaciones en defensa del interés colectivo y el desarrollo integral, sostenible y sustentable de las comunidades; elaborar planes de trabajo para solventar los problemas que la comunidad pueda resolver con sus propios recursos y evaluar sus resultados; organizar el voluntariado social en cada uno de los comités de trabajo; promover la solicitud de transferencias de servicios, participación en los procesos económicos, gestión de empresas públicas y recuperación de empresas paralizadas mediante mecanismos autogestionarios y cogestionarios; promover el ejercicio de la iniciativa legislativa y participar en los procesos de consulta en el marco del parlamentarismo social; promover el ejercicio y defensa de la soberanía e integridad territorial de la Nación; y elaborar el Plan de Desarrollo de la Comunidad a través del diagnóstico participativo, en el marco de la estrategia endógena.

La unidad de gestión financiera del Consejo Comunal, conforme al artículo 10 de la Ley de 2006 fue concebida como un órgano integrado por 5 habitantes de la comunidad electos por la Asamblea de Ciudadanos (art. 12), que debía funcionar como el ente de ejecución financiera de los consejos comunales para administrar recursos financieros y no financieros, servir de ente de inversión y de crédito, y realizar intermediación financiera con los fondos generados, asignados o captados. A tal efecto, la Ley de 2006 denominó a esta unidad de gestión financiera como "Banco Comunal," definido como la forma de organización y gestión económico-financiera de los recursos de los consejos comunales (art. 4,10), del cual debían ser "socios" todos

---

1269   Para 2007 se daba una cifra de entre 18.000 y 20.000 Consejos Comunales. Véase María Pilar García-Guadilla, "La praxis de los consejos comunales en Venezuela: ¿Poder popular o instancia clientelar?," en *Revista Venezolana de Economía y Ciencias Sociales*, abr. 2008, Vol. 14, N° 1, p. 125-151. Véase en http://www.scielo.org.ve/scielo.php?pid=S1315-64112008000100009&script-=sci_arttext. Véase en general sobre el proceso de creación de consejos comunales de acuerdo con la Ley de 2006, en Steve Ellner, "Un modelo atractivo con fallas: los Consejos Comunales de Venezuela", en http://www.rebelion.org/-noticia.php?id=87637; y Miguel González Marregot, "La ley de los consejos comunales: un año después (y II)", Sábado, 21 de abril de 2007, en http://queremoselegir.org/la-ley-de-los-consejos-comunales-un-ano-despues-y-ii/

los ciudadanos que habitasen en el ámbito geográfico definido por la Asamblea de Ciudadanos. Ese Banco Comunal debía adquirir la figura jurídica de cooperativa y regirse por la Ley Especial de Asociaciones Cooperativas, la Ley de Creación, Estímulo, Promoción y Desarrollo del Sistema Microfinanciero y otras leyes aplicables. Estos Bancos Comunales, quedaron exceptuados de la regulación de la Ley General de Bancos y Otras Instituciones Financieras (art. 10).

Conforme al artículo 22 de la Ley de 2006, estos Bancos Comunales tenían entre sus funciones, administrar los recursos asignados, generados o captados tanto financieros como no financieros; promover la constitución de cooperativas para la elaboración de proyectos de desarrollo endógeno, sostenibles y sustentables; impulsar el diagnóstico y el presupuesto participativo, sensible al género, jerarquizando las necesidades de la comunidad; promover formas alternativas de intercambio, que permitan fortalecer las economías locales; prestar servicios no financieros en el área de su competencia; prestar asistencia social; realizar la intermediación financiera; y promover formas económicas alternativas y solidarias, para el intercambio de bienes y servicios.

Por último, la Unidad de Contraloría Social del Consejo Comunal se lo configuró en la Ley de 2006 como un órgano conformado por 5 habitantes de la comunidad electos por la Asamblea de Ciudadanos para realizar la contraloría social y la fiscalización, control y supervisión del manejo de los recursos asignados, recibidos o generados por el consejo comunal, así como sobre los programas y proyectos de inversión pública presupuestados y ejecutados por el gobierno nacional, regional o municipal (art. 11), con las siguientes funciones establecidas en el artículo 23: dar seguimiento a las actividades administrativas y de funcionamiento ordinario del Consejo Comunal en su conjunto; ejercer la coordinación en materia de contraloría social comunitaria; ejercer el control, fiscalización y vigilancia de la ejecución del plan de desarrollo comunitario; y ejercer el control, fiscalización y vigilancia del proceso de consulta, planificación, desarrollo, ejecución y seguimiento de los proyectos comunitarios.

El artículo 25 de la Ley de 2006 enumeró los siguientes recursos que los Consejos Comunales debían recibir de manera directa: los que fueran transferidos por la República, los estados y los municipios; los que provinieran de lo dispuesto en la Ley de Creación del Fondo Intergubernamental para la Descentralización (FIDES) y la Ley de Asignaciones Económicas Especiales derivadas de Minas e Hidrocarburos (LAEE); los que provinieran de la administración de los servicios públicos que les fueran transferidos por el Estado; los generados por su actividad propia, incluido el producto del manejo financiero de todos sus recursos, y los que provinieran de donaciones.

5.　*La organización centralizada de la participación ciudadana*

Los Consejos Comunales fueron articulados en la Ley de 2006 en una organización centralizada tanto desde el punto de vista financiero como de conducción administrativa, la cual en la práctica resultó totalmente inoperante.[1270]

Por una parte, en efecto, la Ley de 2006 creó un Fondo Nacional de los Consejos Comunales, como servicio autónomo sin personalidad jurídica, adscrito al Ministerio de Finanzas (art. 28), con una junta directiva conformada por un presidente, tres miembros principales y tres suplentes, todos designados por el Presidente de la República, en Consejo de Ministros. Este Fondo Nacional de los Consejos Comunales, conforme al artículo 29 de la Ley debía tener por objeto financiar los proyectos comunitarios, sociales y productivos, presentados por la Comisión Nacional Presidencial del Poder Popular en sus componentes financieros y no financieros. La transferencia de los recursos financieros se debía hacer a través de las unidades de gestión financieras, es decir, los Bancos Comunales, creadas por los consejos comunales.

Por otra parte, el artículo 30 de la Ley de 2006 organizó a los Consejos Comunales en diversas Comisiones Presidenciales del Poder Popular establecidas a nivel nacional, regional y municipal.

La Comisión Nacional Presidencial del Poder Popular, que debía ser designada por el Presidente de la República de conformidad con el artículo 71 de la Ley Orgánica de la Administración Pública, tenía por función: orientar, coordinar y evaluar el desarrollo de los Consejos Comunales a nivel nacional, regional y local; fortalecer el impulso del poder popular en el marco de la democracia participativa y protagónica, y el desarrollo endógeno, dando impulso al desarrollo humano integral que eleve la calidad de vida de las comunidades; generar mecanismos de formación y capacitación; recabar los diversos proyectos aprobados por los consejos comunales; tramitar los recursos técnicos, financieros y no financieros necesarios para la ejecución de los proyectos de acuerdo a los recursos disponibles en el Fondo Nacional de los Consejos Comunales; crear en las comunidades donde se amerite o considere necesario, equipos promotores externos para impulsar la conformación de los Consejos Comunales.

Además, el artículo 31 de la Ley de 2006 reguló unas Comisiones Regionales Presidenciales del Poder Popular por cada estado, designadas por la Comisión Na-

---

1270　Sobre esto Miguel González Marregot ha señalado que "El elemento central de las críticas a los consejos comunales es su dependencia y sujeción a una red de Comisiones Presidenciales del Poder Popular, designada "a dedo" desde del Poder Nacional. Sin embargo, las Comisiones Presidenciales del Poder Popular no existen por ahora, en el ámbito municipal. Y su creación no ha sido implementada aún; quizás por una mezcla de la incapacidad operativa oficial con una dosis de cálculo político. Las Comisiones Presidenciales del Poder Popular son una demostración de la visión centralista y concentradora de la gestión pública que va a suprimir las propias posibilidades de participación popular que brindarían los consejos comunales. Una deuda sensible, en este contexto, es la inoperancia del Servicio Autónomo Fondo Nacional de los Consejos Comunales, que estaría adscrito al Ministerio de Finanzas; y cuyo Reglamento Orgánico fue publicado en *la Gaceta Oficial* N° 346.196 de fecha 18 de Mayo de 2006; es decir, hace nueve meses. Por si fuera, poco la Ley de los Consejos Comunales, promulgada en Abril del año pasado, no ha sido aún reglamentada mediante un proceso de consulta pública." En "Consejos Comunales: ¿Para qué?," en *Venezuela Analítica*, Viernes, 9 de febrero de 2007, http://www.analitica.com/va/politica/opinion/7483372.asp

cional Presidencial del Poder Popular previa aprobación del Presidente de la República; y el artículo 32 dispuso que la Comisión Nacional Presidencial del Poder Popular podía designar las Comisiones Locales Presidenciales del Poder Popular por cada municipio, previa aprobación del Presidente de la República.

Por último, en esta estructura centralizada, conforme al artículo 33 de la Ley de 2006, en la Asamblea Nacional también se debía designar una comisión especial para que conjuntamente con las comisiones presidenciales respectivas, realizasen una evaluación del proceso de constitución y funcionamiento de los consejos comunales.

II. LA RECHAZADA REFORMA CONSTITUCIONAL DE 2007 Y EL PROYECTO PARA LA ESTRUCTURACIÓN DEL ESTADO SOCIALISTA DEL PODER POPULAR O PODER COMUNAL

En 2007 el Presidente de la República presentó ante la Asamblea Nacional un proyecto de Reforma Constitucional el cual después de haber sido sancionado por la misma,[1271] una vez que fue sometido a referendo aprobatorio en diciembre de 2007, fue rechazado mayoritariamente por el pueblo. Con la misma se buscaba establecer un Estado Socialista, Centralizado, Policial y Militarista[1272] montado sobre el denominado Poder Popular que se propuso crear, en el cual jugaban importante papel, precisamente, los consejos comunales.

La orientación de la reforma la dio el propio Presidente de la República durante todo el año 2007, y en particular en su "Discurso de Presentación del Anteproyecto de reforma a la Constitución ante la Asamblea Nacional" en agosto de 2007,[1273] en el cual señaló con toda claridad que el objetivo central de la misma era "la construcción de la Venezuela bolivariana y socialista"[1274]; es decir, como lo expresó, se trataba de una propuesta para sembrar "el socialismo en lo político y económico,"[1275] lo que -dijo- no se había hecho en la Constitución de 1999. Cuando ésta se sancionó –dijo el Jefe de Estado– "no proyectábamos el socialismo como camino", agregando, que "así como el candidato Hugo Chávez repitió un millón de veces en 1998, "Vamos a Constituyente", el candidato Presidente Hugo Chávez dijo: "Vamos al

---

1271   Véase Allan R. Brewer-Carías, *La Reforma Constitucional de 2007 (Comentarios al proyecto inconstitucionalmente sancionado por la Asamblea Nacional el 2 de noviembre de 2007)*, Colección Textos Legislativos, N° 43, Editorial Jurídica Venezolana, Caracas 2007, 224 pp.

1272   Véase Allan R. Brewer-Carías, *Hacia la consolidación de un Estado Socialista, Centralizado, Policial y Militarista, Comentarios sobre el sentido y alcance de las propuestas de reforma constitucional 2007*, Colección Textos Legislativos, N° 42, Editorial Jurídica Venezolana, Caracas 2007, 157 pp.

1273   Véase *Discurso de Orden pronunciado por el ciudadano Comandante Hugo Chávez Frías, Presidente Constitucional de la República Bolivariana de Venezuela en la conmemoración del Ducentésimo Segundo Aniversario del Juramento del Libertador Simón Bolívar en el Monte Sacro y el Tercer Aniversario del Referendo Aprobatorio de su mandato constitucional*, Sesión especial del día Miércoles 15 de agosto de 2007, Asamblea Nacional, División de Servicio y Atención legislativa, Sección de Edición, Caracas 2007.

1274   *Idem*, p. 4.

1275   *Idem*, p. 33.

Socialismo", y todo el que votó por el candidato Chávez, votó por ir al socialismo,"[1276] lo que por supuesto no era cierto.

Por ello, el Anteproyecto de Reforma que presentó ante la Asamblea Nacional, era para "la construcción del Socialismo Bolivariano, el Socialismo venezolano, nuestro Socialismo, nuestro modelo socialista"[1277], cuyo "núcleo básico e indivisible" era "la comunidad", "donde los ciudadanos y las ciudadanas comunes, tendrán el poder de construir su propia geografía y su propia historia."[1278] Y todo ello bajo la premisa de que "sólo en el socialismo será posible la verdadera democracia."[1279] pero por supuesto, una "democracia" sin representación que, como lo propuso el Presidente y fue sancionado por la Asamblea Nacional en la rechazada reforma del artículo 136 de la Constitución, se buscaba establecer una "democracia" que "no nace del sufragio ni de elección alguna, sino que nace de la condición de los grupos humanos organizados como base de la población." Es decir, se buscaba establecer una "democracia" que no era democracia, pues en el mundo moderno no hay ni ha habido democracia sin elección de representantes.

En resumen, entre los aspectos esenciales de la reforma propuesta estaba por una parte, transformar el Estado en un Estado Socialista, con una doctrina política oficial de carácter socialista, que se denominaba además como "doctrina bolivariana", con lo cual se eliminaba toda posibilidad de pensamiento distinto al "oficial" y, por tanto, toda disidencia, pues la doctrina política oficial se quería incorporar en la Constitución, como política y doctrina del Estado y la Sociedad, hubiera constituido un deber constitucional de todos los ciudadanos cumplir y hacerla cumplir. Con ello, se buscaba sentar las bases para la criminalización de la disidencia.

Por la otra, también se buscaba transformar el Estado en un Estado Centralizado, de poder concentrado bajo la ilusión del Poder Popular, lo que implicaba la eliminación definitiva de la forma federal del Estado, imposibilitando la participación política y degradando la democracia representativa; todo ello, mediante la supuesta organización de la población para la participación en los Consejos del Poder Popular, como los Comunales, que eran y son instituciones sin autonomía política alguna, cuyos miembros se pretendía declarar, en la propia Constitución, que no fueran elec-

---

1276   *Idem*, p. 4. Lo que no era cierto. En todo caso, se pretendió imponer al 56% de los votantes que no votaron por la reelección del presidente, la voluntad expresada por sólo el 46% de los votantes inscritos en el Registro Electoral que votaron por la reelección del Presidente. Según las cifras oficiales del CNE, en las elecciones de 2006, de un universo de 15.784.777 votantes inscritos en el Registro Electoral, sólo 7.309.080 votaron por el Presidente.

1277   Véase *Discurso...* p. 34.

1278   *Idem*, p. 32.

1279   *Idem*, p. 35. Estos conceptos se recogieron igualmente en la *Exposición de Motivos* para la Reforma Constitucional, Agosto 2007, donde se expresó la necesidad de "ruptura del modelo capitalista burgués" (p. 1), de desmontar la superestructura que le da soporte a la producción capitalista"(p. 2); de "dejar atrás la democracia representativa para consolidar la democracia participativa y protagónica"(p. 2); de "crear un enfoque socialista nuevo" (p. 2) y "construir la vía venezolana al socialismo"(p. 3); de producir "el reordenamiento socialista de la geopolítica de la Nación" (p. 8); de la "construcción de un modelo de sociedad colectivista" y "el Estado sometido al poder popular"(p. 11); de "extender la revolución para que Venezuela sea una República socialista, bolivariana", y para "construir la vía venezolana al socialismo; construir el socialismo venezolano como único camino a la redención de nuestro pueblo"(p. 19).

tos. Dichos Consejos, creados por Ley en 2006, estaban controlados desde la Jefatura del gobierno y para cuyo funcionamiento, el instrumento preciso era el partido único Socialista que el Estado creó también durante 2007.

En ese marco, en la propuesta de reforma constitucional de 2007 se propuso modificar varios artículos fundamentales de la Constitución así:

Primero, en relación con el artículo 16 de la Constitución, se buscaba crear las comunas y comunidades como "el núcleo territorial básico e indivisible del Estado Socialista Venezolano"; con el artículo 70, se definían los medios de participación y protagonismo del pueblo en ejercicio directo de su soberanía mediante todo tipo de consejos, "para la construcción del socialismo", haciéndose mención a las diversas asociaciones "constituidas para desarrollar los valores de la mutua cooperación y la solidaridad socialista"; con el artículo 158, se buscaba eliminar toda mención a la descentralización como política nacional, y definir como política nacional, "la participación protagónica del pueblo, restituyéndole el poder y creando las mejores condiciones para la construcción de una democracia socialista"; con el artículo 168 relativo al Municipio, se buscaba precisar la necesidad de incorporar "la participación ciudadana a través de los Consejos del Poder Popular y de los medios de producción socialista"; con el artículo 184, se buscaba orientar la descentralización de Estados y Municipios para permitir "la construcción de la economía socialista."

Segundo, en relación con el artículo 158 se buscaba eliminar toda referencia a la descentralización política siguiendo la orientación de la práctica política centralista de los últimos años, y centralizar completamente el Estado, eliminando toda idea de autonomía territorial y de democracia representativa a nivel local, es decir, de la unidad política primaria en el territorio. Con la rechazada reforma constitucional, en este campo, se buscaba materializar una supuesta "nueva geometría del poder" donde no había ni podía haber autonomías, con la propuesta de creación de nuevas instancias territoriales, todas sometidas al poder Central, mediante las cuales el Poder Popular[1280] supuestamente iba a desarrollar "formas de agregación comunitaria política territorial" que constituían formas de autogobierno, pero sin democracia representativa alguna, sino sólo como "expresión de democracia directa" (art. 16). Con ello se buscaba, como lo dijo el Presidente de la República, "el desarrollo de lo que nosotros entendemos por descentralización, porque el concepto cuartorepublicano de descentralización es muy distinto al concepto que nosotros debemos manejar. Por eso, incluimos aquí la participación protagónica, la transferencia del poder y crear las mejores condiciones para la construcción de la democracia socialista."[1281]

1280   En la *Exposición de Motivos del Proyecto de Reforma Constitucional* presentado por el Presidente de la República en agosto 2007, se lee que el Poder Popular "es la más alta expresión del pueblo para la toma de decisiones en todos sus ámbitos (político, económico, social, ambiental, organizativo, internacional y otros) para el ejercicio pleno de su soberanía. Es el poder constituyente en movimiento y acción permanente en la construcción de un modelo de sociedad colectivista de equidad y de justicia. Es el poder del pueblo organizado, en las más diversas y disímiles formas de participación, al cual está sometido el poder constituido. No se trata del poder del Estado, es el Estado sometido al poder popular. Es el pueblo organizado y organizando las instancias de poder que decide las pautas del orden y metabolismo social y no el pueblo sometido a los partido políticos, a los grupos de intereses económicos o a una particularidad determinada", *cit.*, p. 11.

1281   Véase *Discurso....*, citado *supra*.

Con ello se pretendía lograr la eliminación de los entes territoriales descentralizados políticamente, sin las cuales no puede haber efectivamente democracia participativa, y la creación en su lugar de Consejos del poder popular que no pasan de ser una simple manifestación de movilización controlada desde el Poder Central. Ello es lo que había ocurrido, precisamente, con los Consejos Comunales creados por Ley en 2006[1282], cuyos miembros no eran electos mediante sufragio sino designados por Asambleas de ciudadanos controladas por el propio Poder Ejecutivo Nacional. Ello era lo que con la rechazada reforma constitucional, se pretendía consolidar en el texto fundamental, al proponerse una "nueva geometría del poder" en la cual se sustituía a los Municipios, por las comunidades, como el "núcleo territorial básico e indivisible del Estado Socialista Venezolano", que debían agrupar a las comunas (socialistas)[1283] como "células sociales del territorio", las cuales se debían agrupar en ciudades que eran las que se pretendía concebir como "la unidad política primaria de la organización territorial nacional". En la rechazada reforma constitucional se buscaba establecer en forma expresa que los integrantes de los diversos Consejos del Poder Popular no nacían "del sufragio ni de elección alguna, sino que nace de la condición de los grupos humanos organizados como base de la población".

Con ello, en definitiva, en nombre de una "democracia participativa y protagónica", lo que se buscaba era poner fin en Venezuela a la democracia representativa a nivel local, y con ello, de todo vestigio de autonomía política territorial que es la esencia de la descentralización.

Tercero, en relación con el artículo 62 de la Constitución que consagra el derecho de los ciudadanos "de participar libremente en los asuntos públicos," con la reforma constitucional se buscaba agregar a los mecanismos de participación enumerados en el artículo 70, a los Consejos del Poder Popular, con los cuales aquella perdía su carácter libre pues se buscaba que quedaran reducidos al único propósito de "la construcción del socialismo", de manera que quien no quisiera construir socialismo alguno, hubiera quedado excluido del derecho a la participación política, que sólo estaba destinado a desarrollar los valores de "la solidaridad socialista" y no era libre como indica el artículo 62.

Por otra parte, en sustitución del concepto amplio de participación ciudadana que establece el artículo 168 de la Constitución y que deben desarrollar los Municipios, con la rechazada reforma constitucional se pretendía establecer la obligación de los Municipios de "incorporar, dentro del ámbito de sus competencias, la participación ciudadana a través de los Consejos del Poder Popular y de los medios de producción socialista", eliminándose toda posibilidad de otras formas de participación, la cual dejaba de ser libre.

1282   Véase los comentarios sobre ello en Allan R. Brewer-Carías, "Introducción General al Régimen del Poder Público Municipal," en, *Ley Orgánica del Poder Público Municipal*, Editorial Jurídica Venezolana, Caracas 2007, pp. 75 y ss.

1283   En la *Exposición de Motivos* del Proyecto de Reforma Constitucional presentado por el Presidente de la República en agosto 2007, a las comunas se las califica como "comunas socialistas", y se la define como "Es un conglomerado social de varias comunidades que poseen una memoria histórica compartida, usos, costumbres y rasgos culturales que los identifican, con intereses comunes, agrupadas entre sí con fines político-administrativos, que persiguen un modelo de sociedad colectiva de equidad y de justicia", *cit.*, p. 12.

Cuarto, en relación con la forma federal del Estado, con la reforma constitucional rechazada de 2007 se buscaba vaciarla totalmente de contenido. En particular, en cuanto a los Estados y Municipios sobre cuya concepción se monta el sistema federal, con la reforma del artículo 16, desaparecía la garantía constitucional de la autonomía municipal y el principio de la descentralización político administrativa que establece la Constitución de 1999 como condición esencial de la división territorial.

En particular, en relación con los Municipios, con la rechazada reforma constitucional se buscaba quitarles el carácter de unidad política primaria que el artículo 168 de la Constitución de 1999 les garantiza, y en su lugar se proponía establecer a "la ciudad" como la unidad política primaria de la organización territorial nacional, entendida como "todo asentamiento poblacional dentro del municipio, e integrada por áreas o extensiones geográficas denominadas comunas". Además, se buscaba definir a estas comunas, como las células sociales del territorio conformadas por las "comunidades", cada una de las cuales se proponía que constituyera "el núcleo territorial básico e indivisible del Estado Socialista Venezolano, donde los ciudadanos y las ciudadanas tendrán el poder para construir su propia geografía y su propia historia". En la rechazada propuesta de reforma constitucional, también se proponía crear la figura de la Ciudad Comunal que debía constituirse cuando en la totalidad de su perímetro, se hubieran establecido las comunidades organizadas, las comunas y el autogobierno comunal, pero asignándose su creación al Presidente de la República en Consejo de Ministros.

A partir de este esquema inicial, en el artículo 16 del proyecto de la rechazado de reforma constitucional, se buscaba cambiar radicalmente la división política del territorio nacional en "entidades políticas" (Estados, Distrito Capital, dependencias federales, territorios federales y Municipios y otras entidades locales) que conforme a la Constitución gozan esencialmente de autonomía política territorial, y deben tener un gobierno "electivo" (art. 6); por una "conformación" del territorio nacional a los fines político-territoriales y de acuerdo con una "nueva geometría del poder", por un Distrito Federal, por los estados, las regiones marítimas, los territorios federales, los municipios federales y los distritos insulares". En ese esquema, se proponía eliminar la exigencia constitucional de que todo el territorio nacional se debe organizar en municipios, por la previsión de que sólo "los Estados se organizan en municipios" (art. 16), los que por tanto se buscaba que desaparecieran, si una parte del territorio se convertía en alguna de las "nuevas" entidades. Por ello es que precisamente, se buscaba que el Municipio desapareciera como unidad política primaria en la organización nacional.

Lo más notorio de la rechazada reforma constitucional es que mediante la misma, se buscaba autorizar al Presidente de la República, en Consejo de Ministros, para que "previo acuerdo aprobado por la mayoría simple de los diputados y diputadas de la Asamblea Nacional", pudiera "decretar regiones marítimas, territorios federales, municipios federales, distritos insulares, provincias federales, ciudades federales y distritos funcionales, así como cualquier otra entidad que establezca esta Constitución y la Ley", con lo que materialmente, la totalidad de la división político territorial de la República se pretendía que dejara de ser una materia de rango constitucional y pasara a ser una materia ni siquiera de regulación legislativa, sino solamente ejecutiva. En fin, lo que se pretendía con la rechazada reforma constitucional era la total centralización del poder, lo que se confirma mediante la asignación que se pretendía hacer al Presidente de la República para designar y remover "las autoridades respectivas" de dichas entidades que hubieran quedado sujetas completamente al Poder Central.

Quinto, con la rechazada propuesta de reforma constitucional, se buscaba agregar a la distribución vertical del Poder Público entre el Poder Municipal, el Poder Estadal y el Poder Nacional (art. 136), a un denominado "Poder Popular," que se pretendía concebir como el medio para que supuestamente "el pueblo" como el depositario de la soberanía, la ejerciera "directamente", pero con la advertencia expresa de que dicho Poder Popular" "no nace del sufragio ni de elección alguna, sino que nace de la condición de los grupos humanos organizados como base de la población", sino mediante la constitución de comunidades, comunas y el autogobierno de las ciudades, a través de toda suerte de consejos comunales y de otra índole.

Se pretendía, así, agregar como un Poder Público más en el territorio, al Poder Popular, cuyos voceros, por ejemplo, con la rechazada reforma constitucional se pretendía que también formaran parte de los Comités de Postulaciones y Evaluaciones para la escogencia de los magistrados del Tribunal Supremo de Justicia, los titulares del Poder Ciudadano y los miembros del Consejo Nacional Electoral (arts. 264, 279 y 295).

SECCIÓN TERCERA:

LA INSTITUCIONALIZACIÓN LEGAL DEL ESTADO COMUNAL O DE CÓMO SE IMPUSO AL PAÍS UN MODELO DE ESTADO COMUNISTA, DE EJERCICIO DEL PODER POPULAR Y DE SOCIEDAD SOCIALISTA POR LOS CUALES NADIE HA VOTADO

I.   EL ESTADO COMUNAL O COMUNISTA Y EL PODER POPULAR

Como se ha dicho, después de que la reforma constitucional de 2007 fue rechazada por el pueblo en el referendo de diciembre de ese mismo año, y después de que el Presidente de la República, su gobierno, la Asamblea Nacional que controlaba y el partido oficial que preside perdieron las elecciones parlamentarias de septiembre de 2010, la Asamblea Nacional ya deslegitimada, bajo el control absoluto del Presidente y en los últimos días de su mandato, en diciembre de 2010, procedió atropelladamente, en fraude a la voluntad popular y a la Constitución, a sancionar el conjunto de Leyes Orgánicas antes mencionados sobre el Poder Popular, las Comunas, el Sistema Económico Comunal, la Planificación Pública y Comunal y la Contraloría Social;[1284] y a reformar la Ley Orgánica del Poder Público Municipal, y de las Leyes de los Consejos Estadales de Planificación y Coordinación de Políticas Públicas, y de los Consejos Locales de Planificación Pública,[1285] completando así el esquema de institucionalización del Estado Comunista, denominado Estado Comunal

1284   Véase en *Gaceta Oficial* N° 6.011 Extra. de 21-12-2010.

1285   Véase en *Gaceta Oficial* N° 6.017 Extra. de 30-12-2010.

que ya se había esbozado en la Ley de los Consejos Comunales de 2006 y en la Ley Orgánica del Consejo Federal de Gobierno.[1286]

Con estas leyes se ha terminado de definir, al margen de la Constitución, el marco normativo de un nuevo Estado, *paralelo al Estado Constitucional*, que se denomina "Estado Comunal" y que si nos atenemos a las experiencias históricas precedentes, todas fracasadas, unas desaparecidas como el de la Unión Soviética, y otros en vías de extinción como el de Cuba, no es otra cosa que un Estado Comunista, para el cual se adopta al Socialismo como doctrina oficial pública, impuesta a los ciudadanos para poder participar, montado sobre un sistema político centralizado, militarista y policial para el ejercicio del poder.

El objetivo fundamental de estas leyes, como se dijo, es la organización del "Estado Comunal" que tiene a la Comuna como a su célula fundamental, suplantando inconstitucionalmente al Municipio en el carácter que tiene de "unidad política primaria de la organización nacional" (art. 168 de la Constitución). A través de la organización de ese Estado Comunal o Comunista, se ejerce el Poder Popular, el cual se concreta en el ejercicio de la soberanía popular sólo directamente por el pueblo, y no mediante representantes. Se trata por tanto, de un sistema político estatal en el cual se ignora la democracia representativa violándose así abiertamente la Constitución de la República.

El Estado Comunista que se busca implantar con estas leyes, denominado Estado Comunal, *en paralelo* al Estado Constitucional, se basa en este simple esquema: como el artículo 5 de la Constitución dispone que "La soberanía reside intransferiblemente en el pueblo, quien la ejerce *directamente* en la forma prevista en esta Constitución y en la ley, e *indirectamente*, mediante el sufragio, por los órganos que ejercen el Poder Público," habiéndose estructurado el Estado Constitucional basado en el concepto de democracia representativa, es decir, el ejercicio de la soberanía en forma indirecta mediante el sufragio; entonces ahora se estructura el Estado Comunal, basado en el ejercicio de la soberanía en forma directa.

Ello incluso ha sido "legitimado" por las sentencias dictadas por la Sala Constitucional del Tribunal Supremo de Justicia cuando al analizar el carácter orgánico de las leyes, como en la dictada en relación con la Ley Orgánica de las Comunas, señaló que la misma se dictó:

> "en desarrollo del principio constitucional de la democracia participativa y descentralizada que postula el preámbulo constitucional y que reconocen los artículos 5 y 6 de la Constitución de la República Bolivariana de Venezuela, de cuyo contenido se extrae el principio de soberanía, cuyo titular es el pueblo, quien está además facultado para ejercerla "*directamente*" y no sólo "*indirectamente*" por los órganos del Poder Público; así como del artículo 62 *ejusdem*, que estatuye el derecho de las personas a la libre participación en los asuntos públicos y, especialmente, el artículo 70 del mismo texto fundamental, que reconoce expresamente medios de autogestión como mecanismos de participa-

---

[1286]   Véase en *Gaceta Oficial* N° 5.963 Extra. de 22-02-2010.

ción popular protagónica del pueblo en ejercicio de su soberanía, medios que son sólo enunciativos en los términos de la predicha norma."[1287]

Es con base en estos principios que en el artículo 8.8 de la LOPP, se define al Estado comunal, como la:

"Forma de organización político social, fundada en el Estado democrático y social de derecho y de justicia establecido en la Constitución de la República, en la cual el poder es ejercido directamente por el pueblo, con un modelo económico de propiedad social y de desarrollo endógeno sustentable, que permita alcanzar la suprema felicidad social de los venezolanos y venezolanas en la sociedad socialista. La célula fundamental de conformación del estado comunal es la Comuna.[1288]

Se busca establecer así, un Estado Comunal en paralelo al Estado Constitucional: el primero basado en el ejercicio de la soberanía directamente por el pueblo; y el segundo, basado en el ejercicio de la soberanía indirectamente por el pueblo, mediante representantes electos por sufragio universal; en un sistema, en el cual el primero irá vaciando progresivamente de competencias al segundo. Todo ello es inconstitucional, particularmente porque en la estructura del Estado Comunal que se monta, el ejercicio de la soberanía en definitiva es indirecta mediante "representantes" que se "eligen" para ejercer el Poder Popular en nombre del pueblo, y que son denominados "voceros" o "vocerías," pero no son electos mediante sufragio.

El sistema que se busca montar, en definitiva, controlado todo por un Ministerio del Ejecutivo Nacional, lejos de ser un instrumento de descentralización –concepto que está indisolublemente unido a la autonomía política– es un sistema de centralización y control férreo de las comunidades por el Poder Central. Por ello la aversión al sufragio.[1289] En ese esquema, una verdadera democracia participativa sería la que garantizaría que los miembros de los Consejos Comunales, las comunas y todas las organizaciones e instancias del Poder Popular fueran electas por sufragio universal, directo y secreto, y no a mano alzada por asambleas controladas por el partido ofi-

---

1287   Véase la sentencia N° 1.330, Caso: Carácter Orgánico de la Ley Orgánica de Comunas, de fecha 17/12/2010. Véase en http://www.tsj.gov.ve/decisiones /scon/Diciembre/1330-171210-2010-10-1436.html

1288   En la Ley Orgánica de las Comunas, sin embargo, se define al Estado Comunal de la siguiente manera: "Forma de organización político-social, fundada en el Estado democrático y social de derecho y de justicia establecido en la Constitución de la República, en la cual el poder es ejercido directamente por el pueblo, a través de los autogobiernos comunales, con un modelo económico de propiedad social y de desarrollo endógeno y sustentable, que permita alcanzar la suprema felicidad social de los venezolanos y venezolanas en la sociedad socialista. La célula fundamental de conformación del estado comunal es la Comuna" (art. 4.10).

1289   Véase lo expuesto en los estudios de José Ignacio Hernández G., "Descentralización y Poder Popular," y Adriana Vigilanza García, "La descentralización política de Venezuela y las nuevas leyes del 'Poder Popular'," en Allan R. Brewer-Carías (Coordinador), Claudia Nikken, Luis A. Herrera Orellana, Jesús María Alvarado Andrade, José Ignacio Hernández y Adriana Vigilanza, *Leyes Orgánicas sobre el Poder Popular y el Estado Comunal (Los Consejos Comunales, las Comunas, la Sociedad Socialista y el Sistema Económico Comunal),* Editorial Jurídica Venezolana, Caracas 2011, pp. 459 ss. y 477 ss., respectivamente.

cial y el Ejecutivo Nacional, en contravención al modelo de Estado democrático y social de derecho y de justicia descentralizado establecido en la Constitución.

Pues bien, es en este contexto, y buscando establecer en paralelo al Estado Constitucional en el cual el pueblo ejerce indirectamente el Poder Público mediante representantes electos por sufragio universal directo y secreto, un Estado Comunal en el cual el pueblo supuestamente ejercería directamente el Poder Popular mediante voceros que no son electos por sufragio universal, directo y secretos, sino en asambleas de ciudadanos, el artículo 2 de la LOPP, define al Poder Popular, como:

"el ejercicio pleno de la soberanía por parte del pueblo en lo político, económico, social, cultural, ambiental, internacional, y en todo ámbito del desenvolvimiento y desarrollo de la sociedad, a través de sus diversas y disímiles formas de organización, que edifican el estado comunal."

Todo lo cual no es más que una falacia, pues en definitiva en ese "edificio" del Estado Comunal se le niega al pueblo el derecho de elegir libremente, mediante sufragio universal, directo y secreto a quienes van a representarlo en todos esos ámbitos, incluyendo el internacional; y además, se niega toda idea de pluralismo al imponerse a los ciudadanos una ideología única compulsiva como es el socialismo. Se trata más bien de un "edificio" de organizaciones para evitar que el pueblo realmente ejerza la soberanía e imponerle mediante férreo control central políticas por las cuales nunca tendrá la ocasión de votar.

Por otra parte, según el artículo 4 de la LOPP, la finalidad de este Poder Popular que se ejerce por los órganos del Estado Comunal,

"garantizar la vida y el bienestar social del pueblo, mediante la creación de mecanismos para su desarrollo social y espiritual, procurando la igualdad de condiciones para que todos y todas desarrollen libremente su personalidad, dirijan su destino, disfruten los derechos humanos y alcancen la suprema felicidad social; sin discriminaciones por motivos de origen étnico, religioso, condición social, sexo, orientación sexual, identidad y expresión de género, idioma, opinión política, nacionalidad u origen, edad, posición económica, condición de discapacidad o cualquier otra circunstancia personal, jurídica o social, que tenga por resultado anular o menoscabar el reconocimiento, goce o ejercicio de los derechos humanos y garantías constitucionales."

Por supuesto todos estos principios de igualdad se rompen desde que el sistema de Estado Comunal o Comunista, paralelo al Estado Constitucional, se monta, como se ha dicho, sobre una concepción única, que es el Socialismo, de manera que quien no sea socialista está automáticamente discriminado y no puede participar. No es posible, por tanto, en el marco de esta Ley, poder conciliar el pluralismo que garantiza la Constitución y el principio de la no discriminación por razón de "opinión política" a que se refiere este artículo, con el resto de las disposiciones de la Ley que persiguen todo lo contrario, es decir, el establecimiento de un Estado Comunista o

Comunal, cuyas instancias sólo pueden actuar en función del Socialismo y en las cuales todo ciudadano que tenga otra opinión queda excluido. [1290]

Es decir, mediante esta Ley Orgánica se ha establecido el marco definitorio de un nuevo modelo de Estado paralelo y distinto al Estado Constitucional, denominado el Estado Comunal basado en forma exclusiva y exclusionista en el socialismo como doctrina y práctica política, que es la organización política a través de la cual se produce el ejercicio del Poder Popular que es a la vez "el ejercicio pleno de la soberanía por parte del pueblo."

Ese Poder Popular se fundamenta, como se declara en el artículo 3 de la LOPP, "en el principio de soberanía y el sentido de progresividad de los derechos contemplados en la Constitución de la República, cuyo ejercicio y desarrollo está determinado por los niveles de conciencia política y organización del pueblo" (art. 3).

Con esta declaración, sin embargo, lejos de la universalidad, prevalencia y progresividad de los derechos humanos que se garantizan la Constitución, lo que se ha establecido es la desaparición total de la concepción universal de los derechos humanos, el abandono a su carácter prevalente y el retroceso ante los principios *pro homines* y *favor libertatis*, al condicionarse su existencia, alcance y progresividad a lo que se determine "por los niveles de conciencia política y organización del pueblo," es decir, por lo que dispongan y prescriban las organizaciones del Poder Popular con las que se busca "organizar" al pueblo, todas sometidas al Socialismo. Con ello desaparece la concepción de los derechos humanos como esferas que son innatas al hombre e inmunes frente al poder; pasándose a una concepción de los derechos humanos dependientes de lo que ordene un poder central, que en definitiva controla todo el "edificio" del Estado Comunal o Estado Socialista, como clara demostración del totalitarismo que está a la base de esta Ley.

En el mismo sentido se dispone en el artículo 5 de la LOPP, que "la organización y participación del pueblo en el ejercicio de su soberanía se inspira en la doctrina del Libertador Simón Bolívar, y se rige por los principios y valores socialistas,"[1291] con lo cual, como se ha dicho, se vincula la organización del Estado Comunal que se

---

1290   En el diario *El Nacional* del 12 de febrero de 2011, se reseñó lo siguiente: "Representantes de 120 consejos comunales del Distrito Capital y de Miranda denunciaron en una asamblea celebrada en presencia del diputado William Ojeda que son víctimas de discriminación por razones políticas. Aseguraron que aunque cumplieron con los requisitos para registrarse en Fundacomunal no pudieron iniciar el proceso porque no presentaron la planilla de inscripción en el PSUV, que es un requisito indispensable. "El Gobierno está aplicando una política de discriminación y exclusión. Está ocurriendo un *apartheid* político. Hay centenares de consejos comunales en el país que están organizados y que no han podido registrarse porque no militan en la tolda roja", indicó Ojeda." Véase en Diana Lozano Parafán, "Consejos Comunales rechazan discriminación. El diputado William Ojeda se reunió con representantes de 120 comunidades que no han podido inscribirse por razones partidistas," en *El Nacional*, Caracas 12-02-2011. Véase en http://impresodigital.el-nacional.com/ediciones/011/02/12/default.asp?cfg=1081FGHH666&iu=757

1291   La misma expresión se utilizó en la Ley Orgánica de las Comunas respecto de la constitución, conformación, organización y funcionamiento de las mismas (art. 2); en la Ley Orgánica de los Consejos Comunales respecto de los mismos (art. 1), en la Ley Orgánica de Contraloría Social (art. 6); en la Ley Orgánica de Planificación Pública y Popular (art. 3), que regula la planificación pública, popular y participativa como herramienta fundamental para construcción de la nueva sociedad (art. 3); y en la Ley Orgánica del Sistema Económico Comunal respecto del mismo (art. 5).

organiza en paralelo al Estado Constitucional, con la ideología política socialista, es decir, con el *socialismo*, el cual se define en el artículo 8.14 como:

> "un modo de relaciones sociales de producción centrado en la convivencia solidaria y la satisfacción de necesidades materiales e intangibles de toda la sociedad, que tiene como base fundamental la recuperación del valor del trabajo como productor de bienes y servicios para satisfacer las necesidades humanas y lograr la suprema felicidad social y el desarrollo humano integral. Para ello es necesario el desarrollo de la propiedad social sobre los factores y medios de producción básicos y estratégicos que permita que todas las familias, ciudadanos venezolanos y ciudadanas venezolanas posean, usen y disfruten de su patrimonio, propiedad individual o familiar, y ejerzan el pleno goce de sus derechos económicos, sociales, políticos y culturales."[1292]

Lo primero que debe observarse respecto de esta norma, es la insostenible pretensión de vincular "la doctrina del Libertador Simón Bolívar" con los principios y valores socialistas. En la obra de Bolívar y en relación con su concepción del Estado nada puede encontrarse al respecto,[1293] no siendo la norma sino una pretensión más de continuar manipulando el "culto" a Bolívar para justificar los autoritarismos, como tantas veces ha ocurrido antes en nuestra historia.[1294] Con la norma, por otra

---

1292   Igual definición se encuentra en el artículo 4.14 de la Ley Orgánica de las Comunas. También en el artículo 3 del Reglamento de la Ley Orgánica del Consejo federal de Gobierno se define el socialismo como "un modo de relaciones sociales de producción centrado en la convivencia solidaria y la satisfacción de las necesidades materiales e intangibles de toda la sociedad, que tiene como base fundamental la recuperación del valor del trabajo como productor de bienes y servicios para satisfacer las necesidades humanas y lograr la Suprema Felicidad Social y el Desarrollo Humano Integral. Para ello es necesario el desarrollo de la propiedad social sobre los factores y medios de producción básicos y estratégicos que permita que todas las familias y los ciudadanos y ciudadanas venezolanos y venezolanas posean, usen y disfruten de su patrimonio o propiedad individual o familiar, y ejerzan el pleno goce de sus derechos económicos, sociales, políticos y culturales."Véase en *Gaceta Oficial* Nº 39.382 del 9 de marzo de 2010. Muchas son las definiciones de socialismo, pero en todas, se pueden identificar sus elementos básicos: (i) un sistema de organización social y económico, (ii) basado en la propiedad y administración colectiva o estatal de los medios de producción, y (iii) en regulación por el Estado de las actividades económicas y sociales y de la distribución de los bienes, (iv) buscando la progresiva desaparición de las clases sociales.

1293   Véase Allan R. Brewer-Carías, "Ideas centrales sobre la organización el Estado en la Obra del Libertador y sus Proyecciones Contemporáneas" en *Boletín de la Academia de Ciencias Políticas y Sociales*, Nº 95-96, enero-junio 1984, pp. 137-151.

1294   Ha sido el caso de Antonio Guzmán Blanco en el siglo XIX y de Cipriano Castro, Juan Vicente Gómez, Eleazar López Contreras y Marcos Pérez Jiménez en el siglo XX. John Lynch ha señalado que: "El tradicional culto a Bolívar ha sido usado como ideología de conveniencia por dictadores militares, culminando con los regímenes de Juan Vicente Gómez y Eleazar López Contreras; quienes al menos respetaron, más o menos, los pensamientos básicos del Libertador, aún cuando tergiversaron su significado." Concluye Lynch señalando que en el caso de Venezuela, en la actualidad, el proclamar al Libertador como fundamento de las políticas del régimen autoritario, constituye una distorsión de sus ideas. Véase John Lynch, *Simón Bolívar: A Life*, Yale University Press, New Haven 2007, p. 304. Véase también, Germán Carrera Damas, *El culto a Bolívar, esbozo para un estudio de la historia de las ideas en Venezuela*, Universidad Central de Venezuela, Caracas 1969; Luis Castro Leiva, *De la patria boba a la teología bolivariana*, Monteávila, Caracas 1987; Elías Pino Iturrieta, *El divino Bolívar. Ensayo sobre una religión republicana*, Alfail, Caracas 2008; Ana Teresa Torres, *La herencia de la tribu. Del mito de la independencia a la Revolución bolivariana*, Editorial Alfa, Ca-

parte y por supuesto, se viola abiertamente la garantía del derecho de propiedad que está en la Constitución (art. 115) que no permite su restricción sólo a la propiedad colectiva o social excluyendo la propiedad privada de los medios de producción

El artículo 5 de la LOPP, por otra parte, define como "principios y valores socialistas" los siguientes:

"democracia participativa y protagónica, interés colectivo, equidad, justicia, igualdad social y de género, complementariedad, diversidad cultural, defensa de los derechos humanos, corresponsabilidad, cogestión, autogestión, cooperación, solidaridad, transparencia, honestidad, eficacia, eficiencia, efectividad, universalidad, responsabilidad, deber social, rendición de cuentas, control social, libre debate de ideas, voluntariedad, sustentabilidad, defensa y protección ambiental, garantía de los derechos de la mujer, de los niños, niñas y adolescentes, y de toda persona en situación de vulnerabilidad, defensa de la integridad territorial y de la soberanía nacional (art. 5).[1295]

Este catálogo de "principios" por supuesto no están vinculados necesariamente al socialismo, ni son exclusivamente "principios y valores socialistas" como se pretende hacer ver, en una apropiación indebida que hace el legislador. El redactor de la norma, en realidad, lo que hizo fue copiar todo el elenco de principios que se encuentran definidos a lo largo de la Constitución, en muchas normas (Preámbulo y arts. 1, 2, 3, 4, 6, 19, 20, 21, 22, 26, 84, 86, 102, 112, 137, 141, 153, 165, 257, 293, 299, 311, 316, 326, por ejemplo), y que son los valores del Estado Constitucional. Sólo en algún caso no se han atrevido a utilizar la terminología clásica como "libertad de expresión," y la han querido sustituir por "libre debate de ideas," lo que por supuesto no es lo mismo, sobre todo porque dicha libertad no se tolera en un Estado Socialista que sólo conoce de una ideología única.

Para desarrollar y consolidar el Poder Popular, ignorando los valores y principios constitucionales básicos que tienen que tener todas las instancias de gobierno en Venezuela que deben ser "electivos, descentralizados, alternativos, responsables, pluralistas y de mandatos revocables" tal como lo exige el artículo 6 de la Constitución, es que se ha dictado la LOPP para supuestamente generar

"condiciones objetivas a través de los diversos medios de participación y organización establecidos en la Constitución de la República, en la ley y los que surjan de la iniciativa popular, para que los ciudadanos y ciudadanas ejerzan el pleno derecho a la soberanía, la democracia participativa, protagónica y corresponsable, así como a la constitución de formas de autogobierno comunitarias y comunales, para el ejercicio directo del poder" (art. 1).

---

racas 2009. Sobre la historiografía en relación con estos libros véase Tomás Straka, *La épica del desencanto*, Editorial Alfa, Caracas 2009.

1295   Estos mismos principios se enumeran en relación con las comunas en el artículo 2 de la Ley Orgánica de las Comunas; en relación con la contraloría social en el artículo 6 de la Ley Orgánica de Contraloría Social; y en relación con la panificación pública y popular el artículo 3 de la ley Orgánica de Planificación Pública y Popular.

Conforme a la Constitución "la creación de nuevos sujetos de descentralización a nivel de las parroquias, las comunidades, los barrios y las vecindades" sólo es posible "a los fines de garantizar el principio de la corresponsabilidad en la gestión pública de los gobiernos locales y estadales y desarrollar procesos autogestionarios y cogestionarios en la administración y control de los servicios públicos estadales y municipales" (art. 184.6). Ello significa que los mecanismos de participación que puedan establecerse conforme a la Constitución no son para vaciar a las estructuras del Estado Constitucional, es decir, de los "gobiernos locales y estadales," sino para reforzarlas en la gestión pública. Por otra parte, conforme a la Constitución, no puede haber gobierno alguno que no sea *electivo, descentralizado y pluralista*; sin embargo, en la LOPP se define un Estado paralelo que es el Estado Comunal, montado sobre "gobiernos" o "autogobiernos" que no son ni electivos, ni descentralizados ni pluralistas.

Sobre estos, el artículo 14 de la LOPP, se limita a definir "el autogobierno comunal y los sistemas de agregación que surjan entre sus instancias" como "un ámbito de actuación del Poder Popular en el desarrollo de su soberanía, mediante el ejercicio directo por parte de las comunidades organizadas, de la formulación, ejecución y control de funciones públicas, de acuerdo a la ley que regula la materia."

En este contexto, además, a la "comunidad" se la define en la LOPP como el "núcleo espacial básico e indivisible constituido por personas y familias que habitan en su ámbito geográfico determinado, vinculadas por características e intereses comunes que comparten una historia, necesidades y potencialidades culturales, económicas, sociales, territoriales y de otra índole" (art. 8.4).[1296]

II. LOS FINES DEL PODER POPULAR

El artículo 7 de la LOPP define los siguientes fines del Poder Popular, es decir, del "ejercicio pleno de la soberanía por parte del pueblo" a través "de sus diversas y disímiles formas de organización, que edifican el Estado Comunal" (art. 2):

1. Impulsar el fortalecimiento de la organización del pueblo, en función de consolidar la democracia protagónica revolucionaria y construir las bases de la sociedad socialista, democrática, de derecho y de justicia.

Se destaca, en relación con lo que dispone la Constitución sobre la organización del Estado, el agregado de "socialista" que impone esta previsión, con lo cual se rompe el principio del pluralismo que garantiza la propia Constitución, abriendo la vía para la discriminación política de todo aquél ciudadano que no sea socialista, a quien se le niega, por tanto, el derecho a la participación política.

2. Generar las condiciones para garantizar que la iniciativa popular, en el ejercicio de la gestión social, asuma funciones, atribuciones y competencias de administración, prestación de servicios y ejecución de obras, mediante la transferencia desde los distintos entes político-territoriales hacia

---

1296   La misma definición se repite en la ley Orgánica de las Comunas (art. 4.4) y en la Ley Orgánica de los Consejos Comunales (art. 4.1).

los autogobiernos comunitarios, comunales y los sistemas de agregación que de los mismos surjan.

Conforme al artículo 184.1 de la Constitución, esta transferencia de competencias sólo se puede referir a "servicios en materia de salud, educación, vivienda, deporte, cultura, programas sociales, ambiente, mantenimiento de áreas industriales, mantenimiento y conservación de áreas urbanas, prevención y protección vecinal, construcción de obras y prestación de servicios públicos" a cuyo efecto se pueden "establecer convenios cuyos contenidos estarán orientados por los principios de interdependencia, coordinación, cooperación y corresponsabilidad.".

3.   Fortalecer la cultura de la participación en los asuntos públicos para garantizar el ejercicio de la soberanía popular.

4.   Promover los valores y principios de la ética socialista: la solidaridad, el bien común, la honestidad, el deber social, la voluntariedad, la defensa y protección del ambiente y los derechos humanos.

Estos, la verdad, no son valores de ninguna "ética socialista," sino como se ha dicho anteriormente, son valores de la democracia y civilización occidental, propios del Estado Constitucional.

5.   Coadyuvar con las políticas de Estado en todas sus instancias, con la finalidad de actuar coordinadamente en la ejecución del Plan de Desarrollo Económico y Social de la Nación y los demás planes que se establezcan en cada uno de los niveles políticos-territoriales y las instancias político- administrativas que la ley establezca.

6.   Establecer las bases que permitan al pueblo organizado el ejercicio de la contraloría social para asegurar que la inversión de los recursos públicos se realice de forma eficiente para el beneficio colectivo; y vigilar que las actividades del sector privado con incidencia social se desarrollen en el marco de las normativas legales de protección a los usuarios y consumidores.

A los efectos de esta norma, el artículo 8.6 de la LOPP, define el control social, como el ejercicio de la función de prevención, vigilancia, supervisión, acompañamiento y control, practicado por los ciudadanos y ciudadanas de manera individual o colectiva sobre la gestión del Poder Público y de las instancias del Poder Popular, así como de las actividades privadas que afecten el interés colectivo (art. 8.6). Sin embargo, nada en la Constitución autoriza a que se asignen a entidades públicas comunitarias dependientes del Ejecutivo Nacional, competencias para ejercer vigilancia o contraloría social sobre las actividades privadas. Esa es una función que sólo pueden ejercer los entes político territoriales del Estado.

III. "PROFUNDIZAR LA CORRESPONSABILIDAD, LA AUTOGESTIÓN Y LA COGESTIÓN."

A los efectos de esta norma, la Ley define la corresponsabilidad, como la "responsabilidad compartida entre los ciudadanos y ciudadanas y las instituciones del Estado en el proceso de formación, ejecución, control y evaluación de la gestión social, comunitaria y comunal, para el bienestar de las comunidades organizadas" (art. 8.7). La autogestión, se la define como el "conjunto de acciones mediante las cuales las comunidades organizadas asumen directamente la gestión de proyectos, ejecución de obras y prestación de servicios para mejorar la calidad de vida en su ámbito geográfico" (art. 8.2). Y la cogestión, se la define como el "proceso mediante el cual las comunidades organizadas coordinan con el Poder Público, en cualquiera de sus niveles e instancias, la gestión conjunta para la ejecución de obras y prestación de servicios necesarios para mejorar la calidad de vida en su ámbito geográfico"(art. 8.3).

Por otra parte, a los efectos de estas normas, la "comunidad organizada" se define en la LOPP como aquella "constituida por las expresiones organizativas populares, consejos de trabajadores y trabajadoras, de campesinos y campesinas, de pescadores y pescadoras y cualquier otra organización social de base, articulada a una instancia del Poder Popular[1297] debidamente reconocida por la ley y registrada en el Ministerio del Poder Popular con competencia en materia de participación ciudadana" (art. 8.5). Por otra parte, en la Ley Orgánica del Consejo Federal de Gobierno[1298] se encuentra otra definición, a los efectos de dicha ley, pero de la "sociedad organizada" que es la "constituida por consejos comunales, comunas y cualquier otra organización de base del Poder Popular" (art. 4); la cual conforme al Reglamento de dicha la Ley Orgánica del Consejo Federal de Gobierno, está "Constituida por consejos comunales, consejos de trabajadores y trabajadoras, de campesinos y campesinas, de pescadores y pescadoras, comunas y cualquier otra organización de base del Poder Popular debidamente registrada en el Ministerio del Poder Popular con competencia en materia de participación ciudadana."[1299]

La Constitución, sin embargo, al referirse a las organizaciones comunitarias para poder ser sujetos de descentralización, las concibe sólo como entidades de carácter territorial, como "las parroquias, las comunidades, los barrios y las vecindades" que son las que pueden asumir conforme al artículo 186,6, "corresponsabilidad en la gestión pública de los gobiernos locales y estadales y desarrollar procesos autogestionarios y cogestionarios en la administración y control de los servicios públicos estadales y municipales."

IV. LAS INSTANCIAS DEL PODER POPULAR

1. Las diversas instancias del poder popular y su personalidad jurídica

Las instancias del Poder Popular para el "ejercicio pleno de la soberanía por parte del pueblo" y que forman las "diversas y disímiles formas de organización, que edifican el Estado Comunal" (art. 2), conforme se precisa en el artículo 8.9 de la LOPP, están "constituidas por los diferentes sistemas de agregación comunal y sus articulaciones, para ampliar y fortalecer la acción del autogobierno comunal: *consejos comunales, comunas, ciudades comunales, federaciones comunales, confedera-*

1297   La definición que se formula sobre la "comunidad organizada," es similar en la Ley Orgánica de las Comunas, como "constituida por las expresiones organizativas populares, consejos de trabajadores y trabajadoras, de campesinos y campesinas, de pescadores y pescadoras y cualquier otra organización de base, articuladas en una instancia del Poder Popular"(art. 4.5).

1298   Véase en *Gaceta Oficial* N° 5.963 Extraordinario del 22 de febrero de 2010.

1299   Véase en *Gaceta Oficial* N° 39.382 del 9 de marzo de 2010.

ciones comunales y las que, de conformidad con la Constitución de la República, la ley que regule la materia y su reglamento, surjan de la iniciativa popular,"[1300] constituyendo las "organizaciones de base del Poder Popular" aquéllas "constituidas por ciudadanos y ciudadanas para la búsqueda del bienestar colectivo" (art. 8.10).[1301]

Todas estas instancias del Poder Popular reconocidas en la LOPP, como lo dispone su artículo 32, adquieren personalidad jurídica mediante el registro ante el Ministerio del Poder Popular de las Comunas, atendiendo a los procedimientos que se establezcan en el Reglamento de la Ley. Con ello, en definitiva, se deja en manos del Ejecutivo Nacional la decisión de registrar o no un consejo comunal, una comuna o una ciudad comunal, y ello lo hará, por supuesto, aplicando la letra de la Ley lo que significa que si no está dominada por "voceros" que no sean socialistas, no cabe su registro ni, por tanto, su reconocimiento como persona jurídica, así sea producto genuino de una iniciativa popular.

2. *Los voceros de las instancias del poder popular y su carácter no representativo*

Ninguna de las personas que ejercen la titularidad de los órganos del Poder Popular, y que se denominan "voceros" tienen su origen en elecciones efectuadas mediante sufragio directo, universal y secreto. Ni siquiera puede decirse que tienen su origen en elecciones indirectas, pues en ningún caso hay elección directa de primer grado.

En efecto, la LOPP no indica la forma de "elección" de los voceros de las instancias del Poder Popular, y lo que se regula en las diferentes leyes dictadas para normar las instancias del Poder Popular es una designación por órganos que no tienen su origen en elecciones directas universales y secretas. En particular, por ejemplo, en la Ley Orgánica de los Consejos Comunales, se dispone que los voceros de los mismos son "electos" por las asambleas de ciudadanos (arts. 4.6 y 11), y no precisamente mediante sufragio universal, directo y secreto como lo prescribe la Constitución, sino mediante una supuesta "votación popular" que no es organizada por el Poder Electoral, y que se realiza en asambleas abiertas en las cuales no hay garantía del sufragio. La Ley, sin embargo, si indica que todas las instancias del Poder Popular que sean "electas por votación popular," son revocables a partir del cumplimiento de la mitad del período de gestión correspondiente, en las condiciones que establece la ley (art. 17).

Debe indicarse, en efecto, que a la base de estas instancias del Poder Popular, están las Asambleas de Ciudadanos que si bien la LOPP no las regula específicamente ni las nombra en artículo alguno, sin embargo, las define como la "máxima instancia de participación y decisión de la comunidad organizada, conformada por la integración de personas con cualidad jurídica, según la ley que regule la forma de participación, para el ejercicio directo del poder y protagonismo popular, cuyas decisiones son de carácter vinculante para la comunidad, las distintas formas de orga-

---

1300   En la Ley Orgánica de las Comunas, sin embargo, se define a las "instancias del Poder Popular como las constituidas "por los diferentes sistemas de agregación comunal: consejos comunales, comunas, ciudades comunales, federaciones comunales, confederaciones comunales y los otros que, de acuerdo a la Constitución de la República y la ley, surjan de la iniciativa popular." (art. 4.12)

1301   Igual definición está contenida en la ley Orgánica del Sistema de Economía Comunal, art. 6.10.

nización, el gobierno comunal y las instancias del Poder Público, de acuerdo a lo que establezcan las leyes que desarrollen la constitución, organización y funcionamiento de los autogobiernos comunitarios, comunales y los sistemas de agregación que de éstos surjan" (art. 8.1).

3. *Sistemas de agregación comunal*

En el artículo 15.4 de la LOPP, se define a los sistemas de agregación comunal, a aquellas instancias que por iniciativa popular surjan entre los consejos comunales y entre las comunas; sobre lo cual el artículo 50 de la LOC precisa que "las instancias del Poder Popular podrán constituir sistemas comunales de agregación entre sí, con el propósito de articularse en el ejercicio del autogobierno, para fortalecer la capacidad de acción sobre aspectos territoriales, políticos, económicos, sociales, culturales, ecológicos y de seguridad y defensa de la soberanía nacional, de conformidad a la Constitución de la República y la ley."

Las finalidades de los sistemas comunales de agregación conforme al artículo 59 de la LOC, son las siguientes:

1. Ampliar y fortalecer la acción del autogobierno comunal.
2. Llevar adelante planes de inversión en su ámbito territorial, atendiendo los lineamientos y requerimientos establecidos en los planes comunales de desarrollo respectivos.
3. Asumir las competencias que mediante transferencias se le otorguen para la administración, ejecución de obras y prestación de servicios públicos.
4. Impulsar el desarrollo del sistema económico comunal, mediante la articulación en redes, por áreas de producción y servicios, de las organizaciones socio-comunitarias de propiedad social comunal directa o indirecta.
5. Ejercer funciones de control social, sobre los diferentes planes y proyectos que en su ámbito territorial ejecuten las instancias del Poder Popular o el Poder Público.

La LOC, sin embargo, nada establece sobre las condiciones para la constitución de los sistemas comunales de agregación y sobre su funcionamiento, lo que se remite a ser establecido en el Reglamento de la LOC y los lineamientos que a tales efectos dicte el Ministerio del Poder Popular de las Comunas.

En todo caso, la LOC enumeró en su artículo 60, los diversos tipos de sistemas de agregación comunal así:

1. El Consejo Comunal: como instancia de articulación de los movimientos y organizaciones sociales de una comunidad.
2. La Comuna: como instancia de articulación de varias comunidades organizadas en un ámbito territorial determinado.
3. La Ciudad Comunal: constituida por iniciativa popular, mediante la agregación de varias comunas en un ámbito territorial determinado.
4. Federación Comunal: como instancia de articulación de dos o más ciudades que correspondan en el ámbito de un Distrito Motor de Desarrollo.

5.   Confederación Comunal: instancia de articulación de federaciones comu-
     nales en el ámbito de un eje territorial de desarrollo.

6.   Las demás que se constituyan por iniciativa popular.

En particular, en cuanto a la Ciudad Comunal, la federación Comunal y la Confederación Comunal, las condiciones para su conformación deben ser desarrolladas
en el Reglamento de cada Ley.

Ahora bien, de todas estas instancias del Poder Popular previstas para "el ejercicio del autogobierno," el artículo 15 de la LOPP sólo se refiere con algún detalle a
los Consejos Comunales y a las Comunas, las cuales por lo demás, son las que han
sido reguladas en la Ley Orgánica de los Consejos Comunales y en la ley Orgánica
de Comunas; y a las Ciudades Comunales.

V. LOS CONSEJOS COMUNALES

Los Consejos Comunales se definen en la Ley como la "instancia de participación, articulación e integración entre los ciudadanos, ciudadanas y las diversas organizaciones comunitarias, movimientos sociales y populares, que permiten al pueblo
organizado ejercer el gobierno comunitario y la gestión directa de las políticas
públicas y proyectos orientados a responder a las necesidades, potencialidades y
aspiraciones de las comunidades, en la construcción de nuevo modelo de sociedad
socialista de igualdad, equidad y justicia social" (art. 15.1).[1302]

Se destaca de esta definición legal, que los Consejos Comunales sólo y exclusivamente pueden tener por objeto contribuir a "la construcción de un nuevo modelo
de sociedad socialista," en violación al principio del pluralismo que establece el
artículo 6 de la Constitución, por lo que todo aquél ciudadano que no siga o acepte
la doctrina socialista no tiene cabida en este nuevo Estado paralelo que se busca
construir con esta Ley.

Esta instancia del Poder Popular constituida por los Consejos Comunales está
regulada en la mencionada Ley Orgánica de los Consejos Comunales,[1303] a cuyos
"voceros," además, mediante la reforma de la Ley Orgánica del Poder Público Municipal de diciembre de 2010, se les ha asignado la función de designar a los miembros de las Juntas Parroquiales, las cuales, en consecuencia, fueron "degradadas"
dejando de ser las "entidades locales" que eran, con gobiernos electos por sufragio
universal directo y secreto, pasando a ser simples órganos "consultivos, de evaluación y articulación entre el Poder Popular y los órganos del Poder Público Municipal" (art. 35), cuyos miembros, además, los deben designar los voceros de los consejos comunales de la parroquia respectiva (art. 35), y sólo de entre aquellos avalados
por la Asamblea de Ciudadanos "de su respectivo consejo comunal"(at. 36). A tal
efecto, en forma evidentemente inconstitucional, la Ley de reforma del Poder Municipal, decretó la "cesación" en sus funciones de "los miembros principales y suplentes, así como los secretarios o secretarias, de las actuales juntas parroquiales, que-

---

1302   Igual definición se establece en el artículo 2 de la ley Orgánica de los Consejos Comunales (art. 2).

1303   Véase en *Gaceta Oficial* N° 39.335 de 28-12-2009.

dando las alcaldías responsables del manejo y destino del personal, así como de los bienes correspondientes" (Disposición Derogatoria Segunda).

Para el estudio del régimen de los Consejos Comunales, véase lo expuesto en la parte IV de esta "Introducción General."[1304]

1. *Las Comunas*

Las Comunas, por su parte, que están concebidas en la LOPP como la "célula fundamental" del Estado Comunal, se las define en el artículo 15.2 como el "espacio socialista que como entidad local es definida por la integración de comunidades vecinas con una memoria histórica compartida, rasgos culturales, usos y costumbres que se reconocen en el territorio que ocupan y en las actividades productivas que le sirven de sustento y sobre el cual ejercen los principios de soberanía y participación protagónica como expresión del Poder Popular, en concordancia con un régimen de producción social y el modelo de desarrollo endógeno y sustentable contemplado en el Plan de Desarrollo, Económico y Social de la Nación."[1305] Esta misma definición de la Comuna como espacio socialista está en el artículo 5 de la Ley Orgánica de las Comunas; noción que implica que la misma está vedada a todo aquél que no sea socialista o que no crea en el socialismo o que no comulgue con el socialismo como doctrina política. La concepción legal de la Comuna, por tanto, es contraria al pluralismo democrático que garantiza la Constitución, siendo abiertamente discriminatoria y contraria a la igualdad que también garantiza el artículo 21 de la Constitución.

Por otra parte, en la norma mencionada de la LOPP se define a la Comuna como una "entidad local," y la misma calificación se encuentra en el artículo 1 de la Ley Orgánica de las Comunas, que las define "como entidad local donde los ciudadanos y ciudadanas en el ejercicio del Poder Popular, ejercen el pleno derecho de la soberanía y desarrollan la participación protagónica mediante formas de autogobierno para la edificación del estado comunal, en el marco del Estado democrático y social de derecho y de justicia" (art. 1). También en la reforma de la ley Orgánica del Poder Público Municipal de diciembre de 2010, se incluyó a las comunas en el listado de las "entidades locales territoriales," disponiéndose que las mismas, al estar reguladas por una legislación diferente como es la relativa al Poder Popular, y al deber

---

1304   Véase en pp. 89 ss. Véase además, el estudio de Claudia Nikken, "La Ley Orgánica de los Consejos Comunales y el derecho a la participación ciudadana en los asuntos públicos," en Allan R. Brewer-Carías (Coordinador), Claudia Nikken, Luis A. Herrera Orellana, Jesús María Alvarado Andrade, José Ignacio Hernández y Adriana Vigilanza, *Leyes Orgánicas sobre el Poder Popular y el Estado Comunal (Los Consejos Comunales, las Comunas, la Sociedad Socialista y el Sistema Económico Comunal),*Editorial Jurídica Venezolana, Caracas 2011, pp. 183 ss.

1305   Igual definición se establece en el artículo 5 de la Ley Orgánica de las Comunas. En el reglamento de la ley Orgánica del Consejo Federal de Gobierno también se define la Comuna como: "Es un espacio socialista definido por la integración de comunidades vecinas con una memoria histórica compartida, rasgos culturales, usos, y costumbres, que se reconocen en el territorio que ocupan y en las actividades productivas que les sirven de sustento y sobre el cual ejercen los principios de soberanía y participación protagónica, como expresión del poder popular, en concordancia con un régimen de producción social y el modelo de desarrollo endógeno, sustentable y socialista contemplado en el Plan Nacional de Desarrollo" (art. 3). Véase en *Gaceta Oficial* N° 39.382 del 9 de marzo de 2010.

constituirse "entre varios municipios," quedan exceptuadas de las disposiciones de la Ley Orgánica del Poder Público Municipal.

Ahora bien, en cuanto a calificar a las Comunas como "entidades locales," el Legislador deslegitimado de diciembre de 2010 olvidó que conforme a la Constitución (arts. 169, 173), esta expresión de entidad local sólo se puede aplicar a las entidades políticas del Estado en las cuales necesariamente tiene que haber "gobiernos" integrados por representantes electos mediante sufragio universal, directo y secreto (arts. 63, 169) ceñidos a los principios establecidos en el artículo 6 de la Constitución, es decir, tiene que ser "siempre democrático, participativo, electivo, descentralizado, alternativo, responsable, pluralista y de mandatos revocables." Conforme a la Constitución, por tanto, no puede haber "entidades locales" con gobiernos que no sean democráticos en los términos mencionados, y menos por "representantes" designados por otros órganos públicos.

Y esto es precisamente lo que ocurre con los llamados "gobiernos de las comunas," que conforme a esta legislación sobre el Poder Popular y sus organizaciones, no se garantiza su origen democrático mediante elección por sufragio universal, directo y secreto, siendo en consecuencia inconstitucional su concepción.

Debe destacarse, además, que en relación a el gobierno de las comunas, que como se establece en el artículo 28 de la LOPP, pueden transferir la gestión, la administración y la prestación de servicios a las diferentes organizaciones del Poder Popular. A tal efecto, las organizaciones de base del Poder Popular deben hacer las respectivas solicitudes formales, cumpliendo con las condiciones previas y requisitos establecidos en las leyes que regulen la materia.

Esta instancia del Poder Popular constituida por las Comunas ha sido regulada en la Ley Orgánica de las Comunas,[1306] a cuyo estudio se dedica la parte V de esta "Introducción General."

2. *Las Ciudades Comunales*

Las ciudades comunales, conforme a la Ley, "son aquellas constituidas por iniciativa popular mediante la agregación de varias comunas en un ámbito territorial determinado" (art. 15.3). Siendo las Comunas, conforme a la Ley, el "espacio socialista" y "célula fundamental" del Estado Comunal, las Ciudades Comunales como agregación de varias comunas o sea de varios espacios socialistas, son concebidas también conforme a la Ley como Ciudades "socialistas" que como tales, están vedadas de hecho a todo aquel ciudadano o vecino que no sea socialista.

VI. LAS ORGANIZACIONES Y EXPRESIONES ORGANIZATIVAS DEL PODER POPULAR

Además de las instancias del Poder Popular, en la LOPP se establecen previsiones tendientes a regular dos formas organizativas específicas del Poder Popular: las organizaciones y las expresiones organizativas del Poder Popular.

1306   Véase en *Gaceta Oficial* N° 6.011 Extra. de 21-12-2010.

1.   *Formas organizativas del Poder Popular*

Conforme al artículo 9 de la LOPP, las organizaciones del Poder Popular "son las diversas formas del pueblo organizado, constituidas desde la localidad o de sus referentes cotidianos por iniciativa popular, que integran a ciudadanos y ciudadanas con objetivos e intereses comunes, en función de superar dificultades y promover el bienestar colectivo, para que las personas involucradas asuman sus derechos, deberes y desarrollen niveles superiores de conciencia política. Las organizaciones del Poder Popular actuarán democráticamente y procurarán el consenso popular entre sus integrantes."

Estas organizaciones del Poder Popular se constituyen por iniciativa de los ciudadanos y ciudadanas, de acuerdo con su naturaleza, por intereses comunes, necesidades, potencialidades y cualquier otro referente común, según lo establecido en la ley que rija el área de su actividad (art. 12).

Estas organizaciones del Poder Popular, al igual que las instancias del Poder Popular, conforme al artículo 32 de la LOPP, adquieren su personalidad jurídica mediante el registro ante el Ministerio del Poder Popular con competencia en materia de participación ciudadana, atendiendo a los procedimientos que se establezcan en el Reglamento de la presente Ley. Queda en manos del Ejecutivo Nacional, por tanto, el reconocimiento formal de estas organizaciones, de mantera que todas aquellas que no sean socialistas por ser contrarias a los fines prescritos en la Ley (art. 1), serían rechazadas. En las registradas, por lo demás, no tendrían cabida los ciudadanos que no compartan la ideología socialista.

En cuanto a las "expresiones organizativas del Poder Popular," conforme se dispone en el artículo 10 de la LOPP, las mismas son "integraciones de ciudadanos y ciudadanas con objetivos e intereses comunes, constituidas desde la localidad, de sus referentes cotidianos de ubicación o espacios sociales de desenvolvimiento, que de manera transitoria y en base a los principios de solidaridad y cooperación, procuran el interés colectivo."

Estas expresiones del Poder Popular se constituyen, por iniciativa popular y como respuesta a las necesidades y potencialidades de las comunidades, de conformidad con la Constitución de la República y la ley (art. 13).

Conforme a la Disposición final Tercera, el ejercicio de la participación del pueblo y el estímulo a la iniciativa y organización del Poder Popular establecidos en la Ley, se deben aplicar en los pueblos y comunidades indígenas, de acuerdo a sus usos, costumbres y tradiciones.

2.   *Los fines de las organizaciones y expresiones organizativas del Poder Popular*

Estas organizaciones y expresiones organizativas del Poder Popular, conforme al artículo 11 de la LOPP, tienen como fines los siguientes:

1.   Consolidar la democracia participativa y protagónica, en función de la insurgencia del Poder Popular como hecho histórico para la construcción de la sociedad socialista, democrática, de derecho y de justicia.

Como antes se dijo, con el agregado de "socialista" que esta previsión impone a la sociedad, se rompe el principio del pluralismo que garantiza la propia Constitu-

ALLAN R. BREWER-CARÍAS

ción, abriendo la vía para la discriminación política de todo aquél ciudadano que no sea socialista, a quien se le niega el derecho político a participar.

2. Impulsar el desarrollo y consolidación del sistema económico comunal, mediante la constitución de organizaciones socio-productivas, para la producción de bienes y servicios destinados a la satisfacción de necesidades sociales, el intercambio de saberes y conocimientos, así como la reinversión social del excedente.

La LOPP, a estos efectos, define como "sistema económico comunal" el conjunto de relaciones sociales de producción, distribución, intercambio y consumo de bienes y servicios, así como de saberes y conocimiento, desarrolladas por las instancias del Poder Popular, el Poder Público, o por acuerdo entre ambos, a través de organizaciones socio-productivas bajo formas de propiedad social comunal"(art. 8.13).

3. Promover la unidad, la solidaridad, la supremacía de los intereses colectivos sobre los intereses individuales y el consenso en sus áreas de influencia.

4. Fomentar la investigación y difusión de los valores, tradiciones históricas y culturales de las comunidades.

5. Ejercer la contraloría social.

VII. ÁMBITOS DEL PODER POPULAR

La LOPP distingue los siguientes "ámbitos del Poder Popular" se definen en la Ley Orgánica y que en la terminología tradicional de derecho público no es otra cosa que competencias que se asignan al Poder Popular: la Planificación de Políticas Públicas, la Economía comunal, la Contraloría social, la Ordenación y gestión del territorio y la Justicia comunal.

1. *Planificación de políticas públicas*

La planificación de políticas públicas en los términos establecidos en la Ley Orgánica de Planificación Pública y Popular,[1307] se define en el artículo 17 de la LOPP como "un ámbito de actuación del Poder Popular que asegura, mediante la acción de gobierno compartida entre la institucionalidad pública y las instancias del Poder Popular, el cumplimiento de los lineamientos estratégicos del Plan de Desarrollo Económico y Social de la Nación, para el empleo de los recursos públicos en la consecución, coordinación y armonización de los planes, programas y proyectos a través de los cuales se logre la transformación del país, el desarrollo territorial equilibrado y la justa distribución de la riqueza."

De esta previsión, llama la atención la distinción entre los órganos del Estado Constitucional que se denominan como "institucionalidad pública" y las instancias del Poder Popular, lo que confirma la intención de la ley de establecer un Estado paralelo, el Estado Comunal, para vaciar de contenido y ahogar en definitiva al Estado Constitucional.

1307   Véase en *Gaceta Oficial* N° 6.011 Extra. de 21-12-2010.

Por otra parte, vinculada a esta competencia de planificación, en cuanto a la "planificación participativa," en la LOPP se la define como la "forma de participación de los ciudadanos y ciudadanas en el diseño, formulación, ejecución, evaluación y control de las políticas públicas" (art. 8.11); y en cuanto al "Presupuesto participativo," se lo define "como el mecanismo mediante el cual los ciudadanos y ciudadanas proponen, deliberan y deciden sobre la formulación, ejecución, control y evaluación de los presupuestos públicos, con el propósito de materializar los proyectos que permitan el desarrollo de las comunidades y el bienestar social general" (art. 8.12).

2. *Economía comunal*

La economía comunal, conforme se define en el artículo 18 de la LOPP, es un "ámbito de actuación del Poder Popular que permite a las comunidades organizadas la constitución de entidades económico-financieras y medios de producción, para la producción, distribución, intercambio y consumo de bienes y servicios, así como de saberes y conocimientos, desarrollados bajo formas de propiedad social comunal, en pro de satisfacer las necesidades colectivas, la reinversión social del excedente, y contribuir al desarrollo social integral del país, de manera sustentable y sostenible, de acuerdo con lo establecido en el Plan de Desarrollo Económico y Social de la Nación y la ley que regula la materia."

Este ámbito de actuación del Poder Público se ha regulado en la Ley Orgánica del Sistema Económico Comunal (LOSEC),[1308] el cual se define en dicha Ley (art. 2) y en la Ley Orgánica de las Comunas como el "conjunto de relaciones sociales de producción, distribución, intercambio y consumo de bienes y servicios, así como de saberes y conocimiento, desarrolladas por las instancias del Poder Popular, el Poder Público, o por acuerdo entre ambos, a través de organizaciones socio-productivas bajo formas de propiedad social comunal" (art. 4.13).

Este sistema económico comunal, como se dijo, está regulado en la Ley Orgánica del Sistema Económico Comunal (LOSEC), que tiene por objeto "desarrollar y fortalecer el Poder Popular, estableciendo las normas, principios, y procedimientos para la creación, funcionamiento y desarrollo del sistema económico comunal, integrado por organizaciones socio-productivas bajo régimen de propiedad social comunal, impulsadas por las instancias del Poder Popular, del Poder Público o por acuerdo entre ambos, para la producción, distribución, intercambio y consumo de bienes y servicios, así como de saberes y conocimientos, en pro de satisfacer las necesidades colectivas y reinvertir social mente el excedente, mediante una planificación estratégica, democrática y participativa" (at. 1). La LOSEC, en particular, tiene por finalidad específica "fomentar el sistema económico comunal en el marco del modelo productivo socialista, a través de diversas formas de organización socio-productiva, comunitaria y comunal en todo el territorio nacional" (Art. 4.3).

En todo caso, en la Ley Orgánica del Sistema Económico Comunal, y en particular en sus artículos 2; 3.2; 3.3; 3.8; 5; 6.12; 6.15 y 9 se adoptan expresa y textualmente para configurar el sistema económico comunal, los más tradicionales postula-

---

1308   Véase en *Gaceta Oficial* Nº 6.011 Extra. de 21-12-2010.

dos marxistas que definen el comunismo, como son la propiedad social de los medios de producción; la eliminación de la división social del trabajo; y la reinversión social del excedente productivo.

Al estudio de dicho sistema comunista tal como ha quedado plasmado en dicha Ley Orgánica del Sistema Económico Comunal, se dedica la parte VII de esta "Introducción General."[1309]

3. *Contraloría social*

En cuanto a la contraloría social, el artículo 19 de la LOPP la define como un "ámbito de actuación del Poder Popular para ejercer la vigilancia, supervisión, acompañamiento y control sobre la gestión del Poder Público, las instancias del Poder Popular y las actividades del sector privado que afecten el bienestar común, practicado por los ciudadanos y ciudadanas de manera individual o colectiva, en los términos establecidos en la ley que regula la materia.

Este ámbito de actuación del Poder Público se ha regulado en la Ley Orgánica del Contraloría Social,[1310] donde se la define como "una función compartida entre las instancias del Poder Público y los ciudadanos, ciudadanas y las organizaciones del Poder Popular, para garantizar que la inversión pública se realice de manera transparente y eficiente en beneficio de los intereses de la sociedad, y que las actividades del sector privado no afecten los intereses colectivos o sociales" (art. 2).

Esta Ley Orgánica al organizar la Contraloría Social e imponer la doctrina socialista como la oficial y obligatoria, lo que ha creado en definitiva es un oscuro sistema general de espionaje y vigilancia social, que se atribuye a individuos o a las organizaciones comunales, basado en la denuncia y persecución contra cualquier persona o empresa privada que pudiera considerarse que no está actuado de acuerdo con la doctrina socialista impuesta, y que por esa razón pudiera considerarse que actúa contra el "bienestar común" o que afecta el "interés social o colectivo."

Al estudio de este sistema de Contraloría Social, tal como se regula en la Ley Orgánica de Contraloría Social, se dedica la VI de esta "Introducción General."[1311]

1309   Véase en Allan R. Brewer-Carías (Coordinador), Claudia Nikken, Luis A. Herrera Orellana, Jesús María Alvarado Andrade, José Ignacio Hernández y Adriana Vigilanza, *Leyes Orgánicas sobre el Poder Popular y el Estado Comunal (Los Consejos Comunales, las Comunas, la Sociedad Socialista y el Sistema Económico Comunal)*, Editorial Jurídica Venezolana, Caracas 2011, pp. 154 ss. Véase además, el estudio de Jesús María Alvarado Andrade, "La 'Constitución económica' y el sistema económico comunal (Reflexiones Críticas a propósito de la Ley Orgánica del Sistema Económico Comunal)," *Idem*, pp. 375 ss.

1310   Véase en *Gaceta Oficial* N° 6.011 Extra. de 21-12-2010

1311   Véase en Allan R. Brewer-Carías (Coordinador), Claudia Nikken, Luis A. Herrera Orellana, Jesús María Alvarado Andrade, José Ignacio Hernández y Adriana Vigilanza, *Leyes Orgánicas sobre el Poder Popular y el Estado Comunal (Los Consejos Comunales, las Comunas, la Sociedad Socialista y el Sistema Económico Comunal)*, Editorial Jurídica Venezolana, Caracas 2011, pp. 147 ss. Véase además, el estudio de Luis A. Herrera Orellana, "La Ley Orgánica de Contraloría Social: Funcionalización de la participación e instauración de la desconfianza ciudadana," *Idem*, pp. 359 ss.

4. *Ordenación y gestión del territorio*

La ordenación y gestión del territorio, conforme al artículo 20 de la LOPP, es un "ámbito de actuación del Poder Popular, mediante la participación de las comunidades organizadas, a través de sus voceros o voceras, en las distintas actividades del proceso de ordenación y gestión del territorio, en los términos establecidos en la ley que regula la materia."

5. *Justicia comunal*

En cuanto a la justicia comunal, el artículo 21 de la LOPP la define como un "ámbito de actuación del Poder Popular, a través de medios alternativos de justicia de paz que promueven el arbitraje, la conciliación, la mediación, y cualquier otra forma de solución de conflictos ante situaciones derivadas directamente del ejercicio del derecho a la participación y a la convivencia comunal, de acuerdo a los principios constitucionales del Estado democrático y social de Derecho y de Justicia, y sin contravenir las competencias legales propias del sistema de justicia ordinario.[1312]

El artículo 22 de la LOPP, remite a una ley especial la regulación de la jurisdicción especial comunal, la cual debe establecer la organización, el funcionamiento, los procedimientos y normas de la justicia comunal, así como su jurisdicción especial. La Ley Orgánica de las Comunas es algo más explícita al señalar que "la ley respectiva establecerá la naturaleza, los procedimientos legales, las normas y condiciones para la creación de una jurisdicción especial comunal, donde se prevea su organización y funcionamiento, así como las instancias con competencia para conocer y decidir en el ámbito comunal, donde los jueces o juezas comunales serán elegidos o elegidas por votación universal, directa y secreta de los y las habitantes del ámbito Comunal mayores de quince años"(art. 57).

La actuación de esta jurisdicción comunal conforme se exige en el artículo 22 de la LOPP, "estará enmarcada dentro de los principios de justicia gratuita, accesible, imparcial, idónea, transparente, autónoma, independiente, responsable, equitativa y expedita, sin dilaciones indebidas y sin formalismos por reposiciones inútiles."

Con estas previsiones se termina de vaciar a los Municipios de una competencia constitucional que tienen asignada (art. 178.7), que se intentó realizar con la rechazada reforma constitucional de 2007, y que corresponde ser ejercida por jueces de paz que conforme al artículo 258 de la constitución deben ser elegidos por votación universal, directa y secreta.[1313].

VIII. LAS RELACIONES ENTRE EL PODER PÚBLICO Y EL PODER POPULAR (O LA TÉCNICA DEL "MATAPALO")

Como hemos señalado, el Estado Comunal que se establece en la LOPP, cuyas manifestaciones ejercen el Poder Popular, se ha establecido como un "Estado paralelo" al Estado Constitucional cuyos órganos electos por votación popular directa universal y secreta ejercen el Poder Público. Se trata de dos Estados establecidos en

---

1312   Esta misma definición se encuentra en el artículo 56 de la Ley Orgánica de las Comunas.

1313   Véase la Ley Orgánica de la Justicia de Paz en *Gaceta Oficial* N° 4.817 Extra. de 21-12-1994).

paralelo, uno en la Constitución y otro en una ley inconstitucional, pero con previsiones en la ley que de llegar a ser aplicadas, permitirán al Estado Comunal ahogar y secar al Estado Constitucional, comportándose como en botánica lo hace el árbol *Ficus benjamina L.*, originario de la India, Java y Bali, conocido como "matapalo" que puede crecer como "estranguladora", como epífitos, rodeando al árbol huésped hasta formar un tronco hueco, destruyéndolo.

A tal efecto, en la LOPP se establecen unas previsiones para regular las relaciones entre el Estado o el Poder Público y el Poder Popular, que en general se dispone que "se rigen por los principios de igualdad, integridad territorial, cooperación, solidaridad, concurrencia y corresponsabilidad, en el marco del sistema federal descentralizado consagrados en la Constitución de la República" (art. 26), y que son las siguientes:

En *primer lugar*, se establece como obligación legal para los órganos, entes e instancias del Poder Público el promover, apoyar y acompañar las iniciativas populares para la constitución, desarrollo y consolidación de las diversas formas organizativas y de autogobierno del pueblo (art. 23).[1314] En particular, incluso, la Ley Orgánica de Comunas dispone que "los órganos integrantes del Poder Ciudadano apoyarán a los consejos de contraloría comunal a los fines de contribuir con el cumplimiento de sus funciones" (art. 48).

En *segundo lugar*, se sujeta a todos los órganos del Estado Constitucional que ejercen el Poder Público, a los mandatos de las organizaciones del Poder Popular, al instaurarse un nuevo principio de gobierno, consistente en "gobernar obedeciendo." El artículo 24 de la LOPP en efecto dispone:

> *Artículo 24.* Actuaciones de los órganos y entes del Poder Público. Todos los órganos, entes e instancias del Poder Público guiarán sus actuaciones por el principio de gobernar obedeciendo, en relación con los mandatos de los ciudadanos, ciudadanas y de las organizaciones del Poder Popular, de acuerdo a lo establecido en la Constitución de la República y las leyes.

Como las organizaciones del Poder Popular no tienen autonomía política pues no sus "voceros" no son electos democráticamente mediante sufragio universal, directo y secreto, sino designados por asambleas de ciudadanos controladas e intervenidas por el partido oficial y el Ejecutivo Nacional que controla y guía todo el proceso organizativo del Estado Comunal, en el ámbito exclusivo de la ideología socialista, sin que tenga cabida vocero alguno que no sea socialista, en definitiva esto de "gobernar obedeciendo" es una limitación a la autonomía política de los órganos del Estado Constitucional electos, como la Asamblea nacional, los Gobernadores y Consejos legislativos de los Estados y los Alcaldes y Concejos Municipales, a quienes se le impone en definitiva la obligación de obedecer lo que disponga el Ejecutivo Nacional y el partido oficial enmarcado en el ámbito exclusivo del socialismo como doctrina política. La voluntad popular expresada en la elección de representantes del Estado Constitucional, por tanto, no tiene valor

---

1314   Una norma similar está en el artículo 62 de la Ley Orgánica de las Comunas, a los efectos de "la constitución, desarrollo y consolidación de las comunas como forma de autogobierno."

alguno, y al pueblo se le confisca su soberanía trasladándola de hecho a unas asambleas que no lo representan.

En *tercer lugar*, en particular, se establece la obligación para el Poder Ejecutivo Nacional, para que "conforme a las iniciativas de desarrollo y consolidación originadas desde el Poder Popular," planifique, articule y coordine "acciones conjuntas con las organizaciones sociales, las comunidades organizadas, las comunas y los sistemas de agregación y articulación que surjan entre ellas, con la finalidad de mantener la coherencia con las estrategias y políticas de carácter nacional, regional, local, comunal y comunitaria"(art. 25).

En *cuarto lugar*, se establece la obligación para los órganos y entes del Poder Público en sus relaciones con el Poder Popular, de dar "preferencia a las comunidades organizadas, a las comunas y a los sistemas de agregación y articulación que surjan entre ellas, en atención a los requerimientos que las mismas formulen para la satisfacción de sus necesidades y el ejercicio de sus derechos, en los términos y lapsos que establece la ley" (art. 29). Igualmente se prevé que los órganos, entes e instancias del Poder Público, en sus diferentes niveles político-territoriales, deben adoptar "medidas para que las organizaciones socio-productivas de propiedad social comunal, gocen de prioridad y preferencia en los procesos de contrataciones públicas para la adquisición de bienes, prestación de servicios y ejecución de obras" (art. 30).[1315]

En *quinto lugar*, se establece la obligación para la República, los estados y municipios, de acuerdo con la ley que rige el proceso de transferencia y descentralización de competencias y atribuciones, la obligación de trasferir "a las comunidades organizadas, a las comunas y a los sistemas de agregación que de éstas surjan; funciones de gestión, administración, control de servicios y ejecución de obras atribuidos a aquéllos por la Constitución de la República, para mejorar la eficiencia y los resultados en beneficio del colectivo" (art. 27).[1316]

Con ello, se dispone legalmente el vaciamiento de competencias de los Estados y Municipios, de manera que queden como estructuras vacías, con gobiernos representativos electos por el pueblo pero que no tienen materias sobre las cuales gobernar.

Este proceso se ha completado en la reforma de la Ley Orgánica de Régimen Municipal (LOPPM) y en la ley Orgánica del Consejo Federal de Gobierno (LOCGR). En efecto, la trasferencia de competencias de los Estados a los Municipios, a las comunidades y a los grupos vecinales que se prevé en la Constitución (art. 184), y que en la LOPPM anterior se atribuía a los Consejos Legislativos de los Estados para establecer el procedimiento a dichos fines, se ha cambiado radicalmente, asignándose esa función al Consejo Federal de Gobierno organizado en la LOCFG,

---

1315   En particular, conforme al artículo 61 de la Ley Orgánica de las Comunas, se dispone que "todos los órganos y entes del Poder Público comprometidos con el financiamiento de proyectos de las comunas y sus sistemas de agregación, priorizarán aquéllos que impulsen la atención a las comunidades de menor desarrollo relativo, a fin de garantizar el desarrollo territorial equilibrado.

1316   Esta misma norma se repite en la Ley Orgánica de las Comunas (art. 64). El 31 de diciembre de 2010, aún estaba pendiente en la Asamblea Nacional la segunda discusión del proyecto de Ley Orgánica del Sistema de Transferencia de Competencias y atribuciones de los Estados y Municipios a las organizaciones del Poder Popular.

la cual se lo ha organizado de manera tal que está completamente controlado por el Ejecutivo Nacional (art. 11). En esta forma se ha limitado inconstitucionalmente la autonomía de los Estados y Municipios que les garantiza la Constitución.

A tal efecto, la LOPPM dispone, en su artículo 281 que "la transferencia de competencias y servicios de los estados a los municipios, y de éstos a las instancias del Poder Popular, se realizará de acuerdo a lo establecido en la Ley Orgánica del Consejo Federal de Gobierno," y en esta LOCFG, se asigna al Consejo, el atender "al establecimiento del régimen para la transferencia de las competencias entre los entes territoriales, y a las organizaciones detentadoras de la soberanía originaria del Estado"(art. 1); siendo por tanto ese órgano ahora el encargado de "de la planificación y coordinación de políticas y acciones para el desarrollo del proceso de descentralización y transferencia de competencias del Poder Nacional a los estados y municipios, " correspondiéndole establecer "los lineamientos que se aplican a los procesos de transferencia de las competencias y atribuciones de las entidades territoriales, hacia las organizaciones de base del Poder Popular" (art. 2). Lineamientos que además, declara esa LOCFG que son "vinculantes para las entidades territoriales (art. 2).

En el Reglamento de la Ley Orgánica del Consejo Federal de Gobierno de 2010, por otra parte, se definió la trasferencia de competencias como el:

"Proceso mediante el cual las entidades territoriales restituyen al Pueblo Soberano, a través de las comunidades organizadas y las organizaciones de base del poder popular, las competencias en las materias que, de acuerdo con lo establecido en el artículo 14 de la Ley Orgánica del Consejo Federal de Gobierno, en concordancia con el artículo 184 de la Constitución de la República Bolivariana de Venezuela, decrete el Presidente o Presidenta de la República en Consejo de Ministros, sin que ello obste para que, por cuenta propia, cualquier entidad territorial restituya al Pueblo Soberano otras competencias, de acuerdo a lo establecido en el correspondiente Plan Regional de Desarrollo y previa autorización de la Secretaría del Consejo Federal de Gobierno."[1317]

En *sexto lugar*, se establece que las instancias y organizaciones de base del Poder Popular contempladas en la LOPP, están exentas de todo tipo de pagos de tributos nacionales y derechos de registro, a cuyo efecto, se podrá establecer mediante leyes y ordenanzas de los estados y municipios, respectivamente, las exenciones aquí previstas para las instancias y organizaciones de base del Poder Popular (art. 31).

IX. LA MARGINALIZACIÓN DEL MUNICIPIO EN RELACIÓN CON LAS ORGANIZACIONES DEL PODER POPULAR

Para establecer el Poder Popular y el Estado Comunal, a los efectos de ahogar y estrangular progresivamente el Estado Constitucional, la primera de las instituciones territoriales afectadas ha sido el Municipio, del cual siendo la unidad política primara de la organización de la república, ha sido desvinculado del proceso de desarrollo comunal y de la participación popular. A tal efecto, diversas reformas se introduje-

1317   Véase en *Gaceta Oficial* N° 39.382 del 9 de marzo de 2010.

ron en diciembre de 2010 a la Ley Orgánica del Poder Público Municipal (LOPP),[1318] y entre ellas se destaca:

En primer lugar, la previsión como objetivo de la Ley además de la regulación de los Municipios y su gobierno, el proceso denominado de "descentralización y la transferencia a las comunidades organizadas, y a las comunas en su condición especial de entidad local, como a otras organizaciones del Poder Popular" (Art. 1). Se entiende que se trata de un proceso de transferencia de "competencias" aún cuando no se indica; sin embargo, la misma no puede calificarse como descentralización, pues está en el marco territorial y político, exige que las entidades receptoras de las competencias a ser transferidas, sean entidades locales como entidades políticas con gobiernos electos democráticamente. Las comunas, que se denominan como Entidades locales especiales" no son gobernadas por órganos cuyos integrantes sean electos por votación universal directa y secreta, y por tanto, no tienen autonomía política ni pueden formar parte del esquema de descentralización territorial del Estado.

En segundo lugar, el artículo 2 de la LOPPM, a pesar de que repite el aserto constitucional de que el Municipio "constituye la unidad política primaria de la organización nacional de la República," ya no habla de que "gozan de autonomía" como lo garantiza el artículo 168 de la Constitución, son que "ejerce sus competencias de manera autónoma." Ello, sin embargo, es contradicho en la propia Ley al establecerse que el artículo 110, que "el municipio se regirá por el Sistema Nacional de Planificación establecido en la ley que regula la materia," que como se sabe es una planificación centralizada.

A tal efecto, en la LOPPM se elimina la iniciativa ejecutiva de la planificación local que se asignaba al Alcalde, quien debía presentar al Consejo Local de Planificación las líneas maestras de su plan de gobierno, y se establece que es el Consejo Local de Planificación Pública "el órgano encargado de diseñar el Plan Municipal de Desarrollo y los demás planes municipales, en concordancia con los lineamientos que establezca el Plan de Desarrollo Económico y Social de la Nación y los demás planes nacionales y estadales, garantizando la participación protagónica del pueblo en su formulación, ejecución, seguimiento, evaluación y control, en articulación con el Sistema Nacional de Planificación"(art. 111). Ese Consejo, además, en la LOPPM, queda encargado de "diseñar el Plan de Desarrollo Comunal, en concordancia con los planes de desarrollo comunitario propuestos por los consejos comunales y los demás planes de interés colectivo, articulados con el Sistema Nacional de Planificación, de conformidad con lo establecido en la legislaciones que regula las comunas, los consejos comunales y la presente Ley; contando para ello con el apoyo de los órganos y entes de la Administración Pública. A tales efectos, es deber de las instancias que conforman la organización del municipio, atender los requerimientos de los diversos consejos de planificación existentes en cada una de las comunas para el logro de sus objetivos y metas" (art. 112)

En tercer lugar, en la reforma de la LOPPM, se encasilla y limita su rol como promotor de la participación del pueblo sólo "a través de las comunidades organizadas," que son las que se regulan en las leyes sobre el Poder Popular identificadas

---

1318   Véase en *Gaceta Oficial* N° 6.015 Extraordinario del 28 de diciembre de 2010.

con el socialismo, en contra de la previsión del artículo 62 de la Constitución que garantiza el carácter libre de la participación. La desvinculación de las comunidades organizadas respecto del Municipio, se asegura en la Ley, al excluirse su registro ante los órganos competentes "del Municipio" como decía la Ley Orgánica anterior que se reformó, previéndose ahora su registro sólo ante "los órganos competentes" (art. 33.3) que en las Leyes del poder Popular es el Ministerio de las Comunas. Es decir, con la reforma de la LOPPM, se produce una total desmunicipalización de las entidades comunales.

En cuarto lugar, a pesar de esta desmunicipalización, a las comunas se las incorpora en el régimen del Poder Público Municipal, como "entidad local territorial" (art. 19) aún cuando de "carácter especial" que conforme al artículo 19, "se rige por su ley de creación, puede constituirse dentro del territorio del Municipio o entre los límites político administrativo de dos o más municipios, sin que ello afecte la integridad territorial de los municipios donde se constituya." Como tal entidades locales de carácter especial, se las excluye completamente del régimen de la LOPPM quedando "reguladas por la legislación que norma su constitución, conformación, organización y funcionamiento" (art. 5). Ello se reafirma en el artículo 33 de la Ley al disponer que "los requisitos para la creación de la comuna, en el marco de su régimen especial como entidad local, se regirán por lo establecido en la Ley Orgánica de las Comunas."

En quinto lugar, se eliminó el carácter de entidad local de las parroquias, y por tanto, se eliminó su carácter democrático representativo. Es más, en la Disposición Transitoria segunda de la Ley se dispuso que a los 30 días siguientes a su publicación, "cesan en sus funciones los miembros principales y suplentes, así como los secretarios o secretarias, de las actuales juntas parroquiales,"

Eliminas las Juntas parroquiales, las cuales en el artículo 35, las pasaron a denominar "juntas parroquiales comunales," estas se regularon sólo como entidades con "facultades consultivas, de evaluación y articulación entre el poder popular y los órganos del Poder Público Municipal," con las funciones enumeradas en el artículo 37, de la cual se eliminó todo vestigio de gobierno local.

Dichas juntas parroquiales comunales, se estableció que deben ser "coordinada por una junta parroquial comunal integrada por cinco miembros y sus respectivos suplentes cuando corresponda a un área urbana y tres miembros y sus respectivos suplentes cuando sea no urbana, elegidos o elegidas para un período de dos años," no por el pueblo mediante sufragio, sino por "por los voceros de los consejos comunales de la parroquia respectiva," quienes "en dicha elección deberán ser fiel expresión del mandato de sus respectivas asambleas de ciudadanos." La norma agrega, que dicha designación, debe ser "validada por la asamblea de ciudadanos."

En la misma norma se estableció el principio de la revocatoria de los mandatos de los integrantes de las juntas parroquiales comunales, mandando a aplicar las condiciones y el procedimiento establecido para la revocación de los voceros de los consejos comunales, conforme a la Ley Orgánica que los regula.

Al desmunicipalizarse las juntas parroquiales comunales, y eliminarse su carácter de entidad política local de orden democrático representativo, el artículo 36 previó que sus miembros que deben ser avalados por la asamblea de ciudadanos, pueden ser menores de edad, aún cuando mayores de quince años, e incluso extranjeros.

SECCIÓN CUARTA:

EL RÉGIMEN DE LOS CONSEJOS COMUNALES O LA RESURRECCIÓN DE LOS SOVIETS EN EL CARIBE, CASI UN SIGLO DESPUÉS

I. LOS CONSEJOS COMUNALES COMO INSTRUMENTOS PARA EL SOCIALISMO

Como se dijo, la propuesta presidencial de reforma constitucional de 2007 fue rechazada por el pueblo en el referendo de diciembre de ese mismo año, en votación mayoritaria, cuyos resultados finales, sin embargo, nunca fueron dados oficialmente por el Consejo Nacional Electoral. No es difícil imaginar la razón de esta abstención.

Sin embargo, a pesar del rechazo, en muchos de sus aspectos la reforma constitucional de 2007 ha venido siendo ilegítimamente implementada por los órganos del Estado, sea mediante leyes, como la de los Consejos Comunales, mediante decretos leyes,[1319] e incluso mediante sentencias del Tribunal Supremo de Justicia.[1320] Precisamente, como se dijo, la Ley relativa a los Consejos Comunales de 2009 es uno de estos intentos de implementar, mediante una ley orgánica, algunos de los postulados esenciales de la rechazada reforma constitucional.

En efecto, la Ley Orgánica de 2009 tiene por objeto regular la constitución, conformación, organización y funcionamiento de los consejos comunales "como una instancia de participación para el ejercicio directo de la soberanía popular" (art. 1); definiéndoselos supuestamente "en el marco constitucional de la democracia participativa y protagónica," como "instancias de participación, articulación e integración entre los ciudadanos, ciudadanas y las diversas organizaciones comunitarias,[1321] movimientos sociales y populares, que permiten al pueblo organizado ejercer el gobierno comunitario y la gestión[1322] directa de las políticas públicas y proyectos orientados a responder a las necesidades, potencialidades y aspiraciones de las comunidades, en la *construcción del nuevo modelo de sociedad socialista* de igualdad, equidad y justicia social (art. 2). Sobre este aspecto insiste el artículo 3, al prescribir que la organización, funcionamiento y acción de los consejos comunales se rige por los principios y valores de "participación, corresponsabilidad, democracia, identidad nacional, libre debate de las ideas, celeridad, coordinación, cooperación, solidaridad, transparencia, rendición de cuentas, honestidad, bien común, humanismo, territoria-

---

1319   Véase los estudios sobre los decretos Leyes de 2008 en *Revista de Derecho Público, Estudios sobre los Decretos Leyes 2008*, N° 116, Editorial Jurídica Venezolana, Caracas 2008.

1320   Véase Allan R. Brewer-Carías, "La fraudulenta mutación de la Constitución en Venezuela, o de cómo el juez constitucional usurpa el poder constituyente originario", en *Anuario de Derecho Público*, Centro de Estudios de Derecho Público de la Universidad e Monteávila, Año 2, Caracas 2009, pp. 23-65.

1321   El artículo 4,4 de la Ley Orgánica define a las Organizaciones comunitarias, como "las organizaciones que existen o pueden existir en el seno de las comunidades y agrupan un conjunto de personas con base a objetivos e intereses comunes, para desarrollar actividades propias en el área que les ocupa."

1322   El artículo 4,10 de la Ley Orgánica define como gestión, "las acciones que exigen el cumplimiento de los objetivos y metas, aprobados por la Asamblea de Ciudadanos y Ciudadanas, de cada una de las unidades de trabajo que integran el Consejo Comunal."

lidad, colectivismo, eficacia, eficiencia, ética, responsabilidad social, control social, libertad, equidad, justicia, trabajo voluntario, igualdad social y de género, *con el fin de establecer la base sociopolítica del socialismo* que consolide un nuevo modelo político, social, cultural y económico."

De estas normas resulta, por tanto, que lo que se quiso establecer en la Ley Orgánica fue un medio de participación política "para el ejercicio directo de la soberanía popular," en el "marco constitucional de la democracia participativa y protagónica," como "instancias de participación, articulación e integración entre los ciudadanos," para "ejercer el gobierno comunitario." Ello, sin duda, corresponde a los ciudadanos, y es distinto a los medios de participación vecinal o comunitaria que no son reservados a los ciudadanos. La Ley Orgánica, por tanto, en forma evidentemente incorrecta e inconstitucional mezcló dos derechos de las personas a la participación: la participación ciudadana con la participación individual o comunitaria.

En todo caso, ha sido en este marco que se ha dictado la Ley Orgánica de los Consejos Comunales de 2009,[1323] la cual, además, tiene por objeto, regular la relación de los mismos "con los órganos y entes del Poder Público para la formulación, ejecución, control y evaluación de las políticas públicas, así como los planes y proyectos vinculados al desarrollo comunitario" (art. 1).

Por otra parte, el marco legal en la Ley Orgánica que regula la participación vinculada necesariamente a "construcción del nuevo modelo de sociedad socialista" y "con el fin de establecer la base sociopolítica del socialismo," es también inconstitucional pues elimina el carácter libre de la participación política que garantiza el artículo 62 de la Constitución, siendo además contrario al derecho constitucional que todos tienen al "libre desenvolvimiento de su personalidad" (art. 20); niega el carácter plural del sistema político que garantizan los artículos 2 y 6 de la Constitución, al encasillar un instrumento de gobierno como es el de los Consejos Comunales, dentro de un marco ideológico único y ahora "oficial," como es el socialismo, de manera que las personas que no crean ideológicamente en esta doctrina o se opongan legítimamente a ella, quedarían excluidos de la posibilidad de participar en aquellos, lo que es contrario a la democracia; y establece un sistema discriminatorio, contrario al principio de igualdad establecido en el artículo 21 de la Constitución.[1324]

1323 Véase además, sobre esta Ley Orgánica el estudio de Claudia Nikken, "La Ley Orgánica de los Consejos Comunales y el derecho a la participación ciudadana en los asuntos públicos," en Allan R. Brewer-Carías (Coordinador), Claudia Nikken, Luis A. Herrera Orellana, Jesús María Alvarado Andrade, José Ignacio Hernández y Adriana Vigilanza, *Leyes Orgánicas sobre el Poder Popular y el Estado Comunal (Los Consejos Comunales, las Comunas, la Sociedad Socialista y el Sistema Económico Comunal),*Editorial Jurídica Venezolana, Caracas 2011, pp. 183 ss.

1324 Sobre esto, contradiciendo lo que se ha previsto en el texto de la Ley Orgánica y en la práctica de los consejos comunales, Marta Harnecker, ha insistido en que "el poder popular no elimina el pluralismo político-ideológico" por lo que "no puede teñirse del color de un partido político, ni de una corriente religiosa; el poder popular debe ser de muchos colores, debe ser un arco iris y debe dar cabida a todas y todos los ciudadanos de Venezuela que deseen participar. Son las personas que habitan en una comunidad, centro de trabajo o estudio las que deben elegir democráticamente sus voceras y voceros y estos naturalmente representan diferentes posiciones políticas e ideológicas, dependiendo de la fuerza que esas posiciones tengan en sus respectivas comunidades." Véase Marta Harnecker, *De los Consejos Comunales a las Comunas. Construyendo el Socialismo del Siglo XXI,* 2 abril 2009, párrafo 268, en   http://www.scribd.com/doc/16299191/Harnecker-Marta-De-los-consejos-comunales-a-las-

Ahora bien, y teniendo en cuenta todas estas violaciones a la Constitución derivadas de tratar de "imponer" a las personas una ideología, al punto de cerrarle las puertas a la participación política a aquellos que no compartan la misma, debe destacarse que el sistema de participación que regula la Ley Orgánica tiene su base fundamental territorial en la unidad social dispuesta para el funcionamiento de los Consejos Comunales, y que la Ley califica como la "Comunidad," la cual se concibe como el "núcleo espacial básico e indivisible constituido por personas y familias que habitan en un ámbito geográfico determinado, vinculadas por características e intereses comunes; comparten una historia, necesidades y potencialidades culturales, económicas, sociales, territoriales y de otra índole." Ese ámbito geográfico donde habitan las personas que conforman la comunidad es "el territorio que ocupan" y "cuyos límites geográficos se establecen o ratifican en Asamblea de Ciudadanos, de acuerdo con sus particularidades y considerando la base poblacional de la comunidad" (art. 4,1 y 2).

La base poblacional para la conformación de una Comunidad a los efectos de la constitución de los Consejos Comunales, es decir, el número de habitantes que debe existir en su ámbito geográfico y que mantiene la "indivisibilidad de la comunidad" y garantiza "el ejercicio del gobierno comunitario y la democracia protagónica," debe oscilar entre 150 y 400 familias en el ámbito urbano; y alrededor de 120 familias en el ámbito rural. En las comunidades indígenas el punto de referencia para la conformación de una Comunidad se estableció en 10 familias; (art. 4,3). Esta referencia poblacional, particularmente en el ámbito de las comunidades urbanas, es muy similar a la que se había establecido en la vieja Ley Orgánica de Régimen Municipal para la constitución de las Asociaciones de Vecinos, a las cuales, en definitiva, los Consejos Comunales han sustituido.[1325]

II. INTEGRACIÓN DE LOS CONSEJOS COMUNALES

Los Consejos Comunales, en esta nueva Ley Orgánica, a los efectos de su funcionamiento, se integran por las siguientes organizaciones: por una parte, por la Asamblea de Ciudadanos del Consejo Comunal, y por la otra, por las tres Unidades

comunas-2009. En el mismo libro la autora ha advertido sobre la necesidad de "evitar la manipulación política" ya que "los consejos comunales deben ser arco iris", indicando que "Se ha insistido mucho en que es necesario evitar toda manipulación política o de otra índole en la conformación de los consejos comunales. No se trata de conformar los consejos comunales sólo con los partidarios de Chávez; estas instituciones comunitarias deben estar abiertas a todos los ciudadanos y ciudadanas, sean del color político que sean." *Idem*, Párrafo 185.

1325 Con razón María Pilar García-Guadilla consideró las Asociaciones de Vecinos como los antecedentes de los Consejos Comunales. Véase en "La praxis de los consejos comunales en Venezuela: ¿Poder popular o instancia clientelar?," en *Revista Venezolana de Economía y Ciencias Sociales*, abr. 2008, Vol. 14, N° 1, p. 125-151. Véase en http://www.scielo.org.ve/scielo.php?pid=S1315-6411200-8000100009&script=sci_arttext. Sin embargo, Marta Harnecker, al analizar algunos de los "problemas" relativos al funcionamiento de los consejos comunales, destaca el hecho de que "se han transformado en una asociación de vecinos más, porque se deja toda la responsabilidad en manos de los voceros y voceras y a veces sólo en alguno de ellos." Véase Marta Harnecker, *De los Consejos Comunales a las Comunas. Construyendo el Socialismo del Siglo XXI*, 2 abril 2009, párrafo 216, en http://www.scribd.com/doc/16299191/Harnecker-Marta-De-los-consejos-comunales-a-las-comunas-2009 .

que los conforman: la Unidad Ejecutiva; la Unidad Administrativa y Financiera Comunitaria; y la Unidad de Contraloría Social (art 19). Además, también integra el Consejo Comunal, el Colectivo de Coordinación Comunitaria que es la instancia de coordinación de las tres Unidades antes mencionadas del Consejo, y una Comisión Electoral Permanente.

1. *Las Asambleas de Ciudadanos*

La Asamblea de Ciudadanos del Consejo Comunal conforme a la Ley Orgánica, es ahora parte integrante de cada Consejo Comunal, concebida como la máxima instancia de deliberación y decisión para el ejercicio del poder comunitario, la participación y el protagonismo popular (art. 20). Conforme a lo dispuesto en el artículo 70 de la Constitución, la Ley Orgánica repite que sus decisiones "son de carácter vinculante" pero sólo "para el Consejo Comunal" (art. 20). De allí la importancia de estas Asambleas de ciudadanos y la obligación que tenía el Legislador de hacerlas junto con los Consejos Comunales real y verdaderamente "representativas" de la Comunidad, y asegurar que en ellas, efectivamente "participen" los habitantes de la misma.

Pero la Ley Orgánica, sin embargo, no ha garantizado nada de esto. En cuanto a la integración de las Asambleas de ciudadanos, conforme al artículo 21 de la Ley Orgánica, las mismas están constituida por "los habitantes de la comunidad mayores de quince años, conforme a las disposiciones de la presente Ley" (art. 21), lo que, como se ha dicho, es una contradicción *in terminis* y además, inconstitucional, pues los extranjeros o menores de 18 años no son ciudadanos. En todo caso, esos habitantes de la comunidad, que sin duda deben formar parte de las familias que conforman la base poblacional de la Comunidad, deben estar inscritos en el registro electoral de la comunidad (art. 37,1), que por lo demás, por su conformación también con no ciudadanos, es diferente del Registro Electoral permanente que debe llevar el Consejo Nacional Electoral.

En efecto, si de lo que se trata es de constituir una Asamblea de "ciudadanos," sólo los "ciudadanos" podrían integrarla, y la ciudadanía, como se sabe, sólo puede ejercerse por los venezolanos conforme a los artículos 39 y 40 de la Constitución y al artículo 50 de la Ley de Nacionalidad y Ciudadanía de 2004,[1326] en la cual, además, se define la ciudadanía, como "la condición jurídica obtenida por la nacionalidad venezolana, la cual permite el goce y el ejercicio de los derechos y deberes políticos previstos en la Constitución de la República Bolivariana de Venezuela y en las leyes" (art. 4,4).

Por tanto, de acuerdo con estas normas constitucionales y legales, sólo los *venezolanos ciudadanos* pueden ser "titulares de derechos y deberes políticos," y entre los derechos políticos establecidos en la Constitución está precisamente el derecho a la participación política, que además, el artículo 62 de la Constitución reserva a los ciudadanos. Por tanto, no todo habitante en el territorio de la República o de una Comunidad es "ciudadano," por lo que como se ha dicho, es inconstitucional otorgar el ejercicio de un derecho político como la participación en las Asambleas de "Ciu-

---

1326   *Gaceta Oficial* N° 37.971 de 01-07-2004.

dadanos" a todos "habitantes" de la comunidad, incluyendo a quienes no sean ciudadanos, como por ejemplo, los extranjeros. Estos, conforme a la Constitución, sólo
tienen excepcionalmente el derecho al sufragio, de acuerdo con la Constitución, en
el ámbito regional y local (art. 64).

Por otra parte, la ciudadanía se ejerce por los venezolanos "en las *condiciones de
edad previstas en esta Constitución*" (art. 39), por lo que no existiendo una previsión constitucional expresa que prevea la posibilidad para los menores de 18 años,
pero mayores de 15 años, para ejercer algún derecho político, ello no podría prever-
lo el Legislador. Este, a lo sumo, lo que podría haber hecho en esta materia era
haber extendido el derecho a participar en las Asamblea de "ciudadanos" a los venezolanos con derecho a la participación ciudadana indirecta, mediante el sufragio,
que son los mayores de 18 años (art. 64). Por tanto, resulta también contrario a la
Constitución el extender legalmente el derecho político de participar en las Asambleas de "ciudadanos" a los menores de 18 años pero mayores de 15 años.

En cuanto al quórum para la adopción de decisiones por parte de las Asambleas
de Ciudadanos, las cuales, como se ha dicho, son obligatorias para el Consejo Comunal, las mismas conforme a la Ley Orgánica se adoptan por mayoría simple de los
asistentes, siempre que concurran a la Asamblea en primera convocatoria, un quórum mínimo del 30% de los habitantes miembros de la Comunidad y del 20% mínimo de los mismos en segunda convocatoria (art. 22). La Ley, por tanto, no garantiza
efectiva la representatividad de la Comunidad en la Asamblea, al permitir que un
órgano con los poderes decisorios que tiene, por ejemplo, de una Comunidad de 400
familias, que implica un universo de aproximadamente 1600 personas, se pueda
constituir con solo la presencia de 320 personas, y pueda tomar decisiones con el
voto de sólo 161 personas; es decir, en definitiva, con el voto del 10% de los habitantes de la Comunidad. Estas previsiones, por otra parte, en lugar de estimular la
participación, lo que fomentan es la ausencia de participación, pues si las decisiones
se pueden adoptar en esa forma, los habitantes no tendrán interés o posibilidad en
participar.[1327]

Estas Asambleas de ciudadanos, así constituidas, a pesar de integrar el Consejo
Comunal, son las que deben aprobar el ámbito geográfico de la Comunidad y del
Consejo Comunal (art. 23,1) así como el acta constitutiva y estatutos del Consejo
Comunal (art. 23,13). Tienen además, dentro de sus funciones: aprobar el Plan Co-
munitario de Desarrollo Integral, que es el documento técnico que identifica las po-
tencialidades y limitaciones, las prioridades y los proyectos comunitarios[1328] que

---

1327 Esto lo ha advertido Marta Harnecker, al destacar que "uno de los problemas que ha habido cuando
se han conformado los consejos comunales, es que las asambleas de ciudadanas y ciudadanos no han
logrado, en muchos casos, convocar a todas las personas que debían convocar. En algunos casos esto
se debe a la apatía de la gente, en otros se debe a los defectos de la convocatoria. Muchas veces hay
sectores de esa comunidad, especialmente los sectores más alejados que nunca han llegado a enterarse
de que existe una asamblea, nunca fueron citados" Véase Marta Harnecker, *De los Consejos Comunales a las Comunas. Construyendo el Socialismo del Siglo XXI*, 2 abril 2009, párrafo 190, en
http://www.scribd.com/doc/16299191/Harnecker-Marta-De-los-consejos-comunales-a-las-comunas-
2009 .

1328 El artículo 4,7 de la Ley Orgánica define los proyectos comunitarios como "el conjunto de actividades concretas orientadas a lograr uno o varios objetivos, para dar respuesta a las necesidades, aspira-

ALLAN R. BREWER-CARÍAS

deben orientar al logro del desarrollo integral de la comunidad (art. 4,9), y demás planes, de acuerdo a los aspectos esenciales de la vida comunitaria, a los fines de contribuir a la transformación integral de la comunidad (art. 23,5); garantizar el funcionamiento del ciclo comunal (art. 23,6); aprobar los proyectos comunitarios, de comunicación alternativa, educación, salud, cultura, recreación, actividad física y deporte, socio-productivos, de vivienda y hábitat, de infraestructura, de funcionamiento, entre otros, y la creación de organizaciones socio-productivas a ser propuestos ante distintos órganos y entes del Poder Público o instituciones privadas (art. 23,7); aprobar las normas de convivencia de la comunidad, sin menoscabo de lo dispuesto en el ordenamiento jurídico vigente (art. 23,9); aprobar la solicitud de transferencia de servicios (art. 23,11).

En cuanto a las diversas Unidades y órganos del Consejo, la Asamblea de ciudadanos debe aprobar la creación de comités de trabajo u otras formas de organización comunitaria, con carácter permanente temporal (art. 23,2); elegir y revocar a los voceros del Consejo Comunal "a través de un proceso de elección popular comunitaria (art. 23,3); designar a los voceros del Consejo Comunal para las distintas instancias de participación popular y de gestión de políticas públicas (art. 23,10); elegir y revocar los integrantes de la comisión electoral (art. 23,4); evaluar la gestión de cada una de las unidades que conforman el Consejo Comunal (art. 23,8); y designar a los y las miembros de la comisión de contratación, conforme a la Ley de Contrataciones Públicas (art. 23,12).

2. La Unidad Ejecutiva y los voceros de la comunidad

La Unidad Ejecutiva es la instancia del Consejo Comunal encargada de promover y articular la participación organizada de los habitantes de la comunidad, organizaciones comunitarias, los movimientos sociales y populares en los diferentes comités de trabajo; se reunirá a fin de planificar la ejecución de las decisiones de la Asamblea de Ciudadanos, así como conocer las actividades de cada uno de los comités y de las áreas de trabajo[1329] (art. 27).

Esta Unidad Ejecutiva está conformada por un número indeterminado y variable de voceros, postulados según la cantidad de comités de trabajo u otras organizaciones comunitarias que existan o se conformen en la comunidad (art. 28).

Esos Comités pueden referirse a las siguientes áreas de actividad enumeradas en el artículo 28 de la Ley Orgánica: salud; tierra Urbana; vivienda y hábitat; economía comunal;[1330] seguridad y defensa integral; medios alternativos comunitarios; recrea-

---

ciones y potencialidades de las comunidades. Los proyectos deben contar con una programación de acciones determinadas en el tiempo, los recursos, los responsables y los resultados esperados."

1329   El artículo 4,8 de la Ley Orgánica define Áreas de trabajo a los "ámbitos de gestión que se constituyen en relación con las particularidades, potencialidades y los problemas más relevantes de la comunidad. El número y contenido de las áreas de trabajo dependerá de la realidad, las prácticas tradicionales, las necesidades colectivas y las costumbres de cada comunidad. Las áreas de trabajo agruparán varios comités de trabajo."

1330   El artículo 4,11 de la ley Orgánica define la economía comunal como "el conjunto de relaciones sociales de producción, distribución, intercambio y consumo de bienes, servicios y saberes, desarrolladas por las comunidades bajo formas de propiedad social al servicio de sus necesidades de manera

ción y deportes; alimentación y defensa del consumidor; mesa técnica de agua; mesa técnica de energía y gas; protección social de niños, niñas y adolescentes; personas con discapacidad; educación, cultura y formación ciudadana; familia e igualdad de género. En los casos en que hubiere otras formas organizativas establecidas en la comunidad, diferentes a las antes señaladas, deberán incorporarse a la constitución, funcionamiento y atribuciones de los comités de trabajo de la Unidad Ejecutiva, de conformidad con la normativa que los regula.

En cuanto a los pueblos y comunidades indígenas, atendiendo a sus culturas, prácticas tradicionales y necesidades colectivas, pueden constituir comités de trabajo, además de los antes indicados, en las siguientes áreas: ambiente y demarcación de tierra en los hábitats indígenas; medicina tradicional indígena; y educación propia, educación intercultural bilingüe e idiomas indígenas.

La Unidad Ejecutiva del Consejo Comunal tiene las siguientes funciones: ejecutar las decisiones de la Asamblea de Ciudadanos y Ciudadanas en el área de su competencia (art. 29,1); crear y organizar el sistema de información comunitario interno (art. 29,2); coordinar y articular todo lo referido a la organización, funcionamiento y ejecución de los planes de trabajo de los comités y su relación con la Unidad de Contraloría Social, la Unidad Administrativa y Financiera Comunitaria y las demás organizaciones sociales de la comunidad (art. 29,3); promover la creación de nuevas organizaciones con la aprobación de la Asamblea de Ciudadanos y Ciudadanas en defensa del interés colectivo y el desarrollo integral de la comunidad (art. 29,4); organizar el voluntariado social como escuela generadora de conciencia y activadora del deber social en cada comité de trabajo[1331] (art. 29,5); promover la participación de los comités de trabajo u otras formas de organización comunitaria en la elaboración y ejecución de políticas públicas, mediante la presentación de propuestas a los órganos y entes del Poder Público (art. 29,6); promover, participar y contribuir, conjuntamente con la Milicia Bolivariana, en la seguridad y defensa integral de la Nación (art. 29,7); coadyuvar con los órganos y entes del Poder Público en el levantamiento de información relacionada con la comunidad, conforme al ordenamiento jurídico vigente (art. 29,8); impulsar y promover la formulación de proyectos comunitarios que busquen satisfacer las necesidades, aspiraciones y potencialidades de la comunidad (art. 29,9); y conocer las solicitudes y emitir las constancias de residencia de los habitantes de la comunidad, a los efectos de las actividades inherentes del Consejo Comunal, sin menoscabo del ordenamiento jurídico vigente (art. 29,10).

3.   La Unidad Administrativa y Financiera Comunitaria

La Unidad Administrativa y Financiera Comunitaria es la instancia del Consejo Comunal que funciona como un ente de administración, ejecución, inversión, crédito, ahorro e intermediación financiera de los recursos y fondos de los consejos co-

---

sustentable y sostenible, de acuerdo con lo establecido en el Sistema Centralizado de Planificación y en el Plan de Desarrollo Económico y Social de la Nación."

1331   El artículo 4, de la Ley Orgánica define el Comité de Trabajo como "el colectivo o grupo de personas organizadas para ejercer funciones específicas, atender necesidades en distintas áreas de trabajo y desarrollar las aspiraciones y potencialidades de su comunidad."

munales, de acuerdo a las decisiones y aprobaciones de la Asamblea de Ciudadanos, "privilegiando el interés social sobre la acumulación de capital." Esta Unidad está integrada por 5 habitantes de la comunidad, electos a través de un "proceso de elección popular" por la Asamblea de ciudadanos (art. 30).

La Unidad Administrativa y Financiera Comunitaria tiene las siguientes funciones: ejecutar las decisiones de la Asamblea de Ciudadanos y Ciudadanas en el área de su competencia (art. 31,1); elaborar los registros contables con los soportes que demuestren los ingresos y egresos efectuados (art. 31,2); presentar trimestralmente el informe de gestión y la rendición de cuenta pública cuando le sea requerido por la Asamblea de Ciudadanos, por el colectivo de coordinación comunitaria o por cualquier otro órgano o ente del Poder Público que le haya otorgado recursos (art. 31,3); prestar servicios financieros y no financieros en el área de su competencia (art. 31,4); realizar la intermediación financiera comunitaria, privilegiando el interés social sobre la acumulación de capital (art. 31,5); apoyar las políticas de fomento, desarrollo y fortalecimiento de la economía social, popular y alternativa (art. 31,6); proponer formas alternativas de intercambio de bienes y servicios para lograr la satisfacción de las necesidades y fortalecimiento de la economía local (art. 31,7); promover el ahorro familiar (art. 31,8); facilitar herramientas que permitan el proceso de evaluación y análisis de los créditos de las organizaciones socio-productivas previstas en la Ley para el Fomento y Desarrollo de la Economía Popular (Decreto N° 6.129)(art. 31,9); consignar ante la Unidad de Contraloría Social del Consejo Comunal, el comprobante de la declaración jurada de patrimonio de los voceros y voceras de la Unidad Administrativa y Financiera Comunitaria al inicio y cese de sus funciones (art. 31,10); administrar los fondos del Consejo comunal con la consideración del colectivo de coordinación comunitaria y la aprobación de la Asamblea de Ciudadanos (art. 31,11); elaborar y presentar el proyecto anual de gastos de los fondos del Consejo Comunal (art. 31,12); y presentar y gestionar ante el colectivo de coordinación comunitaria el financiamiento de los proyectos aprobados por la Asamblea de Ciudadanos (art. 31,13).

Esta Unidad Administrativa y Financiera Comunitaria conforme a la Ley Orgánica de 2007, sustituye a las asociaciones, cooperativas, banco comunal constituidas conforme a la Ley de 2006, las cuales quedan disueltas a partir de la adecuación del Consejo Comunal a la nueva Ley en su carácter de unidad de gestión financiera de los consejos comunales. Por consiguiente, conforme a esa adecuación, deben transferir al Consejo Comunal, en un lapso no mayor a 30 días, los recursos financieros y no financieros, los provenientes de la intermediación financiera con los fondos generados, asignados o captados, bienes, obligaciones, deudas, compromisos, planes, programas, proyectos y cualquier otro adquirido en el ejercicio de sus funciones (Disposición Transitoria Tercera). Una vez efectuada la transferencia por parte de la asociación cooperativa banco comunal, el Consejo Comunal asumirá los compromisos económicos, la ejecución y tramitación de los proyectos y los procesos administrativos y judiciales en curso causados durante la gestión de la asociación cooperativa banco comunal (Disposición Transitoria Cuarta). En todo caso, conforme a la nueva Ley Orgánica, los integrantes de las instancias de gestión financiera de la asociación cooperativa banco comunal deben mantener su condición de voceros en la nueva Unidad Administrativa y Financiera Comunitaria a los efectos del cumplimiento de la continuidad del período para los cuales fueron electos (Disposición Transitoria Sexta).

En todo caso, los voceros de las antiguas instancias de gestión financiera de la asociación cooperativa banco comunal, son responsables civil, penal y administrativamente conforme a la ley, por la omisión, retardo e incumplimiento de la transferencia indicada en la disposición transitoria tercera (Disposición Transitoria Quinta); y los voceros de la Unidad Administrativa y Financiera Comunitaria incurren en responsabilidad civil, penal y administrativa, según sea el caso, por los actos, hechos u omisiones que alteren el destino de los recursos del Consejo Comunal, por lo cual deben ser sancionados conforme a las leyes que regulen la materia (art. 32).

4. La Unidad de Contraloría Social

La Unidad de Contraloría Social es la instancia del Consejo Comunal para realizar la evaluación de la gestión comunitaria y la vigilancia de las actividades, recursos y administración de los fondos del Consejo Comunal. Está integrada por 5 habitantes de la comunidad, electos a través de un "proceso de elección popular" (art. 33). Esta unidad debe realizar sus funciones sin menoscabo del control social que ejerza la Asamblea de Ciudadanos y otras organizaciones comunitarias, de conformidad con el ordenamiento jurídico.

Son funciones de la Unidad de Contraloría Social, ejecutar las decisiones de la Asamblea de Ciudadanos que correspondan a sus funciones (34,1); ejercer seguimiento, vigilancia, supervisión y control de la ejecución de los planes, proyectos comunitarios y socio-productivos, organizaciones socio-productivas, fases del ciclo comunal y gasto anual generado con los fondos y los recursos financieros y no financieros asignados por órganos y entes del Poder Público o instituciones privadas al Consejo Comunal (34,2); rendir anualmente cuenta pública de sus actuaciones (34,3); presentar informes de sus actuaciones cuando les sean solicitados por la Asamblea de Ciudadanos, por el colectivo de coordinación comunitaria o cuando lo considere pertinente (34,4); cooperar con los órganos y entes del Poder Público en la función de control, conforme a la legislación y demás instrumentos normativos vigentes (34,5); conocer y procesar los planteamientos presentados por los ciudadanos y ciudadanas con relación a la gestión de las unidades del Consejo Comunal e informar de manera oportuna a la Asamblea de Ciudadanos (34,6); y remitir ante el Ministerio del Poder Popular para las Comunas con competencia en materia de participación ciudadana, las declaraciones juradas de patrimonio de los voceros de la Unidad Administrativa y Financiera Comunitaria del Consejo Comunal (34,7).

La Unidad de Contraloría Social del Consejo Comunal debe coordinar, en el ejercicio de sus funciones, con los órganos del Poder Ciudadano (art. 35).

5. La coordinación de las Unidades de los Consejos Comunales

El artículo 24 de la Ley Orgánica dispuso la conformación de un "Colectivo de Coordinación Comunitaria" integrado por los voceros de las Unidades Ejecutiva, Administrativa y Financiera Comunitaria y de Contraloría Social del Consejo Comunal, para servir de instancia de articulación, trabajo conjunto y funcionamiento, con las siguientes funciones: realizar seguimiento de las decisiones aprobadas en la Asamblea de Ciudadanos y Ciudadanas (art. 25,1); coordinar la elaboración, ejecución y evaluación del Plan Comunitario de Desarrollo Integral articulado con los planes de desarrollo municipal y estadal de conformidad con las líneas generales del Proyecto Nacional Simón Bolívar (art. 25,2); conocer, previa ejecución, la gestión de la Unidad Administrativa y Financiera Comunitaria del Consejo Comunal (art. 25,3); presentar propuestas aprobadas por la Asamblea de Ciudadanos, para la formulación de políticas públicas (art. 25,4); garantizar información permanente y oportuna sobre las actuaciones de las unidades del Consejo Comunal a la Asamblea de Ciudadanos (art. 25,5); convocar para los asuntos de interés común a las demás unidades del Consejo Comunal (art. 25,6); coordinar la aplicación del ciclo comunal para la elaboración del Plan Comunitario de Desarrollo Integral (art. 25,7); coordinar con la Milicia Bolivariana lo referente a la defensa integral de la Nación (art. 25,8); coordinar acciones estratégicas que impulsen el modelo socio-productivo comunitario y redes socio-productivas[1332] vinculadas al Plan Comunitario de Desarrollo Integral (art. 25,9); promover la formación y capacitación comunitaria en los voceros o voceras del Consejo Comunal y en la comunidad en general (art. 25,10); elaborar propuesta de informe sobre la solicitud de transferencia de servicios y presentarlo ante la Asamblea de Ciudadanos (art. 25,11); coordinar acciones con los distintos comités que integran la Unidad Ejecutiva en sus relaciones con los órganos y entes de la Administración Pública para el cumplimiento de sus fines (art. 25,12); y elaborar los estatutos del Consejo Comunal (art. 25,13).

De acuerdo con el artículo 26 de la ley Orgánica, el Colectivo de Coordinación Comunitaria y las unidades que conforman el Consejo Comunal deben establecer el sistema de trabajo en el reglamento interno, que debe contemplar como mínimo una periodicidad quincenal para las reuniones, sin menoscabo de realizar convocatoria cuando lo estimen necesario, dejando constancia escrita de los acuerdos aprobados.

6.   *La Comisión Electoral Permanente*

En cada Consejo Comunal debe constituirse una Comisión Electoral Permanente que es la instancia encargada de organizar y conducir de forma permanente, los procesos de elección o revocatoria de los voceros del Consejo Comunal y las consultas sobre aspectos relevantes de la vida comunitaria, así como cualquier otro que decida la Asamblea de Ciudadanos (art. 36). Esta Comisión está integrada por 5 habitantes de la comunidad, quienes deben ser electos por la Asamblea de ciudadanos, con sus respectivos suplentes, y duran 2 años en sus funciones, contados a partir de su elección. Quienes integren la comisión electoral no pueden postularse como voceros para las unidades del Consejo Comunal (art. 36).

La Comisión Electoral Permanente del Consejo Comunal, como se especifica en el artículo 37 de la Ley Orgánica, ejerce las siguientes funciones: elaborar y mantener actualizado el registro electoral de la comunidad, conformado por todos los habitantes de la comunidad, mayores de quince años, de acuerdo a lo establecido en la presente Ley (art. 37,1); informar a la comunidad todo lo relativo a la elección, reelección o revocatoria de los voceros del Consejo Comunal, así como los temas objeto de consulta (art. 37,2); elaborar y custodiar el material electoral (art. 37,3); con-

---

1332   El artículo 4,12 de la ley Orgánica define como redes socio-productivas, "la articulación e integración de los procesos productivos de las organizaciones socio-productivas comunitarias, para el intercambio de saberes, bienes y servicios, basados en los principios de cooperación y solidaridad; sus actividades se desarrollan mediante nuevas relaciones de producción, comercio, distribución, cambio y consumo, sustentables y sostenibles, que contribuyen al fortalecimiento del Poder Popular."

vocar a los habitantes de la comunidad para que se postulen como aspirantes a voceros a las unidades del Consejo Comunal (art. 37,4); coordinar el proceso de votación (art. 37,5); verificar los requisitos exigidos a los postulados en las instancias del Consejo Comunal (art. 37,6); escrutar y totalizar los votos, firmando los resultados con los testigos electorales designados (art. 37,7); conocer y decidir sobre las impugnaciones presentadas sobre los procesos electorales o las consultas formuladas (art. 37,8); levantar el acta del proceso de elección y sus resultados (art. 37,9); proclamar y juramentar a los que resulten electos como voceros de las unidades del Consejo Comunal (art. 37,10); organizar y coordinar los procesos electorales en los lapsos establecidos en la presente Ley y en los estatutos del Consejo Comunal (art. 37,11); informar los resultados de las consultas realizadas en la comunidad (art. 37,12); velar por la seguridad y transparencia de los procesos electorales (art. 37,13); cuidar y velar por la preservación de los bienes y archivos electorales de la comunidad (art. 37,14); elaborar y presentar ante el colectivo de coordinación comunitaria un estimado de los recursos, a los fines de llevar los procesos electorales, de revocatoria y las consultas sobre los aspectos relevantes de la comunidad (art. 37,15); notificar al colectivo de coordinación comunitaria, con dos meses de anticipación al cese de las funciones de la comisión electoral, a los fines de la preparación del proceso de elección de sus nuevos integrantes (art. 37,16); y coordinar en el ejercicio de sus funciones con el Poder Electoral (art. 37,17).

Como puede apreciarse, la Ley Orgánica de 2009 ha establecido todo un sistema de administración electoral paralelo al que corresponde al Poder Electoral, para llevar adelante lo que la Ley califica de "elección popular" de los voceros de los Consejos Comunales y los otros órganos comunitarios. La Constitución asigna a los órganos del Poder Electoral, en particular al Consejo Nacional Electoral, la competencia exclusiva para la "organización, administración, dirección y vigilancia de todos los actos relativos a la elección de los cargos de representación popular de los poderes públicos, así como de los referendos" (art. 293), por lo que la elección de los voceros de las Unidades de los Consejos Comunales, que en definitiva, "representan" a los habitantes de la Comunidad, debería también organizarse por dicho Poder Electoral, el cual es el órgano con competencia para llevar el registro electoral, en particular si se trata de elección para integrar entidades estatales, como son los Consejos Comunales. Atribuir la organización, administración, dirección y vigilancia de estos procesos electorales para elegir a los representantes de la Comunidad en los Consejos Comunales, a un órgano distinto al Poder Electoral, sin duda viola la Constitución.

III. LA SUPUESTA "ELECCIÓN" DE LOS VOCEROS DE LAS UNIDADES DE LOS CONSEJOS COMUNALES

Conforme al artículo 4,6 de la Ley, los voceros de las Unidades de los Consejos Comunales son las personas electas mediante "proceso de elección popular," a fin de coordinar el funcionamiento del Consejo Comunal, y la "instrumentación de las decisiones de la Asamblea de Ciudadanos." El ejercicio de las funciones de los voceros del Consejo Comunal tiene carácter voluntario y debe desarrollarse "con espíritu unitario y compromiso con los intereses de la comunidad y de la Patria" (art. 13). Además, conforme al artículo 14 de la Ley, los voceros de los Consejos Comunales tienen como deber, la disciplina, la participación, la solidaridad, la integración, la ayuda mutua, la corresponsabilidad social, la rendición de cuentas, el manejo transparente, oportuno y eficaz de los recursos que dispongan para el funcionamiento del Consejo Comunal.

Con la conformación de estos voceros de los Consejos Comunales, como los agentes a cuyo cargo está la conducción de las actividades de los mismos, en definitiva, lo que la Ley Orgánica ha establecido es una forma de "representación" de la Comunidad para el ejercicio de su derecho a participar, mediante estos voceros de los Consejos Comunales. Siendo esos voceros, en la práctica "representantes"[1333] de la Comunidad, conforme a la Constitución, tendrían que ser electos como tales representantes, mediante votación, no de un número reducido de personas-habitantes que participen en una Asamblea de ciudadanos, que puede ser escuálida, sino de todos los ciudadanos habitantes que forman la Comunidad y que deben estar inscritos en el registro electoral que debe llevar la Comisión Electoral Permanente. Y dicha elección, en todo caso, tendría que realizarse conforme lo exige el artículo 63 de la Constitución mediante votaciones libres, universales, directas y secretas en las cuales se garantice el principio de la personalización del sufragio y la representación proporcional. En contraste con esta previsión constitucional, la supuesta "elección popular" que se establece en la Ley Orgánica de 2009 no es directa ni secreta, ya que incluso podría hacerse "a mano alzada,"[1334] y en cuanto a la elección de los voceros de las unidades Ejecutiva, Administrativa y Financiera Comunitaria y de Contraloría Social, la hace la Asamblea de ciudadanos necesariamente "de manera uninominal" lo que implica que "en ningún caso, se efectuará por plancha o lista electoral" (art. 11), lo que no se ajusta a la previsión constitucional.

Por otra parte, a los efectos de la elección de los voceros, el artículo 11 de la Ley Orgánica establece el derecho de los "ciudadanos" de manera individual o colectiva a participar y postular los candidatos a voceros a las unidades del Consejo Comunal. Este derecho de participar y postular, por tanto, contradictoriamente no se atribuye en la Ley Orgánica a los "habitantes" de la comunidad, que son los supuestos electores, sino sólo a los venezolanos ciudadanos. Pero en cambio, al regular la condición de vocero de las Unidades de los Concejos Comunales, la Ley Orgánica establece que pueden postularse para tales cargos (al igual que para los integrantes de la comisión electoral), los venezolanos o extranjeros residentes, mayores de 15 años, habitantes de la comunidad con al menos un año de residencia en la misma, salvo en los casos de comunidades recién constituidas (at. 15,1). Esto significa que sólo pueden postular a los voceros, quienes sean ciudadanos; pudiendo ser electos como voceros, los extranjeros residentes y, por tanto, no ciudadanos. Sólo en el caso de los voceros

---

1333   A pesar de que en la página web del "Ministerio del Poder Popular para la Participación y Protección Social" se afirmaba que el vocero, a pesar de ser la persona "electa por la asamblea de ciudadanos y ciudadanas para cumplir con los *mandatos* de la comunidad," sin embargo "no es un o una representante a quien le hemos entregado nuestro poder para que decida por nosotros." Véase el anuncio sobre "Consejos Comunales. Base del Poder Popular. ¡Construir el Poder desde Abajo!," en http://gp.cnti.ve/site/minpa-des.gob.ve/view/Consejos%20Comunales.php

1334   Así se informaba por el "Ministerio del Poder Popular para la Participación y Protección Social" en su página web al indicar dentro de las tareas del "equipo promotor" el "recoger ideas para definir con que sistema se va a votar: voto secreto o a mano alzada." Véase el anuncio sobre "Consejos Comunales. Base del Poder Popular. ¡Construir el Poder desde Abajo!," en http://gp.cnti.ve/site/minpades.gob.ve/view/Consejos%20Comunales.php

de las Unidades Administrativa y Financiera Comunitaria y de Contraloría Social se exige que sean mayores de 18 años, no pudiendo formar parte de la comisión electoral (art. 15, in fine).

Para ser postulado como vocero, además, la Ley exige que se presente una carta de postulación o manifestación de voluntad por escrito, identificando nombre, apellido y cédula de identidad (art. 15, 2), y además, que el postulado esté inscrito en el registro electoral de la comunidad (art. 15,4), ser de reconocida solvencia moral y honorabilidad (art. 15,5); tenga capacidad de trabajo colectivo con disposición y tiempo para el trabajo comunitario (art. 15,6), espíritu unitario y compromiso con los intereses de la comunidad (art. 15,7); no posea parentesco hasta el cuarto grado de consanguinidad y segundo grado de afinidad con los demás voceros integrantes de la Unidad Administrativa y Financiera Comunitaria y de la Unidad de Contraloría Social que conforman el Consejo Comunal, salvo las comunidades de áreas rurales y comunidades indígenas (art. 15,8); no ocupe cargos de elección popular (art. 15,9); y no esté sujeto a interdicción civil o inhabilitación política (art. 15,10) ni sea requerido por instancias judiciales (art. 15,11).

Quienes se postulen para voceros sólo pueden hacerlo para una Unidad del Consejo Comunal. En los pueblos y comunidades indígenas la postulación y elección de voceros o voceras se debe hacer según lo previsto en la Ley y tomando en cuenta su uso, costumbres y tradiciones.

Todos los voceros de las unidades que conforman el Consejo Comunal duran 2 años en sus funciones, contados a partir del momento de su elección por la Asamblea de ciudadanos, y podrán ser reelectos (art. 12).

IV. LA CESACIÓN DE LOS VOCEROS COMUNALES

1. *La revocación del mandato de los voceros de las Unidades del Consejo Comunal*

Los cargos de voceros de los Concejos Comunales son revocables por la Asamblea de Ciudadanos (art. 39), mediante decisión tomada por mayoría simple de los asistentes a la Asamblea de Ciudadanos, siempre que la misma cuente con un quórum del 20% de la población mayor de quince años de esa comunidad (art. 41).

El artículo 38 de la Ley Orgánica define por "revocatoria," la separación definitiva de los voceros del Consejo Comunal del ejercicio de sus funciones por estar incurso en alguna de las siguientes causales de revocatoria establecidas en el artículo 39 de la Ley: actuar de forma contraria a las decisiones tomadas por la Asamblea de Ciudadanos o el Colectivo de Coordinación Comunitaria del Consejo Comunal (art. 39,1); faltar evidente a las funciones que le sean conferidas de conformidad con la Ley y los estatutos del Consejo Comunal, salvo que la falta sea por caso fortuito o de fuerza mayor (art. 39,2); omitir o negarse a presentar los proyectos comunitarios decididos por la Asamblea de Ciudadanos, por ante la instancia del Gobierno Nacional, estadal o municipal correspondiente o cualquier otro órgano o ente del Poder Público, a los fines de su aprobación (art. 39,3); presentar los proyectos comunitarios, en orden distinto a las prioridades establecidas por la Asamblea de Ciudadanos (art. 39,4); representar, negociar individualmente asuntos propios del Consejo Comunal que corresponda decidir la Asamblea de Ciudadanos (art. 39,5); no rendir cuentas en el tiempo legal establecido para ello o en el momento exigido por el colectivo de coordinación comunitaria o la Asamblea de Ciudadanos (art. 39,6); incurrir en malversación, apropiación, desviación de los recursos asignados, generados o captados por el Consejo Comunal o cualquier otro delito previsto en la Ley Contra la Corrupción y el ordenamiento jurídico penal (art. 39,7); omisión en la presentación o falsedad comprobada en los datos de la declaración jurada de patrimonio de inicio y cese de funciones (art. 39,8); desproteger, dañar, alterar o destruir el material electoral, archivos o demás bienes electorales del Consejo Comunal (art. 39,9); proclamar y juramentar como electos, a personas distintas de las indicadas en los resultados definitivos (art. 39,10); no hacer la respectiva y amplia publicidad a los fines de la realización de los procesos electorales (art. 39,11); y no llevar el registro electoral, o no actualizarlo conforme con lo establecido en la Ley (art. 39,12).

En todos estos casos, la iniciativa de solicitud para la revocatoria de los voceros del Consejo Comunal, así como los de la Comisión Electoral, corresponde de acuerdo con el artículo 40 de la Ley Orgánica, corresponde a un número de habitantes de la Comunidad que representen el 10% de la población mayor de quince años, habitantes de la comunidad (art. 40,1); y a la Unidad de Contraloría Social del Consejo Comunal (art. 40,2). En estos casos, la correspondiente solicitud de la revocatoria "debe formalizarse por escrito ante el Colectivo de Coordinación Comunitaria del Consejo Comunal" (art. 40).

En los casos de denuncias contra algún vocero formulada por algún miembro de la Comunidad, conforme al artículo 41 de la Ley, "la solicitud de revocatoria de los voceros del Consejo Comunal, así como los de la Comisión Electoral, debe formalizarse ante la Unidad de Contraloría Social," ante la cual debe desarrollarse un procedimiento administrativo de revocatoria en el cual se debe garantizar el derecho a la defensa y al debido proceso. Sin embargo, en caso de que la denuncia sea en contra de un vocero de la Unidad Contraloría Social, la solicitud de revocatoria se debe presentar directamente ante el colectivo de coordinación comunitaria.

La Unidad de Contraloría Social, una vez recibida la solicitud, debe preparar el informe respectivo en un lapso no mayor de 15 días continuos, el cual debe presentar ante el Colectivo de Coordinación Comunitaria para su consideración, el cual, en un lapso no mayor de 15 días continuos, lo debe presentar ante la Asamblea de Ciudadanos para la toma de decisiones correspondiente.

De ser aprobada la revocatoria de un vocero por la Asamblea de ciudadanos, su suplente debe asumir el cargo y la Comisión Electoral debe organizar el proceso para suplir la vacante respectiva. El Colectivo de Coordinación Comunitaria debe informar sobre los resultados de la revocatoria al Ministerio del Poder Popular para las Comunas y Protección Social.

La consecuencia de la revocación del mandato es que los voceras del Consejo Comunal que hayan sido revocados de sus funciones, no pueden postularse a una nueva elección durante los dos períodos siguientes a la fecha de la revocatoria (art. 42).

2.   *La pérdida de condición de vocero de las Unidades de los Consejos Comunales*

Además de por revocación de sus funciones, los voceros de los Consejos Comunales pueden perder tal condición por renuncia; cambio de residencia debidamente comprobado, fuera del ámbito geográfico del Consejo Comunal respectivo; enfermedad que le imposibilite ejercer sus funciones; haber sido electo en un cargo público de elección popular; y "estar sujeto a una sentencia definitivamente firme dictada por los órganos jurisdiccionales" (art. 43), causal esta última que parece absurdo pues puede tratarse de una sentencia en materia civil, laboral o mercantil, y ello no tendría que producir la pérdida de condición de vocero. Quizás el Legislador lo que quiso fue referirse a sentencias en materia penal, lo que hubiera tenido más lógica.

En todos estos casos de pérdida de la condición de vocero de un Consejo Comunal, el suplente debe asumir las respectivas funciones (art. 43).

V. EL CICLO COMUNAL COMO PROCESO DE PARTICIPACIÓN PO- PULAR

El artículo 44 de la LOCC de 2009 define el "Ciclo comunal" en el marco de las actuaciones de los Consejos Comunales, como "un proceso para hacer efectiva la participación popular y la planificación participativa que responde a las necesidades comunitarias y contribuye al desarrollo de las potencialidades y capacidades de la comunidad." A tal efecto, la Ley Orgánica de Planificación Pública y Popular, precisa en especial, que en el marco de las actuaciones inherentes a la planificación participativa, que el consejo comunal "se apoyará en la metodología del ciclo comunal, que consiste en la aplicación de las fases de diagnóstico, plan, presupuesto, ejecución y contraloría social, con el objeto de hacer efectiva la participación popular en la planificación, para responder a las necesidades comunitarias y contribuir al desarrollo de las potencialidades y capacidades de la comunidad" (art. 15).

Ese ciclo también se indica en la LOCC, como una expresión del Poder Popular, a través de la realización de las mismas cinco fases: diagnóstico, plan, presupuesto, ejecución y contraloría social; las cuales conforme al artículo 45, se complementan e interrelacionan entre sí y son definidas en la forma siguiente:

1. Diagnóstico: esta fase caracteriza integralmente a las comunidades, se identifican las necesidades, las aspiraciones, los recursos, las potencialidades y las relaciones sociales propias de la localidad.

2. Plan: es la fase que determina las acciones, programas y proyectos que atendiendo al diagnóstico, tiene como finalidad el desarrollo del bienestar integral de la comunidad.

3. Presupuesto: esta fase comprende la determinación de los fondos, costos y recursos financieros y no financieros con los que cuenta y requiere la comunidad, destinados a la ejecución de las políticas, programas y proyectos establecidos en el Plan Comunitario de Desarrollo Integral.

4. Ejecución: esta fase garantiza la concreción de las políticas, programas y proyectos en espacio y tiempo establecidos en el Plan Comunitario de Desarrollo Integral, garantizando la participación activa, consciente y solidaria de la comunidad.

5. Contraloría social: esta fase es la acción permanente de prevención, vigilancia, supervisión, seguimiento, control y evaluación de las fases del ciclo comunal para la concreción del Plan Comunitario de Desarrollo Integral y, en general sobre las acciones realizadas por el Consejo Comunal, ejercida articuladamente por los habitantes de la comunidad, la Asamblea de Ciu-

dadanos, las organizaciones comunitarias y la Unidad de Contraloría Social del Consejo Comunal.

Todas estas fases del ciclo comunal deben estar avaladas y previamente aprobadas por la Asamblea de Ciudadanos en el Consejo Comunal respectivo.

Por otra parte, los Consejos Comunales, a través de los comités de economía comunal, deben elaborar los proyectos socio-productivos, con base a las potencialidades de su comunidad, impulsando la propiedad social, orientados a la satisfacción de las necesidades colectivas y vinculados al Plan Comunitario de Desarrollo Integral (art. 46).

Debe indicarse que además, en la LOSEC se define un "ciclo productivo comunal" como "sistema de producción, transformación, distribución, intercambio y consumo socialmente justo de bienes y servicios de las distintas formas de organización socio-productivas, surgidas en el seno de la comunidad como consecuencia de las necesidades humanas" (art. 6.3), aun cuando luego en el articulado de la misma ni en las otras leyes del Poder Popular se utiliza la expresión.

VI. LOS RECURSOS DE LOS CONSEJOS COMUNALES Y SU GESTIÓN Y ADMINISTRACIÓN

1. Los recursos de los Consejos Comunales

Los Consejos Comunales tienen los siguientes recursos financieros y no financieros enumerados en el artículo 47 de la Ley Orgánica, que deben recibir de manera directa: los que sean transferidos por la República, los estados y los municipios; los que provengan de lo dispuesto en la Ley que Crea el Fondo Intergubernamental para la Descentralización y la Ley de Asignaciones Económicas Especiales Derivadas de Minas e Hidrocarburos; los que provengan de la administración de los servicios públicos que les sean transferidos por el Estado; los generados por su actividad propia, incluido el producto del manejo financiero de todos sus recursos; los recursos provenientes de donaciones de acuerdo con lo establecido en el ordenamiento jurídico; y cualquier otro generado de actividad financiera que permita la Constitución de la República y la ley.

Los recursos financieros que son los expresados en unidades monetarias propias o asignados, son manejados por el Consejo Comunal orientados a desarrollar las políticas, programas y proyectos comunitarios establecidos en el Plan Comunitario de Desarrollo Integral. Estos recursos, conforme a lo dispuesto en el artículo 48, se clasifican en la siguiente forma:

1. Recursos retornables: son los recursos que están destinados a ejecutar políticas, programas y proyectos de carácter socio-productivo con alcance de desarrollo comunitario que deben ser reintegrados al órgano o ente financiero mediante acuerdos entre los partes; y

2. Recursos no retornables: son los recursos financieros para ejecutar políticas, programas y proyectos con alcance de desarrollo comunitario, que tienen características de donación, asignación o adjudicación y no se reintegran al órgano o ente financiero y a la Unidad Administrativa y Financiera Comunitaria.

En cuanto a los recursos no financieros, que son los que no tienen expresión monetaria y son necesarios para concretar la ejecución de las políticas, planes y proyectos comunitarios, también deben ser manejados por el Consejo Comunal (art. 49).

Todos los recursos aprobados y transferidos para los Consejos Comunales deben siempre ser destinados a la ejecución de políticas, programas y proyectos comunitarios contemplados en el Plan Comunitario de Desarrollo Integral y deben ser manejados de manera eficiente y eficaz para lograr la transformación integral de la comunidad (art. 50).

Cuando se trate de recursos aprobados por los órganos o entes del Poder Público para un determinado proyecto, los mismos no podrán ser utilizados para fines distintos a los aprobados y destinados inicialmente, salvo que sea debidamente autorizado por el órgano o ente del Poder Público que otorgó los recursos, para lo cual el Consejo Comunal debe motivar el carácter excepcional de la solicitud de cambio del objeto del proyecto, acompañada de los soportes respectivos, previo debate y aprobación de la Asamblea de Ciudadanos (art. 50).

Por otra parte, debe advertirse que en la Ley Orgánica de 2009 nada se dispuso directamente en relación con el Fondo Nacional de los Consejos Comunales creado por la Ley de 2006 como servicio autónomo adscrito al Ministerio de Finanzas, y el cual al parecer nunca llegó a ser implementado.[1335] Lo único que se reguló en la Ley es una Disposición Transitoria (Primera) en la cual se dispuso que el Ministerio del Poder Popular con competencia en materia de participación ciudadana debe incorporar en su reglamento orgánico las disposiciones relativas al Fondo Nacional de los Consejos Comunales, en un lapso no mayor de 30 días hábiles siguientes a la entrada en vigencia de la Ley, lo que sugiere que dicho Fondo debería seguir existiendo, pero adscrito al Ministerio del Poder Popular para las Comunas y Protección Social.

2.   *Los fondos de los Consejos Comunales*

La Ley Orgánica de 2009 prevé que el Consejo Comunal, para facilitar el desenvolvimiento armónico de sus actividades y funciones, debe formar cuatro fondos internos: de acción social; de gastos operativos y de administración; de ahorro y crédito social; y de riesgos. Todos estos fondos deben ser administrados por la Unidad Administrativa y Financiera Comunitaria, previa aprobación de la Asamblea de Ciudadanos, con la justificación del colectivo de coordinación comunitaria (art. 51), y se los define en la Ley de la siguiente manera:

a. *Fondo de acción social*, que debe ser destinado a cubrir las necesidades sociales, tales como: situaciones de contingencia, de emergencia o problemas de salud, que no puedan ser cubiertas por los afectados debido a su situación socioeconómica. Se debe presentar una propuesta para la utilización de estos recursos que debe ser aprobada por la Asamblea de Ciudadanos, excepto en los casos de emergencia o fuerza mayor. Este fondo se constituye conforme se indica en el artículo 52 de la Ley Orgánica, mediante: los intereses anuales cobrados de los créditos otorgados con recursos retornables del financiamiento; los ingresos por concepto de los inter-

---

1335   Véase Miguel González Marregot, "Consejos Comunales: ¿Para qué?," en *Venezuela Analítica*, Viernes, 9 de febrero de 2007, http://www.anali-tica.com/va/politica/opinion/7483372.asp

eses y excedentes devengados de los recursos de inversión social no retornables; y los recursos generados de la autogestión comunitaria.

b. *Fondo de gastos operativos y de administración*, que está destinado a contribuir con el pago de los gastos que se generen en la operatividad y manejo administrativo del Consejo Comunal. Este fondo, conforme a lo dispuesto en el artículo 53 de la Ley Orgánica, se constituye mediante tres fuentes: los intereses anuales cobrados de los créditos otorgados con recursos retornables de la línea de crédito o contrato de préstamo; los que sean asignados para estos fines, por los órganos y entes del Poder Público en los respectivos proyectos que le sean aprobados; y los recursos generados por la autogestión comunitaria.

c. *Fondo de ahorro y crédito social*, que debe ser destinado a incentivar el ahorro en las comunidades con una visión socialista y promover los medios socio-productivos mediante créditos solidarios; y está conformado por la captación de recursos monetarios de forma colectiva, unipersonal y familiar, recursos generados de las organizaciones autogestionarias, los excedentes de los recursos no retornables y los propios intereses generados de la cuenta de ahorro y crédito social (art. 54).

d. *Fondo de riesgo*, que debe ser destinado a cubrir los montos no pagados de los créditos socio-productivos, que incidan u obstaculicen el cumplimiento y continuidad de los proyectos comunitarios, en situación de riesgos y asumidos por el Consejo Comunal; el cual, conforme al artículo 55 de la Ley Orgánica, está constituido por los intereses anuales cobrados de los créditos otorgados con recursos retornables del financiamiento;[1336] el interés de mora de los créditos otorgados con recursos retornables; y los recursos generados de la autogestión comunitaria.

VII. EL RÉGIMEN DE ADAPTACIÓN Y CONSTITUCIÓN INICIAL DE LAS ASAMBLEAS DE CIUDADANOS Y DE LOS CONSEJOS COMUNALES

1. *La adecuación de los Consejos Comunales constituidos conforme a la Ley de 2006 a las previsiones de la Ley Orgánica de 2009*

Como se dijo al inicio, los Consejos Comunales fueron creados a partir de la entrada en vigencia de la Ley de los Consejos Comunales de 2006, bajo cuya vigencia se crearon muchos de ellos. Con motivo del nuevo régimen previsto en la Ley Orgánica de 2009, y a los efectos de lograr la uniformidad del régimen legal, la Disposición Transitoria Segunda de la misma estableció la necesidad de que los consejos comunales constituidos bajo el régimen legal anterior (Ley de 2006) sean objeto de un proceso de adecuación de sus estatutos a las disposiciones establecidas en la Ley Orgánica, a los fines de su registro por ante el Ministerio del Poder Popular para las

---

1336   Conforme al artículo 55 de la Ley Orgánica, en esta materia de intereses, la Unidad Administrativa y Financiera Comunitaria debe realizar un informe donde se contemple la voluntad por parte de las organizaciones socio-productivas de no cancelar el saldo adeudado, o cualquier circunstancia que imposibilite el pago del mismo, por situación de emergencia, enfermedad o muerte. La Unidad Administrativa y Financiera Comunitaria está en la capacidad de proponer formas alternativas para el pago de un crédito. Para su trámite administrativo se tendrá una cuenta bancaria en la que se depositará mensualmente el monto.

Comunas y Protección Social creado en 2009, en un lapso no mayor de 180 días contado a partir del 28 de diciembre de 2009 que fue la fecha de publicación de la Ley Orgánica. Durante ese período se debe garantizar la continuidad de sus diferentes instancias en su gestión, para la ejecución de sus planes, programas y proyectos comunitarios aprobados conforme al régimen legal anterior.

A los efectos de realizar la dicha adecuación, en particular de sus Estatutos, el Consejo Comunal debe convocar una Asamblea de Ciudadanos para informar sobre la misma de acuerdo a lo establecido en la Ley Orgánica, sobre la continuidad de la gestión de los voceros hasta cumplir su período, y sobre la liquidación de la asociación cooperativa banco comunal (Disposición Transitoria Séptima).

2. *Régimen para la constitución inicial de los Consejos Comunales*

En todos los casos en los que se vaya a constituir un Consejo Comunal, debe procederse a la convocatoria de una asamblea constitutiva comunitaria; a cuyo efecto, un "equipo promotor" debe constituirse, conformado por un grupo de ciudadanos que deciden asumir la iniciativa de difundir, promover e informar la organización de su comunidad a los efectos de la constitución del Consejo Comunal. En tales casos, el equipo promotor que se constituya "debe notificar su conformación y actuaciones ante el órgano rector" que es el Ministerio del Poder Popular para las Comunas y Protección Social (Art. 5).

Este equipo promotor, conforme al artículo 6 de la Ley Orgánica, tiene las siguientes funciones: difundir entre los habitantes de la comunidad el alcance, objeto y fines del Consejo Comunal; elaborar un croquis del ámbito geográfico de la comunidad; organizar la realización del censo demográfico y socioeconómico de la comunidad; y convocar la primera Asamblea de Ciudadanos, en un lapso no mayor de 60 días a partir de su conformación.

La primera Asamblea de Ciudadanos convocada por el equipo promotor, debe constituirse con la participación mínima del 10% de los habitantes de la comunidad mayores de quince años, lo que sin duda, es una cifra excesivamente baja para asegurar representatividad de la comunidad y participación ciudadana (art. 7).

Esta primera asamblea de ciudadanos se constituye para elegir el equipo electoral provisional y someter a consideración los comités de trabajo que deben ser creados para conformar la Unidad Ejecutiva del Consejo Comunal, dejando constancia en el acta respectiva (art. 7).

El equipo electoral provisional se debe conformar por 3 habitantes de la comunidad electos en la primera Asamblea de Ciudadanos, y es la instancia encargada de regir el proceso electoral para la elección del primer Consejo Comunal (art. 8).

El equipo electoral provisional y al equipo promotor (electo en la primera asamblea de ciudadanos) son las instancias encargadas de realizar la convocatoria de la asamblea constitutiva comunitaria, lo que deben hacer previa notificación al Ministerio del Poder Popular para las Comunas y Protección Social, como órgano rector, en un lapso no mayor de 90 días, contados a partir de la constitución de la primera Asamblea de Ciudadanos (art. 9). Una vez instalada válidamente la asamblea constitutiva comunitaria, el equipo promotor cesa en sus funciones, tal como lo indican los artículos 5 y 9 de la Ley Orgánica.

En cuanto al equipo electoral provisional, le corresponde dirige la asamblea constitutiva comunitaria para la elección de los voceros de las distintas unidades del Consejo Comunal así como los de la comisión electoral permanente (art. 9).

La asamblea constitutiva comunitaria es la Asamblea de Ciudadanos en la cual se eligen por primera vez los voceros del Consejo Comunal. Esta Asamblea se considera válidamente conformada con la participación efectiva del 30% mínimo en primera convocatoria y del 20% mínimo en segunda convocatoria, para los habitantes mayores de quince años de la población censada electoralmente (art. 10).

Una vez electos los voceros se deben realizar el acta constitutiva del Consejo Comunal a los efectos del registro respectivo. El equipo electoral provisional cesa en sus funciones al momento de la constitución definitiva del Consejo Comunal (art. 8).

3. *El registro de los Concejos Comunales*

El acta constitutiva de los Consejos Comunales debe contener: el nombre del Consejo Comunal, y su ámbito geográfico con su ubicación y linderos; la fecha, lugar y hora de la asamblea constitutiva comunitaria, conforme a la convocatoria realizada; la identificación con nombre, cédula de identidad y firmas de los participantes en la asamblea constitutiva comunitaria; los resultados del proceso de elección de los voceros para las unidades del Consejo Comunal; la identificación por cada una de las unidades de los voceros o voceras electos o electas con sus respectivos suplentes (art. 16).

Conforme al artículo 17 de la Ley, los consejos comunales constituidos y organizados conforme a su normativa, adquieren su personalidad jurídica mediante el registro ante el Ministerio del Poder Popular para las Comunas y Protección Social, atendiendo al siguiente procedimiento:

1. Los responsables designados por la asamblea constitutiva comunitaria deben presentar ante la oficina competente del Ministerio del Poder Popular para las Comunas y Protección Social, en un lapso de 15 días posteriores a la constitución y organización del Consejo Comunal, solicitud de registro, acompañada de copia simple con originales a la vista del acta constitutiva, estatutos, censo demográfico y socioeconómico y el croquis del ámbito geográfico. Estos documentos deben pasar a formar parte del expediente administrativo del Consejo Comunal en los términos señalados en la Ley Orgánica de Procedimientos Administrativos. El acta constitutiva y los estatutos deben ir firmados por todos los y las participantes de la asamblea constitutiva comunitaria en prueba de su autenticidad.

2. El funcionario responsable del registro debe recibir los documentos que le hayan sido presentados con la solicitud y en un lapso no superior a 10 días se debe efectuar el registro del Consejo Comunal. Con este acto administrativo de registro, los Consejos adquieren "la personalidad jurídica plena para todos los efectos legales."

3. Si el funcionario encontrare alguna deficiencia, lo debe comunicar a los solicitantes, quienes gozan de un lapso de 30 días para corregirla. Subsanada la falta, el funcionario del Ministerio del Poder Popular para las Comunas y Protección Social debe proceder al registro.

4. Si los interesados no subsanan la falta en el lapso antes señalado, el Ministerio del Poder Popular para las Comunas y Protección Social se debe abstener de registrar al consejo comunal.

5. Contra la decisión del Ministerio del Poder Popular para las Comunas y Protección Social, se puede interponer el recurso jerárquico correspondiente de conformidad con lo previsto en la Ley Orgánica de Procedimientos Administrativos, con lo cual queda agotada la vía administrativa. Los actos administrativos dictados por el Ministerio del Poder Popular para las Comunas y Protección Social podrán ser recurridos ante la jurisdicción contencioso-administrativa.

El Ministerio del Poder Popular para las Comunas y Protección Social, únicamente puede abstenerse del registro de un Consejo Comunal en los siguientes casos: cuando tenga por objeto finalidades distintas a las previstas en la presente Ley; si el Consejo Comunal no se ha constituido con la determinación exacta del ámbito geográfico o si dentro de éste ya existiere registrado un Consejo Comunal; o si no se acompañan los documentos exigidos en la presente Ley o si éstos presentan alguna deficiencia u omisión (art 18).

4. *La nueva adaptación de los Consejos Comunales en 2011*

De acuerdo con la Disposición Transitoria Primera de la LOPP, las instancias y organizaciones del Poder Popular preexistentes a la entrada en vigencia de la presente ley, como fueron los Consejos Comunales, debían adecuar su organización y funcionamiento a las disposiciones de la misma, en un lapso de ciento ochenta días contados a partir de su publicación de la Gaceta Oficial.

VIII. LA CENTRALIZACIÓN DE LA CONDUCCIÓN DEL PROCESO DE PARTICIPACIÓN CIUDADANA A TRAVÉS DE LOS CONSEJOS COMUNALES

La Ley Orgánica de 2009 ha completado el proceso de centralización de la conducción de la participación ciudadana, al haber establecido, en sustitución de las Comisiones Presidenciales del Poder Popular que establecía la Ley de 2006, como "órgano rector" del proceso a uno de los Ministerios del Ejecutivo Nacional, en concreto, el "Ministerio del Poder Popular con competencia en materia de participación ciudadana" al cual le asigna las funciones de dictar las políticas, estratégicas, planes generales, programas y proyectos para la participación comunitaria en los asuntos públicos, el cual debe acompañar a los consejos comunales en el cumplimiento de sus fines y propósitos, y facilitar la articulación en las relaciones entre éstos y los órganos y entes del Poder Público (art. 56).

Mediante Decreto ejecutivo dictado el 17 de junio de 2009, de reforma parcial del Reglamento Orgánico de la Administración Pública, [1337] se reguló en sustitución del Ministerio del Poder Popular para la Participación y la Protección Social, al *Ministerio del Poder Popular para las Comunas y Protección Social*, que es por tanto el que tiene competencia en materia de participación ciudadana. Destaca, sin embargo, que en su denominación se haya eliminado la palabra "participación" y se la

---

1337   *Gaceta Oficial* N° 39.202 de 17-06-2009.

haya sustituido por la palabra "Comunas," particularmente cuando esta instancia territorial no existe en el ordenamiento constitucional ni legal venezolano. Su creación fue una de las propuestas de la Reforma Constitucional de 2007 que fue rechazada por el pueblo, por lo que no se entiende cómo la primera atribución asignada al Ministerio sea "la regulación, formulación y seguimiento de políticas, la planificación y realización de las actividades del Ejecutivo Nacional en materia de participación ciudadana en el ámbito de las *comunas*" (ord. 1).

En todo caso, este Ministerio tiene, además, las siguientes funciones (art. 25):

2. La realización del análisis de la gestión de la economía comunal en el país y formulación de las recomendaciones a los órganos y entes competentes;

3. La regulación, formulación y seguimiento de políticas, la planificación y realización de las actividades del Ejecutivo Nacional en lo atinente a las normas operativas e instrumentos de promoción, autogestión y cogestión de la población en el marco de la economía del Estado, que armonice la acción de los entes involucrados en tal política sectorial, y el uso eficiente de los recursos destinados al financiamiento correspondiente;

4. Participar en la elaboración de los planes y programas tendentes al desarrollo de la economía participativa en todas sus expresiones;

5. Definir los mecanismos para la participación del sector público y privado en la planificación y ejecución de planes y programas relacionados con el desarrollo de la economía comunal. En este sentido, servirá de enlace entre los entes involucrados y las iniciativas populares cuando las circunstancias así lo requieran;

6. Impulsar el desarrollo del sistema microfinanciero en actividades tendentes al desarrollo de la economía comunal;

7. Propender al desarrollo de las actividades de comercialización y explotación en todos los sectores vinculados a la economía comunal, con especial énfasis en el sector rural;

8. Definir las políticas para los programas de capacitación en áreas determinantes para el desarrollo de la economía comunal, en especial la adquisición de conocimientos técnicos para el procesamiento, transformación y colocación en el mercado de la materia prima;

9. Establecer las políticas para el fomento de la economía comunal, estimulando el protagonismo de las cooperativas, cajas de ahorro, empresas familiares, microempresas y otras formas de asociación comunitaria para el trabajo, el ahorro y el consumo de bajo el régimen de propiedad colectiva sustentada en la iniciativa popular;

10. La regulación, formulación y seguimiento de políticas, la planificación estratégica y realización de las actividades del Ejecutivo Nacional en materia de promoción, ejecución y control y articulación de las actividades tendentes a la progresiva cogestión de responsabilidades sociales desde el Estado hacia las comunidades o grupos organizados, así como a la generación de los espacios de la participación protagónica en los asuntos públicos mediante el impulso a la iniciativa popular y otros mecanismos de participación protagónica;

11. Promover la elaboración de planes, programas y proyectos participativos y de base a ejecutarse en todos los ámbitos de la vida social nacional;

12. Diseñar, estructurar y coordinar la formación en las comunidades urbanas y rurales en materia de medios de participación popular y gerencia pública local;

13. Formular y promover políticas de incentivo y fortalecimiento a los movimientos populares que se organicen en los espacios locales;

14. Definir y establecer los parámetros para impulsar la organización del voluntariado social que apoye a los órganos y entes de la Administración Pública;

15. Fomentar la organización de consejos comunales, asambleas de ciudadanos y otras formas de participación comunitaria en los asuntos públicos;

16. Diseñar e instrumentar mecanismos de enlace entre los ciudadanos y la Administración Pública, con los Estados y los Municipios, y las demás expresiones del gobierno local, en aras a generar espacios de cogestión administrativa, y promover el control social de las políticas públicas;

17. Proponer, gestionar y hacer seguimiento, sobre la bese de las propuestas generadas por la participación activa y protagónica de la comunidad organizada, en las mejoras de las condiciones básicas e inmediatas de habitabilidad y convivencia en los sectores populares;

18. Elaborar y ejecutar planes, programas y proyectos orientados a coadyuvar con los municipios en el incremento de su capacidad de gestión en lo concerniente a la prestación de sus servicios públicos, a partir del diseño de modelos de gestión compartida que redunden en la obtención de una mayor calidad de vida para las comunidades;

19. Evaluar, supervisar y controlar los entes que le están adscritos, estableciendo las políticas y mecanismos de coordinación que sena necesarios.

20. Establecer las políticas, directrices y mecanismos para la coordinación de las acciones de los entes que le están adscritos. En este sentido, formulará las políticas sectoriales de asignación de recursos, así como controles de gestión y recuperación de los créditos otorgados;

21. La regulación, formulación y seguimiento de políticas, la planificación estratégica y realización de las actividades del Ejecutivo Nacional en materia de promoción, asistencia y desarrollo social integral y participativo. Dichas políticas estarán dirigidas al fomento del desarrollo humano, especialmente en los grupos sociales más sensibles, así como también a la familia y a la juventud.

22. La formulación, ejecución, seguimiento y control de las políticas y programas de atención y formación integral dirigidas a los niños, niñas y adolescentes, como medios efectivo para el disfrute en sociedad de sus derechos y garantías, así como el acceso a los medios que les permitirán el pleno desarrollo de sus capacidades y destrezas;

23. El diseño, control y seguimiento de las políticas y programas dirigidos a la protección, asistencia y resguardo de los niños, niñas y adolescentes que se encuentren en situación de vulnerabilidad o exclusión, de manera de ase-

gurarles una atención inmediata e integral que posibilite su crecimiento acorde con los derechos y garantías que les corresponden;

24. La elaboración, gestión, coordinación y seguimiento de las acciones tendentes al rescate, protección, integración, capacitación, desarrollo y promoción de los grupos humanos vulnerables o excluidos socialmente, ya se encuentren ubicados en zonas urbanas o rurales;

25. Asistir en la definición de los criterios de asignación de recursos financieros destinados a la población en situación de vulnerabilidad social, que asegure un acceso real y democrático de los beneficiarios a tales recursos; de igual manera, fomentará la elaboración de propuestas de inversión social;

26. Diseñar, proponer e implementar incentivos a la organización y puesta en funcionamiento de redes operativas integradas a un sistemas de información social, el cual contará con el registro de las familias e individuos beneficiarios de programas sociales; también coordinará el establecimiento y ejecución de los sistemas de evaluación a tales programas;

En las Disposiciones Transitorias (Vigésima) del Decreto, se adscribieron al Ministerio los siguientes entes: 1. Banco del Pueblo Soberano, C.A.; 2. Fundación para el Desarrollo de la Comunidad y Promoción del Poder Comunal (FUNDACOMUNAL); 3. Fundación Centro de Estudios sobre el Crecimiento y Desarrollo de la Población Venezolana (FUNDACREDESA); 4. Fondo de Desarrollo Microfinanciero (FONDEMI); 5. Instituto Nacional de Capacitación y Educación Socialista (INCES); 6. Fundación Misión Che Guevara; 7. Fondo para el Desarrollo Endógeno (FONENDOGENO); 8. Instituto Autónomo Fondo Único Social; 9. Instituto Nacional del Menor (en proceso de liquidación); 10. Fundación Fondo de Inversión Social de Venezuela (FONVIS) (en proceso de liquidación); 11. Consejo Nacional para las Personas con Discapacidad (CONAPDIS); 12. Instituto Nacional de Servicios Sociales; 13. Instituto Autónomo Consejo Nacional de Derechos de Niños, Niñas y Adolescentes; y 14. Fundación Misión Negra Hipólita.

El artículo 57 de la Ley Orgánica de 2009, por su parte, específicamente atribuye a este Ministerio del Poder Popular para las Comunas y Protección Social, como "Ministerio del Poder Popular con competencia en materia de participación ciudadana," además, las siguientes atribuciones:

1. Diseñar, realizar el seguimiento y evaluar las políticas, lineamientos, planes y estrategias que deberán atender los órganos y entes del Poder Público en todo lo relacionado con el apoyo a los consejos comunales.

2. El registro de los consejos comunales y la emisión del certificado correspondiente.

3. Diseñar y coordinar el sistema de información comunitario y los procedimientos referidos a la organización y desarrollo de los consejos comunales.

4. Diseñar y dirigir la ejecución de los programas de capacitación y formación de los consejos comunales.

5. Orientar técnicamente en caso de presunta responsabilidad civil, penal y administrativa derivada del funcionamiento de las instancias del Consejo Comunal.

6. Recabar, sistematizar, divulgar y suministrar la información proveniente de los órganos y entes del Poder Público relacionada con el financiamiento y características de los proyectos de los consejos comunales.

7. Promover los proyectos sociales que fomenten e impulsen el desarrollo endógeno de las comunidades articulados al Plan Comunitario de Desarrollo.

8. Prestar asistencia técnica en el proceso del ciclo comunal.

9. Coordinar con la Contraloría General de la República, mecanismos para orientar a los consejos comunales sobre la correcta administración de los recursos.

10. Fomentar la organización de consejos comunales.

11. Financiar los proyectos comunitarios, sociales y productivos presentados por los consejos comunales en sus componentes financieros y no financieros, con recursos retornables y no retornables, en el marco de esta Ley.

Hasta tanto se dicte el reglamento de la Ley Orgánica que el Presidente de la República debe publicar antes de fin de junio de 2010, el Ministerio del Poder Popular para las Comunas y Protección Social debe dictar los lineamientos y elaborar los instructivos que se requieren para hacer efectivo el registro de los consejos comunales, conforme a las Disposiciones Transitorias Octava y Novena de la Ley.

Por otra parte, el Ministerio del Poder Popular para las Comunas y Protección Social, además, debe articular los mecanismos para facilitar y simplificar toda tramitación ante los órganos y entes del Poder Público vinculados a los consejos comunales (art. 58); y los "órganos y entes del Estado" en sus relaciones con los consejos comunales deben dará preferencia a la atención de los requerimientos que éstos formulen y a la satisfacción de sus necesidades, asegurando el ejercicio de sus derechos cuando se relacionen con éstos. Esta preferencia conforme al artículo 59 de la Ley Orgánica comprende: la especial atención de los consejos comunales en la formulación, ejecución y control de todas las políticas públicas; la asignación privilegiada y preferente, en el presupuesto de los recursos públicos para la atención de los requerimientos formulados por los consejos comunales; y la preferencia de los consejos comunales en la transferencia de los servicios públicos.

El artículo 60 de la Ley Orgánica dispone que el Ministerio Público debe contar con fiscales especializados para atender las denuncias y acciones interpuestas, relacionadas con los consejos comunales, que se deriven directa o indirectamente del ejercicio del derecho a la participación.

Por último, debe señalarse que los consejos comunales están exentos de todo tipo de pagos de tributos nacionales y derechos de registro. La Ley Orgánica agrega que "se podrá establecer mediante leyes y ordenanzas de los estados y los municipios las exenciones para los consejos comunales" (art. 61).

SECCIÓN QUINTA:

EL RÉGIMEN DE LAS COMUNAS COMO SOPORTE DEL ESTADO COMUNAL O LA DESMUNICIPALIZACIÓN EL ESTADO CONSTITUCIONAL ME-DIANTE UN SISTEMA DE "AUTOGOBIERNO" NO REPRESENTATIVO MANEJADO POR EL PODER CENTRAL

I. PROPÓSITO Y FINALIDAD DE LAS COMUNAS

El propósito fundamental de las Comunas, tal como se define en el artículo 6 de la Ley Orgánica de las Comunas (LOC), es la "edificación del estado comunal, mediante la promoción, impulso y desarrollo de la participación protagónica y corresponsable de los ciudadanos y ciudadanas en la gestión de las políticas públicas, en la conformación y ejercicio del autogobierno por parte de las comunidades organizadas, a través de la planificación del desarrollo social y económico, la formulación de proyectos, la elaboración y ejecución presupuestaria, la administración y gestión de las competencias y servicios que conforme al proceso de descentralización, le sean transferidos, así como la construcción de un sistema de producción, distribución, intercambio y consumo de propiedad social, y la disposición de medios alternativos de justicia para la convivencia y la paz comunal, como tránsito hacia la sociedad socialista, democrática, de equidad y justicia social" (art. 6).

Además, las Comunas tienen las siguientes finalidades tal como se enumeran en el artículo 7 de la LOC:

1. Desarrollar y consolidar el estado comunal como expresión del Poder Popular y soporte para la construcción de la sociedad socialista.

2. Conformar el autogobierno para el ejercicio directo de funciones en la formulación, ejecución y control de la gestión pública.

3. Promover la integración y la articulación con otras comunas en el marco de las unidades de gestión territorial establecidas por el Consejo Federal de Gobierno.

4. Impulsar el desarrollo y consolidación de la propiedad social.

5. Garantizar la existencia efectiva de formas y mecanismos de participación directa de los ciudadanos y ciudadanas en la formulación, ejecución y control de planes y proyectos vinculados a los aspectos territoriales, políticos, económicos, sociales; culturales, ecológicos y de seguridad y defensa.

6. Promover mecanismos para la formación e información en las comunidades.

7. Impulsar la defensa colectiva y popular de los derechos humanos.

8. Todas aquéllas determinadas en la constitución de la República y en la Ley.

II. ÁMBITO TERRITORIAL DE LAS COMUNAS

1. Ámbito territorial variado

Por otra parte, en cuanto al ámbito de organización político-territorial que puedan tener las comunas, el mismo se formula en términos vagos, sin apuntar a principios de uniformidad algunos, sólo indicando que el mismo dependerá de las "condiciones históricas, integración, rasgos culturales, usos, costumbres y potencialidades económicas, el ámbito geográfico" donde se constituyan, el cual puede "coincidir o no con los límites político-administrativos de los estados, municipios o dependencias federales, sin que ello afecte o modifique la organización político-territorial establecida en la Constitución de la República" (art. 9).

Conforme a esta previsión, por tanto, el ámbito territorial de las comunas, no necesariamente debe estructurarse siguiendo los límites que puedan existir en la demarcación de las entidades políticas de la República; en el sentido de que pueden estar superpuestas a los mismos.

En todo caso, de la normativa de la LOC, dado que las Comunas se constituyen por iniciativa popular que deben adoptar varios Consejos Comunales y otras organizaciones sociales que deben agregarse, sin duda la intención del legislador es que las mismas tengan un ámbito territorial mayor al que puedan tener los Consejos Comunales. En definitiva, las Comunas se conciben, básicamente, como agregaciones de Consejos Comunales y de organizaciones socio productivas.

2. Inserción en ámbitos territoriales centralizados superiores

Por otra parte, las Comunas deben estar integradas en ámbitos territoriales superiores que son determinados por el Poder Ejecutivo, los cuales son los Distritos Motores del Desarrollo y los Ejes Estratégicos de Desarrollo Territorial, establecidos para impulsar y afianzar el socialismo.

Los "Distritos motores del desarrollo" son definidos en la LOC como las "unidades territoriales decretadas por el Ejecutivo Nacional que integran las ventajas comparativas de los diferentes espacios geográficos del territorio nacional, y que responden al modelo de desarrollo sustentable, endógeno y socialista" (art. 4.8).[1338]

En la Ley Orgánica del Consejo Federal de Gobierno[1339] se indica, además, que dichos Distrito Motores tienen la "finalidad de impulsar en el área comprendida en cada uno de ellos un conjunto de proyectos económicos, sociales, científicos y tecnológicos, destinados a lograr el desarrollo integral de las regiones y el fortalecimiento del Poder Popular, en aras de facilitar la transición hacia el socialismo." Di-

---

1338 En el Reglamento de la ley Orgánica del Consejo federal de Gobierno, se definen los Distritos Motores de desarrollo como: "la unidad territorial decretada por el Ejecutivo Nacional que integra las ventajas comparativas de los diferentes ámbitos geográficos del territorio nacional, y que responde al modelo de desarrollo sustentable, endógeno y socialista para la creación, consolidación y fortalecimiento de la organización del Poder Popular y de las cadenas productivas socialistas en un territorio de limitado, como fundamento de la estructura social y económica de la Nación venezolana" (art. 3). Véase en *Gaceta Oficial* N° 39.382 del 9 de marzo de 2010.

1339 Véase en *Gaceta Oficial* N° 5.963 Extraordinario del 22 de febrero de 2010

chos "motores de desarrollo," por tanto se vinculan exclusivamente con la idea de fortalecer el socialismo.

Estos Distritos Motores de desarrollo, por otra parte, se crean conforme se indica en el artículo 6 de la LOCFG por el Presidente de la República en Consejo de Ministros,[1340] "sin perjuicio de la organización política territorial de la República, la competencia para crear Distintos Motores de Desarrollo con la finalidad de impulsar en el área comprendida en cada uno de ellos un conjunto de proyectos económicos, sociales, científicos y tecnológicos, destinados a lograr el desarrollo integral de las regiones y el fortalecimiento del Poder Popular, en aras de facilitar la transición hacia el socialismo." Estos Distritos, conforme se indica en el artículo 24 del Reglamento del Consejo federal de Gobierno, son dirigidos por una Autoridad Única de Área denominada "Autoridad Única Distrital;" y en ellos se debe activar una Misión Distrital y se debe elaborar un plan estratégico de desarrollo integral o plan distrital (art. 22)

Conforme a la LOCFG, además, la vía para lograr el fortalecimiento de las organizaciones de base del Poder Popular y el desarrollo armónico de los Distritos Motores de Desarrollo y regiones del país, es la transferencia de competencias en el marco del Plan de Desarrollo Económico y Social de la Nación (art. 7). En ese contexto el mencionado Consejo Federal es el órgano competente para establecer los lineamientos que se deben aplicar a los procesos de transferencia de las competencias y atribuciones de las entidades territoriales del Estado, es decir, de los Estados y Municipios, hacia las organizaciones de base del Poder Popular; siendo dichos lineamientos de carácter vinculante para las entidades territoriales (art. 2).

En cuanto a los "Ejes estratégicos de desarrollo territorial," están definidos como "las unidades territoriales de carácter estructural supra-local y articuladora de la organización del Poder Popular y de la distribución espacial del desarrollo sustentable, endógeno y socialista, con la finalidad de optimizar las ventajas comparativas locales y regionales, los planes de inversión del Estado venezolano en infraestructura, equipamiento y servicios, la implantación y desarrollo de cadenas productivas y el intercambio de bienes y servicios. (art. 4.9).

III. CONSTITUCIÓN DE LAS COMUNAS

1.   *Iniciativa popular y aprobación de la Carta Fundacional mediante referéndum*

Conforme al artículo 8 de la LOC, las Comunas se constituyen "por iniciativa popular" a través de la agregación de comunidades organizadas. Sin embargo, la Ley nada dispone sobre el número de comunidades organizadas que se requieren para la constitución de una comuna, por lo que la norma su indicación remite al Reglamento, "tanto en el área urbana como en el área rural." A tal efecto, en la Disposición Final Cuarta, se dispuso que el Ejecutivo Nacional debía elaborar y sancionar

---

1340   En el Reglamento del Consejo Federal de Gobierno, el Consejo de Ministros se denomina como "Consejo Revolucionario de Ministros" (art. 21.2). Véase en *Gaceta Oficial* N° 39.382 del 9 de marzo de 2010.

el Reglamento de la Ley, en un lapso no mayor a 180 días continuos a su publicación de la Ley en la Gaceta Oficial, es decir, a partir del 21 de junio del 2011.

La constitución de las Comunas ocurre, en definitiva, conforme al artículo 12 de la LOC, "cuando mediante referendo los ciudadanos y ciudadanas de las comunidades organizadas del ámbito geográfico propuesto" aprueben "por mayoría simple" la Carta Fundacional de la misma, que es el "instrumento aprobado en referendo popular, donde las comunidades expresan su voluntad de constituirse en Comuna, en su respectivo ámbito geográfico, contentiva de la declaración de principios, censo poblacional, diagnóstico sobre los principales problemas y necesidades de su población, inventario de las potencialidades económicas, sociales, culturales, ambientales, y opciones de desarrollo" (art. 4.3).

Este referendo aprobatorio debe tener lugar en un lapso perentorio de 60 días siguientes a la notificación que se haga al Ministerio de las Comunas sobre la conformación de la comisión promotora de constitución de la comuna respectiva (art. 13.3).

La "iniciativa popular" para la constitución de la Comuna, entonces, conforme a la LOC, "corresponde a los consejos comunales y a las organizaciones sociales que hagan vida activa en las comunidades organizadas, quienes deberán previamente conformarse en comisión promotora" (art. 10).

2. *Control centralizado del proceso de constitución por el Ministerio para las Comunas*

Una vez constituida esta comisión promotora, la misma debe notificar dicho acto al "órgano facilitador" (art. 10), que no es otro que "el Ministerio del Poder Popular con competencia en materia de participación ciudadana," es decir, actualmente, el "Ministerio del Poder Popular para las Comunas y Protección Social" (en lo adelante, *Ministerio para las Comunas*) al cual, conforme al artículo 63 de la LOC, se le atribuye competencia para dictar "los lineamientos estratégicos y normas técnicas para el desarrollo y consolidación de las comunas, en una relación de acompañamiento en el cumplimiento de sus fines y propósitos, y facilitando su articulación y sus relaciones con los otros órganos y entes del Poder Público," con lo que se confirma el estricto control que el Ejecutivo Nacional ejerce sobre la edificación del Estado Comunal.

Por otra parte, la Disposición Final Tercera de la LOC dispone que "El Ministerio del Poder Popular con competencia en materia de comunas, desarrollará planes destinados al asesoramiento y acompañamiento de las comunidades para su constitución en comunas, la conformación de sus gobiernos y las relaciones de las mismas entre sí para su agregación en mancomunidades, ciudades comunales y cualquier otra forma de articulación que contribuya a la construcción del estado comunal."

3. *La comisión promotora*

Como se dijo, la comisión promotora para la constitución de una comunas se forma por los consejos comunales y las organizaciones sociales que hagan vida activa en las comunidades organizadas que tomen la iniciativa, la cual en un lapso de 60 días continuos contados a partir de la notificación de su constitución al Ministerio para las Comunas, y conforme se indica en el artículo 11 de la LOC, deben realizar las siguientes actividades:

1. Formular la propuesta del ámbito geográfico de la Comuna.

2. Difundir y promover, en coordinación con las unidades ejecutivas de los consejos comunales, la información y el debate, entre los y las habitantes del ámbito geográfico propuesto, sobre el alcance, objeto y finalidades de la comuna.

3. Coordinar con los voceros y voceras del comité de educación, cultura y formación ciudadana de los consejos comunales, la redacción del proyecto de la carta fundacional de la Comuna a ser sometida a referendo aprobatorio con la participación de los electores y electoras del ámbito geográfico propuesto.

4. Coordinar con las comisiones electorales de los consejos comunales del espacio territorial propuesto, la convocatoria al referendo aprobatorio de la carta fundacional de la Comuna.

5. Coordinar con el órgano facilitador el acompañamiento y apoyo que éste debe prestar en el proceso de constitución de la Comuna.

Como se dijo, incluso, este referendo aprobatorio debe tener lugar en un lapso perentorio de 60 días siguientes a la notificación que se haga al Ministerio de las Comunas sobre la conformación de la comisión promotora de constitución de la comuna respectiva (art. 13.3).

4. *Redacción y difusión del proyecto de Carta Fundacional*

A partir de la conformación de la comisión promotora, la misma tiene un lapso de 30 días continuos para la redacción del proyecto de la carta fundacional de la Comuna (art. 13.1), la cual debe contener los siguientes aspectos enumerados en el artículo 12:

1. Ubicación.

2. Ámbito geográfico.

3. Denominación de la Comuna.

4. Declaración de principios.

5. Censo poblacional para el momento de su constitución.

6. Diagnóstico sobre los principales problemas y necesidades de su población.

7. Inventario de las potencialidades económicas, sociales, culturales, ambientales y opciones de desarrollo.

8. Programa político estratégico comunal, contentivo de las líneas generales de acción a corto, mediano y largo plazo para la superación de los problemas y necesidades de la comuna.

Una vez culminada la redacción del proyecto de Carta Fundacional, la misma debe ser difundida por la comisión promotora y los voceros y voceras de los respectivos consejos comunales entre los habitantes del ámbito territorial propuesto (art. 13.1), en un lapso de 15 días continuos (Jornada de difusión) (art. 13.2).

5. *Referendo aprobatorio*

La aprobación de la Carta Fundacional debe realizarse mediante referendo aprobatorio, que debe tener lugar en un lapso no mayor a los 60 días siguientes a la notificación al Ministerio de las Comunas de la conformación de la comisión promotora (art. 13.3).

Este refrendo aprobatorio, sin embargo, y en contra de lo previsto en la Constitución, no se prevé que deba ser organizado por el Poder Electoral, es decir, el Consejo Nacional Electoral, sino conforme al artículo 14 de la LOC, por "las comisiones electorales permanentes de los consejos comunales del ámbito territorial propuesto para la Comuna, mediante la convocatoria a elecciones en sus respectivas comunidades." Sobre el Poder Electoral, lo que se establece en la LOC es que el mismo "apoyará y acompañará a las comunas en la organización de sus procesos electorales" (art. 65).

A tal efecto, la circunscripción electoral para la realización del referendo aprobatorio de la carta fundacional debe ser el ámbito geográfico propuesto para la Comuna; y los "electores con derecho al voto" serán los que, para el momento de la convocatoria del referendo, se encuentren inscritos en el registro electoral de los consejos comunales del referido ámbito geográfico, de manera que cada consejo comunal se constituye en un centro de votación (art. 15). Ahora bien, de acuerdo con la Ley Orgánica de los Consejos Municipales, como antes se ha dicho, el "registro electoral de la comunidad" en cada Consejo Comunal, está conformado por todos los habitantes de la comunidad, mayores de quince años (art. 37,1), lo que significa que es un registro electoral distinto y paralelo al que lleva el Consejo Nacional Electoral, en el cual están incorporados personas que no son ciudadanos, extranjeros y venezolanos menores de 18 años. Sin embargo, de acuerdo con la Constitución, la participación política mediante referendos está reservada, como todo derecho político, a los "ciudadanos," es decir, a los venezolanos mayores de 18 años inscritos en el Registro Electoral Permanente que lleva el Consejo Nacional Electoral, por lo que en el referendo para aprobar la constitución de las comunas, no sólo lo tendría que organizar el Poder Electoral, sino que en el mismo sólo podrían participar los ciudadanos, siendo inconstitucional que se pudiera organizar al margen del Consejo Nacional Electoral y con la participación de venezolanos que no sean ciudadanos (menores de 18 años) o de extranjeros habitantes de la comunidad.

Ahora bien, conforme al artículo 16 de la LOC, se considera aprobada la carta fundacional y en consecuencia, la constitución de la Comuna, cuando la mayoría de los votos sean afirmativos, siempre y cuando haya concurrido al referendo un número de electores igual o superior al quince por ciento de los electores del ámbito territorial propuesto.

6. *Registro de la Comuna*

En el lapso de los 15 días siguientes a la aprobación de la carta fundacional, la comisión promotora procederá a su registro ante el Ministerio de las Comunas, acompañando dicho documento de las actas de votación suscritas por los integrantes de las respectivas comisiones electorales permanentes. Con este acto la Comuna adquiere su personalidad jurídica (art. 17).

7. *La Gaceta Comunal*

La LOC creó una *Gaceta Comunal*, como órgano informativo oficial de la Comuna, en el cual se deben publicar, además de la Carta Comunal, las decisiones del Parlamento Comunal y las del Banco de la Comuna que posean carácter vinculante para sus habitantes, así como todos aquellos actos que requieran para su validez la publicación en dicho instrumento (art. 4.11).

IV. LAS CARTAS COMUNALES

Cada Comuna, una vez constituida, debe contar con una Carta Comunal, concebida como el instrumento propuesto por los habitantes de la Comuna y aprobado por el Parlamento Comunal, destinado a regular la vida social y comunitaria, coadyuvar con el orden público, la convivencia, la primacía del interés colectivo sobre el interés particular y la defensa de los derechos humanos, de conformidad con la Constitución y las leyes de la República (art. 18).

El artículo 4.2 de la LOC, por su parte al formular las definiciones, define las Cartas comunales, como los:

> Instrumentos donde se establecen las normas elaboradas y aprobadas por los habitantes de la Comuna en el Parlamento Comunal, con el propósito de contribuir corresponsablemente en la garantía del orden público, la convivencia y la primacía del interés colectivo sobre el interés particular, de conformidad con la Constitución y las leyes de la República.

La Ley, sin embargo, remite al Reglamento la determinación de las condiciones para la elaboración, consulta y presentación de proyectos de cartas comunales ante el Parlamento Comunal.

1. *Contenido*

Estas cartas comunales deberán regulaciones sobre los siguientes aspectos que enumera el artículo 19 de la LOC:

1. Título de la carta comunal de acuerdo al ámbito o actividad a regular.
2. Objeto y definición del ámbito y actividad.
3. Desarrollo de la normativa conforme a un articulado bajo los criterios que establecen la técnica legislativa, la Constitución y leyes de la República.

Esta norma está redactada en forma tal que lo único que permitiría deducir es que en las Cartas Comunales podría desarrollar una normativa relativa "al ámbito y actividad" a desarrollar por la Comuna, y que conforme esta LOC sería la tendiente "a regular la vida social y comunitaria, coadyuvar con el orden público, la convivencia, la primacía del interés colectivo sobre el interés particular y la defensa de los derechos humanos."

Sin embargo, la norma es terminante en señalar que ello sólo podría realizarse "de conformidad con la Constitución y las leyes de la República," las cuales no dejan campo regulatorio alguno en esos órdenes que pudiera regularse por cuerpos que no son representativos en el sentido de que no son integrados por representantes electos mediante sufragio universal, directo y secreto. Es decir, de acuerdo con la

Constitución sólo la Asamblea Nacional (art. 187.1 de la Constitución), los Consejos Legislativos de los Estados (art. 162.1 de la Constitución) y los Concejos Municipales de los Municipios (art. 175 de la Constitución) tienen en Venezuela la potestad de legislar, por lo que toda otra "legislación" que se adopte por cuerpos no democráticamente representativos como estos Parlamentos Comunales regulados en la LOC, no sería otra cosa que fruto de una usurpación de autoridad, y por tanto nulos de nulidad absoluta en los términos indicados en el artículo 138 de la Constitución.

No se olvide, por ejemplo, que de acuerdo con la Constitución, en especial, las regulaciones, restricciones y limitaciones a los derechos y garantías constitucionales sólo pueden ser establecidas mediante *ley formal*, y "ley", conforme al artículo 202 de la Constitución, no es otra cosa que "el acto sancionado por la Asamblea Nacional como cuerpo legislador"; es decir, el acto normativo emanado del cuerpo que conforma la representación popular. Por lo demás, en este ámbito de los derechos humanos, la Corte Interamericana de Derechos Humanos ha decidido formalmente en la *Opinión Consultiva OC-6/86* de 9-3-86 que la expresión "leyes" en el artículo 30 de la Convención sólo se refiere a las emanadas de "los órganos legislativos constitucionalmente previstos y democráticamente electos."[1341] Por lo que toda regulación que los afecte sólo puede ser establecida por el órgano colegiado integrado por representantes electos mediante sufragio por el pueblo, es decir, a nivel nacional, por la Asamblea Nacional.

2. *Corrección de estilo*

En el proceso de aprobación de las cartas comunales y atendiendo sólo a razones de estilo y formalidad de redacción, el artículo 20 de la LOC autoriza expresamente al Parlamento Comunal para por acuerdo de por lo menos las dos terceras (2/3) partes de sus integrantes, proceder a modificar las cartas comunales, manteniendo en su contenido el propósito fundamental del proyecto presentado por los habitantes de la Comuna, sin perjuicio de las normas constitucionales y legales.

3. *Publicación*

El Consejo Ejecutivo de la Comuna debe refrendar y publicar en la *Gaceta Comunal* las cartas comunales (art. 29.3).

Las Cartas Fundacionales de las Comunas pueden reformarse sólo mediante referendo popular "a través del voto universal, directo y secreto" de los electores de la Comuna mayores de quince años. A los efectos, la iniciativa para solicitar la reforma corresponde a un número de electores no inferior al quince por ciento (15%) del total de electores y electoras o a las dos terceras partes de los integrantes de los voceros y voceras principales de los consejos comunales de la Comuna (art. 66).

Las reformas de la carta fundacional serán refrendadas por el Consejo Ejecutivo y deberán ser publicadas en la gaceta comunal.

1341   Véase "La expresión 'leyes' en el artículo 30 de la Convención Americana sobre Derechos Humanos" (*Opinión Consultiva, OC-6/86*) Corte Interamericana de Derechos Humanos, en *Revista IIDH*; Instituto Interamericano de Derechos Humanos N° 3, San José 1986, pp. 107 y ss.

V. LA ORGANIZACIÓN Y FUNCIONAMIENTO DE LAS COMUNAS

La LOC establece la organización básica de la Comuna, distinguiendo los siguientes órganos: el Parlamento Comunal, el Consejo Ejecutivo de la Comuna, el Consejo de Planificación Comunal, el Consejo de Economía Comunal, el Banco de la Comuna y el Consejo de Contraloría Social.

1. *El órgano de autogobierno comunal: el Parlamento Comunal*

El Parlamento Comunal, que es el órgano que aprueba la Carta Comunal, está concebido en el artículo 21 de la LOC, como "la máxima instancia del autogobierno en la Comuna."

El mismo artículo le atribuye fundamentalmente dos funciones:

En primer lugar, aprobar la "normativas para la regulación de la vida social y comunitaria, coadyuvar con el orden público, la convivencia, la primacía del interés colectivo sobre el interés particular y la defensa de los derechos humanos";

En segundo lugar, dictar "actos de gobierno sobre los aspectos de planificación, coordinación y ejecución de planes y proyectos en el ámbito de la Comuna."

Se trata, por tanto, de un órgano que se pretende que sea a la vez, "legislador" y de gobierno comunal.

Sobre la pretendida función normativa atribuida a los Parlamentos Comunales, ya hemos señalado que ello es inconstitucional pues de acuerdo con la Constitución y las leyes de la República, normas que pretendan regular esos ámbitos que inciden en los derechos humanos sólo pueden ser producto de órganos representativos y no pueden ser dictados por cuerpos que no son representativos en el sentido de que no estén integrados por representantes electos mediante sufragio universal, directo y secreto. Por ello, la Constitución sólo atribuye la potestad legislativa a la Asamblea Nacional (art. 187.1), a los Consejos Legislativos de los Estados (art. 162.1) y a los Concejos Municipales de los Municipios (art. 175), de manera que toda otra "legislación" que se adopte por cuerpos no democráticamente representativos como serían estos Parlamentos Comunales regulados en la LOC, no sería otra cosa que fruto de una usurpación de autoridad, y por tanto nulos de nulidad absoluta en los términos indicados en el artículo 138 de la Constitución.

2. *Atribuciones del Parlamento Comunal*

El artículo 22 de la LOC, define las siguientes atribuciones de los Parlamentos Comunales "en el ejercicio del autogobierno":

1.   Sancionar materias de sus competencias, de acuerdo a lo establecido en esta Ley, su Reglamento y demás normativas aplicables.

2.   Aprobar el Plan de Desarrollo Comunal.

3.   Sancionar las cartas comunales, previo debate y aprobación por las asambleas de ciudadanos y ciudadanas de las comunidades integrantes de la Comuna.

4.   Aprobar los proyectos que sean sometidos a su consideración por el Consejo Ejecutivo.

5. Debatir y aprobar los proyectos de solicitudes, a los entes político-territoriales del Poder Público, de transferencias de competencias y servicios a la Comuna.

6. Aprobar los informes que le deben presentar el Consejo Ejecutivo, el Consejo de Planificación Comunal, el Consejo de Economía Comunal, el Banco de la Comuna y el Consejo de Contraloría Comunal.

7. Dictar su reglamento interno.

8. Designar a los y las integrantes de los Comités de Gestión.

9. Considerar los asuntos de interés general para la Comuna, propuestos por al menos el equivalente al sesenta por ciento (60%) de los consejos comunales, de la Comuna.

10. Ordenar la publicación en gaceta comunal del Plan de Desarrollo Comunal, las cartas comunales y demás decisiones y asuntos que considere de interés general para los habitantes de la Comuna.

11. Rendir cuenta pública anual de su gestión ante los y las habitantes de la Comuna.

12. Las demás que determine la presente Ley y su Reglamento.

Las decisiones del Parlamento Comunal "que posean carácter vinculante para los habitantes" de la Comuna, así como todos aquellos actos que requieran para su validez la publicación en dicho instrumento, deben publicarse en la *Gaceta Comunal* (art. 4.11).

3. Integración de los Parlamentos Comunales

El Parlamento Comunal no está conformado, en absoluto, por representantes que pudieran ser electos mediante sufragio directo, universal y secreto por todos los ciudadanos con derecho a voto de una Comuna, como sería el caso de tratarse de un cuerpo democráticamente representativo, sino que están integrados, conforme se indica en el artículo 23, por una serie de personas denominadas "voceros" designadas por otros órganos del Poder Popular, de la siguiente manera:

1. Un vocero y su respectivo suplente, electo por cada consejo comunal de la Comuna.

2. Tres voceros y sus respectivos suplentes, electos por las organizaciones socio-productivas, y

3. Un vocero y su respectivo suplente, en representación del Banco de la Comuna.

El período de ejercicio de los voceros ante el parlamento Comunal es de tres años, pudiendo ser reelectos.

Para ser vocero miembro del Parlamento Comunal, conforme se indica en el artículo 24 de la LOC, se requiere ser de nacionalidad venezolana; mayor de quince años; no poseer parentesco hasta el cuarto grado de consanguinidad y segundo de afinidad con quienes representen los entes político-territoriales establecidos en la Ley Orgánica del Consejo Federal de Gobierno; ser habitante del ámbito territorial de la Comuna, con al menos un año de residencia en la misma; hacer vida activa en el ámbito territorial de la Comuna; no desempeñar cargos públicos de elección popular; y no estar sujeto o sujeta a interdicción civil o inhabilitación política.

Sobre esta situación, ya nos hemos referido a su inconstitucionalidad por carecer los menores de 18 años, de acuerdo con la Constitución, de los derechos políticos de la ciudadanía.

4. *Sesiones del Parlamento Comunal*

El Parlamento Comunal debe sesionar ordinariamente una vez al mes; y de forma extraordinaria cuando sea convocado por el Consejo Ejecutivo, el Consejo de Planificación Comunal, la autoridad única del distrito motor o del eje estratégico de desarrollo al que pertenezca, o por el equivalente al setenta (70%) de los consejos comunales de la Comuna (art. 25). En las sesiones ordinarias del Parlamento Comunal se deben tratar los puntos de la agenda previamente establecidos por el Consejo Ejecutivo.

En cuanto a las decisiones del Parlamento Comunal, las mismas se deben tomar por mayoría simple de sus integrantes, cuyos votos deben expresar el mandato de las instancias de las que son voceros (art. 26).

VI. EL ÓRGANO EJECUTIVO DE LA COMUNA: EL CONSEJO EJECUTIVO

1. *Carácter e integración*

La instancia de ejecución de las decisiones del Parlamento Comunal es el Consejo Ejecutivo de la Comuna, el cual está integrado por tres personas: dos voceros, con sus respectivos suplentes, electos por el Parlamento Comunal; y un vocero, con su respectivo suplente, electo de entre los voceros de las organizaciones socioproductivas ante el Parlamento Comunal (art. 27). Dichos voceros del Consejo Ejecutivo duran tres años en sus funciones, pudiendo ser reelectos.

Para ser miembro del Consejo Ejecutivo, conforme al artículo 28 de la LOC se requiere, ser de nacionalidad venezolana; mayor de edad; no poseer parentesco hasta el cuarto grado de consanguinidad y segundo de afinidad con quienes representen los entes político-territoriales establecidos en la Ley Orgánica del Consejo Federal de Gobierno; ser habitante del ámbito territorial de la Comuna, con al menos un año de residencia en la misma; hacer vida activa en el ámbito territorial de la Comuna; no desempeñar cargos públicos de elección popular; y no estar sujeto o sujeta a interdicción civil o inhabilitación política.

2. *Funciones del Consejo Ejecutivo*

El Consejo Ejecutivo conforme al artículo 29 de la LOC. Como la instancia de ejecución de las decisiones del Parlamento Comunal, tiene las siguientes funciones:

1. Ejercer de manera conjunta la representación legal de la Comuna.
2. Refrendar y ejecutar los lineamientos estratégicos y económicos establecidos en el Plan de Desarrollo Comunal, elaborado de conformidad con el Plan de Desarrollo Económico y Social de la Nación, el Plan Regional de Desarrollo y los emanados del Consejo Federal de Gobierno.

3. Refrendar y publicar en la gaceta comunal las cartas comunales, así como las decisiones del Parlamento Comunal que sean de carácter vinculante para los habitantes de la Comuna.

4. Publicar en la gaceta comunal las informaciones del Banco de la Comuna que sean de interés para los habitantes de la Comuna.

5. Formular el presupuesto de la Comuna y someterlo a la consideración del Parlamento Comunal.

6. Convocar al Parlamento Comunal a sesiones extraordinarias.

7. Coordinar con los comités permanentes de gestión la formulación de proyectos a ser sometidos a la consideración del Parlamento Comunal.

8. Promover formas autogestionarias que provengan de la iniciativa de las organizaciones del Poder Popular.

9. Gestionar ante las instancias del Poder Público las transferencias de las atribuciones y servicios que hayan sido aprobados por el Parlamento Comunal.

10. Suscribir los convenios de transferencia de atribuciones y servicios que hayan sido acordados a la Comuna.

11. Someter a la consideración del Parlamento Comunal proyectos y propuestas derivados del estudio de los consejos comunales y sus comités de trabajo.

12. Preparar la agenda de las sesiones ordinarias del Parlamento Comunal.

13. Articular sus actividades con los consejos comunales y sus comités de trabajo.

14. Resguardar el archivo de los documentos fundacionales de la Comuna.

15. Las demás que determine la presente Ley y su Reglamento.

Las decisiones del Comité Ejecutivo para cuya validez se requiera publicación, deben publicarse en la Gaceta Comunal (art. 4.11).

El Consejo Ejecutivo se debe reunir ordinariamente una vez a la semana; y extraordinariamente, cuando así lo decida la mayoría de sus integrantes o sea convocado de acuerdo a lo contemplado en el Reglamento de la Ley (art. 30).

3. *Los Comités de gestión*

El Consejo Ejecutivo debe tener unos Comités de gestión, que son los encargados de articular con las organizaciones sociales de la Comuna de su respectiva área de trabajo, los proyectos y propuestas a ser presentados a través del Consejo Ejecutivo ante el Parlamento Comunal. Los comités de gestión se deben conformar para atender las siguientes áreas:

1. Derechos humanos; 2. Salud; 3. Tierra urbana, vivienda y hábitat; 4. Defensa de las personas en el acceso a bienes y servicios; 5. Economía y producción comunal; 6. Mujer e igualdad de género; 7. Defensa y seguridad integral; 8. Familia y protección de niños, niñas y adolescentes; 9. Recreación y deportes; y 10. Educación, cultura y formación socialista.

En cuanto a las comunas que se conformen en los pueblos y comunidades indígenas, atendiendo a sus culturas, prácticas tradicionales y necesidades colectivas, su
pueden crear, además de los anteriores comités de gestión, los siguientes: a. Comités
de ambiente y ordenación de la tierra; b. Comité de medicina indígena; y c. Comité
de educación propia, educación intercultural bilingüe e idiomas indígenas.

VII. LA PLANIFICACIÓN COMUNAL

1. Plan Comunal de Desarrollo

Conforme al artículo 32 de la LOC, en cada Comuna se debe elaborar un Plan
Comunal de Desarrollo, bajo la coordinación del Consejo de Planificación Comunal,
que también se prevé en la Ley Orgánica de Planificación Pública y Popular (arts.
10.4 y 14), en el cual se deben establecer los proyectos, objetivos, metas, acciones y
recursos dirigidos a darle concreción a los lineamientos plasmados en el Plan de
Desarrollo Económico y Social de la Nación, el Plan Regional de Desarrollo y los
lineamientos del Consejo Federal de Gobierno, tomando en cuenta los patrones de
ocupación del territorio, su cultura, historia, economía y ámbito geográfico.

Dicho plan se debe formular y ejecutar, a partir de los resultados de la aplicación
del diagnóstico participativo, y de lo acordado en el mecanismo del presupuesto
participativo, contando para ello con la intervención planificada y coordinada de las
comunidades que conforman la Comuna (art. 32).

Este Plan Comunal de Desarrollo tal como se define en el artículo 40 de la Ley
Orgánica de Planificación Pública y Popular "es el instrumento de gobierno que
permite a las comunas, establecer los proyectos, objetivos, metas, acciones y recursos dirigidos a darle concreción a los lineamientos plasmados en el Plan de Desarrollo Económico y Social de la Nación, a través de la intervención planificada y coordinada de las comunidades y sus organizaciones, promoviendo el ejercicio directo
del poder, de conformidad con la ley, para la construcción del estado comunal." Los
resultados y metas de este Plan Comunal de Desarrollo, de acuerdo a la misma Ley
Orgánica de Planificación Pública y Popular, debe concretarse en un Plan Operativo
Comunal que es aquel que integra los objetivos, metas, proyectos y acciones anuales
formuladas por cada gobierno comunal (art. 73).

2. El Consejo de Planificación Comunal

El Consejo de Planificación Comunal, conforme se precisa en el artículo 33 de la
LOC, es el órgano encargado de coordinar las actividades para la formulación del
Plan de Desarrollo Comunal, en concordancia con los planes de desarrollo comunitario propuestos por los Consejos Comunales y los demás planes de interés colectivo, articulados con el sistema nacional de planificación, de conformidad con lo establecido en la ley (art. 33).

Por su parte, el artículo 14 de la Ley Orgánica de Planificación Pública y Popular, define al Consejo de Planificación Comunal como "el órgano encargado de la
planificación integral que comprende, al área geográfica y poblacional de una comuna, así como de diseñar el Plan de Desarrollo Comunal, en concordancia con los
planes de desarrollo comunitario propuestos por los consejos comunales y los demás
planes de interés colectivo, articulados con el Sistema Nacional de Planificación, de

conformidad con lo establecido en la Ley de las Comunas y la presente Ley; contando para ello con el apoyo de los órganos y entes de la Administración Pública."

EL Consejo de Planificación Comunal está conformado por las siguientes siete personas: tres voceros electos por los consejos comunales de la Comuna; dos voceros en representación del Parlamento Comunal; un vocero designado por las organizaciones socio-productivas comunitarias; y un vocero de cada consejo comunal, integrante del comité de trabajo en materia de ordenación y gestión del territorio (art. 35).

En el caso de los pueblos y comunidades indígenas, el Consejo de Planificación Comunal se debe conformar de acuerdo con la normativa establecida en la ley respectiva, tomando en cuenta sus usos, costumbres y tradiciones.

El Consejo de Planificación Comunal, al momento de su instalación designará de su seno y por votación de mayoría simple al coordinador del mismo.

3. *Finalidad*

Este Consejo de Planificación Comunal tiene además, como finalidad, conforme se indica en el artículo 34, lo siguiente:

1.   Servir de instancia de deliberación, discusión y coordinación entre las instancias de participación popular y las comunidades organizadas, con miras a armonizar la formulación, aprobación, ejecución y control de los diversos planes y proyectos.

2.   Adecuar el Plan de Desarrollo Comunal al Plan de Desarrollo Económico y Social de la Nación y demás planes estratégicos nacionales, al Plan de Desarrollo Regional y a los lineamientos establecidos en el decreto de creación del Distrito Motor de Desarrollo al que pertenezca la Comuna.

3.   Incentivar a los consejos comunales existentes en el ámbito geográfico de la Comuna, al ejercicio del ciclo comunal en todas sus fases.

4. *Competencias del Consejo*

El Consejo de Planificación Comunal, tendrá las siguientes competencias tal como se enumeran en el artículo 36 de la LOC:

1.   Impulsar la coordinación y participación ciudadana y protagónica en la formulación, ejecución, seguimiento, evaluación y control del Plan de Desarrollo Comunal, así como de otros planes, programas y acciones que se ejecuten o se proyecte su ejecución en la Comuna.

2.   Garantizar que el Plan de Desarrollo Comunal esté debidamente articulado con el Plan de Desarrollo Económico y Social de la Nación, el Plan de Desarrollo Regional y los lineamientos establecidos en el decreto de creación del Distrito Motor al que corresponda.

3.   Formular y promover los proyectos de inversión para la Comuna ante el Parlamento Comunal.

4.   Realizar seguimiento, evaluación y control a la ejecución del Plan de Desarrollo Comunal.

5. Impulsar la coordinación con otros consejos de planificación comunal para coadyuvar en la definición, instrumentación y evaluación de planes para el desarrollo de mancomunidades, formulando propuestas al respecto ante el Parlamento Comunal.

6. Atender cualquier información atinente a sus competencias que le solicite el Parlamento Comunal y sus instancias de ejecución, los consejos comunales y los entes del Poder Público, sobre la situación socio-económica de la Comuna.

7. Elaborar un banco de proyectos que contenga información acerca de los proyectos, recursos reales y potenciales existentes en la Comuna.

8. Estudiar y proponer al Parlamento Comunal la aprobación de los proyectos presentados por las comunidades y organizaciones sociales a ser financiados con recursos provenientes del Fondo de Compensación Interterritorial (regulado en la Ley Orgánica del Consejo Federal de Gobierno) y otros que se les haya acordado.

9. Promover en el desarrollo endógeno y sustentable de la Comuna el sistema de propiedad social.

VIII. EL CONSEJO DE ECONOMÍA COMUNAL

1. *Carácter y composición*

Tal como se define en el artículo 4.6 de la LOC, el Consejo de Economía Comunal es "la instancia encargada de la planificación y coordinación de la actividad económica de la Comuna. Se constituye para la articulación de los comités de economía comunal y las organizaciones socio-productivas con el Parlamento Comunal y el Consejo de Planificación Comunal." Por su parte, el artículo 37 lo define como "la instancia encargada de la promoción del desarrollo económico de la Comuna."

Este Consejo de Economía Comunal, está conformado por cinco voceros y sus respectivos suplentes, electos todos de entre los integrantes de los comités de economía comunal de los consejos comunales de la Comuna (art. 37). Tiene un período de dos años, pudiendo ser reelectos.

Para ser vocero o vocera del Consejo de Economía Comunal conforme al artículo 38 se requiere ser de nacionalidad venezolana; mayor de quince años; no poseer parentesco hasta el cuarto grado de consanguinidad y segundo de afinidad con quienes representen los entes político-territoriales establecidos en la Ley Orgánica del Consejo Federal de Gobierno; ser habitante del Ámbito territorial de la Comuna, con al menos un año de residencia en la misma; ser vocero de un comité de economía comunal de un consejo comunal; hacer vida activa en el ámbito territorial de la Comuna; no desempeñar cargos públicos de elección popular; y no estar sujeto o sujeta a interdicción civil o inhabilitación política.

2. *Funciones del Consejo de Economía Comunal*

El artículo 37 de la LOC, asigna al Consejo de Economía Comunal las siguientes funciones:

1. Promover la conformación de organizaciones socio-productivas para el desarrollo y fortalecimiento del sistema económico comunal.

2. Articular la relación de los comités de economía comunal con el Parlamento Comunal y el Consejo de Planificación Comunal.

3. Seguimiento y acompañamiento a las organizaciones socio-productivas, a los fines de garantizar el cierre del ciclo productivo y la consolidación de redes productivas.

4. Velar para que los planes y proyectos de las organizaciones socio-productivas se formulen en correspondencia con el Plan de Desarrollo Comunal.

5. Gestionar la implementación de programas para la formación, asistencia técnica y actualización tecnológica de las organizaciones socio-productivas.

6. Articular con el órgano coordinador la certificación de saberes y conocimientos de los ciudadanos y ciudadanas integrantes o aspirantes de las organizaciones socio-productivas.

7. Presentar semestralmente, ante el Parlamento Comunal informes sobre los niveles de cumplimiento de los planes de gestión de las organizaciones socio-productivas.

8. Presentar ante el Parlamento Comunal el informe anual sobre la gestión de las organizaciones socio-productivas y los correspondientes planes para el año siguiente.

9. Proponer formas alternativas de intercambio de bienes y servicios, orientadas al desarrollo socio-productivo de la comunidad y la satisfacción de las necesidades colectivas.

10. Organizar en redes de productores y productoras a las organizaciones socio-productivas y a las comunidades organizadas que ejecuten proyectos socio-productivos ubicados en el ámbito geográfico de la Comuna.

IX. EL BANCO DE LA COMUNA

1. *Objeto*

Tal como lo define el artículo 4.1 de la LOC, el Banco de la Comuna es "la organización económico-financiera de carácter social que gestiona, administra, transfiere, financia, facilita, capta y controla, de acuerdo con los lineamientos establecidos en el Plan de Desarrollo Comunal, los recursos financieros y no financieros de ámbito comunal, retornables y no retornables, impulsando las políticas económicas con la participación democrática y protagónica del pueblo, bajo un enfoque social, político, económico y cultural para la construcción del modelo productivo socialista."[1342] Esta definición se complementa en el artículo 4° de la LOC, en la cual se precisa que el Banco de la Comuna "tiene como objeto garantizar la gestión y admi-

---

1342   Igual definición está inserta en el artículo 6.2 de la Ley Orgánica del Sistema Económico Comunal.

nistración de los recursos financieros y no financieros que le sean asignados, así como los generados o captados mediante sus operaciones, promoviendo la participación protagónica del pueblo en la construcción del modelo económico socialista, mediante la promoción y apoyo al desarrollo y consolidación de la propiedad Social para el fortalecimiento de la soberanía integral del país" (art. 40).

Estos Bancos de las Comunas están exceptuados de la regulación prevista en materia de bancos y otras instituciones financieras; y su constitución, conformación, organización y funcionamiento se rige "por los principios de honestidad, democracia participativa y protagónica, celeridad, eficiencia y eficacia revolucionaria, deber social, rendición de cuentas, soberanía, igualdad, transparencia, equidad y justicia social"(art. .41). Igualmente, conforme a la Disposición Final Primera de la LOC, el Banco de la Comuna está exento de todo tipo de pagos de tributos nacionales y derechos de registro. Se previó igualmente que se puede establecer mediante leyes y ordenanzas de los estados y municipios, las exenciones para el Banco de la Comuna aquí previsto.

2. *Propósito*

El Banco de la Comuna conforme se define en el artículo 42 de la LOC, tiene como propósito: gestionar, captar, administrar, transferir, financiar y facilitar los recursos financieros y no financieros, retornables y no retornables de la Comuna, a fin de impulsar a través de la participación popular, la promoción de proyectos comunales, de acuerdo a los lineamientos del Plan de Desarrollo Comunal, en correspondencia con el Plan de Desarrollo Económico y Social de la Nación, el Plan de Desarrollo Regional y lo dispuesto en el decreto de creación de áreas de desarrollo territorial.

3. *Funciones*

El Banco de la Comuna tendrá como funciones las siguientes tal como se enumeran en el artículo 43 de la LOC:

1. Fortalecer el sistema microfinanciero comunal mediante la aplicación de políticas públicas democráticas y participativas en la gestión financiera.

2. Financiar y transferir, previa aprobación por parte del Parlamento Comunal, recursos a proyectos socio-productivos y de inversión social que formen parte del Plan Comunal de Desarrollo, orientados al bienestar social mediante la consolidación del modelo productivo socialista, en aras de alcanzar la suprema felicidad social.

3. Fortalecer y ejecutar una política de ahorro e inversión en el ámbito territorial de la Comuna.

4. Promover la inclusión y activación de las fuerzas productivas de la Comuna para la ejecución de los proyectos a desarrollarse en su ámbito geográfico.

5. Promover la participación organizada del pueblo en la planificación de la producción, distribución, intercambio y consumo a través del impulso de la propiedad colectiva de los medios de producción.

6. Apoyar el intercambio solidario y la moneda comunal.

7. Realizar captación de recursos con la finalidad de otorgar créditos, financiamientos e inversiones, de carácter retornable y no retornable.

8. Las demás que se establezcan en las leyes que rijan el sistema microfinanciero y las disposiciones reglamentarias de la presente Ley.

Las decisiones del Banco de la Comuna "que posean carácter vinculante para los habitantes" de la Comuna, así como todos aquellos actos que requieran para su validez la publicación en dicho instrumento, deben publicarse en la *Gaceta Comunal* (art. 4.11).

4. *Organización*

A los fines de su conformación y funcionamiento, el Banco de la Comuna está integrado por las siguientes unidades indicadas en el artículo 44 de la LOC:

La coordinación administrativa es la cuentadante y responsable de la administración de los recursos del Banco de la Comuna; y está conformada por tres voceros electos de entre los integrantes de las unidades administrativas financieras comunitarias de los consejos comunales de la Comuna.

El comité de aprobación es el órgano responsable de evaluar, para su aprobación o rechazo por parte del Parlamento Comunal, todos los proyectos de inversión, transferencias y apoyo financiero y no financiero que sean sometidos a la consideración del Banco de la Comuna o que éste se proponga desarrollar por su propia iniciativa. Este Comité está conformado por cinco voceros designados por los consejos comunales que formen parte de la Comuna.

El Comité de seguimiento y control tiene la función de velar por el manejo transparente de los recursos financieros y no financieros del Banco de la Comuna, vigilar y supervisar que todas sus actividades se desarrollen con eficiencia y de acuerdo a los procedimientos establecidos, y que los resultados de su gestión se correspondan con los objetivos de la Comuna. Este Comité está integrado por tres voceros, que no posean parentesco hasta el cuarto grado de consanguinidad y segundo de afinidad entre sí ni con los demás voceros y voceras del Banco de la Comuna ni del Consejo de Contraloría Comunal, designados de la siguiente manera: Un vocero, por los consejos comunales que formen parte de la Comuna; un vocero por las organizaciones socio-productivas de la Comuna; y un vocero, designado por el Parlamento Comunal.

Las demás funciones, así como el período de ejercicio de los integrantes de cada una de las instancias antes indicadas deben ser desarrolladas en el Reglamento de la Ley.

X. EL CONSEJO DE CONTRALORÍA COMUNAL

Conforme a los artículos 4.7 y 45 de la LOC, el Consejo de Contraloría Comunal es "la instancia encargada de la vigilancia, supervisión, evaluación y contraloría social, sobre los proyectos, planes y actividades de interés colectivo que en el ámbito territorial de la Comuna, ejecuten o desarrollen las instancias del Poder Popular, del Poder Público y las organizaciones y personas del sector privado con incidencia en los intereses generales o colectivos.

1. *Integración*

Estos Consejo de Contraloría Comunal están conformados por cinco voceros y sus respectivos suplentes, electos de entre los integrantes de las unidades de contraloría social de los consejos comunales de la Comuna (art. 45), por un período de dos años, pudiendo ser reelectos.

Para ser vocero o vocera del Consejo de Contraloría Comunal, conforme se indica en el artículo 46, se requiere ser de nacionalidad venezolana; mayor de edad; no poseer parentesco hasta el cuarto grado de consanguinidad y segundo de afinidad con quienes representen los entes político-territoriales establecidos en la Ley Orgánica del Consejo Federal de Gobierno; ser vocero de una unidad de contraloría social de un Consejo Comunal; ser habitante del ámbito territorial de la Comuna, con al menos un año de residencia en la misma; hacer vida activa en el ámbito territorial de la Comuna; no desempeñar cargos públicos de elección popular; y no estar sujeto o sujeta a interdicción civil o inhabilitación política.

2. *Funciones del Consejo de Contraloría Comunal*

El Consejo de Contraloría Comunal tal como se enumeran en el artículo 47 de la LOC, tiene las siguientes funciones:

1. Ejercer el seguimiento, la vigilancia, supervisión y contraloría social sobre la ejecución de los planes y proyectos ejecutados o desarrollados en el ámbito territorial de la Comuna por las instancias del Poder Popular u órganos y entes del Poder Público.

2. Garantizar que la inversión de los recursos que se ejecuten en el ámbito territorial de la Comuna para beneficio colectivo, se realice de manera eficiente y eficaz, en correspondencia con el Plan de Desarrollo Comunal.

3. Velar por el cumplimiento de las obligaciones colectivas correspondientes a las organizaciones socio-productivas y la reinversión social de los excedentes resultantes de sus actividades.

4. Emitir informes semestralmente, al Parlamento Comunal sobre el funcionamiento del Consejo Ejecutivo, el Banco de la Comuna, el Consejo de Planificación Comunal y el Consejo de Economía Comunal. Dichos informes tendrán carácter vinculante.

5. Recibir y dar curso a las denuncias que se le presente.

6. Presentar informe y solicitar al Parlamento Comunal la revocatoria del mandato de los voceros o voceras de las distintas instancias de la Comuna, con base a las investigaciones sobre denuncias que se le formulen o como resultado de sus propias actuaciones.

7. Ejercer el seguimiento, la vigilancia, supervisión y contraloría social sobre las personas y organizaciones del sector privado que realicen actividades que incidan en el interés social o colectivo, en el ámbito de la Comuna.

8. En el ejercicio de la corresponsabilidad, cooperar con los órganos y entes del Poder Público en las funciones de vigilancia, supervisión y control, de conformidad con las normativas legales aplicables.

Los órganos integrantes del Poder Ciudadano deben apoyar a los consejos de contraloría comunal a los fines de contribuir con el cumplimiento de sus funciones (art. 48).

XI. RÉGIMEN DE LOS VOCEROS DE LOS ÓRGANOS DE LA COMUNA

Como se ha señalado, los titulares de los diversos órganos de la Comuna, se denominan "voceros" y los mismos no tienen su origen en votación popular alguna, sino que son designados por otros órganos del Poder Popular, quienes a su vez, tampoco son electos por votación popular mediante sufragio universal, directo y secreto. Por tanto, ni siquiera se podría decir que los voceros de los órganos de las Comunas son electos en segundo o tercer grado, pues nunca en el origen en el primer grado son electos por votación popular mediante sufragio universal, directo y secreto.

Sin embargo, tales voceros integrantes del Parlamento Comunal, Consejo Ejecutivo, Consejo de Planificación, Consejo de Economía Comunal, Consejo de Contraloría Comunal y Banco de la Comuna, son responsables civil, penal y administrativamente por sus actuaciones (art. 55).

1. *Rendición de cuentas*

En cuanto a los voceros integrantes del Consejo Ejecutivo, Consejo de Planificación, Consejo de Economía Comunal, Consejo de Contraloría Comunal y Banco de la Comuna, conforme se dispone en el artículo 49 de la LOC, deben rendir cuentas anualmente de las actuaciones relativas al desempeño de sus funciones ante el Parlamento Comunal, los consejos comunales, las organizaciones socio-productivas, los ciudadanos de la Comuna. Igualmente, los voceros de las instancias antes indicadas, deben rendir cuenta ante las instituciones, organizaciones y particulares que les hayan otorgado aportes financieros o no financieros, sobre el manejo de los mismos.

2. *Revocatoria del mandato*

Los voceros integrantes del Consejo Ejecutivo, Consejo de Planificación, Consejo de Economía Comunal y Banco de la Comuna, pueden ser revocados por decisión de la mayoría simple del Parlamento Comunal, previo informe del Consejo de Contraloría Comunal. En cuanto a los voceros del Consejo de Contraloría Comunal, pueden ser revocados por decisión de las dos terceras partes del Parlamento Comunal (art. 50).

La decisión sobre la revocatoria del mandato de voceros de las instancias de la Comuna, sin embargo, sólo se puede adoptar, conforme al artículo 51 de la LOC, si se dan alguna de las siguientes causales son las siguientes:

1. Actuar de forma contraria a las decisiones tomadas por el Parlamento Comunal.

2. Falta evidente de las funciones que le sean conferidas de conformidad con la presente Ley y la carta fundacional de la Comuna.

3. Representar y negociar individualmente asuntos propios de la Comuna que corresponda decidir al Parlamento Comunal.

4. No rendición de cuentas en el tiempo establecido para ello.

5. Incurrir en malversación, apropiación, desviación de los recursos asignados, generados o captados por la Comuna o cualquier otro delito previsto en el ordenamiento jurídico aplicable.

6. Improbación del informe de gestión.

7. Desproteger, dañar, alterar o destruir el material electoral, archivos o demás bienes de la Comuna.

En cuanto a los voceros del Parlamento Comunal, la revocatoria de sus mandatos sólo procede mediante referendo que debe ser solicitado por el diez por ciento de los electores de la Comuna. Cuando la mayoría de los electores voten a favor de la revocatoria, los voceros se considerarán revocados, siempre y cuando hayan concurrido al referendo un número de electores mayor al quince por ciento del registro electoral de la Comuna (art. 50). Este registro electoral de la Comuna, en todo caso, está conformado por la sumatoria de los registros electorales de los consejos comunales que la integran (art. 52)

Los voceros de la Comuna que hayan sido revocados de sus funciones, quedan inhabilitados para postularse a una nueva elección por los dos períodos siguientes a la fecha de la revocatoria (art. 53).

Por otra parte, conforme al artículo 54 de la LOC, además de por revocatoria, la condición de vocero de la Comuna se pierde por renuncia, por cambio de residencia debidamente comprobado fuera del ámbito geográfico de la Comuna; por resultar electo en un cargo público de elección popular; por estar sujeto a una sentencia definitivamente firme dictada por los órganos jurisdiccionales; y por muerte.

En cualquiera de estos casos, el suplente asumirá las funciones del vocero o vocera de la instancia comunal que ha perdido tal condición.

SECCIÓN SEXTA:

EL RÉGIMEN DE LA CONTRALORÍA SOCIAL O LA INSTITUCIONALIZACIÓN DE LA TÉCNICA DEL ESPIONAJE SOCIAL Y DE LA DENUNCIA POLÍTICA INDISCRIMINADA PARA IMPONER LA IDEOLOGÍA SOCIALISTA

I. OBJETO, PROPÓSITO Y FINALIDAD DE LA CONTRALORÍA SOCIAL

La contraloría social, a la cual se concibe como función compartida entre las instancias del Poder Público y los ciudadanos, y las organizaciones del Poder Popular, se establece en la Ley Orgánica de Contraloría Social (LOCS) [1343] como un mecanismo generalizado de espionaje social, no sólo "para garantizar que la inversión

---

1343   Véase en *Gaceta Oficial* N° 6.011 del 21 de diciembre de 2010. Véase además, sobre esta Ley Orgánica el estudio de Luis A. Herrera Orellana, "La Ley Orgánica de Contraloría Social: Funcionalización de la participación e instauración de la desconfianza ciudadana," en Allan R. Brewer-Carías (Coordinador), Claudia Nikken, Luis A. Herrera Orellana, Jesús María Alvarado Andrade, José Ignacio Hernández y Adriana Vigilanza, *Leyes Orgánicas sobre el Poder Popular y el Estado Comunal (Los Consejos Comunales, las Comunas, la Sociedad Socialista y el Sistema Económico Comunal),* Editorial Jurídica Venezolana, Caracas 2011, pp. 359 ss.

pública se realice de manera transparente y eficiente en beneficio de los intereses de la sociedad," sino para que "las actividades del sector privado no afecten los intereses colectivos o sociales" (art. 2).

Es evidente que estando concebida legalmente la organización del Poder Popular y las organizaciones del Estado Comunal para el Socialismo, y únicamente para el Socialismo, toda actividad de algún órgano del sector público o de cualquier persona organización o empresa del sector privado no comprometida con los principios del socialismo, afectarían en los términos de la Ley "intereses colectivo o sociales" pudiendo ser objeto de denuncia y sometidas a control popular.

Con ello se atribuye a los órganos del Poder Popular no sólo una función contralora general en relación con el manejo de las inversiones públicas en general, sino más destacadamente respecto de las todas las actividades de los individuos y empresas privadas, de cualquier naturaleza que sean, pues en definitiva, en una forma u otra las mismas siempre "inciden en los intereses colectivos o sociales."

El propósito fundamental de esta labor de control o espionaje social generalizado que se asigna a los órganos del Poder Popular, tal como se precisa en el artículo 3 de la LOCS,

> "es la prevención y corrección de comportamientos, actitudes y acciones que sean contrarios a los intereses sociales y a la ética en el desempeño de las funciones públicas, así como en las actividades de producción, distribución, intercambio, comercialización y suministro de bienes y servicios necesarios para la población, realizadas por el sector público o el sector privado."

A tal efecto, para formalizar esta función de investigación, denuncia y persecución indiscriminada es que se dictó específicamente la LOCS, la cual según se indica en su artículo 1, tiene por objeto desarrollar y fortalecer el Poder Popular, mediante el establecimiento de las normas, mecanismos y condiciones para la promoción, desarrollo y consolidación de la contraloría social como medio de participación y de corresponsabilidad de los ciudadanos, y sus organizaciones sociales, mediante el ejercicio compartido, entre el Poder Público y el Poder Popular, de la función de prevención, vigilancia, supervisión y control de la gestión pública y comunitaria, como de las actividades del sector privado que incidan en los intereses colectivos o sociales (art. 1).

Como se dijo, el ámbito de aplicación de la ley es tan general de manera que no sólo se aplican a "a todos los niveles e instancias político-territoriales de la Administración Pública, a las instancias y organizaciones del Poder Popular y a las organizaciones" sino a todas las "personas del sector privado que realicen actividades con incidencia en los intereses generales o colectivos" (art. 4). Solo se establecen como límites para esta labor de espionaje generalizado, el que deben realizarse "en el marco de las limitaciones legales relativas a la preservación de la seguridad interior y exterior, la investigación criminal, la intimidad de la vida privada, el honor, la confidencialidad y la reputación"(art. 4).

Con los propósitos antes mencionados, la LOCS define en su artículo 5 la finalidad de la LOCS "para la prevención y corrección de conductas, comportamientos y acciones contrarios a los intereses colectivos":

1. Promover y desarrollar la cultura del control social como mecanismo de acción en la vigilancia, supervisión, seguimiento y control de los asuntos públicos, comunitarios y privados que incidan en el bienestar común.

2. Fomentar el trabajo articulado de las instancias, organizaciones y expresiones del Poder Popular con los órganos y entes del Poder Público, para el ejercicio efectivo de la función del control social.

3. Garantizar a los ciudadanos y ciudadanas en el ejercicio de la contraloría social, obtener oportuna respuesta por parte de los servidores públicos y servidoras públicas sobre los requerimientos de información y documentación relacionados con sus funciones de control.

4. Asegurar que los servidores públicos y servidoras públicas, los voceros y voceras del Poder Popular y todas las personas que, de acuerdo a la ley representen o expresen intereses colectivos, rindan cuentas de sus actuaciones ante las instancias de las cuales ejerzan representación o expresión.

5. Impulsar la creación y desarrollo de programas y políticas en el área educativa y de formación ciudadana, basadas en la doctrina de nuestro Libertador Simón Bolívar y en la ética socialista, especialmente para niños, niñas y adolescentes; así como en materia de formulación, ejecución y control de políticas públicas.

A tal efecto, como se ha dicho, en el artículo 6 de la LOCS se precisó que el ejercicio del control social, como herramienta fundamental para construcción de la nueva sociedad, como de todas las otras funciones del Poder Popular supuestamente "se inspira en la doctrina de nuestro Libertador Simón Bolívar, y se rige por los principios y valores socialistas." Lo primero no es cierto, y lo segundo, bajo el prisma de esta LOCS, lo que pone en evidencia es el carácter totalitario del socialismo que se pretende implantar montado sobre la base de la denuncia y de la persecución, particularmente respecto de quienes no sean "socialistas," sobre todo cuando se dispone expresamente en el artículo 7 de la Ley que la contraloría social se ejerce "en todas las actividades de la vida social"

II. EL EJERCICIO Y LOS MEDIOS DE LA CONTRALORÍA SOCIAL

1. *Formas de ejercicio.*

El ejercicio de la contraloría social es una tarea que se regula en la LOCS para ser ejercida en forma completamente indiscriminada, de manera que la misma, conforme al artículo 7 de la Ley, se ejerce "de manera individual o colectiva, en todas las actividades de la vida social, y se integra de manera libre y voluntaria bajo la forma organizativa que sus miembros decidan." Solamente cuando se decida "su conformación sea de manera colectiva, todos y todas sus integrantes tendrán las mismas potestades."

En particular, conforme se dispone en el artículo 9 de la LOCS, y sin perjuicio de cualquier "iniciativa popular que con fundamento en el principio constitucional de la soberanía y de acuerdo a las normativas legales, surjan de la dinámica de la sociedad," el control social se ejerce a través de los siguientes medios:

a.   *Individua:* Cuando la persona formula o dirige una solicitud, observación o denuncia sobre asuntos de su interés particular o se relacione con el interés colectivo o social (Art. 9.1).

En el caso específico de los trabajadores, conforme al artículo 12 de la LOCS, los supervisores inmediatos de la administración pública o empleadores del sector privado, deben garantizarles el ejercicio del control social en su ámbito laboral, sin que se vea afectada la eficacia del funcionamiento de la institución o empresa.

b.   *Colectivamente*: A través de la constitución de organizaciones, por iniciativa popular, conformadas por dos o más personas, para ejercer el control de manera temporal sobre una situación específica y circunstancial; o permanentemente, sobre cualquier actividad del ámbito del control social, debiendo estas últimas cumplir con las formalidades de constitución establecidas en la presente Ley y registrase en el Ministerio del Poder Popular de las Comunas. Las condiciones para la constitución de estas organizaciones de contraloría social deben ser establecidas en el reglamento de la Ley (art. 9.2), que se previó para dictarse en un lapso de 6 meses después de la publicación de la Ley, es decir, antes del 21 de junio de 2011.

En todo caso, para efectos de su operatividad, las organizaciones de contraloría social deben elegir democráticamente en asamblea de sus integrantes, a voceros con sus respectivos suplentes, quienes deben ejercer la expresión de la organización ante el resto de la sociedad y deberán rendir cuenta de sus actuaciones ante los demás integrantes de su colectivo (art. 9).

c.   *Orgánicamente*: Cuando sean creadas mediante ley, estableciéndoseles su forma de organización, integración, funcionamiento y ámbito de actuación

2.   *Condiciones para el ejercicio de la contraloría social*

Para ejercer la contraloría social individualmente o como vocero de alguna organización, el artículo 10 de la LOCS requiere que la persona sea mayor de edad, salvo en los casos previstos en leyes especiales; y sujetar su desempeño a los principios y valores que rigen el control social, previstos en la Ley.

En todo caso, la contraloría social constituye un derecho y un deber constitucional y su ejercicio es de carácter ad honoren, en consecuencia quienes la ejerzan no pueden percibir ningún tipo de beneficio económico ni de otra índole, derivados de sus funciones (art. 11). Esto significa, entonces, que siendo una tarea esencialmente política y ad honorem, la contraloría social sólo podrá realizarse por quienes estén financiados para otras actividades y para otros fines políticos, es decir, por quienes reciben remuneración para la realización de otras acciones políticas. Es claro, entonces, que este control social, siendo además, esencialmente de espionaje y denuncia, quedará en definitiva manos de la militancia del partido oficial, el cual, dada la simbiosis que se ha desarrollado con el Estado, no es descartable que resulte financiada con fondos públicos proveniente del Estado Constitucional, al cual precisamente se quiere ahogar con el esquema organizativo del Estado Comunal.

3.   *Deberes de los voceros para la contraloría social*

En cuanto a los voceros de las organizaciones de contraloría social, los mismos tienen los siguientes deberes enumerados en el artículo 8 de la LOCS:

1. Cumplir sus funciones con sujeción estricta a la normativa de la LOCS y las que regulen la materia o las materias del ámbito de su actuación en el ejercicio del control social.

2. Informar a sus colectivos sobre las actividades, avances y resultados de las acciones de prevención, supervisión, vigilancia, evaluación y control del área o ámbito de actuación de la organización.

3. Presentar informes, resultados y recomendaciones a los órganos y entidades sobre las cuales ejerzan actividades de control social.

4. Remitir informe de avances y resultados de sus actividades a los organismos públicos a los que competa la materia de su actuación y a los órganos de control fiscal.

5. Hacer uso correcto de la información y documentación obtenida en el ejercicio del control social.

Dispone finalmente el artículo 14 de la Ley que los ciudadanos que ejerzan la contraloría social que incurran en hechos, actos u omisiones que contravengan lo establecido la Ley, son responsable administrativa, civil y penalmente conforme a las leyes que regulen la materia (art. 14).

III. EL PROCEDIMIENTO PARA EL EJERCICIO DE LA CONTRALORÍA SOCIAL

Tal como lo dispone el artículo 13 de la LOCS, el procedimiento para el ejercicio de la contraloría social, podrá realizarse "mediante denuncia, noticia criminis o de oficio, según sea el caso, por toda persona natural o jurídica, con conocimiento en los hechos que conlleven a una posible infracción, irregularidad o inacción que afecte los intereses individuales o colectivos de los ciudadanos.

El procedimiento debe realizarse de la manera siguiente, tal como lo precisa el mismo artículo 13 de la LOCS:

1. Notificar directamente al órgano competente local, regional o nacional, para la apertura del inicio de la investigación a los efectos de comprobar la presunta infracción, irregularidad o inacción.

2. Realizada la función de contraloría social y efectivamente presumirse las infracciones, omisiones o hechos irregulares, se levantará un acta suscrita por quien o quienes integren la contraloría social, en la cual se dejará constancia fiel de los hechos, acompañada de la documentación que soporte los mismos, la cual tiene carácter vinculante para los organismos receptores.

3. Remitir el acta vinculante, indicada en el numeral anterior, ante las autoridades administrativas, penales, judiciales o de control fiscal que corresponda.

4. Hacer seguimiento de los procedimientos iniciados ante las autoridades administrativas, penales, judiciales o de control fiscal que corresponda, con el objeto de mantener informado a la organización de contraloría social a la que pertenezca.

De este iter procedimental, sin embargo, no queda claro quién es quien realiza la función de control, si "el órgano competente local, regional o nacional" se entiende

de control (como podría ser el caso de la Contraloría general de la República, o de las contralorías estadales o municipales a los efectos del control fiscal) o la persona u organización que hacen la denuncia o realizan de oficio la contraloría social, y quienes son los que realizada la función de control, deben suscribir el acta para dejar constancia de los hechos, cuyo contenido es la que "tiene carácter vinculante para los organismos receptores" se entiende de la denuncia. Con lo cual, los órganos del Estado Constitucional de Control Fiscal o de otra índole quedan como meros "receptores" de actas de contenido vinculante que provienen de actividades de contraloría social realizadas por individuos o voceros de organizaciones, quedando obligados por lo que en ellas se establece.

Nada indica la Ley, sin embargo, respecto del respeto del debido respeto a las reglas del debido proceso, es decir, los derechos del denunciado o espiado a ser oído, a producir pruebas, en fin, a la defensa que se le debe garantizar antes de que se levante dicha acta vinculante y se remita a "las autoridades administrativas, penales, judiciales o de control fiscal que corresponda." Por otra parte, siendo el acta vinculante, es decir, estando condenado políticamente una persona de antemano por unos individuos u organizaciones de contraloría social, solo con base en una "presunción" establecida en un "acta," no se entiende para que efectos reales se la remite a las autoridades mencionadas y cuál es entonces el sentido de que se inicie otro "procedimientos" ante las "autoridades administrativas, penales, judiciales o de control fiscal que corresponda," de cuyo curso debe mantenerse informada a "la organización de contraloría social a la que pertenezca."

La Ley dispone finalmente que "los informes y denuncias producidos mediante el ejercicio de la contraloría social y hayan sido canalizados antes los órganos competentes del Poder Público deben obtener oportuna y adecuada respuesta," al punto de que no producirse ésta, los funcionarios públicos deben ser sancionados "de conformidad a los procedimientos establecidos en la ley que regula la materia."(art. 15).

La maraña normativa y procedimental que se aprecia en esta función de contraloría social, en forma superpuesta con las funciones de los órganos del Estado Constitucional, es de tal naturaleza que en definitiva lo que producirá será la neutralizarán las funciones de control de las "autoridades administrativas, penales, judiciales o de control fiscal" del mismo, que quedarán condicionadas por actas "vinculantes" que, en definitiva, en la mayoría de los casos sólo quedarán como manifestaciones de control de carácter político producto de la función de espionaje, denuncia y persecución sociales contra todo el que sea disidente de la implantación del socialismo, por supuesto, como este sea entendido por cualquier persona que asuma individualmente esta función "ad honorem" de control social.

IV. LA FORMACIÓN DEL CIUDADANO EN LAS FUNCIONES DE CONTRALORÍA SOCIAL

Precisamente para que las funciones de control social se realicen con conocimiento exacto de sus fines, la LOCS obliga a "las distintas instancias y órganos del Poder Público, así como de todas las expresiones del Poder Popular, desarrollar programas, políticas y actividades orientadas a la formación y capacitación de los ciudadanos, ciudadanas y expresiones del Poder Popular en materia relacionada con el ejercicio de la contraloría social" (art. 16).

En particular, se obliga a los Ministerios del Poder Popular con competencia en materia de educación y educación universitaria para diseñar e incluir en los programas de estudio, "de todos los niveles y modalidades del sistema educativo venezolano, la formación basada en la doctrina de nuestro Libertador Simón Bolívar y valores y principios socialistas relativos al control social" (art. 18). En virtud de que la supuesta doctrina de Simón Bolívar sobre "control social" no es conocida, lo que esta norma pretende es imponer la formación de los jóvenes basada en los "valores y principios socialistas" relativos al control social, que en definitiva, como se aprecia de esta LOCS, no es otra cosa que pretender erigir como valor social y principio de vida social, la práctica del espionaje, la vigilancia y la denuncia entre ciudadanos para forzar e imponer una ideología única.

La Ley, por otra parte y en particular, impone al Ministerio del Poder Popular de las Comunas el deber de diseñar e implementar "programas orientados a crear conciencia en la ciudadanía sobre la utilidad y ventaja del correcto funcionamiento de las instancias del Poder Público y del Poder Popular, así como de las organizaciones del sector público en la realización de sus actividades, para contribuir al desarrollo integral del país" (art. 17). En este aspecto, afortunadamente el Legislador olvidó el aspecto de la contraloría social que regula la LOCS que más afecta a la ciudadanía y que es la que se refiere al control sobre todos los aspectos de la vida social respecto de las actividades del sector privado, sobre las cuales nada se indica sobre cual conciencia ciudadana hay que crear.

SECCIÓN SÉPTIMA:

EL RÉGIMEN DEL SISTEMA ECONÓMICO COMUNAL O DE CÓMO SE DEFINE E IMPONE LEGALMENTE UN SISTEMA ECONÓMICO COMUNISTA POR EL CUAL NADIE HA VOTADO

I. FUNDAMENTOS DEL SISTEMA ECONÓMICO COMUNAL VINCULADO AL SOCIALISMO Y AL MODELO DE PRODUCCIÓN SOCIALISTA

El Sistema Económico Comunal (SEC), tal como se define en el artículo 2 de la Ley Orgánica del Sistema Económico Comunal (LOSEC),[1344] es

"el conjunto de relaciones sociales de producción, distribución, intercambio y consumo de bienes y servicios, así como de saberes y conocimientos, desarrolladas por las instancias del Poder Popular, el Poder Público o por acuerdo en-

---

1344   Véase en *Gaceta Oficial* N° 6.011 Extraordinario del 21 de diciembre de 2010. Véase además, sobre esta Ley Orgánica, el estudio de Jesús María Alvarado Andrade, "La 'Constitución económica' y el sistema económico comunal *(*Reflexiones Críticas a propósito de la Ley Orgánica del Sistema Económico Comunal)," en Allan R. Brewer-Carías (Coordinador), Claudia Nikken, Luis A. Herrera Orellana, Jesús María Alvarado Andrade, José Ignacio Hernández y Adriana Vigilanza, *Leyes Orgánicas sobre el Poder Popular y el Estado Comunal (Los Consejos Comunales, las Comunas, la Sociedad Socialista y el Sistema Económico Comunal)*, Editorial Jurídica Venezolana, Caracas 2010, pp. 375 ss.

tre ambos, a través de organizaciones socio-productivas bajo formas de propiedad social comunal."

Se trata, por tanto, de un sistema económico que se desarrolla exclusivamente "a través de organizaciones socio-productivas bajo formas de propiedad social comunal" que conforme a la Ley son solamente las empresas del Estado Comunal creadas por las instancias del Poder Público, las empresas públicas creadas por los órganos que ejercen del Poder Público, las unidades productivas familiares o los grupos de trueque, donde está excluida toda iniciativa privada y la propiedad privada de los medios de producción y comercialización de bienes y servicios.

Es en consecuencia, un sistema económico socialista que se pretende implantar mediante ley, violentando completamente el sistema de economía mixta que garantiza la Constitución donde se establece, al contrario, como uno de los principios fundamentales del sistema constitucional, por una parte, la libertad económica (art. 112), es decir el derecho de todas las personas de poder dedicarse libremente a la actividad económica de su preferencia, sin más limitaciones que las previstas en la Constitución y las que establezcan las leyes, por razones de desarrollo humano, seguridad, sanidad, protección del ambiente u otras de interés social, a cuyo efecto, el Estado está obligado a promover "la iniciativa privada, garantizando la creación y justa distribución de la riqueza, así como la producción de bienes y servicios que satisfagan las necesidades de la población, la libertad de trabajo, empresa, comercio, industria, sin perjuicio de su facultad para dictar medidas para planificar, racionalizar y regular la economía e impulsar el desarrollo integral del país;" .y por la otra el derecho de propiedad privada (art. 115), al limitarse la materialmente sólo sobre los bienes de uso, es decir, aquellos que una persona utiliza, sobre los bienes de consumo, que no son otros que los bienes fungibles, y sobre los medios de producción estrictamente familiar.

En la LOSEC se regula, por tanto, un sistema económico que cambia la estructura el Estado y cuya aprobación solo podría ser posible a través de la convocatoria de una Asamblea Constituyente (ni siquiera mediante reforma o enmienda constitucional), de un sistema de economía mixta a un sistema económico estatista o controlado por el Estado, mezclado con previsiones propias de sociedades primitivas y lugareñas que en el mundo globalizado de hoy ya simplemente no existen, que presuponen la miseria, como forma de vida, para regular y justificar el trueque como sistema, pensando quizás en sociedades agrícolas, o recolectoras, donde al fin del día se podrían intercambiar unos pescados por una liebre; o una consulta profesional de abogado por planchar una ropa; y para crear una moneda al margen de la de curso legal que es el bolívar, llamando así como "moneda comunal" como medio de intercambio de bienes y servicios, a los viejos "vales" de las haciendas de hace más de un siglo, donde el campesino estaba confinado al ámbito geográfico de la economía que controlaba estrictamente el hacendado.

Por ello es que este sistema económico comunal se lo concibe como la "herramienta fundamental para construcción de la nueva sociedad," que supuestamente debe regirse sólo "por los principios y valores socialistas" que en esta LOSEC también se declara que supuestamente se inspira en la doctrina de Simón Bolívar (art. 5).

A tal efecto, reducida la propiedad privada a la mínima expresión, en la Ley se define la "propiedad social" como:

"El derecho que tiene la sociedad de poseer medios y factores de producción o entidades con posibilidades de convertirse en tales, esenciales para el desarrollo de una vida plena o la producción de obras, bienes o servicios, que por condición y naturaleza propia son del dominio del Estado; bien sea por su condición estratégica para la soberanía y el desarrollo humano integral nacional, o porque su aprovechamiento garantiza el bienestar general, la satisfacción de las necesidades humanas, el desarrollo humano integral y el logro de la suprema felicidad social" (art. 6.15).

Con ello se reafirma que el sistema económico comunal que se regula está basado exclusivamente en la propiedad pública, del Estado (dominio del Estado), sobre los medios de producción, de manera que en la práctica, no se trata de ningún derecho "de la sociedad," sino del aparato Estatal, cuyo desarrollo, regido por un sistema de planificación centralizada, elimina toda posibilidad de libertad económica e iniciativa privada, y convierte a las "organizaciones socio-productivas" en meros apéndices del aparato estatal. El sistema omnicomprensivo que se regula, al contrario está basado en la "propiedad social comunal" y que debe ser desarrollada tanto por el Estado Constitucional (los órganos del Poder Público) como por el Estado Comunal (instancias del Poder Popular), como se dijo, exclusivamente a través de "organizaciones socio-productivas bajo formas de propiedad comunal."

Este sistema económico comunal se había comenzado a regular legalmente, al margen de la Constitución, violentándola, luego de haber sido rechazado en la reforma constitucional que se pretendió implementar en ese sentido en 2007, donde por primera vez se formuló formalmente[1345] mediante el Decreto Ley N° 6.130 de 2008, contentivo de la Ley para el Fomento y Desarrollo de la Economía Popular,[1346] la cual por ello fue derogada y sustituida por esta LOSEC, la cual tiene por finalidad, entre otras, de "impulsar el sistema económico comunal a través de un modelo de gestión sustentable y sostenible para el fortalecimiento del desarrollo endógeno (art. 3.2); "fomentar el sistema económico comunal en el marco del **modelo productivo socialista**, a través de diversas formas de organización socio-productiva, comunitaria y comunal en todo el territorio nacional (art. 3.3); e "incentivar en las comunidades y las comunas los valores y principios **socialistas** para la educación, el trabajo, la investigación, el intercambio de saberes y conocimientos, así como la solidaridad, como medios para alcanzar el bien común.(art. 3.8).

En este contexto socialista, la LOSEC define el "modelo productivo socialista" como el

"modelo de producción basado en la **propiedad social**, orientado hacia la **eliminación de la división social del trabajo** propio del modelo capitalista. El

---

1345   Véase sobre la rechazada reforma constitucional de 2007, en Allan R. Brewer-Carías, "La proyectada reforma constitucional de 2007, rechazada por el poder constituyente originario", en *Anuario de Derecho Público 2007*, Año 1, Instituto de Estudios de Derecho Público de la Universidad Monteávila, Caracas 2008, pp. 17-65.

1346   La LOSEC derogó expresamente la Ley la Ley para el Fomento y Desarrollo de la Economía Popular, publicado en la *Gaceta Oficial de la República Bolivariana de Venezuela* N° 5.890 Extraordinario de fecha 31 de julio de 2008

modelo de producción socialista está dirigido a la satisfacción de necesidades crecientes de la población, a través de nuevas formas de generación y apropiación así como de la **reinversión social del excedente**." (art. 6.12)

Se trata en consecuencia, de una Ley mediante la cual se pretende, además, cambiar el sistema capitalista y sustituirlo a la fuerza por un sistema socialista, imponer un sistema comunista, para lo cual sus redactores, basándose en algún Manual vetusto de revoluciones comunistas fracasadas, han parafraseado en la ley lo que escribieron hace más de 150 años Carlos Marx y Federico Engels, en 1845 y 1846, sobre la sociedad comunista. En el conocido libro *La Ideología Alemana*, en efecto, refiriéndose a la sociedad primitiva de la época, en muchas partes aún esclavista y en todas, preindustrial, después de afirmar que la propiedad es "el derecho de suponer de la fuerza de trabajo de otros" y declarar que la "división del trabajo y la propiedad privada" eran "términos idénticos: uno de ellos, referido a la esclavitud, lo mismo que el otro, referido al producto de ésta," escribieron que:

> "la división del trabajo nos brinda ya el primer ejemplo de cómo, mientras los hombres viven en una sociedad natural, mientras se da, por tanto, una separación entre el interés particular y el interés común, mientras las actividades, por consiguientes no aparecen divididas voluntariamente, sino por modo natural,[1347] los actos propios del hombres se erigen ante él en un poder hostil y ajeno, que lo sojuzga, en vez de ser él quien los domine. En efecto, a partir del momento en que comienza a dividirse el trabajo, cada cual se mueve en un determinado circulo exclusivo de actividad, que le es impuesto y del cual no puede salirse; el hombre es cazador, pescador, pastor o crítico, y no tiene más remedio que seguirlo siendo, si no quiere verse privado de los medios de vida; al paso que en la sociedad comunista, donde cada individuo no tiene acotado un círculo exclusivo de actividades, sino que puede desarrollar sus aptitudes en la rama que mejor le parezca, la sociedad se encarga de regular la producción general, con lo que hace cabalmente posible que yo pueda por la mañana cazar, por la tarde pescar y por la noche apacentar ganado, y después de comer, si me place, dedicarme a criticar, sin necesidad de ser exclusivamente cazador, pescador, pastor o crítico, según los casos."[1348]

Los redactores de la Ley, por tanto, no se han percatado de que en las sociedades contemporáneas ya no se reducen a ser aquellas que vivían de la caza y de la pesca, o de la siembra y cría de animales, y de que en las sociedades globalizadas de la actualidad, es imposible no montar la producción en la división social del trabajo; y además, parece que ni siquiera se han percatado que después de tantos años de estancación y de miseria tratando de imponer la sociedad comunista, el desarrollo del sistema capitalista es el que le ha permitido a China catapultarse económicamente,

---

1347   Esta división "natural" se daba según Marx y Engels "en atención a las dotes físicas (por ejemplo, la fuerza corporal), a las necesidades, las coincidencias fortuitas, etc."

1348   Véase en Karl Marx and Frederick Engels, "The German Ideology," en *Collective Works*, Vol. 5, International Publishers, New York 1976, p. 47. Véanse además los textos pertinentes en http://www.educa.madrid.org/cms_tools/files/0a24636f-764c-4e03-9c1d-6722e2ee60d7/Texto%20-Marx%20y%20Engels.pdf

aún cuando sometida a una dictadura del Estado capitalista, y que en Cuba el régimen comunista clama por su auto eliminación para lo cual en 2011 ha comenzado a lanzar a la calle a decenas de miles de antiguos asalariados o servidores del Estado para forzarlos a desarrollar iniciativas privadas, basadas en la supuesta "esclavitud" de la división del trabajo y en el supuesto producto de esa esclavitud, que es la propiedad, convencidos de que en el mundo contemporáneo no es posible "la eliminación de la división social del trabajo" como en cambio se propugna en el artículo 6.12 de la LOSEC, y de que sólo, precisamente, mediante la división social del trabajo es posible la producción industrial, la generación de empleo y la generación de riqueza.

En cambio, para eliminar toda forma de generar riqueza y con ello de trabajo y empleo, la LOSEC declara como pieza esencial del sistema económico comunal, la necesaria "reinversión social del excedente," como principio esencial que rige las organizaciones socio-productivas, definida como "el uso de los recursos remanentes provenientes de la actividad económica de las organizaciones socio-productivas, en pro de satisfacer las necesidades colectivas de la comunidad o la comuna, y contribuir al desarrollo social integral del país" (art. 6.19). Con este principio, los redactores de la Ley incorporaron a su articulado, otros de los pilares del sistema comunista, tal como fue concebido por Marx y Engels, como contrapuesto al sistema capitalista, y es la necesaria "reinversión social de excedente" producto de la actividad económica. Debe recordarse que las sociedades industriales se desarrollaron económicamente, al contrario, gracias a la acumulación del excedente económico que genera el empresario privado y a la reinversión de este excedente para generar mayor crecimiento, que fue en definitiva lo que generó la industrialización. Un sistema en el cual si bien la reinversión social de parte de ese excedente se logra a través del sistema tributario, está basado en la libre iniciativa generadora de riqueza, que a la vez, es la que puede multiplicar el empleo y el trabajo, y generar mayor crecimiento económico.

Basada por tanto en los principios utópicos comunistas de la "propiedad social de los medios de producción," la "eliminación de la división social del trabajo" y la "reinversión social del excedente," la LOSEC está sin duda concebida para implantar en Venezuela el sistema comunista como contrario al sistema capitalista, a cuyo efecto la misma, como se declara en su artículo 1°, se ha dictado para desarrollar y fortalecer el Poder Popular:

> "estableciendo las normas, principios, y procedimientos para la creación, funcionamiento y desarrollo del sistema económico comunal, integrado por organizaciones socio-productivas bajo régimen de propiedad social comunal, impulsadas por las instancias del Poder Popular, del Poder Público o por acuerdo entre ambos, para la producción, distribución, intercambio y consumo de bienes y servicios, así como de saberes y conocimientos, en pro de satisfacer las necesidades colectivas y reinvertir socialmente el excedente, mediante una planificación estratégica, democrática y participativa (art. 2).

Para implantar el comunismo, la LOSEC establece un ámbito omnicomprensivo de aplicación, al establecer, formalmente, que se aplica, por una parte "a las comunidades organizadas, consejos comunales, comunas y todas las instancias y expresiones del Poder Popular, en especial a las organizaciones socio-productivas que se constituyan dentro del sistema económico comunal," es decir, a todo el ámbito del

Estado Comunal; y por la otra, "de igual manera, a los órganos y entes del Poder Público y las organizaciones del sector privado, en sus relaciones con las instancias del Poder Popular" (Art. 3), es decir, a todos los órganos y entes del Estado Constitucional y a todas las instituciones, empresas y personas del sector privado. Es decir, es una Ley tendiente a implementar el comunismo en todos los órdenes.

II. LAS DIVERSAS ORGANIZACIONES SOCIO-PRODUCTIVAS

Como antes se ha dicho, de acuerdo con esta LOSEC, las organizaciones socio-productivas son los "actores" fundamentales que se han diseñado para dar soporte al sistema económico comunal, pues es a través de ellas que se desarrolla el "modelo productivo socialista" que propugna, las cuales se definen como las:

> "unidades de producción constituidas por las instancias del Poder Popular, el Poder Público o por acuerdo entre ambos, con objetivos e intereses comunes, orientadas a la satisfacción de necesidades colectivas, mediante una economía basada en la producción, transformación, distribución, intercambio y consumo de bienes y servicios, así como de saberes y conocimientos, en las cuales el trabajo tiene significado propio, auténtico; sin ningún tipo de discriminación" (art. 9).[1349]

Esta afirmación legal, que también proviene de los viejos Manuales comunistas basados en las apreciaciones de Marx y Engels en las sociedades anteriores a las europeas de mitades del siglo XIX sobre el trabajo asalariado, su explotación y carácter esclavista y discriminatorio, particularmente en relación con las mujeres,[1350] lo cual no tiene ninguna relación con la actualidad en ningún país occidental, parecería que parte de supuesto de que en Venezuela, el trabajo no ha tenido "significado propio" y no ha sido "auténtico," y además, se ha realizado basado en la "discriminación," lo que no tiene base ni sentido algunos. El trabajo es la tarea desarrollada por el hombre generalmente sobre una materia prima con ayuda de instrumentos con la finalidad de producir bienes y servicios; y es, por tanto, el medio para la producción de la riqueza. Ese es el sentido propio y auténtico del trabajo, en cualquier parte del mundo, y su división es de la esencia de la productividad en una sociedad, pues una sola persona no podría nunca cubrir todas las fases de la producción o comercialización de bienes o de la prestación de servicios. De manera que no se entiende qué es lo que se quiere decir que, con la nueva Ley, el trabajo supuestamente ahora adquirirá un significado "propio y auténtico." Por otra parte, en la definición se sugiere que supuestamente hasta ahora, el trabajo se habría realizado en el país sobre la base

---

1349   La Ley de 2008 las definía como las: "unidades comunitarias con autonomía e independencia en su gestión, orientadas a la satisfacción de necesidades de sus miembros y de la comunidad en general, mediante una economía basada en la producción, transformación, distribución e intercambio de saberes, bienes y servicios, en las cuales el trabajo tiene significado propio y auténtico; y en las que no existe discriminación social ni de ningún tipo de labor, ni tampoco privilegios asociados a la posición jerárquica" (art. 8). Dicha autonomía e independencia desapareció totalmente de la nueva LOSEC.

1350   Al referirse al trabajo en la misma obra la Ideología Alemana, Marx y Engels hablaron de la "explotación del hombre por el hombre": y se refirieron a la "distribución desigual, tanto cuantitativa como cualitativamente, del trabajo y de sus productos," en "The German Ideology," *loc. cit.*

de la explotación y la discriminación, lo que está desmentido por la avanzada legislación laboral que ha habido desde la década de los cuarenta.

Ahora bien, ese trabajo con sentido "propio y auténtico," y "sin discriminación," al que se refiere la LOSEC, es el que supuestamente ahora se va a garantizar a través de las organizaciones socio-productivas que se regulan en la ley, mediante las cuales, en forma exclusiva, se desarrollará la economía del país, y que conforme al artículo 10 de la LOSEC, son sólo cuatro: primero, las empresas del Estado Comunal; segundo, las empresas públicas del Estado Constitucional; tercero, las unidades productivas familiares; y cuarto, los grupos de trueque, variándose sustantivamente las formas que se regulaban en el régimen de la derogada Ley de 2008.[1351] O sea, que del trabajo en empresas privadas en las cuales los trabajadoras tienen herramientas para lograr mejores condiciones que ha sido una de las bases del sistema económico del país, se quiere pasar al trabajo exclusivamente en empresas de carácter público, creadas por las instancias del Estado Comunal y por los órganos y entes del Estado Constitucional, sometidas todas a una planificación centralizada, en las cuales no puede haber movimientos sindicales u organizaciones de trabajadores libres que puedan presionar para el logro de mejores condiciones laborales, y donde el "empresario" en definitiva resultará ser un burócrata de un régimen autoritario que usa el "excedente" para su propio confort, explotando a los asalariados alienados.

1. *Empresas del Estado Comunal (Empresas de propiedad social directa comunal)*

En primer lugar, están las "empresas de propiedad social directa comunal," o empresas del Estado Comunal, concebidas como la "unidad socio-productiva constituida por las instancias de Poder Popular en sus respectivos ámbitos geográficos, destinada al beneficio de los productores y productoras que la integran, de la colectividad a las que corresponden y al desarrollo social integral del país, a través de la reinversión social de sus excedentes." (art. 10.1)

Se trata siempre de empresas de propiedad social directa comunal creadas por las diversas instancias del Poder Popular, cuya gestión y administración es por tanto siempre ejercida la instancia que la constituya, de manera que siempre tienen un ámbito geográfico local limitado, confinadas a una comuna o alguna agregación de comunas.

1351   Debe señalarse que la ley derogada de 2008 establecía además, como unidades socio-productivas, las siguientes unidades de trabajo colectivo para la producción y distribución social y para la autogestión: Primero, la Empresa de Producción Social, que era la "unidad de trabajo colectivo destinada a la producción de bienes o servicios para satisfacer necesidades sociales y materiales a través de la reinversión social de sus excedentes, con igualdad sustantiva entre sus integrantes." (art. 9.3), entendiéndose como "trabajo colectivo" la "actividad organizada y desarrollada por los miembros de las distintas formas organizativas, basada en relaciones de producción no alienada, propia y auténtica, con una planificación participativa y protagónica (art. 5.2). Segundo, la Empresa de Distribución Social, que era la "unidad de trabajo colectivo destinada a la distribución de bienes o servicios para satisfacer necesidades sociales y materiales a través de la reinversión social de sus excedentes, con igualdad sustantiva entre sus integrantes." (art. 9.4). Y tercero, la Empresa de Autogestión, que era la "unidad de trabajo colectivo que participan directamente en la gestión de la empresa, con sus propios recursos, dirigidas a satisfacer las necesidades básicas de sus miembros y de la comunidad." (art. 9.5).

2. Empresas públicas (Empresa de propiedad social indirecta comunal)

En segundo lugar están las "empresa de propiedad social indirecta comunal," o empresas públicas del Estado Constitucional, concebidas como la "unidad socio-productiva constituida por el Poder Público en el ámbito territorial de una instancia del Poder Popular, destinadas al beneficio de sus productores y productoras, de la colectividad del ámbito geográfico respectivo y del desarrollo social integral del país, a través de la reinversión social de sus excedentes." (art. 10.2).

En estos casos se trata siempre de empresas de propiedad social indirecta comunal, constituidas por los órganos del Poder Público (República, Estados y Municipios), es decir, empresas públicas nacionales, estadales y municipales pero siempre creadas en un ámbito geográfico y territorial limitado reducido al de alguna instancia del Poder Popular, y cuya gestión y administración corresponde siempre, como principio, al ente u órgano del Poder Público que las constituya; sin que ello obste para que, progresivamente, la gestión y administración de estas empresas sea transferida a las instancias del Poder Popular, en cuyo caso, se constituirían en empresas de propiedad social comunal directa, es decir, en empresas del Estado Comunal.

3. Unidades productivas familiares

En tercer lugar, están las "unidades productivas familiares," es decir, empresas de carácter netamente familiar, concebidas como "una organización cuyos integrantes pertenecen a un núcleo familiar que desarrolla proyectos socio-productivos dirigidos a satisfacer sus necesidades y las de la comunidad; y donde sus integrantes, bajo el principio de justicia social, tienen igualdad de derechos y deberes" (art. 10.3).

Conforme al artículo 14 de la Ley, el grupo familiar que puede confirmar estas empresas familiares, debe estar "integrado por personas relacionadas hasta el cuarto grado de consanguinidad y segundo de afinidad," y debe estar sustentada "en los saberes y el conocimiento propios del grupo familiar, destinado al beneficio de sus integrantes y a satisfacer necesidades de la comunidad donde el grupo familiar tenga su domicilio." Por tanto, un grupo de amigos y relacionados con intereses comunes, no podría establecer una unidad socio-productiva de esta naturaleza, destinada beneficiar a sus integrantes y a satisfacer necesidades de la comunidad.

4. Organizaciones de trueque (Grupos de intercambio solidario)

Por último, en cuarto lugar, la LOSEC regula como organización socio-productiva a los "grupos de intercambio solidario," como organizaciones de "trueque" concebidas como el "conjunto de prosumidores organizados voluntariamente, con la finalidad de participar en alguna de las modalidades de los sistemas alternativos de intercambio solidario."

A los efectos de estos Grupos, estos llamados "prosumidores" se definen en la LOSEC como las "personas que producen, distribuyen y consumen bienes, servicios, saberes y conocimientos, mediante la participación voluntaria en los sistemas alternativos de intercambio solidario, para satisfacer sus necesidades y las de otras personas de su comunidad" (art. 16.6).

En cuanto a estos sistemas alternativos de intercambio solidario, es decir, de trueque, los mismos deben operar conforme al artículo 43, bajo dos modalidades de trueque: En primer lugar, el "trueque comunitario directo," en las modalidades de intercambio de saberes, conocimientos, bienes y servicios con valores mutuamente equivalentes, sin necesidad de un sistema de compensación o mediación.[1352] Y en segundo lugar, el "trueque comunitario indirecto," en la modalidad de intercambio de saberes, conocimientos, bienes y servicios con valores distintos, que no son mutuamente equivalentes y que requieren de un sistema de compensación o mediación, a fin de establecer de manera explícita relaciones de equivalencias entre dichos valores diferentes.[1353]

Para el desarrollo de estas modalidades de trueque, la Ley define los "mercados de trueque comunitario" como los "espacios físicos destinados periódicamente al intercambio justo y solidario de bienes, servicios, saberes y conocimientos, con el uso de monedas comunales" (art. 6.11); y al "sistema de distribución de trueque comunitario" como el "sistema destinado periódicamente al intercambio justo y solidario de bienes, servicios, saberes y conocimientos" (art. 6.20).

Es imposible leer estas modalidades de "trueque" como uno de los pilares fundamentales del sistema de producción socialista que propugna esta Ley, sin que venga a la memoria, precisamente el esquema utópico descrito por Marx y Engels respecto de una sociedad primitiva en la cual se pudiera, el mismo día, ser cazador, pescador, pastor y crítico, de manera que durante el transcurso del día se pudiera intercambiar liebres o gallinas por unos pescados!! Es posible que ello pudiera aplicarse respecto de grupos o humanos o comunidades aislados que pueda haber en territorios inaccesibles, como forma de vida cotidiana, pero no es más que un disparate pensar que se pueda aplicar en las grandes urbes contemporáneas y en las intercomunicadas áreas rurales del país, salvo que se las reduzca todas, a la miseria.

III. EL RÉGIMEN CENTRALIZADO DEL SISTEMA ECONÓMICO CO-MUNAL

Por otra parte, todo el sistema de producción socialista que se regula en la LOSEC, es un sistema económico sometido a una planificación centralizada, conforme a la cual está proscrita toda iniciativa privada, controlado además por el Ejecutivo nacional directamente.

A tal efecto, en la Ley para el Fomento y Desarrollo de la Economía Popular de 2008, se había establecido que el sistema de economía comunal estaba bajo el control del Ejecutivo Nacional, como "órgano rector," que se ejercía por órgano del Ministerio de las Comunas (art. 6). La LOSEC establece ahora que el Ministerio de las Comunas, "es el órgano coordinador de las políticas públicas relacionadas con la promoción, formación, acompañamiento integral y financiamiento de los proyectos socio-productivos, originados del seno de las comunidades, las comunas o constituidos por entes del Poder Público conforme a lo establecido en el Plan de Desarrollo Económico y Social de la Nación, las disposiciones de la Ley, su Reglamento y demás normativas aplicables" (art 7).

1352   Igual definición se encuentra en el artículo 6.22 de la LOSEC.

1353   Similar definición se establece en el artículo 6.23 de la LOSEC.

Sin embargo, de las competencias que se atribuyen, resulta todo un sistema centralizado que conduce el Ejecutivo Nacional, de manera que al Ministerio de las Comunas corresponde conforme al artículo 8, las siguientes atribuciones:

1. Otorgar la personalidad jurídica a las organizaciones socio-productivas.

2. Dictar las políticas y lineamientos en materia de economía comunal, proyectos socio-productivos, formación, financiamiento, intercambio solidario y distribución que impulsen el desarrollo, consolidación y expansión del sistema económico comunal.

3. Asignar recursos financieros y no financieros, retornables y no retornables, para el desarrollo de las organizaciones socio-productivas que se constituyan en el marco de las disposiciones de la presente Ley.

4. Velar porque los planes y proyectos de sistema económico comunal se formulen en correspondencia con el Plan de Desarrollo Económico y Social de la Nación, adecuados a las necesidades y potencialidades de las comunidades, de las comunas o del ámbito geográfico de los sistemas de agregación que surjan entre éstas.

5. Diseñar e implementar programas, por sí o en articulación con otros órganos y entes públicos, así como del sector privado, para la formación, asistencia técnica y actualización tecnológica de las organizaciones socio-productivas.

6. Coadyuvar a la consolidación de las bases del modelo productivo socialista, como instrumento para alcanzar el desarrollo humano integral, sostenible y sustentable.

7. Dictar normas en materia de recuperación y reestructuración de las organizaciones socio-productivas previstas en la presente Ley.

8. Contribuir a la consecución de la justa distribución de la riqueza mediante el diseño, planificación y ejecución de planes, programas y proyectos tendentes al desarrollo del sistema económico comunal, como instrumento para la construcción del modelo productivo socialista, en correspondencia con los lineamientos del sistema nacional de planificación.

9. Diseñar, en articulación con los órganos y entes con competencia en materia educativa y tecnológica, programas para la formación y capacitación de los integrantes o aspirantes a integrar las organizaciones socio-productivas, así como para la certificación de saberes y conocimientos de los ciudadanos y ciudadanas de las comunidades que formen parte del sistema económico comunal.

10. Hacer seguimiento, evaluación y control de las organizaciones socio-productivas con el fin de asegurar que las actividades de las mismas se correspondan con los respectivos planes, proyectos y programas de cualquiera de los sistemas de agregación comunal.

11. Formular y promover políticas de incentivo y acompañamiento integral a las organizaciones socio-productivas que se constituyan en cualquiera de los sistemas de agregación comunal.

12. Establecer las medidas necesarias para promover el acceso de las organizaciones socio-productivas a los distintos procesos de intercambio socio-productivo, nacionales e internacionales, preferentemente con países latinoamericanos y del Caribe, en el ámbito de la integración comunitaria bolivariana y caribeña, para potenciar el humanismo y la hermandad entre los pueblos.

IV. RÉGIMEN JURÍDICO DE LAS ORGANIZACIONES SOCIO-PRODUCTIVAS

1. Constitución de las organizaciones socio-productivas

Las condiciones para la constitución de las organizaciones socio-productivas se establecen en la LOSEC, diferenciándolas según la forma de las mismas.

En primer lugar, en cuanto a las empresas del Estado Comunal, es decir, aquellas "de propiedad social directa comunal," como se establece en el artículo 12, las mismas deben ser constituidas "mediante documento constitutivo estatutario, acompañado del respectivo proyecto socio-productivo, haciendo este último las veces de capital social de la empresa," el cual debe ser "elaborado con base en las necesidades y potencialidades de las comunidades de la instancia del Poder Popular a la que corresponda, y de acuerdo al plan de desarrollo del correspondiente sistema de agregación comunal."

En segundo lugar, en cuanto a las Empresas públicas constituidas por órganos o entes del Poder Público, que son las "de propiedad social indirecta comunal," dispone el artículo 13, que las mismas son constituidas mediante "documento constitutivo estatutario, de acuerdo a las normativas que rijan al órgano o ente público encargado de su constitución." Se entiende que se refiere al acto ejecutivo por medio del cual se decide en la Administración Central o descentralizada, la creación de una empresa, en los términos de la Ley Orgánica de la Administración Pública.

En *tercer lugar*, en cuanto a las "Unidades productivas familiares," el artículo 14 establece que cada una de las mismas se constituye "por un grupo familiar integrado por personas relacionadas hasta el cuarto grado de consanguinidad y segundo de afinidad, mediante documento constitutivo estatutario y un proyecto socio-productivo sustentado en los saberes y el conocimiento propios del grupo familiar, destinado al beneficio de sus integrantes y a satisfacer necesidades de la comunidad donde el grupo familiar tenga su domicilio."

Por último, en *cuarto lugar*, y en cuanto los Grupos de intercambio solidario, el artículo 15 de la LOSEC dispone que los mismos se constituyen "mediante acta de asamblea de prosumidores y prosumidoras, en la cual toda persona natural o jurídica puede pertenecer a un determinado grupo de intercambio solidario para ofrecer y recibir saberes, conocimientos, bienes y servicios," siempre y cuando cumpla con lo establecido en la Ley y su Reglamento. En este último caso, el acuerdo solidario, conforme se indica en el artículo 44 de la ley, se debe llevar a cabo a través de una asamblea constitutiva de "prosumidores", en la que se debe proponer la denominación del grupo, de "la moneda comunal" que se va a utilizar, así como "la especificación y organización del sistema alternativo de intercambio solidario," el cual se debe regir por lo dispuesto en la Ley y su Reglamento.

Dicha Asamblea de "prosumidores" como se establece en el artículo 47 de la Ley, debe estar integrada por quienes voluntariamente decidan conformar el respectivo grupo de intercambio solidario, con las siguientes atribuciones: 1. Diseñar, denominar, valorar, administrar y decidir sobre cualquier aspecto relativo a la moneda comunal, con autorización del Ministerio de las Comunas y conforme a las resoluciones que dicte al efecto el Banco Central de Venezuela; y 2. Coordinar las actividades de organización y funcionamiento de los diferentes espacios del intercambio solidario.

Las organizaciones socio-productivas conforme se exige en el artículo 11 de la LOSEC, deben tener un determinado espacio geográfico en el país, correspondiente a la instancia del Poder Popular en las que se constituyan, donde deben establecer su domicilio. Sin embargo, en el caso de los grupos de intercambio solidario, los mismos deben tener su domicilio en el lugar donde desarrollen las actividades socio-productivas tendientes a ofrecer y recibir bienes, servicios, saberes y conocimientos.

Los documentos de las empresas de propiedad social comunal deben siempre indicar tal carácter, bien sea con la mención expresa de "Empresa de Propiedad Social" o abreviación mediante las siglas "EPS" (art. 17).

Todas las organizaciones socio-productivas contempladas en la LOSEC, conforme se dispone en el artículo 16 de la Ley, adquieren personalidad jurídica, no mediante la inscripción de su documento constitutivo en el registro mercantil, sino mediante el registro del mismo "ante el órgano coordinador," es decir, ante el Ministerio de las Comunas.

A tal efecto, dicho Ministerio debe establecer una dependencia funcional de verificación, inscripción y registro con el fin de mantener el seguimiento y control de las organizaciones socio-productivas y de los espacios de intercambio solidario del país (art. 19).

El procedimiento para la inscripción ante el Ministerio de las Comunas, a los efectos de la obtención de la personalidad jurídica de las diversas organizaciones socio-productivas, es el siguiente:

1. En los casos de organizaciones socio-productivas de propiedad social comunal directa, es decir, de empresas del Estado Comunal, los responsables designados por la instancia de agregación comunal correspondiente, deben presentar por ante el Ministerio de las Comunas la solicitud de registro, acompañada del acta constitutiva de la organización, acta de la asamblea de productores, así como el proyecto socio-productivo. Cuando se trate de empresas de propiedad social comunal indirecta, es decir, de empresas públicas, el funcionario autorizado del órgano o ente de la Administración Pública correspondiente, es el que debe presentar ante el Ministerio de las Comunas el acta constitutiva, así como los estatutos de la organización.

2. El servidor público responsable en el Ministerio de las Comunas debe recibir los documentos que le hayan sido presentados con la solicitud, debe efectuar el registro en un lapso no mayor a quince días, otorgándole personalidad jurídica a todos los efectos legales.

3. Si se encontrare alguna deficiencia en la documentación presentada, el servidor público competente lo debe comunicar a los solicitantes, quienes tienen un lapso de treinta días para corregirla, de manera que subsanada la falta se debe proceder al registro.

4. Si los interesados no subsanan la falta en el lapso indicado, el órgano coordinador debe abstenerse de registrar la organización, y contra esta decisión puede interponerse el recurso jerárquico correspondiente conforme a lo dispuesto en la Ley Orgánica de Procedimientos Administrativos, con lo cual queda agotada la vía administrativa. Los actos administrativos dictados por el Ministerio de las Comunas como "órgano coordinador" pueden ser recurridos por ante la jurisdicción contencioso administrativa.

El Ministerio de las Comunas, sólo puede abstenerse de registrar una organización socio-productiva, además de cuando no se acompañen los documentos exigidos en la Ley o si éstos presentan alguna deficiencia u omisión no subsanada, "cuando el proyecto socio productivo de la organización tenga por objeto finalidades distintas a las previstas en la Ley." (Art. 18) Por tanto, ninguna organización socio-productiva que no sea socialista o que no responda al modelo productivo socialista podría ser registrada.

2. *Derechos de las organizaciones socio-productivas*

Conforme se establece en el artículo 20 de la LOSEC, las organizaciones socio-productivas gozan de los siguientes derechos:

1. Formación y capacitación integral para el trabajo productivo y técnico, en la formulación, desarrollo y financiamiento de proyectos socio-productivos sustentables por parte de los órganos y entes del Poder Público con competencia en la materia.

2. Acompañamiento integral mediante el otorgamiento de recursos financieros y no financieros, retornables y no retornables, por parte de los órganos y entes del Poder Público.

3. La transferencia de servicios, actividades y recursos, en el área de sus operaciones, de acuerdo con lo establecido en el artículo 184 y 185 de la Constitución de la República, en concordancia con las decisiones del Consejo Federal de Gobierno.

Además, dispone el artículo 22 de LOSEC que los órganos y entes del Poder Público, en sus diferentes niveles político-territoriales, deben establecer entre las condiciones para los procesos de contratación de obras, adquisición de bienes y prestación de servicios, "medidas que favorezcan y otorguen prioridad y preferencia a las organizaciones socio-productivas" establecidas en la Ley.

Por otra parte, en caso de situaciones sobrevenidas no imputables a la organización socio-productiva, que afecte su funcionamiento o capacidad de pago, el artículo 23 de la Ley dispone que el Ejecutivo Nacional, a través del Ministerio de las Comunas, podrá aprobar y aplicar programas de recuperación o reestructuración.

3. *Obligaciones de las organizaciones socio-productivas*

En cuanto a las obligaciones de las organizaciones socio-productivas, las mismas se enumeran en el artículo 24 de la LOSEC, en la siguiente forma:

1. Diseñar y ejecutar planes, programas y proyectos socio-productivos, en coordinación con el Comité de Economía Comunal, el Consejo de Economía

Comunal o la instancia de articulación en materia de economía comunal del sistema de agregación, según sea el caso, dirigidos a consolidar el desarrollo integral de la comunidad o las comunidades del ámbito territorial de la instancia del Poder Popular al que corresponda.

2. Promover y practicar la democracia participativa y protagónica, basada en los principios de la ética socialista, y el desarrollo de actividades socio-productivas, surgidas del seno de la comunidad o las comunidades.

3. Cumplir y hacer cumplir las decisiones emanadas del Comité de Economía Comunal, el Consejo de Economía Comunal o la instancia en materia de economía comunal del sistema de agregación, según sea el caso, en función de articular los planes y proyectos socio-productivos a los lineamientos de planificación de la instancia respectiva.

4. Fomentar, promover e implementar el desarrollo de actividades socio-productivas, políticas, culturales, ecológicas, de defensa de los derechos humanos y de las personas en situación de vulnerabilidad, de acuerdo a los principios y valores contenidos en esta Ley.

5. Rendir cuentas y ejercer la contraloría social, como actividad permanente, en el desarrollo de la gestión comunitaria o comunal.

6. Prever medidas adecuadas para promover la defensa, protección y aseguramiento del ambiente en condiciones óptimas para la realización de sus actividades, a los fines de minimizar el impacto ambiental de las operaciones que realicen.

7. Reinvertir socialmente los excedentes para el desarrollo de las comunidades y contribuir al desarrollo social del país, de acuerdo a lo establecido en el Reglamento de esta Ley y a la planificación de la instancia correspondiente.

8. Dar prioridad a las personas y al trabajo como hecho social sobre el capital, con el fin de garantizar el desarrollo humano integral.

9. Garantizar la igualdad de derechos y obligaciones para los integrantes de las organizaciones socio-productivas.

10. Desarrollar acciones estratégicas de enlace y coordinación, para articularse en red con otras organizaciones socio-productivas, a los fines de garantizar el desarrollo y consolidación del sistema económico comunal, para elevar los niveles de eficiencia en la productividad y la cobertura de bienes y servicios, en beneficio de la colectividad y el desarrollo social integral del país.

11. Incentivar la inserción socio-productiva como elemento fundamental del desarrollo social, impulsando el espíritu emprendedor solidario y la cultura del trabajo colectivo. A tal efecto, la propia Ley define el "trabajo colectivo" como la "actividad organizada, planificada y desarrollada por los integrantes de las distintas formas organizativas de producción de propiedad social, basada en una relación de producción no alienada, propia y auténtica, de manera participativa y protagónica"(art. 6.23).

12. Garantizar un modelo de gestión basado en el aprendizaje permanente y regido por los principios propios de la democracia revolucionaria.

13. Hacer transparente las estructuras de costos y precios, así como participar en la creación de nuevas formas de espacios de integración, mediante el intercambio directo de bienes y servicios entre las organizaciones socio-productivas y las comunidades.

4. *Régimen jurídico de las organizaciones socio-productivas*

Como se aprecia de lo antes señalado, la LOSEC establece toda una precisa regulación sobre la constitución y funcionamiento de las organizaciones socio-productivas, diferentes a las que rigen en el ordenamiento jurídico de la República para las organizaciones económicas o empresariales, particularmente diferentes a las establecidas en el Código de Comercio.

Sin embargo, en todos aquellos casos en los cuales el desarrollo de las actividades de las empresas de propiedad social hubiere que aplicar supletoriamente cualquier disposición contenida en norma distinta a la LOSEC, es decir, en el ordenamiento jurídico de la república, de acuerdo con el artículo 39 de la LOSEC, se debe proceder con arreglo a los siguientes principios:

1. Las personas naturales y sujetos públicos o privados que formen parte de empresas de propiedad social comunal no tienen derecho o participación sobre el patrimonio de las mismas, y el reparto de excedentes económicos, si los hubiere, se hará de conformidad con lo establecido en la Ley.

2. Las empresas de propiedad social comunal pueden realizar cualesquiera actos de comercio, pero tales actos no pueden constituir su único o exclusivo objeto empresarial, por cuanto éste debe comprender, además de las actividades que resulten en un beneficio para sus productores que las conformen, la reinversión social del excedente para el desarrollo de la comunidad y contribución al desarrollo social integral del país.

3. La constitución, operación y administración de las empresas de propiedad social comunal debe atender

"a los principios de desarrollo endógeno, equilibrio territorial, soberanía productiva, sustitución selectiva de importaciones y a un modelo de gestión que consolide la relación de producción socialista, determinándose previamente las necesidades de la población donde se proyecte su constitución, con base al potencial local, cultura autóctona y necesidades colectivas, lo cual determinará el tipo de bienes a producir o los servicios a prestar, de acuerdo a lo establecido en el Plan de Desarrollo Económico y Social de la Nación, así como a los lineamientos del Ejecutivo Nacional por intermedio del Ministerio del Poder Popular con competencia en materia de economía comunal."

4. En caso de conclusión, disolución o liquidación de empresas de propiedad social comunal, los bienes resultantes de la liquidación, si los hubiere, no pueden ser apropiados por ninguna de las personas naturales o jurídicas que conformen la empresa, sino que los mismos deben conservar "la condición de bienes de propiedad social comunal directa o indirecta," según corresponda a la clasificación que se les hubiere otorgado para el momento de la constitución de la empresa.

5. En caso de liquidación de empresas de propiedad social comunal indirecta, los bienes resultantes de la liquidación deben ser revertidos a la República o transferi-

dos a otra empresa de propiedad social comunal indirecta, según se indique en el decreto mediante el cual se establezca la liquidación.[1354]

Por otra parte, conforme se dispone en el artículo 21, las organizaciones socio-productivas están "exentas del pago de todo tipo de tributos nacionales y derechos de registro."

V. ESTRUCTURA ORGANIZATIVA Y FUNCIONAL DE LA ORGANI-ZACIÓN SOCIO-PRODUCTIVA

1. *Las unidades de las organizaciones socio-productivas*

La LOSEC establece detalladas regulaciones absolutamente uniformes sobre las diversas Unidades que deben tener las diversas organizaciones socio-productiva, las cuales conforme al artículo 25, son siempre las siguientes: Unidad de Administración (Art. 27); Unidad de Gestión Productiva (Art. 28); Unidad de Formación (Art. 297); y Unidad de Contraloría Social (Art. 30). La LOSEC establece al efecto detalladas regulaciones sobre las competencias de cada una de dichas Unidades.

2. *Integrantes de las organizaciones socio-productivas*

Las organizaciones socioporductivas están integradas por "productoras o productores" quienes conforme al artículo 6.16, "ejercen el control social de la producción, de manera directa o en conjunto con la representación del Poder Público según la organización, sea de propiedad directa comunal o de propiedad indirecta comunal; y cuyas relaciones de trabajo se basan en la igualdad de derechos y deberes, sin ningún tipo de discriminación ni de posición jerárquica." Es francamente difícil siquiera imaginar cómo una empresa, como organización económica para la producción, pueda funcionar sin posiciones jerárquicas diferenciadas.

Estos productores integrantes de las organizaciones socio-productivas, tienen los siguientes derechos indicados en el artículo 32 de la Ley:

1. Recibir una justa remuneración por el trabajo realizado, de acuerdo a la calidad y cantidad del mismo.

2. Recibir apoyo económico de su organización socio-productiva ante situaciones de contingencia, emergencia o problemas de salud, que no posean capacidad de cubrir.

3. Recibir permanentemente formación y capacitación técnica-productiva y político-ideológica, necesarias para su pleno desarrollo dentro de la organización y del sistema económico comunal.

Por otra parte, dichos integrantes de una organización socio-productiva, tienen los siguientes deberes enumerados en el artículo 33:

1354   El numeral 6 el mismo artículo atribuye al Presidente de la República, en Consejo de Ministros, la potestad de reglamentar los aspectos enumerados en este artículo, así como otros que, con la finalidad de regular el funcionamiento de las empresas de propiedad social comunal, ameriten de normativa administrativa

1. Coadyuvar en el desarrollo del sistema económico comunal, para contribuir con la transformación del modelo productivo tradicional, hacia el modelo productivo socialista.

2. Incentivar la participación y ayuda mutua entre sus compañeros y compañeras de trabajo.

3. Promover la ética y disciplina revolucionaria.

4. Rendir cuenta de su gestión cuando le sea requerido.

5. Manejar con eficacia y eficiencia los recursos de la organización, asignados por el Estado u obtenidos por cualquier otra vía.

6. Actuar conforme a los acuerdos alcanzados en asamblea, ya sea del ámbito de su sistema de agregación comunal o las ordinarias y extraordinarias de la organización productiva.

7. Promover y practicar la democracia participativa y protagónica en el desarrollo de las actividades socio-productivas.

8. Participar en el diseño y ejecución de planes, programas y proyectos socio-productivos dirigidos a consolidar el desarrollo integral de la comunidad.

9. Promover la contraloría social y estar sujeto a la misma.

10. Velar por el buen uso de los activos de propiedad colectiva.

3. *Los Voceros de las unidades de las organizaciones socio-productivas*

Cada una de las cuatro Unidades de las organizaciones socio-productivas (Unidad de Administración, Unidad de Gestión Productiva, Unidad de Formación y Unidad de Contraloría Social) deben estar integradas, por tres voceros, designados en la siguiente forma:

Cuando la organización socio-productiva sea de propiedad social comunal directa, es decir, se trate de una empresa del Estado Comunal, todos los integrantes de la Unidad de Organización deben ser designados por la instancia del Poder Popular a la que corresponda la organización socio-productiva, en consulta con sus integrantes (art. 26).

Cuando se trate de una organización socio-productiva que sea de propiedad social comunal indirecta, es decir, de una empresa pública creada por los órganos o entes del Poder Público, los integrantes de la Unidad de Administración deben ser designados en la siguiente forma: Dos representantes del órgano o ente del Poder Público que constituye la organización, los cuales deben ejercer sus labores en igualdad de condiciones con los demás integrantes de la organización; y un vocero de la asamblea de productores y productoras de la organización. En cambio, en cuanto a los integrantes de las Unidades De Gestión Productiva, Formación y Contraloría Social los mismos deben ser designados por la asamblea de productores y productoras.

4. *Condición para ser productores-integrantes de las organizaciones socio-productivas*

Conforme al artículo 31 de la LOSEC, para ser productor integrante de las organizaciones socio-productivas se requiere:

1. Ser venezolano o extranjero residente, habitante de la comunidad con al menos un año de residencia en la misma, salvo en los casos de las comunidades recién constituidas.

2. Ser mayor de quince años, excepto en los casos de las Unidades De Administración y de Contraloría Social donde se requiere ser mayor de dieciocho años.

3. Estar inscrito en el registro electoral de la instancia de la agregación comunal.

4. De reconocida honorabilidad.

5. Tener capacidad para el trabajo colectivo con disposición y tiempo para el trabajo comunitario.

6. Espíritu unitario y compromiso con los intereses de la comunidad.

7. No poseer parentesco hasta el cuarto grado de consanguinidad y segundo grado de afinidad con los demás integrantes de la Unidad de Administración y de la Unidad de Contraloría Social que conforman la organización socio-productiva, salvo las comunidades de áreas rurales y comunidades indígenas.

8. No ocupar cargos de elección popular.

9. No estar sujeto a interdicción civil o inhabilitación política.

10. No ser requerido o requerida por instancias judiciales.

La condición de integrante de la organización socio-productiva se pierde por las siguientes causales enumeradas en el artículo 34 de la Ley:

1. La renuncia a su condición de integrante de la organización.

2. El cambio de residencia comprobado, fuera del ámbito geográfico al que pertenezca la organización socio-productiva.

3. Enfermedad que imposibilite ejercer sus funciones.

4. Estar sujeto a sentencia definitivamente firmen dictada por los órganos jurisdiccionales, que impida el ejercicio de sus funciones.

5. Ser designado o designada en un cargo público de elección popular.

6. Por disolución y/o liquidación de la organización socio-productiva.

7. Por vencimiento del término de duración de la organización socio-productiva.

8. Incurrir en alguna falta grave o infracción de las establecidas en la presente Ley y las que normen las instancias del Poder Popular.

   Conforme al artículo 35 constituye falta grave, las siguientes: a) Observar mala conducta o realizar actos que se traduzcan en grave perjuicio moral o material para la organización socio-productiva; b) El no cumplimiento de los deberes e irrespeto de los principios y valores fundamentales establecidos en la Ley y su Reglamento; c) Cuando se desvíe el destino de los recursos que le hayan sido entregados para su administración, a un uso distinto al planificado y que dé origen a un hecho previsto en la ley como pu-

nible; o d) Cuando los integrantes de la organización socio-productiva in-
cumplan con la reinversión social del excedente en un periodo de un año.

9. Contravenir las disposiciones establecidas en la carta fundacional de la
comuna, las cartas comunales, relativas a las normas de convivencia, o incurrir en alguna falta calificada como grave por esta Ley.

En todo caso, quien infrinja el normal funcionamiento de los grupos de intercambio solidario, incumpla sus deberes o realice acciones que alteren o
perjudiquen el sistema de intercambio solidario en detrimento de los intereses de la comunidad, debe ser desincorporado del grupo de intercambio
solidario, quedando inhabilitado para participar en otros grupos de intercambio por el lapso de un año, sin perjuicio de la responsabilidad civil, penal y administrativa a que hubiere lugar (art. 51).

10. La muerte.

5.   *Normas sobre la gestión productiva y administración de los recursos de las organizaciones socio-productivas*

La LOSEC trae una extensa y detallada regulación sobre la gestión productiva y
sobre la administración de los recursos de las organizaciones socio-productivas.

A tal efecto, la *gestión productiva*, en el marco de las actuaciones de las organizaciones socio-productivas, se define en el artículo 56 de la LOSEC como un proceso para hacer efectiva la participación popular y la planificación participativa, que
responda a las necesidades colectivas y contribuya al desarrollo de las potencialidades y capacidades de las comunidades.

Esta gestión productiva se concreta como una expresión del ciclo comunal, dirigida a la formulación, ejecución y control del plan de desarrollo de la instancia de
agregación comunal a que corresponda (art. 56). Conforme al artículo 57, al referirse a las fases del ciclo comunal productivo, dispone que la gestión productiva, desarrollada a través del mismo, se conforma por cinco fases, las cuales se complementan e interrelacionan entre sí, y que son: el diagnóstico, el plan, el presupuesto, la
ejecución y la contraloría social.

En cuanto a los *recursos* de las organizaciones socio productivas, los mismos se
regulan en la LOSEC, disponiéndose que los recursos financieros y no financieros
son los siguientes: 1. Los que sean transferidos por la República, los estados y los
municipios, conforme a lo establecido en los artículos 184, 185, 300 y 308 de la
Constitución; 2. Los generados en el desarrollo de su actividad productiva; y 3. Los
provenientes de donaciones. (art. 58). Los Recursos financieros se clasifican en Recursos retornables y Recursos no retornables (art. 59): y los Recursos no financieros
se definen como programas, proyectos, instrumentos y acciones para el adiestramiento, capacitación, asistencia tecnológica, productiva y otros, prestados por los
órganos y entes del Poder Público a las organizaciones socio-productivas, necesarios
para concretar la ejecución de las políticas, planes y proyectos que impulsen al sistema económico comunal (art. 60).

En cuanto a los *fondos* de las organizaciones socio-productivas, en los artículos
62 a 65 de la LOSEC se regulan detalladamente los Fondos internos de las organizaciones socio-productivas; los Fondo de mantenimiento productivo; Fondos de atención a los productores, productoras y prosumidores; y el Fondo comunitario para la

reinversión social. Este último, conforme al artículo 65, está destinado al desarrollo social comunitario, comunal y nacional, constituido por recursos financieros excedentes del proceso socio-productivo que serán transferidos por las organizaciones socio-productivas a la instancia del Poder Popular que corresponda, así como al Ejecutivo Nacional.

VI. EL SISTEMA ALTERNATIVO DE INTERCAMBIO SOLIDARIO

1. *Fines y función del sistema alternativo de intercambio (trueque)*

La LOSEC destina un conjunto de normas para regular, en especial, el "sistema alternativo de intercambio solidario," consistente, como se ha dicho, en el sistema de trueque comunitario directo e indirecto (art. 43), el cual se define en el artículo 40, como:

> "el conjunto de actividades propias que realizan los prosumidores y prosumidoras, dentro y fuera de su comunidad, por un periodo determinado, antes, durante y después del intercambio, con el propósito de satisfacer sus necesidades y las de las comunidades organizadas, de saberes, conocimientos, bienes y servicios, mediante una moneda comunal alternativa; y con prohibición de prácticas de carácter financiero, como el cobro de interés o comisiones."

Este sistema alternativo de intercambio solidario, tal como se indica en el artículo 41 de la Ley, tiene como objetivo primordial facilitar el encuentro de "prosumidores" de los grupos que lo conforman, para desarrollar las actividades propias del sistema, organizado en la forma prescrita en la Ley y su Reglamento, con la finalidad de satisfacer sus necesidades y de las comunidades organizadas, propendiendo al mejoramiento de la calidad de vida del colectivo.

Dicho sistema de intercambio solidario, conforme al artículo 42, se basa en los siguientes principios y valores: 1. La buena fe como base de las operaciones de intercambio. 2. El respeto de las tradiciones sociales y culturales. 3. La responsabilidad en la elaboración de bienes y prestación de servicios. 4. La no discriminación. 5. La coordinación de negociación armónica para el intercambio. 6. El impulso del sistema económico comunal. 7. La satisfacción de necesidades del colectivo. 8. El intercambio de saberes, conocimientos, bienes y servicios de calidad. 9. La reducción de los costos de las transacciones asociadas a los participantes, y 10. El rescate de la memoria histórica local.

Los grupos de intercambio solidario, tal como lo precisa el artículo 46 de la Ley, tienen como función primordial facilitar las relaciones de intercambio entre los "prosumidores", para lo cual deben:

1. Estimular y fortalecer el intercambio justo de saberes, conocimientos, bienes y servicios en cualquiera de los espacios de intercambio solidario.
2. Promover la autogestión comunitaria, incentivando la creación y el desarrollo integral de los prosumidores y prosumidoras.
3. Fomentar el desarrollo endógeno sustentable.
4. Fortalecer la identidad comunal y las relaciones comunitarias.

5. Establecer relaciones con los órganos competentes para el desarrollo de la producción de saberes, conocimientos, bienes y servicios como un medio para alcanzar la soberanía alimentaria.

6. Ejecutar todas aquellas actividades que, en el marco de la Constitución de la República y el ordenamiento legal vigente, determinen los prosumidores y prosumidoras reunidos en asamblea.

2. *Los derechos y deberes de los "prosumidores"*

De acuerdo con el artículo 48 de la Ley, los derechos de los "prosumidores" son los siguientes:

1. Recibir del Ministerio del Poder Popular con competencia en materia de economía comunal, información, formación, capacitación y acompañamiento integral para su efectiva participación en el sistema alternativo de intercambio solidario.

2. Participar en la constitución, gestión y toma de decisiones dentro del grupo de intercambio solidario al cual pertenezcan.

3. Recibir información oportuna e incuestionable sobre los lineamientos del grupo de intercambio solidario en el que participan.

4. Elegir y ser elegidos o elegidas para la conformación de las vocerías de los comités de trabajo del grupo de intercambio solidario.

5. Su publicación en el directorio, que a tales efectos llevará el Ministerio del Poder Popular con competencia en materia de economía comunal, para la identificación de los grupos del sistema alternativo de intercambio solidario, junto con sus ofertas de saberes, conocimientos, bienes y servicios.

6. Los que se reconozcan por decisión de la asamblea de prosumidores y prosumidoras, de conformidad con la Constitución de la República y las leyes.

En cuanto a los deberes de los "prosumidores", conforme al artículo 49 de la LOSEC, son los siguientes:

1. Producir bienes o prestar servicios, saberes y conocimientos para los grupos de intercambio solidario, así como consumir, adquirir bienes y servicios de los otros prosumidores y prosumidoras.

2. Inscribirse ante la unidad de verificación, inscripción y registro del órgano coordinador.

3. Cumplir con las obligaciones y responsabilidades asumidas en su grupo de intercambio solidario.

4. Cumplir y hacer cumplir las decisiones emanadas de la asamblea de su grupo de intercambio solidario.

5. Pertenecer a un comité de trabajo y cumplir las tareas que le sean asignadas.

3. *Los espacios del sistema alternativo de intercambio solidario*

El sistema alternativo de intercambio solidario conforme al artículo 50 de la LOSEC puede ser desarrollado en los siguientes espacios: Primero, el Sistema de producción y suministro para el trueque comunitario. Segundo, en los Centros de acopio, tiendas comunitarias y proveedurías. Tercero, en cualquier lugar que determinen los "prosumidores" en el momento requerido, o en su defecto el lugar acordado por la asamblea de "prosumidores". Y cuarto, todos aquéllos que a tales fines fije el Ejecutivo Nacional a través del Ministerio con competencia en materia de economía comunal.

4. *La moneda comunal*

Como se ha dicho, la LOSEC establece la "moneda comunal," como un "instrumento alternativo a la moneda de curso legal en el espacio geográfico de la República," donde funciona el grupo de intercambio solidario, que permite y facilita el intercambio de saberes, conocimientos, bienes y servicios en los espacios del sistema de intercambio solidario, mediante la cooperación, la solidaridad y la complementariedad, en contraposición a la acumulación individua (art. 52). Corresponde al Banco Central de Venezuela regular todo lo relativo a la moneda comunal dentro del ámbito de su competencia (art. 53).

Cada moneda comunal, por otra parte, tiene una denominación que debe ser escogida por cada grupo de intercambio solidario, "la cual responderá a una característica ancestral, histórica, cultural, social, geográfica, ambiental, patrimonial u otra que resalte los valores, la memoria e identidad del pueblo" (art. 54).

La moneda comunal debe ser administrada por los grupos de intercambio solidario, debidamente registrada y distribuida equitativamente entre los "prosumidores", y sólo tendrá valor dentro del ámbito territorial de su localidad; en consecuencia, no tendrá curso legal ni circulará fuera del ámbito geográfico del grupo de intercambio solidario.

El valor de la moneda comunal debe ser determinado "por equivalencia con la moneda de curso legal en el espacio geográfico de la República," a través de la asamblea de "prosumidores", previa autorización del Ministerio de las Comunas, de conformidad con lo previsto en la Ley y las resoluciones que a tal efecto dicte el Banco Central de Venezuela (art. 55).

Por supuesto, leer estas disposiciones sobre unas monedas comunales, cuyo número puede ser infinito, lo que recuerda es el establecimiento de los viejos "vales" ó moneda de las haciendas que existieron hasta comienzos del siglo XX, donde los campesinos quedaban confinados para sus posibilidades de intercambio, lo que después de tantas décadas de desarrollo se logró superar, primero por la emisión de moneda por los bancos privados; y luego, por la creación de la moneda única, que es el bolívar, luego de la creación del Banco Central de Venezuela al cual se le dio el monopolio de la acuñación. Parecería que con estas regulaciones sobre la moneda comunal, no sólo se ignora la realidad del país y su historia, sino que parece que se quisiera regresar a la Venezuela de hace más de cien años, confinándose la economía a lo local, cuando en el mundo la corriente globalizadora muestra lo contrario. Basta para darse cuenta de ello los esfuerzos por el mantenimiento del Euro en Europa, como moneda supranacional.

En todo caso, sobre este disparate de la moneda comunal, baste recordar lo que recordar lo que escribió Heinz Dieterich, el "ideólogo" del "Socialismo del Siglo

XXI" de Hugo Chávez al referirse al antecedente inmediato de esta Ley Orgánica en 2008:

> "2 *Luzbel y el "dinero comunal."* "Ya, en 2008, la Ley Habilitante sobre el Fomento de la Economía Popular nos había advertido que la Escuela de Teología Económica Bolivariana (ETEB) se había apoderado del Palacio de Miraflores. Para acabar con el capitalismo, aquella ley legisló sobre lo que los economistas clásicos llamaron el "velo monetario" y Marx el "fetichismo del dinero" (*Geldfetischismus*): la quimera que el valor económico reside en el dinero y que la explotación se debe a la existencia de éste. Los espejismos resultantes de Miraflores fueron el "dinero comunal" y las "comunas", dos auténticos monumentos al diletantismo económico."[1355]

5. La red de comercio justo y suministro socialista

Por último, la LOSEC regula la "red de comercio justo y suministro socialista," integrada por "las unidades de suministro socialista" y demás medios de distribución y abastecimiento con que cuenta el Estado para tal fin (art. 69), que deben ser promovidas, fomentadas y estimuladas por el Poder Ejecutivo Nacional, a través del Ministerio del Poder Popular con competencia en materia de comercio, (art. 70). A tal efecto, el mismo Ministerio debe implementar las medidas necesarias "para garantizar el acceso de las organizaciones socio-productivas del sistema de economía comunal a la red de comercio justo y suministro socialista" (Art. 71).

Por otra parte, dispone la Ley que el Ejecutivo Nacional, debe establecer las medidas necesarias para "promover el acceso de las organizaciones socio-productivas del sistema económico comunal a los distintos procesos de intercambio socio-productivos nacionales e internacionales, preferentemente con los países latinoamericanos y del Caribe; y muy especialmente con los países miembros de la Alianza Bolivariana para los Pueblos de Nuestra América (ALBA-TCP), para potenciar el humanismo, el internacionalismo y la unión de los pueblos, bajo los principios de la solidaridad, la complementariedad y el respeto a la soberanía nacional (art. 73). No se entiende cómo funcionando con una moneda comunal, puede siquiera pensarse que las organizaciones socio-productivas puedan acceder al comercio internacional.

VII. EL RÉGIMEN SANCIONATORIO DE ORDEN PENAL

Por último, la LOSEC establece entre sus disposiciones, la tipificación de un conjunto de delitos como consecuencia del régimen compulsivo que se establece sobre el sistema económico comunal o sistema económico comunista, y que son los siguientes:

En primer lugar, se tipifica como conducta delictiva penada con prisión de cuatro a seis años, la realización de "acciones contrarias al normal desenvolvimiento del sistema económico comunal", supuesto que se da conforme al artículo 75 de la Ley, cuando "personas naturales o las responsables de personas jurídicas … conjunta o

---

1355   Véase Heinz Dieterich, "Un simulacro de combate a las "ganancias excesivas" del capital. Milagro económico en Venezuela: La Ley de Costos y Precios Justos," 26 de julio de 2011, en http://www.aporrea.org/ideologia/a127333.html

separadamente, contravengan las medidas, condiciones y controles" previstos en la LOSEC "para lograr el normal y adecuado desenvolvimiento del sistema económico comunal, ya sea almacenando, distribuyendo, comercializando, usando o suministrando bienes de consumo, servicios y saberes del sistema económico comunal."

Las personas naturales o las responsables de personas jurídicas que, conjunta o separadamente, para formar parte del sistema económico comunal o vincularse con sus actividades, de conformidad con la presente Ley, incurran en este supuesto delictivo, serán penados o penadas con prisión de seis a ocho años.

En segundo lugar, también se tipifica como conducta delictiva penada con prisión de dos a cuatro años, la realización de "restricciones u obstáculos a la cadena de producción, distribución y acceso de bienes y servicios," supuesto que se da conforme al artículo 76 de la Ley, cuando "personas naturales o las responsables de personas jurídicas ... conjunta o separadamente, impidan, obstaculicen o restrinjan el normal funcionamiento y resguardo, de la producción, distribución, transporte, comercialización, suministro de los bienes de consumo, servicios y saberes del sistema económico comunal.

Igualmente, incurren en este tipo delictivo, "las personas naturales o las responsables de personas jurídicas que, conjunta o separadamente, impidan el acceso a dichos bienes por partes de los consumidores y consumidoras."

En tercer lugar, por último, también se tipifica como conducta delictiva penada con prisión de dos a cuatro años, la "difusión de propaganda o publicidad subliminal, falsa o engañosa," supuesto que se da conforme al artículo 77 de la LOSEC, cuando "personas naturales o las responsables de personas jurídicas ... conjunta o separadamente, realicen propaganda o publicidad subliminal, falsa o engañosa sobre los bienes, servicios y saberes del Sistema Económico Comunal y sus medios de producción, intercambio, distribución, comercialización y suministro."

EL DESQUICIAMIENTO DE LA ADMINISTRACIÓN PÚBLICA

Esta Quinta Parte del Tomo XV, es el texto ampliado de la Video conferencia sobre "Los condicionantes políticos de la Administración Pública en la Venezuela contemporánea", dictada en las *XIV Jornadas de Derecho Público*, Universidad Monteávila, Caracas 5 de marzo de 2015. Una versión anterior fue preparada para la Video conferencia a dictada a los estudiantes de la materia "Fundamentos de la Administración Pública," Escuela de Estudios Políticos y Administrativos, Facultad de Ciencias Jurídicas y Políticas de la Universidad Central de Venezuela, 20 de noviembre de 2014.

La Administración Pública es ante todo un instrumento esencial del Estado establecido para gerenciar, en su nombre y por su cuenta, la satisfacción de las necesidades colectivas de la sociedad que constitucional y legalmente esté obligado a asumir, por lo que como tal instrumento, su misión esencial es estar al servicio de los ciudadanos o administrados.

Por ello, siendo un instrumento del Estado, por su carácter vicarial o servicial, es evidente que la misma está necesariamente condicionada, en su concepción, organización y funcionamiento, por la propia concepción del Estado de la cual forme parte en un momento dado y en un país determinado, conforme al régimen político existente, y a la práctica política del gobierno que lo conduzca.[1356]

Bajo este ángulo, por tanto, al referirnos a la Administración Pública contemporánea en Venezuela, conforme a sus condicionamientos políticos, trataremos de identificar en primer lugar, cuál es la concepción del Estado que existe en la actualidad en el país, partiendo del que define la Constitución como Estado democrático y social de derecho y de justicia y de economía mixta, pero que en realidad se ha configurado como un Estado totalitario; en segundo lugar, cuáles han sido las conse-

---

[1356] Sobre el tema de los condicionantes políticos de la Administración, ya nos ocupamos desde hace unos buenos años, en Allan R. Brewer-Carías, "Les conditionnements politiques de l'administration publique dans les pays d'Amérique Latine", en *Revue Internationale des Sciences Administratives*, Vol. XLV, N° 3, Institut International des Sciences Administratives, Bruselas 1979, pp. 213-233; y "Los condicionamientos políticos de la Administración Pública en los países latinoamericanos" en *Revista de la Escuela Empresarial Andina*, Convenio Andrés Bello, N° 8, Año 5, Lima 1980, pp. 239-258. Igualmente en nuestro libro *Fundamentos de la Administración Pública*, Tomo I, , Colección Estudios Administrativos, N° 1, Editorial Jurídica Venezolana, Caracas 1980, 386 pp.; 2ª. edición, 1984.

cuencias de la configuración de ese Estado Totalitario sobre la Administración Pública, en particular, el proceso de inflación de la organización administrativa que se ha producido, tanto en la Administración Central como en la Administración descentralizada, y la creación de una Administración paralela, con organizaciones denominadas "Misiones" que sin embargo no están sometidas al régimen de la Ley Orgánica de la Administración Pública; en tercer lugar, cuál es la forma del Estado en el país, partiendo de la fórmula constitucional del Estado federal descentralizado, pero que en realidad se ha configurado como un Estado centralizado con membrete federal, y el impacto que ello ha tenido en la centralización progresiva de la Administración Pública; y en cuarto lugar, cuál es el impacto de la creación de un Estado Comunal o del Poder Popular, en paralelo al Estado Constitucional, sobre éste último y la Administración Pública, en particular, por el ahogamiento progresivo de la Administración Pública Municipal.

SECCIÓN PRIMERA:

LA ADMINISTRACIÓN PÚBLICA Y LA CONCEPCIÓN DEL ESTADO: EL PASO DEL ESTADO DEMOCRÁTICO Y SOCIAL DE DERECHO Y DE JUSTICIA, Y DESCENTRALIZADO PREVISTO EN LA CONSTITUCIÓN, AL ESTADO TOTALITARIO DESARROLLADO AL MARGEN DE LA MISMA

En cuanto al primer aspecto a considerar, sobre la concepción política del Estado, como hay que hacer respecto de cualquier Estado, para precisarla lo primero que debe hacerse es acudir a la fuente suprema del ordenamiento que lo regula, que no es otra que la Constitución, en la cual, además, en el mundo contemporáneo, en casi todos los países se ha progresivamente constitucionalizado no sólo a la propia Administración Pública, sino al derecho que la regula, es decir, al propio derecho administrativo, que ahora encuentra en ella, como ley suprema, la principal de sus fuentes.[1357]

Por ello, es un signo de las Constituciones contemporáneas, del cual no se escapa la Constitución venezolana de 1999, encontrar en sus normas previsiones, por ejemplo, sobre el régimen sobre la organización, funcionamiento y actividad de la Administración Pública como complejo orgánico integrada en los órganos del Poder Ejecutivo; sobre el ejercicio de la función administrativa, realizada aún por otros órganos del Estado distintos a la Administración; sobre las relaciones jurídicas que se establecen cotidianamente entre las personas jurídicas estatales, cuyos órganos son los que expresan la voluntad de la Administración, y los administrados; sobre los fines públicos y colectivos que estas persiguen, situados por encima de los intereses

---

1357   Sobre el proceso de constitucionalización del derecho administrativo en Colombia y en Venezuela, véase Allan R. Brewer-Carías, "El proceso de constitucionalización del Derecho Administrativo en Colombia" en Juan Carlos Cassagne (Director), *Derecho Administrativo. Obra Colectiva en Homenaje al Prof. Miguel S. Marienhoff,* Buenos Aires 1998, pp. 157-172, y en *Revista de Derecho Público,* N° 55-56, Editorial Jurídica Venezolana, Caracas, julio-diciembre 1993, pp. 47-59; y "Algunos aspectos de proceso de constitucionalización del derecho administrativo en la Constitución de 1999" en *Los requisitos y vicios de los actos administrativos. V Jornadas Internacionales de Derecho Administrativo Allan Randolph Brewer-Carías, Caracas 1996,* Fundación Estudios de Derecho Administrativo (FUNEDA), Caracas 2000, pp. 23-37.

particulares; sobre los poderes y prerrogativas de los cuales disponen para hacer prevalecer los intereses generales y colectivos frente a los intereses individuales, y además, de los límites impuestos por normas garantizadoras de los derechos y garantías de los administrados, incluso frente a la propia Administración.

Por tanto, en nuestro caso, para identificar la concepción del Estado que deberíamos tener en Venezuela, y consecuentemente, las características de la Administración Pública que debería existir, lo primero que hay que hacer es acudir al texto mismo de la Constitución de 1999, en particular, sus artículos 2, 3, 4 y 299, que disponen que:

Primero, que "Venezuela se constituye en un *Estado democrático y social de Derecho y de Justicia,* que propugna como *valores superiores de su ordenamiento jurídico y de su actuación, la vida, la libertad, la justicia, la igualdad, la solidaridad, la democracia, la responsabilidad social y, en general, la preeminencia de los derechos humanos, la ética y el pluralismo político"* (Artículo 2)

Segundo, que la República "es un *Estado federal descentralizado* en los términos consagrados en la Constitución, y se rige por los *principios de integridad territorial, cooperación, solidaridad, concurrencia y corresponsabilidad* (Artículo 4).

Tercero, que los *"fines esenciales"* del Estado son: "l*a defensa y el desarrollo de la persona y el respeto a su dignidad, el ejercicio democrático de la voluntad popular, la construcción de una sociedad justa y amante de la paz, la promoción de la prosperidad y bienestar del pueblo y la garantía del cumplimiento de los principios, derechos y deberes* reconocidos y consagrados en la Constitución," siendo "la *educación y el trabajo"* los procesos fundamentales para alcanzar dichos fines (Artículo 3).

Y *cuarto,* que "el *régimen socioeconómico"* de la República, "se fundamenta en los *principios de justicia social, democracia, eficiencia, libre competencia, protección del ambiente, productividad y solidaridad, a los fines de asegurar el desarrollo humano integral y una existencia digna y provechosa para la colectividad,"* a cuyo efecto, *"el Estado, conjuntamente con la iniciativa privada, promoverá el desarrollo armónico de la economía nacional con el fin de generar fuentes dede trabajo, alto valor agregado nacional, elevar el nivel de vida de la población y fortalecer la soberanía económica del país, garantizando la seguridad jurídica, solidez, dinamismo, sustentabilidad, permanencia y equidad del crecimiento de la economía, para lograr una justa distribución de la riqueza mediante una planificación estratégica democrática, participativa y de consulta abierta"* (Artículo 299)

Mejor y más completa definición formal del **Estado democrático y social de derecho y de justicia, de economía mixta y descentralizado** en el texto de una Constitución, ciertamente es casi imposible encontrar.

Si esa definición constitucional del Estado se ajustara a la realidad, en Venezuela tendríamos entonces un Estado Constitucional de derecho, y además, democrático, descentralizado, social, de economía mixta y de justicia, que tendría entonces que responder a los principios democráticos del pluralismo y alternabilidad republicana que tendrían que estar garantizados mediante un sistema de democracia representativa y participativa; donde la Administración Pública tendía que ser una Administración democrática, garante del pluralismo y de la participación de todos; y la misma y todos los órganos del Estado tendrían que estar sometidos al derecho y a la justicia, a través de un riguroso sistema de control judicial contencioso administrativo de la actividad administrativa; en el cual privase la primacía de los derechos y garantías constitucionales de los ciudadanos, y que estuviese montado sobre un sistema económico de economía mixta con la participación conjunta, en un marco de libertad económica, tanto del Estado como de la iniciativa privada, en el cual el derecho que lo regule debería asegurar el punto de equilibrio entre las prerrogativas estatales y los derechos ciudadanos.[1358]

En ese Estado que regula la Constitución con lenguaje florido, la Administración Pública tendría además que ser una Administración social, a cargo de políticas sociales, en la búsqueda, junto con la iniciativa privada, de la justicia social, y una Administración Pública descentralizada, compuesta por diversos niveles administrativos territoriales, dotados de autonomía. Además, dicha Administración Pública debería funcionar, en su tarea de gestionar el interés general y asegurar la satisfacción de las necesidades colectivas, sobre la base de los principios de seguridad jurídica, trasparencia, igualdad e imparcialidad, dando con ello, plena garantía a los derechos de los administrados, en un marco de transparencia gubernamental y de pulcro manejo de los recursos financieros sometidos a escrupulosos controles fiscales. Es decir, un en esa concepción constitucional, estaríamos frente a un Estado donde se debería asegurar que los recursos públicos sean invertidos conforme a los principios de buena administración, con la erradicación o persecución de la corrupción administrativa; con una Administración conducida por un servicio civil basado en la meritocracia, que tendría que estar al servicio exclusivo del Estado y no de una determinada parcialidad política; a la cual los ciudadanos puedan controlar en su funcionamiento mediante mecanismos efectivos de participación y mediante el ejercicio de las acciones judiciales necesarias ante un Poder Judicial independiente que pueda efectivamente asegurar su sometimiento al derecho.

Frente a todo ello, sin embargo, lo que primero corresponde determinar es si realmente, en la práctica política del gobierno del Estado de Venezuela, el Estado que tenemos responde a esa concepción y a esos principios, o si realmente solo se trata de enunciados floridos de lo que debería ser, y nada más; pues es claro que a estas alturas del conocimiento de las ciencias políticas, es evidente que para analizar un régimen político y la estructura de un Estado, no sólo debemos basarnos en las denominaciones y definiciones oficiales de los Estado insertas en las Constituciones.

Y efectivamente al confrontar ese Estado descrito en la Constitución con la realidad, lo que resulta es que el Estado que se ha desarrollado en los últimos quince años no es para nada ni un Estado de derecho, ni es democrático, ni es social, ni es de economía mixta, ni es de justicia, ni es descentralizado, pues más bien, en contra de lo que dice la Constitución, lo que se ha desarrollado al amparo del autoritarismo político ha sido un Estado totalitario

---

1358   Véase Allan R. Brewer-Carías, "El derecho a la democracia entre las nuevas tendencias del Derecho Administrativo como punto de equilibrio entre los Poderes de la Administración y los derecho del administrado," en Víctor Hernández Mendible (Coordinador), *Desafíos del Derecho Administrativo Contemporáneo (Conmemoración Internacional del Centenario de la Cátedra de Derecho Administrativo en Venezuela*, Tomo II, Ediciones Paredes, Caracas 2009, pp. 1417-1439.

No hay que olvidar que lo que dice la Constitución no sólo no existe en la realidad, sino que incluso realidad, ni siquiera fue la intención de implementarlo de quienes asaltaron el poder en 1999, mediante una Asamblea Constituyente que controlaron totalmente, luego del intento de golpe de Estado que procuraron dar en 1992.[1359] El texto constitucional, por lo demás, ante los oídos sordos de quienes obnubilados por el deseo y las promesas de cambio del momento no se percataron de lo que se estaba aprobando, como lo denuncié en su momento, tenía ya el germen para el establecimiento de un Estado autoritario,[1360] que más pronto que tarde derivó en el Estado totalitario y populista de la actualidad;[1361] con el cual lo que se ha

---

[1359]   Así se puede apreciar de los papeles del golpe de Estado de 1992 en los cuales la intención era establecer un Estado totalitario y comunista, publicados en: Kléber Ramírez Rojas, *Historial documental de 4 de febrero*, Colección Alfredo Maneiro, Ministerio de la Cultura, Fundación Editorial El Perro y la Rana, Caracas 2006.

[1360]   En 1999, al propugnar el voto NO por la Constitución de 1999 elaborada por la Asamblea Constituyente y sometida a aprobación popular, advertí que si la Constitución se aprobaba, ello iba a implicar la implantación en Venezuela, de "un esquema institucional concebido para el autoritarismo derivado de la combinación del centralismo del Estado, el presidencialismo exacerbado, la democracia de partidos, la concentración de poder en la Asamblea y el militarismo, que constituye el elemento central diseñado para la organización del poder del Estado." En mi opinión –agregue–, esto no era lo que en 1999 se requería para el perfeccionamiento de la democracia; la cual al contrario, se debió basar "en la descentralización del poder, en un presidencialismo controlado y moderado, en la participación política para balancear el poder del Estado y en la sujeción de la autoridad militar a la autoridad civil" Documento de 30 de noviembre de 1999. *V.* en Allan R. Brewer–Carías, *Debate Constituyente (Aportes a la Asamblea Nacional Constituyente)*, Tomo III, Fundación de Derecho Público, Editorial Jurídica Venezolana, Caracas, 1999, p. 339.

[1361]   Aun cuando no se trata ahora de entrar en la definición del Estado totalitario o del totalitarismo como sistema político de dominación total de la sociedad, estimo que basta recurrir a lo expresado por Raymond Aron en su obra *Démocratie et totalitarisme,* donde destaca los caracteres del totalitarismo, como un régimen político donde la concentración del poder es total; existe un partido único que se fusiona al Estado y que posee el monopolio de la actividad política "legítima" y de la aplicación de la ideología del Estado, que se convierte en verdad oficial del Estado; el Estado asume el monopolio de los medios de persuasión y coacción, y de los medios de comunicación; la economía es totalmente controlada por el Estado y se convierte en parte del mismo; se produce la politización de toda actividad, originándose una confusión entre sociedad civil y Estado, de manera que las faltas cometidas por los individuos en el marco de la actividad política, económica o profesional se conforman simultáneamente como faltas ideológicas, originando un terror ideológico y policial. Véase la edición en castellano: *Democracia y totalitarismo,* Seix Barral, Madrid 1968, La diferencia con el *autoritarismo, es que en éste* la concentración del poder sin aceptación de oposición, no excluye la admisión de un cierto pluralismo en sus apoyos y la carencia de una intención o capacidad de homogeneización total de la sociedad. Véase por ejemplo, José Linz, *Totalitarian and Authoritarian Regimes*, Rienner, 2000. Por ello, en los últimos lustros se podía calificar el régimen político venezolano como autoritario. Ya, sin embargo, comienza a aparecer el totalitarismo con toda su faz. Por ejemplo, la Conferencia Episcopal de Venezuela ha advertido la situación al expresar, sobre lo grave de la situación el panorama político actual, sobre "la pretensión de imponer un modelo político totalitario y un sistema educativo fuertemente ideologizado y centralizado" así como "la criminalización de las protestas y la politización del poder judicial, que se manifiesta, entre otras cosas, en la existencia de presos políticos y en la situación de tantos jóvenes privados de libertad por haber participado en manifestaciones" Véase reportaje de Sergio Mora: "Los obispos de Venezuela: Pretenden imponer un modelo totalitario,", en Zenit. El mundo visto desde *Roma*, Roma, 12 julio 2014, en http://www.zenit.org/es/articles/los-obispos-de-venezuela-pretenden-imponer-un-modelo-totalitario

hecho es desmantelar la democracia,[1362] violándose y moldeándose el orden jurídico tal como los gobernantes han querido, sin control alguno entre los poderes públicos ya que todos responden al unísono a un solo mando, empobreciendo y haciendo miserable a un país otrora próspero,[1363] y donde simplemente se ha eliminado la justicia.

La realidad es entonces que a pesar de que la Constitución nos diga que Venezuela se constituye en un Estado democrático y social de derecho y de justicia, y además, Federal descentralizado, lo que tenemos, luego de un despiadado proceso de desinstitucionalización, de desjuridificación, de desjudicialización, de desdemocratización, de desconstitucionalización y de desadministración,[1364] es un Estado Totalitario caracterizado por una concentración total del poder; donde no hay control ni balance entre los poderes del Estado; donde existe un partido político estatal y militar único, fusionado al propio Estado, que actúa como instrumento facilitador, con una ideología única que se califica como "socialismo," concebida como la actividad política "legítima" u "oficial," contraria al pluralismo; que rechaza la democracia representativa y el parlamentarismo; y en el cual, además, se niegan los derechos individuales y la libertad como valor máximo de la democracia, siendo sustituidos por derechos colectivos respecto de los cuales el Estado supuestamente sería el único presuntamente depositario, desconociéndose con ello, además, la solidaridad social y la primacía de la dignidad de la persona humana; un Estado que si bien desde 1975 controlaba con exclusividad la producción del petróleo, ahora ha asumido el monopolio total de todos los medios de producción, de manera que la economía es ahora totalmente controlada por el Estado y se ha convertido en parte del mismo, dando origen a un extraordinario sistema de Capitalismo de Estado, que ha oprimido a las iniciativas privadas, entre otros medios, además de con limitaciones de toda índole, mediante confiscaciones y requisiciones al margen de la Constitución. Un Estado; además, que ha asumido el control total de los medios de persuasión y coacción, incluso mediante la intervención de las policías locales, y la creación de milicias desordenadas que ahora atentan contra el propio Estado; que,

---

1362   Véase Allan R. Brewer-Carías, *Dismantling Democracy. The Chávez Authoritarian Experiment*, New York, 2010; y "La demolición del Estado de derecho y la destrucción de la democracia en Venezuela (1999-2009)," en José Reynoso Núñez y Herminio Sánchez de la Barquera y Arroyo (Coordinadores), *La democracia en su contexto. Estudios en homenaje a Dieter Nohlen en su septuagésimo aniversario,* Instituto de Investigaciones Jurídicas, Universidad Nacional Autónoma de México, México 2009, pp. 477-517.

1363   Por eso Nelson Castellanos con razón anotó recientemente sobre "la gran mentira bolivariana, esa que prometió un proyecto social y terminó instalando el sistema comunista de los Castro. La que ofreció trabajar para los pobres, cuando su intención era seguir manteniéndolos abajo, para poder manipularlos.// Una banda que se preocupó por enriquecerse rápidamente y por tomar el control de todos los poderes del Estado, afín de no tener que irse nunca. Aunque para ello violara leyes y derechos, reprimiera o persiguiera a los ciudadanos que pretendieron oponerse a sus planes de perennidad." En "La mentira Bolivariana", en Noticiero Digital.com, julio 13, 2014, en http://www.noticierodigital.com/2014/07/la-mentira-bolivariana/.

1364   Véase Jesús María Alvarado Andrade, "Sobre Constitución y Administración Pública ¿Es realmente el Derecho Administrativo en Venezuela un Derecho Constitucional Concretizado?" en HERNÁNDEZ G, José Ignacio (Coord.), *100 Años de Enseñanza del Derecho Administrativo en Venezuela 1909-2009,* Centro de Estudios de Derecho Público de la Universidad Universidad Monteávila- Fundación de Estudios de Derecho Administrativo (FUNEDA), Caracas, 2011, pp. 165-263

además, ha asumido el monopolio de los medios de comunicación, con cuya actividad se ha producido la politización de toda actividad particular, originándose una confusión entre sociedad civil y Estado, de manera que las faltas cometidas por los individuos en el marco de su actividad individual se conforman simultáneamente como faltas ideológicas, procurándose la eliminación de cualquier tipo de opinión disidente a la oficial, sirviéndose para ello de la policía y de los militares.

Por todo ello, lamentablemente, es que se puede afirmar que el Estado que hoy tenemos en Venezuela no ya un Estado democrático y social de derecho y de justicia, descentralizado, sino que es un Estado Totalitario, desvinculado a la democracia y que ha configurado una Administración Pública que pasó de servir al ciudadano a servir al propio Estado, y colocada, por tanto, al margen su misión de garantizar el equilibrio entre los poderes del Estado y los derechos de las personas, atendiendo ahora sólo a velar por la imposición a la población inerme, de políticas autoritarias, incluso violando la Constitución y las leyes.

Ese Estado Totalitario de la actualidad, en efecto:

En *primer lugar*, ha hecho desaparecer todo vestigio del Estado de derecho que prevé la Constitución, lo que ha resultado, primero, de la violación sistemática de la Constitución que ha perdido su carácter de ley suprema y su rigidez; segundo, del sistemático proceso de maleabilidad, mutabilidad y desrigidización constitucional conducido, entre otros, por el Tribunal Supremo,[1365] todo lo cual ha producido una completa desjuridificación del propio Estado; y tercero, de la creación, incluso fuera de la Constitución, de un Estado paralelo al Estado Constitucional, denominado Estado Comunal o Estado del Poder Popular, [1366] lo que ha provocado la completa desconstitucionalización del mismo.

En *segundo lugar*, el Estado totalitario ha hecho desaparecer, igualmente, todo vestigio del Estado democrático que regula la Constitución, lo que ha resultado primero, de la distorsión de la representatividad política en la legislación electoral, de manera que con minoría de votos se obtenga mayoría de representantes;[1367] segundo, de las fallas en la implementación de la democracia participativa, que ha resulta-

---

1365   Véase por ejemplo, lo expuesto en Allan R. Brewer-Carías, *Crónica sobre la "in" justicia constitucional. La Sala Constitucional y el autoritarismo en Venezuela*, Colección Instituto de Derecho Público, Universidad Central de Venezuela, N° 2, Caracas 2007; *Práctica y distorsión de la justicia constitucional en Venezuela (2008-2012)*, Colección Justicia N° 3, Acceso a la Justicia, Academia de Ciencias Políticas y Sociales, Universidad Metropolitana, Editorial Jurídica Venezolana, Caracas 2012.

1366   Véase lo expuesto en Allan R. Brewer-Carías, "La desconstitucionalización del Estado de derecho en Venezuela: del Estado Democrático y Social de derecho al Estado Comunal Socialista, sin reformar la Constitución," *en Libro Homenaje al profesor Alfredo Morles Hernández, Diversas Disciplinas Jurídicas*, (Coordinación y Compilación Astrid Uzcátegui Angulo y Julio Rodríguez Berrizbeitia), Universidad Católica Andrés Bello, Universidad de Los Andes, Universidad Monteávila, Universidad Central de Venezuela, Academia de Ciencias Políticas y Sociales, Vol. V, Caracas 2012, pp. 51-82; en Carlos Tablante y Mariela Morales Antonorzzi (Coord.), *Descentralización, autonomía e inclusión social. El desafío actual de la democracia*, Anuario 2010-2012, Observatorio Internacional para la democracia y descentralización, En Cambio, Caracas 2011, pp. 37-84; y en *Estado Constitucional*, Año 1, N° 2, Editorial Adrus, Lima, junio 2011, pp. 217-236.

1367   Véase Allan R. Brewer-Carías, *El golpe a la democracia dado por la Sala Constitucional*, Colección Estudios Políticos N° 8, Editorial Jurídica venezolana, Caracas 2014.

do ser un esquema de movilización popular basada en repartos controlados por el Poder central; [1368] tercero, de la ausencia de separación de poderes en la organización del Estado, en particular, de la ausencia de autonomía e independencia del Poder Judicial; [1369] cuarto, de la distorsión de la Administración Pública que dejó de estar al servicio del ciudadano; quinto, de la militarización avasallante de la sociedad y del Estado; sexto, de la eliminación de la libertad de expresión y comunicación; y séptimo, de la eliminación y violación del principio democrático, al hacer imposible la iniciativa popular de revocación de mandatos, pero permitiendo la revocación de mandaos populares por parte del Tribunal Supremo, en contra de la Constitución. [1370]

En *tercer lugar*, el Estado totalitario también ha hecho desaparecer todo vestigio del Estado Social y de Economía Mixta que regula la Constitución, primero, mediante la eliminación de la libertad económica, el ahogamiento de la iniciativa privada y la eliminación de la garantía del derecho de propiedad; segundo, por la política que ha castigado toda generación de riqueza, resultando la configuración de un Estado montado sobre una política de subsidios y repartos directos; tercero, mediante la formulación de un esquema de economía comunista donde el Estado ha acaparado la totalidad de la actividad económica, basado en sistema de Capitalismo de Estado;[1371] cuarto, mediante la total burocratización del Estado, que se ha convertido en el principal empleador, a costa de haber hecho desaparecer el servicio civil basado en la meritocracia; y quinto, mediante el desarrollo de un Estado Populista, con la forma ahora de Estado Comunal y del Poder Popular, que lo conforme, en todo caso, como un Estado Clientelar.

En *cuarto lugar*, el Estado totalitario adicionalmente ha hecho desaparecer todo vestigio del Estado de Justicia que regula la Constitución, lo que ha resultado prime-

1368   Véase Allan R. Brewer-Carías, "La necesaria revalorización de la democracia representativa ante los peligros del discurso autoritario sobre una supuesta "democracia participativa" sin representación," en *Derecho Electoral de Latinoamérica. Memoria del II Congreso Iberoamericano de Derecho*, Bogotá, 31 agosto-1 septiembre 2011, Consejo Superior de la Judicatura, ISBN 978-958-8331-93-5, Bogotá 2013, pp. 425-449.

1369   Véase por ejemplo, Allan R. Brewer-Carías, "La justicia sometida al poder [La ausencia de independencia y autonomía de los jueces en Venezuela por la interminable emergencia del Poder Judicial (1999-2006)]" en *Cuestiones Internacionales. Anuario Jurídico Villanueva 2007*, Centro Universitario Villanueva, Marcial Pons, Madrid 2007, pp. 25-57; y "Sobre la ausencia de independencia y autonomía judicial en Venezuela, a los doce años de vigencia de la constitución de 1999 (O sobre la interminable transitoriedad que en fraude continuado a la voluntad popular y a las normas de la Constitución, ha impedido la vigencia de la garantía de la estabilidad de los jueces y el funcionamiento efectivo de una "jurisdicción disciplinaria judicial"), en *Independencia Judicial*, Colección Estado de Derecho, Tomo I, Academia de Ciencias Políticas y Sociales, Acceso a la Justicia org., Fundación de Estudios de Derecho Administrativo (Funeda), Universidad Metropolitana (Unimet), Caracas 2012, pp. 9-103.

1370   Véase Allan R. Brewer-Carías, Véase Allan R. Brewer-Carías, *El golpe a la democracia dado por la Sala Constitucional*, Colección Estudios Políticos N° 8, Editorial Jurídica venezolana, Caracas 2014.

1371   Véase Allan R. Brewer-Carías, "Sobre la Ley Orgánica del Sistema Económico Comunal o de cómo se implanta en Venezuela un sistema económico comunista sin reformar la Constitución," en *Revista de Derecho Público*, N° 124, (octubre-diciembre 2010), Editorial Jurídica Venezolana, Caracas 2010, pp. 102-109.

ro, de la ausencia de leyes justas y la multiplicación de leyes inconsultas; [1372] segundo, de una extrema inflación de la inseguridad jurídica, con reformas de las leyes que se realizan mediante su simple republicación en la *Gaceta Oficial*, sin que sean producto de la voluntad popular; [1373] tercero, del sometimiento político del Poder Judicial al Poder Ejecutivo y la Asamblea Nacional, habiendo desaparecido todo vestigio de autonomía e independencia del mismo; cuarto, del hecho de que el Estado se ha escapado de la justicia interna, al no existir materialmente control contencioso administrativo, ni posibilidad de condena al Estrado por responsabilidad, y además, de haberse escapado también de la justicia internacional, al denunciar la Convención Americana de Derechos Humanos [1374] tornándose en un Estado irresponsable; quinto, de haberse puesto la Justicia al servicio del autoritarismo, al punto de que áreas de actividad social carecen de justicia, como es la justicia de paz; y sexto, de haberse desarrollado un sistema de injusticia como consecuencia de la impunidad.

Y por último, en *quinto lugar*, el Estado totalitario también ha hecho desaparecer todo vestigio del Estado descentralizado que bajo una concepción centralista de la llamada "federación descentralizada" reguló la Constitución, lo que se ha consolidado primero, con el desbalance introducido a favor de los órganos del nivel nacional de gobierno en la distribución territorial de competencias; segundo, con un Municipio que no se llegó a configurar efectivamente como la unidad primaria de la organización nacional, pero que ahora tiende a desaparecer con la política de desmunicipalización resultante de la estructuración del Estado Comunal; tercer, con la creación, en paralelo a las entidades políticas territoriales previstas en la Constitución, pero fuera de sus regulaciones, de mencionado Estado Comunal o del Poder Popular, estructurando Comunas [1375] para acabar con los Estados y Municipios, los cuales han sido vaciados de competencia a favor de las mismas; y por último, cuarto, con el ahogamiento y neutralización de las mismas entidades políticas territoriales en paralelo, por parte de los órganos del Poder Ejecutivo Nacional.

Todo ello incluso se ha hecho mediante leyes orgánicas que han pretendido regular supuestamente mecanismos de ejercicio de directo de la soberanía, como son las

---

1372   Véase Allan R. Brewer-Carías, El fin de la llamada "democracia participativa y protagónica" dispuesto por la Sala Constitucional en fraude a la Constitución, al justificar la emisión de legislación inconsulta en violación al derecho a la participación política, *Revista de Derecho Público*, N° 137 (Primer Trimestre 2014, Editorial Jurídica Venezolana, Caracas 2014, pp. 157-164.

1373   Véase Allan R. Brewer-Carías, "Autoritarismo e inseguridad jurídica en Venezuela. O sobre la irregular forma utilizada para "reformar" la Constitución y las leyes," en Rafael Valim, José Roberto Pimenta Oliveira, e Augusto Neves Dal Pozzo (Coordinadores), *Tratado sobre o princípio da segurança jurídica no Direito Administrativo*, Editora Fórum, Sao Paulo, 2013.

1374   Véase Allan R. Brewer-Carías, "La reciente tendencia hacia la aceptación del arbitraje en la contratación estatal en el derecho venezolano," en Jaime Rodríguez Arana, Miguel Ángel Sendín, Jorge E. Danós Ordóñez, Jorge Luis Cáceres Arce, Verónica Rojas Montes, Neil Amador Huáman Paredes (Coordinadores), *Contratación Pública. Doctrina Nacional e Internacional*, Volúmen II, XII Foro Iberoamericano de Derecho Administrativo, Adrus Editores, Arequipa 2013, pp. 803-830.

1375   Véase Allan R. Brewer-Carías, Claudia Nikken, Luis A. Herrera Orellana, Jesús María Alvarado Andrade, José Ignacio Hernández y Adriana Vigilanza, *Leyes Orgánicas sobre el Poder Popular y el Estado Comunal (Los Consejos Comunales, las Comunas, la Sociedad Socialista y el Sistema Económico Comunal)*, Editorial Jurídica Venezolana, Caracas 2011.

Asambleas de ciudadanos y Comunas, sin sufragio ni representación, controladas por el partido oficial de gobierno y dependientes directamente del Poder Ejecutivo Nacional; que lejos de ser instrumentos de participación política, por la ausencia de descentralización, lo que han hecho es configurar un sistema de centralización y control férreo de las comunidades por parte el Poder Central. Se trata más bien de un "edificio" de organizaciones para evitar que el pueblo efectivamente participe y ejerza la soberanía, y para imponerle, mediante férreo control central, políticas por las cuales nunca ha votado ni tendrá la ocasión de votar, basado en una concepción única, que es el socialismo, de manera que quien no sea socialista está automáticamente discriminado, desplazado e impedido de "participar."

No es posible, por tanto, en el marco de esas Leyes Orgánicas del Poder Popular poder conciliar el pluralismo que garantiza la Constitución y el principio de la no discriminación por razón de "opinión política," con las disposiciones de dichas leyes que persiguen todo lo contrario, es decir, el establecimiento de un Estado Comunal, cuyas instancias sólo pueden actuar en función del socialismo y de las cuales todo ciudadano que tenga otra opinión, queda automáticamente excluido.

En esta forma, al fraude a la Constitución,[1376] y además, en fraude a la voluntad popular, que votó en contra de esas reformas que se quisieron introducir en la Constitución en 2007, se le ha impuesto a los venezolanos mediante leyes orgánicas, y por tanto, inconstitucionales, un modelo de Estado totalitario, comunista y centralizado por el cual nadie ha votado, con lo que se ha cambiado radical e inconstitucionalmente el texto de la Constitución de 1999, que no ha sido reformado conforme a sus previsiones, en abierta contradicción y desprecio, se insiste, al rechazo popular mayoritario que se expresó en diciembre de 2007 a la reforma constitucional que entonces se intentó realizar incluso violando la propia Constitución. [1377]

Es a ese marco de Estado totalitario y de desconstitucionalización del Estado, bien alejado al modelo de Estado democrático y social de derecho y de justicia, descentralizado, del cual habla la Constitución, al cual hoy responde la Administración Pública que es su instrumento, y que nos la muestran ya como una institución que dejó de estar al servicio del ciudadano, que abandonó su rol de servir de punto de equilibrio entre los poderes y prerrogativas del Estado y las garantías de derechos de los particulares, pasando, en un marco de su desquiciamiento, a servir ahora, sin seguridad jurídica alguna, exclusivamente al Estado, a sus poderes y prerrogativas, en la medida en que los gobernantes decidan, sin control judicial de naturaleza alguna; siendo su misión el servir de medio de imposición de la voluntad del Estado y de los funcionarios, a los ciudadanos.

Es decir, la Administración se ha convertido en una estructura burocrática discriminadora, sin garantía alguna de imparcialidad, con la cual los ciudadanos ahora sólo pueden entrar en relación en dos formas: por una parte, los que son privilegia-

1376   Véase Allan R. Brewer-Carías, *Reforma constitucional y fraude a la Constitución (1999-2009)*, Academia de Ciencias Políticas y Sociales, Caracas 2009; *Dismantling Democracy. The Chávez Authoritarian Experiment*, Cambridge University Press, New York 2010.

1377   Véase Allan R. Brewer-Carías, *La reforma constitucional de 2007 (Comentarios al proyecto inconstitucionalmente sancionado por la Asamblea Nacional el 2 de noviembre de 2007)*, Colección Textos Legislativos, N° 43, Editorial Jurídica Venezolana, Caracas 2007.

dos del poder, como consecuencia de la pertenencia política al régimen o a su partido único, con todas las prebendas y parcialidades de parte de los funcionarios; y por otra parte, los que como marginados del poder acuden a la Administración por necesidad ciudadana, a rogar las más elementales actuaciones públicas, como es por ejemplo solicitar autorizaciones, licencias, permisos o habilitaciones, las cuales no siempre son atendidas y más bien tratadas como si lo que se estuviera requiriendo fueran favores y no derechos o el cumplimiento de obligaciones públicas, con el consecuente "pago" por los servicios recibidos, y no precisamente a través de timbres fiscales que es lo propio de las tasas legalmente establecidas. En ambas situaciones, lamentablemente, el equilibrio entre poderes del Estado y derechos ciudadanos de los administrados ha desaparecido, sin que existan elementos de control para restablecerlo, de manera que se privilegia y se margina, sin posibilidad alguna de control.

La consecuencia de todo este esquema de ausencia de Estado Social y de Estado de economía mixta, y el establecimiento en su lugar del Estado comunista, burocratizado, populista y clientelar, ha sido que en nombre del "socialismo," Venezuela hoy tiene el record de ser el país que ocupa el primer lugar en el índice de miseria del mundo,[1378] y la sociedad con el más alto riesgo de América Latina.[1379] Esa es la hazaña o el milagro de la política económica del gobierno durante los pasados quince años, que tanto va a costar superar en el futuro,[1380] lo que se suma el indicado primer lugar en criminalidad, falta de transparencia e inflación.

Todo lo cual, sin duda, ha sido uno de los objetivos del gobierno durante los últimos quince años de manera que como lo ha expresado Pedro Palma, la explicación de lo incomprensible, es decir, del "milagro económico" de destrucción a mansalva de la economía y de la creación de miseria, está en que para el gobierno lo importante es mantener la condición de pobreza:

"pues ella crea dependencia del Estado y abona el terreno para el clientelismo político, asegurándose el apoyo incondicional de una amplia masa poblacional a través de la manipulación informativa y de la explotación descarada de su ignorancia y buena fe. Eso, a su vez, facilita el logro e uno de los objetivos

---

1378   Venezuela tiene el "ignominioso" primer lugar en el Índice de miseria del mundo. Véase el Informe de Steve H. Hanke, "Measury Misery arround the World," publicado en mayo 2104, en *Global Asia*, en http://www.cato.org/publications/commentary/measuring-misery-around-world Véase igualmente *Índice Mundial de Miseria*, 2014, en http://www.razon.com.mx/spip.php?ar-ticle215150; y en http://vallartaopina.net/2014/05/23/en-indice-mundial-de-miseria-venezuela-ocupa-primer-lugar/

1379   Véase en http://www.elmundo.com.ve/noticias/actualidad/noticias/infografia-riesgo-pais-de-venezuela-cerro-el-201.aspx.

1380   Pedro Carmona Estanga ha resumido la hazaña económica del régimen explicando que: "Por desgracia para el país, a lo largo de estos 16 años se han dilapidado unos US$ 1,5 billones que no volverán, de los cuales no quedan sino la destrucción del aparato productivo, el deterioro de la calidad de vida, de la infraestructura, de la institucionalidad, y distorsiones macroeconómicas y actitudinales en la población de una profundidad tal, que costará sudor y sangre superar a las generaciones venideras. Esa es la hazaña histórica lograda y cacareada por el régimen." Véase Pedro Carmona Estanga, "La destrucción de Venezuela: hazaña histórica," 19 de octubre de 2014, en http://pcarmonae.blogspot.com/2014/10/la-destruccion-de-venezuela-hazana.html.

buscados, cual es la eliminación de la vieja oligarquía del anterior sistema, para sustituirlo por otra, pero revolucionaria."[1381]

Por eso se ha hablado, con razón, de que la política de Estado en Venezuela es la de una "una fábrica de pobres,"[1382] o como lo ha resumido Leandro Area, al referirse a la noción del "Estado Misional":

"El consumo, por su parte, en un país que no produce nada, viene determinado por la oferta restringida de quien monopoliza, petroliza, en todos los sentidos, los productos de la cesta de las mercancías de consumo social entre los que destacan el trabajo, la salud, la educación, la vivienda, etc. Populismo, demagogia, asistencialismo, plebeyismo, "peronismo", cultura de la sumisión, degradación de la civilidad, desesperanza aprehendida, envilecimiento, etc., son expresiones, realidades, cercanas a la idea del Estado misional." [1383]

Este Estado Misional, Comunista, Burocrático, Populista, Comunal y del Poder Popular y Clientelar, acaparador de toda la actividad económica, en definitiva, es el que ha sustituido al Estado Social y de Economía Mixta que está en la Constitución, conduciendo a su negación total, pues se ha convertido como observa Isaac Villamizar, es un "Estado inepto, secuestrado por la élite de la burguesía corrupta gubernamental, que niega todos los derechos sociales y económicos constitucionales, y que manipula la ignorancia y pobreza de las clases sociales menos favorecidas," argumentando al contrario, que:

"Si Venezuela fuera un Estado Social, no habría neonatos fallecidos por condiciones infecciosas en hospitales públicos. Si Venezuela fuera un Estado Social, toda persona tendría un empleo asegurado o se ejercería plenamente la libertad de empresa y de comercio. Si Venezuela fuera un Estado Social no exhibiríamos deshonrosamente las tasas de homicidios más altas del mundo. Si Venezuela fuera un Estado Social no estaría desaparecida la cabilla y el cemento y las cementeras intervenidas estarían produciendo al máximo de su capacidad instalada. Si Venezuela fuera un Estado Social todos los establecimientos de víveres y artículos de primera necesidad estarían abarrotados en sus anaqueles. Si Venezuela fuera un Estado Social las escuelas no tendrían los techos llenos de filtraciones, estarían dotadas de materiales suficientes para la enseñanza-aprendizaje y los maestros y profesores serían el mejor personal pagado del país. Si Venezuela fuera un Estado Social no habría discriminación por razones

1381   Véase Pedro Palma, "Las Revoluciones fatídicas,", en *El Nacional*, Caracas, 8 de septiembre de 2014, en http://www.el-nacional.com/pedro_palma/Revoluciones-fatidicas_0_478752208.html

1382   En tal sentido, Brian Fincheltub, ha destacado que "Las misiones se convirtieron en fábrica de personas dependientes, sin ninguna estabilidad, que confiaban su subsistencia exclusivamente al Estado. Nunca hubo interés de sacar a la gente de la pobreza porque como reconoció el propio ministro Héctor Rodríguez, se "volverían escuálidos". Es decir, se volverían independientes y eso es peligrosísimo para un sistema cuya principal estrategia es el control." Véase Brian Fincheltub, "Fabrica de pobres," en *El Nacional*, Caracas, 5 de junio de 2014, en http://www.el-nacional.com/opinion/Fabrica-pobres_0_421757946.html

1383   Véase Leandro Area, "El 'Estado Misional' en Venezuela," en *Analítica.com*, 14 de febrero de 2014, en http://analitica.com/opinion/opinion-nacional/el-estado-misional-en-venezuela/

políticas e ideológicas para tener acceso a cualquier servicio, beneficios y auxilios públicos y bienes de primera necesidad. Si Venezuela fuera un Estado Social el problema de la basura permanente en las grandes ciudades ya estaría resuelto con los métodos más modernos, actualizados y pertinentes a la protección ambiental."[1384]

En ese panorama se entiende entonces, la magnitud y significado del condicionamiento político que ese Estado Totalitario ha ocasionado en la Administración Pública, la cual básicamente ha abandonado el parámetro de su misión establecido en el artículo 141 de la Constitución, que al contrario, requeriría que la misma estuviese al servicio de los ciudadanos, fundamentada "en los principios de honestidad, participación, celeridad, eficacia, eficiencia, transparencia, rendición de cuentas y responsabilidad en el ejercicio de la función pública, con sometimiento pleno a la ley y al derecho," nada de lo cual se cumple.

SECCIÓN SEGUNDA:

EL IMPACTO DEL ESTADO TOTALITARIO SOBRE LA ADMINISTRACIÓN PÚBLICA: LA INFLACIÓN DE LA ORGANIZACIÓN ADMINISTRATIVA Y LA CREACIÓN DE LAS "MISIONES" NO SOMETIDAS A LA LEY ORGANICA DE LA ADMINISTRACIÓN PÚBLICA

Ese Estado Totalitario que hoy tenemos, y que como se dijo, es la negación del Estado democrático y social de derecho y de justicia, descentralizado del que nos habla la Constitución, si en alguna organización ha tenido un impacto directo ha sido en la Administración Pública, la cual para responder a políticas populistas, primero, se ha convertido en una Administración burocrática y burocratizada, producto de la desaparición, persecución y estigmatización de la iniciativa privada, y con ello, de toda posibilidad de efectiva generación de riqueza y de empleo en el país, el cual sólo la iniciativa privada puede asegurar; con la lamentable generación de altas tasas de desempleo o de empleo informal; segundo, ha sufrido una inflación inusitada, tanto en los órganos de la Administración Ministerial como en las entidades descentralizadas; y tercero, ha sido objeto de la creación de una Administración paralela, con la creación de las "Misiones," lo que globalmente ha provocado una colosal indisciplina presupuestaria.

I.   LA BUROCRATIZACIÓN DE LA ADMINISTRACIÓN PÚBLICA

Al perseguirse al sector privado y destruirse el aparato productivo, buena parte de la política social del gobierno, como solución al desempleo, lamentablemente ha conducido a la total burocratización de la Administración Pública, lo que ha provocado el aumento del empleo público a niveles nunca antes vistos, por supuesto bien lejos de la meritocracia que prescribe la Constitución, conforme a la cual el ingreso a la función pública debería ser sólo mediante concursos públicos (art. 146). La consecuencia de esta política ha sido que la Administración Pública en Venezuela, des-

---

1384   Véase Isaac Villamizar, "Cuál Estado Social?," en *La Nación*, San Cristóbal, 7 de octubre de 2014, en http://www.lanacion.com.ve/columnas/opinion/cual-estado-social/

pués de quince años de estatizaciones, hoy tiene casi el mismo número de empleados públicos civiles que los que, por ejemplo, existen en toda la Administración Federal de los Estados Unidos.[1385] Ello significa que durante los últimos 10 años el número de empleados públicos aumentó en un 156%, pero con una disminución lamentablemente, quizás en proporción mayor, respecto de la eficiencia de la Administración en la prestación de los servicios sociales.[1386]

En ese esquema de burocracia estatal, por otra parte, quedó simplemente en el papel la norma constitucional que prescribe que "los funcionarios públicos están al servicio del Estado y no de parcialidad política alguna," y de que su "nombramiento o remoción no pueden estar determinados por la afiliación u orientación política" (art. 145), pues en la práctica gubernamental actual sucede todo lo contrario, de manera que para ingresar y permanecer en la función pública, el interesado tiene que haber demostrado lealtad al gobierno y a la doctrina oficial, obligándoseles a estar al servicio del partido de gobierno, de manera que quien no se adapte a ese principio, es simplemente removido de su cargo, sin contemplación. Esta "nueva" función pública es la antítesis de lo que antes se conocía como el estatuto de la función pública, que tenía una Ley que la regulaba, la cual incluso establece concursos para ingresar a la carrera administrativa, y causales de destitución, todo lo cual, en realidad, cayó en desuso.

II. LA INFLACIÓN ORGANIZATIVA EN LA ADMINISTRACIÓN PÚBLICA CENTRAL

La implementación de las políticas populistas por parte del Estado Totalitario ha tenido también un fuerte y directo impacto en la organización de la Administración Pública, que lejos de obedecer a criterios racionales de reforma administrativa, lo que ha provocado es una desusada inflación organizacional que ha originado un desquiciamiento de la organización administrativa en su conjunto.

Ello se ha evidenciado, ante todo, en la organización ministerial, que constituye el grueso de la Administración Pública Central, originado particularmente por el ejercicio incontrolado y sin plan de naturaleza alguna, de la atribución que la Ley Orgánica de la Administración Pública,[1387] siguiendo lo prescrito en la Constitución,

---

1385   En ésta última, por ejemplo, en 2012 existían aproximadamente 2.700.000 de empleados públicos civiles que sirven a 316 millones de personas, y Venezuela, que tiene una población de 30 millones de personas, en 2012 contaba con cerca de 2.470.000 (comparado con los 90.000 que había en 1998). Véase la información de la Office of Personal Management, en http://www.opm.gov/policy-data-oversight/data-analysis-documentation/federal-employment-reports/historical-tables/total-government-employment-since-1962/. Véase Víctor Salmerón, "A ritmo de 310 por día crecen los empleados públicos," en *El Nacional*, Caracas 2 de diciembre de 2012, en http://www.eluniversal.com/econo-mia/121202/a-ritmo-de-310-por-dia-crecen-los-empleados-publicos

1386   Véase Jairo Márquez Lugo, "Venezuela tiene más empleados que Estados Unidos," en http://entresocios.net/ciudadanos/venezuela-tiene-mas-empleados-publicos-que-estados-unidos. Véanse también los datos en: "1999 versus 2013: Gestión del Desgobierno en números,", en https://twitter.com/sushidavid/status/451006280061046784.

1387   La Ley Orgánica der la Administración Pública fue dictada inicialmente en 2001, reformada en 2008 y vuelta a reformar en 2014. Véase el Decreto Ley 1424 de 17 de noviembre de 2014, *Gaceta Oficial* N° 6147 Extra de 17 de noviembre de 2014.

desde 2001 asignó al Presidente de la República en Consejo de Ministros, para fijar, mediante decreto, "el número, denominación, competencia y organización de los ministerios y otros órganos de la Administración Pública Nacional, así como sus entes adscritos, con base en parámetros de adaptabilidad de las estructuras administrativas a las políticas públicas que desarrolla el Poder Ejecutivo Nacional y en los principios de organización y funcionamiento establecidos en la presente ley" (art. 61).

Fue precisamente, conforme a dicha atribución constitucional, que en los últimos quince años se fueron dictado innumerables decretos ejecutivos cambiando, sin orden ni concierto, sobre la organización ministerial a medida que surgían nuevas y circunstanciales exigencias administrativas, creando ministerios, eliminándolos, fusionándolos, dividiéndolos y recreándolos, a medida que además se quería dar algún cargo ministerial a determinadas personas. Así, luego de sancionare la reforma de la Ley Orgánica de la Administración Pública de 2008, mediante el Decreto N° 6.670 de 22 de abril de 2009[1388] se reguló la organización y funcionamiento de la Administración Pública Central, estableciéndose veintiséis (26) Ministerios, enumerándose sus competencias, denominándoselos – siguiendo la pauta ya establecida en el Decreto similar de marzo de 2007[1389] como "Ministerios del Poder Popular,", pero sin base constitucional alguna, sin duda en la búsqueda de implementar una de las rechazadas reformas constitucionales de 2007, que fue la creación del Estado del Poder Popular. Luego de la reforma de la Ley Orgánica de la Administración Pública de 2009, y con la creación sucesiva y en forma aislada de nuevos Ministerios, para 2014 ya la Administración Ministerial había adquirido una dimensión monstruosa, formada en su cúspide por treinta y seis (36) Ministerios del Despacho Ejecutivo (de los 16 que eran en 1999), pero adicionalmente con ciento siete (107) Viceministros designados.[1390]

En septiembre de 2014, el Presidente de la República procedió de nuevo a suprimir y fusionar varios ministerios,[1391] incluso alguno de la importancia como el Ministerio del Ambiente y de los Recursos Naturales Renovables, y además, creó y designó seis (6) Vicepresidentes sectoriales, [1392] además de la Vicepresidencia Ejecutiva. Es esa forma, el Gabinete ejecutivo quedó integrado con los siguientes veintisiete (27) Ministerios: Ministerio del Poder Popular del Despacho de la Presidencia y Seguimiento de la gestión de Gobierno; Ministerio del Poder Popular para Rela-

---

1388   *Gaceta Oficial* N° 39.163 de 22-04-2009.

1389   Decreto 5.246 de 20 -03-2007 en *Gaceta Oficial* N° 38.654 de 28-03-2007.

1390   Véanse el reportaje "Venezuela rompió récord mundial con la mayor cantidad de ministerios," en *Notitarde.com*, 3 de julio de 2014, en http://www.notitarde.com/Pais/Venezuela-rompio-record-mundial-con-la-mayor-cantidad-de-ministerios-2189733/2014/07/03/336113. Véase además, los datos en "1999 versus 2013: Gestión del Desgobierno en números", en https://twitter.com/sushidavid/status/451006280061046784. Véase también la información en Nelson Bocaranda, "Runrunes del jueves 21 de agosto de 2014," en http://www.lapa-tilla.com/site/2014/08/21/runrunes-del-jueves-21-de-agosto-de-2014/.

1391   Véase Decretos N° 1226, 1227 y 1228 de 2 de septiembre de 2014, en Gaceta Oficial No. 40.489 de 3 de septiembre de 2014.

1392   Véanse el Decreto N° 1213 de 2 de septiembre de 2014, en *Gaceta Oficial* N° 40489 de 3 de septiembre de 2014.

ciones Interiores, Justicia y Paz; Ministerio del Poder Popular para Relaciones Exteriores; Ministerio del Poder Popular para la Economía, Finanzas y Banca Pública; Ministerio del Poder Popular para la Planificación; Ministerio del Poder Popular para la Defensa; Ministerio del Poder Popular para Comercio; Ministerio del Poder Popular para las Industrias; Ministerio del Poder Popular para el Turismo; Ministerio del Poder Popular para la Agricultura y Tierras; Ministerio del Poder Popular para la Educación Universitaria, Ciencia y Tecnología; Ministerio del Poder Popular para la Educación; Ministerio del Poder Popular para la Salud; Ministerio del Poder Popular para el proceso social del Trabajo; Ministerio del Poder Popular para Transporte Terrestre y Obras Públicas; Ministerio del Poder Popular para Trasporte Acuático y Aéreo; Ministerio del Poder Popular para Petróleo y Minería; Ministerio del Poder Popular para la Vivienda, el Habitat y el Ecosocialismo; Ministerio del Poder Popular para la Comunicación y la Información; Ministerio del Poder Popular para las Comunas y Movimientos Sociales; Ministerio del Poder Popular para la Alimentación; Ministerio del Poder Popular para la Cultura; Ministerio del Poder Popular para la Juventud y el Deporte; Ministerio del Poder Popular para los Pueblos Indígenas; Ministerio del Poder Popular para la Energía Eléctrica; Ministerio del Poder Popular para la Mujer y la Igualdad de Género; y Ministerio del Poder Popular para el servicio Penitenciario. [1393]

El 17 de noviembre de 2014, mediante Decreto Ley N° 1424, se reformó una vez más la Ley Orgánica de la Administración Pública,[1394] consistiendo dicha reforma, básicamente en los siguientes aspectos:

En *primer lugar*, si bien se conservó la orientación de regular a la "Administración Pública" como una sola organización que comprende la de la República (nacional), la de los estados y la municipal (art. 1), en forma centralizada, sometida toda a los lineamientos de la planificación centralizada, bajo la dirección del Presidente de la República (art. 46) y la coordinación del Vicepresidente ejecutivo (art. 49,3), en cuanto al ámbito de aplicación de la misma se estableció que es respecto de la "Administración Pública Nacional, *así como* de las de los estados, distritos metropolitanos, el Distrito capital, el territorio federal Miranda y las de los municipios"(art. 2).

En *segundo lugar*, en el texto de la Ley se incorporó formalmente la denominación de Ministerios "del Poder Popular" (arts. 49, 50, 52, 60, 64, 68, 79, 85, 94, 123) que hasta entonces sólo se había establecido de hecho en la práctica gubernamental para denominar los despachos ministeriales, sin base legal alguna.

En *tercer lugar*, se eliminó la inclusión entre los Órganos Superiores del Nivel Central de la Administración Pública Nacional (art. 44), de la Comisión Central de Planificación, la cual sin embargo se continuó regulando como un órgano del Nivel Central de la Administración Pública Nacional (arts. 60).

En *cuarto lugar*, se creó como órgano superior de dirección del Nivel Central de la Administración Pública Nacional, a las "Vicepresidencias Sectoriales," eliminándose las anteriores "juntas sectoriales" (arts. 44, 49-51), establecidas para la supervi-

---

1393   *Idem.*
1394   *Gaceta Oficial* Extra N° 6147 de 17-11-2014.

sión y control de los ministerios que se agrupen en los sectores. Ésta en realidad puede considerarse como la única reforma realmente sustantiva introducida en 2014, regulándose dichas Vicepresidencias Sectoriales como órganos encargados de la supervisión y control funcional, administrativo y presupuestario de los ministerios del poder popular que determine el Presidente de la república, quien además debe fijar el número, denominación, organización, funcionamiento y competencias de dichas Vicepresidencias (art. 49).

En *quinto lugar*, se incorporó en la regulación de la Ley a una figura nueva denominada "jefe de gobierno" (art. 34, 41) que está relacionada con la figura de las "autoridades regionales" como integrantes de "los órganos superiores de dirección del Nivel Central de la Administración Pública nacional" (art. 44, 71).

En *sexto lugar*, la reincorporación en el texto de la ley de la noción de "autonomía", para calificar a los "institutos públicos" denominándose ahora "institutos públicos y autónomos" (arts. 98-102, 107).

En *séptimo lugar*, se estableció el régimen de la desconcentración administrativa mediante la creación de órganos y servicios desconcentrados, no sólo en el seno de los ministerios, sino de la Vicepresidencia ejecutiva, de las vicepresidencias sectoriales, y de las oficinas nacionales (arts. 92 ss.).

Y en *octavo lugar*, la previsión de posibilidad de la adscripción de los "entes" no sólo a "órganos" de la Administración, sino también a otros "entes" (arts. 118, 119, 120).

Ahora bien, en cuanto a la organización y funcionamiento de los Ministerios, de acuerdo con la nueva reforma de la Ley Orgánica de noviembre de 2014, mediante el Decreto N° 1.612 de 18 de febrero de 2015[1395] sobre organización y funcionamiento de la Administración Pública Central, se establecieron los siguientes veintisiete (27) Ministerios y se enumeraron sus competencias, denominándoselos, siguiendo la pauta ya establecida en los Decretos similares de 2007 y 2009,[1396] como "Ministerios del Poder Popular" pero ahora con base legal: 1. Ministerio del Poder Popular del Despacho de la Presidencia y Seguimiento de la gestión de Gobierno; 2. Ministerio del Poder Popular para Relaciones Interiores, Justicia y Paz; 3. Ministerio del Poder Popular para Relaciones Exteriores; 4. Ministerio del Poder Popular para Economía y Finanzas; 5. Ministerio del Poder Popular para la Defensa; 6. Ministerio del Poder Popular para el Comercio; 7. Ministerio del Poder Popular para las Industrias; 8. Ministerio del Poder Popular para el Turismo; 9. Ministerio del Poder Popular para la Agricultura y Tierras; 10. Ministerio del Poder Popular para la Educación; 11. Ministerio del Poder Popular para la Salud; 12. Ministerio del Poder Popular para el Proceso Social del Trabajo; 13. Ministerio del Poder Popular para Ecosocialismo, Hábitat y Viviendas; 14. Ministerio del Poder Popular de Petróleo y Minería; 15. Ministerio del Poder Popular de Planificación; 16. Ministerio del Poder Popular para Educación Universitaria, Ciencia y Tecnología; 17. Ministerio del Poder Popular para la Comunicación y la Información; 18. Ministerio del Poder Popu-

---

1395   *Gaceta Oficial* N° 1.612 de 18-02-2015.

1396   Decreto N° 1.612 6.670 de 22 de abril de 2009 en *Gaceta Oficial* N° 39.163 de 22-04-2009; y Decreto 5.246 de 20 -03-2007 en *Gaceta Oficial* N° 38.654 de 28-03-2007.

lar para las Comunas y los Movimientos Sociales; 19. Ministerio del Poder Popular para la Alimentación; 20. Ministerio del Poder Popular para la Cultura; 21. Ministerio del Poder Popular para la Juventud y el Deporte; 22. Ministerio del Poder Popular para los Pueblos Indígenas; 23. Ministerio del Poder Popular para la Mujer y la Igualdad de Género 24. Ministerio del Poder Popular para el Servicio Penitenciario; 25. Ministerio del Poder Popular para el Transporte Acuático y Aéreo; 26. Ministerio del Poder Popular para el Transporte Terrestre y Obras Públicas; 27. Ministerio del Poder Popular para la Energía Eléctrica. [1397].

En todo caso, de acuerdo con el artículo 17 del decreto de Organización y Funcionamiento de la Administración Pública, conforme a la Ley Orgánica, la estructura organizativa básica de cada Ministerio, está integrada por el Despacho del Ministro y los Despachos de los Viceministros; y además por los siguientes órganos: En el *nivel de apoyo*, por las Direcciones Generales, y las siguientes unidades con rango de Dirección general: Oficinas Estratégicas de Seguimiento y Evaluación de Políticas Públicas; Consultorías Jurídicas; Oficinas de Auditoría Interna; Oficinas de Atención Ciudadana; Oficinas de Gestión Comunicacional; Oficinas de Planificación y Presupuesto; Oficinas de gestión Humana; Oficinas de Gestión Administrativa; y Oficinas de Tecnología de la Información y la Comunicación. En el *nivel sustantivo*, cada Ministerio está integrado por los Despachos de los Viceministros, Direcciones Generales, Direcciones, y las Divisiones dependientes jerárquicamente de las mismas. Y en el *nivel desconcentrado territorialmente,* por las unidades que ejerzan representación del Ministerio a nivel regional, estadal, municipal o comunal.

Cada Ministerio debe estar regulado internamente por un Reglamento Orgánico dictado por el Presidente en Consejo de Ministros, en el cual se deben determinar la estructura y las funciones de los Viceministros y de las demás dependencias que integran cada Ministerio. [1398] En los mencionados Reglamentos Orgánicos, de acuerdo con el artículo 65 del Decreto de Organización y Funcionamiento de 2015, dictados con la participación de los Vicepresidentes Sectoriales, se deberá establecer la adscripción de los entes descentralizados a los diversos Ministerios.

1397   Sobre la evolución del número y competencias de los Ministerios antes de la reforma constitucional de 1999, véase Allan R. Brewer-Carías, *Principios del Régimen Jurídico de la Organización Administrativa... cit.,* pp. 127 y ss. Sobre la misma materia con posterioridad a 1999 véase Jesús María Alvarado Andrade, "Consideraciones sobre la evolución de la Administración Ministerial", en este libro.

1398   Véase los Decretos N° 1.614 a 1.629, mediante los cuales se dictan los Reglamentos Orgánicos de los Ministerios del Poder Popular para Industrias; para Energía Eléctrica; de Economía y Finanzas; para el Proceso Social del Trabajo; para las Comunas y los Movimientos Sociales; de Planificación; de Petróleo y Minería; para la Agricultura y Tierras; para el Servicio Penitenciario; para la Defensa; para Relaciones Interiores, Justicia y Paz; del Despacho de la Presidencia y Seguimiento de la Gestión de Gobierno; para los Pueblos Indígenas; para Educación Universitaria, Ciencia y Tecnología; para la Mujer y la Igualdad de Género; y para la Cultura.- (Véase *Gaceta Oficial* N° 6.176 Extra. De 20 de febrero de 2015.

III. LA INFLACIÓN ORGANIZATIVA EN LA ADMINISTRACIÓN PÚBLICA DESCENTRALIZADA FUNCIONALMENTE

Pero el desquiciamiento de la Administración Pública no sólo ha afectado a la Administración Central, sino también a la Administración descentralizada la cual ha sufrido también un proceso de inflación organizativa inusitada, derivada de la intervención total del Estado en la economía, y de la estatización de todo tipo de empresas otrora privadas, dando origen a la creación de cientos y cientos de empresas pública, incluso de Empresas del Estado, sin control ni coordinación alguna, todo lo cual ha complicado en demasía el aparato burocrático del Estado. Por todo eso, con toda razón, *The Economist* estimaba en septiembre de 2014, que Venezuela era "probablemente la economía peor gerenciada del mundo," donde "el precio de la sobrevivencia de la revolución parece ser la muerte lenta del país;"[1399] gerencia de la economía que durante más de una década estuvo a cargo de un ingeniero mecánico, y que en 2014, se ha entregado a un militar general del ejército,[1400] teniendo ambos, en común, la formación que deriva de haber sido sólo burócratas durante los tres últimos lustros. Ello ha provocado que en el país se haya producido lo que se ha calificado como "un milagro económico a la inversa, de los que se registran tan pocos en el devenir de los pueblos," y es el de haber convertido "en país miserable el más rico de América."[1401]

Ahora, en cuanto a la regulación de dichas empresas del Estado debe observarse que el artículo 100 de la Ley Orgánica de 2001 las definía como "las sociedades mercantiles en las cuales la República, los estados, los distritos metropolitanos y los municipios, o alguno de los entes descentralizados funcionalmente regulados en la Ley Orgánica, solos o conjuntamente, tuvieran una participación mayor al 50% del capital social."[1402] En la reforma de la Ley Orgánica de 2008, lo que se ha ratificado en la reforma de la Ley Orgánica de 2014, esta definición se eliminó del artículo 103, e ignorando la "forma de derecho privado" conceptualmente esencial de las empresas del Estado conforme a los principios de la descentralización establecidos en el artículo 29 de la misma Ley, se las definió eliminándose toda referencia a su carácter "de sociedades mercantiles," calificándolas en forma totalmente contradictoria, como *"personas jurídicas de derecho público* constituidas de acuerdo a las normas de derecho privado," en los entes públicos tengan una participación mayor al cincuenta por ciento del capital social. Frente a tamaña contradicción, si bien se podría concluir que se podría tratar de un error de la Ley, sin embargo, por la forma del cambio, no pasa de ser obra de la ignorancia en materia de organización administrativa. Solo eso explica que se califique en forma contradictoria a las empresas

---

1399   Véase "Venezuela's Economy. Of oil and coconut wáter. Probably the world's managed economy," en *The Economist*, N° 8905, September 20th. 2014, pp. 31-32.

1400   *Idem.*

1401   Véase Fernando Londoño en el diario *El Tiempo* de Bogotá, reproducido por el Jefe de Redacción (Elides Rojas) del diario *El Universal* de Caracas el 24 de mayo de 2014. "Fernando Londoño en *El Tiempo*: Venezuela en llamas. Santos calla," en *El Universal*, Caracas 24 de mayo de 2014, en http://www.eluniversal.com/blogs/sobre-la-marcha/140524/fernando-londono-en-el-tiempo-venezuela-en-llamas-santos-calla.

1402   Véase Allan R. Brewer-Carías, *Régimen de las Empresas Públicas en Venezuela*, Caracas 1981.

del Estado, como entes "con forma de derecho privado" (art. 29) y, a la vez, como "personas de derecho público" (art. 103).

Ello, por lo demás, explica la aversión que los redactores de la reforma de la Ley Orgánica de 2008 tuvieron con respecto a la noción y palabra "autonomía," lo que se reflejó por ejemplo, en la transformación de los "servicios autónomos sin personalidad jurídica" en "servicios desconcentrados" (art. 93), y en la creación de los "institutos públicos" en lugar de los "institutos autónomos," como entes descentralizados funcionalmente, aun cuando sin poder eliminar los últimos por tratarse de una institución que tiene rango constitucional (art. 96). En la reforma de la Ley Orgánica de 2014, sin embargo, se estructuró el régimen de los "institutos públicos" y de los "institutos autónomos" bajo una sola denominación de "institutos públicos o autónomos" (arts. 98 ss.).

IV. LA CREACIÓN DE UNA ADMINISTRACIÓN PÚBLICA PARALELA: LAS "MISIONES"

Además de la hiperinflación que se ha presentado en la Administración ministerial y en la Administración descentralizada, la política social populista del Estado basada en la configuración de todo tipo de subsidios, como si los recursos del petróleo fuesen ilimitados e invariables, ha conducido a la definición de programas de políticas públicas denominados "Misiones," que después de varios años de implementación encontraron cabida expresa en la reforma de la Ley Orgánica de la Administración Pública de 2008, pero paradójicamente para quedar excluidas de sus regulaciones;[1403] es decir, como una Administración paralela a la Administración Central; todo lo cual se ha ratificado en la reforma de la Ley Orgánica de la Administración Pública dictada mediante Decreto Ley 1.424 de 17 de noviembre de 2014.[1404]

La consecuencia ha sido, entonces, que además de la existencia de entes y de los órganos en la organización de la Administración Pública, ahora se han insertado en la misma a las "Misiones" –que en realidad no son nada distinto, en su forma jurídica de los tradicionales entes y órganos administrativos, pero con la diferencia de que se los denomina "Misiones,"– pero con la absurda característica, como se dijo, de que las mismas quedan fuera de la regulación de dicha Ley Orgánica de la Administración Pública, como una especie de Administración Paralela.[1405].

La consecuencia de este signo del Estado populista en relación con la Administración Pública es ostensible, pues implica que el derecho administrativo, cuyo obje-

1403   Véase Allan R. Brewer-Carías, "Una nueva tendencia en la organización administrativa venezolana: las "misiones" y las instancias y organizaciones del "poder popular" establecidas en paralelo a la administración pública," en *Retos de la Organización Administrativa Contemporánea, X Foro Iberoamericano de Derecho Administrativo* (26-27 de septiembre de 2011), Corte Suprema de Justicia, Universidad de El Salvador, Universidad Doctor José Matías Delgado, San Salvador, El Salvador, 2011.

1404   Decreto Ley 1424 de 17 de noviembre de 2014, *Gaceta Oficial* N° 6147 Extra de 17 de noviembre de 2014.

1405   Véase José Ignacio Hernández, "La administración paralela como instrumento del Poder Público," en *Revista de Derecho Público*, N° 112, Editorial Jurídica Venezolana, Caracas 2007, 175 ss.

to es regular a la Administración Pública, integrado en la Ley Orgánica de la Administración Pública, simplemente no la regula totalmente pues no se aplica a estas "Misiones" que, por tanto, pueden actuar al margen del derecho de la organización administrativa, a pesar de que son las que manejan fuera de la disciplina fiscal y presupuestaria, ingentes recursos del Estado, con el consecuente desquiciamiento de la Administración Pública y del derecho administrativo.

Pero por otra parte del tema jurídico, desde el punto de vista social, si bien la tarea de las "Misiones" de "administrar" el sistema extendido de subsidios directos a las personas de menos recursos contribuyó efímeramente y con una carga electoral conocida, a aumentar el ingreso de una parte importante de la población, éste sin embargo, con el fomento del consumismo exagerado que eliminó espacio para el ahorro, y con la inflación galopante que para mayo de 2014 ya alcanzaba el 60%,[1406] dicho incremento se ha disipado, dejando como secuela el deterioro de los valores fundamentales de toda sociedad, como consecuencia de recibir beneficios sin enfrentar sacrificios o esfuerzos, como por ejemplo, el valor del trabajo productivo como fuente de ingreso, que materialmente se ha eliminado, sustituido por el que encuentra, que es preferible recibir sin trabajar.

Este Estado Populista ha sido lo Leandro Area ha calificado acertadamente como un "Estado Misional," por estar montado sobre dichas Misiones "como actores colectivos no formales de política pública, que manejan un oscuro e inmenso mar de recursos," resultando ser un "espécimen no incluido aún en las tipologías de la Ciencia Política," entendiendo por tal:

> "aquel Estado que haciendo uso de sus recursos materiales y simbólicos le impone, por fuerza u operación de compra-venta o combinación de ambas a la sociedad, un esquema de disminución, de minusvalía consentida, en sus capacidades y potencialidades de crecimiento a cambio de sumisión. [...] Se encarama sobre ella en su ayer, hoy y mañana, amaestrándola con la dieta diaria cuyo menú depende del gusto del gobernante. Confisca, privatiza, invade, expropia, conculca, controla, asfixia, acoquina hasta decir basta, poniendo en evidencia lo frágil del concepto de propiedad privada creando así miedo, emigración, desinversión, fuga de capitales. Y aunque usted no lo crea esas son metas o simples desplantes o locura u obscura necesidad de auto bloqueo como forma de amurallarse para obtener inmunidad e impunidad para sus tropelías, frente a la mirada de una época que no los reconoce sino como entes del pasado, objeto de museo o de laboratorio, insectos atrapados en el ámbar del tiempo; fracaso, derrota."[1407]

A lo anterior agrega el mismo Leandro Area, que dicho Estado Misional en definitiva es un tipo de Estado Socialista, que nada tiene que ver con el Estado Social del cual habla la Constitución, concebido en paralelo al Estado Constitucional, "con la intención de acabarlo o mejor, de extinguirlo." Para ello, indica Area:

1406   Véase César Miguel Rondón, "Cada vez menos país," en *Confirmado*, 16-8-2014, en http://confirmado.com.ve/opinan/cada-vez-menos-pais/

1407   Véase Leandro Area, "El 'Estado Misional' en Venezuela," en *Analítica.com*, 14 de febrero de 2014, en http://analitica.com/opinion/opinion-nacional/el-estado-misional-en-venezuela/

"El gobierno crea misiones a su antojo que son estructuras burocráticas y funcionales "sui generis" y permanentes, con un control jurisdiccional inexistente y que actúa con base a los intereses de dominio. Además si el gobernante se encuentra por encima del bien y del mal, como es el caso venezolano, nadie es capaz de controlar sus veleidades y apetitos. En ese sentido el Estado es un apéndice del gobernante que es el repartidor interesado de los bienes de toda la sociedad y que invierte a su gusto, entre otras bagatelas, en compra de conciencias y voluntades de acólitos y novicios aspirantes. Por su naturaleza, todo Estado misional es un Estado depredador sin comillas. Vive de la pobreza, la estimula, la paga, organiza, la convierte en ejercito informal y también paralelo. El gobierno y su partido los tiene censados, chequeados, uniformados de banderas, consignas y miedos. Localizados, inscritos, con carnet, lo que quiere decir que fotografiados, listos para la dádiva, la culpa, castigos y perdones." [1408]

Por todo ello, por tanto, las misiones, sujetas como lo observa Heinz Sonntag, a un "patrón de organización destinado a darles dadivas a los sectores pobres y garantizar así su adhesión a la Revolución Bolivariana," [1409] además de haber provocado más miseria y control de conciencia sobre una población de menos recursos totalmente dependiente de la burocracia estatal y sus dádivas, en las cuales creyó encontrar la solución definitiva para su existencia, también provocó el deterioro de otra parte de la población, particularmente la clase media, que junto con todos los demás componentes de la misma ha visto desaparecer su calidad de vida, y sufren en conjunto los embates de la inflación y de la escases. [1410] Y todo ello, con un deterioro ostensible y trágico de los servicios públicos más elementales como los servicios de salud y atención médica.

Dichas 'Misiones," como se dijo, encontraron cabida en el propio texto de la reforma de la Ley Orgánica de la Administración Pública de 2008, establecidas, además de los "órganos" y "entes," como una "nueva" figura organizativa de la Administración Pública (arts. 15 y 132), pero con la peculiaridad contradictoria mencionada de que se las excluye, en general, de la aplicación de las normas de la propia Ley Orgánica que las creó, la cual básicamente, como se ha ratificado en la reforma de 2014, continúa destinada a regular sólo a los "órganos y entes" de la Administración. En esta forma, por primera vez se reguló legislativamente una forma

---

1408   *Idem.*

1409   Véase Heinz Sonntag "¿Cuántas Revoluciones más?" en El *Nacional*, Caracas 7 de octubre de 2014, en http://www.el-nacional.com/heinz_sonntag/Cuantas-Revoluciones_0_496150483.html

1410   Como el mismo Area lo ha descrito en lenguaje común y gráfico, pero tremendamente trágico: "Vivimos pues "boqueando" y de paso corrompiéndonos por las condiciones impuestas por y desde el poder que nos obligan a vivir como "lateros", "balseros", "abasteros" mejor dicho, que al estar "pelando" por lo que buscamos y no encontramos, tenemos que andar en gerundio, ladrando, mamando, haciendo cola, bajándonos de la mula, haciéndonos los bolsas o locos, llevándonos de caleta algo, caribeando o de chupa medias, pagando peaje, tracaleando, empujándonos los unos contra los otros, en suma, degradándonos, envileciéndonos, para satisfacer nuestras necesidades básicas de consumo. Es asfixia gradual y calculada, material y moral. Desde el papel toilette hasta la honestidad. ¡Pero tenemos Patria! Falta el orgullo, la dignidad, el respeto, el amor a uno mismo." Véase en "El 'Estado Misional' en Venezuela," en *Analítica.com*, 14 de febrero de 2014, en http://analitica.com/opinion/opinion-nacional/el-estado-misional-en-venezuela/

de organización administrativa, que no tiene "sin forma" organizativa precisa, y que desde 2003 se había venido utilizando para atender programas concretos de la Administración Pública.

Sobre ellas, en todo caso, lo único que se establece en la Ley Orgánica es la atribución al Presidente de la República en Consejo de Ministros, de la potestad de crear dichas "misiones" cuando circunstancias especiales lo ameriten, "destinadas a atender a la satisfacción de las necesidades fundamentales y urgentes de la población, las cuales estarán bajo la rectoría de las políticas aprobadas conforme a la planificación centralizada," debiendo, en el decreto de creación, determinar el órgano o ente de adscripción o dependencia, formas de financiamiento, funciones y conformación del nivel directivo encargado de dirigir la ejecución de las actividades encomendadas (art. 132).

Debe recordarse, por otra parte, que las mencionadas "misiones," como integrando la Administración Pública, fue uno de los aspectos que se pretendió constitucionalizar en el proyecto de Reforma Constitucional de 2007 que fue rechazado por el pueblo en el referendo de diciembre de 2007,[1411] en la cual se propuso una nueva redacción del artículo 141 constitucional, que se buscaba que pasara de regular un régimen universal aplicable a toda "la Administración Pública," a establecer varias "administraciones públicas", las cuales, incluso, contra toda técnica legislativa, se las buscaba "clasificar" en el texto mismo de la Constitución en las siguientes dos "categorías": "las *administraciones públicas burocráticas o tradicionales*, que son las que atienden a las estructuras previstas y reguladas en esta Constitución"; y "las *misiones*, constituidas por organizaciones de variada naturaleza, creadas para atender a la satisfacción de las más sentidas y urgentes necesidades de la población, cuya prestación exige de la aplicación de sistemas excepcionales, e incluso, experimentales, los cuales serán establecidos por el Poder Ejecutivo mediante reglamentos organizativos y funcionales".

Es decir, con el rechazado proyecto de reforma constitucional de 2007, en lugar de corregirse el descalabro administrativo que se había producido a partir de 2003 por el desorden organizativo y la indisciplina presupuestaria derivada de fondos asignados a programas específicos del gobierno a través de las "misiones", concebidas en general fuera del marco de la organización general del Estado, lo que se buscaba era constitucionalizar dicho desorden administrativo, calificándose en el propio texto constitucional a las estructuras administrativas del Estado Constitucional como "burocráticas o tradicionales", renunciando a que las mismas fueran reformadas para convertirlas en instrumentos para que, precisamente, pudieran atender a la satisfacción de las más sentidas y urgentes necesidades de la población.

Posteriormente, con la reforma de la Ley Orgánica de 2008, ratificado en la Ley Orgánica de 2014, como se dijo, se regularizó legislativamente a las "misiones,"[1412]

1411   Véase Allan R. Brewer-Carías, *La Reforma Constitucional de 2007 (Comentarios al proyecto inconstitucionalmente sancionado por la Asamblea Nacional el 2 de noviembre de 2007)*, Editorial Jurídica Venezolana, Caracas 2007.

1412   Véase Cosimina G. Pellegrino Pacera, "La reedición de la propuesta constitucional de 2007 en el Decreto N° 6.217 con rango, valor y fuerza de Ley Orgánica de la Administración Pública," en en *Re-*

pero precisamente para no regularlas, pues la Ley, como hemos dicho, se destina íntegramente a regular exclusivamente a los "órganos y entes," dejando fuera de sus regulaciones a las "misiones," estando sin embargo, todas, en común, solo sujetas a "los lineamientos dictados conforme a la planificación centralizada" (art. 15).

Sobre esta "novedad legislativa" de estas misiones, como se indicó en la Exposición de Motivos del Decreto Ley de la Ley Orgánica de 2008, las mismas "nacieron como organismo de ejecución de políticas públicas, obteniendo niveles óptimos de cumplimiento de los programas y proyectos asignados, y se conciben dentro del proyecto, como aquellas destinadas a atender a la satisfacción de las necesidades fundamentales y urgentes de la población, que pueden ser creadas por el Presidente de la República en Consejo de Ministros, cuando circunstancias especiales lo ameriten."

La consecuencia de ello es que se estableció en la Ley la misma distinción que se quiso establecer en la Constitución en 2007, entre una Administración Pública "tradicional" conformada por órganos y entes del Estado Constitucional que es la regulada precisamente en la Ley Orgánica, y otra Administración Pública paralela, supuestamente "no tradicional," conformada por las misiones, destinada "a atender a la satisfacción de las necesidades fundamentales y urgentes de la población", como si la primera no tuviera esa función, pero con la diferencia de que la primera está sometida estrictamente a todas las prescripciones de la Ley Orgánica, y la segunda no está sometida a todas dichas previsiones. Es decir, se creó una nueva organización en la Ley para excluirla de su régimen, el cual como se puede apreciar del conjunto de su normativa, en su casi totalidad sólo rige para los "órganos y entes."[1413],

En todo caso, con anterioridad a la entrada en vigencia de la Ley Orgánica de 2008, y con la denominación de "misiones" lo que se fue creando fue una serie de organizaciones administrativas como Administraciones paralelas,[1414] con el objeto de atender programas puntuales, utilizándose para ello, muy desordenadamente, las más variadas "formas" organizativas autorizadas en la Ley Orgánica, en algunos casos de órganos, como son las Comisiones Presidenciales o Interministeriales, o de entes, como las fundaciones del Estado. A tal efecto, por ejemplo, utilizándose la figura de las *Comisiones Presidenciales o Interministeriales*, se establecieron las siguientes "misiones": -Misión Ribas,[1415] Misión Alimentación (Mercal),[1416] Misión Guaicaipuro,[1417] Misión Árbol,[1418] Misión Robinson,[1419] Misión Villanueva,[1420] y

vista de Derecho Público N° 115 *(Estudios sobre los decretos leyes)*, Editorial Jurídica Venezolana, Caracas 2008, pp. 163 ss.

1413   En igual sentido, las "misiones" también quedan excluidas de la aplicación de la Ley Orgánica de Simplificación de Trámites Administrativos, pues la misma solo se aplica a "los órganos y entes" de la misma (art. 2). *Gaceta Oficial* N° 5.891 *Extraordinaria* de 22-7-2008.

1414   Véase Manuel Rachadell, "La centralización del poder en el Estado federal descentralizado," en *Revista de Derecho Público* N° 115 *(Estudios sobre los decretos leyes)*, Editorial Jurídica Venezolana, Caracas 2008, pp. 115-116, 125.

1415   *Gaceta Oficial* N° 37.798 del 16 de octubre de 2003

1416   *Gaceta Oficial* N° 38.603 del 12 de enero de 2007

1417   *Gaceta Oficial* N° 38.758 del 30 de agosto de 2007

1418   *Gaceta Oficial* N° 38.445 del 26 de mayo de 2006

Misión Madres Del Barrio "Josefa Joaquina Sánchez."[1421] Por su parte, utilizándose la figura de las *fundaciones del Estado*, se establecieron las siguientes "misiones": *Misión Barrio Adentro,*[1422] *Misión Che Guevara*, que sustituyó a la "Misión Vuelvan Caras," "dentro del objetivo supremo de alcanzar la Misión Cristo: Pobreza y Miseria Cero,"[1423] *Misión Identidad,*[1424] *Misión Milagro,*[1425] *Misión Sucre,*[1426] *Misión Negra Hipólita,*[1427] y *Misión Piar.*[1428]

Como se puede apreciar, hasta la promulgación de la Ley Orgánica de 2008, las "misiones" se crearon adoptando la forma de "órganos" como las Comisiones Presidenciales o Interministeriales, o la forma de "entes" descentralizados, conforme a la forma de derecho privado de las Fundaciones del Estado, mostrando en todo caso, una falta total de coherencia, particularmente en cuanto al manejo presupuestario, ya que las mismas han manejado ingentes recursos públicos. En los casos de las Misiones configuradas como Comisiones Presidenciales o Interministeriales, las previsiones presupuestarias establecidas en los decretos de creación en general se refieren solo a los gastos administrativos que ocasione el funcionamiento de las mismas, agregándose muchas veces, que los gastos de la ejecución de las misiones están a cargo del presupuesto de respectivo Ministerio, conforme a la competencia en la materia específica.

En los casos de las Fundaciones del Estado, como entes descentralizados, en los decretos de creación en general se han dispuesto los aportes públicos al patrimonio de las mismas, que deben asignarse en Ley de Presupuesto; o mediante el aportes de bienes muebles e inmuebles propiedad de la República.

En todo caso, sea que se trate de Fundaciones o de Comisiones, en la mayoría de los casos, la actividad desplegada forma parte de las competencias asignadas a los Ministerios, pero desarrolladas sin relación efectiva con os mismos.

V.   LA REGULACIÓN LEGISLATIVA DE LAS "MISIONES".

Después de seis años de su insuficiente regulación en la Ley Orgánica de la Administración Pública de 2008, que no se corrigió en la reforma de 2014, el 13 de noviembre de 2014 se dictó el Decreto Ley de la Ley Orgánica de Misiones, Grandes Misiones y Micro misiones,[1429] con el objeto regular los "mecanismos a través de los cuales el Estado Venezolano, conjunta y articuladamente con el Poder Popu-

---

1419   *Gaceta Oficial* N° 37.711 del 13 de junio de 2003

1420   *Gaceta Oficial* N° 38.647 del 19 de marzo de 2007

1421   *Gaceta Oficial* N° 38.549 del 25 de octubre de 2006

1422   *Gaceta Oficial* N° 38.423 del 25 de abril de 2006

1423   *Gaceta Oficial* N° 38.819 del 27 de noviembre de 2007

1424   *Gaceta Oficial* N° 38.188 del 17 de mayo de 2005

1425   *Gaceta Oficial* N° 38.632 del 26 de febrero de 2007

1426   *Gaceta Oficial* N° 38.188 del 17 de mayo de 2005

1427   *Gaceta Oficial* N° 38.776 del 25 de septiembre de 2007

1428   *Gaceta Oficial* N° 38.282 del 28 de septiembre de 2005

1429   Véase en *Gaceta Oficial* N° 6.154 Extra. de 19 de noviembre de 2014.

lar bajo sus diversas formas de expresión y organización, promueven el desarrollo social integral; así como la protección social de los ciudadanos" mediante el establecimiento de las mencionadas misiones "orientadas a asegurar el ejercicio universal de los derechos sociales consagrados en la Constitución"(Art. 1).

Entre los fines de la Ley se destaca el de establecer los criterios para la creación, desarrollo, supresión o fusión de las Misiones, el "Sistema Nacional de Misiones, Grandes Misiones y Micro-misiones como la estructura orgánica del Estado y del Poder Popular," y "garantizar las condiciones para el financiamiento de las Misiones, Grandes Misiones y Micro-misiones (art. 6).

Las disposiciones de la Ley se declararon como "de orden público" siendo sus normas aplicables "en todo el territorio de la República a la Administración Pública Nacional, Estadal y Municipal, a las organizaciones del Poder Popular, así como a todas las personas naturales o jurídicas de derecho público o privado que tengan responsabilidades, obligaciones, derechos y deberes vinculados al ejercicio de los derechos sociales de las personas y del pueblo. (art. 5); y además, la ley declaró como "de interés general" y con el "carácter de servicio público" todas las actividades vinculadas a la prestación de bienes y servicios a la población objeto de las Misiones (art. 7).

1   *La Misión como política pública:*

Siguiendo la orientación que se adoptó en la Ley Orgánica de la Administración Pública, la ley Orgánica de Misiones las reguló, exclusivamente, una "política pública destinada a materializar de forma masiva, acelerada y progresiva las condiciones para el efectivo ejercicio y disfrute universal de uno o más derechos sociales de personas o grupos de personas, que conjuga la agilización de los procesos estatales con la participación directa del pueblo en su gestión, en favor de la erradicación de la pobreza y la conquista popular de los derechos sociales consagrados en la Constitución," (art. 4.1) que por tanto, se ejecuta por los órganos y entes que se determine en el acto de su creación (art. 36).

A tal efecto, el artículo 8 de la Ley enumera entre los derechos sociales a ser desarrollados y atendidos por las Misiones, además de los consagrados en la ley y en los tratados y acuerdos suscritos y ratificados por la República, los derechos a la alimentación, a la protección de la familia, a la identidad, a la vivienda y al hábitat, a la salud, a la seguridad social, al trabajo, a la educación, a la cultura, al deporte y la recreación, a los servicios básicos, a la seguridad personal, y de los pueblos y comunidades indígenas.

Además de los cometidos por los que fueren creadas, las Misiones, conforme al artículo 13 de la ley, deben atender al desarrollo de proyectos socio-productivos que contribuyan al fortalecimiento de la soberanía del país, a la satisfacción de las necesidades de la población y "a la construcción de la Venezuela potencia."

A los efectos de la ejecución de la Ley, como actor en la política pública denominada Misión, la Ley identifica al "Misionero" que son tanto "los ciudadanos que desde su accionar diario contribuyen al desarrollo de los planes y acciones en favor del cumplimiento de los objetivos de cada misión desde el ámbito institucional, así como a los grupos y personas sujetos de atención específicos de las Misiones, Grandes Misiones y Micro-misiones, quienes se organizan en los territorios para empoderarse de sus derechos y contribuir a la transformación de la sociedad a través del poder popular"(Art. 4.4). Los artículos 9 y 10 de la Ley enumeran los derechos y deberes de dichos misioneros.

2. *Prestaciones de bienes y servicios a cargo de las Misiones*

Conforme se indica en el artículo 11 de la Ley, corresponde a las Misiones las siguientes prestaciones de bienes y servicios: 1. Programas de atención a grupos y personas en situación de vulnerabilidad. 2. Atención en los diversos niveles del Sistema Público Nacional de Salud. 3. Establecimientos de servicios sociales, entre los que se incluyen centros educativos, de salud, deportivos, de alimentación, culturales, recreativos y de protección especial. 4. Transferencias dinerarias condicionadas. 5. Pensiones no contributivas. 6. Subsidios. 7. Ayudas técnicas para personas con discapacidad. 8. Suministro de medicamentos. 9. Desarrollo de equipamiento urbano. 10. Jornadas de atención de los servicios sociales. 11. Desarrollo de actividades educativas, culturales, deportivas y recreativas. 12. Suministro de bienes esenciales para el disfrute de los derechos a la educación, la salud, el deporte, la cultura, entre otros. 13. Suministro de servicios básicos, entre los que se incluye el agua, la electricidad, el gas, la telefonía, el internet, aseo urbano, vialidad, transporte público y saneamiento ambiental. 14. Financiamiento de proyectos socio-productivos. 15. Financiamiento y subsidio de la vivienda.

En ese marco de prestaciones, uno de los objetivos del Sistema Nacional de Misiones es "erradicar la pobreza" (art. 15.2); para cuyo efecto se dispone que a los efectos del desarrollo de sus actividades prestacionales en estas áreas de actividad, los órganos y entes que participen en la ejecución de las Misiones se deben regir para la definición, identificación y medición de la pobreza, por los lineamientos y criterios que establezca el Consejo Nacional de Política Social y el Instituto Nacional de Estadística, sin menoscabo del uso de otros datos que se estimen convenientes. 12

3. *La Administración de las Misiones o el aparataje burocrático de las Misiones*

Aparte de las previsiones generales de la Ley, lo que la misma ha hecho es organizar un aparataje burocrático, que podría denominarse la "Administración de la Misiones" que dirigido por un "Alto Mando del Sistema" integrado por el Presidente de la República, Vicepresidentes y Ministros, se integra en un Sistema Nacional de Misiones compuesto por órganos de Dirección del mismo en los niveles político-territoriales; una Coordinación General del Sistema; un Consejo Nacional de Política Social; un Servicio Nacional de Información Social; el Fondo Nacional de Misiones (art.43), las organizaciones de las diversas Misiones, Grandes Misiones y Micromisiones, y un Consejo Nacional de Misioneros (art. 16).

Además, en los niveles estadales, el Sistema debe contar con "Coordinaciones Estadales" (art. 24) como sus instancias de dirección a nivel estadal; y con "Coordinaciones Municipales, como instancias de dirección del Sistema a nivel municipal (art. 26), las cuales deben crear instancias de articulación comunal denominadas Mesas de Misiones de la Comuna, (art. 28), y donde un haya Comuna, se denominarán "comités de trabajo del Consejo Comunal" (art. 29).

En el Sistema, además, se establecen las "Bases de Misiones" "como espacios para la prestación de servicios de las Misiones y de otros servicios públicos, destinados a la atención y protección integral de las comunidades y familias" (art. 32), desde donde las Misiones desarrollarán los siguientes ámbitos de atención: 1. Promoción y fortalecimiento de las organizaciones del Poder Popular. 2- Atención Primaria en Salud, incluyendo visitas domiciliarias y seguimiento nutricional. 3. Desarrollo de los programas de abastecimiento y comercialización de alimentos. 4. Promoción de la inserción y de la permanencia escolar de todos los niños, niñas y adolescentes. 5. prestación de servicios de identificación, registro civil y trámites de servicios públicos. 6. Promoción de actividades y emprendimientos productivos. Y 7. Desarrollo de programación cultural, deportiva y recreativa. (art. 35)

4.   *Principios para la creación de Misiones*

La Ley Orgánica, por otra parte ha establecido una serie de principios para la creación de las Misiones por parte del Presidente de la República en Consejo de Ministros, "bajo la rectoría de las políticas aprobadas conforme a la planificación centralizada," para lo cual debe "estar precedida por un estudio diagnóstico y un análisis prospectivo de la situación y problema que se busca atender o resolver elaborado por el Consejo Nacional de Política Social."

Tratándose de una política pública, las Misiones deben atribuirse en el Decreto de su creación, a un determinado órgano o ente de la Administración 'Pública, en los términos dela ley Orgánica de la Administración Pública, al cual se atribuye la responsabilidad de la ejecución de la misma, las formas de financiamiento, funciones y la conformación del nivel directivo encargado de dirigir la ejecución de las actividades encomendadas (art. 36). En caso de supresión de las Misiones, el Decreto respectivo, en caso que se hayan creado órganos o entes para la ejecución de las mismas debe disponer el cumplimiento de las formalidades legales para su supresión y liquidación (art. 37).

El Presidente igualmente puede resolver la fusión de las mismas estableciendo las reglas básicas para su funcionamiento (art. 38), y podrá, igualmente modificar el objeto de las mismas estableciendo las nuevas reglas para su funcionamiento (art. 39).

5.   *La organización popular en el marco de las Misiones*

La Ley Orgánica, por otra parte, ha regulado los principios de organización popular en el marco de las Misiones, estableciendo las siguientes instancias de participación y organización comunitaria: 1. El Consejo de Planificación Comunal. 2. El Consejo de Contraloría Comunal. 3. El Consejo Nacional de Misioneros y Misioneras. 4. El Comité de trabajo de la Comuna y del Consejo Comunal. Y 5. El Área de trabajo (art. 45).

Entre estos órganos, se destaca el Consejo Nacional de Misioneros, creado como una instancia de encuentro, evaluación y de formulación de propuestas de los voceros de las Misiones, en el cual además deben participar las autoridades de los órganos y entes responsables de la ejecución de las Misiones (art. 46); y tendrá como objetivo generar un espacio nacional para el debate, la evaluación y el fortalecimiento de las Misiones (art. 47). Dicho Consejo está conformado por el Presidente de la República, los voceros nacionales de cada una de las Misiones, que hayan sido electos por las organizaciones de base que congregan a los Misioneros, por los Jefes de las Misiones, y por los Ministros o Viceministros de los órganos que tienen rectoría sobre las Misiones (art. 48).

6. *El Fondo Nacional de Misiones y el financiamiento de las Misiones*

El artículo 43 de la ley Orgánica "creó" el Fondo Nacional de Misiones "para la gestión, asignación y administración de recursos destinados a las mismas" pero sin establecer si se trata de un órgano o de un ente, dejando al Presidente de la República la determinación eventual mediante Reglamento de "la naturaleza jurídica del ente u órgano que administrara los recursos asignados a este fondo y su patrimonio," lo cual excluye la posibilidad de que se trate de un ente de derecho público (instituto autónomo o público), que solo podría ser creado por Ley conforme a la Constitución y a la Ley Orgánica de la Administración Pública.

Dicho Fondo, en todo caso, conforme al artículo 44 de la ley Orgánica de Misiones, tiene a su cargo administrar, centralizar y sistematizar la gestión y asignación de los recursos destinados a los subsidios, transferencias dinerarias condicionadas y financiamientos de proyectos socio-productivos de las Misiones.

En cuanto al financiamiento de las Misiones la Ley Orgánica declaró los recursos destinados para su desarrollo como "prioritarios y de interés público," estableciendo que los mismos "no podrán sufrir disminuciones en sus montos presupuestarios, excepto en los casos y términos que establezca la Ley de Presupuesto" (art. 50). Igualmente La Ley estableció el principio de progresividad de la inversión social, lo que implica que las asignaciones presupuestarias destinadas a la misma "no podrán ser inferiores, en términos reales, al del ejercicio económico financiero anterior, por lo cual tendrá carácter progresivo y sustentable, con base en la disponibilidad de recursos a partir de los ingresos previstos en la Ley de Presupuesto y en los fondos de inversión administrados por el Poder Ejecutivo" (art. 50).

La distribución de los recursos previstos para las Misiones debe ser recomendada por el Consejo Nacional de Política Social al Alto Mando del Sistema Nacional de Misiones antes de su incorporación en la Ley de Presupuesto (art. 52); estableciendo la Ley, además, los siguientes criterios para la distribución de los recursos: Primero, la inversión social per cápita no debe ser menor en términos reales al asignado el año inmediato anterior; y segundo, la misma se debe destinar de forma prioritaria a las personas y comunidades en situación de pobreza y pobreza extrema; se debe basar en indicadores y lineamientos generales de eficacia y de cantidad y calidad en la prestación de los servicios sociales, establecidos por el Consejo Nacional de Política Social; y debe estar orientada a la promoción de un desarrolle regional equilibrado.

SECCIÓN TERCERA:

LA FORMA FEDERAL DEL ESTADO, Y LA CENTRALIZACIÓN PROGRESIVA DE LA ADMINISTRACIÓN PÚBLICA

El otro condicionante político esencial de la Administración Pública, además de la concepción del Estado, es la forma del Estado, según se trate de un Estado unitario centralizado o de un Estado descentralizado, y entre éstos, de un Estado federal.

Ello originará una Administración Pública centralizada o descentralizada territorialmente, en este último caso, abierta a la participación política.

I.   EL ESTADO CONSTITUCIONAL EN VENEZUELA, COMO FEDE-
RACIÓN CENTRALIZADA, LA CENTRALIZACIÓN DE LA ADMI-
NISTRACIÓN PÚBLICA

En cuanto a la forma del Estado venezolano, si nos atenemos a la definición de la
Constitución de 1999, en la misma, además de declarar que se establece un Estado
democrático y social de derecho y de justicia, el cual, como se ha indicado, no existe
en la realidad, también prevé que la República se organiza como "un Estado federal
descentralizado" que "se rige por los principios de integridad territorial, cooperación,
solidaridad, concurrencia y corresponsabilidad" (art. 4).

Esa debería ser la forma del Estado Constitucional en Venezuela, la de un Estado
Federal descentralizado, derivado de un sistema de distribución vertical del Poder
Público en tres niveles territoriales, entre el Poder Nacional, el Poder de los Estados y
el Poder Municipal (art. 136), cada uno debiendo tener siempre un gobierno de carácter "electivo, descentralizado, alternativo, responsable, pluralista y de mandatos revocables," tal como lo exige el artículo 6 de la Constitución; y cada nivel territorial
con su respectiva Administración Pública.

La realidad de las propias disposiciones constitucionales, sin embargo, lo que
muestra es un Estado con un régimen "centralista" a pesar del calificativo de "descentralizado," siendo esa contradicción el signo más característico de la Constitución al regular el régimen de las entidades territoriales,[1430] pues en paralelo, a regular la autonomía política, normativa y administrativa de los Estados y Municipios, el
texto la niega al remitir a la Ley para su regulación, con lo que la garantía constitucional de la misma desapareció; a lo que se agrega un marcado desbalance en la
distribución de competencias.

En efecto, la autonomía de los entes territoriales, es decir, de los Estados y de los
Municipios, ante todo, como sucede en toda federación o Estado descentralizado,
exigía la previsión de su garantía constitucional, en el sentido de que los límites a la
misma sólo podían estar en la propia Constitución, y no podía ser remitida su regulación por ley nacional posterior. La Constitución de 1999, sin embargo, al regular
el funcionamiento y la organización de los Consejos Legislativos Estadales remitió
su regulación a la ley nacional (art. 162), que se dictó en 2001, como Ley Orgánica
de los Consejos Legislativos de los Estados,[1431] lo cual, además de contradictorio

---

1430   Ello lo advertimos apenas se sancionó la Constitución en Allan R. Brewer-Carías, *Federalismo y
        municipalismo en la Constitución de 1999 (Alcance de una reforma insuficiente y regresiva)*, Cua-
        dernos de la Cátedra Allan R. Brewer-Carías de Derecho Público, N° 7, Universidad Católica del
        Táchira, Editorial Jurídica Venezolana, Caracas-San Cristóbal 2001; y "El Estado federal descentrali-
        zado y la centralización de la federación en Venezuela. Situación y perspectiva de una contradicción
        constitucional" en *Federalismo y regionalismo,* Coordinadores Diego Valadés y José María Serna de
        la Garza, Universidad Nacional Autónoma de México, Tribunal Superior de Justicia del Estado de
        Puebla, Instituto de Investigaciones Jurídicas, Serie Doctrina Jurídica N° 229, México 2005, pp. 717-
        750

1431   *Gaceta Oficial* N° 37.282 del 13 de septiembre de 2001.

con la atribución a los mismos de dictarse su propia Constitución para organizar sus poderes públicos (art. 164.1), se configuró como una intromisión inaceptable del Poder Nacional en el régimen de los Estados.

En cuanto a los Municipios, la autonomía municipal tradicionalmente garantizada en la propia Constitución, también se interfirió en la Constitución, al señalarse que los Municipios gozan de la misma, no sólo "dentro de los límites" establecidos en la Constitución, sino de los establecidos en la ley nacional (art. 168), con lo cual el principio descentralizador básico, que es la autonomía, quedó minimizado.

La centralización, por otra parte ha sido el signo característico regularse constitucionalmente a la Administración Pública, mediante la incorporación de una sección específica dedicada a la misma en el Título IV del Poder Público, cuyas normas se aplican a todos los "órganos" y "entes" que conforman las Administraciones Públicas en los tres niveles territoriales, es decir, en la República (administración pública nacional), los Estados (administración pública estadal), y los Municipios (administración pública municipal). Conforme a esas normas, dicho universo de la Administración Pública encontró regulación global en la Ley Orgánica de la Administración Pública de 2001, la cual, siendo una ley nacional, sus disposiciones fueron básicamente "aplicables a la Administración Pública Nacional" (art. 2), pero disponiéndose, en relación con los órganos de los otros Poderes públicos estadales y municipales, que los principios y normas de la Ley Orgánica que se refirieran "en general a la Administración Pública, o expresamente a los Estados, Distritos Metropolitanos y Municipios," serían de "obligatoria observancia por éstos, quienes desarrollarán los mismos dentro del ámbito de sus respectivas competencias". Con ello, se respetaba la autonomía administrativa de los Estados y Municipios, y de sus propias Administraciones Públicas, que debía ejercerse dentro de un marco legal común. En cuanto a las demás regulaciones de la Ley Orgánica, regía el mismo principio de su posible aplicación supletoria a las Administraciones Públicas de los Estados y Municipios (art. 2).

En esta definición del ámbito de aplicación de la Ley Orgánica de la Administración Pública, sin embargo, con la reforma de la Ley Orgánica de 2008, se produjo una centralización administrativa al regularse entonces legalmente una sola "Administración Pública," "nacionalizándose" totalmente el régimen de la misma, al disponer que sus normas se aplican a la Administración Pública que abarca los tres niveles de distribución vertical del poder, es decir, "incluidos los estados, distritos metropolitanos y municipios, quienes deberán desarrollar su contenido dentro del ámbito de sus respectivas competencias" (art. 2). En la reforma de 2014, se ratificó el régimen único a pesar de hacer referencia a la "Administración Pública Nacional": al establecerse que sus normas "serán aplicables a la Administración Pública Nacional, así como a las de los estados, distritos metropolitanos, el Distrito capital, el Territorio Insular Miranda y las de los municipios, quienes deberán desarrollar su contenido dentro del ámbito de sus respectivas competencias"(art. 2).

Además, la Ley Orgánica centraliza totalmente la Administración Pública, al someterla (incluyendo la de los Estados y Municipios) a los lineamientos dictados por la Comisión Nacional de Planificación o conforme con la planificación centralizada (arts. 15, 18, 23, 32, 57, 78, 88, 93, 101, 120, 122, 132), a la dirección del Presidente de la República (art. 46) y a la coordinación del Vicepresidente de la República (art. 48,3). Es decir, la Ley Orgánica de 2008 reformada en 2014 no es que establece un régimen normativo común para todas las Administraciones Públicas, sino que regula una sola Administración Pública, totalmente centralizada, sin que los Gobernadores y Alcaldes tengan autonomía alguna en sus Administraciones Públicas, ya que las mismas están bajo la dirección del Presidente de la República, la coordinación del Vicepresidente ejecutivo y sometidas a los lineamientos de la planificación centralizada a cargo de un Ministerio del Poder Popular y una Comisión Central de Planificación que es un órgano de coordinación y control nacional.

Por otra parte, en cuanto al carácter supletorio de la Ley, sólo se refiere a las Administraciones de los demás órganos del Poder Público nacional, al disponer que "las disposiciones de la presente Ley se aplicarán supletoriamente a los demás órganos y entes del Poder Público" (art. 2).

II. EL DESBALANCE HACIA EL NIVEL NACIONAL EN LA DISTRIBU-CIÓN TERRITORIAL DEL PODER

La progresiva centralización de la Administración Pública también ha sido consecuencia del sistema de distribución de competencias del Poder Público entre los entes político territoriales que se adoptó en la Constitución, que ha atentado contra la descentralización política, lo que ha conducido a que casi todas las competencias públicas quedaron en el Poder Nacional. Los Estados, en la Constitución, materialmente carecen de materias sobre las cuales actuar como competencia exclusiva de los mismos, a pesar de que el artículo 164 hable, precisamente, de "competencias exclusivas."[1432] Las pocas indicadas en dicha norma, en realidad, son en su mayoría materias de competencia parcial de los Estados, en algunos casos concurrentes con el Poder Nacional o con el Poder Municipal, y en cuanto a las competencias que se habían descentralizado y convertido en "exclusiva" de los Estados, como la de la administración y manejo de los aeropuertos y puertos nacionales ubicados en cada Estado, como se dijo, fue centralizada o nacionalizada por la Sala Constitucional del Tribunal Supremo de Justicia en 2008, mutándose a tal efecto la Constitución.[1433]

En materia de competencias concurrentes, que los Estados hubieran podido haber asumido mediante ley estadal, las mismas, en la Constitución, quedaron sujetas a lo dispuesto en unas leyes nacionales denominadas "de base," con lo que pueden quedar condicionadas (art. 165), quedando en todo caso sujetas a lo dispuesto en la ley nacional. Y si bien en la Constitución se estableció la garantía de participación previa de los Estados en el proceso de elaboración de leyes nacionales que los puedan afectar (art. 206), que podía permitir a los Estados expresar su opinión sobre leyes que los afecten, ello nunca se ha garantizado en la práctica legislativa.

1432   Véase Allan R. Brewer-Carías, "La distribución territorial de competencias en la Federación venezolana" en *Revista de Estudios de Administración Local. Homenaje a Sebastián Martín Retortillo,* N° 291, enero-abril 2003, Instituto Nacional de Administración Pública, Madrid 2003, pp. 163-200.

1433   Véase sentencia de la Sala Constitucional, N° 565 de 15 de abril de 2008 (*caso Procuradora General de la República, recurso de interpretación del artículo 164.10 de la Constitución de 1999*) en http://www.tsj.gov.ve/decisiones/scon/Abril/565-150408-07-1108.htm. Véase los comentarios sobre esta sentencia, en Allan R. Brewer-Carías, "La Sala Constitucional como poder constituyente: la modificación de la forma federal del estado y del sistema constitucional de división territorial del poder público, en *Revista de Derecho Público,* N° 114, (abril-junio 2008), Editorial Jurídica Venezolana, Caracas 2008, pp. 247-262.

Y así las leyes nacionales dictadas en relación con materias de competencias concurrentes, en todo caso, lo que han producido es más bien una acentuada centralización, casi total, de las mismas, como ha ocurrido en materia de policía, respecto de la cual, los Estados y Municipios han sido vaciados casi completamente.[1434]

Por otra parte, en cuanto a la distribución de competencias entre los entes territoriales, el proceso de descentralización exigía, además, la asignación efectiva de competencias tributarias a los Estados, sobre todo en materia de impuestos al consumo, como sucede en casi todas las Federaciones. Los avances que se discutieron incluso en la Asamblea Constituyente en esta materia, sin embargo, se abandonaron, quitándosele a los Estados todas las competencias tributarias que se le habían asignado, con lo que incluso se retrocedió aún más respecto del esquema que existía en la Constitución de 1961.

Por tanto, en realidad, la Constitución de 1999 terminó de vaciar totalmente a los Estados de competencias tributarias, estableciéndose incluso en la Constitución una competencia residual, no a favor de los Estados como ocurre en las federaciones, sino en forma contraria al principio federal, a favor del Poder Nacional, en materia de impuestos, tasas y rentas no atribuidas a los Estados y Municipios por la Constitución o por la ley (art. 156,12). En consecuencia, a los Estados sólo les quedaron las competencias en materia de papel sellado, timbres y estampillas como se había establecido en la Ley Orgánica de Descentralización, Delimitación y Transferencia de Competencias del Poder Público de 1989,[1435] y nada más, pues incluso las materias que se les había transferido como las relativas a la atención de la salud, han sido progresivamente centralizadas.[1436]

La consecuencia de todo ese proceso de centralización es que los Estados y sus Administraciones Públicas han seguido siendo totalmente dependientes de los aportes provenientes del Presupuesto Nacional (Situado Constitucional), habiéndose atribuido la coordinación de la inversión de sus ingresos a un Consejo Federal de Gobierno (art. 185), que conforme a la Ley que lo reguló, lo que ha hecho es reforzar el control de los mismos por parte de los órganos nacionales. En efecto, en dicha la Ley Orgánica que regula el Consejo Federal de Gobierno de 2010,[1437] además de

---

1434   Lo que comenzó a realizarse con la Ley de Coordinación de Seguridad Ciudadana, en *Gaceta Oficial* N° 37.318 del 6 de noviembre de 2001. Véase además, la Ley Orgánica del Servicio de Policía y del Cuerpo de Policía Nacional, y la Ley Orgánica de la Función Policial en *Gaceta Oficial* N° 5940 de 7 de diciembre de 2009.

1435   Véase Allan R. Brewer-Carías, "Bases legislativas para la descentralización política de la federación centralizada (1990: El inicio de una reforma", en Allan R. Brewer-Carías (Coordinador y editor), Carlos Ayala Corao, Jorge Sánchez Meleán, Gustavo Linares y Humberto Romero Muci, *Leyes para la Descentralización Política de la Federación*, Colección Textos Legislativos, N° 11, Editorial Jurídica Venezolana, Caracas 1990, pp. 7-53; y "La descentralización política en Venezuela: 1990. El inicio de una reforma" en Dieter Nohlen (editor), *Descentralización Política y Consolidación Democrática Europa-América del Sur*, Madrid-Caracas 1991, pp. 131-160.

1436   Véase por ejemplo el Decreto N° 6.543, "mediante el cual se decreta la transferencia al Ministerio del Poder Popular para la Salud, de los Establecimientos y las Unidades Móviles de Atención Médica adscrito a la Gobernación del estado Bolivariano de Miranda," en *Gaceta Oficial* N° 39.072 de 3-12-2008.

1437   Véase en *Gaceta Oficial* N° 5.963 Extra. de 22-2-2010.

preverse su organización y funcionamiento, se establecen "los lineamientos de la planificación y coordinación de las políticas y acciones necesarias para el adecuado desarrollo regional," e igualmente, "el régimen para la transferencia de las competencias entre los entes territoriales, y a las organizaciones detentadoras de la soberanía originaria del Estado" (art. 1). En este último caso, además, haciendo referencia, sin duda, a los órganos del llamado Poder Popular o Estado Comunal, lo que significa que además del centralismo por asunción de poderes de intervención por parte del Poder Central, se ha previsto otro mecanismo de centralización pero por "vaciamiento" de competencias hacia las entidades del llamado Poder Popular que están controlados precisamente por el Poder Nacional.

Conforme a dicha Ley Orgánica, en efecto, dicho Consejo Federal es el órgano encargado de la planificación y coordinación de las políticas y acciones para el desarrollo del proceso de descentralización y transferencia de competencias del Poder Nacional a los Estados y Municipios, teniendo los lineamientos que dicte en materia de transferencia de competencias, carácter "vinculantes para las entidades territoriales" (art. 2). La Ley Orgánica estableció, además, que dicha transferencia de competencias "es la vía para lograr el fortalecimiento de las organizaciones de base del Poder Popular y el desarrollo armónico de los Distritos Motores de Desarrollo y regiones del país," (art. 7), órganos todos que por lo demás, como se ha dicho, son dependientes del Ejecutivo Nacional.

III. EL AHOGAMIENTO Y NEUTRALIZACIÓN DE LAS ENTIDADES TERRITORIALES POR PARTE DE LA ADMINISTRACIÓN PÚBLICA NACIONAL

Pero el proceso de centralización de la Administración Pública no sólo se ha producido los el desbalance en el régimen de distribución de competencias entre los entes territoriales, a favor del ámbito nacional, sino por la acción de los propios órganos del Poder Nacional, que han venido, a la vez, ahogando directamente a las entidades territoriales.

Ello ha ocurrido, por ejemplo, mediante el establecimiento de una estructura organizativa de la Administración Pública nacional, dependiente del Vicepresidente Ejecutivo de la República, en forma paralela y superpuesta a la Administración de los Estados, denominada como "Órganos Desconcentrados de las Regiones Estratégicas de Desarrollo Integral (REDI),"[1438] a cargo de funcionarios denominados "Autoridades Regionales," las cuales además, tienen "Dependencias" en cada Estado de la República, que están a cargo de Delegaciones Estadales, todos del libre nombramiento del Vicepresidente de la República.

Estos Delegados, que ejercen sus funciones "dentro del territorio del Estado que le ha sido asignado" (art. 19), se los ha concebido como los canales de comunicación de los Gobernadores de Estado con el Poder Nacional y viceversa, del Poder Nacional con los Estados, teniendo además como misión "realizar las acciones ten-

---

1438   Véase Resolución N° 031 de la Vicepresidencia de la República, mediante la cual se establece la Estructura y Normas de Funcionamiento de los órganos Desconcentrados de las Regiones Estratégicas de Desarrollo Integral (REDI), en *Gaceta Oficial* N° 40.193 de 20-6-2013.

dentes a impulsar la integración y operación de las comunidades organizadas, instancias del poder popular, organizaciones del poder popular, los consejos de economía y contraloría comunal bajo su demarcación, en términos de la normatividad aplicable, cumpliendo con los criterios establecidos por la Autoridad Regional de las Regiones Estratégicas de Desarrollo Integral (REDI)"(art. 20). En definitiva, estas Autoridades nacionales Regionales y los Delegados Estadales, son los órganos administrativos del Poder Nacional montados en paralelo a las autoridades estadales, con el objeto de asegurar el vaciamiento de sus competencias y la neutralización del poder de los Gobernadores de Estado, particularmente si no son miembros del partido oficial; todo ello dentro de un proceso de planificación centralizada que se ha regulado en la Ley de la Regionalización Integral para el Desarrollo Socio productivo de la Patria de 2014,[1439] que establece zonas económicas especiales de desarrollo, buscándose "regularizar" las estructuras administrativas nacionales de intervención y sometimiento de las entidades político territoriales.

En todo caso, un ejemplo del proceso de ahogamiento y neutralización de las entidades territoriales de la República, particularmente de las existentes en la Región Capital, ocurrió en 2008, con la creación de autoridades en el Distrito Capital totalmente dependientes del Poder Ejecutivo, violándose la Constitución. En efecto, en la Constitución de 1999 se había buscado cambiar radicalmente la concepción del viejo Distrito Federal creado desde 1863 como entidad dependiente del Poder Nacional, estableciéndose el Distrito Capital como una entidad política más de la República (art. 16), con sus propios órganos legislativo y ejecutivo de gobierno democrático, es decir, integrado por funcionarios electos popularmente, que debía ser regulado por el Poder Nacional (art. 156,10). Debe mencionarse que ese esquema de autonomía territorial también se pretendió reformar en la rechazada Reforma Constitucional de 2007, en la cual se buscaba eliminar el Distrito Capital y recrear la desaparecida figura del Distrito Federal como entidad totalmente dependiente del Poder Nacional, en particular del Presidente de la República, sin gobierno propio.

Después del rechazo popular a dicha reforma constitucional, sin embargo, esta reforma se ha implementado en fraude a la Constitución, y por supuesto a la voluntad popular, mediante la Ley Especial Sobre la Organización y Régimen del Distrito Capital,[1440] en la cual se lo ha regulado como una dependencia del Poder Nacional, con el mismo ámbito territorial del extinto Distrito Federal; y con un supuesto "régimen especial de gobierno," conforme al cual, la función legislativa en el Distrito está a cargo de la Asamblea Nacional, y el órgano ejecutivo es ejercido por un Jefe de Gobierno (art. 3), que de acuerdo con el artículo 7 de la Ley Especial, es "de libre nombramiento y remoción" por parte del Presidente de la República; es decir, un "régimen especial de gobierno" dependiente del Poder Central.

Con ello, en el mismo territorio del Municipio Libertador y de parte del territorio del Distrito metropolitano a cargo de un Alcalde y un Consejo Metropolitanos de Caracas, se le ha superpuesto una estructura nacional, como entidad dependiente funcionalmente del Ejecutivo nacional, sin gobierno democrático ni autonomía polí-

---

1439   Véase en *Gaceta Oficial* N° 6.151 de 18 de noviembre de 2014.
1440   Véase en *Gaceta Oficial* N° 39.156 de 13 de abril de 2009.

tico territorial, ignorando además la existencia del régimen municipal metropolitano a dos niveles previsto en la Constitución, duplicando las funciones del mismo, dispuesto para ahogarlo y controlarlo.

Como consecuencia de todo lo anteriormente expuesto, puede decirse entonces que la Federación que se plasmó en la Constitución de 1999 no sólo siguió siendo, más acentuadamente, la misma Federación centralizada desarrollada en las décadas anteriores, sino que los pocos elementos que podían contribuir a su descentralización política, fueron desmontados progresivamente en los últimos tres lustros.

En esta perspectiva, el Estado venezolano que nunca ha sido ni ha tenido realmente las características de un " Federal descentralizado," expresión que sólo fue una etiqueta contradictoria e ilusa inserta en una Constitución centralista, progresivamente se ha centralizado aún más, ubicándose todo el poder público en el Estado nacional, que ahora está configurado como un Estado Totalitario y centralizado. Esa centralización ha sido el resultado de un progresivo desbalance hacia el nivel nacional en la distribución territorial del Poder, en el cual se ha vaciado a los Estados de toda competencia sustantiva, y a los Municipios se les ha quitado su carácter de unidad primaria en la organización nacional, montándose en paralelo y en contra de la Constitución, una organización del llamado Poder Popular Estado Comunal, integrada por Comunas y Consejos Comunales, que han venido neutralizando y ahogando a los Municipios, como instrumentos realmente del Poder nacional. Con ese esquema estatal, sin duda, el derecho público y administrativo que se ha desarrollado es un derecho propio de un Estado centralizado.

SECCIÓN CUARTA:

LA CREACIÓN DEL ESTADO COMUNAL O DEL PODER POPULAR, EN PARALELO AL ESTADO CONSTITUCIONAL Y EL AHOGAMIENTO PROGRESIVO DE LA ADMINISTRACIÓN MUNICIPAL

I. LA CREACIÓN DEL ESTADO COMUNAL EN PARALELO AL ESTADO CONSTITUCIONAL

Conforme a las previsiones de la Constitución, así ese haya concebido al Estado, realmente, como una "federación centralizada" montada en un sistema desbalanceado de distribución de competencias entre los tres niveles territoriales (nacional, estadal y municipal), el régimen constitucional impide crear por ley instancias políticas que vacíen de competencias a los órganos del Estado (la República, los Estados, los Municipios y demás entidades locales) y menos aún establecerlos con funciones políticas sin que se asegure su carácter electivo mediante la elección de representantes del pueblo a través de sufragio universal, directo y secreto; sin que se asegure su autonomía política propia del carácter "descentralizado" del Estado; y sin que se garantice su carácter pluralista, en el sentido de que no pueden estar vinculados a una sola ideología determinada como es el Socialismo.

El modelo de Estado Constitucional, sin embargo, como se ha dicho, se intentó cambiar mediante la mencionada Reforma Constitucional sancionada por la Asamblea Nacional en noviembre de 2007, con el objeto de establecer un Estado Socialista, Centralizado, Militarista y Policial[1441] denominado "Estado del Poder Popular" o "Estado Comunal,"[1442] la cual sin embargo, una vez sometida a consulta popular, fue rechazada por el pueblo el 7 de diciembre de 2007.[1443]

Sin embargo, en burla a la dicha voluntad popular, y en fraude a la Constitución, desde antes de que se efectuara dicho referendo, la Asamblea Nacional en abierta violación a la Constitución, comenzó a desmantelar el Estado Constitucional para sustituirlo por un Estado Socialista mediante la estructuración *paralela* de un Estado del Poder Popular o Estado Comunal, lo que comenzó a hacer a través de la sanción de la Ley de los Consejos Comunales de 2006,[1444] reformada posteriormente y elevada al rango de ley orgánica en 2009.[1445] Posteriormente, puede decirse que el empeño por implantar en Venezuela un Estado Socialista fue rechazado de nuevo con ocasión de las elecciones legislativas efectuadas el 26 de septiembre de 2010, las cuales fueron planteadas por el Presidente de la República de entonces y por la mayoría oficialista de la propia Asamblea Nacional, quienes hicieron una masiva campaña a favor de sus candidatos, como un "plebiscito" respecto al propio Presidente, su actuación y sus políticas socialistas ya previamente rechazadas por el pueblo en 2007; "plebiscito" que el Presidente de la República y su partido perdieron abrumadoramente pues la mayoría del país votó en contra de las mismas.

Sin embargo, al haber perdido el Presidente y su partido, a raíz de dichas elecciones parlamentarias, el control absoluto que ejercían sobre la Asamblea Nacional, lo que a partir de entonces les debía impedir imponer sin límites cualquier ley, en diciembre de 2010, unos días antes de que la nueva Asamblea Nacional se constituyera y los nuevos diputados electos pudieran tomar posesión de sus cargos en enero de 2011, atropelladamente y de nuevo en fraude a la voluntad popular y a la Constitución, la ya deslegitimada Asamblea Nacional procedió a sancionar un conjunto de Leyes Orgánicas del Poder Popular, de las Comunas, del Sistema Económico Comunal, de Planificación Pública y Comunal y de Contraloría Social,[1446] mediante las cuales se buscó terminar de definir, al margen de la Constitución, el marco normativo de un nuevo Estado, *paralelo al Estado Constitucional*, que no es otra cosa que un Estado Comunista, es decir, Socialista, Centralizado, Militarista y Policial, denominado "Estado Comunal," que

1441   Véase Allan R. Brewer-Carías, *Hacia la Consolidación de un Estado Socialista, Centralizado, Policial y Militarista. Comentarios sobre el sentido y alcance de las propuestas de reforma constitucional 2007*, Colección Textos Legislativos, N° 42, Editorial Jurídica Venezolana, Caracas 2007.

1442   Véase Allan R. Brewer-Carías, *La reforma constitucional de 2007 (Comentarios al Proyecto inconstitucionalmente sancionado por la Asamblea Nacional el 2 de noviembre de 2007)*, Colección Textos Legislativos, N° 43, Editorial Jurídica Venezolana, Caracas 2007.

1443   Véase Allan R. Brewer-Carías, "La proyectada reforma constitucional de 2007, rechazada por el poder constituyente originario", en *Anuario de Derecho Público 2007*, Año 1, Instituto de Estudios de Derecho Público de la Universidad Monteávila, Caracas 2008, pp. 17-65.

1444   Véase en *Gaceta Oficial* N° 5.806 Extra. de 10-04-2006.

1445   Véase en *Gaceta Oficial* N° 39.335 de 28-12-2009.

1446   Véase en *Gaceta Oficial* N° 6.011 Extra. de 21-12-2010.

ha originado otra "nueva" Administración Pública paralela a la Administración Pública que regula en la Ley Orgánica de la Administración Pública.[1447]

Además de dichas Leyes Orgánicas, en el mismo marco de estructuración del "Estado Comunal" montado sobre el "Poder Popular" se reformó de la Ley Orgánica del Poder Público Municipal, y las Leyes de los Consejos Estadales de Planificación y Coordinación de Políticas Públicas, y de los Consejos Locales de Planificación Pública.[1448] En diciembre de 2010, además, se trató de aprobar la Ley Orgánica del Sistema de Transferencia de Competencias y Atribuciones de los Estados y Municipios a las Organizaciones del Poder Popular, la cual sin embargo no llegó a ser sancionada,[1449] aun cuando en 2012 se materializó con la la Ley Orgánica para la Gestión Comunitaria de Competencias, Servicios y Otras Atribuciones (Decreto Ley N° 9.043),[1450] habiendo sido reformada en 2014, por la Ley Orgánica para la Transferencia al Poder Popular de la Gestión y Administración Comunitaria de Servicios.[1451]

El Estado Comunal, mediante la progresiva desconstitucionalización del Estado Constitucional, al margen y en contra de las instituciones previstas en la Constitución, ha venido configurando "nuevos" órganos y entes como si fueran las "unidades primarias en la organización nacional" para supuestamente garantizar la participación de los ciudadanos en la acción pública, pero suplantando a los Estados y Municipios como entes descentralizados del Estado federal. Esta estructuración del Estado Comunal, además, se ha hecho negándole recursos financieros a los propios del Estado Constitucional (Estados y Municipios), montando un sistema de entidades denominadas del Poder Popular, creadas al margen de la Constitución y en paralelo a los órganos del Poder Público. Estas son básicamente los antes mencionadas Comunas y Consejos Comunales, creadas como instrumentos para la recepción de subsidios directos y reparto de recursos presupuestarios públicos, pero con un grado extremo de exclusión, lo que deriva de su propia existencia que sólo se puede materializar con el registro de las mismas ante el "Ministerio del Poder Popular para las Comunas y Movimientos Sociales" que además depende del "Vicepresidente del Consejo de Ministros para Desarrollo del Socialismo Territorial," por supuesto, siempre que estén controlados y manejados por el partido de gobierno, sean socialistas y comprometidas con la política socialista del Estado; condición indispensable para poder ser aceptados como instrumentos de supuesta "participación protagónica," y de recepción de subsidios dinerarios directos, que por lo demás se están sometidos a control fiscal alguno.

1447   Véase sobre estas leyes Allan R. Brewer-Carías, Claudia Nikken, Luis A. Herrera Orellana, Jesús María Alvarado Andrade, José Ignacio Hernández y Adriana Vigilanza, *Leyes Orgánicas sobre el Poder Popular y el Estado Comunal (Los Consejos Comunales, las Comunas, la Sociedad Socialista y el Sistema Económico Comunal),* Editorial Jurídica Venezolana, Caracas 2011.

1448   Véase en *Gaceta Oficial* N° 6.015 Extra. de 30-12-2010.

1449   El proyecto de esta Ley fue aprobado en Primera Discusión en la Asamblea Nacional el 21 de diciembre de 2010. Para el 31 de diciembre de 2010 quedó en discusión en la Asamblea Nacional.

1450   Véase en *Gaceta Oficial* N° 6.097 Extra. de 15 de junio de 2012.

1451   Véase en *Gaceta Oficial* N° 40.540 de 13 de noviembre de 2014.

En efecto, la práctica legislativa y gubernamental desarrollada después del rechazo popular a la reforma constitucional de 2007 que pretendía consolidar un Estado totalmente centralizado, y además, crear en paralelo al Estado Constitucional, a una estructura denominada como "Estado del Poder Popular" o "Estado Comunal," ha originado que el mismo haya sido efectivamente crearlo al margen de la Constitución con el propósito de desmantelar el Estado Constitucional federal, centralizando hacia el nivel nacional competencias estadales, y transfiriendo competencias estadales y municipales hacia los Consejos Comunales, que a su vez como se ha dicho, dependen del Ejecutivo Nacional.[1452]

En ese esquema, el proceso de desconstitucionalización, centralismo y desmunicipalización en Venezuela, en los últimos años se ha llevado a cabo, en *primer lugar*, mediante el establecimiento como obligación legal para los órganos, entes e instancias del Poder Público, es decir del Estado Constitucional, de promover, apoyar y acompañar las iniciativas populares para la constitución, desarrollo y consolidación de las diversas formas organizativas y de autogobierno del pueblo, es decir, del llamado Estado Comunal (art. 23).[1453]

En *segundo lugar*, la desconstitucionalización del Estado se ha impuesto mediante la sujeción de todos los órganos del Estado Constitucional que ejercen el Poder Público, a los mandatos de las organizaciones del Poder Popular, al instituirse un nuevo principio de gobierno, consistente en "gobernar obedeciendo" (artículo 24).[1454] Como las organizaciones del Poder Popular no tienen autonomía política pues sus "voceros" no son electos democráticamente mediante sufragio universal, directo y secreto, sino designados por asambleas de ciudadanos controladas e intervenidas por el partido oficial y el Ejecutivo Nacional que controla y guía todo el proceso organizativo del Estado Comunal, en el ámbito exclusivo de la ideología socialista, sin que tenga cabida vocero alguno que no sea socialista; en definitiva, esto de "gobernar obedeciendo" es una limitación a la autonomía política de los órganos del Estado Constitucional electos, como la Asamblea Nacional, los Gobernadores y Consejos Legislativos de los Estados y los Alcaldes y Concejos Municipa

---

1452   Véase en general sobre este proceso de desconstitucionalización del Estado, Allan R. Brewer-Carías, "La desconstitucionalización del Estado de derecho en Venezuela: del Estado Democrático y Social de derecho al Estado Comunal Socialista, sin reformar la Constitución," *en Libro Homenaje al profesor Alfredo Morles Hernández, Diversas Disciplinas Jurídicas,* (Coordinación y Compilación Astrid Uzcátegui Angulo y Julio Rodríguez Berrizbeitia), Universidad Católica Andrés Bello, Universidad de Los Andes, Universidad Monteávila, Universidad Central de Venezuela, Academia de Ciencias Políticas y Sociales, Vol. V, Caracas 2012, pp. 51-82; en Carlos Tablante y Mariela Morales Antonorzzi (Coord.), *Descentralización, autonomía e inclusión social. El desafío actual de la democracia,* Anuario 2010-2012, Observatorio Internacional para la democracia y descentralización, En Cambio, Caracas 2011, pp. 37-84; y en *Estado Constitucional,* Año 1, N° 2, Editorial Adrus, Lima, junio 2011, pp. 217-236.

1453   Una norma similar está en el artículo 62 de la Ley Orgánica de las Comunas, a los efectos de "la constitución, desarrollo y consolidación de las comunas como forma de autogobierno."

1454   El artículo 24 de la Ley Orgánica del Poder Popular, en efecto, sobre dispone sobre las "Actuaciones de los órganos y entes del Poder Público" que "Todos los órganos, entes e instancias del Poder Público guiarán sus actuaciones por el principio de gobernar obedeciendo, en relación con los mandatos de los ciudadanos, ciudadanas y de las organizaciones del Poder Popular, de acuerdo a lo establecido en la Constitución de la República y las leyes."

les, a quienes se le impone en definitiva la obligación de obedecer lo que disponga el Ejecutivo Nacional y el partido oficial enmarcado en el ámbito exclusivo del socialismo como doctrina política, con la máscara del Poder Popular. La voluntad popular expresada en la elección de representantes del Estado Constitucional, por tanto, en este esquema del Estado Comunal no tiene valor alguno, y al pueblo se le confisca su soberanía trasladándola de hecho a unas asambleas que no lo representan.

En *tercer lugar*, la desconstitucionalización del Estado Constitucional se ha reforzado con el establecimiento de la obligación para los órganos y entes del Poder Público en sus relaciones con el Poder Popular, de dar "preferencia a las comunidades organizadas, a las comunas y a los sistemas de agregación y articulación que surjan entre ellas, en atención a los requerimientos que las mismas formulen para la satisfacción de sus necesidades y el ejercicio de sus derechos, en los términos y lapsos que establece la ley" (art. 29). Igualmente se ha previsto que los órganos, entes e instancias del Poder Público, es decir, del Estado Constitucional, en sus diferentes niveles político-territoriales, deben adoptar "medidas para que las organizaciones socio-productivas de propiedad social comunal, gocen de prioridad y preferencia en los procesos de contrataciones públicas para la adquisición de bienes, prestación de servicios y ejecución de obras" (art. 30).[1455]

En *cuarto lugar*, la desconstitucionalización del Estado también ha derivado de la previsión de la obligación para la República, los Estados y Municipios, de acuerdo con la ley que rige el proceso de transferencia y descentralización de competencias y atribuciones, de trasferir "a las comunidades organizadas, a las comunas y a los sistemas de agregación que de éstas surjan; funciones de gestión, administración, control de servicios y ejecución de obras atribuidos a aquéllos por la Constitución de la República, para mejorar la eficiencia y los resultados en beneficio del colectivo" (art. 27).[1456] Con ello, se dispuso legalmente el vaciamiento de competencias de los Estados y Municipios, de manera que queden como estructuras vacías, con gobiernos representativos electos por el pueblo pero que no tienen materias sobre las cuales gobernar.

II. LAS COMUNAS VERSUS LA ADMINISTRACIÓN MUNICIPAL

La estructuración paralela del Estado Comunal o del Poder Popular, con la creación de las Comunas, ha tenido un impacto fundamental en la Administración Municipal, con la creación, al margen de la Constitución, de las Comunas, que han sido concebidas en la Ley Orgánica del Poder Popular, precisamente para suplantar al

---

1455   En particular, conforme al artículo 61 de la Ley Orgánica de las Comunas, se dispone que "todos los órganos y entes del Poder Público comprometidos con el financiamiento de proyectos de las comunas y sus sistemas de agregación, priorizarán aquéllos que impulsen la atención a las comunidades de menor desarrollo relativo, a fin de garantizar el desarrollo territorial equilibrado.

1456   Esta misma norma se repite en la Ley Orgánica de las Comunas (art. 64). El 31 de diciembre de 2010, aún estaba pendiente en la Asamblea Nacional la segunda discusión del proyecto de Ley Orgánica del Sistema de Transferencia de Competencias y atribuciones de los Estados y Municipios a las organizaciones del Poder Popular.

Municipio constitucional, como la "célula fundamental" de dicho Estado Comunal.[1457]

Para ese efecto, a la Comuna se la definió en el artículo 15.2 de esta Ley Orgánica del Poder Popular, como el "espacio socialista que como entidad local es definida por la integración de comunidades vecinas con una memoria histórica compartida, rasgos culturales, usos y costumbres que se reconocen en el territorio que ocupan y en las actividades productivas que le sirven de sustento y sobre el cual ejercen los principios de soberanía y participación protagónica como expresión del Poder Popular, en concordancia con un régimen de producción social y el modelo de desarrollo endógeno y sustentable contemplado en el Plan de Desarrollo, Económico y Social de la Nación." Esta misma definición de la Comuna como "espacio socialista," está también en el artículo 5 de la Ley Orgánica de las Comunas; noción que implica que la misma está vedada a todo aquél que no sea socialista o que no crea en el socialismo, o que no comulgue con el socialismo como doctrina política. La concepción legal de la Comuna, por tanto, es contraria al pluralismo democrático que garantiza la Constitución (art. 6), siendo abiertamente discriminatoria y contraria a la igualdad que también garantiza el artículo 21 de la Constitución.

Pero para consolidar la institución, aún en forma contraria al pluralismo, en la Ley Orgánica del Poder Popular se define a la Comuna como una "entidad local," y la misma calificación se encuentra en el artículo 1 de la Ley Orgánica de las Comunas, que la define "como entidad local donde los ciudadanos y ciudadanas en el ejercicio del Poder Popular, ejercen el pleno derecho de la soberanía y desarrollan la participación protagónica mediante formas de autogobierno para la edificación del estado comunal, en el marco del Estado democrático y social de derecho y de justicia" (art. 1). También en la reforma de la Ley Orgánica del Poder Público Municipal de diciembre de 2010, se incluyó a las comunas en el listado de las "entidades locales territoriales" (art. 19) disponiéndose que las mismas, al estar reguladas por una legislación diferente como es la relativa al Poder Popular, y al poder constituirse "entre varios municipios," quedan exceptuadas de las disposiciones de la Ley Orgánica del Poder Público Municipal.

Ahora bien, en cuanto a calificar a las Comunas como "entidades locales," el Legislador olvidó que conforme a la Constitución (arts. 169, 173), esta expresión de "entidad local" sólo se puede aplicar a las "entidades políticas" del Estado en las cuales necesariamente tiene que haber gobiernos integrados por representantes electos mediante sufragio universal, directo y secreto (arts. 63, 169), ceñidos a los principios establecidos en el artículo 6 de la Constitución, es decir, que ser "siempre democrático, participativo, electivo, descentralizado, alternativo, responsable, pluralista y de mandatos revocables."

1457   Véase en *Gaceta Oficial* Nº 6.011 Extra. de 21-12-2010. Véase sobre esta Ley el libro de Allan R. Brewer-Carías, Claudia Nikken, Luis A. Herrera Orellana, Jesús María Alvarado Andrade, José Ignacio Hernández y Adriana Vigilanza, *Leyes Orgánicas sobre el Poder Popular y el Estado Comunal (Los Consejos Comunales, las Comunas, la Sociedad Socialista y el Sistema Económico Comunal)*, Colección Textos Legislativos Nº 50, Editorial Jurídica Venezolana, Caracas 2011. Véase además, Allan R. Brewer-Carías, "La Ley Orgánica del Poder Popular y la desconstitucionalización del Estado de derecho en Venezuela," en *Revista de Derecho Público*, Nº 124, (octubre-diciembre 2010), Editorial Jurídica Venezolana, Caracas 2010, pp. 81-101.

Conforme a la Constitución, por tanto, no puede haber "entidades locales" con gobiernos que no sean democráticos representativos en los términos mencionados, y menos "gobernadas" por "voceros" designados por otros órganos públicos. Y esto es precisamente lo que ocurre con los llamados "gobiernos de las comunas," que conforme a esta legislación sobre el Poder Popular y sus organizaciones, no se garantiza su origen democrático mediante elección por sufragio universal, directo y secreto, siendo en consecuencia inconstitucional su concepción. Por ello, con razón, Héctor Silva Michelena se ha referido al Estado Comunal como un "Estado de siervos," indicando que:

"El establecimiento de las comunas es la demolición de la República porque la República está asentada sobre el municipio que es su célula primaria. Las gobernaciones, consejos municipales, asambleas legislativas, alcaldes son la base de una República democrática. En esta estructura el voto es universal, directo y secreto. En las leyes aprobadas para las comunas se deja ese tema abierto sin mayor precisión, solo se menciona que habrá una elección popular, pero es a mano alzada, consulté con constitucionalistas y personas que han estado en consejos comunales en varios estados del país y es así. Después no hay más elecciones, la votación es de segundo o tercer grado.

Este es un sistema que sirve para que el chavismo continúe en el poder, la idea es que los voceros elegidos a mano alzada sean representantes del partido."[1458]

III. EL ESTADO COMUNAL Y EL AHOGAMIENTO DE LA ADMINISTRACIÓN PÚBLICA MUNICIPAL

En este esquema de establecimiento del Estado del Poder Popular y el Estado Comunal, a los efectos de ahogar y estrangular progresivamente el Estado Constitucional, por tanto, la primera de las instituciones territoriales afectadas ha sido el Municipio, el cual, siendo la unidad política primaria dentro la organización de la República, ha quedado desvinculado totalmente del proceso de desarrollo comunal y de la llamada participación popular. A tal efecto, además de la sanción de las Leyes Orgánicas del Poder Popular, en fraude a la Constitución y a la voluntad popular que había rechazado la reforma constitucional de 2007, en el mismo mes de diciembre de 2010, se introdujeron diversas reformas la Ley Orgánica del Poder Público Municipal (LOPP),[1459] en la cual, entre otros aspectos, se reguló lo siguiente:

En primer lugar, la previsión, como objetivo de la Ley, además de la regulación de los Municipios y su gobierno, del denominado proceso de "descentralización y la transferencia de competencias a las comunidades organizadas, y a las comunas en su condición especial de entidad local, como a otras organizaciones del Poder Popular" (Art. 1). Se entiende que se trata de un proceso de transferencia de "competencias,"

1458   Véase en Víctor Salmerón, "La comuna es una sociedad de súbditos," Entrevista a Héctor Silva Michelena, en *Prodavinci*, 25 de septiembre de 2014, en http://prodavinci.com/2014/09/25/actualidad/la-comuna-es-una-sociedad-de-subditos-entrevista-a-hector-silva-michelena-por-victor-salmeron/1nm. Véase además, Héctor Silva Michelena, *Estado de Siervos. Desnudando al Estado Comunal*, bid & co., Caracas 2014.

1459   Véase en *Gaceta Oficial* N° 6.015 Extraordinario del 28 de diciembre de 2010.

pero la misma no puede calificarse como "descentralización," pues ésta, conceptualmente en el derecho administrativo y en el marco territorial y político, exige que
las entidades receptoras de las competencias a ser transferidas, sean entidades locales concebidas como entidades políticas con gobiernos electos democráticamente. Es
decir, no puede haber conceptualmente descentralización política cuando la transferencia de competencias se conduce a órganos dependientes del Poder Central; y las
Comunas, a pesar de que se las denomine como "entidades locales especiales," no
son gobernadas por órganos cuyos integrantes sean electos por votación universal
directa y secreta. Las mismas, por tanto, no tienen autonomía política ni pueden
formar parte del esquema de descentralización territorial del Estado, sino que son
conducidas por "voceros" designados a mano alzada por asambleas controladas por
el partido oficial, sujetas al gobierno nacional.

En segundo lugar, el artículo 2 de la Ley Orgánica del Poder Municipal, a pesar
de que repite el principio constitucional de que el Municipio "constituye la unidad
política primaria de la organización nacional de la República," ya no habla de que
"gozan de autonomía" como lo garantiza el artículo 168 de la Constitución, sino de
que "ejerce sus competencias de manera autónoma." Ello, sin embargo, es contradicho con lo que la propia Ley establece al disponer de que "el municipio se regirá por
el Sistema Nacional de Planificación establecido en la ley que regula la materia,"
(art. 110) que en Venezuela, muy anacrónicamente es una planificación centralizada
y obligatoria regulada en la Ley que creó la Comisión Central de Planificación,[1460] y
desarrollada en la ley Orgánica de Planificación Pública y Popular.[1461]

A tal efecto, en la Ley Orgánica del Poder Público Municipal, además, se eliminó la iniciativa ejecutiva de la planificación local que se asignaba al Alcalde,
quien debía presentar al Consejo Local de Planificación las líneas maestras de su
plan de gobierno, y se establece, en cambio, que el Consejo Local de Planificación
Pública es "el órgano encargado de diseñar el Plan Municipal de Desarrollo y los
demás planes municipales, en concordancia con los lineamientos que establezca el
Plan de Desarrollo Económico y Social de la Nación y los demás planes nacionales
y estadales, garantizando la participación protagónica del pueblo en su formulación,
ejecución, seguimiento, evaluación y control, en articulación con el Sistema Nacional de Planificación" (art. 111).

Ese Consejo, además, en la Ley Orgánica, quedó encargado de "diseñar el Plan
de Desarrollo Comunal, en concordancia con los planes de desarrollo comunitario
propuestos por los Consejos Comunales y los demás planes de interés colectivo,
articulados con el Sistema Nacional de Planificación, de conformidad con lo establecido en la legislaciones que regula a las Comunas y los Consejos Comunales;"
contando para ello con el apoyo de los órganos y entes de la Administración Pública. A tales efectos, agrega la norma, "es deber de las instancias que conforman la

---

1460   Véase Allan R. Brewer-Carías, "Comentarios sobre la inconstitucional creación de la Comisión Cen-
        tral de Planificación, centralizada y obligatoria", en *Revista de Derecho Público*, N° 110, (abril-junio
        2007), Editorial Jurídica Venezolana, Caracas 2007, pp. 79-89.

1461   Véase en *Gaceta Oficial* N° 6.011 Extraordinario del 21 de diciembre de 2010. Dicha Ley ha sido
        reformada de nuevo en noviembre de 2014. Véase en *Gaceta Oficial* N° 6.148 Extra de 18 de no-
        viembre de 2014. Al concluir la redacción de este texto, dicha Gaceta no había circulado.

organización del municipio, atender los requerimientos de los diversos consejos de planificación existentes en cada una de las comunas para el logro de sus objetivos y metas" (art. 112)

En tercer lugar, en la reforma de la Ley Orgánica del Poder Púbico Municipal se encasilló y limitó el rol del Municipio como promotor de la participación del pueblo sólo "a través de las comunidades organizadas," que son las que se regulan en las Leyes Orgánicas del Poder Popular como dependientes del Poder Ejecutivo nacional y orientadas exclusivamente a desarrollar el socialismo, en contra de la previsión del artículo 62 de la Constitución que garantiza el carácter libre de la participación, y en contra del pluralismo que también establece la Constitución. La desvinculación de las comunidades organizadas respecto del Municipio, se aseguró además, en la propia Ley, al excluirse su registro ante los órganos competentes "del Municipio" como decía la Ley Orgánica anterior que se reformó, previéndose ahora su registro sólo ante "los órganos competentes" (art. 33.3) que en las Leyes Orgánica del Poder Popular es uno de los Ministerios del Ejecutivo Nacional, el Ministerio del Poder Popular para las Comunas y Movimientos Sociales.

Es decir, con la reforma de la Ley Orgánica del Poder Municipal se produjo la total desmunicipalización de las entidades locales, y su total control por el Poder central. Se recuerda, además, que de acuerdo con la Ley Orgánica del Poder Popular (art. 32), los Consejos Comunales y las Comunas adquieren personalidad jurídica mediante el registro ante el Ministerio del Poder Popular de las Comunas y Movimientos Sociales, con lo que, en definitiva, se deja en manos del Ejecutivo Nacional la decisión de registrar o no un Consejo Comunal, una Comuna o una Ciudad comunal, y ello debe hacerse, por supuesto, aplicando la letra de la Ley, lo que significa que si está dominada por "voceros" que no sean socialistas, no cabe su registro ni, por tanto, su reconocimiento como persona jurídica, así sea producto genuino de una iniciativa popular.

En cuarto lugar, como parte de ese proceso de desmunicipalización de la vida local, a las Comunas, se las buscó incorporar en el régimen del Poder Público Municipal como "entidad local territorial" (art. 19) aun cuando de "carácter especial," pues conforme al artículo 19, "se rige por su ley de creación," y pueden constituirse "dentro del territorio del Municipio o entre los límites político administrativo de dos o más municipios, sin que ello afecte la integridad territorial de los municipios donde se constituya." Pero a pesar de ser tales "entidades locales" de carácter especial, sin embargo, se las excluyó completamente del régimen de la Ley Orgánica del Poder Municipal quedando "reguladas por la legislación que norma su constitución, conformación, organización y funcionamiento" (art. 5). Ello se reafirmó en el artículo 33 de la Ley, al disponer que "los requisitos para la creación de la comuna, en el marco de su régimen especial como entidad local," son los establecidos en la propia Ley Orgánica de las Comunas.

Es precisamente hacia las Comunas, además de hacia las Comunidades, Consejos Comunales, empresas de propiedad social y otras entidades de base del Poder Popular, hacia las cuales se prevé que se deben vaciar a los Municipios de sus competencias, lo cual se concretó en 2012 al dictarse la Ley Orgánica para la Gestión

Comunitaria de Competencias, Servicios y Otras Atribuciones, [1462] reformada en 2014, pasando a denominarse Ley Orgánica para la Transferencia al Poder Popular de la Gestión y Administración Comunitaria de Servicios, bienes y otras atribuciones, [1463] precisamente con el objeto de implementar la "transferencia de la gestión y administración de servicios, actividades, bienes y recursos del Poder Público a las Comunidades, Comunas, Consejos Comunales, Empresas de propiedad Social Directas o Indirectas y otras organizaciones de base del Poder Popular legítimamente registradas. Ni más ni menos que la destrucción de los Municipios, siendo lo más grave la "motivación" legal que se dio en la ley Orgánica de 2012 para dicha transferencia, que era la peregrina idea de que los Municipios, que son los que están gobernados por representantes electos mediante sufragio universal, directo y secreto, supuestamente – así lo decía la letra de la Ley - , supuestamente "usurparon lo que es del pueblo soberano;" es decir, los órganos representativos locales "usurparon lo que es del pueblo," y por tanto, supuestamente con el establecimiento del Estado Comunal, se "restituyen al Pueblo Soberano, a través de las comunidades organizadas y las organizaciones de base del poder popular, aquellos servicios, actividades, bienes y recursos que pueden ser asumidas, gestionadas y administradas por el pueblo organizado" (art. 5.3, Ley Orgánica de 2012). Esta redacción absurda fue sin embargo modificada en la reforma de 2014, eliminándose la noción de "usurpación" como motivación de la transferencia y limitándose la idea de "restitución al pueblo soberano" sólo al supuesto de que una entidad territorial por cuenta propia, decida hacer la transferencia pero conforme al Plan Regional de Desarrollo y autorización del Consejo Federal de Gobierno (art. 5.3).

En todo caso, se destaca que la transferencia de la gestión y administración de servicios, actividades, bienes y recursos del Poder Público a las Comunidades, Comunas, Consejos Comunales, Empresas de propiedad Social Directas o Indirectas y otras organizaciones de base del Poder Popular, debe hacerse conforme a los lineamientos que a tal efecto dicte el Consejo Federal de Gobierno (art. 20), que es un órgano controlado por el Poder Central, siendo los mecanismos de transferencia "de obligatorio cumplimiento a todas las instituciones del poder público para reivindicar al pueblo, su poder para decidir y gestionar su futuro y formas de organización" (art. 3). La transferencia a dichas organizaciones, además debe hacerse a las mismas siempre que sean "legítimamente registradas" (art. 2), por supuesto, por el gobierno central, a través del Ministerio del Poder Popular para las Comunas y los movimientos sociales, lo que sólo es posible si son socialistas. Y lo más insólito es que las áreas prioritarias para dicha transferencia son las de "atención primaria de salud, mantenimiento de centros educativos, producción de materiales y construcción de vivienda, políticas comunitarias de deporte y mantenimiento de instalaciones deportivas, actividades culturales y mantenimiento de instalaciones culturales, administración de programas sociales, protección del ambiente y recolección de desechos sólidos, administración y mantenimiento de áreas industriales, mantenimiento y conservación de áreas urbanas, prevención y protección comunal, construcción de obras comunitarias y administración y prestación de servicios públicos, financieros, pro-

---

1462   Véase en *Gaceta Oficial* N° 6.097 Extra. de 15 de junio de 2012;

1463   Véase en *Gaceta Oficial* N° 40.540 de 13 de noviembre de 2014

ducción, distribución de alimentos y de bienes de primera necesidad, entre otras" (art. 27),[1464] es decir, materialmente de todo lo imaginable como acción de gobierno local. Con ello, como se dijo, es claro que lo que se busca vaciar totalmente de competencias a los entes políticos territoriales, específicamente a los Municipios[1465] y ahogarlos financieramente, para lo cual, como lo afirmó la Sala Constitucional en la sentencia que analizó el carácter orgánico de la Ley, la misma "incide de forma evidente en la estructura orgánica o institucional de un Poder Público como es el Poder Ejecutivo, y a su vez los distintos entes político-territoriales quienes *están sujetos* a los planes de transferencia planteados en sus normas."[1466]

Por supuesto, este proceso de transferencia no es, en absoluto, un proceso de "descentralización," por más que así se lo califique expresamente en el artículo 20 de la Ley Orgánica, y en el artículo 5.3 de la misma se invoque el artículo 184 de la Constitución, pues para descentralizar es necesario que los entes recipiendarios de las competencias sean entidades políticas locales, con gobiernos democráticos a cargo de personas electas mediante sufragio universal directo y secreto. En este caso, todas las llamadas "organizaciones de base del Poder Popular" en definitiva son entidades dependientes y controladas por el Poder Ejecutivo nacional, por lo que la transferencia de competencias a las mismas en realidad es un procedo una "centralización administrativa." Como lo destacó José Ignacio Hernández, "la descentralización no se concibe aquí como la transferencia de competencias a favor de Estados y Municipios para democratizar el Poder acercándolo al ciudadano," pues "la transferencia de competencias del Poder Nacional, Estadal y Municipal –así como por parte de los Distritos– a favor de las instancias del Poder Popular, [...] desnaturaliza el concepto constitucional de descentralización, pues el Poder Popular, como quedó

1464   Véase sobre la Ley Orgánica de 2012, los comentarios de: José Luis Villegas Moreno, "Hacia la instauración del Estado Comunal en Venezuela: Comentario al Decreto Ley Orgánica de la Gestión Comunitaria de Competencia, Servicios y otras Atribuciones, en el contexto del Primer Plan Socialista-Proyecto Nacional Simón Bolívar 2007-2013"; de Juan Cristóbal Carmona Borjas, "Decreto con rango, valor y fuerza de Ley Orgánica para la Gestión Comunitaria de Competencias, Servicios y otras atribuciones;" de Cecilia Sosa G., "El carácter orgánico de un Decreto con fuerza de Ley (no habilitado) para la gestión comunitaria que arrasa lentamente con los Poderes estadales y municipales de la Constitución;" de José Ignacio Hernández, "Reflexiones sobre el nuevo régimen para la Gestión Comunitaria de Competencias, Servicios y otras Atribuciones;" de Alfredo Romero Mendoza, "Comentarios sobre el Decreto con rango, valor y fuerza de Ley Orgánica para la Gestión Comunitaria de Competencias, Servicios y otras Atribuciones;" y de Enrique J. Sánchez Falcón, "El Decreto con Rango, Valor y Fuerza de Ley Orgánica para la Gestión Comunitaria de Competencias, Servicios y otras Atribuciones o la negación del federalismo cooperativo y descentralizado," en *Revista de Derecho Público*, Nº 130, Editorial Jurídica Venezolana, Caracas 2012, pp. 127 ss.

1465   Como observó Cecilia Sosa Gómez, para entender esta normativa hay que "aceptar la desaparición de las instancias representativas, estadales y municipales, y su existencia se justicia en la medida que año a año transfiera sus competencias hasta que desaparezcan de hecho, aunque sigan sus nombres (Poderes Públicos Estadal y Municipal) apareciendo en la Constitución. El control de estas empresas, las tiene el Poder Público Nacional, específicamente el Poder Ejecutivo, en la cabeza de un Ministerio." Véase Cecilia Sosa G., "El carácter orgánico de un Decreto con fuerza de Ley (no habilitado) para la gestión comunitaria que arrasa lentamente con los Poderes estadales y municipales de la Constitución," en *Revista de Derecho Público*, Nº 130, Editorial Jurídica Venezolana, Caracas 2012, p. 152.

1466   Véase sentencia Nº 821 de la Sala Constitucional (Exp. Nº AA50–T–2012–0702) de 18 de junio de 2012, en http://www.tsj.gov.ve/decisiones/scon/junio/821-18612-2012-12-0704.HTML.

regulado en las Leyes del Poder Popular, es en realidad el conjunto de instancias reguladas y controladas por el Poder Ejecutivo Nacional cuyo objetivo único, exclusivo y excluyente es el socialismo, que pasa a ser así a ser doctrina de Estado." [1467]

En quinto lugar, también debe observarse, como antes se indicó, que se eliminó el carácter de entidad local que en la Constitución tienen las parroquias, y por tanto, se eliminó su carácter democrático representativo. Es más, en la Disposición Transitoria segunda de la Ley Orgánica se dispuso que unos días después de la promulgación de la Ley, los miembros principales y suplentes, así como los secretarios de las actuales juntas parroquiales, cesaron en sus funciones. En esta forma, eliminadas las Juntas parroquiales, las cuales en el artículo 35 de la Ley Orgánica pasaron a denominarse "juntas parroquiales comunales," las mismas se regularon sólo como entidades con "facultades consultivas, de evaluación y articulación entre el poder popular y los órganos del Poder Público Municipal," con las funciones enumeradas en el artículo 37 de la Ley Orgánica, de la cual se eliminó todo vestigio de gobierno local representativo.

En esta forma, cada una de dichas juntas parroquiales comunales debe ser "coordinada por una junta parroquial comunal integrada por cinco miembros y sus respectivos suplentes cuando corresponda a un área urbana y tres miembros y sus respectivos suplentes cuando sea no urbana, elegidos o elegidas para un período de dos años," pero no por el pueblo mediante sufragio universal, directo y secreto, sino "por los voceros de los consejos comunales de la parroquia respectiva," quienes "en dicha elección deberán ser fiel expresión del mandato de sus respectivas asambleas de ciudadanos." La norma prevé que dicha designación, debe ser "validada por la asamblea de ciudadanos," quedando eliminado, en esta forma, toda suerte de sufragio universal, directo y secreto y con ello, la democracia representativa.

Al desmunicipalizarse las juntas parroquiales comunales, y eliminarse su carácter de entidad política local de orden democrático representativo, el artículo 36 previó que sus miembros, que deben ser avalados por la asamblea de ciudadanos, incluso pueden ser menores de edad, aun cuando mayores de quince años, e incluso extranjeros.

IV. LAS ORGANIZACIONES Y EXPRESIONES ORGANIZATIVAS DE LA ADMINISTRACIÓN PÚBLICA DEL PODER POPULAR

Además de las instancias del Poder Popular, en la LOPP se establecen previsiones tendientes a regular dos formas organizativas específicas del Poder Popular: las organizaciones y las expresiones organizativas del Poder Popular, que originarán, por supuesto, sendas nuevas Administraciones Públicas, las cuales tienen conforme al artículo 11.1 de la LOPP, como fin esencial," Consolidar la democracia participativa y protagónica, en función de la insurgencia del Poder Popular como hecho histórico para la construcción de la sociedad socialista, democrática, de derecho y de justicia." En esta forma, con el agregado de "socialista" que esta previsión impone a

---

1467   Véase José Ignacio Hernández, "Reflexiones sobre el nuevo régimen para la Gestión Comunitaria de Competencias, Servicios y otras Atribuciones," en *Revista de Derecho Público*, N° 130, Editorial Jurídica Venezolana, Caracas 2012, pp. 157.

la sociedad, se rompe el principio del pluralismo que garantiza la propia Constitución, abriendo la vía para la discriminación política de todo aquél ciudadano que no sea socialista, a quien se le niega el derecho político a participar.

Ahora bien, en cuanto a las organizaciones del Poder Popular, conforme al artículo 9 de la Ley Orgánica del Poder Popular, las mismas "son las diversas formas del pueblo organizado, constituidas desde la localidad o de sus referentes cotidianos por iniciativa popular, que integran a ciudadanos y ciudadanas con objetivos e intereses comunes, en función de superar dificultades y promover el bienestar colectivo, para que las personas involucradas asuman sus derechos, deberes y desarrollen niveles superiores de conciencia política. Las organizaciones del Poder Popular actuarán democráticamente y procurarán el consenso popular entre sus integrantes." Estas organizaciones del Poder Popular se constituyen por iniciativa de los ciudadanos y ciudadanas, de acuerdo con su naturaleza, por intereses comunes, necesidades, potencialidades y cualquier otro referente común, según lo establecido en la ley que rija el área de su actividad (art. 12).

Estas organizaciones del Poder Popular, al igual que las instancias del Poder Popular, conforme al artículo 32 de la Ley Orgánica del Poder Popular, adquieren su personalidad jurídica mediante el registro ante el Ministerio del Poder Popular con competencia en materia de participación ciudadana, atendiendo a los procedimientos que se establezcan en el Reglamento de la presente Ley. Queda entonces en manos del Ejecutivo Nacional, por tanto, el reconocimiento formal de estas organizaciones, de mantera que todas aquellas que no sean socialistas por ser contrarias a los fines prescritos en la Ley (art.1), serían rechazadas. En las registradas, por lo demás, no tendrían cabida los ciudadanos que no compartan la ideología socialista.

En cuanto a las "expresiones organizativas del Poder Popular," conforme se dispone en el artículo 10 de la Ley Orgánica del Poder Popular, las mismas son "integraciones de ciudadanos y ciudadanas con objetivos e intereses comunes, constituidas desde la localidad, de sus referentes cotidianos de ubicación o espacios sociales de desenvolvimiento, que de manera transitoria y en base a los principios de solidaridad y cooperación, procuran el interés colectivo."

Estas expresiones del Poder Popular se constituyen, por iniciativa popular y como respuesta a las necesidades y potencialidades de las comunidades, de conformidad con la Constitución de la República y la ley. (art. 13).

Conforme a la Disposición final Tercera, el ejercicio de la participación del pueblo y el estímulo a la iniciativa y organización del Poder Popular establecidos en la Ley, se deben aplicar en los pueblos y comunidades indígenas, de acuerdo a sus usos, costumbres y tradiciones.

V. LAS DIVERSAS ORGANIZACIONES SOCIO-PRODUCTIVAS DE LA "ADMINISTRACIÓN PÚBLICA" DEL SISTEMA ECONÓMICO CO-MUNAL

En particular, en el marco del Estado Comunal paralelo, como consecuencia de la estructuración de un "sistema económico comunal," la Ley Orgánica del Sistema

Económico Comunal,[1468] buscando sustituir el sistema económico de economía mixta consagrado en la Constitución de 1999, por un sistema económico comunista, basado en la propiedad social de los medios de producción, la eliminación de la división social del trabajo y la reinversión social del excedente, ha regulado las "organizaciones socioproductivas" como los "actores" fundamentales que se han diseñado para dar soporte al sistema económico comunal, pues es a través de ellas que se desarrolla el "modelo productivo socialista" que propugna. Dichas organizaciones socioproductivas, que se configuran como una "nueva" Administración Pública económica, se definen como las:

> "unidades de producción constituidas por las instancias del Poder Popular, el Poder Público o por acuerdo entre ambos, con objetivos e intereses comunes, orientadas a la satisfacción de necesidades colectivas, mediante una economía basada en la producción, transformación, distribución, intercambio y consumo de bienes y servicios, así como de saberes y conocimientos, en las cuales el trabajo tiene significado propio, auténtico; sin ningún tipo de discriminación" (art. 9).[1469]

Esta afirmación legal, que proviene de los mismos viejos manuales comunistas basados en las apreciaciones de Marx y Engels en las sociedades anteriores a las europeas de mitades del siglo XIX sobre el trabajo asalariado, su explotación y carácter esclavista y discriminatorio, particularmente en relación con las mujeres,[1470] lo cual no tiene ninguna relación con la actualidad en ningún país occidental, parecería que parte de supuesto de que en Venezuela, el trabajo hasta ahora no habría tenido "significado propio" y no habría sido "auténtico," y además, se habría realizado basado en la "discriminación," lo que no tiene base ni sentido algunos. El trabajo es la tarea desarrollada por el hombre generalmente sobre una materia prima con ayuda de instrumentos con la finalidad de producir bienes y servicios; y es, por tanto, el medio para la producción de la riqueza. Ese es el sentido propio y auténtico del trabajo, en cualquier parte del mundo, y su división es de la esencia de la productividad en una sociedad, pues una sola persona no podría nunca cubrir todas las fases de la producción o comercialización de bienes o de la prestación de servicios. De manera que no se entiende qué es lo que se quiere decir que, con la nueva Ley, el trabajo supuestamente ahora adquirirá un significado "propio y auténtico." Por otra parte, en la definición se sugiere que supuestamente hasta ahora, el trabajo se habría realizado en el país sobre la base de la explotación y la discriminación, lo que está

1468   Véase en *Gaceta Oficial* N° 6.011 Extra. de 21 de diciembre de 2010.

1469   La Ley de 2008 las definía como las: "unidades comunitarias con autonomía e independencia en su gestión, orientadas a la satisfacción de necesidades de sus miembros y de la comunidad en general, mediante una economía basada en la producción, transformación, distribución e intercambio de saberes, bienes y servicios, en las cuales el trabajo tiene significado propio y auténtico; y en las que no existe discriminación social ni de ningún tipo de labor, ni tampoco privilegios asociados a la posición jerárquica" (art. 8). Dicha autonomía e independencia desapareció totalmente de la nueva LOSEC.

1470   Al referirse al trabajo en la misma obra la Ideología Alemana, Marx y Engels hablaron de la "explotación del hombre por el hombre": y se refirieron a la "distribución desigual, tanto cuantitativa como cualitativamente, del trabajo y de sus productos." *Idem.*

desmentido por la avanzada legislación laboral que ha habido desde la década de los cuarenta.

Ahora bien, ese trabajo con sentido "propio y auténtico," y "sin discriminación," al que se refiere la Ley Orgánica del Sistema Económico Comunal, es el que supuestamente ahora sería garantizado a través de las "organizaciones socioproductivas" que se regulan en la ley, mediante las cuales, en forma exclusiva, se desarrollará la economía del país, y que conforme al artículo 10 de la Ley Orgánica del Sistema Económico Comunal, son sólo cuatro: primero, las empresas del Estado Comunal; segundo, las empresas públicas del Estado Constitucional; tercero, las unidades productivas familiares; y cuarto, los grupos de trueque, variándose sustantivamente las formas que se regulaban en el régimen de la derogada Ley de 2008.[1471]

O sea, que del trabajo en empresas privadas en las cuales los trabajadoras tienen herramientas para lograr mejores condiciones que ha sido una de las bases del sistema económico del país, se quiere pasar al trabajo exclusivamente en empresas de carácter público, creadas por las instancias del Estado Comunal y por los órganos y entes del Estado Constitucional, sometidas todas a una planificación centralizada, en las cuales no puede haber movimientos sindicales u organizaciones de trabajadores libres que puedan presionar para el logro de mejores condiciones laborales, y donde el "empresario" en definitiva resultará ser un burócrata de un régimen autoritario que usa el "excedente" para su propio confort, explotando a los asalariados alienados.

En *primer lugar*, están las "empresas de propiedad social directa comunal," o empresas del Estado Comunal, concebidas como la "unidad socioproductiva constituida por las instancias de Poder Popular en sus respectivos ámbitos geográficos, destinada al beneficio de los productores y productoras que la integran, de la colectividad a las que corresponden y al desarrollo social integral del país, a través de la reinversión social de sus excedentes." (art. 10.1)

Se trata siempre de empresas de propiedad social directa comunal creadas por las diversas instancias del Poder Popular, cuya gestión y administración es por tanto siempre ejercida la instancia que la constituya, de manera que siempre tienen un ámbito geográfico local limitado, confinadas a una comuna o alguna agregación de comunas.

1471   Debe señalarse que la Ley derogada de 2008 establecía además, como unidades socioproductivas, las siguientes unidades de trabajo colectivo para la producción y distribución social y para la autogestión: Primero, la Empresa de Producción Social, que era la "unidad de trabajo colectivo destinada a la producción de bienes o servicios para satisfacer necesidades sociales y materiales a través de la reinversión social de sus excedentes, con igualdad sustantiva entre sus integrantes." (art. 9.3), entendiéndose como "trabajo colectivo" la "actividad organizada y desarrollada por los miembros de las distintas formas organizativas, basada en relaciones de producción no alienada, propia y auténtica, con una planificación participativa y protagónica (art. 5.2). Segundo, la Empresa de Distribución Social, que era la "unidad de trabajo colectivo destinada a la distribución de bienes o servicios para satisfacer necesidades sociales y materiales a través de la reinversión social de sus excedentes, con igualdad sustantiva entre sus integrantes." (art. 9.4). Y tercero, la Empresa de Autogestión, que era la "unidad de trabajo colectivo que participan directamente en la gestión de la empresa, con sus propios recursos, dirigidas a satisfacer las necesidades básicas de sus miembros y de la comunidad." (art. 9.5).

Estas empresas del Estado Comunal, es decir, aquellas "de propiedad social directa comunal," como se establece en el artículo 12, deben ser constituidas "mediante documento constitutivo estatutario, acompañado del respectivo proyecto socioproductivo, haciendo este último las veces de capital social de la empresa," el cual debe ser "elaborado con base en las necesidades y potencialidades de las comunidades de la instancia del Poder Popular a la que corresponda, y de acuerdo al plan de desarrollo del correspondiente sistema de agregación comunal." En los documentos de las empresas de propiedad social comunal deben siempre indicarse tal carácter, bien sea con la mención expresa de "Empresa de Propiedad Social" o abreviación mediante las siglas "EPS" (art. 17).

En *segundo lugar* están las "empresa de propiedad social indirecta comunal, "o empresas públicas del Estado Constitucional, concebidas como la "unidad socioproductiva constituida por el Poder Público en el ámbito territorial de una instancia del Poder Popular, destinadas al beneficio de sus productores y productoras, de la colectividad del ámbito geográfico respectivo y del desarrollo social integral del país, a través de la reinversión social de sus excedentes." (art. 10.2). En estos casos se trata siempre de empresas de propiedad social indirecta comunal, constituidas por los órganos del Poder Público (República, Estados y Municipios), es decir, empresas públicas nacionales, estadales y municipales pero siempre creadas en un ámbito geográfico y territorial limitado reducido al de alguna instancia del Poder Popular, y cuya gestión y administración corresponde siempre, como principio, al ente u órgano del Poder Público que las constituya; sin que ello obste para que, progresivamente, la gestión y administración de estas empresas sea transferida a las instancias del Poder Popular, en cuyo caso, se constituirían en empresas de propiedad social comunal directa, es decir, en empresas del Estado Comunal.

En cuanto a estas empresas públicas constituidas por órganos o entes de la Administración Pública, es decir, del Poder Público, que son las "de propiedad social indirecta comunal," dispone el artículo 13, que las mismas son constituidas mediante "documento constitutivo estatutario, de acuerdo a las normativas que rijan al órgano o ente público encargado de su constitución." Se entiende que se refiere al acto ejecutivo por medio del cual se decide en la Administración Central o descentralizada, la creación de una empresa, en los términos de la Ley Orgánica de la Administración Pública .

En *tercer lugar*, están las "unidades productivas familiares," es decir, empresas de carácter netamente familiar, concebidas como "una organización cuyos integrantes pertenecen a un núcleo familiar que desarrolla proyectos socioproductivos dirigidos a satisfacer sus necesidades y las de la comunidad; y donde sus integrantes, bajo el principio de justicia social, tienen igualdad de derechos y deberes." (art. 10.3).

Conforme al artículo 14 de la Ley, el grupo familiar que puede confirmar estas empresas familiares, debe estar "integrado por personas relacionadas hasta el cuarto grado de consanguinidad y segundo de afinidad," y debe estar sustentada "en los saberes y el conocimiento propios del grupo familiar, destinado al beneficio de sus integrantes y a satisfacer necesidades de la comunidad donde el grupo familiar tenga su domicilio." Por tanto, un grupo de amigos y relacionados con interesess comunes, no podría establecer una unidad socioproductiva de esta naturaleza, destinada beneficiar a sus integrantes y a satisfacer necesidades de la comunidad.

En cuanto a estas "unidades productivas familiares," el artículo 14 establece que cada una de las mismas se constituye "por un grupo familiar integrado por personas relacionadas hasta el cuarto grado de consanguinidad y segundo de afinidad, mediante documento constitutivo estatutario y un proyecto socioproductivo sustentado en los saberes y el conocimiento propios del grupo familiar, destinado al beneficio de sus integrantes y a satisfacer necesidades de la comunidad donde el grupo familiar tenga su domicilio."

Por último, en *cuarto lugar*, la Ley Orgánica del Sistema Económico Comunal regula como organización socioproductiva a los "grupos de intercambio solidario," como organizaciones de "trueque" concebidas como el "conjunto de prosumidores y prosumidoras organizados voluntariamente, con la finalidad de participar en alguna de las modalidades de los sistemas alternativos de intercambio solidario."A los efectos de estos Grupos, estos llamados "prosumidores y prosumidoras" se definen en la Ley Orgánica como las "personas que producen, distribuyen y consumen bienes, servicios, saberes y conocimientos, mediante la participación voluntaria en los sistemas alternativos de intercambio solidario, para satisfacer sus necesidades y las de otras personas de su comunidad" (art. 16.6). Es imposible leer estas modalidades de "trueque" como uno de los pilares fundamentales del sistema de producción socialista que propugna esta Ley, sin que venga a la memoria, precisamente, el esquema utópico descrito por Marx y Engels respecto de una sociedad primitiva en la cual como decían, se pudiera, el mismo día, ser cazador, pescador, pastor y crítico, de manera que durante el transcurso del día incluso se pudiera intercambiar liebres o gallinas por unos pescados !! Es posible que ello pudiera aplicarse respecto de grupos o humanos o comunidades aislados que pueda haber en territorios inaccesibles, como forma de vida cotidiana, pero no es más que un disparate pensar que se pueda aplicar en las grandes urbes contemporáneas y en las intercomunicadas áreas rurales del país, salvo que se las reduzca todas, a la miseria.

Estos grupos de intercambio solidario, conforme al artículo 15 de la Ley Orgánica del Sistema Económico Comunal, se constituyen "mediante acta de asamblea de prosumidores y prosumidoras, en la cual toda persona natural o jurídica puede pertenecer a un determinado grupo de intercambio solidario para ofrecer y recibir saberes, conocimientos, bienes y servicios," siempre y cuando cumpla con lo establecido en la Ley y su Reglamento. En este último caso, el acuerdo solidario, conforme se indica en el artículo 44 de la ley, se debe llevar a cabo a través de una asamblea constitutiva de prosumidores, en la que se debe proponer la denominación del grupo, de "la moneda comunal" que se va a utilizar, así como "la especificación y organización del sistema alternativo de intercambio solidario," el cual se debe regir por lo dispuesto en la Ley y su Reglamento.

Todas estas organizaciones socioproductivas que contempla la Ley Orgánica del Sistema Económico Comunal, conforme se dispone en el artículo 16 de la misma, no adquieren personalidad jurídica mediante la inscripción de su documento constitutivo en el registro mercantil, sino mediante el registro del mismo "ante el órgano coordinador" que no es otro que el Ministerio de las Comunas (art. 8.1), donde debe establecerse una dependencia funcional de verificación, inscripción y registro con el fin de mantener el seguimiento y control de las organizaciones socioproductivas y de los espacios de intercambio solidario del país (art. 19). Nada se indica en la Ley, sin embargo, sobre la publicidad de este registro, es decir, sobre el acceso del público al mismo, ni sobre la potestad del funcionario innominado a cargo de la inscripción de dar fe pública o autenticidad a los documentos registrados. Parecería que se trata de desmantelar el sistema registral general, sin reformar la ley respectiva.

El Ministerio de las Comunas, sólo puede abstenerse de registrar una organización socioproductiva, además de cuando no se acompañen los documentos exigidos en la Ley o si éstos presentan alguna deficiencia u omisión no subsanada, "cuando el proyecto socio productivo de la organización tenga por objeto finalidades distintas a las previstas en la Ley." (Art. 18) Por tanto, ninguna organización socioproductiva que no sea socialista o que no responda al modelo productivo socialista podría ser registrada.

APRECIACIÓN GENERAL

De todo lo anteriormente expuesto, se confirma que uno de los condicionantes de mayor importancia que tiene la Administración Pública en cualquier país, lo constituyen los condicionantes políticos, sin cuya consideración no es posible determinar las características, modalidades de organización, principios de funcionamiento y los objetivos de la misma.; siendo dichos condicionamientos, en primer lugar, la concepción del Estado del cual la Administración es el instrumento para gerenciar el interés general y satisfacer las necesidades colectivas; y en segundo lugar, la forma del Estado que es la que contribuye a conformar a la Administración Pública en todo el territorio del Estado.

Si bien es cierto que para identificar uno y otro condicionante político de la Administración Pública hay que acudir a las previsiones constitucionales que rigen al Estado, es evidente que ello no es suficiente, y en muchas veces es más bien engañoso, pues en la práctica política los Estados responden a otros principios distintos a los plasmados en las Constituciones.

Es el caso de Venezuela, donde a pesar de que la Constitución define al Estado como un Estado democrático y social de derecho y de justicia, en mismo, en la práctica política de los últimos lustros, se ha configurado como un Estado totalitario, que impide que la Administración Pública, pueda ser una Administración democrática y social, que asegure el equilibrio entre los poderes públicos y las derechos de los administrados, sometida al derecho, y controlada por un poder judicial independiente. Más bien se ha configurado como una Administración burocrática que dejó de estar al servicio del ciudadano, y que sirve a la burocracia estatal misma, y cuyas acciones hacia los ciudadanos sólo son consecuencia de políticas populistas, que persiguen las iniciativas privadas, signadas por una ideología oficial que es la antítesis al pluralismo, donde se discrimina políticamente.

Esa Administración Pública burocratizada, consecuencia de las políticas del Estado totalitario, ha sufrido un proceso de inflación organizativa, tanto en la Administración Central por la multiplicación sin plan ni control de los Ministerios, de los cargos de viceministros y de Vicepresidencias sectoriales; como en la Administración descentralizada funcionalmente con la creación de cientos y cientos de empresa públicas y otras entidades estatales, sin concierto alguno. Además, esa Administración Pública tradicional, ha visto crecer una nueva Administración paralela, configurada por las Misiones, reguladas en la Ley Orgánica de la Administración Pública pero para que no se rijan por sus normas, las cuales sólo en 2014 parecen encontrar un cuerpo normativo que las rige.

Por otra parte, a pesar también de que la Constitución defina al Estado como un Estado federal descentralizado, en la práctica política de los últimos lustros, se ha configurado como un Estado centralizado, con un desbalance evidente de competencias a favor del Poder nacional, y un debilitamiento competencial progresivo de los niveles estadales y municipales, lo que impide que la Administración Pública, pueda ser una Administración descentralizada con los tres niveles territoriales (nacional, estadal y municipal) de los que habla el texto constitucional. Más bien se ha configurado como una Administración centralizada, que deriva, en primer lugar del régimen mismo unitario regulado en la Ley Orgánica de la Administración Pública, aplicable a todos las entidades territoriales, que incluso se las sujetan a las instrucciones de los órganos de los niveles superiores de la Administración nacional; en segundo lugar, del proceso de centralización de competencias en desmedro de las de los Estados hacia el nivel nacional; y en tercer lugar, por la estructuración a nivel de la Administración nacional, de órganos nacionales incluso llamados "jefes de gobierno" con competencia regional y estadal, en paralelo y superpuestas a las Administraciones de los Estados o de la Administración municipal metropolitana de Caracas.

Y por último, a pesar de que la Constitución regula un Estado que podemos denominar Estado Constitucional, al cual debería responder la propia Administración Pública, a partir de 2010, mediante un proceso de desconstitucionalización del Estado Constitucional, mediante legislación ordinaria se ha creado un nuevo Estado paralelo, denominado Estado Comunal o del Poder Popular, totalmente al margen de la Constitución, con el objeto de vaciar progresivamente de competencias a los órganos del Estado Constitucional, mediante su transferencia obligatoria a las Comunidades, Consejos Comunales y Comunas, que son órganos dirigidos por "voceros" que no son electos popularmente mediante sufragio, y cuya existencia depende exclusivamente de lo que decida un Ministerio del Ejecutivo nacional, que es el que las registra para que incluso puedan tener personalidad jurídica.

La misión última del Estado Comunal, en un proceso conducido y controlado por el poder central, mediante el partido de gobierno que actúa como facilitador, es asegurar el vaciamiento progresivo de las competencias municipales y su total transferencia a entes que controla el poder central, con la consecuente desmunicipalización del país, y la centralización total del Estado y consecuentemente de su administración pública.

En ese proceso de estructuración del Estado Comunal, por último, una nueva Administración pública está en proceso de configurarse, integrada por organizaciones socioproductivas, básicamente, empresas públicas, en el universo del sistema económico comunal que se ha previsto legalmente, conforme a la más clásica ortodoxia comunista que se regula en la Ley Orgánica de dicho sistema, montado sobre los tres pilares utópicos de la propiedad social de los medios de producción, la eliminación de la división social del trabajo, y la reinversión social del excedente.

New York, 26 de Noviembre 2014.

SEXTA PARTE:

CONSTITUTIONAL LAW. VENEZUELA (2015)

DERECHO CONSTITUCIONAL. VENEZUELA (2015)

Esta Sexta-Parte del Tomo XV de la Colección Tratadod de Derecho Constitucional, es el texto actualizado (a febrero 2015) del libro *Constitutional Law. Venezuela*, publicado en la International Encyclopaedia of Laws, Kluwer Law International, 2012.

GENERAL INTRODUCTION

Chapter 1. An Outline of Venezuelan Constitutional History

1. The Venezuelan State, located in the northern territories of South America, was created in 1811 after a General Congress of the representatives of the 'United Provinces of *Caracas, Cumaná, Barinas, Margarita, Barcelona, Mérida y Trujillo*' on 5 July 1811 solemnly proclaimed the 'Declaration of the Independence', establishing the 'American Confederation of Venezuela in the Meridian Continent'. The work of the Congress,[1472] after almost one year, resulted in the sanctioning on 21 December 1812 of the 'Federal Constitution for the United States of Venezuela'.[1473] Venezuela was, thus, the first country in modern constitutionalism to adopt the federal form of State following the principles adopted a few decades before in the United States of America.

2. These initial constituent decisions were the immediate outcome of the political rebellion initiated the previous year on 19 April 1810 in the Province of Caracas

---

1472   See Ramón Díaz Sánchez (ed.), *Libro de Actas del Supremo Congreso de Venezuela 1811–1812* (Caracas: Academia Nacional de la Historia, 1959).

1473   See Caraccciolo Parra Pérez (ed.), *La Constitución Federal de Venezuela de 1811 y Documentos afines* (Caracas: Academia Nacional de la Historia, 1959), 79 et seq.; and Allan R. Brewer-Carías, *Las Constituciones de Venezuela*, vol. I (Caracas: Academia de Ciencias Políticas y Sociales, 2008), 553–581.

(created in 1528),[1474] against the authority of the Spanish Crown. Among the facts that ignited such rebellion was the extreme political instability affecting the Spanish government since 1808, due to the absence of Ferdinand VII from Spain, who with his father, the former Carlos IV, was held captive in France by Emperor Napoleon Bonaparte. The invasion of the Peninsula by the French Army, and the appointment of Joseph Bonaparte as King of Spain by the Emperor after enacting a new Constitution for the Realm, in Bayonne, was another contributory factor. This situation and the war of independence that spread all over the Spanish Peninsula, originated a de facto political situation affecting the government of the Monarchy, provoking the creation of provisional provincial governments (*Juntas*) spontaneously established during the war. The Central board (*Junta Suprema*) of these provisional local governments by 1810 was forced to be concentrated in the Island of Cádiz, in the extreme south of Andalucía, and there it appointed a Regency board to govern the Realm in the absence of the Monarch, convening the elections for the *Cortes* (Parliament) in order to draft a new Constitution, which is known as the 1812 Cádiz Constitution.

This situation, and the fear to be subjected to France, originated the political rebellion in the Colonies, in particular in the Municipality of Caracas, whose councilmen decided to ignore the Spanish colonial authorities, and to establish in substitution of the colonial Governor and the Provincial Council (*Ayuntamiento*), a *Junta Suprema de Venezuela Conservadora de los Derechos de Fernando VII*, following the same pattern of the *Juntas* that were established in almost all the provinces of Spain during the war of independence. The example given by the Province of Caracas was immediately followed by almost all the Provinces that since 1777 were integrated for military purposes in the General Captaincy of Venezuela. These Provinces were *Cumaná* (created in 1568), *Barinas* (created in 1786), *Margarita* (created in 1525), *Barcelona* (created in 1810), *Mérida* (created in 1676) and *Trujillo* (created in 1810). All of them during 1810 and 1811 declared their independence and adopted their own provincial constitutions.[1475]

The 21 December 1811 Federal Constitution, adopted by the elected representatives of these Provinces in General Congress,[1476] left open the possibility for the other Provinces which, although having been part of the General Captaincy of Venezuela, had not participated in the independence movement, as was the case of the provinces of *Maracaibo* (created in 1676) and the city of Coro, and of *Guayana* (created in 1568), to seek their future incorporation in the new State (Article 128).

1474   See the relevant documents in *El 19 de Abril de 1810* (Caracas: Instituto Panamericano de Geografía e Historia, 1957). See Juan Garrido Rovira, *La Revolución de 1810* (Caracas: Universidad Monteávila, 2009); Enrique Viloria Vera & Allan R. Brewer-Carías, *La Revolución de Caracas de 1810* (Caracas: Centro de Estudios Ibéricos y Americanos de Salamanca, 2011).

1475   See Ángel F. Brice (ed.), *Las Constituciones Provinciales* (Caracas: Academia Nacional de la Historia, 1959); Allan R. Brewer-Carías, *La constitución de la Provincia de Caracas de 31 de enero de 1812* (Caracas: Academia de Ciencias Políticas y Sociales, 2011).

1476   See Juan Garrido R, *El Congreso Constituyente de Venezuela, Bicentenario del 5 de julio de 1811* (Caracas: Universidad Monteávila, 2010).

3. By the time in which this independent and constituent process began in Venezuela, the political and constitutional effects of the American (1776) and French (1789) Revolutions had begun to spread to many of the Hispanic American Colonies, directly influencing the drafting of the 1811 Constitution.[1477] Consequently, modern constitutionalism principles were adopted in Venezuela before the sanctioning of the March 1812 Cádiz Constitution of the Spanish Monarchy.[1478] Nonetheless, this Constitution, although not having had influence in the initial constitution-making process of Venezuela, had important influence in other constitution-making processes held after 1820 in other former Spanish colonies of Latin America and in Italy and Portugal.[1479]

Consequently, it can be said that Venezuela was the first country in constitutional history that, after the American and French Revolutions, sanctioned a modern constitution based on the principles of constitutional supremacy, sovereignty of the people, political representation and republicanism. An extended declaration of fundamental rights of Man and Society[1480] that organized the State according to the principle of separation of power with a system of checks and balances and the superiority of the law as expression of the general will were also key to its formation. This has resulted in a presidential system of government and elected representatives to the senate and the representatives chamber (*diputados*). The government is of a federal form, according to which the former colonial Provinces became federated sovereign states, within which the Constitution set forth the establishment of a local government system. The Judicial Power is integrated by judges imparting justice in the name of the nation with judicial review powers.

4. Since the 1811 Constitution, and during the last 200 years, the Venezuelan independent State has been subjected to twenty-six Constitutions sanctioned successively in 1811, 1819, 1821, 1830, 1857, 1858, 1864, 1874, 1881, 1891, 1893, 1901, 1904, 1909, 1914, 1922, 1925, 1928, 1929, 1931, 1936, 1945, 1947, 1953, 1961 and 1999.[1481] This excessive number of 'constitutions' was the product of the absence of the 'amendment' constitutional revision technique, so in their great majority they were mere partial and punctual reforms generally provoked by circumstantial politi-

---

1477   See Pedro Grases (Compilador), *El pensamiento político de la Emancipación Venezolana* (Caracas: Ediciones Congreso de la República, 1988); Tulio Chiossone, *Formación Jurídica de Venezuela en la Colonia y la República* (Caracas: Universidad Central de Venezuela, 1980).

1478   See Allan R. Brewer-Carías, *Los inicios del proceso constituyente Hispano y Americano, Caracas 1811 – Cádiz 1812*, (Caracas: bid & co. Editor, 2012); Allan R. Brewer-Carías, *Sobre el constitucionalismo hispanoamericano pre-gaditano 1811-1812* (Caracas: Editorial Jurídica Venezolana, 2013) 25 et seq.

1479   See Allan R. Brewer-Carías, *Reflexiones sobre la Revolución Norteamericana (1776), la Revolución Francesa (1789) y la Revolución Hispanoamericana (1810–1830) y sus aportes al constitucionalismo moderno* (Bogotá: Universidad Externado de Colombia, 2008), 204 et seq.

1480   See Allan R. Brewer-Carías, *Las declaraciones de derechos del pueblo y del hombre de 1811* (Caracas: Academia de Ciencias Políticas y Sociales, 2011).

1481   See the texts of all the Venezuelan Constitutions since 1811, in Ulises Picón Rivas, *Índice Constitucional de Venezuela* (Caracas, 1944); Luis Mariñas Otero, *Las Constituciones de Venezuela* (Madrid, 1965); Allan R. Brewer-Carías, *Las Constituciones de Venezuela*, 2 vols (Caracas: Academia de Ciencias Políticas y Sociales, 2008).

cal factors. That is, this number of constitutions does not correspond to similar number of fundamental political pacts originating new political regimes and forms of constitutional government. The fact has been, on the contrary, that in Venezuelan history, between 1811 and 2011 *four* great constitutional periods and political changes can be distinguished, each one distinct in its political characteristic, form of government, leadership and programs.[1482] Each of these periods developed according to a new leadership that assumed the government, reached exhaustion after entering into decay and inexorably arrived at a final crisis. This, in each case, needed the work of more than a generation in order to build and establish a new political project in lieu of the previous institutional collapsed framework. Since 1999, a *fifth* constitutional period is in the process of being conformed, after the approval of the currently in force 1999 Constitution, a period that nonetheless, is still in the first phase of being shaped. The political crisis initiated in 1989, which provoked the collapse of the previous period, has not yet concluded.[1483]

§1. *First Constitutional Period (1811–1864): The Independent, Autonomous, Semi-Decentralized State*

5. The *first* of these great political-constitutional periods in the history of the country is the one of the *Independent Semi-Decentralized State* established by the 'Federal Constitution for the Venezuelan States' of 21 December 1811 that lasted up to 1864, which was dominated by the generation that fought for independence from Imperial Spain. The defining political project that characterized this historical period was the effort to create a brand new State on the former Spanish colonial territory,[1484] organizing the government in a federal state with the former colonial Provinces integrated in 1777, for military purposes, in the General Captaincy of Venezuela. The territories of Venezuela, being very poor, had no other colonial integration and were under the general authority of two Viceroyalties (New Spain and Peru) and of two *Audiencias* (*Santo Domingo* and *Nueva Granada*) that were the most important instruments of colonial government. Consequently, the Captaincy General created only thirty years before the Independence, was composed of highly autonomous and decentralized provincial entities developed under the Spanish Crown to govern these extremely isolated and poor provincial colonies. It was precisely because of the dispersion and autonomy of the government and the territorial organization of these

---

1482   See Allan R. Brewer-Carías, *Historia Constitucional de Venezuela*, (Caracas, 2 vols. Editorial Alfa, 2008). Second edition (Caracas, Colección Tratado de Derecho Constitucional, Vol. I, Editorial Jurídica Venezolana, 2013).

1483   See on the identification of these five political periods in Venezuelan history, in *Informe sobre la descentralización en Venezuela 1993, Memoria del Dr. Allan R. Brewer-Carías, Ministro de Estado para la Descentralización (junio 1993 – febrero 1994)* (Caracas, 1994), 17 et seq.; and Allan R. Brewer Carías, *Instituciones Políticas y Constitucionales, Vol. I, Evolución histórica del Estado* (Caracas, 1996); 'La conformación político-constitucional del Estado Venezolano', in *Las Constituciones de Venezuela, cit.*, vol. I, 23–526; and in *Historia Constitucional de Venezuela*, vol. I (Caracas: Editorial Alfa, 2008), 220 et seq.

1484   See Tomás Polanco, 'Interpretación jurídica de la Independencia', in *El Movimiento Emancipador de Hispanoamérica, Actas y Ponencias* (Caracas: Academia Nacional de la Historia, 1961). See the relevant text in *Textos oficiales de la Primera República de Venezuela*, vol. I (Caracas: Academia Nacional de la Historia, 1959), 105.

former Provinces that a federal constitutional system was chosen in 1811 to create the Venezuelan State.

However, it must be borne in mind that by the time of the independence of Venezuela and the adoption of the federal form of government, the Republic had already been suppressed in France (1808), and no other form of government, different to the Monarchical regime against which the revolution of independence was conducted, could inspire the framing of the new State except the new Republican Federal one that at that time had begun to be shaped in North America, allowing former colonies to gain independence within a new State. The 'Confederation de Venezuela' was therefore based on a scheme taken from the experience of the United States in order to try to unify territories that had never before been united, except militarily during the previous thirty years through the Captaincy General. As aforementioned, in all other aspects, the Venezuelan provinces experienced no other form of integration, remaining isolated provinces, virtually without communication between one another.

6. This constitutional period developed between 1811 and 1864 through various stages marked by constitutional changes: first, with the Constitution of the primary process of constitution building of the State, the 1811 Constitution, that as aforementioned was preceded by Provincial Constitutions adopted by each Province between 1810 and 1811, configuring what was called the 'First Republic',[1485] as a civic Republic, ruled by civilians until the military Spanish invasion in 1812;[1486] second, the constitution-making process that developed since 1813 during the liberation wars against Spain, influenced by the ideas of Simón Bolívar, the Liberator and political and military leader of the country's struggle for liberation and independence;[1487] third, with the 1819 Constitution, adopted after a prolonged seven years wars against another important expeditionary Spanish Army that was sent in 1814 to crush the rebellion, called the *Angostura* Constitution, drafted by Simón Bolívar himself;[1488] fourth, with the Constitution of 1821, the first Constitution of the 'Colombian' State formed by the Venezuelan territories and those of the former provinces of the *Virreinato de Nueva Granada*, following the proposals made by Simón Bolívar;[1489]

1485   See Caracciolo Parra Pérez, *Historia de la Primera República de Venezuela*, vol. I (Caracas: Academia Nacional de la Historia, 1959).

1486   See Allan R. Brewer-Carías, *Documentos Constitucionales de la Independencia/Constitucional Documents of the Independence 1811*, Colección Textos Legislativos No 52 (Caracas, Editorial Jurídica Venezolana, 2012); and 'La independencia de Venezuela y el inicio del constitucionalismo hispanoamericano en 1810-1811, como obra de civiles, y el desarrollo del militarismo a partir de 1812, en ausencia de régimen constitucional,' *Revista de Historia Constitucional*, 14, (Oviedo, Revista Electrónica, http://hc.rediris.es 2013), 405-424

1487   See Simón Bolívar, *Escritos Fundamentales* (Caracas: Monte Ávila Editores, 1982); *Proclamas y Discursos del Libertador* (Caracas, 1939); *Los Proyectos Constitucionales de Simón Bolívar, El Libertador 1813–1830* (Caracas, 1999); Pedro Grases & Tomás Polanco (eds), *Simón Bolívar y la Ordenación del Estado en 1813* (Caracas, 1979).

1488   See Pedro Grases (ed.), *El Libertador y la Constitución de Angostura de 1819* (Caracas, 1970).

1489   See Allan R. Brewer-Carías, "Cádiz y los orígenes del constitucionalismo en Venezuela. Después de Caracas (1811): Angostura (1819), Cúcuta (1821) y Valencia (1830)," en Andrea Romano y Francesco Vegara Caffarelli (Coord.) *1812: fra Cadice e Palermo - entre Cádiz y Palermo. Nazione, rivolu-*

and fifth, with the 1830 Constitution that re-established the Venezuelan State separated from the State of Colombia that the same year adopted its own Constitution. This 1830 Constitution was the one with the longest period of continuous enforcement (1830–1857) with two reforms made to it in 1857 and in 1858, particularly because of the struggle between the central and provincial governments.[1490]

7. The most distinguished trend of this first constitutional period (beginning with the 1811 Constitution) was the configuration of a more or less decentralized State resulting from a 'federative pact' entered by sovereign and independent provinces after having also approved their own provincial constitutions. During this first period (except during the wars of liberation), the dominant pattern of the government was the important local-federated power which was even designed in 1830 against the ideas of Simón Bolívar, with the political power located at the Province-Cities level with a very weak central government (see *infra* paragraphs 180 et seq.). This feature, at the beginning of the institution building of the country, initiated its also long process of institutional disarticulation, mainly provoked by the regional *caudillos* that governed the country during all the nineteenth century. This pattern was only eliminated at the beginning of the twentieth century when the *Caudillista* federation was definitively buried.

8. Also in this period the bitter war fought since 1813 to liberate from Spain the territories of the new State and consolidate the independence (1813–1821), was not only a political one but a social one between the dominant Creole white population that had control over the local government and the economy, and the lower working classes including the former slaves instigated by the caudillos supporting the Royalist forces. After changing the pattern of the war through extreme measures (*Decreto de Guerra a Muerte*), gaining the control of the territory, and having sanctioned the 1819 Constitution in Angostura, Simón Bolivar proposed the conformation of a great State integrating the territories of what today is Venezuela, Colombia, Panama and Ecuador. In this framework Venezuela disappeared as an independent State up to 1830, and was a Department of the so-called Great Colombia.

9. The separation of Venezuela from that great State took place in 1830, in a secessionist process lead by José Antonio Páez, one of the distinguished military leaders of the independence, which coincided with the death of Bolívar. It was a political reaction of the military *caudillos* of Venezuela against the centralized government of Bogotá, provoking the sanctioning of the 1830 Constitution of Venezuela, which was the result of a central-federal pact. The resulting 'centralized federation' (see infra paragraphs 183 et seq.) has been one of the main trends of the subsequent constitutional history of the country.

10. Thus, from the beginning of constitutionalism in 1811, in one way or another, the federal form of the State and the pendulum movement between centralization and decentralization have marked the entire political history of Venezuela, even

zione, constituzione, representanza politica, libertà garantite, autonomie,(Palermo-Messina Università degli Strudi di Messina, 2012), 167-195

1490 See Eleonora Gabaldón, *La Constitución de 1830 (El debate parlamentario y la opinión de la prensa)* (Caracas: Instituto Biblioteca Nacional, ed. Turnes, 1991).

in current times. With such form, the regional political *caudillismo* found its place in the Constitution, and even if in the years after 1819 the term 'federal' disappeared from the constitutional texts, the same political trend of regional and local autonomy continued assuring the authority of the military *caudillos*. Thus, towards the end of the decade of the 1850s, the struggle between the central Power, which had itself been built by the regional leaders, and regional Powers, provoked a rupture of the constitutional system culminating in the Federal Wars of 1858–1863, or *Guerras Federales*.[1491]

11. The 1830 Constitution was reformed in 1857 in a constitution-making process that did not satisfy the regional political claims against the central government that had begun to take shape during the previous two decades. This provoked a *coup d'état*, the first in Venezuelan constitutional history, that led to the sanction in 1858 of a new Constitution by a Constituent Assembly with more federal elements than the previous one.[1492] As has been the general pattern in Venezuelan history, these reforms were a prelude to the collapse of the constitutional order.

After these constitutional reforms of 1857 and 1858, in the midst of war, it appeared that there was no other solution to the political crisis than to bring out one of the leaders of the independence war who had been present and active in the political life of the country since Independence, and had completely dominated it after Bolívar. This was José Antonio Páez who was called in as the 'saviour' of the country. Although invested with dictatorial powers, the reality is that he did not last as President more than a few months. The first political period of Venezuelan constitutional history definitively concluded with the Federal Wars, which like the independence war, were also wars of social character, which left profound consequences in the political history of the country. From the political point of view it resulted in the triumph of regional and local powers regarding central government, being the federation the political form used to reaffirm the power of the regional *caudillos* and the politico-federal disintegration of the Republic. Also from the social point of view, the wars gave rise to a second social revolution, in continuation of the one that took place with the war of independence, but still more anarchic that the latter, even provoking the physical disappearance of the land owner class, under popular resentment, but giving rise to social equalitarianism that was later reaffirmed by the *mestizaje*.

§2. *Second Constitutional Period (1864–1901): The Federal State and the United States of Venezuela*

12. With the end of the independent semi-decentralized state government period, in the aftermath of the federal wars a new political cycle began with a new form of government, a new leadership, and a new political programme, giving rise to the period of the *Federal State* (1864–1901). The change was a radical one, although a few years earlier the new leaders of the *Federación* were only hardly recognized as

---

1491   See José S. Rodríguez, *Contribución al Estudio de la Guerra Federal en Venezuela,* 2 vols (Caracas, 1960); Emilio Navarro, *La Revolución Federal, 1859 a 1863* (Caracas, 1963).

1492   See Eleonora Gabaldón, *La Convención de Valencia (la idea federal), 1858* (Caracas, 1988).

local leaders, with no national projections. Moreover, Antonio Guzmán Blanco himself, who dominated this period but was not seen at that time as the leader, called to command the second great constitutional historical period as he effectively did, defining the cast of national politics from 1863 up to the beginning of the twentieth century.[1493]

In 1863, through a constitution-making process developed by a Constituent Assembly[1494] the remains of the prior state system had vanished and the new order was being built, formally covered with the form of a federal State based on an extreme system of territorial distribution of public power. This system was based on autonomous federal entities or states with their own governments elected by universal and direct suffrage, and confined the 'National Power' to a Federal District, a neutral territory that was 'temporarily' placed in Caracas.

13. The Constitution of 14 April 1864 established the 'United States of Venezuela', 'reuniting' twenty provinces that declared themselves 'independent', recognizing reciprocally their 'autonomy', and adopting the denomination of 'States'.[1495] Antonio Guzmán Blanco was elected President of the Republic, acting as *primus inter pares* regarding the regional *caudillos* in a political system initially controlled by the latter. In the first years of his tenure, among other governing institutions, Guzmán Blanco made use of 'Conferences of Plenipotentiaries' which were nothing more than formal meetings of the regional *caudillos* in Caracas to resolve common political problems of a national scope. He also tried to define a 'bolivarian doctrine' in order to attain, through the cult of Bolivar some sort of political unity to his regime (see *infra* paragraphs 17, 35, 42, 247, 335, 545). The country continued to be very poor, with a large public debt, and increasingly subjected to the new autocracy installed in the Central Power led by Guzmán Blanco, named the 'Great Civilizator'.[1496] He established the complete separation between the Catholic Church and the State regarding public affairs (see *infra* paragraphs 106 et seq.) After twice reforming the Constitution, in 1874 and in 1881, the latter called the 'Swiss Constitution' because of the creation of a 'Federal Council',[1497] mainly tending to accommodate it to his way of exercising power, he converted many of the traditional states (former Provinces) into 'Sections' of larger new states with aggregated territories, one of them called 'Great Guzman Blanco State'. In 1881 he retired to France, progressively contributing to the deterioration and weakening of his own authority.

1493   See Germán Carrera Damas, *Formulación definitiva del Proyecto Nacional: 1870–1900* (Caracas: Cuadernos Lagoven, 1988).

1494   See Rafael Lugo Felice, 'Proceso Constituyente de 1863', in *Procesos Constituyentes y Reformas Constitucionales en la Historia de Venezuela: 1811–1999*, ed. Elena Plaza y Ricardo Combellas (Coord.), vol. I (Caracas: Universidad Central de Venezuela, 2005), 225–264.

1495   See J. Gabaldón Márquez (ed.), *Documentos Políticos y Actos Ejecutivos y Legislativos de la Revolución Federal* (Caracas, 1959).

1496   See R.A. Rondón Márquez, *Guzmán Blanco. El Autócrata Civilizador o Parábola de los Partidos Políticos Tradicionales en la Historia de Venezuela*, 2 vols. (Caracas, 1944).

1497   See Elide Rivas, 'El proceso constituyente y la Constitución de 1881. Un federalismo a la Suiza', in *Procesos Constituyentes y Reformas Constitucionales en la Historia de Venezuela: 1811–1999*, ed. Elena Plaza y Ricardo Combellas (Coord.) vol. I (Caracas: Universidad Central de Venezuela, 2005), 317–339.

14. The last decade of the nineteenth century was also marked by constitutional reforms in 1892 and 1893, initiating a frequent historical constitutional change recurrence of seeking to extend the tenure of the President of the Republic. However, the political crisis derived from the interminable struggles between the Central Power and the regional *caudillos* could not be stemmed by just constitutional reforms, particularly because of the general degradation of the political system, which eventually provoked its collapse.

This period came to an end with the *Revolución Liberal Restauradora* (23 October 1899) lead by Cirpiano Castro, one of the Andean *caudillos*,[1498] which originated in defence of the sovereignty of states and as a reaction against the decision of the Congress to give the National Executive the power to provisionally appoint its Governors, once the traditional territories of the traditional states were restored.

§3. *Third Constitutional Period (1901–1945): The Centralized Autocratic State*

15. This Liberal Restoration Revolution of 1899, launched in defence of federalism, ironically consolidated Cipriano Castro into power as President of the Republic, by means of the approval of a new Constitution by a Constituent Assembly in 1901 which reversed all of the remaining general trends of a federal State.[1499] During his tenure he resisted the attempts of European Navies (Great Britain, Germany and Italy) to blockade the Venezuelan coast seeking payment of debts by the country (see *infra* paragraphs 100, 328). His Vice President, Juan Vicente Gómez, was his revolutionary companion, who at the beginning of the twentieth century led the last war against the remaining regional *caudillos*, consolidating the hegemonic presence of the Andean rulers in the central national government. He concluded with the traditional nineteen century Liberal and Conservative political parties and with the basis of the federal form of the State. Gómez also initiated the process of political integration of the country after forming, for the first time in the country's history, a National Army substituting the former traditional States' militias, and got rid of Castro, using for such purpose a ruling of the Federal and Cassation Court accusing Castro of criminal offences.[1500] He controlled State and military power from 1908 up to his death in 1935, consolidating the new political period of the *Centralized Autocratic State,* which finished in 1945.[1501]

1498   See Domingo A. Rangel, *Los Andinos en el Poder* (Caracas, 1964); Ramón J. Velásquez, *La Caída del Liberalismo Amarillo, Tiempo y Drama de Antonio Paredes* (Caracas, 1973).

1499   See Mariano Picón Salas, *Los días de Cipriano Castro* (Caracas: Barquisimeto, 1955); Ángel Zerpa Aponte, 'El primer proceso constituyente del Siglo XX: La Constituyente de 1901', in *Procesos Constituyentes y Reformas Constitucionales en la Historia de Venezuela: 1811–1999*, ed. Elena Plaza y Ricardo Combellas (Coord.), vol. II (Caracas: Universidad Central de Venezuela, 2005), 419–449.

1500   See R.J. Velásquez, *La caída del Liberalismo Amarillo. Tiempo y Drama de Antonio Paredes* (Caracas, 1973), 206 et seq., and 242 et seq.

1501   See Ramón J. Velásquez (Director), *El Pensamiento Político Venezolano en el Siglo XX*, 10 vols (Caracas, 1983); Ángel Ziemn, *El Gomecismo y la formación del Ejército Militar* (Caracas, 1979); Allan R. Brewer-Carías, 'El desarrollo institucional del Estado Centralizado en Venezuela (1899–1935) y sus proyecciones contemporáneas', in *Revista de Estudios de la Vida Local y Autonómica*

ALLAN R. BREWER-CARÍAS

16. During this period the true integration among the regions of the nation began, and the Nation State was consolidated, a process which had occurred in many Latin American nations far earlier, towards the mid-nineteenth century. After the initial 1901 Constitution, various constitutional reforms took place in 1904, 1909, 1914 and 1922, ending this first part of the period with the 1925 Constitution, in which the autocratic centralized State was consolidated, although without abandoning the federal framework. This latter Constitution was subsequently also reformed, due to Gómez political and military circumstantial motives, in 1928, 1929 and 1931, and after his death, in 1936 and 1945, without changing substantially the constitutional provisions regarding the progressive centralization of State powers at the national level in all its scopes: political, military, fiscal, administrative and legislative. In this task, the dictatorship of Gómez was decisive, inspired in the authoritarian idea of the 'necessary guardian' (*Gendarme Necesario*),[1502] fed with the new public income wealth that precisely began to pour into the public coffers due to the beginning of the oil exploitation in the country, through concessions given to foreign companies.

17. After the death of Gómez, with a constitutional reform sanctioned by Congress in 1936, his Defence Minister, Eleazar López Contreras, succeeded him in the Presidency of the Republic, and a gradual process of transition from autocracy to democracy began, which was continued within the Presidency of Isaías Medina Angarita, also Lopez's Minister of Defence. López Contreras was the other political ruler in the country's history that profited from the 'Bolivarian' doctrine in order to give some basis to his policies (see *supra* paragraph 13; *infra* paragraphs 35, 42, 244, 247, 335, 545).

This period witnessed the birth of workers' and mass movements, and of political organizations that initiated the contemporary political parties which had originated in the student movements of 1928.[1503] Nonetheless, after finishing centralizing power and progressively finishing with the federal vestiges, except for the use of the term, eventually the Andean political leadership did not fully understand the changes that had been taking place in the Venezuelan society, and also in the world as a consequence of the World Wars, particularly regarding the general democratizing tendencies. In this regard, for instance, the two successors of Juan Vicente Gómez failed to understand that in 1945 and after the Second World War, direct elections, and secret and universal suffrage were essential elements in the consolidation of the democracy that was beginning to be born.

The Constitution was finally reformed in 1945,[1504] but despite the clamour of new political actors, who were the products of nascent syndicalism and the democra-

---

(Madrid, 1985), no. 227, 483–514; and no. 228, 695–726; and Naudy Suárez Figueroa (ed.), *Programas Políticos Venezolanos de la Primera Mitad del siglo XX* (Caracas, 1977).

1502 See Laureano Vallenilla Lanz, *Cesarismo Democrático. Estudios sobre las bases sociológicas de la Constitución efectiva de Venezuela* (Caracas, 1952); *El sentido americano de la democracia. Cesarismo democrático y otros textos* (Caracas: Biblioteca Ayacucho, 1991).

1503 See Vicente Magallanes, *Los Partidos Políticos en la Evolución Histórica Venezolana* (Caracas, 1973).

1504 See Linda Núñez, 'El reforma constitucional del 1945', in *Procesos Constituyentes y Reformas Constitucionales en la Historia de Venezuela: 1811–1999*, ed. Elena Plaza y Ricardo Combellas (Coord.), vol. II (Caracas: Universidad Central de Venezuela, 2005), 563–585.

tic opening, direct elections and universal suffrage were not established. Instead, the Constitution sanctioned only a limited form of 'universal' suffrage in which women were excluded from all national elections and restricted to municipal voting, and the indirect system for the election of the National President was left unchanged. Such a timid democratic opening was not sufficient, so despite the extremely important legal reforms promoted by Medina to organize the mining and petroleum industries and ensure that the oil concessions were really taxed, and despite the fact that Venezuela was a country more open to the world on the eve of the wave of contemporary democratization that followed the Second World War, the *Medenista* leadership still failed to see the significance of the need for a direct and universal presidential election for the succession of Medina Angarita. Unfortunately, here again, as in so many instances in history, the incomprehension of the historical juncture blinded the leadership, which was lost in trying to impose succession by an Andean candidate through the three-tiered system of indirect Congressional elections, while being overshadowed by López Contreras who threatened them with his own candidacy.

18. In the 1945 constitutional reform the key components of the regime remained untouched, with the result that the constitutional text together with the remaining of the authoritarian political system initiated at the beginning of the twentieth century, lasted only a few more months until the October Revolution of 1945. This was led by the social-democratic party, *Acción Democratica*, beginning the democratization process not only of the State, but of society; and sweeping away the autocratic regime with its leadership and the generation that undertook its political program at the beginning of the twentieth century. As it can be clearly deduced from the Constituent Act of the Revolutionary *Junta,* the principal constitutional idea motivating the Revolution, among its other causes, was the institution of secret, direct and universal suffrage.

§4. *Fourth Constitutional Period (1945–1999): The Democratic Centralized State of parties*

19. In 1945, and as a consequence of the democratic revolution that followed, a new political period was opened, the one of the *Democratic Centralized State of Parties* that found its foundations in the Constitution of 5 July 1947, sanctioned by a Constituent Assembly.[1505] This Constitution laid the foundations of the democratic regime that lasted until 1999, based in two fundamental pillars: the democratic regime through political parties but based in a dominant party; and a centralized constitutional structure of the State. The Constitution was only in force for one year (1947–1948), when the system was broken by a military coup, which led to one decade of dictatorship conducted by General Marcos Pérez Jimenez (1948–1958), who

---

1505   See Ingrid Jiménez Monsalve, 'Asamblea Nacional Constituyente 1946–1947. Logros y fracasos de un programa político', in *Procesos Constituyentes y Reformas Constitucionales en la Historia de Venezuela: 1811–1999*, ed. Elena Plaza y Ricardo Combellas (Coord.), vol. II (Caracas: Universidad Central de Venezuela, 2005), 587–621.

promoted in 1953 the sanctioning of a new Constitution[1506] that eliminated the denomination itself of the State as 'United States of Venezuela'.

20. After trying to be re-elected in 1957, Pérez Jiménez was overthrown by a new democratic revolution that took place in 1958, restoring again the democratic system. That year the leaders of the political parties signed a very important political pact known as '*Pacto de Punto Fijo*',[1507] which formed the basis for the restoration of democracy in the country. Unfortunately, a decade of military dictatorship had to be suffered in order for the political leadership to arrive at the conclusion that a pluralistic system of parties and political compromises and consensus was needed in order to establish democracy; and for Rómulo Betancourt,[1508] who was the leader of the failed October 1945 Revolution, to admit and understand that democracy could not and cannot function on the basis of the hegemony of a single party excluding all other political groups. The *Pacto de Punto Fijo* of 1958 was the profoundly distilled product of the painful experience of militarism of the 1950s, and its focused objective was precisely to implant a democracy that would amply bear fruit in the following decades.[1509]

21. This Pact conditioned the drafting of the 1961 Constitution, which has been the one with the longest term in force in the country from 1961 to 1999.[1510] In this Constitution the main role was given to the political parties who monopolized political representation, political participation, and State power, following the principles of the electoral system of proportional representation (d'Hondt model), which remained unaltered until after the electoral reform of 1993.[1511] The resulting political project conditioned the life of the generations that led the country during the last four decades of the twentieth century, based on the compromise to establish and maintain a democratic government, and to promote the democratization of the society and of the economy. During the period, the country lived under a democratic representative regime, with a succession of nine Presidents who for the first time in the Venezuelan political history were all elected by universal, direct and secret suffrage.

1506   See Andrés Stambouli, *Crisis Política Venezuela 1945–1958* (Caracas, 1980); José Rodríguez Iturbe, *Crónica de la Década Militar* (Caracas, 1984).

1507   See Juan Carlos Rey, 'El sistema de partidos venezolano', in *Problemas socio políticos de América Latina* (Caracas, 1980), 255 a 338; Naudy Suárez Figueroa, *Punto Fijo y otros puntos. Los grandes acuerdos políticos de 1958*, Serie Cuadernos de Ideas Políticas N° 1 (Caracas: Fundación Rómulo Betancourt, 2006).

1508   See R. Betancourt, *La Revolución Democrática en Venezuela* (Caracas, 1968); Roberto J. Alexander, *The Venezuela Democratic Revolution. A profile of the Regime of Rómulo Betancourt* (New Jersey, 1964).

1509   See D.H. Blank, *Politics in Venezuela* (1973).

1510   See *La Constitución de 1961 y la evolución constitucional de Venezuela*, 2 vols (Caracas: Ediciones del Congreso de la República, 1972–1973); *Estudios sobre la Constitución. Libro Homenaje a Rafael Caldera*, 4 vols. (Caracas: Universidad Central de Venezuela, 1980); and Allan Brewer-Carías, *La Constitución y sus Enmiendas* (Caracas: Editorial Jurídica venezolana, 1991).

1511   See Allan R. Brewer-Carías, *Cambio Político y Reforma del Estado en Venezuela*, ed. Tecnos (Madrid, 1975), 178 et seq.

22. Regarding the form of the State, the federal form was kept, but covering a very centralized state in which the states were kept but lacked effective political power, due to the fact that all power; political, economic, legislative, taxing, administrative and labour, was concentrated at the national level of government. This centralism of the state was accompanied by other centralisms, that of the political parties, internally organized in a 'centralized democratic' scheme, similar to the one developed in the labour unions, which became another fundamental element of the system.[1512] Nonetheless, the Constitution, due to its democratic foundations, expressly established the possibility to promote the decentralization of the Federation by empowering the National Assembly to revert the centralization framework of the country, by transferring powers and competencies from the national level to the states. At the beginning of the political crisis of the 1990s, that process began through the sanctioning of the Organic Law on the Transfer, Distribution and Decentralization of competencies among public entities,[1513] which began to be implemented.[1514] Unfortunately since 1994 and particularly after 1999, the decentralization efforts were abandoned (see *infra* paragraph 183 et seq.).

23. The 1961 Constitution, when enacted, was one of the more advanced of its time, having served as a model in many aspects to later Latin American constitutions. As aforementioned, its text was the result of a consensus attained among the various political actors, being considered as an authentic political pact of the Venezuelan society, conceived by the leaders of a generation that at the time had more than two decades of political struggle, and in an historical moment in which the spirit of unity and concord prevailed, resulting from the overthrow of the Perez Jimenez dictatorship.

During the last four decades of the twentieth century, the political parties dominated the political scene. This meant that when they entered, during the 1990s, into the profound political crisis that affected their leadership,[1515] particularly because they failed to understand the democratic advances they helped to complete, the poli-

---

1512   See Allan R. Brewer-Carías, *El Estado. Crisis y Reforma* (Caracas: Academia de Ciencias Políticas y Sociales, 1983); *El Estado Incomprendido. Reflexiones sobre el sistema político y su reforma* (Caracas: Vadell hermanos, 1985); *Problemas del Estado de Partidos* (Caracas: Editorial Jurídica Venezolana, 1989); *Cinco siglos de Historia y un País en Crisis* (Caracas: Academia de Ciencias Políticas y Sociales y Comisión Presidencial del V Centenario de Venezuela, 1998), 95 a 117.

1513   The Law was sanctioned in 1989. See Allan R. Brewer-Carías et al., *Leyes y reglamentos para la Descentralización Política de la Federación* 94 (Caracas, 1990). See in *Gaceta Oficial* N° 39.140 of 17 Mar. 2009.

1514   See *Informe sobre la descentralización en Venezuela 1993. Informe del Ministro de Estado para la Descentralización* (Caracas, 1994).

1515   See Pedro Guevara, *Estado v. Democracia* (Caracas, 1997); Miriam Kornblith, *Venezuela en los 90. Crisis de la Democracia* (Caracas, 1998); and Allan R. Brewer-Carías, *El Estado, Crisis y Reforma* (Caracas: Academia de Ciencias Políticas y Sociales, 1983); *El Estado Incomprendido. Reflexiones sobre el sistema político y su reforma* (Caracas, 1985); *La crisis de las instituciones: responsables y salidas Revista de la Facultad de Ciencias Jurídicas y Políticas*, N° 64 (1985), 129–155; *Problemas del Estado de Partidos* (Caracas: Editorial Jurídica Venezolana, 1989); and 'Reflexiones sobre la crisis del sistema político, sus salidas democráticas y la convocatoria a una Constituyente', in *Los Candidatos Presidenciales ante la Academia* (Caracas: Academia de Ciencias Políticas y Sociales, 1998), 11 a 66.

tical vacuum they left provoked the takeover of the State and its institutions by an authoritarian and militaristic government. This government was led by an anti-party leader that appeared in the middle of the political vacuum, the late Hugo Chávez Frias, a former Lieutenant-Colonel who led a military attempt of a *coup d'état* in 1992. Chávez was elected in 1998 promoting the collapse of the democratic political system designed in 1958, and tried to begin a new political system that nonetheless is still in the process of being conformed, characterized by a status of permanent coup d'Etat given by all the Branches of Government[1516] (see *infra* paragraph 23, 26, 141, 238).

§5. *The Beginning of a Fifth Constitutional Period after 1999: The Centralized, Military and Authoritarian State*

24. The main political offer Chávez made during the 1998 presidential campaign, beside the anti-party slogans and the promise of change, was the convening of a Constituent Assembly in order to 'redound' the State and to sanction a new Constitution with a new democratic and participatory order, in substitution of the 1961 Constitution and of the *Pacto de Punto Fijo* framework (see *supra* paragraph 2; *infra* paragraph 169). For the sanctioning of the new Constitution, after bitter political and legal disputes, a National Constituent Assembly, not established in 1961 as a constitutional review procedure, was convened and elected in 1999, exclusively promoted by the new President of the Republic. This became the main institutional tool he used to materialize a complete takeover of all the branches of government of the State, and to reinforce the centralization of the Federation. According to the then in force 1961 Constitution, the only way to elect such Assembly in 1999 was after a previous constitutional reform incorporating it in the Constitution, unless a constitutional judicial interpretation of the 1961 Constitution allowed the election. The latter was precisely what the Supreme Court of Justice did in January 1999, although in a very ambiguous way,[1517] trying to resolve the then existing dilemma between popular sovereignty willing to be expressed and constitutional supremacy. It eventually decided in favour of the former.[1518]

25. The Constituent Assembly was then elected in July 1999 after a consultative referendum that took place in April 1999, which was completely controlled by

---

1516   See for instance, Allan R. Brewer-Carías, Golpe de Estado y proceso constituyente (México, Instituto de Investigaciones Jurídicas, 2002); *Golpe de Estado Constituyente, Estado Constitucional y Democracia*, Caracas: Editorial Jurídica Venezolana, Colección Tratado de Derecho Constitucional, Vol. VIII, 2015; *El golpe a la democracia dado por la Sala Constitucional,*. (Caracas, Editorial Jurídica Venezolana, 2014); "El golpe de Estado dado en diciembre de 2014, con la inconstitucional designación de las altas autoridades del poder público," *Revista de Derecho Público*, 140 (Caracas, Editorial Jurídica Venezolana, 2014).

1517   See Allan R. Brewer-Carías, 'La configuración judicial del proceso constituyente en Venezuela de 1999 o de cómo el guardián de la Constitución abrió el camino para su violación y para su propia extinción', in *Revista de Derecho Público*, N° 77–80 (Caracas: Editorial Jurídica Venezolana, 1999), 453–514. See the text of the Supreme Court rulings in the same *Revista*.

1518   See Allan R. Brewer-Carías, 'El desequilibrio entre soberanía popular y supremacía constitucional y la salida constituyente en Venezuela en 1999', in *Revista Anuario Iberoamericano de Justicia Constitucional, N° 3 1999* (Madrid: Centro de Estudios Políticos y Constitucionales, 2000), 31–56.

Chávez supporters with more than 95% of its seats. This method of constitution-making process was not the first of its kind in Venezuelan constitutional history. After the two initial ones creating the independent and autonomous State of Venezuela (1811 and 1830), seven other constitution-making processes were carried out in 1858, 1863, 1893, 1901, 1914, 1946 and 1953 through Constituent Assemblies or Constituent Congresses, but in each case, as a consequence of a de facto rejection of the existing constitution, through a *coup d'état*, a revolution, or a civil war.

The constitution-making process of 1999, in contrast, had a peculiarity that made it different from all the previous ones in Venezuelan history, in the sense that it was not the result of a de facto rejection of the 1961 Constitution, through a revolution, a war or a *coup d'état*. Rather it had its origin in a democratic process without involving a rupture of the previous political regime.[1519]

However, it took place in the context of a severe political crisis that was affecting the functioning of the democratic regime's centralized political parties established in 1958, resulting from the lack of its evolution. That is why the call for the referendum consulting the people on the establishment of the Constituent National Assembly, as expressed in the February 1999 Decree issued by the President, intended to ask the people their opinion on a Constituent National Assembly 'aimed at transforming the State and creating a new legal order that allows the effective functioning of a social and participative democracy'. That was the formal *raison d'être* of the constitutional process of 1999, and that is why, with few exceptions, it would have been difficult to find anyone in the country who could have disagreed with those stated purposes.

26. The Constituent Assembly, far from dedicating itself to write off the new Constitution, was the main tool the newly elected President had, in order to assault and control all the branches of government, violating the same 1961 Constitution whose interpretation helped to create it. Consequently, the elected Constituent Assembly technically gave a *coup d'état*, [1520] unfortunately with the consent and complicity of the former Supreme Court of Justice, which as it always happens in these illegitimate institutional complicity cases, was inexorably the first victim of the authoritarian government which it had helped to grab power. Just a few months later, in December 1999, that Supreme Court was erased from the institutional scene.

However, unfortunately, Chavez did not formally conceive the constitutional process conducted by the National Assembly as an instrument of conciliation aimed at reconstructing the democratic system and assuring good governance. That would have required the political commitment of all components of society and the participation of all sectors of society in the design of a new, functioning democracy, which did not occur. The constitutional process of 1999, on the contrary, served to facilitate the total takeover of State power by a new political group that crushed all the others, including the then existing political parties. As a result, almost all of the oppor-

---

1519   See Allan R. Brewer-Carías, 'On the making process and the 1999 Constitution in Venezuela, en el Symposium on 'Challenges to Fragile Democracies in the Americas: Legitimacy and Accountability', *Texas International Law Journal* 36 (Austin: University of Texas at Austin, 2001), 333–338.

1520   See Allan R. Brewer-Carías, *Golpe de Estado y proceso constituyente en Venezuela* (México, Guayaquil: Universidad Nacional Autónoma de México, 2002, 2006).

ALLAN R. BREWER-CARÍAS

tunities for inclusion and public participation vanished and the constitution-making process became an endless *coup d'état* when the Constituent Assembly, elected in July of 1999, began violating the existing Constitution of 1961 by intervening and assuming all branches of government, over which it had no power, according to the referendum mandate that created the Assembly. The Constituent Assembly also intervened in the federated states without any legitimate authority, by eliminating the States Legislative Assemblies.

27. The general result of the 1999 constitution-making process[1521] was its failure as an instrument for political reconciliation, and the stated democratic purposes of the process were not accomplished. No effective reform of the State was accomplished, except for the purpose of authoritarian institution building, and for the election of a populist government that has concentrated all branches of government and crushed political pluralism. Thus, if it is true that political changes of great importance were made, some of them have contributed to the aggravation of the factors that provoked the crisis in the first place. New political actors assumed power, but far from implementing a democratic conciliation policy, they have accentuated the differences among Venezuelans, worsening political polarization, and making conciliation increasingly difficult. The seizure of power which characterized the process has opened new wounds, making social and political rivalries worse than they have been for more than a century. Despite Venezuela's extraordinary oil wealth during the first years of the twenty-first century, the social problems of the country have increased.

28. The violations of the 1961 Constitution that continued to be in force at the time the National Constituent assembly was elected were subsequently followed by the violation of the new 1999 Constitution voted on November 1999 by the same Constituent Assembly, and approval by referendum was held on 15 December 1999.[1522] The violation began on 22 December 1999, a week later, when the Constituent Assembly enacted a 'Transitional Constitutional Regime' Decree, which was not authorized in the new Constitution, and which was not submitted to, nor approved by, popular vote.[1523] It was that extra constitutional regime which allowed the Constituent Assembly to continue the endless *coup d'état* initiated a few months earlier, affecting the separations of powers, and allowing the new National Assembly elected in 2000 to legislate outside the constitutional framework.

The final result of that 1999 constitution-making process was the omission of provisions in the new Constitution to undertake the democratic changes that were most needed in Venezuela, namely, the effective separation of powers, the political

---

1521   See Allan R. Brewer-Carías, 'Constitution Making in Defraudation of the Constitution and Authoritarian Government in Defraudation of Democracy. The Recent Venezuelan Experience', *Lateinamerika Analysen* 19, N° 1 (2008), GIGA, Germa Institute of Global and Area Studies, Institute of latin American Studies, Hamburg 2008, 119–142; *Asamblea Constituyente y Proceso Constituyente 1999*, *Colección Tratado de Derecho Constitucional, Tomo VI*, Fundación de Derecho Público, Editorial Jurídica Venezolana, Caracas 2013.

1522   See in *Gaceta Oficial* N° 5.453 Extra. of 24 Mar. 2000. The text was originally published in *Gaceta Oficial* N° 36.860 of 30 Dec. 1999. Arts 160, 162, 174, 192 and 230 of the 1999 Constitution were amended by referendum held on 14 Feb. 2009. See *Gaceta Oficial* N° 5.908 Extra. of 19 Feb. 2009.

1523   *Gaceta Oficial* N° 36.859 of 29 Dec. 1999.

decentralization of the Federation and the reinforcement of states and municipal political powers.[1524]

Nonetheless, and in spite of these absence of democratic reforms, in 1999 a new constitutional period in Venezuelan history began to be configured, establishing the framework of an *Authoritarian and Centralized State,* based in populist policies of socialist trends, which have been developing during the first decade of the twenty-first century. This State has been erected by demolishing the rule of law principles, the separation of powers and the federation; by the weakening of the effectiveness of the protection of constitutional rights; by subjecting the judicial review system and other check and balance institutions to the Executive, and by progressively destroying representative democracy itself in the name of a supposedly 'participatory democracy'. Nonetheless, the Constitution formally establishes a general framework of a democratic political regime and rule of law, which in political practice has been distorted.

29. But the 1999 constitution-making process governed by the National Constituent Assembly did not finish with the final proclamation of the new Constitution on 20 December 1999, and the Constituent Assembly continued to act as a constituent power, even ignoring the new Constitution, particularly sanctioning the aforementioned constitutional transitory regime after the popular approval of the Constitution.

In effect, the text approved by the National Constituent Assembly in November of 1999, and submitted to a referendum for popular approval on 15 December 1999, contained just twenty-eight Transitory Provisions intended to assure the immediate legal effect of the Constitution, and to regulate the legislative program to execute the Constitution. These were the provisions approved by the people, in which no solution was given with respect to the possible immediate transition of titular officials of the State organs elected a year before, under the 1961 Constitution, in relation to the new organs established under the Constitution of 1999. That is, the people when approving the Constitution did not vote for any termination of the mandate of the previous elected authorities. The consequence of this omission was that in order, for instance, to substitute the former Congress by the new National Assembly, their members needed to be elected according to the new Constitution. After the election of the new National Assembly it could begin to elect the new head of the Branches of Government, like the Supreme Tribunal or the Officers of the Citizen and Electoral power. The only transitory provision of the 1999 Constitution on these matters of electing new officers to high public offices was the immediate provisional appointment of the People's Defender, an office created by the new Constitution (Ninth Transitory Provision) until the new National Assembly to be elected in 2000 could made the definitive election.

1524   See on the initial critical comments of the Constitution in Allan R. Brewer-Carías, 'Reflexiones críticas sobre la Constitución de Venezuela de 1999' in *Constitucionalismo Iberoamericano del Siglo XXI,* ed. Diego Valadés & Miguel Carbonell (Coordinadores) Cámara de Diputados. LVII Legislatura (México: Universidad Nacional Autónoma de México, 2000), 171–193; in *Revista Facultad de Derecho, Derechos y Valores* III, N° 5 (Universidad Militar Nueva Granada, Santafé de Bogotá, D.C., Colombia, Julio 2000), 9–26; in the collective book, *La Constitución de 1999* (Caracas: Academia de Ciencias Políticas y Sociales, 2000), 63–88; and in *Revista de Derecho Público,* N° 81 (Caracas: Editorial Jurídica Venezolana, 2000), 7–21.

30. Notwithstanding, the Constituent Assembly without having any power for such purpose, as aforementioned, a week after the Constitution was approved by the people, on 22 December 1999 sanctioned the Decree on 'The Regimen of Transition for the Public Powers', creating a constitutional vacuum by dismissing the senators and representatives to the former Congress, the representatives to the State Legislative Assemblies and intervening in the Municipal Councils, all elected in 1998; the magistrates of the former Supreme Court of Justice, the General Comptroller of the Republic, the members of the former Supreme Electoral Council and of the then existing Council of the Judiciary, and the General Prosecutor of the Republic.

The consequence of the created institutional vacuum was the 'need' for the same Constituent Assembly to fill it, and without any power to do so, it 'created' a new organ, not provided for in the new Constitution. In order to act as Legislative Power, the 'National Legislative Commission' called the 'Little Congress' (Congresillo), 'until representatives to the National Assembly are elected and in office' (Article 5), appointed its members in a discretionary way. The same happened at the states level, with the dismissals of the former representatives to the Legislatives Assemblies and the subsequent appointment of members of new organs not established in the Constitution, the State Legislative Commissions. Regarding the Municipal Councils, they were subjected to the supervision and control of the National Constituent Assembly or the National Legislative Commission, violating their autonomy.

The Constituent Assembly also determined the number of Magistrates of each of the Chambers of the new Supreme Tribunal of Justice, appointing them, due to the vacuum that the same Assembly, without any constitutional authority created, by dismissing the Magistrates of the former Supreme Court of Justice; and creating a new organ that existed until 2010, the 'Commission on the Functioning and the Re-structuring of the Judicial System (Article 21) that substituted the former Council of the Judiciary'. In 2010 this Commission was eliminated, once the Judicial Disciplinary Jurisdiction began to function (see *infra* paragraph 402).

The result of this usurpation of the popular will by the National Constituent Assembly was the beginning of an endless constitutional transitory regime in defraudation of the new Constitution, governed by new provisional authorities designated by the Assembly, which in many cases, as is the case of the Judiciary, continues to exist one decade after the sanctioning of the Constitution.

§6. *The Outgoing Constitutional Process in Defraudation of the Constitution and of Democracy (1999–2015)*

31. After the sanctioning of the 1999 Constitution by the National Constituent Assembly through a constitution-making process that began with the violation of the 1961 Constitution and finished with the violation of the new 1999 Constitution by the same Constituent Assembly, after its popular approval, the constitutional process in Venezuela during the first fifteen years of the twenty-first century, unfortunately can be globally characterized as a process developed in continuous defraudation of the Constitution and of the democratic regime.

As aforementioned, the 1999 National Constituent Assembly was the instrument used by the new elected President to dissolve and intervene in all branches of government (particularly the Judiciary) and to dismiss all the public officials that had been elected just a few months before (November 1998) with the sole exception of the President of the Republic itself. In addition, the Constitutional Assembly intervened in all the other branches of government, among them, and above all, the Judiciary, whose autonomy and independence was progressive and systematically demolished.[1525] The result has been the tight Executive control over the Judiciary, particularly regarding the new appointed Supreme Tribunal of Justice, with its Constitutional Chamber the most ominous instrument for the consolidation of authoritarianism in the country[1526] (see *infra* paragraphs 62, 222, 401, 666).

32. After the initial defraudation of the Constitution in order to control all the State branches of government, another defraudation process began, this time of democracy, led by the authoritarian government that emerged from the 1999 constituent process, who used representative democracy for the purpose of progressively eliminating it, and supposedly substituting it by a 'participative democracy', among others aspects, based on the establishment of popular councils of a new Popular Power controlled by the Head of the State (see *infra* paragraphs 158, 258, 627).

33. But notwithstanding the purpose, the outcome has been that all the essential elements of democracy (see *infra* paragraphs 41, 212) are precisely the ones that have unfortunately been ignored or fractured in Venezuela, in the name of that supposed participative democracy. Never before, has there been more violation of human rights as can be deduced from the numerous petitions filed before the Inter-American Commission on Human Rights. The access to power has been achieved contrary to the rule of law, by violating the separation and independence of the Judicial, Citizen and Electoral powers, and the last political reforms creating the Communal Councils, tend to substitute electoral representation by supposed citizens assemblies and councils whose members are not elected but appointed from the summit of the Popular Power controlled by the National Executive.[1527] The plural regime of parties has been destroyed and an official single Socialist Party has been created by the State itself, completely imbricated in its apparatus and controlled by the President of the Republic. Since everything depends on the oil rich State, only those

---

1525   See Allan R. Brewer-Carías, 'The Government of Judges and Democracy. The Tragic Situation of the Venezuelan Judiciary,' in *Venezuela. Some Current Legal Issues 2014, Venezuelan National Reports to the 19th International Congress of Comparative Law, International Academy of Comparative Law, Vienna, 20-26 July 2014*, (Caracas, Academia de Ciencias Políticas y Sociales, 2014), 13-42; La progresiva y sistemática demolición de la autonomía e independencia del Poder Judicial en Venezuela (1999-2004)', in *XXX Jornadas J.M Domínguez Escovar, Estado de derecho, Administración de justicia y derechos humanos* (Barquisimeto: Instituto de Estudios Jurídicos del Estado Lara, 2005), 33–174.

1526   See Allan R. Brewer-Carías, *Authoritarian Government v. The Rule Of Law. Lectures and Essays (1999-2014) on the Venezuelan Authoritarian Regime Established in Contempt of the Constitution*, (Caracas, Fundación de Derecho Público, Editorial Jurídica Venezolana, 2014); *Estado Totalitario y desprecio a la ley. La desconstitucionalización, desjuridificación, desjudicialización y desdemocratización de Venezuela*, (Caracas, Fundación de Derecho Público, Editorial Jurídica Venezolana, 2014).

1527   See Allan R. Brewer-Carías, 'El inicio de la desmunicipalización en Venezuela: La organización del Poder Popular para eliminar la descentralización, la democracia representativa y la participación a nivel local', in *AIDA, Opera Prima de Derecho Administrativo. Revista de la Asociación Internacional de Derecho Administrativo* (Universidad Nacional Autónoma de México, Facultad de Estudios Superiores de Acatlán, Coordinación de Postgrado, Instituto Internacional de Derecho Administrativo 'Agustín Gordillo', Asociación Internacional de Derecho Administrativo, México, 2007), 49 a 67.

who are part of the Single Party are able to have a political, administrative, economic and social life.

One crucial step in this process took place in December 2010, through the sanctioning by the National Assembly, in contempt of the Constitution, of a group of Organic Laws establishing in parallel to the Constitutional State, of a so-called Communal State. This State exercised not the Public Power as established in the Constitution, but a so-called Popular Power, through the organization of Communes, Communal Councils, Social Control entities, and socio-productive entities. All these entities work within an economic system of 'communal economy' that has affected the constitutional structure of the State[1528] (see *infra* paragraphs 216 et seq. and 625 et seq.) implementing through statutes, what the government could not achieved through a constitutional reform that was rejected by the people in 2007 (see *infra* paragraphs 36 et seq. and 236 et seq., 675).

This entire institutional distortion has been established without the existence of separation or independence between the public powers, not only in their horizontal division due to the control that the Executive Power has over them; but in their vertical distribution, where the Federation has been progressively dismantled. Consequently, the federated states and the municipalities have been minimized, by means of eliminating every trace of political decentralization, that is, of autonomous entities in the territory, preventing any real possibility for democratic participation.

Another crucial step in the process of dismantling the rule of law took place in January 2013, after the announcement of the death of President Hugo Chávez, through the appointment to succeed him by means of an unconstitutional interpretation made by the Constitutional Chamber of the Supreme Tribunal, of a non-democratic elected official, as was the Executive-Vice-president, Nicolás Maduro, who was later elected as President of the Republic. [1529]

34. The result has been that , the fundamental components of democracy (see *infra* paragraphs 40, 150) have also been ignored or fractured, in the sense that the governmental activity deployed by the rich and suddenly wealthy State ceased to be transparent due to the lack of any sort of control and check and balance, it not being possible to demand any kind of accountability or responsibility from the government for the public interests management, so a rampant corruption has developed in a way never seen before. In addition, the freedom of speech and press has been systemati-

---

1528   See. these Organic Laws on the Popular Power, the Communes, the Communal Counils, the Communal Economic System, and the Social Comprollership in *Gaceta Oficial* N° 6.011 Extra. of 21 Dec. 2010. See the comments in Allan R. Brewer-Carías et al., *Leyes Orgánicas sobre el Poder Popular y el Estado Comunal (Los Consejos Comunales, las Comunas, la Sociedad Socialista y el Sistema Económico Comunal)* (Caracas: Editorial Jurídica Venezolana, 2011).

1529   See Allan R. Brewer-Carías, 'El juez constitucional y la demolición del principio democrático de gobierno. O de cómo la Jurisdicción Constitucional en Venezuela impuso arbitrariamente a los ciudadanos, al inicio del período constitucional 2013-2019, un gobierno sin legitimidad democrática, sin siquiera ejercer actividad probatoria alguna, violentando abiertamente la Constitución,' *Revista de Derecho Público*, N° 133 (Caracas, Editorial Jurídica Venezolana, 2013), 179-212.

cally threatened, imposing in many cases self-censorship, as reporters and dissidents are persecuted.[1530]

The consequence has been that all the essential elements and fundamental components of democracy have been progressively dismantled, particularly the separation of powers. On the contrary, what the country is facing is an excess of concentration and centralization of power, as it occurs in any authoritarian government, despite the electoral origin they can have. In such cases, as history has shown, an inevitable tendency toward tyranny develops, particularly when there are no efficient controls over those who govern, and even worse, if they have or believe to have popular support. In the case of Venezuela, the authoritarian government that has taken roots during the last decade against the principle of separation of powers, has led to the concentration of all powers in the hands of the Executive Power which in its turn controls the National Assembly, and consequently all the other branches of government (see *infra* paragraphs 199 et seq., 221).

35. All these authoritarian trends were intended to be constitutionalized through a Constitutional Reform proposal in 2007, aimed to radically transform the Decentralized, Democratic, Pluralistic rule of law and Social State into a Socialist, Centralized, Repressive and Militaristic State, grounded in a so-called Bolivarian doctrine, identified with 'XXI Century Socialism', and a communal economic system of State capitalism.[1531] These constitutional reforms were proposed in defraudation of the Constitution due to the fact that the proposed changes, because of their importance regarding the structure of the State, needed the convening of a national Constituent Assembly (Article 347), and not just to be approved by the constitutional reform procedure. The intention was to consolidate a Communist and Socialist State based in a State capitalism or, as was announced by the then Vice President of the Republic in January 2007, the instalment of 'the dictatorship of democracy';[1532] of course a contradiction in itself because in democracy no dictatorship is acceptable, whether of democracy or 'of the proletariat' as was proposed ninety years ago (1918) in the old Soviet Union through the same sort of 'councils' then called 'soviets' of soldiers, workers and countrymen.

But even without succeeding in the proposed constitutional reform, the fact is that in defraudation of democracy, since 2010 a new model of authoritarian State of a supposed Popular Power has taken shape in Venezuela, having its immediate origin in popular elections, providing the regime with a camouflage suit with 'constitu-

---

1530   See as an example, the case of the shout down of *Radio Caracas Televisión*, in Allan R. Brewer-Carías, 'El juez constitucional en Venezuela como instrumento para aniquilar la libertad de expresión y para confiscar la propiedad privada: el caso RCTV' (I de III), in *Gaceta Judicial* (mayo: Santo Domingo, República Dominicana, 2007), 24–27.

1531   See Allan R. Brewer-Carías, *La Reforma Constitucional de 2007 (Comentarios al proyecto inconstitucionalmente sancionado por la Asamblea Nacional el 2 de noviembre de 2007)* (Caracas: Editorial Jurídica Venezolana, 2007); Manuel Rachadell, *Socialismo del Siglo XXI. Análisis de la Reforma Constitucional propuesta por el Presidente Chávez en agosto de 2007* (Caracas: FUNEDA, 2007).

1532   Jorge Rodríguez, Vice President of the Republic, in January 2007, expressed: 'Of course we want to install a dictatorship, the dictatorship of the true democracy and the democracy is the dictatorship of everyone, you and us together, building a different country. Of course we want this dictatorship of democracy to be installed forever', in *El Nacional* (Caracas, 2 Jan. 2007), A-2.

ALLAN R. BREWER-CARÍAS

tional' and 'elective' shapes, designed for the destruction of the representative democracy itself.[1533]

36. In effect, in August 2007, the President of the Republic filed before the National Assembly, at his own initiative, a 'Constitutional Reform' draft that after the corresponding discussions was sanctioned by the Assembly on 2 November 2007, formally approving to 'Reform' the 1999 Constitution, in the following aspects: abandoning the Democratic Rule of Law State, a Centralized, Socialist and Militaristic State, based on a Socialist Bolivarian Doctrine; changing the Armed Force into a Bolivarian Armed Force, and creating a new component of it, the Bolivarian Popular Militia; dismantling the Federation and all that remained of political decentralization by giving the President and his regional authorities power over the states; dismantling the Municipal government by consolidating below them the Communal Councils for the Popular Power, controlled directly by the President of the Republic and composed by non-elected members, eliminating representative democracy at the lower lever of the State; reinforcing Presidentialism, concentrating all powers in the hands of the President, establishing the possibility of his indefinite re-election, and expanding his powers in 'states of exception' (emergency situations); eliminating economic freedom, establishing the pre-eminence of public property over private property, and consolidating the State capitalism already in place; eliminating the autonomy of the Central Bank; and limiting political participation of civil society in the election of High officials of the non-elected branches of government and of Citizenship in the referendums, and reducing participation to institutions with socialist purposes.[1534]

All these reform proposals were formulated and discussed by the National Assembly in defraudation of the Constitution, due to the fact that they seek to modify essential elements of the State and political system that could only be transformed through the constitutional review procedure of a 'National Constituent Assembly' and not by means of the 'constitutional reform' procedure (Articles 342, 347). (See *infra* paragraphs 116 et seq.). It was an attempt, proposed by the President of the Republic and approved by the National Assembly, to introduce essential changes in the Constitution evading the procedure established in the 1999 Constitution for such fundamental changes; that is, a constitutional review proposed in defraudation of the Constitution, being sanctioned through a procedure established for other purposes, in order to deceive the people.

1533   See Allan R. Brewer-Carías, *Authoritarian Government v. The Rule Of Law. Lectures and Essays (1999-2014) on the Venezuelan Authoritarian Regime Established in Contempt of the Constitution*, (Caracas, Fundación de Derecho Público, Editorial Jurídica Venezolana, 2014); 'El autoritarismo establecido en fraude a la Constitución y a la democracia y su formalización en Venezuela mediante la reforma constitucional. (De cómo en un país democrático se ha utilizado el sistema eleccionario para minar la democracia y establecer un régimen autoritario de supuesta 'dictadura de la democracia' que se pretende regularizar mediante la reforma constitucional)', in *Temas constitucionales. Planteamientos ante una Reforma* (Caracas: Fundación de Estudios de Derecho Administrativo, FUNEDA, 2007), 13–74.

1534   See Allan R. Brewer-Carías, 'El sello socialista que se pretendía imponer al Estado', in *Revista de Derecho Público*, N° 112 *(Estudios sobre la Reforma Constitucional)* (Caracas: Editorial Jurídica Venezolana, 2007), 71–76.

A change of the nature of the one that was proposed, according to Article 347 of the 1999 Constitution, required the convening and election of a National Constituent Assembly, and could not be undertaken by means of the 'constitutional reform' procedure, which as it has been mentioned, is exclusively reserved for a 'partial revision of the Constitution and a substitution of one or several of its norms without modifying the structure and fundamental principles of the Constitutional text' Consequently, by following this procedure in order to achieve substantial constitutional changes, was to act fraudulently with respect to the Constitution, in a process that can be considered as accomplished in defraudation of the Constitution. This occurs when existing institutions are used in a manner that appears to adhere to constitutional form and procedure in order to proceed towards the creation of a new political regimen, a new constitutional order, without altering the established legal system.

Fortunately, the 2007 Constitutional Reform, although sanctioned by the National Assembly, was rejected by popular vote in the referendum held on 2 December 2007,[1535] but again, in a new defraudation of the Constitution, during the following six months in the first half of 2008, the President of the Republic implemented many of the popularly rejected constitutional reforms, but this time by means of decree-laws issued under delegate legislation according to a January 2007 enabling law, which of course did not authorize to modify the Constitution.[1536] This was, of course, completely contrary to the Constitution, but the absence of an independent Constitutional Chamber of the Supreme Tribunal made futile any judicial review action.

37. The main constitutional consequence of the popular rejection of a constitutional reform proposed at the initiative of the President of the Republic, in accordance to Article 345, is that it 'cannot be submitted again before the Assembly in the same constitutional term' (see *infra* paragraphs 85, 672), which in the case of the President, having been elected in 2006 endures up to 2012. Nonetheless, after the official party lost regional and local elections in the most important state and municipal entities of the country on November 2008, the President of the Republic formally announced that he was going to seek again for the review of the Constitution, in order to establish the possibility of his indefinite re-election, first by 'authorizing' his official Party to formulate a 'constitutional amendment' proposal by popular initiative, and after, due to the celerity problems of this review procedure, asking the National Assembly to take the initiative to formulate again proposal for a reform of the Constitution in order to allow his indefinite re-election.[1537] The Assembly approved the 'amendment' on January 2009, eliminating the limits for re-election of all elected public officials established in Articles 160, 162, 174, 192 and 230 of the Constitution, and again, in defraudation of the Constitution, an already popular re-

1535   Allan R. Brewer-Carías, 'La reforma constitucional en Venezuela de 2007 y su rechazo por el poder constituyente originario', in *Revista Peruana de Derecho Público*, Año 8, N° 15 (Lima, Julio-Diciembre 2007), 13–53.

1536   See the comments on the 2008 Decree-laws, in *Estudios sobre los decretos leyes Julio-Agosto 2008*, *Revista de Derecho Público*, N° 115 (Caracas: Editorial Jurídica Venezolana, 2008). See Allan R. Brewer-Carías, '¿Reforma constitucional o mutación constitucional?: La experiencia venezolana,' *Revista de Derecho Público*, N° 137 (Caracas, Editorial Jurídica Venezolana, 2014), 19-65.

1537   See the President speeches in *El Universal* (Caracas, 30 Nov.–5 Jan. 2008.

jected reform was submitted to a new referendum held on 14 February 2009, in the same constitutional period, contrary to Article 345 of the Constitution, using fraudulently this time the constitutional 'amendment' procedure.[1538] (See *infra* paragraph 85, 672).

38. Two questions with constitutional implication resulted from this new 'amendment' proposal that were the object of constitutional discussions: first, the possibility to use a 'constitutional amendment' procedure through which no fundamental constitutional principle can be changed, in order to alter and change the principle of alternating government that is a fundamental republican principle formulated in Article 6 of the Constitution; and second, the possibility to use the 'constitutional amendment' procedure to include the continuous election of the President of the Republic, changing the limits imposed in the Constitution (re-election only once, for the next period), which was a proposal previously submitted to referendum in December 2007, and rejected by the people. On these matters, the Constitutional Chamber of the Supreme Tribunal of Justice on 3 February 2009 issued two decisions (No. 46 and 53)[1539] in which a binding interpretation of the Constitution was established: first, regarding the possibility of submitting to popular vote a modification of the Constitution via 'constitutional amendment' on the same matter already rejected by the people in a 'constitutional reform' procedure held during the same constitutional term. The Constitutional Chamber argued that the limit imposed in the Constitution was directed only to the National Assembly to discuss again a constitutional reform on the same subject once rejected by the people, without considering the substantive aspect of the prohibition regarding the limits to ask again and again the people, to express in an endless way their will, through referenda (see *infra* paragraph 116). Second, regarding the possibility of using the 'constitutional amendment' procedure in order to change the fundamental principle of alternating (*alternabilidad*) government, which means that public offices must be occupied by turns, and not continuously by the same elected person, the Constitutional Chamber said that what the principle of *alternabilidad* imposed was 'for the people as sovereign to have the possibility to periodically elect their representatives', confusing alternating government (*gobierno alternativo*) with 'elected government' (*gobierno electivo*), that is, the principle that elected public offices must be occupied by turns, with the principle of election of representatives, considering that the principle of alternating (*alternabilidad*) government can only be infringed if the possibility to have elections is impeded. With these decisions, what the Supreme Tribunal made, in addition to resolving the constitutional challenges to the 15 February 2009 referendum was, through a constitutional interpretation, to modify or mutate the text of the Constitution, changing the sense of the prohibition of subsequent calling for referendum on

---

1538   The amendment was approved in the referendum by 54% of the votes, and was published in *Gaceta Oficial* N° 5.908 Extra. of 19 Feb. 2009.

1539   See the Constitutional Chamber of the Supreme Tribunal of Justice Decision N° 53, of 3 Feb. 2009 (*Interpretation of Arts 340,6 and 345 of the Constitution* Case), in <www.tsj.gov.ve/ decisions/scon/Febrero/53-3209-2009-08-1610.html>. See the comments on that decision in Allan R. Brewer-Carías, 'El Juez Constitucional vs. La alternabilidad republicana (La reelección continua e indefinida)', in *Revista de Derecho Público*, N° 117 (enero-marzo 2009) (Caracas, 2009), 205–211. Also published in <www.analitica.com/va/politica/opinion/6273405.asp>.

the same matters, and also changing the sense of a constitutional principle like the principle of alternating government considering it alike to the principle of elective government, ignoring the difference established in the Constitution (Article 6) (see *infra* paragraph 116, 672).

Chapter 2. Some Basic Aspect of the Political System of Government According to the 1999 Constitution and Its Distortions

39. According to the Constitution of 1999, Venezuela has been formally organized as a democratic Republic that is expressly qualified as 'The Bolivarian Republic of Venezuela', conceived as an '*Etat de droit*', in the sense of the English expression 'rule of law', with an elected government organized according to the principles of separation of powers, a presidential system of government, and vertical division of powers following the federal form of government; all their actions being subjected to judicial review by the Courts when unconstitutional or illegal.

§1. The Democratic Republic

40. The 1999 Constitution, following the tradition initiated in 1811 has been politically organized as a Republic, where the 'sovereignty resides untransferibly in the people', who exercise it 'directly' by means of referendum and other instruments established in the Constitution, 'and indirectly, through suffrage, by the organs that exercise State Powers' (Article 5). This provision consecrates the principles of popular sovereignty and the democratic regime, in particular the concept of political representation, adding in Article 62 the rights of all Citizens 'to participate freely in public matters directly or by means of their representatives'.

The important aspect to be stressed is the expression that sovereignty resides 'untransferable' *(intransferiblemente)* in the people, it resides only and always in the people, so that no man or entity may assume it, not even a Constituent Assembly, which of course could never be 'sovereign'. That is why the Constitution also indicates, when regulating the 'National Constituent Assembly' as a mean for constitutional review, that 'the people of Venezuela are the repository of the original constituent power', (Article 347) which, for that reason, could never be transferred to an Assembly.

Of course, the consecration of the principle of popular sovereignty and its untransferability led in the modern world, to the development of the principle of representative democracy, in the sense that the people, who are the holders of sovereignty, normally exercise it through representatives. Popular sovereignty and representative democracy are then consubstantial and indivisible principles.

41. However, as it has been conceived in the Inter-American Democratic Charter *(Carta Democratica Interamericana)* adopted by the Organization of American States (OAS) in 2001, after so many anti-democratic, militarist and authoritarian regimes disguised as democratic because of their electoral origin, democracy is not only a matter of electing governments, in the sense that it has many other *essential elements of the representative democracy.* That is, in addition to having periodic, fair and free elections, based on the universal and secret vote as expression of the will of the people; democracy means the respect for human rights and fundamental liberties; the access to power and its exercise with subjection to the rule of law; the plural regime of the political parties and organizations; and the separation and inde-

pendence of public powers (Article 3), that is, the possibility to control the different branches of government. In addition, democracy also has other *fundamental components*, like the transparency of governmental activities; the integrity, responsibility of governments in the public management; the respect of social rights and freedom of speech and press; the constitutional subordination of all institutions of the State to the legally constituted civil authority, and the respect to the rule of law of all the entities and sectors of society.[1540]

Without all such essential elements and fundamental components in force, it is difficult to consider that a political system is really a democratic one, notwithstanding the formal declarations in the Constitutions.

42. Consequently, even though democracy as a political system of government and social life is much more than just representative democracy, the latter is an essential part of it and cannot be substituted by a supposedly 'participatory democracy', as it was intended to be drafted in the 1999 Constitution with the elimination of the word 'representative' from Article 6, which in order to characterize the democratic government, only uses the expressions: 'participative, elective, decentralized, alternating, pluralist, and of revocable mandates'. Notwithstanding, democracy is always 'representative',[1541] and in addition, it can be more or less 'participative' according to the degree of direct participation of the people in public decision making[1542] (see *infra* paragraphs 143, 145, 150, 168).

1540   See Allan R. Brewer-Carías, *La crisis de la democracia venezolana. La Carta Democrática Inter-americana y los sucesos de abril 2002* (Caracas: Ediciones El Nacional, 2002).

1541   See Pedro L. Bracho Grand y Miriam Álvarez de Bozo, 'Democracia representativa en la Constitución Nacional de 1999', in *Estudios de Derecho Público: Libro Homenaje a Humberto J. La Roche Rincón*, vol. I (Caracas: Tribunal Supremo de Justicia, 2001), 235–254; and Ricardo Combellas, 'Representación vs. Participación en la Constitución Bolivariana. Análisis de un falso dilema', en *Bases y principios del sistema constitucional venezolano (Ponencias del VII Congreso Venezolano de Derecho Constitucional realizado en San Cristóbal del 21 al 23 de Noviembre de 2001)*, vol. II San Cristóbal, 383–402.

1542   See Manuel Feo La Cruz, 'La participación de la sociedad civil en el proceso de gestión pública. Retos y desafíos', in *El Derecho Público a comienzos del siglo XXI. Estudios homenaje al Profesor Allan R. Brewer-Carías*, vol. I (Madrid: Instituto de Derecho Público, UCV, Civitas Ediciones, 2003), 415–429; Yusby S. Méndez-Apolinar, 'La obligación ciudadana de participar en los asuntos públicos, como expresión de la cultura democrática', in *El Derecho Público a comienzos del siglo XXI. Estudios homenaje al Profesor Allan R. Brewer-Carías*, vol. I (Madrid: Instituto de Derecho Público, UCV, Civitas Ediciones, 2003), 431–437; Ana P. Deniz, 'La participación ciudadana en la Constitución de 1999', in *Revista de Derecho Constitucional*, N° 7 (enero-junio) (Caracas: Editorial Sherwood, 2003), 115–124; Fernando Flores Jiménez, 'La participación ciudadana en la Constitución venezolana de 1999', in *Revista de Derecho Constitucional*, N° 5 (julio-diciembre) (Caracas: Editorial Sherwood, 2001), 75–88; Luis Salamanca, 'La Constitución venezolana de 1999: de la representación a la hiper-participación ciudadana', in *Revista de Derecho Público*, N° 82 (abril-junio) (Caracas: Editorial Jurídica Venezolana, 2000), 85–105; Humberto Njaim, 'Las implicaciones de la democracia participativa: un tema constitucional de nuestro tiempo', in *Constitución y Constitucionalismo Hoy* (Caracas: Editorial Ex Libris, 2000), 719–742; Allan R. Brewer-Carías, 'Democracia participativa, descentralización política y régimen municipal', in *Tendencias actuales del derecho público en Iberoamérica*, ed. Miguel Alejandro López Olvera y Luis Gerardo Rodríguez Lozano (Coordinadores) (México: Editorial Porrúa, 2006), 1–23; Ricardo Combellas, 'La democracia participativa y la Constitución de la República Bolivariana de Venezuela', in *Derecho Constitucional. General y Particular. Actualizado con la Constitución de la República Bolivariana de Venezuela del 24-03-2000*, vol. I (Caracas: Universidad Santa María), 279–305.

Nonetheless, the drafters of the Constitution of 1999 pretended to install a supposedly 'participative democracy', by confounding participation with direct democracy instruments like the referenda, that are established in all its forms: consultative, approbatory, abrogating, and revoking (Articles 78 et seq.); and by defining a government political project based on a supposedly direct relation between the President of the Republic and the people, giving rise to an illusory 'participative' mechanism that is controlled from above (see *infra* paragraphs 126, 258 et seq.). Nonetheless, the fact is that the project monopolizes power and consolidates it hegemonically, in a concentrated and authoritarian manner, completely contrary to that which is required of a democratic regime.

The fact is that participation in democratic systems is only possible in a developed system of local government, with their own autonomous governments elected democratically; not in supposed 'communal councils' conceived in parallel to the municipalities, directly dependent on the President of the Republic, and directed by non-elected public officials, as it has been regulated by statute[1543] (see *infra* paragraphs 168, 264). That is, political participation is only effectively possible in a decentralized system of government based on local authorities; which is contrary to the concentration of Power and centralism as it has been developed in Venezuela during the past years (see *infra* paragraphs 53, 219 et seq.).

§2. *The 'Bolivarian' Republic of Venezuela*

43. But regarding the Republic, one of the innovations incorporated in Article 1° of the Constitution, was the re-naming of the Republic, changing the traditional expression 'Republic of Venezuela', for the 'Bolivarian Republic of Venezuela'; a change that can yield multiple interpretations. At the beginning, the motivation for the new name given to the country was formally to refer to the ideas and actions of Simón Bolívar, who as mentioned was not only the 'Liberator' of Venezuela at the beginning of the nineteenth century in the wars of independence against Spain (see *supra* paragraphs 1, 2), but also of other Latin American countries such as Colombia, Ecuador, Bolivia and Peru which were historically called the 'Bolivarian' Republics.

Although it has not been the first time in Venezuela's political history that rulers, mainly of military and authoritarian roots, have evoked Simón Bolívar to attract followers and to give some 'doctrinal' basis to their regimes,[1544] never before had

---

1543   Communal Councils Law, *Gaceta Oficial* Extra N° 5.806 of 10 Apr. 2006.

1544   It was the case of Antonio Guzmán Blanco in the nineteenth century and of Cipriano Castro, Juan Vicente Gómez, Eleazar López Contreras, and Marcos Pérez Jiménez in the twentieth century. John Lynch has pointed out: 'The traditional cult of Bolivar has been used as a convenient ideology by military dictators, culminating with the regimes of Juan Vicente Gómez and Eleazar López Contreras; these had at least more or less respected the basic thought of the Liberator, even when they misrepresented its meaning.' See John Lynch, *Simón Bolívar: A Life* (New Haven, CT: Yale University Press, 2007), 304. See also Germán Carrera Damas, *El culto a Bolívar, esbozo para un estudio de la historia de las ideas en Venezuela* (Caracas: Universidad Central de Venezuela, 1969); Luis Castro Leiva, *De la patria boba a la teología bolivariana* (Caracas: Monteávila, 1987); Elías Pino Iturrieta, *El divino Bolívar. Ensayo sobre una religión republicana* (Caracas: Alfail, 2008); Ana Teresa Torres, *La herencia de la tribu. Del mito de la independencia a la Revolución bolivariana* (Caracas, Editorial

the adherence to Bolivar led to changing the Republic's name and to the invention of a 'Bolivarian doctrine' to justify the government's policies, as Chávez did regarding his 'XXI century Socialism' one[1545] (see *infra* paragraph 247, 335).

In Venezuelan constitutional history, strictly speaking, the only 'Bolivarian Republic' that has existed as a State, has been the one resulting from the 'union of the peoples of Colombia' proposed by Simón Bolívar in 1819, and materialized in the 1821 Constitution of the Republic of Colombia (comprising the territories of today's Venezuela, Nueva Granada and Ecuador). With that constitution the Republic of Venezuela just disappeared as an autonomous State,[1546] a situation that endured up to 1830, until Bolivar's death.

44. Consequently, the re-naming of the Republic in 1999, this time without affecting the country's sovereignty, was explained as intent to give the Republic, although ignoring the past 200 years of history, a 'definitive' national doctrine supposedly based on the thoughts of Bolívar. Nonetheless, as it can now be appreciated after twelve years, the truth was otherwise, being just a label used by the new rulers of the country in order to impose their own socialist doctrine disguised as a Bolivarian one.

For that purpose, the first step taken in order to give to the country the name of Bolivar was an exclusive political or partisan one based on the name initially given in 1982 to the political movement used by the late President of the Republic (H. Chávez) to gain power, the 'Bolivarian Revolutionary Movement 200 (MBR-200).' Because such an organization could not continue as a formal political party in order to lead the 'Bolivarian' revolution due to the legal prohibition for parties to use in their denomination symbols of the motherland,[1547] the decision was to incorporate

---

Alfa, 2009). See also the historiography study on these books in Tomás Straka, *La épica del desencanto* (Caracas: Editorial Alfa, 2009).

1545   John Lynch has pointed out: 'In 1999 Venezuelans were astonished to learn that their country had been renamed "the Bolivarian Republic of Venezuela" by decree of President Hugo Chávez, who called himself a "revolutionary Bolivarian". Authoritarian populist, or neocaudillos, or Bolivarian militarists, whatever their designation, invoke Bolívar no less ardently than did previous rulers, though it is doubtful whether he would have responded to their calls...But the new heresy, far from maintaining continuity with the constitutional ideas of Bolívar, as was claimed, invented a new attribute, the populist Bolívar, and in the case of Cuba gave him a new identity, the socialist Bolívar. By exploiting the authoritarian tendency, which certainly existed in the thought and action of Bolívar, regimes in Cuba and Venezuela claim the Liberator as patron for their policies, distorting his ideas in the process.' See John Lynch, *Simón Bolívar: A Life* (New Haven, CT: Yale University Press, 2007), 304. See also A.C. Clark, *The Revolutionary Has No Clothes: Hugo Chávez's Bolivarian Farce* (New York: Encounter Books, 2009), 5–14. The last attempt to completely appropriate Simón Bolívar for the 'Bolivarian Revolution', was the televised exhumation of his remains that took place at the National Pantheon in Caracas on 26 Jul. 2010, conducted by President Chávez himself and other high officials, including the Prosecutor General, among other things, for the purpose of determining if Bolivar died of arsenic poisoning in Santa Marta in 1830, instead of from tuberculosis. See Simon Romero, 'Building a New History By Exhuming Bolívar', *The New York Times,* 4 Aug. 2010, A7.

1546   See the texts of all these Laws in Allan R. Brewer-Carías, *Las Constituciones de Venezuela*, vol. 1 (Caracas: Academia de Ciencias Políticas y Sociales, 2008), 643–46.

1547   According to the Political Parties Law, *Gaceta Oficial* N° 27.725, of 30 Apr. 1965, political parties cannot use the name of the founders of the country or homeland symbols. The political organization the President formed before campaigning for the 1998 election was Movimiento Bolivariano 200. That name could not be used to identify the political party he founded, which became Movimiento V República.

the name in the Constitution by labelling the country,[1548] and the party became the Fifth Republic Movement (*Movimiento V República,* MVR) which was later transformed into the United Socialist Party of Venezuela (PSUV), which declared itself as a 'Marxist' party following the 'Bolivarian doctrine.'[1549]

The consequence of the constitutional reform on this matter has been that everything related to the new political regime has been called Bolivarian, beginning, for instance, with the creation ten years ago of the 'Bolivarian Circles' that were the first social or communal organizations promoted and supported by the government in order to react against any opposition to the government and to threaten anybody with views contrary to it.[1550]

The fact has been that the partisan character of the use of Bolivar's name applied to the Republic and to the government policies has initiated a bitter polarization of the country, between those who are 'Bolivarian' and those who are not and, consequently, supposedly, between patriots and anti-patriots, good people and bad people, pure people and corrupt people, revolutionary and anti-revolutionary or oligarchs; all that by manipulating history and popular feelings regarding the image of Bolivar.

45. The constant promotion of the 'Bolivarian Revolution' even led the President of the Republic himself, in 2007, to draft and propose a constitutional reform before the National Assembly,[1551] (see *infra* paragraphs 33, 36, 236 ff., 242) in order to express and formally incorporate in the text of the Constitution the socialist 'Bolivarian doctrine' as the fundamental doctrine of the State. For such purpose, the 'Bolivarian socialism' was proposed to be incorporated in the Constitution as the State's guiding doctrine, even for international relations. This constitutional reform based on then so-called twenty-first century socialism,[1552] failed to be implanted, being

---

1548   *Mutatis mutandi,* in a certain way it happened with the use of the name of Augusto C. Sandino in the name of the *Frente Sandinista de Liberación* and of the Sandinista Republic of Nicaragua.

1549   See 'Declaration of Principles' of the United Socialist Party of Venezuela (23 Apr. 2010), available at <http://psuv.org.ve/files/tcdocumentos/Declaracion-de-principios-PSUV.pdf>.

1550   The general assembly of the Organization of American States, in its Report of 18 Apr. 2002, said about the Bolivarian Circles, that they 'are groups of citizens or grassroots organizations which support the President's political platform. Many sectors consider them responsible for the human rights violations, acts of intimidation and looting.' See the reference in Allan R. Brewer-Carías, *La crisis de la democracia en Venezuela* (Caracas: Libros El Nacional, 2002).

1551   See on the constitutional reforms proposals, Allan R. Brewer-Carías, *Hacia la consolidación de un Estado socialista, centralizado, policial y militarista. Comentarios sobre el sentido y alcance de las propuestas de reforma constitucional 2007* (Caracas: Editorial Jurídica Venezolana, 2007); *La reforma constitucional de 2007 (Comentarios al proyecto inconstitucionalmente sancionado por la Asamblea Nacional el 2 de noviembre de 2007)* (Caracas: Editorial Jurídica Venezolana, 2007).

1552   See Rogelio Pérez Perdomo, 'La Constitución de papel y su reforma', in *Revista de Derecho Público* 112 *(Estudios sobre la reforma constitucional)* (Caracas: Editorial Jurídica Venezolana, 2007), 14; G. Fernández, 'Aspectos esenciales de la modificación constitucional propuesta por el Presidente de la República. La modificación constitucional como un fraude a la democracia', *id.,* 22; Alfredo Arismendi, 'Utopía Constitucional', in *id.,* 31; Manuel Rachadell, 'El personalismo político en el Siglo XXI', in *id.,* 66; Allan R. Brewer-Carías, 'El sello socialista que se pretendía imponer al Estado', in *id.,* 71–75; Alfredo Morles Hernández, 'El nuevo modelo económico para el Socialismo del Siglo XXI', in *id.,* 233–36.

rejected by the people through popular votes in the 2 December 2007 referendum.[1553]

Nonetheless, and despite its rejection by the peoples votes, in the following year (2008), the 2007 constitutional reform proposals began to be implemented by the authoritarian government in violation of the Constitution through a massive amount of decree-laws issued by the President and by means of Organic Laws sanctioned by the National Assembly, changing in this way the Constitution but without formally reforming it. The last set of unconstitutional legislation implementing the 2007 rejected reform were approved in December of 2010, by formally creating a Communal State (or Socialist or Communist State) based upon the exercise of a Popular Power that has no constitutional basis, in parallel to the existing Constitutional decentralized State based upon the Public Power (National, state, municipal) expressly established in the Constitution.[1554]

46. For such purpose, after the set of unconstitutional laws approved between 2008 and 2009 related to the implantation of Socialism as the doctrine of the new Communal State, in January 2010, Chávez himself confessed that the supposedly 'Bolivarian revolution', was no more than the phantasmagorical resurrection of the historically failed 'Marxist revolution', but in this case led by a President who has never even read Marx's writings.[1555] This announcement provoked in April 2010, that the governmental United Socialist Party of Venezuela of which the President presides, in its First Extraordinary Congress then adopted its 'Declaration of Principles' in which it officially declared itself as a 'Marxist', 'Anti-imperialist' and 'Anti-capitalist' party. According to the same document, the party's actions are to be based on 'scientific socialism' and on the 'inputs of Marxism as a philosophy of praxis', in order to substitute the 'Capitalist Bourgeois State' with a 'Socialist State' based on the Popular Power and the socialization of the means of production.[1556] Of course, none of these ideas can be found in the works of Simón Bolivar, his name only being used as a pretext to continue to manipulate the Bolivar 'cult' to justify authoritarianism, as has occurred so many times before in the history of the country.[1557]

1553   The definitive voting figures in such referendum have never been informed to the country by the government-controlled National Electoral Council. See Allan R. Brewer-Carías, 'Estudio sobre la propuesta de Reforma Constitucional para establecer un estado socialista, centralizado y militarista (Análisis del anteproyecto presidencial, Agosto de 2007)', *Cadernos da Escola de Direito e Relações Internacionais da UniBrasil* 7 (Curitiba, 2007), 265–308.

1554   See Gustavo Linares Benzo, 'Sólo un Poder Público más. El Poder Popular en la reforma del 2007', in *Revista de Derecho Público* 112 *(Estudios sobre la reforma constitucional)* (Caracas: Editorial Jurídica Venezolana, 2007), 102–105; Arturo Peraza, 'Reforma, Democracia participativa y Poder Popular', in *id.*, 107–113.

1555   In his annual speech before the National Assembly on 15 Jan. 2010, in which Chávez declared to have 'assumed Marxism', he also confessed that he had never read Marx's works. See María Lilibeth Da Corte, 'Por primera vez asumo el marxismo', in *El Universal* (Caracas, 16 Jan. 2010), <www.eluniversal.com/2010/01/16/pol_art_por-primera-vez-asu_1726209.shtml>.

1556   See 'Declaración de Principios, I Congreso Extraordinario del Partido Socialista Unido de Venezuela', 23 Apr. 2010, at <http://psuv.org.ve/files/tcdocumentos/Declaracion-de-principios-PSUV.pdf>.

1557   In Bolívar's writings, nothing can be found that could allow to identify his thoughts with any socialist ideas. Otherwise, Karl Marx himself would have detected it, in 1857, ten years after writing on Socialism and Communism in his book with Friedrich Engels, *The German Ideology* (See in

With these declarations it can be said, finally, that the so-called Bolivarian Revolution has been unveiled; a revolution for which nobody in Venezuela has voted except for its rejection in the 2 December 2007 referendum, in which the President's proposals for constitutional reforms in order to establish a Socialist, Centralized, Police and Militaristic State received a negative popular response.[1558]

§3.   *The Social and Democratic Rule of Law and Justice State*

47. According to Article 2 of the Constitution of 1999, Venezuela is defined as an '*Estado democrático y social de derecho y de justicia*', that is, a 'social democratic rule of law and justice State'.[1559]

Yet, the rule of law in the Venezuelan constitutional system is not only a deduction of the constitutional framework establishing the conception of the State as submitted to the Constitution and the law in which the Citizens are not subjected to arbitrary rules. It is the result of an express provision of the Constitutions which have been included in it, following the contemporary constitutional trend as expressed in the Constitution of the Federal Republic of Germany (Article 20.1), in the Spanish Constitution (Article 1) and in the Constitution of Colombia (Article 1).

In this regard, the rule of law implies the subordination of the State and its officials to the authority of the law (Preamble), in the sense that all branches of government and the organs of the State are subjected to the 'Constitution and laws' (Article 137) and Public Administration must act completely subjected to the law (Article 141). This principle implies the existence in the Constitution of the systems of judicial review of legislation (Articles 334 y 336) and of administrative actions *(contencioso administrativo)* (Article 259) (see *infra* paragraphs 631, 702).

48. But in addition, the Constitution not only declared that Venezuela is a rule of law State (*Estado de derecho*), but that it is also a democratic and social justice State, which implies three different additional qualifications: social State, democratic State and justice State.

The idea of a 'social State' is that of a State with social obligations, established to procure social justice, an objective which brings the State to intervene in social

---

<www.educa.madrid.org/cms_tools/files/0a24636f-764c-4e03-9c1d-6722e2ee60d7/Texto%20Marx%20y%20Engels.pdf>), when writing the very critical entry on 'Bolívar y Ponte, Simón', for the *The New American Cyclopaedia*, vol. III, 1858., in which he observed nothing regarding possible socialists ideas that could be had derived from the writings of Bolívar. See the text in <www.marxists.org/archive/marx/works/1858/01/bolivar.htm>.

1558   See on the 2007 constitutional reforms proposals, Allan R. Brewer-Carías, *Hacia la consolidación de un Estado socialista, centralizado, policial y militarista. Comentarios sobre el sentido y alcance de las propuestas de reforma constitucional 2007* (Caracas: Editorial Jurídica Venezolana, 2007); *La reforma constitucional de 2007 (Comentarios al proyecto inconstitucionalmente sancionado por la Asamblea Nacional el 2 de noviembre de 2007)* (Caracas: Editorial Jurídica Venezolana, 2007).

1559   See Luis Enrique Useche Díaz, 'El Estado Social y Democrático de Derecho y de Justicia. Utopía y Frustración', in *Tendencias Actuales del Derecho Constitucional. Homenaje a Jesús María Casal Montbrun*, ED. Jesús María Casal, Alfredo Arismendi & Carlos Luis Carrillo Artiles (Coords.), vol. I (Caracas: Universidad Central de Venezuela/Universidad Católica Andrés Bello, 2008), 129–160; José M. Delgado Ocando, 'El estado social de derecho' en *Lex. Revista del Colegio de Abogados del Estado Zulia* (Colegio de Abogados del Estado Zulia., 236, Maracaibo 2000, 17–27.

and economic activity as a welfare State. That is why this Social State must seek for the application of the fundamental values of equality and solidarity, the pre-eminence of human rights (Preamble, Articles 1 and 21) and the achievement of 'social justice' as one of the basis of the economic system (Article 299)[1560] (see *infra* paragraph 47, 73, 82, 627).

Regarding the 'democratic State', the expression refers to the grounds of the po-litical organization of the Nation according to democratic principles (Articles 2, 3, 5 and 6), as a 'democratic society' (Preamble), of representative and participatory character. (see *infra* paragraphs 41, 71, 143, 148, 150, 168)

Finally the 'State of justice' refers to a State that must tend towards guaranteeing justice, specifically beyond procedural formalities. That is why, the value of justice is expressly proclaimed (Preamble and Article 1), for which the right of having ac-cess to justice is declared as well as the right to obtain the effective protection of persons' rights and interests (Article 26),[1561] the courts being obligated to guarantee the provision of justice without cost, assuring constant accessibility, impartiality, adequacy, transparency, autonomy, independence, responsibility, equanimity and expediency, absence of dilatory practices, and unnecessary formalities or annul-ments. (Article 26) (see *infra* paragraphs 367 et seq.).

Unfortunately, the authoritarian government that took shape during the past years conducting the so called 'Bolivarian Revolution,' instead of developing the 'social democratic rule of law and justice State' formally declared in the Constitution, has consolidated an Totalitarian State that is in contradiction with what is provided in the Constitution.[1562]

1560   On the social values in the Constitution see Jacqueline Lejarza A., 'El carácter normativo de los principios y valores en la Constitución de 1999', in *Revista de Derecho Constitucional,* N° 1 (sep-tiembre-diciembre) (Caracas: Editorial Sherwood, 1999), 195–220; Liliana Fasciani 'De la Justicia a la Justicia Social', in *Tendencias Actuales del Derecho Constitucional. Homenaje a Jesús María Ca-sal Montbrun,* ed. Jesús María Casal, Alfredo Arismendi & Carlos Luis Carrillo Artiles Coords, vol. I (Caracas: Universidad Central de Venezuela/Universidad Católica Andrés Bello, 2008), 161–196.

1561   See José R. Duque Corredor, 'El acceso a la justicia como derecho fundamental en el contexto de la democracia y de los derechos humanos', in *Revista de derecho del Tribunal Supremo de Justicia,* N° 6 (Caracas, 2002), 379 a 389; Judith Useche, 'El acceso a la justicia en el nuevo orden constitucional venezolano', in *Bases y principios del sistema constitucional venezolano (Ponencias del VII Congre-so Venezolano de Derecho Constitucional realizado en San Cristóbal del 21 al 23 de Noviembre de 2001),* vol. II, 29–76; Lourdes Cortes de Arangon, 'El acceso de los administrados al sistema jurídico: ¿un derecho vivo?', in *Estudios de Derecho Administrativo: Libro Homenaje a la Universidad Cen-tral de Venezuela,* vol. I (Caracas: Imprenta Nacional, 2001), 275–305.

1562   See Allan R. Brewer-Carías, 'El Estado Totalitario y la ausencia de Estado democrático y social de derecho y de justicia, de economía mixta y descentralizado,' in Ramsis Ghazzaoui (Coordinador), *XVII Jornadas Centenario Internacionales. Constitución, derecho administrativo y proceso: vigen-cia, reforma e innovación,* (Valencia, Colegio de Abogados del Estado Carabobo, Instituto de Estu-dios Jurídicos Dr. José Ángel Castillo Moren, 2014), 31-151; *Estado Totalitario y desprecio a la ley. La desconstitucionalización, desjuridificación, desjudicialización y desdemocratización de Venezue-la,* (Caracas, Fundación de Derecho Público, Editorial Jurídica Venezolana, 2014).

§4. *Separation of Powers*

49. Article136 of the Constitution establishes a double system of checks and balances regarding State powers and the branches of government. First, the vertical distribution of State power on a territorial basis, between the municipal, states and national powers, giving form to the Federal form of Government, organized in three levels of governments constituting the Republic at the national level, the states at the state level and the municipal at the local government level. The State, accordingly, is qualified in Article 4 as a Federal Decentralized State. (see *infra* paragraphs 186 et seq.)

However, the same Article 136 establishes the horizontal separation of powers regarding the National Public Power, which is divided between the traditional Legislative, Executive and Judicial Powers, to which the Constitution now has added two new branches: the Citizen and the Electoral Powers, in a system of penta separation of powers (see *infra* paragraphs 214 et seq.). These branches of Public Power have their own functions, but the respective organs that exercise them must collaborate between them in the prosecution of the State aims.[1563]

50. It must be mentioned that since the 1947 Constitution, as in many other Latin American countries, the Constitution began to directly create new bodies with some kind of autonomy, beyond the three traditional powers, not subjected to the Legislative, the Executive or the Judiciary, conceived to accomplish certain control functions. These have included the Comptrollers General, Peoples' or Human Rights Defenders, Public Prosecutors or General Prosecutors, Judicial Councils or Councils of the Judiciary, and special organs for the control and administration of elections. This evolution of constitutional autonomous organs was the one that formally gained an important foothold in the Constitution of 1999, which not only regulates such entities, but affords them the status of a constitutional 'power' or branch of government, thereby creating a penta separation of powers in which the Legislative Power is exercised by the National Assembly; the Executive Power by the President of the Republic and other officers of the government and its Administration; the Judicial Power by the Supreme Tribunal of Justice and other Courts; the Citizen Power by the Comptroller General of the Republic, the Prosecutor General (Public Prosecutor) and the Peoples' Defender; and the Electoral Power by the National Electoral Council and other organs of electoral power.

51. The essence of the principle of the separation of powers in the Constitution is that each constitutionally established organ of the State exercises its respective function with independence and autonomy, in a system of checks and balances in which no branch of government is to be or can be subject to that of another, except on matters of judicial review, audit controls or protection of human rights. Nonetheless, on

---

1563   See Carlos Luis Carrillo Artiles, 'La composición del poder público en la Constitución de la República Bolivariana de Venezuela', in *Libro Homenaje a Enrique Tejera París, Temas sobre la Constitución de 1999* (Caracas: Centro de Investigaciones Jurídicas (CEIN), 2001), 51 a 76; Allan R. Brewer-Carías, 'Consideraciones sobre el régimen de distribución de competencias del Poder Público en la Constitución de 1999', in *Estudios de Derecho Administrativo. Libro Homenaje a la Universidad Central de Venezuela*, ed. Fernando Parra Aranguren y Armando Rodríguez García Editores, vol. I (Caracas: Tribunal Supremo de Justicia, 2001), 107–136.

the contrary, the penta division of powers under the Constitution of 1999 is deceiving because it, in fact, conceals the subjection of some of the principal branches of government to the legislator, in a very dangerous system regarding democracy and the rule of law that leaves an open door to the concentration of power in the State and to authoritarianism,[1564] to which the Constitutional Chamber of the Supfreme Tribunal of Justice has contributed[1565]. (see *infra* paragraphs 610, 666).

The Constitution, in fact, contains an absurd distortion of the separation of power principle by giving to the National Assembly the authority not only to elect, but to dismiss the Judges of the Supreme Tribunal of Justice, the Prosecutor General, the General Comptroller, the People's Defender and the Members of the National Electoral Council from their positions (Articles 265, 279 and 296); and in some cases established through legislation, even by simple majority of votes (see *infra* paragraph 375). Even this latter solution was proposed to be formally constitutionalized in the rejected 2007 Constitutional reform proposals, which seek to eliminate the guarantee of the qualified majority of the members of the National Assembly for such dismissals, and to establish a simple majority for that purpose.

52. It is really impossible to talk about independence of separate powers, and of mutual control when the tenure of the Head officials of the institutions depends on the political will of one of the branches of government.[1566] The sole fact of the provision of such possibility for the National Assembly to dismiss makes futile the formal consecration of the independence of powers, since the High officials of the State are aware that they can be removed at any time precisely when they act effectively with independence. In Venezuela, in political practice, this has converted to a system of concentration of powers in the National Assembly, and because the political control that the President of the Republic exercises upon the Assembly, to the concentration of powers in the hands of the former (see *infra* paragraphs 610, 666) The consequence has been the total absence of fiscal or audit control made by the General Comptroller Office over the huge disposal of the oil wealth not always in accordance with Budget discipline rules; the total absence of protection assured by the People's Defender, which has been perceived more as a defender of State power than of the people; and the indiscriminate use by the Public Prosecutor of the Judiciary and of judicial procedures as a tool to persecute any political dissidence; and the absolute control exercised by the Executive over the Judiciary.

1564   See Gustavo Tarre, *Solo el poder detiene al poder, La teoría de la separación de los poderes y su aplicación en Venezuela,* (Caracas, Editorial Jurídica Venezolana, 2014).

1565   See Allan R. Brewer-Carías, 'Sobre la mutación del principio de la separación de poderes en la jurisprudencia constitucional,' *Revista de Derecho Público,* N° 132 (Caracas, Editorial Jurídica Venezolana, 2012), 201-213; 'El principio de la separación de poderes como elemento esencial de la democracia y de la libertad, y su demolición en Venezuela mediante la sujeción política del Tribunal Supremo de Justicia,' *Revista Iberoamericana de Derecho Administrativo, Homenaje a Luciano Parejo Alfonso,* 12, (San José, Costa Rica, Asociación e Instituto Iberoamericano de Derecho Administrativo Prof. Jesús González Pérez, 2012), 31-43.

1566   See Allan R. Brewer-Carías, 'Democracia: sus elementos y componentes esenciales y el control del poder', *Grandes temas para un observatorio electoral ciudadano,* Vol. I, *Democracia: retos y fundamentos (Compiladora Nuria González Martín)* (México: Instituto Electoral del Distrito Federal, 2007), 171-220.

53. Beside the vertical distribution of State Powers (national power, states power and municipal power) and the horizontal Separation of Powers (Legislative, Executive, Judicial, Citizens and Electoral Powers), according to the Constitution, no other State Power can be conceived. In 2007, a proposed Constitutional Reform was rejected, proposing the creation of a new State Power, called the 'Popular Power', to be established in parallel to the Constitutional State and its Powers. Nonetheless, despite such rejection, the National Assembly in December 2010, by-passing the Constitution has sanctioned a set of organic laws through which it has defined the legislative framework of a'new State' called the 'Communal State', in parallel to the Constitutional State, conceived as a socialist, centralized, military and police State, acting in exercise of a so-called Popular Power.[1567] (See *infra* paragraphs 258, 264). This new State, for whose creation nobody has voted, is supposedly based on the exercise of the sovereignty of the people but exclusively in a 'direct' manner through the exercise of the 'Popular Power' and subjected to a new 'socialist principle of legality'. For the organization of this 'Communal State' the communes are established as the fundamental unit, unconstitutionally supplanting the municipalities as the 'primary political units of the national organization' (Article 168 of the Constitution). Through the organization of such Communes, the Popular Power is exercised, as expression of the 'popular sovereignty' although not through representatives. It is therefore a political system in which representative democracy is ignored, openly violating the Constitution.

§5. *Presidential System of Government*

54. The Venezuelan system of government, following the general feature in Latin America, since the beginning of the Republic in 1811, has always been the Presidential system, which remains in the 1999 Constitution. The President of the Republic is then, at the same time, the Head of State and the Head of the Executive and of the Public Administration, and is elected by universal, direct and secret suffrage (Articles 226, 228). Nonetheless, in the relationship between the National Executive and the National Assembly, the Constitution has adopted some elements of parliamentarianism already introduced since the 1961 Constitution.[1568]

1567   See the Organic laws on the Popular Power; the Communes; the Communal Economic System; the Public and Communal Planning; and the Social Comptrollership, in *Gaceta Oficial* N° 6.011 Extra. 21 Dec. 2010.

1568   See Donato Lupidii, 'El sistema presidencial y la Constitución venezolana de 1999', in *El Derecho Público a comienzos del siglo XXI. Estudios homenaje al Profesor Allan R. Brewer-Carías*, vol. I (Madrid: Instituto de Derecho Público, UCV, Civitas Ediciones, 2003), 819–835; Miguel A. Gómez Ortiz, 'El régimen presidencial en Venezuela', in *Bases y principios del sistema constitucional venezolano (Ponencias del VII Congreso Venezolano de Derecho Constitucional realizado en San Cristóbal del 21 al 23 de Noviembre de 2001)*, vol. II, 299–336; José Peña Solis, 'Notas sobre los Sistemas de Gobierno parlamentario y Presidencial. Breve Referencia al Sistema Venezolano', in *Tendencias Actuales del Derecho Constitucional. Homenaje a Jesús María Casal Montbrun*, ed. Jesús María Casal, Alfredo Arismendi y Carlos Luis Carrillo Artiles (Coord.), vol. I (Caracas: Universidad Central de Venezuela/Universidad Católica Andrés Bello, 2008), 405–430; Alfredo Arismendi A., 'El fortalecimiento del Poder Ejecutivo Nacional en la Constitución venezolana de 1999', in *El Derecho Público a comienzos del siglo XXI. Estudios homenaje al Profesor Allan R. Brewer-Carías*, vol. I (Madrid: Instituto de Derecho Público, UCV, Civitas Ediciones, 2003), 837–865; Ricardo Combellas, 'El Poder Ejecutivo en la Constitución de 1999', in *Revista UGMA Jurídica de la Facul-*

But in the 1999 Constitution, the presidential framework of government has been exacerbated[1569] by the combination of a few factors: first, by the extension of the presidential term from five to six years, and by the possibility for the immediate re-election of the President (Article 230), which before was traditionally prohibited, now limiting the republican principle of alternate representation in government, allowing the possibility for a long period of presidential incumbency of up to twelve years. The remedy for this long tenure was the provision of the possibility of a re-pealing referendum but conceived in such a complicated and complex way (Article 72) that it is nearly inapplicable (see *infra* paragraph 161). Second, the loss of the checks and balances between the Executive and the Legislative branches of govern-ment, among other factors due to the elimination of the Senate, that is, the elimina-tion of the traditional legislative bicameralism that had existed in the country since 1811. Third, the possibility for the President of the Republic to dissolve the National Assembly, even in exceptional cases when three votes for the parliamentary censure of the Vice President of the Republic, (Article 240) have been approved. Fourth, the possibility that through the approval of enabling laws (*leyes habilitantes*) the Natio-nal Assembly can delegate the legislative power to the Executive, by means of which through Executive Decrees-Laws *(Decretos-leyes)*, the President without any limits can legislate (Article 203), resulting in practice that with the enabling laws of 2001, 2002, 2007 and 2014 all the important statutes in the country have been sanc-tioned by the President of the Republic, although he has completely controlled the National Assembly. In the 1961 Constitution, the possibility for legislative delega-tion was limited to only economic and financial matters and in extraordinary cir-cumstances (see *infra* paragraphs 100 et seq.)

55. The President of the Republic has the power to dissolve the National Assem-bly, even in exceptional cases when three votes for the parliamentary censure of the Vice President of the Republic have been passed, (Article 240) (see *infra* paragraph 255). However, Presidential power has been reinforced in other ways, such as the passing of aforementioned enabling laws (*leyes habilitantes*) allowing the delegation of legislative power to the Executive by means of Decrees-Laws, without limiting this executive 'law-making' power to matters in the economic and financial spheres (Article 203), as was provided in the 1999 Constitution (see *infra* paragraphs , 133, 253).

Another element that should be mentioned with respect to the relations between the powers of the State is the attribution to decree, 'the removal from office of the President of the Republic', (Article 233) to the Supreme Tribunal of Justice without significant specific delineation or definition of conditions for exercising that power.

---

tad de Derecho de la Universidad Gran Mariscal de Ayacucho, N° 1 (mayo-agosto) (Barcelona-Venezuela, 2002), 9–24.

1569   See Allan R. Brewer-Carías, 'El sistema presidencial de gobierno en la Constitución de Venezuela de 1999', in Allan R. Brewer-Carías, *Estudios sobre el Estado Constitucional (2005-2006)* (Caracas: Editorial Jurídica Venezolana, 2007), 475–624.

§6. *Alternating Government*

56. Since the beginning of the Republic, the general restriction for elected officials to be re-elected in a continuous way, without limits, has been a tradition within the presidential system of government. The restriction to presidential re-election was first established in the 1830 Constitution, as a reaction to continuity in office (*continuísmo*), precisely in order to confront individuals' anxieties to perpetuate themselves in power, and to avoid the advantages that public officials in office could have in electoral processes.[1570]

This principle of limiting the term of elected officials called as the principle of '*alternabilidad*', (alternating),[1571] means that the public offices must be occupied by turns, and not continuously by the same elected person. It is in this same sense that the Supreme Tribunal of Justice of Venezuela in a decision of 2002 issued by its Electoral Chamber, said that *alternabilidad* means 'the successive exercise of public offices by different persons' (Decision No. 51 of 18 March 2002.)[1572] The principle, consequently, is not the same as the 'elective' principle or to be elected for public offices. To be elected is one thing, and another is to occupy public offices by turns. The principle has always been established as a 'rock-like' or immutable constitutional clause (*Cláusula pétrea*), in the sense that it can never be changed. That is why Article 6 of the Constitution says that 'The government of the Republic and of its political entities is and will always be alternating' *(alternativo)*, in addition to 'democratic, participatory, elective, decentralized, responsible, plural and of repeal mandates', which mean that it cannot be changed.

The principle was included in almost all the Venezuelan Constitutions since 1830 (1830, 1858, 1864, 1874, 1881, 1891, 1893, 1901, 1904, 1909, 1936, 1845 and 1947), establishing a general prohibition for the immediate re-election of the President of the Republic for the next term. In the 1961 Constitution the prohibition for re-election was extended up to two terms (ten years), and it was in the 1999 Constitution that the provision was made more flexible, by establishing for the first time in more than a century the possibility for the immediate re-election of the President, but only once, for the next term (Article 230). This limit was proposed to be eliminated in the rejected 2007 Constitutional Reform, and was finally eliminated, after a

---

1570   The reaction against continuity in power was clearly expressed by Simón Bolívar in his famous Angostura Speech (1819) when he said: 'The continuation of the authority in the same individual has frequently been the end of democratic governments. Repeated elections are essentials in popular systems, because nothing is more dangerous than to leave for a long term the same citizen in power. The people get used to obey him, and he gets used to command them; from were usurpation and tyranny is originated....Our citizens must fear with more than enough justice that the same Official, who has governed them for a long time, could perpetually command them.' See in Simón Bolívar, *Escritos Fundamentales* (Caracas, 1982).

1571   From the Latin word '*alternatium*', which means 'interchangeably' or 'by turns'.

1572   Quoted in the Dissenting Vote to the Constitutional Chamber of the Supreme Tribunal of Justice Decision N° 53, of 2 Feb. 2009 (*Interpretation of Arts 340,6 and 345 of the Constitution* Case), in <www.tsj.gov.ve/decisions/scon/Febrero/53-3209-2009-08-1610.html>.

constitutional interpretation of the alternating principle,[1573] through a constitutional amendment approved by referendum on February 2009 (see *infra* paragraph 233), as well as the limits established for the re-election of the representatives to the National Assembly and the States Legislative Councils, and for the re-election of the Governors of the states and the Mayors of the municipalities (Articles 160, 162, 174, 192) (see *infra* paragraphs 1155, 233, 672).

§7. The Centralized Federation

57. Venezuela was the first country to adopt since 1811, after the United States of America, a federal form of government politically uniting former colonial provinces (see *supra* paragraph 2). Those provinces were progressively transformed into the twenty-three states in (see *infra* paragraph 103) which the territory of the Republic is divided, adding to them, a Capital District (the former Federal District, covering parts of the city of Caracas) (see *infra* paragraph 103, 209), and federal dependencies that comprise almost all the islands located along the country's coast in the Caribbean Sea (see *infra* paragraph 103).

The consequence of the federal form of the State has been the establishment in the text of the constitutions a system of vertical distribution of State power in three tier levels, as it is prescribed in the 1999 Constitution by setting forth that 'The Powers of the State shall be distributed between the Municipal Powers, the State Powers and the National Powers' which must collaborate and cooperate in the pursuit of the State objectives (Article 136) see *infra* 196 et seq.).

58. The constitutional and political tendency since the beginning of the twentieth century has been a process of centralization of powers at the national level, so the territorial distribution of power and territorial autonomy of the states has almost disappeared (see *infra* paragraphs 202 et seq.) Nonetheless, according to the provisions of the 1961 Constitution, an initial political decentralization process sparked by the democratic practice began in 1989 with the transfer of powers from the central government to the federal states, and for the first time since the nineteenth century, with the direct elections of Governors of the states and Mayors, which provoked for regional political life the beginning of playing an important role in the country (see *infra* paragraph 184). But the 1999 Constitution, instead of undertaking the changes that were needed for reinforcing democracy, namely the effective political decentralization of the federation and the reinforcement of state and municipal political powers, has caused the pendulum to swing back, and to reinforce the centralization process[1574] (see *infra* paragraph 186).

1573   Véase Allan R. Brewer-Carías, 'El Juez Constitucional vs. La alternabilidad republicana (La reelección continua e indefinida)', in *Revista de Derecho Público*, N° 117, Editorial Jurídica Venezolana, Caracas 2009, 205–211.

1574   See Allan R. Brewer-Carías, 'El Estado federal descentralizado y la centralización de la federación en Venezuela. Situación y perspectiva de una contradicción constitucional', in *Federalismo y regionalismo*, ed. Diego Valadés y José María Serna de la Garza (Coordinadores) (Universidad Nacional Autónoma de México, Tribunal Superior de Justicia del Estado de Puebla, Instituto de Investigaciones Jurídicas, Serie Doctrina Jurídica N° 229, México 2005), 717–750; Allan R. Brewer-Carias and Jan Kleinheisterkamp, 'Venezuela: The End of federalism?,' in Daniel Halberstam and Mathias Rei-

§8. *Judicial Review System*

59. Following a general Latin American feature, the judicial review system established in Venezuela since the nineteenth century has been mixed in nature, in which the concentrated method of judicial review is applied conjunctly with the diffuse method.[1575] On the one hand, all courts are entitled to decide upon the constitutionality of legislation and of its inapplicability in a particular case, with *inter partes* effects; and on the other hand, the Supreme Court or a Constitutional Court or Tribunal are empowered to declare the total nullity of statutes contrary to the Constitution (see *infra* paragraph631).

60. Article 7 of the 1999 Constitution declares that its text is 'the supreme law' of the land and 'the ground of the entire legal order'. This provision assigns to all judges the duty 'of guaranteeing the integrity of the Constitution' (Article 334) with the power to decide not to apply a statute that is deemed to be unconstitutional when deciding a concrete case. Article 335 of the Constitution also assigns the Supreme Tribunal of Justice the duty of guaranteeing 'the supremacy and effectiveness of the constitutional rules and principles', as 'the maximum and final interpreter of the Constitution', with the duty to seek for 'its uniform interpretation and application'.

61. Additionally, the Constitutional Chamber of the Supreme Tribunal of Justice (Articles 266.1° and 336) is the 'Constitutional Jurisdiction', exclusively empowered to declare the nullity of statutes and other State acts with similar rank and effects or issued in direct execution of the Constitution. The Tribunal also is empowered to judge the unconstitutionality of the omissions of the legislative organ.

Other State acts, such as administrative acts and regulations, are also subject to judicial review by the 'Contentious Administrative Jurisdiction' whose courts are empowered to annul administrative acts because of their illegality or unconstitutionality (Article 259) (see *infra* paragraph 702).

Also, according to Article 29 of the Constitution, the courts have a duty to protect all persons in their constitutional rights and guarantees when deciding an action for protection, or '*amparo*'. Such an action can be brought before the court against any illegitimate harm or threat to such Rights (see *infra* paragraphs 686 et seq.).

62. Of course judicial review, above all, is an institutional tool which is essentially linked to democracy; democracy understood as a political system not just reduced to the fact of having elected governments, but where separation and control of power and the respect and enforcement of human rights is possible through an independent and autonomous judiciary. It has been precisely because of this process of reinforcement of democracy that judicial review of the constitutionality of legisla-

---

mann (Editors), *Federalism and Legal Unification: A Comparative Empirical Investigation of Twenty Systems*, (London, Springer, 2014), 523-543.

1575   See Allan R. Brewer-Carías, *La Justicia Constitucional (Procesos y procedimientos constitucionales)* (México: Instituto Mexicano de Derecho Procesal Constitucional, ed. Porrúa), 2007; *Judicial Review in Comparative Law* (Cambridge: Cambridge Studies in International and Comparative Law. New Series, Cambridge University Press, 1989), 406; *Études de droit public comparé* (Bruxelles: Académie International de Droit Comparé, Bruylant, 2001), 526–934; *Judicial Review. Comparative Constitucional Law Essays, Lectures and Courses (1985-2011)*, (Caracas, Fundación de Derecho Público, Editorial Jurídica Venezolana, 2014).

tion and other governmental actions has become an important tool in order to guarantee the supremacy of the Constitution, the rule of law, and the respect of human rights. It is in this sense that judicial review of the constitutionality of State acts has been considered as the ultimate result of the consolidation of the *rule of law*, when precisely in a democratic system the courts can serve as the ultimate guarantor of the Constitution, effectively controlling the exercise of power by the organs of the State.

On the contrary, as happens in all authoritarian regimes even having elected governments, if such control is not possible, the same power can constitute the most powerful and diabolical instrument for the consolidation of authoritarianism, the destruction of democracy, and the violation of human rights.[1576] Unfortunately this is what has been happening in Venezuela, where after decades of democratic ruling through which we constructed one of the most formally complete systems of judicial review in South America, since 2000 that same system has been the instrument through which the politically controlled judiciary, and particularly the subjected Constitutional Chamber of the Supreme Tribunal, have been consolidating the authoritarian regime installed in the country.

Chapter 3. Global Values in the Constitution

63. As has been aforementioned, the 1999 Venezuelan Constitution contains not only an extensive amount of articles devoted to enumerating human rights (120), but also a rich text full of values, principles and global declarations. The Constitutional Chamber of the Supreme Tribunal of Justice has said that the Constitution is 'an instrument with legal spirit that connects, according to the nature of the applicable precept, both the bodies of the State and the individuals'; and that imposes constitutional juridical situations 'with reference to indispensable values for the assurance of human freedom, equality and dignity' guaranteed by the judiciary.[1577]

Constitutional values in the Venezuelan Constitution[1578] are expressed not only in its Preamble but in many of its articles, as goals intending to guide the state, society and general conduct of individuals.[1579] Consequently, in Venezuela, global values and principles do not derive from the sole interpretation and application of the Constitution by the courts, but from provisions in the Constitution itself.[1580] Nonetheless, by means of constitutional judicial decisions, the sense, the scope and the

---

1576   See Allan R. Brewer-Carías, *Crónica de la 'In' Justicia Constitucional. La Sala Constitucional y el autoritarismo en Venezuela* (Caracas: Editorial Jurídica Venezolana, 2007); *Práctica y distorsión de la justicia constitucional en Venezuela (2008-2012)*, (Caracas, Editorial Jurídica Venezolana, 2012); and *La Patología De La Justicia Constitucional*,(Caracas, Tercera edición ampliada, Editorial Jurídica Venezolana, 2014). .

1577   See Decision N° 963 dated June 5, 2001. *José A Guía y otros v Ministerio de Infraestructura*, *Revista de Derecho Público*, N° 85–88 (Caracas, Editorial Jurídica Venezolana, 2001) 447.

1578   See on the subject of these Part: Allan R. Brewer-Carías, 'Global values in the Venezuelan Constitution,' in Dennis Davis, Alan Richter and Cheryl Saunders, *An Inquiry into the Existence of Global Values: Through the Lens of Comparative Constitutional Law*, (2015)..

1579   See Allan R Brewer-Carías, 'La constitucionalización del derecho administrativo', *Derecho Administrativo*, Vol. I (Bogotá, Universidad Externado de Colombia, 2005) 215ff.

1580   See Allan R Brewer-Carías, *Principios fundamentales del derecho público* (Caracas, Editorial Jurídica Venezolana, 2005).

priority character of many of these constitutional principles and values have been defined and enriched; and also, unfortunately, in many cases, some constitutional incongruence have been established between the constitutional text and the political practice of government.

§1   Constitutional Values and their Prioritisation

64. The Preamble to the Constitution began by declaring that it was adopted by the representatives of the Venezuelan people, having in mind the achievement of a series of goals 'guided by social, economic, political and judicial values',[1581] in order to inspire the action of the state, 'which must respond to equalitarian, international, democratic, moral and historical principles'.

In this context, the state is defined as a 'state of justice, federal and decentralised', that must develop its action to enforce the values of 'freedom, independence, peace, solidarity, common good, territorial integrity, cohabitation and the empire of the law for these and all future generations', in a society that is qualified as 'democratic, participatory, multi-ethnic and pluri-cultural', which is confirmed, for instance, by the express recognition in the Constitution of the indigenous populations' status (articles 119 et seq).

These goals represent the fundamental principles and constitutional values that inspire the constitutional text as a whole. They have the same binding quality as constitutional provisions, and consequently are enforceable. As affirmed by the Constitutional Chamber of the Supreme Tribunal, 'the statutes must have those values as their guide, so those that do not follow them or that are contrary to those objectives become unconstitutional'.[1582]

65. Besides the values guiding the configuration of the state declared in the Preamble, the Constitution also enumerates as superior values of the legal system and of the whole state activity: 'life, freedom, justice, equality, solidarity, democracy, social responsibility and, in general, the pre-eminence of human rights, ethics and political pluralism' (article 2).

Additionally, the Constitution identifies 'the defence and the development of the individual and the respect of his/her dignity, the democratic exercise of the popular will, the construction of a fair and peace loving society, the promotion of the prosperity and wellbeing of the people and the guarantee of the fulfilment of all principles, rights and duties recognised and enshrined in the Constitution' as essential goals of the state, considering 'education and work' as fundamental processes to achieve those ends (article 3).

The constitutional text also gave form to a series of social ends specified in the Preamble with the object of ensuring 'the right to a life, work, culture, education, social justice and equality without discrimination nor subordination of any kind'.

1581   Regarding the nature of the Preamble and its constitutional value, see the decision of the former Supreme Court of Justice in its Political-Administrative Chamber, dated August 8, 1989, *Revista de Derecho Público* N° 39 (Caracas, Editorial Jurídica Venezolana, 1989) 102.

1582   See *Deudores hipotecarios v Superintendencia de Bancos, Revista de Derecho Público*, N° 89–92 (Caracas, Editorial Jurídica Venezolana, 2002) 94ff.

Reference is also made in the Constitution regarding the social goals of society and of the state in order to achieve 'social justice'. The assurance of 'equality without discrimination nor subordination of any kind' is also specified as a fundamental social goal.

66. Referring to the Republic, particular further fundamental values are expressly emphasised in the Constitution: the principle that the nation's rights ('independence, freedom, sovereignty, immunity, territorial integrity and the national self-determination') cannot be renounced or abandoned (article 1).

The Preamble sets out as one of the goals of the state, the 'peaceful cooperation between nations', which implies the commitment to look for the peaceful solution of controversies, and the rejection of war. This peaceful cooperation must be executed in accordance with the 'principle of the non-intervention' in the affairs of other countries, and the principle of 'self-determination of the people'. Also, it specifies that international cooperation must be carried out 'according to the universal and indivisible guarantee of human rights and the democratisation of the international society'.

References are also made in the Constitution to other values that must guide the international relations of the Republic, including 'nuclear disarmament, the ecological balance and the environment considered as a common and non-renouncable patrimony of humanity'. In particular, according to the Preamble, another fundamental goal that must serve as guidance of the state's actions is 'the impulse and consolidation of Latin-American integration' (article 153).

67. Some of the values declared in the Constitution have been prioritised in political practice and through judicial decisions, in the sense that they have been considered as having some kind of superior hierarchy regarding other principles that are governed by the former. This is the case for human dignity; fairness/justice/rule of law/state of justice; equality/respect/tolerance/diversity/multiculturalism; democracy/participation/decentralization /inclusion; compassion/caring/solidarity/social justice/social state; community/civil society; family; life; honesty/integrity; learning/education; freedom/ liberty/ independence; security; responsibility/ accountability/transparency; environment.

68. *Human Dignity*: The value of 'human dignity' is considered by the courts 'as inherent to the human condition' that exists 'before the state' and imposes on all branches of government the need to be 'at the service of the human being.'[1583] This implies not only the existence of constitutional rights considered 'inherent to human beings' but the emergence of the 'principle of progressiveness' in their interpretation and enforcement. According to the criteria set out by the Constitutional Chamber of the Supreme Tribunal, the courts have an obligation 'to interpret the entire legal system in the light of the Right of the Constitution ... which also means, that they have to interpret the system congruently with the fundamental rights or human

---

1583   See Decision of the First Court of the Administrative Jurisdiction dated June 1, 2000, *Julio Rocco A*, *Revista de Derecho Público*, N° 82 (Caracas, Editorial Jurídica Venezolana, 2000) 287 ff.

rights, that must be respected above all, making a progressive and complete interpretation'.[1584]

The Constitution refers to this value in many articles, when guaranteeing to anybody deprived of liberty the right to be 'treated with respect due to the inherent dignity of the human being' (article 46); when guaranteeing that the judicial seizure of a person's home must be made 'always respecting human dignity' (article 47); when imposing the obligation on the state's security offices to always 'respect the human dignity and rights of all persons' (article 55); when establishing the duty of the state to protect senior citizens and disabled persons, always respecting their 'human dignity' (articles 80, 81); and when guaranteeing that the salary of every worker must be 'sufficient to enable him or her to live with dignity' (article 91).

The Constitutional Chamber of the Supreme Tribunal has considered human dignity as 'one of the values on which the Social rule of law and Justice State is based, and around which all the legal system and all the actions of the branches of government (public powers) must turn.' Based on this approach, the Chamber defined human dignity as 'the supremacy that persons have as an inherent attribute of their rational being, which imposes on public authorities the duty to watch for the protection and safe-conduct of the life, freedom and autonomy of men and women for the sole fact of their existence, independently of any other consideration.' Thus, 'the sole existence of man grants him the right to exist and to obtain all the guarantees needed to assure him a dignified life, that is, his own existence, proportional and rational to the recognition of his essence as a rational being.' This concept of human dignity implies the imposition 'upon the State of the duty to adopt the necessary protective measures to safeguard the legal assets that define man as a person, that is, life, integrity, freedom, autonomy.'[1585]

The Political-Administrative Chamber of the Supreme Tribunal of Justice has also emphasised the pre-eminent character of dignity, considering it the 'axiological' element representing 'the ideological base that supports the dogmatic order of the current Constitution', limiting the exercise of public power and establishing an effective judicial guarantee system.' Hence this 'prevalent position of human dignity' is considered as a 'superior value of the legal system'. It implies 'the obligation of the State and of all its bodies to protect and guarantee human rights as the main purpose and objective of its public action'. Consequently, the development of human dignity is considered by the Supreme Tribunal as 'one of the superior values of the legal system', seeing its 'defence and development' as 'one of the essential objectives of the State' (articles 2 and 3).[1586]

1584   *Ibid.*

1585   With this purpose, the Constitution, in its art 3, 'establishes that the recognition of the human dignity constitutes a structural principle of the Social rule of law State and for that, it forbids, in its Title III, Chapter III, the forced disappearances, the degrading treatments, the tortures or cruel treatments that could harm the life as an inviolable right, the degrading punishments and all other inherent rights of the human person (articles 43 ff)' See Decision N° 2442, dated September 1, 2003, *Alejandro Serrano López*, *Revista de Derecho Público*, No 83–96 (Caracas, Editorial Jurídica Venezolana, 2003) 183 ff.

1586   See Decision N° 224 dated February 24, 2000, *Revista de Derecho Público*, N° 81 (2000, Editorial Jurídica Venezolana, Caracas) 131 ff. See also, decision of the Constitutional Chamber of the Supre-

Human dignity also promotes the idea of the 'pre-eminence of human rights' (Preamble); which according to the 'principle of progressiveness' (article 19) imposes the need for the interpretation of statutes in the most favourable way for their enjoyment. In this regard, article 19 of the 1999 Constitution begins the Title on 'Duties, Rights and Constitutional Guarantees' by setting forth that the state must guarantee every person, 'according to the progressiveness principle and without discrimination whatsoever, the enjoyment and non-renounceable, indivisible and interdependent exercise of human rights'. The provision adds that 'the respect and the guarantee of the rights are mandatory to all State bodies in accordance with the Constitution, the treaties on human rights signed and ratified by the Republic and the statutes.'[1587] As affirmed by the courts, 'the interpretation of the corresponding constitutional provisions and any future constitutional revision must be performed in the most favourable way for the exercise and enjoyment of the rights', adding that 'this principle is so important that its application obliges the State to update legislation in favour of the defence of the human rights and in view to dignify the human condition, adapting the interpretation of the norms "to the sensibility, thought and needs of the new times in order to adapt them to the new established order and to reject any anachronistic precept that opposes their effective force".'[1588]

In order to give human dignity its complete application, article 23 of the 1999 Constitution ensured that international treaties on human rights signed and ratified by Venezuela, 'prevail in the internal order when containing more favourable provisions regarding their enjoyment than those contained in the Constitution and the laws of the Republic.' The same article provides for the immediate and direct application of these treaties by state bodies, particularly the courts.[1589]

---

me Tribunal N° 3215 dated June 15, 2004, *Revista de Derecho Público*, N° 97–98 (Caracas, Editorial Jurídica Venezolana, 2004) 428.

1587   About this principle, the Constitutional Chamber of the Supreme Tribunal of Justice, quoting art 2 of the American Convention on Human Rights, in Decision N° 1154, dated June 29, 2001, based on the same principle, has ruled that it is necessary 'to adapt the legal system in order to ensure the efficiency of said rights, being unacceptable the excuse of the inexistence or unsuitability of the means provided in the internal order for their protection and application.' *Revista de Derecho Público*, N° 85–88 (Caracas, Editorial Jurídica Venezolana, 2001) 111ff.

1588   In this sense the First Court of the Administrative Jurisdiction has considered as its obligation 'to interpret the entire legal system in the light of the Right of the Constitution, even more, when acting in exercise of the constitutional power for protection, which also means, that we have to interpret the system congruently with the fundamental rights or human rights, that must be respected above all, making a progressive and complete interpretation.' See Decision dated June 1, 2000, *Julio Rocco A*, *Revista de Derecho Público*, N° 82 (Caracas, Editorial Jurídica Venezolana, 2000) 287ff.

1589   The Constitutional Court of the Supreme Tribunal has for instance applied this provision regarding due process rights, preferentially applying art 8 of the American Convention on Human Rights. See Decision dated March 14, 2000 *CA Electricidad del Centro and CA Electricidad de los Andes*, *Revista de Derecho Público*, N° 81 (Caracas, Editorial Jurídica Venezolana, 2000) 157–58; quoted also in Decision N° 328 dated March 9, 2001, of the same Chamber, *Revista de Derecho Público*, N° 85–88 (Caracas, Editorial Jurídica Venezolana, 2001) 108. The Political-Administrative Chamber of the Supreme Tribunal interpreted and developed the criteria established by the Constitutional Chamber regarding the lack of application of art 185 of the Organic Law of the Supreme Court of Justice in Decision N° 802 dated April 13, 2000, *Elecentro v Superintendencia Procompetencia*, *Revista de Derecho Público* N° 82 (Caracas, Editorial Jurídica Venezolana, 2000) 270. On a similar matter, see also, Decision N° 449 dated March 27, 2001, *Dayco de Construcciones v INOS*, *Revista de Derecho*

On the other hand, in order to reinforce the constitutional value of human dignity, the human rights that are guaranteed and protected are not only the ones enumerated in the Constitution, but also those considered 'inherent to the human person' (article 22)[1590]. The last phrase of article 22 of the Constitution established that 'the lack of regulatory statutes regarding human rights do not diminish their exercise'; that is, their application 'cannot be conditioned by the existence of a statute developing it; and on the contrary, the lack of legal instruments regulating them does not diminish their exercise, being such rights 'of immediate and direct application by the courts and all other bodies of the State' (articles 22, 23 Constitution).[1591]

69. *Fairness/Justice/Rule Of Law/State of Justice:* 'Justice' has also been considered as a global and 'fundamental value' that must contribute to 'the construction of a just and peace-loving society resulting from the democratic exercise of popular will' (article 3). The Constitutional Chamber has considered that 'the power to administer justice must be exercised in the name of the Republic and come from the citizens (article 253)', and 'must be executed with independence and impartiality' by judges 'free from subordinations and inadequate pressures' (articles 254 and 256 of the Constitution). This has been considered as 'a new paradigm about values and constitutional principles connected to the justice', which has led to the conception of the 'State of Justice', considering the judiciary not just one more branch of government but 'the integrating and stabilising State power with authority to control and even dissolve the rest of the branches of government' (Judicialist State).[1592]

This conception of the 'State of Justice' (*Estado de Justicia*) not only flows from the provisions of the Preamble and of article 1 that declares justice as a constitutional value, but from the constitutional provisions establishing 'the prevalence of the notion of material justice over formalities and technicalities';[1593] and providing for the 'effective judicial protection' of human rights by means of a system of justice that must be 'free, available, impartial, idoneous, transparent, autonomous, independent, responsible, fair and expeditious, without improper delays, formalisms or use-

---

Público, N° 85–88 (Caracas, Editorial Jurídica Venezolana, 2001). Nonetheless, the Political-Administrative Chamber has denied giving prevalence to art 8 of the American Convention regarding the requests made by corporate persons, understanding that the Convention only refers to the 'human' rights of individuals. See Decision N° 278 dated March 1, 2001, *Revista de Derecho Público*, N° 85–88 (Caracas, Editorial Jurídica Venezolana, 2001) 104.

1590   This open clause is more extensive in comparison with the original wording of the North American Constitution (Ninth Amendment), in the sense that it refers not only to the rights and guarantees not enumerated in the Constitution but also in the international instruments on human rights, which conforms a truly unlimited cast of unstated, but protected rights that are inherent to the human person.

1591   See Decision N° 723, dated May 15, 2001, *Revista de Derecho Público*, N° 85–88 (Caracas, Editorial Jurídica Venezolana, 2001) 111.

1592   See Decision N° 659 of the Political-Administrative Chamber dated March 24, 2000, *Rosario Nouel v Consejo de la Judicatura y Comisión de Emergencia Judicial*, *Revista de Derecho Público* N° 81 (Caracas, Editorial Jurídica Venezolana, 2000) 103–04.

1593   See Supreme Tribunal of Justice, Decision N° 949 of the Political-Administrative Chamber dated April 26, 2000, *Revista de Derecho Público*, N° 82 (Caracas, Editorial Jurídica Venezolana, 2000) 163ff.

less repositions' (article 26).[1594] To that effect, the procedural laws must establish the 'simplification, uniformity and efficiency of the proceedings and adopt a brief, oral and public procedure, without sacrificing justice because of omission of non-essential formalities' (article 257).

70. *Equality/Respect/Tolerance/Diversity/Multiculturalism:* The Preamble to the Constitution also declares as a fundamental social value, 'equality without discrimination or subordination of any kind', which results from the traditional and historical egalitarian character of Venezuelan society, which rejects any kind of discrimination or servility (articles 19, 21). This has also been considered 'as a fundamental principle of democracy'.[1595]

The principle of equality has been defined in a very explicit way in article 21 of the Constitution, stating that all persons are equal before the law, and consequently, no discrimination can be allowed based on race, sex, religion, social condition, or any other cause having the purpose or consequence of annulling or harming the recognition, enjoyment and exercise of rights and liberties in conditions of equality. For such purpose, the Constitution provides for the juridical and administrative conditions in order to effectively guarantee equality before the law; for instance providing for positive measures in favour of persons or groups that could be discriminated, marginalised or vulnerable; protecting persons located in circumstance of manifest weakness and punishing abuses and harms inflicted against them.

On matters of religion and belief, the Constitution expressly declares that the state must guarantee the freedom of 'cult and religion' (article 50); everybody having the right to profess religious faith and cults, and to express their beliefs in private or in public by teaching and other practices, provided that such beliefs are not contrary to moral, good customs or public order. No one shall invoke religious beliefs or discipline as a means for evading the compliance with the laws or preventing another person from the exercising of his rights. The autonomy and independence of religious confessions and churches is likewise guaranteed in the Constitution, subject only to such limitations as may derive from the Constitution and the law. The Constitution also entitles parents to determine the religious education to be given to their children in accordance with their convictions.

The Constitution guarantees freedom of conscience, although conscientious objections cannot be invoked in order to evade compliance with laws or prevent others from complying with it or exercising their rights (article 60).

Finally, the Preamble of the Constitution expressly declares the Venezuelan Society to be multi-ethnic and pluri-cultural.

1594   This conception of the 'State of Justice' has also been analysed by the Constitutional Chamber of the Supreme Tribunal of Justice, particularly in Decision N° 389 dated March 7, 2002, in which the principle of the informality of the process was repeated, also asserting the principle of *pro actione* as another principle of the State of Justice. See *Revista de Derecho Público*, N° 89–92 (Caracas, Editorial Jurídica Venezolana, 2002) 175ff.

1595   See Decision N° 439 of the Political-Administrative Chamber dated October 6, 1992, *Revista de Derecho Público*, N° 52 (Caracas, Editorial Jurídica Venezolana, 1992) 91–92.

71. *Democracy/Participation/Decentralisation/Inclusion:* The Constitution gua-rantees 'democracy' (Preamble), not only as a political regime and as a condition of government, but also as a way of life, founded in the ideas of political pluralism and equal 'participation' of everyone in the political processes. In this sense, the concept of the 'democratic state' (*Estado democrático*) is also identified as a constitutional principle that gives roots to the political organisation of the nation, as it derives from the Preamble ('democratic society') and from articles 2, 3, 5 and 6 of the Constitu-tion. Democracy is also established in article 6 of the Constitution as an immutable regime of the government of the Republic and of its political entities (states and municipalities), by declaring that it is and always will be 'democratic, participative, elective, decentralised, alternative, responsible, pluralist, and of revocable manda-tes.'

The Constitutional Chamber of the Supreme Tribunal of Justice, in a decision N° 23 dated January 22, 2003 held that the intention of the 1999 Constitution was to 'establish a democratic, participative and protagonist society, which implies that it is not just the State who has to adopt and submit its institutions to the ways and princi-ples of democracy, but it is also the society (formed by Venezuelan citizens) who must play a decisive and responsible role in the conduct of the Nation'.[1596]

By establishing the concept of participation as a fundamental principle of demo-cracy, the Constitution regulates it as a political constitutional right 'considering individuals as member of a determined political community, in order to take part in the formation of public decisions or of the will of the public institutions'; a right that is related to other political rights established in the Constitution, like the right to vote (article 63), to petition (article 51), to have access to public offices (article 62), to political association (article 67), to demonstration (article 68), and to be informed in due time and truthfully by public administration (article 143). It is also related to the social rights, like the right to health (article 84), educational rights (article 102) and environmental rights (article 127).[1597]

'Participative democracy', in addition to 'representative' and 'direct' democracy, is promoted in other constitutional instruments established for the direct intervention of citizens in the decision making process of public affairs, and in particular, 'in political matter: the election of public office, the referendum, the revocation of the term of office, the initiative for legislation, for constitutional reforms and for the constituent process, the open municipal council and the citizens' assembly whose decisions will be of binding force' (article 70).

72. The Constitution directly regulates some mechanisms in order to guarantee direct participation of the representatives of the different sectors of the society in the adoption of some public decisions, particularly through the integration of 'Nomina-ting Committees' for the proposal of candidates for the election by the National As-sembly of high public officials not popularly elected, namely, the Prosecutor Gene-ral, the General Comptroller, the judges of the Supreme Court, and the members of

---

1596   See *Interpretación del artículo 71 de la Constitución* in *Revista de Derecho Público,* N° 93–96 (Caracas, Editorial Jurídica Venezolana, 2003) 530ff.

1597   *Idem.*

the Electoral National Council, seeking to avoid the traditional agreements between political parties.[1598] This was considered by the Constitutional Chamber of the Supreme Tribunal of Justice, in a decision N° 23 dated January 23, 2003, as a result of the 'struggles to change the negative political culture generated by decades of a centralised state of political parties (Cfr. Allan R. Brewer-Carias, *Problemas del Estado de Partidos*, Caracas 1988, pp. 39) that interfered with the development of democratic values, through the participation of the people which is no longer limited to electoral processes,' recognising their 'intervention in the formation, formulation and execution of public politics as a means to overcome the deficits of governability that have affected our political system due to the lack of harmony between the State and the society'; and radically changing 'from the root, the relations between State and society in which the latter receives back its legitimate and undeniable protagonist role by means of the exercise of its fundamental political rights.'[1599]

In order to ensure the enforcement of citizens' right to political participation, the principle of federalism is promoted so that public power is territorially distributed among various levels of government, each of them with autonomous, democratic political institutions.

Article 4 of the 1999 Constitution formally defines the Republic of Venezuela 'as a decentralised Federal State under the terms set out in the Constitution' governed by the principles of 'territorial integrity, solidarity, concurrence and coresponsibility'. In practice, Venezuela continues to be a contradictory 'centralised federation'. [1600]

Article 136 of the 1999 Constitution states that 'public power is distributed among the municipal, state and national entities', establishing a federation with three levels of political governments and autonomy: a national level exercised by the Republic (federal level); the states level, exercised by the 23 states and a Capital District; and the municipal level, exercised by the 338 existing municipalities. At each of these levels, the Constitution requires government that is 'democratic, participatory, elected, decentralised, alternative, responsible, plural and with revocable mandates' (article 6). Regarding the Capital District, this has substituted the former Federal District which was established in 1863, with the elimination of traditional federal interventions that existed regarding the authorities of the latter.

73. *Compassion/Caring/Solidarity/Social Justice /Social State:* Article 2 of the 1999 Constitution defines the Venezuelan state as a social and democratic rule of law state, in which the principle of 'social responsibility' (Preamble) prevails in guiding public policies, configuring the state as a 'Social State', with specific social duties regarding society. In particular, the Constitution refers to the social goal of society and of the state in order to ensure 'social justice', guaranteeing the equitable

---

1598   See, eg, Allan R Brewer-Carías, *Los problemas del Estado de Partidos* (Caracas, Editorial Jurídica Venezolana, 1988).

1599   See *Interpretación del artículo 71 de la Constitución* in *Revista de Derecho Público*, N° 93–96 (Caracas, Editorial Jurídica Venezolana, 2003) 530 ff.

1600   See Allan R Brewer-Carías, *Federalismo y Municipalismo en la Constitución de 1999* (Caracas, Universidad Católica del Táchira-Editorial Jurídica Venezolana, 2001); 'Centralized Federalism in Venezuela' (2005) 43(4) *Duquesne Law Review* 629–43.

participation of all in the enjoyment of wealth, preventing its concentration in a few hands, avoiding unfair income differences, and seeking the guarantee of a dignified and prosperous existence for the collectivity (articles 112, 299).

This idea of a 'Social State' (*Estado Social*) refers to a sState with social obligations that strives for social justice, which allows its intervention in social and economic activities, as a welfare state. Such social character mainly derives from the fundamental constitutional value of 'equality and non-discrimination' that comes from the Preamble, and from article 1 of the Constitution which, besides declaring it as a fundamental right (article 21), is the criterion of the performance of the state (article 2), and of the principle of 'social justice' as the base of the economic system (article 299).

This concept of a 'Social State' has been defined by the Constitutional Chamber of the Supreme Tribunal in a decision N° 85 dated January, 24, 2002, thus:

> The Social State must protect people or groups that regarding others are in a situation of legal weakness, regardless of the principle of equality before the law, which in practice does not resolve anything, because unequal situations cannot be treated with similar solutions. In order to achieve the balance, the Social State not only intervenes in the labour and social security factor, protecting the salaried workers not related to the economic or political power, but it also protects their health, housing, education and economic relations. That is why the Economic Constitution must be seen from an essentially social perspective.

> ... The State is obligated to protect the weak, defend their interests protected by the Constitution, particularly through the courts; and regarding the strong, its duty is to watch that their freedom is not a load for everybody. As a juridical value, there cannot be constitutional protection at the expense of the fundamental rights of others...

> The Social State tries to harmonise the antagonistic interests of society, without allowing unlimited actions from social forces based on the silence of the statutes or their ambiguities, because otherwise that would lead to the establishment of an hegemony over the weak by those economically and socially stronger, in which the private power positions become an excessive diminution of the real freedom of the weak, in a subjugation that constantly encourages the social crisis.[1601]

74. *Community/Civil Society*: The Constitution contains specific provisions that refer to the community, the family and civil society, implying the existence, in addition to personal and individual rights, of collective rights. These have been analysed by the Constitutional Chamber of the Supreme Tribunal in decision N° 1395 dated November 21, 2000, as corresponding to the organised community (article 84), like the right to participate in the decision-making process of the public health institutions; to the Venezuelan people (articles 99 and 347), like the right to cultural values; to the community (article 118), like the right to develop associations of social

---

1601 *Deudores hipotecarios v Superintendencia de Bancos, Revista de Derecho Público*, N° 89–92 (Caracas, Editorial Jurídica Venezolana, 2002) 94ff.

and participative character; to the indigenous people (articles 121, 123, and 125), like the right to maintain their ethnic and cultural identity, and to maintain their own economic practices and to political participation. These are, according to the Chamber's doctrine, differentiated entities that are considered as holders of collective rights by express order of the Constitution.[1602]

75. *Family*: The Constitution has established several personal rights to be protected by the state, beginning with the protection of the family and of families. Article 75 imposes on the state the obligation to protect families as a natural association in society, and as the fundamental space for the overall development of human beings. According to the same constitutional provision, family relationships must be based on equality of rights and duties, solidarity, common effort, mutual understanding and reciprocal respect among family members. In order to protect families, the state must guarantee protection to the mother, father or other person acting as head of a household.

76. Children and adolescents have the right to live, be raised and develop in their original family. When this proves to be impossible or contrary to their best interests, they shall have the right to have a substitute family, in accordance with law. Article 76 of the Constitution provides for the full protection of motherhood and fatherhood, whatever the marital status of the mother or father. Couples have the right to decide freely and responsibly how many children they wish to conceive, and are entitled to access to information and means necessary to guarantee the exercise of this right. The state guarantees overall assistance and protection for motherhood, in general, from the moment of conception, throughout pregnancy, delivery and the puerperal period, and guarantees full family planning services based on ethical and scientific values. The implication of this provision, particularly when protecting maternity from the moment of conception limits abortion as a right.

Article 77 of the Constitution also expressly 'protects marriage between a man and a woman, based on free consent and absolute equality of rights and obligations of the spouses'; consequently, same-sex 'marriages' are not protected in the Constitution, and only a stable de facto union between a man and a woman that meets the requirements established by law shall have the same effects as marriage.

Children and adolescents are considered as full legal persons whose rights are shall be protected by specialised courts, organs and legislation. The rights flow from the Constitution, the Convention on Children's Rights and other international treaty that may have been executed and ratified by the Republic in this field. The state, families and society shall guarantee their full protection as an absolute priority, taking into account their best interest in actions and decisions concerning them. The state shall promote their progressive incorporation into active citizenship, and shall create a national guidance system for the overall protection of children and adolescents (article 78).

77. Regarding senior citizens, article 80 of the Constitution imposes on the state the duty to guarantee the full exercise of their rights and guarantees; providing that the state, with the participation of families and society, is obliged to respect their

---

1602   *Revista de Derecho Público*, No 84 (Caracas, Editorial Jurídica Venezolana, 2000) 331ff.

human dignity, autonomy and to guarantee them full care and social security benefits to improve and guarantee their quality of life. Pension and retirement benefits granted through the social security system shall not be less than the urban minimum salary. Senior citizens shall be guaranteed the right to proper work if they indicate a desire to work and are capable of work.

78. *Life*: The most important civil right according to the Constitution is the right to life, article 43, as 'inviolable'. The Constitution thus prohibits the death penalty, providing that 'no law shall provide for the death penalty and no authority shall apply the same.' In addition, the article obliges the state to 'protect the life of persons who are deprived of liberty, are in military or civil services, or are subject to its authority in any other manner.' The right to life, therefore, is an absolute right that cannot be 'suspended' nor restricted in cases of states of exception decreed by the President of the Republic.

79. *Learning/Education:* A chapter in the Constitution is devoted to educational rights. In this respect, article 102 establishes that 'education is a human right and a fundamental social duty that is democratic, cost-free, and mandatory.' The consequence of this provision is an obligation imposed on the state to provide education as a function of greatest interest, at all levels and in all modes, as an instrument of scientific, humanistic and technical knowledge at the service of society. Every person has the right to a full, high-quality, ongoing education under conditions and circumstances of equality, subject only to personal aptitude, vocation or aspiration limitations. According to the Constitution, education is obligatory at all levels from day-care to the diversified secondary level.

Education is constitutionally declared to be a public service (article 102), although it states that, 'the State will stimulate and protect private education imparted which accords with the principles established in this Constitution and the Laws.' The Constitution establishes that education offered in state institutions is free of charge up to the undergraduate university level. The state shall create and maintain institutions and services sufficiently equipped to ensure the admission process, ongoing education and programme completion in the education system (article 103). The communications media, public and private, shall contribute to civil education. The state guarantees public radio and television services and library and computer networks, with a view to allowing universal access to information (article 108).

80. *Honesty/Integrity:* The Preamble to the Constitution refers to the values of 'ethics'. Ethical values are expressly mentioned in the provisions regarding education. Consequently, beyond the legal provisions referred to public ethics in public administration, there is a set of ethical norms that must guide society and state officials in the task of transforming the state and creating a new legal system. As for public administration, which must be 'at the service of the people', the Constitution also enumerates the principles and values on which it must be based: 'honesty, participation, celerity, efficiency, effectiveness, transparency, the accounting and responsibility in the execution of the public function, with complete subjection to the statutes and to the Law' (article 141).

81. *Impartiality*. As for elections, the Constitution enumerates the following principles that must be guaranteed regarding the electoral processes: 'equality, reliability, impartiality, transparency and efficiency', besides the 'personalisation of the vote and proportional representation' (article 293);

Regarding public services, the Constitution enumerates a series of governing principles in this respect: regarding the national public health system, it states that it must be 'inter-sectorial, decentralised and participative, and managed by the principles of gratuitousness, universality, integrality, impartiality, social integration and solidarity' (article 84); in respect of the social security system, it indicates that the system must be 'universal, integral, unified [*solidario*], unitary, efficient and participative financing, from direct or indirect contributions' (article 86); and as for the education, the Constitution expresses that it must be

> democratic, free and mandatory, based on the respect to all thought tendencies, in order to develop the creative potential of every human being and the complete exercise of his/her personality inside a democratic society based on the ethical valuation of labour and the active, conscientious and unified [*solidario*] participation in the processes of social transformation related with the values of the national identity and with a Latin-American and universal vision. (Article 102)

82. *Social Economic Justice*. Regarding the socioeconomic regime of the Republic, the Constitution enumerates the following principles on which the system must be based:

> social justice, democracy, efficiency, free competition, environmental protection, productivity and solidarity, in order to guarantee the integral human development, a dignified and prosperous existence for the collectivity, the generation of labour sources, high national added value, elevation of the standard of living of the people and to strengthen the economical supremacy of the country, guaranteeing juridical security, stability, dynamism, supportability, permanence and equity of the economic growth, in order to achieve a fair distribution of the wealth by means of a democratic, participative and of open consultation strategic planning. (Article 299)

83. *Freedom/Liberty/Independence:* The Constitution establishes certain rights that cannot be renounced or waived, being 'independence, freedom, sovereignty, immunity, territorial integrity and national self-determination' (article 1).

Regarding independence, in the provisions referred to the territorial organisation of the state, particularly regarding the 'decentralised federal state' (article 4), it is established that it must be configured following the principles of 'territorial integrity, cooperation, solidarity, concurrence and co-responsibility' (article 4). As for the national statutes that can be sanctioned by the National Assembly regarding concurrent competences between the national, the states and the municipal levels, the Constitution prescribes that they must be oriented by 'the principles of independence, coordination, cooperation, co-responsibility and subsidiary' (article 165).

'Independence' is also affirmed in the Preamble, in the sense of reaffirming the existence of the Republic itself, which attained its independence from the Spanish monarchy in 1810, not subjected to any nature of foreign domination. Consequently, the 'territorial integrity' of the nation is also conceived as another fundamental value of the country, which impedes the modification of its borders in any way. Regarding the aims of 'peace', as a fundamental value, it implies the existential rejection of war.

On the other hand, 'freedom', according to the Preamble, is also one of the most fundamental values, understood in its most classical expression as the right of every individual to do anything that does not harm others; to not be obliged to do what the law does not order nor to be impeded from doing what it does not forbid; that is, the right to the 'free development of the personality', which is also expressly regulated (article 20) without any other limitation than those derived from the rights of others and the public and social order.

84. *Security*: According to article 55 of the Constitution, every person has the right to be protected by the state, through the entities established by law for the protection of citizens from situations that constitute a threat, vulnerability or risk to the physical integrity of individuals, their properties, and the enjoyment of their rights or the fulfilment of their duties. The citizens' participation in programmes for purposes of prevention, citizen safety and emergency management shall be regulated by a special law.

The Constitution guarantees that the state's security entities shall respect the human dignity and rights of all persons, and sets forth expressly that the use of weapons or toxic substances by police and security officers shall be limited by the principles of necessity, convenience, opportunity and proportionality in accordance with law.

The Constitution enumerates the following principles regarding the Nation's security: 'independence, democracy, equality, peace, freedom, justice, solidarity, promotion and conservation of the environment, the affirmation of the human rights and the progressive satisfaction of all individual and collective needs of the Venezuelan people' (article 326).

85. *Responsibility /Accountability/Transparency:* The Constitution establishes the general principle providing for state liability, incorporated in an express way in article 140, that 'The State is liable for the damages suffered by individuals in their goods and rights, provided that the injury be imputable to the functioning of Public Administration', being possible to comprise in the expression 'functioning of Public Administration' its normal or abnormal functioning. The Constitution provides for elected public officials to be subject to accountability (*rendición de cuentas*), establishing the possibility for them being subjected to repeal referendums for the revocation of mandates (article 6), which according to article 72 can only take place at the mid-point of a term in office. The corresponding petition for a repeal referendum can only be one of popular initiative that must be signed by at least 20 per cent of the registered voters in the corresponding jurisdiction. In order for a mandate to be repealed or revoked, the concurrence of a number of voters equal to or greater than the number that originally elected the official is needed, and the voters must total at least 25 per cent of the registered voters in the corresponding jurisdiction. If the repeal petition is approved, the substitute officer must be elected immediately according to the electoral procedures established in the Constitution and laws. This repeal referendum was distorted in 2004 regarding its application to the President of the

Republic, and was transformed against the constitutional provision into a 'ratifying' referendum.[1603]

Article 143 of the Constitution guarantees the rights of citizens to be informed and to have access to administrative information. In the first place, it provides for the right of citizens to be promptly and truly informed by public administration regarding the situation of the procedures in which they have a direct interest, and to know about the definitive resolutions therein adopted, to be notified of administrative acts and to be informed on the courses of the administrative procedure.

The constitutional article also establishes for the individual right everybody has to have access to administrative archives and registries, without prejudice of the acceptable limits imposed in a democratic society related to the national or foreign security, to criminal investigation, to the intimacy of private life, all according to the statutes regulating the matter of secret or confidential documents classification. The same article provides for the principle of prohibition of any previous censorship referring to public officials regarding the information they could give referring to matters under their responsibility.

86. *Environment*: The Constitution regulates the environment, declaring that each generation has the right and duty to protect and maintain the environment for its own benefit and that of the world of the future; and that everyone has the right, individually and collectively, to enjoy a safe, healthful and ecologically balanced life and environment.

The state shall protect the environment, biological and genetic diversity, ecological processes, national parks and natural monuments, and other areas of particular ecological importance. The genome of a living being shall not be patentable, and the field shall be regulated by the law relating to the principles of bioethics.

It is a fundamental duty of the state, with the active participation of society, to ensure to people their development in a pollution-free environment in which air, water, soil, coasts, climate, the ozone layer and living species receive special protection, in accordance with law (article 127).

In order to guarantee the protection of the environment, article 129 of the Constitution prescribes that any activities capable of generating damage to ecosystems must be preceded by environmental and socio-cultural impact studies. The state shall prevent toxic and hazardous waste from entering the country, as well as preventing the manufacture and use of nuclear, chemical and biological weapons. A special law shall regulate the use, handling, transportation and storage of toxic and hazardous substances.

As a matter of public policy, article 128 of the Constitution imposes on the state the duty to develop a land-use policy taking into account ecological, geographic, demographic, social, cultural, economic and political realities, in accordance with the premises of sustainable development, including information, consultation and

---

1603   See Allan R Brewer-Carías, 'El secuestro del Poder Electoral y la confiscación del derecho a la participación política mediante el referendo revocatorio presidencial: Venezuela 2000–2004' *Boletín Mexicano de Derecho Comparado* 112, (México, Instituto de Investigaciones Jurídicas, Universidad Nacional Autónoma de México, 2005), 11–73.

male/female participation by citizens. An organic law shall develop the principles and criteria for this zoning.

Article 106 of the Constitution ensures that environmental education is obligatory in the various levels and modes of the education system, as well as in informal civil education.

§2. *The Incongruences between Declared Values and Political and Judicial Practice*

I.   *Superior Values of the Constitution and the 'Political Project'*

87. The superior character of the values enshrined in the Constitution has been transformed by the Constitutional Chamber of the Supreme Tribunal of Justice, in its decision N° 23 of January 22, 2003. Thus, the universal meaning of the values has been eschewed by the Tribunal which has said that 'to interpret the legal system according to the Constitution, means to protect the Constitution itself from every diversion of principles and from every separation from the political project that it embodies by will of the people'. It added:

> "[A] system of principles, assumed to be absolute and supra historical, cannot be placed above the Constitution, nor that its interpretation could eventually contradict the political theory that supports it. From this perspective, any theory that proposes absolute rights or goals must be rejected and ... the interpretation or integration [of the Constitution] must be done according to the living cultural tradition whose sense and scope depends on the specific and historical analysis of the values shared by the Venezuelan people. Part of the protection and guarantee of the Constitution is established then, in an *in fieri* politic perspective, reluctant to the ideological connection with theories that can limit, under pretext of universal validities, the supremacy and the national self-determination, as demanded in article 1° *eiusdem*."[1604]

This doctrine of subjection of the global constitutional values to a political project was ratified in Decision N° 1.939 of December 18, 2009 (*Gustavo Álvarez Arias y otros*) in which the Constitutional Chamber declared a decision of the Inter American Court of Human Rights as non-enforceable in Venezuela, rejecting the existence of superior values which may trump government policy. The Chamber argued that the legal order 'is a normative theory at the service of politic defined in the axiological project of the Constitution'; that the standard in order to resolve conflicts between principles and provisions must be 'compatible with the political project of the Constitution', and such provisions 'cannot be affected with interpretations that could give prevalence to individual rights or that could give prevalence to the international order regarding the national one affecting the State sovereignty'; that no system of principles 'supposedly absolute and supra-historic can be placed above the Constitu-

---

[1604]   *Interpretación del article 71 de la Constitución, Revista de Derecho Público*, N° 93–96 (Caracas, Editorial Jurídica Venezolana, 2003) 530ff.

tion', and that 'theories based on universal values that pretend to limit the sovereignty and national auto-determination are unacceptable.'[1605]

This rejection of superior and universal values has been followed by the rejection of the constitutional rank that the Constitution has given to international instruments of human rights and to their direct and immediate application by all courts.

In effect, article 23 of the 1999 Constitution, one of the most important provisions for the protection of human rights, provides for constitutional ranking of international treaties on human rights and their prevalence when containing provisions more favourable to their enjoyment than those established in the internal legal order. Its inclusion in the new Constitution was a significant advance in the completion of the protective framework of human rights.

88. Nonetheless, in the judicial practice and particularly regarding the provisions of the American Convention of Human Rights, the doctrine of the Supreme Tribunal in this case has been progressively restrictive, eventually rejecting the constitutional ranking of the international instruments of human rights. This restrictive approach by the Constitutional Chamber, that has affected the role of the Inter American institutions for the protection of human rights, began with a decision dated May 5, 2000, in which the Constitutional Chamber objected to the 'quasi-jurisdictional' powers of the Inter American Commission when issuing provisional protective measures regarding a state, qualifying it as 'unacceptable', stating that they 'imply a gross intrusion in the country's judiciary, like the suspension of the judicial proceeding against the plaintiff, measures that can only be adopted by the judges exercising their judicial attributions and independence, according to what is stated in the Constitution and the statutes of the Republic'.[1606]

The restrictive approach regarding the role and value of international institutions for the protection of human rights was also applied in Decision N° 1.942 of July 15, 2003 (*Impugnación de artículos del Código Penal, Leyes de desacato*),[1607] in which the Constitutional Chamber, when referring to International courts, stated that 'in Venezuela, in general, in relation to article 7 of the Constitution, no jurisdictional organ could exist above the Supreme Tribunal of Justice, and even in such case, its decisions when contradicting constitutional provisions are inapplicable in the country.'

This approach was extended in the decision of the Constitutional Chamber N° 1.939 of December 18, 2008 (*Abogados Gustavo Álvarez Arias y otros*), in which it declared a decision of the Inter American Court on Human Rights as non enforceable in Venezuela. The decision of the former of August 5, 2008 (*Apitz Barbera y otros ('Corte Primera de lo Contencioso Administrativo') v Venezuela*)[1608] condemned the Venezuelan state for the violation of the judicial guarantees of three former

---

1605   See at www.tsj.gov.ve/decisiones/scon/Diciembre/1939–181208–2008–08–1572.html.

1606 See *Faitha M Nahmens L and Ben Ami Fihman Z (Revista Exceso)*, Exp n° 00–0216, Decisión n° 386 dated May 17, 2000. See the reference in Carlos Ayala Corao, 'Recepción de la jurisprudencia internacional sobre derechos humanos por la jurisprudencia constitucional' *Revista del Tribunal Constitucional* 6, (Lima, 2004), 275ff.

1607   See en *Revista de Derecho Público*, N° 93–96 (Caracas, Editorial Jurídica Venezolana, 2003) 136ff.

1608   See in www.corteidh.or.cr. Excepción Preliminar, Fondo, Reparaciones y Costas, Serie C N° 182.

judges of a First Contentious Administrative Court that were dismissed by a Special Commission of the Supreme Tribunal. The Constitutional Chamber in its decision rejected the supra-constitutional character of the provisions of the American Convention, considering that in the event of contradiction of a provision of the Constitution and a provision of an international treaty, the judiciary should have the attribution to determine the applicable provisions.[1609] The non-enforceability in Venezuela of the decisions of the Inter American Court of Human Rights was ratified by the Supreme Tribunal of Venezuela in decision N° 1547 of October 17, 2011 (*Estado Venezolano vs. Corte Interamericana de Derechos Humanos*),[1610] in which the Constitutional Chamber decided on the 'unconstitutionality' of the decision of the Inter American Court on Human Rights of September 1, 2011 (*Leopoldo López v Estado de Venezuela*). [1611]

The problem with the interpretative role of the Court is that the Constitutional Chamber, unfortunately is overly controlled by the Executive.[1612] This has resulted in the rejection of the power of all courts to apply in a direct and immediate way, international instruments on human rights for the resolution of judicial cases.

II.   *Erosion of Public Participation in Political Decision Making*

89 The goal of participation requires some form of decentralisation, the inclusion of instruments of direct democracy in a representative democratic framework and the possibility for the people to express their opinion on political decisions.

Referendums can be useful instruments in order to perfect democracy, but by themselves cannot satisfy the aim of participation. This is illustrated in the 2002–04 process concerning the Venezuelan presidential repeal referendum (see *infra* paragraphs 91, 161, 177, 179, 342), which was converted into a presidential 'ratification' referendum of a plebiscitary nature.[1613] A repeal referendum is a vote asking the people if the mandate of an elected official must be revoked or not; it is not a vote asking if the elected official must remain or not in office. In the first case, the vote of the people for YES, if reached the percentage established in the Constitution, it is the decision to revoke, independently of the number of people that could have vote

---

1609   Available at www.tsj.gov.ve/decisiones/scon/Diciembre/1939–181208–2008–08–1572.html.

1610   Available at www.tsj.gov.ve/decisiones/scon/Octubre/1547–171011–2011–11–1130.html.

1611   Available at www.corteidh.or.cr/docs/casos/articulos/resumen_233_esp.pdf. See the comments in Allan R Brewer-Carías, 'El ilegítimo "control de constitucionalidad" de las sentencias de la Corte Interamericana de Derechos Humanos por parte la Sala Constitucional del Tribunal Supremo de Justicia de Venezuela: el caso *Leopoldo López vs Venezuela, septiembre 2011,'Revista de Derecho Público* 128 (Caracas, Editorial Jurídica Venezolana, 2011) 227–50.

1612   See Allan R Brewer-Carías, 'El juez constitucional al servicio del autoritarismo y la ilegítima mutación de la constitución: el caso de la Sala Constitucional del Tribunal Supremo de Justicia de Venezuela (1999–2009),' *Revista de Administración Pública,* 180, (Madrid, Centro de Estudios Constitucionales, 2009), 383–418.

1613   See Allan R Brewer-Carías, 'El secuestro del Poder Electoral y de la Sala Electoral del Tribunal Supremo y la confiscación del derecho a la participación política mediante el referendo revocatorio presidencial: Venezuela: 2000–2004' *Revista Costarricense de Derecho Constitucional,* Tomo V (San José, Costa Rica, Instituto Costarricense de Derecho Constitucional, Editorial Investigaciones Jurídicas SA, 2004) 167–312; and in *Revista Jurídica del Perú* 55 (Lima, 2004), 353–96.

for NO. In the second case, it would be a "plebiscite," based only on the majority of votes for the YES or the NO that is not established in the Constitution. But in the 2004 repeal referendum, the National Electoral Council, when giving the voting results, converted it into a plebiscite ratifying the President.

The result of the implementation of the 1999 Constitution is that Venezuelan democracy transformed from being a representative democracy with more or less competitive and pluralist parties which alternated in government (1958–98), into a centralised plebiscite democracy, in which effectively all power lies with the President, supported by politically partisan votes of the National Assembly and the military, and more appropriate to a one-party system.

This plebiscite democracy system has created an illusion of popular participation, particularly by means of the uncontrolled distribution of state oil income among the poor through governmental social programmes that are not tailored to the promotion of investment and the creation of meaningful employment. This plebiscite democracy is less representative and less participatory than the traditional representative party democracy, which, notwithstanding all the warnings[1614] that were raised, the traditional parties have failed to preserve.

90. On the other hand, the only two constitutional provisions establishing means for direct participation of the people in political decisions process, in practice have been neutralized. This applies for the election of high officials of the Branches of Government (Prosecutor General, Comptroller General, People's Defender, National Electoral Council, Justices of the Supreme Court), that according to the Constitution must be nominated by specific Committees composed of 'representatives of the various sectors of society' (articles 270,279, 295) (see *infra* paragraphs 151, 224, 286,393 ff.,420, 423, 433). Nonetheless the different statutes regulating their composition have organized such Committees as "parliamentary commissions" subjected to the political party that control the majority if the National Assembly.[1615]

The other provision for the direct participation of the people established in the 1999 Constitution, in decision making processes, is the obligatory public consultation that has to be organized before the sanctioning the statutes (article 211) (see *infra* paragraph 161). This provision, in practice, has generally being ignored, because since 2001 almost all the statutes in the country have been issued by means of decree-laws, or delegate legislation, and the Executive Branch has never organized any sort of popular participation in order hear the opinion of the people. Even worst,

---

1614   See in general Allan R Brewer-Carías, *El Estado. Crisis y reforma* (Caracas, Academia de Ciencias Políticas y Sociales, 1982); and *Problemas del Estado de partidos* (Caracas, Editorial Jurídica Venezolana, 1988); Allan R Brewer-Carías, 'La crisis de las instituciones: responsables y salidas,' *Revista del Centro de Estudios Superiores de las Fuerzas Armadas de Cooperación,* 11 (Caracas, 1985), 57–83; *Revista de la Facultad de Ciencias Jurídicas y Políticas,* 64 (Caracas, Universidad Central de Venezuela, 1985), 129–55. Also see Allan R Brewer-Carías, *Instituciones Políticas y Constitucionales,* Vol I, Evolución histórica del Estado (San Cristóbal-Caracas, Universidad Católica del Táchira, Editorial Jurídica Venezolana, 1996) 523–41.

1615   See Allan R. Brewer-Carías, "La participación ciudadana en la designación de los titulares de los órganos no electos de los Poderes Públicos en Venezuela y sus vicisitudes políticas", en *Revista Iberoamericana de Derecho Público y Administrativo,* (San José, Costa Rica, Asociación Latinoamericana de Derecho Administrativo, 2005), 76-95

the Constitutional Chamber of the Supreme Tribunal has expressly ruled in decision N° 203, March 25, 2014 (*Impugnación del Decreto de la Ley Orgánica de la Administración Pública*), that popular participation is not guaranteed in the Constitution when the statutes are issued by the President of the Republic, but only when sanctioned by the National Assembly.[1616]

III. *The Erosion of the Democratic Principle*

91. The democratic principle embedded in the Constitution as one of its most important values, means that all high officials of the State must be elected by direct or indirect popular vote, and hat the will of the people manifested through an election must be respected, corresponding only to the people, directly or indirectly revoke the election made.

This implies that according to the Constitution, the representatives (*diputados*) to the National Assembly and the President of the Republic must always be elected by popular vote through direct, secret and universal vote cast by the people (articles 186, 228), and that only the vote of the people cast in a referendum organized by popular initiative, can revoke the democratic mandate of those elected to the Executive and Legislative Branches of Government (articles 72, 198, 233). The same democratic principle applies regarding the election of the high official of the other Branches of Government (Judicial, Citizens and Electoral) in the sense that they only can be elected by indirect popular vote made by a qualified majority of the elected representatives to the National Assembly acting as an electoral body, and that their mandates can only be revoked by the same Assembly eith the same qualify vote (articles 265, 279, 296) (see *infra* paragraphs 42, 224).

Nonetheless, the incongruence in this case between the constitutional provisions and the practice of government has been notorious, basically resulting from decisions of the Constitutional Chamber of the Supreme Tribunal[1617] that, for instance, in January 2013 imposed a non elected official (the then acting Executive Vice-President) to act as President of the Republic;[1618] in 2014 revoked the popular electoral mandate of an elected representative to the National Assembly,[1619] and of two

---

1616   Available in *Revista de Derecho Público, Revista de Derecho Público,* 137 (Caracas, Editorial Jurídica Venezolana, 2014), 100-103. See the comments on the decisión in Allan R. Brewer-Carías, "El fin de la llamada "democracia participativa y protagónica" dispuesto por la Sala Constitucional en fraude a la Constitución, al justificar la emisión de legislación inconsulta en violación al derecho a la participación política," in *Idem*, 157-164. See also Allan R. Brewer-Carías, "El derecho ciudadano a la participación popular y la inconstitucionalidad generalizada de los decretos leyes 2010-2012, por su carácter inconsulto," *Revista de Derecho Público,* N° 130, (Caracas, Editorial Jurídica Venezolana, 2012), 85-88.

1617   See in general on the Supreme Tribunal decisions: Allan R. Brewer-Carías, *El golpe a la democracia dado por la Sala Constitucional*, (Caracas, Editorial Jurídica Venezolana, 2014)

1618   Decisions N° 2 of January 9, 2013, available at http://www.tsj.gov.ve/decisio-nes/scon/Enero/02-9113-2013-12-1358.html, and N° 141 of March 8, 2013, available at http://www.tsj.gov.ve.decisio-nes/scon/Marzo/141-9313-2013-13-0196.html. See the comments in Asdrúbal Aguiar (Compilador), *El Golpe de Enero en Venezuela (Documentos y testimonios para la historia)*, (Caracas, Editorial Jurídica Venezolana, 2013), 85-90. 97-106, 133-148 y 297-314

elected municipal mayors; [1620] and in 2014, it allowed the 'indirect election' of the Justices of the Supreme Tribunal, the Prosecutor General, the General Comptroller and the People's Defender by only simple majority of votes of the representatives present in the session of the Assembly, and even worst, the same Constitutional Chamber designated the members of the National Electoral Council, usurping the role of the National Assembly[1621] (see *infra* paragraphs 411, 412,413).

IV. *The Contradictory State Intervention in the Internal Life of Civil Society Entities*

92. In some cases, the incongruence between constitutional provisions is not the product of judicial rulings or of political application of the Constitution, but of norms contained in the Constitution. In this context, the Constitution, contrary to its participative phraseology, creates scope for intervention in the organisations of civil society by establishing the jurisdiction of the National Electoral Council for 'the organisation of the elections of trade unions, professional associations and organisations with political objectives' and in general, to guarantee 'the equality, reliability, impartiality, transparency and efficiency of the electoral processes' (article 293,6).

According to this provision, the Constitution provides that the internal elections that can take place within political parties, trade unions and professionals associations of any kind, must be organised by the state through one of the branches of government. This represents a contradiction with the participatory feature attributed to the Constitution and with its declared goal of promoting citizens' participation.

Consequently, all the internal electoral processes within the political parties in Venezuela from 2000 are to be organised by the National Electoral Council, although this has not always been the case in practice.

State intervention has been active regarding civil society organisations. For example, even though the trade unions are considered as not being 'inside the struc-

1619   Decision N° 207 de 31 de marzo de 2014, available at en http://www.tsj.gov.ve/decisiones/scon/marzo/162546-207-31314-2014-14-0286.HTML Also published in *Official Gazette* N° 40385 of April 2, 2014. See the comments in Allan R. Brewer-Carías, 'La revocación del mandato popular de una diputada a la Asamblea Nacional por la Sala Constitucional del Tribunal Supremo de oficio, sin juicio ni proceso alguno (El caso de la Diputada María Corina Machado),' *Revista de Derecho Público*, 137 (Caracas, Editorial Jurídica Venezolana, 2014), 165- 189

1620   Decision N° 138 of March 17, available at http://www.tsj.gov.ve/decisiones/scon/marzo/162025-138-17314-2014-14-0205.HTML 2014; and Decision N° 245 of April, 9, 2014, available at: http://www.tsj.gov.ve/decisiones/scon/abril/162860-245-9414-2014-14-0205.HTML See also in *Official Gazette*, 40.391 de 10 de abril de 2014. See the comments in Allan R. Brewer-Carías, 'La ilegítima e inconstitucional revocación del mandato popular de alcaldes por la Sala Constitucional del Tribunal Supremo, usurpando competencias de la jurisdicción penal, mediante un procedimiento "sumario" de condena y encarcelamiento (El caso de los Alcaldes Vicencio Scarano Spisso y Daniel Ceballo),' *Revista de Derecho Público*, 138 (Caracas, Editorial Jurídica Venezolana, 2014), 176-210

1621   Decision N° 1864 of December 22, 2014, available at: http://historico.tsj.gov.ve/decisiones/scon/diciembre/173494-1864-221214-2014-14-1341.HTML; and decision N° 1865 of December 26, 2014, available at: http://historico.tsj.gov.ve/decisiones/scon/diciembre/173497-1865-261214-2014-14-1343.HTML. See the comments in Allan R. Brewer-Carías, 'El golpe de Estado dado en diciembre de 2014, con la inconstitucional designación de las altas autoridades del Poder Público," *Revista de Derecho Público*, N° 40 (Caracas, Editorial Jurídica Venezolana, 2014).

ture of the Venezuelan public organisation',[1622] the Electoral Chamber of the Supreme Court, in Ddecision N° 46 dated March 11, 2002, justified state intervention and supervision regarding social organisations, arguing that it tends:

> To guarantee [internal] democracy in said organisations through the transparency and celerity of their electoral processes and the selection of the legitimate authorities that are called to represent the interests and rights of those affiliated in the negotiations and collective conflicts of labour; in the procedures of conciliation and arbitrage; in the promotion, negotiation, celebration, revision and modification of collective labour conventions, and in everything necessary for the guarantee of the patrimony and the interests of the trade union organisation.[1623]

The Electoral Chamber of the Supreme Tribunal of Justice has decided in many cases to participate in the internal functioning of other forms of civic associations, as happened within neighbourhood associations. In a Decision N° 61 dated May 29, 2001, the Constitutional Chamber considered that the matter was about organisations 'that the constitutional text, itself, refers to as "civil society", being able to request, from the National Electoral Council, its intervention in order to organise their internal elections.'[1624] In a decision dated November 1, 2000, in which the Electoral Chamber ruled against the electoral regulations issued by the Electoral Commission of a social club, considering that, even though the club was an association, 'the constitutional text itself refers to as forming part of "civil society", with authority to be freely constituted by its members, providing for their own organisation, being nonetheless able to request the intervention of the National Electoral Council for the organisation of their internal elections.'[1625]

As for other civil associations, such as businesses and industrial or commercial chambers, the Electoral Chamber of the Supreme Tribunal, in Decision N° 18, dated February 15, 2001, considered that a civil association called 'Cámara de Comercios e Industrias del Estado Aragua' by virtue of its objectives to 'encourage for the economic development and the social progress of the region, providing the collective effort of the sectors that form it', as well as 'the defence and the strengthening of the free initiative and the freedom of the enterprise', constituted an indirect participative mechanism – both economically and socially – of a sector of the people in national society life; thus 'even if the referred civil association is of a private character, its objectives transcend the core particular interest'. For this reason, the Chamber considered that it was 'justified to include it as one of the organisations of the "civil society" implicitly stated in article 293,6 of the Constitution', a reason for which it

---

1622   *Revista de Derecho Público*, 84 (Caracas, Editorial Jurídica Venezolana, 2000) 132ff.

1623   *Revista de Derecho Público*, N° 89–92 (Caracas, Editorial Jurídica Venezolana, 2000) 148–49.

1624   See Exp 000064, *Asociación de Residentes de la Urbanización La Trinidad*. See the reference in Allan R Brewer-Carías, *Derecho Administrativo*, vol. I (Bogotá, Universidad Externado de Colombia, 2005) 413ff.

1625   See Exp 0115, *Asociación Civil Club Campestre Paracotos*. See the reference in Allan R Brewer-Carías, *Derecho Administrativo*, vol I (Bogotá, Universidad Externado de Colombia, 2005) 413ff.

declared its jurisdiction to resolve a dispute challenging the election held in the association 'independently of the nature of the entity from which these proceed'.[1626]

But in other cases, the Electoral Chamber has recognised the obligatory intervention of the National Electoral Council in the electoral processes of civil associations like those of university professors, as occurred regarding internal elections in the professors' association of the Universidad Central de Venezuela. Regarding these associations, the Electoral Chamber ruled in a Decision No 51 dated May 19, 2000, that article 293.6 refers to those 'groups of people that in their condition of professionals, unite to defend their common interests and to achieve improvements also of common character, independently from the fact that their conformation is not done by expressed disposition of a statute, but by common agreement from its members, under a form of private right'. The Electoral Chamber thus included associations established inside the Universities, formed by the professionals of diverse disciplines or knowledge areas that are part of the institution in their condition of professors, teachers or instructors, imposing on them the intervention of the state to organise their internal electoral processes.[1627]

V. *The Dangerous Expansion of Security and Defence Values*

93. The Constitution made substantial departures from the provisions of the earlier 1961 Constitution regarding national security and defence and the military. The earlier Constitution contained only three provisions on the subject: article 133, establishing restrictions regarding the possession of arms; article 131, prohibiting the simultaneous exercise of civilian and military authority by any public official other than the President of the Republic as Commander in Chief of the Armed Forces; and article 132, referring to the general regulation of the Armed Forces.

By contrast, the Constitution promotes a markedly militarist shape to the state, with particular provisions regarding not only the military but the security and defence establishment (see *infra* paragraphs 247,338).

Article 322 of the Constitution begins by stating that the security of the nation falls within the essential competence and responsibility of the state, founded upon the state's 'integral development;' the defence of the state being the responsibility of Venezuelans, and of all natural and legal persons, whether of public or private law, within the geographic territory of the state.

In addition, article 326 provides for general principles of national security, declaring that its preservation in 'economic, social, political, cultural, geographic, environmental and military areas' mutually corresponds ('co-responsibility') to the state and to civil society, in order to fulfil the principles of 'independence, democracy, equality, peace, liberty, justice, solidarity, promotion and conservation of the envi-

---

1626   See Exp 000017, *Cámara de Comercios e Industrias del Estado Aragua*. This jurisprudence was ratified by the same Chamber according to verdict N° 162, Exp 2002–000077 dated 10–17–02 (Cámara de Comercio e Industrias del Estado Bolívar). See the reference in Allan R Brewer-Carías, *Derecho Administrativo*, Vol I (Bogotá, Universidad Externado de Colombia, 2005) 413ff.

1627   See *Asociación de Profesores de la Universidad Central de Venezuela*, in *Revista de Derecho Público*, N° 82 (Caracas, Editorial Jurídica Venezolana, 2000) 92 ff.

ronment, the affirmation of human rights, and, the progressive satisfaction of the individual and collective needs of Venezuelans on the basis of sustainable and productive development fully covering the national community.' All of these principles are enumerated in the opening articles 1, 2, and 3 of the Constitution of 1999.

For this purpose, the Constitution created a new council, the National Council of Defence (article 323), as the nation's highest authority for defence planning, advice, and consultation to the state (public powers) on all matters related to the defence and security of the nation's sovereignty, territorial integrity, and strategic thinking. This Council is presided over by the President of the Republic, and integrated by the Executive Vice-President, the President of the National Assembly, the President of Supreme Tribunal of Justice, the President of the Moral Republican Council (Citizen Branch of government, article 237), the Ministers of the defence sectors: interior security, foreign relations, and planning, and others whose participation is considered pertinent.

Under the Constitution, the traditional national armed forces (comprised of the Army, the Navy, the Air Force, and the National Guard) have become integrated into a single institution, named the 'National Armed Force', which nonetheless, according to article 328, is comprised of the Army, the Navy, the Air Force, and the National Guard, each working within its area of competence to fulfil its mission, and with its own system of social security, as established by its respective organic legislation.

All these constitutional provisions reinforce a normative framework with clear marks of a militarist structure, which when combined with the centralisation of state power and the concentration of state power in the President by his control over the National Assembly.   The result is a system that has shown authoritarian tendencies. In particular, the Constitution's provisions on military matters, the idea of the subjection or subordination of military authority to civilian authority has disappeared. Instead what has been created is a greater autonomy of the National Armed Forces, whose four branches (since 2008, five branches) have been unified into one institution with the possibility of intervention in civilian functions.

This militaristic tendency is evidenced by the following constitutional rules: first, the elimination of the traditional prohibition that military and civilian authority be exercised simultaneously, as was established by article 131 of the 1961 Constitution; second, the elimination of control by the National Assembly of senior military promotions, as provided in article 331 of the 1961 Constitution and throughout the country's traditional constitutionalism; third, the elimination of the constitutionally 'non-deliberative and apolitical' character of the military institution, as established in article 132 of the 1961 Constitution, which has opened the way for the Armed Force, as a military institution, to deliberate politically, intervene, and give its opinion on matters under resolution within the civil organs of the state; fourth, the elimination of the obligation of the Armed Force to ensure the stability of democratic institutions required by article 132 of the 1961 Constitution; fifth, the elimination of the obligation of the Armed Force to respect the Constitution and laws 'the adherence to which will always be above any other obligation' as was set forth in article 132 of the 1961 Constitution; sixth, the express right of suffrage granted to members of the military in article 330 of the 1999 Constitution, which in many cases has been politically incompatible with the principle of obedience; seventh, the submission of authority over the use of all weapons, for war or otherwise, to the Armed Force, while removing this authority from the civil administration of the state (article 324); eighth, the general attribution of police administrative functions to the Armed Force (article 329); ninth, the establishment of procedural privilege for generals and admirals in the sense that in order for them to be tried, the Supreme Tribunal of Justice must declare in advance of trial whether or not the proceeding has merit (article 266,3); and tenth, the adoption in the Constitution of the concept of the 'doctrine of national security,' as a global, totalistic, and omni-comprehensive doctrine in the sense that everything that happens in the state and in the nation concerns the security of the state, including economic and social development (article 326); with the duty for the Armed Force to have an 'active participation in national development' (article 328). All these provisions create a picture of militarism, unique in Venezuelan constitutional history, not found even in former military regimes.

As can be appreciated from the above mentioned, the Venezuelan Constitution incorporated in its text an express and extensive list of constitutional values and principles defined as goals intended to guide the conduct and activities of the state, society and individuals. Thus, those global values and principles do not derive from the process of interpretation and application of the Constitution, particularly by the courts, but are expressly established in the text of the Constitution.

By means of constitutional interpretation, mainly through the Constitutional Chamber of the Supreme Tribunal of Justice, the sense, the scope and the priority character of many of many of the constitutional principles and values have been defined and enriched, even giving some of them a priority vis-à-vis others. Unfortunately, in practice these have been distorted by legislative practice and by the same Supreme Tribunal decisions[1628] originating some constitutional incongruence between what is provided for in the Constitution and what has been decided in the political practice of government.

Chapter 4. State Territory

94. Venezuela is one of the largest Latin American countries located in the northern part of South America with an area of 916,445 square kms. Its boundaries are with Colombia to the west; with Brazil and Colombia to the south and with Guyana to the east. To the north, it has 2,813 km of coast on the Caribbean Sea and the Atlantic Ocean.

95. The territory is defined in Article 10 of the Constitution, in similar terms as in all the previous Constitutions since 1821, by referring to the one that appertained to the General Captaincy of Venezuela (see *supra* paragraphs 2, 5) before the 19 April 1810 political transformation (independence) began (see *supra* paragraph 2), with the modifications resulting from the treaties and arbitral rulings not affected of nullity. The previous 1961 Constitution only referred to the modifications resulting from treaties 'validly adopted by the Republic' (Article 7), a phrase that was added

---

1628   See Allan R Brewer-Carías, *La patología de la justicia constitucional* (San José, Costa Rica, Investigaciones Jurídicas, 2012; (Third edition: Caracas, Editorial Jurídica Venezolana, 2014); *Golpe a la democracia dado por la Sala Constitucional* (Caracas, Editorial Jurídica Venezolana, 2014).

'in order to demonstrate in an unequivocal manner, the will of the Republic to only accept those modifications to its territorial *status* resulting from a free and valid determination'.[1629] These provisions were the consequence of many boundaries the country had with its neighbors.

96. Since the separation of Venezuela from the Great Colombia in 1830 (see *supra* paragraph 9), boundary problems were always present between the two countries, up to 1881 when the disputed boundaries were settled by means of an Arbitral Treaty (14 September 1881), in which, due to the fact that both countries 'could not reach an agreement regarding their respective rights or *uti possidetis juris,* of 1810', they agreed to submit the matter to the judgment and ruling by the Spanish King, as legal arbitrator, in order to establish the territory appertaining before 1810 to the General Captaincy of Venezuela, and to the Viceroyalty of Nueva Granada. Consequently, in March 1891, an Arbitral decision was signed establishing the respective boundaries, which was executed by a pact of 30 December 1898.

97. Regarding Brazil, on 5 May 1859 Venezuela signed a Boundary and River Navigation Treaty with the then Emperor of Brazil, in which the boundaries were determined, being later marked between 1879 and 1905.

98. Also, on 5 August 1857 an Arbitral Convention was signed between Venezuela and the Netherlands regarding the sovereignty over the Aves Island in the Caribbean, a matter that was submitted to the decision of Queen Elizabeth II of Spain, who ruled in 1865 that the island appertained to Venezuela.

99. Regarding the boundaries with the former British colony of Guyana, the aforementioned 1961 Constitution provision (Article 7) that opened the possibility for the country to formally challenge the validity of treaties or arbitral awards concerning its borders, acquired particular significance, particularly regarding the 1899 Arbitration decision that established the border with British Guiana, which Venezuela considered had ignored its territorial rights derived from the incorporation of the Province of Guyana, created in 1868, in the General Captaincy of Venezuela.

In effect, after the 13 August 1814, Anglo–Dutch Treaty, the colonial possessions of the Dutch in the Americas were returned to what they were at the beginning of the war in 1803, with the exceptions of the Cape of Good Hope and the South American settlements of Demerara, Essequibo and Berbice, which were ceded to the United Kingdom, being consolidated in 1831 as British Guiana. The Treaty did not define the western boundary of the British colony regarding the newly re-establish Venezuelan State (1830) (see *supra* paragraph 9), and particularly with its province of Guyana, so after the British commissioned Robert Schomburgk to delineate that boundary (1835), the Venezuelan–Guyana Boundary Dispute officially began when in 1840 the Venezuelan Government protested British encroachment on Venezuelan

---

1629   See José A. Zambrano Velazco, *Sumario Jurídico de la territorialidad* (Maracaibo-San Cristóbal, 1983); Allan R. Brewer-Carías, 'Territorio de Venezuela. Período Republicano', in *Diccionario de Historia de Venezuela*, vol. II (Caracas: Fundación Polar, 1989), 867–874.

territory, considering that the borders of the former Guyana Province of the General Captaincy of Venezuela extended as far east as the Essequibo River.[1630]

After claims and protests, and due to the United States' threats of intervention, the United Kingdom agreed in 1897, by means of the Treaty of Washington entered into by the United Kingdom and Venezuela, to let an international tribunal arbitrate the boundary. On 3 October 1899, the Tribunal issued a decision determining the boundary line between the Colony of British Guiana and the United States of Venezuela, and without any written opinion or explanation, awarded more than 90% of the disputed territory of British Guiana to the United Kingdom, with Venezuela receiving the mouth of the Orinoco River and a short strait of the Atlantic coastline just to the east.

100. The 1899 Arbitral award coincided with one of the main nineteenth century internal political struggles of Venezuela, in which a Revolution (the Liberal Restorative Revolution) seized State power and consolidated the authoritarian government that controlled the country for almost the entire first half of the twentieth century (see *supra* paragraphs 15, 16). The newly established government was also involved in a bitter international struggle which arose because of unpaid loans; provoking Great Britain, Germany and Italy to send a joint naval expedition to the Venezuelan coast to blockade seaports and capture Venezuelan gunboats (see *supra* paragraph 15; *infra* 328).

101. In 1949 the *American Journal of International Law*,[1631] published after his death, a Memorandum written by Severo Mallet-Prevost (11 August 1944), a lawyer who had acted as a junior counsel for Venezuela at the Paris 1899 Tribunal, adducing that the Arbitral Tribunal's president had coerced several of its members into assenting to the final decision, that was the result of a political deal between Britain and Russia. Consequently, under the 1961 Constitution, Venezuela claimed that their rights to the Essequibo territory had been ignored by a tribunal which had settled the frontier based not on a judicial process, but on a political deal, filing in 1962 a formal territorial reclaim before the United Kingdom.

In 1966, an 'Agreement to resolve the controversy between Venezuela and the United Kingdom of Great Britain and Northern Ireland regarding the Venezuela and British Guiana Borders' was signed in Geneva, in consideration that the independence of British Guiana was going to be proclaimed as it happened that same year. Venezuela recognized the new State of Guyana with the stipulation that it 'does not imply recognition or in any way renouncement or diminishment of the territorial rights that Venezuela is claiming'. Afterward, Guyana became a State party of the Geneva Agreement (Article VII), Venezuela reiterated its claim that the Paris Tribunal Arbitral decision of 1899 was 'null and void', considering that the *Guayana* Essequibo territory claimed by Venezuela 'has its east border with the new State of

1630   See Tomás E. Carrillo Batalla (Coord.), *La Reclamación Venezolana sobre la Guayana Esequiba* (Caracas: Academia de Ciencias Políticas y Sociales, 2009); Allan R. Brewer-Carías, 'Guyana-Venezuela Border Dispute', in *Max Planck Encyclopedia of Public International Law* (Oxford University Press, 2008).

1631   N° 43 (3), July 1949, 528–530.

Guyana, on the Essequibo river line, from its origins to its discharge on the Atlantic Ocean'.

On 18 June 1970, the governments of Venezuela, Britain, and Guyana signed the Protocol of Port-of-Spain, which suspended for a period of twelve years the application of Article IV of the Geneva Agreement, providing for the parties to explore the possibility of improving their understanding and to create a more convenient environment to continue with the procedures set forth in the Geneva Agreement. The protocol was to end on 18 July 1982, but one year before, the Venezuelan Government publicly announced its decision not to extend its term, provoking the reactivation of the Geneva Agreement provisions, in the sense that the claim would be regulated by its Article IV, which refers to the peaceful settlement means set forth in Article 33 of the United Nations Charter. Accordingly, the matter was eventually referred to the Secretary General of the United Nations, for the selection of a peaceful settlement mean, being the dispute settlement since 1985, in his hands, through a United Nations-based Good Officer process.

102. Regarding the delimitation of Venezuelan territorial waters, the first Treaty on the matter in international history was the Treaty on Maritime Waters of the Paria Gulf signed by Venezuela and Great Britain on 26 February 1942, establishing the delimitation of waters between the continental territory of Venezuela and the Island of Trinidad. This Treaty was later substituted by the Treaty signed between Venezuela and Trinidad and Tobago on Maritime and Submarines Waters in November 1990.

The national statutes related to Territorial Water, Contiguous Zone, and Continental Shell of 1956 and to Exclusive Economic Zone of 1978, set forth that in cases in which the limits established according to its provisions caused superposition regarding foreign waters, the matter must be resolved according to international law. Consequently Venezuela has subscribed to International Treaties for the delimitation of maritime and submarines areas with all the States with boundaries of waters, except Colombia: on 28 March 1978, with the United States of America regarding the Islands of Puerto Rico and Saint Croix (Law 20 July 1978); on 30 March 1978, with the Netherlands regarding the Netherlands Antilles (Aruba, Bonaire and Curaçao) (Law 20 July 1978); on 3 March 1979, with Dominican Republic (Law 26 July 1979); on 19 July 1980, with France regarding the Islands of Guadalupe and Martinique and the Island of Aves (Law 15 July 1982).

103. The national territory, being the State organized as a Federal Decentralized one, is politically organized according to Article 16 of the Constitution, and divided into twenty-three states, one Capital District where the capital city of Caracas is located (see *infra* paragraphs 209), Federal Dependencies that are the Venezuelan Islands in the Caribbean Sea, and Federal Territories.[1632] The twenty-three states are

---

1632   See Armando Rodríguez, 'Las nuevas bases constitucionales de la estructura político territorial en Venezuela', in *Revista de Derecho Administrativo*, N° 10 (septiembre-diciembre) (Caracas: Editorial Sherwood, 2001), 169–200; Ramón Crazut, 'Comentarios al Título II de la Constitución de 1999 sobre el espacio geográfico y la división política', in *Revista de Derecho Público*, N° 81 (Caracas: Editorial Jurídica Venezolana, 2000), 40–46;. Tulio Álvarez, 'El concepto de territorio y su integración en el caso venezolano', in *Estudios de Derecho Público*, ed. en Román Duque Corredor, y Jesús María Casal (Coord.), vol. II (Caracas: Universidad Católica Andrés Bello, 2004), 1–50.

the following: Amazonas, Anzoátegui, Apure, Aragua, Barinas, Bolívar, Carabobo, Cojedes, Delta Amacuro, Falcón, Guárico, Lara, Mérida, Miranda, Monagas, Nueva Esparta, Portuguesa, Sucre, Táchira, Trujillo, Vargas, Yaracuy and Zulia. The Capital District exists, which in 2000 substituted the former traditional Federal District founded in 1863, comprising part of the City of Caracas, which is the Capital of the Republic. In 2009 the Capital District was organized but contrary to the Constitution, just as a 'national' entity dependent from the Central Government.[1633] The Constitution also establishes Federal Dependencies, which comprise the Venezuelan islands in the Caribbean Sea, except those integrating the state of Nueva Esparta (Islands of Margarita, Coche and Cubagua). Following a tradition also initiated in 1864, the Constitution also provided for the Federal Territories (Article 16), which nonetheless are currently non-existent. The last two Federal Territories were the Delta Amacuro Federal territory in the Orinoco Delta and the Amazonas Federal territory in the south of the country, which were transformed into states in 1991 and 1992.[1634] In 2011 the creation of a new federal territory was announced by the Government comprising some of the Islands near the coast (*Territorio Insular Miranda*).

Chapter 5. Population (Demographic Data)

104. The national population census of 2011 shows a total Venezuelan population of 28,946,101 (2014 estimated 30,206,307), mainly being concentrated in the coastal and mountain zones, which represents approximately 20% of the territory and more than 80% of the population. The region of the plains, with 30% of the territory has only 10.2% of the total population, and the Guayana region with 50% of the territory of the country, only has 6% of the population.

The density of the population is of 25.2 inhabitants per Km^2, being the highest one in the Capital District (4,240 inhabitants per Km^2), followed by the states of Carabobo, Nueva Esparta, Miranda and Aragua. The lowest density is located in the southern states of Amazonas, Delta Amacuro, Apure and Bolivar, where the indigenous people population (less than 1.5% of the total population) (see *infra* paragraphs 556 et seq.), is mainly concentrated.

The Venezuelan population is characterized by being an aggregation of mixed races, a product of the historical *mestizaje* of the country, whose origin are to be found in the colonial times with the unions of Indians and Spaniards and since the sixteenth century, with the African population. After World War II, an important process of migration took place in the country and the country received many Spanish, Portuguese and Italian migrants who were rapidly integrated in the country. During the 1970s, a similar process of migration took place with people from South

---

1633   See the Special Law on the Organization and Regime of the Capital District, *Gaceta Oficial* N°
       39.156 of 13 Apr. 2009. See Allan R. Brewer-Carías, 'La problemática del régimen jurídico del 'Distrito Capital' en la estructura federal del Estado en Venezuela, y su inconstitucional regulación legal',
       AIDA Opera Prima de Derecho Administrativo, N° 5 (México: Universidad Nacional Autónoma de
       México, enero-junio 2009, 2009), 81–119; and Allan R. Brewer-Carías et al., *Leyes sobre el Distrito
       Capital y el Área metropolitana de Caracas* (Caracas: Editorial Jurídica Venezolana, 2009).

1634   See Allan R. Brewer-Carías, 'El régimen de los Territorios y Dependencias Federales', in *Revista de
       Derecho Público*, N° 18 (Caracas, Editorial Jurídica Venezolana, 1984), 85–98.

American countries, mainly due to the development of the Venezuelan economy compared to the recession in other counties. Currently all those processes of migration have given rise to a completely integrated population without any sort of inter racial conflicts, in spite of the recurrent efforts made by the government since 2000 to provoke social class conflicts.

1055. The official language of the country is 'Castilian' (Spanish). Nonetheless, according to Article 9 of the Constitution, the indigenous languages, are also of official use for the indigenous peoples and being part of national and humanity cultural heritage, must be respected in all the national territory[1635] (see *infra* paragraph 558).

Chapter 6. Constitutional Relationship between Church and State

106. The most important religion in Venezuela has always been the Roman Catholic one. Nonetheless, except in the 1811 Constitution where the Catholic, Apostolic and Roman Religion was declared the only and exclusive one of the population as well as the State's religion (Article 1), in no other Constitution has such a provision been included. In the 1857 constitutional reform, a provision establishing that the State was to protect the Catholic religion (Article 5) was in effect only for a few months (see *supra* paragraph 11). Since the 1864 Constitution (Articles 14, 13), religious freedom has been expressly declared and guarantee in the country (see *infra* paragraphs 446, 502).

107. However, the separation between Church and State is the principle established in Venezuela since the nineteenth century, after decades in which the State had the right to be involved in Church affairs. In effect, since the Independence, the new independent State assumed the Right to *Patronato Eclesiastico* that the Spanish Crown used to have regarding the Catholic Church. Consequently, on 25 July 1824, the Congress of the Republic of Colombia passed an Ecclesiastic *Patronato* Law, conferring to the State the power to be involved in the administration and organization of the Catholic Church, and even regarding the discipline of the Church and the administration of the Church properties.

During the presidency of Antonio Guzmán Blanco (see *supra* paragraph 13), the traditional conflicts between the State and the Church were exacerbated, when the government suspended the Seminars, imposing thelaic character of education. In 1873, the civil marriage was formally decreed, and the civil registry was organized out of the reach of the Church. All these provisions were incorporated in the first Civil Code approved that same year, substituting the former ecclesiastic provisions, and since then, have been the general regime of civil law applied in the country. In 1874 all Convents and Cloisters were dissolved, and the ecclesiastic properties taken by the State.

108. Later, in 1911, a Decree was adopted on the Supreme Inspection of Cults, where references were made to the Ecclesiastic *Patronato* Law. These inspection powers were also included in the 1961 Constitution, in which after establishing the freedom of religion (Article 65), expressly regulated the Ecclesiastic *Patronato* right, establishing with the same trend as the 1947 Constitution, that nonetheless,

---

1635 Indigenous Languages Law, *Gaceta Oficial* N° 38.981 of 28 Jul. 2008.

international agreements could be signed to regulate the relations between the Church and the State (Article 130).[1636]

Based on this provision, a *Modus Vivendi* was signed in 1964 between the Saint Siege and the Venezuelan State regulating the relations between the Church and the State, substituting the old provisions referred to the Ecclesiastic *Patronato*. In the 1999 Constitution, no reference at all is made to these matters, being limited to establishing the freedom of religion and cult that the State must guarantee. The Constitution also proclaimed the independence and autonomy of all churches and religions (Article 59).

Chapter 7. Constitutional Principles Regarding International Relations

109. The Preamble of the Constitutions establishes the political, social, cultural and international goals of the State and the Society, and among the latter it defined as an essential goal of the State to pacifically cooperate with all nations, through pacific solution of controversies, rejecting war. The international cooperation must be governed by the principles of non-intervention in other countries' affairs, and of the self-determination of peoples, according to the universal and indivisible international guarantee of human rights and the democratization of international society.

The Preamble also refers to the values that must govern the International relations of the Republic, like nuclear disarmament, environmental equilibrium as well as the healthy environment as a common and non-renounceable human heritage.

Another of the main goals of the State mentioned in the Preamble that must govern the action of the State, is the promotion and consolidation of the Latin American integration, which at that moment was referring to the Andean Community of Nations of which Venezuela was a member up to 2006.

110. In addition to the Preamble, Article 152 of the Constitution also refers to the international relations of the Republic, pointing out that they must coincide with the goals of the State regarding the exercise of its sovereignty and the peoples' interest. Those relations must be governed by the principles of independence, equality between States, free determination and non-intervention in internal matters of other States, the pacific solution of controversies, cooperation, human rights respect, solidarity among the people in their fight for emancipation and the welfare of human kind.[1637] In addition, the same Article 152 provides that the Republic must maintain the most firm and decided defence of these principles and of the democratic practice in all international organs and institutions.

111. Regarding the Latin American integration process, the 1999 Constitution incorporated a major reform providing for constitutional basis for such process, giving foundations to the possibility of the transfer of State powers to supra-national

---

1636   See José Rodríguez Iturbe, *Iglesia y Estado en Venezuela 1824–1964* (Caracas, 1968); and Jesús Leopoldo Sánchez, 'El convenio Eclesiástico, las Constituciones Hispanoamericanas y los Códigos Nacionales', in *Estudios sobre la Constitución. Libro Homenaje a Rafael Caldera*, vol. III (Caracas: Universidad Central de Venezuela, 1979), 1723 y ss.

1637   See in general, Juan Carlos Sainz Borgo, 'Régimen internacional de la Constitución de 1999', in *Revista de la Facultad de Ciencias Jurídicas y Políticas,* N° 121 (Caracas, 2001), 143–209.

entities. The previous constitutional situation was precarious, due to the provision of Article 108 of the 1961 Constitution, which in fact impeded Venezuela's ability to decisively enter with clear constitutional solutions into the process of integration.[1638] On the contrary, and with the purpose of giving specific constitutional grounding to any supra-national integration process, Article 153 of the 1999 Constitution incorporated a new express clause on the subject, in which, in addition to imposing on the Republic the duty to promote and favour the Latin American and Caribbean integration in order to advance towards the creation of a Community of Nations, it established the possibility for the Republic to participate by means of treaties, in the creation of supra-national organizations, to which powers may be attributed or transferred to conduct the processes of integration that the Constitution assigns to the branches of government. Accordingly, the same constitutional provision establishes that the resulting communitarian law *(derecho comunitario)*, not only have direct and immediate effect in internal law, because it is considered to be an integral part of the existing legal order, but it also has to be preferred over national laws with which they could be in conflict.[1639]

These provisions of the Constitution were very important regarding the only integration process in Latin America with a supra-national organization, that is the Andean Community of Nations, which had its origin in the Cartagena Agreement (*Andean Pact*) of 1969, initially signed by Bolivia, Chile, Colombia, Ecuador and Perú, and to which Venezuela adhered to in 1973 as a Member State. In 1996 the Andean Pact of sub regional integration was transformed into the Andean Community of Nations, conformed by supra-national organs such as the Commission, the Andean Court of Justice and the Andean Parliament.[1640] Unfortunately Venezuela

---

1638   See Allan R. Brewer-Carías, *Implicaciones constitucionales del proceso de integración económica regional* (Caracas, 1997); 'Las exigencias constitucionales de los procesos de integración y la experiencia latinoamericana', in *Congreso de Academias Iberoamericanas de Derecho* (Córdoba: Academia Nacional de Derecho y Ciencias Sociales de Córdoba, 1999), 279–317; 'Las implicaciones constitucionales de la integración económica regional', in *El Derecho Venezolano a finales del Siglo XX* (Caracas: Academia de Ciencias Políticas y Sociales, 1998), 407–511.

1639   See in general, Jorge L. Suárez, 'La Constitución venezolana y el Derecho Comunitario', in *El Derecho Público a comienzos del siglo XXI. Estudios homenaje al Profesor Allan R. Brewer-Carías,* vol. III (Madrid: Instituto de Derecho Público, UCV, Civitas Ediciones, 2003), 253–276; Marianella Zubillaga, 'Los fundamentos del Derecho Comunitario y su soporte constitucional: la experiencia europea y andina', *id.,* 281–307; Jorge L. Suárez M., 'La Comunidad Andina, la responsabilidad del Estado y la Constitución venezolana', in *Estudios de Derecho Público: Libro Homenaje a Humberto J. La Roche Rincón,* vol. II (Caracas: Tribunal Supremo de Justicia, 2001), 489–648; Jorge L. Suárez M., 'La Constitución venezolana de 1999 y la integración regional', in *Estudios de Derecho Administrativo: Libro Homenaje a la Universidad Central de Venezuela,* vol. I (Caracas: Imprenta Nacional, 2001), 440–472; Nelly Herrera Bond, 'El Derecho Comunitario en la nueva Constitución', in *Comentarios a la Constitución de la República Bolivariana de Venezuela* (Caracas: Vadell Hermanos Editores, 2000), 7–10; Jorge Petit, 'Los principios de auto–ejecutividad e inmediatez de los tratados internacionales en materia de integración a la luz de la Constitución Venezolana de 1999, en el marco de la Comunidad Andina de Naciones', in *Revista de la Facultad de Ciencias Jurídicas y Políticas de la UCV,* N° 122 (Caracas, 2001), 153–168; and Juan Carlos Sainz Borgo, 'La regulación constitucional del proceso de Integración Andino', in *Libro Homenaje a Enrique Tejera París, Temas sobre la Constitución de 1999* (Caracas: Centro de Investigaciones Jurídicas (CEIN), 2001), 241 a 271.

1640   See Allan R. Brewer-Carías, 'El largo camino para la consolidación de las bases constitucionales de la integración regional andina y su abandono por el régimen autoritario de Venezuela', in André Sad-

withdrew from the Andean Community in 2006, and since then has asked to be incorporated in the Mercosur process without success.

112. Finally, it must be mentioned that according to Article 155 of the Constitution, in all international treaties, covenants and agreements signed by the Republic, a clause must be inserted according to which the parties are obliged to resolve the controversies that could arise between them, derived from their interpretation or execution, by the pacific means recognized in International law provided that it is possible in the procedure followed by the signing.

SELECTED BIBLIOGRAPHY

Alfredo Arismendi. *Contribución a la Bibliografía del Derecho Constitucional y su Historia.* Caracas: Editorial Jurídica Venezolana, 2005.

1.1. *Constitutional History of Venezuela*

Allan R. Brewer-Carías. *Instituciones Políticas y Constitucionales.* 7 Vols. San Cristóbal-Caracas: Universidad Católica del Táchira, Editorial Jurídica Venezolana, 1996.

Allan R. Brewer-Carías. *Las Constituciones de Venezuela.* 2 Vols. Caracas: Academia de Ciencias Políticas y Sociales, 2008.

Allan R. Brewer-Carías. *Historia Constitucional de Venezuela.* 2 Vols. Caracas: Editorial Alfa, 2008; Second edition, Caracas, Editorial Jurídica Venezolana, Colección Tratado de Derecho Constitucional, Vol. I, 2013.

Ambrosio Oropeza. *Evolución Constitucional de nuestra República.* Caracas, 1944; *Evolución constitucional de nuestra República, y otros textos.* Caracas: Biblioteca de la Academia de Ciencias Políticas y Sociales, 1985.

Ambrosio Perera. *Historia Orgánica de Venezuela.* Caracas: Editorial Venezuela, 1943.

Elena Plaza y Ricardo Combellas (Coordinadores). *Procesos Constituyentes y Reformas Constitucionales en la Historia de Venezuela: 1811–1999.* Caracas: Universidad Central de Venezuela, 2005.

José Gil Fortoul. *Historia Constitucional de Venezuela.* 2 Vols. Berlín: Carl Heyman, 1907; 3 Vols. Caracas: Ministerio de Educación, 1953.

LuisMariñas Otero. *Las Constituciones de Venezuela.* Madrid: Instituto de Estudios Políticos, 1965.

Ulises Picón Rivas. *Índice Constitucional de Venezuela.* Caracas: Editorial Elite, 1944.

Mariano Picón Salas et al. *Venezuela Independiente 1810–1960.* Caracas Fundación Mendoza, 1962.

---

dy (Coordinador), *Dereito Público Econômico Supranacional* (Rio de Janeiro: Methoius Consultoría Jurídica Internacional, 2009).

Pablo Ruggeri Parra. *Historia Política y Constitucional de Venezuela.* 2 Vols. Caracas, 1949.

R.J. Velásquez et al. *Venezuela Moderna, Medio Siglo de Historia 1926–1976.* Barcelona: Fundación Eugenio Mendoza, 1979.

Pedro Vivas. *Guía de Historia Constitucional.* Caracas: Universidad Santa María, 1985.

2 2. *1999 Constitution Making-Process*

Allan R. Brewer-Carías. *Asamblea Constituyente y Ordenamiento Constitucional.* Caracas: Academia de Ciencias Políticas y Sociales, 1998.

Allan R. Brewer-Carias. *Poder constituyente originario y Asamblea Nacional Constituyente (Comentarios sobre la interpretación jurisprudencial relativa a la naturaleza, la misión y los límites de la Asamblea Nacional Constituyente).* Caracas: Editorial Jurídica Venezolana, 1999.

Allan R. Brewer-Carías. *Debate Constituyente, Aportes a la Asamblea Nacional Constituyente.* 3 Vols. Caracas: Fundación de Derecho Público, Editorial Jurídica Venezolana, 1999.

Allan R. Brewer-Carías. *Golpe de Estado y Proceso Constituyente en Venezuela.* México: Universidad Nacional Autónoma de México, 2002.

Allan R. Brewer-Carías. *Asamblea Constituyente y Proceso Constituyente.* Caracas: Editorial Jurídica Venezolana, Colección Tratado de Derecho Constitucional, Vol. VI, 2014

Carlos M. Escarrá Malavé. *Proceso Político y Constituyente. Papeles Constituyentes.* Maracaibo, 1999.

Claudia Nikken. *La Cour Suprême de Justice et la Constitution vénézuélienne du 23 Janvier 1961.* (Paris II), Paris: Thése Docteur de l'Université Panthéon Assas, 2001.

Hermánn Escarrá Malavé. *Democracia, reforma constitucional y asamblea constituyente.* Caracas, 1995.

Lolymar Hernández Camargo. *La Teoría del Poder Constituyente. Un caso de estudio: el proceso constituyente venezolano de 1999.* San Cristóbal: Universidad Catóilica del Táchira, 2000.

Lolymar Hernández Camargo. *El Proceso Constituyente Venezolano de 1999.* Caracas: Academia de Ciencias Políticas y Sociales, 2008.

Juan M. Raffalli Arismendi. *Revolución, Constituyente y Oferta Electoral.* Caracas, 1998.

Ricardo Combellas. *¿Qué es la Constituyente?, Voz para el futuro de Venezuela.* Caracas, 1998.

Ricardo Combellas. *Poder Constituyente.* Caracas, 1999.

Ricardo Combellas (coordinador). *Constituyente. Aportes al Debate.* COPRE, Konrad Adenauer Stiftung. Caracas, 1999.

Roberto Viciano Pastor y Rubén Martínez Dalmau. *Cambio político y proceso constituyente en Venezuela (1998-2000).* Valencia, 2001.

Asamblea Constituyente: Salida democrática a la crisis, Folletos para la Discusión N° 18. Caracas: Comisión Presidencial para la Reforma del Estado, 1992.

Tulio Álvarez. *La Constituyente. Todo lo que Usted necesita saber.* Caracas: Libros de El Nacional, 1998.

3. *1999 Constitution and Constitutional Texts*

Alfredo Arismendi. *Derecho Constitucional.* 2 Vols. Caracas: Universidad Central de Venezuela, 2002.

Allan R. Brewer-Carías. *La Constitución de 1999.* Caracas: Editorial Jurídica Venezolana, 2000.

Allan R. Brewer-Carías. *La Constitución de 1999. Derecho Constitucional Venezolano.* 2 Vols. Caracas: Editorial Jurídica Venezolana, 2004.

Allan R. Brewer-Carías. *La Constitución de 1999 y la Enmienda Constitucional No. 1.* Caracas: Editorial Jurídica Venezolana, 2011.

Allan R. Brewer-Carías. *La Constitución de 1999: El Estado Democrático y Social de Derecho,* Caracas: Editorial Jurídica Venezolana, Colección Tratado de Derecho Constitucional, Vol. VII, 2014.

Alfonso Rivas Quintero. *Derecho Constitucional.* Valencia, 2002.

Hildegard Rondón de Sansó. *Análisis de la Constitución venezolana de 1999.* Caracas: Editorial Ex Libris, 2001.

José Peña Solís. *Lecciones de Derecho Constitucional General, Volumen I, Tomo I y II.* Caracas: Universidad Central de Venezuela, 2008.

AAVV, La Constitución de 1999. Caracas: Academia de Ciencias Políticas y Sociales, 2000.

Ricardo Combellas. *Derecho Constitucional: una introducción al estudio de la Constitución de la República Bolivariana de Venezuela.* Caracas: Mc Graw Hill, 2001.

Román Duque Corredor. *Temario de Derecho Constitucional y de Derecho Público.* Caracas: Legis, 2008.

Tulio Alberto Álvarez. *Instituciones Políticas y Derecho Constitucional.* Caracas: Tomo I, Ediciones Liber, 2008.

4. *Proposed and Rejected 2007 Constitutional Reform*

Allan R. Brewer-Carías. *Hacia la consolidación de un Estado Socialista, Centralizado y Militarista. Comentarios sobre el alcance y sentido de las propuestas de reforma Constitucional 2007.* Caracas: Editorial Jurídica Venezolana, 2007.

Allan R. Brewer-Carías. *La reforma constitucional de 2007 (Comentarios al proyecto inconstitucionalmente sancionado por la Asamblea Nacional el 2 de noviembre de 2007).* Caracas, Editorial Jurídica Venezolana, 2007.

Estudios sobre la Reforma Constitucional, Revista de Derecho Público. N° 112 (octubre-diciembre 2007). Caracas: Editorial Jurídica Venezolana, 2007.

Héctor Turupial Cariello. *Texto Oculto de la Reforma.* Caracas: Fundación de Estudios de Derecho Administrativo, 2008.

Manuel Raachadell. *Socialismo del Siglo XXI. Análisis de la reforma Constitucional propuesta por el Presidente Chávez en agosto de 2007.* Caracas: Fundación de Estudios de Derecho Administrativo, Editorial Jurídica Venezolana, 2008.

5.   *Other Constitutional Law Texts*

Allan R. Brewer-Carías. *Instituciones Políticas y Constitucionales.* 8 Vols. San Cristóbal-Caracas: Universidad Católica del Táchira, Editorial Jurídica Venezolana, 1996–1998.

Allan R. Brewer-Carías. *Reflexiones sobre el Constitucionalismo en América.* Caracas: Editorial Jurídica Venezolana, 2001.

Allan R. Brewer-Carías. *Estudios sobre el Estado Constitucional (2005-2006).* Caracas: Editorial Jurídica Venezolana, 2007.

Ernesto Wolf. *Tratado de derecho constitucional.* 2 Vols. Caracas: Tipografía Americana, 1945.

Humberto J. La Roche. *Derecho Constitucional.* Valencia: Parte general, Vadell Ed, 1991.

José Guillermo Andueza. *Apuntes de Derecho Constitucional.* 2 vols. Caracas: Editorial Inquietud, 1982.

PART I. SOURCES OF CONSTITUTIONAL LAW

Chapter 1. The Constitution

§1.   *Supremacy and Rigidity*

113. The principle of constitutional supremacy is expressly established in Article 7 of the 1999 Constitution setting forth that 'the Constitution is the supreme norm and the foundation of the legal order', and that, 'all persons and organs that exercise public power are subject to this Constitution'. For such purpose, the provisions of the Constitution as superior law are always directly enforceable and applicable; and the Constitution is essentially the ground norm for the interpretation of the entire legal order.

This character of the Constitution as supreme norm and the foundation of the legal order is also accompanied by the express prescription that its provisions are obligatory for all branches of government as well as for individuals. The most important consequence of this express consecration of the principle of constitutional supremacy is the establishment of the system of judicial review and particularly the obligation of all judges to assure the integrity of the Constitution (Article 334) (see *supra* paragraph 59; *infra* paragraph 640).

However, the supreme law character of the Constitution implies that it has derogatory power regarding any other norm sanctioned prior to its enactment; and in addition, that any act approved after the enactment of the Constitution that could contradict its provisions are considered null and void.

Finally, the supreme character of the Constitution means that it is accompanied by the principle of rigidity in the sense that the constitutional text is out of the reach of the ordinary legislator and that it cannot be modified by the procedure of forma-tion of the ordinary laws, but only by means of the specific procedures set forth in the Constitution for its revision with popular participation.[1641]

§2. *Procedure for Constitutional Review*

114. In effect, the rigidity of the Constitution materialized through the provision of special procedures and institutional channels for constitutional review,[1642] implies that the National Assembly through the procedure for enacting ordinary legislation, may in no case modify the Constitution or perform constitutional review.

The Constitution of 1999 contains three institutional mechanisms for constitutio-nal review, distinguishable according to the importance and magnitude of the chan-ges proposed, which includes the Amendment, the Constitutional Reform, and the National Constituent Assembly.[1643]

I. *Constitutional Amendment*

115. The first constitutional review procedure is the 'Constitutional Amendment' which has been established for the purpose of adding or of modifying one or more provisions to the Constitution without altering the text's fundamental structures (Ar-ticle 340).

According to Article 341.1, this amendment procedure can be initiated by a peti-tion signed by 15% of Citizens inscribed in the civil and electoral register; by 30% of the members of the National Assembly; or, by the President of the Republic in a decision that must be adopted in the Council of Ministers.

When the initiative stems from the National Assembly, the amendment proposi-tion requires the approval of a majority of its members, and the draft must be deba-ted and approved, following the procedures constitutionally established for the pas-sage of legislation. (Article 341.2). This means that a legislative debate of a propo-sed amendment only takes place when the amendment procedure is initiated by the National Assembly which, in that case, must approve it. Thus, if an Amendment is proposed by popular initiative or is initiated by the President of the Republic, that

---

1641 See Allan R. Brewer-Carías, 'La intervención del pueblo en la revisión constitucional en América latina', in *El derecho público a los 100 números de la Revista de Derecho Público 1980-2005* (Ca-racas: Editorial Jurídica Venezolana, 2006), 41–52.

1642 See Allan R. Brewer-Carías, 'Los procedimientos de revisión constitucional en Venezuela', in *I Procedimenti di revisione costituzionale nel Diritto Comparato*, ed. Eduardo Rozo Acuña (Coord.) (Urbino, Italia, 1999), 137–181; 'Modelos de revisión constitucional en América Latina', in *Boletín de la Academia de Ciencias Políticas y Sociales*, enero-diciembre 2003, N° 141 (Caracas, 2004), 115–156.

1643 Véase Claudia Nikken, 'Breves consideraciones sobre el ejercicio del poder de revisión en Venezuela: a partir de la vigente constitución', in *Revista de Derecho Público*, N° 109 (Caracas: Editorial Jurídi-ca Venezolana, 2007), 27–34; Lolymar Hernández Camargo, 'El Poder Constituyente como principio legitimador de la Constitución', in *El Derecho Público a comienzos del siglo XXI. Estudios homena-je al Profesor Allan R. Brewer-Carías*, vol. I (Madrid: Instituto de Derecho Público, UCV, Civitas Ediciones, 2003), 113–130; José Vicente Haro, 'Sobre los límites materiales de la enmienda y la re-forma constitucional', in *Estudios de Derecho Público*, ed. Román Duque Corredor y Jesús María Casal (Coord.), vol. II (Caracas: Universidad Católica Andrés Bello, 2004), 373–420.

proposal is the one to be directly submitted to popular approval by referendum (Article 341.3), without any kind of debate or approval by the National Assembly. In the referendum at least 25% of registered voters must concur, and in order to approve the proposal, it must be voted for by a simple majority of those voting (Article 73).

Once approved by the people, the President of the Republic is obligated to promulgate Amendments within ten days of their approval (Article 346).

The Constitution requires that Amendments once approved by referendum, be numbered consecutively, and published as a continuation of the Constitution without altering the original text. However, articles amended are to be annotated with a footnote corresponding to the number and date of their amendments.

Up to 2015, the only Constitutional Amendment to the Constitution was sanctioned and approved by the people in 2009, regarding articles 160, 162, 174, 192 and 230, providing for the possibility of indefinite re-election of all public elected officials. [1644]

II. *Constitutional Reforms*

1116. The second constitutional review procedure established in the 1999 Constitution is the 'Constitutional Reforms', which in Article 342 is designed for partial revisions of the Constitution and for the substitution of one or several provisions but without modifying the structure and fundamental principles of the constitutional text.

The differences between an 'Amendment' and a 'Reform' are thus subtle. The former enables, 'the addition or modification of one or several articles of the Constitution, without altering its fundamental structure' (Article 342), while the latter has as its objective, 'the substitution of one or several of its provisions which do not modify the structure and principles of the constitutional text' (Article 340).

From these provisions, it can be said that the 'Amendment' procedure is designed to 'add or modify' articles of the Constitution, while the 'Reform' procedure is designed to 'substitute' articles, but in neither case can the fundamental structure of the Constitution be altered. That is why the 'constitutional reform' proposed and sanctioned in 2007, which was rejected by the people by referendum held in December 2007, was formulated in defraudation of the Constitution (see *infra* paragraphs 250 ff., , 625 ff.), because it was seeking to modify essential elements of the State through a procedure established for other purposes (see *infra* paragraph 36).

Nonetheless, the procedure for the 'Constitutional Reform' is more complicated, and requires that a proposed reform be debated and approved by the National Assembly before it can be submitted to referendum. The initiative of the 'Reform' is assigned to the National Assembly when approved by a Resolution approved by a majority of its members; to the President of the Republic in a decision adopted in a Council of Ministers; or, to the people through a petition signed by no less than 15%

[1644]   See *Official Gazette* N° 5,908 Extra. Of Feb. 19, 2009.

of the registered voters (Article 342). In all these cases, the initiative must be brought before the National Assembly.

117. Once the 'Reform' proposal is filed before the National Assembly, according to Article 343, the draft must be submitted to debate, and have three discussions: a first discussion in the period of the Assembly corresponding to the period of the filing of the draft; a second discussion by Titles or by chapters, depending on the draft; and a third discussion, article by article. The Assembly must approve the 'Reform' draft in a term of no more that two years since the draft was filed and accepted. The 'reform' proposal must be considered as approved if voted by two-third of the members of the Assembly.

Once the Reform draft is approved, within thirty days it must be submitted to referendum (Article 344), in which the people are generally required to vote on the Reform in its entirety, that is, as a whole. However, up to one-third of the Reform draft could be submitted to separate vote when one-third of the National Assembly so decides, or if it is requested by the President of the Republic in his initiative of the Reform, or is requested by no less than 5% of registered voters in case of popular initiative.

A 'Constitutional Reform' must be declared approved if the number of affirmative votes exceeds the number of negative votes (Article 345). The President of the Republic is required to promulgate a reform within ten days of its approval. If the President fails to do so according to the provisions of Article 216 of the Constitution, the President of the Assembly must proceed to promulgate it (Article 346).

In the event that a constitutional reform fails to be approved, that is, when rejected by popular vote in the referendum, Article 345 prohibits it from being filed again before the Assembly in the remainder of the constitutional term. Nothing is established in the Constitution regarding the effects of the rejection of 'constitutional amendments', and also, nothing is established regarding the possibility to file the same rejected 'constitutional reform' proposal, through the procedure of a 'constitutional amendment', as it is now occurring. The case is a matter of interpretation and of determining the intention of the Constituent power, which was to establish a limit regarding the possibility of repeatedly asking the direct expression of the will of the people by referenda. That is, once the people have expressed their popular will through a referendum, it is not possible to ask the people again and again, without limits, on the same matters in the same constitutional term.

For instance, the matter of the continuous presidential re-election in 2007 was proposed through a 'constitutional reform' draft formulated by the President of the Republic in 2007 and was rejected by the people in the Referendum held on December 2007. Nonetheless, in spite of this prohibition, in December 2008, the President of the Republic proposed again to modify the Constitution, using the 'Amendment' seeking his indefinite re-election, although the same proposal was already rejected in his same constitutional term in the Constitutional reform referendum held in December 2007. The National Assembly proposed then a constitutional amendment of Articles 160, 162, 174, 192 and 230 of the Constitution, which was approved in the referendum of 14 February 2009, eliminating all the limits established for the re-election of public officials.[1645] (see *infra* paragraphs 155, 233, 672).

III. *The National Constituent Assembly*

118. The 1999 Constitution, which was a product of a National Constituent Assembly not foreseen nor regulated as an institution for constitutional review by the then in force 1961 Constitution, now precisely provides for that institution in cases when the constitutional review proposals seek for 'transforming the State, creating a new legal order, and writing a new Constitution' (Articles 347 et seq.). In these cases, no constitutional amendment or reform procedures can be used.

119. When establishing the National Constituent Assembly procedure, Article 347 begins by setting forth an essential principle of modern constitutionalism: that the people are the bearers of the 'original constituent power'; so it is in the exercise of that power that the people can convene a National Constituent Assembly with the purpose of transforming the State, creating a new legal order, and drafting a new Constitution.

This mean that in the 1999 Constitution, and contrary to the practice when the 1999 Constituent Assembly was convened, the National Constituent Assembly cannot be considered in itself as an 'original constituent power', a power that is reserved for the people in an untransferable way. Thus, the people being the only title-holder of the original constituent power, it is for the people to establish the framework of action of the Constituent Assembly. If it is true that in the constitutional provision no reference is expressly made to the need for a referendum in order to approve the convening of the National Constituent Assembly, it is evident that such referendum must take place in order for the people to express its will regarding the statute of the National Constituent Assembly, that is its composition, the system of election of its members, its powers and duration, and its limits.

120. The initiative for convening a referendum in order to convene a National Constituent Assembly is assigned to the President of the Republic in a decision adopted in Ministers' Council; to the National Assembly by means of a resolution approved by two-thirds of its members; to two-third of the Municipal Councils of the country expressing its votes in open Town Halls (*Cabildos abiertos*); or to a petition signed by 15% of registered voters (Article 348).

Once the initiative for convening the Assembly is formulated, the National Electoral Council must convene the referendum in order for the people to convene the Assembly; and once decided by the people, the election of its members must be made. According to Article 349 of the Constitution, once the Constituent Assembly is installed, the constituted powers of the State may in no way impede any of its deci-

---

1645   The question submitted to referendum and approved by the people was the following: *'Do you appro-ve of the amendment of Articles 160,162,174,192 and 230 of the Constitution of the Republic prepa-red by initiative of the National Assembly, which extends the political rights of the people in order to allow any citizen in exercise of a public office by popular election to become a candidate to the sa-me office for the constitutionally established term, his or her election depending exclusively from the popular vote?'* See the text in *Official Gazette* N° 5.908 Extra. Of Feb. 19, 2009.

sions, which imply that even if it is a decision suspending the constituted powers of government, they cannot obstruct them.

On the one hand, once the new Constitution is approved by the National Constituent Assembly, the President of the Republic cannot object to it and must publish it in the *Official Gazette*. The 1999 Constitution failed to subject the new Constitution to an approbatory referendum, although it is regulated in its Articles 73 and 74, and specifically is established for the approval of constitutional amendments and reforms (Articles 341, 344). On the other hand, the 1999 Constitution itself, after being sanctioned by a National Constituent Assembly, was approved through a referendum on 15 December 1999, in order for it to enter into effect (see *supra* paragraphs 28, 29).

IV. *Limits to the Constitutional Review Powers*

121. The 1999 Constitution does not establish in an express way the so-called immutable principles or clauses found in many of the modern constitutions when stating that some provisions cannot ever be changed.[1646]

Nonetheless, in an indirect way it is possible to identify some of those immutable clauses derived from the wording of the constitutional provisions. For instance, when Article 1 of the Constitution proclaims that the Republic is 'irrevocably' free and independent, it means that in no way can the Republic lose its freedom and independence, so no constitutional review can be initiated for such purpose, thus that declaration is an immutable one.

In the same sense, when the same Article 1 of the Constitution declares that independence, freedom, sovereignty, immunity, territorial integrity and national auto determination are non-renounced rights of the Nation, that is, that those principles cannot be changed in any way, these declarations can be considered as immutable clauses.

Article 5 of the Constitution establishes that sovereignty resides 'untransferably' in the people, which means that that character cannot be changed and that the people in no way can transfer its sovereignty, so no constitutional revision can establish such transfer.

Also when Article 6 of the Constitution establishes that the government of the Republic and its territorial entities will always be democratic, participatory, elective, decentralized, alternative, responsible, pluralistic and of revocable mandates, that means that in no way a constitutional review process could change or eliminate any of those characteristics of the government, because if they must always be as mentioned, they are immutable.

§3. *The Sub-national Constitutions*

122. According to Article 164 of the 1999 Constitution, the Legislative Councils of the states have the power to enact their own Constitution in order to organize the

---

1646   See Allan R. Brewer-Carías, 'La reforma constitucional en América Latina y el control de constitucionalidad', en *Reforma de la Constitución y control de constitucionalidad. Congreso Internacional* (Pontificia Universidad Javeriana, Bogotá Colombia, junio 14 al 17 de 2005, Bogotá 2005), 108–159.

state branches of government in accordance with what is established in the national Constitution.

This provision follows a traditional constitutional trend regarding the existence of sub-national constitutions sanctioned by each state, as has been the tradition since the 1811 initial Provincial Constitutions (see *supra* paragraph 6). The scope and contents of these states' constitutions, nonetheless, is now completely limited to provide for the organization of the branches of government of the states, which are only two: the legislative branch of government corresponding to the Legislative Councils, and the Executive branch of government, assigned to the state Governors. There is no judicial power at the states level, and they have no powers to incorporate in their Constitutions other matters like for instance, constitutional rights, which are of national jurisdiction.

But even in this limited scope of the sub-national constitutions, the content that can be established in the states constitutions has being additionally reduced, by attributing to the National Assembly the power to enact a national law on the organization and functioning of one of their main organs, the Legislative Councils (Article 162);[1647] and by directly regulating the main aspects of states' executive organization, particularly their Public Administration, which has been the object of various national laws,[1648] that are directly applicable to the states' executive branch of government (see *supra* paragraph 316).

Consequently, in practice, if it is true that all the twenty-three states of the Republic have their own Constitutions, the content is very similar, repeating what is already established in the national Constitution or in the laws enacted by the National Assembly. Nothing original is possible to be found in such 'constitutions'.

Chapter 2. The Treaties

§1. *Incorporation to Internal Law*

123. Article 154 of the Constitution set forth that the Treaties entered by the Republic must be approved by the National Assembly before their ratification by the President of the Republic. Thus, international Treaties and conventions must be incorporated in internal law before their ratification by means of their approval by statutes by the National Assembly, which like all statutes must be published in the *Official Gazette* in order to have effect (Article 215). This is then the general provision regarding the incorporation of Treaties to internal Law.

The legislative approval of international treaties, conventions or agreements must be made through statutes (Article 156.18) following the general procedure established in the Constitution for the 'formation of laws' (Article 202 et seq.). After the approval, the ratification of the treaties corresponds to the Executive, and can only refer to the content of the text approved by the National Assembly. Consequently, any change or variation of the approved text in the act of ratification nullifies it.

1647   Organic Law on the States Legislative Councils, *Official Gazette* N° 37.282 of 13 Sep. 2001.

1648   For Instance, the Organic Law on Public Administration, *Gaceta Oficial* N° 5.890 Extra. of 31 Jul. 2008.

In the case of approbatory laws of international treaties, the President has the discretion to determine the opportunity in which the said Law must be promulgated and published in the *Official Gazette* (Article 215), according to international conventions and the convenience of the Republic (Article 217).

14. Regarding this general provision on the legislative approval of international treaties, the Constitution establishes a few exceptions where Treaties do not need to be approved by the Legislator in order to be incorporated in internal law. These exceptions refers to those Treaties tending to execute or to improve pre-existent obligations of the Republic; those seeking to apply principles expressly recognized by the Republic; those called to execute ordinary international relations acts; and those through which the Executive exercise powers that are expressly given to it by statute.[1649]

125. In the process of incorporating Treaties to internal law, the President of the Republic, before ratifying a Treaty and even when the Treaty has been already approved by the National Assembly, is entitled to file a request before the Constitutional Chamber of the Supreme Tribunal for the verification of the constitutionality of the Treaty (Article 336.5) (see *infra* paragraph 651).

126. Treaties, conventions, or other international agreements which can compromise national sovereignty or transfer national powers or competencies to supranational entities, as for example, in the case of treaties for economic integration, may be subject to approbatory referendum (Article 73). The initiative for such referendum can be filled by the President of the Republic in a decision adopted in the Council of Ministers; by the National Assembly in a motion approved by the vote of at least two-thirds of its members; or by popular petition signed by at least 15% of registered voters.

Nonetheless, approbatory laws of international treaties cannot be submitted to referenda intended to abrogate them (Article 74).

§2. *Hierarchy*

127. The general constitutional consequence of the process of incorporation of international treaties and conventions into internal law by means of statutory approval by the National Assembly is that as a matter of principle treaties have the same rank as statutes in the internal order. Nonetheless, three main exceptions can be identified regarding this hierarchical position of treaties.

The first derives from the general principle established in Article 8 of the Civil Procedure Code referring to matters of private international law regarding which courts are obliged in relation to the specific issue in question to apply first to the international treaties between Venezuela and the respective State.

1649   See Larys Hernández Villalobos, 'Rango o jerarquía de los tratados internacionales en el ordenamiento jurídico de Venezuela (1999)', in *Revista del Tribunal Supremo de Justicia*, N° 3 (Caracas, 2001), 110–131; Boris Bunimov Parra, 'La entrada en vigor de los acuerdos internacionales en Venezuela', in *Libro Homenaje a Antonio Linares* (Caracas: Instituto de Derecho Público. Universidad Central de Venezuela, 1999), 19–26.

The second refers to treaties or conventions on human rights, which have constitutional hierarchy; this being one of the important innovations of the 1999 Constitution on matters of human rights (Article 23) (see *infra* paragraphs 442, 443, 682). This means that treaties, pacts and conventions ratified by Venezuela must be preferred over internal law (*orden interno*) if they have more favourable provisions regarding the enjoyment or exercise of rights. In addition, the same article points out that those international treaties and conventions on human rights are immediately and directly applicable by the courts and any other organ exercising Public Powers.[1650] This meant, for instance, that the American Convention of Human Rights ratified by Venezuela in 1977, in addition to its aforementioned constitutional hierarchy in internal law, was a fundamental tool for the international protection of human rights violated, by the State by the Inter-American Court on Human Rights, until Venezuela withdrawal from the Convention in 2012.This governmental decision fallowed previous judicial decisions issued by the Constitutional Chamber of the Supreme Tribunal of Justice, not only diminishing the mentioned hierarchy, but requesting the Government to withdrawal from the Convention.[1651] The third exception regarding the hierarchy of treaties refers to the treaties and norms derived from the processes of Latin American and Caribbean integration, in which is set forth that the communitarian law resulting from them must prevail over the internal laws; that is, communitarian treaties and norms have a superior hierarchy regarding statutes (see *supra* paragraph 111).

Chapter 3. The Legislation

§1. *Types of Laws at the National Level*

I. *Ordinary Laws*

128. According to Article 202 of the Constitution, 'law' (statute) on the national level is that act sanctioned by the National Assembly acting as a legislative body through the procedure of laws formation, which imposes the need to have at least two sets of debates regarding the draft (Article 205) (see *infra* paragraph 358). The statutes that systematically gather norms concerning a specific subject may be termed 'codes' (*Códigos*), as is the case for example, of the Civil, Commercial and Criminal Codes (see *infra* paragraph 145).

1650   See Allan R. Brewer-Carías, 'Nuevas reflexiones sobre el papel de los tribunales constitucionales en la consolidación del Estado democrático de derecho: defensa de la Constitución, control del poder y protección de los derechos humanos', in *Dignidad de la persona, Derechos Fundamentales, Justicia Constitucional*, ed. Francisco Fernández Segado (coordinador) (Madrid: Dykinson, 2008), 761–826.

1651   See Allan R. Brewer-Carías, 'La ilegítima mutación de la Constitución por el juez constitucional mediante la eliminación del rango supra constitucional de los tratados internacionales sobre derechos humanos, y el desconocimiento en Venezuela de las sentencias de la Corte Interamericana de Derechos Humanos,' in *Libro Homenaje al Capítulo Venezolano de la Asociación Mundial de Jóvenes Juristas y Estudiantes de Derecho: Recopilación de artículos que desarrollan temas de actualidad jurídica relacionados con el derecho público y el derecho privado*, (Caracas, Asociación Mundial de Jóvenes Juristas y Estudiantes de Derecho, 2012).

II.   Organic Laws

129. However, Article 203 identified one specific type of statutes called 'organic laws' (*leyes orgánicas*),[1652] distinguishing four categories:

First, those statutes that are expressly termed in the Constitution as organic law, as is the case, for instance, of the Organic Law on Boundaries (*Fronteras*) (Article 15), the Organic Law on Territorial Division (Article 16), the Armed Force Organic Law (Article 41), the Social Security System Organic Law (Article 86), the Land Use Organic Law (*Ordenación del Territorio*) (Article 128), the Municipal Public Power Organic Law (Article 169), the Organic Law on Metropolitan Districts (Articles 171, 172), the Organic Law reserving the State activities, industries and services (Article 302), the Organic Law on the Council for National Defence (Article 323), the Organic Law on Judicial Review (Article 336), the Organic Law on the States of Exception (*Estados de Excepción*) (Article 338), the Organic Law on Asylum and Refugees (Transitory Provision -T.P.-, 4,2), the Public Defence Organic Law (T.P. 4,5), the Education Organic Law (T.P. 6), the Organic Law on Indigenous Peoples (T.P. 7) or the Labour Organic Law (T.P. 4,3).

Second, the Constitution qualifies as organic laws those enacted by the National Assembly to organize the various branches of government, as is the case, for instance, of the Public Administration Organic Law (Article 236, 20); the Attorney General Organic Law (Article 247), the Judiciary Organic Law and the Supreme Tribunal of Justice Organic Law (Article 262); the Electoral Power Organic Law (Article 292); the Citizen Power Organic Law, the General Comptroller Office Organic Law, the Public Prosecutor Organic Law, the Peoples' Defender Organic Law (T. P 9); the Municipal Regime Organic Law (Article 169) and the States Legislative Councils Organic Law (Article 162).

Third, also considered as organic laws are those enacted in order to develop the regulation of constitutional rights, which opens an enormous field of matters in the sense that all the statutes enacted to regulate any of the constitutional rights declared in Articles 19–129 must be organic laws.

Fourth, the Constitution also considers as organic laws those enacted for the purpose of serving as a normative framework to other laws, as is the case, for instance, of the Taxation Organic Code which serves as the framework to all the specific tax laws, or the Financial Public Administration Law, that serves as the general framework for all the specific annual budget laws of all the public debts authorizations laws.

130. Except for the first category of organic laws, in all the others cases the corresponding draft must be admitted by the National Assembly by a vote of the two-third of the present members before beginning the debate of the project; a majority that also applies in cases of reforms to organic laws (Article 203).

1652   See José Peña Solís, 'La nueva concepción de las leyes orgánicas en la Constitución de 1999', in *Revista del Tribunal Supremo de Justicia*, N° 1 (Caracas, 2000), 73–111; Milagros López Betancourt, 'Una aproximación a las Leyes Orgánicas en Venezuela', in *Libro Homenaje a Enrique Tejera París, Temas sobre la Constitución de 1999* (Caracas: Centro de Investigaciones Jurídicas (CEIN), 2001), 109 a 157.

Also, except for the first aforementioned category, the qualification of a law, as an 'organic law' by the National Assembly, must be reviewed regarding the constitutionality of such qualification by the Constitutional Chamber of the Supreme Tribunal of Justice (Article 203). For such purpose the statutes must be sent to the Constitutional Chamber before their promulgation, and if the Chamber considers that the statute is not an organic law, it will lose this character.

III. *Other Laws: Enabling and Cadre Laws*

131. According to Article 203 of the Constitution, enabling laws (*leyes habilitantes*) are statutes of legislative delegation, that is, those sanctioned by the National Assembly by a vote of three-fifth of its members, in order to establish the guidelines, the purposes and the framework of the matters that are delegated to the President of the Republic, in order for him to regulate them through decree-laws (decrees with rank and value of laws) during a certain period of time (Articles 203, 236.8).

This possibility for legislative delegation by means of enabling laws can be considered as an innovation of the 1999 Constitution, without precedents in modern constitutionalism regarding its scope. It substituted the previous provisions of the 1961 Constitution, which limited the authorization by enabling laws to the President, to adopt extraordinary measures exclusively on economic and financial matters (Article 190.8). In contrast, in the 1999 Constitution, the possibility of legislative delegation has been established in an extended way, without limits regarding the matters that can be regulated by the Executive, which contradicts the general constitutional guarantee of certain matters that must be reserved to the legislator (as body composed by elected representatives) (*reserva legal*), like the establishing of limits to the exercise of human rights, the approval of taxes (no taxation without representation) and the creation of criminal offences.[1653] (see *infra* paragraph 454).

132. Regarding the cadre laws (*leyes de bases*) they are established in order to empower the National Assembly to regulate matters of concurrent character between the national and states level that once enacted by the National Assembly then can be developed in each state by the corresponding State Legislative Council (Article 165).[1654] (see *infra* paragraph 193).

IV. *Decree-Laws*

133. The President of the Republic is authorized in the Constitution to enact in three cases decrees-laws, that is, decrees with rank and value of statutes:[1655]

1653   See Pedro Nikken, 'Constitución venezolana de 1999: La habilitación para dictar decretos ejecutivos con fuerza de ley restrictivos de los derechos humanos y su contradicción con el derecho internacional', *Revista de Derecho Público*, N° 83 (julio-septiembre) (Caracas: Editorial Jurídica Venezolana, 2000), 5–19.

1654   See José Peña Solís, 'Dos nuevos tipos de leyes en la Constitución de 1999: leyes habilitantes y leyes de bases', in *Revista de la Facultad de Ciencias Jurídicas y Políticas de la UCV*, N° 119 (Caracas, 2000), 79–123.

1655   See Eloisa Avellaneda Sisto, 'El régimen de los Decretos-Leyes, con especial referencia a la Constitución de 1999', in *Estudios de Derecho Administrativo, Libro Homenaje a la Universidad Central de Venezuela*, ed. F. Parra Aranguren y A. Rodríguez G., vol. I (Caracas: Tribunal Supremo de Justicia,

First, when the National Assembly approves a legislative delegation through an enabling law authorizing the President to regulate the matters specified in it, through decree-laws, for which purpose the President must conform its legislative acts to the guidelines, the purposes and the framework established in the enabling law, and to the period established for such purpose (see *infra* paragraphs 234, 253, 301, 455). These decree-laws can be the object of abrogate referendum, as it is expressly set forth in Article 74 of the Constitution, when a popular petition is filed supported by no less than 5% of the registered electors.

Second, when in cases of state of exceptions, that is, in situations that seriously threaten the security of the Nation, its institutions and persons, the President of the Republic considers it necessary to restrict the guarantees of some constitutional rights, in which case, he must establish the rules regarding the exercise of the res-tricted guarantee (Article 339). In these cases these decrees, due to the content and object of their regulations referred to constitutional rights (which can only be regula-ted by statutes), can be considered as decree-laws (see *infra* paragraphs 285, 291 ff., 457, 645).

The third type of decree-laws refers to those enacted by the President of the Re-public regarding the organization of Public Administration. In this respect, Article 236.20 of the Constitution authorizes the President to 'set forth the number, organi-zation and attributions of the Ministries and the organs of National Public Adminis-tration, as well as the organization and functioning of the Council of Ministers' (see *infra* paragraph 316). Even though this presidential power is established in the Constitution, its exercise by the Executive, particularly when referred to the creation or suppression of Ministries, and to their organization and attributions, always im-plies the modification of some substantive legislation.

§2. *Equivalent Legislative Rules: The States Laws and the Municipal Ordinances*

134. As the Venezuelan State is organized according to a federal form of go-vernment, with a system of vertical division of powers, in addition to the legislative powers of the national (federal) level of government, the states and the municipali-ties also have legislative powers regarding the matters attributed to them in the Constitution.

Regarding the states, Article 162 of the Constitution assigns them the attribution of 'legislate' on matters assigned to the states, as well as to sanction the 'Budget Law of the state.' In this regard the legislative acts of the Legislative Councils are also called 'laws' (statutes). The Legislative Councils, as aforementioned, are also empowered to sanction the states' constitutions in order to organize the branches of governments (Article 164.1) (see *infra* paragraph 191).

In the municipal level, also regarding the matters attributed to the municipalities, Article 175 assigns to the Municipal Councils the 'legislative function', which is

2001), 69 a 106; Allan R. Brewer-Carías, 'El régimen constitucional de los Decretos-Leyes y de los Actos de Gobierno', in *Bases y principios del sistema constitucional venezolano (Ponencias del VII Congreso Venezolano de Derecho Constitucional realizado en San Cristóbal del 21 al 23 de No-viembre de 2001)*, vol. I, 25–74.

exercised through 'Municipal Ordinances' that have always been considered as 'local laws' (see *infra* paragraph 208).

States laws and Municipal Ordinances can be challenged before the Constitutional Chamber of the Supreme Tribunal on grounds of their unconstitutionality (see *infra* paragraph 644).

§3. *Hierarchy*

135. The legislative function in the three levels of government (national, states, municipal) is exercised according to the federal division of power system, and according to the matters assigned to each level. Consequently, in principle, the laws passed in each level are autonomously sanctioned by each legislative body (National Assembly, States Legislative Councils, Municipal Councils) referring only to the matters assigned in the distribution of powers framed in the Constitution (see *infra* paragraphs 196, 204, 208). Any encroachment in the matters reserved to other levels implies usurpation of power, affecting the law as unconstitutional.

136. Due to the centralized form of the Venezuelan federation, almost all matters of public action and policy have been assigned to the national level, so the national laws have general and comprehensive scope and application in all the country. The states scarcely have exclusive matters attributed to their authority, so the states laws are very few and mainly refer to organizational matters. When the matter is assigned in a concurrent way to the national and state level of government, the states' laws on the matter must be subjected to the national legislation which can also consist in a Cadre Law (Article 165) (see *infra* paragraph 203).

The same occurs at the Municipal level, although in this case the Constitution assigns more matters in an exclusive way to local governments. Only when matters have been assigned to different levels of government in a concurrent way must the legislation at the local level be subject to the national or states' laws.

137. Any conflict between the different legislative entities, and any encroachment regarding legislative attributions of the different level of government, can be subjected to judicial review before the Constitutional Chamber of the Supreme Tribunal of Justice, which is empowered to decide conflicts between legal provisions and to declare which must prevail (Article 336.8); as well as to decide constitutional controversies between the different branches of government, not only in the horizontal sense (separation of powers) but in the vertical sense (territorial distribution of powers) (Article 336.9) (see *infra* paragraph 656).

Chapter 4. The Jurisprudence

§1. *The Obligatory Character of the Decisions of the Constitutional Jurisdiction*

138. The Constitutional Chamber of the Supreme Tribunal of Justice, as Constitutional Jurisdiction, exercising powers of judicial review of constitutionality of legislation and of all State acts with rank of statute or issued in direct application of constitutional provisions (Articles 334, 336), has the task of guaranteeing the supremacy and effectiveness of the constitutional provisions and principles. It is named as the highest and last interpreter of the Constitution, being charged with wat-

ching over for its uniform interpretation and application (Article 335). Accordingly, the 1999 Constitution set forth that 'the interpretations established by the Constitutional Chamber regarding the content and scope of the constitutional provisions and principles are binding for the other Chambers of the Supreme Tribunal and all the courts of the Republic' (Article 335)[1656] (see *infra* paragraph 658).

This provision regarding the effects of judicial review rulings on interpretations of the Constitution by the Constitutional Jurisdiction is an innovation introduced in the 1999 Constitution, complementing the traditional general and obligatory (*erga omnes*) effects of the judicial review rulings when annulling laws. In both cases, the jurisprudence of the Constitutional Jurisdiction is obligatory and binding (see *infra* paragraph 645).

The Judicial Review of Administrative Action Jurisdiction decisions have the same *erga omes* effects, when annulling executive regulations and administrative acts (Article 259), being in these cases the jurisprudence obligatory and binding (see *infra* paragraph 702).

In a similar sense it must be noted that the decisions adopted by the Civil, Criminal and Social Cassation Chambers of the Supreme Tribunal of Justice when hearing a cassation recourse (Article 266.8), have the effect of annulling the judicial decisions submitted for their review, and also have obligatory and binding effects regarding the courts that issued the reviewed decisions.

§2. *The General Value of Jurisprudence*

139. Except in the specific aforementioned cases of obligatory and binding jurisprudence derived from judicial decisions issued on judicial review rulings on constitutional (Constitutional Jurisdiction), administrative (Judicial Review of Administrative Action Jurisdiction) and judicial matters (Cassation), the value of the jurisprudence derived from judicial decisions is of an auxiliary character, as a very important tool for the correct interpretation and application of laws. Nonetheless, the courts are not subjected to precedents, except, as aforementioned, on matters of judicial review of constitutionality of legislation and constitutional interpretation, when the Constitutional Chamber gives to its decision binding effects (see *infra* paragraph 638).

Chapter 5. The Unwritten Law

§1. *Constitutional Principles and Values*

140. The 1999 Venezuelan Constitution is one of the Constitutions in the contemporary world containing not only an impressive number of Articles (350), but also a very rich and numerous declaration of values and principles.

1656   See in general, Rubén J. Laguna Navas, *La Sala Constitucional del Tribunal Supremo de Justicia: su rol como máxima y última intérprete de la Constitución* (Caracas: Universidad Central de Venezuela, 2005); Nancy Carolina Granadillo Colmenares, *Sentencias Vinculantes de la Sala Constitucional del tribunal Supremo de Justicia 2000-2007* (Caracas: Paredes Libros, 2008).

They can be found not only in the Preamble of the Constitution but also in many of its articles, where in a very enumerative and express way, an extensive list of constitutional values and principles are enshrined, as goals intending to guide the State, the Society and the individuals' general conduct. Consequently, in Venezuela, the global values and principles not only derive from the interpretation and application of the Constitution by the courts, but from what it is set forth in a precise and express way in the text of the Constitution.[1657] By means of constitutional judicial decisions, of course, the sense, the scope and the priority character of many of these constitutional principles and values have been defined and enriched; and also, unfortunately, in other cases, they have also been distorted, originating in many cases some constitutional incongruence between what is said in the constitutional text and what is decided in the political practice of government (see *infra* paragraphs 87 et seq.).

In any case, since the Constitution is a text in which the generally shared values of a society are reflected, the declarations of intent contained in it are of indubitable value, both for the State bodies, who must be guided by them, as for the judges, specially the Supreme Tribunal of Justice as its superior judicial guardian.

141. All these constitutional values expressly mentioned in the Constitution, and also those interpreted by the Constitutional Jurisdiction, refer to the State (the Republic, the Nation), its organization (distribution of State powers and branches of government) and functioning (government and Public Administration); to the legal system; to human rights; and to the content and scope of the concept of the democratic and social rule of law and justice state' regulated by the Constitution. These values have the same constitutional rank as the express provisions of the Constitution. Consequently, those principles have been an important tool for judicial review of constitutionality exercise by the Constitutional Jurisdiction, to the point that the binding interpretations that can be establish by the Constitutional Chamber of the Supreme Tribunal, not only can be referred to the content and scope of the constitutional provisions but also to the 'constitutional principles' (Article 335).

§2. *General Principles of Law*

142. Article 4 of the Civil Code that lays out the basic rules for the interpretation of laws, sets forth that the sense that must be attributed to the law must be the one that evidently appears from the significance of words, in accordance with their connection and to the intention of the Legislator. When no precise legal provision exists, the provisions regulating similar cases or analogous matters must be taken into account; and if doubts remain, the general principles of law must be applied.

Consequently, the general principles of law are always a source of law for the interpreter, when no express provision exists, and no similar or analogous rules can be applied.

They are also referred to in the Civil Procedure Code, on matters of international private law regarding which the courts must first apply what is established in inter-

---

1657   See Allan R. Brewer-Carías, *Principios fundamentales del derecho público* (Caracas: Editorial Jurí-
        dica Venezolana, 2005).

national treaties between Venezuela and the respective State. When no treaty exists, they must apply what is provided on the matter in the laws of the Republic or what can be deducted from the mind of national legislation, and finally, they must be guided by the principles of law generally accepted (Article 8).

Chapter 6. The Executive Regulations and Administrative Acts

§1. National, States and Municipal Regulations

143. An essential part of the administrative functions is the power assigned to the Executive branch of government to enact regulations in order to develop and facilitate the application of statutes. Consequently, in each of the three levels of government: the President of the Republic in the national level (Article 156.10); the Governors in the states level, and the Mayors in the municipal level, have the power to issue regulations referring to the respective national, states or municipal laws.

In addition, the other branches of government have been empowered in the Constitution to issue regulations in order to develop specific statutes, like the National Electoral Council regarding the Electoral Laws (Article 293.1). In other cases it is in specific statutes that the regulatory powers have been established, like the case of the Comptroller General of the Republic regarding his fiscal control functions according to the Organic Law on the General Comptroller of the Republic (Article 13.1). Regulatory power has also been assigned to the Ministers by the Organic Law on Public Administration,[1658] and to specific independent administrative or regulatory authorities by the corresponding statute creating them, like the Superintendence of Banks and Financial Institutions, Superintendence of Insurance, Superintendence on Free Competition protection, Stock Exchange control Commission (see *infra* paragraph 381). Also, the Supreme Tribunal of Justice has regulatory powers regarding the organization and functioning of the Judiciary (Article 267, Constitution).

§2. Limits to the Executive Regulatory Powers

144. In all cases, the principal limit to the regulatory powers are those established in Article 156.10 of the Constitution when assigning it to the President of the Republic in the sense that they must always be exercised, regarding statutes, 'without altering its spirit, purpose and reason'.

The consequence of this principle is that regulations are always administrative acts, although of general content, and consequently always subjected to the statutes whose contents always prevail over the regulations. Nonetheless, it is possible for administrative organs to issue 'autonomous regulations', in the sense of regulations that are not intended to specifically develop a particular statute, and are generally referred to organizational matters. In these cases, the limit is always its sub-legal character, and that their validity ceases if the matters are later regulated in a statute passed by the National Assembly.

1658   *Gaceta Oficial* N° 5.890 Extra. of 31 Jul. 2008.

Regulations, as all administrative acts, are subjected to judicial review by the Judicial Review of Administrative Action Courts (Article 259) (see *infra* paragraph 702).

Chapter 7. Codification, Interpretation and Publication

§1. *The Codes*

145. As defined in Article 203 of the Constitution, 'codes' are the statutes that systematically gather norms concerning a specific subject, so it is for the National Assembly to sanction codes, that being a competence reserved for the national level of government. No code exists at the states or municipal levels.

The most important Codes are the Civil Code,[1659] the Commercial Code,[1660] the Criminal Code,[1661] and the Procedural Codes: Civil Procedure Code,[1662] Criminal Organic Procedure Code,[1663] and the Military Justice Code.[1664]

As an organic law, the taxation one has been named Taxation Organic Code;[1665] and on Administrative Law matters, the Organic Law on Administrative Procedures[1666] has always been considered as an important sign of the codification of Administrative Law.

§2. *Interpretation*

146. The main rule on law interpretation, which applies to all laws, including Codes, as aforementioned, has been set forth in Article 4 of the Civil Code that provides that the sense that must be attributed to the law must be the one that evidently appears from the significance of words, in accordance to their connection and to the intention of the Legislator. When no precise legal provision exists, the provisions regulating similar cases or analogous matters must be taken into account; and if doubts remain, the general principles of law must be applied.

Nonetheless, in addition to the literal sense of the legal provisions, in order to interpret them, according to the doctrine established by the Supreme Tribunal of Justice, summarized in decision N° 895 of the Politico-Administrative Chamber of 30 July 2008, the interpretation of laws must always consider three other elements. Consequently, for the interpretation of laws, the interpreter must take into consideration the following four basic elements: first, the literal, grammatical or philological element, which is the initial point from where must depart any interpretation of laws following the provision of Article 4 of the Civil Code; second, the logical, rational

---

1659   *Gaceta Oficial* N° 2.990 Extra. of 26 Jul. 1982.

1660   *Gaceta Oficial* N° 475 Extra. of 21 Dec. 1955.

1661   *Gaceta Oficial.* N° 5.768 Extra. of 13 Apr. 2005.

1662   *Gaceta Oficial* N° 3.694 Extra. of 22 Jan. 1986.

1663   *Gaceta Oficial* N° 5.930 Extra. of 4 Sep. 2009.

1664   *Gaceta Oficial* N° 5.263 Extra. of 17 Sep. 1998.

1665   *Gaceta Oficial* N° 37.305 of 17 Oct. 2001.

1666   *Gaceta Oficial* N° 2.818 Extra. of 1 Jul. 1981.

or reasonable element; third, the historical element, in the sense that any legal provision must be inserted within a reality that has its origins and evolution, whose comprehension through its historical paths is important in order to give the provision an actual sense; and four, the systematic element, or the integral comprehension of law as a social life regulatory system. The Chamber has said, consequently that any law interpretation must have all four elements, in the sense that there are not four types of interpretation in order to choose one according to the interpreter's choice, but four different operations whose gathering is indispensable for the interpretation of the law, even in the event that one of such elements could have more importance. Consequently, in the interpretative task, it is not possible to rest only in the literal, grammatical or philological element. In addition there are other relevant elements that the authors have added, like the teleological element, that is, to understand that the law is sanctioned in order to attain certain social goals within the State organization; and the sociological element, that helps to understand the provision from the comprehension of the social, economical, political and cultural reality where the text is going to be applied.[1667]

In the same sense, the Constitutional Chamber has also pointed out in a decision of 9 December 2002 that the interpretation of laws has to be made '*in totum*', that is, that the provision must be interpreted within the legal order as a whole.[1668] That is, within the whole positive law, because otherwise it is impossible to get to the bottom of the sense and scope of the legal provision, necessary in order to determine what has been the will of the Legislator.

Regarding matters related to international private law, according to the Civil Procedure Code, the courts on the subject to be decided must first pay attention to what is established in international treaties between Venezuela and the respective State. In the absence of treaties, they must apply what on the matter is provided in the laws of the Republic or what can be deducted from the mind of national legislation. Finally, they must decide according to generally accepted principles of law (Article 8).

§3. *Publication and Derogatory Effects*

147. In order to have effect all statutes and regulations must be published in the *Official Gazette* (*Gaceta Oficial*) (Article 215).

Statutes can be total or partially reformed, and in the latter case, they must be published in one single text in which the approved modifications must be incorporated.[1669]

1667   See in *Revista de derecho Público*, N° 115 (Caracas: Editorial Jurídica Venezolana, 2008), 468 et seq.

1668   See File N° 02-2154, case: *Fiscal General de la República*, quotet in decision N° 2152 of 14 Dec. 2007, in *Revista de Derecho Público*, N° 112 (Caracas, Editorial Jurídica Venezolana, 2007), 446.

1669   Official Publications Law, *Gaceta Oficial* N° 20.546 of 22 Jul. 1941.

STATUTES, ACCORDING TO ARTICLE 218 OF THE CONSTITUTION, CAN ONLY BE ABROGATED BY OTHER STATUTES OR BY MEANS OF REFERENDUM WITH EXCEPTIONS ESTABLISHED IN THE CONS-TITUTION (ARTICLE 74). STATUTES, HOWEVER, HAVE DEROGATO-RY EFFECTS REGARDING PREVIOUS STATUTES OR REGULATIONS

PART II. BASIC ELEMENTS OF THE REPRESENTATIVE AND PARTI-CIPATORY DEMOCRATIC POLITICAL SYSTEM

148. The 1999 Constitution proclaims that the government of the Republic of Venezuela is and shall always be democratic, participatory, elective, decentralized, alternating, responsible, plural and of revocable mandates (Article 6), establishing in addition, provisions regarding the need to be subject to accountability (*rendición de cuentas*), particularly of the elected officers, and establishing the possibility for all of them to be subjected to repeal referendums.

In order to establish the democratic government with all such elements, that are defined in the sense of 'rock-like clauses'(*cláusulas pétreas*) in the sense that they must always exist, Article 5 of the Constitution, after setting forth that 'sovereignty resides in an non-transferable way in the people', declares that it can be exercised in two ways: on the one hand, in a 'direct' way by means of referendum and other ins-truments for direct democracy established in the Constitution; and on the other hand, in an indirect way, 'through suffrage, by the organs that exercise State Powers' (Ar-ticle 5). These same enunciations are contained in Article 62 of the same Constitu-tion that sets forth the citizens' political right to freely participate in all public affairs, that is, to participate in the formation, execution, and control of public activities in order to achieve their complete collective and individual development, being an obligation of the State and of society to facilitate and create the most favourable conditions for such participation. This political participation, being an essential cha-racteristic of any democracy although not always accomplished, according to the same provision of the Constitution is exercised in two ways: in a direct way, through instruments of direct democracy; and in an indirect way, through elected representa-tives, which is one of the essential elements of representative democracy (Article 62).

149. For the purpose of guaranteeing this right to political participation, Article 70 of the Constitution enumerates the following political means for the citizens' rights to participate in the exercise of their sovereignty: on the one hand, regarding representative democracy, the election of representatives to public office; and on the other hand, regarding direct democracy, the vote in referenda and in the referendum for the revocation of mandates of elected officers; participation in popular consulta-tions; the legislative or constitutional initiative; participation in open town meeting, and in Citizens' assemblies whose decisions are binding.

According to these constitutional provisions, the Venezuelan representative and participatory democratic political system is characterized by the following elements: representative democracy and its electoral system; direct democracy instruments and its voting system; plural political parties' regime; alternating system of government, and government accountability instruments.

Chapter 1. Representative Democracy

150. Representative democracy, consequently, is one of the basic components of the Democratic System of Venezuela through which citizens exercise its sovereignty electing representatives to the State organs. It is an indirect mean of exercising sovereignty, precisely 'through suffrage, by the organs that exercise State Powers' (Article 5).[1670]

But suffrage and periodical, fair and free elections, based on the universal and secret vote expressing the will of the people, do not exhaust representative democracy, which in addition has the other following essential elements: respect for human rights and fundamental liberties; access to power and its exercise with subjection to the rule of law; plural regime of the political parties and organizations; and separation and independence of public powers.

151. Regarding the exercise of sovereignty through representatives by means of elections not only is it the most common element of representative democracy, but it is an irreplaceable one, implying that all the Head Officials of the Executive Branches of Government and the members of Legislative Branches of Government, in all levels of government (see *infra* paragraphs 204, 208, 269) are elected by popular, direct and secret vote. In the National level of government, the President of the Republic is elected for a term of six years by popular, universal, direct and secrete vote by all the Citizens registered in the Electoral Registry by a simple majority of votes (Articles 228, 230).

The members or representatives to the National Assembly are also elected for a term of five years (Article 192) by the Citizens registered in the Electoral Registry by popular, universal, direct, secret vote. In this case, the electoral system applied is a mixed one, combining personalized vote with proportional representation in a number fixed according to a population base of 1.1% of the total population of the country (Article 186) (see *infra* paragraph 341). In addition, three additional national representatives in each State of the Federation must be elected. Also, the indigenous people have the right to elect three national representatives taking into account their traditions and customs (Article 125). Each representative must have a substitute member, also elected in the same process, who is called to act in cases of temporal or absolute absence of the principal (Article 186) (see *infra* paragraph 340).

All the other high public officials of the other national Branches of Government (Justices of the Supreme Tribunal of Justice, General Comptroller of the Republic,

---

1670   See Pedro L. Bracho Grand y Miriam Álvarez de Bozo, 'Democracia representativa en la Constitución Nacional de 1999', in *Estudios de Derecho Público: Libro Homenaje a Humberto J. La Roche Rincón*, vol. I (Caracas: Tribunal Supremo de Justicia, 2001), 235–254; and Ricardo Combellas, 'Representación vs. Participación en la Constitución Bolivariana. Análisis de un falso dilema', en *Bases y principios del sistema constitucional venezolano (Ponencias del VII Congreso Venezolano de Derecho Constitucional realizado en San Cristóbal del 21 al 23 de Noviembre de 2001)*, vol. II, 383–402; Juan De Stefano, 'El sufragio, el mandato político y su doctrina en la Constitución de 1961 y 1999 y de los Estados Socialistas', in *Tendencias Actuales del Derecho Constitucional. Homenaje a Jesús María Casal Montbrun*, ed. Jesús María Casal, Alfredo Arismendi y Carlos Luis Carrillo Artiles (Coord.), vol. I (Caracas: Universidad Central de Venezuela/Universidad Católica Andrés Bello, 2008), 563–576.

General Prosecutor of the Republic, Peoples' Defender, and the members of the National Electoral Council) are not elected in direct popular elections, but in an indirect popular election made by the elected representatives to the the National Assembly (Articles 265, 279, 296), acting in this case, as an electoral body by the vote of a qualified majority (see *infra* paragraph 224, 286,393 ff.,420, 423, 433). This indirect election must be made with the active participation of representatives of the various sectors of society that must integrate the Nominating Committees that are the only ones that can nominate the cadidaes, which must be established for such purposes.[1671] Unfortunately, these latter provisions of the Constitution have been distorted by the National Assembly reducing the participation scope of civil society by incorporating in such Committees, representatives of the National Assembly, being transformed, in fact, into common parliamentary commissions controlled by the political party that control the Assembly(see *infra* paragraph *194*). In addition, the election of the high public officials has been made by the Assembly through a simple majority of the votes of the representatives participating in the session, which occurred in 2014, ignoring the qualify majority rule imposed in the Constitution (see *infra* paragraphs 224, 286,393 ff., 420, 423, 433). In the case of the election of the members of the National Electoral Coincil, the violation of the Constitution has been even more chocking, because in 2004 and 2014 it was made by the Constitutional Chamber of the Supreme Tribunal, usurping the functions of the Assembly as electoral body, supposedly supplying the omission of the Assembly (see *infra* paragraph 401).[1672]

152. On the state level, the Governors of each of the states are also elected for a term of four years by popular, universal, direct and secret vote of the Citizens registered in the Electoral Registry of the constituency of the respective state by a relative majority of votes, (Article 160). The members of the Legislative Councils of each state are elected every four years, in a number of not more that fifteen or less than seven, also by the Citizens registered in the Electoral Registry of the respective state. In this case, the same rules for the election of the representatives to the National Assembly must be followed (Article 162) (see *infra* paragraph 316).

153. On the municipal level, Mayors and members of the Municipal Councils are also elected every four years by popular, universal, direct and secret vote of the majority of Citizens registered in the Electoral Registry of the constituency of the respective municipality (Articles 174, 175) (see *infra* paragraph 205).

1671   See Allan R. Brewer-Carías, 'La participación ciudadana en la designación de los titulares de los órganos no electos de los Poderes Públicos en Venezuela y sus vicisitudes políticas', in *Revista Iberoamericana de Derecho Público y Administrativo*, Año 5, N° 5-2005 (San José, Costa Rica, 2005), 76–95.

1672   See Constitutional Chamber Decisions N° 1864 of December 22, 2014 (available at: http://historico.tsj.gov.ve/decisiones/scon/diciembre/173494-1864-221214-2014-14-1341.HTML); and N° 1865 of December 26, 2014 (available at: http://historico.tsj.gov.ve/decisiones/scon/diciembre/173497-1865-261214-2014-14-1343.HTML). See the comments in Allan R. Brewer-Carías, 'El golpe de Estado dado en diciembre de 2014, con la inconstitucional designación de las altas autoridades del Poder Público," *Revista de Derecho Público*, 40 (Caracas, Editorial Jurídica Venezolana, 2014).

154. From the aforementioned, it can be said that according to the Constitution, the general principle is that all public officials that are to occupy positions in public offices representing the people, must always be elected by universal, direct and secret suffrage. The unconstitutional exception to this constitutional rule has been established since 2006 and in particular, after the rejection of the 2007 Constitutional reform Project, in the 2010 legislative creation of the 'Communal State' framework (see *infra* paragraph 258), in which no popular suffrage is established – in fact is rejected – providing in substitution for the appointment of the members of the Communal Councils and other 'representatives' only through Citizens Assembly duly controlled by the Central Government and the Official Party.[1673]

155. The 1999 Constitution initially established that the President of the Republic, the states' Governors and the municipal Mayors could be re-elected only once for the following immediate constitutional term (Articles 160, 174, 230); and that the members of the National Assembly and the members of the States Legislative Councils could be re-elected for two consecutives constitutional terms at a maximum (Article 162, 192). All these limits to re-election of elected officials, established as a consequence of the principle of alternating government according to what is established in Article 6 of the Constitution, were eliminated through a constitutional amendment approved by referendum on 14 February 2009 (see *supra* paragraph 37; *infra* paragraph 233).

Chapter 2. Electoral System

156. For the purpose of guaranteeing representative democracy, the electoral system has been established in the Constitution according to the elected officials.[1674] The President of the Republic, the Governors of the states and the Mayors of the municipalities are elected by simple majority of the voters in universal, direct and secret elections (Articles 160, 174, 228). The constitutional term of the President of the Republic is of six years (Article 230), and those of the Governors of the states and the Mayors (Article 174) are of four years (Articles 160, 174). At the end of their term, the Constitution established that they could be re-elected only once for the subsequent constitutional term; a limit that was eliminated with the constitutional amendment approved by referendum on 14 February 2009 (see *infra 168, 115, 233*).

1673   See Allan R. Brewer-Carías, 'El inicio de la desmunicipalización en Venezuela: La organización del Poder Popular para eliminar la descentralización, la democracia representativa y la participación a nivel local', en *AIDA, Opera Prima de Derecho Administrativo. Revista de la Asociación Internacional de Derecho Administrativo* (Universidad Nacional Autónoma de México, Facultad de Estudios Superiores de Acatlán, Coordinación de Postgrado, Instituto Internacional de Derecho Administrativo 'Agustín Gordillo', Asociación Internacional de Derecho Administrativo, México, 2007), 49–67; Allan R. Brewer-Carías, *Ley de los Consejos Comunales* (Caracas: Editorial Jurídica Venezolana, 2010), 16 et seq.; Antonio Canova González, '¿Extinción de los Municipios? Una propuesta más en el afán de centralizar el poder', in *Erga Omnes. Revista Jurídica de la Sindicatura Municipal de Chacao* (Caracas: Ediciones Sindicatura Municipal de Chacao, N° 1 (julio-diciembre, 2006), 239–252.

1674   See Allan R. Brewer-Carías, 'Reforma electoral en el sistema político de Venezuela', in *Reforma Política y Electoral en América Latina 1978-2007*, ed. Daniel Zovatto y J. Jesús Orozco Henríquez (Coordinadores) (México: Universidad Nacional Autónoma de México-IDEA internacional, 2008), 953–1019.

In the case of the representatives to the National Assembly, to the Legislative Councils of the states and to the Municipal Councils, the electoral system is also based on universal, direct and secret vote (Article 63). The constitutional term of the National Assembly is of five years (Article 230), and those of the Legislative Councils of the states and the Municipal Councils are of four years (Articles 162, 174).

For the election of the representatives and members of the National Assembly, Legislative Councils and Municipal Councils, the electoral system traditionally applied according to the 1961 Constitution was governed by the d'Hondt proportional representation method. In 1993, the Organic Law on Suffrage and Political Participation,[1675] seeking to guarantee more representativeness in the elections, introduced a combination of methods, adding to the proportional representation one a majority elections method in uninominal or plurinominal constituencies that were finally constitutionalized in the 1999 Constitution as a 'personalized proportional representation method' (Article 63).[1676] This system, following the trends of the Organic Law on Suffrage and Political Participation of 1993, modified in 1998[1677] was initially regulated in the Electoral Statute approved by the National Constituent Assembly for the 2000 elections,[1678] in which it was established that 60% of all representatives had to be elected un uninominal constituencies following the personalized principle; and 40% of them, through the list system, following the proportional representation principle (Article 15). This mixed system imposed the need to begin with the adjudication of those elected through the proportional representation method, in order to deduct to the Parties those obtained in the uninominal constituencies, in order to preserve the proportional representation system. This mixed system, nonetheless, was deformed in 2006 by means of an interpretation of the Constitution made by the Constitutional Chamber of the Supreme Tribunal of Justice before the election of the members of the National Assembly in 2006, through which the defrauding method applied by the parties supporting the government name as 'Las Morochas' was legitimized.[1679] The method consisted in allowing the various parties supporting official candidates to enter into agreements in order for some to only file nominations for the uninominal constituencies and others only for the plurinominal constituencies, so being formally 'different' parties (although being part of the same coalition) no deduction of the elected candidates was to be applied.[1680] In this way, the system tur-

---

1675   *Gaceta Oficial* N° 5.233 Extra. of 28 May 1998.

1676   See decision of the Constitutional Chamber of the Supreme Tribunal of Justice, N° 74 of 25 Jan. 2006 in *Revista de Derecho Público*, N° 105 (Caracas: Editorial Jurídica Venezolana, 2006), 122–144.

1677   See *Gaceta Oficial* N° 5.233 Extra. of 28 May 1998.

1678   See *Gaceta Oficial* N° 36.884 of 3 Feb. 2000. See Allan R. Brewer-Carías, 'Reforma electoral en el sistema político de Venezuela', in *Reforma Política y Electoral en América Latina 1978-2007*, ed. en Daniel Zovatto y J. Jesús Orozco Henríquez (Coord.) (México: Universidad Nacional Autónoma de México-IDEA internacional, 2008), 953–1019.

1679   Decision N° 74 (Case: *Acción Democrática v. National Electoral Council* and other electoral authorities). See in *Revista de Derecho Público*, N° 105 (Caracas: Editorial Jurídica Venezolana, 2006), 122–144.

1680   See Allan R. Brewer-Carías, 'El juez constitucional vs. El derecho al sufragio mediante la representación proporcional', in *Crónica sobre la 'In' Justicia Constitucional. La Sala Constitucional y el autoritarismo en Venezuela* (Caracas, 2007), 337 et seq.

ned to be in practice a preponderant majority system distorting proportional representation. In 2009, a new Organic Law on the Electoral Processes was sanctioned
'legalizing' this electoral distorting method.[1681]

157. Regarding the election of the high official of the other Branches of Government (Judicial, Citizens and Electoral), the Constitution has establishe a system
of popular indirect election, attributed to the National Assembly, not acting as a
'legislative' body but as an electoral body, and only by the vote of a qualified majority of the elected representatives to the National Assembly. This is expressly provided in articles 265, 279,296 of the Constitution for the election of the Justices of the
Supreme Tribunal of Justice, the Prosecutor General, the Comptroller General, the
People's Defender and the members of the National Electoral Council; election that
can only be made based on the exclusive proposal of candidates by the corresponding Nominated Committees that in each case are to be integrated exclusively by
representatives of the various sectors of society (articles 270, 279, 295 of the Constitution.

Chapter 3. Direct Democracy Institutions and the Referenda Voting System

158. Regarding direct democracy, the 1999 Constitution has also established various mechanisms for its exercise in order to promote direct popular participation in
conducting public affairs. In this context, Article 70 of the Constitution, referring to
the need for prominent participation of the people, as aforementioned, enumerates as
means for direct democracy: the referendums; the popular consultation; the repealing of public mandate; the legislative, constitutional and constituent initiatives; the
open town hall meetings (*cabildos abiertos*), and the Assemblies of Citizens 'whose
decisions shall have a binding character'.

§1. *Referenda*

159. In particular, regarding referenda, the Venezuelan Constitution expressly set
forth for the following: consultative referendum; repeal referendum for the revocation of mandates; approbatory referendum of statutes and of constitutional revisions
and referendum to abrogate statutes.[1682]

160. Regarding the consultative referendum, they can be convened for questions
regarding matters of pre-eminent national, state or municipal importance. According
to Article 71 of the Constitution, at the national level the initiative for their convening belongs either to the President of the Republic in Council of Ministers; to the

---

1681   *Gaceta Oficial* No. 5928 Extra. of 12 Aug. 2009. See Manuel Rachadell, 'El sistema electoral en la
Ley Orgánica de Procesos Electorales', in *Ley Orgánica de los Procesos Electorales*, ed. Juan M.
Matheus (Coord.) (Caracas: Editorial Jurídica Venezolana, 2010), 15 et seq.; Juan M. Matheus, 'Re-
presentación proporcional de las minorías y Ley Orgánica de Procesos Electorales', *id.,* 41 et seq.

1682   See Cosimina G. Pellegrino Pacera, 'Una introducción al estudio del referendo como mecanismo de
participación ciudadana en la Constitución de 1999', in *El Derecho Público a comienzos del siglo
XXI. Estudios homenaje al Profesor Allan R. Brewer-Carías*, vol. I (Madrid: Instituto de Derecho
Público, UCV, Civitas Ediciones, 2003), 441–481; Hildegard Rondón de Sansó, 'El referendo en la
Constitución de Venezuela de 1999', in *Estudios de Derecho Público*, ed. Román Duque Corredor y
Jesús María Casal (Coords), vol. II (Caracas: Universidad Católica Andrés Bello, 2004), 163–212.

National Assembly by means of a Resolution approved by a majority of its members; or to the citizens by means of a petition signed by at least 10% of registered voters. At local levels of government (parish, municipal, states) the consultative referendums can be convened by the Municipal Councils or by the State Legislative Councils on the initiative of two-thirds of their members, respectively; by the Mayor or the State Governor; or by the people through a petition signed by no less than 10% of the registered voters in the specific district or jurisdiction.

161. However, regarding revocation or repeal referendums, they are the consequence of the principle established in the Constitution in the sense that all popular elected public officials are subjected to revocation of their mandate (Article 6).[1683] For such purpose, Article 72 establishes the repeal referendum or referendum of revocation, which can only take place at the mid-point of the term in office. The corresponding petition for a repeal referendum can only be one of popular initiative that must be signed by at least 20% of the registered voters in the corresponding jurisdiction. In order for a mandate to be repealed or revoked, it is enough that the number of votes for the revocation be equal to or greater than the number that originally elected the official; and the voters must total at least 25% of the registered voters in the corresponding jurisdiction. If the repeal petition is approved, the substitute officer must be elected immediately according to the electoral procedures established in the Constitution and laws (see *infra* paragraph 341). This repeal referendum was distorted in 2004 regarding its application to the President of the Republic,[1684] and was transformed against the constitutional provision through a constitutional interpretation by the Constitutional Chamber of the Supreme Tribunal into a 'ratifying' referendum.[1685]

1683   See. Ricardo Antela, *La revocatoria del mandato (Régimen Jurídico del referéndum revocatorio en Venezuela)* (Caracas: Editorial Jurídica Venezolana, 2011); Carlos Ayala Corao, 'Antecedentes del Referendo Revocatorio', in *Estudios de Derecho Público*, ed. Román Duque Corredor y Jesús María Casal (Coord.), vol. II (Caracas: Universidad Católica Andrés Bello, 2004), 213–240.

1684   See Allan R. Brewer-Carías, 'El secuestro del Poder Electoral y la confiscación del derecho a la participación política mediante el referendo revocatorio presidencial: Venezuela 2000-2004', in *Derecho Constitucional para el Siglo XXI. Actas del Congreso Iberoamericano de Derecho Constitucional*, ed. Juan Pérez Royo, Joaquín Pablo Urías Martínez, Manuel Carrasco Durán, vol. I (Madrid: Thomson-Aranzadi, 2006), 1081–1126; and *Boletín Mexicano de Derecho Comparado*, Instituto de Investigaciones Jurídicas, Universidad Nacional Autónoma de México, Nº 112. México, enero-abril 2005 11–73.

1685   Decision Nº 2750 of 21 Oct. 2003 (Case: *Carlos E. Herrera Mendoza, Interpretación del artículo 72 de la Constitución*), in *Revista de Derecho Público*, Nº 93–96 (Caracas: Editorial Jurídica Venezolana, 2003), 229 et seq. This illegitimate 'mutation' of the Constitution had the precise purpose of avoiding the revocation of the mandate of the President of the Republic (H. Chávez F.) in 2004. He had been elected in August 2000 with 3,757,774 votes, and in the 2004 repeal referendum 3,989,008 votes were cast for the revocation of its mandate, so that from the constitutional point of view the mandate was revoked *ex constitutione*. Nonetheless, because 5,800,629 votes were cast for the 'no revocation', the National Electoral Council, following the Constitutional Chamber interpetation, resolved to 'ratify' the Presidente de la República up to 2007 (See in *El Nacional*, Caracas, 28 Aug. 2004, A-1 y A-2). Consequently, in an illegitimate way, a repeal referendum was transformed into a 'ratificatory referendum' or Plebiscite that is not provided in the Constitution. See Allan R. Brewer-Carías, 'La Sala Constitucional vs. el derecho ciudadano a la revocatoria de mandatos populares: de cómo un referendo revocatorio fue inconstitucionalmente convertido en un 'referendo ratificatorio',

162. Another referendum established in the Constitution is the approval referendum referred to as Draft statutes which are debated before the National Assembly, which according to Article 73 of the Constitution proceeds when at least two-thirds of the members of the Assembly so decide. In such a case, if the referendum results in the approval of the statute provided that at least 25% registered voters have concurred, the corresponding bill is to be sanctioned as law. The approbatory referendum can also be proposed by popular initiative (Article 204.7) when the National Assembly fails to take up debate on bills that also were proposed by popular initiative (Article 205).

Also, according to Article 73 of the Constitution, treaties, conventions or other international agreements that can compromise national sovereignty or transfer national powers or competencies to supra-national entities, as is the case of treaties for regional economic integration (see *supra* paragraph 126), may also be subject to approbatory referenda. In this case, the initiative corresponds to the President of the Republic in Council of Ministers, to the National Assembly when approved by a vote of at least two-thirds of its members, or to popular initiative through a petition signed by at least 15% of registered voters.

163. The Constitution also regulates the referendum for the abrogation of statutes that can be convened regarding all laws, except budgetary laws, tax laws, public debts laws, amnesty laws, human rights laws and those laws approving international treaties (Article 74). The abrogation referendums can be convened on the initiative of at least 10% of registered voters, or on the initiative of the President of the Republic in Council of Ministers. Decrees-laws issued by the President of the Republic (Article 236.8) may also be subjected to abrogation referendum, in which case the initiative to convene it can only be a popular one through a petition signed by at least 5% of registered voters.

In all cases of abrogation referendums the concurrence of at least 40% of registered voters is necessary to approve the abrogation of a statute or decree law.

§2. *Popular consultation of statutes*

164. Regarding the popular consultation, in addition to the representatives of the different sectors of society in the Nominating Committees for the elections of High-ranking officials of the Citizen, Judicial and Electoral Branches of Government (see *supra* paragraph 151; *infra* paragraphs 393 et seq.), in reference to the sanctioning of statutes by the National Assembly Article 211 of the Constitution imposes on the National Assembly the obligation to always submit draft legislation to public consultation, asking the opinion of Citizens and the organized society.This provision has been distorted by the Constitutional Chamber of the Supreme Tribunal of Justice in Decision No. 203, of March 25, 2014 (*Impugnación del Decreto de la Ley Orgánica de la Administración Pública*), by expressly exluding from the obligatory popular consultation, the statutes approved through decree-law by the President of the Repu-

---

in *Crónica sobre la 'In' Justicia Constitucional. La Sala Constitucional y el autoritarismo en Venezuela* (Caracas: Editorial Jurídica Venezolana, 2007), 349–378.

blic resulting from delegate legislation, eventhough almost all the statutes issued in the country since 1999 have been approved by decree-laws..[1686]

Also, according to Article 206, the States must be consulted by the National Assembly, through their Legislative Councils, when legislation regarding them is being considered in the National Assembly. In addition, in all the statutes that have been sanctioned under the 1999 Constitution, a chapter has always been included regarding popular participation by means of consultations on public policies.

165. The Constitution also guarantees popular initiative not only for the introduction of Draft legislation before the National Assembly by means of petitions signed by no less that the 0.1% of the registered voters (Article 204.7), but also for the purpose of convening consultative, approbatory and abrogation referenda (see *supra* paragraph 158 et seq.). Regarding the revocation or repeal referendum, it is an exclusive right of the people to convene them by popular initiative (the Popular initiative (see *supra* paragraph 161).

§3. *Local participation*

166. The municipalities are conceived in the Constitution as the primary political unit in the national organization (Article 168), thus disposed as the main institutional channel for political participation in the matters belonging to local life. This principle was ratified in all the municipal organization statutes up to 2010 as was provided in Article 1 of the 2006 Organic Law on the Municipal Public Power.[1687] This Law specifically established that the municipalities and the other local entities were the primary areas for citizens' participation in the planning, design, execution, control and evaluation of public policies, imposing on them the duty to create the needed mechanisms in order to guarantee the participation of communities and social groups (Article 7), being obliged to promote them (Article 56). For such purpose, the Organic Law enumerated all the aspects of the citizens participatory rights (Articles 255, 260), and for such purposes established that the parishes were to be the information, production and promotion centres for participatory processes, for identifying budgetary priorities, and for the promotion of citizens' participation in public affairs (Article 37).

All these provisions were eliminated in 2010, by incorporating in the Organic Law on Municipal Public Power[1688] the unconstitutional framework of the 'Communal State' and the 'Popular Power' (see *infra* paragraph 258 ff., 264), depriving the municipalities of their constitutional role of being the primary entities in the national organization of the country, and assigning such character to the Communes and to the Communal Councils (composed by non-elected officials), extinguishing the Pa-

---

1686   Available in *Revista de Derecho Público, Revista de Derecho Público,* 137 (Caracas, Editorial Jurídica Venezolana, 2014), 100-103. See the comments in Allan R. Brewer-Carías, "El fin de la llamada "democracia participativa y protagónica" dispuesto por la Sala Constitucional en fraude a la Constitución, al justificar la emisión de legislación inconsulta en violación al derecho a la participación política," in *Idem*, 157-164.

1687   *Official Gazette* N° 38.421 of 21 Apr. 2006. See Allan R. Brewer-Carías et al., *Ley Orgánica del Poder Público Municipal* (Caracas: Editorial Jurídica Venezolana, 2006).

1688   *Official Gazette* N° 6.015 Extra. 28 Dec. 2010.

rishes as local organizations for political participation composed, as they were, of elected officials.[1689]

167. Within the municipal means for political participation, Article 70 of the Constitution specifically refers to the Town Hall Meetings, also regulated in the Municipal Power Organic Law, which can be convened by the Municipal Councils, by the Parish councils and by popular initiative according to what is established in the Municipal Ordinances. The decisions adopted in such Meetings are valid if approved by the majority of the persons present provided that they refer to matters concerning the municipal life.

168. The other direct democracy participative means established in the Constitution are the Citizens Assemblies (Article 70) that were conceived in the Municipal Organic Law as local entities within the municipal framework for participation, with deliberative character, established in order to enforce governance, impulse planning and the decentralization of services and resources, in which all citizens have the right to participate. Their decisions have obligatory character (Article 70, Constitution), provided, that they are not contrary to legislation and to the community and State interest. Since 2006 and in particular, with the 2010 reforms on the Popular Power, these *Asambleas de Ciudadanos*, have been attached to the Communal State based on the 'Communes' and the 'Communal Councils', and completely taken from the Municipal Power (see *infra* paragraph 258). In this regard, the specific regulation concerning these Citizens Assemblies was initially established in the 2006 Communal Councils Law[1690] where the Citizens' Assemblies were assigned with the duty of creating the Communal Councils at the communal level without any relation with the municipalities, except for the latter to transfer activities or services to the former. However, although being organs of the State, the members of the Communal Councils are not elected by suffrage, but only appointed by Assemblies of Citizens, which have been directly controlled by the official political party, and from the institutional and financial point of view, directly dependent on the President of the Republic through a Ministry for the Communes and Citizens participation.[1691] (see *infra* paragraph 238). The result of all these reforms has been the complete demunicipalization of the country, and the erasement of the municiopalities as the primary political entities in its political organization. [1692]

1689　　*Gaceta Oficial* N° 6.015 Extra. of 28 Dec. 2010. See Allan R. Brewer-Carías et al., *Leyes Orgánicas del Poder Popular* (Caracas: Editorial Jurídica Venezolana, 2011).

1690　　*Gaceta Oficial* Extra N° 5.806 of 10 Apr. 2006.

1691　　See the Communal Councils Law in *Gaceta Oficial* Extra N° 39.335 of 28 Dec. 2009. See Allan R. Brewer-Carías, *Ley Orgánica de los Consejos Comunales* (Caracas: Editorial Jurídica Venezolana, 2009).

1692　　See Allan R. Brewer-Carías, 'El inicio de la desmunicipalización en Venezuela: La organización del Poder Popular para eliminar la descentralización, la democracia representativa y la participación a nivel local, in *AIDA, Opera Prima de Derecho Administrativo. Revista de la Asociación Internacional de Derecho Administrativo*, (México, Universidad Nacional Autónoma de México, 2007), 49 a 67

Chapter 4. The Plural Political Parties Regime

169. A democratic regime cannot exist without political parties and pluralism. That is why, after a short experiment of a dominant party system in the 1940s (1945–1948) (see *supra* paragraph 18) the democratic parties that in 1958 signed the *Pacto de Punto Fijo* after the Democratic Revolution which was initiated that same year against the Military dictatorship (see *supra* paragraph 20, 24); compromised themselves to establish a competitive and pluralistic multi-party democratic system that functioned up to 1999 (see *supra* paragraphs 21 et seq.).

The democratic period that according to those goals developed in the country during the second half of the twentieth century, was characterized from the beginning as being one with a notorious pre-eminence of the political parties that dominated all aspects of political life, and particularly participation and representation (Party State).[1693] It was their crisis and the crisis of their leadership because of the lack of reforms and of up dating the functioning of the democratic system that eventually provoked the collapse of the democratic system itself in 1998 (see *supra* paragraphs 24 et seq.). After forty years of controlling political power and having democratized the country, the parties underestimated the need the country had for more means of representation and political participation and failed to open the democratic system through, for instance, political decentralization to allow effective participation. At the end of the twentieth century, the fact was that all of the political ills of the Republic were attributed to the political parties, to the 1958 *Pacto de Punto Fijo* (see *supra* paragraph 20, 24) and to the Constitution of 1961, and political discussion ignited by the new authoritarian military and populist leadership that took control of the State centred on the anathema against them and on their destruction.

170. The result was that the presidential election of that year and the election of the National Constituent Assembly the next year (1999) were characterized by an anti-party trend that was reflected in the drafting of the new 1999 Constitution, to the point that it can be said that it was conceived as an anti-party instrument, where the expression itself of 'political party' was eliminated from its text, being substituted by the general expression of 'organizations with political purposes' (Article 67).[1694] Of course, what in 1998 and in 1999 tended to be ignored were the traditional political parties that up to then had been in control of power.

171. The constitution-making process of 1999 and the sanctioning of the new Constitution unfolded in this context, and gave way to new political parties mainly

---

1693   See Allan R. Brewer-Carías, *Problemas del Estado de Partidos* (Caracas: Editorial Jurídica Venezolana, 1989).

1694   See Lolymar Hernández Camargo, 'Los Partidos Políticos en la Constitución de la República Bolivariana de Venezuela de 1999', in *Tendencias Actuales del Derecho Constitucional. Homenaje a Jesús María Casal Montbrun*, ed. Jesús María Casal, Alfredo Arismendi y Carlos Luis Carrillo Artiles (Coord.), vol. I (Caracas: Universidad Central de Venezuela/Universidad Católica Andrés Bello, 2008), 577–590; Roberto V. Pastor; Rubén Martínez Dalmau, 'La configuración de los partidos políticos en la Constitución venezolana', in *Revista de Derecho Constitucional*, N° 4 (enero-julio) (Caracas: Editorial Sherwood, 2001), 375–389; Allan R. Brewer-Carías, 'Regulación jurídica de los partidos políticos en Venezuela', in *Regulación jurídica de los partidos políticos en América Latina*, ed. Daniel Zovatto (Coordinador) (México: Universidad Nacional Autónoma de México, International IDEA, 2006), 893–937.

constituted for electoral purposes and from the government, crushing the old and then marginalized political parties which abstained from participating in that process. During the subsequent years, these new political parties continued to act supportive of the new government and its President, and eventually resulted in being more centralized that the traditional ones, with internal governing centralized structures linked to the President of the Republic. The final result of this process was the presidential initiative, in 2006, to promote the constitution of a single United Socialist Party, using the State structures and services, which the President of the Republic presides, intending to unite in it all the various political parties that have supported his tenure. The total unification failed, because the Communist Party refused to disappear, which did not prevent the official United Socialist Party from declaring itself in 2010 as a 'Marxist' party following the 'Bolivarian docrine.'[1695]

This official United Socialist Party was in charge of supporting the presidential Constitutional Reform Draft submitted to referendum in 2007, which nonetheless was rejected by popular vote, and was also the supporting instrument of the Government candidates to the regional and municipal elections in November 2008, in which the Government's candidates lost the elections in the most important and populated states and municipalities of the country where opposition candidates to Governors and Mayors were elected.

In any case, the result of the first decade of the political life under the 1999 Constitution, which seems to ignore political parties in its regulations, has been to increase partisanship and 'party-autocracy', particularly regarding the official party that has been embodied in the State structures, in a way never before seen.

172. However, regarding the 1999 Constitution provisions related to political organizations, the traditional lack of internal democracy within the parties with their traditional pattern of leaders in perpetuity, led to a provision according to which not only the members of governing boards have to be elected by the members of each party, but also the choosing of party candidates for elections to representative offices must also be made through democratic internal elections (Article 67). To this end, the Constitution imposed the obligation that the National Electoral Council must organize such internal elections (Article 293.6), which in practice, due to the lack of statutory development of the constitutional provisions has not occurred during the first decade of the Constitution.

173. In addition, also as a reaction against the problems stemming from the public funding of political parties that was regulated under the 1998 Organic Law of Suffrage and Political Participation,[1696] which led to a cornering and monopolizing of those funds by the traditional dominant parties, the drafters of the new 1999 Constitution simply prohibited public funding of organizations with political purposes and established new controls for their private financing (Article 67). This was a regression in addressing what is a constant problem in the democratic world: the possibility for public funding of political parties in order to avoid irregular and ille-

---

1695   See 'Declaration of Principles' of the United Socialist Party of Venezuela (23 Apr. 2010), available at
        <http://psuv.org.ve/files/tcdocumentos/Declaracion-de-principios-PSUV.pdf>.

1696   *Gaceta Oficial* N° 5.233 Extra. of 28 May 1998.

gitimate funding, particularly of governing parties.[1697] Nonetheless, in a 2008 decision of the Constitutional Chamber of the Supreme Tribunal interpreting Article 67 of the Constitution, the Chamber has mutated the Constitution, concluding in a way contrary to the constitutional provision, ruling that what the Article intended was to prohibit the public financing only regarding the 'internal activities' of the parties, and not their electoral activities, which consequently since 2008 has then been accepted.[1698]

However, Article 67 of the Constitution refers to a statute the task of regulating the scope of private contributions to and finances of 'organizations with political purposes', including mechanisms to oversee the origins and management of these funds. This statute must regulate political and elections campaigns, overseeing their duration and spending limits, and inclining them towards democratization. These matters previously regulated in the 1998 Organic Law of Suffrage and Political Participation, since 2009 are regulated in the Organic Law on Electoral Processes.[1699]

174. In the same trend of reacting against political parties, the Constitution also established the principle that the members of the National Assembly are representatives of the whole of the people and 'are not to be subject to mandates or instructions other than their own conscience' (Article 200), seeking to eliminate parliamentary party groups. Nonetheless, in practice, the parliamentary factions have only changed their names and since 2000 have been called 'opinion groups'. In any case, and particularly regarding the governing party, its board presided by the President of the Republic itself, has had a more centralized control over the representatives to the National Assembly than the traditional parties before 1999.

The result of all these provisions, constitutional distortions and absence of legislation has been that in political practice, under the new Constitution, the parties have greater presence than they ever had, to the point that as aforementioned, since 1999 the President of the Republic is the President of the governing Party, which since 2007 has been the Venezuelan Unique Socialist Party, and almost all the Ministers are also members of the party's National Coordination Board. As never before, the symbiosis between the governing political party and the State and its Public Administration has been organically sealed in Venezuela, opening lines of communication and financial channels as could not have been seen in the golden age of 'party-autocracy' of the 1980s. The result has been that the same 'Party State' has continued, with the same vices of clientism, and the same control by officials sitting in governing boards at the helm of the parties who have not been chosen in free and democratic internal elections.

1697   See Juan Carlos Rey y otros, *El financiamiento de los partidos políticos y la democracia en Venezuela* (Caracas, 1981); Allan R. Brewer-Carías, 'Consideraciones sobre el financiamiento de los partidos políticos en Venezuela', in *Financiamiento y democratización interna de partidos políticos. Memora del IV Curso Anual Interamaricano de Elecciones* (San José, Costa Rica, 1991), 121 a 139.

1698   Decision of the Constitutional Chamber of the Supreme Tribunal of Justice, N° 780, of 8 May 2008 (Interpretaton of Art. 67 of the Constitucion), in *Revista de Derecho Público*, N° 114 (Caracas: Editorial Jurídica Venezolana, 2008), 126 et seq. See Allan R. Brewer-Carías, 'El juez constitucional como constituyente: el caso del financiamiento de las campañas electorales de los partidos políticos en Venezuela', in *Revista de Derecho Público*, N° 117 (Caracas, 2009, 195–203).

1699   See in *Gaceta Oficial* N° 5.928 Extra. of 12 Aug. 2009.

175. Finally, it should be emphasized that the Constitution conferred to one of the national braches of government, the Public Electoral Power through the National Electoral Council, the duty not only to organize all electoral processes but also to 'organize elections in the organizations with political purposes' (Article 293.6), establishing an intolerable principle of State intervention in the internal functioning of political parties (see *infra* paragraph 431).

Chapter 5. Institutions for Governmental Accountability

176. As aforementioned, the 1999 Constitution, in addition to qualifying the government of the Republic as democratic, participatory, elective, decentralized, alternating, responsible, plural and of revocable mandates (Article 6), has established that the officials are subject to accountability (*rendición de cuentas*), which in particular applies to elected officers, which can be subjected to repeal referendums.

Regarding the President of the Republic, the Constitution imposes on him the duty to formulate before the National Assembly in ordinary sessions of the National Assembly, each year during the first ten days of its instalment, a State of the Republic message giving account of the political, economic, social and administrative aspect of his actions during the previous year (Article 237). Regarding the Governors of states, they must give account of their actions, not before the Legislative Councils, but only before the Comptroller General of each state, having only to formulate before the Councils a report (Article 161). Regarding the representatives to the National Assembly, the Constitution imposes on them the duty to give an annual account of their actions to their electors, being subjected to repeal referendum (Article 197).

177. Within the institutions of accountability, the most distinguishing feature of the Venezuelan constitutional system is the express establishment of the repeal referendum as an institution of direct democracy (see *supra* paragraph 161) referred to all elective officials, in the sense that the mandates of all elected officers are essentially revocable (Article 72). In this regard, the popular revocation of mandates is one of the means for direct political participation of the people in exercise of its sovereignty (Article 70). The revocation of mandates, consequently, can only take place by means of the revocation referendum, which according to Article 72 of the Constitution must be made according to the following rules: First, the repeal referendum can only be convened once half of the term of the elected officer has been elapsed.Second, the request for convening a repeal referendum can only be made by popular initiative, signed by no less than the 25% of the registered electors in the corresponding constituency and filed before the National Electoral Council (Article 293,5). There cannot be more that one request for repeal referendum during the same constitutional term of the elected official.Third, in the convened repeal referendum, a number equal or superior than the equivalent to the 25% of the registered electors must concur as voting persons.Fourth, in order for a repeal of a mandate to be approved, it is sufficient that a number of voters equal or superior to those that have elected the officer must have voted in the referendum for the revocation of the mandate. In this case, the mandate of the officer must be considered as revoked, and a new election must take place immediately in order to fill the absolute absence according to the Constitution (Article 72, 233).

178. Regarding the President of the Republic, since the revocation of his mandate has the effect of an absolute absence, in case a revocation occurs, his replacement must be done as follows: if the revocation takes place during the first four years of his mandate, a new election must be made in order for the newly elected to complete the revoked President's term. If the revocation takes place during the last two years of the presidential term, the Executive Vice President must assume the position up to the end of the term (Article 233).

However, the Constitution only provided for the effects of the mandate revocation regarding the revoked official in the cases of the representatives to the National Assembly, in which case, the revoked representatives cannot seek a new election in the next constitutional term (Article 198). Nothing in this regard was established regarding the mandate revoking the other public elected officers.

179. On these matters of repeal referendums, the only experience the country had during the first decade of the 1999 Constitution was the repeal referendum of the President of the Republic (who was elected in 2000 by 3,757,774 votes), convened in 2004 by popular initiative signed by more that three and a half million signatures, which was held in August 2004.[1700] In it, 3,989,008 voters voted YES for the repeal of its mandate, that is, a number of votes superior to the ones that elected him in 2000. The consequence of that voting result, according to express provision of the Constitution, was to consider the mandate of the President revoked and to call for a new election. Nonetheless, the National Electoral Council, following a phrase in a Constitutional Chamber of the Supreme Tribunal decision, converted the repeal referendum of the President into a 'ratification referendum'[1701] that does not exist in the Constitution, just because a superior number of voters cast a NO vote, a condition or situation not established in the Constitution.

1700   See Allan R. Brewer-Carías, 'El secuestro del Poder Electoral y la confiscación del derecho a la participación política mediante el referendo revocatorio presidencial: Venezuela 2000-2004', in *Revista Jurídica del Perú*, Año LIV N° 55 (Lima, March–April 2004), 353–396; 'El secuestro del Poder Electoral y de la Sala Electoral del Tribunal Supremo y la confiscación del derecho a la participación política mediante el referendo revocatorio presidencial: Venezuela: 2000-2004', in *Revista Costarricense de Derecho Constitucional*, vol. V (Instituto Costarricense de Derecho Constitucional, Editorial Investigaciones Jurídicas S.A., San José, 2004), 167–312; 'El secuestro del poder electoral y la confiscación del derecho a la participación política mediante el referendo revocatorio presidencial: Venezuela 2000-2004', *Stvdi Vrbinati*, Rivista trimestrale di Scienze Giuridiche, Politiche ed Economiche, Year LXXI –2003/04 Nuova Serie A– N. 55,3, Università degli studi di Urbino, Urbino, 2004, 379–436; 'El secuestro del Poder Electoral y la confiscación del derecho a la participación política mediante el referendo revocatorio presidencial: Venezuela 2000-2004', in *Boletín Mexicano de Derecho Comparado* (Instituto de Investigaciones Jurídicas, Universidad Nacional Autónoma de México, N° 112. México, January–April 2005), 11–73.

1701   See Allan R. Brewer-Carías, 'La Sala Constitucional vs. el derecho ciudadano a la revocatoria de mandatos populares: de cómo un referendo revocatorio fue inconstitucionalmente convertido en un 'referendo ratificatorio', in *Crónica sobre la 'in' justicia constitucional. La Sala Constitucional y el autoritarismo en Venezuela*, ed. Allan R. Brewer-Carías (Caracas: Colección Instituto de Derecho Público, Universidad Central de Venezuela, N° 2, 2007), 349–378.

PART III. THE FEDERATION AND THE TERRITORIAL DISTRIBUTION OF STATE POWERS

180. The Venezuelan State has always been organized as a Federation. The federal form of Government was adopted in 1811 (see *supra* paragraph 2) when an elected General Congress adopted on 21 December 1811, the first Constitution of any Latin American country, the '*Federal Constitution for the States of Venezuela*', which declared the former colonial provinces as sovereign States, all of which in 1810–1811 had declared independence from Spain and adopted their own provincial constitutions or forms of government. By means of this 1811 Constitution, the country adopted a federal form of government, following the influence of the United States' Constitution, at a time when the Federation was the only new constitutional instrument recently invented, different to the centralized monarchical States. That invention was followed by the Venezuelan framers of the new State in order to unite the former Spanish Colonial Provinces that formed the Venezuelan State, which had never been previously united. In those territories there were no Viceroyalties or *Audiencias* (until 1786), and a General Captaincy exclusively for military purposes integrating the Provinces was only established in 1777. Thus, it can be said that Venezuela was the second country in constitutional history to adopt federalism.[1702]

181. The federation was later reaffirmed in the 1864 Constitution organizing the Republic as the United States of Venezuela (see *supra* paragraph 12). Even though this latter denomination was eliminated in the 1953 Constitution, the federal form of the State was kept in the following 1961 and 1999 Constitutions, in which the national Territory is divided into twenty-three states, a Capital District exists, Federal Dependencies and Federal Territories (Article 16) (see *supra* paragraph 103).

182. But in practice, with all this territorial division and the State named in the Constitution as a 'Federal Decentralized State' (Article 4), federalism in Venezuela reveals a very contradictory form of government. In effect, a Federation is a politically decentralized State organization based on the distribution of State power in a two or three level of territorial political entities functioning with some sort of autonomy. Nonetheless, in Venezuela, with a Federation organized in a three level of government (national, states and municipal), the competencies of the states and municipal level are scarce, and the autonomy of them very weak, lacking effective public policies and even of substantive sub-national constitutions. Consequently, in contrast to many Federations, what has been established in Venezuela in a very contradictory way is a Centralized Federation. Nonetheless, this situation has not always been like it is now. The process of centralization really began and developed during the twentieth century (see *supra* paragraph 57), being particularly more accentuated precisely during the first decade after the approval of the 1999 Constitution.[1703]

1702   After the North American independence (1776) and Federation (1777), the first Latin American Country to declare independence and adopt a Constitution was Venezuela in 1811, adopting the federal form of State.

1703   See Allan R. Brewer-Carías, 'El 'Estado Federal descentralizado' y la centralización de la Federación en Venezuela. Situación y Perspectiva de una contradicción constitucional', in *Revista de Estudios de la Administración Local (REAL)*, 292–293, mayo-diciembre 2003 (Madrid, 2003), 11–43; 'La descentralización política en la Constitución de 1999: Federalismo y Municipalismo (una reforma insufi-

Chapter 1. The Centralization Process of the Federation

183. In effect, the centralization process of the Federation began with the installment of the authoritarian government resulting from the 1899 Liberal Restorative Revolution, and particularly under the almost three decades of Juan Vicente Gómez dictatorship, spanning the first half of the twentieth century. During these years no democratic institutions were developed (see *supra* paragraph 16). So it was after the endless civil conflict that marked the history of Venezuela during the nineteenth century that the federal form of government began to be limited. The conflict stemmed from the permanent struggles between the regional *Caudillos* and the weak central power that had been formed, giving rise to the centralizing tendencies derived from the consolidation of the Nation State, a process that was particularly reinforced during the first half of the twentieth century.

During these decades, the autocratic regimes of the country, aided by the income derived from the new exploitation of oil by the national State (oil and the subsoil always has been the public property of the State), contributed to the consolidation of the Nation State in all aspects, based on the creation of a national army, a centralized public administration, a central taxation system, and national legislation. These centralizing tendencies almost provoked the disappearance of the Federation, the territorial distribution of power, and the effective autonomy of the twenty-three states and of the Federal District.

184. The transition from autocracy to democracy began with the death of Gómez, and later, between 1945 and 1958, when a democratic regime, in accordance with the democratic Constitution of 1961, was progressively developed in which the Federal form of the State was kept, but with a highly centralized national organization. This democratic Constitution was the longest Constitution in force in all Venezuelan history, assuring the dominance of a very centralized political party system. During its forty years of functioning, this democratic centralized political party system, without doubts, restrained the development of effective federal institutions. Nonetheless, due to the democratization process of the country and according to express constitutional provisions, a political decentralization process was forced to be applied in order to politically decentralize the federation with the transfer of powers and services from the national level of government to the state level. The process began in 1989 when the party system crisis exploded, and was forced by the democratic pressure exercised against the political parties, all of which were in the middle of a severe leadership crisis. One of the most important reforms then adopted was the provision of the direct election of the states' Governors which, until that year, were just public officials appointed by the President of the Republic.[1704] In December 1989, for the first time since the nineteenth century, states' Governors were elec-

---

ciente y regresiva)' in *Boletín de la Academia de Ciencias Políticas y Sociales*, N° 138, Año LXVIII, enero-diciembre 2001 (Caracas, 2002), 313–359, and in *Provincia. Revista Venezolana de Estudios Territoriales*, N° 7, julio-diciembre 2001, II Etapa, Centro Iberoamericano de Estudios Provinciales y Locales (CIEPROL) (Mérida: Universidad de los Andes, 2001), 7–92.

1704   See Allan R. Brewer-Carías, 'Problemas de la Federación centralizada (A propósito de la elección directa de Gobernadores)', *IV Congreso Iberoamericano de Derecho Constitucional* (México: Universidad Nacional Autónoma de México, 1992), 85–131.

ted by universal, direct and secret suffrage,[1705] and regional political life began to play an important role in the country, initializing the increasing appearance of regional and local political leaders, many of whom were from outside the traditional political parties.

Nonetheless, after important efforts in 1993, the process to politically decentralize the federation was later abandoned, mainly due to the crisis of the centralized party system, and to the consequential political void it produced in the country.

185. Ultimately, it was this crisis in the centralized party system that gave rise to the covenant of a National Constituent Assembly not regulated in the 1961 Constitution, resulting in the sanctioning of a new Constitution, the 1999 Constitution of the 'Bolivarian Republic of Venezuela' approved by referendum (15 December 1999). This new Constitution, if it is true that it provoked a radical change in the political players nationwide, also started the reversal of the decentralizing political efforts that were being made. The new Constitution continued with the same centralizing foundation embodied in the previous Constitution and, in some cases, centralizing even more aspects. For instance, although defining the decentralization process as a 'national policy devoted to strengthened democracy' (Article 158), in contrast the national public policy executed during the past decade can be characterized as a progressive centralization of government, without any real development of local and regional authorities.

Consequently, in Venezuela, federalism has been postponed and democracy has been progressively weakened; and the Constitution covers with a democratic veil an authoritarian regime, regulating a very centralized system of government where all powers of the State can be concentrated, as they now are. The Constitution has excellent declarations, including the one referring to the 'Decentralized Federal State', the enumeration of human rights, and the 'penta separation' of State branches of government. However, each of these declarations is contradicted by other regulations in the same Constitution, which allow a contrary result.

Chapter 2. The Contradictory 'Decentralized Federation' in the 1999 Constitution

§1. Constitutional Provisions Relating to Federalism in the 1999 Constitution

186. A Federation, above all, is a form of government in which public power is territorially distributed among various levels of government each of them with autonomous democratic political institutions. That is why in principle, federalism and political decentralization are intimately related concepts. Specifically, decentralization is the most effective instrument not only for the guaranteeing of civil and social rights, but to allow effective participation of the citizens in the political process. In this context, the relation between local government and the population is essential.

1705   Election and Remotion of States' Governors Law, *Gaceta Oficial* N° 4.086 Extra of 14 Apr. 1989. See the comments in Allan R. Brewer-Carías, 'Los problemas de la federación centralizada en Venezuela', in *Revista Ius et Praxis* (Universidad de Lima, N° 12, 1988), 49 a 96; and 'Bases legislativas para la descentralización política de la federación centralizada (1990: El inicio de una reforma', in *Leyes y reglamentos para la descentrlización política de la Federación*, ed. Allan R. Brewer-Carías et al. (Caracas: Editorial Jurídica Venezolana, 1994), 7–53.

That is why all consolidated democracies in the world today are embodied in clearly decentralized forms of governments, such as Federations, or like the new Regional states, as is the case of countries like Spain, Italy and France. That is why it can be said that the strong centralizing tendencies developing in Venezuela in recent years are contrary to democratic governance and political participation.

187. According to Article 4 of the 1999 Constitution, the Republic of Venezuela is formally defined 'as a decentralized Federal State under the terms set out in the Constitution' governed by the principles of 'territorial integrity, solidarity, concurrence and co-responsibility'. Nonetheless, 'the terms set out in the Constitution', are without a doubt centralizing, and Venezuela continues to be a contradictory 'Centralized Federation'.[1706]

Article 136 of the 1999 Constitution states that 'public power is distributed among the municipal, state and national entities', establishing a Federation with three levels of political governments and autonomy: *a national level* exercised by the Republic (federal level); the *States level*, exercised by the twenty-three states and a Capital District; and the *municipal level,* exercised by the 338 existing municipalities. On each of these three levels, the Constitution requires 'democratic, participatory, elected, decentralized, alternating, responsible, plural and with revocable mandates' governments (Article 6). Regarding the Capital District, it has substituted the former Federal District which was established in 1863, with the elimination of traditional federal interventions that existed regarding the authorities of the latter.

188. The organization of the political institutions in each of the territorial level is formally guided by the principle of the organic separation of powers, but with different scope. On the *national level*, with a presidential system of government, the national public power is separated among five branches of government, including: the 'Legislative, Executive, Judicial, Citizen and Electoral' (Article 136). Thus, the 1999 Constitution has surpassed the classic tripartite division of power by adding to the traditional Legislative, Executive and Judicial branches, the Citizen branch, which includes the Public Prosecutor Office, the General Comptrollership Office, and the People's Rights Defender Office, as well as an Electoral branch of government controlled by the National Electoral Council (see *infra* paragraph 417 et seq.).

The new Citizen and Electoral branches, as well as the Judiciary, are reserved only to the national or federal level of government. Therefore, Venezuela does not have a Judiciary at the state level. In fact, since 1945, the Judicial branch has been reserved to the national level of government, basically due to the national character of all major legislation and Codes (Civil, Commercial, Criminal, Labour and Procedural Codes) (see *supra* paragraphs 128, 145). Consequently, since Courts are national (federal), there is no room for state constitution regulations on these matters.

1706   See Allan R. Brewer-Carías, *Federalismo y Municipalismo en la Constitución de 1999* (Caracas: Universidad Católica del Táchira-Editorial Jurídica Venezolana, 2001); 'Centralized Federalism in Venezuela', in *Duquesne Law Review*, vol. 43, no. 4, summer 2005. Duquesne University, Pittsburgh, Pennsylvania, 2005, 629–643. See also Allan R. Brewer-Carias and Jan Kleinheisterkamp, 'Venezuela: The End of federalism?,' in Daniel Halberstam and Mathias Reimann (Editors), *Federalism and Legal Unification: A Comparative Empirical Investigation of Twenty Systems*, (London, Springer, 2014), 523-543.

Regarding judicial review, the Constitutional Chamber of the Supreme Tribunal of Justice is the constitutional organ with power to review and annul with *erga omnes* effects (Article 336) all laws (national, state and municipal) including state constitutions when contrary to the national constitution (see *infra* paragraphs 644 et seq.), so there are no state courts or judicial organization.

189. Pertaining to the Legislative branch, it must be noted that the Constitution of 1999 established a one-chamber National Assembly, thus ending the country's federalist tradition of bicameralism by eliminating the Senate. As a result, Venezuela has also become a rare federal State without a federal chamber or Senate where the states, through their representatives, can be equal in the sense of equal vote. In the National Assembly there are no representatives of the states, and its members are global representatives of the citizens and of all the states collectively. Theoretically, these global representatives are not subject to mandates or instructions, but only subject to the 'dictates of their conscience' (Article 201). This has effectively eliminated all vestiges of territorial representation.

190. Regarding the states' branch of government, the 1999 Constitution established that each state has a Governor who must be elected by a universal, direct and secret vote (Article 160). Each state must also have a Legislative Council comprised of representatives elected according to the principle of proportional representation (Article 162). According to the Constitution, it is the responsibility of each states' Legislative Council to enact their own Constitution in order 'to organize their branches of government' along the guidelines of the national Constitution, which in principle guarantees the autonomy of the states (Article 159).

§2. *Limits to the Contents of the Sub-national Constitutions*

191. Consequently, each state has constitutional power to enact its own sub-national constitution in order to organize the state's Legislative and Executive branches of government, and to regulate the state's own organ for audit control. But in spite of these regulations on the organization and functioning of the state branches of government, the scope of states' powers has also been seriously limited by the 1999 Constitution, particularly due to the fact that for the first time in federal history, the Constitution refers to a national legislation for the establishment of the general regulation on this matter.

192. In effect, and in relation to the states' Legislative branch of government, the 1999 Constitution states that the organization and functioning of the states' Legislative Councils must be regulated by a *national statute* (Article 162), a manifestation of centralism never before envisioned, according to which the national Legislative power has the power to enact legislation in order to determine the organization and functioning of all of the state legislatures.

According to this power, the National Assembly has sanctioned an *Organic Law for the State Legislative Councils* (2001)[1707] in which detailed regulations are established regarding their organization and functioning, and in addition, even without constitutional authorization, regarding the statutes and attributions of the Legislative

---

1707   *Gaceta Oficial* N° 37.282 of 13 Sep. 2001.

Council members, as well as regarding the general rules for the exercise of the legislative functions, or the law enacting procedure itself. With this national regulation, the effective contents of the state constitutions regarding their Legislative branch have been voided, and are limited to repeat what is established in the said national organic law or statute.

193. Additionally, the possibility of organizing the Executive branch of government of each state was also limited by the 1999 Constitution, which has established the basic rules concerning the Governors as head of the executive branch. The Constitution has additional regulations referring to the public administration (national, states and municipal), public employees (civil service), and the administrative procedures and public contracts in all of the three levels of government. All of these rules have also been developed in two 2001 national *Organic Laws on Public Administration* [1708] *and on Civil Service.* [1709] Therefore, state constitutions have also been voided of real content in these matters, have limited scope, and their norms tend to just repeat what has been established in the national organic laws or statutes.

194. Finally, regarding other state organs, in 2001, the National Assembly also sanctioned a *Law on the appointment of the States' Controller,* [1710] limiting the powers of the State Legislative Councils on the matter without constitutional authorization. [1711] In addition, the national intervention regarding the various state constitutions and their respective regulations in relation to their own state organizations, has been completed by the Constitutional Chamber of the Supreme Tribunal of Justice. Specifically, the Constitutional Chamber of the Supreme Tribunal of Justice's rulings during the past years (2001–2002) included the annulment of the articles of three state constitutions creating an Office of the Peoples' Defender, on the grounds that Citizens rights is a matter reserved to the national (federal) level of government. [1712]

195. As mentioned, the National Constitution establishes three levels of territorial autonomy and regulates the distribution of state powers, directly regulating the local or municipal government in an extensive manner. Therefore, the states' constitutions and legislations can regulate municipal or local government only according to what is established in the national Constitution, and in the *National Organic Law on Municipal Power,* [1713] which leaves very little room for the state regulation.

Thus, without any possibility for the state legislatures to regulate anything related to civil, economic, social, cultural, environmental or political rights; and with the

---

1708   *Gaceta Oficial* N° 6.147 Extra. of 17 Nov. 2014.

1709   *Gaceta Oficial* N° 37.522 of 6 Sep. 2002.

1710   *Gaceta Oficial* N° 37.304 of 16 Oct. 2001.

1711   This Law was specifically abrogated by Law published in *Gaceta Oficial* N° 39.217 of 9 Jul. 2009, and a specific Regulation on the matter was issued by the Comptroller General of the Republic.

1712   See decisions N° 1182 of 11 Oct. 2000, N° 1395 of 7 Aug. 2001 and N° 111 of 12 Feb. 2004 (States of Mérida, Aragua and Lara), in *Revista de Derecho Público*, N° 84 (Caracas: Editorial Jurídica Venezolana, 2000), 177 et seq.; and in *Revista de Derecho Público* N° 85–88 (Caracas: Editorial Jurídica Venezuela, 2001).

1713   *Gaceta Oficial* N° 6.015 Extra. of 28 Dec. 2010.

limited powers to regulate their own branches of government, as well as other state organizations including the General Comptroller and Peoples' Defender, very little scope has been left for the contents of sub-national constitutions.[1714]

§3. *The Constitutional System of Distribution of Powers within the National, State and Municipal Levels of Government*

196. Federalism is based on an effective distribution of powers within the various levels of government, and in Venezuela, between the national, state and municipal levels. Accordingly, the National Constitution enumerates the competencies attributed in an exclusive way to the national (Article 156), state (Article 154), and municipal (Article 178) levels of government, but in fact, under these regulations, these exclusive matters are almost all reserved for the national level of government, an important portion attributed to the municipalities, and very few of the exclusive matters are attributed to the states.[1715]

197. According to Article 156, the National Power has exclusive competencies in the following matters: international relations; security and defence; nationality and alien status; national police; economic regulations; mining and oil industries; national policies and regulations on education, health, the environment, land use, transportation, industrial, and agricultural production; post, and telecommunications; and legislation concerning constitutional rights; civil law, commercial law, criminal law, the penal system, procedural law and private international law; electoral law; expropriations for the sake of public or social interests; public credit; intellectual, artistic, and industrial property; cultural and archaeological treasures; agriculture; immigration and colonization; indigenous people and the territories occupied by them; labour and social security and welfare; veterinary and phytosanitary hygiene; notaries and public registers; banks and insurances; lotteries, horse racing, and bets in general; and the organization and functioning of the organs of the central authori-

---

1714   See. Michael Penfold-Becerra, 'Federalism and Institutional Change in Venezuela', in *Federalism and Democracy in Latin America*, ed. Edward L. Gibson (Baltimore, 2004) 197–225; Rafael J. Chavero Gazdik, 'La forma de Estado prevista en la Constitución de 1999 (¿Un canto de sirenas?)', in *Revista de Derecho Público*, N° 81 (Caracas: Editorial Jurídica Venezolana, 2000), 29–39; José Peña Solís, 'Aproximación al proceso de descentralización delineado en la Constitución de 1999', in *Estudios de Derecho Público: Libro Homenaje a Humberto J. La Roche Rincón*, vol. II. (Caracas: Tribunal Supremo de Justicia, 2001), 217–282.

1715   See Gustavo J. Linares Benzo, 'El sistema venezolano de repartición de competencias', in *El Derecho Público a comienzos del siglo XXI. Estudios homenaje al Profesor Allan R. Brewer-Carías*, vol. I (Madrid: Instituto de Derecho Público, UCV, Civitas Ediciones, 2003), 702–713; Manuel Rachadell, 'La distribución del poder tributario entre los diversos niveles del Poder Público según la Constitución de 1999', in *Revista de Derecho Administrativo*, N° 8 (enero-abril) (Caracas: Editorial Sherwood, 2000), 179–205; and Allan R. Brewer Carías, 'Consideraciones sobre el régimen de distribución de Competencias del Poder Público en la Constitución de 1999', in *Estudios de Derecho Administrativo: Libro Homenaje a la Universidad Central de Venezuela*, vol. I (Caracas: Imprenta Nacional, 2001), 107–138, and 'La distribución territorial de competencias en la Federación venezolana', in *Revista de Estudios de la Administración Local, Homenaje a Sebastián Martín Retortillo*, N° 291, enero-abril 2003 (Madrid: Instituto Nacional de Administración Pública, 2003), 163–200; and 'Consideraciones sobre el régimen constitucional de la organización y funcionamiento de los Poderes Públicos', in *Revista Derecho y Sociedad de la Universidad Monteávila*, N° 2 (abril) (Caracas, 2001), 135–150.

ty and the other organs and institutions of the State. The administration of justice, as mentioned, also falls within the exclusive jurisdiction of the national government (Article 156.31).

Article 156.32 of the Constitution also specifies that the national level of government also has legislative attributions on all matter of 'national competence', which explicitly attributes to the National Assembly power to legislate regarding the following matters: armed forces and civil protection; monetary policies; the coordination and harmonization of the different taxation authorities; the definition of principles, parameters, and restrictions, and in particular the types of tributes or rates of the taxes of the states and municipalities; as well as the creation of special funds that assure the inter-territorial solidarity; foreign commerce and customs; mining and natural energy resources like hydrocarbon, fallow and waste land; and the conservation, development and exploitation of the woods, grounds, waters, and other natural resources of the country; standards of measurement and quality control; the establishment, coordination, and unification of technical norms and procedures for construction, architecture, and urbanism, as well as the legislation on urbanism; public health, housing, food safety, environment, water, tourism, and the territorial organization; navigation and air transport, ground transport, maritime and inland waterway transport; post and telecommunication services and radio frequencies; public utilities such as electricity, potable water, and gas. Furthermore, the Constitution attributes to the national power the powers to conclude, approve and ratify international treaties (Article 154); and legislate on antitrust and the abuse of market power (Articles 113 and 114).

198. Regarding local governments, Article 178 assigns the municipalities power to govern and administrate the matters attributed to them in the Constitution and the national laws with respect to local life, and within them, the ones related to urban land use, historic monuments, social housing, local tourism, public space for recreation, construction, urban roads and transport, public entertainment, local environmental protection and hygiene, advertising regulations, urban utilities, electricity, water supply, garbage collection and disposal, basic health and education services, municipal police, funerals services, child care and other community matters. Only the matters related to local public events and funerals can be regarded as exclusive powers of the municipalities, and the rest are concurrent with the national government. Nonetheless, these matters can always be regulated by national legislation, as the municipal autonomy is essentially limited (Article 168).

199. Regarding state competencies, the National Constitution fails to enumerate substantive matters within exclusive state jurisdiction, and only assigns as matters corresponding to them, generally in a concurrent way, the municipal organizations, the non-metallic mineral exploitation, the police, the state roads, the administration of national roads, and the commercial airports and ports (Article 164). Nonetheless, for instance, in the Constitution, the possibility for the state legislature to regulate its own local government is also very limited, being subjected to what is established in the national Organic Municipal Law.

According to the Constitution, State Legislative Councils can enact legislation on matters that are in the states' scope of powers (Article 162). However, these powers are referred to concurrent matters, and according to the National Constitution their exercise depends on the previous enactment of national statutes and regulations (framework laws) (see *supra* paragraphs 101, 106). As a result, the legislative powers of the states are also very limited, and in any event, the resulting states legislation on concurrent matters must always adhere to the principles of 'interdependence, coordination, cooperation, co-responsibility and subsidiary' (Article 165).

200. However, regarding residual competencies, the principle of favouring the states as in all federations, although being a constitutional tradition in Venezuela, in the 1999 Constitution has also been limited by expressly assigning the national level of government a parallel and prevalent residual taxation power in matters not expressly attributed to the states or municipalities (Article 156.12). Furthermore, Article 156.33 provides for the jurisdiction of the national power 'in all other matters that correspond to it due to their nature or kind', establishing an implicit powers clause in favour of the federal government[1716] that has been strengthened by the Constitutional Chamber jurisprudence.[1717] In summary, the general residual power allocated to the states is a rather theoretical one, and in practice, in case of doubt, the presumption in favour of federal powers will virtually always prevail.

201. Another aspect that must be mentioned regarding the distribution of competencies between the national and state levels is the provision in the 1999 Constitution, following the same provision of the 1961 Constitution, allowing the possibility of decentralizing competencies via their transfer from the national level to the states.[1718] This process was regulated in the 1989 Law on Delimitation, Transfer and Decentralization Competencies between public entities, and even though important efforts for decentralization were made between 1990 and 1994 in order to revert the centralizing tendencies,[1719] the process, unfortunately was later abandoned. Since 2003, the transfers of competencies that were made, including health services, started the reversion process, which has been completed in 2008,[1720] in particular with the reform of the aforementioned 1989 Decentralization Law, sanctioned by the National Assembly on 17 March 2009, reverting to the national level the 'exclusive' competence of the states for the management and making use of national highways, bridges and commercial ports located in the states, established in Article 164.10 of the Constitution.[1721] This reform was also proposed by the President of the Republic in the rejected 2007 Constitutional Reform.

1716   See. C. Ayala Corao, 'Naturaleza y Alcance de la Descentralización Estadal', in *Leyes y reglamentos para la Descentralización Política de la Federación* 94, ed. Allan R. Brewer-Carías et al. (Caracas, 1990), referring to the *Exposición de Motivos* of the 1961 Constitution.

1717   See decision of the Constitutional Chamber of the Supreme Tribunal of 15 Apr. 2008, in *Revista de Derecho Público*, N° 114 (Caracas: Editorial Jurídica Venezolana, 2008), 164.

1718   See José Peña Solís, 'Aproximación al proceso de descentralización delineado en la Constitución de 1999', in *Estudios de Derecho Público: Libro Homenaje a Humberto J. La Roche Rincón*, vol. II (Caracas: Tribunal Supremo de Justicia, 2001), 217–282.

1719   See Allan R. Brewer-Carías et al., *Leyes y reglamentos para la Descentralización Política de la Federación* (Caraca: Editorial Jurídica Venezolana, 1990); *Informe sobre la descentralización en Venezuela 1993. Informe del Ministro de Estado para la Descentralización* (Caracas, 1994).

1720   See Decree N° 6.543, on the renationalization of the Health Care services in Miranda State, *Gaceta Oficial* N° 39.072 of 3 Dec. 2008.

1721   *Gaceta Oficial* N° 39.140 of 17 Mar. 2009. For the purpose of this reform, the Constitutional Chamber previously issued decision N° 565 of 15 Apr. 2008 'interpreted' the Constitution changing the

Chapter 3. The Organization of Public Power in the Territory

§1. The States

I. The Limited States Autonomy

202. The territorial distribution of state power within the framework of a federation implies a decentralized structure of political entities that must be essentially autonomous. For this reason, Article 159 of the Constitution establishes that the twenty-three states (see *supra* paragraph 186) are 'politically autonomous and equal' entities with full legal personality. The states are required to uphold the independence, sovereignty and integrity, as well as the Constitution and laws of the Republic, and to ensure that these are obeyed within their territory.

This states' autonomy is, of course, political (in the election of its authorities), organizational (in drafting of their own Constitutions), administrative (in the investment of their revenue), legal (in the non-reviewing of state actions except through the courts of law) and taxing (in the creation of state taxes); aspects that in principle must not be regulated by national legislation, but only in the national Constitution.

203. Nonetheless, as aforementioned, state autonomy is limited in the Constitution corresponding, for instance, to a national statute to establish the organic and functional regime of states' Legislative Councils (Article 162), which should be the exclusive competence of states, and be regulated according to the state drafted Constitutions (Article 164.1).

Similar limitations are established by the 1999 Constitution with respect to the exercise of other states' competencies. For example, in the area of taxation, not only has the Constitution left the matter to future *national* legislation, but it has also definitively established that it is to be the National Power that will coordinate state and municipal taxing authority (Article 156.13).

In regards to concurrent powers between state and national governments, these, according to the Constitution of 1999, are to be exercised by the states only in conformity to 'framework laws' *(leyes de base)* pre-enacted on the national level (Article 165). In some cases, as in the area of police, the functioning of state police may only be exercised in accord with applicable national legislation (Article 164, Order 6).

II. The States' Executive and Legislative Powers

204. According to Article 160, the government and administration of each state is the responsibility of a Governor who is elected for a term of four years by a majority of the voters. According to the Constitution, the Governor could be re-elected for a consecutive second term; a limit that was eliminated with the constitutional amendment approved by referendum on 14 February 2009 (see *supra* paragraph 37).

---

character of such 'exclusive' competency into a 'concurrent' one. See in <www.tsj.gov.ve/decisiones/scon/Abril/565-150408-07-1108.htm>. See Allan R. Brewer-Carías, 'La Sala Constitucional como poder constituyente: la modificación de la forma federal del estado y del sistema constitucional de división territorial del poder público', in *Revista de Derecho Público*, N° 114 (April–June 2008) (Caracas: Editorial Jurídica Venezolana, 2008), 247–262.

Legislative powers are exercised in each state by a Legislative Council constituted by no more than fifteen and no less than seven members who proportionally represent the population of the states as well as municipalities (Article 162).

As mentioned, the Constitution undermines the autonomy of the states by attributing to the National Assembly the power to establish the organization and functions of states' Legislative Councils (Article 162) when this ought to correspond to state constitutions drafted by State Legislative Councils under Article 164. In all events, with respect to competency, State Legislative Councils have been attributed the powers to legislate on matters within state competence; to approve the state budget; and to exercise the other powers conferred to the states by the Constitution and the statutes (Article 162).

§2. The Municipalities

I. The Municipal Autonomy

205. According to Article 168 of the Constitution, municipalities are the primary political units in the organization of the nation, having legal personality and autonomy within constitutional and legal limits. Municipal organization is to be, in all events, democratic and possess the characteristics of local government (Article 169).[1722]

Municipal autonomy entails the following under Article 168: the election of municipal authorities; the administration and governance of matters falling within municipal jurisdiction; and the creation, collection, and investment of municipal taxes. In addition, except through designated courts of law, municipal actions may not be impugned or otherwise reviewed on the national and state levels.[1723] The organizational regime of municipalities and other local entities is to be governed by the legislation enacted according to the principles laid down in the Constitution, by national organic legislation, and by laws sanctioned by the State Legislative Councils (Article 169).

As aforementioned, Article 168 of the Constitution establishes the principle of participation providing that actions carried out by municipalities within their jurisdiction are to be undertaken while incorporating citizens' participation in the definition, execution, regulation and evaluation of the results of public business, according to law, in an adequate, effective and opportune manner.

206. One of the most important problems of the system of municipal government in Venezuela has been the excessive uniformity in the organization of municipal governments, provoking the almost inapplicability of the Organic Law of Municipal

---

1722   See Argenis Urdaneta, 'El Poder Público Municipal en el Estado federal descentralizado', in *El Derecho Público a comienzos del siglo XXI. Estudios homenaje al Profesor Allan R. Brewer-Carías*, vol. I (Madrid:Instituto de Derecho Público, UCV, Civitas Ediciones, 2003), 731–744.

1723   See José L. Villegas Moreno, 'La autonomía local y su configuración en la Constitución venezolana de 1999', in *El Derecho Público a comienzos del siglo XXI. Estudios homenaje al Profesor Allan R. Brewer-Carías*, vol. I (Madrid: Instituto de Derecho Público, UCV, Civitas Ediciones, 2003), 715–729.

Power[1724] particularly in many small municipal entities. To avoid this situation, Article 169 of the Constitution establishes the principle that the legislation passed to develop and apply constitutional principles regarding municipalities and other local entities must create diverse organizational regimes for their administration and government, taking into account such local factors as population, economic development, capacity for generating revenue, geographic situation and other historic and cultural factors that may have relevance to government. In particular, such legislation is to establish options for the organization of local government and administration suitable to municipalities containing indigenous populations. Unfortunately none of these aspects have been regulated in the Organic Law.

27. However, it must be pointed out that municipalities, according to Article 168 of the Constitution, are the 'primary political unit of the national organization', and the basis for political participation. Nonetheless, this has been virtually rendered moot by the creation, since 2006, of the parallel structure of the Communal Councils,[1725] which are designated by local 'assemblies of the Citizens' (Article 70), which can be formed by interested citizens. These Assemblies, since 2010, have been organized as one of the main organizations of the 'Communal State' for the exercise of the 'Popular Power' that has been established by-passing the Constitution[1726] (see *infra* paragraph 238, 239, 242, 258 ff.,264), having jurisdiction to 'approve the rules of the communal living of the community' (Article 6.1). The 'Community' is defined as 'the social conglomerate of families and citizen which live in a specific geographic area, which share a common history and interests, which know each other and have relations with each other, use the same public utilities and share similar economic, social, urban and other necessities and potentials' (Article 4.1). Although these structures are supposed to allow self-governance of local communities, this is contradicted due to the high degree of centralization set forth by their organization being directly coordinated, supervised and financed by the National Executive through a Ministry of the Communes and Citizens Participation, without the participation of the states or the municipalities. In addition, the Communal Councils have been created outside the municipal organization of the country.

II. *The Municipal Executive and Legislative Powers*

208. Municipal government and administration corresponds to the Mayors, who according to the terms of the Civil Code (Article 446, et seq.*)* are the primary civil

---

1724   *Official Gazette* N° 6.015 Extra. 28 Dec. 2010. On the previous 2006 Law (*Gaceta Oficial* N° 38.421 of 21 Apr. 2006), see Allan R. Brewer-Carías et al., *Ley Orgánica del Poder Público Municipal* (Caracas: Editorial Jurídica venezolana, 2006).

1725   *Gaceta Oficial* N° 5.806 Extra. of 10 Apr. 2006. See Allan R. Brewer-Carías, 'El inicio de la desmunicipalización en Venezuela: La organización del Poder Popular para eliminar la descentralización, la democracia representativa y la participación a nivel local', in *Revista de la Asociación Internacional de Derecho Administrativo* (México, 2007), 49–67.

1726   Organic Law on the Communal Councils in *Gaceta Oficial* N° 39.335 of 28 Dec. 2009. See Allan R. Brewer-Carías et al., *Ley Orgánica de los Consejos Comunales* (Caracas, Editorial Jurídica venezolana, 2010). See also Organic Law on the Popular Power, in *Oficial* N° 6.011 Extra. 21 Dec. 2010. See Allan R. Brewer-Carías et al., *Leyes Orgánicas sobre el Poder Popular y el Estado Comunal* (Caracas: Editorial Jurídica Venezolana, 2011).

authority (Article 174). The Mayors are elected for a term of four years, by a majority of those who vote in an election, and the Constitution established that they could be re-elected for a single second consecutive term; a limit that was eliminated with the constitutional amendment approved by referendum on 14 February 2009 (see *supra* paragraph 37).

Article 175 of the Constitution confers the legislative functions of municipalities to the Municipal Councils composed of members elected by universal, secret and direct suffrage in a number, and according to conditions, established in the national legislation based on the system of proportional representation and personalized vote (see *supra* paragraph 151). These Municipal Councils are empowered to enact Municipal Ordinances that are 'local laws' related to the matters assigned to the municipalities (see *supra* paragraph 208).

§3. *The Capital District and the Metropolitan Municipal Government of Caracas*

209. According to Article 16 of the Constitution, in addition to the twenty-three states, the national territory has also a Capital District and Federal Dependencies that are the Venezuelan Islands in the Caribbean Sea. Since 1992 there have been no Federal Territories.

The Capital District was established in the 1999 Constitution in substitution of the Federal District that existed since 1863 with a very dependent configuration regarding the President of the Republic, who used to be the highest authority in the District. He exercised his powers through an appointed Governor (Article 190.17, 1961 Constitution). With the 1999 Constitution, the Capital District was conceived as an additional political entity in the territory, independent from the National Executive that needs to have a democratic government of its own. Nonetheless, and in spite of such new democratic configuration, the National Assembly passed on April 2009 a Special Law on the Organization and regime of the Capital District,[1727] establishing just an administrative entity dependent upon the national level of government, so the Chief Executive of the capital District is freely appointed and dismissed by the President of the Republic, and the legislative functions in the District corresponds to the National Assembly (Article 7). In the rejected 2007 Constitutional Reform, the President of the Republic proposed this same configuration of the Capital District with the patterns of the former Federal District established in 1863.

210. The municipal government in the territory of the Capital District, where part of the City of Caracas as the capital of the Republic is located, has been organized in the Constitution with two levels of local government organization: at the metropolitan level, the Metropolitan Government of Caracas (Article 18), with a Head Mayor (*Alcalde Mayor*) and a Metropolitan Council, both elected by popular vote; and at the municipal level, with their corresponding Mayors and Municipal Councils in the various municipalities of the city (*Libertador, Baruta, Chacao, Sucre, El Hatillo*) elected by the people. This metropolitan organization was established according to

---

1727   *Gaceta Oficial* N° 39.156 of 13 Apr. 2009. See Allan R. Brewer-Carías et al., *Leyes sobre el Distrito Capital y el Área Metropolitána de Caracas* (Caracas: Editorial Jurídica Venezolana, 2009).

the Special Law on the Metropolitan District Regime sanctioned by the National Constituent Assembly in March 2000.[1728]

Chapter 4. The Financing System of the Federation

211. Regarding the financing of the federation, virtually everything in the 1999 Constitution concerning the taxation system is more centralized than in the previous 1961 Constitution, and the powers of the states in tax matters are essentially eliminated.

The National Constitution lists the national government competencies with respect to basic taxes, including income tax; inheritance and donation taxes; taxes on capital and production; value added tax; taxes on hydrocarbon resources and mines; taxes on the import and export of goods and services, taxes on the consumption of liquor, alcohol, cigarettes and tobacco (Article 156.12). The National Constitution also expressly allocates local taxation powers to the municipalities including property, commercial and industrial activities taxes (Article 179). The National Constitution gives the national government residual competencies in tax matters (Article 156.12).

In contrast, the Constitution does not grant the states competencies in matters of taxation, except with respect to official stationery and revenue stamps (Article 164.7). Thus, the states can only collect taxes when the National Assembly expressly transfers the power to them by a statute, which contains specific taxation powers (Article 167.5). No such statute has yet been approved (see *infra* paragraph 602).

212. Lacking their own resources from taxation, state financing is accomplished by the transfer of national financial resources through three different channels, which are all politically controlled by the national government. The first channel is by means of the 'Constitutional Contribution' (*Situado Constitucional*) which is an annual amount established in the National Budget Law (see *infra* paragraph 608) equivalent to a minimum of 15% and a maximum of 20% of total ordinary national income, estimated annually (Article 167.4), which must be distributed among the states according to their population. The second channel is through a nationally established system of special economic allotments for the benefit of those states in the territories of which mining and hydrocarbon projects are being developed. The benefits that accompany this statute have also been extended to include other non-mining states (Article 156.16).[1729] The third channel of financing for states and mu-

---

1728   *Gaceta Oficial* N° 36.906 of 8 Mar. 2000. See Manuel Rachadell, '¿Distrito Capital o Distrito Metropolitano?', in *El Derecho Público a comienzos del siglo XXI. Estudios en homenaje al Profesor Allan R. Brewer-Carías,* vol. III (Madrid: Instituto de Derecho Público, UCV, Civitas Ediciones, 2003), 3271 a 3311; Alfredo De Stefano Pérez, 'Aproximación al estudio del Distrito Metropolitano de Caracas', in *Temas de Derecho Administrativo: Libro Homenaje a Gonzalo Pérez Luciani,* vol. II (Caracas, Editorial Torino, 2002), 553–592; Allan R. Brewer-Carías, 'Consideraciones sobre el régimen constitucional del Distrito Capital y del sistema de gobierno municipal de Caracas', in *Revista de Derecho Público,* N° 82 (abril-junio) (Caracas: Editorial Jurídica Venezolana, 2000), 5–17; and in *Revista Iberoamericana de Administración Pública (RIAP),* Ministerio de Administraciones Públicas, N° 5, julio-diciembre 2000 (Madrid: 2000), 17–39.

1729   See Law on Special Economic Allotments derived from Mines and Hydrocarbons to the States and the Metropolitan District of Caracas, *Gaceta Oficial* N° 37086 of 27 Nov. 2000; substituted by the

nicipalities also comes from national funds. The most important source was the Intergovernmental Fund for Decentralization, created by statute in 1993[1730] as a consequence of the national regulation of VAT, which was to be substituted by an Interstate Compensation Fund established in the National Constitution (Article 167.6), and that has been created in 2010, in the Law establishing the Federal Council of Government.[1731] This Council was conceived in the 1999 Constitution as an intergovernmental entity for the purpose of planning and coordinating the policies and actions for the development of the decentralization process and transfer of powers from the central government to the component states and municipalities. It is headed by the Vice President of the Republic and integrated by Ministers, Governors of the component states and one Mayor from each component state, as well as of representatives of the civil society (Article 185). Nonetheless, in the 2010 Law such entity has only been organized as an instrument controlled by the Central Government, designed to reinforce the centralization process through a central planning system.

However, following a long tradition, the states and municipalities cannot borrow nor have public debt due to the requirement of a special national statute to approve state borrowing.

213. As it can be deduced from what has been said, the declaration of Article 4 of the 1999 Constitution regarding the 'Federal Decentralized' form of the Venezuelan government is mere wording, being a formula that is contradicted by all the other regulations regarding the federalism contained in the Constitution, which, on the contrary, shows that the Federation in Venezuela is a very Centralized Federation. This situation, of course, affects the democratic regime and governance deeply.

Federalism and decentralization in the contemporary world are matters of democracy. There are no decentralized autocracies, and there have never been decentralized authoritarian governments, only democracies can be decentralized. Autocracies and authoritarian governments have been, and will remain, centralized. Thus, the reality of the political situation in Venezuela is that democracy is very weak. Although democracy is based on elections, it cannot be consolidated without a real separation of powers, and without the real possibility of political participation due to the lack of decentralization.

Law on Special Economic Allotments derived from Mines and Hydrocarbons, *Gaceta Oficial* N°
5991 Extra. of 29 Jul. 2010. See Adriana Vigilanza García, *La Federación descentralizada. Mitos y realidades en el reparto de tributos y otros ingresos entre los entes políticos territoriales de Venezuela* (Caracas, 2010).

1730   See in *Gaceta Oficial* N° 5.805 Extra. of 22 Mar. 2006.

1731   See in *Gaceta Oficial* N° 5.963 Extra. of 22 Feb. 2010. See Manuel Rachadell, 'El Consejo Federal de Gobierno y el Fondo de Compensación', in *Revista de Derecho del Tribunal Supremo de Justicia*, N° 7 (Caracas, 2002), 417 a 457; Emilio Spósito Contreras, 'Reflexiones sobre el Consejo Federal de Gobierno como máxima instancia de Participación administrativa', in *Temas de derecho administrativo, Libro Homenaje a Gonzalo Pérez Luciani*, vol. II, Tribunal Supremo de Justicia, Colección Libros Homenaje, N° 7 (Caracas, 2002), 827 a 863; José V. Haro, 'Aproximación a la noción del Consejo Federal de Gobierno previsto en la Constitución de 1999', in *Revista de Derecho Constitucional*, N° 7 (enero-junio) (Caracas: Editorial Sherwood, 2003), 161–166.

PART IV. THE CONSTITUTIONAL SYSTEM OF SEPARATION OF POWERS

Chapter 1. The Principle of Separation of Powers

§1. The Venezuelan Constitutional Tradition

214. The principle of separation of powers, following the provisions of the Constitution of Virginia of 1776 (section 3.1), and of the French Declaration of Rights of Man and Citizens of 1789, (Article 16), was incorporated in the first modern Constitution adopted in all Latin America, which as aforementioned, was the 1811 Federal Constitution of the States of Venezuela, setting forth in its Preamble that:

> The exercise of authority conferred upon the Confederation could never be reunited in its respective functions. The Supreme Power must be divided in the Legislative, the Executive and the Judicial, and conferred to different bodies independent between them and regarding its respective powers.

To this proposition, Article 189 of the Constitution added that:

> The three essential Departments of government, that is, the legislative, the Executive and the Judicial, must always be kept separated and independent one from the other according to the nature of a free government, which is convenient in the connection chain that unites all the fabric of the Constitution in an indissoluble way of Friendship and Union.

Consequently, since the beginning of modern constitutionalism, the principle of separation of constitutional power was also adopted in Venezuela, in particular, according to the trends of the presidential system of government within a check and balance conception, granting the Judiciary specific powers of judicial review. The latter, according to the objective guarantee of the Constitution established in Article 227 of the same 1811 Constitution, in the sense that 'The laws sanctioned against the Constitution will have no value except when fulfilling the conditions for a just and legitimate revision and sanction [of the Constitution]'; and in Article 199, in the sense that any law sanctioned by the federal legislature or by the provinces contrary to the fundamental rights enumerated in the Constitution 'will be absolutely null and void'.

215. Since 1811, all the Constitutions in Venezuelan history have established and guaranteed the principle of separation of powers, particularly between the three classical Legislative, Executive and Judicial branches of government (powers) in a system of check and balance, and always giving the Judiciary, judicial review power. For such purpose, the independence and autonomy of the branches of government have been the most important aspects regulated in the Constitutions, particularly during democratic regimes, due to the fact that the principle of separation of powers in contemporary constitutionalism has become one of the basic conditions for its existence, and for the possibility of guaranteeing the enjoyment and protection of fundamental rights. On the contrary, without separation of powers, and without autonomy and independence between the branches of government, no democratic regime can be developed and no guarantee of fundamental rights can exist.

§2. *Separation of Powers and Democracy*

216. In effect, the essential components of democracy are much more than the sole popular or circumstantial election of government officials, as is now formally recognized in the Inter-American Democratic Charter *(Carta Democratica Inter-americana)* adopted by the OAS in 2001,[1732] after so many anti-democratic, militarist and authoritarian regimes disguised as democratic because of their electoral origin that Latin American countries have suffered.

The Charter, in effect, enumerates among the *essential elements of the representative democracy,* in addition to having periodic, fair and free elections based on the universal and secret vote as expression of the will of the people; the following: respect for human rights and fundamental liberties; access to power and its exercise with subjection to the rule of law; plural regime of the political parties and organizations; and what is the most important of all, *'separation and independence of public powers'* (Article 3), that is, the possibility to control the different branches of government. The *Inter-American Charter* in addition, also defined the following *fundamental components of the democracy*: transparency of governmental activities; integrity, responsibility of governments in the public management; respect of social rights and freedom of speech and press; constitutional subordination of all institutions of the State to the legally constituted civil authority, and respect to the rule of law of all the entities and sectors of society.

The principle of separation and independence of powers is so important, as one of the 'essential elements of democracy', that it is the one that can allow all the other 'fundamental components of democracy' to be politically possible. To be precise, democracy, as a political regime, can only function in a constitutional rule of law system where the control of power exists; that is, check and balance based on the separation of powers with their independence and autonomy guaranteed, so that power can be stopped by power itself.

217. Consequently, without separation of powers and the possibility of control of power, any of the other essential factors of democracy cannot be guaranteed, because only by controlling Power, can free and fair elections and political pluralism exist; only by controlling Power, can effective democratic participation be possible, and effective transparency in the exercise of government be assured; only by controlling Power can there be a government submitted to the Constitution and the laws, that is, the rule of law; only by controlling Power can there be an effective access to justice functioning with autonomy and independence; and only by controlling Power can there be a true and effective guarantee for the respect of human rights.[1733]

1732   See on the Inter-American Democratic Charter, in Allan R. Brewer-Carías, *La crisis de la democracia venezolana. La Carta Democrática Interamericana y los sucesos de abril de 2002* (Caracas: Ediciones El Nacional, 2002), 137 et seq.; Asdrúbal Aguiar, *El Derecho a la Democracia* (Caracas: Editorial Jurídica Venezolana, 2008).

1733   See Allan R. Brewer-Carías, 'Democracia: sus elementos y componentes esenciales y el control del poder', in *Grandes temas para un observatorio electoral ciudadano, Vol. I, Democracia: retos y fundamentos*, ed. Nuria González Martín (Compiladora) (México: Instituto Electoral del Distrito Federal, 2007), 171–220.

218. The constitutional situation in Venezuela since the constitution-making process that took place in 1999, which resulted in the complete takeover of all powers of the State and the sanctioning of the current 1999 Constitution, unfortunately has been of a very weak democracy, precisely because of the progressive demolishing of the principle of separation of powers. [1734] In it, a process of concentration of powers has taken place, first with the 1999 constitution-making process itself, which intervened in all branches of government before sanctioning the new constitution (see *supra* paragraph 25); and after, due to the provisions of the 1999 Constitution, which do not guarantee the effective independence and autonomy of the branches of government.

Chapter 2. Concentration of Powers and Authoritarianism in Defraudation of the Constitution

219. The result has been that in 2011, Venezuela still has an authoritarian government which is not the result of a classical Latin American military *coup d'état*, but of a systematic process of destruction and dismantling of all the basic principles of democracy and of the Constitution.[1735] This process, as aforementioned, began with the 1998 election of Hugo Chávez Frías as President of the Republic, a position that a decade later he still holds, being in 2011 the President with the longest continued tenure in all the Venezuelan constitutional history.

220. The 1999 Constitution, if it is read in a vacuum, ignoring the political reality of the country, can mislead any elector. As aforementioned, it is the only Constitution in the contemporary world that has established, not only a tripartite separation of powers between the traditional Legislative, Executive and Judicial branches of government, but a *penta* separation of powers, adding to the latter two more branches of government: the Electoral Power, attributed to the National Electoral Council, in charge of the organization and conduct of the elections; and the Citizen Power, attributed to three different State entities: the General Prosecutor Office (Public Prosecutor) (*Fiscalía General de la República*), the General Comptroller Office (*Contraloría General de la República*), and the Peoples' Defender (*Defensor del Pueblo*) (Article 136) (see *infra* paragraph 416 et seq.).[1736] This *penta* separation of powers, in any case, was the culmination of a previous constitutional process and tendency initiated in the 1961 Constitution that consolidated the existence of State organs with constitutional rank not dependent on the classical powers, as was for

---

1734   See Allan R. Brewer-Carías, "El principio de la separación de poderes como elemento esencial de la democracia y de la libertad, y su demolición en Venezuela mediante la sujeción política del Tribunal Supremo de Justicia," *Revista Iberoamericana de Derecho Administrativo, Homenaje a Luciano Parejo Alfonso,* 12, (San José, Costa Rica, Asociación e Instituto Iberoamericano de Derecho Administrativo Prof. Jesús González Pérez, 2012), 31-43.

1735   See Allan R. Brewer-Carías, *Dismantling Democracy. The Chávez Authoritarian Experiment* (New York: Cambridge University Press, 2010).

1736   See Cecilia Sosa Gómez, 'La organización política del estado venezolano: El Poder Público Nacional', in *Revista de Derecho Público,* N° 82 (abril-junio) (Caracas: Editorial Jurídica Venezolana, 2000), 71–83; C. Kiriadis Iongui, 'Notas sobre la estructura orgánica del Estado venezolano en la Constitución de 1999', in *Temas de Derecho Administrativo: Libro Homenaje a Gonzalo Pérez Luciani,* vol. I (Caracas: Editorial Torino, 2002), 1031–1082.

instance the case of the Public Prosecutor Office, the Council of the Judiciary, and the Comptroller General Office.

But as mentioned, in spite of this *penta* division of powers, the fact is that the autonomy and independence of the branches of government is not completely and consistently assured in the Constitution, its application leading, on the contrary, to a concentration of State powers in the National Assembly, and through it, in the Executive power.

§1. *The Constitutional Supremacy of the National Assembly*

221. In effect, in any system of separation of powers, even with five separate branches of government (Legislative, Executive, Judicial, Citizen and Electoral), in order for such separation to become effective, the independence and autonomy among them has to be assured in order to allow check and balance, that is, the limitation and control of power by power itself. This was the aspect that was not designed as such in the 1999 Constitution, and notwithstanding the aforementioned penta separation of powers, an absurd distortion of the principle was introduced by giving the National Assembly the authority not only to appoint, but to dismiss the Magistrates of the Supreme Tribunal of Justice, the Prosecutor General, the General Comptroller, the People's Defender and the Members of the National Electoral Council (Articles 265, 279 and 296); and in some cases, even by simple majority of votes. This latter solution was even proposed to be formally introduced in the rejected 2007 Constitutional reform proposals, seeking to eliminate the guarantee of the qualified majority of the members for the approval of the National Assembly for such dismissals.

222. It is simply impossible to understand how the autonomy and independence of separate powers can function and how they can exercise mutual control, when the tenure of the Head officials of the branches of government (except the President of the Republic) depend on the political will of one of the branches of government, that is, the National Assembly. The sole fact of the possibility for the National Assembly to dismiss the head of the other branches makes futile the formal consecration of the autonomy and independence of powers since the High officials of the State are aware that they can be removed from office at any time precisely if they effectively act with independence.[1737]

Unfortunately, this has happened in Venezuela during the past decade, so when there have been minimal signs of autonomy from some holders of State institutions who have dared to adopt their own decisions distancing themselves from the Executive will, they have been dismissed. This occurred, for instance, in 2001 with the People's Defender and with the Prosecutor General of the Republic, originally appointed in 1999 by the Constituent National Assembly, who were separated from

---

1737   See 'Democracia y control del poder', in Allan R. Brewer-Carías, *Constitución, democracia y control de poder* (Mérida: Centro Iberoamericano de Estudios Provinciales y Locales. Universidad de Los Andes, 2004); and 'Los problemas del control del poder y el autoritarismo en Venezuela', in *El control del poder. Homenaje a Diego Valadés,* Instituto de Investigaciones Jurídicas, ed. Peter Häberle and Diego García Belaúnde (Coords.), vol. I (México: Universidad Nacional Autónoma de México, 2011), 159–188.

their positions[1738] for failing to follow the dictates of the Executive power; and this also happened with some Judges of the Supreme Tribunal who dared to vote on decisions that could question the Executive action, who were immediately subjected to investigation and some of them were removed or duly 'retired' from their positions.[1739]

223. The consequence resulting from this factual 'dependency' of the State organs regarding the National Assembly has been the total absence of fiscal or audit control regarding all the State entities. The General Comptroller Office has ignored the results of the huge and undisciplined disposal of the oil wealth that has occurred in Venezuela, not always in accordance with Budget discipline rules. But on the contrary, the most important decisions taken by the Comptroller General have been those directed to disqualify many opposition candidates from the November 2008 regional and municipal elections, based on 'administrative irregularities', although the Constitution establishes that the constitutional right to run for office can only be suspended when a judicial criminal decision is adopted (Articles 39, 42);[1740] which the Constitutional Chamber of the Supreme Tribunal has upheld in defraudation of the Constitution.[1741]

1738   In the case of the General Prosecutor of the Republic, appointed in December of 1999, he thought he could initiate a criminal impeachment proceeding against the then Minister of the Interior; and in the case of the People's Defendant, also appointed in December of 1999 she also thought that she could challenge the Special Law of the 2001 National Assembly on appointment of Judges of the Supreme Tribunal without complying with the constitutional requirements. They were both duly dismissed in 2001.

1739   It was the case of the First Vice President of the Supreme Tribunal of Justice, who delivered a decision of the Supreme Tribunal dated 14 Aug. 2002 regarding a criminal process against the generals who acted on 12 Apr. 2002, when the President of the Republic resigned to his position, declaring that there were no grounds to judge them due to the fact that in said occasion no military coup took place; and that of the President and two more members of the Electoral Chamber of the Supreme Tribunal who undersigned decision N° 24 of 15 Mar. 2004 (Case: *Julio Borges, Cesar Perez Vivas, Henry Ramos Allup, Jorge Sucre Castillo, Ramón Jose Medina and Gerardo Blyde vs. the National Electoral Council*), that suspended the effects of Resolution N° 040302-131, dated 2 Mar. 2004 of the National Electoral Council which, in that moment, stopped the realization of the presidential recall referendum.

1740   In October 2008, the European Parliament approved a Resolution asking the Venezuelan government to end with these practices (political incapacitation in order to impede the presence of opposition leaders in the regional and local elections) and to promote a more global democracy with complete respect of the principles established in the 1999 Constitution. See <http://venezuelanoticia.com/ archives/8298>. See Allan R. Brewer-Carías, 'El derecho político de los ciudadanos a ser electos para cargos de representación popular y el alcance de su exclusión judicial en un régimen democrático (O de cómo la Contraloría General de la República de Venezuela incurre en inconstitucionalidad e inconvencionalidad al imponer sanciones administrativas de inhabilitación política a los ciudadanos)', en *Libro homenaje a Francisco Cumplido* (Santiago de Chile: Asociación Chilena de Derecho Constitucional, 2011).

1741   Teodoro Petkoff has pointed out that with this decision 'the authoritarian and autocratic government of Hugo Chávez has clearly shown its true colors in this episode', explaining that 'The political rights to run for office is only lost when a candidate has received a judicial sentence that has been upheld in a higher court. The recent sentence by the Venezuelan Supreme Court, upholding the disqualifications, as well as the constitutionality of Art. 105 [of the Organic Law of the Comptroller General Office], constitute a defraudation of the Constitution and the way in which the decision was handed down was an obvious accommodation to the president's desire to eliminate four significant opposition

Regarding the People's Defender, it has been perceived more as a defender of State powers than of the peoples' rights, even if the Venezuelan State never before has been denounced so many times as has happened during the past years before the Inter-American Commission on Human Rights. Finally, the Public Prosecutor has been characterized by using its powers to prosecute using, in an indiscriminate way, the controlled Judiciary as a tool to persecute any political dissidence.

§2. *The Defraudation of Political Participation in the Election of High Governmental Officers*

224. But the process of concentration of powers that Venezuela has experienced during the past decade has also been the result of a process of defraudation of the Constitution, particularly ignoring the limits the 1999 Constitution established to reduce the former complete discretional power of the National Assembly in the process of the indirect electiion of the non-popularly direct elected Heads of the different branches of government, which before the drafting of the Constitution had been highly criticized.[1742]

In effect, independently of the constitutional provisions regarding the possible dismissal by the National Assembly of the Heads of the Citizens, Judicial and Electoral branches of government, and its distortions, one of the mechanism established in the 1999 Constitution in order to assure their independence was the establishment of an indirect electoral system t in charge of the National Assembly, acting in this case as an electoral body with the vote of a majority of two third of its members, limited by the necessary participation of special collective bodies called Nominating Committees that must be integrated with representatives of the different sectors of society (Articles 264, 279, 295). Those Nominating Committees are in charge of selecting and nominating the candidates, guaranteeing the political participation of the Citizens in the process.

Consequently, the indirect election of the Justices of the Supreme Tribunal, of the Members of the National Electoral Council, of the Prosecutor General of the Republic, of the People's Defender and of the Comptroller General of the Republic can only be made by the National Assembly among the candidates proposed by the corresponding 'Nominating Committees', which are the ones in charge of selecting and nominating the candidates before the Assembly. These constitutional provisions, as mentioned, were designed in order to limit the discretional power the political legislative organ traditionally had to elect those high officials through political party agreements, by assuring political Citizenship participation.[1743]

---

candidates from the electoral field'. See Teodoro Petkoff, 'Election and Political Power. Challenges for the Opposition', in *Revista. Harvard Review of Latin America* (Harvard University:David Rockefeller Centre for Latin American Studies, Fall 2008), 11.

1742 Véase Allan R. Brewer-Carías, *Los problemas del estado de partidos* (Caracas: Editorial Jurídica Venezolana, 1988).

1743 See Allan R. Brewer-Carías, 'La participación ciudadana en la designación de los titulares de los órganos no electos de los Poderes Públicos en Venezuela y sus vicisitudes políticas', in *Revista Iberoamericana de Derecho Público y Administrativo*, Año 5, N° 5-2005 (San José, Costa Rica, 2005), 76–95.

225. Unfortunately, these exceptional constitutional provisions have not been applied, due to the fact that the National Assembly during the past years, also defrauding the Constitution, has deliberately 'transformed' the said Committees into simple 'parliamentary Commissions' reducing the civil society's right to political participation. The Assembly in all the statutes sanctioned regarding such Committees and the election process, has established the composition of all the Nominating Committees with a majority of parliamentary representatives (who by definition cannot be representatives of the 'civil society'), although providing, in addition, for the incorporation of some other members chosen by the National Assembly itself from strategically selected 'non-governmental Organizations'.[1744]

The result has been the complete political control of the Nominating Committees, and the persistence of the discretional political and partisan way of electing the official heads of the non-directly elected branches of government, which the provisions of the 1999 Constitution intended to limit, by a National Assembly that since 2000 has been completely controlled by the Executive.In addition, the indirect electoral process has been completely distorted in December of 2014, by the election of the aforementioned head of the branches of government by the National Assembly, acting as a simple legislative body and not as the electoral body established in the Constitution, applying a simple majority of votes instead of the qualified majority set forth in the Constitution; which was accepted unconstitutionally by the Constitutional Chamber.[1745]

This practice even pretended to be constitutionalized through the rejected Constitutional Reform of 2007 with the proposal to formally establish exclusively parliamentary Nomination Committees, instead of being composed of representatives of the various sectors of civil society.

§3. The Catastrophic Dependence and Subjection of the Judiciary

226. The effects of the dependency of the branches of government subjected to the Legislative Power and through it to the Executive, have been particularly catastrophic regarding the Judiciary, which after being initially intervened by the Constituent National Assembly in 1999 (see *supra* paragraph 31), continued to be intervened with the unfortunate consent of the Supreme Tribunal of Justice itself. In this

---

1744   See regarding the distortion of the 'Judicial Nominating Committee' in Allan R. Brewer-Carías, *Ley Orgánica del Tribunal Supremo de Justicia* (Caracas: Editorial Jurídica Venezolana, 2004); the distortion on the 'Citizen Power Nominating Committee' in Allan R. Brewer-Carías et al., *Ley Orgánica del Poder Ciudadano* (Caracas: Editorial Jurídica Venezolana, 2005); and in 'Sobre el nombramiento irregular por la Asamblea Nacional de los titulares de los órganos del poder ciudadano en 2007, in Revista *de Derecho Público*, N° 113 (Caracas: Editorial Jurídica Venezolana, 2008), 85–88; and the distortion on the Electoral Nominating Committee in Allan R. Brewer-Carías, *Crónica sobre la 'in' justicia constitucional. La Sala Constitucional y el autoritarismo en Venezuela*, N° 2 (Caracas: Colección Instituto de Derecho Público, Universidad Central de Venezuela, 2007), 197–230.

1745   See Constitutional Chamber Decisions N° 1864 of December 22, 2014 (available at: http://historico.tsj.gov.ve/decisiones/scon/diciembre/173494-1864-221214-2014-14-1341.HTML); and N° 1865 of December 26, 2014 (available at: http://historico.tsj.gov.ve/decisiones/scon/diciembre/173497-1865-261214-2014-14-1343.HTML). See the comments in Allan R. Brewer-Carías, 'El golpe de Estado dado en diciembre de 2014, con la inconstitucional designación de las altas autoridades del Poder Público," Revista de Derecho Público, 40 (Caracas, Editorial Jurídica Venezolana, 2014).

matter, in the past decade the country has witnessed a permanent and systematic demolition process of the autonomy and independence of the judicial power, aggravated by the fact that according to the 1999 Constitution, the Supreme Tribunal that is completely controlled by the Executive is in charge of administering all the Venezuelan judicial system, particularly, by appointing and dismissing judges.[1746] (see *infra* paragraph 380 et seq.).

227. The process began with the appointment, in 1999, of new Magistrates of the Supreme Tribunal of Justice without complying with the constitutional conditions, made by the National Constituent Assembly itself, by means of a Constitutional Transitory regime sanctioned after the Constitution was approved by referendum (see *supra* paragraph 29). From there on, the intervention process of the Judiciary continued up to the point that the President of the Republic has politically controlled the Supreme Tribunal of Justice and, through it, the complete Venezuelan judicial system.

228. For that purpose, the constitutional conditions needed to be elected Magistrate of the Supreme Tribunal and the procedures for their nomination with the participation of representatives of the different sectors of civil society, were violated since the beginning. First, as aforementioned, in 1999 by the National Constituent Assembly itself once it dismissed the previous Justices, appointing new ones without receiving any nominations from any Nominating Committee, and many of them without compliance with the conditions set forth in the Constitution to be Magistrate. Second, in 2000, by the newly elected National Assembly by sanctioning a Special Law in order to elect the Magistrates, in a transitory way, without compliance with those constitutional conditions.[1747] Third, in 2004, again by the National Assembly by sanctioning the Organic Law of the Supreme Tribunal of Justice, increasing the number of Justices from 20 to 32, and distorting the constitutional conditions for their election and dismissal, allowing the government to assume an absolute control of the Supreme Tribunal, and in particular, of its Constitutional Chamber.[1748] Fourth, in 2010, once more, the National Assembly reformed the Organic

---

1746   See Rafael J. Chavero Gazdik, *La Justicia Revolucionaria. Una década de reestructuración (o involución) Judicial en Venezuela* (Caracas: Editorial Aequitas, 2011); Laura Louza Scognamiglio, *La revolución judicial en Venezuela* (Caracas: FUNEDA, 2011); Allan R. Brewer-Carías, 'La progresiva y sistemática demolición de la autonomía e independencia del Poder Judicial en Venezuela (1999–2004)', in *XXX Jornadas J.M. Domínguez Escovar, Estado de derecho, Administración de justicia y derechos humanos* (Barquisimeto: Instituto de Estudios Jurídicos del Estado Lara, 2005), 33–174; and 'La justicia sometida al poder (La ausencia de independencia y autonomía de los jueces en Venezuela por la interminable emergencia del Poder Judicial (1999–2006)' in *Cuestiones Internacionales. Anuario Jurídico Villanueva 2007* (Madrid: Centro Universitario Villanueva, Marcial Pons, 2007), 25–57.

1747   For this reason, in its 2003 *Report on Venezuela,* the Inter-American Commission on Human Rights, observed that the election of Judges of the Supreme Court of Justice did not apply to the Constitution, so that 'the constitutional reforms introduced in the form of the election of these authorities established as guaranties of independence and impartiality were not used in this case'. See Inter-American Commission of Human Rights, 2003 *Report on Venezuela;* para. 186.

1748   *Gaceta Oficial* N° 37.942 of 20 May 2004. See the comments in Allan R. Brewer-Carías, *Ley Orgánica del Tribunal Supremo de Justicia* (Caracas: Editorial Jurídica Venezolana, 2004).

Law of the Supreme Tribunal of Justice, first in a regular way,[1749] and subsequently in an irregular manner,[1750] in order to pack the Tribunal with new government-controlled members. Finally, in 2014 by the election of he Magistrates by the National Assembly, by simple majority of votes, distorting the character of the election as an indirect popular election by the Assambly acting as an electoral body, with the vote of the two third of its members. [1751]

229. After the 2004 reform of the Organic Law of the Supreme Tribunal, the process of selection of new Justices has been openly subjected to the President of the Republic's will, as was publicly admitted by the President of the parliamentary Commission in charge of selecting the candidates for Magistrates of the Supreme Tribunal Court of Justice, who later was appointed Minister of the Interior and Justice. On December 2004, he said the following:

> Although we, the representatives, have the authority for this selection, the President of the Republic was consulted and his opinion was very much taken into consideration.' He added: 'Let's be clear, we are not going to score auto-goals. In the list, there were people from the opposition who comply with all the requirements. The opposition could have used them in order to reach an agreement during the last sessions, but they did not want to. We are not going to do it for them. There is no one in the group of postulates that could act against us.[1752]

This configuration of the Supreme Tribunal, as highly politicized and subjected to the will of the President of the Republic has been reinforced in 2010,[1753] eliminating all autonomy of the Judicial Power and even the basic principle of the separation of power, as the corner stone of the rule of law and the base of all democratic institutions.

230. However, as aforementioned, according to Article 265 of the 1999 Constitution, the Magistrates can be dismissed by the vote of a qualified majority of the National Assembly, when grave faults are committed, following a prior qualification by the Citizen Power (see *infra* paragraph 400). This qualified two-thirds majority was

---

1749   *Gaceta Oficial* N° 39.483 of 9 Aug. 2010 and N° 39.522 of 1 Oct. 2010. See the comments in Allan R. Brewer-Carías & Víctor Hernández Mendible, *Ley Orgánica del Tribunal Supremo de Justicia* (Caracas: Editorial Jurídica Venezolana, 2010).

1750   See the comments Víctor Hernández Mendible, 'Sobre la nueva reimpresión por "supuestos errores" materiales de la Ley Orgánica del Tribunal Supremo, octubre 2010', and Antonio Silva Aranguren, 'Tras el rastro del engaño, en la web de la Asamblea Nacional', in *Revista de Derecho Público*, No. 124 (Caracas: Editorial Jurídica Venezolana, 2010), 10–113.

1751   See Allan R. Brewer-Carías, 'El golpe de Estado dado en diciembre de 2014, con la inconstitucional designación de las altas autoridades del Poder Público," *Revista de Derecho Público*, 40 (Caracas, Editorial Jurídica Venezolana, 2014).

1752   See in *El Nacional* (Caracas, 13 Dec. 2004). That is why the Inter-American Commission on Human Rights suggested in its Report to the General Assembly of the OAS corresponding to 2004 that 'these regulations of the Organic Law of the Supreme Court of Justice would have made possible the manipulation, by the Executive Power, of the election process of judges that took place during 2004'. See Inter-American Commission on Human Rights, 2004 *Report on Venezuela*; para. 180.

1753   See Hildegard Rondón de Sansó, *'Obiter Dicta*. En torno a una elección', in *La Voce d'Italia* (Caracas, 14 Dec. 2010).

established to avoid leaving the existence of the heads of the judiciary in the hands of a simple majority of legislators. Unfortunately, this provision was also distorted by the 2004 Organic Law of the Supreme Tribunal of Justice, in which it was established in an unconstitutional way that the Magistrates could be dismissed by simple majority when the 'administrative act of their appointment' is revoked (Article 23.4). This distortion, contrary to the independence of the Judiciary, although eliminated in the reform of the Law in 2010, also pretended to be constitutionalized with the rejected 2007 Constitutional reform, which proposed to establish that the Magistrates of the Supreme Tribunal could be dismissed in case of grave faults, but just by the vote of the majority of the members of the National Assembly.

231. The consequence of this political subjection is that all the principles tending to assure the independence of judges at any level of the Judiciary have been postponed. In particular, the Constitution establishes that all judges must be selected by public competition for the tenure; and that the dismissal of judges can only be made through disciplinary trials carried out by disciplinary judges (Articles 254 and 267). Unfortunately, none of these provisions have been implemented, and on the contrary, since 1999, the Venezuelan Judiciary has been composed by temporal and provisional judges,[1754] lacking stability and being subjected to the political manipulation, altering the people's right to an adequate administration of justice. Also regarding the disciplinary jurisdiction of the judges, it was only in 2010[1755] that it was established. Until then, with the authorization of the Supreme Tribunal, a 'transitory' Reorganization Commission of the Judicial Power created since 1999, continued to function, removing judges without due process.[1756] (see *infra* paragraph 402)

The worst of this irregular situation is that since 2006 the problem of the provisional status of judges has been 'regularized' through a 'Special Programme for the Regularization of Tenures', addressed to accidental, temporary or provisional judges, by-passing the entrance system constitutionally established by means of public competitive exams (Article 255), by consolidating the effects of the provisional appointments and their consequent power dependency.

1754   The Inter-American Commission on Human Rights said: 'The Commission has been informed that only 250 judges have been appointed by opposition concurrence according to the constitutional text. From a total of 1772 positions of judges in Venezuela, the Supreme Court of Justice reports that only 183 are holders, 1331 are provisional and 258 are temporary', *Informe sobre la Situación de los Derechos Humanos en Venezuela*; OAS/Ser.L/V/II.118. d.C. 4rev. 2; 29 Dec. 2003; para. 11. The same Commission also said that 'an aspect linked to the autonomy and independence of the Judicial Power is that of the provisional character of the judges in the judicial system of Venezuela. Today, the information provided by the different sources indicates that more than 80% of Venezuelan judges are 'provisional'. *Id.*, para. 161.

1755   The Law on the Ethics Code of the Venezuelan Judges *Gaceta Oficial* N° 39.494 of 24 Aug. 2010, created the expected Disciplinary Judicial Jurisdiction. In 2011 the corresponding tribunal was appointed.

1756   See Allan R. Brewer-Carías, 'La justicia sometida al poder y la interminable emergencia del poder judicial (1999-2006)', *in Derecho y democracia. Cuadernos Universitarios*, N° 11 (Caracas: Órgano de Divulgación Académica, Vicerrectorado Académico, Universidad Metropolitana, Año II, septiembre 2007), 122–138.

§4. *The Factual Political Supremacy of The Executive and the Absence of Check and Balance*

232. But if the supremacy of the National Assembly over the Judicial, Citizen and Electoral Powers is the most characteristic sign of the implementation of the Constitution of 1999 during the last decade, the distortion of the separation of powers principle transformed into a power concentration system, also derives from the supremacy that, from a political party's point of view, the Executive Power has over the National Assembly.

233. In the Constitution of 1999, the presidential system has been reinforced, among other factors, because of the extension to six years of the presidential term; the authorization of the immediate re-election for an immediate following period of the President of the Republic (Article 203), and the maintaining of it in election by simple majority (Article 228) (see *infra* paragraph 269). In the rejected Constitutional Reform of 2007, the term of the President was even proposed to be extended up to seven years, and the indefinite re-election of the President of the Republic was one of the main proposals contained in it. In 2008, again, and by-passing the prohibition established in the Constitution to propose again within the same constitutional term a reform already rejected by the people, the National Assembly approved the proposal for a 'constitutional amendment' allowing the indefinite and continuous re-election of all elected public officials, that was submitted to referendum and approved by the people in February 2009 (see *supra* paragraph 37).

With this presidential model, to which the possibility of the dissolution of the National Assembly by the President of the Republic is added, although in exceptional cases (Articles 236.22 and 240), the presidential system has been reinforced. No check and balance possibility exists, for instance, from the Senate, which was eliminated in 1999.[1757]

234. Also, the presidential system has been reinforced with other reforms, like the provision for legislative delegation to authorize the President of the Republic by means of 'delegating statutes' (enabling laws), to issue decree-laws and not only in economic and financial matters (Article 203). According to this provision, the fact is that the fundamental legislation of the country sanctioned during the past decade has been contained in these decree-laws, which have been approved without assuring the mandatory constitutional provision for public hearings, established in the Constitution (Article 211) to take place before the sanctioning of all statutes (see *supra* paragraph 161).

235. In order to enforce this constitutional right of the Citizens to participation (see *infra* paragraph 164), the Constitution specifically set forth that the National Assembly is compelled to submit draft legislation to public consultation, asking the opinion of Citizens and the organized society (Article 211). This is the concrete way by which the Constitution tends to assure the exercise of the political participation

---

1757   See María M. Matheus Inciarte y María Elena Romero Ríos, 'Estado Federal y unicameralidad en el nuevo orden constitucional de la República Bolivariana de Venezuela', in *Estudios de Derecho Público: Libro Homenaje a Humberto J. La Roche Rincón,* vol. I (Caracas: Tribunal Supremo de Justicia, 2001), 637–676.

right in the process of drafting legislation. This constitutional obligation, of course, must also be accomplish by the President of the Republic when a legislative delegation takes place. But nonetheless, in 2007, 2008, 2011 and 2014, the President of the Republic, following the same steps adopted in 2001,[1758] has extensively legislated without any public hearing or consultation. In this way, in defraudation of the Constitution, by means of legislative delegation, the President has enacted decree-laws without complying with the obligatory public hearings, violating the Citizens' right to political participation (see *infra* paragraph 90).

Chapter 3. The Rupture of the Rule of Law, the Rejected 2007 Constitutional Reform and Its Illegitimate Implementation

236. As it can be deducted from the aforementioned, in order for a democratic rule of law State to exist, the declarations contained in constitutional texts on separation of power are not enough, an effective check and balance system between the State powers being indispensable. This is the only way to assure the enforcement of the rule of law and democracy, and the effective enjoyment of human rights.

And check and balance and control of State Powers in a democratic rule of law State can only be achieved by dividing, separating and distributing Public Power, either horizontally by means of the guarantee of the autonomy and independence of the different branches of government to avoid the concentration of power; or vertically, by means of its distribution or spreading in the territory, creating autonomous political entities with representatives elected by votes to avoid its centralization. The concentrations of power, as well as its centralization, then, are essentially antidemocratic State structures.

237. It is precisely there where the problems of the formally declared rule of law and of democracy in Venezuela begin, due to the fact that its deformation lies in the same constitutional text of 1999, whose institutional framework unfortunately was established to encourage authoritarianism, affecting the possibility of controlling power. This has permitted the centralization of power, provoking the dismantling process of federalism and municipalism (see *supra* paragraph 163) and twisting the possibility of the effective political participation in spite of the direct democracy mechanisms established.

This process of centralization of powers was also proposed to be constitutionalized in 2007 by means of a Constitutional Reform draft submitted by the late President Hugo Chávez, and sanctioned by the National Assembly, in which the intention was to transform the Democratic Rule of Law and Decentralized Social State established in the 1999 Constitution, into a Socialist, Centralized, Repressive and Militaristic State, grounded in a so-called 'Bolivarian doctrine', which was identified with 'XXI Century Socialism', and an economic system of State capitalism (see *supra* paragraphs 35, 43).

1758   See the comments in Allan R. Brewer-Carías, 'Apreciación general sobre los vicios de inconstitucionalidad que afectan los Decretos Leyes Habilitados' in *Ley Habilitante del 13-11-2000 y sus Decretos
        Leyes* (Caracas: Academia de Ciencias Políticas y Sociales, 2002), 63–103.

§1. *The Sense and Objectives of the Reform Proposals*

238. In effect, in order to formally consolidate in the Constitution an authoritarian government and a socialist, centralized and communal State, the President of the Republic proposed to the National Assembly in 2007 the sanctioning of a Constitutional Reform[1759] based on the configuration of a so-called State of the 'Popular Power' or 'Communal State'. As aforementioned, nevertheless, once it was put to popular vote, it was rejected by the people on 2 December 2007.

That constitutional reform was intended to transform the most essential and fundamental aspects of the State,[1760] making it one of the most important reforms proposals in all of Venezuelan constitutional history. With it, the decentralized, democratic, pluralistic and social State built and consolidated since the Second World War would have been radically changed to create a socialist, centralized, repressive and militaristic State grounded in a so-called Bolivarian doctrine, which at the time was identified with 'twenty-first-century socialism' and a socialist economic system of State capitalism. This reform was sanctioned evading the procedure established in the Constitution for such fundamental change, which imposes the convening of a Constituent Assembly. The reform defrauded the Constitution[1761] as one more step of the 'permanent *coup d'état'* that since 1999 has occurred in Venezuela.[1762]

The most important consequence of this draft reform from the citizens' perspective was that, with it, an official State ideology and doctrine was to be formally established in Venezuela, which was the socialist and supposedly 'Bolivarian' doctrine, implying if approved by the people, the duty for all citizens to actively contribute to its implementation, eliminating any vestige of political pluralism, and allowing for the formal criminalization of any dissidence regarding the unique and official way of thinking.

239. Guidelines for the proposed reforms emerged from various discussions and speeches of the President. These pointed to, on the one hand, the formation of a State of 'popular power' or of 'communal power', or a 'communal state' (*Estado del*

1759   See Allan R. Brewer-Carías, *Hacia la Consolidación de un Estado Socialista, Centralizado, Policial y Militarista. Comentarios sobre el sentido y alcance de las propuestas de reforma constitucional 2007*, Colección Textos Legislativos, N° 42 (Caracas: Editorial Jurídica Venezolana, 2007).

1760   See Rogelio Pérez Perdomo, 'La Constitución de papel y su reforma', in *Revista de Derecho Público* 112 *(Estudios sobre la reforma constitucional)* (Caracas: Editorial Jurídica Venezolana, 2007), 14; Alfredo Arismendi, 'Utopía Constitucional', in *id.*, 31; Manuel Rachadell, 'El personalismo político en el Siglo XXI', in *id.*, 66; Allan R. Brewer-Carías, 'El sello socialista que se pretendía imponer al Estado', in *id.*, 71–75; Alfredo Morles Hernández, 'El nuevo modelo económico para el Socialismo del Siglo XXI', in *id.*, 233–236.

1761   See Gerardo Fernández, 'Aspectos esenciales de la modificación constitucional propuesta por el Presidente de la República. La modificación constitucional en fraude a la democracia', in *Revista de Derecho Público* N° 112 *(Estudios sobre la reforma constitucional)* (Caracas, Editorial Jurídica Venezolana, 2007), 21–25; Fortunato González, 'Constitución histórica y poder constituyente', in *id.*, 33–36; Lolymar Hernández Camargo, 'Los límites del cambio constitucional como garantía de pervivencia del Estado de derecho', in *id.*, 37–45; Claudia Nikken, 'La soberanía popular y el trámite de la reforma constitucional promovida por iniciativa presidencial el 15 de agosto de 2007', in *id.*, 51–58.

1762   See José Amando Mejía Betancourt, 'La ruptura del hilo constitucional', in *id.*, 47. The term was first used by Francois Mitterand, *Le coup d'État permanent*, Éditions 10/18 (Paris, 1993).

poder popular o del poder communal, o Estado comunal) built on the communal councils (*consejos comunales*) as primary political units or social organizations. The communal councils, whose members are not elected by means of universal, direct and secret suffrage, in a way contrary to the democratic principles established in the Constitution, had already been created by statute in 2006,[1763] parallel to the municipal entities, supposedly to channel citizen participation in public affairs. However, since their creation, they have operated within a system of centralized management by the national executive power and without any political or territorial autonomy.[1764]

On the other hand, the guidelines for reform also referred to the structuring of a socialist State and the substitution of the existing system of economic freedom and mixed economy with a State and collectivist socialist economic system subject to centralized planning, which minimizes the role of individuals and eliminates any vestige of economic liberties or private property as constitutional rights.

240. In accordance with these orientations, the 2007 rejected reform intended to radically transform the State by creating a completely new juridical order. A change of that nature, according to Article 347 of the 1999 Constitution, required the convening and election of a Constituent Assembly and could not be undertaken by means of mere constitutional reform procedures. This procedure for constitutional reform is applicable only to 'a partial revision of the Constitution and a substitution of one or several of its norms without modifying the structure and fundamental principles of the Constitutional text'. (See *supra* paragraph 87). In such a case, the limited constitutional change is achieved through debate and sanctioning in the National Assembly, followed by approval in popular referendum.

241. Nonetheless, despite these constitutional provisions, with the rejected reform proposals, a political tactic that has been a common denominator in the actions of the authoritarian regime since 1999 was repeated: acting fraudulently with respect to the Constitution. As was ruled in other matters by the Constitutional Chamber of the Supreme Tribunal of Justice in a decision N° 74 of 25 January 2006, a defraudation of the Constitution (*fraude a la Constitución*) occurs when democratic principles are destroyed 'through the process of making changes within existing institutions while appearing to respect constitutional procedures and forms'. The Chamber also ruled that a 'falsification of the Constitution' (*falseamiento de la Constitución*) occurs when 'constitutional norms are given an interpretation and a sense different from those that they really possess: this is in reality an informal modification of the Constitution itself'. The Chamber concluded by affirming that 'A Constitutional reform not subject to any type of limitations would constitute a defraudation of the constitution.'[1765] This is to say, a defraudation of the Constitution occurs when the

---

1763   Communal Councils Law, *Gaceta Oficial*, Extra. 5.806, of 10 Apr. 2006. This statute was replaced by Organic Law on the Communal Councils. See *Gaceta Oficial* N° 39.335 of 28 Dec. 2009.

1764   See Allan R. Brewer-Carías, 'El inicio de la desmunicipalización en Venezuela: La organización del poder popular para eliminar la descentralización, la democracia representativa y la participación a nivel local', in *AIDA, Revista de la Asociación Internacional de Derecho Administrativo* (Mexico City: Universidad Nacional Autónoma de México, Asociación Internacional de Derecho Administrativo, 2007), 49–67.

1765   See in *Revista de Derecho Público*, N° 105 (Caracas: Editorial Jurídica Venezolana, 2006), 76 et seq.

existing institutions are used in a manner that appears to adhere to constitutional forms and procedures in order to proceed, as the Supreme Tribunal warned, 'towards the creation of a new political regimen, a new constitutional order, without altering the established legal system'.[1766]

That is, existing institutions were used in a manner that appeared to adhere to constitutional form and procedure to proceed, as the Supreme Tribunal had warned, 'towards the creation of a new political regime, a new constitutional order, without altering the established legal system'.[1767] This occurred in February 1999 in the convening of a consultative referendum on whether to convene a Constituent Assembly when that institution was not prefigured in the then existing Constitution of 1961.[1768] (see *supra* paragraph 25). It occurred with the December 1999 Decree on the Transitory Regime of the Public Powers, with respect to the 1999 Constitution, which was never the subject of an approbatory referendum[1769] (see *supra* paragraph 28). It has continued to occur in subsequent years with the progressive destruction of democracy through the exercise of power eliminating all effective separation of powers, and the sequestering of successive public rights and liberties, all supposedly based on legal and constitutional provisions.[1770]

In this instance, once again, constitutional provisions were fraudulently used for ends other than those for which they were established; they were used to radically transform the State, thus disrupting the civil order of the social-democratic State to convert the State into a socialist, centralized, repressive and militarist State in which representative democracy, republican alternation in office and the concept of decentralized power would have disappeared, with all power instead concentrated in the decisions of the head of State.[1771]

1766   *Ibid.*

1767   See the decision of the Constitutional Chamber of the Supreme Tribunal of Justice N° 74 (25 Jan. 2006), in *Revista de Derecho Público* 105 (Caracas: Editorial Jurídica Venezolana, 2006), 76 et seq.

1768   See Allan R. Brewer-Carías, *Asamblea constituyente y ordenamiento constitucional* (Caracas: Academia de Ciencias Políticas y Sociales, 1999).

1769   See Allan R. Brewer-Carías, *Golpe de estado y proceso constituyente en Venezuela* (México City: Universidad Nacional Autónoma de México, 2002).

1770   See Allan R. Brewer-Carías, 'Constitution-Making Process in Defraudation of the Constitution and Authoritarian Government in Defraudation of Democracy: The Recent Venezuelan Experience', paper presented at the VII International Congress of Constitutional Law, Athens, June 2007. See also Allan R. Brewer-Carías, 'El autoritarismo establecido en fraude a la Constitución y a la democracia y su formalización en Venezuela mediante la reforma constitucional. (De cómo en un país democrático se ha utilizado el sistema eleccionario para minar la democracia y establecer un régimen autoritario de supuesta 'dictadura de la democracia' que se pretende regularizar mediante la reforma constitucional)', in *Temas constitucionales. Planteamientos ante una reforma* (Caracas: Fundación de Estudios de Derecho Administrativo, 2007), 13–74.

1771   As is constitutionally proscribed, and as the Constitutional Chamber of the Supreme Tribunal of Justice summarized in Decision N° 74 (25 Jan. 2006), a symbolic case, it occurred 'with the fraudulent use of powers conferred by martial law in Germany under the *Weimar* Constitution, forcing the Parliament to concede to the fascist leaders, on the basis of terms of doubtful legitimacy, plenary constituent powers by conferring an unlimited legislative power'. See the Constitutional Chamber of the Supreme Tribunal of Justice, Decision N° 74 (25 Jan. 2006) in *Revista de Derecho Público* 105 (Caracas: Editorial Jurídica Venezolana, 2006), 76 et seq.

This was constitutionally proscribed, and as the Constitutional Chamber of the Supreme Tribunal of Justice summarized it, in its aforementioned decision Nº 74 of 25 January 2006, referring to a symbolic case, it occurred 'with the fraudulent use of powers conferred by martial law in Germany under the *Weimar* Constitution, forcing the Parliament to concede to the fascist leaders, on the basis of terms of doubtful legitimacy, plenary constituent powers by conferring an unlimited legislative power'.[1772] Nonetheless, in the case of the constitutional reform of 2007, the Supreme Tribunal deliberately refused to take any decision on judicial review regarding the unconstitutional procedure that was followed by the President of the Republic, the National Assembly and the National Electoral Council.[1773]

242. In the case of the 2007 reforms, the various acts adopted (the presidential initiative, the sanction by the National Assembly, the convening of referendum by the National Electoral Council) were all challenged through judicial review actions of unconstitutionality and actions of *amparo* and, in all cases, the Supreme Tribunal, completely controlled by the Government, diligently declared all as inadmissible.[1774]

Nonetheless, the fraud on the Constitution was initially evidenced in the proposals elaborated by the President's Council for Constitutional Reform that began to circulate in June 2007, despite the President's ordered 'pact of confidentiality',[1775] and which were later given concrete form in the first draft constitutional reforms, which the President presented to the National Assembly on 15 August 2007,[1776] proposing a radical transformation of the State to create a new juridical order.[1777]

1772   See in *Revista de Derecho Público,* Nº 105 (Caracas: Editorial Jurídica Venezolana, 2006), 76 et seq.

1773   See Allan R. Brewer-Carías, 'El juez constitucional vs. la supremacía constitucional. O de cómo la Jurisdicción Constitucional en Venezuela renunció a controlar la constitucionalidad del procedimiento seguido para la "reforma constitucional" sancionada por la Asamblea Nacional el 2 de noviembre de 2007, antes de que fuera rechazada por el pueblo en el referendo del 2 de diciembre de 2007', in *Revista de Derecho Público,* Nº 112 (Caracas: Editorial Jurídica venezolana, 2007), 661 et seq.

1774   On these decisions, see Allan R. Brewer-Carías, 'El juez constitucional vs. la supremacía constitucional. O de cómo la jurisdicción constitucional en Venezuela renunció a controlar la constitucionalidad del procedimiento seguido para la "reforma constitucional" sancionada por la Asamblea Nacional el 2 de noviembre de 2007, antes de que fuera rechazada por el pueblo en el referendo del 2 de diciembre de 2007', in *Revista de Derecho Público* 112 *(Estudios sobre la reforma constitucional)* (Caracas: Editorial Jurídica Venezolana, 2007), 661–694.

1775   The document circulated in June 2007 under the title *Consejo Presidencial para la Reforma de la Constitución de la República Bolivariana de Venezuela, 'Modificaciones propuestas.'* The complete text was published as *Proyecto de reforma constitucional. Versión atribuida al Consejo Presidencial para la reforma de la Constitución de la República Bolivariana de Venezuela* (Caracas: Editorial Atenea, 2007), 146.

1776   The full text was published as *Proyecto de Reforma Constitucional. Elaborado por el ciudadano Presidente de la República Bolivariana de Venezuela, Hugo Chávez Frías* (Caracas: Editorial Atenea, 2007).

1777   In this sense, the director of the National Electoral Council, Vicente Díaz, stated on 16 Jul. 2007, 'The presidential proposal to reform the constitutional text modifies fundamental provisions and for that reason it would be necessary to convene a National Assembly to approve them.' This council member was consulted on this matter on Unión Radio, 16 Aug. 2007, at <www.unionradio.com.ve/Noticias/No-ticia.aspx?noticiaid=212503>. The initiation of the reform process in the National Assembly could have been challenged before the Constitutional Chamber of the Supreme Tribunal on the basis of unconstitutionality. Nonetheless, the president of the Constitutional Chamber – who was also a member of the Presidential Council for the Reform of the Constitution – made clear

Finally, the defrauding of the Constitution was consummated in November 2007 with the National Assembly's sanctioning of the reform,[1778] in which:

243. *First,* the State was to be converted into a centralized State of concentrated power under the illusory guise of a popular power, implying definitive elimination of the federal form of the State,[1779] rendering political participation impossible, and degrading representative democracy. For such purpose, the reform established a new 'popular power' (*poder popular*) (Article 16), composed by communities (*comunidades*), each of which 'shall constitute a basic and indivisible spatial nucleus of the Venezuelan Socialist State, where ordinary citizens will have the power to construct their own geography and their own history'; which were to be grouped into communes (*comunas*).[1780] The main aspect of these reforms was that they provided that the popular power 'is expressed through the constitution of communities, communes, and the self-government of the cities, by means of the communal councils, workers' councils, peasant councils, student councils, and other entities established by law'. However, although 'the people' (*el pueblo*) were designated as the 'depositary of sovereignty', to be 'exercised directly through the popular power', it was expressly stated that the popular power 'does not arise from suffrage or from any election, but arises from the condition of the organized human groups that form the base of the population'. Consequently, representative democracy at the local level and territorial political autonomy was to disappear, substituted with a supposed participatory and protagonist democracy that would, in fact, be controlled by the President and that proscribed any form of political decentralization and territorial autonomy.[1781] Even anticipating the constitutional reform proposal, perhaps being sure of its approval, in

---

that 'no legal action related to modifications of the constitutional text would be heard until such modifications had been approved by citizens in referendum', adding that 'any action must be presented after a referendum, when the constitutional reform has become a norm, since we cannot interpret an attempted norm. Once a draft reform has become a norm we can enter into interpretations of it and hear nullification actions'. See Juan Francisco Alonso, *El Universal* (Caracas, 18 Aug. 2007).

1778   On the reform proposals, see Allan R. Brewer-Carías, *Hacia la consolidación de un estado socialista, centralizado, policial y militarista. Comentarios sobre el sentido y alcance de las propuestas de reforma constitucional 2007,* Colección Textos Legislativos N° 42 (Caracas: Editorial Jurídica Venezolana, 2007); *La reforma constitucional de 2007 (Comentarios al proyecto inconstitucionalmente sancionado por la Asamblea Nacional el 2 de noviembre de 2007),* Colección Textos Legislativos N° 43 (Caracas: Editorial Jurídica Venezolana, 2007). See also all the articles published in *Revista de Derecho Público* 112 *(Estudios sobre la reforma constitucional)* (Caracas: Editorial Jurídica Venezolana, 2007).

1779   See Manuel Rachadell, 'El personalismo político en el Siglo XXI', in *Revista de Derecho Público* 112 *(Estudios sobre la reforma constitucional)* (Caracas: Editorial Jurídica Venezolana, 2007), 67; Ana Elvira Araujo, 'Proyecto de reforma constitucional (agosto a noviembre 2007). Principios fundamentales y descentralización política', in *id.,* 77–81; José Luis Villegas, 'Impacto de la reforma constitucional sobre las entidades locales', in *id.,* 119–123.

1780   The communes were created in the statute on the Federal Council of Government. See Organic Law on the Federal Council of Government, *Gaceta Oficial* N° 5.963 Extra. of 22 Feb. 2010.

1781   This fundamental change, as the President stated on 15 Aug. 2007, constituted 'the development of what we understand by decentralization, because the Fourth Republic concept of decentralization is very different from the concept we must work with. For this reason, we have here stated "the protagonist participation of the people, transferring power to them, and creating the best conditions for the construction of social democracy"'. See *Discurso de orden pronunciado por el ciudadano Comandante Hugo Chávez Frías, supra,* 50.

2006 the Law on the Councils of the Popular Power (*Consejos del Poder Popular*) was sanctioned.[1782] In the same trend of such Law, the reforms proposals conceived 'the communes and communities' (*comunas y comunidades*) as 'the basic and indivisible spatial nucleus of the Venezuelan Socialist State' (Article 15); adding that the only objective of the constitutional provision for political participation, was 'for the construction of socialism', requiring that all citizens' political associations be devoted 'to develop the values of mutual cooperation and socialist solidarity' (Article 70).

244. *Second*, the State was to be converted into a socialist State, being obligated to 'promote people's participation as a national policy, devolving its power and creating the best conditions for the construction of a Socialist democracy' (Article 158); thus establishing a political official doctrine of socialist character – Bolivarian doctrine. The consequence of this would be that any thoughts different from the official one were to be rejected, as the official political doctrine was incorporated into the Constitution itself, establishing a constitutional duty for all citizens to ensure its compliance, imposing the teaching in the schools of the '*ideario bolivariano*' (Bolivarian ideology), and stating that the primary investment of the State in education was to be done 'according to the humanistic principles of the Bolivarian socialism'. As a consequence, the basis for criminalizing all dissidence was formally established.

245. *Third*, the economic system was to be converted into a State-owned, socialist, centralized economy by means of eliminating economic liberty and private initiative as constitutional rights, as well as the constitutional right to private property (see *infra* paragraphs 581 ff.);colliding with the ideas of liberty and solidarity proclaimed in the 1999 Constitution and established a State that substitutes itself for society and private economic initiative.

246. *Fourth*, the State was to be converted into a repressive (police) State, given the regressive character of the regulations established in the reform regarding human rights, particularly civil rights, and the expansion of the President's emergency powers, under which he was authorized to indefinitely suspend constitutional rights.

247. *Fifth*, and finally, the State was to be converted into a militarist State, on the basis of the role assigned to the 'Bolivarian Armed Force' (*Fuerza Armada Bolivariana*), which was configured to function wholly under the President, and the creation of the new 'Bolivarian National Militia' (*Milicia Nacional Bolivariana*). All were to act 'by means of the study, planning and execution of Bolivarian military

---

1782   See Giancarlo Henríquez Maionica, 'Los Consejos Comunales (una breve aproximación a su realidad y a su proyección ante la propuesta presidencial de reforma constitucional)', in *Revista de Derecho Público* 112 *(Estudios sobre la reforma constitucional)* (Caracas: Editorial Jurídica Venezolana, 2007), 89–99; Allan R. Brewer-Carías, 'El inicio de la desmunicipalización en Venezuela: La organización del poder popular para eliminar la descentralización, la democracia representativa y la participación a nivel local', in *AIDA, Opera Prima de Derecho Administrativo. Revista de la Asociación Internacional de Derecho Administrativo* (Mexico City: Universidad Nacional Autónoma de México, Asociación Internacional de Derecho Administrativo, 2007), 49–67. The 2006 law was replaced by Organic Law on Communal Councils, *Gaceta Oficial* N° 39.335 of 28 Dec. 2009. See the comments on this Law in Allan R. Brewer-Carías, *Ley Orgánica de los Consejos Comunales* (Caracas: Editorial Jurídica Venezolana, 2010).

doctrine' – that is, according to socialist doctrine. All the reforms implied the radical transformation of the Venezuelan political system; sought to establish a centralized socialist, repressive and militaristic State of popular power; and departed fundamentally from the concept of a civil social-democratic State under the rule of law and justice based on a mixed economy.

248. The motives for the reforms were all very explicitly expressed by the President of the Republic in 2007, beginning with his speech of presentation of the draft reforms before the National Assembly, in which he said that the reforms' main objective was 'the construction of a Bolivarian and socialist Venezuela' – that is, to sow 'socialism in the political and economic realms'.[1783] He clearly expressed that in his presidential campaign in 1999, he did not propose such thing as 'projecting the road of socialism' to be incorporated in the Constitution, but conversely in 2006, as candidate for re-election, he said: 'Let us go to Socialism', deducting from that that 'everyone who voted for [re-electing] candidate Chávez then, voted to go to socialism'.[1784]

This was then the motivation for the drafting of the constitutional reforms in 2007, aiming to construct 'Bolivarian Socialism, Venezuelan Socialism, our Socialism, and our socialist model', having 'the community' (*la comunidad*), a 'basic and indivisible nucleus', and considering that 'real democracy is only possible in socialism'. However, the democracy referred to was not at all a representative democracy because it was 'not born of suffrage or from any election, but rather is born from the condition of organized human groups as the base of the population'.[1785]

The President in that speech summarized the aims of his reform proposals explaining that on the political ground, the purpose was to 'deepen popular Bolivarian democracy'; and on the economic ground, to 'create better conditions to sow and construct a socialist productive economic model', which he considered 'our model'. That is, 'in the political field: socialist democracy; on the economic, the productive socialist model; in the field of public administration, incorporate new forms in order to lighten the load, to leave behind bureaucracy, corruption, and administrative inefficiency, which are heavy burdens of the past still upon us like weights, in the political, economic and social areas'.[1786]

249. All his proposals to construct socialism were linked by the President to Simón Bolívar's 1819 Constitution of Angostura, which he considered 'perfectly

---

1783   See *Discurso de orden pronunciado por el ciudadano Comandante Hugo Chávez Frías, Presidente Constitucional de la República Bolivariana de Venezuela en la conmemoración del ducentécimo segundo aniversario del juramento del Libertador Simón Bolívar en el Monte Sacro y el tercer aniversario del referendo aprobatorio de su mandato constitucional*, special session, 15 Aug. 2007, Asamblea Nacional, División de Servicio y Atención legislativa, Sección de Edición (Caracas, 2007), 4, 33.

1784   *Ibid.*, 4. That is, it sought to impose the wishes of only 46% of registered voters who voted to re-elect the President on the remaining 56% of registered voters who did not vote for presidential re-election. According to official statistics from the National Electoral Council, of 15,784,777 registered voters, only 7,309,080 voted to re-elect the President.

1785   See *Discurso de orden pronunciado por el ciudadano Comandante Hugo Chávez Frías, supra*, 32, 34, 35.

1786   *Ibid.*, 74.

applicable to a socialist project' in the sense of considering that it was possible to 'take the original Bolivarian ideology as a basic element of a socialist project'.[1787] Of course, this assertion has no serious foundations: it is enough to read Bolívar's 1819 Angostura discourse on presenting the draft constitution to realize that it has nothing to do with a 'socialist project' of any kind.[1788]

The rejected constitutional reform, without doubt, would have altered the basic foundations of the State.[1789] This is true particularly with respect to the proposals on the constitutional amplification of the Bolivarian doctrine; the substitution of the democratic, social State with the socialist State; the elimination of decentralization as a policy of the State designed to develop public political participation; and the elimination of economic freedom and the right to property.[1790]

All these constitutional reforms, approved by the National Assembly defrauding the Constitution, as aforementioned, were submitted to popular vote, and were all rejected by the people in the referendum that took place on 2 December 2007.[1791]

§2. *The Irregular and Illegitimate Implementation in 2008 of the Rejected Reform Proposals Through Ordinary Legislation*

250. Inspite of which the popular rejection of the 2007 constitutional reform was a very important step back to the authoritarian government of President Chávez, in 2008 he announced his intention to seek for the imposition of the rejected constitutional reform, again, in defraudation of the Constitution. First, in January 2008 he suggested that in order to assure the possibility for his indefinite re-election, he was willing to propose a repeall referendum of himself, seeking to convert the eventual

---

1787   *Ibid.*, 42. Only one month before the President's speech on the proposed constitutional reforms, the former minister of defence, General in Chief Raúl Baduel, who was in office until 18 Jul. 2007, stated on leaving the Ministry of Popular Power for the Defence that the President's call to 'construct socialism for the twenty-first century, implied a necessary, pressing and urgent need to formalize a model of Socialism that is theoretically its own, autochthonous, in accord with our historical, social, political and cultural context'. He added, 'Until this moment, this theoretical model does not exist and has not been formulated.' It is hard to imagine that it could have been formulated just one month later.

1788   See Simón Bolívar, *Escritos fundamentales* (Caracas, 1982). See also Pedro Grases (ed.), *El Libertador y la Constitución de Angostura de 1819* (Caracas, 1969); José Rodríguez Iturbe (ed.), *Actas del Congreso de Angostura* (Caracas, 1969). The contrary at least would have been noticed by Karl Mark who, on the contrary, in 1857 wrote a very critical entry regarding Bolivar, without discovering any socialist trends in his life, for the *The New American Cyclopaedia*, vol. III (1858), on 'Bolivar y Ponte, Simón.' Available at <www.marxists.org/archive/marx/works/1858/01/bolivar.htm>.

1789   See Eugenio Hernández Bretón, 'Cuando no hay miedo (ante la Reforma Constitucional)', in *Revista de Derecho Público* 112 *(Estudios sobre la reforma constitucional)* (Caracas: Editorial Jurídica Venezolana, 2007), 17–20; Manuel Rachadell, 'El personalismo político en el Siglo XXI', in *id.*, 65–70.

1790   See on these reforms, Allan R. Brewer-Carías, *Dismantling Democracy. The Chávez Authoritarian Experiment* (Cambridge University Press, 2010).

1791   See Allan R. Brewer-Carías, 'La proyectada reforma constitucional de 2007, rechazada por el poder constituyente originario', in *Anuario de Derecho Público 2007*, Año 1 (Caracas: Instituto de Estudios de Derecho Público de la Universidad Monteávila, 2008), 17–65. According to information from the National Electoral Council on 2 Dec. 2007, of 16,109,664 registered voters, only 9,002,439 voted (44.11% abstention); of voters, 4,504,354 rejected the proposal (50.70%). This means that there were only 4,379,392 votes to approve the proposal (49.29%), so only 28% of registered voters voted for the approval.

rejection of such referendum into a plebiscite for his re-election;[1792] and second, as mentioned in December 2008 he formally asked the National Assembly to approve a constitutional amendment in order to establish the possibility of the indefinite re-election of the President of the Republic which was submitted and approved by refe-rendum on 14 February 2009 (see *supra* paragraph 37), in spite of the constitutional prohibition to ask the people to vote about the same constitutional reform already rejected by popular vote (see *supra* paragraph 116).

251. It must also be noted that during the months before the Constitutional Re-form was submitted to the National Assembly, during July and August 2007, the President of the Republic, exercising the powers to legislate by decree that were delegated upon him by his completely controlled National Assembly in January 2007,[1793] sanctioned twenty-six very important new Statutes with the intention of beginning with the implementation, beforehand and in a fraudulent way, with the constitutional reform proposals that eventually were rejected by the people in the 2007 December referendum.[1794] Unfortunately, even though all were unconstitutio-nal, those Decree-Laws were enacted and applied without any possibility of control or judicial review. The President was sure that no Constitutional Chamber judicial review decision was to be issued, being such Chamber is a wholly controlled entity that has proved to be his most effective tool for the consolidation of his authoritarian government. This dependence of the Supreme Tribunal regarding the President of the Republic was admitted by himself in 2007, when he publicly complained about the fact that the Supreme Tribunal had issued an important ruling in which it 'modi-fied' the Income Tax Law, without previously consulting the 'leader of the Revolu-tion'.[1795]

1792   See *El Universal*, Caracas 27 Jan. 2008.

1793   See the January Enabling Law of January 2007, in *Gaceta Oficial*, 38.617 of 1 Feb. 2007.

1794   Regarding these 2008 Decree Laws, see *Revista de Derecho Público*, N° 115, *Estudios sobre los Decretos leyes Julio-Agosto*, 2008 (Caracas: Editorial Jurídica venezolana, 2008). Referring to these Decree Laws, Teodoro Petkoff has pointed out that: 'In absolute contradiction to the results of the 2 Dec. 2007 referendum in which voters rejected constitutional reforms, in several of the laws promul-gated the president presents several of the aspects of the rejected reforms almost in the same terms. The proposition of changing the name of the Venezuelan Armed Forces to create the Bolivarian Na-tional Militia was contained in the proposed reforms; the power given to the President to appoint na-tional government officials over the Governors and Mayors to, obviously, weaken those offices and to eliminate the last vestiges of counterweight to the executive in general and the presidency in particu-lar, was also contained in the reforms; the recentralization of the national executive branch of powers that today belong to the states and decentralized autonomous institutes was also part of the reforms; the enlargement of government powers to intervene in economic affairs was also contained in the re-form. To ignore the popular decision about the 2007 proposal to reform the constitution in conformity with the will and designs of an autocrat, without heed to legal or constitutional norms, is, *stricto sen-su*, a tyrannic act'. See Teodoro Petkoff, 'Election and Political Power. Challenges for the Opposi-tion', in *Revista. Harvard Review of Latin America* (Harvard University: David Rockefeller Centre for Latin American Studies, Fall 2008), 12.

1795   The case was a very polemic and discussed one, decided by the Constitutional Chamber of the Su-preme Tribunal in decision N° 301 of 27 Feb. 2007, regarding which the President of the Republic said: 'Many cases arrive when the Revolutionary Government wants to take a decision against somet-hing that for instance, deals with or has to pass through judicial decisions, and then they begin to mo-ve themselves in contrary sense in the shadow, and in many cases they attain to neutralize the deci-sions of the Revolution yon by means of a judge, or a court, and even through the own Supreme Tri-

252. All this situation is the only explanation a constitutional lawyer can find to understand why a Head of State of our times, as was the case of President Chávez in Venezuela, can say, challenging his opponents in a political rally held on 28 August 2008, 'I am the Law' and 'I am the State.'[1796] Anyway, this was not the first time that the President of the Republic used this expression. In 2001, when he approved more than forty-eight Decree-laws, also via delegate legislation, he also said, although in a different way: 'The law is me. The State is me.'[1797] This phrase, which although attributed to Luis XIV was never delivered by him,[1798] expressed by a Head of State of our times, is enough to realize and understand the tragic institutional situation of Venezuela in the period 1999–2009, precisely characterized by a complete absence of separation of powers and consequently, of a democratic government.[1799]

253. This legislative delegation was sanctioned by the National Assembly parallel to the announcement by the President at the beginning of the 2007 constitutional reform process. As aforementioned, perhaps assuming that the presidential constitutional reform proposal was to be approved by the people, the President began implementing it through the enabling law (delegate legislation) sanctioned in 2007 that was later also used fraudulently to implement the rejected reforms,[1800] particularly in

---

bunal of Justice, behind the *backs of the Leader of the Revolution,* acting from inside, against the Revolution. This is, I insist, treason to the people, treason to the Revolution.' (emphasis added). *Discurso en el Primer Evento con propulsores del Partido Socialista Unido de Venezuela desde el teatro Teresa Carreño, 24 marzo 2007.*

1796   He said: 'I warn you, group of Stateless, putrid opposition. Whatever you do, the 26 Laws will go ahead! And the other 16 Laws,...also. And if you go out in the streets, like on 11 Apr. (2002)...we will sweep you in the streets, in the barracks, in the universities. I will close the golpista media; I will have no compassion whatsoever...This Revolution came to stay, forever ! You can continue talking stupidities...I am going to intervene all communications and I will close all the enterprises I consider that are of public usefulness or of social interest! Out [of the country] Contractors and Forth Republic corrupt people ! *I am the Law...I am the State'* (*Yo soy la Ley..., Yo soy el Estado!!).* See in Gustavo Coronel, *Las Armas de Coronel,* 15 de octubre de 2008: <http://lasarmasdecoronel. blogspot.com/2008/10/yo-soy-la-leyyo-soy-el-estado.html>.

1797   '*La ley soy yo. El Estado soy yo*'. See in *El Universal* (Caracas, 12 Apr. 2001), 1,1 and 2,1.

1798   This famous phrase was attributed to Louis XIV, when in 1661 he decided to govern alone after the death of Cardinal Mazarin, but was never pronounced by him. See Yves Giuchet, *Histoire Constitutionnelle Française (1789–1958),* ed. Erasme (Paris, 1990), 8.

1799   This situation was summarized by Teodoro Petkoff, editor and founder of *Tal Cual,* one of the important newspapers in Caracas, as follows: 'Chavez controls all the political powers. More that 90% of the Parliament obey his commands; the Venezuelan Supreme Court, whose number were raised from 20 to 32 by the parliament to ensure an overwhelming officialist majority, has become an extension of the legal office of the Presidency...The Prosecutor General's Office, the Comptroller's Office and the Public Defender are all offices held by "yes persons", absolutely obedient to the orders of the autocrat. In the National Electoral Council, four of five members are identified with the government. The Venezuelan Armed Forces are tightly controlled by Chávez. Therefore, from a conceptual point of view, the Venezuelan political system is autocratic. All political power is concentrated in the hands of the President. There is no real separation of Powers.' See Teodoro Petkoff, 'Election and Political Power. Challenges for the Opposition', in *ReVista. Harvard Review of Latin America* (Harvard University: David Rockefeller Centre for Latin American Studies, Fall 2008), 12.

1800   See Lolymar Hernández Camargo, 'Límites del poder ejecutivo en el ejercicio de la habilitación legislativa: Imposibilidad de establecer el contenido de la reforma constitucional rechazada vía habilitación legislativa', in *Revista de Derecho Público* 115 *(Estudios sobre los Decretos Leyes)* (Caracas:

economic and social matters, in order to structure a socialist centralized State.[1801] This process, however, was developed in absolute secrecy with no public consultation and participation in violation of Article 210 of the Constitution.[1802]

254. Regarding the 2007 rejected constitutional reforms related to eliminating local level representative democracy, as aforementioned, the same began to be implemented in 2006, even before its formal proposal, with the sanctioning of the Communal Councils Law, which created them as social units and organizations not directed by popularly elected officials, without any sort of territorial autonomy, supposedly devoted to channelling citizens' participation but in a centralized conducted system from the apex of the national executive.[1803] This Law was later reformed and elevated to organic law rank in 2009.[1804]

A primary purpose of the 2007 constitutional reforms was to complete the dismantling of the federal form of the State by centralizing power attributions of the States, creating administrative entities to be established and directed by the national executive, attributing powers to the President to interfere in regional and local affairs, and voiding state and municipal competency by means of compulsory transfer of that competency to communal councils.[1805] The implementation of the rejected constitutional reforms regarding the organization of the 'Popular Power' based on the strengthening of the communes and communal councils was completed with the approval in 2010 of the Law on the Federal Council of Government.[1806]

Editorial Jurídica Venezolana, 2008), 51 et seq.; Jorge Kiriakidis, 'Breves reflexiones en torno a los 26 Decretos-Ley de julio-agosto de 2008, y la consulta popular refrendaría de diciembre de 2007', in *id.*, 57 et seq.; José Vicente Haro García, 'Los recientes intentos de reforma constitucional o de cómo se está tratando de establecer una dictadura socialista con apariencia de legalidad (A propósito del proyecto de reforma constitucional de 2007 y los 26 decretos leyes del 31 de julio de 2008 que tratan de imponerla)', in *id.*, 63 et seq.

1801 See Ana Cristina Núñez Machado, 'Los 26 nuevos Decretos-Leyes y los principios que regulan la intervención del Estado en la actividad económica de los particulares', in *id.*, 215–20.

1802 See Aurilivi Linares Martínez, 'Notas sobre el uso del poder de legislar por decreto por parte del Presidente venezolano', in *id.*, 79–89; Carlos Luis Carrillo Artiles, 'La paradójica situación de los Decretos Leyes Orgánicos frente a la Ingeniería Constitucional de 1999', in *id.*, 93–100; Freddy J. Orlando S., 'El 'paquetazo', un conjunto de leyes que conculcan derechos y amparan injusticias', in *id.*, 101–104.

1803 Ley Orgánica de los Consejos Comunales, *Gaceta Oficial* N° 39.335, 28 Dec. 2009. See Juan M. Raffali A., 'Límites constitucionales de la Contraloría Social Popular', in Revista de Derecho Público, 115 *(Estudios sobre los Decretos Leyes)* (Caracas: Editorial Jurídica Venezolana, 2008), 133–147.

1804 See *Gaceta Oficial* N° 39.335 of 12 Dec. 2009. See decision N° 1.676 12 Mar. 2009 Constitutional Chamber, Supreme Tribunal of Justice about the constitutionality of the organic character of the Communal Councils Organic Law, in <www.tsj.gov.ve/deci-siones/scon/diciembre/1676-31209-2009-09-1369.html>. See Allan R. Brewer-Carías, *Ley Orgánica de los Consejos Comunales* (Caracas: Editorial Jurídica Venezolana, 2010).

1805 See Manuel Rachadell, *'La centralización del poder en el Estado federal descentralizado'*, in *Revista de Derecho Público*, 115 *(Estudios sobre los Decretos Leyes)* (Caracas: Editorial Jurídica Venezolana, 2008), 111–131.

1806 See Organic Law on the Federal Council of Government, *Gaceta Oficial* N° 5.963 Extra. of 22 Feb. 2010.

To implement these reforms, not only the last mentioned aspect was achieved, forcing the states and municipalities to transfer its attributions to local institutions controlled by the central power (communal councils), but also by means of Decree Law N° 6217 of 15 July 2008, on the Organic Law of Public Administration[1807] that began to bedirectly applicable to the states' and municipalities' Public Administrations, the national executive has implemented the principle of centralized planning, subjecting regional and local authorities to the Central Planning Commission. This Organic Law also assigns to the President, as proposed in the 2007 reforms, the power to appoint regional authorities with powers to plan, execute, follow up on and control land use and territorial development policies, thus subjecting all programmes and projects to central planning approval.

255. Regarding the vertical distribution of State attributions between the national level and the states, one of the general purposes of the rejected 2007 constitutional reform was to change the federal form of the State and the territorial distribution of the competencies established in Articles 156 and 164 of the Constitution, thus centralizing the State even more by concentrating almost all competencies of the public power at the national level. Particularly, 'nationalizing' the competency set forth in Article 164.10 of the Constitution, which attributed to the State's exclusive jurisdiction on the conservation, administration and use of national highways, roads, ports and airports.[1808] Despite the rejection of the constitutional reforms in the December 2007 referendum in order to change such provision, the Constitutional Chamber of the Supreme Tribunal, in Decision N° 565 (15 April 2008),[1809] issuing an abstract constitutional interpretation at the request of the Attorney General of the Republic, modified the content of the constitutional provision, arguing that the 'exclusive' attribution 'was not exclusive' but 'concurrent' – meaning that the national government could also exercise that competency interfering with the states' powers. With that interpretation, the Chamber illegitimately modified the Constitution, usurping popular sovereignty, and changed the federal form of the State by misrepresenting the territorial distribution system of powers between the national power and the sta-

---

1807   *Gaceta Oficial* N° 5.890, Extra. of 31 Jul. 2008. See Allan R. Brewer-Carías, 'El sentido de la reforma de la Ley Orgánica de la Administración Pública', in *Revista de Derecho Público* 115 *(Estudios sobre los Decretos Leyes)* (Caracas: Editorial Jurídica Venezolana, 2008), 155–161; Cosimina G. Pellegrino Pacera, 'La reedición de la propuesta constitucional de 2007 en el Decreto N° 6.217, con Rango, Valor y Fuerza de Ley Orgánica de la Administración Pública', in *id.*, 163–68; Jesús Caballero Ortíz, 'Algunos comentarios sobre la descentralización funcional en la nueva Ley Orgánica de la Administración Pública', in *id.* 169–174; Alberto Blanco-Uribe Quintero. 'Afrenta a la Debida Dignidad frente a la Administración Pública. Los Decretos 6.217 y 6.265', in *id.*, 175–179.The Organic Law has been reformed in 2014. See *Gaceta Oficial* N° 6.147, Extra. of 17 Dec 2014

1808   See Allan R. Brewer-Carías, *Hacia la consolidación de un estado socialista, centralizado, policial y militarista. Comentarios sobre el sentido y alcance de las propuestas de reforma constitucional 2007* (Caracas: Editorial Jurídica Venezolana, 2007), 41 et seq.; and *La Reforma Constitucional de 2007 (Comentarios al proyecto inconstitucionalmente sancionado por la Asamblea Nacional el 2 de noviembre de 2007)* (Caracas: Editorial Jurídica Venezolana, 2007), 72 et seq.

1809   See Decision N° 565 of the Constitutional Chamber (15 Apr. 2008) (Case: *Procurador General de la república, Interpretación del artículo 164.10 de la Constitución)*, available at <www.tsj.gov.ve/decisio-nes/scon/Abril/565-150408-07-1108.htm>.

tes.[1810] The Chamber, consequently, urged the National Assembly to issue legislation against the provisions of the 1999 Constitution, which was effectively accomplished in May 2009 by reforming the Organic Law on Decentralization, Delimitation, and Transfer of Public Attributions,[1811] eliminating the aforementioned exclusive attribution of the states.[1812]

256. The rejected 2007 constitutional reforms also sought to eliminate the Capital District that the 1999 Constitution had created as a political entity in substitution of the former Federal District, which was dependent on the national level of government. Notwithstanding popular rejection of the 2007 reform proposals, in April 2009, such reform was unconstitutionally implemented by the National Assembly, defrauding once more the Constitution by sanctioning the Special Law on the Organization and Regime of the Capital District.[1813] In it, instead of organizing a democratic political entity to govern the capital district, in Caracas, the capital of the Republic, the law established an organization completely dependent on the national level of government in the same territorial jurisdiction that 'used to be one of the extinct Federal District'. According to this law, the capital district, contrary to what is provided for in the Constitution, has no elected authorities of government and is governed by the national level by means of a 'special regime' consisting of the exercise of the legislative function by the National Assembly itself and a chief of government as the executive branch (Article 3) appointed by the President. This means that through a national statute, in the same territory of Caracas, a new national structure has been unconstitutionally imposed.

257. Finally, although the 2007 constitutional proposed reforms regarding the military and the Armed Force that sought to transform them into the Bolivarian Armed Force organized for the purpose of reinforcing socialism were rejected in the December 2007 referendum, the radical changes it contained have been implemented by the President, also usurping the constituent power, by means of a Decree Law reforming the Organic Law on the Armed Force,[1814] creating the 'Bolivarian National Armed Force' subjected to a 'military Bolivarian Doctrine', and creating in it the

---

1810   See Decision N° 565 of the Constitutional Chamber (15 Apr. 2008) (Case: *Procurador General de la República, Interpretación del artículo 164.10 de la Constitución)*, available at <www.tsj.gov.ve/decisio-nes/scon/Abril/565-150408-07-1108.htm>.

1811   *Gaceta Oficial* N° 39.140 of 17 Mar. 2009.

1812   See Allan R. Brewer-Carías, 'La Sala Constitucional como poder constituyente: La modificación de la forma federal del estado y del sistema constitucional de división territorial del poder público', in *Revista de Derecho Público* 114 (Caracas: Editorial Jurídica Venezolana, 2008), 247–262; Manuel Rachadell, *'La centralización del poder en el Estado federal descentralizado'*, in *Revista de Derecho Público*, N° 115 (Estudios sobre los Decretos Leyes) (Caracas: Editorial Jurídica Venezolana, 2008), 120.

1813   *Gaceta Oficial* N° 39.156 of 13 Apr. 2009. See the comments on this Law in Allan R. Brewer-Carías et al., *Leyes sobre el Distrito Capital y el Área Metropolitana de Caracas* (Caracas: Editorial Jurídica Venezolana, 2009).

1814   Decree Law N° 6.239, on the Organic Law of the National Bolivarian Armed Force, in *Gaceta Oficial* N° 5.933, Extra. of 21 Oct. 2009.

'National Bolivarian Militia' – all of this according to what was proposed and rejected by the people in the 2007 Constitutional Reform.[1815]

§3. *The Unconstitutional Implementation in 2010–2011 of the Rejected Reform Proposals Through Organic Laws*

258. On 26 September 2010 a parliamentary election was held in the country, the result of which being that the opposition to the government won the popular vote, although not the majority of seats in the National Assembly, due to distorting electoral regulations. This result meant, in fact, that the majority of popular vote expressed was against the proposals debated in the electoral campaign for the establishment of a socialist State in Venezuela, a matter that the President and the governmental majority of the National Assembly, with a massive campaign for their candidates, posed as a 'plebiscite' on the President, his performance and his socialist policies.

259. In disdain of the popular will expressed ratifying the previous rejection by the people of the reforms in the 2007 referendum, the President and his party, having lost the absolute control they used to have since 2005 over the National Assembly, before the newly elected deputies to the Assembly could have taken possession of office in January 2011, in December 2010 forced the National Assembly to proceed to sanction a set of organic laws through which they have finished defining the legislative framework for a new State. In this way, by-passing the Constitution and in parallel to the Constitutional State, the National Assembly regulated a socialist, centralized, military and police State, called the 'Communal State' of the 'Popular Power' already rejected by the people in 2007.

The organic laws that were approved on 21 December 2010 are the laws on the Popular Power; the Communes; the Communal Economic System; the Public and Communal Planning; and the Social Comptrollership.[1816] Furthermore, in the same framework of organizing the Communal State, based on the Popular Power, the reform of the Organic Law of Municipal Public Power and the Public Policy Planning and Coordination of the State Councils,[1817] and of the Local Council Public Planning Laws stand out. The delegitimized National Assembly also passed an enabling Law authorizing the President, through delegated legislation, to enact laws on all imaginable subjects, including laws of organic nature, emptying the new National Assembly of matters on which to legislate for a period of eighteen months until 2012.

260. However, the general defining framework of the Socialist State imposed on Venezuelans through such unconstitutional legislation, and for which nobody has

---

1815   See Alfredo Arismendi A., 'Fuerza Armada Nacional: Antecedentes, evolución y régimen actual', in *Revista de Derecho Público*, N° 115 (Estudios sobre los Decretos Leyes) (Caracas: Editorial Jurídica Venezolana, 2008), 187–206; Jesús María Alvarado Andrade, 'La nueva Fuerza Armada Bolivariana (Comentarios a raíz del Decreto N° 6.239, con rango, valor y fuerza de Ley Orgánica de la Fuerza Armada Nacional Bolivariana)', in *id.*, 207–214.

1816   See the text of all these Laws in *Gaceta Oficial* N° 6.011 Extra. 21 Dec. 2010. See on all these organic laws, Allan R. Brewer-Carías et al., *Leyes Orgánicas sobre el Poder Popular y el Estado Comunal* (Caracas: Editorial Jurídica Venezolana, 2011), 361 et seq.

1817   See *Gaceta Oficial* N° 6.015 Extra. Of 28 Dec. 2010.

voted, is supposedly based on the exercise of the sovereignty of the people but exclusively in a 'direct' manner through the exercise of the Popular Power and the establishment of a Communal State. This is contained in the Organic Law for Popular Power, which is to be applied to everyone and everything as an essential part of the new 'socialist principle of legality' in the creation, implementation and control of public management.

261. The main purpose of these laws is the organization of the 'Communal State' which has the commune as its fundamental unit, unconstitutionally supplanting the municipalities as the 'primary political units of the national organization' (Article 168 of the Constitution), through whose organization the Popular Power is exercised, and which is manifested in the exercise of popular sovereignty although not through representatives. It is therefore a political system in which representative democracy is ignored, openly violating the Constitution.

The Socialist State or Communal State sought to be established through these laws, in parallel to the Constitutional State, is supposedly based on Article 5 of the Constitution that provides that 'Sovereignty resides untransferably in the people, who exercise it directly as provided in this Constitution and the Law, and indirectly, by suffrage, through the organs exercising Public Power', but by-passing the basic rule of the Constitutional State structure grounded on the concept of representative democracy, that is, the exercise of sovereignty indirectly through the vote. The Communal State is now structured based only on the supposedly direct exercise of sovereignty[1818] through the Communes, 'with an economic model of social property and endogenous sustainable development that allows reaching the supreme social happiness of the Venezuelan people in a socialist society' (Article 8.8),[1819] called the ' Communal Economic System' (see *infra* par.627).

262. What is being sought is to establish a Socialist or Communal State alongside the Constitutional State: the first one based on the direct exercise of sovereignty by the people; and the second, based also on the indirect exercise of sovereignty by the people through elected representatives by universal suffrage; in a system in which the former will gradually strangle and empty competencies from the second. All of this is unconstitutional, particularly because in the structure of the Communal State that is established, in the end, the exercise of sovereignty is factually indirect, through supposed 'representatives' that are not popularly elected through universal and direct suffrage, but 'elected' in Citizens' Assemblies. They are the ones called to exercise Popular Power in the name of the people, with the name of 'spokespersons',

---

1818   This has even been 'legitimized' by the Supreme Tribunal Constitutional Chamber's decisions analysing the organic character of the laws, such as the one issued in connection with the Organic Law of Municipalities. See decision N° 1.330, Case: Organic Character of the Law of the Communes 12/17/2010, in <www.tsj.gov.ve/decisiones/scon/Diciembre/1330-171210-2010-10-1436.html>.

1819   The Organic Law of Municipalities, however, defines the Communal State as follows: 'Form of sociopolitical organization, based on the democratic and social state of law and justice established in the Constitution of the Republic, whose power is exercised directly by the people through communal self goverments, with an economic model of social property and endogenous and sustainable development that achieves the supreme social happiness of the Venezuelan people in a socialist society. Forming the basic unit of the Communal State is the commune' (Art. 4.10).

but that as already mentioned, are not elected by the people through universal, secret and direct suffrage.

This system that is being structured, directly controlled by a Ministry from the National Executive Branch of Government, far from being an instrument of participation and decentralization – a concept that is indissolubly linked to political autonomy – is a centralized and tightly controlled system of the communities by the central power, in which the members of the communal councils, the communes and all organizations of the Popular Power are not elected but 'appointed' through a show of hands by assemblies controlled by the official party and the executive branch.

263. This Communal State system, parallel to the Constitutional State, is structured on a unique concept which is socialism, so that anyone who is not a socialist is automatically discriminated. It is not possible, therefore, under the framework of these laws to reconcile pluralism and the principle of non-discrimination on grounds of 'political opinion' guaranteed by the Constitution, with the provisions of these Laws pursuing the opposite, that is, the establishment of a Communal State whose bodies can only act on the basis of socialism and in which any citizen who has another opinion is excluded. That is, through these Organic Laws, the defining framework of a new model of a State parallel and different from the Constitutional State has been established called the Communal State based exclusively on Socialism as the political doctrine and practice.

In this regard, Article 5 of the Organic Law on the Popular Power states, in addition, that 'people's organization and participation in exercising its sovereignty is based on Simon Bolivar the Liberator's doctrine, and is based on socialist principles and values',[1820] – a link that, as aforementioned, is untenable – matching the organization of the Communal State (established in parallel to the Constitutional State) with the socialist political ideology.

Article 7 of the same Organic Law on the Popular Power defines as a purpose of the Popular Power, to strengthen 'the organization of the people in order to consolidate the revolutionary democracy and build the bases of a socialist society, democratic, of law and justice', and to 'establish the bases that allow organized communities to exercise social comptrollership to ensure that the investment of public resources is efficiently performed for the collective benefit; and monitor that the activities of the private sector with social impact develop within legal rules that protect users and consumers'. This, of course, is a well known procedure established in other authoritarian regimes in order to construct a general system of social espionage to be developed among people in order to institutionalize the denunciation and persecution of any deviation regarding the socialist framework imposed on the citizenship.[1821]

1820   The same expression was used in the Organic Law of the Communes with respect to their constitution, shaping and functioning (Art. 2), in the Communal Council's Law (Art. 1) and in the Organic Law of Social Comptrollership (Art. 6).

1821   See Luis A. Herrera Orellana, 'La Ley Orgánica de Contraloría Social: Funcionalización de la participación e instauración de la desconfianza ciudadana', in Allan R. Brewer-Carías et al., *Leyes Orgánicas sobre el Poder Popular y el Estado Comunal* (Caracas: Editorial Jurídica Venezolana, 2011), 361 et seq.

According to the Law of the Communes[1822] these communes are conceived as a 'local entity' or 'socialist space' of the Communal State, where citizens exercise the 'Popular Power' (Article 1). Nonetheless, according to the Constitution, this expression of 'local entity' can only be applied to local political entities of the Constitutional State with self-governments composed of elected representatives by universal, direct and secret ballot (Article 169), so there can be no 'local entities' directed by persons that are not elected by the people but appointed by other bodies. On the contrary, the origin of the so-called governments of the communes, this legislation on Popular Power and its organizations, according to is not guaranteed through democratic representative election by universal, direct and secret suffrage, thus being an unconstitutional conception.

§4. *The 'Communal State' conceived in Parallel to the 'Constitutional State'*

264. This Communal State, regulated on the fringes of the Constitution, has been established as a 'Parallel State' to the Constitutional State, but with provisions that, if implemented, will enable the Communal State to drown the Constitutional State, for which purpose the Law has provided that all organs of the Constitutional State that exercise Public Power are subjected to the mandates of the organizations of Popular Power, establishing a new principle of government, so-called in the Law, the principle of 'govern obeying', no other than obeying the wishes of the central government.[1823]

As the Popular Power organizations have no political autonomy, since their 'spokespersons' are not democratically elected by universal, direct and secret ballot, but appointed by citizen Assemblies politically controlled and operated by the governing party and the National Executive who controls and guides all the organizational process of the Communal State in the sphere of socialist ideology, there is no way there can be a spokesperson who is not a socialist.

Consequently, this 'govern obeying' principle is a limitation to the political autonomy of the elected bodies of the Constitutional State such as the National Assembly, Governors and Legislative Councils of states and Mayors and Municipal Councils, upon whom ultimately is imposed an obligation to obey any provision made by the National Government and the ruling party, framed exclusively in the socialist sphere as a political doctrine.

Therefore, in the unconstitutional framework of these Popular Power Laws, the popular will expressed in the election of representatives of the Constitutional State bodies has no value whatsoever, and the people have been confiscated of their sovereignty by transferring it to assemblies who do not represent them.

1822   See *Gaceta Oficial* N° 6.011 Extra. Of 21 Dec. 2010.

1823   Article 24 of the Law establishes the following principle: 'Proceedings of the bodies and entities of Public Power. All organs, entities and agencies of Public Power will govern their actions by the principle of "govern obeying", in relation to the mandates of the people and organizations of Popular Power, according to the provisions in the Constitution of the Republic and the laws.'

265. With this Organic Law of Popular Power framework, there is no doubt about the political decision taken on 21 December 2010 by the completely delegitimized National Assembly that was elected in 2005, and that no longer represented the majority of the popular will as it was expressed in the 26 September 2010 legislative election, against the President of the Republic, the National Assembly itself and socialist policies they have developed. These policies are aimed to impose on Venezuelans, against popular will and defrauding the Constitution, a Socialist State model, called 'the Communal State' and conceived as a Socialist State, in order to supposedly exercise Popular Power directly by the people, as an alleged form of direct exercise of sovereignty, which isnot true because it is exercised through 'spokespersons' who supposedly 'represent' them but without being elected in universal, direct and secret suffrage.

266. By regulating this Communal State of the Popular Power through ordinary legislation, in addition to defrauding the Constitution, a technique that has been consistently applied by the authoritarian regime in Venezuela since 1999 to impose its decisions outside of the Venezuelan Constitution,[1824] it now adds fraud to the popular will by imposing on Venezuelans through organic laws a State model for which nobody has voted.

The new State framework radically and unconstitutionally changes the text of the 1999 Constitution, which has not been reformed as the regime had wished in 2007, and in open contradiction to the popular rejection that the majority expressed in the attempt the regime developed to reform the Constitution in the referendum of 2 December 2007, even in violation of the Constitution, and the popular rejection that the majority of the people expressed regarding the socialist policies of the President to the Republic and his National Assembly on the occasion of the parliamentary elections of 26 September 2010.

What is clear about all this is that there are no masks to deceive anyone, or by reason of which someone pretends to be deceived or fooled about what essentially the 'Bolivarian revolution' is; nothing else but a communist Marxist revolution, carried out deliberately by misusing and defrauding constitutional institutions.

1824   See Allan R. Brewer-Carías, *Reforma constitucional y fraude a la Constitución (1999-2009)* (Caracas: Academia de Ciencias Políticas y Sociales, 2009); *Dismantling Democracy. The Chávez Authoritarian Experiment* (New York: Cambridge University Press, 2010).

PART V. THE GOVERNMENT

267. Within the presidential system of government[1825] (see *supra* paragraph 54), according to Article 255 of the Constitution, the Executive Power is exercised by the President of the Republic, the Executive Vice President, the Ministers, and the other officials as determined by the Constitution and by statutes.

Chapter 1. The National Executive

§1. *The President of the Republic*

I.   *Head of State and of the Government*

268. Article 226 of the Constitution provides that the President of the Republic is both the Chief of State, and the Chief of the National Executive branch, and in which capacity he directs the government.

The President of the Republic is elected through direct, secret and universal suffrage, by relative majority of votes (Article 228). To be elected President, the candidate must be Venezuelan by birth, possess no other nationality, be older than 30 years of age, and not be convicted of a crime (Article 227). Those that on the day of the nomination for President or on any date between that date and the day of the election, are or have been acting as Executive Vice President, Governor of a state or municipal Mayor, may not lawfully be elected to the Presidency of the Republic (Article 229).

269. The President's constitutional term is of six years. For the first time since the nineteenth century, after forbidding presidential elections, the 1999 Constitution provided that the President could be re-elected for the consecutive term, although only once (Article 230). This limit was eliminated in 2009, first by means of a constitutional interpretation on the alternating principle of government,[1826] and second, through a constitutional amendment approved by referendum on 14 February 2009 (see *supra* paragraph 37). President Hugo Chávez Frias, after being elected in 1998 and subsequently in 2000 once the new Constitution was approved, was re-elected

---

1825   See in general, Donato Lupidii, 'El sistema presidencial y la Constitución venezolana de 1999', en *El Derecho Público a comienzos del siglo XXI. Estudios homenaje al Profesor Allan R. Brewer-Carías*, vol. I (Madrid: Instituto de Derecho Público, UCV, Civitas Ediciones, 2003), 819–835; Miguel A. Gómez Ortiz, 'El régimen presidencial en Venezuela', en *Bases y principios del sistema constitucional venezolano (Ponencias del VII Congreso Venezolano de Derecho Constitucional realizado en San Cristóbal del 21 al 23 de Noviembre de 2001)*, vol. II, 299–336; José Peña Solis, 'Notas sobre los Sistemas de Gobierno parlamentario y Presidencial. Breve Referencia al Sistema Venezolano', en *Tendencias Actuales del Derecho Constitucional. Homenaje a Jesús María Casal Montbrun*, vol. I, ed. Jesús María Casal, Alfredo Arismendi y Carlos Luis Carrillo Artiles (Coord.) (Caracas: Universidad Central de Venezuela/Universidad Católica Andrés Bello, 2008), 405–430; Alfredo Arismendi, 'La Separación de Poderes y el Sistema Presidencial', en *Tendencias Actuales del Derecho Constitucional. Homenaje a Jesús María Casal Montbrun*, ed. Jesús María Casal, Alfredo Arismendi y Carlos Luis Carrillo Artiles (Coord.), vol. I (Caracas: Universidad Central de Venezuela/Universidad Católica Andrés Bello, 2008), 465–484.

1826   See Allan R. Brewer-Carías, 'El Juez Constitucional vs. La alternabilidad republicana (La reelección continua e indefinida)', en *Revista de Derecho Público*, N° 117 (Caracas, 2009), 205–211.

in 2006. In 2007 he proposed a Constitutional Reform Draft seeking for the establishment in the Constitution of the possibility for the indefinite re-election of the President of the Republic, which was rejected by the people in the referendum held on December 2007. Nonetheless, as aforementioned, in January 2008, he announced that he was going to seek for a constitutional amendment, and in December 2008 after important defeats in the regional and municipal elections, he asked the National Assembly to approve a constitutional amendment draft on the same matter of indefinite presidential election, which was approved by referendum on February 2009.

270. It must also be mentioned that the Constitution has established the possibility for the Supreme Tribunal of Justice to decide 'the removal from office of the President of the Republic' (Article 233) without any other significant specific delineation or definition of the conditions for exercising that power.

II.   *The Absences of the President of the Republic and Its Substitutions*

271. The Constitution distinguishes two kinds of absences of the President from his tenure: absolute and temporal, and the ways to replace him.

According to Article 233, absolute absence of the President of the Republic is produced in cases of death; resignation; dismissal by the Supreme Tribunal; physical or mental incapacity certified by a medical panel appointed by the Supreme Tribunal with the approval of the National Assembly; the abandonment of the office declared by the National Assembly, and the repeal of his mandate by referendum.

In such cases, if the absolute absence is produced before his inauguration, a new universal, direct and secret election must be convened within the following thirty days. In this case, in the mean time, the President of the National Assembly must take charge of the Presidency of the Republic. If the absolute absence takes place within the first four years of the constitutional term, a new universal and direct election must be convened within the following thirty days. In this case, in the mean time, the Executive Vice President must take charge of the Presidency of the Republic. In all these situations, the new President must finish the constitutional term of the absent President.

If the absolute absence is produced during the last two years of the constitutional term of the President, the Executive Vice President must assume the Presidency of the Republic up to the end of the term.

272. Regarding the temporary absences of the President, such as for instances when travelling abroad, Article 234 establishes that in such cases, he must be replaced by the Executive Vice President up to ninety days, which can be extended by the National Assembly for another ninety days. If the temporary absence exceeds the latter ninety days, the National Assembly can decide by a majority vote of its members to consider it as an absolute absence of the President.

Regarding travels of the President outside the national territory, only trips abroad for more than five days require the authorization of the National Assembly (Article 235).

All these constitutional provisions were openly violated during the last years of Chávez, who was submitted to intermitent medical treatment in La Habana, Cuba, until his death in December 2012, but without the government even considering that a temporal absence occured.[1827] Not to mention the absolute absence situation produced by the death of President Chavez and the unconstitutional sucssesion in the Presidency decree by the Constitutional Chamber of the Supreme Tribunal in January 2013.[1828]

§2. *The Executive Vice President*

273. One of the innovations in the Constitution of 1999 was the creation of the office of the Executive Vice President, which is a non-elected organ appointed by the President and directly tied to his office, which has the power to freely appoint or dismiss him. The Executive Vice President must meet the same qualifications for office as the President, and must have no blood or marriage relation with the President.

The Executive Vice President is thus an immediate collaborator of the President in his capacity as Chief Executive (Article 238). Consequently, its creation in the Constitution does not alter the nature of the presidential system of government.[1829] Its main attributions are the following (Article 239): to collaborate with the President in the direction of Government action; to coordinate National Public Administration according to the President's instructions; to propose to the President the appointment and dismissal of Ministers; to preside over the Council of Ministers, with prior authorization of the President (Article 242); to coordinate the relations of the National Executive with the National Assembly; and to fill the temporal absences of the President (Article 234).

274. As mentioned, the Executive Vice President is appointed and dismissed by the President of the Republic. Nonetheless, according to Article 240 of the Constitution, a motion to censure the Vice President, arising from a vote of at least three-fifths of the members of the National Assembly, will result in his removal from office. In such a case the Executive Vice President may not occupy that office or that of a Minister for the remainder of the President's term in office. However, three removals of Executive Vice Presidents due to legislative motion to censure approved

---

1827   See Allan R. Brewer-Carías, 'La extraña situación constitucional respecto del funcionamiento del gobierno en Venezuela, durante la falta temporal del Presidente de la República, por su ausencia del territorio nacional entre el 5 de junio y el 4 de julio de 2011,' *Revista de Derecho Público*, 126, (Caracas, Editorial Jurídica Venezolana, 2011, 59-75; 'Comentario sobre la bizarra situación constitucional y administrativa derivada de la ausencia temporal del Presidente de la República entre el 17 y 24 de julio de 2011 por encontrarse en tratamiento médico en La Habana, Cuba,' *Revista de Derecho Público* 127 (Caracas, Editorial Jurídica Venezolana 2011), 47-54.,

1828   See Allan R. Brewer-Carías, '"Crónicas Constitucionales sobre el régimen constitucional en Venezuela con motivo de la ausencia del territorio nacional del Presidente (re-electo) de la República, a partir del 9 de diciembre de 2012 (Crónicas I-IX: 29-1-2012 / 12-1-2013)," *Revista digital "Elementos de juicio. Temas Constitucionales* (Bogotá, José Gregorio Galindo Publicaciones y medios, 2013), pp. 99-165.

1829   See Carlos Ayala Corao, *El Régimen Presidencial en América Latina y los planteamientos para su Reforma* (Caracas, 1992).

during the same constitutional term of the Legislature, authorizes the President of the Republic to dissolve the National Assembly.

Thisis the only situation in which the President is entitled to dissolve the National Assembly, such a situation being difficult to conceive, unless the Assembly itself 'provoked' its own dissolution by voting to approve a third motion to censure. In such case, the Executive Decree dissolving the Assembly implies the need to convene new elections for the National Assembly that must take place within sixty days of its dissolution. In no case can the Assembly be dissolved during the last year of its constitutional term.

§3. *The Ministers*

275. The Ministers' offices are also directly linked to the President of the Republic, being directly under his control. The Ministers, sitting together with the President and the Executive Vice President, constitute the Council of Ministers (Article 242).

The Ministers are usually the head of the Ministries, which are the most important executive organs of the Government. They are freely appointed and dismissed by the President (Article 236.3). Nonetheless, Article 246 of the Constitution establishes the possibility for the National Assembly to approve motions to censure the Minister, and when the motion arises from a vote of not less than three-fifth of the members present in the National Assembly, the decision will result in the Minister's removal. The Minister may not then occupy any other office of Minister or of Executive Vice President for the remainder of the Presidential term.

276. The number, organization and functions of the Ministries are establish by the President of the Republic, by Executive Decree (Article 236.20) according to the general provisions established in the Organic Law of Public Administration.[1830] In accordance with Article 243 of the Constitution, the President of the Republic may also name Ministers of State, who, in addition to forming part of the Council of Ministers and without a Ministerial Office, assist the President and Vice President in certain functions.

277. The Ministers have the right to speak before the National Assembly (Article 211); and they can take part in its debates, although without vote (Article 245). However, the National Assembly can convoke the Ministers to its sessions, with the Assembly having the right to question them. The Ministers, as well as any public official, are also obliged to appear before the Assembly and to give them all the information and documents it requires for its legislative and control functions (Article 223). The National Assembly has the power to declare political responsibility of the Ministers, and can ask the Citizen Power to prosecute them. As already mentioned, the Assembly can also approve motions of censure of the Ministers (Article 246).

Finally, the Ministers must deliver before the National Assembly, within the first sixty days of each year, a motivated sufficient memoir referring to their activities in the previous year (Article 224).

1830   *Gaceta Oficial* N° 6.47 Extra. of 17 Nov. 2014.

§4. *The Council of Ministers*

278. As indicated, when sitting together with the President and the Executive Vice President, the Ministers constitute the Council of Ministers (Article 242). According to Article 236 of the Constitution, the President of the Republic, sitting in Ministers' Council, is required to exercise a set of functions designated in sections 7, 8, 9, 10, 12, 13, 14, 18, 20, 21, 22 of that article, as well as those imposed by statutes. Within these attributions that the President must always exercise in Council of Ministers are the following: declaration of states of exception and the suspension of constitutional guarantees; issuing of decrees-laws according to the legislative delegation made by the National Assembly; convening of the National Assembly to extraordinary sessions; issuing of regulations to statutes; approval of the National Plan for Development; the fixation of the number and organization of the Ministries; ordering the dissolution of the National Assembly, and convening referendums.

The Council of Ministers is presided over by the President of the Republic, although the President may authorize the Executive Vice President to preside when unable to attend. In all events, decisions of the Ministers' Council must always be ratified by the President.

§5. *Other Constitutional Executive Organs*

279. The Attorney General of the Republic is also an Executive organ of the Government and is required to attend the Council of Ministers but only with the right to speak, without the vote (Article 250). It is defined in the Constitution as an organ of the National Executive Branch that assists, defends and represents the interests of the Republic in judicial and non-judicial matters (Article 247). In particular, the Constitution requires the advice of the Attorney General with respect to the approval of contracts of national public interest to be signed by the executive (Article 247).

280. One of the innovations of the Constitution of 1999 was the creation of the Council of State as a superior advisory organ of the Government and of the National Public Administration (Article 251). The Council of State is formally charged with making policy recommendations regarding matters of national interest that the President of the Republic recognizes as being of special importance, requiring the Council's point of view.

The Council of State's specific functions and attributes must be determined by law, which up to 2011 had not been sanctioned. Anyway, regarding the constitutional provisions, the Executive Vice President must preside over the Council of State, which must be integrated, in addition, by five individuals named by the President of the Republic, a representative designated by the National Assembly, a representative designated by the Supreme Tribunal of Justice, and a Governor collectively designated by the chief executives of the states (Article 252). In practice, during the first decade of the 1999 Constitution, the Council of State has not been integrated and has not functioned.

281. Another innovation in the 1999 Constitution was the creation of the Federal Council of Government in charge of planning and coordinating the policies and actions for the process of decentralization and transfer of competencies from the national level of government to the states and municipalities. As aforementioned, this Council is presided over by the Executive Vice President, and integrated by the

Ministers, the state Governors, one municipal Mayor from each state and by representatives of the organized society; and is in charge of managing the Inter-territorial
Compensatory Fund (Article 185), in order to finance the public investments to
promote the equitable development of the regions, the cooperation and complemen-
tation of development policies and initiatives of the public territorial entities.[1831]

In 2010 the Organic Law on the Federal Council of Government was approved,
following the centralistic character of the Government developed during the first
decade of the Constitution (see *supra* paragraph 57), creating the Inter-territorial
Compensatory Fund in substitution of the former Intergovernmental Fund on Decentralization established in 1993.[1832]

282. Finally, Article 323 of the Constitution has also created the Council of Nation's Defence, presided over by the President of the Republic, as the country's highest authority for defence planning, advice and consultation regarding all public
entities (Public Powers) on all matters related to the defence and security of the Nation's sovereignty, territorial integrity and strategic thinking (see *supra* paragraph
334).

Chapter 2. Constitutional Powers of the National Executive

283. The President of the Republic is at the same time the Head of the State and
the Head of Government and of Public Administration, and as such, directs the Government actions (Article 226). Thus, the two basic functions of the National Executive are political and administrative, being subjected in both cases to the control of
the National Assembly.

§1. *The Political Functions of Government in the Constitution and the Parlia-
mentary Control*

284. As aforementioned, the President of the Republic directs the Government
actions (Articles 226; 236.2), and for such purpose, the Constitution directly assigns
him a series of political attributions. Among these, for instance, are the direction of
foreign relations, the convening of extraordinary sessions of the National Assembly,
and the declaration of states of exception, or the restriction of constitutional guarantees, in the latter case according to the corresponding Organic Law (Article 338).

In all these cases of political acts enumerated in Article 236 of the Constitution,
the Executive decisions must be counter signed by the Vice President and by the
corresponding Ministers, except the acts of the appointment of the Vice President
and of the Ministers, and the decrees of pardon.

1831   See Manuel Rachadell, 'El Consejo Federal de Gobierno y el Fondo de Compensación', in *Revista de
        derecho del Tribunal Supremo de Justicia,* N° 7 (Caracas, 2002), 417 a 457; Emilio Spósito Contre-
        ras, 'Reflexiones sobre el Consejo Federal de Gobierno como máxima instancia de Participación ad-
        ministrativa', in *Temas de derecho administrativo, Libro Homenaje a Gonzalo Pérez Luciani* II, no.
        7 (Caracas: Tribunal Supremo de Justicia, Colección Libros Homenaje, 2002), 827 a 863,; and José
        V. Haro, 'Aproximación a la noción del Consejo Federal de Gobierno prrevisto en la Constitución de
        1999', in *Revista de Derecho Constitucional,* N° 7 (enero-junio) (Caracas: Editorial Sherwood, 2003),
        161–166.

1832   See in *Gaceta Oficial* N° 5.963 Extra. of 22 Feb. 2010.

285. In these matters, the National Assembly 'exercises its control functions over the Government' (Article 187.3); according to which it can approve motions to censure the Vice President and the Ministers, which can lead to their removal when approved by three-fifth of the representatives (Articles 187.10; 240). As already mentioned, the National Assembly must also decide certain cases of absolute absence of the President because of physical or mental incapacity or abandonment of the Office, or the conversion of a temporal absence into an absolute one (Articles 233, 234) (see *supra* paragraph 271). The National Assembly can also authorize criminal processes against the President (Article 266.2) and must always review the Decrees of State of Exception (Articles 338, 339).

286. The National Assembly also has important attributions in political matters like the indirect election, as electoral body representing the people, of the Magistrates of the Supreme Tribunal of Justice and the High officials of the Citizen and Electoral branches of government, (Prosecutor General, Peoples' Defender, Comptroller General, and Members of the National Electoral Council) and their removal or dismissal (Articles 265, 279, 296) (see *infra* paragraph 420).

I.   *The Direction of Foreign Relations*

287. The President of the Republic has within his attributions 'to direct the foreign relations of the Republic and to sign and ratify international treaties, covenants and agreements' (Article 236.4). Regarding the latter, they must be approved by special statute (Article 187.18), before their ratification by the President, except when they execute or perfect pre-existent obligations of the Republic; they apply principles expressly recognized by it; they execute international relations ordinary acts; or they exercise attributions expressly assigned by statute to the President (Article 154) (see *supra* paragraph 123).

However, as mentioned before, the National Assembly must authorize the President's trips abroad when they exceed more than five days (Article 187.17).

II.   *The Executive Initiatives on Matters of Constitutional Review and of Referendum*

288. The President of the Republic in Council of Ministers has the initiative to propose amendments (Article 341) and reforms (Article 342) to the Constitution, as well as to convene a National Constituent Assembly for major constitutional changes to it (Article 348). The National Assembly also has initiative rights regarding constitutional review (Articles 341, 342, 348), and in the case of constitutional reforms, the draft must always be debated before it (Article 343) (see *supra* paragraph 116).

The President of the Republic, also in Council of Ministers (Article 236.22) has the initiative to submit to consultative referendum matters he considers as of special national interest (Article 71); to submit to approbatory referendum, international treaties, covenants or agreements that could compromise the national sovereignty or that could imply the transfer of State attributions to supra-national organs (Article 73); and to submit statutes to total or partial abrogate referendum (Article 74). However, the National Assembly has the initiative for the approbatory referendums of statutes (Article 73).

ALLAN R. BREWER-CARÍAS

III. *The Military Powers of the President of the Republic*

289. According to Article 236 of the Constitution, the President of the Republic in his position of Commander in Chief, has the attribution of directing the National Armed Force, to exercise the supreme authority upon it and to fix its contingent (Article 236.5). In such position, the President exercises the supreme command of the National Armed Force, and has the power to promote its officers from the rank of colonel or navy captain, and to appoint them for their corresponding positions (Article 236.6). In case of use of military missions abroad, or in case of foreign military missions in the country, the National Assembly must always give the corresponding authorization (Article 187.11).

IV. *Executive Powers Regarding the National Assembly*

290. The President of the Republic has legislative initiative and can send to the National Assembly Draft statutes for its discussion (Article 304.1). He also has, in Council of Ministers, the power to convene the National Assembly to extraordinary sessions, and to dissolve the Assembly in case of its approval of three motions of censure against the Executive Vice President (Articles 236.21; 240) (see *infra* paragraph 340). The President of the Republic can personally or through the Executive Vice President, direct reports or special messages to the National Assembly (Article 236.17).

V. *Executive Powers in Situations of Exception*

291. Chapter II of the Constitution, titled 'Protection of the Constitution' regulates cases of exceptional circumstances provoking 'situation of exception' that can seriously threaten the security of the Nation, and of its institutions and persons, in which the adoption of special political-constitutional measures to confront them are necessary.

Article 337 of the Constitution defines these 'states of exception'[1833] as the circumstances affecting the social, economic, political or natural order regarding which ordinary powers of government are considered insufficient to confront; as well as those gravely affecting the security of the Nation, and its institutions and Citizens. These are exceptional circumstances whose characteristics exceed the possibility of being attended to by the State through the institutional mechanisms established for normal situations. In these cases, the President of the Republic, in Council of Ministers, can decree the state of exceptions and also restrict some constitutional guarantees (Article 236.7).

292. According to the Organic Law on the States of Exception, which was sanctioned according to Article 338 of the Constitution,[1834] the following states of ex-

---

1833   See in general Jesús M. Casal H., 'Los estados de excepción en la Constitución de 1999', in *Revista de Derecho Constitucional*, N° 1 (septiembre-diciembre) (Caracas: Editorial Sherwood, 1999), 45–54; Salvador Leal W., 'Los estados de excepción en la Constitución', in *Revista del Tribunal Supremo de Justicia*, N° 8 (Caracas, 2003), 335–359; María de los Ángeles Delfino, 'El desarrollo de los Estados de Excepción en las Constituciones de América Latina', in *Constitución y Constitucionalismo Hoy* (Caracas: Editorial Ex Libris, 2000), 507–532.

1834   See the Organic Law on States of Exception, *Gaceta Oficial* N° 37.261 of 15 Aug. 2001.

ception can be decreed: The 'state of alarm' that can be decreed in cases of 'catastrophes, public calamities or similar events' exposing the Nation or its Citizens to serious danger. This state of exception is to have a duration of thirty days, which may be extended for an additional period of equal length. The 'state of economic emergency' that can be decreed when 'extraordinary economic circumstances arise' that 'gravely affect the Nation's economic life'. The permitted duration of this exceptional situation is sixty days, a term that may again be extended for an equal period. The 'state of interior or exterior commotion' that can be decreed in cases of 'interior or exterior conflict that seriously endangers the security of the Nation, its Citizens or institutions'. Here, the state of exception can last up to ninety days, and may be extended for an equal period.

293. In the above exceptional circumstances, the President of the Republic, sitting in Council of Ministers, is the one that has the prerogative and responsibility to decree these States of Exception (Article 337). Article 339 of the Constitution requires that within eight days of being issued, the decree must be sent to the consideration and approval by the National Assembly or to its Delegated Commission, and to the Constitutional Chamber of the Supreme Tribunal of Justice which must decide whether the decree is constitutional (Article 336.6)) (see *supra* paragraph 648). The decree must be in compliance with the requirements, principles and guarantees of the International Covenant on Civil and Political Rights[1835] and the American Convention on Human Rights.[1836]

The President of the Republic may also request the National Assembly to extend the duration of a decree for a term equal to its original constitutional one. The decree may be revoked by the National Executive, the National Assembly or its Delegated Commission before the completion of the decree's term should the causes that motivated its declaration cease. In all cases, however, the National Assembly must approve any extension of the duration of a decree (Article 338).

294. In addition, when a state of exception is decreed, the President of the Republic, sitting in Council of Ministers, is authorized in the Constitution to temporarily restrict constitutional guarantees, with the exception of those referring to the right to life, the right against *incomunicado* detentions and torture, the right to due process of law, the right to information, and those considered untouchable (intangibles) human rights (Article 377). In the latter category can be identified those human rights provided in the International Covenant on Civil and Political Rights (Article 4), and in the American Convention on Human Rights (Article 27), like the guarantee of equality before the law and non-discrimination; the guarantee against being imprisoned for contract obligations; the guarantee against retroactive or *ex post facto* laws; the right to individual personality; religious liberty; the guarantee to be free of slavery or involuntary servitude; the right to physical integrity of the person; the principle of legality; the protection of the family; the rights of children; the guarantee against arbitrary deprivation of nationality and the political rights to suffrage, and the guarantee of public access in government affairs.

1835   International Covenant on Civil and Political Rights of 16 Dec. 1966.

1836   American Convention on Human Rights, San José, Costa Rica, of 22 Nov. 1969.

The consequence of these provisions is that *in the first place*, the Constitution has here eliminated the possibility of 'suspending' individual constitutional rights or guarantees, which on the contrary was authorized by the Constitution of 1961 (Articles 241; 190.6), contributing to innumerable institutional abuses. By contrast, in the 1999 Constitution the President is left with only the power to 'restrict' (Article 236.7) constitutional guarantees. In the second place, the Constitution now expressly requires that an Executive Decree declaring a state of emergency that 'restricts' a constitutional guarantee must 'regulate the exercise of the right whose guarantee is restricted' (Article 339). Thus, it is no longer constitutionally possible for the President to simply 'restrict' a constitutional guarantee, but it is now indispensable that the text of the decree itself expressly sets forth the specific normative regulation and concrete limitations of the exercise of the right.

295. Finally, it must be mentioned that the declaration of a state of exception cannot in any event interrupt the functioning of the branches of governments and other organs of the State (Article 339). Moreover, the declaration of a state of emergency does not alter the liability of the President of the Republic, those of the Executive Vice President, nor of the Ministers, in conformity with the Constitution and laws (Article 232).

VI. *Executive Pardon Powers*

296. The President of the Republic has the power to give pardons (*indultos*) (Article 236.19); although the National Assembly is the one empowered to decree amnesties (Article 187.5).

VII. *The Legislation Veto Powers of the President of the Republic*

297. The President of the Republic must promulgate all statutes sanctioned by the National Assembly within ten days of having received the statute's approval (Article 214); and legislation is considered promulgated and producing effects once published in the *Gaceta Oficial de la República* (Article 215) with the corresponding order that it be put into effect.

The President may, however, within the ten day period, in a decision adopted in Council of Ministers, and on the basis of a reasoned exposition, request that the National Assembly modify some aspect of the legislation or reverse the approval of all or a part of it.

The National Assembly must decide on the President's proposal through a vote by an absolute majority of representatives present, and must then send the statute for promulgation. The President must then promulgate the law within five days of receiving it, and may not propose new changes.

298. However, when the President of the Republic considers that a statute or certain of its articles are unconstitutional, he must request a declaration on the matter from the Constitutional Chamber of the Supreme Tribunal of Justice during the ten day period in which the law must be promulgated or returned to the Assembly(see *supra* paragraph 653). The Constitutional Chamber must then issue its decision within fifteen days of receiving the communication from the President. If the Tribunal denies the unconstitutionality of the law or fails to decide within the allotted time period, the President must promulgate the law within five days (Article 214).

299. If the President of the Republic fails to promulgate statutes according to the abovementioned rules, the President and the two Vice Presidents of the National Assembly must proceed to promulgate the statute as indicated, without prejudice to the responsibility incurred by the President of the Republic for his omission (Article 216).

300. In the case of statutes approving international treaties, agreements or conventions, they may be promulgated at the moment determined at the discretion of the National Executive, according to international custom and the national interest (Article 217).

VIII. Delegate Legislation301. As aforementioned, the President of the Republic can be authorized by the National Assembly, by means of an 'enabling law' approved by the vote of three-fifth of its members, to enact legislation by means of delegate legislation. In these cases, the enabling law must fix the guidelines, purpose and framework of the matters that are delegated to the President's legislative powers, and the term for the issuing of the corresponding Decrees-Laws (Articles 203; 236.8) (see *supra* paragraphs 54, 133, 234, 253).

§2. *The Administrative Functions of Government in the Constitution and the Parliamentary Control*

I.   *The President of the Republic as Head of Public Administration*

302. According to Article 236.11 of the Constitution, the President is the head of the Public Administration, which he administers. In all his acts in these matters the Ministers must always countersign the corresponding executive acts. In particular, the President is empowered in Article 236.20 of the Constitution to determine the numbers, competencies and organization of the Ministries and other organs of Public Administration.

In all these administrative matters the National Assembly also exercises its control over Public Administration (Article 187.3), being competent to discuss and approve the national budget and all public debt statutes (Articles 187.6; 314; 317).

303. In his position of Head of Public Administration, Article 236 of the Constitution assigns the President with the following attributions: to appoint and dismiss the Executive Vice President and the Ministers (Article 236.3); to appoint, after parliamentary approval, the Attorney General of the Republic as well as the ambassadors and head of permanent diplomatic missions (Article 236.15; Article 187.14); and in general, to appoint all other public officials when attributed in the Constitution by statutes (Article 236.16).

304. On matters of public contracts, the same Article 236 of the Constitution assigns the President of the Republic in Council of Ministers, the power to negotiate public national debt (Article 236.12); and to sign national interest contracts according to the Constitution (Article 236.14). For the signing of these contracts, the National Assembly must approve them only when it is expressly required by a statute (Article 150), except in cases of contracts to be signed with foreign States or official foreign entities, or enterprises not domiciled in the country, in which cases the parliamentary approval is necessary (Article 187.9). Also a parliamentary authorization

is required in cases of public contracts selling public immoveable property (Article 187.12).

II. *The Formulation of the National Development Plan*

305. Article 236.18 of the Constitution assigns the President of the Republic in Council of Ministers the attribution to formulate the national Development Plan and direct its execution. The National Assembly must approve the general guidelines of the economic and social development plan, which the National Executive must file before the Assembly within the first trimester of the first year of the constitutional term (Article 236.18).

III. *The Regulatory Powers of the President of the Republic*

306. According to Article 236.10 of the Constitution, the President of the Republic in Council of Ministers has extensive powers to issue regulations to totally or partially develop statutory provisions, 'without altering the spirit, purpose and ratio' of the statute (see *supra* paragraph 143).

§3. *Liabilities*

307. The President of the Republic is responsible for his acts and for the accomplishment of his duties. He is specifically obliged to seek for the guarantee of the Citizens' rights and liberties, as well as for the independence, integrity, sovereignty of the territory and the defence of the Republic (Article 232). The declaration of states of exception does not modify the liability principles regarding the President, or the Executive Vice President and the Ministers (Article 232).

308. However, the Executive Vice President and the Ministers are also individually, civilly, criminally and administratively responsible for their actions (Articles 241, 244). They are also politically responsible before the President of the Republic, as head of Government, and before the National Assembly that can censure them.

309. According to Article 242 of the Constitution, the Executive Vice President and all the Ministers that have concurred in a decision of the Council of Ministers are jointly liable for their decisions. Only those that have formally expressed a dissenting or negative vote are excluded from this liability. The President of the Republic is, of course, also subject to joint liability for the Council's decisions, when he presides over it.

Chapter 3. Public Administration

§1. *The Constitutional Principles Related to Public Administration and Administrative Activities*

310. In the title referred to as the 'Public Power', the 1999 Constitution includes a section related to 'Public Administration',[1837] whose provisions have been develo-

---

1837 See Antonieta Garrido de Cárdenas, 'La Administración Pública Nacional y su organización administrativa en la Constitución de 1999', in *Estudios de Derecho Administrativo: Libro Homenaje a la Universidad Central de Venezuela*, vol. I (Caracas: Imprenta Nacional, 2001), 427–471.

ped by the Organic Law on Public Administration of 2001, reformed in 2008 and 2014.[1838] These provisions are applicable to all the organs and entities of all branches of government exercising administrative functions, and not only of the Executive branch, and to the national, states and municipal public administrations.[1839]

The Constitution sets forth a series of principles related to Public Administration, and within them, those that are common to all of the organs of the branches of government: principle of legality, principle of liability of the State and of its officials, and principle of finality.

311. The *first* principle related to Public Administration and to all State organs is the principle of legality enunciated in Article 137 of the Constitution when establishing that 'The Constitution and the law would define the attributions of the organs exercising Public Power, to which they must subject all the activities they perform.' This provision imposes the necessary submission of Public Administration to the law, being the consequence of it, that all administrative activities contrary to it can be reviewed by the Constitutional Jurisdiction (Article 334) and by the Administrative Jurisdiction (Article 259), whose courts have the power to annul illegal acts (see *infra* paragraph 702).

The principle of legality is also declared in the Constitution as one of the foundations of Public Administration, defined as the 'complete subjection to the law' (Article 141), being one of the basic missions of the organs of the Citizen Power, to assure 'the complete subjection of the administrative activities of the State to the law' (Article 274).

312. The *second* general principle of Public administration is the principle of State liability, incorporated in an express way in the 1999 Constitution (Article 140), setting forth that 'The State is liable for the damages suffered by individuals in their goods and rights, provided that the injury be imputable to the functioning of Public Administration', being possible to comprise in the expression 'functioning of Public Administration', its normal or abnormal functioning.[1840] Although doubts can result

---

1838   See *Gaceta Oficial* N° 6.147 Extra. of 17 Nov. 2014. The 2008 Law was published in *Gaceta Oficial* N° 5.890 Extra. of 31 Jul. 2008. Allan R. Brewer-Carías & Rafael Chavero Gazdik y Jesús María Alvarado Andrade, *Ley Orgánica de la Administración Pública, Decreto Ley N° 4317 de 15-07-2008* (Caracas: Editorial Jurídica Venezolana, 2009); Gustavo Briceño Vivas, 'Principios constitucionales que rigen la Administración en la nueva Ley Orgánica de la Administración Pública', in *Temas de derecho administrativo, Libro Homenaje a Gonzalo Pérez Luciani* vol. I, no. 7 (Caracas: Tribunal Supremo de Justicia, Colección Libros Homenaje, 2002), 351 a 372.

1839   See Allan R. Brewer-Carías, *Principios del Régimen Jurídico de la Organización Administrativa Venezolana* (Caracas, 1994), 11 y 53.

1840   See Jesús Caballero Ortiz, 'Consideraciones fundamentales sobre la responsabilidad administrativa en Francia y en España y su recepción en la Constitución venezolana de 1999', in *Estudios de Derecho Público: Libro Homenaje a Humberto J. La Roche Rincón,* vol. II (Caracas: Tribunal Supremo de Justicia, 2001), 255–271; Luis A. Ortiz-Álvarez, 'La responsabilidad patrimonial del Estado y de los funcionarios públicos en la Constitución de 1999', in *Estudios de Derecho Administrativo: Libro Homenaje a la Universidad Central de Venezuela,* vol. II (Caracas: Imprenta Nacional, 2001), 149–208, and in *Revista de Derecho Constitucional,* N° 1 (septiembre-diciembre) (Caracas: Editorial Sherwood, 1999), 267–312; María E. Soto, 'Régimen constitucional de la responsabilidad extracontractual de la Administración Pública', in *Revista LEX NOVA del Colegio de Abogados del Estado Zulia,* N° 239 (Maracaibo, 2001), 49–72; Ana C. Núñez Machado, 'La nueva Constitución y la res-

from the wording of the article regarding the liability of the State caused by legislative actions that nonetheless are derived from the general principles of public law,[1841] regarding the liability caused by judicial acts, it is clarified by the express provisions of Articles 49.8 and 255 of the Constitution, in which it is established, in addition, the State liability caused because of 'judicial errors or delay'.[1842]

313. The *third* general constitutional principle regarding Public Administration is the principle of liability of public officials in the exercise of public functions established in Article 139 of the Constitution, based on the 'abuse or deviation of powers or the violation of the Constitution or of the law'. In addition, Article 25 of the Constitution, following a long constitutional tradition, expressly establishes the specific civil, criminal and administrative liability of any public officials when issuing or executing acts violating human rights guarantees in the Constitution and the statutes, any excuse due to superior orders not being acceptable.

314. The *fourth* principle of Public Administration incorporated in the 1999 Constitution is the principle of finality (Article 141), emphasizing that 'Public Administration is at the service of Citizens', and as an organ of the State, it must also 'guaranty the inalienable, indivisible and interdependent enjoyment and exercise of human rights to all persons, according to the principle of progressiveness and without discrimination'.

315. And *fifth,* Article 141 of the Constitution also enumerates in an express way the general principles concerning administrative activities, providing that all activities of Public Administration are founded in the principles of 'honesty, participation, celerity, efficacy, efficiency, transparency, accountability and liability in the exercise of public functions, with complete subjection to the law'.

All these principle have been developed in the Organic Law on Public Administration (Article 12), adding to them, the principles of economy, simplicity, objectivity, impartiality, good faith and confidence (Article 12), and in the Administrative Procedure Organic Law.[1843]

ponsabilidad patrimonial del Estado', in *Comentarios a la Constitución de la República Bolivariana de Venezuela* (Caracas: Vadell Hermanos Editores, 2000), 35–64; and 'Reflexiones sobre la interpretación constitucional y el artículo 140 de la Constitución sobre responsabilidad patrimonial del Estado', in *Revista de Derecho Administrativo,* N° 15 (mayo-diciembre) (Caracas: Editorial Sherwood, 2002), 207–222.

1841   See Carlos A. Urdaneta Sandoval, 'El Estado venezolano y el fundamento de su responsabilidad patrimonial extracontractual por el ejercicio de la función legislativa a la luz de la Constitución de 1999', in *Revista de Derecho Constitucional,* N° 5 (julio-diciembre) (Caracas: Editorial Sherwood, 2001), 247–301.

1842   See Abdón Sánchez Noguera, 'La responsabilidad del Estado por el ejercicio de la función jurisdiccional en la Constitución venezolana de 1999', in *Revista Tachirense de Derecho,* N° 12 (enero-diciembre) (San Cristóbal: Universidad Católica del Táchira, 2000), 55–74.

1843   *Gaceta Oficial* N° 2818 Extra. of 7 Jul. 1981. See Allan R. Brewer-Carías et al., *Ley Orgánica de Procedimientos Administrativos,* 13 edición (Caracas: Editorial Jurídica Venezolana, 2006), 175 y ss.

§2. *Constitutional Provisions Related to the Organization of Public Administration: Centralized and Decentralized Public Administration*

316. The Constitution establishes the basic principles for the organization of Public Administration, distinguishing between the Central Public Administration and the Decentralized Public Administration.

Regarding Central Public Administration, it is conformed by the Executive organs of the State in each of the three levels of government, according to the federal form of the State: at the national level, the President of the Republic is the head of National Public Administration; at the states level, the Governors of the states are the head of their states' Public Administrations (Article 160); and at the municipal level, the Mayors are the Heads of the Municipal Public Administrations (Article 174).

Regarding the Central National Public Administration, as aforementioned, it is basically organized around the Ministries, being the President of the Republic the competent organ, following the general principles established in the Organic Law on Public Administration, to determine their number, attributions and organization as well as of the other entities of Central Public Administration (Article 236.20).[1844]

317. Regarding the National Decentralized Public Administration, the Constitution basically refers to the creation of autonomous institutions (public corporations), which is a power reserved to statutes (Article 142), and such institutions are always subjected to State control. Other forms of administrative functional decentralization, like public enterprises or public foundations, are regulated in the Organic Law on Public Administration, except for Petróleos de Venezuela S.A., the State-owned oil company, which is regulated in Article 302 of the Constitution as a nationalized entity.

Regarding independent Regulatory Administrations, they are all regulated by statutes (Banking Superintendence, Insurance Superintendence, Free competition Superintendence, Stock Exchange Commission), except for the Central Bank that is also regulated as an autonomous entity in the Constitution (Article 320).

§3. *Constitutional Principles Regarding Administrative Information*

318. Finally, Article 143 of the Constitution is also innovative regarding Citizens Rights to be informed and to have access to administrative information. In the first place, it provides for the right of Citizens to be promptly and truly informed by Public Administration regarding the situation of the procedures in which they have direct interest, and to know about the definitive resolutions therein adopted, to be notified of administrative acts and to be informed on the courses of the administrative procedure.

1844   See Decree N° 1.612, *Official Gazette* N° 6.173 Extra. Of 18 Feb. 2015. See on this matter:Daniel Leza Betz, 'La organización y funcionamiento de la administración pública nacional y las nuevas competencias normativas del Presidente de la República previstas en la Constitución de 1999. Al traste con la reserva legal formal ordinaria en el Derecho Constitucional venezolano', in *Revista de Derecho Público*, N° 82 (abril-junio) (Caracas: Editorial Jurídica Venezolana, 2000), 18–55.

The constitutional article also establishes that for the individual right everybody has to have access to administrative archives and registries, without prejudice of the acceptable limits imposed in a democratic society related to the national or foreign security, to criminal investigation, to the intimacy of private life, all according to the statutes regulating the matter of secret or confidential documents classification. The same article provides for the principle of prohibition of any previous censorship referring to public officials regarding the information they could give referring to matters under their responsibility.[1845]

The Constitutional Chamber of the Supreme Tribunal in 2010, through constitutional interpretation, restricted the scope of this right to have access to administrative information, denying the request made by a non-governmental organization regarding the salary of the Comptroller General of the Republic, arguing that on the matter the privacy of the economic rights of the latter prevailed.[1846]

§4. *Constitutional Principles Regarding Civil Service*

319. In the 1999 Constitution, also in an innovative way, the general principles of the organization of civil service are established (Article 144 et seq.), which have been developed by the Statute on the Civil Service.[1847] In the first place, Article 145 establishes the general principle that all public officials are at the State service, and that they cannot serve any political group, providing also that their appointment and dismissal cannot be determined by political affiliation or orientation. Unfortunately, this constitutional principle has not been respected, due to the authoritarian government that has developed during the last decade (2000–2011) in the country, characterized by political discrimination in Public Administration regarding those citizens that signed petitions for presidential repeal referendums in 2003–2004 (see *supra* paragraph 131), the absence of pluralism, and the interrelation between the official party and Public Administration) (see *supra* paragraph 177, 179).

320. In the second place, the Constitution distinguishes between two sorts of public officials: those following career position and those in positions of free appointment and dismissals (Article 146), establishing in an express way that all career po-

---

1845   See Orlando Cárdenas Perdomo, 'El derecho de acceso a los archivos y registros administrativos en la Constitución de 1999', in *Estudios de Derecho Administrativo: Libro Homenaje a la Universidad Central de Venezuela*, vol. I (Caracas: Imprenta Nacional, 2001), 177–217; Manuel Rodríguez Costa, 'Derecho de acceso a los archivos y registros de la Administración Pública', in *El Derecho Público a comienzos del siglo XXI. Estudios homenaje al Profesor Allan R. Brewer-Carías*, vol. II (Madrid: Instituto de Derecho Público, UCV, Civitas Ediciones, 2003), 1483–1505; Javier T. Sánchez Rodríguez, 'La libertad de acceso a la información en materia del medio ambiente', in *Revista de derecho del Tribunal Supremo de Justicia*, N° 7 (Caracas, 2002), 459 a 495.

1846   See Allan R. Brewer-Carías, 'De la Casa de Cristal a la Barraca de Hierro: el Juez Constitucional vs. El derecho de acceso a la información administrativa', en *Revista de Derecho Público*, N° 123 (julio-septiembre 2010) (Caracas: Editorial Jurídica Venezolana, 2010), 197–206.5.

1847   *Gaceta Oficial* N° 37.522 of 6 Sep. 2002. See Jesús Caballero Ortíz, 'Bases constitucionales del derecho de la función pública', in *Revista de Derecho Constitucional*, N° 5, julio-diciembre-2001 (Caracas: Editorial Sherwood, 2002), 21 a 46; Antonio de Pedro Fernández, 'Algunas consideraciones sobre la función pública en la Constitución de la República Bolivariana de Venezuela', in *Estudios de Derecho Administrativo: Libro Homenaje a la Universidad Central de Venezuela*, vol. I (Caracas: Imprenta Nacional, 2001), 307–342.

sitions in the Public Administration must always be filed through public competition (*concurso público*), based on honesty, competence and efficiency considerations. Also the promotions must be subjected to scientific methods based on a merit system, and the transfer, suspension and dismissals must be decided according to their performance. Unfortunately, due to the strict political control of all the bureaucracy, neither of these constitutional provisions factually are in force.

321. In the third place, the Constitution also establishes the general principle of discipline in public spending regarding the provisions of public official positions, in the sense that being remunerated, they can only be provided when there are enough budget provisions for funds (Article 147). The scale of remunerations for public officials must be established by statute, and the National Assembly has been empowered to establish limits to municipal, states and national public officers (Article 229). The regime for pensions and retirements are also attributed in the Constitution to be established by the National Assembly.[1848]

322. In addition, other constitutional provisions are established regarding public officers. For instance, the principle of incompatibility to occupy more than one remunerated position (Article 148), except in cases of academic, transitory, assistant or teaching positions. In any case of acceptance of a new position, it implies the renunciation of the first, except in cases of deputies, up to the definitive replacement of the principal. In addition, the Constitution provides that a public officer cannot benefit from more than one pension (Article 148).

The Constitution also establishes the prohibition for public officers to sign contracts with the municipalities, the states, the Republic and with any other public law or State-owned entity (Article 145).

§5. *Constitutional Principles Regarding Public Contracts*

I.   *The Public Interest Contracts*

323. The 1999 Constitution, following a previous constitutional tradition, identifies as public interest contracts those signed by all the State entities (national, states or municipalities), which can then be national public interest contracts, states' public interest contracts or municipal public interest contracts (Article 150). The expression 'administrative contracts' in order to identify public contracts, is not used in the Constitution or in the legal system.[1849]

1848   Law on the Remuneration, Pensions and Retrat of High Public Officials of Public Power, *Gaceta Oficial* N° 39.592 of 12 Jan. 2011.

1849   The legal regime on public contracts was established in the the Public Contracting Law of 2010 (*Official Gazette*, N° 39.503 of 6 Sep. 2010), reformed in 2014 (*Official Gazette*, N° 6.154 Extra. of 19 Nov. 2014). See Allan R. Brewer-Carías et al., *Ley de Contrataciones Públicas* (Caracas: Editorial Jurídica venezolana, 2011). See on the matter of 'administrative contracts' Jesús Caballero Ortiz, 'Los contratos administrativos, los contratos de interés público y los contratos de interés nacional en la Constitución de 1999', in *Estudios de Derecho Administrativo: Libro Homenaje a la Universidad Central de Venezuela*, vol. I (Caracas: Imprenta Nacional, 2001), 139–154, and '¡Deben subsistir los contratos administrativos en una futura legislación', in *El Derecho Público a comienzos del siglo XXI. Estudios homenaje al Profesor Allan R. Brewer-Carías*, vol. II (Madrid: Instituto de Derecho

In this matter, the 1999 Constitution has completed the traditional constitutiona-lization of public contracts regime,[1850] also regulating some inter-administrative public contracts, that is, those signed between public entities. This is the case of the intergovernmental contracts entered by the Republic and the states or between the states, or entered by the states and the municipalities, particularly as consequence of the process of transfer of competencies derived from the decentralization process (Article 170).[1851] The 1999 Constitution provides, in this regard, for contracts to be entered between the states and the municipalities, for the transfer of services and competencies to them (Article 165); and for contracts that can be signed by the mu-nicipalities (*mancomunidades*) in order to develop activities together (Article 170). The Constitution also has provisions regarding contracts signed between the states and the municipalities with the organized community for the transfer of services to them (Article 184).

324. The Constitution also establishes some prohibitions regarding public con-tracts, for instance, on territorial matters, due to the constitutional principle that 'the national territory could never be ceded, trespassed, leased or in any way sold, even temporally or partially to Foreign States or international law entities' (Article 13). The only constitutional exception on this regard refers to the land needed for foreign embassies (Article 13).

These prohibitions also refer to all the cases of public domain declared in the Constitution, regarding which the State cannot sign any contracts that could signify the loss of such character. It occurs with the subsoil, mines and hydrocarbons (Arti-cle 12); with the maritime coast (Article 12); with all waters (Article 304); with war weapons (Article 324); and with the shares of Petróleos de Venezuela S.A., the Sta-te-owned oil company (Article 303). Nonetheless, regarding natural resources and their exploitation, the Constitution establishes the possibility for the State to subscri-be temporal concession contracts with private parties (Article 113), with the express prohibition to sign for mines concessions for indefinite term (Article 156.16).

Regarding private law immoveable property of public entities, some of those lands have also a constitutional prohibition to be sold, as is the case of national land located on islands (Article 13) and municipal lands in urban areas that can only be sold for urban development (Article 181).

The same restriction regarding public contracts exists in all the cases in which the State has reserved by statute some services, exploitations or industries for natio-nal interest motives (Article 302), as is the case of the oil industry, the iron mining

Público, UCV, Civitas Ediciones, 2003), 1765–1777; Allan R. Brewer-Carías, *Contratos Administra-tivos* (Caracas: Editorial Jurídica Venezolana, 1992), 28 et seq.

1850   See Allan R. Brewer-Carías, 'Algunos aspectos del proceso de constitucionalización del Derecho administrativo en Venezuela', in *V Jornadas internacionales de Derecho Administrativo Allan Ran-dolph Brewer Carías, Los requisitos y vicios de los actos administrativos* (Caracas: FUNEDA 2000), 21 a 37.

1851   For instance as was initially established in the Organic Law on Decentralization, Delimitation and Transfer of attributions among public entities. *Gaceta Oficial* N° 37.753 of 14 Aug. 2003.

industry, and the natural gas industry all nationalized since 1975.[1852] This implies, for instance, regarding the oil industry, that since the sanctioning of the 2001 Organic Law on Hydrocarbons,[1853] the only way in which the private companies can participate in the exploitation of the oil industry is through their participation in mixed public enterprises, with State-owned majority of shares(see *infra* paragraph 624).

II. *Obligatory Constitutional Clauses in Public Interest Contracts*

325. Following the trends of the 1961 Constitution, the 1999 Constitution has also established in its norms, a series of contractual clauses that must always be incorporated in all public contracts, particularly, the jurisdiction immunity clause, the 'Calvo' clause; and the environmental protection clause.

A. *The Jurisdiction Immunity Clause*

326. Article 151 of the Constitution establishes that in all public interest contracts, if it were not unsuitable according to their nature, a clause must be considered as incorporated even if not expressly provided, according to which all doubts and controversies that could arise from such contracts and that could not be amicably resolved by the contracting parties, must be decided by the competent courts of the Republic according to its laws.

It is thus, an obligatory constitutional clause that follows the relative jurisdiction immunity system,[1854] according to which, for example, in contracts with commercial purposes, like (*ius gestionis*), the Venezuelan State can accept to submit contractual controversies to be resolved by arbitration and even subjected to foreign law.[1855]

1852   Organic Law reserving the State the Industry and Commerce of Hydrocarbon, *Gaceta Oficial* N° 35.754 of 17 Jul. 1975. See *Régimen jurídico de las Nacionalizaciones en Venezuela, Homenaje del Instituto de Derecho Público al Profesor Antonio Moles Caubet*, Archivo de Derecho Público y Ciencias de la Administración, vol. VIII (1972–1979) (Caracas: Instituto de Derecho Público, Universidad Central de Venezuela, 1981).

1853   The Law was reformed in 2006. *Gaceta Oficial* N° 38.493 of 4 Aug. 2006.

1854   See Allan R. Brewer-Carías, *Debate Constituyente (Aporte a la Asamblea Nacional Constituyente)*, vol. II (Caracas: Fundación de Derecho Público, 1999), 175 a 177; 'Comentarios sobre la doctrina del acto de gobierno, del acto político, del acto de Estado y de las cuestiones políticas como motivo de inmunidad jurisdiccional de los Estados en sus Tribunales nacionales', in *Revista de Derecho Público*, N° 26 (Caracas: Editorial Jurídica Venezolana, abril-junio 1986), 65–68.

1855   See Tatiana Bogdanowsky de Maekelt, 'Inmunidad de Jurisdicción de los Estados', in *Libro Homenaje a José Melich Orsini*, vol. 1 (Caracas, 1982), 213 et seq.; Allan R. Brewer-Carías, *Contratos Administrativos*, Colección Estudios Jurídicos N° 44 (Caracas: Editorial Jurídica Venezolana, 1992), 262–265; Allan R. Brewer-Carías, 'Principios especiales y estipulaciones obligatorias en la contratación administrativa', in *El Derecho Administrativo en Latinoamérica*, vol. II (Bogotá: Ediciones Rosaristas, Colegio Mayor Nuestra Señora del Rosario, 1986), 345–378; Allan R. Brewer-Carías, 'Algunos comentarios a la Ley de Promoción y Protección de Inversiones: contratos públicos y jurisdicción' in *Arbitraje comercial interno e internacional. Reflexiones teóricas y experiencias prácticas* (Caracas: Academia de Ciencias Políticas y Sociales, 2005), 279–288; 'El arbitraje y los contratos de interés nacional' in *Seminario sobre la Ley de Arbitraje Comercial*, N° 13 (Caracas: Biblioteca de la Academia de Ciencias Políticas y Sociales, Serie Eventos, 1999), 169–204.

B.   The 'Calvo' Clause

327. The second obligatory clause that is considered incorporated in all public interest contracts according to the Constitution is the so-called Calvo Clause which implies that their execution in any case can originate foreign claims by the States on behalf of its citizens or nationals (Article 151).[1856] The origin of this clause is to be found in the 1893 Constitution as a consequence of the international diplomatic claims the European countries initiated by force against Venezuela as a consequence of contracts signed by the country with foreign citizens. Its conception was the work of Carlos Calvo in his book *Tratado de Derecho Internacional*, initially edited in 1868, after studying the Franco–British intervention in Rio de la Plata and the French intervention in Mexico.[1857] This Calvo clause also helps the adoption of the so-called *Drago Doctrine* conceived in 1902 by the then Argentinean Minister of Foreign Relations, Luis María Drago, who regarding the threats of using force made by Germany, Great Britain and Italy against Venezuela, formulated its thesis condemning the compulsory collection of public debts by the States.[1858]

C.   The Environmental Protection Clause

328. Article 129 of the Constitution also imposes the obligation for Public Administration to include an environment protection clause in any national public contract whose execution could affect natural resources,[1859] providing for the obligation of the private party to the contract to preserve the ecological equilibrium, to allow the access and transfer of environmental protection technology, and to restore the environment to its natural state if altered.

III.   The Parliamentary Approval of Public Interest Contracts

329. The constitutional system of Venezuela, has traditionally provided for the intervention of the Legislature regarding the approval of public interest contracts. In the 1961 Constitution this legislative approval was established in a general way as a condition for their validity (Article 126), having raised many discussions and interpretations. This provision was radically changed in Article 150 of the 1999 Constitution, by providing that the legislative approval of a national public interest contract is only required when a specific statute so establishes (see *infra* paragraph 329).

Consequently, only when a statute expressly determines that a national public contract must be submitted to the approval of the National Assembly, such condition is considered as a efficacy condition regarding the contract (Article 182.9). Nonet-

---

1856   See Allan R. Brewer-Carías', Algunos aspectos de la inmunidad jurisdiccional de los Estados y la cuestión de los actos de Estado (*act of state*) en la jurisprudencia norteamericana' in *Revista de Derecho Público*, N° 24 (Caracas: Editorial Jurídica Venezolana, octubre-diciembre 1985), 29–42.

1857   See Carlos Calvo, *Tratado de Derecho Internacional*, vol. I, para. 205, *supra*, by L.A. Podestá Costa, *Derecho Internacional Público*, vol. I (Buenos Aires, 1955), 445–446.

1858   See Victorino Jiménez y Núñez, *La Doctrina Drago y la Política Internacional* (Madrid, 1927).

1859   See Alberto Blanco-Uribe Quintero, 'La tutela ambiental como derecho-deber del Constituyente. Base constitucional y principios rectores del derecho ambiental', in *Revista de Derecho Constitucional*, N° 6 (enero-diciembre) (Caracas: Editorial Sherwood, 2002), 31–64.

heless, the Constitution, in the same Articles 150 and 182.9, directly imposes the need for legislative approval regarding public interest contracts when signed with foreign States, foreign official entities or societies not domiciled in Venezuela, as well as the transfer of public interest contracts to such entities.

IV. *Principles Related to the State's Contractual Liabilities*

330. In parallel to the provision of the general regime of State liability (Article 140) (see *supra* paragraph 307), the 1999 Constitution also establishes the general basis and conditions for the contractual liability of the State, providing that it will only recognize as contracted obligations those entered by legitimate organs of the State; a constitutional provision that had its origin in the nineteenth century when the State was sued because of damages caused in civil wars by rebels who claimed to be acting as the legitimate government.

In any case, the legitimacy for contracting obligations is related to the competency of the respective public officer to sign the contract, for which purpose the Constitution assigns, for instance, the President of the Republic power to enter into national public contracts (Article 236.14) and to negotiate national public debt (Article 236.12); powers that of course are not exclusive, because such attributions can and are assigned to the corresponding Ministries as its direct organs (Article 242).

However, the Constitution imposes some budget restrictions in the execution of contracts by providing that no spending can be made if not established in the budget's annual statute (Article 314).

§6. *Prerogatives of the Administration*

331. The Constitution does not provide for prerogative or privilege of the Republic regarding other legal persons, having then the same rights and obligation as them in their legal relations, which as aforementioned is particularly important on matters of State responsibility and liability (see *supra* paragraph 307).

Nonetheless, on procedural matters regarding the position of public entities in judicial processes, the Organic Law of the Attorney General,[1860] provide specific procedural prerogatives for public entities, related to the time set for them to be considered notified or summoned, to the effects of their failure to appear in court to answer a claim, to the exception established for public entities not to impose any bail of guarantee for procedural purposes, or to the privilege for public property not to be the object of procedural preventive or executive seizure measures.

Chapter 4. *The Military and the National Security System*

332. The 1999 Constitution made substantial departures from the provisions of the 1961 Constitution regarding the National Security and Defence system and the Military. The latter Constitution contained only three provisions on the subject: Article 133, establishing restrictions regarding the possession of arms; Article 131 prohibiting the simultaneous exercise of civilian and military authority by any public

---

1860   *Gaceta Oficial* N° 5.892 Extra. of 31 Jul. 2008.

official other than the President of the Republic as Commander in Chief of the Armed Forces; and, Article 132, referring to the general regulation of the Armed Forces.

333. In the 1999 Constitution, on the contrary, a marked militarist shape was given to the State, with board provisions regarding not only the Military but the security and defence system, without precedent in Venezuelan constitutionalism.

Article 322 of the Constitution of 1999 begins by stating that the security of the nation falls within the essential competence and responsibility of the State, founded upon the State's 'integral development'; the defence of the State being the responsibility of Venezuelans, and of all natural and legal persons, whether of public or private law, founded within the geographic territory of the State.

In addition, Article 326 sets forth the general principles of National Security declaring that its preservation in 'economic, social, political, cultural, geographic, environmental and military areas', mutually corresponds (co-responsibility) *to* the State and to Civil Society, in order to fulfil the principles of 'independence, democracy, equality, peace, liberty, justice, solidarity, promotion and conservation of the environment, the affirmation of human rights, and, the progressive satisfaction of the individual and collective needs of Venezuelans on the basis of sustainable and productive development fully covering the national community'. All of these principles are also those enumerated in the opening Articles 1, 2, and 3 of the Constitution of 1999. For the purposes of implementing these principles of national security in the country's territorial border regions, Article 327 provides for the establishment of a special regime.

334. Also for such purposes, the Constitution created a new council, the 'National Council of Defense' (Article 323), as the nation's highest authority for defence planning, advice and consultation to the State (Public Powers) on all matters related to the defence and security of the Nation's sovereignty, territorial integrity and strategic thinking. This Council is presided over by the President of the Republic, and integrated by the Executive Vice President, the President of the National Assembly, the President of Supreme Tribunal of Justice, the President of the Moral Republican Council (Citizen Branch of government, Article 237), the Ministers of the defence sectors: interior security, foreign relations and planning, and others whose participation is considered pertinent.

335. According to the Constitution, the traditional National Armed Forces (which is comprised of the Army, the Navy, the Air Force and the National Guard) have become integrated into a single institution, named the 'National Armed Force', which nonetheless, according to Article 328, is comprised of the Army, the Navy, the Air Force and the National Guard, each working within its area of competence to fulfil its mission, and with its own system of social security, as established by its respective organic legislation.

It must be mentioned that the 2007 constitutional reform project that was rejected by popular referendum, the proposal of the President of the Republic was to change the name of the National Armed Force to the 'Bolivarian Armed Force', to create a 'Bolivarian Military Doctrine'; to create the 'Bolivarian Popular Militia', as a new component of the Armed Force, and to eliminate the character of the Armed Force as an 'essential professional institution, without political militancy', converting it into 'an essentially patriotic, popular and anti-imperialist corp'. As mentioned, the people, through referendum rejected all such Constitutional Reforms, but nonetheless, the President of the Republic approved them all, six months after the popular rejection, in July 2008, through delegate legislation.[1861]

336. According to Article 329, the Army, Navy, Air Force and National Guard each has essential responsibilities for planning, execution and control of military operations necessary to ensure the defence of the Nation. The National Guard, however, only has a cooperative role in these functions and basic responsibility to carry out operations necessary for the maintenance of internal order in the country. The Constitution also establishes that the National Armed Force can carry out police administrative activities and criminal investigation as authorized by law.

337. Article 328 defines the character of the Armed Forces as an essentially professional institution, without a militant political function, organized by the State to guarantee the independence and sovereignty of the Nation, and to ensure the integrity of the Nation's geographic space by means of military defence and cooperation in the maintenance of internal order, as well as active participation in national development. According to the wording of this article, in order to fulfil these functions, the Armed Force is at the exclusive service of the Nation and in no case may be at the service of any particular person or political partiality. The foundations of the Armed Forces are discipline, obedience and subordination.

Nonetheless, the 1999 Constitution failed to provide for the 'apolitical and nondeliberative' character of the Armed Force that was established in Article 132 of the Constitution of 1961; and it has no provision establishing the essential obligation of the Armed Force to ensure 'the stability of the democratic institutions' and to 'respect the Constitution and laws, the adherence which is above any other obligation', as was declared in Article 132 of the 1961 Constitution. What the 1999 Constitution was innovative on these matters was in giving the military the right to vote (Article 325).

In addition, the Constitution established the general regime applicable to military promotions, providing that they are to be based on merit, seniority and the availability of vacancies, and are the exclusively competence of the National Armed Forces (Article 331). Consequently, the traditional intervention of the Legislature to approve the promotions of high-ranking military officials (Article 150.5, 1961 Constitution) was eliminated.

338. All these constitutional provisions conform a normative framework with clear marks of a militarist structure, which when combined with the centralization tendency of State Power and the concentration of State Power in the President of the Republic by his control over the National Assembly, the result is a system that unfortunately has led to authoritarianism. In particular, in the 1999 Constitution's pro-

---

1861   See Organic Law on the Bolivarian Armed Force, *Gaceta Oficial* N° 5.891 Extra. of 31 Jul. 2008. See Jesús María Alvarado Andrade, 'La nueva Fuerza Armada Bolivariana (comentarios a raíz del Decreto N° 6.239, con rango, valor y fuerza de Ley Orgánica de la Fuerza Armada Nacional Bolivariana)', en *Revista de Derecho Público*, N° 115 *(Estudios sobre los Decretos Leyes 2008)* (Caracas: Editorial Jurídica Venezolana, 2008), 205 ss.; Alfredo Arismendi, 'Fuerza Armada Nacional: Antecedentes, evolución y régimen actual', en *Revista de Derecho Público*, N° 115 *(Estudios sobre los Decretos Leyes 2008)* (Caracas: Editorial Jurídica Venezolana, 2008), 187–206.

visions on military matters, the idea of the subjection or subordination of military authority to civilian authority has disappeared; and instead what has been consecrated is a greater autonomy of the National Armed Force, whose four branches (and since 2008, five branches) have been unified into one institution with the possibility of intervention in civilian functions. This militaristic tendency is evidenced by the following constitutional rules, as already indicated: *first,* the elimination of the traditional prohibition that military and civilian authority be exercised simultaneously, as was established by the Article 131 of the 1961 Constitution; *second*, the elimination of control by the National Assembly of military promotions in the top brass, as provided in Article 331 of the 1961 Constitution and throughout the country's traditional constitutionalism; *third,* the elimination of the constitutionally 'non-deliberative and apolitical' character of the military institution, as established in Article 132 of the 1961 Constitution, which has opened the way for the Armed Force, as a military institution, to deliberate politically, intervene, and give its opinion on matters under resolution within the civil organs of the State; *fourth,* the elimination of the obligation of the Armed Force to ensure the stability of democratic institutions required by Article 132 of the 1961 Constitution; *fifth,* the elimination of the obligation of the Armed Force to respect the Constitution and laws 'the adherence to which will always be above any other obligation' as was set forth in Article 132 of the 1961 Constitution; *sixth,* the express right of suffrage granted to members of the military in Article 330 of the 1999 Constitution, which in many cases has been politically incompatible with the principle of obedience; *seventh,* the submission of authority over the use of all weapons, for war or otherwise, to the Armed Force, while removing this authority from the civil Administration of the State (Article 324); *eighth,* the general attribution of police administrative functions to the Armed Force (Article 329); *ninth,* the establishment of procedural privilege for generals and admirals in the sense that in order for them to be tried, the Supreme Tribunal of Justice must declare in advance of trial whether or not the proceeding has merit (Article 266.3); and *tenth*, the adoption in the Constitution of the concept of the 'doctrine of national security', as a global, totalistic and omni-comprehensive doctrine in the sense that everything that happens in the State and in the Nation concerns the security of the State, including economic and social development (Article 326); with the duty for the Armed Force to have an 'active participation in national development' (Article 328). All these provisions, sets forth a picture of militarism, unique in Venezuelan constitutional history, not even found in former military regimes.

PART VI. THE LEGISLATURE

Chapter 1. The National Assembly

§1. The Unicameral Parliamentary System

339. In 1999, and contrary to the previous 200 years parliamentary bicameral tradition, the new Constitution eliminated the Senate and established a National Assembly following the unicameral parliamentary trend, exercising the National

Legislative Power.[1862] The consequence being that although the State is configured as a federation, no federal chamber exists representing the states in which they could really be equals, in the sense of having equal vote. Consequently, the clause contained in Article 159 of the Constitution pointing out that states of the federation are *equal* political entities cannot effectively materialize. However, and in spite of this wording, from the point of view of their territory, population and economic and social development, the states are very different.

340. According to Article 186 of the Constitution, the National Assembly is composed of representatives (*diputados*) elected within each state and the Capital District (the former Federal District) by universal, direct and secret vote according to a mixed system combining personalized nomination and proportional representation scrutiny. The number of representatives is based on national population, calculating one representative per 1.1% of the total population of the country. Each representative must have a substitute member, also elected in the same process, who is called to act in cases of temporal or absolute absence of the principal (Article 186).

Each of the twenty-three states and the Capital District, in addition, has the right to elect three additional representatives to the National Assembly. The indigenous people's communities in the Republic have the right to elect three representatives according to the prescriptions of the electoral law, observing their traditions and customs (Article 125) (see *infra* paragraph 556). In all cases, each representative must have an alternate representative also elected through the same process.

The constitutional term of office for representatives is five years, according to Article 193, with the possibility of consecutive re election for a maximum of two additional terms. Nonetheless, this limit was eliminated through a constitutional amendment approved by referendum on February 2009, providing for the possibility of the continuous election of the representatives (see *infra* paragraphs 234, 672). However, the President of the Republic has, in Council of Ministers, the power to dissolve the Assembly in case of its approval of three motions of censure against the Executive Vice President (Articles 236.21; 240).

§2. *The Representatives*

I.   *Eligibility Conditions*

341. Article 188 of the Constitution establishes the following conditions of eligibility for the representatives to the National Assembly: to be a Venezuelan citizen, and in case of naturalized citizens, with fifteen years of residence in the Venezuelan territory; to be at least 21 years of age; and to have resided for at least four consecutive years in the territory of the state where the election will take place.

1862   See Allan R. Brewer-Carías, *Debate Constituyente (Aportes a la Asamblea Nacional Constituyente)*, vol. III (18 octubre-30 noviembre 1999) (Caracas: Fundación de Derecho Público-Editorial Jurídica Venezolana, 1999), 196–198; María M. Matheus Inciarte y María Elena Romero Ríos, 'Estado Federal y unicameralidad en el nuevo orden constitucional de la República Bolivariana de Venezuela', in *Estudios de Derecho Público: Libro Homenaje a Humberto J. La Roche Rincón*, vol. I (Caracas: Tribunal Supremo de Justicia, 2001), 637–676.

In addition, Article 189 establishes the cases of ineligibility for representatives, excluding the President of the Republic, the Executive Vice President, the Ministries, the Secretary of the President Office, the Presidents of Public Corporations and public enterprises, the Governors and Secretaries of government of the states from the possibility of running for such position up to three months after their separation from office. Also, all the national, states or municipal public officers, as well as those serving in public corporations of public enterprises, cannot be elected representatives if the election take place in their respective jurisdictions, except in cases of provisional, health, teaching or academic positions. Other situations of ineligibility can also be established by statutes.

II. *Tenure, Incompatibilities, Accountability and Revocation of Mandate*

342. The tenure of the representatives, as provided in Article 197 of the Constitution, is a full time job that must be accomplished for benefit of the people. That is why the same article imposes upon them the duty to maintain permanent relations with their electors, paying attention to their opinions and informing them of their accomplishment and of the work of the Assembly (Article 197).

In addition, representatives must annually inform their electors about their activities[1863] and can be subjected to repeal referendum (Article 72). In such cases, the representative whose mandate is repealed cannot be re-elected as representative for the next term (Article 198).Except in case of repeal referendum expressing the will of the people, the democratic principle means that in no other way, except for criminal reasons, the representatives can be removed. Nonetheless, in 2014, the Supreme Tribunal, in an unconstitutional way, decided to revoke the mandate of one representative, based on exclusively political reasons. [1864]

343. However, the Constitution forbids the representatives the possibility of being owners, administrators or directors of enterprises that have entered in contracts with public entities, and cannot develop private activities with lucrative interest. On matters that are discussed before the Assembly, in which economic interest conflicts could exist, the involved representative must abstain from participating (Article 190).

344. Regarding public sector activities, the representatives cannot accept or exercise public offices without losing their tenure, except in cases of teaching, academic, provisional or health activities, provided that they do not imply a full time job (Article 191). Consequently, with the 1999 Constitution, the possibility for the representatives to be appointed Ministers in the executive without losing

---

1863   See María E. León Álvarez, 'La rendición de cuentas en la gestión de los asuntos públicos en el nuevo orden constitucional venezolano', in *Revista de Derecho Público,* N° 84 (octubre-diciembre) (Caracas: Editorial Jurídica Venezolana, 2000), 70–81.

1864   See Decision N° 207 de 31 de marzo de 2014, available at en http://www.tsj.gov.ve/decisiones/scon/marzo/162546-207-31314-2014-14-0286.HTML Also published in *Official Gazette* N° 40385 of April 2, 2014. See the comments in Allan R. Brewer-Carías, "La revocación del mandato popular de una diputada a la Asamblea Nacional por la Sala Constitucional del Tribunal Supremo de oficio, sin juicio ni proceso alguno (El caso de la Diputada María Corina Machado)," *Revista de Derecho Público,* 137 (Caracas, Editorial Jurídica Venezolana, 2014), 165- 189

their legislative tenure, as established by the 1961 Constitution (Article 141) was expressly eliminated.

III. *Liability and Immunity*

345. The members of the National Assembly represent the people as a whole and also represent the states where they were elected. In their legislative activities they are not bound to the instructions of any other than their own conscience, their vote being a personal one (Article 201). This provision is another of the series established in the Constitution, based on the anti-partisan spirit inspiring it, for the purpose of supposedly protecting the votes in the Assembly against the formation of partisan and other parliamentary factions (see *supra* paragraph 33). Nonetheless, the fact is that never before has the country witnessed an official party controlling its representatives in the Legislature in a stricter way than the way experienced during the years of enforcement of the 1999 Constitution (1999–2011).

346. Regarding responsibility, representatives to the National Assembly are not liable for their votes and opinions given in the exercise of their functions. They are only responsible before their electors and before the National Assembly according to the Constitution and the Assembly's internal regulations (Article 199).

347. On criminal matters, during their tenure, representatives have immunity from their inauguration up to the end of their tenure or their resignation (Article 200); and all public officers that violate parliamentary immunity, are criminally liable and must be punished accordingly. Only in cases of flagrant crime committed by a representative can the corresponding authority put him in custody in his residence and must immediately inform the facts to the Supreme Tribunal of Justice, which is the competent court to order, with the authorization of the National Assembly, their detention and to continue their judicial prosecution.

§3. *Organization and Commissions*

348. The National Assembly has a Board of Directors integrated by its President and two Vice Presidents elected within the representatives, and a Secretary and a Deputy Secretary designated from outside the members of the Assembly; all appointed for a one year term (Article 194). The President and the two Vice Presidents of the Assembly must be Venezuelan by birth and without other nationality (Article 41).

348. The Assembly has ordinary and special Permanent Commissions. The latter can be created in the various activities sectors, by the favourable vote of two-third of the representatives, composed by no more that fifteen representatives each. The Assembly can also create temporal commissions for the investigation or study of determined matters (Article 193).

§4. *Sessions of the National Assembly and Its Delegate Commission*

350. The Assembly has two periods of ordinary sessions, from January to August and from September to December. The first session must begin without any previous notification on 5 January of each year or the following immediate and possible day enduring up to 15 August; and the second, on 15 September or the following immediate and possible day enduring up to 15 December (Article 219). The National As-

sembly can also have extraordinary sessions in order to consider the matters expressed in the convening and the related ones. It can also consider those matters declared urgent by its members (Article 220).

351. The conditions for the instalment of the Assembly and for its sessions, as well as for the functioning of its Commissions, must be established in the internal parliamentary regulation, except the quorum conditions that are provided in the Constitution establishing that in all cases it cannot be less than the absolute majority of the representatives composing the Assembly (Article 221).

352. During the periods of when the National Assembly is not in session (15 December–5 January, and 15 August–15 September), a Delegate Commission must function, integrated by the President, the Vice Presidents and the Presidents of the Permanent Commissions (Article 195). This Commission, which exists in almost all Latin American countries, has the following attributions: to convene the National Assembly for extraordinary sessions, when needed; to authorize the trips of the President abroad; to authorize the National Executive to decree additional credits to the budget; to designate temporal Commissions of the Assembly; to exercise the investigative functions of the Assembly; and to authorize the National Executive, by a vote of two-thirds of the representatives, to create, modify and suspend public services in cases of confirmed urgency (Article 196).

§5. *The Attributions of the National Assembly*

353. The National Assembly, as the Legislature, has the power to legislate on matters of national character (Article 187.1) (see *supra* paragraph 353) and, in particular, to discuss and approve the Budget Law and all taxation and public debt laws (Articles 187,6; 314, 317, 312); and to sanctioned laws for the approval of international treaties and conventions (Article 187.19; 154).

In addition to these legislative functions, according to Article 187, the Assembly has another series of powers on constitutional, political and administrative matters that gives it, its pre-eminent character in the political system of separation of powers (see *supra* paragraph 221).

354. On constitutional matters, the Assembly can propose amendments and reforms to the Constitution, and must discuss and approve all constitutional reforms drafts (Articles 341, 343, 344) (see *supra* 116). Also on constitutional matters, the National Assembly have the constitutional character of being an electoral body in order to elect, in an indirect way in representation of the people, by a qualified majority of two third of its members, the High Officials Head of the Citizen's, Electoral and Judicial Branches of Government (articles 264, 279, 296) (see *supra* 151, 224, 286 ; *infra* 393 ff.,420, 423, 433)355. On political matters, the Assembly is empowered to decree amnesties (Article 187.5); to approve censure vote to the Executive Vice President and to the Ministers (Article 187.10); to authorize the use of Venezuelan military missions abroad and foreign military missions in the country (Article 187.11); to watch over the interests and autonomy of the states of the federation (Article 187.16); to authorize the trips abroad of the President of the Republic for more than five days (Article 235); to decide cases of absolute and temporal absence of the President (Articles 233, 234) (see *supra* paragraph 271); to authorize the criminal processing of the President of the Republic (Article 266.2) and to debate on the Decrees of States of Exception (Articles 338, 339) (see *supra* paragraph 308).

Also on political matters, the Assembly is empowered to elect and remove the head of the Judicial, Citizen and Electoral Branches of Government (see *infra* paragraph 422), that is, to elect and remove from office the Magistrates of the Supreme Tribunal of Justice (Article 265), the Comptroller General of the Republic, the Prosecutor General of the Republic, the Peoples' Defender (Article 279), and the members of the National Electoral Council (Article 296). These are powers that give preeminence to the Legislature, which, as aforementioned, basically contradict the principle of the independence of the Judicial, Citizen and Electoral powers, respectively (see *supra* paragraph 221).

356. On administrative matters, the Assembly must authorize the appointment of the Attorney General of the Republic (see *supra* paragraph 279) and the Head of diplomatic missions (Article 187.14); and most importantly, exercise control powers regarding the Government and the National Public Administration (Article 187.3), being competent to authorize additional credits to the budget (Article 187.7), to approve the general guidelines of the Economic and Social Development Plan formulated by the President of the Republic within the first year of each constitutional term (Articles 187.8; 236.18); to authorize the National Executive to sign national public interest contracts when required by statute, and in any case, public interest contracts when signed with foreign State or foreign public entities with enterprises non-domiciled in Venezuela (187,9; 150); and authorize the national executive to sell immovable State properties (Article 187.12).

357. On internal parliamentary matters, the National Assembly has its own powers to organize and promote citizens participation in legislative matters (Article 187.4); to approve its own internal regulations, to organize its own internal security services, to establish and execute its own budget and to regulate its own civil service[1865] (Article 187.19, .21, .22). The Assembly is also empowered to qualify its own members and to receive their resignations (Article 187.20).

Chapter 2. Legislative Procedure

358. The initiative to introduce draft legislation (Codes, Organic Laws, ordinary laws) (see *supra* paragraphs 128 et seq.) before the National Assembly was expanded in Article 204 of the 1999 Constitution, conferring that power to: the National Executive, the Commissions of the National Assembly; three or more members of the National Assembly; the Supreme Tribunal of Justice in the case of legislation relating to the Judiciary and to procedural matters; the Citizen Power with respect to legislation relating to the Comptroller General, the Prosecutor General or the Peoples Defender; to the Electoral Power in electoral matters; the State Legislative Councils in matters relating to the states; and to the citizens by means of a petition supported by no less than 0.1% of the registered voters. In this latter case, the debate in the Assembly must begin no later than in the legislative session following the session in which the proposed legislation was introduced. If debate does not begin within this time, the popular proposed legislation must be submitted to an approbatory referendum (Article 205) (see *supra* paragraph 159).

1865   Estatute of National Assembly Public emporyees, *Gaceta Oficial* N° 37.598 of 26 Dec. 2002.

359. All draft legislation in order to acquire the status of a statute must be submitted to two discussions (Article 205), on different days, according to the rules established in the Assembly's internal regulation. Once the draft is approved, the President of the Assembly must declare the statute sanctioned (Article 207).

The first discussion, according to Article 208, must refer to the motives of the proposed legislation and its purpose, scope and viability, in order to determine its pertinence. In addition, a global discussion on its articles must take place. Once approved in first discussion, the draft must be sent directly to the Commission related with its content, in order for it to study the draft and to prepare a report that must be completed within a period of thirty days.

The second discussion must be held once the Commission's Report is received by the Assembly. In this case, discussion then must be made article by article. If the draft is approved without modification, the statute will be sanctioned. If modifications are introduced, the draft must be returned to the corresponding Commission, who must prepare a new report. This report must be read in plenary session of the Assembly, which must decide by majority of votes. If approved, the President of the Assembly must declare the statute sanctioned.

360. In order to allow peoples' participation, the 1999 Constitution establishes the obligation for the National Assembly or its Commissions during the debate of the legislative draft, to consult with other entities of government, with the citizens, and with organizations of society in order to hear their point of view with respect to such legislation (Article 211). Also, according to Article 206, the states must be consulted by the National Assembly, through their Legislative Councils, when legislation regarding them is being considered in the Assembly. Nonetheless, all these provisions regarding popular participation have been bypassed in cases of legislative delegations to the Executive, and decree-laws have been enacted without any sort of consultation, as happened from 2000 to 2014, a period in which the most important legislation of the country was enacted through decree-laws (see *supra* paragraphs133, 234, 253, 301).

361. During the discussions of the drafts' legislation, and according to the regulations established by the National Assembly, the Ministers of the Executive branch have the right to express their views in the legislative debate (see *supra* paragraph 277), as do the Magistrates of the Supreme Tribunal of Justice, the representatives of the Citizen Power; the members of the Electoral Power; the states, through a representative designated by the Legislative Council of each, and representatives of social organizations (Article 211).

362. Once a statute is sanctioned by the National Assembly, it must be promulgated by the President of the Republic within ten days of having received it from the National Assembly (Article 214). Legislation is considered promulgated once published in the *Official Gazette* of the Republic (Article 215) with the corresponding presidential order that it be put into effect. The President may, however, within the said period, in a decision taken in Council of Ministers, and on the basis of a reasoned report, request the National Assembly to modify some aspect of the sanctioned legislation or reverse its approval of all or a part of it (presidential veto).

The National Assembly must decide on the President's arguments by absolute majority of members present, and must send the law for promulgation. In these cases, the President must promulgate the law within five days of receiving it, without proposing new changes.

363. However, when the President of the Republic considers that legislation or certain articles of a statute are unconstitutional, during the ten day period in which the law must be promulgated, he can request the matter to be reviewed by the Constitutional Chamber of the Supreme Tribunal of Justice. This is one of the *a priori* judicial review means provided in the Constitution (see *infra* paragraph 653). The Constitutional Chamber must decide within fifteen days of receiving the request from the President.

If the Tribunal denies the unconstitutionality presidential argument, or fails to decide within the allotted time period, the President must promulgate the law within five days.

364. If the President of the Republic fails to promulgate a statute according to all these rules, the President and the two Vice Presidents of the National Assembly must proceed to promulgate the law as indicated, without prejudice of the President of the Republic's liability for his omission (Article 216).

Only legislation approving international treaties, accords or conventions may be promulgated at the opportune time determined within the discretion of the National Executive, according to international custom and the national interest (Article 217).

Chapter 3. Political and Administrative Legislative Control Procedures

365. As set forth in Article 222 of the Constitution, the National Assembly may exercise its powers of control in political and administrative matters through the questioning (*interpelación*) procedure, in which a Minister or other official is summoned to the Assembly to answer specific questions with respect to his actions. In addition the Assembly and its Commissions can also make investigations or inquiries (Article 223).

366. In exercising parliamentary control, the Assembly can declare the political responsibility of government officials[1866] and request the Citizen Power to initiate the necessary legal actions to enforce such responsibility.

All public officials are obligated, subjected to sanctions, to appear before the Assembly's Commissions, and to furnish them with any information and documentation they may require to fulfil their functions. This obligation is also imposed upon private individuals, but cannot refer to those matters protected by Constitutional guarantees.[1867]

1866   On this subject, see Allan R Brewer-Carías 'Aspectos del control político sobre la Administración Pública, in *Revista de Control Fiscal*, 101 (Caracas: Contraloría General de la República, 1981), 107–130.

1867   See Allan R. Brewer-Carías, 'Los poderes de investigación de los cuerpos legislativos y sus limitaciones, con particular referencia a los asuntos secretos', 10 (Caracas, *Revista de Derecho Público,*), 1982), 25–42.

In no case could the exercise of the Assembly's investigatory power affect the powers of the other branches of government. Nonetheless, judges are required to provide evidence to the Assembly and its Committees when ordered to do so (Article 224).

PART VII. THE JUDICIARY

Chapter 1. General Constitutional Regime Referred to the Judiciary

§1. *Justice and the Judicial System*

I.   *Justice and the Components of the Judicial System*

367. The power to render or administer justice according to Article 253 of the Constitution emanates from the citizenry and is imparted in the name of the Republic and by the authority of the law. For such purposes, Article 26 of the Constitution provides that the State must guarantee a 'cost-free, accessible, impartial, adequate, transparent, autonomous, independent, accountable, equitable, and expeditious justice, without undue or dilatory delay, formalism, or unnecessary replication of procedures'.[1868]

The system of justice, according to the same Article 253 of the Constitution, is composed not only by the organs of the Judicial Branch (Supreme Tribunal of Justice and all the other courts established by law), but by the offices of the Prosecutor General, the Peoples' Defender, the criminal investigatory organs, the penitentiary system, the alternative means of justice, the citizens who participate in the administration of justice as provided in the law and the attorneys authorized to practice law.[1869]

II. *Independence and Autonomy of the Judicial Branch*

368. The principle of the independence of the Judicial Power is set forth expressly in Article 254 of the Constitution, which, in addition, establishes its financial autonomy,[1870] and assigns 'functional, financial, and administrative autonomy' to the Supreme Tribunal. As mentioned, unfortunately, the independence and autono-

---

1868   See Gustavo Urdaneta Troconis, 'El Poder Judicial en la Constitución de 1999', in *Estudios de Derecho Administrativo: Libro Homenaje a la Universidad Central de Venezuela*, vol. I (Caracas: Imprenta Nacional, 2001), 521–564.

1869   See the Law on the Judicial System, *Gaceta Oficial* N° 39.276 of 1 Oct. 2009. See in general Gustavo Urdaneta Troconis, 'El Poder Judicial en la Constitución de 1999', en *Estudios de Derecho Administrativo: Libro Homenaje a la Universidad Central de Venezuela*, vol. I (Caracas: Imprenta Nacional, 2001), 521–564; Román J. Duque Corredor, 'El sistema de Justicia', en *Tendencias Actuales del Derecho Constitucional. Homenaje a Jesús María Casal Montbrun*, ed. Jesús María Casal, Alfredo Arismendi y Carlos Luis Carrillo Artiles (Coord.), vol. II (Caracas: Universidad Central de Venezuela/Universidad Católica Andrés Bello, 2008), 87–112.

1870   See Juan Rafael Perdomo, 'Independencia y competencia del Poder Judicial', in *Revista de derecho del Tribunal Supremo de Justicia,* N° 8 (Caracas, 2003), 483 a 518.

my of the Judiciary in general has been neutralized due to the Executive political control over the National Assembly and the Supreme Tribunal (see *supra* paragraph 226 ff., 229; *infra* , 401 ff., 406).

In any case, the Constitution provides that within the National general annual budget, an appropriation of at least 2% of the ordinary national budget is established for the judiciary, a percentage amount that cannot be changed without prior approval by the National Assembly.

Article 26 of the Constitution guarantees 'cost-free justice'; consequently, the Constitution denies the Judiciary the power to establish court costs or fees, or to require payment for services (Article 254).

369. With the purpose of guaranteeing the impartiality and independence of judges in the exercise of their duties, Article 256 of the Constitution requires that magistrates, judges and prosecutors of the Public Prosecutor and the Public Defenders' offices may not, from the time of entering their respective jobs until they step down, engage in partisan political activity other than voting. This includes political party activism, union, guild and similar activities. Magistrates, judges and prosecutors are also prohibited from engaging in private or business activities that are incompatible with their judicial functions, on their own behalf or on the behalf of others, and they may not undertake any other public functions other than educational activities.

Judges are prohibited from associating with one another (Article 256), which is a limit regarding the constitutional right of association set forth in Article 52 of the Constitution.

III. *Judicial Process as the Instrument for Justice*

370. According to Article 257 of the Constitution, the fundamental instrument for the realization of justice is the judicial process; regarding which the procedural laws must establish simplified, uniform and effective procedures, and adopt brief, public and oral proceedings, through which in no case justice should be sacrificed based on the omission of non-essential formalities. These provisions are complemented by Article 26 of the Constitution that set forth that the State must guarantee expeditious justice without undue delay, formalisms or useless procedural repositions. In addition, being the alternative means of justice part of the judicial system (Article 253), Article 258 of the Constitution imposes on the Legislator the duty to promote arbitration, conciliation, mediation and other alternative means for conflicts resolution.

IV. *Judicial Liability*

371. According to Article 255 of the Constitution, judges are personally responsible for unjustified errors, delays or omissions, for substantial failures to observe procedural requirements, for abuse of or refusal to apply the law (*denegación*), for bias, for the crime of graft (*cohecho*) and for criminally negligent or intentional injustice (*prevaricación*) effectuated in the course of performing their judicial functions.

§2. *Judicial Jurisdictions in the Constitution*

372. In addition to the basic civil, commercial, labour, agrarian and criminal Jurisdictions established in the legal order to fulfil the realization of justice through the judicial processes, the 1999 Constitution has specifically included express provisions regarding jurisdictions in constitutional matters (Article 334), matters related to discipline in the judiciary (Article 267), judicial review of administrative actions matters (Article 259), electoral matters (Article 297), criminal military matters (Article 261), justices of the peace (Article 258), and justice within the Indigenous Peoples (Article 260).[1871]

373. In particular, Article 334 of the Constitution has created the Constitutional Chamber of the Supreme Tribunal of Justice with the exclusive power to exercise jurisdiction on constitutional matters (Constitutional Jurisdiction), including the power to declare the nullity of legislation or other acts of State organs issued in direct and immediate execution of the Constitution or that have the same rank of Statutes (Article 334) (see *infra* paragraph 644). This Jurisdiction is regulated in the Organic Law of the Supreme Tribunal.[1872]

374. Concerning the Judicial review of administrative action jurisdiction, Article 259 of the Constitution attributed it to the Supreme Tribunal of Justice and to all the other courts established by law; assigning them the power to annul general and individual administrative acts contrary to the legal order, including those issued with abuse of public power (*desviación de poder*). These courts are also competent to condemn the State to pay sums of money, and to repair injuries or damages caused by the Administration, to hear claims concerning the rendering of public services, and to rule as necessary to re-establish subjective legal rights affected by administrative acts. This Jurisdiction is regulated in the 2010 Organic Law on the Contentious Administrative Jurisdiction[1873] (see *infra* paragraph 702).

In addition, on contentious administrative matters, Article 297 of the Constitution has established a specific Jurisdiction on electoral matters attributed to the Electoral Chamber of the Supreme Tribunal and all the other courts determined by law.[1874] (see *infra* paragraph 702).

1871   See María E. León Álvarez, 'El sistema de justicia en la Constitución de Venezuela de 1999. Estudio crítico acerca de la jurisdicción especial indígena', in *Revista del Tribunal Supremo de Justicia*, Nº 4 (Caracas, 2002), 369–377.

1872   See in *Gaceta Oficial* Nº 39.522 of 1 Oct. 2010.

1873   Véase en *G. O.* Nº 39.451 de 22 Jun. 2010. See Allan R. Brewer-Carías y Víctor Hernández Mendible, *Ley de la Jurisdicción Contencioso Administrativa* (Caracas: Editorial Jurídica venezolana, 2011); María L. Acuña López, 'Algunas notas relacionadas con los principios constitucionales que regulan el sistema de justicia venezolano y su alcance en la jurisdicción contencioso-administrativa', en *Estudios de Derecho Administrativo: Libro Homenaje a la Universidad Central de Venezuela*, vol. I (Caracas: Imprenta Nacional, 2001), 521–564.

1874   See Miguel A. Torrealba Sánchez, 'Notas sobre la jurisdicción contencioso electoral en la Constitución de 1999', in *Revista de Derecho Administrativo*, Nº 12 (mayo-agosto) (Caracas: Editorial Sherwood, 2001), 165–192. The Electoral Jurisdiction is regulated in the Organic Law of the Supreme Tribunal of Justice, *Gaceta Oficial* Nº 39.522 of 1 Oct. 2010.

375. Regarding the disciplinary regime of the judges, Article 276 of the Constitution establishes the Judicial Disciplinary Jurisdiction, which implies the need to create disciplinary tribunals to judge the judges.It was only in 2010 when the Disciplinary Jurisdiction was created, with judges appointed by the National Assembly in 2011, conforming a Court with competence on this matter.[1875] (see *supra* paragraph 231).

376. Article 261 of the Constitution establishes the rules for a criminal military jurisdiction as an integral part of the Judicial Branch, whose judges are to be selected competitively. Its sphere of competence, organization and forms of functioning is governed by the accusatory (adversarial) system of criminal procedure, as provided in the Organic Code of Military Justice.[1876] In all events, the Constitution expressly provides that ordinary civil crimes, human rights violations, and crimes against humanity by military personnel are to be adjudicated in the ordinary courts, while the competence of military tribunals is limited to military crimes.

377. Following the orientation of the Organic Law of Justice of the Peace,[1877] Article 258 refers to the election of the Judges of the Peace by universal, direct and secret vote, being the only elected judges in the country (Article 261).

378. Article 260 of the Constitution also authorizes the legitimate authorities of indigenous peoples to apply their own jurisdiction, laws and procedure based upon their ancestral traditions within their territory and with effect only with respect to their members. Indigenous law must not, however, be in violation of the Constitution or laws of the country and the means of coordination of this special jurisdiction with the national legal system is to be established by national law.[1878]

379. All the other jurisdiction within the Judiciary are established by statute, as is the case of the Civil and Commercial Jurisdiction, the Criminal Jurisdiction, the Labor Jurisdiction, the Juvenile Jurisdiction, and the Agrarian Jurisdiction.[1879]

§3. *Governance and Administration of the Judicial Branch*

380. One of the innovations of the 1999 Constitution was to confer to the Supreme Tribunal of Justice 'the Governance and Administration of the Judicial Branch', while eliminating the former Council of the Judiciary (*Consejo de la Judicatura*) which exercised these functions under Article 217 of the Constitution of 1961, as one of the organs with functional autonomy separate and independent from all the branches of government, including the former Supreme Court of Justice.

1875   See the Law in the Ethics Code of the Venezuelan Judge, *Gaceta Oficial* N° 39.494 of 24 Aug. 2010. This Code expressly abrogated the regulation concerning the Commission on the Functioning of the Judiciary established in 1999. The members of the Disciplinary Judicial Court were appointed by the Nacional Assembly in June 2011, *Gaceta Oficial* N° 39.693 of 10 Jun. 2011. The Court was organized on 28 Jun. 2011, *Gaceta Oficial* N° 39.704 of 29 Jun. 2011.

1876   *Gaceta Oficial* Extra. N° 5.263 of 17 Sep. 1998.

1877   *Gaceta Oficial* Extra. N° 4.817 21 Dec. 1994.

1878   See María E. León Álvarez, 'El sistema de justicia en la Constitución de Venezuela de 1999. Estudio crítico acerca de la jurisdicción especial indígena', en *Revista del Tribunal Supremo de Justicia,* N° 4 (Caracas, 2002), 369–377.

1879   Organic Law on the Judiciary, *Gaceta Oficial* Extra. N° 5.262 11 Sep. 1998.

Consequently, since 2000, as provided in Article 267 of the Constitution, the Supreme Tribunal of Justice is charged with the direction, governance and administration of the Judicial Branch, including inspection and oversight of the other courts of the Republic as well as the offices of the Public Defenders.[1880] For such purposes the Supreme Tribunal is in charge of drafting and putting into effect its own budget and the budget of the Judicial Branch in general, according to principles set out in Article 254.

381. In order to perform these functions, the plenary Supreme Tribunal of Justice has created an Executive Directorate of the Judiciary (*Dirección Ejecutiva de la Magistratura*) with regional offices. Judicial Circuits are to be established and organized by statute, as are the creation of jurisdictions of tribunals and regional courts in order to promote administrative and jurisdictional decentralization of the Judicial Power (Article 269).

382. As mentioned, jurisdiction for judicial discipline is to be carried out by disciplinary tribunals as determined by law (Article 267), which as has been previously mentioned, was eventually established in 2010–2011 after the sanctioning of the Code of Ethics of the Venezuelan Judge. Disciplinary proceedings must be public, oral and brief, in conformity with due process of law.

§4. *Regimen Governing the Judicial Career and the Stability of Judges*

383. The basic constitutional provision in order to guarantee the independence and autonomy of courts and judges is established in Article 255, which provides for a specific mechanism to assure the independent appointment of judges, and to guarantee their stability.

38. In this regard, the judicial tenure is considered as a judicial career, in which the admission as well as the promotion of judges within it must be the result of a public competition or examinations to assure the excellence and adequacy of qualifications of the participants, who are to be chosen by panels from the judicial circuits (Article 255). The naming and swearing-in of judges is to be done by the Supreme Tribunal of Justice, and the citizens' participation in the selection procedure and designation of judges are to be guaranteed by law. Unfortunately, up to 2011, all these provisions have not been applicable because of a lack of legislation implementing them.

385. The Constitution also creates a Judicial Nominations Committee (Article 270) as an organ for the assistance of the Judicial Branch in selecting not only the Magistrates for the Supreme Tribunal of Justice (Article 264) (see *supra* paragraph

1880   See the Organic Law of the Supreme Tribunal of Justice *Gaceta Oficial* N° 39.522 of 1 Oct. 2010, See Allan R. Brewer-Carías and Víctor Hernández Mendible, *Ley Orgánica del Tribunal Supremo de Justicia 2010* (Caracas: Editorial Jurídica Venezolana, 2010); Laura Louza, 'El Tribunal Supremo de Justicia en la Constitución de la República Bolivariana de Venezuela', en *Revista del Tribunal Supremo de Justicia,* N° 4 (Caracas, 2002), 379–437; Nélida Peña Colmenares, 'El Tribunal Supremo de Justicia como órgano de dirección, gobierno, administración, inspección y vigilancia del Poder Judicial venezolano', in *Revista de derecho del Tribunal Supremo de Justicia,* N° 8 (Caracas, 2003), 391 a 434; and Olga Dos Santos, 'Comisión Judicial del Tribunal Supremo de Justicia', in *Revista de derecho del Tribunal Supremo de Justicia,* N° 6 (Caracas, 2002), 373 a 378.

224 et seq.), but also to assist judicial colleges in selecting judges for the courts including those of the jurisdiction in Judicial Discipline. This Judicial Nominations Committee is to be composed of representatives from different sectors of society, as determined by law. The law is required to promote the professional development of judges, to which end universities are to collaborate with the judiciary by developing training in judicial specialization in law school curricula.

As aforementioned, none of these provisions have been implemented, and on the contrary, since 1999, the Venezuelan Judiciary has been almost completely composed by temporal and provisional judges,[1881] lacking stability and being subjected to political manipulation, altering the people's right to an adequate administration of justice.

386. However, in order to guarantee the stability of judges according to the express provision of the Constitution, they can only be removed or suspended from office through judicial procedures or trails expressly established by statutes, led by Judicial Disciplinary Judges (Article 255). Nonetheless, up to 2011, because of the lack of implementing the Disciplinary Jurisdiction, judges were removed without due process guarantees by a 'transitory' Reorganization Commission of the Judicial Power in charge of the disciplinary procedures, that if it is true that it was eliminated in June 2011 (see *infra* paragraph402), it was substituted by courts but whose judges are appointed by the political organ of the State, the National Assembly, instead of by the Supreme Tribunal of Justice.

Chapter 2. The Supreme Tribunal of Justice

§1. Composition

387. The Constitution of 1999 created the Supreme Tribunal of Justice in substitution of the former Supreme Court of Justice established in the 1961 Constitution. The Supreme Tribunal is composed of six Chambers: Constitutional, Politico-Administrative, Electoral, Civil Cassation, Criminal Cassation and Social Chambers. The Supreme Tribunal can also seat and function in Plenary Session (*Sala Plena*).[1882]

The Constitution did not expressly provide for the number of Justices integrating the Supreme Tribunal of Justice or each of its Chambers, a matter that was left to the

---

1881   The Inter-American Commission on Human Rights said: 'The Commission has been informed that only 250 judges have been appointed by opposition concurrence according to the constitutional text. From a total of 1772 positions of judges in Venezuela, the Supreme Court of Justice reports that only 183 are holders, 1331 are provisional and 258 are temporary', *Informe sobre la Situación de los Derechos Humanos en Venezuela*; OAS/Ser.L/V/II.118. d.C. 4rev. 2; 29 Dec. 2003; para. 11. The same Commission also said that 'an aspect linked to the autonomy and independence of the Judicial Power is that of the provisional character of the judges in the judicial system of Venezuela. Today, the information provided by the different sources indicates that more than 80% of Venezuelan judges are 'provisional'. *Id.*, para. 161.

1882   See Laura Louza, 'El Tribunal Supremo de Justicia en la Constitución de la República Bolivariana de Venezuela', in *Revista del Tribunal Supremo de Justicia*, N° 4 (Caracas, 2002), 379–437.

provisions of the Organic Law of the Supreme Tribunal which was only sanctioned in 2004[1883] (see *supra* paragraph 226).

§2. *Jurisdiction*

388. According to the express provision of Article 266 of the Constitution, the Supreme Tribunal of Justice exercises in an exclusive way the Constitutional Jurisdiction (Article 334) (see *infra* paragraph 594); is the highest court within the Administrative Jurisdiction (judicial review of administrative actions (Article 295) (see *infra* paragraph 702); and exercises the Electoral Jurisdiction (judicial review of electoral acts, Article 297). The Tribunal also has competence to decide conflicts between superior courts of justice; has the exclusive power to interpret statutes by means of recourses of interpretation (see *infra* paragraph 685); decides in an exclusive way recourses of cassation; has competence to declare that there are merits for the prosecution of High officials of the State; has attributions to decide on the dismissal of the President of the Republic (A233), and to express its opinion on the dismissal of the Comptroller General, the Prosecutor General, the Peoples' Defender and the members of the National Electoral Council (Articles 296, 297).

389. In addition, the Constitution establishes some provisions related to attributions of the Constitutional, Politico-Administrative and Electoral Chambers, as well as of the Social Chamber particularly in agrarian, labour and juvenile matters (Article 262). According to these provisions, the Supreme Tribunal of Justice exercises jurisdiction on constitutional matters (judicial review) exclusively through its Constitutional Chamber (Article 334); through the Politico-Administrative Chamber which is the highest judicial court on judicial review of administrative action proceedings (contentious administrative jurisdiction) (Article 259); and through the Social and Cassation Chambers which hears cases in cassation. The Supreme Tribunal, through the two first Chambers, is also competent to decide constitutional and administrative conflicts between territorial entities; and through all the Chambers decide recourses of interpretation regarding the content and scope of statutes. In Plenary Session, the Supreme Tribunal is in charge of deciding whether there are or not grounds to prosecute high government officials (Article 266).

390. In addition to its jurisdictional attributions, as aforementioned, the Supreme Tribunal of Justice, according to the Constitution of 1999, is in charge of the 'governance and administration of the Judiciary' (Article 267), through the Executive Board of the Judiciary (see *supra* paragraph 380).

§3. *Status of the Supreme Tribunal Magistrates*

I.   *Conditions to be Magistrate of the Supreme Tribunal Justice*

391. Article 263 of the Constitution is very precise in establishing in detail the conditions for being elected Magistrate to the Supreme Tribunal of Justice, leaving

---

1883   *Gaceta Oficial* N° 37.942 of 20 May 2004. See Allan R. Brewer-Carías, *Ley Orgánica del Tribunal Supremo de Justicia. Procesos y procedimientos constitucionales y contencioso-administrativos* (Caracas, 2004). The Law was reformed in 2010, *Gaceta Oficial* N° 39.522 of 1 Oct. 2010.

the procedures for election of Magistrates on the Tribunal to be determined by law (Article 264).

The conditions to be Magistrate are the following: to be a Venezuelan national by birth, without any other nationality (Article 41); a citizen of recognized honourability; a recognized jurist, with professional practice of at least fifteen years, having university postgraduate degree; or with university teaching career of at least fifteen years; or with judicial positions in courts of appeal in jurisdictions related with the attributions of the corresponding Chamber, for at least fifteen years; and having recognized prestige in his functions.

392. These strict conditions to be Magistrates of the Supreme Tribunal were by-passed in 1999, when the first provisional 'election' of Magistrates was made by the Constituent Assembly (see *supra* paragraph 226), and again in 2000 when the then newly elected National Assembly also made election of Magistrates without sanctioning the Organic Law of the Tribunal, and without complying with the constitutional conditions, in execution of a Special Law sanctioned specifically for such election purposes.[1884]

This statute was challenged for judicial review by means of an action of unconstitutionality filed by the then Peoples' Defender, that has never been decided. Nonetheless, when deciding on the admissibility of the action, and particularly of a petition for protection of constitutional rights (*amparo*),[1885] the Constitutional Chamber explaining that since 2000 two constitutional regimes were in effect: the one established in the 1999 Constitution and the one established in the Transitory Constitutional Regime Decree of the same year 1999 (see *supra* paragraph 30), decided to ask the Peoples' Defender to clarify its petition, although incidentally ruling that the conditions established in the Constitution to be magistrated were not applicable to themselves, those that were deciding the case, because they were not to be elected but to be ratified (see *infra* paragraph 396).

II.   *The Nomination and Election Procedure*

393. The Constitution attributed the election of Magistrates for a single term of twelve years to the National Assembly (Article 264), specifically limiting the discretionary power that the former Congress had in this regard. For such purpose, the Constitution provides that the Assembly can only elect magistrates that are nominated by a specific Judicial Nominations Committee, which is the organ to receive the nominations presented whether by own initiative of the candidate or by organizations related to the judicial activities. This Judicial Nominations Committee, according to express constitutional provision, is to be integrated only by 'representatives of the different sectors of society' (Article 270).

1884   *Gaceta Oficial* N° 37.077 of 14 Nov. 2000. See Carlos Luis Carrillo Artiles, 'El desplazamiento del principio de supremacía constitucional por la vigencia de los interregnos temporales', *Revista de Derecho Constitucional,* N° 3 (Caracas, 2000), 86 y ss.

1885   Decision of 12 Dec. 2000, in *Revista de Derecho Público,* N° 84 (octubre-diciembre) (Caracas: Editorial Jurídica Venezolana, 2000), 108 y ss. See Allan R. Brewer-Carías, *Golpe de Estado y Proceso Constituyente en Venezuela* (México: UNAM, 2002), 395 y ss.

According to the same Article 264 of the Constitution, for the purpose of proposing candidates before the National Assembly, the Committee, having heard the opinion of the community, must pre-select a group of nominees that must be presented before the Citizen Power (Prosecutor General, Comptroller General, Peoples' Defender), which must make a second pre-selection of nominees that is the one to be submitted to the National Assembly. Finally, the Constitution also provides for the rights of any Citizens to file well-founded objections to any of the nominees before the Judicial Nominations Committee or before the National Assembly. As mentioned, the main purpose of this constitutional procedure was to limit the discretional power the former Congress had in the election of Magistrates to the Supreme Court, based on political agreements and without any sort of Citizens or society control.

394. But as aforementioned, ignoring all these provisions, and of course, without the previous sanctioning of the Supreme Tribunal Organic Law, the 1999 National Constituent Assembly, in a 'Decree on the Regimen for the Transition of Public Powers', issued on 22 December 1999, one week after the Constitution was already approved by popular vote (15 December 1999) (see *supra* paragraph 30), dismissed the then existing fifteen Justices of the former Supreme Court of Justice that were still in their tenure. It appointed in substitution twenty new Justices for the new Supreme Tribunal of Justice, although in a transitory way. In the absence of constitutional or legal provisions regarding the number of Magistrates, the Constituent Assembly provided for the appointment of three Justices for each of the five: Political-Administrative, Electoral, Civil Cassation, Criminal Cassation and Social Chambers, and five Justices for the Constitutional Chamber. These appointments, as mentioned, had no constitutional or legal basis due to the fact that the Constitution or the Law did not specify the number of Justices of each Chamber of the Supreme Tribunal. In addition, the National Constituent Assembly had no power to enact constitutional provisions without popular approval by referendum, and the Constitutional Transitory Constitutional Regime Decree was enacted after the Constitution approbatory referendum of 15 December 1999; thus without popular approval. The appointments made on December 1999, however, were made by the Constituent Assembly without complying with the provisions regarding the ineludible need for a Judicial Nomination Committee integrated by representatives of the different sectors of the society, to select and propose the candidates in order to guarantee the Citizens' participation.[1886]

395. After the election of the new National Assembly in 2000 and according to the provisions of the new Constitution, it was suppose to enact the Organic Law of the Supreme Tribunal of Justice in order to determine the number of Magistrates of each of its Chambers, and to provide for the integration, organization and functioning of the Judicial Nominating Committee so as to elect in a definitive way the Justices of the Supreme Tribunal. But the Assembly, as aforementioned, instead of passing such Organic Law, on 14 November 2000 sanctioned a 'Special Law for the

---

1886   See Allan R. Brewer-Carías, 'La participación ciudadana en la designación de los titulares de los
        órganos no electos de los Poderes Públicos en Venezuela y sus vicisitudes políticas', in *Revista Ibe*
        roamericana de Derecho Público y Administrativo. Year 5. N° 5-2005 (San José, Costa Rica, 2005),
        76–95.

ratification or election of the High Officials of the Citizen Power and of the Magistrates of the Supreme Tribunal of Justice for the first constitutional term',[1887] creating a Parliamentary Commission integrated by a majority of representatives as 'Nominating Committee' to select the Magistrates, by-passing the constitutional provision and imposing the need to create and regulate the Judicial Nominating Committee integrated exclusively with representatives of different sectors of society. The Assembly, in fact, appointed 'a Commission integrated by fifteen deputies, that shall act as the Committee for the Evaluation of Nominations' (Article 3), that was to select 'a list of twelve representatives of the different sectors of the society by means of mechanisms of consultation', and present the list to the National Assembly so that it may choose, by an absolute majority, six persons to sit on the Commission (Article 4).

396. The Peoples' Defender at the time (who had been provisionally appointed in December 1999), filed an action of unconstitutionality with an *amparo* petition against this Special Law, in order to protect the rights of political participation,[1888] a process that the Supreme Tribunal has never decided. The response to that sign of independence was the Legislator's decision not to ratify the titleholder of that position, and in a preliminary ruling in the case, the Constitutional Chamber deciding the *amparo* petition, ruled that the eligibility conditions for the election of the Magistrates of the Tribunal set forth in a very precise way in Article 263 of the Constitution, were not applicable to those Magistrates sitting in the Supreme Tribunal that were precisely deciding the matter. The Magistrates considered that according to the Special Law they could be 'ratified' in their positions by the National Assembly even without compliance with the constitutional conditions to be Magistrates, arguing that the 'ratification' was a concept not foreseen in the Constitution (that only provided for the nomination). Therefore, Article 263 was to be applied only to *ex novo* elections of Magistrates but not to those that were already in the position that were going to be 'ratified'.[1889] In this way, the Constitutional Chamber simply decided that the Constitution was inapplicable precisely with respect to its own Magistrates and particularly to those of the Constitutional Chamber that were the deciding judges in this case itself. The Magistrates eventually decided in their own case.[1890]

397. The result of this process was that civil society was marginalized, and the Magistrates, as well as the High officials of the Citizen Power and of the Electoral

---

1887   *Gaceta Oficial* N° 37.077 of 14 Nov. 2000.

1888   See, *El Universal,* Caracas 13 Dec. 2000, 1–2.

1889   The Tribunal ruled: 'The consequence of the Regimen for the Transition of the Public Powers – of constitutional rank as this Chamber has pointed out – is that the concept of ratification is applied only to Magistrates of the Supreme Tribunal of Justice, since the concept is not foreseen by the Constitution itself. Because of this, the phrase in *Art. 21 of the Regimen for the Transition of Public Powers* that states that definitive ratifications or appointments *shall be done according to the Constitution,* is inapplicable, since as this Chamber stated out previously, the current Constitution did not provide for ratification of Magistrates to the Supreme Tribunal of Justice.' See decision of 12 Dec. 2000 in *Revista de Derecho Público,* N° 84 (Caracas: Editorial Jurídica Venezolana, 2000), 108 et seq.

1890   That is why the Peoples' Defendant announced that she was going to ask for the inhibition of the Magistrates of the Constitutional Chamber in the case. See *El Universal* (Caracas, 16 Dec. 2000), 1–4.

Power were elected by the National Assembly in a discretionary way, as before, even without complying in all cases with the constitutional conditions required to be a magistrate. Through the Special Law the political control of the Branches of government was consolidated,[1891] a situation that has persisted, particularly regarding the election of the Magistrates of the Supreme Tribunal.

398. The subsequent step in this regard, was made in 2004, with the enactment of the Organic Law of the Supreme Tribunal of Justice, in which the Judicial Nominating Committee was regulated, but instead of being integrated by representatives of the different sectors of society as imposed by the Constitution, it was established that it was to be integrated by'eleven members, from which five must be elected from the National Assembly, and the other six from the other sectors of society elected in a public proceeding' (Article 13, paragraph 2). In practice, this Committee has been a Parliamentary Commission with additional non-parliamentary members that functions within the Assembly (Article 13).

399. The 2004 Organic Law, in addition, for the first time since the approval of the Constitution (1999), established the number of the Magistrates of the Chambers of the Supreme Tribunal, extending it to a total of thirty-two Justices, whose nomination by the new Nominating Committee was completely controlled by the government. This was publicly announced by the President of the Parliamentary Nominating Commission in charge of selecting the candidates for Magistrates of the Supreme Tribunal Court of Justice (who a few months later was appointed Minister of the Interior and Justice), when he publicly declared on December 2004 that none of the elected Magistrates were to decide against the government interests.[1892]

1891   This constitutional problem was pointed out by the Secretary General of the Organization of American States, in its Report to the General Assembly of 18 Apr. 2002, and was highlighted with emphasis by the Inter-American Commission of Human Rights in a press Communiqué N° 23/02 of 10 May 2002, which referred to the questioning it has received 'related to the legitimacy of the process of selecting of the Highest Titleholders of the Judiciary..., [by means of] proceedings not stipulated in the Venezuelan Constitution. The received information pointed out that those officials were not nominated by the Committees provided in the Constitution but instead based on a statute sanctioned by the National Assembly after the approval of the Constitution...' (N° 7). The matter was more precisely referred to by the same Inter American Commission in the Preliminary Remarks of 10 May 2002, in which it said that: 'The constitutional reforms established regarding the way to appoint those authorities were not used in this case. Those provisions precisely seek to limit the undue interventions, assuring more independenence and impartiality, allowing diverse society opinions to be heard in the election of such high authorities' (N° 26).

1892   This is what the representative said: 'Although we, the representatives, have the authority for this selection, the President of the Republic was consulted and his opinion was very much taken into consideration.' He added: 'Let's be clear, we are not going to score auto-goals. In the list, there were people from the opposition who comply with all the requirements. The opposition could have used them in order to reach an agreement during the last sessions, be they did not want to. We are not going to do it for them. There is no one in the group of postulates that could act against us...' See in *El Nacional* (Caracas, 13 Dec. 2004). That is why the Inter-American Commission on Human Rights suggested in its Report to the General Assembly of the OAS corresponding to 2004 that 'these regulations of the Organic Law of the Supreme Court of Justice would have made possible the manipulation, by the Executive Power, of the election process of judges that took place during 2004'. See Inter-American Commission on Human Rights, 2004 *Report on Venezuela*; para. 180.

The last expression of this executive control on the Judiciary occurred in 2010, after an illegitimate 'reform' of Organic Law of the Supreme Tribunal of Justice, by means of its 'reprinting' due to a supposed printing (material) error,[1893] allowing the election of new Magistrates of the Tribunal before the new National Assembly elected in September 2010 convened in January 2011.[1894]

III. *The Removal and Dismissal of the Magistrates*

400. However, according to Article 265 of the Constitution, the Magistrates of the Supreme Tribunal of Justice although elected for a twelve years tenure, can be dismissed by the National Assembly by a vote of two-thirds of its members following a hearing in cases of serious or major offences as determined by the Citizen Power. This sole possibility for the Legislative Power to dismiss the Head of the Judiciary contradicts the principle of separation of powers and the independence of the Judiciary.[1895] Nonetheless, the qualified two-thirds majority vote was established to avoid leaving the existence of the Heads of the Judiciary in the hands of a simple majority of Legislators.

For such purpose, Article 12, paragraph 1 of the 2004 Organic Law of the Supreme Tribunal of Justice defines as grave faults of a magistrate, among others, not to be impartial or independent in the exercise of his functions; to have political activism on party or trade-union matters; to exercise private activities or activities incompatible with their functions; not to accomplish their functions of being manifestly negligent of it; to publicly act against the respectability of the Judiciary and its organs; to endanger the credibility and impartiality of their position, compromising the dignity of the office; to act with abuse or excess of power; or to commit grave and inexcusable errors, prevarication or denials of justice.

But the 2004 Organic Law of the Supreme Tribunal, in an evident fraud to the Constitution, established another way to dismiss Magistrates of the Supreme Court, by-passing the qualified majority required in the Constitution, by adding the possibility for the National Assembly to approve by just a simple majority of votes, to 'annul the administrative act of appointment of the Magistrate', in cases of them have given false information when nominated; of public attitude that could harm the pres-

---

1893   See the comments of Víctor Hernández Mendible, 'Sobre la nueva reimpresión por "supuestos errores" materiales de la Ley Orgánica del Tribunal Supremo, octubre de 2010', y Antonio Silva Aranguren, 'Tras el rastro del engaño, en la web de la Asamblea Nacional', in *Revista de Derecho Público*, No. 124 (Caracas: Editorial Jurídica Venezolana, 2010), 110–113.

1894   A former member of the Supreme Court of Justice, regarding such reform, said that 'the Nomination Judicial Committee was unconstitutionally converted into an appendix of the Legislative Power'. See Hildegard Rondón de Sansó, *'Obiter Dicta. En torno a una elección'*, in *La Voce d'Italia* (Caracas, 14 Dec. 2010).

1895   See Allan R. Brewer-Carías, *Separation of Powers and Authoritarian Government in Venezuela*, Lecture given in the Seminar on Separation of Powers in the Americas and Beyond, Duquesne University, School of Law, Pittsburgh, 7 and 8 Nov. 2008, in <www.allanbrewercarías.com> (I,1,982,2008); 'La justicia sometida al poder y la interminable emergencia del poder judicial (1999–2006)', in *Derecho y democracia. Cuadernos Universitarios*, Órgano de Divulgación Académica, Vicerrectorado Académico (Caracas: Universidad Metropolitana, Año II, N° 11, septiembre 2007), 122–138.

tige of the Supreme Tribunal, its Chambers and Magistrates; and of actions against the functioning of the Tribunal (Article 234). Although the National Assembly used this power to dismiss Magistrates after deciding on some particular sensible questions not according with the government's willingness,[1896] such provision was eliminated in the 2010 reform of the Organic Law of the Supreme Tribunal.

Chapter 3. The dependence of the Judiciary and factual absence of judicial autonomy and independence

401. The progressive process of centralization and concentration of powers (see *supra* paragraphs 219 ff.) developed in Venezuela since 1999, by means of a continuous, persistent, and deliberate process of demolishing the rule of law institutions[1897] and of destroying democracy in a way never before experienced in all the constitutional history of the country,[1898] has lead to the configuration of a highly politicized Supreme Tribunal, subjected to the will of the President of the Republic; which was reinforced with the election of Magistrates in 2010,[1899] and in 2014, eliminating all autonomy of the Judicial Power and even the basic principle of the separation of power, as the corner stone of the Rule of Law and the base of all democratic institutions.

1896   It was the case of the Vice President of the Supreme Tribunal of Justice, who delivered the decision of the Supreme Tribunal of 14 Aug. 2002 regarding the criminal process against the generals who acted on 12 Apr. 2002, declaring that there were no grounds to judge them due to the fact that in said occasion no military coup took place; and that of Alberto Martini Urdaneta, President of the Electoral Court, and Rafael Hernandez and Orlando Gravina, Judges of the same Court who undersigned decision N° 24 of 15 Mar. 2004 (Case: *Julio Borges, Cesar Perez Vivas, Henry Ramos Allup, Jorge Sucre Castillo, Ramón Jose Medina and Gerardo Blyde v. the National Electoral Council*), that suspended the effects of Resolution N° 040302-131, dated 2 Mar. 2004 of the National Electoral Council which, in that moment, stopped the realization of the presidential recall referendum.

1897   See in *general*, Allan R. Brewer-Carías, 'La progresiva y sistemática demolición de la autonomía e independencia del Poder Judicial en Venezuela (1999-2004),' *XXX Jornadas J.M Dominguez Escovar, Estado de Derecho, Administración de Justicia y Derechos Humanos*, (Barquisimeto, Instituto de Estudios Jurídicos del Estado Lara, 2005), 33-174; Allan R. Brewer-Carías, 'El constitucionalismo y la emergencia en Venezuela: entre la emergencia formal y la emergencia anormal del Poder Judicial,' in Allan R. Brewer-Carías, 2007. *Estudios Sobre el Estado Constitucional (2005-2006)*, (Caracas: Editorial Jurídica Venezolana, 2007), 245-269; and Allan R. Brewer-Carías 2007. 'La justicia sometida al poder. La ausencia de independencia y autonomía de los jueces en Venezuela por la interminable emergencia del Poder Judicial (1999-2006),' *Cuestiones Internacionales. Anuario Jurídico Villanueva, (*Centro Universitario Villanueva, Madrid: Marcial Pons, 20070, 25-57. See also Allan R. Brewer-Carías, 2008. *Historia Constitucional de Venezuela*, Vol II. Caracas, Editorial Alfa, pp. 402-454.

1898   See, in general, Allan R. Brewer-Carías, 2007. El autoritarismo establecido en fraude a la Constitución y a la democracia y su formalización en "Venezuela mediante la reforma constitucional. (De cómo en un país democrático se ha utilizado el sistema eleccionario para minar la democracia y establecer un régimen autoritario de supuesta "dictadura de la democracia" que se pretende regularizar mediante la reforma constitucional), *Temas constitucionales. Planteamientos ante una Reforma*, Fundación de Estudios de Derecho Administrativo, Caracas FUNEDA, pp. 13-74; and Allan R. Brewer-Carías, 2009. La demolición del Estado de Derecho en Venezuela Reforma Constitucional y fraude a la Constitución (1999-2009), *El Cronista del Estado Social y Democrático de Derecho*, N° 6, Madrid, Editorial Iustel, pp. 52-61.

1899   See Hildegard Rondón de Sansó, 2010. *Obiter Dicta. En torno a una elección*, *La Voce d'Italia*, Caracas December 14, 2010.

§1. *The Judiciary packed by Temporal and Provisional Judges and the use of the Judiciary for Political Persecution*

402. It has been through the Supreme Tribunal, which is in charge of governing and administering the Judiciary, that the political control over all judges has been assured, reinforced by means of the survival until 2011, of the 1999 "provisional" Commission on the Functioning and Restructuring of the Judicial System, which was legitimized by the same Tribunal, making completely inapplicable the 1999 constitutional provisions seeking to guarantee the independence and autonomy of judges.

In effect, as aforementioned (see *supra* paragraph 383), according to the text of the 1999 Constitution, judges can only enter the judicial career by means of public competition that must be organized with citizens' participation. Nonetheless, this provision has not yet been implemented, being the judiciary almost exclusively made up of temporary and provisional judges, without any stability. Regarding this situation, for instance, since 2003 the Inter-American Commission on Human Rights repeatedly expressed concern about the fact that provisional judges are susceptible to political manipulation, which alters the people's right to access to justice, reporting cases of dismissals and substitutions of judges in retaliation for decisions contrary to the government's position.[1900] In its *2008 Annual Report*, the Commission again verified the provisional character of the judiciary as an "endemic problem" because the appointment of judges was made without applying constitutional provisions on the matter –thus exposing judges to discretionary dismissal– which highlights the "permanent state of urgency" in which those appointments have been made.[1901]

403. Contrary to these facts, according to the words of the Constitution in order to guarantee the independence of the Judiciary, judges can be dismissed from their tenure only through disciplinary processes, conducted by disciplinary courts and judges of a Disciplinary Judicial Jurisdiction. Nonetheless, as aforementioned, that jurisdiction was only created in 2011, corresponding to that year the disciplinary judicial functions to the already mentioned transitory Commission,[1902] which, as reported by the same Inter-American Commission in its *2009 Annual Report*, "in addition to being a special, temporary entity, does not afford due guarantees for ensuring the independence of its decisions,[1903] since its members may also be appointed or removed at the sole discretion of the Constitutional Chamber of the Supreme

---

1900   See *Informe sobre la Situación de Derechos Humanos en Venezuela*; OAS/Ser.L/V/II.118. doc.4rev.2; December 29, 2003, Paragraphs 161, 174, available at http://www.cidh.oas.org/countryrep/Venezuela2003eng/toc.htm.

1901   See *Annual Report 2008* (OEA/Ser.L/V/II.134. Doc. 5 rev. 1. 25 febrero 2009), paragraph 39.

1902   The Politico Administrative Chamber of the Supreme Tribunal has decided that the dismiss of temporal judges is a discretionary power of the Commission on the Functioning and Reorganization of the Judiciary, which adopts its decision without following any administrative procedure rules or due process rules. See Decision N° 00463-2007 of March 20, 2007; Decision N° 00673-2008 of April 24, 2008 (cited in Decision N° 1.939 of December 18, 2008, p. 42). The Chamber has adopted the same position in Decision N° 2414 of December 20, 2007 and Decision N° 280 of February 23, 2007.

1903   See Decisión N° 1.939 of December 18, 2008 (Caso: *Gustavo Álvarez Arias et al.*)

Tribunal of Justice, without previously establishing either the grounds or the procedure for such formalities."[1904]

The Commission then "cleansed" the Judiciary of judges not in line with the authoritarian regime, removing judges in a discretionary way when they have issued decisions not within the complacency of the government.[1905] This lead the Inter-American Commission on Human Rights, to observe in its *2009 Annual Report,* that "in Venezuela, judges and prosecutors do not enjoy the guaranteed tenure necessary to ensure their independence." [1906]

404. One of the leading cases showing this situation took place in 2003, when a High Contentious Administrative Court ruled against the government in a politically charged case regarding the hiring of foreign physicians (not licensed in Venezuela) for medical social programs. In response to a provisional judicial measure suspending the hiring procedures, due to discrimination allegations made by the Council of Physicians of Caracas, [1907] the government after declaring that the decision was not going to be accepted [1908] seized the Court using secret police officers, and dismissed its judges after being offended by the President of the Republic.[1909] The case was brought before the Inter-American Court of Human Rights and after it ruled in 2008 that the dismissal effectively violated the American Convention on Human Rights,[1910] the Constitutional Chamber of the Supreme Tribunal response to the Inter-American Court ruling, at the request of the government, was that the decision of the Inter-American Court could not be enforced in Venezuela,[1911] showing the subordination of the Venezuelan judiciary to the policies, wishes, and dictates of the President.

1904   Véase *Annual Report 2009*, Par. 481, en http://www.cidh.org/annualrep/2009eng/Chap. IV.f.eng.htm.

1905   Decision N° 1.939 (Dec. 18, 2008) (Case: *Abogados Gustavo Álvarez Arias y otros*), in which the Constitutional Chamber declared the non-enforceability of the decision of the Inter American Court of Human Rights of August 5, 2008, Case: *Apitz Barbera y otros ("Corte Primera de lo Contencioso Administrativo") vs. Venezuela* Serie C, N° 182.

1906   See *Informe Anual de 2009*, paragraph 480, available at http://www.cidh.oas.org/annual-rep/2009eng/Chap.IV.f.eng.htm

1907   See Decision of August, 21 2003, in *Revista de Derecho Público*, n° 93-96, (Caracas: Editorial Jurídica Venezolana, 2003), 445 ff. See the comments in Claudia Nikken,'El caso "Barrio Adentro": La Corte Primera de lo Contencioso Administrativo ante la Sala Constitucional del Tribunal Supremo de Justicia o el avocamiento como medio de amparo de derechos e intereses colectivos y difusos,' *Revista de Derecho Público*, n° 93-96, (Caracas: Editorial Jurídica Venezolana, 2003), pp. 5 ff.

1908   The President of the Republic said: "*Váyanse con su decisión no sé para donde, la cumplirán ustedes en su casa si quieren ...*" (You can go with your decision, I don't know where; you will enforce it in your house if you want ...). See *El Universal*, Caracas, August 25, 2003 and *El Universal*, Caracas, August 28, 2003.

1909   See in *El Nacional*, Caracas November 5, 2004, p. A2.

1910   *See* Inter-American Court of Human Rights, case: *Apitz Barbera et al. (Corte Primera de lo Contencioso Administrativo) v. Venezuela,* Decision of August 5, 2008, available at www.corteidh.or.cr. *See also, El Universal,* Caracas, October 16, 2003; and *El Universal,* Caracas, September 22, 2003.

1911   Supreme Tribunal of Justice, Constitutional Chamber, Decision N° 1.939 of December 18, 2008 (Case: *Abogados Gustavo Álvarez Arias et al.*) (Exp. N° 08-1572), available at http://www.tsj.gov.ve/deci-siones/scon/Diciembre/1939-181208-2008-08-1572.html

405. In December 2009, another astonishing case was the detention of a criminal judge for having ordered, based on a previous recommendation of the UN Working Group on Arbitrary Detention, the release of an individual in order for him to face criminal trial while in freedom, as guaranteed in the Constitution. The same day of the decision, the President of the Republic publicly asked for the judge to be incarcerated asking to apply her a 30–year prison term, which is the maximum punishment in Venezuelan law for horrendous or grave crimes. The fact is that the judge remained for years in detention without trial. The UN Working Group described these facts as "a blow by President Hugo Chávez to the independence of judges and lawyers in the country," demanding "the immediate release of the judge," concluding that "reprisals for exercising their constitutionally guaranteed functions and creating a climate of fear among the judiciary and lawyers' profession, serve no purpose except to undermine the rule of law and obstruct justice."[1912]

406. The fact is that in Venezuela, no judge can adopt any decision that could affect the government policies, or the President's wishes, the state's interest, or public servants' will, without previous authorization from the same government.[1913] That is why the Inter-American Commission on Human Rights, after describing in its *2009 Annual Report* "how large numbers of judges have been removed, or their appointments voided, without the applicable administrative proceedings," noted "with concern that in some cases, judges were removed almost immediately after adopting judicial decisions in cases with a major political impact," concluding that "The lack of judicial independence and autonomy vis-à-vis political power is, in the Commission's opinion, one of the weakest points in Venezuelan democracy." [1914]

407. In this context of political subjection, the Constitutional Chamber of the Supreme Tribunal, since 2000, far from acting as the guardian of the Constitution, has been the main tool of the authoritarian government for the illegitimate mutation of the Constitution, by means of unconstitutional constitutional interpretations, [1915] not only regarding its own powers of judicial review, which have been enlarged, but also regarding substantive matters. The Supreme Tribunal has distorted the Constitution through illegitimate and fraudulent "constitutional mutations" in the sense of changing the meaning of its provisions without changing its wording. And all this,

---

1912   Case María Lourdes Afiuni Mora. See the text of the UN Working Group in http://www.unog.ch/unog/website/news_media.nsf/%28httpNewsByYear_en%29/93687E8429BD53 A1C125768E00529DB6?OpenDocument&cntxt=B35C3&cookielang=fr . In October 14, 2010, the same Working Group asked the venezuelan Government to subject the Judge to a trail ruled by the due process guaranties and in freedom." See *in El Universal*, October 14, 2010, available at http://www.eluniversal.com/2010/10/14/pol_ava_instancia-de-la-onu_14A4608051.shtml

1913   See Antonio Canova González, *La realidad del contencioso administrativo venezolano (Un llamado de atención frente a las desoladoras estadísticas de la Sala Político Administrativa en 2007 y primer semestre de 2008)*, (Caracas: FUNEDA, 2008) p. 14.

1914   See in ICHR, *Annual Report 2009*, paragraph 483, available at http://www.cidh.oas.org/-annualrep/2009eng/Chap.IV.f.eng.htm .

1915   See Allan R. Brewer-Carías, *Crónica sobre la "In" Justicia Constitucional. La Sala Constitucional y el autoritarismo en Venezuela*, (Caracas: Editorial Jurídica Venezolana. 2007)

of course, without any possibility of being controlled, [1916] so the eternal question arising from the uncontrolled power, – *Quis custodiet ipsos custodes* –, in Venezuela also remains unanswered.

408. On the other hand, regarding some fundamental rights essentials for a democracy to function, like the freedom of expression, contrary to the principle of progressiveness established in the Constitution, it has been the Supreme Tribunal of Justice the State organ in charge of limiting its scope. First, in 2000, it was the Political-Administrative Chamber of the Supreme Tribunal that ordered the media not to transmit certain information, eventually admitting limits to be imposed to the media, regardless of the general prohibition of censorship established in the Constitution.

The following year, in 2001, it was the Constitutional Chamber of the Supreme Tribunal, the one that distorted the Constitution when dismissing an *amparo* action filed against the President of the Republic by a citizen and a nongovernmental organization asking for the exercise of their right to response against the attacks made by the President in his weekly TV program. The Constitutional Chamber reduced the scope of freedom of information, eliminating the right to response and rectification regarding opinions in the media when they are expressed by the president in a regular televised program. In addition, the tribunal excluded journalists and all those persons that have a regular program in the radio or a newspaper column, from the right to rectification and response. [1917]

In addition, in 2003, the Constitutional Chamber dismissed an action of unconstitutionality filed against a few articles of the Criminal Code that limit the right to formulate criticism against public officials, considering that such provisions could not be deemed as limiting the freedom of expression, contradicting a well-established doctrine in the contrary ruled by the Inter-American Courts on Human Rights. The Constitutional Chamber also decided in contradiction with the constitutional prohibition of censorship, that through a statute it was possible to prevent the diffusion of information when it could be considered contrary to other provisions of the Constitution. [1918]

Regarding other cases in which the Judiciary has been used for political persecution, they are referred to the exercise of freedom of expression, concluding in the

---

1916   See Allan R. Brewer-Carías, *Quis Custodiet ipsos Custodes*: De la interpretación constitucional a la inconstitucionalidad de la interpretación, *VIII Congreso Nacional de Derecho Constitucional*, (Arequipa: Fondo Editorial Colegio de Abogados de Arequipa, 2005), 463-89; and Allan R. Brewer-Carías, *Crónica de la "In" Justicia constitucional: La Sala constitucional y el autoritarismo en Venezuela*, (Caracas: Editorial Jurídica Venezolana, 2007), 11-44 and 47-79.

1917   See Allan R. Brewer-Carías, 'La libertad de expresión del pensamiento y el derecho a la información y su violación por la Sala Constitucional del Tribunal Supremo de Justicia,' in Allan R. Brewer-Carías et al., 2001. *La libertad de expresión amenazada (Sentencia 1013), (*Caracas/San José: Instituto Interamericano de Derechos Humanos - Editorial Jurídica Venezolana, 2002), 17-57; and Jesús A. Davila Ortega, 'El derecho de la información y la libertad de expresión en Venezuela (Un estudio de la sentencia 1.013/2001 de la Sala Constitucional del Tribunal Supremo de Justicia),' *Revista de Derecho Constitucional* 5, (Caracas: Editorial Sherwood 2002), 305-25.

1918   See *Revista de Derecho Público*, 93–94, (Caracas: Editorial Jurídica Venezolana, 2003), 136 ff. and 164ff. See comments in Alberto Arteaga Sánchez et al., *Sentencia 1942 vs. Libertad de expresión*, (Caracas, 2004)

shutdown of TV stations that had a line of political opposition regarding the government and the persecution of their main shareholders. One leading case was the *Radio Caracas Televisión* case, referred to a TV station that, in 2007, was the most important television station of the country, critical of the administration of President Hugo Chavez. In that case, it was the Supreme Tribunal in 2007, the State organ that materialized the State intervention in order to terminate authorizations and licenses of the TV station, whose assets were confiscated and its equipment assigned to a state-owned enterprise through an illegitimate Supreme Tribunal decision. [1919] The case is the most vivid example of the illegitimate collusion or confabulation between a politically controlled Judiciary and an authoritarian government in order to reduce freedom of expression, and to confiscate private property. For such purpose, it was the Constitutional Chamber of the Supreme Tribunal of Justice and the Political Administrative Chamber of the same Tribunal that in May 2007, instead of protecting the citizens' right of freedom of expression, conspired as docile instruments controlled by the Executive, in order to kidnap and violate them. In this case, it was the highest level of the Judiciary that covered the governmental arbitrariness with a judicial veil, executing the shout down of the TV Station, reducing the freedom of expression in the country, and with total impunity, proceeded to confiscate private property in a way that neither the Executive nor the Legislator, could have done, because being forbidden in the Constitution (art. 115). In the case, it was the Supreme Tribunal, which violated the Constitution, with the aggravating circumstance that the conspirators knew that their actions could not be controlled. This case has also been recently submitted before the Inter American Court of Human Rights.

Other cases of political persecution, also related to freedom of expression are the cases against the principal shareholders of Globovisión, the other independent TV station that after the takeover of Radio Caracas Television, remained with a critic line of opinion regarding the government. They both were harassed by the Public Prosecutor Office and by the Judiciary; accused of different common crimes that they did not commit; they were detained without any serious base, their enterprises were occupied and their property confiscated. They both had to leave the country, without any possibility of obtaining Justice. Their cases have also been submitted before the Inter American Commission of Human Rights. [1920]

409. The Judiciary, particularly on criminal matters, has also been used as the government instrument to pervert Justice, distorting the facts in specific cases of political interest, converting innocent people into criminals, and liberating criminals of all suspicion. It was the unfortunate case of the mass killings committed by government agents and supporters as a consequence of the enforcement of the so-

---

1919   See the Constitutional Chamber Decision N° 957 (May 25, 2007), in *Revista de Derecho Público* 110, (Caracas, Editorial Jurídica Venezolana, 2007), 117 ff. See the comments in Allan R. Brewer-Carías,. El juez constitucional en Venezuela como instrumento para aniquilar la libertad de expresión plural y para confiscar la propiedad privada: El caso RCTV,' *Revista de Derecho Público*, N° 110, (Caracas: Editorial Jurídica Venezolana, 2007), 7-32.

1920   Case Globovisión (Guillermo Zuloaga and Nelson Mezerhane). See PRESS RELEASE. N° R119/10. SPECIAL RAPPORTEURSHIP EXPRESSES CONCERN REGARDING VENEZUELAN STATE INTERVENTION IN GLOBOVISIÓN, Dec. 8. 2010, available at http://www.oas.org/en/iachr/expression/showarticle.asp?artID=827&lID=1

called Plan Avila, a military order that encouraged the shooting of peoples participating in the biggest mass demonstration in Venezuelan history which on April 11, 2002, was asking for the resignation of the late President Chávez. The soothing provoked a general military disobedience by the high commanders, in a way witnessed by all the country in TV, which ended with the military removal of the President, although just for a few hours, until the same military reinstated him in office. Nonetheless, in order to change history, the shooting and mass killing were re-written, and those responsible that everybody saw in live in TV, because being government supporters were gratified as heroes, and the Police Officials trying to assure order in the demonstration, were blamed of crimes that they did not commit, and condemned of murder with the highest term of 30 years of prison.[1921]

§2. *The use of the Judiciary to facilitate the Concentration of Power and the Dismantling of Democracy*

410. The Constitutional Chamber of the Supreme Tribunal, on the other hand, has been one of the most important instruments used by the government in order to reinforce the concentration of powers, not only adopting decisions, at the request of the Government, through which the Constitution has been "mutated,"(see *supra* paragraph 404; *infra* Paragraphs 420, 433) that is, changed by means of interpretation made by the Constitutional Chamber of the Supreme Tribunal of Justice as Constitutional Jurisdiction,[1922] without a constitutional review procedure (see *supra* paragraphs 114 ff.); but through which the government has assume direct control of other branches of government, as happened in 2002 with the take-over of the Electoral Power, which since then has been completely controlled by the Executive.

1921   Cases *Simonovic and Forero*. A former Chief Justice of the Criminal Chamber of the Supreme Tribunal of Justice, general Eladio Aponte Aponte, confessed last year 2012 in a TV Program (SolTV)in Miami, when answering about if there were "political persons in prison in Venezuela, saying "Yes, there are people regarding which there is an order not to let them free," referring particularly to "the Police Officers," mentioning Officer Simonovic. The same former Justice, answering a question about *"Who gives the order,"* simply said: "The order comes from the President's Office downwards," adding that "we must have no doubts, in Venezuela there are no sewing point if it is not approved by the President." He finally said, answering a question if he *"received the order not to let free Simonovis"* he explained that: "the position of the Criminal Chamber" was "To validate all that arrived already done; that is, in a few words, to accept that these gentlemen could not be freed." To hear this answers given by one who until recently was the highest Justice in the Venezuelan Criminal System, produce no other than indignation, because it was him, as Chief Criminal Justice, the one in charge of manipulating justice, in the way he confessed; condemning the Police Officers to 30 years in prison, just because obeying orders from the Executive. See the text of the statement on, in *El Universal*, Caracas 18-4-2012, available at: http://www.eluniversal.com/nacional-y-politica/120418/historias-secretas-de-un-juez-en-venezuela

1922   See Allan R. Brewer-Carías, "El juez constitucional al servicio del autoritarismo y la ilegítima mutación de la Constitución: el caso de la Sala Constitucional del Tribunal Supremo de Justicia de Venezuela (1999-2009)", in *Revista de Administración Pública*, N° 180, Madrid 2009, pp. 383-418; "La fraudulenta mutación de la Constitución en Venezuela, o de cómo el juez constitucional usurpa el poder constituyente originario,", in *Anuario de Derecho Público*, N° 2 Caracas, Centro de Estudios de Derecho Público de la Universidad Monteávila, 2009), 23-65; José Vicente Haro, "La mutación de la Constitución 'Bolivariana'," in Gonzalo Pérez Salazar and Luis Petit Guerra, *Los retos del derecho procesal constitucional en Latinoamérica, I Congreso Internacional de Derecho Procesal Constitucional, 19 y 20 Octubre de 2011*, Vol I, (Caracas, Universidad Monteávila Funeda, 2011), 93-141.

This began in 2002 after the Organic Law of the Electoral Power[1923] was sanctioned and the National Assembly was due to elect, as electoral body, the new members of the National Electoral Council. Because the representatives supporting the government did not have the qualified majority to approve such election by themselves, and did not reached agreements on the matter with the opposition, when the National Assembly failed to elect the members of the National Electoral Council, that task was assumed, without any constitutional power, by the Constitutional Chamber of the Supreme Tribunal itself. Deciding an action that was filed against what was considered as an unconstitutional legislative omission, the Chamber instead of urging the Assembly to comply with its constitutional duty, directly elected the members of the Electoral Council, usurping the Assembly's functions as electoral body, but without complying with the conditions established in the Constitution for such election. [1924] With this decision, the Chamber assured the government's complete control of the Council, kidnapping the citizen's rights to political participation, and allowing the official governmental party to manipulate the electoral results. The same was repeated in December 2014, when the Constitutional Chamber again usurped the roll of the National Assembly as electoral body, and appointed new members of the Electoral Council all related to the official political party. [1925]

Consequently, the elections held in Venezuela during the past years have been organized by a politically dependent branch of government, without any guarantee of independence or impartiality.

411. The Constitutional Chamber of the Supreme Tribunal has also been the instrument in order to erode the democratic principle, limiting the right to be elected, imposing non elected officials as Head of State, or revoking the popular mandate of elected officials without having competency or jurisdiction. As aforementioned (see *supra*, paragraoh 91 ff.), between January and March 2013, the Constitutional Chamber of the Supreme Tribunal, openly violated the democratic principle by imposing a non elected official as head of State, during the illness of former President Chávez and after his death, in two decisions adopted, in addition, without proving anything. The decisions were issued after deciding interpretations recourses of the Constitution: The first decision, N° 2 of January 9, 2013, was issued to resolve the legal situation of the non attendance by the President elected to his Inauguration for the presidential term 2013-2019, refusing the Constitutional Chamber to consider

---

1923   See *Gaceta Oficial* N° 37.573 of November 19, 2002

1924   See Decision N° 2073 of August 4, 2003, Case: *Hermánn Escarrá Malaver y oros)*, and Decision N° 2341 of August 25, 2003, Case: *Hemann Escarrá y otros*. See in Allan R. Brewer-Carías, 2003/2004. El secuestro del poder electoral y la conficación del derecho a la participación política mediante el referendo revocatorio presidencial: Venezuela 2000-2004, *Stvdi Vrbinati, Rivista tgrimestrale di Scienze Giuridiche, Politiche ed Economiche*, Año LXXI –(Urbino: Università degli Studi di Urbino, 2003), 379-436

1925   Decision N° 1864 of December 22, 2014, available at: http://historico.tsj.gov.ve/decisiones/scon/diciembre/173494-1864-221214-2014-14-1341.HTML; and decision N° 1865 of December 26, 2014, available at: http://historico.tsj.gov.ve/decisiones/scon/diciembre/173497-1865-261214-2014-14-1343.HTML. See the comments in Allan R. Brewer-Carías, 'El golpe de Estado dado en diciembre de 2014, con la inconstitucional designación de las altas autoridades del Poder Público," *Revista de Derecho Público,* 40 (Caracas, Editorial Jurídica Venezolana, 2014).

that the situation was one of absolute absence of the elected President, and instead constructing, without proving anything on the heath condition of the elected and ill President, a supposed "administrative continuity" of Chávez, affirming that even been absent of the country (he was said to be in an Hospital in La Habana), he was supposedly effectively in charge of the Presidency, so his nonelected Vice President (N. Maduro) was to be in charge of the Presidency. [1926] The second decision, N° 141, of March 8, 2013, was issued after the announcement of the death of President Chávez, but without proving such fact or when it did effectively occurred, in order to assure that the Vice President (N. Maduro), already imposed as President in charge by the same Supreme Tribunal, was to continue in charge of the Presidency; and additionally allowing him, contrary to the text of the Constitution, to be candidate to the same position in the subsequent election, without leaving the post.[1927]

412. In other decisions, also contrary to the democratic principle, the Constitutional Chamber of the Supreme Tribunal revoked the popular mandate of two mayors, a decision that according to the Constitution only can be adopted by the people that elected the officials by means of a referendum (art. 74). The Supreme Tribunal, ignoring such principle and provision, without having constitutional competency and usurping the jurisdiction of the criminal courts that are the only competent to impose criminal sanctions to officials for not obeying judicial decisions, issued decision N° 138 of March 17, 2014, condemning the Mayors by considering that they had committed a crime (not to obey a preliminary injunction), and imprisoning them, without guarantying a due process of law. [1928] The common trend in this case was that both Mayors were from the opposition to the government

413. In another case, the Constitutional Chamber of the Supreme Tribunal also revoked the popular mandate of a representative to the National Assembly, which also can only be revoked by the people through a referendum, issuing decision N° 207 of March 31, 2014, in a case that the Tribunal had already concluded because the action was declared inadmissible, proceeding the Tribunal to act ex officio, and interpret an article of the Constitution (Article 93), that prevent representatives to accept another public positions without losing their elected one. The initial petition that was declared inadmissible was a requested for the Tribunal to condemn the *the facto* actions of the President of the National Assembly to strip out the elected condition of one representative; being the result of the case, once declared the petition

---

1926   See the text of the decision in http://www.tsj.gov.ve/decisiones/scon/Enero/02-9113-2013-12-1358.html

1927   See the text of the decision in http://www.tsj.gov.ve.decisioes/scon/Marzo/141-9313-2013-13-0196.html

1928   Decision N° 138 of March 17, available at http://www.tsj.gov.ve/decisiones/scon/marzo/162025-138-17314-2014-14-0205.HTML 2014; and Decision N° 245 of April, 9, 2014, available at: http://www.tsj.gov.ve/decisiones/scon/abril/162860-245-9414-2014-14-0205.HTML Véase también en *Gaceta Oficial* N° 40.391 de 10 de abril de 2014. See the comments in Allan R. Brewer-Carías, 'La ilegítima e inconstitucional revocación del mandato popular de alcaldes por la Sala Constitucional del Tribunal Supremo, usurpando competencias de la jurisdicción penal, mediante un procedimiento "sumario" de condena y encarcelamiento (El caso de los Alcaldes Vicencio Scarano Spisso y Daniel Ceballo),' *Revista de Derecho Público,* 138 (Caracas, Editorial Jurídica Venezolana, 2014), 176-210

inadmissible, for the Tribunal, to *ex officio* decide to revoke the popular mandate to the representative that was supposed to be protected by the Tribunal. The reason for such decision was that the representative, had talked as such representative, before the Permanent Council of the Organization of American States, in a session devoted to analyze the political situation of Venezuela, from the site of the representative of Panama that had invited her to do so. [1929]

414. Finally, in another decision, the Supreme Tribunal, also in violation of the democratic principle, accepted that the right of a citizen to be elected, which is a constitutional right, could be limited by an administrative body as the General Audit Office, when issuing decisions imposing public officials the sanction of disqualifying them to run for elected positions. In decision N° 1265 of August 5, 2008, [1930] the Supreme Tribunal refused to declare that such disqualification for the exercise of a political right was contrary to the American Convention of Human Rights, that in Venezuela had constitutional hierarchy (Article 23). The lack of justice in Venezuela, lead the interested person, a former Mayor, to filed a petition before the Inter American Court of Human Right, seeking the protection of his political right, the result being a decision of such Court of September 1ˢᵗ, 2011 (case *López Mendoza vs. Venezuela*), condemning the Venezuelan State for the violation of the Convention. Nonetheless, the response of the State was to fie before the Supreme Tribunal of Justice, at the initiative of the Attorney General, an action for "judicial review" of the Inter American Court decision, which was astonishingly admitted by the Constitutional Chamber, which through decision N° 1547 of October 17, 2011, [1931] declared the Inter American Court of Human Rights as "non enforceable" in Venezuela, recommending the Government to denounce the Convention,. This eventually happened in 2012.

415. Unfortunately, the political control over the Supreme Tribunal of Justice that can be appreciated in these examples, has permeated to all the judiciary, due mainly to the already mentioned fact that in Venezuela, it is the Supreme Tribunal the one in charge of the government and administration of the Judiciary. This has affected gravely the autonomy and independence of judges at all levels of the Judiciary, which has been aggravated by the fact that during the past years the Venezuelan Judiciary has been composed primarily of temporary and provisional judges, without career or stability, appointed without the public competition process of selection established in the Constitution, and dismissed without due process of law, for

---

1929   See Decision N° 207 de 31 de marzo de 2014, available at en http://www.tsj.gov.ve/decisiones/scon/marzo/162546-207-31314-2014-14-0286.HTML Also published in *Official Gazette* N° 40385 of April 2, 2014. See the comments in Allan R. Brewer-Carías, "La revocación del mandato popular de una diputada a la Asamblea Nacional por la Sala Constitucional del Tribunal Supremo de oficio, sin juicio ni proceso alguno (El caso de la Diputada María Corina Machado)," *Revista de Derecho Público,* 137 (Caracas, Editorial Jurídica Venezolana, 2014), 165- 189

1930   See the text of the decision in http://www.tsj.gov.ve:80/decisiones/scon/Agosto/1265-050808-05-1853.htm

1931   See the text of the decision in http://www.tsj.gov.ve/decisiones/scon/Octubre/1547-171011-2011-11-1130.htmll

political reasons.[1932] This reality amounts to political control of the Judiciary, as demonstrated by the dismissal of judges who have adopted decisions contrary to the policies of the governing political authorities.

PART VIII. OTHER BRANCHES OF GOVERNMENT

416. Another innovation in the Constitution of 1999 (see *supra* paragraph 49) was to formally declare that the distribution of the Powers of the State, at the national level, that is the National Branches of government, are not only between the National Legislative Power, the National Executive Power, and the Judicial Power, but also between two new additional branches: the Citizen Power and the Electoral Power (Article 136).[1933]

Chapter 1. The Citizen Power

417. The Citizen Power is exercised by three traditional constitutional organs of the State: two established in the Constitutions since the 1940s, the Office of the Comptroller General of the Republic (General Audit Office) and the Office of the Public Prosecutor; and another one created by the 1999 Constitution, the Office of the Peoples' Defender, following the general trend of similar institutions existing in many Latin American countries for the purpose of protecting human rights.[1934]

The Citizen Power, as a branch of government, is to be independent, and its organs are conferred functional, financial and administrative autonomy, having a variable assignation within the annual budget (Article 273).

§1. The Republican Moral Council

418. According to Article 273 of the Constitution, the Head Officials of the three organs of the Citizen Power, sitting together, conform the Republican Moral Council (Article 274), which has the following attributions: to prevent, investigate and sanction facts against the public ethics or the administrative morals; to seek for the

---

1932   See Inter-American Commission on Human Rights, *Report on the Situation of Human Rights in Venezuela*, OEA/Ser.L/V/II.118, doc. 4 rev. 2, December 29, 2003, par. 174, *available at* http://www.cidh.oas.org/countryrep/Venezuela2003eng/toc.htm.

1933   See Roxana Orihuela Gonzatti, 'El nuevo Poder Ciudadano', in *El Derecho Público a comienzos del siglo XXI. Estudios homenaje al Profesor Allan R. Brewer-Carías,* vol. I (Madrid: Instituto de Derecho Público, UCV, Civitas Ediciones, 2003), 933–980; María A. Correa de Baumeister, 'El Poder Ciudadano y el Poder Electoral en la Constitución de 1999', in *El Derecho Público a comienzos del siglo XXI. Estudios homenaje al Profesor Allan R. Brewer-Carías,* vol. I (Madrid: Instituto de Derecho Público, UCV, Civitas Ediciones, 2003), 982–995; José L. Morantes Mago, 'El Poder Ciudadano y sus órganos en la Constitución de 1999', in *Revista de Control Fiscal,* N° 142 (enero-abril) (Caracas: Contraloría General de la República, 2000), 15–51; Celia Poleo de Ortega, 'El Poder Ciudadano en la Constitución venezolana de 1999', in *Revista de Control Fiscal,* N° 143 (mayo-agosto) (Caracas: Contraloría General de la República, 2000), 15–46.

1934   Organic Law on the Citizen Power, *Gaceta Oficial* N° 37.310 of 25 Oct. 2001. See Allan R. Brewer-Carías et al., *Leyes Orgánicas del poder ciudadano (Ley Orgánica del Poder Ciudadano, Ley Orgánica de la Defensoría del Pueblo, Ley Orgánica del Ministerio Público, Ley Orgánica de la Contraloría General de la República)* (Caracas: Editorial Jurídica Venezolana, 2005).

maintenance of good business practices by the State, and assure that the use of public property is made in adherence to legality, and to seek for the respect of the principle of legality in any administrative activity of the State. The Council is also empowered to promote education as a means to develop citizenship, solidarity, liberty, democracy, social responsibility and work (Article 274).

419. The members of the Republican Moral Council are required to inform the authorities and officials of the Public Administration of any breaches in the fulfilment of their legal duties. In a case of a continuous failure to conform to the Moral Council's admonition, the President of the Republican Moral Council is to send information to the organ or government agency in which the offending official is assigned or employed, so that those corrective measures may be taken by that entity (Article 275).

In conformity with Article 278, the Moral Republican Council must also promote pedagogical activities directed towards developing knowledge and study of the Constitution, love of one's country, civic and democratic virtues, the most important values of the Republic, and the observance and respect for human rights.

§2. *Election of the Head of the Organs of the Citizen Power*

420. The election of the Comptroller General of the Republic, the Prosecutor General, and the Peoples' Defender is assigned to the National Assembly, acting as electoral body for such indirect popular election, which nonetheless, has no discretion for the elections, because they can only be made from candidates nominated by a 'Committee for Evaluation of Nominations to the Citizen Power'. This Committee is to be convened by the Republican Moral Council, and according to the Constitution must be exclusively composed by 'representatives from different sectors of society' (Article 279).

For the purpose of making the nominations, the Committee must initiate and lead a public process to select three names for each of the organs of the Citizen Power, to be proposed to the National Assembly. The Assembly, through a favourable vote of at least two-thirds of its members, must then elect one of each triad of nominees within a period of no more than thirty consecutive days. If this period elapses with no agreement reached by the Assembly, the Electoral Power will submit the triads to a popular vote for selection (Article 279).

Article 279 of the Constitution states, nonetheless, that in a case when the Committee for Evaluation of Nominations has not been convened, the National Assembly must proceed to elect the heads of the organs of the Citizen Power, but of course, as electoral body by the same qualified majority. Nonetheless, in Dcember 2014, this provision was "mutated" by the Constitutional Chamber of the Supreme Tribunal, which interpreted that the National Assembly in such cases could elect the high officials by simple majority of votes of the representatives present in the corresponding session, as a legislative body, ignoring its character in this case, of indirect electoral body.[1935]

1935   Decision N° 1864 of December 22, 2014, available at: http://historico.tsj.gov.ve/decisiones/scon/diciembre/173494-1864-221214-2014-14-1341.HTML   available   at:

421. Regarding the Nominating Committee for the proposal of candidates for the election of the head of the organs of the Citizen Power, the same as occurred regarding the Judicial Nominating Committee in the case of the Magistrates of the Supreme Tribunal (see *supra* paragraph 224) has happened, in the sense that its composition has been distorted by the 2001 Organic Law of the Citizen Power, and contrary to the participatory sense of the Constitution, has been composed with a majority of representatives of the National Assembly and not exclusively by representatives of the various sectors of society, as provided in the Constitution. In this case, the Committee has also resulted in just a parliamentary commission with some additional members designated by the same Assembly from non-governmental entities.[1936]

422. However, as happens with all the non-directed elected heads of the branches of government, the Constitution states that following a declaration of the Supreme Tribunal of Justice, members of the Citizen Power may be removed from their positions by the National Assembly in cases of grave faults (Article 279). In the 2007 rejected constitutional reform, it was proposed to allow the National Assembly to approve such dismissals with only a majority of votes.

§3. *The Peoples' Defender*

423. The Office of the Peoples' Defender is in charge of promoting, defending and maintaining human rights and guarantees declared in the Constitution and international treaties, as well as over 'legitimate collective and diffuse interests of Citizens' (Article 280).[1937] The activities of the Office of the Peoples' Defence are to be executed in accordance with the principles of cost-free service, public accessibility, celerity, informality andself initiative (Article 283).[1938]

---

http://historico.tsj.gov.ve/decisiones/scon/diciembre/173497-1865-261214-2014-14-1343.HTML. See the comments in Allan R. Brewer-Carías, 'El golpe de Estado dado en diciembre de 2014, con la inconstitucional designación de las altas autoridades del Poder Público," *Revista de Derecho Público,* 40 (Caracas, Editorial Jurídica Venezolana, 2014).

1936   See Allan R. Brewer-Carías, 'Sobre el nombramiento irregular por la Asamblea Nacional de los titulares de los órganos del poder ciudadano en 2007', in Revista *de Derecho Público*, N° 113 (Caracas: Editorial Jurídica Venezolana, 2008), 85–88.

1937   See José L. Villegas Moreno, 'Los intereses difusos y colectivos en la Constitución de 1999', in *Revista de Derecho Constitucional*, N° 2 (enero-junio) (Caracas: Editorial Sherwood, 2000), 253–269; Ana E. Araujo García, 'El principio de la tutela judicial efectiva y los intereses colectivos y difusos', in *El Derecho Público a comienzos del siglo XXI. Estudios homenaje al Profesor Allan R. Brewer-Carías*, vol. III (Madrid: Editorial Thompson Civitas, 2003), 2703–2717, and in *Revista de derecho del Tribunal Supremo de Justicia*, N° 4 (Caracas, 2002), 1 a 29; Mariolga Quintero Tirado, 'Aspectos de una tutela judicial ambiental efectiva', in *Nuevos estudios de derecho procesal, Libro Homenaje a José Andrés Fuenmayor*, vol. II, no. 8 (Caracas: Tribunal Supremo de Justicia, Colección Libros Homenaje, 2002), 189 a 236; Flor M. Ávila Hernández, 'La tutela de los intereses colectivos y difusos en la Constitución venezolana de 1999', in *El Derecho Público a comienzos del siglo XXI. Estudios homenaje al Profesor Allan R. Brewer-Carías*, vol. III, *supra*, 2719–2742.

1938   See Alberto Baumeister Toledo, 'Algunos aspectos de derecho comparado de especial consideración sobre la figura del defensor del pueblo en la Constitución de 1999', in *Tendencias Actuales del Derecho Constitucional. Homenaje a Jesús María Casal Montbrun*, ed. Jesús María Casal, Alfredo Arismendi y Carlos Luis Carrillo Artiles (Coord.), vol. II (Caracas: Universidad Central de Venezuela/Universidad Católica Andrés Bello, 2008), 53–64; Gustavo Briceño Vivas, 'La protección de los derechos humanos y su inserción en la Constitución de 1999', in *Estudios de Derecho Público*, ed.

424. The Head of the Office is the People's Defender, who is designated by the National Assembly for a term of seven years (Article 280), and cannot be re-elected. The elected must be Venezuelan by birth without any other nationality (Articles 41, 280), with manifest and demonstrated skill in human rights matters. Its functions have been regulated in the 2004 Organic Law on the Peoples' Defender.[1939]

425. Within its attributions, the Peoples' Defender has powers to watch over the effective guarantee of human rights, investigating ex officio or at party request, the complaints filed before his office; to seek for the good functioning of public services, and protect the people's rights and legitimate interest, collective or diffuse, against arbitrariness, abuse of power or errors in their rendering, filing the necessary actions, if needed, in order to ask the State to pay the citizens damages caused by the functioning of public services; to fill actions of unconstitutionality, of *amparo*, of habeas corpus, of habeas data regarding the aforementioned attributions; to request the Public Prosecutor to file actions against public officials responsible for the violations of human rights; to request from the Republican Moral Council to adopt the needed measures regarding public officials responsible for the violations of human rights; and to watch over the rights of the indigenous peoples and exercise the necessary actions for their guarantee and effective protection (Article 281).

526. The Peoples' Defender, according to Article 282 of the Constitution, is immune in the exercise of its functions, and cannot be persecuted, detained or prosecuted because of actions taken in the exercise of its functions. The Supreme Tribunal of Justice is in charge of deciding over the prosecution of the Peoples' Defender.

§4. *The Prosecutor General of the Republic*

427. The Public Prosecutor is under the guidance of the Prosecutor General of the Republic (Article 284), who is elected for a term of six years by the National Assembly and must comply with the same conditions established in order to be elected Magistrate of the Supreme Tribunal (see *supra* paragraph 391). Its functions have been regulated in the 2007 Organic Law on the Public Prosecutor.[1940]

428. Within the attributions of the Prosecutor General, the following must be mentioned: to guarantee in the judicial process the respect of human rights and guarantees; to guarantee celerity and good development of justice and the respect of due process of law rules; to order and direct criminal investigations for crimes committed, in order to register the facts, circumstances and authors; to file in the name of the State the corresponding criminal actions and persecutions; and to file the necessary actions to make effective the civil, labour, military, criminal, administrative or disciplinary liability of public officials, because of the exercise of their functions (Article 285).

Román Duque Corredor y Jesús María Casal (Coords), vol. II (Caracas: Universidad Católica Andrés Bello, 2004), 51–86; Gustavo Briceño Vivas, 'El Defensor del Pueblo en la nueva Constitución. Análisis y crítica', in *Revista de Derecho Público*, N° 82 (Caracas: Editorial Jurídica Venezolana, 2000), 57–69; Jesús M. Casal H., 'La Defensoría del Pueblo en Venezuela', in *Revista de Derecho Constitucional*, N° 3 (julio-diciembre) (Caracas: Editorial Sherwood, 2000), 345–358.

1939   Organic Law on the Public Defendant Office, *Gaceta Oficial* N° 37.995 of 5 Aug. 2004.

1940   *Gaceta Oficial* n° 38.647 of 19 Mar. 2007.

§5. *The Comptroller General of the Republic*

429. The Office of the Comptroller General of the Republic (Audit Office) is the auditing State organ responsible for the control, oversight and investigation of public revenue and disbursements, national public assets and property, and all transactions referred to them. The Comptroller General Office has functional, administrative and organizational autonomy, and is oriented towards the inspection of entities and organs subjected to control (Article 287).[1941]

The Office of the Comptroller General of the Republic is under the direction, and is the responsibility of the Comptroller General of the Republic, who is also elected by the National Assembly for a term of seven years, and must be Venezuelan by birth without any other nationality (Articles 43, 288). Its functions have been regulated in the 2001 Organic Law on the Office of the Comptroller General of the Republic.[1942]

430. Within the attributions of the Comptroller General Office, are the following: to exercise control, to watch and to supervise public revenues, expenses and property, as well as the operation related with them; to control public debt; to inspect and supervise the public sector entities subjected to control, to execute the inspections, and to impose the corresponding administrative sanctions in cases of corruption; to request the Public Prosecutor to initiate the corresponding judicial actions regarding the faults and crimes against the public assets; to control public management and to evaluate the accomplishment of the public policies and decisions (Article 289); and to direct the national system of fiscal control (Article 290).

Chapter 2. The Electoral Power

431. Another innovation of the 1999 Constitution was the creation of the Electoral Power as another branch of government, by giving constitutional hierarchy to the organ assigned to oversight and control over electoral matters.[1943] For such purpose, Article 292 of the Constitution provides that the Electoral Power will be exercised by the National Electoral Council, as the governing entity of this branch of government, as well as by the National Electoral Board, the Commission for Civil and Electoral Registry, and the Commission for Political Participation and Financing. Its functions have been regulated in the 2002 Organic Law on the Electoral Power.[1944]

432. The functions of the Electoral Power under Article 293, in addition to the organization, administration, direction and oversight of all activities concerning

---

1941 See José Ignacio, Hernández G., 'La Contraloría General de la República', in *Revista de Derecho Público,* N° 83 (julio-septiembre) (Caracas: Editorial Jurídica Venezolana, 2000), 21–38.

1942 *Gaceta Oficial* N° 37.347 of 17 Dec. 2001.

1943 See María A. Correa de Baumeister, 'El Poder Ciudadano y el Poder Electoral en la Constitución de 1999', in *El Derecho Público a comienzos del siglo XXI. Estudios homenaje al Profesor Allan R. Brewer-Carías,* vol. I (Madrid: Instituto de Derecho Público, UCV, Civitas Ediciones, 2003), 982–995; Rafael Méndez García, 'Estudio del Poder Electoral (controles)', in *Bases y principios del sistema constitucional venezolano (Ponencias del VII Congreso Venezolano de Derecho Constitucional realizado en San Cristóbal del 21 al 23 de Noviembre de 2001),* vol. II, 355–383; Alfonso Rivas Quintero, *Derecho Constitucional* (Valencia-Venezuela: Paredes Editores, 2002), 517 et seq.

1944 *Gaceta Oficial* N° 37.573 of 19 Nov. 2002.

elections for State public offices, include the power to organize labour union elections, as well as the elections held in professional guilds and associations, and organizations with political purposes. In the same way, the Electoral Power may organize elections for civil society organizations that so request it, or, upon the order of the Electoral Chamber of the Supreme Tribunal of Justice. This constitutes an inconvenient interference by organizations of the State into intermediary organizations of society.

433. Article 296 establishes that the National Electoral Council is to be composed of five persons with no ties to political organizations, elected by the National Assembly for a seven year term, by a vote of two-thirds of its members. Three of them must be nominated by civil society, one by Law and Political Science Divisions of national universities, and one by the Citizen Power. The three members nominated by civil society are to have six alternates sequentially ordered, and each member designated by the Universities and Citizen Power are to have two alternates respectively.

For the purpose of nominating before the Assembly the candidates to the Electoral Council, Article 295 of the Constitution also creates, in this case a Committee for Electoral Nominations that must also be constituted of representatives from different sectors of society. Also in this case, as happened with the Judicial Nominating Committee and with the Nominating Committee for the Members of the Citizen Power, the Committee for Electoral Nominations has been distorted in the Organic Law of the Electoral Power, regulating it without compliance with the constitutional provision tending to guarantee political participation of civil society, converting the Committee into a parliamentary commission, with some additional members appointed by the same Assembly.

434. In any case, in 2002, after the sanctioning of the Organic Law of the Electoral Power, the National Assembly was due to elect the members of the National Electoral Council, but failed in such duty basically because the representatives supporting the government could not achieve the majority required and did not want to agree on the matter with the opposition. The consequence of this omission was that the Constitutional Chamber of the Supreme Tribunal of Justice, when deciding an action filed against such unconstitutional legislative omission, directly elected the Members of the Electoral Council, substituting the National Assembly in its duty and usurping its functions as indirect electoral body, without complying with the conditions established in the Constitution. Since then the complete control by the government of such an important State organ has been assured,[1945]being such control

---

1945   See decisions N° 2073 of 4 Aug. 2003 (Caso: *Hermánn Escarrá Malaver y oros*) and N° 2341 of 25 Aug. 2003 (Caso: *Hermánn Escarrá M. y otros*) in Allan R. Brewer-Carías, *La Sala Constitucional versus el Estado Democrático de Derecho. El secuestro del poder electoral y de la Sala Electoral del Tribunal Supremo y la confiscación del derecho a la participación política* (Caracas: Los Libros de El Nacional, Colección Ares, 2004), 172; 'El secuestro del Poder Electoral y la confiscación del derecho a la participación política mediante el referendo revocatorio presidencial: Venezuela 2000-2004', in *Boletín Mexicano de Derecho Comparado*, N° 112 (México: Instituto de Investigaciones Jurídicas, Universidad Nacional Autónoma de México, enero-abril 2005 1) 1–73, and in Rafael Chavero G. et al., *La Guerra de las Salas del TSJ frente al Referéndum Revocatorio* (Caracas: Editorial Aequitas, 2004), C.A., 13–58.

reinforced in December 2014, by the election of the new members of the Electoral Council, again, by the Constitutional Chamber of the Supreme Tribunal, usurping the indirect electoral character of the National Assembly for such purpose. [1946]

435. Finally, also in this case, the Members of the National Electoral Council can be removed from office by the National Assembly following a declaration by the Supreme Tribunal of Justice (Article 296). In the 2007 rejected constitutional reform, it was also proposed to allow the National Assembly to approve such dismissals with only a majority of votes.

PART IX. THE CONSTITUTIONAL SYSTEM OF HUMAN RIGHTS AND GUARANTEES

436. After a long tradition on matters of human rights,[1947] the Venezuelan 1999 Constitution, as in all recent Latin American Constitutions, introduced notable innovations not only by expanding the list of constitutional rights, adding to the more traditional civil and political rights, the social, economic (see *infra* 505 et seq.), cultural, environmental and indigenous peoples' rights as fundamental ones, but also by establishing general principles to assure the guarantee of all such rights.[1948] The Constitution also provides for constitutional duties.

[1946]   N° 1865 of December 26, 2014, available at: http://historico.tsj.gov.ve/decisiones/scon/diciembre/173497-1865-261214-2014-14-1343.HTML. See the comments in Allan R. Brewer-Carías, 'El golpe de Estado dado en diciembre de 2014, con la inconstitucional designación de las altas autoridades del Poder Público," *Revista de Derecho Público,* 40 (Caracas, Editorial Jurídica Venezolana, 2014).

[1947]   Which was initiated in 1811, with the 'Declaration of the Rights of the People' approved by the general Congress of the Independent provinces. See Allan R. Brewer-Carías, *Los Derechos Humanos en Venezuela: Casi 200 Años de Historia,* N° 38 (Caracas: Academia de Ciencias Políticas y Sociales, Serie Estudios, 1990); *Las Declaraciones de Derechos del Pueblo y del Hombre de 1811 (Bicentenario de la Declaración de 'Derechos del Pueblo' de 1° de julio de 1811 y de la 'Declaración de Derechos del Hombre' contenida en la Constitución Federal de los Estados de Venezuela de 21 de diciembre de 1811)* (Caracas: Academia de Ciencias Políticas y Sociales, 2011).

[1948]   See Jesús María Casal H., *Los derechos fundamentales y sus restricciones* (Caracas: Legis, 2010); Josefina Calcaño de Temeltas, 'Notas sobre la constitucionalización de los Derechos Fundamentales en Venezuela', in *El Derecho Público a comienzos del siglo XXI. Estudios homenaje al Profesor Allan R. Brewer-Carías,* vol. I (Madrid: Civitas Ediciones, 2003), 2489–2535; Rafael Ortiz-Ortiz, 'Los Derechos Humanos en la República Bolivariana de Venezuela. Apreciaciones generales y principios orientadores de su ejercicio', in *Revista de la Facultad de Derecho de la Universidad de Carabobo,* N° 1 (Valencia, 2002), 339–369; Agustina Y. Martínez, 'Los Derechos Humanos en la Constitución Venezolana: consenso y disenso', in *Estudios de Derecho Público: Libro Homenaje a Humberto J. La Roche Rincón,* vol. I (Caracas: Tribunal Supremo de Justicia, 2001), 549–572; Élida Aponte Sánchez, 'Los Derechos Humanos: fundamentación, naturaleza y universalidad', in *Estudios de Derecho Público: Libro Homenaje a Humberto J. La Roche Rincón,* vol. I (Caracas: Tribunal Supremo de Justicia, 2001), 85–108; Luis A. Herrera Orellana, 'Sobre el concepto y fundamento de los derechos humanos', en *Revista de Derecho,* N° 12 (Caracas: Tribunal Supremo de Justicia, 2004), 31–58.

Chapter 1. General Principles Regarding Human Rights and Constitutional Guaranties

§1. The Basic Principles Regarding Human Rights

437. Among the innovations of the Constitution on matters of human rights, it is important to highlight the inclusion in the constitutional text of express provisions regarding the principle of progressive interpretation of the constitutional rights; the open clause of rights and freedoms; the constitutional hierarchy given to international treaties on human rights; the principle of personal liberty and the principle of equality and non-discrimination.

I.   Principle of Progressive Interpretation of Constitutional Rights

438. The first of the articles of the 1999 Constitution contained in the title devoted to 'Constitutional Duties, Rights and Guarantees', which is Article 19, proclaims as a duty of the State to 'guarantee to every individual, in accordance with the progressiveness principle, and without discrimination of any kind, the not renounceable, indivisible and interdependent enjoyment and exercise of human rights. Their respect and guarantee are obligatory for the organs of Public Power, in accordance with the Constitution, the human rights treaties signed and ratified by the Republic and any laws developing the same'.

This principle of progressiveness means that no interpretation of statutes related to human rights can be admitted if the result of the interpretation is to diminish the effective enjoyment, exercise or guarantee of constitutional rights (see *supra* paragraph 68); and also that in cases involving various provisions, the one that should prevail is the one that contains the more favourable regulation. This principle of progressiveness has also been called as the *pro homines* principle of interpretation, which implies that in resolving a case, 'the courts must always prefer the provisions that are in favour of man (*pro homine*)'.[1949]

The principle also implies that if a constitutional right is regulated with different contexts in the Constitution and in international treaties, then the most favourable provision must prevail and be applicable to the interested party.[1950]

II.   The Declarative Nature of the Constitutional Declarations of Rights and Freedoms and the Open Constitutional Clauses

439. The second general principle that must be highlighted is the express provision in the Constitution that human rights protected and guaranteed are not limited to those listed or enumerated in its text, and in the international instruments on

---

1949   See Pedro Nikken, *La protección internacional de los derechos humanos: su desarrollo progresivo* (Madrid, 1987).

1950   See for instance regarding the protection of rights of a pregnant public employee not to be unjustifiably dismissed of her job during pregnancy, the former Supreme Court of Justice of Venezuela on 3 Dec. 1990, in *Revista de Derecho Público*, N° 45 (Caracas: Editorial Jurídica venezolana, 1991), 84–85 and in *Revista de Derecho Público*, N° 97–98 (Caracas: Editorial Jurídica Venezolana, 1996), 170.

human rights, but also includes other rights that are 'inherent' to human being (persons) not expressly mentioned in them.[1951]

This principle, which was contained in Article 50 of the 1961 Constitution, allowed the incorporation in it, by means of judicial decisions, of many rights non-enumerated in the Constitution, assigning them constitutional rank. This clause has also been incorporated and broadened in Article 22 of the 1999 Constitution.

440. These rights inherent to human persons, for instance, have been defined by the former Supreme Court of Justice of Venezuela in 1991, as: 'natural, universal rights which find their origin and are a direct consequence of the relationships of solidarity among men, of the need for the individual development of mankind and for the protection of the environment'. The same Court concluded by stating that:

> such rights are commonly enshrined in universal declarations and in national and supra-national texts, and their nature and content as human rights shall leave no room for doubt since they are the very essence of a human person and shall therefore be necessarily respected and protected.[1952]

In the case of Venezuela, the open clause allows for the identification of rights inherent to human persons, not only regarding those not listed in the Constitution, but also not listed in international human rights instruments, thus considerably broadening their scope. According to this open clause, for instance, the former Supreme Court of Justice of Venezuela, on judicial review annulled statutes founding its rulings on rights not listed in the Constitution but listed in the American Convention on Human Rights, considering them as rights inherent to human beings.[1953]

441. In addition, because of the incorporation of this open clause in the Constitution regarding human rights, the absence of statutory regulation of such rights cannot be invoked to deny or undermine its exercise by the people.

III. *The Constitutional Rank of International Human Rights Treaties*

442. The third important principle on the progressive protection of fundamental rights and freedom has been the process of constitutionalization of international law

---

1951   See Agustina Yadira Martínez e Innes Faría Villarreal, 'La Cláusula Enunciativa de los Derechos Humanos en la Constitución venezolana', in *Revista de derecho del Tribunal Supremo de Justicia*, Nº 3 (Caracas, 2001), 133 a 151.

1952   See decision of 31 Jan. 1991, Case: *Anselmo Natale*, in Carlos Ayala Corao, 'La jerarquía de los instrumentos internacionales sobre derechos humanos', in *El nuevo derecho constitucional latinoamericano, IV Congreso venezolano de Derecho constitucional*, vol. II (Caracas, 1996), and in *La jerarquía constitucional de los tratados sobre derechos humanos y sus consecuencias* (México, 2003).

1953   In this sense in 1996, the Supreme Court annulled an Amazon State Act regarding territorial divisions sanctioned without the participation and consultation of the indigenous peoples organization, considering that it violated the American Convention on Human Rights, Decision of 5 Dec. 1996, Case: *Antonio Guzmán, Lucas Omashi ey al.*, in *Revista de Derecho Público*, Nº 67–68 (Caracas: Editorial Jurídica Venezolana, 1996), 176 et seq. Other cases regarding discrimination and the application of the International Covenant on Civil and Political Rights, in *Revista de Derecho Público*, Nº 71–72 (Caracas: Editorial Jurídica Venezolana, 1997), 177 et seq.; and on political participation as a non-enumerated right inherent in the human person, in *Revista de Derecho Público*, Nº 77–80 (Caracas: Editorial Jurídica Venezolana, 1999), 67.

in matters of human rights. In this sense the 1991 Constitution has expressly established the value and rank of international instruments on human rights, regarding the same Constitution as well as regarding statutes, even determining which shall prevail in the event of there being a conflict among them.[1954]

This process has resulted in the incorporation in the Constitutions of a provision giving the international instruments on human rights regarding internal law, not only the traditional statutory rank or a supra-legal rank, but most importantly, constitutional rank and even supra-constitutional rank.[1955] For such purposes Article 23 of the Constitution, as one of the 1999 constitution-making process innovations, provides that:

> Treaties, covenants and conventions referring to human rights, signed and ratified by Venezuela, shall have constitutional hierarchy and will prevail over internal legal order, when they contain more favorable regulations regarding their enjoyment and exercise, than those established in this Constitution and in the statutes of the Republic.

According to this provision, constitutional rank has been given to treaties, pacts, and conventions on human rights, having preference over the national Constitution and statutes if they should establish more favourable provisions. In addition, they have immediate and direct application by all courts and authorities of the country.[1956]

443. This supra-constitutional rank given to international treaties, for instance, has allowed the Supreme Tribunal of Justice through its Constitutional Chamber to decide cases by directly applying the American Convention. In this regard, for instance, the Constitutional Chamber, in 2000, gave prevalence to the American Convention regulations referring to the 'the right to appeal judgments before a higher court' (Article 8,2,h), considered as forming part of internal constitutional law of the country, regarding the provision of the Supreme Court of Justice 1976 Statute, which excluded the appeal in certain cases on Administrative Jurisdiction courts' decisions, interpreting 'that the latter is incompatible with the former, because it

---

1954   See Allan R. Brewer-Carías, *Debate Constituyente (Aportes a la Asamblea Nacional Constituyente)*, vol. II (Caracas: Fundación de Derecho Público, 1999), 111–115; Carlos M. Ayala Corao, 'La jerarquía constitucional de los tratados relativos a Derechos Humanos y sus consecuencias', in *Bases y principios del sistema constitucional venezolano (Ponencias del VII Congreso Venezolano de Derecho Constitucional realizado en San Cristóbal del 21 al 23 de Noviembre de 2001)*, vol. I, 167–240, and Lorena Rincón Eizaga, 'La incorporación de los tratados sobre derechos humanos en el derecho interno a la luz de la Constitución de 1999', in *Revista de la Facultad de Ciencias Jurídicas y Políticas de la UCV*, N° 119 (Caracas, 2000), 87–108; Innes Faria Villarreal, 'Los tratados Internacionales sobre derechos humanos en la Constitución venezolana', in *Revista de Derecho*, N° 13 (Caracas: Tribunal Supremo de Justicia, 2004), 297–326.

1955   On this classification, see Allan R. Brewer-Carías, *Mecanismos nacionales de protección de los derechos humanos, Instituto Internacional de Derechos Humanos* (San José, 2004), 62 et seq.

1956   See Larys Hernández Villalobos, 'Rango o jerarquía de los tratados internacionales en el ordenamiento jurídico de Venezuela (1999)', in *Revista del Tribunal Supremo de Justicia*, N° 3 (Caracas, 2001), 110–131.

denies in absolute terms, the right that the Convention guarantees'.[1957] Based on the aforementioned, the Constitutional Chamber concluded its ruling by stating that the right to appeal recognized in Article 8.1 and 2.h of the American Convention on Human Rights, which is 'part of the Venezuelan constitutional order', is more favourable regarding the exercise of such right in relation to what is set forth in Article 49.1 of the Constitution; and that such provisions are of 'direct and immediate application by courts and authorities'.

444. But in spite of the constitutional provision, and of its application by the Constitutional Chamber of the Supreme Tribunal, in a decision No. 1.939 issued in 18 December 2008 (Case *Gustavo Álvarez Arias y otros*),[1958] the same Constitutional Chamber after declaring as 'non-enforceable' in Venezuela the decision of the Inter-American Court on Human Rights of 5 August 2008[1959] (see supra paragraph. 82; *infra* paragraph 682) in which the Venezuelan State was condemned for violations of the judicial guarantees of various magistrates of the First Court of the Contentious Administrative Jurisdiction, has declared that the aforementioned:

> Article 23 of the Constitution does not assign supra-constitutional rank to international treaties on human rights, so that in case of contradiction between a constitutional provision and a provision of an international covenant, it is the competence of the Judicial Power to determine which is the applicable provision.

IV. *The Principle of Freedom*

445. Article 20 of the Constitution establishes the general principle of freedom as the basis of the whole system in matters of human rights (see *supra* paragrah 83), by stating that 'each person has the right to the free development of his personality, without limitation other than those deriving from the rights of others and from social and public order'.[1960] This enunciation, as indicated in the explaining document of the 1961 Constitution, which contained the same provision, substituted the traditional norm contained in previous constitutions setting forth that everyone may do

---

1957   See decision N° 87 of 13 Mar. 2000. Case: *C.A. Electricidad del Centro (Elecentro) y otra v. Superintendencia para la Promoción y Protección de la Libre Competencia. (Procompetencia)*, in *Revista de Derecho Público*, N° 81 (Caracas: Editorial Jurídica Venezolana, 2000), 157 et seq.

1958   See in <www.tsj.gov.ve/decisiones/scon/Diciembre/1939-181208-2008-08-1572.html>.

1959   See Case(*Apitz Barbera y otros ('Corte Primera de lo Contencioso Administrativo') v. Venezuela*), in See in <www.corteidh.or.cr>. Excepción Preliminar, Fondo, Reparaciones y Costas, Serie C N° 182.

1960   See María C. Domínguez Guillen, 'Alcance del artículo 20 de la Constitución de la República Bolivariana de Venezuela (Libre desenvolvimiento de la personalidad)', en *Revista de Derecho*, N° 13 (Caracas: Tribunal Supremo de Justicia, 2004), 13–40; Rafael Ortiz-Ortiz, 'Los derechos de la personalidad como derechos fundamentales en el nuevo orden constitucional venezolano', in *Estudios de Derecho Público: Libro Homenaje a Humberto J. La Roche Rincón*, vol. I (Caracas: Tribunal Supremo de Justicia, 2001), 39–82; María C. Domínguez Guillén, 'Innovaciones de la Constitución de 1999 en materia de derechos de la personalidad', in *Revista de la Facultad de Ciencias Jurídicas y Políticas de la UCV*, N° 119 (Caracas, 2000), 17–44; María Candelaria Domínguez Guillén, 'Aproximación al estudio de los derechos de la personalidad', *Revista de derecho del Tribunal Supremo de Justicia*, N° 7 (Caracas, 2002), 49 a 311.

anything that does not harm others and no one is obliged to do anything that the law does not require, nor can be impeded from doing what the law does not prohibit.

V. The Principle of Equality and Non-discrimination

446. The principle of equality is another of the main principles regarding human rights in the 1999 Constitution, which has been included in a very explicit way[1961] in Article 21, stating that all persons are equal before the law, and consequently, no discrimination could be permitted based on race, sex, religion, social condition or any other motive that in general terms could have the objective or the consequence of annulling or harming the recognition, enjoyment and exercise by everybody of the rights and liberties in conditions of equality (see supra paragraph 70).

447. For such purpose, the same Article 21 of the Constitution provides that the law must guarantee the juridical and administrative conditions in order to guarantee that equality before the law could be real and effective, and must provide for positive measures in favour of persons or groups that could be discriminated, marginalized or vulnerable; must specially protect those persons that due to any of the abovementioned conditions could be in a circumstance of manifest weakness and must sanction the abuses and harms inflicted against them. In addition, the Constitution prescribes that no nobility titles and hereditary distinctions are recognized in Venezuela.

§2. General Principles Regarding Constitutional Guarantees

448. The 1999 Constitution has also incorporated a very important set of norms concerning the constitutional guarantee of human rights, that is, the legal instruments that are designed to implement and permit the effective exercise of these protected rights.

I. Prohibition of the Retroactive Effects of Law

449. The Constitution expressly establishes the prohibition for legislative provisions of having retroactive effects, except when they impose a lesser penalty. In the case of procedural laws, they shall apply from the moment they go into effect, even to proceedings already in progress; however, in criminal proceedings, evidence already admitted shall be weighed in accordance with the laws that were in effect when the evidence was admitted, insofar as this benefits the defendant. When there are doubts as to the statute that is to be applied, the most beneficial to the defendant will prevail (Article 24).

II. Nullity of Acts Contrary to the Constitution

450. However, the 1999 Constitution, also following a long constitutional tradition, has established the objective guarantee of the Constitution by providing that any State act that violates or encroaches upon the rights guaranteed by the Constitu-

---

1961   See Luis Beltrán Guerra, 'Algunas consideraciones respecto a la igualdad y a la libertad como valores protegidos en el régimen de los derechos fundamentales', in *Temas de Derecho Administrativo: Libro Homenaje a Gonzalo Pérez Luciani,* vol. I (Caracas: Editorial Torino, 2002), 815–876.

tion and by law is null and void, and the public officials ordering or implementing the same shall incur criminal, civil and administrative liability, as applicable in each case, with no defence on grounds of having followed superior orders (Article 25).

III. *Due Process of Law Rules and the Right to Have Access to Justice*

451. The Constitution has also expressly enumerated the rules of the due process of law guarantees, and the right to have access to the system of justice. For such purposes, Article 26 of the Constitution establishes the general right of everyone to access the organs comprising the justice system for the purpose of enforcing his rights and interests, including those of a collective or diffuse nature to the effective protection of the aforementioned and to obtain the corresponding prompt decision. In this regard, the State must guarantee a free-of-charge justice, which in addition must be accessible, impartial, suitable, transparent, autonomous, independent, responsible, equitable and expeditious, without undue delays and superfluous formalities.

452. Regarding due process of law rules, requiring justice to be imparted according to the norms established within the Constitution and laws, Article 49 of the Constitution requires that 'due process shall be applied in all judicial and administrative acts', and consequently, declares legal assistance and defence as inviolable rights at all stages and levels during the investigation and process. Consequently, the same article establishes that every person has the right to be notified of the charges for which he or she is being investigated, to have access to the evidence and to be afforded the necessary time and means to conduct his or her defence. Any evidence obtained in violation of due process shall be null and void. Any person declared guilty shall have the right to appeal, except in the cases established by the Constitution and by the law (Article 49.1).

453. In addition, the same Article 49 of the Constitution enumerates the following other rules of due process of law rights: Any person shall be presumed innocent until proven otherwise. Every person has the right to be heard in proceedings of any kind, with all due guarantees and within such reasonable time limit as may be legally detained, by a competent, independent and impartial court established in advance. Anyone who does not speak Spanish or is unable to communicate verbally is entitled to an interpreter. Every person has the right to be judged by his or her natural judges of ordinary or special competence, with the guarantees established in the Constitution and by law. No person shall be put on trial without knowing the identity of the party judging him or her, nor be adjudged by exceptional courts or commissions created for such purpose. No person shall be required to confess guilt or testify against himself or herself or his or her spouse or partner, or any other relative within the fourth degree of consanguinity or the second degree of affinity. A confession shall be valid only if given without coercion of any kind. No person shall be punished for acts or omissions not defined under pre-existing laws as a crime, offence or infraction (*Nullum crimen nulla poena sine lege*). No person shall be placed on trial based on the same facts for which such person has been judged previously (*Non bis in idem*). Every person shall request from the State the restoration or re-establishment of the legal situation adversely affected by unwarranted judicial errors, and unjustified delay or omissions. This right is established without prejudice

to the right of the individual to seek to hold the magistrate or judge personally liable, and that of the State to take action against the same.[1962]

IV. *Guarantee for Rights to Only Be Limited or Restricted by Statutes*

454. Among all of the constitutional guarantees of human rights, without a doubt, one of the most important is the guarantee imposing the need for a statute to establish limitations and restrictions upon these rights;[1963] that is, that only through formal legislation can limitations be established regarding the enjoyment of human rights. And 'legislation' in the terms of this constitutional guarantee can only be an act emanating from the National Assembly acting in its capacity as the Legislative Body (Article 202). Thus, statutes are the only form of government action which can restrict or limit constitutional guarantees under Article 30 of the American Convention on Human Rights.

Nonetheless, this guarantee has been contradicted in the same 1999 Constitution, due to the broad provision it contains regarding the possibility for the National Assembly to delegate legislative power to the President of the Republic through the so-called enabling laws (Article 203), authorizing it to dictate 'decree-laws' with the same legal rank and effect of national legislation in any subject area (Article 236.8)[1964] (see *supra* paragraphs, 54, 133, 253).

V. *State Obligations to Investigate*

455. Among the constitutional guarantees of human rights, Article 29 obliges the State to investigate and legally punish offences against human rights committed by its authorities. In cases of actions to punish the offence against humanity, serious violations of human rights and war crimes shall not be subject to statute of limitation.

Human rights violations and the offence of violating humanity rights shall be investigated and adjudicated by the courts of ordinary competence. These offences are excluded from any benefit that might render the offenders immune from punishment, including pardons and amnesty.

456. Article 30 of the Constitution sets forth the obligation of the State to make full reparations to the victims of human rights violations for which it may be held

---

1962   See Antonieta Garrido de Cárdenas, 'La naturaleza del debido proceso en la Constitución de la República Bolivariana de Venezuela de 1999', in *Revista de Derecho Constitucional*, N° 5 (julio-diciembre) (Caracas: Editorial Sherwood, 2001), 89–116; Antonieta Garrido de Cárdenas, 'El debido proceso como derecho fundamental en la Constitución de 1999 y sus medios de protección', in *Bases y principios del sistema constitucional venezolano (Ponencias del VII Congreso Venezolano de Derecho Constitucional realizado en San Cristóbal del 21 al 23 de Noviembre de 2001)*, vol. I, 127–144.

1963   See Allan R Brewer-Carías, 'Consideraciones sobre la suspensión o restricción de las garantías constitucionales', *Revista de Derecho Público*, N° 37 (Caracas, 1989), 6–7.

1964   See Pedro Nikken, 'Constitución venezolana de 1999: La habilitación para dictar decretos ejecutivos con fuerza de ley restrictivas de los derechos humanos y su contradicción con el derecho internacional', *Revista de Derecho Público*, N° 83 (julio-septiembre) (Caracas: Editorial Jurídica Venezolana, 2000), 5–19.

responsible and to the legal successors to such victims, including payment of damages. The State is also obliged to adopt the necessary legislative measures and measures of other nature to implement the aforementioned reparations and damage compensation. In any case, the State shall protect the victims of ordinary crimes and endeavour to make the guilty parties provide reparations for the inflicted damages.

VI. *The Regime of Restricting Constitutional Guaranties in States of Exception*

457. As aforementioned, another important guarantee of human rights set forth in the 1999 Constitution is the impossibility to 'suspend' fundamental rights and their guaranties in cases of States of Exception, the President of the Republic being authorized ,in such cases, only to temporarily restrict them, with the exception of those relating to the right to life, prohibition of incommunicative detention or torture, the right to due process, the right to information and other intangible human rights. In any case of restriction, the President is obliged to enact the corresponding regulation of the restricted guarantee[1965] (see *supra* paragraph 294).

VII. *Judicial Guarantees of Human Rights*

458. Finally, the Constitution also regulates the judicial guarantees for the protection of constitutional rights by means of the actions of *amparo,* and habeas corpus (Article 27), which have been developed in the Organic Law of Amparo of Constitutional Rights and Guarantees.[1966] (see *infra* paragraph 687). The Constitution also guarantees the action of habeas data, in order to guarantee the peoples' right to have access to the information and data concerning the claimant contained in official or private registries or data banks, as well as to know about the use made of the information and about its purpose, and to petition before the competent court for the updating, rectification or destruction in cases of erroneous records and those that unlawfully affect the petitioner's rights (Article 28).

VIII. *International Guarantees of Human Rights*

459. The international scope of the constitutional guarantees is established in Article 31 of the Constitution which provides for everybody, on the terms established by the human rights treaties, pacts and conventions ratified by the Republic, the right to address petitions and complaints to the international organs created for such purpose, in order to ask for protection of his human rights.[1967] This is the case of the Inter-American Court on Human Rights created by the American Convention on

---

1965   See Jesús M. Casal H., 'Condiciones para la limitación o restricción de derechos fundamentales', in *El Derecho Público a comienzos del siglo XXI. Estudios homenaje al Profesor Allan R. Brewer-Carías,* vol. III (Madrid: Editorial Thomson-Civitas, 2003), 2515–2534.

1966   *Gaceta Oficial* N° 34.060 of 27 Sep. 1988. See Allan R. Brewer-Carías & Carlos M. Ayala Corao, *Ley Orgánica de Amparo sobre derechos y garantías constitucionales* (Caracas: Editorial Jurídica Venezolana, 1988).

1967   See Carlos M. Ayala Corao, *Del amparo constitucional al amparo Interamericano como Institutos para la protección de los Derechos Humanos* (Caracas: Editorial Jurídica Venezolana, 1998).

Human Rights (1969), whose jurisdiction has been recognized by the Venezuelan State.

The Constitution also obliges the State, in accordance with the procedures established under the Constitution and by the law, to adopt such measures as may be necessary to enforce the decisions emanating from the corresponding international organs. Nonetheless, the Constitutional Chamber of the Supreme Tribunal in decision N° 1939 of December 18, 2008 (Case: *Abogados Gustavo Álvarez Arias y otros*)[1968] declared that the Inter-American Court on Human Rights decision of 5 Aug. 2008, Case: *Apitz Barbera y otros 'Corte Primera de lo Contencioso Administrativo' v. Venezuela*) condemning the State for violations of human rights of a group of judges (see *supra* paragraph 88; *infra* paragraphs 682, 684) was non-enforceable (*inejecutable*) in Venezuela, and asked the Executive to denounce the American Convention of Human Rights, accusing the Inter-American Court of having usurped powers of the Supreme Tribunal. The same occurred with the Constitutional Chamber decision No. 1547 of Oct. 17, 2011 (Caso *Estado Venezolano vs. Corte Interamericana de Derechos Humanos*),[1969] also rejected the decision of the Inter-American Court on Human Rights of Sep. 1°, 2011 (case *Leopoldo López vs. Estado de Venezuela)* that condemned the State for violating the political rights of a citizen, considering it as non-executable in Venezuela. In this decision, the Supreme Tribunal also asked the Executive to denounce the American Convention of Human Rights, which eventually occurred when the Executive formally comunicate to the Organization of American States the withdrawl of Venezuela from the Convention on Sep. 6, 2012. .

Chapter 2. The Status of Persons and Citizens

460. The rights and guarantees declared in the Constitution in general terms correspond to every person. Nonetheless, there are some rights that only correspond to Venezuelans, or nationals. For such purpose, the Constitution has established the general status of persons distinguishing between Venezuelans or nationals and foreigners, and within the former, those that are considered citizens and therefore, able to exercise political rights. In this regard, Citizenship and Nationality is one of the fundamental elements of the political organization of the State, regulated in the Constitution.

1968   See in *Revista de Derecho Público*, N° 116, Editorial Jurídica Venezolana, Caracas 2008, pp. 88 ss. Also available at: http://www.tsj.gov.ve/decisiones/scon/Diciembre/1939-181208-2008-08-1572.html See the comments in Allan R. Brewer-Carías, "La interrelación entre los Tribunales Constitucionales de América Latina y la Corte Interamericana de Derechos Humanos, y la cuestión de la inejecutabilidad de sus decisiones en Venezuela," in Armin von Bogdandy, Flavia Piovesan y Mariela Morales Antonorzi (Coodinadores), *Direitos Humanos, Democracia e Integraçao Jurídica na América do Sul*, (rio de janeiro, Lumen Juris Editora, 2010), 661-70; and in *Anuario Iberoamericano de Justicia Constitucional* No. 13, (Madrid, Centro de Estudios Políticos y Constitucionales, 2009), 99-136.

1969   Available at http://www.tsj.gov.ve/decisiones/scon/Octubre/1547-171011-2011-11-1130.html. See the comments in Allan R. Brewer-Carías, "El ilegítimo "control de constitucionalidad" de las sentencias de la Corte Interamericana de Derechos Humanos por parte la Sala Constitucional del Tribunal Supremo de Justicia de Venezuela: el caso de la sentencia *Leopoldo López vs. Venezuela, 2011*," en *Constitución y democracia: ayer y hoy. Libro homenaje a Antonio Torres del Moral*, Vol. I,. (Madrid, Editorial Universitas, 2013), 1.095-1124

In this context, Venezuelans or nationals are the persons that have a fundamental legal bond to the State and the country allowing them to be part of its political life. Consequently, in spite of the equality general principle established in the Constitution (see *supra* paragraph 446), foreigners do not have all the rights that Venezuelans have, particularly regarding political rights. That is why although the provision of Article 45 of the 1961 Constitution that established that 'Foreigners have the same duties and rights as Venezuelans, subject to the limitations and exceptions established by this Constitution and the laws', was not included in the 1999 Constitution, the same principle subsists within the provisions related to Nationality, Citizenship and Foreigners.

§1. *The Constitutional Rules on the Venezuelan Nationality*

461. The 1999 Constitution distinguishes two sorts of nationals: nationals by birth and nationals by naturalization (acquisition of the Venezuelan nationality);[1970] and regarding the former the Constitution also distinguishes the two classical ways of acquiring the Venezuelan nationality by birth, according to the principles of *jus soli* and of *jus sanguinis*.[1971]

I.   *Venezuelan by Birth*

462. In this regard, Article 32 of the Constitution declares that people who are Venezuelan by birth are, any person born within the territory of the Republic; any person born in a foreign territory, and is the child of a father *and* a mother who are both Venezuelans by birth; any person born in a foreign territory, and is the child of a father *or* a mother, who is Venezuelan by birth, provided they have established residence within the territory of the Republic or declared their intention to obtain the Venezuelan nationality; and any person who was born in a foreign territory, and is the child of a father or a mother who is Venezuelan by naturalization, provided that prior to reaching the age of 18, they establish their residence within the territory of the Republic, and before reaching the age of 25 declare their intention to obtain the Venezuelan nationality.

463. According to this provision, the *jus soli* principle remains in an absolute way, in the sense of being born on Venezuelan soil is enough for having the Venezuelan nationality by birth, even if it is accidental, and no relation in the future is established regarding the country. According to this same provision, the *jus sanguinis* principle also remains in an absolute way, in the sense that the Venezuelan nationality by birth corresponds to those born in foreign countries from father and

---

1970   See Allan R. Brewer-Carías, *Régimen legal de la Nacionalidad, Ciudadanía y Extranjería (Ley de Nacionalidad y Ciudadanía, Ley de Extranjería y Migración, Ley Orgánica sobre Refugiados y Asilados)* (Caracas: Editorial Jurídica Venezolana, 2005); Allan R. Brewer-Carías, *El régimen jurídico administrativo de la Nacionalidad y Ciudadanía venezolana* (Caracas, 1965).

1971   See Eugenio Hernández Bretón, 'Nacionalidad, ciudadanía y extranjería en la Constitución de 1999', in *Revista de Derecho Público*, N° 81 (enero-marzo) (Caracas: Editorial Jurídica Venezolana, 2000), 47–59; Juan De Stefano, 'El principio de la nacionalidad', in *Temas de Derecho Administrativo: Libro Homenaje a Gonzalo Pérez Luciani*, vo. I (Caracas: Editorial Torino, 2002), 593–608.

mother who are Venezuelan by birth, even if they do not establish any subsequent relation with the country.

II.   *Venezuelan by Naturalization*

464. With respect to the regime of the nationality by acquisition (naturalization), the regimen of the 1999 Constitution also follows the previous tradition, establishing that foreigners can acquire the Venezuelan nationality by obtaining a 'naturalization letter', providing they have at least ten years of uninterrupted residence immediately preceding the application date. Nonetheless, the Constitution provides that this period of residence shall be reduced to five years in the case of foreign nationals whose original nationality is that of Spain, Portugal, Italy, or a Latin American or Caribbean country.

465. The 1999 Constitution also expanded the cases of naturalization based on marriage, in the sense that it benefits not only women married to Venezuelan men as established in the 1961 Constitution, but also men married to Venezuelan women, upon declaring their wish to adopt the Venezuelan nationality, which may be done at least five years after the date of marriage. Also minors of foreign nationality, on the date of the naturalization of one of his/her parent who exercises parental authority, provided that such minor declares his or her intention of adopting the Venezuelan nationality before reaching the age of 21, and has resided in Venezuela without interruption throughout the five-year period preceding such declaration.

III.   *Dual Nationality*

466. The most important constitutional innovation in these matters has been the acceptance of the possibility for Venezuelans to have dual nationality, in the sense that Venezuelans by birth and naturalization may now have another nationality without losing their Venezuelan nationality. This principle, established in Article 34, prescribes that 'Venezuelan nationality is not lost upon choosing or acquiring another nationality' and radically changes the preceding rule, under which according to Article 39 of the 1961 Constitution, Venezuelan nationality was lost upon voluntarily choosing or acquiring another nationality. In accord with the spirit and purpose of the new regimen, which was of course, that if Venezuelan nationality was made available through naturalization, there ought not be a requirement that the interested party renounce his or her nationality of origin, insofar as Venezuela is concerned in such cases, the nationality of origin is retained in conformity with the requirements of that country.

467. The constitutional progress of permitting Venezuelans to have dual nationality is nonetheless limited with respect to the holding of certain high public offices, for which not only Venezuelan nationality by birth is required, but not having another nationality is also required. It is the case, according to Article 41, of the offices of President of the Republic, Executive Vice President, President and Vice Presidents of the National Assembly, Magistrates of the Supreme Tribunal of Justice, President of the National Electoral Council, the Attorney General of the Republic, Comptroller General of the Republic, Prosecutor General of the Republic (Public Prosecutor), the Peoples' Defender, Ministers in matters of National Security, Finances, Energy and Mining, Education; Governors and Mayors of frontier states and

municipalities, and those regarding military positions established in the Organic Law of the Armed Forces.

IV. *Loss and Recuperation of Venezuelan Nationality*

468. As aforementioned, Article 34 of the Constitution sets forth that the Venezuelan nationality is not lost upon electing or acquiring another nationality; and Article 35 establishes that Venezuelans by birth cannot be deprived of their nationality. Nonetheless, the Venezuelan nationality by naturalization can be revoked only by a judgment handed down by a court in accordance with law.

469. However, Venezuelan nationality may be renounced; but the person who renounces it when by birth, may regain such nationality if he or she establishes a residence within the territory of the Republic for a period of at least two years, and expresses the intention of regaining the Venezuelan nationality. Naturalized Venezuelans who renounce the Venezuelan nationality may regain it by again meeting the requirements prescribed under Article 33 of this Constitution (Article 36).

§2. *The Constitutional Rules on Citizenship*

I.   *Citizenship and Political Rights*

470. Citizenship is the political bond established between the person and the State that allows that person to participate in the political system. For this reason, according to the Constitution, a citizen is essentially a Venezuelan national. On this basis, Article 39 of the Constitution states that Venezuelans with the required age who are not subject to political impediment or civil interdiction, can exercise citizenship and therefore are entitled to political rights and duties in accordance to the Constitution.[1972]

471. The age conditions for exercising citizenship differ regarding the corresponding political right to be exercised. For example, to vote, it is enough to have reached the age of 18 (Article 64), but to be elected Governor of a State of the federation, it is necessary to be over the age of 25 (Article 160); to be Congressmen to the National Assembly and to a State Legislative Council, it is necessary to be over the age of 21 (Articles 188 and 162); to be Mayor of any municipality, it is necessary to be over the age of 25 (Article 174); to be President and Vice President of the Republic, it is necessary to be over the age of 30 (Articles 227 and 238); as well as to be People's Defender (Article 280) and General Controller of the Republic (Article 288); and to be Minister, it is necessary to be over the age of 25 (Article 244). Furthermore, as regards the Justices to the Supreme Tribunal of Justice (Article 263), the Attorney General (Article 249) and the Prosecutor General of the Republic

---

1972   This provision has been repeated in Art. 50 of the 2004 Nationality and Citizenhip Law specifying that 'Citizen are those Venezuelans not subject to political impedment or to civil interdiction and fulfil the age requirements foreseen in the Constitution and in the statutes.' See *Official Gazette*, N° 37971 of 1 Jul. 2004. See Allan R. Brewer-Carías, *Régimen Legal de la Nacionalidad, Ciudadanía y Extranjería. Ley de Nacionalidad y Ciudadanía, Ley de Extranjería y Migración, Ley Orgánica sobre Refugiados y Asilados* (Caracas: Editorial Jurídica Venezolana, 2005).

(Public Prosecutor) (Article 284), the Constitution requires to be over the age of 35, which is set forth in the conditions to exercise such positions.

472. The condition of Citizenship implies the exercise of political rights, like the right to vote, the right to be elected, the right to exercise public functions, which are reserved to Venezuelans. The only exception to this rule, according to Article 64 of the Constitution is the right to vote given to foreigners in state, municipal and parish elections, who have reached the age of 18 and have resided in Venezuela for more than ten years, subject to the limitations established in the Constitution and by law, and provided they are not subject to political disablement or civil interdiction.

473. According to Article 42, anyone who loses or renounces Venezuelan nationality loses citizenship. In addition, the Constitution establishes the guarantee that the exercise of citizenship or any political rights can be suspended only by final judicial decision in the cases provided by law.

II. *Equality between Venezuelans by Birth and by Naturalization*

474. With respect to the exercise of political rights, the constitutional principle of equality between those who are Venezuelan by birth and those who are naturalized is derived from Article 40 of the Constitution, with the exceptions established in the aforementioned Article 41 of the Constitution, which requires in order to be elected or to be appointed for some public offices, to be Venezuelan by birth without having any other nationality. Also, in order to be elected representative to the National Assembly, or to be appointed Minister, Governors and Mayors of non-frontier states and municipalities, naturalized citizens must have been domiciled in Venezuela with uninterrupted residency not less than fifteen years (Article 41).

475. Nonetheless, all these exceptions establishing some distinction between Venezuelan by birth and naturalized Venezuelans disappear in the cases of Naturalized Venezuelans who have entered the country prior to reaching the age of 7 years and have resided permanently in Venezuela until reaching legal age shall enjoy the same rights as Venezuelans by birth (Article 40).

§3. *Constitutional Condition of Foreigners*

476. All other persons in Venezuela not being Venezuelans are legally considered aliens or foreigners, as is expressly set forth in Article 3 of the 2004 Aliens and Migration Statute,[1973] which provides that all those who are not considered to be Venezuelans, are legally considered to be foreigners or aliens.

I. *Migrant and Non-migrant Aliens*

477. Aliens, according to this same Statute, and regarding their access and permanency in the territory of the Republic, can be admitted in two categories: as non-migrants or as migrants. Non-migrant aliens are the people who enter the territory of

---

1973   See in *Official Gazette* N° 37.944 of 24 May 2004. See in Allan R. Brewer-Carías, *Régimen Legal De La Nacionalidad, Ciudadanía Y Extranjería. Ley de Nacionalidad y Ciudadanía, Ley de Extranjería y Migración, Ley Orgánica sobre Refugiados y Asilados* (Caracas: Editorial Jurídica Venezolana, 2005), 101 et seq.

the Republic to remain in it for a limited period of ninety days, without having the intention to establish with their family permanent residence in it. These non-migrant aliens cannot perform activities that involve remuneration or profit.

478. Migrants aliens are those who enter the territory of the Republic to reside in it, temporarily or permanently (Article 3), being classified in two categories: temporary migrants and permanent migrants (Article 6). Temporary migrants are those entering the territory of the Republic with the intention of residing in it temporarily while the activities that have originated their admission last (migrant workers, border migrants). Permanent migrants are those who have authorization to remain indefinitely in the territory of the Republic.

II. *Asylum and Refugee Aliens*

479. In addition to the status of migrant and non-migrant aliens, Article 69 of the Constitution sets forth in the section related to political rights, 'that the Bolivarian Republic of Venezuela acknowledges and guarantees the right of asylum and of refuge'. Therefore, in addition to the non-migrant and migrant aliens, two other categories of aliens can be identified: refugees and asylees aliens, with a status that according to Article 2 of the 2001 Organic Statute on Refugees and Asylees,[1974] is governed by the following rules:

(1)   Every person is able to file a refugee protection claim in the Republic, based on a well-founded fear to be persecuted by the reasons and the conditions set forth in the 1967 Protocol on the Refugee Statutes.

(2)   Every person is able to make a refugee protection claim in the Republic as well as in its diplomatic missions, warships and military aircrafts abroad, when persecuted for political reasons or crimes in the conditions set forth in that Law.

(3)   No person claiming asylum or refugee protection shall be neglected or subjected to any measure that forces him or her to be repatriated to the territory where his or her life, physical integrity or freedom is jeopardized due to the reasons set forth in that Law.

(4)   Authorities shall impose no punishment due to the irregular entrance or stay in the territory of the Republic on persons that claim refugee protection or asylum, pursuant to the terms set forth in the Constitution.

(5)   Discrimination based on race, gender, religion, political opinions, social condition, country of origin or those that in general lessen or annul the acknowledgement, enjoyment or exercise in equal situation of the refugee's or asylee's condition shall not be permitted.

1974   See in *Official Gazette* N° 37.296 of 3 Oct. 2001. See Allan R. Brewer-Carías, *Régimen Legal de la Nacionalidad, Ciudadanía y Extranjería. Ley de Nacionalidad y Ciudadanía, Ley de Extranjería y Migración, Ley Orgánica sobre Refugiados y Asilados* (Caracas: Editorial Jurídica Venezolana, 2005), 117 et seq.

(6)   The unity of a refugee's or asylee's family shall be guaranteed, and specially, the protection of child refugees and teenagers without company or separated from the family, in the terms set forth in the Law.

480. Consequently, pursuant to Article 38 of this Statute, the asylum status is granted to aliens the State considers to be persecuted due to their beliefs, opinions, or political affinities, or due to acts that might be considered as political crimes, or to common crimes but committed with political purposes. Asylum cannot be granted to a person accused, processed or convicted before ordinary competent Courts due to common crimes, or having committed crimes against peace, war crimes or crimes against mankind, as defined in international treaties (Article 41 of the Organic Law).

481. Asylum can be granted within the territory of the Republic, once the nature of such is qualified (Article 39) (territorial asylum); or can be granted to persons seeking it before diplomatic missions, Venezuelan warships, or military aircrafts according to the applicable international treaties and conventions on the matter (Article 40) (Diplomatic asylum). All these provisions related to asylum, according to Article 24 of the Organic Law, shall be construed pursuant to the 1948 Universal Declaration of Human Rights, and the 1954 Caracas Convention on Territorial Asylum and other provisions of international treaties on human rights, duly executed and ratified by the Government of Venezuela.

482. The same Organic Statute on Refugees and Asylees establishes, regarding the refugee status, that the Venezuelan State shall grant it 'to every person recognized as such by the competent authority, in virtue of having entered in the national territory due to persecution because of his or her race, gender, religion, nationality, membership in a social group or political opinion, and is outside his or her home country and shall not or does not want to be protected by that country, or that, having no nationality, shall not or does not want to return to the country where he or she has his residence' (Article 5). The main legal trend regarding the refugee status is that according to the Law, no person asking refugee protection shall be punished due to illegal entrance or stay in the national territory, provided that he or she appears without delay before the national authorities, and pleads just cause (Article 6). Additionally, a person making a refugee protection claim shall not be denied admission or be subject to a measure forcing him or her to return to the country where his or her life, physical integrity or personal freedom is jeopardized. However, these benefits shall not be granted to aliens considered, due to well-founded reasons, a danger for the Republic's security or that having been convicted of a serious crime, he or she represents a threat to the community (Article 7).

483. According to the same Statute, every alien claiming Venezuelan State protection as refugee, shall be admitted in the national territory and shall be authorized to stay in it until his or her claim is decided, including a reconsideration period. However, an alien considered due to well-founded reasons, a danger for the Republic's safety or a threat to the community because convicted of a serious crime, cannot claim these benefits (Article 2).

484. The refugee protection shall not be granted to aliens in the following cases: when the alien committed a crime against peace, war crimes or crimes against mankind, as defined in international treaties; when the alien committed common crimes outside the country granting refugee protection that are not compatible with the refugee status; and when the alien committed acts against the principles of the United

Nations Organization (Article 9). All these internal provisions related to the refugee status, according to Article 4 of the Organic Law, shall be construed pursuant to the 1948 Universal Declaration of Human Rights, 1967 Protocol on the Status of Refugees, the 1969 American Convention on Human Rights, and other provisions of international treaties on human rights, duly executed and ratified by the Government of Venezuela.

Chapter 3. Civil Rights

§1. Right to Life

485. Chapter IV, Title III of the Constitution enumerates the 'civil rights' of all persons, also called 'individual rights,' begining with the right to life (see *supra* paragraph 70), which is set forth in Article 43, as 'inviolable', and therefore, the prohibition of the death penalty is expressly declared, in the sense that 'no law shall provide for the death penalty and no authority shall apply the same'. In addition, the article obliges the State to 'protect the life of persons who are deprived of liberty, are in military or civil services, or are subject to its authority in any other manner'.

§2. Right to Own Name and to Be Identified

486. Article 56 establishes the right of every person to have his own name, to have the name of his father and of his mother, and to know their identity. For this purpose, the State guarantees the right of everyone to investigate maternity and paternity situations. All persons have the right to be registered free of charge with the Civil Registry Office after birth, and to obtain public documents constituting evidence of their biological identity, in accordance with law. Such documents shall not contain any mention classifying the parental relationship.

§3. Personal Freedom

487. Personal freedom is declared in Article 44 as inviolable, and in order to guarantee such inviolability, the following rights of everyone are enumerated: no person shall be arrested or detained except by virtue of a court order, unless such person is caught *in fraganti*. In the latter case, such person must be brought before a judge within forty-eight hours of his or her arrest. He or she shall remain free during trial, except for reasons determined by law and assessed by the judge on a case-by-case basis. Any officer taking measures involving the deprivation of liberty must identify himself. The bail, as required by law, for the release of a detainee shall not be subject to tax of any kind. Any person under arrest has the right to communicate immediately with members of his or her family, an attorney or any other person in whom he or she reposes trust, and such persons in turn have the right to be informed where the detainee is being held, to be notified immediately of the reasons for the arrest and to have a written record inserted into the case file concerning the physical or mental condition of the detainee, either by himself or herself, or with the aid of specialists. The competent authorities shall keep a public record of every arrest made, including the identity of the person arrested, the place, time, circumstances and the officers who made the arrest. In the case of the arrest of foreign nationals, applicable provisions of international treaties concerning consular notification shall also be observed. The penalty shall not extend beyond the person of the convicted indi-

vidual. No one shall be sentenced to perpetual or humiliating penalties. Penalties consisting of deprivation of liberty shall not exceed thirty years. (7) No person shall remain under arrest after a release order has been issued by the competent authority or such person's sentence has been served.

488. In this same regard related to personal freedom, Article 45 expressly prohibits public authorities, whether military, civilian or of any other kind, even during a state of exception, exception or restriction or guarantees, from effecting, permitting or tolerating the forced disappearance of persons. An officer receiving an order or instruction to carry it out, has the obligation not to obey, and to report the order or instruction to the competent authorities. The intellectual and physical perpetrators, accomplices and those covering up the crimes of forced disappearance of a person, as well as any attempt to commit such offence, shall be punished in accordance with law.

§4. *Personal Integrity*

489. The right to personal integrity is established in Article 46, as the right everyone is entitled to respect for his or her physical, mental and moral integrity. Therefore, according to the same provision, no person shall be subjected to cruel, inhuman or degrading penalties, tortures or treatment. Every victim of torture or cruel, inhumane or degrading treatment effected or tolerated by agents of the State has the right to rehabilitation. Any person deprived of liberty shall be treated with respect due to the inherent dignity of the human being. No person shall be subjected without his or her freely given consent to scientific experiments or medical or laboratory examinations, except when such person's life is in danger, or in any other circumstances as may be detained by law. Any public official who, by reason of his official position, inflicts mistreatment or physical or mental suffering on any person or instigates or tolerates such treatment, shall be punished in accordance with law.

490. Article 54 of the Constitution establishes the guarantee of everyone not to be subjected to slavery or servitude. Traffic of persons, in particular women, children and adolescents, in any form, shall be subject to the penalties prescribed by law.

§5. *Inviolability of Person's Home*

491. Article 47 of the Constitution, also following the tradition of prior constitutions, guarantees the inviolability of a person's home and any of his private premises. They may not be forcibly entered except by court order, and only to prevent the commission of a crime or carry out the decisions handed down by the courts in accordance with law, always respecting human dignity in all cases. Any health inspections carried out in accordance with law shall be performed only after notice from the officials ordering or carrying it out.

§6. *Inviolability of Private Communications*

492. The Constitution also guarantees the secrecy and inviolability of private communications in all forms. The same may not be interfered with except by order of a competent court, with observance of applicable provisions of law and preserving the secrecy of the private issues unrelated to the pertinent proceedings (Article 48).

§7. *Right to Petition Before Public Authorities and to Obtain Due Answer*

493. Article 51 of the Constitution sets forth the right of everyone to petition or make representations before any authority or public official concerning matters within their competence, and to obtain a timely and adequate response. Whoever violates this right shall be punished in accordance with law, including the possibility of dismissal from office.[1975]

§8. *Right of Association*

494. The right of everyone to assemble or associate with others for lawful purposes is also provided in the Constitution (Article 52), the State being obliged to facilitate its exercise. The right is, however, limited in Article 256 of the Constitution that prohibits judges from associating with one another, and in Article 294 that establishes the intervention of the State (National Electoral Council) in the internal elections of professional associations (guilds).

§9. *Right of Meeting*

495. Article 53 of the Constitution establishes the right of everyone to meet publicly or privately, without obtaining permission in advance, for lawful purposes and without weapons. Meetings in public places may be regulated by law.

§10. *Freedom of Movement*

496. Article 50 of the Constitution establishes the right of everyone to freely transit by any means throughout the national territory, to change his domicile and residence, to leave and return to the Republic, to move his goods or belongings within the country and to bring his goods into or remove them from the country, subject only to such limitations as may be prescribed by law. In addition, Venezuelans shall enter the country without need for authorization of any kind and no act of the State may establish against Venezuelans the penalty of banishment from the national territory. According to Article 69, extradition of Venezuelans is prohibited.

§11. *Freedom of Expression and of Information*

497. The right to free expression without censorship is guarantied in Article 57 of the Constitution, which states that:

> Everyone has the right to express freely his or her thoughts, ideas or opinions orally, in writing or by any other form of expression, and to use for such purpose any means of communication and diffusion, and no censorship shall be established.

1975   See Carlos L. Carrillo Artiles, 'El derecho de petición y la oportuna y adecuada respuesta en la Constitución de 1999', in *Estudios de Derecho Administrativo: Libro Homenaje a la Universidad Central de Venezuela,* vol. I (Caracas: Imprenta Nacional, 2001), 219–251; and Lubín Aguirre, 'Garantías procesales frente a la inacción administrativa' in *Estudios de Derecho Administrativo: Libro Homenaje a la Universidad Central de Venezuela,* vol. I (Caracas: Imprenta Nacional, 2001), 35–41.

Anyone making use of this right assumes full responsibility for everything expressed. Anonymity, war propaganda, discriminatory messages or those promoting religious intolerance are not permitted. Also, the same Article 57 of the Constitution provides that censorship restricting the ability of 'public officials' (*funcionarios públicos*) to report on matters for which they are responsible is prohibited; a provision that is not applicable to judges.

For such purposes, Article 58 of the Constitution guarantees that communications are free and plural, and involve the duties and responsibilities indicated by law.

§12. *Right to Be Informed and to Reply and Rectification*

498. Article 58 of the Constitution also establishes the right of everybody to be 'timely, truthful and impartially' informed, without censorship, in accordance with the principles of the Constitution. In this regard, the use of these adjectives were widely debated in the 1999 National Constituent Assembly due to the dangers they could raise regarding the State's temptation to control or monopolize what 'truthful, opportune and impartial' is, and with this, the possible creation of some 'official truth'.[1976] This matter has been regulated in the 2005 Radio and Television Social Responsibility Law.[1977]

The same Article 58 also guarantees the right of everyone to reply and to ask for rectification when they are directly affected by inaccurate or offensive information.[1978] Children and adolescents have the right to receive adequate information for purposes of their overall development.

1976   See Allan R. Brewer-Carías, 'La libre expresión del pensamiento y el derecho a la información en la Constitución venezolana de 1999', in *Anuario de Derecho Constitucional Latinoamericano* (Edición, 2002, Konrad Adenauer Stiftung, Montevideo, 2002), 267 a 276; Fernando Flores Gimenez, 'Las libertades de expresión e información en la Constitución de Venezuela: Análisis de una confusión', in *Revista de Derecho Constitucional*, N° 7 (Caracas: Editorial Sherwood, enero-junio 2003), 125 a 135; Jesús A. Davila Ortega, 'El Derecho De la información y la libertad de expresión en Venezuela (Un estudio de la sentencia 1.013/2001 de la Sala Constitucional del Tribunal Supremo de Justicia)', in *Revista de Derecho Constitucional*, N° 5 julio-diciembre-2001 (Caracas: Editorial Sherwood, 2002), 305 a 325; María Candelaria Domínguez Guillén, 'Las libertades de expresión e información', in *Revista de derecho del Tribunal Supremo de Justicia*, N° 5 (Caracas, 2002), 19 a 72; Héctor Faúndez Ledesma, 'Las condiciones de las restricciones a la libertad de expresión', in *El Derecho Público a comienzos del siglo XXI. Estudios homenaje al Profesor Allan R. Brewer-Carías*, vol. III (Madrid: Instituto de Derecho Público, UCV, Civitas Ediciones, 2003), 2598–2664; Rafael Ortiz-Ortiz, 'Las implicaciones jurídico positivas del derecho a la información y a la libertad de expresión en el nuevo orden constitucional', in *Revista de la Facultad de Derecho de la Universidad de Carabobo*, N° 1 (Valencia, 2002), 163–246.

1977   *Gaceta Oficial* N° 38.333 of 12 Dec. 2005. See Allan R. Brewer-Carías et al., *Ley de Responsabilidad Social de Radio y Televisión (Ley Resorte)* (Caracas: Editorial Jurídica Venezolana, 2006). and Carolina Puppio, 'Libertad de Expresión vs. Ley de Contenidos. Reflexiones de cara a la aprobación de una Ley de Contenido en Venezuela', in *Revista de Derecho Constitucional*, N° 6, enero-diciembre-2002 (Caracas: Editorial Sherwood, 2003), 165 a 190.

1978   See Allan R. Brewer-Carías et al., *La libertad de expresión amenazada (sentencia 1.013)* (Caracas: Editorial Jurídica Venezolana, 2001).

§13. *Right to Have Access to Personal Information*

499. Article 28 of the Constitution guarantees the right of anyone to have access to the information and data concerning him or her or his or her goods which are contained in official or private records, with the exceptions only established by law, as well as the right to know what use is being made of the same and the purpose thereof. This right implies in particular, the right to petition (habeas data recourse) (see *supra* paragraph 458) before the competent courts for the updating, correction or destruction of any records that are erroneous or that can unlawfully affect the petitioner's right.

500. According to the same provision of the Constitution, everybody also has the right to have access to documents of any nature containing information of interest to communities or groups of persons. The foregoing right is without prejudice to the confidentiality of sources from which information is received by journalists, or secrecy in other professions as may be determined by law.

§14. *Right to the Protection of Honour and Private Life*

501. According to Article 60 of the Constitution, every person is entitled to protection of his or her honour, private life, intimacy, self-image, confidentiality and reputation. The use of electronic information shall be restricted by law in order to guarantee the personal and family intimacy and honour of citizens and the full exercise of their rights.[1979]

§15. *Freedom of Religion and Cult*

502. The Constitution expressly declares in Article 59 that the State guarantees the freedom of cult and religion. Consequently, all persons have the right to profess their religious faith and cults, and express their beliefs in private or in public by teaching and other practices, provided such beliefs are not contrary to moral, good customs and public order. Nonetheless, no one shall invoke religious beliefs or discipline as a means of evading compliance with law or preventing another person from exercising his or her rights.[1980]

The autonomy and independence of religious confessions and churches is likewise guaranteed in the Constitution, subject only to such limitations as may derive from this Constitution and the law.

Fathers and mothers are entitled to have their sons and daughters receive religious education in accordance with their convictions.

1979   See Rafael Ortiz, 'Configuración del derecho a la intimidad como derecho civil fundamental', in *Revista del Tribunal Supremo de Justicia,* N° 5 (Caracas, 2002), 87–149; Cosimina Pellegrino Pacera, 'El derecho a la intimidad en la nueva era informática, el derecho a la autodeterminación informativa y el hábeas data a la luz de la Constitución venezolana de 1999', in *Estudios de Derecho Público: Libro Homenaje a Humberto J. La Roche Rincón,* vol. I (Caracas: Tribunal Supremo de Justicia, 2001), 143–216.

1980   See Josefina Calcaño de Temeltas, *Aproximación a la libertad de conciencia, religión y culto en derecho comparado y en Venezuela* (Caracas: FUNEDA, 2011); Carmen Vallarino Bracho, 'Libertad de religión y derechos humanos en Venezuela', en *Revista de Derecho,* N° 30 (Caracas: Tribunal Supremo de Justicia, 2009), 309–319.

§16. *Freedom of Conscience*

503. All persons have the right to freedom of conscience, and to express the same, provided that its practice does not affect his personality or constitute criminal offence. Objections of conscience may not be invoked in order to evade compliance with law or prevent others from complying with law or exercising their rights.

§17. *Right to Personal Security and to Be Protected by the State*

504. Finally, according to Article 55 of the Constitution, every person has the right to be protected by the State, through the entities established by law for the protection of citizens, from situations that constitute a threat, vulnerability or risk to the physical integrity of individuals, their properties, the enjoyment of rights or the fulfilment of their duties. The citizens' participation in programmes for purposes of prevention, citizen safety and emergency management shall be regulated by a special law.

The Constitution guarantees that the State's security corps shall respect the human dignity and rights of all persons; and set forth in an express way that the use of weapons or toxic substances by police and security officers shall be limited by the principles of necessity, convenience, opportunity and proportionality in accordance with law.

Chapter 4. Social and Cultural Rights

505. The 1999 Constitution contains very extensive declarations of social rights,[1981] including family and social protection rights, right to health and social security, labour rights, educational and cultural rights, environmental rights and the indigenous peoples' rights; although in many cases, the declarations are more of aims or public policy regarding social welfare than specific justiciable rights.

§1. *Family Rights and Rights to Social Protection*

I. *Right to Family Protection*

506. The Constitution has established a series of social rights as people's 'rights to protection' or to be protected by the State, beginning by the protection of families. In this regard, Article 75 imposes on the State the obligation to protect families as a natural association in society, and as the fundamental space for the overall development of persons. According to the same constitutional provision, family relationships must be based on equality of rights and duties, solidarity, common effort, mutual understanding and reciprocal respect among family members. In order to protect

---

1981   See Mercedes Pulido de Briceño, 'La Constitución de 1999 y los derechos sociales', in *La cuestión social en la Constitución Bolivariana de Venezuela* (Caracas: Editorial Torino, 2000), 15–28; Carlos Aponte Blank, 'Los derechos sociales y la Constitución de 1999', *id.*, 113–134; and Emilio Spósito Contreras, 'Aproximación a los derechos sociales en la Constitución de la República Bolivariana de Venezuela', in *Revista de derecho del Tribunal Supremo de Justicia*, N° 9 (Caracas, 2003), 381 a 398.

families, the State must guarantee protection to the mother, father or other person acting as head of a household.

507. Children and adolescents have the right to live, be raised and develop in the bosom of their original family. When this is impossible or contrary to their best interests, they shall have the right to a substitute family, in accordance with law. Adoption has effects similar to those of parenthood, and is established in all cases for the benefit of the adoptee, in accordance with law. International adoption shall be subordinated to domestic adoption.

II. *Right to Motherhood and Fatherhood Protection*

508. Article 76 of the Constitution provides for the full protection of motherhood and fatherhood, whatever the marital status of the mother or father. Couples have the right to decide freely and responsibly how many children they wish to conceive, and are entitled to access to the information and means necessary to guarantee the exercise of this right. The State guarantees overall assistance and protection for motherhood, in general, from the moment of conception, throughout pregnancy, delivery and the puerperal period, and guarantees full family planning services based on ethical and scientific values. This provision, particularly when protecting maternity from the moment of conception, implies limits to configured abortion as a right.

III. *Right to Marriage Protection*

509. Article 77 of the Constitution also expressly 'protects marriage between a man and a woman, based on free consent and absolute equality of rights and obligations of the spouses'. Also, a stable de facto union between a man and a woman that meets the requirements established by law shall have the same effects as marriage.[1982] From this provision, according to the Venezuelan constitutional system, no same sex 'marriage' is admissible.

IV. *Rights of Children and Adolescents*

510. Regarding children and adolescents, Article 78 of the Constitution considers them as full legal persons that shall be protected by specialized courts, organs and legislation, which shall respect, guarantee and develop the contents of the Constitution, the law, the Convention on Children's Rights and any other international treaty that may have been executed and ratified by the Republic in this field. The State,

---

1982   See Anabella Del Moral, 'Contenido y alcance del artículo 77 de la Constitución de la República Bolivariana de Venezuela, según sentencia de la Sala Constitucional del 15 de julio de 2005', in *Revista de Derecho*, Nº 27 (Caracas: Tribunal Supremo de Justicia, 2008), 111–131; María C. Domínguez Guillen, 'Más sobre las uniones estables de hecho, según la Sala Constitucional del Tribunal Supremo de Justicia', in *Revista de Derecho*, Nº 27 (Caracas: Tribunal Supremo de Justicia, 2008), 133–167; Gilberto Guerrero Quintero, 'La interpretación de la Sala Constitucional del Tribunal Supremo de Justicia del artículo 77 de la Carta Magna', in *Revista de Derecho*, Nº 27 (Caracas: Tribunal Supremo de Justicia, 2008), 169–237; José Peña Solís, 'Análisis crítico de la sentencia de la Sala Constitucional Nº 0190, de 28 de febrero de 2008: Interpretación de los artículos 21 y 77 constitucionales: derecho a la igualdad, uniones estables de hecho y extensión de los efectos del matrimonio a uniones concubinarias', in *Revista de Derecho*, Nº 27 (Caracas: Tribunal Supremo de Justicia, 2008), 287–322.

families and society shall guarantee their full protection as an absolute priority, taking into account their best interest in actions and decisions concerning them. The State shall promote their progressive incorporation into active citizenship, and shall create a national guidance system for the overall protection of children and adolescents.

511. However, Article 79 of the Constitution guarantees the right and duty of young people to be active participants in the development process. For such purpose, the State, with the joint participation of families and society, shall create opportunities to stimulate their productive transition into adult life, including in particular, training for and access to their first employment, in accordance with law.

V. *Rights of Elderly Protection*

512. Regarding senior citizens, Article 80 of the Constitution imposes on the State the duty to guarantee the full exercise of their rights and guarantees; providing that the State, with the participation of families and society, is obligated to respect their human dignity, autonomy and to guarantee them full care and social security benefits to improve and guarantee their quality of life. Pension and retirement benefits granted through the social security system shall not be less than the urban minimum salary. Senior citizens shall be guaranteed to have the right to a proper work, if they indicate a desire to work and are capable of it.

VI. *Rights of Disabled Protection*

513. Article 81 of the Constitution sets forth that any person with disability or special needs has the right to the full and autonomous exercise of his abilities and to its integration into the family and community. The State, with the participation of families and society, must guarantee them respect for their human dignity, equality of opportunity and satisfactory working conditions, and shall promote their training, education and access to employment appropriate to their condition, in accordance with law. It is recognized that deaf persons have the right to express themselves and communicate through the Venezuelan sign language,[1983] and the televised media must carry sub-titles and sign language translations for persons with hearing impairments (Article 101).

§2. *Right to Dwelling*

514. Article 82 of the Constitution also establishes the right of every person to adequate, safe and comfortable, hygienic housing, with appropriate essential basic services, including a habitat such as to humanize family, neighbourhood and community relations. The progressive meeting of this requirement is the shared responsibility of citizens and the State in all areas. The State shall give priority to families, and shall guarantee them, especially those with meagre resources, the possibility of

---

1983 See María C. Domínguez Guillén, 'La protección constitucional de los incapaces', in *Temas de Derecho Administrativo: Libro Homenaje a Gonzalo Pérez Luciani*, vol. I, no. 7 (Caracas: Tribunal Supremo de Justicia, Colección Libros Homenaje, 2002), 609 a 658.

access to social policies and credit for the construction, purchase or enlargement of dwellings.

§3. *Right to Health*

515. The Constitution also provides expressly for the right to health, as a fundamental social right, being an obligation of the State to guarantee it as part of the right to life (Article 83).[1984] Consequently, the State shall promote and develop policies oriented toward improving the quality of life, common welfare and access to services; and all persons have the right to protection of health, as well as the duty to participate actively in the furtherance and protection of the same, and to comply with such health and hygiene measures as may be established by law, and in accordance with international conventions and treaties signed and ratified by the Republic.

516. In order to guarantee the right to health, Article 84 sets forth that the State must create, exercise guidance over and administer a national public health system that crosses sector boundaries, and is decentralized and participatory in nature, integrated with the social security system and governed by the principles of gratuity, universality, completeness, fairness, social integration and solidarity. The public health system gives priority to promoting health and preventing disease, guaranteeing prompt treatment and quality rehabilitation. Public health assets and services are the property of the State and shall not be privatized. The organized community has the right and duty to participate in the making of decisions concerning policy planning, implementation and control at public health institutions. This is to say the health service is constitutionally conceived as being integrated to the system of social security, as a sub-system of it, and is conceived as being cost-free for its users and universally available. Moreover, the Constitution itself establishes that public health related property and services cannot be privatized.

517. Accordingly, the financing of the public health system is the responsibility of the State, which shall integrate the revenue resources, mandatory Social Security contributions and any other sources of financing provided for by law. The State guarantees a health budget such as to make possible the attainment of health policy objectives. In coordination with universities and research centres, a national professional and technical training policy and a national industry to produce health care supplies shall be promoted and developed. Finally, Article 85 concludes its regulation in the area by stating that, the State must 'regulate public and private institutions of health'. This is the only place in which private health institutions are mentioned, but for the purpose of regulating them.

1984   See Jesús Ollarves Irazábal, 'La vigencia del derecho a la salud', in *El Derecho Público a comienzos del siglo XXI. Estudios homenaje al Profesor Allan R. Brewer-Carías,* vol. III (Madrid: Instituto de Derecho Público, UCV, Civitas Ediciones, 2003), 2867–2886; Oscar Feo, 'La salud en la nueva Constitución', in *La cuestión social en la Constitución Bolivariana de Venezuela* (Caracas: Editorial Torino, 2000), 29–46; Belén Anasagasti, 'Caracterización de los principales rasgos del derecho a la salud dentro del marco constitucional de los derechos sociales del texto de 1961 y de 1999', in *La cuestión social en la Constitución Bolivariana de Venezuela* (Caracas: Editorial Torino, 2000), 135–152.

§4. *Right to Social Security*

518. Regarding social security, it is also considered in Article 86 of the Constitution as a constitutional right,[1985] providing for it as a non-profit public service to guarantee health and protection in contingencies of maternity, fatherhood, illness, invalidity, catastrophic illness, disability, special needs, occupational risks, loss of employment, unemployment, old age, widowhood, loss of parents, housing, burdens deriving from family life and any other social welfare circumstances. The Constitution imposes upon the State the obligation and responsibility of ensuring the efficacy of this constitutional right, creating a universal and complete Social Security system, with joint, unitary, efficient and participatory financing from direct and indirect contributions. Nonetheless, the lack of ability to contribute shall not be ground for excluding persons from protection by the system.

519. The Constitution also establishes that Social Security financial resources shall not be used for other purposes. The mandatory assessments paid by employees to cover medical and health care services and other Social Security benefits shall be administered only for social purposes, under the guidance of the State. Any net remaining balances of capital allocated to health, education and Social Security shall be accumulated for distribution and contribution to those services. The Social Security system is ruled by a special organic law.[1986]

§5. *Labour Rights*

I.   *Right to Work and State's Obligations*

520. The chapter of the Constitution of 1999 containing social and family rights also incorporated a set of labour rights, following the orientation of the 1961 Constitution, but amplifying and making them even more rigid, by constitutionalizing many rights which by nature could exist at the level of ordinary law. Thus, the right and duty to work is expressly set forth (Article 87); work is considered as a social fact and shall enjoy the protection of the State (Article 89), and freedom to work shall be subject only to the restrictions established by statutes.[1987]

1985   See María Bernardoni de Govea, 'Reforma de la seguridad social en Venezuela: un proceso inconcluso', in *Derecho y Sociedad. Revista de Estudiantes de Derecho de la Universidad Monteávila*, N° 3 (Caracas: Universidad Monteávila, Facultad de Ciencias Jurídicas y Políticas, 2002), 193–213; Pablo Pérez Herrera, 'El sistema venezolano de seguridad social', in *Revista Tachirense de Derecho*, N° 14 (San Cristóbal: Universidad Católica del Táchira, 2002), 143–158; Allan R. Brewer-Carías, 'Consideraciones sobre el régimen constitucional del derecho a la seguridad social, el Sistema de Seguridad Social y la Administración Privada de Fondos de Pensiones', in *Libro Homenaje a Fernando Parra Aranguren*, vol. I (Caracas: Facultad de Ciencias Jurídicas y Políticas, Universidad Central de Venezuela, 2001), 73–85.

1986   See Organic Law on the Social Security System, and Social Security Law, *Gaceta Oficial* N° 5.891 Extra., 31 Jul. 2008.

1987   See Napoleón Goizueta H., 'Aspectos laborales en la Constitución Bolivariana de Venezuela y normas concordantes con la legislación del trabajo', in *Revista Gaceta Laboral* 8, no. 2 (mayo-agosto) (Maracaibo: Ediciones Astro Data, 2002), 251–282; Héctor A. Jaime Martínez, 'La nueva Constitución venezolana y su influencia en la Ley Orgánica del Trabajo', in *Revista Tachirense de Derecho*, N° 12 (San Cristóbal: Universidad Católica del Táchira, 2000), 151–178; Gabriela Santana González,

521. The State must guarantee the adoption of the necessary measures so that every person shall be able to obtain productive work providing them with a dignified and decorous living and guarantee him or her the full exercise of the right to work and of being employed. The State must also promote employment, and measures tending to guarantee the exercise of the labour rights of self-employed persons must be adopted by statutes.

522. However, every employer shall guarantee employees adequate safety, hygienic and environmental conditions on the job, and the State shall adopt measures and create institutions such as to make it possible to control and promote these conditions.

523. Article 88 of the Constitution guarantees the equality and equitable treatment of men and women in the exercise of the right to work. The same provision recognizes work at home as an economic activity that creates added value and produces social welfare and wealth; and declares that housewives are entitled to Social Security in accordance with law.

II.   Rights to Have Work Protected

524. The Constitution establishes that by statute the necessary provisions must be established for improving the material, moral and intellectual conditions of workers. In order to fulfil this duty of the State, Article 89 of the Constitution enumerates the following principles: (1) No law shall establish provisions that affect the intactness and progressive nature of labour rights and benefits. In labour relations, reality shall prevail over forms or appearances. (2) Labour rights are not renounceable; consequently, any action, agreement or convention involving a waiver of or encroachment upon these rights is null and void. Concessions and settlements are possible only at the end of the employment relationship, in accordance with the requirements established by law. (3) When there are doubts concerning application or conflicts among several rules or in the interpretation of a particular rule, that most favourable to the worker shall be applied. The rule applied must be applied in its entirety. (4) Any measure or act on the part of an employer in violation of this Constitution is null and void, and of no effect. (5) All types of discrimination because of political reasons, age, race, creed, sex or any other characteristic is prohibited. (6) Work by adolescents at tasks that may affect their overall development is prohibited. The State shall protect them against any economic and social exploitation.

III. Working Hours

525. However, the Constitution (Article 90) has also established provisions regarding working hours that shall not exceed eight hours per day or forty-four hours per week. Where permitted by law, night work shall not exceed seven hours per day or thirty-five hours per week. No employer shall have the right to require employees

'Normas constitucionales en materia laboral. De moribundas a bolivarianas', in *Revista Syllabus,* N° 1 (Caracas: Escuela de Derecho, Facultad de Ciencias Jurídicas y Políticas. Universidad Central de Venezuela, noviembre, 2000), 39–55; María C. Torres Seoane, 'Las normas laborales en la Constitución', in *Comentarios a la Constitución de la República Bolivariana de Venezuela* (Caracas: Vadell Hermanos Editores, 2000), 149–176.

to work overtime. An effort shall be made to reduce working hours progressively in the interest of society and in such sphere as may be determined, and appropriate provisions shall be adopted to make better use of free time for the benefit of the physical, spiritual and cultural development of workers. Workers are entitled to weekly time off and paid vacations on the same terms as for days actually worked.

IV. *Right to Salary and other Benefits*

526. Regarding salary, Article 91 of the Constitution establishes that every worker has the right to a salary sufficient to enable him or her to live with dignity and cover basic material, social and intellectual needs for himself or herself and his or her family. The payment of equal salary for equal work is guaranteed, and the share of the profits of a business enterprise to which workers are entitled shall be determined. Salary is not subject to seizure, and shall be paid periodically and promptly in legal tender, with the exception of the food allowance, in accordance with law.

527. The State guarantees workers in both the public and the private sector a vital minimum salary which shall be adjusted each year, taking as one of the references the cost of a basic market basket. The form and procedure to be followed shall be established by law.

528. Article 92 of the Constitution declares that all workers have the right to benefits to compensate them for length of service and protect them in the event of dismissal.

529. Salary and benefits are labour obligations due and payable immediately upon accrual. Any delay in payment of the same shall bear interest, which also constitutes a debt and shall enjoy the same privileges and guarantees as the principal debt.

530. The liability of the natural or juridical person for whose benefit services are provided through an intermediary or contractor shall be determined by law, without prejudice to the job and severance liability of the latter. The State shall establish, through the competent organ, the liability to which employers in general are subject in the event of simulation or fraud for the purpose of distorting, disregarding or impeding the application of labour legislation (Article 94).

V. *Stability Rights*

531. The stability of employment is regulated in Article 93 of the Constitution, setting forth that it shall be guaranteed by law, with provisions as appropriate to restrict any form of unjustified dismissal. Dismissals contrary to this Constitution are null and void.

VI. *Trade-Unions Rights*

532. Article 95 of the Constitution guarantees workers, without distinction of any kind and without need for authorization in advance, the right to freely establish such union organizations as they may deem appropriate for the optimum protection of their rights and interests, as well as the right to join or not to join the same, in accor-

dance with law.[1988] These organizations are not subject to administrative dissolution, suspension or intervention. Workers are protected against any act of discrimination or interference contrary to the exercise of this right. The promoters and the members of the board of directors of the union enjoy immunity from dismissal from their employment for the period and on the terms required to enable them to carry out their functions. For purposes of the exercise of union democracy, the bylaws and regulations of union organizations shall provide for the replacement of boards of directors and representatives by universal, direct and secret suffrage. Any union leaders and representatives who abuse the benefits deriving from union freedom for their personal gain or benefit shall be punished in accordance with law. Boards of directors of union organizations shall be required to file a sworn statement of assets.

533. With respect to this right to unionize, the intervention of the State into labour union functions must be mentioned, through the provision in Article 294.6 of the Constitution of the jurisdiction of the National Electoral Council, an organ of the State (Electoral Power), to 'organize elections in unions and professional associations'. As a result, in Venezuela, unions are not free to organize their own elections of representatives and authorities, since these elections now are organized by the State.

VII. *Right to Collective Bargaining Agreements*

534. Article 96 of the Constitution guarantees all employees in both public and the private sector to have the right to voluntary collective bargaining and to enter into collective bargaining agreements, subject only to such restrictions as may be established by law. The State guarantees this process, and shall establish appropriate provisions to encourage collective relations and the resolution of labour conflicts. Collective bargaining agreements cover all workers who are active as of the time they are signed, and those hired thereafter.

VIII. *Right to Strike*

535. Finally, regarding the right to strike, Article 97 of the Constitution guarantees it to all workers in the public and private sector, subject to such conditions as may be established by law.

§6. *Cultural Rights*

536. Cultural creation is considered in the Constitution as a free action, including as provided in Article 98 of the Constitution, the right to invest in, produce and disseminate the creative, scientific, technical and humanistic work, as well as legal protection of the author's rights in his works. The State recognizes and protects intellectual property rights in scientific, literary and artistic works, inventions, innovations, trade names, patents, trademarks and slogans, in accordance with the conditions and exceptions established by law and the international treaties executed and ratified by the Republic in this field.

1988   See León Arismendi; 'Libertad sindical y elecciones sindicales en la Constitución de 1999', in *Revista Gaceta Laboral* 8, no. 1 (enero-abril) (Maracaibo: Ediciones Astro Data, 2002), 79–98.

537. In addition, Article 99 of the Constitution declares cultural values as the un-renounceable property of the Venezuelan people and a fundamental right to be encouraged and guaranteed by the State, efforts being made to provide the necessary conditions, legal instruments, means and funding. The autonomy of the public administration of culture is recognized, on such terms as may be established by law.

538. The State must guarantee the protection and preservation, enrichment, conservation and restoration of the cultural tangible and intangible heritage and the historic memories of the nation. The assets constituting the cultural heritage of the nation are inalienable, not subject to seizure or to statute of limitations. Penalties and sanctions for damage caused to these assets shall be provided for by law.

539. The folk cultures comprising the national identity of Venezuela enjoy special attention, with recognition of and respect for intercultural relations under the principle of equality of cultures. Incentives and inducements shall be provided for by law for persons, institutions and communities which promote, support, develop or finance cultural plans, programmes and activities within the country and Venezuelan culture abroad. The State guarantees cultural workers inclusion in the social security system to provide them with a dignified life, recognizing the idiosyncrasies of cultural work, in accordance with law (Article 100).

540. Regarding cultural information, the State must guarantee its issuance, reception and circulation; the communications media having the duty of assisting in the dissemination of the values of folk traditions and the work of artists, writers, composers, motion-picture directors, scientists and other creators of culture of the country. The television media shall include sub-titles and translation into Venezuelan sign language for persons with hearing problems. The terms and modalities of these obligations shall be established by law. (Article 101).

§7. *Educational Rights*

I.   *Right to Education*

541. With respect to the right to education, Article 102 of the Constitution begins by establishing, as a general matter, that 'education is a human right and a fundamental social duty, it is democratic, cost-free, and mandatory'.[1989] The consequence of the foregoing is that Article 102 itself imposes upon the State the obligation to

---

1989   See Gustavo J. Linares Benzo, 'Bases constitucionales de la educación', in *Revista Derecho y Socie-dad de la Universidad Monteávila*, N° 2 (abril) (Caracas, 2001), 217–252; Gustavo J. Linares Benzo, 'La educación en el texto constitucional', in *Estudios de Derecho Administrativo: Libro Homenaje a la Universidad Central de Venezuela*, vol. II (Caracas: Imprenta Nacional, 2001), 91–120 and in *Revista de Derecho Público*, N° 84 (octubre-diciembre) (Caracas: Editorial Jurídica Venezolana, 2000), 5–25; and Mabel Mundó, 'El derecho a la educación en las Constituciones de 1999 y 1961: reflexio-nes sobre principios, recursos y aprendizajes para la elaboración de la política educativa', in *La cues-tión social en la Constitución Bolivariana de Venezuela* (Caracas: Editorial Torino, 2000), 47–74; Suying Olivares García, 'El derecho a la educación como un derecho humano fundamental a la luz de la Constitución de 1999', in *Frónesis. Revista de Filosofía Jurídica, Social y Política* (Maracaibo: Universidad del Zulia, Facultad de Ciencias Jurídicas y Políticas, Instituto de Filosofía del Derecho Dr José M. Delgado Ocando, Ediciones Astro Data, N° 14, 2 (mayo-agosto), 2007), 11–36.

assume responsibility as an irrevocable function of the greatest interest, at all levels and in all modes, as an instrument of scientific, humanistic and technical knowledge at the service of society.

Accordingly, every person has the right to a full, high-quality, ongoing education under conditions and circumstances of equality, subject only to such limitations as derive from such persons own aptitudes, vocation and aspirations. Education is obligatory at all levels from maternal to the diversified secondary level.

II. *Education As a Public Service*

52. Education is constitutionally declared to be a public service (Article 102), although the Constitution also states that, 'the State will stimulate and protect private education that is imparted according with the principles established in this Constitution and the Laws'. As a public service, education is grounded on the respect for all currents of thought, to the end of developing the creative potential of every human being and the full exercise of his or her personality in a democratic society based on the work ethic value and on active, conscious and joint participation in the processes of social transformation embodied in the values which are part of the national identity, and with a Latin American and universal vision. The State, with the participation of families and society, must promote the process of civic education in accordance with the principles contained in this Constitution and in the laws.

543. Education offered at State institutions is free of charge up to the undergraduate university level. To this end, the State shall make a priority investment in accordance with United Nations recommendations. The State shall create and sustain institutions and services sufficiently equipped to ensure the admission process, ongoing education and programme completion in the education system (Article 103).

544. The law shall guarantee equal attention to persons with special needs or disabilities, and to those who have been deprived of liberty or do not meet the basic conditions for admission to and continuing enrolment in the education system. The contributions of private individuals to public education programmes at the secondary and university levels shall be tax deductible in accordance with the pertinent law (Article 103).

545. Regarding the content of education, Article 106 of the Constitution sets forth that environmental education is obligatory in the various levels and modes of the education system, as well as in informal civil education. Spanish, Venezuelan geography and history and the principles of the Bolivarian thought shall be compulsory courses at public and private institutions up to the education diversified level.

However, the Constitution also declares that physical education and sports play a fundamental role in the overall education of childhood and adolescents. Instruction in the same is obligatory at all levels of public and private education up to the education diversified level, with such exceptions as may be established by law (Article 111).

546. The communications media, public and private, shall contribute to civil education. The State guarantees public radio and television services and library and computer networks, with a view to permitting universal access to information. Education centres are to incorporate knowledge and application of new technologies and

the resulting innovations, in accordance with such requirements as may be establis-hed by law to this end (Article 108).

III. *Right to Educate*

547. Article 106 of the Constitution guarantees every natural or juridical person subject to demonstration of its ability and provided it meets at all times the ethical, academic, scientific, financial, infrastructure and any other requirements that may be established by law, to be permitted to fund and maintain private educational institu-tions under the strict inspection and vigilance of the State, with the prior approval of the latter.

548. For such purposes, only persons of recognized good moral character and proven academic qualifications shall be placed in charge of education (Article 104). The State shall encourage them to remain continuously up-to-date, and shall guaran-tee stability in the practice of the teaching profession, whether in public or private institutions, in accordance with this Constitution and the law, with working condi-tions and a standard of living commensurate with the importance of their mission. Admissions, promotion and continued enrolment in the education system shall be provided for by law, and shall be responsive to evaluation criteria based on merit, to the exclusion of any partisan or other non-academic interference.

IV. *Principle of the University Autonomy*

549. The Constitution establishes and recognizes the principle of the autonomy of universities, as a principle and status that allows teachers, students and graduates from its community, to devote themselves to the search for knowledge through rese-arch in the fields of science, humanities and technology, for the spiritual and mate-rial benefit of the Nation (Article 109).

550. Autonomous universities shall adopt their own rules for their governance and operation and the efficient management of their property, under such control and vigilance as may be established by law to this end. Autonomy of universities is established in the planning, organization, preparation and updating of research, tea-ching and extension programmes. The inviolability of the university campus is esta-blished. Experimental national universities shall attain their autonomy in accordance with law (Article 109).

V. *Science and Technology System*

551. Article 110 of the Constitution recognizes as being in the public interest science, technology, knowledge, innovation and the resulting applications, and the necessary information services, the same being fundamental instruments for the country's economic, social and political development, as well as for national sove-reignty and security.

In order to promote and develop these activities, the State shall allocate sufficient resources and shall create a national science and technology system in accordance with law. The private sector shall contribute with resources as well.[1990] The State

---

1990   Organic law on Science, Technology and Innovation, *Gaceta Oficial* N° 39.575 of 16 Dec. 2010.

shall guarantee the enforcement of the ethical and legal principles that are to govern research activities in science, humanism and technology. The manners and means of fulfilling this guarantee shall be determined by law.

VI. *Right to Sport*

552. The right to sport and the right to recreation are also declared in the Constitution, as well as the right to recreation as activities beneficial to individual and collective quality of life. For such purpose, the State assumes responsibility for sports and recreation as an education and public health policy, and guarantees the resources for the furtherance thereof (Article 111).

The State guarantees full attention to athletes without discrimination of any kind, as well as support for high-level competitive sports and evaluation and regulation of sports organizations in both the public and the private sector, in accordance with law. Incentives and inducements shall be established for the persons, institutions and communities that promote athletes and develop or finance sports activities, plans and programmes in the country.

§8. *Environmental Rights*

I. *Right to the Protection of Environment*

553. The Constitution of 1999 is also innovative with respect to its regulation of constitutional rights concerning the environment,[1991] declaring that each generation has the right and duty to protect and maintain the environment for its own benefit and that of the world of the future; and that everyone has the right, individually and collectively, to enjoy a safe, healthful and ecologically balanced life and environment.

The State shall protect the environment, biological and genetic diversity, ecological processes, national parks and natural monuments, and other areas of particular ecological importance. The genome of a living being shall not be patentable, and the field shall be regulated by the law relating to the principles of bioethics.

It is a fundamental duty of the State, with the active participation of society, to ensure that the populace develops in a pollution-free environment in which air, water, soil, coasts, climate, the ozone layer and living species receive special protection, in accordance with law (Article 127).

1991   See Fortunato González Cruz, 'El ambiente en la nueva Constitución venezolana', in *El Derecho Público a comienzos del siglo XXI. Estudios homenaje al Profesor Allan R. Brewer-Carías*, vol. III (Madrid: Instituto de Derecho Público, UCV, Civitas Ediciones, 2003), 2917–2923; Germán Acedo Payarez, 'La Constitución de la República Bolivariana de Venezuela de 1999 y los denominados 'Derechos Ambientales', *id.*, vol. III, 2925–2978; Alberto Blanco-Uribe Quintero, 'La tutela ambiental como derecho-deber del Constituyente. Base constitucional y principios rectores del derecho ambiental', in *Revista de Derecho Constitucional*, N° 6 (enero-diciembre) (Caracas: Editorial Sherwood, 2002), 31–64, and 'El ciudadano frente a la defensa jurídica del ambiente en Venezuela', in *El Derecho Público a comienzos del siglo XXI. Estudios homenaje al Profesor Allan R. Brewer-Carías*, vol. III (Madrid: Instituto de Derecho Público, UCV, Civitas Ediciones, 2003), 2995–3008.

504. In order to guarantee the protection of environment, Article 129 of the Constitution prescribes that any activities capable of generating damage to ecosystems must be preceded by environmental and socio-cultural impact studies. The State shall prevent toxic and hazardous waste from entering the country, as well as preventing the manufacture and use of nuclear, chemical and biological weapons. A special law shall regulate the use, handling, transportation and storage of toxic and hazardous substances.

II.   The Land Use Planning

555. As a matter of public policy, Article 128 of the Constitution imposes on the State the duty to develop a land use policy taking into account ecological, geographic, demographic, social, cultural, economic and political realities, in accordance with the premises of sustainable development, including information, consultation and male/female participation by citizens. An organic law shall develop the principles and criteria for this zoning.

§9.   The rights of Indigenous Peoples

556. Another innovation in the 1999 Constitution, was the incorporation in its text of a set of provisions concerning the rights of indigenous peoples,[1992] which constitutes an ethnic group not exceeding 1.5% of the population.

The chapter begins with a declaration that the State shall recognize the existence of indigenous peoples and communities, their social, political and economic organization, their cultures, habits and customs, languages and religions, their habitat and original rights to the territories they ancestrally and historically occupy and that are necessary to develop and guarantee their ways of life. It is incumbent upon the National Executive, with the participation of the indigenous peoples, to mark the boundaries of and guarantee the property collective rights of their territories, which will be inalienable, imprescriptible, unseizable, and untransferable in accord with the Constitution and laws (Article 119).

This declaration is a recognition of the existence of political communities within the State, in the sense of recognizing that there can be *a people* in the country, with its own *political organization* and its own geographic *territory*, being these elements (people, government, and territory) the essential components of every State. Nonetheless, in order to avoid problems with respect to the integrity of national territory, Article 126 of the Constitution states that the indigenous peoples, as cultures with ancestral roots, form a part of the Nation, the State and the Venezuelan people, which is unique, sovereign and indivisible. Consequently, the indigenous peoples have the duty to protect national integrity and sovereignty, and in no case, the term 'people' shall be interpreted in the sense that it has in international law.

557. According to Article 120, the State's use of natural resources within indigenous peoples' territories must be undertaken without violating the integrity of the

1992 See Ricardo Colmenares Olívar, 'Constitucionalismo y derechos de los pueblos indígenas en Venezuela', in *Revista LEX NOVA del Colegio de Abogados del Estado Zulia,* N° 237 (Maracaibo, 2000), 13–46.

inhabitants' culture, social and economic life. The use of natural resources within indigenous peoples' territories requires prior information and consulting with the relevant indigenous population.

558. Article 121 of the Constitution declares the right of indigenous peoples to maintain and develop their ethnic and cultural identities, their cosmology, values, spirituality, sacred locations and religion. To this end, the State is obliged to promote the value and distribution of indigenous cultural manifestations. In addition, indigenous people have the right to their own form of education as well as to an intercultural and bilingual education, giving specific attention to their particular socio-cultural characteristics, values and traditions.

509. Similarly, Article 122 establishes the right of indigenous peoples to comprehensive health, while taking into account their own practices and culture. As a consequence, the State is obliged to recognize their traditional medicine and therapies, subject to principles of medical ethics.

560. With respect to economic activities, Article 123 of the Constitution establishes the right of indigenous peoples to maintain and promote their own economic practices based upon reciprocity, solidarity, and trade, their traditional productive activities, and in addition their participation in the national economy, while defining their priorities for themselves. However, the State is also obliged to guarantee the enjoyment of rights conferred by labour law to indigenous workers.

561. Article 124 of the Constitution guarantees and protects the collective intellectual property of the knowledge, technologies and innovations produced by indigenous peoples and requires that all activities related to their genetic resources and the associated knowledge be linked to the collective benefit of the indigenous people who produce it. The Constitution prohibits the registration of patents on such ancestral resources and knowledge.

According to Article 260 of the Constitution the legitimate authorities of the indigenous peoples could apply in their habitat, according to their ancestral traditions, and following their own rules and procedures, judicial means that could only affect their members, providing that they are not contrary to the Constitution, the law or the public order.[1993]

562. Finally, Article 125 of the Constitution consecrates the right of indigenous peoples to political participation, which in particular is established in Article 182 guaranteeing, 'indigenous representation in the National Assembly and deliberating bodies of federal entities and of local entities where indigenous populations exist, in accordance with law'[1994] (see *supra* paragraph 556).

1993   See María E. León Álvarez, 'El sistema de justicia en la Constitución de Venezuela de 1999. Estudio crítico acerca de la jurisdicción especial indígena', en *Revista del Tribunal Supremo de Justicia*, N° 4 (Caracas, 2002), 369–377.

1994   See Ricardo Colmenares Olivar, 'El derecho de participación y consulta de los pueblos indígenas en Venezuela', in *Revista del Tribunal Supremo de Justicia*, N° 8 (Caracas, 2003), 21–48.

Chapter 5. Political Rights

§1. Right to Political Participation

563. The 1999 Constitution also declares a series of political rights that in principle are reserved to Citizens (see *supra* paragraph 420), beginning with the right to free political participation in all public affairs, either directly or by means of their elected representatives (Article 62), considering such participation in the formation, execution, and control of public affairs as necessary to achieve their complete development, collectively and individually, being an obligation of both the State and society to facilitate the creation of conditions most favourable for the practice of this participation.

564. Article 70 of the Constitution enumerates the means of the people's participation in the exercise of their sovereignty, as follows: *in political matters,* election of representatives to public office, vote in referenda, popular consultations, revocation of the mandate of elected officials, legislative or constitutional initiative, open town meeting, and Citizens' assemblies whose decisions are binding; in *social and economic matters,* people's complaints means, workers participation in the management of enterprises, all forms of cooperatives, including financial cooperatives, cooperative savings banks, communitarian businesses, and other 'forms of associations guided by values of mutual cooperation and solidarity'.

§2. Right to Vote and Electoral Principles

565. The right to vote is declared in Article 63, but without qualifying it as a duty as was conceived in the 1961 Constitution (Article 110). This right to vote belongs to all Venezuelans who have reached the age of 18, and not subject to civil interdiction or political incapacity (Article 64). The Constitution has also specifically conferred the right to vote to members of the armed forces in active duty, although military personnel my not participate in propaganda, political militancy or proselytizing (Article 330). This was an innovation in the Venezuelan political process, in which the military traditionally did not have the right to vote.

566. The election of representatives must always be done by means of free, universal, direct and secret voting, combining the principles of the 'personalization of suffrage' and proportional representation (see *supra* paragraphs 151, 341). Citizens, on their own initiative, and associations for political purposes, shall be entitled to participate in the electoral process, putting forward candidates (Article 67).

In this regard, Article 63 establishes two elements for the configuration of the electoral system of representatives: on the one hand, the 'personalization of suffrage', which requires nominal voting, that is, the voting for a named person, whether votes are counted from single constituency districts, in which case there is no possibility other than voting in nominal or personified way; or whether votes are cast in plurinominal constituencies, by means of lists, where voters cast nominal ballots for multiple persons to represent a single district. At the same time, the article also guarantees proportional representation, as a system that absolutely requires a plurinominal constituency in which ballots are cast for more than one candidate per electoral district. Proportional representation *excludes* the possibility of single district representation for representative assemblies, implying the need of an electoral system where elections are carried out through lists, where multiple candidates are selected for each district, in a nominal form (see *supra* paragraph 156).

567. Being the political rights of Citizens, and thus, of the Venezuelan nationals, foreigners in principle do not have such right. Nonetheless, Article 64 of the Constitution extends an exception to the rule, providing that foreigners who have reached the age of 18, and are not subject to civil interdiction or political incapacity, and who have lived in the country for more than ten years, can vote in the states in municipal elections.

§3. *Right to Be Elected and to Exercise Public Offices*

568. The text of the 1999 Constitution contains no equivalent provision to Article 112 of the 1961 Constitution that established the right of the citizen to be elected and perform duties of public office, that is, to hold public office. On these matters, the Constitution only establishes restrictions and prohibitions. Article 65 of the Constitution establishes that a person who has been convicted of an offence while exercising public office, or convicted of an offence involving public funds, may not be a candidate to any popular election, during a time period based upon the gravity of the offence. Also, Members of the armed forces in active duty are not permitted to run in popular elections (Article 330).

569. Regarding the right to be elected, according to Article 67 of the Constitution, nominations for all elective offices may be made by own initiative (self-initiated) or at proposals made by political associations. In this way, all Citizens have the right to participate in electoral processes nominating candidates.

However, Article 66 of the Constitution consecrates the citizens' right to have their representatives to render periodic and transparent accounts for their work in office 'according to the programme submitted in the election' (Article 66). This implies that all candidates to elections must present to the electors their corresponding programme.

§4. *Right to Be Associated to Political Parties*

570. All Citizens have the right to be associated for political purposes, in political associations that must be governed by democratic means of organization, functioning and direction (Article 67) (see *supra* paragraph 169 et seq.).

§5. *Right to Demonstrate*

571. Citizens have also the right to participate in demonstrations, peacefully without weapons, subject only to such requirements as may be established by law (Article 68). The same provision establishes limits to police interventions regarding demonstration, in the sense that they cannot use firearms or toxic substance to control peaceful demonstrations. The activity of police and security corps in maintaining public order shall be regulated by law.

Chapter 6. Constitutional Duties

572. In addition to the enunciation of rights, the Constitution also enumerates constitutional duties, in some cases of Venezuelans, and in general of all persons. In this sense, Venezuelans have the duty to honour and defend their native land symbols and cultural values and to guard and protect the sovereignty, nationhood, territorial integrity, self-determination and interests of the nation (Article 130); but everyone has the duty to comply with and obey the Constitution and the laws and other official acts of the public entities (Article 131); to fulfil his or her social responsibilities and participate together in the political, civic and community life of the country, promoting and protecting human rights as the foundation of democratic coexistence and social peace (Article 132); to contribute with public expenditures by paying such taxes, assessments and contributions as may be established by law (Article 133); of rendering its services in the electoral functions assigned to them by law; and to perform such civilian or military service as may be necessary for the defence, preservation and development of the country, or to deal with situations involving a public calamity. Nonetheless, a guarantee is established in the sense that no one shall be subjected to forcible recruitment (Article 134).

573. In addition, the Constitution declares education as a fundamental social duty; therefore, it is free of charge and obligatory. For such purpose, the State must assume the responsibility for it as an irrevocable function of the greatest interest, at all levels and in all modes, as an instrument of scientific, humanistic and technical knowledge at the service of society (Article 102). In Article 87 of the Constitution, work is also considered as a duty of all persons, imposing upon the State the need to adopt the necessary measures so that every person could be able to obtain productive work providing a dignified and decorous living (Article 87).

574. Finally, Article 76 of the Constitution also imposes duties related to family; providing that the father and mother have the shared and inescapable obligation of raising, training, educating, maintaining and caring for their children; and also that the latter has the duty to provide care when the former is unable to do so by themselves. The necessary and proper measures to guarantee the enforceability of the obligation to provide alimony shall be established by law.

575. In all cases of obligations imposed upon the State according to the general social welfare objectives, according to Article 135, these obligations do not preclude the ones which, by virtue of solidarity, social responsibility and humanitarian assistance, corresponds to private individuals according to their abilities. Appropriate provisions shall be enacted by law to compel the fulfilment of these obligations when necessary. Those aspiring to practice any profession have a duty to perform community service for such period, in such place and on such terms as may be provided for by law.

PART X. THE CONSTITUTIONAL REGIME OF THE ECONOMY

576. The 1999 Constitution, also following the general trend of the 1961 Constitution,[1995] in addition to the political and social constitutions, contains an economic constitution in which are established the principles governing the economy, including the respective roles played by private initiative and the State in this field. According to these provisions, since the beginning of the oil exploitation, and particularly during the second half of the twentieth century, the economic system that has been developed in Venezuela is one of mixed economy or of 'social market economy',[1996] which combines economic freedom, private initiative and a free market economic model (as opposed to the model of a State-directed economy), and the possibility of State intervention in the economy in order to uphold principles of social justice. This has been possible, particularly because of the special position of the State as owner of the subsoil and of the oil industry which since 1975 was nationalized[1997] (see *infra* paragraph 623). This has made the State the most powerful economic entity in the nation, leading it to intervene in the country's economic activity in important ways.

Chapter 1. Principles of the Economic System

577. It is precisely within this context that Article 299 of the 1999 Constitution sets forth that the social-economic regime of the Republic shall be based on the principles of social justice, democratization, efficiency, free competition, protection of the environment, productivity and solidarity, with a view to ensuring overall human development and a dignified and useful existence for the community. For these purposes, this very Article of the Constitution expressly sets forth that the State must, 'jointly with private initiative', promote:

the harmonious development of the national economy for the purpose of generating sources of employment, a high national level of added value, in order

---

1995 See Allan R. Brewer-Carías, 'Reflexiones sobre la Constitución Económica', in *Estudios sobre la Constitución Española. Homenaje al Profesor Eduardo García de Enterría* (Madrid, 1991), 3839–3853; Ignacio de León, 'A cinco años de la Constitución Económica de 1999. Un balance de la gestión', in *Tendencias Actuales del Derecho Constitucional. Homenaje a Jesús María Casal Montbrun*, ed. Jesús María Casal, Alfredo Arismendi y Carlos Luis Carrillo Artiles (Coord.), vol. II (Caracas: Universidad Central de Venezuela/Universidad Católica Andrés Bello, 2008), 379–406.

1996 See Henrique Meier, 'La Constitución económica', in *Revista de Derecho Corporativo*, 1, no. 1 (Caracas, 2001), 9–74; Ana C. Nuñez Machado, 'Los principios económicos de la Constitución de 1999', in *Revista de Derecho Constitucional*, Nº 6 (enero-diciembre) (Caracas: Editorial Sherwood, 2002), 129–140; Claudia Briceño Aranguren y Ana C. Núñez Machado, 'Aspectos económicos de la nueva Constitución', in *Comentarios a la Constitución de la República Bolivariana de Venezuela* (Caracas: Vadell Hermanos, Editores, 2000), 177 y ss.; Jesús Ollarves Irazábal, 'La vigencia constitucional de los Derechos Económicos y Sociales en Venezuela', in *Libro Homenaje a Enrique Tejera París, Temas sobre la Constitución de 1999* (Caracas: Centro de Investigaciones Jurídicas (CEIN), 2001), 159 a 192.

1997 See Organic Law that reserves to the State the Industry and Commerce of Hydrocarbons, *Gaceta Oficial* Extra, Nº 1.769 of 29 Aug. 1975. See Allan R. Brewer-Carías, 'Introducción al Régimen Jurídico de las Nacionalizaciones en Venezuela', in *Archivo de Derecho Público y Ciencias de la Administración*, vol. I, vol. III, 1972–1979 (Caracas: Instituto de Derecho Público, Facultad de Ciencias Jurídicas y Políticas, Universidad Central de Venezuela, 1981), 23–44.

to elevate the standard of living of the population and strengthen the nation's economic sovereignty, guaranteeing legal certainty, solidity, dynamism, sustainability, permanence, and economic growth with equity, in order to guarantee a just distribution of wealth by means of strategic democratic, participative and open planning.

578. The economic system is therefore based upon economic freedom, private initiative and free competition, although in combination with the participation of the State as a promoter of economic development, a regulator of economic activity, and a planner, together with civil society. As the Constitutional Chamber of the Supreme Tribunal of Justice stated in its decision No. 117 of 6 February 2001[1998] this is 'a socioeconomic system that is in between a free market (in which the State acts as a simple programmer (*programador*) for an economy that is dependent upon the supply and demand of goods and services) and an interventionist economy (in which the State actively intervenes as the 'primary entrepreneur')'. The Constitution promotes, 'joint economic activity between the State and private initiative in the pursuit of, and in order to concretely realize the supreme values consecrated in the Constitution', and in order to pursue 'the equilibrium of all the forces of the market, and, joint activity between the State and private initiative'. In accord with this system, the Courts ruled, the Constitution:

> advocates a series of superior normative values with respect to the economic regimen, consecrating free enterprise within the framework of a market economy and, fundamentally, within the framework of the Social State under the Rule of Law (the Welfare State, the State of Well-being or the Social-Democratic State). This is a social State that is opposed to authoritarianism.'[1999]

Nonetheless, in practice, particularly during the past decade (2000–2011), this framework has been changed, due to the authoritarian government that has been developed, inclining the balance toward the State participation in the economy, through a process of progressively 'statization' of the economy, reducing economic freedom and increasing the dependency of the country on oil exploitation.[2000]

1998   See in *Revista de Derecho Público*, N° 85–88 (Caracas: Editorial Jurídica Venezolana, 2001), 212–218.

1999   The values that are alluded to, according to the doctrine of the Constitutional Chamber, 'are developed through the concept of free enterprise' (*libertad de empresa*) which encompasses both the notion of a subjective right 'to dedicate oneself to the economic activity of one's choice', and a principle of economic regulation according to which the will of the business (*voluntad de la empresa*) to make its own decisions is manifest. The State fulfils its role of intervention in this context. Intervention can be direct (through businesses) or indirect (as an entity regulating the market)'. *Id.* See on the decision, José Ignacio Hernández, 'Constitución económica y privatización (Comentarios a la sentencia de la Sala Constitucional del 6 de febrero de 2001)', en *Revista de Derecho Constitucional*, N° 5, julio-diciembre-2001 (Caracas: Editorial Sherwood, 2002), 327–342.

2000   As reported by Simón Romero in 'Chávez Reopens Oil Bids to West as Prices Plunge', published in *The New York Times* on 12 Jan. 2009, 1, in 2009 Venezuela 'reliant on oil for about 93% of its export revenue in 2008, up from 69% in 1998'.

§1. *Private Economic Rights*

I. *Right to Exercise Economic Activities*

579. Title III of the 1999 Constitution on constitutional rights and guarantees also contains a declaration of the economic rights (Chapter VII, Articles 112–118), including, economic freedom, and the right to private property.

Regarding economic freedom, Article 112 of the Constitution declares the right of all persons to develop the economic activity of his choice, without other limits than those established by statute for reasons of human development, security, sanitation, environment protection and others of social interest. In any case, the State must promote private initiative, guaranteeing the creation of wealth and its just distribution, as well as the production of goods and services in order to satisfy the needs of the population, freedom to work, and the free enterprise, commerce and industry, without prejudice to the power of the State to promulgate measures to plan, rationalize and regulate the economy and promote the overall development of the country.

580. In 2007, by means of the Constitutional Reform Draft that was rejected by referendum held on December that same year, the President of the Republic proposed to eliminate this constitutional provision guaranteeing economic freedom, substituting it with one only defining as a matter of State policy, the obligation to promote:

> the development of a Productive Economic Model, that is intermediate, diversified and independent...founded upon the humanistic values of cooperation and the preponderance of common interests over individual ones, guaranteeing the meeting of the people's social and material needs, the greatest possible political and social stability, and the greatest possible sum of happiness.

The proposal added that the State, in the same way, 'shall promote and develop different forms of businesses and economic units from social property, both directly or communally, as well as indirectly or through the state', According to this norm, additionally, the State was to promote, 'economic units of social production and/or distribution, that may be mixed properties held between the State, the private sector, and the communal power, so as to create the best conditions for the collective and cooperative construction of a Socialist Economy'.

The 2007 Constitutional reform proposals on economic matters, although rejected by the people in the referendum of December 2007, were nonetheless implemented in 2010, of course violating the Constitution, through the Organic Law on the Communal Economic System. [2001] (see *infra* paragraph 625 ff.).

2001   See. Organic Law on the Communal Economic System, *Gaceta Oficial* N° 6.011 Extra. of 21 Dec. 2010. See the comments in Allan R. Brewer-Carías, 'Sobre la Ley Orgánica del Sistema Económico Comunal o de cómo se implanta en Venezuela un sistema económico comunista sin reformar la Constitución', in *Revista de Derecho Público*, N° 124 (Caracas: Editorial Jurídica Venezolana, 2010), 102–109

II. Property Rights

581. Regarding the right to property, Article 115 of the Constitution, although following the orientation of the previous 1961 Constitution,[2002] in the sense of guaranteeing the right to property, did not establish private property as having a 'social function' to be accomplished, as did the 1961 Constitution. Nonetheless, it provides that property shall be subject to such contributions, restrictions and obligations as may be established by law in the service of the public or general interest. However, Article 115 defines the attributes of the right to property that traditionally were only enumerated in the Civil Code (Article 545), that is, the right to use, the enjoyment and the disposition of property are now in the Constitution.[2003]

This constitutional regime regarding property rights was proposed to be radically changed in the 2007 rejected Constitutional Reforms, in which the President of the Republic sought to eliminate private property as a constitutionally protected right, and substituting the right's conception by a recognition of private property only referred to 'assets for use and consumption or as means of production', altogether with other forms of properties, and in particular, public property. The proposed reform regarding Article 115 of the Constitution tended to recognize and guarantee 'different forms of property' instead of guaranteeing the right to private property, enumerating them as follows: public property, as the one that belongs to State entities; social property, as the one that belongs to the people jointly and to future generations; collective property, as the one pertaining to social groups or persons, exploited for their common benefit, use, or enjoyment, that may be of social or private origin; mixed property, as the one constituted between the public sector, the social sector, the collective sector and the private sector, in different combinations, for the exploitation of resources or the execution of activities, subject always to the absolute economic and social sovereignty of the nation; and private property, as the one owned by 'natural or legal persons, only regarding assets for use or consumption, or as means of production legitimately acquired'.

582. Regarding expropriation, Article 115 of the Constitution establishes that it can be decreed regarding any kind of property only for reasons of public benefit or social interest, by means of a judicial process and payment of just compensation.[2004] Consequently, the Constitution prohibits confiscation (expropriation without com-

---

2002   See Allan R. Brewer-Carías 'El derecho de propiedad y libertad económica. Evolución y situación actual en Venezuela', in *Estudios sobre la Constitución. Libro Homenaje a Rafael Caldera,* vol. II (Caracas, 1979), 1139–1246.

2003   See, José L. Villegas Moreno, 'El derecho de propiedad en la Constitución de 1999', in *Estudios de Derecho Administrativo: Libro Homenaje a la Universidad Central de Venezuela,* vol. II (Caracas: Imprenta Nacional, 2001), 565–582.

2004   See the Law on Expropriation because public and social needs, *Gaceta Oficial* Nº 37.475 of 1 Jul. 2002. See Allan R. Brewer-Carías et al., *Ley de expropiación por causa de utilidad pública o social* (Caracas, 2003); Eloísa Avellaneda Sisto, 'La expropiación en la legislación venezolana', in *Tendencias Actuales del Derecho Constitucional. Homenaje a Jesús María Casal Montbrun,* ed. Jesús María Casal, Alfredo Arismendi y Carlos Luis Carrillo Artiles (Coord.), vol. II (Caracas: Universidad Central de Venezuela/Universidad Católica Andrés Bello, 2008), 407–442; Karina Anzola Spadaro, 'La expropiación y la ocupación temporal en Venezuela', in *Revista de Derecho n 26* (Caracas: Tribunal Supremo de Justicia, 2008), 201–222.

pensation), except in cases permitted by the Constitution itself, regarding property of persons responsible for crimes committed against public property, or who have illicitly enriched themselves exercising public offices. Confiscations may also take place regarding property deriving from business, financial or any other activities connected with illicit trafficking of psychotropic or narcotic substances (Article 116 y 271).

583. Article 307 of the Constitution declares the regimen of large private real estate holdings (*latifundio*) to be contrary to social interests, charging the legislator to tax idle lands, and establish the necessary measures to transform them into productive economic units, as well as to recover arable land. The same constitutional provision entitle peasants to own land, constitutionalizing the obligation of the State to protect and promote associative and private forms of property in order to guarantee agricultural production, and oversee sustainable arrangements on arable lands to guarantee its food-producing potential. In exceptional cases, the same Article requires that the legislature must establish federal tax revenue to provide funds for financing, research, technical assistance, transfer of technology and other activities aimed to raise productivity and competitiveness of the agricultural sector.

III. *Quality Services and Good Rights*

584. However, Article 117 contains a constitutional innovation in the economic area, providing for the right of all persons to access to goods and services of good quality, as well as to adequate and non-misleading information regarding the content and characteristics of the products and services they consume; to freedom of choice with respect to them; and to be treated fairly and with dignity. The mechanisms necessary to guarantee these rights, the standards of quality and quantity for goods and services, consumer protection procedures, compensation for damages caused and appropriate penalties for the violation of these rights shall be established by law.[2005]

IV. *Popular Economy Rights*

585. Article 118 of the Constitution also recognized the right of workers and of the community to develop associations of social and participative nature such as cooperatives, savings funds, mutual funds and other forms of association, in order to develop any kind of economic activities in accordance with the law. The law shall recognize the specificity of these organizations, especially those relating to the cooperative, the associated work and the generation of collective benefits. The State shall promote and protect these associations destined to improve the popular economic alternative.[2006]

[2005]   Law on the Venezuelan System of Quality, *Gaceta Oficial* N° 37.555 of 23 Oct. 2002; Law on the Persons'Access to Goods and Services Defence, *Gaceta Oficial* N° 39.358 of 1 Feb. 2010.

[2006]   The Law on the Promotion and Development of Popular Economy of 2008, *Gaceta Oficial* N° 5.890 Extra. of 31 Jul. 2008. was substituted by the Organic Law on the Communal Economic System, *Gaceta Oficial* N° 6.011 Extra. of 21 Dec. 2010.

V. Limits to Private Economic Activities

586. Article 113 of the Constitution prohibits monopolies. Consequently, any act, activity, conduct or agreement of private individuals which is intended to establish a monopoly or which leads by reason of its actual effects to the existence of a monopoly, regardless of the intentions of the persons involved, and whatever the form it actually takes, is declared contrary to the fundamental principles of this Constitution. Also contrary to such principles is the abuse of a position of dominance which a private individual, a group of individuals or a business enterprise or group of enterprises acquires or has acquired in a given market of goods or services, regardless of what factors caused such position of dominance; or the case of a concentration of demand. In all of the cases indicated, the State shall be required to adopt such measures as may be necessary to prevent the harmful and restrictive effects of monopoly, abuse of a position of dominance and a concentration of demand, with the purpose of protecting consumers and producers and ensuring the existence of genuine competitive conditions in the economy.

587. In the case of the exploitation of natural resources which are the property of the Nation or in the case of public services rendered by private entities, on an exclusive basis or otherwise, the State shall grant concessions for a certain period, in all cases ensuring the existence of adequate compensation regarding public interest (Article 113).

§2. State Participation in the Economy Regime

I State Promotion of Economic Activities

588. The Constitution also regulates various forms of State economic intervention that have developed in Venezuela in the last decades. In this regard, the Constitution regulates the State as a promoter, that is, without substituting private initiatives, to foster and order the economy in order to ensure the development of private initiative. In this regard, Article 112 sets forth that in any case, the State must promote private initiative, guaranteeing the creation of wealth and its just distribution, as well as the production of goods and services in order to satisfy the needs of the population, freedom to work, and the free enterprise, commerce and industry, without prejudice to the power of the State to promulgate measures to plan, rationalize and regulate the economy and promote the overall development of the country.

589. In this same regard, Article 299 sets forth that the State, jointly with private initiative, shall promote the harmonious development of the national economy, to the end of generating sources of employment, a high rate of domestic added value, raising the standard of living of the population and strengthening the economic sovereignty of the country; and guaranteeing the reliability of the law, as well as the solid, dynamic, sustainable, continuing and equitable growth of the economy, to ensure a just distribution of wealth through participatory democratic strategic planning with open consultation.

5940. Specifically regarding the agricultural activities, Article 305 of the Constitution establishes that the State shall promote sustainable agriculture as the strategic basis for overall rural development, and consequently shall guarantee the population a secure food supply, defined as the sufficient and stable availability of food within the national sphere and timely and uninterrupted access to the same for consumers. A secure food supply must be achieved by developing and prioritizing internal agricultural and livestock production, understood as production deriving from the activities of agriculture, livestock, fishing and aquaculture. Food production is in the national interest and is fundamental to the economic and social development of the Nation. To this end, the State shall promulgate such financial, commercial, technological transfer, land tenancy, infrastructure, manpower training and other measures as may be necessary to achieve strategic levels of self-sufficiency. In addition, it shall promote actions in the national and international economic context to compensate for the disadvantages inherent to agricultural activity. The State shall protect the settlement and communities of non-industrialized fishermen, as well as their fishing banks in continental waters and those close to the coastline, as defined by law.

591. Regarding rural development, Article 306 imposes on the State the duty to promote conditions for overall rural development, for the purpose of generating employment and ensuring the rural population an adequate level of well-being, as well as their inclusion in national development. It shall likewise promote agricultural activity and optimum land use by providing infrastructure projects, supplies, loans, training services and technical assistance.

592. Regarding industrial activities, the Constitution (Article 308) imposes on the State the role to protect and promote small and medium-sized manufacturers, cooperatives, savings funds, family-owned businesses, small businesses and any other form of community association for purposes of work, savings and consumption, under an arrangement of collective ownership, to strength the country's economic development, based on the initiative of the people. Training, technical assistance and appropriate financing shall be guaranteed. However, Article 309 provides that typical Venezuelan crafts and folk industries shall enjoy the special protection of the State, in order to preserve their authenticity, and they shall receive credit facilities to promote production and marketing.

593. On commercial matters, Article 301 reserves to the State the use of trade policy to protect the economic activities of public and private Venezuelan enterprises. In this regard, more advantageous status than those established for Venezuelan nationals shall not be granted to foreign persons, enterprises or entities. Foreign investment is subject to the same conditions as domestic investment.

544. Finally, Article 310 of the Constitution declares tourism as an economic activity of national interest, and of high priority in the country's strategy of diversification and sustainable development. As part of the foundation of the socio-economic regime contemplated by the Constitution, the State shall promulgate measures to guarantee the development of tourism and shall create and strengthen a national tourist industry.

II.   *State Economic Planning*

595. Regarding economic planning, Article 112 empowers the State to promulgate measures to plan, rationalize and regulate the economy and promote the overall development of the country. The President of the Republic must formulate the National Plan of Development and, once approved by the National Assembly, direct its execution (Article 187.8; 236.18). Since 2007 a centralized system of planning has

been established in the country[2007] followed by the structuring of the Communal Economic System (see *infra* paragraphs 625 ff.).

III. *State Direct Assumption of Economic Activities*

596. No provisions are established in the Constitution in order for the State to promote highly qualified or heavy industries, and what is established is for the State the possibility to reserve for its own exploitation, through an organic law and by reasons of national convenience, the petroleum industry (already nationalized since 1975) and other industries, operations and goods and services which are in the public interest and of a strategic nature. The State shall promote the domestic manufacture of raw materials deriving from the exploitation of non-renewable natural resources, with a view to assimilating, creating and inventing technologies, generating employment and economic growth and creating wealth and well-being for the people (Article 302).

597. As aforementioned, based on a similar constitutional provision establishing the power of the State to reserve for its own exploitation services or resources (Article 97, 1961 Constitution), the oil industry was nationalized in 1975, being managed by a State-owned enterprise, *Petróleos de Venezuela S.A.*, regarding which, Article 303 of the 1999 Constitution set forth that for economic and political sovereignty and national strategy reasons, the State shall retain all shares of such public enterprise, but with the exception of its subsidiaries, strategic joint ventures, enterprises and any other ventures established or to be established as a consequence of the carrying on of the business of *Petróleos de Venezuela, S.A.* This last possibility has been considered as a loosening of the strict nationalization process carried out through the 1975 Organic Law that reserves to the State the Industry and Commercialization of Hydrocarbons.[2008] In this regard, the 2000 Organic Law on Hydrocarbons allowed the establishment of mixed companies for the exploitation of primary hydrocarbons activities, although with the State as majority shareholder,[2009] which has been implemented in 2006–2007.[2010]

2007   See the Organic Law on Popular Planning *Gaceta Oficial* N° 6.011 Extra. of 21 Dec. 2010; and the Law on Creation of the Central Planning Commission, *Gaceta Oficial* N° 5.990 Extra. of 29 Jul. 2010. See on this planning centralized system Allan R. Brewer-Carías, 'Comentarios sobre la inconstitucional creación de la Comisión Central de Planificación, centralizada y obligatoria' in *Revista de Derecho Público*', N° 110 (Caracas: Editorial Jurídica Venezolana, 2007), 79–89.

2008   See Allan R. Brewer-Carías, 'El régimen de participación del capital privado en las industrias petrolera y minera: Desnacionalización y regulación a partir de la Constitución de 1999', in *VII Jornadas Internacionales de Derecho Administrativo Allan R. Brewer-Carías, El Principio de Legalidad y el Ordenamiento Jurídico-Administrativo de la Libertad Económica* (Caracas, noviembre 2004). Fundación de Estudios de Derecho Administrativo FUNEDA, Caracas Noviembre, 2004 15–58.

2009   Ley Orgánica de Hidrocarburos, *Gaceta Oficial* N° 38.493 of 4 Aug. 2006.

2010   See Allan R. Brewer-Carías, 'The "Statization" of the Pre 2001 Primary Hydrocarbons Joint Venbture Exploitations: Their Unilateral termination and the Assets'Confiscation of Some of the Former Private parties' in Oil, Gas & Energy Law Intelligence, <www.gasandoil.com/ogel/ ISSN: 1875-418X>, issue, vol 6, issue 2 (OGEL/TDM Special Issue on Venezuela: The battle of Contract Sanctity vs. Resource Sovereignty, ed. By Elizabeth Eljuri), April 2008; and 'La estatización de los convenios de asociación que permitían la participación del capital privado en las actividades primarias de hidrocarburos sucritos antes de 2002, mediante su terminación anticipada y unilateral y la confiscación de los bienes

598. However, regarding public enterprises in general, Article 300 of the Constitution refers to the statutes to determine the conditions for the creation of functionally decentralized entities to carry out social or entrepreneurial activities, with a view to ensuring the reasonable economic and social productivity of the public resources invested in such activities.

599. All the aforementioned provisions regarding the participation of the State in the economy were proposed to be radically changed in the rejected 2007 Constitutional Reform Draft, in which the whole economic role of the State pretended to be reduced to promote and develop economic and social activities 'under the principles of the socialist economy' (Article 300). Nonetheless, this has been achieved through an extended process of nationalization and confiscation of private assets executed during the past years (see *supra* paragraph 623ff.), and by the formal enacting of a Communal Economic System based on the social property of all means of production (see *infra* paragraph 625).

Chapter 2. Taxation Regimen

600. The Constitution also establishes the general principles of the taxation regimen, providing in Article 316 that the tax system must seek for a fair distribution of public burden (taxation), following the principle of progressive taxation according to the economic capacity of taxpayers; for the protection of the national economy and the raising of the standard of living of the population, sustaining itself through efficient collections.[2011]

601. The Constitution also establishes the general principle of 'tributary legality', that is, that all taxes must always be created by statute approved by the representatives of the people, which must also be the one to provide for exemptions, reductions and any other incentives (Article 317).[2012] In addition, the principle that taxes shall never have confiscatory effect is also expressly established.[2013]

---

afectos a los mismos', in *Nacionalización, Libertad de Empresa y Asociaciones Mixtas*, ed. Víctor Hernández Mendible (Coordinador) (Caracas: Editorial Jurídica Venezolana, 2008), 123–188.

2011   See Gabriel Ruán Santos, 'Principios substantivos de la tributación en la Constitución de 1999', in *Revista de Derecho Corporativo* 1, no. 2 (Caracas, 2001), 11–38; Moisés Ballenilla Tolosa y otros, 'El régimen tributario constitucional', in *Comentarios a la Constitución de la República Bolivariana de Venezuela* (Caracas: Vadell Hermanos Editores, 2000), 117–148; Alejandro R. Van Der Velde; Antonio Planchart Mendoza; Adriana Vigilanza García, 'El poder tributario antes y después de la Constitución de 1999', in *Revista de Derecho Constitucional*, N° 3 (julio-diciembre) (Caracas: Editorial Sherwood, 2000), 187–228; Juan D. Alfonzo Paradisi, 'El Poder Tributario y los derechos y garantías constitucionales como límites a su ejercicio', in *El Derecho Público a comienzos del siglo XXI. Estudios homenaje al Profesor Allan R. Brewer-Carías*, vol. III (Madrid: Instituto de Derecho Público, UCV, Civitas Ediciones, 2003), 3151–3184.

2012   See Eduardo E. Meier García, 'Reflexiones sobre el sistema tributario y el principio de legalidad tributaria en la Constitución de 1999', in *Revista de Derecho Corporativo* 2, no. 1 (Caracas, 2002), 73–124.

2013   See Allan R. Brewer-Carías, 'Les protections constitutionnelles et légales contre les impositions confiscatoires', in *Rapports Generaux. XIII Congrès International de Droit Comparé* (Montreal, 1990), 795–824.

602. Almost all taxation powers have been attributed to the national (federal level of government) but in addition, Article 156.13 of the Constitution assigns the National Assembly the power to enact legislation in order to guarantee the coordination and harmonization of the different national, state and municipal government taxation power. Such legislation shall define appropriate principles, parameters and limitations; determine the types of taxes or aliquots of state and municipal taxes; and establish specific funds for the purpose of ensuring inter-territorial solidarity.[2014]

603. But the Constitution also establishes some prohibitions for the states and municipalities in taxation matters. For instance, on matters of agriculture, animal husbandry, fisheries and forest activities, the states and municipalities can only tax them at the opportunity, in the form prescribed by, and through measures permitted by national statute. This is confirmed in Article 183 of the Constitution that prohibits states and municipalities from creating taxes on matters reserved to the national level of government; from creating customs or from taxing the import, export or transit of national or foreign goods; from taxing consumption goods before entering in their territories; from taxing them in a different way as those produced in their territory. The Constitution also prohibits the states and municipalities to forbid the consumption of goods produced outside their territory.

Chapter 3. Budgetary System

604. Within the innovations of the 1999 Constitution are a set of provisions governing fiscal and budgetary issues, the monetary system, and macro-economic coordination, not only applicable to the national level of government, but also to the states and municipalities (Article 311).

§1. Principles of Fiscal Policy

605. Article 311 of the Constitution established the general principles governing the fiscal policy, which must be based on efficiency, solvency, transparency, liability and fiscal balance. Fiscal policy is to be balanced over a multi-year budget framework, in such manner that ordinary revenues shall be sufficient to cover ordinary expenses. The National Executive must submit for enactment by the National Assembly a multi-year framework for budgeting that establishes the maximum limits of expenditures and indebtedness to be contemplated in national budgets. The characteristics of this framework, the requirements for modifying the same and the terms for carrying out are established in the Organic Law of State Financial Administration.[2015] The Constitution also establishes the principle that any revenues generated

---

2014   See Manuel Rachadell, 'La distribución del poder tributario entre los diversos niveles del Poder Público según la Constitución de 1999', in *Revista de Derecho Administrativo*, N° 8 *(enero-abril)* (Caracas: Editorial Sherwood, 2000), 179–205; Adriana Vigilanza García, 'Menú para la armonización y coordinación de la potestad tributaria de Estados y Municipios. Algunas reflexiones', in *Revista de Derecho Tributario*, N° 99 (abril-junio) (Caracas: Legislec Editores, 2003), 9–26, and in *Revista de Derecho Constitucional*, N° 6, enero-diciembre-2002 (Caracas: Editorial Sherwood, 2003), 213 a 230.

2015   Organic Law on the Financial Administration of the Public Sector, *Gaceta Oficial* N° 39.556 of 19 Nov. 2010.

by exploiting underground wealth (hydrocarbon) and minerals, in general, shall be used to finance real productive investment, education and health. All these principles and provisions established for national, economic and financial management shall also govern that of the states and municipalities, to the extent applicable.

§2. *Principles of Public Debt Policy*

606. According to Article 312 of the Constitution, public debt limits shall be set by law in accordance with a prudent level in terms of the size of the economy, reproductive investment and the ability to generate revenues to cover public debt service. In order to be valid, public credit transactions shall always require a special law authorizing them, with the exceptions established under the Organic Law on State Financial Administration. The special law shall indicate the modalities of the transactions and authorize the appropriate budget credits in the pertinent budget law. The annual special indebtedness law shall be submitted to the National Assembly together with the budget law. The State shall not recognize any obligations other than those assumed by lawful National Authority organs in accordance with law.

§3. *Principles of Budget*

607. Regarding budget, in particular Article 313 of the Constitution establishes the general principle that the economic and financial management of the State shall be governed by a budget approved annually by law. The National Executive shall submit the draft Budget Law or statute to the National Assembly at the time prescribed by the same Organic Law on State Financial Administration. Nonetheless, if the Executive Power fails for any reason to submit the budget bill within the time limit established by law, or the bill is rejected, the budget for the then current fiscal year shall be applicable.

608. Regarding the Budget draft law, the National Assembly has the power to alter budget items, but shall not authorize measures leading to a decrease in public revenues or to expenses exceeding the estimated revenue amounts in the budget bill (Article 313). In the annual public expense budgets at all levels of government, the specific objective to which each credit item in the budget is addressed shall be clearly established, as well as the concrete results expected and the public officials responsible for achieving these results. The latter shall be established in quantitative terms, by means of performance indicators, where this is technically possible (Article 315). Also, in each annual budget the Constitutional Contribution to the States (*Situado Constitucional*) must be calculated in an amount equivalent to a minimum of 15% and a maximum of 20% of total ordinary national income (Article 167.4) (see *supra* paragraph 212).

609. In submitting the multi-year budget framework, the special indebtedness law and the annual budget, the National Executive Branch shall explicitly state the long-term objectives of fiscal Policy and explain how these objectives are to be achieved, in accordance with principles of responsibility and a fiscal balance (Article 313).

610. According to Article 314, a balanced budget is a constitutional principle, so no expense of any kind shall be disbursed unless the same has been provided for in the budget law. Additional budget credit items may be ordered to cover essential unforeseen expenses or items that had not been adequately funded only if the treasu-

ry has resources to cover the expenditure concerned; this shall be done only following a vote in favour by the Council of Ministers and authorization by the National Assembly, or in its absence, by the Delegated Commission. The Executive Power shall submit to the National Assembly within six months of the close of the fiscal year the annual accounting and budget implementation balance sheet for such fiscal year (Article 315).

Chapter 4. Monetary System and the Macro-economic Policies

611. In addition to the abovementioned provisions on the State economic regime, for the first time in Venezuelan constitutional history, the text of the Constitution incorporates a set of norms regulating the monetary system, and in particular, the autonomy and role of the Central Bank of Venezuela, as well as the State's macro-economic policies (Articles 318–321).[2016]

§1. Autonomy of the Central Bank of Venezuela Regarding the Monetary Policy

612. The monetary policy of the State, according to Article 318 of the Constitution, is attributed in an exclusive way to the Venezuelan Central Bank, whose fundamental objective is to achieve price stability and preserve the internal and foreign exchange value of the monetary unit. The Venezuelan Central Bank is conceived in the Constitution as a public law juridical person with autonomy to formulate and implement policies within its sphere of competence. The Venezuelan Central Bank shall perform its functions in coordination with general economic policy, in the interest of attaining the higher objectives of the State and the Nation. In order to provide for the adequate attainment of its objective, the functions of the Venezuelan Central Bank shall include those of formulating and implementing monetary policy, participating in the design of and implementing foreign exchange policy, currency regulation, credit and interest rates, administrating international reserves and any others established by law.[2017]

613. According to Article 319 of the Constitution, the Venezuelan Central Bank shall be governed by the principle of public responsibility, to which end it shall render an accounting of its actions, goals and the results of its policies to the National Assembly, in accordance with law. It shall also issue periodic reports on the behaviour of the country's macro-economic variables and on any other matters concerning which reports may be requested, including sufficient analysis to permit its evaluation. Failure to meet the objective and goals, without justifiable cause, shall result in removal of the Board of Directors and imposition of administrative penalties, in accordance with law.

614. The Venezuelan Central Bank shall be subject to oversight after the fact by the Office of the General Comptroller of the Republic and inspection and supervision by the public entity that supervises banking, which shall send to the National

---

2016   See Isabel C. Medina Ortiz, 'Comentarios acerca de las normas constitucionales y legales que regulan el funcionamiento del Banco Central de Venezuela', in *Revista del Tribunal Supremo de Justicia*, N° 8 (Caracas, 2003), 357–389.

2017   Central Bank of Venezuela Law, *Gaceta Oficial* N° 39.419 of 7 May 2010.

Assembly reports on the inspections it conducts. The budget of operating expenses of the Venezuelan Central Bank shall require discussion and approval by the National Assembly, and its accounts and balance sheets shall be subjected to independent audits on such terms as may be established by law.

615. Nonetheless, in the 2007 Constitutional Reform which was proposed by the President of the Republic and rejected by referendum, the purpose of it on these matters was to eliminate the Bank's competencies and autonomy, and render the Bank totally and directly dependent upon the National Executive. To this end, the following reforms were proposed and sanctioned by the National Assembly regarding Article 318 of the Constitution: to require that the national monetary system be directed towards the achievement of the essential ends of the 'Socialist State'; to attribute the conduction of monetary policies to the National Executive and the Central Bank; to eliminate the autonomy of the Bank, proposing to establish that it was to be subordinated to general economic policy and to the National Development Plan in order to achieve the 'superior objectives of the Socialist State'; and to remove from the Central Bank the exclusive competency to administer international reserves, by proposing to place it under the administration and direction of the President of the Republic as administrator of the National Public Treasury. Although the 2007 Reform was rejected by the people on December 2007 (see *supra* paragraph 36), the fact is that because of the political and legislative practice of the authoritarian government that has been consolidated during the past decade (2000–2011), the Central Bank has been completely controlled. In addition, all such reforms have been implemented in 2010 through the establishing by Organic Law of the Economic Communal System,[2018] based on a centralized planning economy and the State ownership of the means of production (see *infra* paragraph 623)

§2. *National Currency*

616. The monetary unit of the Bolivarian Republic of Venezuela is the Bolívar. Nonetheless, the Constitution provides that in the event a common currency is instituted within the framework of Latin American and Caribbean integration, it shall be permissible to adopt the currency provided for by a treaty signed by the Republic (Article 318). Nonetheless, the Law on the Communal Economic System has provided in a way contrary to the Constitution, for the existence of 'communal currencies' at the communal level of the Communal State.[2019]

§3. *Macro-economic Policies*

617. Regarding macro-economic policies, the Constitution also innovated by providing the general framework for it coordination. In this regard, Article 320 establishes the general principle that the State must promote and defend economic stability, avoid its vulnerability, and watch over the monetary and price stability, in order

---

2018   *Gaceta Oficial* N° 6.011 Extra. of 21 Dec. 2010.

2019   *Gaceta Oficial* N° 6.011 Extra. of 21 Dec. 2010. See Allan R. Brewer-Carías, 'Sobre la Ley Orgánica del Sistema Económico Comunal o de cómo se implanta en Venezuela un sistema económico comunista sin reformar la Constitución', in *Revista de Derecho Público*, No. 124 (Caracas: Editorial Jurídica Venezolana, 2010), 102–109.

to assure social welfare (Article 320). In order to facilitate the attaining of such objectives, the Minister of Finances and the Central Bank must contribute to the harmonization of the fiscal and monetary policies, although the Central Bank in the exercise of its functions shall not be subordinated to the Executive directives and would not avail or finance fiscal deficits.

The coordination between the National Executive and the Central Bank must be formalized in an annual agreement of policies, in which the final objectives of growth and its social repercussion must be expressed, as well as the external balance and inflation, regarding the fiscal, exchange and monetary policies. It must also include the levels of intermediate variables and required instruments in order to attain the final objectives. The agreement must be signed by the President of the Central Bank and the Minister of Finance, and must be published once the Budget is approved by the National Assembly. They are responsible that the policy actions to be taken be consistent with its objectives, so the agreement must specify the attained results, and the policies and actions to be achieved.

618. The Constitution also created a Macro-economic Stabilization Fund in charge of guaranteeing the stability of the public expenses in all National, state and municipal levels, regarding the ordinary income fluctuations. The Law on the Macro-economic Stabilization Fund,[2020] has defined the basic principles the Constitution enumerated for its functioning: efficiency, equity and non-discrimination between the public entities that contribute to it with resources (Article 321).

Chapter 5. Constitutional Provisions on Public Domain

619. The 1999 Constitution declares all mining and hydrocarbons deposits, of any nature, including those under the ocean floor in territorial waters, within Venezuela's exclusive economic zone, and on the continental shelf, as 'public domain' or public property (Article 12).[2021] Consequently, according to the terms of Article 453 of the Civil Code, this property is inalienable and not subject to status of limitation.[2022]

620. The same provision of Article 12 of the Constitution sets forth that the nation's sea coasts are within the public domain, meaning those of the nation's shores that touch the ocean, that is the beaches between high and low tides.[2023]

2020   *Gaceta Oficial* N° 38.846 of 9 Jan. 2008.

2021   See Isabel Boscán de Ruesta, 'La propiedad de los yacimientos de los hidrocarburos. Evolución histórica', in *El Derecho Público a comienzos del siglo XXI. Estudios homenaje al Profesor Allan R. Brewer-Carías*, vol. III (Madrid: Instituto de Derecho Público, UCV, Civitas Ediciones, 2003), 3061–3105.

2022   The principle has also been established in the Mining Law (Art. 2), *Gaceta Oficial* N° 5382 of 28 Sep. 1999, and in the Organic Law on Gaseous Hydrocarbons (Art. 1), *Gaceta Oficial* N° 36.793 of 23 Sep. 1999. See Armando Rodríguez García, 'Comentarios sobre el régimen de los bienes públicos en la Constitución de 1999', in *Revista de Derecho Público*, N° 84 (octubre-diciembre) (Caracas: Editorial Jurídica Venezolana, 2000), 63–68.

2023   Costal Zones Law, *Gaceta Oficial* N° 37.349 of 19 Dec. 2001. See Allan R. Brewer-Carías, 'El nuevo régimen de las zonas costeras. Inconstitucionalidades, dominio público, limitaciones a la propiedad privada e insuficiencias normativas' in *Ley Habilitante del 13-11-2000 y sus Decretos Leyes*, N° 17 (Caracas: Academia de Ciencias Políticas y Sociales, Serie Eventos, 2002), 245–294.

621. Article 304 of the Constitution provides, further, that all waters constitute property in the national public domain, irreplaceable for life and development. The Constitution provides that legislation is to be enacted as necessary to guarantee: the protection of national waters, and their productive use and recuperation, while respecting the phases of the hydrological cycle, and criteria pertaining to territorial order.[2024]

622. Municipal land (*ejidos*) is considered in the Constitution as inalienable and imprescriptible. The Constitution establishes the presumption that all land without specific owner located in urban areas are considered as such *ejidos* (Article 181), although without prejudice to the legitimate and validly constituted rights of third parties.

Chapter 6. The Progressive Nationalization and State Ownership of the Economy

623. Within the general framework of the economic mixed system established in the Constitution, and due to the importance of oil exploitation, and of oil income in the Venezuelan economy, during almost all the past hundred years the State has been the most powerful component of the economic system. In 1975, the Oil Industry was nationalized (see *supra* paragraph 623).

As aforementioned, this explains why the Constitution is not only manifestly statist in its economic provisions, but also establishes extended State responsibility for the management and provision of health, education, and social security services, as well as that of public utilities including water, electricity and gas. The State has derived, through the regulation of these tasks, a complete set of powers to plan and control the economy, with wide possibilities of intervention in the private sector in some aspects, missing the necessary equilibrium between the public and private sectors. The only protected or privileged economic activities in the private sector are those that are *not* basic to the generation of wealth and employment in the country, such as agriculture (Article 305); handicraft and craft work (Article 309); small and medium business enterprises (Article 308), and tourism (Article 310). Added to this are the constitutional rules of control and sanctioning, such as those norms governing monopoly and other economic offences (Articles 113, 114); the declaration of the country's subsoil, sea coasts and waters to be within the public domain (Articles 112, 304); the State's reservation of rights in the oil industry; the possibility of similar State control in other exploitations, activities and services of a 'strategic nature'; and finally, the constitutional provisions that provide for the planning powers of the State, on the national (Articles 112, 299) and local (Article 178) levels. As a result, the State, is responsible for nearly everything, and can regulate everything, and private initiative and investment seems both marginal and marginalized.

624. The result of the implementation of the constitutional text by an authoritarian government in the area of the economy, from a comprehensive viewpoint, has been the increase of the economic intervention by the State, with for instance the almost complete State ownership of the whole economy, by means of nationaliza-

---

2024   Waters Law, *Gaceta Oficial* N° 38.595 of 2 Jan. 2007. See, Allan R. Brewer-Carías, *Ley de Aguas* (Caracas: Editorial Jurídica Venezolana, 2007).

tions and expropriations of industries and private enterprises, in many cases without compensation.

For instance, regarding the private enterprise participation in the exploitation of the Oil industry, after its nationalization in 1975, through the policy known as the 'Oil Opening' (Operating Agreements and Association Agreements), such participation was allowed by the 1975 Organic Law Reserving to the State the Industry and Commerce of Hydrocarbons.[2025] Nonetheless, in 2006–2007[2026] through the Decree Law N° 5.200 on the Migration to Mixed Companies of the Association Agreements of the Orinoco Oil Belt and of the Shared-Risk-and-Profit Exploration Agreements of February 2007,[2027] and the Law on the Effects of the Process of Migration to Mixed Companies of the Orinoco Oil Belt Association Agreements and the Shared-Risk-and-Profit Exploration Agreements of 11 September 2007,[2028] the private sector participation in the oil industry was reduced to being minority shareholders on public mixed enterprises controlled by the State, following the provisions of the 2001 Organic Hydrocarbons Law,[2029] which was then applied retroactively to the Agreements entered into in the 1990s.

Inaddition, all the electricity companies, and the telephone company were assumed by the State, the Steel industry and the cement industry were nationalized,[2030] as well as all the assets and services related to the hydrocarbon industry were also reserved for the State.[2031] Finally, in September 2011, the activities of exploration and exploitation of gold, and its related and ancillary activities were also reserved for the state.[2032]

Chapter 7. The Implementation of the Rejected 2007 Constitutional Reform through Legislation in Order to Establish a Communal Economic System

625. As aforementioned (see*supra* paragraph 236 ff), the 2007 Constitutional Reform Draft that was rejected by the people through a referendum held on December that same year, pretended to convert the mixed economic system established in

---

2025   *Gaceta Oficial* N° 1.769 Extra. of 29 Aug. 1975.

2026   See Allan R. Brewer-Carías, 'The 'Statization' of the Pre 2001 Primary Hydrocarbons Joint Venbture Exploitations: Their Unilateral termination and the Assets'Confiscation of Some of the Former Private parties' in Oil, Gas & Energy Law Intelligence, <www.gasandoil.com/ogel/ ISSN: 1875-418X>, issue vol 6, issue 2 (OGEL/TDM Special Issue on Venezuela: The battle of Contract Sanctity vs. Resource Sovereignty, ed. By Elizabeth Eljuri), April 2008; and 'La estatización de los convenios de asociación que permitían la participación del capital privado en las actividades primarias de hidrocarburos suscritos antes de 2002, mediante su terminación anticipada y unilateral y la confiscación de los bienes afectos a los mismos', in Víctor Hernández Mendible et al., *Nacionalización, Libertad de Empresa y Asociaciones Mixtas* (Caracas: Editorial Jurídica Venezolana, 2008), 123–188.

2027   *Gaceta Oficial* N° 38.632 of 26 Feb. 2007.

2028   *Gaceta Oficial* N° 38.785 of 8 Oct. 2007.

2029   *Gaceta Oficial* N° 37.323 of 13 Nov. 2001. See Isabel Boscán de Ruesta, *La actividad petrolera y la nueva Ley Orgánica de Hidrocarburos* (Caracas: FUNEDA, 2002).

2030   *Gaceta Oficial* N° 38.928 of 12 May 2008; and See in Víctor Hernández Mendible et al., *Nacionalización, Libertad de Empresa y Asociaciones Mixtas* (Caracas: Editorial Jurídica Venezolana, 2008).

2031   *Gaceta Oficial* N° 39.173 of 7 May 2009.

2032   *Gaceta Oficial* N° 39.759 of 16 September 2011.

the Constitution into a State-owned, socialist, centralized economy in which economic liberty and private initiative as constitutional rights were to be eliminated, as well as the constitutional right to private property. In substitution, it sought to confer the means of production only to the State, to be centrally managed. In such framework, the State was to be configurated as an institution on which all economic activity depended and to whose bureaucracy the totality of the population was to be subject.

In this sense, the reform established that the socialist economic model created was to achieve 'the best conditions for the collective and cooperative construction of a Socialist Economy' (Article 112), through 'socialist means of production' (Article 168) by constituting 'mixed corporations and/or socialist units of production' (Article 113), or 'economic units of social production' as to 'create the best conditions for the collective and cooperative construction of a socialist economy', or 'different forms of businesses and economic units from social property, both directly or communally, as well as indirectly or through the state' (Article 112).

The reforms sought simply to derogate and eliminate the right to the free exercise of economic activities as a constitutional right and economic freedom itself.[2033] The reforms then referred to the 'socialist principles of the socioeconomic system' (Article 229) and to the 'socialist state' and the 'socialist development of the nation' (Articles 318, 320). All the reforms collided with the ideas of liberty and solidarity proclaimed in the 1999 Constitution and established a State that substitutes itself for society and private economic initiative.

626. As aforementioned, although the 2007 Constitutional Reform was rejected by the people, the government proceed to implemented in an illegitimate way by means of legislation (see *supra* paragraph 250). Specifically on economic matters, this implementing process began even before the draft reforms were even submitted to the National Assembly, when Decree Law N° 5,841 was enacted on 12 June 2007,[2034] containing the organic law creating the Central Planning Commission. This was the first formal State act devoted to building the socialist State.[2035] Later, once the 2007 Constitutional Reform was rejected in referendum, on 13 December 2007, the National Assembly approved the 2007–2013 Economic and Social Deve-

2033 See Gerardo Fernández, 'Aspectos esenciales de la modificación constitucional propuesta por el Presidente de la República. La modificación constitucional como un fraude a la democracia', in *Revista de Derecho Público* 112 *(Estudios sobre la reforma constitucional)* (Caracas: Editorial Jurídica Venezolana, 2007), 24; Alfredo Arismendi, 'Utopía Constitucional', in *id.*, 31; José Antonio Muci Borjas, 'La suerte de la libertad económica en el proyecto de Reforma de la Constitución de 2007', in *id.*, 203–208; Tamara Adrián, 'Actividad económica y sistemas alternativos de producción', in *id.*, 209–214; Víctor Hernández Mendible, 'Réquiem por la libertad de empresa y derecho de propiedad', in *id.*, 215–218; Alfredo Morles Hernández, 'El nuevo modelo económico para el Socialismo del Siglo XXI', in *id.*, 233–236.

2034 *Gaceta Oficial* N° 5.841, Extra., of 22 Jun. 2007.

2035 See Allan R. Brewer-Carías, 'Comentarios sobre la inconstitucional creación de la Comisión Central de Planificación, centralizada y obligatoria', in *Revista de Derecho Público* 110 (Caracas: Editorial Jurídica Venezolana, 2007), 79–89; Luis A. Herrera Orellana, 'Los Decretos-Leyes de 30 de julio de 2008 y la Comisión Central de Planificación: Instrumentos para la progresiva abolición del sistema político y del sistema económico previstos en la Constitución de 1999', in *Revista de Derecho Público* 115 *(Estudios sobre los Decretos Leyes)* (Caracas: Editorial Jurídica Venezolana, 2008), 221–232.

lopment National Plan, established in Article 32 of the Decree Law enacting the Planning Organic Law,[2036] in which the basis of the 'planning, production and distribution system oriented towards socialism' is established, providing that 'the relevant matter is the progressive development of social property of the production means'. For such purpose, the proposed 2007 rejected constitutional reforms to assign the State all powers over farming, livestock, fishing and aquaculture, and in particular the production of food, was then materialized in the Decree Law on the Organic Law on Farming and Food Security and Sovereignty.[2037] That law assigned to the State power not only to authorize food imports but also to prioritize production and directly assume distribution and commercialization. The law also expanded expropriation powers of the executive violating the constitutional guarantee of the previous declaration of a specific public interest or public utility involved, and allowing the State occupation of industries without compensation –[2038] what has repeatedly occurred during the past years.[2039]

627. Another Decree Law, N° 6,130 of 3 June 2008, enacted the Popular Economy Promotion and Development Law, establishing a 'socio-productive communal model', with different socio-productive organizations following the 'socialist model'.[2040] In the same openly socialist orientation, Decree Law N° 6,092 was also issued enacting the Access to Goods and Services Persons Defence Law,[2041] which derogated the previous Consumer and Users Protection Law,[2042] with the purpose of regulating all commercialization and different economic aspects of goods and servi-

---

2036   *Gaceta Oficial* N° 5.554 of 13 Nov. 2001.

2037   *Gaceta Oficial* N° 5.889, Extra., of 31 Jul. 2008. See José Ignacio Hernández G., 'Planificación y soberanía alimentaria', in *Revista de Derecho Público* 115 *(Estudios sobre los Decretos Leyes)* (Caracas: Editorial Jurídica Venezolana, 2008), 389–394; Juan Domingo Alfonso Paradisi, 'La constitución económica establecida en la Constitución de 1999, el sistema de economía social de mercado y el decreto 6.071 con rango, valor y fuerza de Ley Orgánica de seguridad y soberanía agroalimentaria', in *id.*, 395–415; Gustavo A. Grau Fortoul, 'La participación del sector privado en la producción de alimentos, como elemento esencial para poder alcanzar la seguridad alimentaria (Aproximación al tratamiento de la cuestión, tanto en la Constitución de 1999 como en la novísima Ley Orgánica de soberanía y seguridad alimentaria)', in *id.*, 417–424.

2038   See Carlos García Soto, 'Notas sobre la expansión del ámbito de la declaratoria de utilidad pública o interés social en la expropiación', in *id.*, 149–151.

2039   See, in general, Antonio Canova González, Luis Alfonso Herrera Orellana & Karina Anzola Spadaro, *¿Expropiaciones o vías de hecho? (La degradación continuada del derecho fundamental de propiedad en la Venezuela actual* (Caracas: Funeda, Universidad Católica Andrés Bello, 2009).

2040   *Gaceta Oficial* N° 5.890, Extra., of 31 Jul. 2008. See Jesús María Alvarado Andrade, 'La desaparición del bolívar como moneda de curso legal (Notas críticas al inconstitucional Decreto N° 6.130, con rango, valor y fuerza de la ley para el fomento y desarrollo de la economía comunal, de fecha 3 de junio de 2008', in *Revista de Derecho Público* 115 *(Estudios sobre los Decretos Leyes)* (Caracas: Editorial Jurídica Venezolana, 2008), 313–320.

2041   *Gaceta Oficial* N° 5,889 Extra of 31 Jul. 2008; José Gregorio Silva, 'Disposiciones sobre el Decreto-Ley para la defensa de las personas en el acceso a bienes y servicios', in *id.*, 277–279; Carlos Simón Bello Rengifo, 'Decreto N° 6.092 con rango, valor y fuerza de la ley para la defensa de las personas en el acceso a los bienes y servicios (Referencias a problemas de imputación)', in *id.*, 281–305; Alfredo Morles Hernández, 'El nuevo modelo económico del socialismo del siglo XXI y su reflejo en el contrato de adhesión', in *id.*, 229–232.

2042   *Gaceta Oficial* N° 37.930, of 4 May 2004.

ces, extending the State powers of control to the point of establishing the possibility of confiscating goods and services by means of their takeover and occupation of private industries and services through administrative decisions,[2043] which has also repeatedly occurred during the past years.[2044]

628. Finally, in December 2010 as aforementioned (see *supra* paragraphs 258 ff., 264), the National Assembly approved a set of organic laws through which it has not only defined a legislative framework for a new Communal State, exercising the Popular Power, by-passing the Constitution and in parallel to the Constitutional State, but also a new economic system called the Communal Economic System, based on the Socialist doctrine and subjected to a centralized system of Public and Communal Planning. For such purpose, in addition to the Laws on the Popular Power, the Communes and the Communal Council, an Organic Law on the Communal Economic System was sanctioned.[2045]

This Communal State is then structured through the Communes,'with an economic model of social property and endogenous sustainable development that allows reaching the supreme social happiness of the Venezuelan people in a socialist society' (Article 8.8),[2046] with the socialist political ideology, for which purpose the Law defined socialism, as:

> a mode of social relations of production, centered in coexistence with solidarity and the satisfaction of material and intangible needs of all of society, which has as fundamental basis, the recuperation of the value of work as a producer of goods and services to meet human needs and achieve supreme social happiness and integral human development. This requires the development of social ownership of the basic and strategic means of production, so that all families, Venezuelan citizens, possess, use and enjoy their patrimony, individual

---

2043   See Juan Domingo Alfonso Paradisi, 'Comentarios en cuanto a los procedimientos administrativos establecidos en el Decreto N° 6.092 con rango, valor y fuerza de Ley para la defensa de las personas en el acceso a los bienes y servicios', in *Revista de Derecho Público* 115 *(Estudios sobre los Decretos Leyes)* (Caracas: Editorial Jurídica Venezolana, 2008), 245–260; Karina Anzola Spadaro, 'El carácter autónomo de las 'medidas preventivas' contempladas en el artículo 111 del Decreto-Ley para la defensa de las personas en el acceso a los bienes y servicios', in *id.*, 271–276.

2044   See, in general, Antonio Canova González, Luis Alfonso Herrera Orellana & Karina Anzola Spadaro, *¿Expropiaciones o vías de hecho? (La degradación continuada del derecho fundamental de propiedad en la Venezuela actual* (Caracas: Funeda, Universidad Católica Andrés Bello, 2009).

2045   See in *Gaceta Oficial* N° 6.011 Extra. of 21 Dec. 2010. See Allan R. Brewer-Carías, 'Sobre la Ley Orgánica del Sistema Económico Comunal o de cómo se implanta en Venezuela un sistema económico comunista sin reformar la Constitución', in *Revista de Derecho Público*, No. 124 (Caracas: Editorial Jurídica Venezolana, 2010), 102–109. On the Laws referred to the Popular State, see Allan R. Brewer-Carías et al., *Leyes Orgánicas sobre el Poder Popular y el Estado Comunal* (Caracas: Editorial Jurídica Venezolana, 1911) (should this be 1991?), 361 et seq.

2046   The Organic Law of Municipalities, however, defines the Communal State as follows: 'From of sociopolitical organization, based on the democratic and social state of law and justice established in the Constitution of the Republic, whose power is exercised directly by the people through communal self goverments, with an economic model of social property and endogenous and sustainable development that achieves the supreme social happiness of thethe Venezuelan people in a socialist society. Forming the basic unit of the Communal State is the commune' (Art. 4.10).

or family property, and exercise full enjoyment of their economic, social, political and cultural rights (Article 8.14).[2047]

Within the areas of communal power, the Law has specifically regulated the Communal economy that must be developed 'under communal forms of social ownership, to satisfy collective needs, social reinvestment of the surplus, and contribute to the country's overall social development in a sustainable manner' (Article 18). This area of Public Power has been regulated by the Organic Law of the Communal Economic System,[2048] that must be exclusively developed through 'socio-productive organizations under communal social property forms' created as public enterprises, family productive units or bartering groups, in which private initiative and private property are excluded. This system radically changes the mixed economic system of the 1999 constitutional framework, substituting it with a State-controlled economic system, mixed with provisions belonging to primitive societies, and even allowing the creation of local or 'communal' currencies in a society that must be ruled only 'by socialist principles and values' that the Law declares to be inspired, without any historical support, on the 'Simón Bolívar's doctrine' (Article 5).

629. The socialist productive model established in the Law (Article 3.2), is precisely defined as a 'production model based on social property, oriented towards the elimination of the social division of work that appertains to the capitalist model', directed to satisfy the increasing needs of the population through new means of generation and appropriation as well as the reinvestment of social surplus' (Article 6.12).

This is nothing different than to legally impose a communist system by copying isolated paragraphs perhaps of a forgotten old manual of a failed communist revolution paraphrasing what Karl Marx and Friedrich Engels wrote 150 years ago (1845–1846) on the 'communist society',[2049] precisely based upon those three basic concepts: the social property of production means, the elimination of social division of work, and the social reinvestment of surplus (Article 1).

PART XI. RULE OF LAW AND JUDICIAL REVIEW

630. The formal consolidation in the Constitution of the principles of the rule of law (*Estado de Derecho*), following the general trends of modern constitutionalism, has led to the reinforcement in the Constitution not only of the aforementioned principle of its supremacy, considered as the foundation of the juridical order (Article 7)

2047   The same definition is found in Art. 4.14 of the Organic Law of the Communes. Many are the definitions of socialism, but in all, its basic elements can be identified: (i) a system of social and economic organization (ii) based on collective or State ownership and administration of the means of production, and (iii) State regulation of economic and social activities and distribution of goods (iv) seeking the gradual disappearance of social classes.

2048   See *Gaceta Oficial* N° 6.011 Extra. of 21 Dec. 2010.

2049   See in Karl Marx & Frederich Engels',The German Ideology', en *Collective Works*, vol. 5 (New York: International Publishers, 1976), 47. Véanse además los textos pertinentes en <www.educa.madrid.org/cms_tools/files/0a24636f-764c-4e03-9c1d-6722e2ee60d7/Texto%20Marx%20y%20Engels.pdf>.

(see *supra* paragraph 113), but also of various judicial means in order to guarantee such supremacy. In this regard, the 1999 Constitution follows a long tradition on the matter and the general trends already set forth in the previous 1961 Constitution,[2050] by establishing a system of judicial review of the constitutionality of legislation; a specific means for the judicial protection of human rights, known as the *amparo* action or recourse; and a system of judicial review of administrative action.

Chapter 1. Judicial Review System

631. As aforementioned (see *supra* paragraph 59), Article 334 of the Constitution provides for the diffuse method of judicial review allowing any court to apply the Constitution in any case of incompatibility between its provisions and a statute. In addition to the diffuse method, in Venezuela there also exists the concentrated method of judicial review being attributed to the Supreme Tribunal of Justice, as Constitutional Jurisdiction, exercised by its Constitutional Chamber, which has the exclusive powers to declare the nullity of statutes and other State acts issued in direct and immediate execution of the Constitution, or that have the force of law (statute) (Article 334).

632. These provisions of the Constitution established the general framework of the judicial review of constitutionality system in Venezuela, which was particularly developed since the democratic system was consolidated during the second half of the twentieth century. It is important to insist that judicial review is above all an institutional tool essentially linked to democracy, understood as a political system not just reduced to the fact of having elected governments, but where separation and control of power and the respect and enforcement of human rights is possible through an independent and autonomous judiciary. It has been precisely because of this process of reinforcement of democracy in Latin American countries that judicial review of the constitutionality of legislation and other governmental actions has become an important tool in order to guarantee the supremacy of the Constitution, the rule of law and the respect of human rights. It is in this sense that judicial review of the constitutionality of State acts has been considered as the ultimate result of the consolidation of the *rule of law*, when precisely in a democratic system the courts can serve as the ultimate guarantor of the Constitution, effectively controlling the exercise of power by the organs of the State.

On the contrary, as happens in all authoritarian regimes even having elected governments, if such control is not possible, the same power vested, for instance, upon a politically controlled Supreme Court or Constitutional Court, can constitute the most powerful instrument for the consolidation of authoritarianism, the destruction

---

2050   See Allan R. Brewer-Carías, *Instituciones Políticas y Constitucionales*, vol VI: *La Justicia Constitucional* (San Cristóbal-Caracas: Universidad Católica del Táchira, Editorial Jurídica Venezolana, 1998); *Estado de Derecho y Control Judicial* (Madrid: Instituto de Administración Pública, 1985); *Judicial Review in Comparative Law* (Cambridge: Cambridge University Press, 1989); *El Sistema de Justicia Constitucional en la Constitución de 1999: Comentarios sobre su desarrollo jurisprudencial y su explicación a veces errada, en la Exposición de Motivos* (Caracas: Editorial Jurídica Venezolana, 2000); *Justicia Constitucional. Procesos y Procedimientos constitucionales* (México: Ed. Porrúa, 2007).

of democracy and the violation of human rights.[2051] With this important warning, the following are the general trends governing the very comprehensive judicial review system established in Venezuela, in many aspects, since the nineteenth century.[2052]

§1. *A General Overview of the Systems of Judicial Review and the Venezuelan System*

633. Judicial review can always be analysed according to the criteria established a few decades ago by Mauro Cappelletti[2053] who, following the trends of the so-called North American and European systems, distinguished between the 'diffuse' (decentralized) and 'concentrated' (centralized) methods of judicial review of the constitutionality of legislation. The former is exercised by all the courts of a given country, while the latter is only assigned to a Supreme Court or to a court specially created for that purpose such as a Constitutional Court or Tribunal.

634. In the diffuse, or decentralized, method, all the courts are empowered to judge upon the constitutionality of statutes, as is the case in the United States of America, where the 'diffuse method' was born. That is why it is also referred as the 'American model' initiated with *Marbury v. Madison,* 5 U.S. 137 (1803), later followed in many countries with or without a common law tradition. It is called 'diffuse' or decentralized because judicial control is shared by all courts, from the lowest level up to the Supreme Court of the country. In Latin America, the only country that has kept the diffuse method of judicial review as *the only* judicial review method available is Argentina. In other Latin American countries, the diffuse method

---

2051   See Allan R. Brewer-Carías, *'Quis Custodiet ipsos Custodes*: De la interpretación constitucional a la inconstitucionalidad de la interpretación', in *VIII Congreso Nacional de derecho Constitucional, Perú* (Fondo Editorial, 2005), Colegio de Abogados de Arequipa, Arequipa, September 2005, 463–489.

2052   See Jesús M. Casal H., *Constitución y justicia constitucional: los fundamentos de la justicia constitucional en la nueva Carta Magna* (Caracas: Universidad Católica Andrés Bello, 2000); Jesús M. Casal H., 'Hacia el fortalecimiento y racionalización de la justicia constitucional', in *Revista de Derecho Constitucional,* N° 2 (enero-junio) (Caracas: Editorial Sherwood, 2000), 215–242; Antonio Canova González, 'La futura justicia constitucional en Venezuela', in *Revista de Derecho Constitucional,* N° 2 (enero-junio) (Caracas: Editorial Sherwood, 2000), 93–181; María A. Bonnemaison, 'El control constitucional de los Poderes Públicos', in *Bases y principios del sistema constitucional venezolano* (Ponencias del VII Congreso Venezolano de Derecho Constitucional realizado en San Cristóbal del 21 al 23 de Noviembre de 2001*),* vol. II, 233–260; Carla Crazut Jiménez, 'Progreso de la protección constitucional en Venezuela', in *Libro Homenaje a Enrique Tejera París, Temas sobre la Constitución de 1999* (Caracas: Centro de Investigaciones Jurídicas (CEIN), 2001), 273–289; José Vicente Haro G., 'La justicia constitucional en Venezuela y la Constitución de 1999', in *Revista de Derecho Constitucional,* Editorial Sherwood, N° 1 (Caracas, sep-dic. 1999), 137–146; Allan R. Brewer-Carías, *El Sistema de Justicia Constitucional en la Constitución de 1999: Comentarios sobre su desarrollo jurisprudencial y su explicación a veces errada, en la Exposición de Motivos* (Caracas: Editorial Jurídica Venezolana, 2000); 'La Justicia Constitucional en la Nueva Constitución' in *Revista de Derecho Constitucional,* N° 1 (Caracas: Editorial Sherwood, Septiembre-Diciembre 1999), 35–44, in *Derecho Procesal Constitucional,* Colegio de Secretarios de la Suprema Corte de Justicia de la Nación, A.C. (México: Editorial Porrúa, 2001), 931–961, and in *Reflexiones sobre el Constitucionalismo en América* (Caracas: Editorial Jurídica Venezolana, 2001), 255–285.

2053   See Mauro Cappelletti, *Judicial Review in the Contemporaly World* (Indianapolis, 1971); 'El control judicial de la constitucionalidad de las leyes en el derecho comparado', in *Revista de la Facultad de Derecho de México,* N° 61 (México, 1966).

coexists with the concentrated method (Brazil, Colombia, the Dominican Republic, Ecuador, Guatemala, Mexico, Nicaragua, Perú and Venezuela).

635. The 'concentrated' or centralized method of judicial review, in contrast with the diffuse method, empowers only one single court to control the constitutionality of legislation, utilizing annulatory powers. This can be achieved by a Supreme Court or a constitutional court created specially for that particular purpose. The concentrated or centralized system is also called the 'Austrian' or 'European' model because it was first established in Austria in 1920, and later developed in Germany, Italy, Spain, Portugal and France. This method has also been adopted in many Latin American countries, in some cases as *the only* form of judicial review applied (Costa Rica, El Salvador, Bolivia, Chile, Honduras, Panama, Paraguay and Uruguay). In other countries, as mentioned, it is applied conjunctly with the diffuse method.

636. It has been this mixture, or parallel functioning, of the diffuse and concentrated methods, which has given rise to what can be considered the 'Latin American' model of judicial review. This model can be identified in Brazil, Colombia, the Dominican Republic, Ecuador, Guatemala, Mexico, Nicaragua, Perú and Venezuela. On the one hand, all courts are entitled to decide upon the constitutionality of legislation by autonomously deciding upon a statute's inapplicability in a particular case, with *inter partes* effects; and on the other hand, the Supreme Court or a Constitutional Court or Tribunal has been empowered to declare the total nullity of statutes contrary to the Constitution.[2054] The Venezuelan judicial review system is precisely one of the latter, combining the diffuse and the concentrated methods of judicial review since the nineteenth century[2055] that in addition can also be exercised through a variety of other means.

637. According to the express provision of Article 335 of the 1999 Constitution, the Supreme Tribunal and specifically its Constitutional Chamber, has the duty to guarantee the supremacy and effectiveness of constitutional norms and principles, and is the final and authoritative interpreter of the constitutional text. For this reason, it is the Tribunal's duty to oversee the maintenance of uniformity in the Constitution's interpretation and application.

2054   See Allan R. Brewer-Carías, 'La jurisdicción constitucional en América Latina', in *La jurisdicción constitucional en Iberoamérica*, ed. Domingo García Belaúnde & Francisco Fernández Segado (Madrid: Edit. Dickinson, 1997), 117–161.

2055   See Allan R. Brewer-Carías, *El sistema mixto o integral de control de la constitucionalidad en Colombia y Venezuela* (Bogotá, 1995); Manuel Arona Cruz, 'El control de la constitucionalidad de los actos jurídicos en Colombia ante el Derecho Comparado', in *Archivo de Derecho Público y Ciencias de la Administración*, vol. VII (1984–1985), *Derecho Publico en Venezuela y Colombia* (Caracas: Instituto de Derecho Público, UCV, 1986), 39–114; Antonio Canova González, 'Rasgos generales de los modelos de justicia constitucional en derecho comparado: Estados Unidos de América', in *Temas de Derecho Administrativo: Libro Homenaje a Gonzalo Pérez Luciani*, vol. I (Caracas: Editorial Torino, 2002), 373–411; Antonio Canova González, 'Rasgos generales de los modelos de justicia constitucional en Derecho Comparado: (2) Kelsen', in *Revista de Derecho Constitucional*, N° 6, enero-diciembre-2002 (Caracas: Editorial Sherwood, 2003), 65 a 88; Antonio Canova González, 'Rasgos generales de los modelos de justicia constitucional en Derecho Comparado: (3) Europa Actual', in *Revista de Derecho Constitucional*, N° 7 (Caracas: Editorial Sherwood, enero-junio 2003), 75 a 114.

638. However, it must be pointed out that the constitutional interpretations made by the Constitutional Chamber have binding effects upon all the other Chambers of the Supreme Tribunal of Justice and all other courts of the Republic (Article 334). This is particularly true with respect to the content and scope of constitutional norms and principles. Thus, these constitutional interpretations have the weight and value of precedent, and, as such, are mandatory in the other Chambers of the Supreme Tribunal, as well as in all tribunals or courts in Venezuela.

The constitutional interpretation of the Constitution, of course, is normally established by the Constitutional Chamber when deciding any of the aforementioned actions or petitions for judicial review that the Constitution has expressly enumerated.

639. Based on all the aforementioned constitutional provisions, judicial review of constitutionality in Venezuela can be exercised not only through the diffuse and concentrated methods, but also through a variety of other means. Judicial review may occur through any of the following means: (1) The diffuse method of judicial review of the constitutionality of statutes and other normative acts, exercised by all courts; (2) The concentrated method of judicial review of the constitutionality of certain State acts, exercised by the Constitutional Chamber of the Supreme Tribunal of Justice; (3) The protection of constitutional rights and guarantees through the actions for *amparo*; (4) The concentrated method of judicial review of Executive regulations and administrative actions, exercised by special courts controlling their unconstitutionality and illegality (*contencioso adminsitrativo*); (5) The judicial review powers to control the constitutionality of legislative omissions; (6) The concentrated judicial review power to resolve constitutional conflicts between the State organs; (7) The protection of the Constitution through the abstract recourse for interpretation of the Constitution; and (8) The Constitutional Chamber's power to remove from ordinary courts jurisdiction over particular cases.

§2. *The Diffuse Method of Judicial Review*

640. Since 1897, the Venezuelan Civil Procedure Code has regulated the diffuse method of judicial review,[2056] which is currently set forth in Article 20. This article prescribes that 'In the case in which a law in force, whose application is requested, collides with any constitutional provision, judges shall apply the latter with preference.' The principle of the diffuse method of judicial review also has been more recently set forth in Article 19 of the Criminal Procedure Organic Code, as follows: '*Control of the Constitutionality*. The control of the supremacy of the Constitution corresponds to the judges. In case that a statute whose application is requested would collide with it, the courts shall abide [by] the constitutional provision.'[2057]

2056   Expressly established in the Civil Procedure Code of 1897. See Allan R. Brewer-Carías, *Judicial Review in Comparative Law* (Cambridge: Cambridge University Press, 1989), 127 et seq.

2057   See Allan R. Brewer-Carías, 'El método difuso de control de constitucionalidad de las leyes en el derecho venezolano', in *Derecho Procesal Constitucional Americano y Europeo*, ed. Víctor Bazán (coord.) Edit. Abeledo-Perrot, 2 Vols. Buenos Aires, Rep. Argentina, 2010, Vol. I, 671–690; José Vicente Haro García, 'El Control Difuso de la Constitucionalidad en Venezuela. El estado actual de la cuestión', in *Tendencias Actuales del Derecho Constitucional. Homenaje a Jesús María Casal*

641. Article 334 of the 1999 Constitution consolidated the diffuse method of judicial review of the constitutionality of legislation by setting forth that:

> In case of incompatibility between this Constitution and a law or other legal provision, constitutional provisions shall be applied, corresponding to all courts in any case whatsoever, even at their initiative, the pertinent decision.

Through this Article, the diffuse method of judicial review acquired constitutional rank in Venezuela as a judicial power that can even be exercised ex officio by all courts, including the different Chambers of the Supreme Tribunal of Justice.

This constitutional provision follows the general trends shown in comparative law regarding the diffuse method: it is based on the principle of constitutional supremacy, according to which unconstitutional acts are considered void and hold no value. Therefore, each and every judge is entitled to decide the unconstitutionality of the statute they are applying in order to resolve the case. This power can be exercised at the judge's own initiative, or ex officio. The decision of the judge has only an *inter partes* effect in each specific case and, therefore, is declarative in nature.

642. The general judicial procedural system in Venezuela is governed under the 'by-instance principle', so that judicial decisions resolving cases on judicial review are subject to ordinary appeal. Therefore, the cases could only reach the Cassation Chambers of the Supreme Tribunal through cassation recourses (Article 312 Civil Procedure Code). Since this situation could lead to possible dispersion of the judicial decision on constitutional matters, the 1999 Constitution specifically set forth a corrective procedure. The Constitution granted the Constitutional Chamber of the Supreme Tribunal of Justice the power to review final judicial decisions issued by the courts of the Republic on *amparo* suits and when deciding judicial review of statutes in the terms established by the respective organic law (Article 336.10).

Regarding this provision, it must be pointed out that it is neither an appeal nor a general second or third procedural instance. Instead, it is an exceptional faculty of the Constitutional Chamber to review, upon its judgment and discretion, through an extraordinary recourse, similar to a writ of certiorari. Such review is exercised against last instance decisions in which constitutional issues are decided by means of judicial review, or in *amparo* suits. It is a reviewing, non-obligatory power that can be exercised optionally. The Constitutional Chamber is empowered to choose the cases in which it considers convenient to decide due to the constitutional importance of the matter. The Chamber also has the power to give a general binding effect to its interpretation of the Constitution, similar to the effect of *stare decisis* (Article 335).

643. Nonetheless, the Constitutional Chamber has distorted its review power regarding judicial decisions, extending it far beyond the precise cases of judicial review and *amparo* established in the Constitution. The Chamber has extended its

---

Montbrun, ed. Jesús María Casal, Alfredo Arismendi y Carlos Luis Carrillo Artiles (Coord.), vol. II (Caracas: Universidad Central de Venezuela/Universidad Católica Andrés Bello, 2008), 129–156; Jesús María Casal H., 'El control difuso de la Constitucionalidad y sus perspectivas en el derecho venezolano', in *Estudios de Derecho Público*, ed. Román Duque Corredor y Jesús María Casal (Coord.), vol. II (Caracas: Universidad Católica Andrés Bello, 2004), 303–336.

review power over any other judicial decision issued in any matter when it considers it contrary to the Constitution, a power that the Chamber has proceeded to exercise without any constitutional authorization, even ex officio and regarding the Constitutional Chamber's interpretation of the Constitution, or in cases in which it has considered that the decision is affected by a grotesque error regarding constitutional interpretation.[2058]

§3. *The Concentrated Method of Judicial Review: The Popular Action*

644. The second traditional method of judicial review in Venezuela is the judicial power to annul unconstitutional statutes and other State acts of similar rank, which has been granted exclusively to the Supreme Court of the country since 1858. According to the 1999 Constitution, this power is now attributed to one of the Chambers of the Supreme Tribunal of Justice – the Constitutional Chamber – as Constitutional Jurisdiction (Articles 266.1; 334 and 336).[2059]

For the purpose of implementing the concentrated method of judicial review, the Constitution has provided for different judicial means and, in particular, for the *a posteriori* popular action of unconstitutionality that can be filed directly against statutes before the Constitutional Chamber by any citizen. In addition to this main judicial review action, the Constitution also provides for various *a apriori* judicial review means. Consequently, this method of judicial review can be exercised in three ways: (1) when the Chamber is requested through a popular action to decide upon the unconstitutionality of statutes already in force, (2) in some cases, in an obligatory way, or (3) when deciding on the matter in a preventive way before the publication of the challenged statute. In all of these cases, the Constitutional Chamber has the power to annul the unconstitutional challenged statutes with *erga omnes* effects.

645. The second traditional method of exercising judicial review in Venezuela has been the judicial power to annul statutes and other State acts of similar rank issued in direct and immediate execution of the Constitution. This power is granted solely to the Constitutional Chamber of the Supreme Tribunal of Justice, as the Constitutional Jurisdiction (Articles 266.1; 334 and 336).[2060]

According to Article 334 of the Constitution of 1999, following a tradition that began in 1858, the court retains competence 'to declare the nullity of the statutes and

---

2058   See Allan R. Brewer-Carías, *Justicia Constitucional. Procesos y Procedimienos constitucionales* (México: Ed. Porrúa, 2006), 389 et seq.

2059   See Román J. Duque Corredor, 'La Sala constitucional contemplada en la Constitución de 1999', in *Estudios de Derecho Público: Libro Homenaje a Humberto J. La Roche Rincón,* vol. I (Caracas: Tribunal Supremo de Justicia, 2001), 289–301; Rafael Badell Madrid, 'Competencias de la Sala Constitucional', in *Nuevos estudios de derecho procesal, Libro Homenaje a José Andrés Fuenmayor,* vol. I, no. 8 (Caracas: Tribunal Supremo de Justicia, Colección Libros Homenaje, 2002), 61 a 119; Rafael Badell Madrid, 'Las competencias de la Sala Constitucional', in *Derecho y Sociedad. Revista de Estudiantes de Derecho de la Universidad Monteávila,* N° 3 (Caracas: Universidad Monteávila, Facultad de Ciencias Jurídicas y Políticas, 2002), 13–48.

2060   The Constitutional Jurisdiction is regulated in the Organic Law on the Supreme Tribunal of Justice, *Gaceta Oficial* N° 39.522, of 1 Oct. 2010, See Allan R. Brewer-Carías & Víctor Hernández Mendible, *Ley Orgánica del Tribunal Supremo de Justicia 2010* (Caracas: Editorial Jurídica Venezolana, 2010).

other acts of the organs exercising public power issued in direct and immediate execution of the Constitution or being ranked equal to a law, [which] corresponds exclusively to the Constitutional Chamber of the Supreme Court of Justice'. This judicial review power to annul State acts on the grounds of their unconstitutionality refers to: (1) National laws or statutes and other acts which have the force of laws; (2) State constitutions and statutes, municipal ordinances, and other acts of the legislative bodies issued in direct and immediate execution of the Constitution; (3) State acts with rank equal to statutes issued by the National Executive; and (4) State acts issued in direct and immediate execution of the Constitution by any State organ exercising the public power. The judicial decisions declaring the nullity of statutes and the other State acts have *erga omnes*, general effects, and in principle *ex nunc* or *pro futuro* effects, unless the Constitutional Chamber disposes in an express way its retroactive effects.

646. Since the 1858 Constitution, constitutional jurisdiction was assigned to the Supreme Court of Justice in Plenary Session. Therefore, one of the novelties of the 1999 Constitution was to assign constitutional jurisdiction to just one of the Chambers of the Supreme Court of Justice, namely the Constitutional Chamber (Articles 262; 266,1). This chamber, like all of the other chambers, has the mission of 'Guaranteeing the supremacy and effectiveness of the constitutional rules and principles: it shall be the last and maximum interpreter of the Constitution and guardian of its standard interpretation and application' (Article 335). The specificity of the Constitutional Chamber in these cases, according to Article 335 of the Constitution, is that, 'The interpretations made by the Constitutional Chamber on the content or the scope of the constitutional rules are binding [on] the other Chambers of the Supreme Court and other courts of the Republic.'

647. The most important feature of the concentrated method of judicial review under the Venezuelan system is that the standing necessary to raise an action resides in all individuals, being an *actio popularis*.[2061] Consequently, any individual or corporation with legal capacity is entitled to file a nullification action against the abovementioned State acts on grounds of the act's unconstitutionality. According to the doctrine of the Supreme Tribunal, the objective of the popular action is that anybody with legal capacity has the necessary standing to sue.

This concentrated method of judicial review has traditionally been used in an extensive way, particularly by states and municipalities against national statutes, and conversely, by the Federal government against state and municipal legislation. Also, individuals have used this method against national, state and municipal statutes for the protection of individual rights.

§4. *Other Concentrated Judicial Review Means*

I.   *The Obligatory Judicial Review of 'State of Exception' Decrees*

648. Under the concentrated method of judicial review, particular emphasis must be made regarding the 'state of exception' decrees that can be issued by the Presi-

---

2061   See Allan R. Brewer-Carías, *La Justicia Constitucional* (México: Ed. Porrúa, 2006).

dent of the Republic. Pursuant to Article 339 of the Constitution, these executive decrees declaring a 'state of emergency' shall be submitted by the President of the Republic before the Constitutional Chamber of the Supreme Tribunal in order for its constitutionality to be reviewed. Additionally, Article 336.6 sets forth that the Constitutional Chamber is entitled to, 'Review, in any case, even ex officio, the constitutionality of decrees declaring states of exception issued by the President of the Republic' (Article 336.6).

This judicial power of obligatory judicial review is also a novelty introduced by the 1999 Constitution. This model followed the precedent of Colombia (Article 241.7) but added the Constitutional Chamber's power to exercise judicial review ex officio.

649. By exercising this control, the Constitutional Chamber can decide not only the constitutionality of the decrees declaring 'states of exception', but also the constitutionality of its content. This control is exercised pursuant to the provisions of Article 337 and the Constitution. In particular, in case of restriction of constitutional guarantees, the Chamber must verify that the decree effectively contains a *regulation* regarding 'the exercise of the right whose guarantee is restricted' (Article 339).

II.   *The Preventive Judicial Review*

650. In addition to the *actio popularis* and these cases of obligatory review, the concentrated method of judicial review can also be exercised by the Constitutional Chamber of the Supreme Tribunal in a preventive way regarding statutes that have been sanctioned but are not yet published. This preventive control can occur in three cases established as an innovation in the 1999 Constitution: (1) cases regarding international treaties, (2) cases involving organic laws, and (3) cases regarding non-promulgated statutes, at the request of the President of the Republic.

In the traditional system of judicial review in Venezuela, the sole mechanism of preventive concentrated judicial review of statutes was the Supreme Tribunal of Justice's power to decide the unconstitutionality of a statute that is already sanctioned, but not yet promulgated because of a presidential veto.

Presently, the Constitution of 1999 has expanded preventive control of constitutionality to cover treaties, organic laws and non-promulgated statutes when requested by the President of the Republic.

A.   *Preventive Judicial Review of International Treaties*

651. With regard to international treaties, there is the preventive judicial review method, foreseen in Article 336.5 of the Constitution, which grants the Constitutional Chamber faculty to:

> Verify, at the President of the Republic's or the National Assembly's request, conformity with the Constitution of the international treaties subscribed by the Republic before their ratification.

It is important to point out that this provision originated in the European constitutional systems, like those existing in France and Spain, and subsequently adopted in Colombia. This system is now incorporated in the Venezuelan system of judicial review, and permits the preventive judicial review of international treaties subscribed by the Republic, thereby avoiding the possibility of subsequent challenge of the statutes approving the treaty.

In this case, if the treaty turns out not to be in conformity with the Constitution, it cannot be ratified, and an initiative for constitutional reform to adapt the Constitution to the treaty may result. However, if the Constitutional Chamber decides that the international treaty conforms to the Constitution, then a popular action of unconstitutionality against the approving statute could not subsequently be raised.

B. *The Preventive Judicial Review of the Organic Laws*

652. The second mechanism of the preventive judicial review method refers to organic laws. According to Article 203 of the Constitution, the Constitutional Chamber must decide, before their promulgation, the constitutionality of the 'organic' character of the *organic laws* when qualified this way by the National Assembly.

Article 203 of the Constitution defines the organic laws in five senses (see *supra* paragraph 129): (1) those named as such in the Constitution; (2) the organic laws issued in order to organize public branches of government (Public Powers); (3) those intended to 'develop the constitutional rights', which implies that all laws issued to develop the content of Articles 19–129 shall be Organic Laws; (4) those organic laws issued to 'frame other laws'; and (5) those Organic Laws named 'organic' by the National Assembly, when they are admitted by two-third votes of the present members before initiating the discussion.

This last case of laws qualified as such by the National Assembly, are those that shall be *automatically* sent, before their promulgation, to the Constitutional Chamber of the Supreme Tribunal of Justice. The Tribunal will make a decision regarding the constitutionality of the laws' organic character.

C. *Judicial Review of Statutes Sanctioned before Their Promulgation*

653. The third mechanism of preventive judicial review of constitutionality set forth in Article 214 of the Constitution is established in cases when the President of the Republic raises before the Constitutional Chamber the constitutional issue against sanctioned statutes before their promulgation. Thus, control over the constitutionality of sanctioned but not promulgated statutes is set forth in a different way than the traditional so-called presidential veto of statutes, which involves a devolution to the National Assembly (Article 214).

III. *Judicial Review of Legislative Omissions*

654. The fifth judicial review method established in the 1999 Constitution refers to legislative omissions, empowering the Constitutional Chamber to review the unconstitutional omissions of the legislative organ.[2062] This is another new institution

---

2062   This institution has its origins in the Portuguese system. See Allan R. Brewer-Carías, *Judicial Review in Comparative Law* (Cambridge: Cambridge Univ. Press, 1989), 269.

in matters of judicial review established by the 1999 Constitution. In Article 336, the Constitution grants the Constitutional Chamber faculty:

> To declare the unconstitutionality of municipal, state or national legislative organ omissions, when they failed to issue indispensable rules or measures to guarantee the enforcement of the Constitution, or when they issued them in an incomplete way; and to establish the terms, and if necessary, the guidelines for their correction.

This provision has given extended judicial power to the Constitutional Chamber, which surpasses the trends of the initial Portuguese antecedent on the matter, where only the President of the Republic, the Ombudsman or the Presidents to the Autonomous Regions had standing to require such decisions. On the contrary, the Venezuelan Constitution of 1999 does not establish any condition whatsoever for standing; whereby regarding normative omissions,[2063] standing has been treated similarly as in *popular actions*.

655. In many cases, the Chamber has been asked to rule on omissions of the National Assembly in sanctioning statutes, like the Organic Law on Municipalities which, according to the Transitory dispositions of the 1999 Constitution, was due to be sanctioned within two years following its approval. Even though the Chamber issued two decisions in the case, the National Assembly failed to sanction the statute until 2005.[2064] In these cases, fortunately, the Chamber has not itself decided (in this case to legislate) in place of the legislative body, as it has done regarding the election of the National Electoral Council. There, due to the failure of the National Assembly to elect those members with the needed two-thirds majority vote, the Constitutional Chamber, which has been completely controlled by the Executive, directly elected them in violation of the Constitution. Through that decision, the Constitutional Chamber guaranteed the complete control of the Electoral body by the Executive.[2065]

IV. *Judicial Review of the Constitutional Controversies*

656. The sixth judicial review method refers to the power attributed to the Constitutional Chamber of the Supreme Tribunal to 'decide upon constitutional controversies aroused between any organ of the branches of government (public power)' (Article 336).

2063   It has been called by the Constitutional Chamber: 'legislative silence and the legislative abnormal functioning', decision N° 1819 of 8 Aug. 2000, of the Political-Administrative Chamber, case: *Rene Molina v. Comisión Legislativa Nacional*.

2064   See the reference in Allan R. Brewer-Carías et al., *Ley Orgánica del Poder Público Municipal* (Caracas: Editorial Jurídica Venezolana, 2005).

2065   See decisions N° 2073 of 4 Aug. 2003 (Caso: *Hermánn Escarrá Malaver y oros*) and N° 2341 of 25 Aug. 2003 (Caso: *Hermánn Escarrá M. y otros*) in Allan R. Brewer-Carías, in 'El secuestro del Poder Electoral y la confiscación del derecho a la participación política mediante el referendo revocatorio presidencial: Venezuela 2000-2004', in *Boletín Mexicano de Derecho Comparado*, N° 112 (México: Instituto de Investigaciones Jurídicas, Universidad Nacional Autónoma de México, enero-abril 2005), 11–73.

This judicial review power refers to controversies between any of the organs that the Constitution foresees, whether in the horizontal or vertical distribution of the public power. In particular, 'constitutional' controversies – those whose decision depends on the examination, interpretation and application of the Constitution – refers to the distribution of powers between the different State organs, especially those distributing the power between the national, state and municipal levels.

657. The 'administrative' controversies that can arise between the Republic, the states, municipalities or other public entities are to be decided by the Political-Administrative Chamber of the Supreme Tribunal (Article 266.4) as an Administrative Jurisdiction.

As the Supreme Court of Justice specified, in order to identify the constitutional controversy, it is required:

> that the parties of the controversy are those who have been expressly assigned faculties for those actions or provisions in the constitutional text itself, that is, the supreme state institutions, whose organic regulation is set forth in the Constitution, different from others, whose concrete institutional frame is established by the ordinary legislator.[2066]

In any case, the standing to raise a remedy in order to settle a constitutional controversy only corresponds to one of the branches of government (public power) party to the controversy.

V. *Recourse of Constitutional Interpretation*

658. Finally, regarding the jurisdiction of the Constitutional Chamber, mention must be made of the faculty to decide abstract recourses of interpretation of the Constitution. This is a judicial means that the Constitutional Chamber has created from the interpretation of Article 335 of the Constitution, which grants the Supreme Tribunal the character of 'maximum and final interpreter of the Constitution', in order for the Citizenship to seek from the Constitutional Chamber an abstract interpretation of the Constitution without referring to any particular case or controversy.[2067]

In effect, before the 1999 Constitution was sanctioned, the only recourse of interpretation existing in the Venezuelan legal order was the recourse of interpretation of statutes in cases expressly provided for them, formerly established in 42,24 of the Organic Law of the Supreme Court of Justice, and exclusively attributed to the Politico-Administrative Chamber of such former Supreme Court of Justice.

2066 Decision of the Political-Administrative Chamber N° 1468 of 27 Jun. 2000 of the Political-Administrative Chamber, in *Revista de Derecho Público*, N° 82 (Caracas: Editorial Jurídica Venezolana, 2000), 744 et seq.

2067 See Allan R. Brewer-Carías, '*Quis Custodiet Ipsos Custodes*: De la interpretación constitucional a la inconstitucionalidad de la interpretación', in *Revista de Derecho Público*, No 105 (Caracas: Editorial Jurídica Venezolana, 2006), 7–27; 'Le recours d'interprétation abstrait de la Constitution au Vénézuéla', in *Le renouveau du droit constitutionnel, Mélanges en l'honneur de Louis Favoreu* (Paris: Dalloz, 2007), 61–70.

It was according to this previous regulation that the 1999 Constitution also attributed to the Supreme Tribunal the same power to decide the recourses of interpretation regarding the content and scope of statutes (Article 266.6) but attributing it, not only to the Politico-Administrative Chamber of the new Supreme Tribunal, but to all its Chambers according to their respective competencies (Article 266.6). This attribution was later repeated in the 2004 Organic Law of the Supreme Tribunal of Justice (Article 5, paragraphs 1, 52).

659. In the 1999 Constitution, therefore, no recourse for abstract interpretation of the Constitution was established to be filed before the Supreme Tribunal of Justice. Nonetheless, in the absence of any constitutional provision, the Constitutional Chamber of the Supreme Tribunal, interpreting its character of 'maxim and last interpreter of the Constitution' (Article 335), created an autonomous recourse to seek for the interpretation of the Constitution in an abstract way, founded on Article 26 of the Constitution, which established the right to access justice, from which it was deduced that although said action was not set forth in any statute, it was not forbidden, either. Therefore, it was decided that 'Citizens do not require statutes establishing the recourse for constitutional interpretation, in particular, to raise it.'[2068] Based on such preposition, the Chamber considered that no constitutional or legal provision was necessary to allow the development of such recourse.[2069] This power of the Constitutional Chamber of the Supreme Tribunal to decide recourses of abstract interpretation of the Constitution, even though created by the Chamber, was not incorporated in the 2004 Organic Law of the Supreme Tribunal of Justice. Nonetheless, its main rules have been developed by the Constitutional Chamber in subsequent decisions on the matter, as a recourse of the same nature to the one provided for the interpretation of statutes, that is, as having the purpose of obtaining a declarative ruling of mere certainty on the scope and content of constitutional norms.

660. Regarding the standing to file such recourses on constitutional interpretation, the Chamber has only required for the petitioner to invoke an actual, legitimate and juridical interest based on a particular and specific situation in which he stands, which necessarily requires the interpretation of a constitutional applicable provision, in order to put an end to the uncertainty that impedes the development and effects of such juridical situation. In the petition, the plaintiff must always argue on 'the obscurity, the ambiguity or contradiction between constitutional provisions' justifying the filing of the recourse. The petition, if applicable, must also specify 'the nature and scope of the applicable principles', or 'the contradictory or ambiguous situations aroused between the Constitution and the rules of its transitory regime'.[2070] The interpretation of the Constitution made by the Constitutional Chamber in these cases has binding effects.[2071]

2068   This criterion was ratified later in decision (N° 1347 dated 11 Sep. 2000), in *Revista de Derecho Público*, N° 84 (Caracas: Editorial Jurídica Venezolana, 2000), 264 et seq.

2069   See Decision N° 1077 of the Constitutional Chamber of 22 Sep. 2000, Case: *Servio Tulio León Briceño*, in *Revista de Derecho Público*, N° 83 (Caracas, 2000), 247 y ss.

2070   *Ibid.*

2071   Decision N° 1347 of the Constitutional Chamber dated 9 Nov. 2000, in *Revista de Derecho Público*, N° 84 (Caracas: Editorial Jurídica Venezolana, 2000), 264 et seq.

661. Even though this recourse for constitutional interpretation must result in the opening of a constitutional process in order to confront the different criteria on the interpretation of a constitutional provision, and thus the need to a public call for any interested party to participate in the process, the Chamber denied such contradictory character of the process, arguing that the conditions established for the standing are only to justify the filing of the recourse and to avoid the use of the recourse only as a means to seek advisory opinions from the Chamber. Nonetheless, the Chamber has the discretion to call to the process all those that could have something to say on the matter, according to their right to participate, extended to the judicial activities, due to the binding and *erga omnes* effects of the decision.[2072] In addition, the Constitutional Chamber decision on these matters of deciding abstract recourses of constitutional interpretation, according to Article 335 of the Constitution, have the character of a 'true *jurisdatio,* providing that it declares *erga omnes* and *pro futuro* the content and scope of the constitutional principles and norms whose constitutional interpretation is requested by means of the corresponding extraordinary action'. The Chamber added that 'the general norm produced by the abstract interpretation has *erga omnes* effects, and is, as a true *jurisdatio,* a quasi authentic or para constituent, that declares the constitutional content declared in the fundamental text'.[2073]

This extraordinary interpretive power, although theoretically an excellent judicial means for the interpretation of the Constitution, unfortunately has been extensively abused by the Constitutional Chamber to distort important constitutional provisions, to interpret them in a way contrary to the text, or to justify constitutional solutions according to the will of the Executive. This was the case, for instance, with the various Constitutional Chamber decisions regarding the consultative and repeal referendums between 2002 and 2004, where the Chamber confiscated and distorted the peoples' constitutional right to political participation.[2074]

VI. *The Constitutional Chamber's Power to Assume Any Cause from Lower Courts*

662. Finally, mention must be made to the figure of the '*avocamiento*', that is, the authority of the Constitutional Chamber to remove cases from the jurisdiction of lower courts, at any stage of the procedure, in order for the cases to be decided by the Chamber itself.

This extraordinary judicial power was initially established in the 1976 Organic Law of the Supreme Court of Justice as a competence attributed only to the Politico-

---

2072   Decision N° 2651 of October, 2003 (Caso: *Ricardo Delgado (Interpretación artículo 174 de la Constitución).*

2073   Decision N° 1.309 of 19 Jun. 2001 (case: *Hermann Escarrá*) ratified in decision N° 1684 of 4 Nov. 2008 (Caso: *Carlos Eduardo Giménez Colmenárez,* Expediente N° 08-1016).

2074   See decisions: N° 1139 of 5 Jun. 2002 (Caso: *Sergio Omar Calderón Duque y William Dávila Barrios*); N° 137 of 13 Feb. 2003 (Caso: *Freddy Lepage y otros*); N° 2750 of 21 Oct. 2003 (Caso: *Carlos E. Herrera Mendoza*); N° 2432 of 29 Aug. 2003 (Caso: *Luis Franceschi y otros*); and N° 2404 of 28 Aug. 2003 (Caso: *Exssel Alí Betancourt Orozco, Interpretación del artículo 72 de la Constitución*), in Allan R. Brewer-Carías, *La Sala Constitucional versus el Estado Democrático de Derecho. El secuestro del poder electoral y de la Sala Electoral del Tribunal Supremo y la confiscación del derecho a la participación política* (Caracas: Los Libros de El Nacional, Colección Ares, 2004).

Administrative Chamber of the Supreme Court, which the Chamber used in a self-restricted way.[2075] However, the Constitutional Chamber has now assumed for itself the *avocamiento* power in matters of *amparo* cases,[2076] and eventually annulled the former Organic Law provision.[2077]

In 2004, the new Organic Law of the Supreme Tribunal granted to all the Chambers of the Tribunal a general power to remove cases from the jurisdiction of lower courts, ex officio or through a party petition, and when convenient, to decide the cases (Articles 5,1.48; 18.11).

663. This power has been highly criticized as a violation of due process rights, and particularly, the right to a trial on a by-instance basis by the courts. It has allowed the Constitutional Chamber to intervene in any kind of process, including cases being tried by the other Chambers of the Supreme Tribunal, with very negative effects. For instance, this Constitutional Chamber power was used to annul a decision issued by the Electoral Chamber of the Supreme Tribunal,[2078] which protected the Citizens' rights to political participation. There, the Electoral Chamber suspended the effects of a National Electoral Council decision,[2079] objecting the presidential repeal referendum petition of 2004.

In this way,[2080] the Constitutional Chamber interrupted the process which was normally developing before the Electoral Chamber of the Supreme Tribunal, took the case away from that Chamber, and annulled its ruling. Instead, the Constitutional Chamber decided the case according to the will of the Executive, restricting the peoples' right to participate through petitioning referendums.[2081]

2075   See Roxana Orihuela, *El avocamiento de la Corte Suprema de Justicia* (Caracas:Editorial Jurídica Venezolana, 1998).

2076   See decisión N° 456 of 15 Mar. 2002 (Case: *Arelys J. Rodríguez v. Registrador Subalterno de Registro Público, Municipio Pedro Zaraza, Estado Carabobo*), in *Revista de Derecho Público*, N° 89–92 (Caracas: Editorial Jurídica Venezolana, 2002).

2077   See decisión N° 806 of 24 Apr. 2002 (Case: *Sindicato Profesional de Trabajadores al Servicio de la Industria Cementera),* in *Revista de Derecho Público*, N° 89–92 (Caracas: Editorial Jurídica Venezolana, 2002), 179 y ss.

2078   See decisions N° 24 of 15 Mar. 2004) (Exp. AA70-E 2004-000021; Exp. x-04-00006); and N° 27 of 29 Mar. 2004 (Case*: Julio Borges, César Pérez Vivas, Henry Ramos Allup, Jorge Sucre Castillo, Ramón José Medina Y Gerardo Blyde v. Consejo Nacional Electoral*) (Exp. AA70-E-2004-000021-AA70-V-2004-000006).

2079   See Resolution N° 040302-131 of 2 Mar. 2004.

2080   See Decision N° 566 of 12 Apr. 2004.

2081   See Allan R. Brewer-Carías, *La Sala Constitucional versus el Estado Democrático de Derecho. El secuestro del poder electoral y de la Sala Electoral del Tribunal Supremo y la confiscación del derecho a la participación política* (Caracas: Los Libros de El Nacional, Colección Ares, 2004); and 'El secuestro del Poder Electoral y la confiscación del derecho a la participación política mediante el referendo revocatorio presidencial: Venezuela 2000-2004', in *Boletín Mexicano de Derecho Comparado*, Instituto de Investigaciones Jurídicas, N° 112 (México: Universidad Nacional Autónoma de México, enero-abril 2005), 11–73.

§5. Some General Conclusions

664. As abovementioned, judicial review has played a very important role in the contemporary world and can be considered as the ultimate result of the consolidation of the *rule of law*. Judicial review can contribute to the consolidation of democracy, which ensures control over the exercise of State powers and guarantees the respect of human rights. When exercised for those purposes, judicial review powers are the most important instruments for a Supreme Court or a Constitutional Tribunal to guarantee the supremacy of the Constitution.

But when used against democratic principles for circumstantial political purposes, the judicial review powers attributed to a Supreme Court or to a Constitutional Tribunal can constitute the most powerful instrument for the consolidation of an authoritarian government.

Consequently, the provision of various methods of judicial review and the corresponding actions and recourses established in a Constitution is not, alone, a guarantee of constitutionalism and of the enjoyment of human rights. Nor does the mere existence of such provisions guarantee that there will be control of State powers, particularly, that there will be the division and separation of powers, which today still remains the most important principle of democracy.

665. The most elemental condition for this control is inevitably the existence of an independent and autonomous judiciary and, in particular, the existence of adequate institutions for controlling the constitutionality of State acts (Constitutional Courts or Supreme Tribunals), which are the institutions capable of controlling the exercise of political power and of annulling unconstitutional State acts.

Unfortunately, in Venezuela – notwithstanding the marvellous, formal system of judicial review enshrined in the Constitution, combining all the imaginable instruments and methods for that purpose – due to the concentration of all State power in the National Assembly and in the Executive branch of government, and due to the very tight political control that is exercised over the Supreme Tribunal of Justice, the *rule of law* has been progressively demolished with the complicity of the Constitutional Chamber. Consequently, the authoritarian elements that were enshrined in the 1999 Constitution have been progressively developed and consolidated, precisely through the decisions of the Constitutional Chamber, weakening the democratic principle.[2082]

That is why, unfortunately, the politically controlled Constitutional Chamber of the Supreme Tribunal of Justice in Venezuela, instead of being the guarantor of constitutionalism, of democracy, and of the *rule of law*, has instead been a façade of 'constitutionality' or 'legality', camouflaging the authoritarian regime we now have installed in the country.[2083]

[2082]   See Allan R. Brewer-Carías, "La ilegítima mutación de la Constitución por el juez constitucional y la demolición del Estado de derecho en Venezuela.," *Revista de Derecho Político*, N° 75-76, Homenaje a Manuel García Pelayo (Madrid, Universidad Nacional de Educación a Distancia, 2009), 291-325

[2083]   See Antonio Canova González, Luis Alfonso Herrera, Rosa Rodríguez and Giussepe Graterol, *El Tribunal Supremo de Justicia al servicio de la Revolución*, (Caracas 2015); Allan R. Brewer-Carías,"El juez constitucional al servicio del autoritarismo y la ilegítima mutación de la Constitución:

Chapter 2. The distortion of Judicial Review and Constitutional Mutations

666. In accordance with the aforementioned previsions, the Venezuelan Constitutional Chamber of the Supreme Tribunal of Justice is, without a doubt, the most powerful instrument designed to ensure the supremacy of the Constitution and the Rule of Law, which, of course, as guardian of the Constitution, must be submitted, as well, to the Constitution. As such guardian, and as it occurs in any Rule of Law system, the submission of the Constitutional Court to the Constitution is an absolutely understood preposition and is not subjected to discussion, since it would be inconceivable that the constitutional judge can violate the Constitution he is called to apply and warrant. As a matter of principle, it could be violated by other bodies of the State, but not by the guardian of the Constitution. For such purpose and in order to ensure that this does not occur, the Constitutional Court must of course have absolute independence and autonomy, because on the contrary, a Constitutional Court submitted to the will of the political power, instead of being the guardian of the Constitution becomes the most atrocious instrument of authoritarianism. Thus, the best constitutional justice system, in the hands of a judge submitted to political power, is a dead letter for individuals and is an instrument for defrauding the Constitution.

Unfortunately, the latter is what has been occurring in Venezuela during the last few years since 2000, where the Constitutional Chamber of the Supreme Tribunal, as Constitutional Judge, far from acting within the expressed constitutional attributions, has been adopting decisions in some cases containing unconstitutional constitutional interpretation,[2084] not only about its own powers of judicial review, but regarding substantive matters, changing or modifying constitutional provisions, in may cases in order to legitimize and support the progressive building of the authoritarian State. That is to say, it has distorted the content of the Constitution, through illegitimate and fraudulent "mutation."[2085] These illegitimate modifications to the Constitution, of course, have been made by its maximum guardian, who has no one to guard him, assuming a derived constituent power that does not belong to it, and is not regulated in the constitutional text. The eternal question arising from the uncontrolled power, *Quis custodiet ipsos custodes* has also acquired in this case all its meaning.

---

el caso de la Sala Constitucional del Tribunal Supremo de Justicia de Venezuela (1999-2009)",180, *Revista de Administración Pública*, Madrid, Centro de Estudios Constitucionales, 2009), 383-418.

2084   See Allan R. Brewer-Carías, *"Quis Custodiet Ipsos Custodes*: De la interpretación constitucional a la inconstitucionalidad de la interpretación," in *VIII Congreso Nacional de Derecho Constitucional, Perú*, (Arequipa, Fondo Editorial Colegio de Abogados de Arequipa, 2005), pp. 463-489; and in *Revista de Derecho Público*, N° 105, (Caracas, Editorial Jurídica Venezolana, 2006), 7-27. See also, Allan R. Brewer-Carías, *Crónica sobre la "In" Justicia Constitucional. La Sala Constitucional y el autoritarismo en Venezuela*, (Caracas, Editorial Jurídica Venezolana, 2007).

2085   A constitutional mutation occurs when the content of a constitutional standard is modified in such a way that, even when said standard maintains its content, it receives a different significance. See Néstor Pedro Sagüés, *La interpretación judicial de la Constitución*, (Buenos Aires 2006), 56-59, 80-81, 165 ff.; Salvador O. Nava Gomar, "Interpretación, mutación y reforma de la Constitución. Tres extractos" in Eduardo Ferrer Mac-Gregor (Coordinator), *Interpretación Constitucional*, Vol. II, (México, Ed. Porrúa, Universidad Nacional Autónoma de México, 2005), 804 ff.; and Konrad Hesse, "Límites a la mutación constitucional", in *Escritos de derecho constitucional*, Madrid, Centro de Estudios Constitucionales, 1992).

§1. *The Acceptance of a Transitory Constitutional Regime not Approved by the People*

667. The first constitutional mutation regarding the 1999 Constitution was decided by the Constitutional Chamber of the Supreme Tribunal of Justice, a few weeks after the approval of the Constitution, by admitting the existence of "Constitutional Transitory" provisions different to those approve by popular vote and embodied in the text of the Constitution. The 1999 Constitution was approved by referendum held on December 15, 1999, with a text that included transitory provisions. With the popular the approval of the Constitution in principle concluded the mission of the Constituent National Assembly.

However, one week after the approval of the Constitution, on December 22, 1999, the Constituent National Assembly sanctioned a Decree of the "Regime of Transition of the Public Power,"[2086] in order "to give effect to the transition process towards the regime established in the Constitution of 1999", in which it decided without any attribution foreseen in the new Constitution, to eliminate the prior Congress along with its Senators and Deputies, and instead, to assign Legislative power to a National Legislative Commission not established in the Constitution; to dissolve the Legislative Assemblies of the States, and to assign legal attributions in their place, to State Legislative Commissions which were not provided either in the Constitution; to take control of the Mayor's Offices and Municipal Councils; to eliminate the former Supreme Court of Justice, create new Chambers of the new Supreme Tribunal and to assign them a fixed number of judges -not established in the Constitution- and to elect them without complying with what the Constitution demanded; to create a Commission for the Reorganization and Functioning of the Judiciary in order to take it over, removing judges from office without due process which, even in 2009, still coexists with the Supreme Tribunal, with its complicity; to elect the high officials of the different Branches of government; and to dictate an Electoral Statute without any constitutional provision supporting it.

None of these reforms were constitutional because they were not approved by the people. Consequently the Transition Regime Decree was challenged before the Constitutional Chamber created in it, based in the violation of the Constitution recently approved by the people. The result was that the same Constitutional Chamber decided in its own cause, considering that the National Constituent Assembly supposedly had supra-constitutional power to create "constitutional provisions" without the popular approval, and that in consequence, in Venezuela there were two transitional constitutional regimes: the one contained in the Transitory Provisions approved by the people when they approved the Constitution via referendum; and those approved by the National Constituent Assembly without said popular appro-val.

668. In decision N° 6, of January 27, 2000, the Constitutional Chamber decided that, since the Transition Regime of December 22, 1999 was adopted by the Constituent Assembly prior to the publication of the Constitution on December 31, 1999 it was not subjected to this, or to the previous Constitution of 1961 still in force.[2087]

2086   *Official Gazette*, N°. 36.859 dated 12-29-1999.

2087   See in *Revista de Derecho Público*, N° 81, (Caracas, Editorial Jurídica Venezolana, 2000), 81 ff.

Later, in decision of No 186 of March 28, 2000 (case: *Allan R. Brewer-Carías* and others), when deciding the challenging of the Electoral Statute of the Public Power also adopted by the Constituent Assembly on January 30, 2000,[2088] the Constitutional Chamber ratified his criteria that in order to create a new legal order and adopt a new Constitution, the Constituent Assembly supposedly had several alternatives to regulate the transitory constitutional regime: *One*, to incorporate Transitory Dispositions that would be part of the Constitution to be approved by the people via referendum; and *the other*, to dictate separate constituent acts, of constitutional scope and value, that would originate a parallel constitutional transitory regime, not approved by the people.

With these decisions, it was the Constitutional Judge the one that proceeded to illegitimately mutate the Constitution, violating popular sovereignty, by admitting that supposedly, the National Constituent Assembly could dictate constitutional provisions not approved by the people through referendum, in this way beginning a long period of constitutional instability that, ten years later, has not ended; as it can be evidenced, for instance, with the survival of Judiciary interference Commission, exercising disciplinary functions over the judges, which the Constitution expressly demands to be exclusively done by "disciplinary judges" members of a "disciplinary jurisdiction" and through a "disciplinary procedure" (article 267). Thus, Venezuela has been under a constitutional transitory regime not approved by the people, by the grace of the Constitutional Judge who legitimized the usurpation of the popular will.

§2. *The transformation of the repeal referenda into a 'ratifying' referenda*

669. As aforementioned, in Venezuela, article 72 of the Constitution established, as a political right of the people, the revocation of mandates of all popular election offices, when the repeal is required after half of the term for which the official was elected, by popular initiative of a number no lesser than 20% of the electors registered in the corresponding constituency. The Constitution determined that when a number of electors, equal or higher than 25% of the registered electors have attend to the referendum and *"a number of electors equal or higher* than that of those who elected the official, vote in favour of the revocation," its mandate is considered as revoked and the absolute void must be covered immediately through by a new election.

That is to say, the necessary votes to proceed with the revocation of a mandate must be of a number *equal or higher than the votes of the electors who elected the officer*, independently from the number of votes cast against the revocation; as it was even ratified by the Constitutional Chamber in several decisions.[2089] The matter provided in the Constitution is about a "revocation" referendum of popular election mandates and not of a "ratifying" referendum (plebiscites) of said mandates, which

---

2088   See in *Official Gazette,* N° 36,884 of February 3, 2000.

2089   See decision N° 2750 of October 21, 2003, Case: *Carlos Enrique Herrera Mendoza, (Interpretación del artículo 72 de la Constitución (*Exp. 03-1989; and decision N° 1139 of June 5, 2002, Case: *Sergio Omar Calderón Duque and William Dávila Barrios,* in *Revista de Derecho Público,* N° 89-92, (Caracas, Editorial Jurídica Venezolana, 2002), 171. The same criterium was followed in decision N° 137 of February 13, 2003, Case: *Freddy Lepage Scribani et al.* (Exp. 03-0287).

does not exist in the constitutional text. Precisely for this reason, there is nothing in the Constitution regarding the case where a number of electors, higher than the number of votes obtained by the official at the time of his election, could vote against the revocation, that is, for the "no revocation." This could occur, but according to the Constitutional text, it would have no effect at all, because what the constitutional regulation establishes is revocation referendum: it is enough for the votes for the revocation to be equal, or greater, than those obtained by the official at the time of his election in order to be revoked.

670. Nevertheless, clearly in an unconstitutional way, in 2003 when a repeal referendum was first call by popular initiative for the revocation of the President mandate, the National Electoral Council issued a Regulation on the matter[2090], in which even though it was established that a mandate is considered to be revoked "if the number of votes in favour of the revocation is equal or higher to the number of the electors that vote for the officer", the phrase: "*and does not result to be lower than the number of electors that voted against the revocation*" was added (article 60), changing the constitutional provisions on the matter. With this addition –in a Regulation of sub-legal scope– the right of the people to politically participate through the revocation of popular mandates was restricted, when establishing a condition not included in the Constitution regarding the vote for the "no revocation", disrupting the "revocation" nature of the referendum regulated by article 72 of the Constitution, and in an evident fraud to the Constitution, turning it into a "ratifying" referendum of mandates of popular election.

671. What was without precedent in this constitutional fraud, was that said illegitimate constitutional "reform" was endorsed by the Constitutional Chamber of the Supreme Court when it decided on an abstract interpretation recourse of the Constitution in decision N° 2750 of October 21, 2003 (Case: *Carlos E. Herrera Mendoza, Interpretación del artículo 72 de la Constitución*) stating that:

> It has to do with some kind of re-legitimating the officer and, even, in this democratic process of majorities, **if the option of his permanence obtains more votes in the referendum, he should remain in office**, even if a sufficient number of people vote against him to revoke his mandate.[2091]

In this way, an illegitimate "mutation" of the Constitution was adopted by the Constitutional Judge. Actually, in a "revocation" referendum there can not be votes "in favour" of "the permanence" of the officer; what can exist are votes in favour of the "revocation" of the mandate and votes for the "no revocation". The vote "in favour" of the "no revocation" of the mandate is a negative vote (No); and a negative vote can not be turned into a positive one (Yes) for the permanence of the officer. With this mutation of the Constitution, the Constitutional Chamber changed the nature of the revocation referendum, ratifying the disruption of the nature of the revocation of mandate, turning it into a vote to "re-legitimate" or to "ratify" manda-

---

2090   See *Normas para regular los procesos de Referendos Revocatorios de mandatos de Elección Popular*, of September 25, 2003. Resolution N° 030925-465 of September 25, 2003.

2091   Exp. 03-1989.

tes of popular election, when this was not the intention of the Constituent. The only issue regulated in article 72 of the Constitution is the "revocation" of mandates, and for that, the only thing it demands in regards to the voting process is that "*a number of electors equal or higher* than that of those who elected the official, vote in favour of the revocation."

This illegitimate mutation of the Constitution, nonetheless, had a precise objective: to avoid the revocation of the mandate of the President of the Republic, Hugo Chavez, in 2004. He was elected in August 2000 with 3,757,744 votes; being enough for the vote in favour of the revocation to surpass this number in order to revoke his mandate. As announced by the National Electoral Council in August 27, 2004, the number of votes in favour of the revocation of the mandate of the President of the Republic, obtained in the referendum that took place on August 15, 2004, was of 3,989,008; reason for which his mandate had been constitutionally revoked.

However, the Constitution had already been illegitimately mutated, and regardless of the fraud accusations formulated, the National Electoral Council (on August 27, 2004), because the option for vote "No" obtained more votes (5.800.629) it decided to "ratify" the President of the Republic in his position until the culmination of the constitutional term in January 2007.[2092]

§3. *The elimination of the constitutional principle of the alternate government abd the limits to the continuous re-electionas*

672. Article 6 of the Constitution establishes the fundamental principles of republican government, in a clause pertaining to those denominated "rocklike", that states

Article 6. "The government of the Bolivarian Republic of Venezuela and its political entities **is and will always be** democratic, participative, elective, decentralized, alternate, responsible, pluralist and of revocable mandates"

Consequently, among the fundamental principles of the constitutional system that can not be modified neither by means of constitutional reform or amendment are

---

2092   In fact, on the web page of the National Electoral Council of August 27, 2004, the following note appeared: "Francisco Carrasquero Lopez, President of the National Electoral Council, addressed the country in national broadcast, to announce the definite and official results of the electoral act that took place on August 15th, *which ratified* Hugo Rafael Chavez Frias, *as President of the Republic* with a total of 5 million 800 thousand 629 votes in favour of the option "NO". 9 million 815 thousand 631 electors participated in the election, of which 3,989,008 voted in favour of the option "YES" to revoke the mandate of President Chavez. The total showed that the option "NO" represented 59.25% of the ballot, while the option "YES" achieved 40.74% of the grand total, with a 30.02% of non-participation. It must be said that for these elections, the Electoral Registry increased significantly, reaching a universe of 14,027,607 electors with the right to vote in the Revocation Referendum. On this Friday, August 27, based on the expression of the popular will, the National Electoral Council *will ratify* Hugo Chavez Frias *in the Presidency of the Bolivarian Republic* of Venezuela, whose constitutional term will culminate in the year 2006." And in fact, during a solemn act that took place on the same day, the National Electoral Council agreed to "ratify" the President of the Republic in his position, despite the fact that a number of electors, greater than those who elected him had voted in favour of the revocation of his mandate. See *El Nacional*, Caracas, 28 Aug. 2004, pp A-1 and A-2.

these principles of government, and within them, the principle that the government must not only "democratic" but "elective" and also "alternate" (see *supra* paragraphs 38, 56, 117, 155, 233).

This latter principle was incorporated for the first time in Venezuela constitutional history as a reaction to communism in power and, among other aspects, based on the very "doctrine of Simon Bolivar", in which the Republic is based according to article 1 of the Constitution, when expressing, in one of its statements, that:

> "... There is nothing as dangerous as to allow the long term permanence in office of a single citizen. The people gets used to obeying him and he gets used to rule over them... our citizens must fear, with abundant justice, that the same Magistrate who has ruled them for a long time, rules them forever".[2093]

According to this doctrine, which as a "Bolivarian" one must be considered part of the values of the constitution itself (article 1), in the Venezuelan constitutionalism the word used of "alternate" government referring to "alternation" in power regarding the public positions, has always had the meaning of the people having to **take successive turns** in said positions or that the positions had to be carried out **in turns** (Spanish Royal Academy Dictionary). As stated by the Electoral Chamber of the Supreme Tribunal of Justice in decision N° 51 of March 18, 2002, the alternate principle means **"the successive exercise of a position by different persons, belonging or not to the same party."**

673. This principle of alternate government was historically conceived to face the perpetuation desires to remain in power, that is to say, "continuism;" and to avoid the advantages in the electoral processes of those occupying positions when being candidates to occupy the same positions. The principle of "alternate government", thus, is not equivalent that of "elective government". Election is one thing, but the need for people to take turns in office is another, and thus the principle has always been reflected in the establishment of limits to the re-election of elected officials, which is proper of the presidential government systems. This is what happened in the Constitutions of 1830, 1858, 1864, 1874, 1881, 1891, 1893, 1901, 1904, 1909, 1936, 1845 and 1947 in which it was established the prohibition of the re-election of the President of Republic for the immediate constitutional term.[2094]

This prohibition, on the contrary, regarding the President of the Republic, during the democratic period that began in 1958 was extended in the Constitution of 1961 for the two following terms (10 years). The softening of the principle occurred in the 1999 Constitution, in which the possibility of the immediate presidential re-election was allowed, only once, for a new term. That is why President Chávez, after being "ratified" in 2004, was re-elected in 2006.

The alternation of government, thus, is a principle of constitutionalism that contests continuism or the permanence in power by the same person; for this reason,

---

2093   See Simon Bolivar, "Discurso de Angostura" (1819), in *Escritos Fundamentales* (Caracas, 1982).

2094   Actually, in the constitutional history of the country, the prohibition of the immediate presidential re-election only stopped being established in the Constitutions of the authoritarian governments, that is, the Constitution of 1857; Constitutions of Juan Vicente Gomez of 1914, 1922, 1925, 1928, 1929, and 1931; and the Constitution of Marcos Perez Jimenez of 1953.

any provision that would allow this from happening, would be contrary to it. Thus the principle can not be confused with the "elective" principle of government or with the most general "democratic" principle established by article 6 of the Constitution. One thing is to be able to elect government officials, and another is the principle of alternation that impedes the succesive election of the same government official.

674. Thus, it is contrary to the Constitution to interpret, as it was done by the Constitutional Chamber in its decision N° 53 of February 3rd, 2009; that the principle of alternation "demands that the people, as the holder of sovereignty, has the periodical possibility to choose its government officials or representatives", confusing "alternate government" with "elective government". For this, what the Constitutional Chamber stated was wrong when deciding that the principle "would only be violated" if the possibility of election is impede. With its decision, what the Constitutional Chamber has done, once more, is to illegitimately mutate the text of the Constitution, and contrary to what has been said, the elimination of the ineligibility cause for the exercise of public positions derived from its previous exercise by any citizen, does misrepresent the alternation principle in the exercise of power.

Thus, contrary to what was decided by the Constitutional Chamber, the possibility of the continuous re-election does alter the fundamental principle of the "alternate" government, which is one of the democratic values that inform our juridical order. Said principle, would be altered if the possibility of the continuous re-election of elective positions was to be established, and which is different from the principle of the "elective" government. Because having a "rocklike" formulation in article 6 of the Constitution ("is and always will be") it can not be the object of any constitutional reform, and in the event that it could be modified, that could not be carried out neither by the proceedings of Constitutional Amendment nor Reform, but only by means of the invitation of a Constituent National Assembly.

The Constitutional Chamber, in its decision N° 53 of February 2009, actually mutated the Constitution by means of an interpretation, illegitimately modifying the sense of the principle of the "alternate" government that the Venezuelans decided must always rule their governments. In any case, with this decision, what the Constitutional Chamber did was to smooth out the road so the Referendum held a few days later on February 15, 2009 could take place in order for the people to vote for the approval or the rejection of a "Constitutional Amendment" project proposed by the National Assembly regarding articles 160, 162, 174, 192 and 230 of the Constitution to establish, in Venezuela, the principle for the possibility of continuous re-election of elective positions, antagonizing the constitutional principle of the republican alternation (article 6). The 2009 Amendment was approved in the said Referendum, and after the illegitimate "mutation" introduced by the Constitutional Chamber, the Constitution was then formally changed eliminating the effects of the principle of "alternate" government that has just remained void and ineffective in article 6 of the Constitution.

§4. *The modification of the prohibition to repeat referenda on constitutional reforms on the same matter during the same constitutional term*

675. In the aforementioned decision of the Constitutional Chamber, N° 53 of February 2009 regarding the illegitimate change of the principle of alternate govern-

ment, another illegitimate mutation to the Constitution was adopted, loosing the prohibition set forth in the Constitution to call for a popular referendum regarding reforms to the Constitution already rejected by the people during the same constitutional term (article 345).

Article 345 of the Constitution, in effect, regarding "constitutional reform" procedures, establishes an express prohibition to submit to the National Assembly during the same constitutional term an initiative for constitutional reform when its matter has already been rejected by referendum. Notwithstanding, the Constitution nothing establishes regarding the effects of the rejection of a "Constitutional Amendment", or if it is possible in case a rejected "constitutional reform" to submit the matter again to referendum but through the "constitutional amendment" procedure.

In December 2007, a Constitutional Reform proposal sanctioned by the National Assembly was rejected by popular vote, in which one of the aspects that was proposed was the elimination of the prohibition established in the Constitution for the possible continuous re election of the President of the Republic. Being the expressed popular will the rejection of the proposal for a constitutional modification, according to article 345 of the Constitution it was not possible to submit during the same constitutional term, once more, the same reform to popular vote. Nonetheless, and notwithstanding this popular rejection, the same National Assembly on January 2009, took the initiative and approved this time "Constitutional Amendment" with the same specific purpose of modifying article 230 of the Constitution regarding the limits to presidential re-election, and also of modifying articles 160, 162, 174, and 192 of the Constitution regarding the re-election of the other elective officials, also eliminating the limits established.

676. This constitutional conflict was another of the topics interpreted by the Constitutional Chamber in its aforementioned decision N° 53 of February 2009, and instead of looking for the intention of the Constituent when establishing the rules for the non repetition of multiple referendum on the same constitutional issues (article 345), the Constitutional Chamber, confusing the sense of the prohibition, sustained that the provision established was not directed to fix limits to successive popular votes on the same matter, but only to provide limits regarding the National Assembly in the sense that it could not be asked to discuss twice in the same constitutional term modifications already rejected. The Constitutional Chamber forgot the fact that the constitutional restrictive principle was addressed to regulate popular expression of will in matters modification of the Constitution and their effects, and not regarding debates within the National Assembly.

In fact, the purpose of the constitutional prohibition to re-submit a rejected constitutional reform to multiple referendums is related to the effects of the expression of the will of the people in the sense that it cannot be asked, again and again in the same constitutional term about the same constitutional modification once it has already being rejected. Consequently, the importance of the prohibition established in a Title of the Constitution devoted to "Constitutional Reform" which, in Venezuela, can only refer to the effects of the peoples' expression as original constituent power, and not to the effects of the debate that could have taken place in the National Assembly on the matter, a body that is not a constituent power, not even derived, since it can not approve by itself any constitutional modification.

In this case, the decision N° 53 of February 2009 of the Constitutional Chamber can be considered as another one defrauding the Constitution, because the fact was that in 2007 a constitutional reform was sanctioned by the National Assembly trough the "constitutional reform" procedure in order to establish the continuous and indefinite re-election of the President of the Republic, which was rejected by the people; and that in the same constitutional term, in 2009, the same National Assembly also sanctioned a constitutional reform for the same purpose, this time trough the "constitutional amendment" procedure, only adding to the original proposal, perhaps in order to try to differentiate both proposals, all the other elected representatives.

The result was then that although the people rejected in 2007 the proposal for the continuous and indefinite re-election of the President, this modification same rejected modification of the Constitution was submitted again to referendum in 2009, and was approved. For such purpose the Constitutional Chamber issued a constitutional interpretation of article 345 of the Constitution ignoring that it has the purpose that once the people has expressed their choice, rejecting a modification to the constitutional text, citizens cannot be summoned during the same constitutional term, consecutively and without limits, to express its will on the same matter.

§5. *Illegitimate transformation federal system, changing "exclusive" attributions into "concurrent" ones*

677. Article 4 of the Constitution of 1999 establishes that the Republic "is a decentralized federal State in the terms expressed in this Constitution", a wording that contradicts the real sense of the constitutional provisions that allow the qualification of the State as that of a "Centralized federation."[2095] But in spite of this limits, and notwithstanding the contradiction, the Constitution has expressly distributed some State powers between the various public and different territorial levels of government, that is to say, the Municipalities, the States and the National government, which can not be changed but by means of a constitutional reform (articles 136, 156, 164, 178 and 179).[2096]

Specifically, regarding the infrastructure for circulation and transport, the Constitution provides that the conservation, administration and use of roads and national highways, as well as of national ports and airports of commercial use, exclusively

---

2095   See Allan R. Brewer-Carías, *Federalismo y Municipalismo en la Constitución de 1999 (Alcance de una reforma insuficiente y regresiva)*, (Caracas-San Cristóbal, Editorial Jurídica Venezolana, 2001); "El Estado federal descentralizado y la centralización de la federación en Venezuela. Situación y perspectiva de una contradicción constitucional," in Diego Valadés and José María Serna de la Garza (Coordinators), *Federalismo y regionalismo,* (México, Universidad Nacional Autónoma de México, Supreme Court of Justice of the State of Puebla, Instituto de Investigaciones Jurídicas, 2005), 717-750.

2096   See Allan R. Brewer-Carías, "Consideraciones sobre el régimen de distribución de competencias del Poder Público en la Constitución de 1999" in Fernando Parra Aranguren and Armando Rodríguez García (Editors), *Estudios de Derecho Administrativo. Libro Homenaje a la Universidad Central de Venezuela, Facultad de Ciencias Jurídicas y Políticas, con ocasión del Vigésimo Aniversario del Curso de Especialización en Derecho Administrativo,* Vol. I, (Caracas, Supreme Tribunal of Justice, 2001), 107-136.

correspond to the States; competency that they must exercise in "coordination with the National Power."

In the rejected Constitutional Reform proposed in 2007, one of its general purposes was to change the federal form of the State and of the territorial distribution of the competencies established in articles 156 and 164 of the Constitution, centralizing the State even more by concentrating almost all the competencies of the Public Power on the national level. Particularly, one of the purposes of the reform was to "nationalize" the referred attribution set forth in article 164.10 of the Constitution attributing the States the matters of the conservation, administration and use of national highways, roads ports and airports.[2097]

678. As it has been said, the 2007 Constitutional Reform was rejected by the people in the referendum of December 2nd, 2007, for which the attribution of the States established is the aforementioned article 164.10 of the Constitution, remained without modification. However, the Constitutional Chamber ogf the Supreme Tribunal, in decision N° 565 of April 15, 2008[2098] deciding an autonomous recourse for constitutional interpretation filed by the Attorney General of the Republic ruled modifying the content of the aforementioned constitutional provision disposing that the "exclusive attribution" established in it *is not such exclusive attribution*, but a concurrent one that even the National Government can revert it in its favour, eliminating it from the States level. The Attorney General of the Republic considered that the provision "was not clear enough to establish, in an efficient and precise way, the scope and performance of the National Executive, regarding the coordination with the States about the administration, conservation and use of national roads and highways, as well as ports and airports of commercial use." The Constitutional Chamber decided, acordingly, that the National Public Administration "in exercise of its coordination authority can directly assume the conservation, administration and use of the national roads and highways, as well as all ports and airports of commercial use," and that it corresponds to the National Executive (the President of the Republic in Ministers Cabinet), to decree its intervention and assume the rendering of services and assets when considering deficient or inexistent.

With this interpretation, what the Constitutional Judge did was to illegitimately mutate the Constitutional in the sense proposed in the 2007 rejected Constitutional Reform, usurping popular sovereignty, changing the federal form of the State by misrepresenting the territorial distribution system of powers between the National Power and the States, and particularly "nationalizing" against what expressly establishes the Constitution, attributions that are exclusively assigned to the States. The result of the interpretation requested has been that the Constitutional Chamber, has

---

2097   See Allan R. Brewer-Carías, *Hacia la Consolidación de un Estado Socialista, Centralizado, Policial y Militarista. Comentarios sobre el sentido y alcance de las propuestas de reforma constitucional 2007*, Editorial Jurídica Venezolana, Caracas 2007, pp. 41 ff.; and *La Reforma Constitucional de 2007 (Comentarios al Proyecto Inconstitucionalmente sancionado por la Asamblea Nacional el 2 de Noviembre de 2007)*, (Caracas, Editorial Jurídica Venezolana, 2007), 72 ff.

2098   See decision of the Constitutional Chamber, N° 565 of April 15, 2008, Case: Attorney *General of the Republic, interpretation recourse of article 164,10 of the 1999 Constitution of 1999*, available at http://www.tsj.gov.ve/decisio-nes/scon/Abril/565-150408-07-1108.htm

"reformed" the Constitution and has eliminated the exclusive competency of the States in the matter, turning it into a concurrent one, subjecting it to be possibly "decentralized," and in such cases with the possibility to be reverted and reassumed by the National Government. The Chamber, in order to decide, has forgotten that if it is true that the specific attribution of the States according to the Organic Law for Decentralization, Delimitation and Competency Transfer of the Public Power, was decentralized in 1989, such attribution was transformed into an "exclusive" one in the 1999 Constitution," which constitutionalized what the said Organic Law established in 1989. Nonetheless, the Constitutional Chamber without any constitutional or legal basis, disposed that "it corresponds to the National Executive, to decree the intervention in order to assume the rendering of services and assets of national roads and highways, as well as ports and airports of commercial use, in those cases where, even though said competencies had been transferred, the rendering of the service, either by the States, is deficient or inexistent."

679. After an illegitimate "constitutional modification" of this nature carried out through a judicial interpretation, as the very Constitutional Chamber said in its decision, it "generated a necessary revision and modification of great scope and magnitude of the current legal system," warning the National Assembly to "proceed to the revision and corresponding modification of the legal provisions related to the obligatory interpretation established in this decision, and sanctioned statutes congruent with the constitutional principles derived from the interpretation established by this Chamber in exercise of its competencies." That is to say, the Chamber forced the legislator to issue legislation against the provisions of the 1999 Constitution, and according to the illegitimate constitutional modification imposed. This provoked that, after the electoral triumph of opposition Governors and Mayors in key States and Municipalities in the elections of December 2008, substituting pro Government ones, the National Assembly in March 2009, diligently reformed, among other, the said Organic Law for Decentralization,[2099] in order to eliminate the exclusive attribution of the States established in article 11, 3 and 5 of said Law; adding two new provisions allowing the National Executive to "revert, for strategic reasons, of merit, opportunity or convenience, the transfer of attributions to the States, for the conservation, administration and use of assets and services considered to be of general public interest" (article 8); and that the National Executive, could decree the intervention of the said assets and rendering of public services transferred in order to ensure users and consumers a quality service (article 9). With this, the defraudation of the Constitution made by the Constitutional Chamber was completed by the national Assembly, resulting that a constitutional assigned "exclusive" attribution was changed into a concurrent one.

§6. *The illegitimate reform of the constitutional prohibition to finance electoral activities of political parties with government funds*

680. Article 67 of the Constitution of 1999 expressly establishes that the "the financing of political associations with Government funds will not be allowed," a provision that emphatically changed in a radical way the previous regime of public

---

2099   *Official Gazette* N° 39 140 of March 17, 2009.

financing to the political parties, established in article 230 of the Organic Law of Suffrage and Political Participation of 1998. This Law sought to establish a greater balance and impartiality for the participation of the parties in democratic life and, especially, in electoral campaigns trying to mitigate the unbalances and perversions that could arise just with the private financing of the parties, with the risk, for instance, of the presence of "drug-financing", and the eventual indirect, irregular and corrupt public financing, just intended for government parties,[2100] which can magnify in a system where there is no fiscal nor parliamentary effective control of the exercise of power. The constitutional prohibition, by derogating such article of the Organic Law, eliminated any the public funding of political parties, abandoning the inverse technique that predominates in the comparative law.[2101]

This express constitutional prohibition regarding the public financing of political parties, was also one of the matters referred to in the 2007 rejected Constitutional Reform[2102], in which it was proposed to modify article 67, providing the opposite, that "the State will be able to finance electoral activities." As already mentioned, the aforementioned 2007 Constitutional Reform proposal was rejected by popular vote in the referendum of December 2, 2007;[2103] with which the governmental financing of political parties regarding their electoral activities continued to be prohibited in the Constitution.

681. However, in spite of said constitutional prohibition and of the popular rejection of its modification, the Constitutional Chamber of the Supreme Court of Justice, in decision N° 780 of May 8, 2008 (File N° 06-0785), by means of an obligatory constitutional interpretation, has illegitimately mutated the Constitution; substituting itself to the popular will and of the original constituent power, disposing that "regarding the scope of the prohibition of public financing of political associations" contained in said norm, it only "limits the possibility to provide resources for the internal expenses of the different forms of political associations, but… said limitation, is not extensive to the electoral campaign, as a fundamental stage of the electoral process".

That is, the Constitutional Chamber, even facing a clear although censurable constitutional provision as the one contained in article 67 of the Constitution, whose

---

2100   See Allan R. Brewer-Carías, "Consideraciones sobre el financiamiento de los partidos políticos en Venezuela" in *Financiamiento y democratización interna de partidos políticos. Memoria del IV Curso Anual Interamericano de Elecciones,* (San José, Costa Rica, Instituto Interamericano de Derechos Humanos, 1991), 121 to 139.

2101   See in Allan R. Brewer-Carías, "Regulación jurídica de los partidos políticos en Venezuela" in *Estudios sobre el Estado Constitucional (2005-2006),* Cuadernos de la Cátedra Fundacional Allan R. Brewer Carías de Derecho Público No. 9, (Caracas, Universidad Católica del Táchira, Editorial Jurídica Venezolana. 2007), 655-686

2102   See *Proyecto de Exposición de Motivos para la Reforma Constitucional, Presidencia de la República, Proyecto Reforma Constitucional. Propuesta del presidente Hugo Chávez Agosto 2007; Proyecto de Reforma Constitucional. Prepared by the President of the Bolivarian Republic of Venezuela, Hugo Chávez Frías,* (Caracas, Editorial Atenea, 2007), 19.

2103   See Allan R. Brewer-Carías, "La proyectada reforma constitucional de 2007, rechazada por el poder constituyente originario," in *Anuario de Derecho Público 2007,* (Caracas, Universidad Monteavila, 2008).

reform was attempted without success in 2007, in this precise decision has usurped the constituent power, substituting the people, and has ruled reforming the provision by means of its interpretation, in the same sense that it was intended in the rejected Constitutional Reform, expressly allowing the governmental financing of the electoral activities of the political parties and associations, that is, in the opposite of what is provided in the Constitution.

Therefore, the Constitutional Judge simply decided that the Constitution does not say what it says, but says completely the opposite; that when it says that "the financing of political associations with Government funds will not be allowed," it is not what the Constitution establishes, but what it prohibits is solely "the financing of current and internal expenses of the political associations with resources coming from the State"; and, on the contrary, that the expenses of the electoral campaigns of said political associations, can be financed with funds coming form the State. In order to arrive to this conclusion, in a decision unnecessarily packed with author quoting about interpretation techniques, the notion of democracy, and the advantages of the public financing of the electoral campaigns of political parties, concluded in the aforementioned distinction, that one things is that the State finances "current and internal expenses" of political parties, and another is that it finances "their electoral campaigns," deducing, without any foundation, that what the Constitution prohibits is the first and not the latter.

It is an absurd conclusion, which against any democratic logic, derives from a false premise, in which, supposedly, in democratic systems it could happen that the State could finance the current and internal expenses of the parties. The latter is not conceived in democracies, reason for which it does not require of any prohibition. In democracies, what is financed is the operation of the parties, but always, with a view to the electoral campaigns, to the point of cancelling the financing if the parties do not obtain a certain percentage of votes in the elections.

The decision of the Constitutional Judge can be very commendable, allowing the financing of the electoral campaigns of the political parties with funds belonging to the State, but since it was expressly prohibited by the Constitution, just by reforming it is that the opposite could be achieved. And, in that case, that was what the Constitutional Judge did in Venezuela, that is, to reform the Constitution, usurping the original constituent power which corresponds to the people and, even against its own will expressed five months earlier by rejecting, precisely, said constitutional reform, establishing now the possibility to finance with public funds the electoral campaigns of the political parties.

§7. *The illegitimate elimination of the supra-constitutional rank of international treaties in matters human rights*

682. Following a contemporary universal trend, which has allowed constitutional courts the direct application of international treaties in matters of human rights for their protection, progressively widening their cast, in the text of contemporary Constitutions, the normative scope of said treaties has been progressively recognized,

being possible to distinguish four different ranks recognized in the internal law: supra-constitutional, constitutional, supra-legal or legal rank.[2104]

In the case of the Venezuelan Constitution of 1999, article 23 expressly disposes the following:

> Article 23. Treaties, pacts and conventions regarding to human rights, subscribed and ratified by Venezuela, have constitutional rank and prevail in the internal order, as long as they contain norms about their enjoyment and exercise, more favourable than those established in this Constitution and in the laws of the Republic, and are to be direct and immediate applicable, by the courts and other bodies of the State.

Without a doubt, this norm is one of the most important ones in matters of human rights in the country, unique in its conception in Latin-America, because first it grants international treaties in matters of human rights, not only constitutional rank, but *supra-constitutional* rank; that is, a superior rank regarding the Constitution itself, which must prevail over it in cases they contain more favourable regulations for their exercise. The article also establishes the principle of the direct and immediate application of said treaties by the courts and other authorities of the country. This provision of the Constitution was, without a doubt, a significant advance in the construction of the human rights protection framework, which has been applied by the courts for instance declaring the prevalence of the norms of the American Convention of Human Rights regarding legal and constitutional provisions. It was the case, for instance, of the right to appeal before a second judicial instance invoked before the contentious administrative jurisdiction in which in some cases (autonomous institutions or independent Administrations acts) it was excluded in the former Organic Law of the Supreme Court of Justice of 1976.

The Constitution of 1999 only establishes as a constitutional right, the right to appeal in matters of criminal procedures in favour of the person declared as guilty (article 40.1); so regarding the aforementioned contentious administrative suit, there was no express constitutional guaranty for the appeal, having been always the appeal of the First Court of Contentious Administrative decisions as inadmissible. Nonetheless, the application of article 23 of the Constitution in these cases finally leads the Constitutional Chamber of the Supreme Court to rule in 2000, on the prevailing application of the Inter-American Convention on Human Rights, considering:

> "that article 8.1 and 8. 2, h of the American Convention on Human Rights, are part of the Venezuelan constitutional order; that its dispositions, containing

---

2104 Regarding this general classification, see Rodolfo E. Piza R., *Derecho internacional de los derechos humanos: La Convención Americana*, (San José 1989); and Carlos Ayala Corao, "La jerarquía de los instrumentos internacionales sobre derechos humanos", in *El nuevo derecho constitucional latinoamericano*, IV Congreso Venezolano de Derecho constitucional, Vol. II, (Caracas 1996), and *La jerarquía constitucional de los tratados sobre derechos humanos y sus consecuencias*, (México, 2003); Humberto Henderson, "Los tratados internacionales de derechos humanos en el orden interno: la importancia del principio pro homine", in *Revista IIDH*, 39, (San José, Instituto Interamericano de Derechos Humanos, 2004), 71 and ss. See also, Allan R. Brewer-Carías, *Mecanismos nacionales de protección de los derechos humanos*, (San José, Instituto Internacional de Derechos Humanos, 2004), 62 ff.

the right to appeal judicial decision are more favourable, concerning the benefit and exercise of said right, than that foreseen in article 49.1 of said Constitution; and that are of immediate and direct application by the courts and other State bodies."[2105]

However, in decision N° 1.939 of December 18th 2008 (Case: Gustavo Alvarez Arias and others), by declaring in executable a decision of the Inter-American Court on Human Rights of August 5th 2008 referred to the case of the former judges of the First Court on the Contentious Administrative matters *(Apitz Barbera and others ("First Court on the Contentious Administrative matters") vs. Venezuela)*, the Constitutional Chamber has definitely resolved that:

> "the aforementioned article 23 of the Constitution **does not** grant "supra-constitutional rank to international treaties on human rights, thus, in case of antinomy or contradiction between one disposition of the Constitution and a provision of an international pact, it would correspond to the Judicial Power to determine which would be applicable, considering both what is established in the referred provision, and in the jurisprudence of this Constitutional Chamber of the Supreme Court of Justice, paying attention to the content of articles 7, 266.6, 334, 335, 336.11 *ejusdem* and to decision N° 1.077/2000 of this Chamber."

In order to base its decision, and reject the existence of superior values not modifiable by the authoritarian political project, the Chamber clarified the following concepts:

> "On this subject, the decision N° 1309/2001 of this Chamber, among others, clarifies that law is a normative theory at the service of politics that underlines behind the axiological project of the Constitution, and that the interpretation must be engaged, if we want to maintain the supremacy of the Constitution when exercising the constitutional jurisdiction assigned to the judges, with the best political theory that underlines behind the system interpreted or integrated and with the institutional morality that serves as its axiological base *(interpretatio favor Constitutione)*. The decision adds: "in this order of ideas, the standards to resolve the conflict between the principles and the provisions have to be compatible with the political project of the Constitution (Democratic and Social State of Law and Justice) and can not affect the force of said project with ideological interpretative elections that privilege individual rights decisively, or that welcome the supremacy of the international judicial order over national law at the sacrifice of the sovereignty of the State".

The decision concludes that: "a system of principles, supposedly absolute and supra-historic, can not be above the Constitution" and that the theories that pretend to limit "under the pretext of universal legalities, the sovereignty and the national auto-determination" are unacceptable.

2105   Decision N° 87 of March 13th, 2000. Case: *C.A. Electricidad del Centro (Elecentro) y otra vs. Superintendencia para la Promoción y Protección de la Libre Competencia. (Procompetencia)*, in *Revista de Derecho Público*, N° 81, (Caracas, Editorial Jurídica Venezolana, 2000), 157 ff.

In the same sense, the decision of this Chamber (N° 1265/2008) established that when a contradiction is evidenced between the Constitution and an international convention or treaty, "the constitutional provision that privilege the general interest and the common wellbeing must prevail, applying the dispositions that privilege the collective interests... (...) over particular interests..."[2106]

With this decision, the Constitutional Chamber accomplished an illegitimate constitutional mutation, reforming article 23 of the Constitution when eliminating the supra-national rank of the American Convention on Human Rights, in the cases containing more favourable previsions for the benefit and exercise of human rights regarding those foreseen in the very Constitution.

The matter has been so about an illegitimate constitutional reform, that it was one of the express reform proposals made in 2007 by the "Presidential Council for the Constitutional Reform,"[2107] in which, regarding article 23 of the Constitution, the intention was to completely eliminate the constitutional hierarchy of the previsions of the international treaties on human rights, and their prevalence over the internal order, proposing the reformulation of the provision just in the sense that: "treaties, pacts and conventions related to human rights, subscribed and ratified by Venezuela, as long as they remain current, are part of the internal order, and are of immediate and direct application by the bodies of the Public Power".

This proposal for constitutional reform, which luckily was filled before the national Assembly by the President of the Republic, was a hard blow to the principle of progressivity in the protection of the rights established in article 19 of the Constitution, which does not allow regressions in their protection.[2108] However, what the authoritarian regime was not able to accomplish through a constitutional reform process, which at the end was in 2007 rejected by the people, was carried out by the Constitutional Chamber of the Supreme Court throughout its long carrier at the service of authoritarianism.[2109]

§8. *The elimination of judges' power to immediately and directly apply international treaties on human rights*

683. In matters of human rights, article 23 of the Constitution not only grants supra-constitutional rank to the provisions of the international treaties, pacts and conventions regarding human rights, "as long as they contain provisions more favourable to their enjoyment and exercise as those established in this Constitution and in

---

2106   See in http://www.tsj.gov.ve/decisiones/scon/Diciembre/1939-181208-2008-08-1572.html

2107   See *Consejo Presidencial para la Reforma de la Constitución de la República Bolivariana de Venezuela, "Modificaciones propuestas"*. The compelte text was Published as *Proyecto de Reforma Constitucional. Versión atribuida al Consejo Presidencial para la reforma de la Constitución de la República Bolivariana de Venezuela*, (Caracas, Editorial Atenea, 2007), 146 pp.

2108   See in Allan R. Brewer-Carías, *Hacia la consolidación de un Estado Socialista, Centralizado, Policial y Militarista. Comentarios sobre el sentido y alcance de las propuestas de reforma constitucional 2007*, (Caracas, Editorial Jurídica Venezolana, 2007), 122 ss.

2109   See Allan R. Brewer-Carías, *Crónica sobre la "In" Justicia Constitucional. La Sala Constitucional y el autoritarismo en Venezuela*, Colección Instituto de Derecho Público No. 2, (Caracas, Universidad Central de Venezuela, 2007).

the laws of the Republic", which, as it has been seen, it had been illegitimately mutated; but it also expressly declare that they are "of direct and immediate application by the courts and other bodies of the State" (article 23).

Regarding this provision, the Constitutional Chamber of the Supreme Court, by reaffirming its role of maximum and ultimate interpreter of the Constitution and the treaties on human rights, has established in decision N° 1492 of July 15, 2003 (Case: *Impugnación de diversos artículos del Código Penal*), that because those treatises having constitutional rank, the only one capable of their interpretation, of determine which one of their provisions prevail in the internal legal order; and of deciding which human rights, not contemplated in said international instruments, have force in Venezuela, is the Constitutional Chamber of the Supreme Tribunal.[2110] With this unconstitutional decision, the Constitutional Chamber has also illegitimately mutated the Constitution, because according to its article 23, the authority to do so n not only corresponds to the Constitutional Chamber, but to all the courts of the Republic when acting as constitutional judges, for instance, when exercising the diffused control of the constitutionality of statutes or when deciding cases of amparo. The intention of the Constitutional Chamber to concentrate all constitutional justice procedures is not in accordance to the Constitution and to the judicial review system it establishes.

§9. *The denial of the peoples' right for the international protection of the human rights and the non enforceability of the decisions of the interamerican court on human rights*

684. But besides the unawareness regarding the supra constitutional scope of the American Convention on Human Rights, the Constitutional Chamber, in decision N° 1.939 of December 18, 2008 (Case: *Gustavo Álvarez Arias and others*, or more accurate, *Case: Venezuelan Government vs. Inter-American Court on Human Rights*), has ignored the effects of the decisions of the Inter-American Court on Human Rights, declaring them as un enforceable in Venezuela, contradicting the international regime of the treaties.

With said decision, issued in a proceedings initiated by the Attorney General of the Republic as a dependant organ of the National Executive, the Constitutional Chamber declared that the decision of the Inter American Court on Human Rights issued on August 5, 2008 in the case of the former judges of the First Court on Contentious Administrative that were illegitimately dismissed without any sort of judicial guaranties (Case *Apitz Barbera and others ("First Court on Contentious Administrative matters) vs. Venezuela),* was non enforceable in Venezuela. In that decision, the Inter American Court decided that the Venezuelan State had violated the judicial guarantees of the said judges established in the American Convention, by removing them form their offices without due process, and condemned the State to pay for compensations, to reinstate the judges to their former positions or to some similar, and to publish the verdict in Venezuelan newspapers.[2111]

2110   See *Revista de Derecho Público*, N° 93-96, (Caracas, Editorial Jurídica Venezolana, 2003), 135 ff.

2111   See www.corteidh.or.cr . Excepción Preliminar, Fondo, Reparaciones y Costas, Serie C N° 182.

Of course, in the case of the American Convention of Human Rights, once a Member State recognized the jurisdiction from the Inter American Court on Human Rights, according to article 68.1 of the Convention, they must "commit themselves to comply with the decisions of the Court in every case in which they are a part of."[2112] In addition, the Venezuelan Constitution expressly contains the right to have access to the international protection in matters of human rights, with the obligation for the State to carry out the decisions of the international bodies. To that effect, article 31 of the Constitution establishes:

> Article 31. Every person has the right, within the terms established by the treaties, pacts and conventions on human rights ratified by the Republic, to file petitions or complaints before the international bodies established for such purposes, in order to ask for the protection of their human rights.
>
> The State shall adopt, in accordance with the proceedings established in this Constitution and statutes, the necessary measures for the enforcement of the decisions issued by the international bodies indicated in this article.

There have been States, however, who have resisted against the decisions of the Inter-American Court, and have intended to avoid their responsibility in their enforcement. The decision of the Inter American Court on the *Case: Castillo Petruzzi*, of May 30, 1999 (Series C, number 52), is proof of that, since after declaring that the Peruvian State had violated during a proceeding, articles 20; 7.5; 9; 8.1; 8.2.b,c,d and f; 8.2.h; 8.5; 25; 7.6; 5; 1.1 and 2,[2113] the Plenary Chamber of the Supreme Council of Military Justice of Peru refused to enforce the verdict, considering that it had ignored the Political Constitution of Peru, subjecting it to "the American Convention on Human Rights in the interpretation that the judges of said Court can carry out *ad-libitum*."[2114]

2112   As stated by the Inter-American Court on Human Rights in the decision of *Case Castillo Petruzzi*, on "Enforcement decision" of November 17, 1999 (Series C, number 59), "the conventional obligations of the State party entail all the powers and bodies of the State;" (paragraph 3) adding "That this obligation corresponds to a basic principle of international responsibility right of the State, endorsed by the international jurisprudence, according to which the States must comply with their conventional duties in good faith (*pacta sunt servanda*) and, as it has been mentioned by this Court, can not, due to reasons of internal order, stop complying with the established international responsibility" (paragraph 4). See in Sergio García Ramírez (Coord.), *La Jurisprudencia de la Corte Interamericana de Derechos Humanos*, (México, Universidad Nacional Autónoma de México, Corte Interamericana de Derechos Humanos, 2001), 628-629.

2113   Consequently, in the decision, the Inter-American Court declared "the nullity, of the process against Mr. Jaime Francisco Sebastián Castillo Petruzzi and others, for been incompatible with the Convention" ordering "the guaranty of a new trial with the complete observance of the legal due process," and also, "the State to adopt the necessary measures in order to reform the provisions that had been declared to be against the American Convention of Human Rights in the present decision, and to ensure the benefit of the rights established in the American Convention on Human Rights to all the people under its jurisdiction, without any exception". Available at http://www.tsj.gov.ve/ decisiones/scon/Diciembre/1939-181208-2008-08-1572.html

2114   It is precisely, because of this decision of the Plenary Chamber of the Supreme Council of Military Justice of Peru regarding the non enforceability of the decision of the Inter-American Court on Human Rights in Peru, issued on May 30, 1999, that the same Inter-American Court ruled its subsequent decision of November 7, 1999, declaring that "the State has the duty to promptly fulfil the deci-

In 1999 Venezuela has followed the same steps of the authoritarian regime of President Fujimori in Peru, and the Constitutional Chamber of the Supreme Court in the aforementioned decision N° 1.939 of December 18, 2008 (*Case: Attorneys Gustavo Álvarez Arias and others*), has also declared the Inter American Court on Human Rights of August 5, 2008 issued in the case *Apitz Barbera and others (First Court on Contentious Administrative matters) vs. Venezuela*, as "un enforceable" in Venezuela, accusing the Inter American Court of usurping the power of the Supreme Court.[2115]

The Constitutional Chamber in its decision, quoting a previous decision N° 1.942 of July 15, 2003, and considering that it was about an interpretation request formulated by the Republic, ruled that the Inter American Court on Human Rights could not "intend to exclude or ignore the internal constitutional order," and that it had ruled "guidelines on the government and administration of the Judiciary w matter that is of exclusive and excluding attributions of the Supreme Tribunal of Justice, and has established "rules for the Legislature in matters of judicial responsibility of the judges, transgressing the sovereignty of the Venezuelan State in its organization and in the selection of its officials; which it considered as inadmissible. The Constitutional Chamber even accused the Inter American Court of having used its decision "to intervene, unacceptably, in the judicial government and administration, which exclusively corresponds to the Supreme Tribunal," arguing that with the questioned decision, the Inter-American Court intended to "ignore the strength and force of judicial and administrative decisions that have acquired the *res judicata*, by demanding the reincorporation of the judges that have been removed from office." In order to make these affirmations, the Constitutional Chamber turned, precisely, to the aforementioned decision of 1999 of the Plenary Chamber of the Supreme Council of Military Justice of Peru, which considered un enforceable in Peru the decisions of the Inter-American Court of May 30, 1999 (Case: *Castillo Petruzzi and other*).

But the Constitutional Chamber did not stop there, but in an evident usurpation of powers -since the international relations are a matter of exclusive attribution of

---

sion of May 30, 1999 ruled by the Inter-American Court in the case Castillo Petruzzi and others." See, in Sergio García Ramírez (Coord.), *La Jurisprudencia de la Corte Interamericana de Derechos Humanos*, (México, Universidad Nacional Autónoma de México, Corte Interamericana de Derechos Humanos, 2001), 629. This occurred during the authoritarian regime in Peru, during the mandate of President Fujimori, and which, two months after the decision of the Inter American Court of May 30, 1999, drove the Congress of Peru to approve the withdraw the recognition of the contentious competency of the Court; which was submitted the following day before the General Secretariat of the OAS. This withdrawal was declared inadmissible by the Inter American Court, in ts decision in the case *Ivcher Bronstein* of September 24, 1999, considering that "a State party can only remove itself to the competency of the Court through the formal complaint of the complete treaty." *Idem*, pp. 769-771. In any case, Peru, later in 2001, derogated the Resolution of July 1999, completely re-establishing for the State the competency of the Inter American Court.

2115   The issue had been affirmed by the Constitutional Chamber in its known decision N° 1.942 of July 15, 2003 in which, when referring to the International Courts, began stating that in Venezuela, "above the Supreme Court of Justice and according to article 7 of the Constitution, there is no jurisdictional body, unless stated otherwise by the Constitution or the law, and even in this last possible case, any decision contradicting the Venezuelan constitutional order, lacks of application in the country." See Case: *Impugnación de artículos del Código Penal, Leyes de desacato*, in *Revista de Derecho Público*, N° 93-96, (Caracas, Editorial Jurídica Venezolana, 2003), 136 ff.

the Executive- requested "the National Executive to proceed to denounce the Convention, in view of the evident usurpation of functions in which the Inter American Court on Human Rights has incurred into with the ruling object of this decision." With this, the Venezuelan State concluded its process of separation from the American Convention on Human Rights, and of the jurisdiction of the Inter-American Court on Human Rights, using it very own Supreme Court of Justice for this purpose.

We must recall in fact that, in this same matter, the Constitutional Chamber has also decided adopt another illegitimate constitutional mutation, by reforming article 23 of the Constitution in the way intended in 2007 proposal for Constitutional reform formulated by the "Presidential Council for the Reform of the Constitution," by suggesting to add to article 23 of the Constitution, also in a regressive manner, that it "corresponds to the courts of the Republic to be decide upon the violations on matters established in said treaties", proposing the establishment a constitutional prohibition impeding the Inter American Court on Human Rights to decide on the violations of the American Convention on Human Rights. That is, with a provision of that kind, Venezuela would have been constitutionally excluded from the jurisdiction of said International Court, and of the Inter American protection human rights system.[2116]

On this matter, also, what the authoritarian regime could not do by means of a constitutional reform process like the one initiated in 2007, which at the end was rejected by the people, was done by the Constitutional Chamber of the Supreme Court throughout its long carrier at the service of authoritarianism.

§10. The ilegitimate creation of an autonomous recourse for the abstract interpretation of the constitution

685. Almost all of the aforementioned illegitimate mutations of the Constitutions, that have been adopted by the Constitutional Chamber of the Supreme Tribunal, have been made when deciding autonomous recourses for the abstract interpretation of the Constitution, which at its turn have their origin, also, in an illegitimate mutations to the Constitution made by the same Constitutional Chamber. In other words, it has been this autonomous recourse for the abstract interpretation of the Constitution, which is not established either in the Constitution or in any statute, the one that has served as the main tool for the adoption of some of the most distinguishable and illegitimate mutations to the Constitution, which have not their origin in constitutional interpretations made by the Constitutional Judge when deciding a particular case or action of unconstitutionality or another mean to of judicial review. Instead, they have its origin in the decision on autonomous requests for the abstract interpretation of the Constitution, in many cases filed by the National Executive through the Attorney General of the Republic.

2116   See Allan R. Brewer-Carías, *Hacia la consolidación de un Estado Socialista, Centralizado, Policial y Militarista. Comentarios sobre el sentido y alcance de las propuestas de reforma constitucional 2007,* (Caracas Editorial Jurídica Venezolana, 2007), 122.

In this regard, notwithstanding that a recourse or action for the interpretation of statutes is the only established in the Constitution, the Constitutional Chamber of the Supreme Tribunal in decision N° 1.077 of September 22, 2001, formally created its own power in order to decide "autonomous recourses for the abstract interpretation in the Constitution," establishing an unconstitutional interpretation of article 335 of the Constitution, which assigns the Supreme Tribunal and not solely to the Constitutional Chamber, its character of being the "maximum and last interpreter of the Constitution."[2117] This recourse, according to the criteria followed by the Constitutional Chamber, has similarities in nature to the one expressly established for interpretation of statutes, but in these cases in order to obtain a mere declarative decision about the scope and content of a constitutional provision. The Chamber recognized standing to file this recourse to anybody when alleging an actual, personal and legitimate interest, derived from a particular and specific legal situation which necessarily requires the interpretation of a Constitution provision applicable to it, in order to put an end to the uncertainty that impedes the development and effects of said legal situation. The main condition for the admissibility of such recourse is the obscurity or ambiguity of the particular constitutional provision that must apply to the legal situation, or the contradiction that could exist between constitutional provisions and principles including those contained in the transition constitutional provisions adopted by the National Constituent Assembly in 1999.

As was decided by the Constitutional Chamber, notwithstanding the constitutional process that in originated when a recourse for constitutional interpretation in filed, there is not need to open a contradictory hearing in order to allow the participation in the debate of people with judicial interest in a particular interpretation of the Constitution, and in decision N° 2651 of October 2, 2003 it denied the character of constitutional process to the procedure stating that in these cases "there is no *litis*, confrontation between parts, regarding which their defence has to be secured."[2118] In any case, the result of the procedure is the binding character of the decision adopted by the Constitutional Chamber, particularly regarding the nucleus of the case in study.[2119]

The creation by the Constitutional Chamber of this instrument for the abstract interpretation of the Constitution, without doubts, has produced a constitutional mutation, amplifying the constitutional powers of the Constitutional Chamber, by attributing to itself the power to decide a recourse that is not established in the Constitution. On the other hand, this autonomous recourse for the abstract interpretation of the Constitution has no precedent in comparative law.[2120]

2117   See decision N° 1077 of the Constitutional Chamber dated September 22, 2000, Case: *Servio Tulio León Briceño*. See in *Revista de Derecho Público*, N° 83, Caracas, Editorial Jurídica Venezolana, 2000), 247 ff. This criteria was then confirmed in decisions of November 9, 2000 (N° 1347), November 21, 2000 (N° 1387), and April 5, 2001 (N° 457), among others.

2118   See Case: *Ricardo Delgado. Interpretation of article 174 of the Constitution.*

2119   See decision N° 1347, of November 9, 2000

2120   See Allan R. Brewer-Carías, "Le recours d'interprétation abstrait de la Constitution au Vénézuéla", in *Le renouveau du droit constitutionnel, Mélanges en l'honneur de Louis Favoreu*, Dalloz, Paris, 2007, pp 61-70.

As we have mentioned, an autonomous recourse for the abstract interpretation of the Constitution, in the hands of an autonomous and independent Constitutional Judge, can be, without a doubt, an efficient instrument to adapt the norms of the Constitution to the changes operated in the constitutional order of a country at a point in time. However, a recourse of that nature in the hands of a Constitutional Judge absolutely dependant of the Executive Power, in an authoritarian regime like the one structured in Venezuela during the last 10 years; deciding, particularly, the interested requests filed by the Executive through the Attorney General of the Republic, is an instrument for illegitimate mutation of the Constitution, used to modify it and adapt at will, in order to strengthen authoritarianism. That is what has happened in Venezuela.

Chapter 3. Judicial Protection of Constitutional Rights: The Amparo Proceeding

686. Constitutional declarations of rights, in the Constitutions or in international treaties and covenants, would be of no use at all if those rights were not supported by a set of constitutional guarantees for their protection, and particularly, by the judicial guarantee, that is to say, the set of judicial means established in benefit of persons in order to assure not only the supremacy of the Constitution but the effective exercise and protection of the rights therein contained.

For that purpose, an effective Judiciary has to be built upon the principle of separation of powers. So, on the contrary, if the Government controls the courts and judges, no effective guarantee can exist regarding constitutional rights, particularly when the offending party is a governmental agency. In this case, and in spite of all constitutional declarations, it is impossible to speak of rule of law, as happens in many Latin American countries, and as has been the case of Venezuela during the past decade (2000–2011).

687. Nonetheless, regarding the general provisions of the Constitution and the means for protection of constitutional rights and freedoms, their judicial protection and guarantee in general terms can be achieved in two ways: first, by means of the general established ordinary or extraordinary suits, actions, recourses or writs regulated in procedural law; and second, in addition to those general means, by means of specific judicial suits, actions or recourses of *amparo* seeking remedies specifically and particularly established in order to protect and enforce constitutional rights and freedoms and to prevent and redress wrongs regarding those rights.[2121]

2121   On the action of *amparo* in Venezuela, in general, see Allan R. Brewer-Carías, 'The Amparo Proceeding in Venezuela: Constitutional Litigation and Procedural Protection of Constitutuonal Rughts and Guaratiees', in *Duquesne Law Review* 49, no. 2 (Srping 2011), 161–241; Gustavo Briceño V., *Comentarios a la Ley de Amparo* (Caracas: Editorial Kinesis, 1991); Rafael J. Chavero Gazdik, *El nuevo régimen del amparo constitucional en Venezuela* (Caracas, 2001); Gustavo José Linares Benzo, *El Proceso de Amparo* (Caracas: Universidad Central de Venezuela, Facultad de Ciencias Jurídicas y Políticas, 1999); Hildegard Rondón De Sansó, *Amparo Constitucional* (Caracas, 1988); Hildegard Rondón De Sansó, *La acción de amparo contra los poderes públicos* (Caracas: Editorial Arte, 1994); Carlos M. Ayala Corao & Rafael J. Chavero Gazdik, 'El amparo constitucional en Venezuela' in *El derecho de amparo en el mundo*, ed. Héctor Fix-Zamudio & Eduardo Ferrer Mac-Gregor (Coordinadores) (México: Universidad Nacional Autónoma de México, Editorial Porrúa, 2006), 649–692; Hildegard Rondón de Sansó, 'La acción de amparo constitucional a raíz de la vigencia de la Constitución de 1999', in *Revista de la Facultad de Ciencias Jurídicas y Políticas de la UCV*, N° 119 (Cara-

That is, the judicial guarantee of constitutional rights can be achieved through the general procedural regulations that are established in order to enforce any kind of personal or proprietary rights and interest, or it can also be achieved by means of a specific judicial proceeding established only and particularly for the protection of the rights declared in the Constitution. In this regard, it can be considered as a general trend in Latin America to establish these specific means of *amparo*,[2122] mainly because of the traditional insufficiencies of the general judicial means for granting effective protection to constitutional rights.

688. The habeas corpus recourse is also considered as an *amparo* proceeding regarding the protection of personal freedom; and in addition, the Constitution has set forth for the habeas data recourse in order to guarantee the right to have access to the information and data concerning the claimant contained in official or private registries, as well as to know about the use that has been made of such information and about its purpose, and to petition the competent court for the updating, rectification or destruction of erroneous records and those that unlawfully affect the petitioner's right (Article 28).

§1. *The Right of Amparo (to Be Protected)*

689. The action or suit for protection, or *amparo*, as a specific judicial means for the protection of all constitutional rights and guarantees has been constitutionalized in Venezuela since the 1961 Constitution. This provision implies the obligation of all the courts to protect persons in the exercise of their constitutional rights and guarantees. In the *amparo* suit decisions, judicial review of the constitutionality of legislation can also be exercised by the courts as part of their rulings.

Article 27 of the Constitution of 1999 establishes:

> Every individual is entitled to be protected by the courts in the enjoyment and exercise of rights, even those which derive from the nature of man that are not expressly set forth in this Constitution or in the international treaties on human rights.

> The amparo suit is governed by an informal, oral proceeding that shall be public, brief and free of charge. The judge is entitled to immediately restore the affected legal situation, and the court shall issue the decision with preference to all other matters.

---

cas, 2000), 147–172; Richard D. Henríquez Larrazábal, 'El problema de la procedencia del amparo constitucional en el Derecho venezolano', in *Bases y principios del sistema constitucional venezolano (Ponencias del VII Congreso Venezolano de Derecho Constitucional realizado en San Cristóbal del 21 al 23 de Noviembre de 2001)*, vol. II, 403–475; Víctor R. Hernández-Mendible, 'El amparo constitucional desde la perspectiva cautelar', in *El Derecho Público a comienzos del siglo XXI. Estudios homenaje al Profesor Allan R. Brewer-Carías*, vol. I, *supra*, 1.219–1.301.

2122   See Allan R. Brewer-Carías, *Constitutional Protection of Human Rights in Latin America. A Comparative Study of Amparo Proceedings* (New York: Cambridge University Press, 2008).

As per the Organic Law on A*mparo* of Constitutional Rights and Guarantees of 1988,[2123] in principle, all courts of first instance are competent to decide *amparo* suits.

690. Standing to file the action of *amparo* corresponds to every individual whose constitutional rights and guarantees are affected (whether individual, political, social, cultural, educative, economic, Indigenous peoples' or environmental rights), even those inherent rights that are not expressly provided for in the Constitution or in the international treaties on human rights that are ratified by the Republic. In Venezuela, such treaties rank on the same level as the Constitution, and they even prevail in the internal order as long as they establish more favourable rules on the enjoyment and exercise of rights than those established under the Constitution and other laws (Article 23) (see *supra* paragraph 442, 443, 682).

691. In Venezuela, the action of *amparo* may be instituted against State organs, against corporations and even against individuals whose actions or omissions may infringe or threaten constitutional rights and guarantees. In all cases of *amparo* proceedings, if the alleged violation of the constitutional right involves a statutory provision, in his decision, the *amparo* judge can decide that the statute is unconstitutional and not apply it to the case.

692. Generally, the individual directly affected by the infringement of the constitutional rights and guarantees has standing in an action for *amparo*. But by virtue of the constitutional acknowledgement of the legal protection of diffuse or collective interests, the Constitutional Chamber of the Supreme Court has admitted the possibility of exercising the action of *amparo* to enforce collective and diffuse rights. For instance, those rights related to an acceptable quality of life and also those pertaining to the political rights of voters, admitting precautionary measures with *erga omnes* effects.[2124]

In such cases the Constitutional Chamber has admitted that:

> any individual with legal capacity to bring suit, who is going to prevent damage to the population or parts of it to which he belongs, is entitled to bring the [amparo] suit grounded in diffuse or collective interests...This interpretation, based on Article 26, extends standing to companies, corporations, foundations, chambers, unions and other collective entities, whose object be the defense of the society, as long as they act within the boundaries of their corporate object, aimed at protecting the interests of their members regarding their object.[2125]

2123   See *Gaceta Oficial* N°33.891 of 22 Jan. 1988. See Allan R. Brewer-Carías & Carlos M. Ayala Corao, *Ley Orgánica de Amparo sobre Derechos y Garantías Constitucionales* (Caracas, 1988). See also Allan R. Brewer-Carías, *El derecho y la acción de amparo, vol. V, Instituciones Políticas y Constitucionales* (Caracas: Editorial Jurídica venezolana, 1998), 163 et seq.

2124   Decision of the Constitutional Chamber N° 483 of 29 May 2000 (Case: *'Queremos Elegir' y otros*), *Revista de Derecho Público*, N° 82 (Caracas: Editorial Jurídica Venezolana, 2000), 489–491. In the same sense, decision of the same Chamber N° 714 of 13 Jul. 2000 (Case: *APRUM*), in *Revista de Derecho Público*, N° 83 (Caracas: Editorial Jurídica Venezolana, 2000), 319 et seq.

2125   See decision of the Constitutional Chamber N° 487 of 6 Apr. 2001, Case: *Glenda López*, in *Revista de Derecho Público*, N° 85–88 (Caracas: Editorial Jurídica Venezolana, 2001), 453 et seq. In these cases (are there more than one case in this decisión?) If so 'these cases' is fine. If not, should just be 'this

However, regarding the general defence and protection of diffuse and collective interests, the Constitutional Chamber has also admitted the standing of the Defender of the People.[2126]

693. In order to seek uniformity of the application and interpretation of the Constitution, Article 336 of the Constitution also grants the Constitutional Chamber of the Supreme Tribunal the power to review, in a discretionary way, all final decisions issued in *amparo* suits. The extraordinary recourse can also be raised against judicial decisions applying the diffuse method of judicial review, being the review power of the Constitutional Chamber of facultative, non-obligatory character.

§2. *The Various Judicial Means for Amparo*

694. This *right to amparo* can be exercised through an 'autonomous action for amparo'[2127] that in principle is filed before the first instance court; or by means of pre-existing ordinary or extraordinary legal actions or recourses to which an *amparo* petition is joined, being the judges empowered to immediately re-establish the infringed legal situation. In all such cases, it is not that the ordinary means substitute the constitutional right of protection (or diminish it), but that they can serve as the judicial mean for protection since the judge is empowered to protect fundamental rights and immediately re-establish the infringed legal situation.

This last possibility does not presuppose in Venezuela that for the filing of an autonomous *amparo* action all other pre-existing legal judicial or administrative means have to be exhausted, as is the case for instance, of the recourse for *amparo* or the 'constitutional complaint' developed in Europe, particularly in Germany and in Spain.

695. This right for *amparo* has been regulated in the 1988 Organic Law of Amparo,[2128] expressly providing for its exercise, as aforementioned, not only by means of an autonomous action for *amparo*, but also through other pre-existing actions or recourses already established in the legal system. This main characteristic of the

---

case', as stated by the Constitutional Chamber in a decision dated 17 Feb. 2000 (N° 1.048, Case: *William O. Ojeda O. v. Consejo Nacional Electoral*), in order to enforce diffuse or collective rights or interests, it is necessary that the following elements be combined: (1) That the plaintiff sues based not only on his personal right or interest, but also on a common or collective right or interest; (2) That the reason for the claim filed on the action of *amparo*, be the general damage to the quality of life of all the inhabitants of the country or parts of it, since the legal situation of all the members of the society or its groups has been damaged when their common quality of life was unimproved; (3) That the damaged goods are not susceptible of exclusive appropriation by one subject (such as the plaintiff); (4) That the claim concerns an indivisible right or interest that involves the entire population of the country or a group of it [and] that a necessity of satisfying social or collective interests exists, before the individual ones.' See in *Revista de Derecho Público*, N° 83 (Caracas: Editorial Jurídica Venezolana, 2000), 375 et seq.

2126   See decision of the Constitutional Chamber N°487 of 6 Apr. 2001, Case: *Glenda López*, in *Revista de Derecho Público*, N° 85–88 (Caracas: Editorial Jurídica Venezolana, 2001), 453 et seq.

2127   See Allan R. Brewer-Carías, 'El derecho de amparo y la acción de amparo', in *Revista de Derecho Público*, N° 22 (Caracas: Editorial Jurídica Venezolana, 1985), 51 et seq.

2128   See *Gaceta Oficial* N° 33.891 of 22 Jan. 1988.

Venezuelan *amparo* was summarized in a decision by the former Supreme Court of 7 July 1991 (*Case Tarjetas Banvenez*), as follows:

> The Amparo Law sets forth two adjective mechanisms: the (autonomous) action for amparo and the joint filing of such action with other actions or recourses, which differs in their nature and legal consequences. Regarding the latter, that is to say, the filing of such action of amparo jointly with other actions or recourses, the Amparo Law distinguishes three mechanism: a) the action of amparo filed jointly with the popular action of unconstitutionality against statutes and State acts of the same rank and value (Article 3); b) The action of amparo filed jointly with the judicial review of administrative actions recourses against administrative acts or against omissions from Public Administration (Article 5); and c) the amparo action filed jointly with another ordinary judicial actions (Article 6,5).[2129]

The same Supreme Court also ruled that in these latter cases, the action for *amparo* is not an autonomous action, 'but a subordinate one, ancillary to the action or recourse to which it has been joined, thus subject to its final decision. Being joint actions, the case must be heard by the competent court regarding the principal one'.[2130]

696. Regarding the first mean for protection, that is, the autonomous action for *amparo*, in principle it can be brought before the first instance courts, and has a re-establishing nature in order to return things to the situation they had when the right was violated and to definitively make the offending act or fact disappear. For such purposes the plaintiff must invoke and demonstrate that it is a matter of flagrant, vulgar, direct and immediate constitutional harm, and the courts must decide based on the violation of the Constitution and not only on the violation of statutes, because on the contrary, it will not be a constitutional action for *amparo* but rather another type of recourse, for instance, the judicial review action against administrative acts whose annulatory effects do not correspond with the restitutory effects of the *amparo*.

697. Regarding the second mean for protection, the right to *amparo* can also be enforced by filing an *amparo* petition conjunctly with other pre-existing actions, recourses and proceedings, for which the Amparo Law provides the following possibilities:

> First, according to Article 3 of the Amparo Law, it is possible to file an amparo petition against statutes, bringing the petition together or jointly with the popular action of unconstitutionality of statutes exercised before the Constitutional Chamber of the Supreme Tribunal of Justice. In these cases, when the popular action is founded on the violation of a constitutional right or guaranty by the statute, the Organic Law authorizes the Supreme Tribunal to suspend the effects of the disputed statute regarding the specific case and in some cases with general effects, pending the issue of the requested decision on the nullity of the

---

2129   See the text in *Revista de Derecho Público*, N° 47 (Caracas: Editorial Jurídica Venezolana, 1991), 169–174.

2130   See in *Revista de Derecho Público*, N° 50 (Caracas: Editorial Jurídica Venezolana, 1992), 183–184.

statute. Since the amparo petition is subordinate to the nullity action against statutes, the amparo decision in the proceeding has a preliminary character of suspending the effects of the challenged statute pending the Court's decision on the merits of the nullity of the statute.

698. Second, according to Article 5 of the Amparo Law, as already mentioned, it expressly establishes that the petition for *amparo* against administrative acts and against Public Administration omissions may also be brought before the corresponding courts of the Administrative Jurisdiction (*Jurisdicción contencioso-administrativa*) jointly with the judicial review of administrative actions' recourses (see *infra* paragraph 702).

In such cases, when the recourse is founded in the violation of a constitutional right by the challenged administrative act, the general admissibility conditions of the *contencioso administrativo* nullity recourse have been made more flexible, in particular referring to the need to previously exhaust the existing administrative procedures, and to the term for the filing of the recourse; conditions that have been eliminated when the petition for *amparo* is filed jointly with the nullity recourse. In such cases, in addition, the courts are allowed to adopt immediate steps for the reduction of procedure terms, and also have the power to suspend the effects of the challenged administrative acts while the nullity action is decided (Articles 5, and 6.5). Also in these cases, the *amparo* protection is reduced to the suspension of the effects of the challenged administrative act pending the court's decision on the nullity of the challenged act.

699. Third and finally, according to Article 6.6 of the same Amparo Law, it is implicitly recognized that the claim for *amparo* may also be brought before the courts jointly with any other 'ordinary judicial procedures' or with the 'pre-existing judicial means', through which the 'violation or threat of violation of a constitutional right or guaranty may be alleged'. In these cases, for instance, the *amparo* petition can be filed jointly with the recourse of cassation when the claim against the challenged judicial decision is based on violations of a constitutional right or guarantee. In such cases, the Cassation Chambers of the Supreme Tribunal shall follow the procedure and terms established in the Organic Law of Amparo (Article 6.5) and the recourse will anyway have the effect of suspending the challenged decision.

All these cases of *amparo* petitions in Venezuela, do not substitute the ordinary or extraordinary judicial means allowing the *amparo* claim to be filed jointly with those other judicial means.

§3. *The Universal Character of the Amparo Proceeding*

700. From all these regulations, the Venezuelan right for *amparo* has certain peculiarities that distinguish it from the other similar institutions for the protection of the constitutional rights and guarantees established in Latin America. Beside the adjective consequences of the *amparo* being a constitutional right, it can be characterized by the following trends:[2131]

2131   See Allan R. Brewer-Carías, 'La acción de amparo en Venezuela y su universalidad', in *Génesis, Desarrollo y Actualidad de Amparo en América Latina*, ed. José de Jesús Naveja Macía (Coord.),

First, the right of *amparo* can be exercised in Venezuela for the guarantee of *all* constitutional rights, not only of civil rights, freedoms or individual rights. Consequently, the social, economic, cultural, environmental, political and indigenous peoples rights declared in the Constitution and in international treaties are also justiciables and protected by means of *amparo*. The habeas corpus *action* is an aspect of the right to constitutional protection, or one of the expressions of the *amparo*.

Second, the right to *amparo* seeks to assure protection of constitutional rights and guarantees against *any disturbance* in their enjoyment and exercise, whether originated by *public* authorities or by *private* individuals, without distinction. In the case of disturbance by public authorities, the *amparo* is admissible in Venezuela against statutes, and also against legislative, administrative and judicial acts, as well as against material or factual courses of action of Public Administration or public officials.

Third, the judicial adjudication on *amparo* matters as a consequence of the exercise of this right to *amparo*, whether through the pre-existing actions or recourses or by means of the autonomous action for *amparo*, is not limited to be of a precautionary or preliminary nature, but is conceived to re-establish the infringed legal situation by deciding on the merits, that is, the legality and legitimacy of the alleged disturbance of the constitutional right or guarantee.

Fourth, since the Venezuelan system of judicial review is a mixed one (see *supra* paragraph 639), judicial review of legislation can also be exercised by the courts when deciding action for *amparo*. This can happen, for instance, when the alleged violation of the right is based on a statute deemed unconstitutional. In such cases, if the protection requested is granted by the courts, it must previously declare the statute inapplicable on the grounds of it being unconstitutional. Therefore, in such cases, judicial review of the constitutionality of legislation (diffuse method) can also be exercised when an action for *amparo* of fundamental rights is filed.

701. Finally, it must also be mentioned that in the Venezuelan systems of judicial review and of *amparo*, the 1999 Constitution introduced an extraordinary means of review recourse which allows the Constitutional Chamber of the Supreme Court to issue final judgments in all cases of constitutional importance decided by lower courts. This extraordinary review recourse can be filed, in effect, against judicial final decisions issued in *amparo* suits and also, against any judicial decision issued when the diffuse judicial review method is exercised resolving the inapplicability of statutes because they are considered unconstitutional (Article 336.10).

The essential trend of this attribution of the Constitutional Chamber is its discretionary character that allows it to choose the cases to be reviewed. As the same Constitutional Chamber of the Supreme Tribunal pointed out in its decision N° 727 of 8 April 2003:

vol. I (Tijuana México: Ediciones Ilcsa), 109–141; 'El proceso constitucional de amparo en Venezuela: su universalidad y su inefectividad en el régimen autoritario', in *Horizontes Contemporáneos del Derecho Procesal Constitucional. Liber Amicorum Néstor Pedro Sagüés* (Lima: Centro de Estudios Constitucionales del Tribunal Constitucional, 2011).

in the cases of the decisions subject to revision, the Constitution does not provide for the creation of a third instance. What has set forth the constitutional provision is an exceptional and discretional power of the Constitutional Chamber that as such, must be exercised with maxim prudence regarding the admission of recourses for reviewing final judicial decisions.[2132]

Chapter 4. Judicial Review of Administrative Action Jurisdiction (Administrative Contentious Jurisdiction)

702. The most important consequence of the rule of law and of the principle of legality applied to Public Administration is the provision in the same Constitution of the existence of the Administrative Contentious Jurisdiction *(Jurisdicción contenciosa administrativa)* (Article 259) as well as the Electoral Contentious Jurisdiction (Article 297), both integrated in the general organization of the Judiciary for the purpose of controlling administrative actions.

With these constitutional provisions the Constitution adopted the judicial system regarding the Judicial Review of Administrative Action (Contentious Administrative) Jurisdiction, departing from the French model and reaffirming the traditional tendency in the national legislation to assign to the Judicial Branch the power to control the legality of administrative acts.[2133]

703. The difference between the 'Constitutional Jurisdiction' attributed to the Constitutional Chamber of the Supreme Court of Justice, and the 'Administrative Contentious Jurisdiction' attributed to the Politico-Administrative and Electoral Chambers of the Supreme Tribunal and to other special courts for judicial review of administrative actions, resides on the State's acts subjected to control: the Constitu-

---

2132   Case: *Revisión de la sentencia dictada por la Sala Electoral en fecha 21 de noviembre de 2002*, in *evista de Derecho Público*, N° 93–96 (Caracas: Editorial Jurídica Venezolana, 2003).

2133   See Luis Torrealba Narváez, 'Consideraciones acerca de la Jurisdicción Contencioso Administrativa, su Procedimiento y Algunas Relaciones de éste con el de la Jurisdicción Judicial Civil', in *Anales de la Facultad de Derecho* (Caracas: Universidad Central de Venezuela, 1951); Hildegard Rondón de Sansó, *El Sistema Contencioso administrativo de la Carrera Administrativa. Instituciones, Procedimiento y Jurisprudencia* (Caracas: Ediciones Magón, 1974); José Araujo Juárez, José, *Derecho Procesal Administrativo* (Caracas: Vadell Hermanos editores, 1996); Allan R. Brewer-Carías, *Instituciones Fundamentales del Derecho Administrativo y la Jurisprudencia Venezolana* (Caracas: Universidad Central de Venezuela, 1964), 451 et seq.; *Estado de derecho y Control Judicial* (Madrid, 1985), 281 et seq., and *Contencioso Administrativo, vol. VII* of *Instituciones Políticas y Constitucionales* (Caracas-San Cristóbal: Editorial Jurídica Venezolana, 1997); Antonio Canova González, *Reflexiones para la reforma del sistema contencioso administrativo venezolano* (Caracas: Editorial Sherwood, 1998). See also, *El Control Jurisdiccional de los Poderes Públicos en Venezuela* (Caracas,: Instituto de Derecho Público, Facultad de Ciencias Jurídicas y Políticas, Universidad Central de Venezuela, 1979); *Contencioso Administrativo en Venezuela* (Caracas: Editorial Jurídica Venezolana, tercera edición, 1993); *Derecho Procesal Administrativo* (Caracas: Vadell Hermanos editores, 1997); *8ª Jornadas 'J.M. Domínguez Escovar' (Enero 1983), Tendencias de la jurisprudencia venezolana en materia contencioso administrativa* (Caracas: Facultad de Ciencias Jurídicas y Políticas, U.C.V., Corte Suprema de Justicia; Instituto de Estudios Jurídicos del Estado Lara, Tip. Pregón, 1983); *Contencioso Administrativo, I Jornadas de Derecho Administrativo Allan Randolph Brewer-Carías* (Caracas: Funeda, 1995); *XVIII Jornadas 'J.M. Domínguez Escovar, Avances jurisprudenciales del contencioso–administrativo en Venezuela*, 2 vols (Instituto de Estudios Jurídicos del Estado Lara, Diario de Tribunales Editores, S.R.L. Barquisimeto, 1993).

tional Jurisdiction is in charge of annulling unconstitutional statutes and other acts of similar rank or issued in direct and immediate execution of the Constitution; and the Administrative Contentious Jurisdiction is in charge of annulling unconstitutional or illegal administrative acts or regulations, with general *erga omnes* effects.

704. The courts of this Jurisdiction have the power to annul general and individual administrative acts when contrary to the legal order, including those issued with abuse of public power (*desviación de poder*). They are also competent to order the State to pay sums of money, and to repair injuries or damages caused by the Administration, to hear claims concerning the rendering of public services, and to rule as necessary to re-establish subjective legal rights affected by administrative acts (Article 259).

705. Regarding the standing to challenge administrative acts on the grounds of unconstitutionality and illegality, when referring to normative administrative acts or regulations, anybody can bring an action before the court by means of the popular action of nullity. Consequently, a simple interest in the legality or constitutionality is enough for any citizen to be sufficiently entitled to raise the nullity action for unconstitutionality or illegality against regulations and other normative administrative acts. This simple interest has been defined, as 'the general right granted by law upon every citizen to access the competent courts to raise the nullity of an unconstitutional or illegal administrative general act'.[2134]

706. As to the administrative acts of particular effects, the standing to challenge such acts before the Administrative Jurisdiction courts corresponds solely to those who have a personal, legitimate and direct interest in the annulment of the act (Article 5, Law). This has been the general rule on the matter even though some decisions have been issued by the Politico-Administrative Chamber of the Supreme Tribunal, giving standing to any person with only a legitimate interest.[2135]

Additionally, in the case of the Administrative Jurisdiction, even before the new Constitution took effect in 1999, the possibility of protecting collective interests was also made available. In particular, it is now widely accepted that a collective or diffuse right exists against city-planning acts.

Nonetheless, despite very impressive advances regarding judicial review of administrative actions experienced in the past decades, due to the political control of the Judiciary during the past seven years, the role of the Administrative Jurisdiction in controlling Public Administration has dramatically diminished in Venezuela, affecting the rule of law.[2136]

2134   See decision of the First Administrative Court dated 22 Mar. 2000, case: *Banco de Venezolano de Crédito v. Superintendencia de Bancos, Revista de Derecho Público*, N° 81 (Caracas: Editorial Jurídica Venezolana, 2000), 452–453.

2135   See decision of the Supreme Court of Justice in Political-Administrative Chamber of 13 Apr. 2000, case: *Banco Fivenez v. Junta de Emergencia Financiera, Revista de Derecho Público*, N° 82 (Caracas: Editorial Jurídica Venezolana, 2000), 582–583.

2136   See Allan R. Brewer-Carías, 'La progresiva y sistemática demolición institucional de la autonomía e independencia del Poder Judicial en Venezuela 1999-2004', in *XXX Jornadas J.M Domínguez Escovar, Estado de derecho, Administración de justicia y derechos humanos* (Barquisimeto: Instituto de Estudios Jurídicos del Estado Lara, 2005), 33–174.

707. The procedure and organization of the Administrative Contentious Jurisdiction, since 1976, had been transitorily regulated in the statute referred to the Supreme Tribunal: first, by the 1976 Organic Law of the Supreme Court of Justice in 1976,[2137] and after the sanctioning of the 1999 Constitution by the 2004 Organic Law of the Supreme Tribunal of Justice. This transitory regime was substituted in 2010 by the Organic Law on the Administrative Contentious Jurisdiction[2138] in which the judicial competence on the matter was distributed among the Politico-Administrative Chamber of the Supreme Tribunal, and the National Tribunals, the States Tribunals and the Municipal Tribunals of Administrative Contentious Jurisdiction. In addition, other special statutes attributed to other courts with special aspects of the Administrative Contentious Jurisdiction, as has happened with the Taxation Superior Courts for the taxation contentious recourses; and with the Agrarian Superior Courts, with the agrarian contentious actions.

708. The Constitution assigns to the Politico-Administrative Chamber of the Supreme Tribunal exclusive jurisdiction to totally or partially annul Executive regulations and other general or individual administrative acts issued by the National Executive; to decide administrative controversies between the Republic, a state, a municipality and other public entities, when the other party involved is one of them, except controversies between municipalities that can be attributed to other courts; and to decide recourses of interpretation of statutes (Article 266.5). Consequently, competencies to decide actions challenging administrative acts of the states and of the municipalities and any other public corporations of entity are assigned to the other courts of the Jurisdiction.

709. According to the provision of Article 259 of the Constitution, the Administrative Contentious Jurisdiction in Venezuela is governed by the following general principles:[2139]

(1) First, the universal character of the judicial control of constitutionality and illegality exercised over any regulations and administrative acts, which means that it is made without exception regarding the challenged act and no matter the motive of the challenging action. The Constitution allows the challenging of those acts when 'contrary to the law'.

(2) Second, the multiplicity of recourses or means of actions to be filed against administrative acts seeking to nullify unconstitutional or illegal executive regulations and administrative acts, to which must be added those recourses of *amparo* seeking to obtain constitutional protection of human rights violated by the challenged administrative act; the actions against administrative omis-

---

2137   Organic Law Supeme Court of Justice, *Gaceta Oficial* N° 1.893, Extra, of 30 Jul. 1976. See Allan R. Brewer-Carías and Josefina Calcaño de Temeltas, *Ley Orgánica de la Corte Suprema de Justicia* (Caracas: Editorial Jurídica Venezolana, 1994).

2138   *Gaceta Oficial* N° 39.451 of 22 Jun. 2010. See Allan R. Brewer-Carías y Víctor Hernández Mendible, *Ley Orgánica de la Jurisdicción Contencioso Administrativa* (Caracas: Editorial Jurídica Venezolana, 2010).

2139   Véase Allan R. Brewer-Carías, *Nuevas Tendencias en el Contencioso Administrativo en Venezuela* (Caracas: Editorial Jurídica Venezolana, 1993).

sions particularly regarding responses to administrative petitions (see *supra* paragraph 698); the recourse of interpretation of statutes; the various actions that can be filed against Public Administration seeking liability and compensation for damages caused by its functioning (see *supra* paragraph 257); the recourse for the solution of administrative conflicts between public entities; the recourses for the solution of conflicts regarding public contracts, whether between the parties to the contracts or in cases of actions filed by any interested person seeking the annulment of public contracts; and the actions filed because of the malfunctioning of public services.

(3) Third, the broad and extended power of control assigned to the administrative contentious judges of extended powers of control, not only to annul administrative acts, but to decide on the various subjective rights or interests that the individuals could have regarding Public Administration.

Consequently, the administrative contentious system in Venezuela has not only been conceived as an objective process against administrative acts, but also as a subjective process for the protection of personal subjective rights and interest of persons regarding Public Administration, including the protection of fundamental rights. That is why administrative contentious judges not only have power to annul administrative acts, but to restore subjective individual situations harmed by administrative authorities.

710. Nonetheless, and unfortunately, the authoritarian regime instauled in the country during the past years since 1999, in practice, due to the political control of the courts, has neutralized the possibility of judicial control of administrative action, to the point that only a very small percentage of cases have been decided condemning the State or annulling illegal administrative acts. [2140]

2140   Véase Antonio Canova González, *La realidad del contencioso administrativo venezolano (Un llamado de atención frente a las desoladoras estadísticas de la Sala Político Administrativa en 2007 y primer semestre de 2008)*, (Caracas, Funeda, 2008).

SÉPTIMA PARTE

LA CONSTITUCIÓN COMO PROMESA INCUMPLIDA

Esta Primera parte es el texto redactado para mi exposición sobre el mismo tema del título en el *Congreso de Derecho Constitucional, 20 años de la Constitución de 1991*, **Universidad Javeriana, Bogotá, febrero 2016.**

I. EL SENTIDO DE LA CONSTITUCIÓN: UN PACTO SUPREMO Y RÍGIDO COMO PROMESA DE SER CUMPLIDA

En el mundo moderno, después de que la soberanía le fue arrebatada a los Monarcas y la misma se trasladó al pueblo, las Constituciones se sancionan con participación popular, como normas supremas y rígidas plasmando el pacto de una sociedad, como promesa para ser cumplida, en el cual se definen los principios de la organización del Estado, el rol que se le asigna en relación con la sociedad, y los derechos y garantías de los ciudadanos declarados y reconocidos por el Estado; promesas signadas por los principios de supremacía y rigidez de la Constitución, que solo el mismo pueblo puede modificar, quedando fuera del alcance del legislador ordinario.[2141]

Para ello, las Constituciones expresan, como es el caso de la de Venezuela de 1999, que son "la norma suprema y el fundamento del ordenamiento jurídico" (art. 7) asignando a todos los jueces "la obligación de asegurar la integridad de esta Constitución," y de aplicar sus previsiones con preferencia a cualquier otra norma (art. 334),[2142] y en particular al Tribunal Supremo de Justicia como Juez Constitucional, la de garantizar "la supremacía y efectividad de las normas y principios constitucionales" (art. 335).

La misma Constitución dispone, además, sobre la garantía de su rigidez para asegurar que siendo producto de la voluntad popular, su reforma o modificación esté

2141   Véase Allan R. Brewer-Carías, *Reflexiones sobre la Revolución Americana (1776), la Revolución Francesa (1789) y la revolución Hispanoamericana (1810-1830) y sus aportes al constitucionalismo moderno*, Colección Derecho Administrativo Nº 2, Universidad Externado de Colombia, Bogotá 2008.

2142   Me correspondió proponer en la Asamblea Nacional Constituyente de 1999 la consagración en forma expresa de dichos principios constitucionales en los artículos 7 y 334. Véase Allan R. Brewer-Carías, *Debate Constituyente, (Aportes a la Asamblea Nacional Constituyente)*, Tomo II, (9 septiembre-17 octubre 1999), Fundación de Derecho Público-Editorial Jurídica Venezolana, Caracas, 1999, p. 24.

fuera del alcance del legislador ordinario, los mecanismos y procedimientos específicos para las reformas y enmiendas constitucionales, y para la reforma total mediante una Asamblea Constituyente, que sólo pueden realizarse con participación popular (arts. 340-349).

Estas declaraciones dan origen, ante todo, al que quizás es el principal derecho ciudadano que es el derecho a la Constitución misma y a su supremacía,[2143] lo que implica el derecho a que el texto fundamental no pierda vigencia, ni sea violado; el derecho a que no pueda ser reformado o modificado sino mediante los procedimientos previstos en la Constitución; y el derecho a poder controlar la constitucionalidad de todos los actos estatales que atenten contra dichos derechos.[2144]

Estos derechos conforman la principal promesa contenida en la Constitución, como Constitución de Garantías, que complementa el otro conjunto de promesas que la conforman, y que se estructuran en la Constitución Política, la Constitución Económica y la Constitución Social. Y hablamos de promesas porque ello es lo que debe constituir necesariamente no sólo el marco del programa de acción de los gobiernos, sino el límite de acción de los mismos. Éstos pueden hacer todo lo que necesiten para ejecutar sus políticas, dentro de la Constitución, y nada fuera de ella.

En Venezuela, después del proceso constituyente que se desarrolló en 1999, con todos sus problemas, y la lamentable conformación de una Asamblea Constituyente dominada mayoritariamente por una sola corriente política, que dio un golpe de Estado contra los poderes entonces constituidos,[2145] se sancionó una nueva Constitución que es la de 30 de diciembre de 1999, la cual sin duda, luego de aprobada por el pueblo mediante referendo del 15 de diciembre de 1999, debió ser en su globalidad y en cada una de sus regulaciones, la promesa que el pueblo impuso a los gobernantes para ser cumplida.

Dicha promesa, particularmente en cuanto a la conformación del Estado, se basó en la consagración de un Estado Democrático y Social de derecho y de Justicia, con

---

2143   Al tema me he referido en diversos trabajos, y entre ellos, en el libro Allan R. Brewer-Carías, *Mecanismos nacionales de protección de los derechos humanos (Garantías judiciales de los derechos humanos en el derecho constitucional comparado latinoamericano),* Instituto Interamericano de Derechos Humanos, San José, 2005, pp. 74 ss.; y "Sobre las nuevas tendencias del derecho constitucional: del reconocimiento del derecho a la Constitución y derecho a la democracia", en *VNIVERSITAS, Revista de Ciencias Jurídicas (Homenaje a Luis Carlos Galán Sarmiento),* Pontificia Universidad Javeriana, facultad de Ciencias Jurídicas, N° 119, Bogotá 2009, pp. 93-111

2144   Como lo visualizó Alexander Hamilton en *El Federalista* (1788) en los inicios del constitucionalismo moderno: "Una Constitución es, de hecho, y así debe ser vista por los jueces, como ley fundamental, por tanto, corresponde a ellos establecer su significado así como el de cualquier acto proveniente del cuerpo legislativo Si se produce una situación irreconocible entre los dos, por supuesto, aquel que tiene una superior validez es el que debe prevalecer; en otras palabras, la Constitución debe prevalecer sobre las leyes, *así como la intención del pueblo debe prevalecer sobre la intención de sus agentes,*" en *The Federalist* (ed. por B.F. Wrigth), Cambridge, Mass. 1961, pp. 491-493.

2145   Véase Allan R. Brewer-Carías, *Golpe de Estado y proceso constituyente en Venezuela,* Universidad Nacional Autónoma de México, México 2002.

forma Federal y descentralizada,[2146] sobre la base de tres pilares político constitucionales:

En primer lugar, un sistema de control de poder, al establecer el principio fundamental de la separación de poderes (entre cinco y no sólo tres poderes del Estado, pues además de los clásicos Legislativo, Ejecutivo y Judicial, se han incluido el Poder Electoral y el Poder Ciudadano, regularizándose la autonomía de viejos órganos constitucionales; y un sistema de distribución vertical del Poder Público en tres niveles territoriales, entre el Poder Nacional, el Poder de los Estados y el Poder Municipal (art. 136), cada uno con autonomía política y debiendo tener siempre un gobierno de carácter "electivo, descentralizado, alternativo, responsable, pluralista y de mandatos revocables."

En segundo lugar un sistema político democrático, de democracia representativa mediante la elección directa de los representantes por sufragio directo, universal y secreto, es decir, de democracia indirecta de los titulare de los Poderes Ejecutivo y Legislativo, que siempre posibilita la participación política, enriquecida con elementos de democracia directa, al preverse todos los tipos imaginables de referendos (aprobatorios, abrogatorios y revocatorios), las consultas populares y las asambleas de ciudadanos; así como de la elección indirecta de los altos titulares de los Poderes Judicial, Electoral y Ciudadano.

En tercer lugar, un sistema económico conforme a un modelo económico de economía mixta, basado en el principio de la libertad como opuesto al de economía dirigida, similar al que existe en todos los países contemporáneos desarrollados de Occidente,[2147] con la participación del Estado como promotor del desarrollo económico, regulador de la actividad económica, y planificador con la participación de la sociedad civil. En definitiva, es un sistema de economía social de mercado que se basa en la libertad económica, pero que debe desenvolverse conforme a principios de justicia social.

Transcurridos tres lustros desde que se aprobó la Constitución por el pueblo, sin embargo, lo que se constata es que la promesa contenida en la misma ha sido incumplida, pudiendo entonces considerarse a la Constitución venezolana de 1999 como la muestra más vívida en el constitucionalismo contemporáneo de una Consti-

---

2146   Véase el estudio de la Constitución en cuanto a la regulación de este modelo de Estado Constitucional en Allan R. Brewer-Carías, *La Constitución de 1999. Derecho Constitucional venezolano*, 2 tomos, Caracas 2004.

2147   Véase sobre la Constitución Económica, lo que hemos expuesto en Allan R. Brewer-Carías, *La Constitución de 1999. Derecho Constitucional Venezolano*, Tomo II, Editorial Jurídica venezolana, Caracas 2004 pp. 53 ss.; y en "Reflexiones sobre la Constitución Económica" en *Estudios sobre la Constitución Española. Homenaje al Profesor Eduardo García de Enterría*, Madrid, 1991, pp. 3.839 a 3.853. Véase, además, Henrique Meier, "La Constitución económica", en *Revista de Derecho Corporativo*, Vol. 1, N° 1. Caracas, 2001, pp. 9-74; Dagmar Albornoz, "Constitución económica, régimen tributario y tutela judicial efectiva", en *Revista de Derecho Constitucional*, N° 5 (julio-diciembre), Editorial Sherwood, Caracas, 2001, pp. 7-20; Ana C. Nuñez Machado, "Los principios económicos de la Constitución de 1999", en *Revista de Derecho Constitucional*, N° 6 (enero-diciembre), Editorial Sherwood, Caracas, 2002, pp. 129-140; Claudia Briceño Aranguren y Ana C. Núñez Machado, "Aspectos económicos de la nueva Constitución", en *Comentarios a la Constitución de la República Bolivariana de Venezuela*, Vadell Hermanos, Editores, Caracas, 2000, pp. 177 y ss.

tución que ha sido violada y vulnerada desde antes incluso que fuera publicada, siendo el lamentable ejemplo de una Constitución como promesa incumplida.

II. EL INICIO DEL INCUMPLIMIENTO DE LA PROMESA: UN RÉGIMEN TRANSITORIO NO APROBADO POR EL PUEBLO QUE SUSPENDIÓ LA VIGENCIA DE MUCHAS NORMAS CONSTITUCIONALES

Los hechos, en la historia, con frecuencia se olvidan, y ello impide que se conozcan las causas de males posteriores. Por ello, cuando se constata la violación sistemática de la Constitución de 1999 durante los dieciséis años de su vigencia entre 1999 y 2015, lo primero que debe recordarse en que ello fue así pues la pauta que marcó el régimen que se instaló en el país cuando fue puesta en vigencia, la comenzó a violar antes de que incluso entrara en vigencia.

La Constitución, como se dijo, se aprobó por el pueblo el 15 de diciembre de 1999, no conteniendo su texto previsión alguna que estableciera un régimen transitorio que permitiera, por ejemplo, la remoción y designación de los titulares de los poderes públicos constituidos en forma distinta a lo establecido en su texto. Sin embargo, contra lo establecido en el texto aprobado por el pueblo, y aún antes de que el mismo fuera publicado en *Gaceta Oficial*, la Asamblea Nacional Constituyente que ya había terminado la misión para la cual fue elegida, dictó un Decreto sobre Régimen Transitorio, no aprobado popularmente, violando lo previsto tanto en la Constitución entonces vigente (1961) como en la nueva sancionada (1999), designando sin cumplir con lo establecido en la misma a los titulares de los Poderes Judicial (Magistrados del Tribunal Supremo), Ciudadano (titulares de la Contraloría General de la República, de la Fiscalía General de la República y de la Defensoría del Pueblo), Electoral (rectores del Consejo Supremo Electoral), y designando una "Comisión Legislativa Nacional" que usurpó las funciones del Poder Legislativo, no prevista en la Constitución.[2148]

Ello fue el origen de la Constitución como promesa incumplida, a lo que se agrega que su propio texto fue "modificado" o "reformado" con ocasión de la publicación en la *Gaceta Oficial*, con "correcciones de estilo" no aprobadas popularmente, no sólo en diciembre de 1999, sino en marzo de 2000, agregándose al texto constitucional, de paso, una "exposición de motivos" ilegítima que ni siquiera la Asamblea Constituyente discutió.[2149]

El Régimen "constitucional" transitorio impuesto sin aprobación popular, dio origen al primer incumplimiento general de la promesa de la garantía de rigidez de la Constitución, la cual también incumplió el Tribunal Supremo de Justicia en Sala Constitucional, el cual actuando como juez y parte, consideró que el decreto de régimen transitorio que lo había creado y nombrado a los magistrados que estaban decidiendo, tenía un rango supraconstitucional que nadie le había dado. Así, a partir de 2000 y por lustros, en Venezuela existieron dos textos constitucionales en parale-

2148   Véase Allan R. Brewer-Carías, *Golpe de Estado y proceso constituyente en Venezuela*, Universidad Nacional Autónoma de México, México 2002.

2149   Véase Allan R. Brewer-Carías, "Comentarios sobre la ilegítima "Exposición de Motivos" de la Constitución de 1999 relativa al sistema de justicia constitucional", en la *Revista de Derecho Constitucional*, Nº 2, Enero-Junio 2000, Caracas 2000, pp. 47-59.

lo: una Constitución que se incumplía, y un Decreto de régimen constitucional transitorio, que suspendió buena parte de sus normas.

Así, de entrada, antes de que la Constitución de 1999 siquiera fuera publicada, el régimen incumplió dos de las promesas políticas de mayor importancia y publicitación que se pregonaron como fueron la de la democracia participativa, además del incumplimiento de la promesa de la rigidez constitucional.

La Constitución impone que los titulares de los Poderes Públicos, todos, sean electos popularmente, unos en forma directa en primer grado por el pueblo (Poderes Ejecutivo y Legislativo), y otros en forma indirecta, en segundo grado, por la Asamblea Nacional actuando, no como cuerpo legislados, sino como Cuerpo Electoral con el voto de una mayoría calificada de las 2/3 partes de sus miembros (Poderes Judicial, Ciudadano y Electoral).

Adicionalmente, en cuanto a la elección popular de segundo grado de los titulares de los Poderes Judicial, Ciudadano y Electoral, la Constitución impuso la necesaria e ineludible participación ciudadana, al exigir que los nominados para esos cargos tengan que ser seleccionados por sendos Comités de Postulaciones que tienen que estar integrados por 'representantes de los diversos sectores de la sociedad."

Ambas promesas no sólo fueron violadas desde el inicio, al hacerse por la Asamblea Nacional Constituyente las primeras designaciones en diciembre de 1999, después de aprobada popularmente la Constitución y en contra de su texto, incluso antes de su publicación, sin que la elección hubiese sido hecha por la Asamblea Nacional como Cuerpo Electoral de segundo grado que debía elegirse, y sin que se hubiesen constituido siquiera los Comités de Postulaciones para asegurar la participación ciudadana.[2150]

Y ese vicio inicial de incumplimiento de la promesa constitucional, lamentablemente no fue un hecho circunstancial, sino que marcó la pauta para el sucesivo incumplimiento de la promesa de la Constitución.

III. EL INCUMPLIMIENTO DE LA PROMESA CONSTITUCIONAL DEL ESTABLECIMIENTO DE UN RÉGIMEN POLÍTICO DEMOCRÁTICO Y PARTICIPATIVO

La Constitución de 1999, está montada sobre una promesa fundamental que fue configurar al Estado como un Estado democrático, con un gobierno que además de democrático, tiene que además ser participativo, electivo y alternativo (art. 6), basado en la legitimidad democrática representativa de los órganos del Poder Público, producto del ejercicio de la soberanía popular mediante el sufragio (art. 5).

Esta promesa constitucional, lamentablemente ha sido incumplida, pues si bien la elección directa de los órganos del Poder Ejecutivo y del Poder Legislativo se ha realizado conforme a la Constitución, en cambio en materia de representatividad democrática, la promesa de la elección popular indirecta de los titulares de los Pode-

---

2150   Véase Allan R. Brewer-Carías, "La participación ciudadana en la designación de los titulares de los órganos no electos de los Poderes Públicos en Venezuela y sus vicisitudes políticas", en *Revista Iberoamericana de Derecho Público y Administrativo*, Año 5, N° 5-2005, San José, Costa Rica 2005, pp. 76-95.

res Judicial, Ciudadano y Electoral, en segundo grado con el voto calificado de la representación popular en el Parlamento, ha sido incumplida, habiendo en muchos casos sido hecha la elección sin la mayoría calificada exigida en la Constitución y sin asegurarse la participación ciudadana en la postulación de los nominados, contrariando la Constitución; en materia de democracia participativa, además, por una parte, por la falta de consulta popular de las leyes durante el proceso de su formación, habiéndose menospreciado la participación ciudadana; y por la otra, por la creación de mecanismos engañosos del llamado Estado Comunal, que la han hecho desaparecer las instancias de participación política que solo un gobierno democrático representativo puede garantizar; minimizado; y en materia de gobierno democrático, por la violación del principio de alternabilidad republicana en el ejercicio del gobierno, que fue deliberadamente olvidado.

1. *La promesa de la elección popular de los titulares de los Poderes Públicos y su incumplimiento*

La legitimidad democrática de los gobernantes la asegura la Constitución de 1999, como se dijo, con la elección directa por el pueblo respecto de los titulares de los Poderes Ejecutivo (Presidente de la República) y Legislativo (diputados a la Asamblea Nacional), sino que con la también elección popular indirecta de los titulares de los otros poderes públicos como son los Poder Judicial, es decir, de los Magistrados del Tribunal Supremo de Justicia (art. 264, 265); del Poder Ciudadano, es decir, del Contralor General de la República, del Fiscal General de la República y del Defensor del Pueblo (art. 279); del Poder Electoral, es decir, de los Rectores del Consejo Nacional Electoral (art. 296); efectuada en este caso, en forma indirecta, por la Asamblea nacional, actuando como Cuerpo elector (no actuando como cuerpo legislativo), con las garantías de máxima participación política que establece la Constitución al exigir la mayoría calificada de votación de sus miembros y la participación ciudadana en la selección de los nominados

En Venezuela, sin embargo, luego de la pauta inicial dada con el inconstitucional régimen "transitorio" de 1999, a partir de 2004 se comenzó a desconocer esta promesa de elección democrática, habiendo asumido el Tribunal Supremo la inconstitucional decisión de "designar" a los miembros del Consejo Nacional Electoral, lo que se ratificó posteriormente en 2014. Y en cuanto a los titulares de los otros Poderes Públicos, comenzaron a ser "designados" (no "electos") por la Asamblea Nacional como simple cuerpo legislativo, con el voto de la mayoría simple de los presentes (no de la mayoría calificada de sus miembros), como ocurrió en violación de la Constitución en diciembre de 2014[2151] y en diciembre de 2015,[2152] todo en violación

---

2151   Véase Allan R. Brewer-Carías, "El golpe de Estado dado en diciembre de 2014 en Venezuela con la inconstitucional designación de las altas autoridades del Poder Público," en *El Cronista del Estado Social y Democrático de Derecho*, N° 52, Madrid 2015, pp. 18-33; José Ignacio Hernández, "La designación del Poder Ciudadano: fraude a la Constitución en 6 actos;" en *Prodavinci*, 22 de diciembre, 2014, en http://prodavinci.com/blogs/la-designacion-del-poder-ciudadano-fraude-a-la-constitucion-en-6-actos-por-jose-i-hernandez/;

2152   Véase Allan R. Brewer-Carías, "El golpe de Estado dado en diciembre de 2014, con la inconstitucional designación de las altas autoridades del Poder Público," en *Revista de Derecho Público*, N° 140 (Cuarto Trimestre 2014, Editorial Jurídica Venezolana, Caracas 2014, pp. 495-518.

de la Constitución. Esta inconstitucionalidad, además, llegó a ser incorporada en la Ley Orgánica del Tribunal Supremo de Justicia de 2004 para "legitimar" la inconstitucional "designación" (no elección) de los magistrados del Tribunal Supremo.

Así, la primera promesa de la Constitución, de asegurar la legitimidad democrática de los titulares de los Poderes Públicos ha sido sistemáticamente incumplida desde el inicio de la entrada en vigencia de la Constitución.

2. *La promesa de la participación popular en el funcionamiento del Estado y su incumplimiento*

La Constitución de 1999, aparte de utilizar la expresión "participación" y "participativa" en múltiples artículos, como promesa general, directamente estableció, además de los mecanismos de participación a través de la elección o de votaciones en referendos e instituciones locales (asambleas de ciudadanos), dos mecanismos de participación ciudadana en asuntos públicos, que son los únicos que tienen su fuente en la propia Constitución, y ambos han sido sistemáticamente violados e ignorados durante toda su vigencia.

El primero, es el de la participación ciudadana en el proceso de elección popular indirecta, de los titulares de los Poderes Públicos Judicial, Ciudadano y Electoral, por la Asamblea Nacional actuando como cuerpo elector, al exigir que los candidatos respectivos deben ser postulados o nominados por sendos Comités de Postulaciones regulados constitucionalmente, todos los cuales deberían estar integrados únicamente y exclusivamente "por representantes de los diversos sectores de la sociedad" (Comité de Postulaciones Judiciales, art. 270; Comité de Evaluación de Postulaciones del Poder Ciudadano, art. 279; y Comité de Postulaciones Electorales art. 295).

Esa promesa de participación política ha sido sistemáticamente incumplida desde 2000, habiendo sido violada la exigencia constitucional de la participación ciudadana al haberse integrado los referidos Comités de Postulaciones, no exclusivamente por representantes de los diversos sectores de la sociedad, sino por una mayoría de diputados, los cuales por esencia no son "representantes" de la sociedad civil, que es lo que exige la Constitución.[2153] Ello se estableció así inconstitucionalmente en la Ley Especial para la Designación de los Titulares de los Poderes Públicos de 2000,[2154] y se repitió en las Leyes Orgánicas del Poder Electoral,[2155] del Poder Ciudadano[2156] y del Tribunal Supremo de Justicia sancionadas a partir de 2004, donde que-

---

2153   Véase los comentarios sobre la inconstitucional práctica legislativa reguladora de los Comités de Postulaciones integradas, cada uno, con una mayoría de diputados, convirtiéndolas en simples "comisiones parlamentarias ampliadas," en Allan R. Brewer-Carías, "La participación ciudadana en la designación de los titulares de los órganos no electos de los Poderes Públicos en Venezuela y sus vicisitudes políticas", en *Revista Iberoamericana de Derecho Público y Administrativo*, Año 5, N° 5-2005, San José, Costa Rica 2005, pp. 76-95.

2154   *Gaceta Oficial* N° 37.077 de 14 de noviembre de 2000. La impugnación por inconstitucional de dicha Ley en 2000, hay que recordarlo, le costó el cargo a la primera Defensora del Pueblo que había electo la Asamblea Constituyente en 1999.

2155   *Gaceta Oficial* N° 37.573 de 19 de noviembre de 2002.

2156   *Gaceta Oficial* N° 37.310 de 25 de octubre de 2001.

daron configurados los mencionados Comités controlados por la Asamblea, como simples "comisiones parlamentarias ampliadas," totalmente controladas por la fracción mayoritaria de la Asamblea Nacional. La consecuencia ha sido que todas las "designaciones" de los titulares de los Poderes Electoral, Ciudadano y Judicial durante los últimos quince años, han sido hechas incumpliendo la promesa de la garantía constitucional de la participación ciudadana mediante unos Comités de Postulaciones integrados únicamente por representantes de los diversos sectores de la sociedad.

3. *La promesa de la participación popular en el proceso de formación de las leyes y su incumplimiento*

Pero además de este mecanismo de participación ciudadana, el otro directamente establecido en la Constitución, es el que deriva del derecho constitucional de los ciudadanos y de la sociedad organizada a participar en el procedimiento de formación de las leyes al preverse en la misma la Constitución, la obligación de la Asamblea Nacional de someter los proyectos de leyes, durante el proceso de su discusión y aprobación, a consulta pública, para conocer de los ciudadanos y de la sociedad organizada su opinión sobre los mismos (art. 211).

La promesa de participación popular contenida en la Constitución, en esta materia, sin embargo, también ha sido sistemáticamente incumplida, y el derecho ciudadano a la participación política en este caso permanentemente violado, no sólo por la propia Asamblea Nacional, la cual hasta 2015 legisló sin asegurar mecanismo alguno de consulta popular de los proyectos de leyes,[2157] sino lo más grave, por el Presidente de la república en todos los casos en los que emitió legislación delegada.

La misma obligación de asegurar la participación ciudadana que impone el artículo 211 de la Constitución a la Asamblea Nacional para la sanción de leyes, la tiene también el Presidente de la República cuando en ejercicio del Poder Ejecutivo emite, en virtud de una delegación legislativa, decretos con valor de ley, debiendo siempre en el proceso de su elaboración, someter el proyecto de ley previamente a consulta pública, en particular, a los ciudadanos y a la sociedad organizada. La obligación de consulta para asegurar la participación no se establece en razón del órgano que emite la ley, sino del proceso mismo de formación de la ley que por concernir a todos, debe consultarse popularmente. Sin embargo, reafirmando la violación a la Constitución la Sala Constitucional del Tribunal Supremo, en lugar de garantizar el derecho y darle primacía a los derechos humanos, mediante sentencia No. 203 de 25 de marzo de 2014,[2158] más bien lo que hizo fue declarar que los ciudadanos solo

---

2157   Véase por ejemplo, "El derecho ciudadano a la participación popular y la inconstitucionalidad generalizada de los decretos leyes 2010-2012, por su carácter inconsulto," en *Revista de Derecho Público,* N° 130, (abril-junio 2012), Editorial Jurídica Venezolana, Caracas 2012, pp. 85-88. Además finalmente, basta solo constatar que durante las sesiones extraordinarias celebradas entre el 23 y el 30 de diciembre de 2015, en plena fiestas navideñas, la Asamblea "discutió" y sancionó 20 leyes, sin que se hubiese hecho consulta popular alguna. Véase por ejemplo *Gaceta Oficial* N° 40.819 de diciembre de 2015.

2158   Véase Caso *Síndica Procuradora Municipal del Municipio Chacao del Estado Miranda, impugnación del Decreto Ley de Ley Orgánica de la Administración Pública de 2008,* en http://www.tsj.gov.ve/de-

tienen derecho constitucional a participar en el proceso de formación de las leyes sólo cuando las dicta la Asamblea Nacional, pero que no existe cuando las leyes las dicta el Poder Ejecutivo mediante una delegación legislativa, lo que sin duda es contrario al espíritu y propósito de la Constitución, es decir, es una forma de burlar el derecho ciudadano a la participación política, configurándose como un fraude a la Constitución.[2159] Ello lo que significa es que en Venezuela se puede impunemente violar el derecho ciudadano a la participación política mediante consulta pública de los proyectos de leyes, si estos se dictan mediante decretos leyes, lo que en la práctica ha ocurrido porque en los últimos quince años materialmente toda la legislación básico del país se ha dictado mediante decretos leyes.

4. *La promesa de la democracia participativa y protagónica como ejercicio democrático cotidiano, y su incumplimiento*

Si hay una Constitución en el mundo contemporáneo donde se haya utilizado la palabra "participación" y la frase "democracia participativa y protagónica" del pueblo, es sin duda la Constitución de Venezuela, cuya promesa esencial desde el punto de vista de la democracia fue, además de asegurar (a pesar de que el término "representativo" se eliminó del texto y se sustituyó por la expresión "electiva" que no es su equivalente), asegurar una democracia participativa y protagónica.

Lamentablemente dicha promesa ha sido otra de las que han sido totalmente incumplidas, no solo por no haberse asegurado, como se ha dicho, los únicos dos mecanismos de participación ciudadana establecidos directamente en la Constitución,[2160] sino porque en la práctica del gobierno no se ha establecido ningún sistema real y efectivo de democracia participativa, y aún menos "protagónica." En los últi-

---

cisiones/scon/marzo/162349-203-25314-2014-09-0456.HTML   La Ley impugnada fue publicada en *Gaceta Oficial* N° 5.890 Extra. de 31 de julio de 2008.

2159   Véase Allan. Brewer-Carías, "El fin de la llamada "democracia participativa y protagónica" dispuesto por la Sala Constitucional en fraude a la Constitución, al justificar la emisión de legislación inconsulta en violación al derecho a la participación política," en *Revista de Derecho Público*, N° 137 (Primer Trimestre 2014, Editorial Jurídica Venezolana, Caracas 2014, pp. 157-164.

2160   Como se dijo, los mecanismos de participación ciudadana directamente previstos en la Constitución le fueron arrebatados al pueblo, al distorsionarse en la legislación la integración de los Comités de Postulaciones Judiciales, Electorales y del Poder Ciudadano, que quedaron bajo el control político de la mayoría oficialista de la Asamblea Nacional sin que el ciudadano y sus organizaciones pueda participar (Véase Allan R. Brewer-Carías, "La participación ciudadana en la designación de los titulares de los órganos no electos de los Poderes Públicos en Venezuela y sus vicisitudes políticas", en *Revista Iberoamericana de Derecho Público y Administrativo*, Año 5, N° 5-2005, San José, Costa Rica 2005, pp. 76-95; y "Sobre el nombramiento irregular por la Asamblea Nacional de los titulares de los órganos del poder ciudadano en 2007", en *Revista de Derecho Público*, N° 113, Editorial Jurídica Venezolana, Caracas 2008, pp. 85-88.) y al haberse vaciado, por la Sala Constitucional, la norma constitucional que prevé la consulta popular necesaria e indispensable antes de la sanción de las leyes, al haber dispuesto, en fraude a la Constitución, que ello no se aplica a la legislación delegada, dictada mediante decretos leyes, que en definitiva se ha convertido en la forma normal de legislación en el país (Véase Allan R. Brewer-Carías, "Apreciación general sobre los vicios de inconstitucionalidad que afectan los Decretos Leyes Habilitados" en *Ley Habilitante del 13-11-2000 y sus Decretos Leyes*, Academia de Ciencias Políticas y Sociales, Serie Eventos N° 17, Caracas 2002, pp. 63-103; y "El derecho ciudadano a la participación popular y la inconstitucionalidad generalizada de los decretos leyes 2010-2012, por su carácter inconsulto," en *Revista de Derecho Público*, N° 130, (abril-junio 2012), Editorial Jurídica Venezolana, Caracas 2012, pp. 85-88.

mos quince años, la participación del pueblo en política, como en la más típica de las democracias formales, en la práctica y contrario a lo que se prometió, se redujo a la sola participación ciudadana mediante el voto en las elecciones. Los mecanismos de democracia directa que se establecieron en la Constitución, como otra forma de participación mediante el voto, como los referendos, se hicieron de hecho y de derecho de imposible ejercicio, por las condiciones y requisitos legales impuestos para que por iniciativa popular pudieran convocarse como lo exige la Constitución.[2161]

Pero la ausencia de participación política también queda evidenciada con el proceso de centralización del poder que materialmente desdibujó al Estado federal que dejo de ser "descentralizado" como lo exige la Constitución (art. 4), y con el proceso de desmunicipalización que se operó en el país.[2162]

En efecto, la promesa de democracia participativa solo puede ser cumplida cuando un Estado cuando el mismo se configura como un Estado descentralizado. Aparte de en la participación en procesos de elecciones y mediante votación popular, en los Comités de Postulaciones para la elección de altos cargos nacionales, y en la consulta popular de las leyes, no hay otra forma cómo el ciudadano pueda efectivamente pueda participar en la gestión de los asuntos públicos que no sea acercando el poder al ciudadano, y ello no puede hacerse en otra forma que no sea descentralizando políticamente el ejercicio del poder.[2163] Todas las democracias contemporáneas están montadas sobre esquemas de descentralización política,[2164] basados en la creación de instancias de gobierno local, en los municipios y en las demás entidades locales, en las cuales de manera necesaria e ineludiblemente tiene que haber gobiernos electos popularmente mediante sufragio universal y secreto.

Para cumplir la promesa constitucional de la participación política y protagónica del pueblo, debió por tanto reforzarse las instancias regionales y locales de gobierno,

---

2161   Véase Allan R. Brewer-Carías, *La Sala Constitucional versus el Estado democrático de derecho. El secuestro del Poder Electoral y de la Sala Electoral del Tribunal Supremo y la confiscación del derecho a la participación política*, Los Libros de El Nacional, Colección Ares, Caracas 2004; "El secuestro del Poder Electoral y la confiscación del derecho a la participación política mediante el referendo revocatorio presidencial: Venezuela 2000-2004", en *Boletín Mexicano de Derecho Comparado*, Instituto de Investigaciones Jurídicas, Universidad Nacional Autónoma de México, N° 112. México, enero-abril 2005 pp. 11-73.

2162   Véase Allan R. Brewer-Carías, "El inicio de la desmunicipalización en Venezuela: La organización del Poder Popular para eliminar la descentralización, la democracia representativa y la participación a nivel local", en *AIDA, Opera Prima de Derecho Administrativo. Revista de la Asociación Internacional de Derecho Administrativo*, Universidad Nacional Autónoma de México, Facultad de Estudios Superiores de Acatlán, Coordinación de Postgrado, Instituto Internacional de Derecho Administrativo "Agustín Gordillo", Asociación Internacional de Derecho Administrativo, México, 2007, pp. 49 a 67.

2163   Véase por ejemplo, Allan R. Brewer-Carías, "Democracia participativa, descentralización política y régimen municipal", en Miguel Alejandro López Olvera y Luis Gerardo Rodríguez Lozano (Coordinadores), *Tendencias actuales del derecho público en Iberoamérica*, Editorial Porrúa, México 2006, pp. 1-23.

2164   Véase Allan R. Brewer-Carías, "La descentralización del poder en el Estado democrático contemporáneo", en Antonio María Hernández (Director) José Manuel Belisle y Paulina Chiacchiera Castro (Coordinadores), *La descentralización del poder en el Estado Contemporáneo*, Asociación Argentina de derecho constitucional, Instituto Italiano de Cultura de Córdoba, Instituto de derecho constitucional y derecho público provincial y municipal Joaquín V. González, Facultad de Derecho y Ciencias Sociales Universidad nacional de Córdoba, Córdoba Argentina, 2005, pp. 75-89

federalizándose y municipalizándose todos los rincones del país.[2165] Sin embargo, ello no se hizo, y más bien, a la concentración del poder que caracterizó la política del gobierno durante los últimos quince años, se sumó en Venezuela, el proceso de centralización del mismo, desmantelándose progresivamente a Federación y desmunicipalizándose su territorio, paradójicamente mediante la estructurado de un denominado Estado del Poder Popular o Estado Comunal, sobre la base de unos Consejos Comunales establecidos única y exclusivamente para desarrollar el socialismo, por tanto, ausentes totalmente de pluralismo político, comandados por voceros que no son electos sino impuestos por el partido de gobierno a través de supuestas asambleas de ciudadanos (asociaciones de vecinos) que los controla y financia directamente desde uno de los Ministerios del Poder Ejecutivo, sin cuya anuencia ni siquiera pueden obtener reconocimiento legal.[2166] Esa "participación" sin gobiernos locales electos mediante sufragio, que encubre el llamado "Poder Popular" regula no es más que una falacia engañosa.[2167]

Ello, en realidad no ha pasado de ser una falacia de participación,[2168] pues se trata de instituciones usadas para el populismo de Estado, que maneja el Poder Central, para repartir recursos fuera de los canales regulares del Estado y particularmente fuera de los gobiernos locales, vaciando en paralelo a los Municipios de competencias, y que más bien contribuyen al centralismo de Estado al depender totalmente, incluso en su propia existencia, de una decisión del Ejecutivo Nacional. En esos Consejos Comunales, en realidad, el único que "participa" es el partido de gobierno y los derivados de su clientelismo, y si alguna participación se le da a la población local en el proceso de inversión de los recursos repartidos, por supuesto es sólo parcial, solo para los sectores que se identifican con el socialismo como doctrina oficial. De resto, lo que hay es exclusión y marginamiento, y con ello, el olvido total de la promesa constitucional de estructurar como "alternativa" a la democracia representativa, una participación democrática y protagónica del pueblo.

2165   Véase Allan R. Brewer-Carías, "La descentralización política en la Constitución de 1999: Federalismo y Municipalismo (una reforma insuficiente y regresiva" en *Boletín de la Academia de Ciencias Políticas y Sociales*, N° 138, Año LXVIII, Enero-Diciembre 2001, Caracas 2002, pp. 313-359

2166   Véase Allan R. Brewer-Carías, *Ley Orgánica de Consejos Comunales*, Colección Textos Legislativos, N° 46, Editorial Jurídica Venezolana, Caracas 2010.

2167   Véase sobre esto Allan R. Brewer-Carías, "La necesaria revalorización de la democracia representativa ante los peligros del discurso autoritario sobre una supuesta "democracia participativa" sin representación," en *Derecho Electoral de Latinoamérica. Memoria del II Congreso Iberoamericano de Derecho*, Bogotá, 31 agosto-1 septiembre 2011, Consejo Superior de la Judicatura, ISBN 978-958-8331-93-5, Bogotá 2013, pp. 457-482.

2168   Véase Allan R. Brewer-Carías, "La necesaria revalorización de la democracia representativa ante los peligros del discurso autoritario sobre una supuesta "democracia participativa" sin representación," en *Derecho Electoral de Latinoamérica. Memoria del II Congreso Iberoamericano de Derecho*, Bogotá, 31 agosto-1 septiembre 2011, Consejo Superior de la Judicatura, ISBN 978-958-8331-93-5, Bogotá 2013, pp. 425-449. Véase además, el texto de la Ponencia: "La democracia representativa y la falacia de la llamada "democracia participativa," *Congreso Iberoamericano de Derecho Electoral*, Universidad de Nuevo León, Monterrey, 27 de noviembre 2010.

5.   *La promesa de que el gobierno debía ser siempre alternativo y su incumplimiento*

Pero además, otra de las promesas constitucionales incumplidas en cuanto al establecimiento de un Estado democrático, fue el olvido del postulado que como principio pétreo se estableció en el artículo 6 de la Constitución de 1999, del carácter alternativo del gobierno ("El gobierno *es y será siempre...* alternativo..."), en el sentido de que la voluntad popular que lo estableció fue que nunca podría ser alterado.

Con la consagración de este principio como promesa constitucional, se siguió una larga tradición histórica, que se recoge en general en los sistemas presidenciales de gobierno,[2169] y que en Venezuela data desde la Constitución de 1830, con base en la doctrina definida por Simón Bolívar en su Discurso de Angostura cuando expresó que:

> "...La continuación de la autoridad en un mismo individuo frecuentemente ha sido el término de los gobiernos democráticos. Las repetidas elecciones son esenciales en los sistemas populares, porque nada es tan peligroso como dejar permanecer largo tiempo en un mismo ciudadano el poder. El pueblo se acostumbra a obedecerle y él se acostumbra a mandarlo; de donde se origina la usurpación y la tiranía. ... nuestros ciudadanos deben temer con sobrada justicia que el mismo Magistrado, que los ha mandado mucho tiempo, los mande perpetuamente."[2170].

De acuerdo con esta doctrina, el término usado para calificar el gobierno como "alternativo" y expresar el principio de la "alternabilidad" en el ejercicio del poder, siempre ha tenido el significado basado en la idea de que las personas deben turnarse sucesivamente en los cargos o que los cargos deben desempeñarse por turnos (*Diccionario de la Real Academia Española),*[2171] en el sentido de ejercicio sucesivo de un cargo por personas distintas,[2172] con el objeto de -enfrentar las ansias de perpetuación en el poder, es decir, el continuismo, y evitar las ventajas en los procesos electorales de quienes ocupan cargos y a la vez puedan ser candidatos para ocupar los mismos cargos. El principio de "gobierno alternativo," por tanto, no es equivalente al de "gobierno electivo." La elección es una cosa, y la necesidad de que las personas se turnen en los cargos es otra.

Este principio pétreo, impuso siempre como consecuencia, que en todas las Constituciones se hubieran establecido limitaciones para la posibilidad de reelección en cargos electivos, como por ejemplo sucedió en casi todas las Constituciones de

---

2169   Las restricciones a la reelección presidencial son tradicionales en los sistemas presidenciales de gobierno, como son los de América Latina, y no en los sistemas parlamentarios como los que existen en Europa. Véase, Allan R. Brewer-Carías, *Reflexiones sobre la Revolución Norteamericana (1776), la Revolución Francesa (1789) y la Revolución Hispanoamericana (1810-1830) y sus aportes al constitucionalismo moderno,* Universidad Externado de Colombia, Bogotá 2008, pp. 106 ff.

2170   Véase en Simón Bolívar, *Escritos Fundamentales,* Caracas, 1982.

2171   Véase el Voto Salvado a la sentencia n° 53, de la Sala Constitucional de 2 de febrero de 2009 (Caso: *Interpretación de los artículos 340,6 y 345 de la Constitución),* en http://www.tsj.gov.ve/decisions/scon/Febrero/53-3209-2009-08-1610.html

2172   Véase la sentencia de la Sala Electoral del Tribunal Supremo de Justicia N° 51 de 18 de marzo de 2002

Venezuela entre 1830 y 1947,[2173] respecto de la reelección del Presidente de la República para el período constitucional inmediato, que solo fue relajado en las Constituciones de los gobiernos autoritarios.[2174] En la Constitución de 1961 la prohibición se extendió a los dos períodos siguientes (10 años); y en contraste con toda la tradición, en la Constitución de 1999, en cambo se permitió la posibilidad de reelección presidencial de inmediato y por una sola vez, para un nuevo período. Esa fue la promesa constitucional plasmada por voluntad popular: un gobierno alternativo con la posibilidad única de reelección presidencial solo por un nuevo período.

La promesa constitucional, sin embargo, fue rota por el Presidente de la República en 2007, al formular una propuesta de reforma constitucional que incluía la eliminación de la alternabilidad democrática del gobierno, para en cambio permitir la reelección indefinida, la cual sin embargo fue rechazada por el pueblo en referendo de diciembre de 2007, reafirmando la promesa constitucional de la alternabilidad.

Pero no pasó sino algo más de un año, para que la Sala Constitucional del Tribunal Supremo, como "supremo interprete de la Constitución," la "interpretara" precisamente para acabar con la promesa popular de siempre tener gobiernos alternativos, para lo cual en sentencia N° 53 de 3 de febrero de 2009, distorsionó las previsiones constitucionales llegando a afirmar que el principio de la alternabilidad "lo que exige es que el pueblo como titular de la soberanía tenga la posibilidad periódica de escoger sus mandatarios o representantes", confundiendo deliberada y maliciosamente "gobierno alternativo" con "gobierno electivo." De allí la falsedad de la conclusión de la Sala Constitucional al afirmar que "sólo se infringiría el mismo si se impide esta posibilidad al evitar o no realizar las elecciones."[2175] La sentencia, simplemente mutó ilegítimamente el texto de la Constitución, y al contrario de lo que preveía su artículo 6 sobre alternabilidad republicana, despejó el camino "constitucional" para justificar la posibilidad de reelección inmediata e indefinida de los gobernantes, eliminando el carácter pétreo de la disposición, y por tanto permitiendo que el régimen pudiera someter a referendo una "Enmienda Constitucional" en la materia, cuando el cambio de un principio pétreo solo podía realizarse mediante la convocatoria a una Asamblea Nacional Constituyente.

Y así, todo fue "preparado" por el Juez Constitucional para que la Asamblea Nacional, a pesar del rechazo de la reforma constitucional de diciembre de 2007, propusiera efectuar un referendo aprobatorio de una Enmienda Constitucional, el cual fue convocado para el 15 de febrero de 2009 a los efectos de votar por la aprobación de la eliminación del principio de la alternabilidad republicana, no sólo respecto de la elección presidencial, sino ahora respecto de todos los cargos electivos, enmendándose así los artículos 160, 162, 174, 192 y 230 de la Constitución, estable-

---

2173   Véase el texto de todas las Constituciones en Allan R. Brewer-Carías, *Las Constituciones de Venezuela*, 2 vols., Academia de Ciencias Políticas y Sociales, Caracas 2008.

2174   Así se reguló en la efímera Constitución de 1857; en las Constituciones de Juan Vicente Gómez de 1914, 1922, 1925, 1928, 1929 y 1931, y en la Constitución de Marcos Pérez Jiménez de 1953.

2175   Véase Allan R. Brewer-Carías, "El Juez Constitucional vs. La alternabilidad republicana (La reelección continua e indefinida), en *Revista de Derecho Público*, N° 117, (enero-marzo 2009), Caracas 2009, pp. 205-211.

ciéndose en cambio el principio de la reelección continua de cargos electivos, incumpliéndose totalmente la promesa constitucional de la alternabilidad republicana.

IV. EL INCUMPLIMIENTO DE LA PROMESA CONSTITUCIONAL DEL ESTABLECIMIENTO DE UN ESTADO DEMOCRÁTICO DE DERECHO Y DE JUSTICIA

En la Constitución de 1999, en lo que se refiere a la configuración del Estado, la principal promesa que se formula en ella, es por el establecimiento de un Estado democrático y social de derecho y de justicia "que propugna como valores superiores de su ordenamiento jurídico y de su actuación, la vida, la libertad, la justicia, la igualdad, la solidaridad, la democracia, la responsabilidad social y, en general, la preeminencia de los derechos humanos, la ética y el pluralismo político" (art. 2).

Dicha promesa, sin embargo, en los últimos quince años, en particular la relativa al establecimiento y consolidación de un Estado de derecho y de Justicia, ha sido otra de las promesas constitucionales que ha sido totalmente incumplida en Venezuela, habiéndose consolidado más bien en su lugar, por la práctica del ejercicio del poder hasta 2015, un Estado Totalitario en el cual ninguno de los elementos esenciales y de los componentes de la democracia se ha asegurado.

Para que pueda decirse que existe un Estado democrático, solo utilizando los parámetros contenidos en la *Carta Democrática Interamericana* de 2001, debería concurrir, al menos los siguientes *elementos esenciales:* 1) respeto a los derechos humanos y las libertades fundamentales; 2) acceso al poder y su ejercicio con sujeción al Estado de derecho; 3) celebración de elecciones periódicas, libres, justas y basadas en el sufragio universal y secreto, como expresión de la soberanía del pueblo; 4) un régimen plural de partidos y organizaciones políticas y 5) separación e independencia de los poderes públicos (art. 3); y adicionalmente los siguientes *componentes fundamentales:* 1) transparencia de las actividades gubernamentales; 2) probidad y la responsabilidad de los gobiernos en la gestión pública; 3) respeto de los derechos sociales; 4) respeto de la libertad de expresión y de prensa; 5) subordinación constitucional de todas las instituciones del Estado a la autoridad civil legalmente constituida y 6) respeto al Estado de derecho de todas las entidades y sectores de la sociedad (art. 4).

Excepto la realización de elecciones periódicas, durante los pasados quince años, ninguno de esos elementos esenciales y componentes fundamentales de la democracia se han encontrado garantizados en Venezuela, por haberse desarrollado un régimen totalitario caracterizado por la ausencia total de controles respecto del ejercicio del poder. Ello en particular, derivó del incumplimiento de la promesa de establecer un sistema de gobierno basado en el principio de la separación de poderes, en particular, de una Justicia autónoma e independiente que es la única que puede garantizar que el Estado de derecho sea además un Estado de justicia; y además, asegurar el necesario equilibrio que debe haber entre los poderes y prerrogativas de la Administración del Estado y los derechos ciudadanos.[2176]

2176   Véase sobre el tema Gustavo Tarre Briceño, *Solo el poder detiene al poder, La teoría de la separación de los poderes y su aplicación en Venezuela,* Colección Estudios Jurídicos Nº 102, Editorial

La importancia de ese principio es de tal naturaleza para el Estado de derecho que solo controlando al Poder mediante su separación, es que puede haber democracia, es decir, verdaderas elecciones libres, justas y confiables; pluralismo político; acceso al poder conforme a la Constitución; efectiva participación en la gestión de los asuntos públicos; transparencia administrativa en el ejercicio del gobierno; rendición de cuentas por parte de los gobernantes; sumisión efectiva del gobierno a la Constitución y las leyes, así como de los militares al gobierno civil; efectivo acceso a la justicia; y real y efectiva garantía de respeto a los derechos humanos, incluyendo la libertad de expresión y los derechos sociales. [2177]

En cambio, por el abandono de la separación de poderes nada de ello se ha podido asegurar en Venezuela, por haberse concentrado la totalidad del Poder, que durante quince años fueron manejados por el binomio establecido entre Poder Legislativo y Poder Ejecutivo, situación que sólo ha comenzado a cambiar en enero de 2016 con la elección de una Asamblea nacional controlada por la oposición.

1. *La ausencia de separación de poderes*

La promesa establecida en la Constitución está basada en la existencia no de tres poderes del Estado separados e independientes, sino de cinco poderes públicos que además de los poderes Legislativo, Ejecutivo, Judicial comprenden a los Poderes, Ciudadano y Electoral. Como se ha dicho, los dos primeros, tienen su origen en elecciones populares directas de sus titulares (Presidente de la República diputados a la Asamblea Nacional), correspondiendo a la Asamblea Nacional como Cuerpo Elector de segundo grado, elegir en forma indirecta y con mayoría calificada con participación popular, a los titulares de los otros poderes. El incumplimiento de este rol de Cuerpo Electoral por parte de la Asamblea, al haber "designado" como común cuerpo legislativo por simple mayoría a los titulares de los mismos fue el germen para incumplir la promesa constitucional y establecer un sistema de concentración del poder por obra de la Asamblea Nacional, en manos del Poder Ejecutivo, que la controló hasta 2015. Con ello, progresivamente, durante los pasados quince años, los otros Poderes Públicos, y particularmente el Poder Judicial, el Poder Ciudadano y el Poder Electoral quedaron sometidos a la voluntad del Ejecutivo.[2178]

Esta dependencia de todos los órganos de los poderes del Estado respecto del Ejecutivo y del Legislativo, y en especial en lo que se refiere a los órganos de control, ha sido lo que ha originado hasta el presente la abstención total de los mismos de ejercer las potestades que le son atribuidas, y con ello, la práctica política de con-

Jurídica Venezolana, Caracas 2014; y Jesús María Alvarado Andrade, "División del Poder y Principio de Subsidiariedad. El Ideal Político del Estado de Derecho como base para la Libertad y prosperidad material" en Luis Alfonso herrera Orellana (Coord.), *Enfoques Actuales sobre Derecho y Libertad en Venezuela*, Academia de Ciencias Políticas y Sociales, Caracas, 2013, pp. 131-185.

2177   Véase Allan R. Brewer-Carías, "Prólogo" al libro de Gustavo Tarre Briceño, *Solo el poder detiene al poder, La teoría de la separación de los poderes y su aplicación en Venezuela*, Colección Estudios Jurídicos Nº 102, Editorial Jurídica Venezolana, Caracas 2014, pp. 13-49.

2178   Véase Allan R. Brewer-Carías, El sistema presidencial de gobierno en la Constitución de Venezuela de 1999 (Bogotá, junio 2005), *Estudios sobre el Estado Constitucional (2005-2006)*, Cuadernos de la Cátedra Fundacional Allan R. Brewer Carías de Derecho Público, Universidad Católica del Táchira, Nº 9, Editorial Jurídica Venezolana, Caracas, 2007, pp. 475-624.

centración total del poder en manos del Ejecutivo, dado el control político partidista que ejercía sobre la Asamblea Nacional, y por con ello, la configuración de un modelo político autoritario. Con ello, la designación de los titulares de dichas instituciones de control quedó a la merced de la Asamblea Nacional, por la violación sistemática a la cuan antes nos referimos, de la previsión garantizadora del derecho a la participación política en la designación de los mismos, mediante unos Comités de postulaciones que debían estar integrados exclusivamente por representantes de los diversos sectores de la sociedad. Desde 2000 hasta 2015, dichos Comités, se conformaron como simples "comisiones parlamentarias ampliadas" controladas completamente por el partido de gobierno mientras controló la Asamblea.[2179]

En ese contexto, entonces, a pesar de que hay un Poder Ciudadano supuestamente autónomo e independiente, dentro del mismo, la Contraloría General de la República en Venezuela dejó de ejercer control fiscal alguno de la Administración Pública, y ello a pesar de la inflación de las prácticas de corrupción que han impedido que en el país siquiera se pueda obtener el más simple de los servicios administrativos sin pago ilegítimo previo, lo que ha ubicado al país en el primer lugar del índice de corrupción en el mundo, según las cifras difundidas por Transparencia Internacional.[2180]

Por su parte, el Defensor del Pueblo, desde cuando la primera persona designada para ocupar el cargo en 2000 fue removida por haber ejercido un recurso judicial contra la Ley especial que discutía la Asamblea Nacional para la "designación" de los titulares del poder público, precisamente en defensa del derecho colectivo a la participación en la designación de los mismos que estimó se violaba con la misma,[2181] dicho órgano perdió completamente la orientación, y sin brújula alguna, abandonando toda idea de defensa de derechos humanos, se convirtió en un órgano oficial para avalar la violación de los mismos por parte de las autoridades del Estado.[2182]

2179   Véase Allan R. Brewer-Carías, "La participación ciudadana en la designación de los titulares de los órganos no electos de los Poderes Públicos en Venezuela y sus vicisitudes políticas", en *Revista Iberoamericana de Derecho Público y Administrativo*, Año 5, N° 5-2005, San José, Costa Rica 2005, pp. 76-95.

2180   Véase el Informe de la ONG alemana, Transparencia Internacional de 2013, en el reportaje: "Aseguran que Venezuela es el país más corrupto de Latinoamérica,", en El Universal, Caracas 3 de diciembre de 2013, en http://www.eluniversal.com/nacional-y-politica/131203/aseguran-que-venezuela-es-el-pais-mas-corrupto-de-latinoamerica. Igualmente véase el reportaje en BBC Mundo, "Transparencia Internacional: Venezuela y Haití, los que se ven más corruptos de A. Latina," 3 de diciembre de 2013, en   http://www.bbc.co.uk/mundo/ultimas_noticias/2013/12/131203_ultnot_transparencia_corrupcion_lp.shtml. Véase al respecto, Román José Duque Corredor, "Corrupción y democracia en América Latina. Casos emblemáticos de corrupción en Venezuela," en *Revista Electrónica de Derecho Administrativo*, Universidad Monteávila, 2014.

2181   Véase los comentarios en Allan R. Brewer-Carías, "La participación ciudadana en la designación de los titulares de los órganos no electos de los Poderes Públicos en Venezuela y sus vicisitudes políticas", en *Revista Iberoamericana de Derecho Público y Administrativo*, Año 5, N° 5-2005, San José, Costa Rica 2005, pp. 76-95.

2182   Por ejemplo, ante la crisis de la salud denunciada por la Academia Nacional de Medicina en agosto de 2014, reclamando la declaratoria de emergencia del sector, la respuesta de la Defensora del Pueblo fue simplemente que en Venezuela no había tal crisis. Véase el reportaje: "Defensora del Pueblo Gabriela Ramírez afirma que en Venezuela no existe ninguna crisis en el sector salud," en *Noticias Ve-*

Y la Fiscalía General de la República, el otro órgano del Poder Ciudadano que ejerce el Ministerio Público, en lugar de haber sido la parte de buena fe del proceso penal y de la vindicta pública, se lo convirtió en el principal instrumento para la prevalencia de la impunidad en el país, y para asegurar la persecución política y la extorsión gubernamental. Como se destacó en el Informe de la Comisión Internacional de Juristas sobre *Fortalecimiento del Estado de Derecho en Venezuela*, publicado en Ginebra en marzo de 2014, "El incumplimiento con la propia normativa interna ha configurado un Ministerio Público sin garantías de independencia e imparcialidad de los demás poderes públicos y de los actores políticos, con el agravante de que los fiscales en casi su totalidad son de libre nombramiento y remoción, y por tanto vulnerables a presiones externas y sujetos órdenes superiores."[2183]

Por su lado, el Consejo Nacional Electoral, configurado en la Constitución como el quinto de los Poderes Públicos, como se ha dicho, al haber sido integrado por militantes del partido de gobierno en violación de la Constitución, en lugar de haber sido el árbitro independiente en las elecciones, desde cuándo comenzó a ser secuestrado por el Poder Ejecutivo a partir de 2004,[2184] utilizando para ello como instrumento del plagio a la Sala Constitucional, ignorándose la norma constitucional que exige que esté integrado por personas no vinculadas a organizaciones políticas; ha actuado más bien como su agente político electoral oficial, minando la credibilidad en la posibilidad efectiva de la realización de elecciones libres; lo que solo pudo vencerse al producirse materialmente una rebelión popular de rechazo al régimen mediante el voto, como sucedió el 6 de diciembre de 2015, con resultados tan abrumadores que ninguna posibilidad efectiva de fraude pudo materializarse.

2.   *La ausencia de autonomía e independencia del Poder Judicial*

Pero es la ausencia de autonomía e independencia del Poder Judicial, lo que en cualquier sistema de gobierno y Estado, quiebra el principio de separación de poderes. Si el Poder Judicial está controlado por el Ejecutivo o el Legislativo, por más separados que incluso éstos puedan estar, no existe el principio de la separación de poderes, y en consecuencia, no se puede hablar de Estado de derecho.

---

nezuela, 20 agosto de 2014, en http://noticiasvene-zuela.info/2014/08/defensora-del-pueblo-gabriela-ramirez-afirma-que-en-venezuela-no-existe-ninguna-crisis-en-el-sector-salud/; y el reportaje: "Gabriela Ramírez, Defensora del Pueblo: Es desproporcionada petición de emergencia humanitaria en el sector salud," en *El Universal*, Caracas 20 de agosto de 2014, en http://m.eluniversal.com/nacional-y-politica/140820/es-desproporcionada-peticion-de-emergencia-humanitaria-en-el-sector-sa. Por ello, con razón, el Editorial del diario *El Nacional* del 22 de agosto de 2014, se tituló: "A quien defiende la defensora?" Véase en http://www.el-nacional.com/opinion/editorial/defiende-defensora_19_46874-3123.html.

2183   Véase en http://icj.wpengine.netdna-cdn.com/wp-content/uploads/2014/06/VENEZUELA-Informe-A4-elec.pdf

2184   Véase Allan R. Brewer–Carías, "El secuestro del Poder Electoral y la confiscación del derecho a la participación política mediante el referendo revocatorio presidencial: Venezuela 2000–2004,", en *Boletín Mexicano de Derecho Comparado*, Instituto de Investigaciones Jurídicas, Universidad Nacional Autónoma de México, Nº 112. México, enero–abril 2005 pp. 11–73; *La Sala Constitucional versus el Estado Democrático de Derecho. El secuestro del poder electoral y de la Sala Electoral del Tribunal Supremo y la confiscación del derecho a la participación política*, Los Libros de El Nacional, Colección Ares, Caracas, 2004, 172 pp.

Y esa es la situación en Venezuela. En la Constitución de 1999, una de las promesas constitucionales de mayor relevancia para asegurar el Estado de derecho y la vigencia de la separación de poderes que contiene, fue no sólo la declaración del principio de la independencia y autonomía del Poder Judicial (art. 254), sino la previsión de precisos y adecuados mecanismos para lograrlo: primero, con el aseguramiento de la elección de los magistrados del Tribunal supremo, en segundo grado, por la Asamblea nacional, actuando como Cuerpo Elector con el voto de una mayoría calificada de sus miembros (para asegurar la mayor representatividad democrática de la elección), y sólo mediante la postulación de candidatos por parte de un Comité de Postulaciones Judiciales integrado solo por representantes de los diversos sectores de la sociedad (para lograr la mayor participación ciudadana); segundo, previendo el ingreso de todos los jueces a la carrera judicial mediante la realización de concursos públicos de oposición que aseguren la idoneidad y excelencia de los participantes, debiendo además garantizarse la participación ciudadana en el procedimiento de selección y designación de los jueces (art. 255); y tercero, disponiendo la permanencia y estabilidad de los jueces en sus cargos, al imponer que los mismos sólo pueden ser removidos o suspendidos de sus cargos mediante juicios disciplinarios, llevados a cabo por jueces disciplinarios mediante un proceso disciplinario judicial con las debidas garantías (art. 255).

Una promesa constitucional mejor que esta es imposible conseguir en constitución alguna. Sin embargo, la misma, en Venezuela, durante los pasados quince años no se ha cumplido, siendo ello uno de los más graves atentados al Estado de derecho, con el resultado de un Poder Judicial, que en su conjunto, quedó sometido a los designios y control político por parte del Poder Ejecutivo;[2185] habiendo comenzado ese proceso desde la inconstitucional intervención del Poder Judicial por parte de la Asamblea Nacional Constituyente en 1999. Con ello, desde que la propia promesa se formuló en la Constitución, en paralelo comenzó a ser incumplida. Primero, con la destitución masiva de Magistrados y jueces sin garantías judiciales;[2186] y segundo, con el apoderamiento por parte del partido de gobierno, desde 2000, a través de la Asamblea Nacional, del proceso de designación de los Magistrados del Tribunal Supremo, sacrificándose la previsión que exigía la participación en ello de represen-

---

2185   Véase Allan R. Brewer–Carías, "La progresiva y sistemática demolición de la autonomía en independencia del Poder Judicial en Venezuela (1999–2004)", en *XXX Jornadas J.M Domínguez Escovar, Estado de derecho, Administración de justicia y derechos humanos,* Instituto de Estudios Jurídicos del Estado Lara, Barquisimeto, 2005, pp. 33–174; y "La justicia sometida al poder [La ausencia de independencia y autonomía de los jueces en Venezuela por la interminable emergencia del Poder Judicial (1999–2006)]" en *Cuestiones Internacionales. Anuario Jurídico Villanueva 2007,* Centro Universitario Villanueva, Marcial Pons, Madrid, 2007, pp. 25–57; "La demolición de las instituciones judiciales y la destrucción de la democracia: La experiencia venezolana," en *Instituciones Judiciales y Democracia. Reflexiones con ocasión del Bicentenario de la Independencia y del Centenario del Acto Legislativo 3 de 1910,* Consejo de Estado, Sala de Consulta y Servicio Civil, Bogotá 2012, pp. 230-254.

2186   Véase nuestro voto salvado a la intervención del Poder Judicial por la Asamblea Nacional Constituyente en Allan R. Brewer–Carías, *Debate Constituyente, (Aportes a la Asamblea Nacional Constituyente),* Tomo I, (8 agosto–8 septiembre), Caracas 1999; y las críticas formuladas a ese proceso en Allan R. Brewer–Carías, *Golpe de Estado y proceso constituyente en Venezuela,* Universidad Nacional Autónoma de México, México, 2002.

tantes de la sociedad civil. Ello se consolidó en 2004, con el aumento del número de Magistrados del Tribunal Supremo en la Ley Orgánica del Tribunal Supremo de Justicia, los cuales además quedaron con posibilidad de ser removidos por simple mayoría de votos de los diputados en la Asamblea Nacional, que entonces alcanzaba la bancada oficialista;[2187] y en 2010, con la irregular "reforma" de la Ley Orgánica del Tribunal Supremo de Justicia mediante la "re-publicación" de la Ley,[2188] para impedir que en la designación pudieran participar con su voto los diputados de oposición, llenándose el Tribunal Supremo de jueces incluso con militancia abierta del partido de gobernó,[2189] lo que se consolidó luego en diciembre de 2015. Y mediante el control y asalto al Tribunal Supremo de Justicia, que es el órgano que en Venezuela tiene a su cargo todo el gobierno y administración del sistema de Justicia, la totalidad del Poder Judicial quedó controlado políticamente.

En cuanto a los jueces, durante los tres lustros de vigencia del texto fundamental, nunca se desarrollaron los concursos púbicos con participación ciudadana para asegurar su ingreso de manera de garantizar su autonomía, habiendo sido llenado el poder Judicial con jueces provisorios o temporales,[2190] dependientes del Poder y sin garantía alguna de estabilidad; y por lo que respecta a la promesa de garantizar su estabilidad, la jurisdicción disciplinaria (art. 255), nunca llegó a ser implementada. A partir de 1999,[2191] más bien se regularizó una ilegítima transitoriedad constitucional, la existencia de una Comisión de Funcionamiento del Poder Judicial creada ad hoc para "depurar" el poder judicial, removiéndolos sin garantías judiciales;[2192] y si bien en 2011 se crearon unos tribunales de la llamada "Jurisdicción Disciplinaria

---

2187   Véase en *Gaceta Oficial* N° 37942 de 20 de mayo de 2004. Sobre dicha Ley y las reformas introducidas véase, Véase Allan R. Brewer-Carias *Ley Orgánica del Tribunal Supremo de Justicia*, Caracas 2010.

2188   Véase en *Gaceta Oficial* N° 39483 de 9-8-2010. Véase Allan R. Brewer-Carías y Víctor Hernández Mendible, *Ley Orgánica del Tribunal Supremo de Justicia*, Caracas 2010. Sobre la reforma efectuada mediante la re-publicación de la Ley Orgánica, véase Víctor Hernández Mendible, "Sobre la nueva reimpresión por "supuestos errores" materiales de la Ley Orgánica del Tribunal Supremo, octubre de 2010," y Antonio Silva Aranguren, "Tras el rastro del engaño en la web de la Asamblea Nacional," en *Revista de Derecho Público*, N° 124, Editorial Jurídica Venezolana, Caracas 2010, pp. 110-114.

2189   Véase los comentarios de Hildegard Rondón de Sansó, "*Obiter Dicta*. En torno a una elección," en *La Voce d'Italia*, Caracas 14-12-2010.

2190   En el *Informe Especial* de la Comisión sobre Venezuela correspondiente al año 2003, la misma también expresó, que "un aspecto vinculado a la autonomía e independencia del Poder Judicial es el relativo al carácter provisorio de los jueces en el sistema judicial de Venezuela. Actualmente, la información proporcionada por las distintas fuentes indica que más del 80% de los jueces venezolanos son "provisionales". *Informe sobre la Situación de los Derechos Humanos en Venezuela 2003*, cit. párr. 161.

2191   Véase nuestro voto salvado a la intervención del Poder Judicial por la Asamblea Nacional Constituyente en Allan R. Brewer–Carías, *Debate Constituyente, (Aportes a la Asamblea Nacional Constituyente), Tomo I, (8 agosto–8 septiembre), Caracas 1999; y las críticas formuladas a ese proceso en Allan R. Brewer–Carías, *Golpe de Estado y proceso constituyente en Venezuela*, Universidad Nacional Autónoma de México, México, 2002.

2192   Véase Allan R. Brewer–Carías, "La justicia sometida al poder y la interminable emergencia del poder judicial (1999–2006)", en *Derecho y democracia. Cuadernos Universitarios*, Órgano de Divulgación Académica, Vicerrectorado Académico, Universidad Metropolitana, Año II, N° 11, Caracas, septiembre 2007, pp. 122–138.

Judicial," la misma quedó sujeta a la Asamblea Nacional, que como órgano político, es la que designó a los "jueces disciplinarios."[2193] Solo fue, luego de que el gobierno perdió la mayoría en la Asamblea Nacional, que la saliente Asamblea en unas ilegítimas sesiones extraordinarias celebradas en diciembre de 2015, reformó la Ley del Código de Ética del Juez, pero para quitarle a la nueva Asamblea la competencia para nombrar dichos jueces (que por supuesto nunca debió tener), y pasarlos al Tribunal Supremo,[2194] y así ahora a través de éste, seguir ejerciéndose el control político en la materia.

La consecuencia de todo este proceso de quince años es que Venezuela carece completamente de un Poder Judicial autónomo e independiente, estando, el que existe, completamente al servicio del gobierno del Estado y de su política autoritaria, como lo han incluso declarado expresamente sus Magistrados.[2195] El resultado es que, como lo destacó la Comisión Internacional de Juristas, en un *Informe* de marzo de 2014, que resume todo lo que en el país se ha venido denunciando en la materia, al dar "cuenta de la falta de independencia de la justicia en Venezuela," se destaca que "el Poder Judicial ha sido integrado desde el Tribunal Supremo de Justicia (TSJ) con criterios predominantemente políticos en su designación. La mayoría de los jueces son "provisionales" y vulnerables a presiones políticas externas, ya que son de libre nombramiento y de remoción discrecional por una Comisión Judicial del propio Tribunal Supremo, la cual, a su vez, tiene una marcada tendencia partidista;" concluyendo sin ambages afirmando que:

> "Un sistema de justicia que carece de independencia, como lo es el venezolano, es comprobadamente ineficiente para cumplir con sus funciones propias. En este sentido en Venezuela, un país con una de las más altas tasas de homicidio en Latinoamérica y en el de familiares sin justicia, esta cifra es cercana al 98% en los casos de violaciones a los derechos humanos. Al mismo tiempo, el poder judicial, precisamente por estar sujeto a presiones externas, no cumple su función de proteger a las personas frente a los abusos del poder sino que por el contrario, en no pocos casos es utilizado como mecanismo de persecución contra opositores y disidentes o simples críticos del proceso político, incluidos diri-

---

2193   Ley del Código de Ética del Juez Venezolano en *Gaceta Oficial* N° 39.493, de 23 de agosto de 2010. Véase Allan R. Brewer-Carías, "Sobre la ausencia de independencia y autonomía judicial en Venezuela, a los doce años de vigencia de la constitución de 1999 (O sobre la interminable transitoriedad que en fraude continuado a la voluntad popular y a las normas de la Constitución, ha impedido la vigencia de la garantía de la estabilidad de los jueces y el funcionamiento efectivo de una "jurisdicción disciplinaria judicial"), en *Independencia Judicial*, Colección Estado de Derecho, Tomo I, Academia de Ciencias Políticas y Sociales, Acceso a la Justicia org., Fundación de Estudios de Derecho Administrativo (Funeda), Universidad Metropolitana (Unimet), Caracas 2012, pp. 9-103.

2194   Véase en *Gaceta Oficial* N° 6204 Extra de 30 de diciembre de 2015.

2195   Véase por ejemplo lo expresado por el magistrado Francisco Carrasqueño, en la apertura del año judicial en enero de 2008, al explicar que : "no es cierto que el ejercicio del poder político se limite al Legislativo, sino que tiene su continuación en los tribunales, en la misma medida que el Ejecutivo", dejando claro que la "aplicación del Derecho no es neutra y menos aun la actividad de los magistrados, porque según se dice en la doctrina, deben ser reflejo de la política, sin vulnerar la independencia de la actividad judicial". *V.* en *El Universal*, Caracas, 29–01–2008.

gentes de partidos, defensores de derechos humanos, dirigentes campesinos y sindicales, y estudiantes."[2196]

Con todo esto, no sólo la promesa constitucional de la separación de poderes y sobre todo de la autonomía e independencia del Poder Judicial, quedó incumplida, habiendo el Poder Judicial abandonado su función fundamental de servir de instrumento de control y de balance respecto de las actividades de los otros órganos del Estado para asegurar su sometimiento a la Constitución y a la ley; sino que, además, materialmente desapareció el derecho ciudadano a la tutela judicial efectiva y a controlar el poder, produciéndose una desjusticiabilidad del Estado, al disiparse la posibilidad de que el Poder Judicial pueda ser utilizado para enjuiciar la conducta de la Administración y frente a ella, garantizar los derechos ciudadanos.

V.   EL INCUMPLIMIENTO DE LA PROMESA CONSTITUCIONAL DEL ESTABLECIMIENTO DE UN ESTADO FEDERAL DESCENTRALIZADO

Otra de las promesas constitucionales fundamentales incorporada en la Constitución de 1999, fue la de consolidad un "Estado federal descentralizado," regido por los principios de integridad territorial, cooperación, solidaridad, concurrencia y corresponsabilidad (art. 7), respondiendo así, no sólo a una tradición histórica pues la Federación como forma de Estado se adoptó en el constitucionalismo venezolano desde 1811, sino a las exigencias de la democracia que imponían la necesidad de descentralizar el poder, al punto de que la propia Constitución al referirse a la descentralización como política de Estado (arts. 16, 84, 166, 184, 185, 269, 272, 285, 300), la definió con el propósito de "profundizar la democracia, acercando el poder a la población y creando las mejores condiciones, tanto para el ejercicio de la democracia como para la prestación eficaz y eficiente de los cometidos estatales" (art. 158).

1.   Los intentos de desmantelar al Estado federal

Todo ello, sin embargo, fue deliberadamente olvidado e incumplida la promesa constitucional, desarrollándose en su lugar en los últimos tres lustros, una política para centralizar completamente el Estado, eliminándose todo vestigio de descentralización como organización y política pública, de autonomía territorial y de democracia representativa a nivel local, particularmente en el municipio como la unidad política primaria en el territorio del cual habla la Constitución (art. 168).

Ello, incluso se pretendió formalizar en 2007 con la rechazada reforma constitucional que se propuso ese año,[2197] y que fue rechazada por el pueblo, tendiente a eliminar toda posibilidad de autonomías territoriales, creando en cambio instancias

2196   Véase en http://icj.wpengine.netdna-cdn.com/wp-content/uploads/2014/06/VENEZUELA-Informe-A4-elec.pdf.

2197   Véase Allan R. Brewer-Carías, *La reforma constitucional de 2007 (Comentarios al proyecto inconstitucionalmente sancionado por la Asamblea Nacional el 2 de noviembre de 2007)*, Colección Textos Legislativos, Nº 43, Editorial Jurídica Venezolana, Caracas 2007; y *Hacia la consolidación de un Estado socialista, centralizado, policial y militarista. Comentarios sobre el sentido y alcance de las propuestas de reforma constitucional 2007*, Colección Textos Legislativos, Nº 42, Editorial Jurídica Venezolana, Caracas 2007.

territoriales solo sometidas al poder central, mediante las cuales un Poder Popular supuestamente iba a desarrollar "formas de agregación comunitaria política territorial" que constituían formas de "autogobierno," pero sin democracia representativa alguna, sino sólo como supuesta "expresión de democracia directa" (art. 16). Con ello se buscaba, como lo dijo el Presidente de la República en 2007, "el desarrollo de lo que nosotros entendemos por descentralización, porque el concepto cuartorepublicano de descentralización es muy distinto al concepto que nosotros debemos manejar. Por eso, incluimos aquí la participación protagónica, la transferencia del poder y crear las mejores condiciones para la construcción de la democracia socialista,"[2198] pero a entidades sin autonomía política controladas por el poder central.

Acompañando a aquella propuesta de reforma constitucional, se buscaba además, alterar la distribución de competencias públicas prevista en la Constitución entre los tres niveles territoriales de gobierno (nacional, estadal y municipal), de manera de centralizar materialmente todas las competencias del Poder Público en el nivel nacional (arts. 156, 164), vaciándose de competencias a los Estados y obligándose a los Municipios a transferir sus competencias a unos Consejos Comunales integrados por "voceros" no electos y sin representatividad democrática, con lo que en definitiva se buscaba que aquellos quedasen como entelequias vacías.

Entre las reformas propuestas para abandonar definitivamente la promesa constitucional de la descentralización política, estuvo además la propuesta de recread el Distrito Federal sin representación democrática y de establecer otras instancias no descentralizadas de "provincias federales, regiones estratégicas de defensa, territorios federales, municipios federales, ciudades federales y comunales, distritos funcionales, regiones marítimas y distritos insulares" (Artículo 156,11), eliminando a los Estados y Municipios como "entidades políticas" perdiendo efectiva autonomía, haciéndolos pasar a depender totalmente del Poder Nacional, como simples órganos u administraciones periféricas del Poder Central sometidas a la ordenación y gestión que establezca el Poder Nacional.

En cuanto a la forma federal del Estado, con aquella reforma desaparecía totalmente incluso al eliminar la tradicional competencia residual de los Estados (art. 164,11) –que existe en todas las federaciones del mundo-, invirtiéndola a favor del Poder Central.

En cuanto a los municipios, se buscaba eliminar totalmente su autonomía, e incluso su carácter de unidad política primaria que prometió la Constitución, y en su lugar establecer a la ciudad, a las comunas, y a las comunidades, como "el núcleo territorial básico e indivisible del Estado Socialista Venezolano."

Si bien todas estas reformas constitucionales fueron rechazadas por el pueblo, lo cierto es que implementadas a partir de 2008 por supuesto inconstitucionalmente mediante reformas legales, que materializaron el incumplimiento del compromiso constitucional que estaba a la base de la Constitución de 1999.

2198   Véase *Discurso del Presidente Chávez de Presentación del Anteproyecto de Constitución ante la Asamblea Nacional*, Caracas 2007.

2. *Las propuestas de creación del Estado Comunal o del Poder Popular sin representatividad democrática para ahogar al Estado federal*

La primera medida en tal sentido, fue la reversión de la reforma que se hizo en 1999 en aras de la descentralización que había eliminado el antiguo Distrito Federal, estableciendo en su lugar el Distrito Capital y un régimen de gobierno municipal a dos niveles en la ciudad de Caracas, como entidades políticas con gobiernos democráticos, mediante una Ley de Creación del Distrito Capital que simplemente eliminó el carácter de entidad local autónoma que tiene conforme a la Constitución,[2199] con autoridades de "gobierno" totalmente dependientes del Poder Ejecutivo, reviviéndose precisamente al viejo Distrito Federal, aun cuando con otro nombre.

Adicionalmente, como segunda medida, se reformó la Ley Orgánica del Poder Público Municipal de 2010, para olvidar el carácter del Municipio como la "unidad política primaria de la organización nacional," sustituyéndoselo por comunas; eliminándose de paso en carácter representativo de las "parroquias" que como entidades locales están en la Constitución (art. 178).

La tercera medida, para abandonar la promesa constitucional por reforzar el Estado federal descentralizado fue minar las bases del Estado constitucional, montado sobre la idea de gobiernos democrático representativos con legitimidad electoral, estableciéndose mediante Ley para que supuestamente "el pueblo," como el depositario de la soberanía, la ejerciera "directamente," pero con la advertencia expresa como se indicó en el proyecto de reforma constitucional rechazado de 2007, de que dicho Poder Popular "no nace del sufragio ni de elección alguna, sino que nace de la condición de los grupos humanos organizados como base de la población", sino mediante la constitución de comunidades, comunas y el autogobierno de las ciudades, no electos democráticamente. Todo ello se hizo mediante la reforma de la Ley de los Consejos Comunales en 2009;[2200] la sanción, en 2010, del conjunto de Leyes Orgánicas del Poder Popular, de las Comunas, del Sistema Económico Comunal, de Planificación Pública y Comunal y de Contraloría Social,[2201] y de Ley de la Comisión

---

2199   Véase en *Gaceta Oficial* N° 39.156, de 13 de abril de 2009. Véase en general, Allan R. Brewer-Carías et al., *Leyes sobre el Distrito Capital y el Área Metropolitana de Caracas*, Editorial Jurídica Venezolana, Caracas 2009.

2200   Véase en *Gaceta Oficial* N° 39.335 de 28-12-2009. Véase la sentencia N° 1.676 de 03-12-2009 de la Sala Constitucional del Tribunal Supremo de Justicia sobre la constitucionalidad del carácter orgánico de esta Ley Orgánica de los Consejos Comunales, en http://www.tsj.gov.ve/decisiones/scon/diciembre/1676-31209-2009-09-1369.html . Véase sobre esta Ley: Allan R. Brewer-Carías, *Ley Orgánica de los Consejos Comunales*, Editorial Jurídica Venezolana, Caracas 2010

2201   Véase en *Gaceta Oficial* N° 6.011 Extra. de 21-12-2010. Véase en general sobre estas leyes, Allan R. Brewer-Carías, Claudia Nikken, Luis A. Herrera Orellana, Jesús María Alvarado Andrade, José Ignacio Hernández y Adriana Vigilanza, *Leyes Orgánicas sobre el Poder Popular y el Estado Comunal (Los consejos comunales, las comunas, la sociedad socialista y el sistema económico comunal)* Colección Textos Legislativos N° 50, Editorial Jurídica Venezolana, Caracas 2011; Allan R. Brewer-Carías, "La Ley Orgánica del Poder Popular y la desconstitucionalización del Estado de derecho en Venezuela," en *Revista de Derecho Público*, N° 124, Editorial Jurídica Venezolana, Caracas 2010, pp. 81-101,

de Planificación Centralizada;[2202] y la reforma el mismo año de la Ley Orgánica del Poder Público Municipal de 2010, y de las Leyes de los Consejos Estadales de Planificación y Coordinación de Políticas Públicas, y de los Consejos Locales de Planificación Pública;[2203] produciéndose además la desconstitucionalización del Estado

Esa desconstitucionaliación, deriva precisamente, de haberse establecido mediante leyes, en paralelo al Estado Constitucional, y en fraude a la voluntad popular que lo había rechazado, del llamado "Estado del Poder Popular" o "Estado Comunal," para vaciarlo de contenido, dejándolo sólo como una entelequia, para lo cual se dictó en 2012 una Ley Orgánica para la Gestión Comunitaria de Competencias, Servicios y Otras Atribuciones (Decreto Ley N° 9.043),[2204] transformada en 2014, en la Ley Orgánica para la Transferencia al Poder Popular de la Gestión y Administración Comunitaria de Servicios,[2205] todo con el objeto, supuestamente, de garantizar la participación de los ciudadanos en la acción pública, pero suplantando a los Estados y Municipios como entes descentralizados del Estado federal.

Con dicha estructura, además, se le han negado recursos financieros a los Estados y Municipios, a favor de Comunas y los Consejos Comunales, que creados como instrumentos para la recepción de subsidios directos y reparto de recursos presupuestarios públicos, pero con un grado extremo de exclusión, pues sólo pueden ejecutar la política socialista del Estado, que dependen del Poder Ejecutivo y que son controlados y manejados por el partido de gobierno. A eso quedó reducida la publicitada "participación protagónica," para recibir subsidios dinerarios directos, que por lo demás no están sometidos a control fiscal alguno.[2206]

La desconstitucionalización del Estado federal descerntralizado, para asegurar el incumplimiento de la promesa constitucional, además, se montó con una idea de sujetar obligatoriamente a todos los órganos del Estado Constitucional que ejercen el Poder Público, a los mandatos de las organizaciones del Poder Popular, al instituirse un nuevo principio de gobierno, consistente en "gobernar obedeciendo" (artí-

---

2202   Véase en *Gaceta Oficial* N° 5.841, Extra. de 22 de junio de 2007. Véase Allan R. Brewer-Carías, "Comentarios sobre la inconstitucional creación de la Comisión Central de Planificación, centralizada y obligatoria", *Revista de Derecho Público*", N° 110, (abril-junio 2007), Editorial Jurídica Venezolana, Caracas 2007, pp. 79-89.

2203   Véase en *Gaceta Oficial* N° 6.015 Extra. de 30 de diciembre de 2010.

2204   Véase en *Gaceta Oficial* N° 6.097 Extra. de 15 de junio de 2012.

2205   Véase en *Gaceta Oficial* N° 40.540 de 13 de noviembre de 2014.

2206   Véase en general sobre este proceso de desconstitucionalización del Estado, Allan R. Brewer-Carías, "La desconstitucionalización del Estado de derecho en Venezuela: del Estado Democrático y Social de derecho al Estado Comunal Socialista, sin reformar la Constitución," *en Libro Homenaje al profesor Alfredo Morles Hernández, Diversas Disciplinas Jurídicas,* (Coordinación y Compilación Astrid Uzcátegui Angulo y Julio Rodríguez Berrizbeitia), Universidad Católica Andrés Bello, Universidad de Los Andes, Universidad Monteávila, Universidad Central de Venezuela, Academia de Ciencias Políticas y Sociales, Vol. V, Caracas 2012, pp. 51-82; en Carlos Tablante y Mariela Morales Antonorzzi (Coord.), *Descentralización, autonomía e inclusión social. El desafío actual de la democracia,* Anuario 2010-2012, Observatorio Internacional para la democracia y descentralización, En Cambio, Caracas 2011, pp. 37-84; y en *Estado Constitucional,* Año 1, N° 2, Editorial Adrus, Lima, junio 2011, pp. 217-236

culo 24).[2207] Como las organizaciones del Poder Popular no tienen autonomía política pues sus "voceros" no son electos democráticamente mediante sufragio universal, directo y secreto, sino designados por asambleas de ciudadanos controladas e intervenidas por el partido oficial y el Ejecutivo Nacional que controla y guía todo el proceso organizativo del Estado Comunal, en el ámbito exclusivo de la ideología socialista, sin que tenga cabida vocero alguno que no sea socialista; este mandato legal de "gobernar obedeciendo" no es sino una limitación inconstitucional a la autonomía política de los órganos del Estado Constitucional electos, como la Asamblea Nacional, los Gobernadores y Consejos Legislativos de los Estados y los Alcaldes y Concejos Municipales, a quienes se les buscó imponer dicha obligación de "obedecer" lo que disponga el Ejecutivo Nacional y el partido oficial enmarcado en el ámbito exclusivo del socialismo como doctrina política, cuando utilicen con la máscara del Poder Popular. La voluntad popular expresada en la elección de representantes del Estado Constitucional, por tanto, en este esquema del Estado Comunal no tendría valor alguno, y al pueblo se le confisca su soberanía trasladándola de hecho a unas asambleas que no lo representan. Nada distinto, pero afortunadamente en forma tardía, pretendió el Presidente de la Asamblea Nacional saliente en diciembre de 2015, al perder el gobierno la elección parlamentaria, con la creación de un supuesto "Parlamento Comunal" instalándolo además en la sede de la propia Asamblea nacional (palacio federal legislativo), para pretender someter a la nueva Asamblea nacional que se instaló el 5 de enero de 2016, y que por supuesto desalojó dicha inexistente instancia de su sede.

En todo caso, sigue vigente la obligación impuesta por ley –aún cuando inconstitucional– a los órganos y entes del Poder Público en sus relaciones con el Poder Popular, de dar "preferencia a las comunidades organizadas, a las comunas y a los sistemas de agregación y articulación que surjan entre ellas," que no son otras que las que el propio Poder Central disponga desde el Poder Ejecutivo (art. 30);[2208] y de transferir sus competencias y atribuciones en materialmente todas las materias que tienen asignadas ("atención primaria de salud, mantenimiento de centros educativos, producción de materiales y construcción de vivienda, políticas comunitarias de deporte y mantenimiento de instalaciones deportivas, actividades culturales y mantenimiento de instalaciones culturales, administración de programas sociales, protección del ambiente y recolección de desechos sólidos, administración y mantenimiento de áreas industriales, mantenimiento y conservación de áreas urbanas, prevención y protección comunal, construcción de obras comunitarias y administración y prestación de servicios públicos, financieros, producción, distribución de alimentos y de

---

2207   El artículo 24 de la Ley Orgánica del Poder Popular, en efecto, sobre dispone sobre las "Actuaciones de los órganos y entes del Poder Público" que "Todos los órganos, entes e instancias del Poder Público guiarán sus actuaciones por el principio de gobernar obedeciendo, en relación con los mandatos de los ciudadanos, ciudadanas y de las organizaciones del Poder Popular, de acuerdo a lo establecido en la Constitución de la República y las leyes."

2208   En particular, conforme al artículo 61 de la Ley Orgánica de las Comunas, se dispone que "todos los órganos y entes del Poder Público comprometidos con el financiamiento de proyectos de las comunas y sus sistemas de agregación, priorizarán aquéllos que impulsen la atención a las comunidades de menor desarrollo relativo, a fin de garantizar el desarrollo territorial equilibrado."

bienes de primera necesidad, entre otras" (art. 27)),[2209] "a las comunidades organizadas, a las comunas y a los sistemas de agregación que de éstas surjan;[2210] buscándose legalmente el vaciamiento de competencias de los Estados y Municipios,[2211] de manera que queden como estructuras vacías, con gobiernos representativos electos por el pueblo pero que no tienen materias sobre las cuales gobernar, lo que se buscó consolidar con la Ley Orgánica del Poder Público Municipal (LOPP).[2212]

3. La desmunicipalización del país al margen de la Constitución

Esta estructuración paralela del Estado Comunal o del Poder Popular, en particular ha tenido un impacto fundamental en la Administración Municipal, buscando suplantar con las comunas, concebidas en la Ley Orgánica del Poder Popular, al margen de la Constitución, como la "célula fundamental" de dicho Estado Comunal,[2213] para suplantar definitivamente al Municipio constitucional como la única "entidad local" regulada en la Constitución (arts. 169, 173), como "entidad política" del Estado que implica tener gobierno integrado por representantes electos mediante

---

2209   Véase sobre la Ley Orgánica de 2012, los comentarios de: José Luis Villegas Moreno, "Hacia la instauración del Estado Comunal en Venezuela: Comentario al Decreto Ley Orgánica de la Gestión Comunitaria de Competencia, Servicios y otras Atribuciones, en el contexto del Primer Plan Socialista-Proyecto Nacional Simón Bolívar 2007-2013"; de Juan Cristóbal Carmona Borjas, "Decreto con rango, valor y fuerza de Ley Orgánica para la Gestión Comunitaria de Competencias, Servicios y otras atribuciones;" de Cecilia Sosa G., "El carácter orgánico de un Decreto con fuerza de Ley (no habilitado) para la gestión comunitaria que arrasa lentamente con los Poderes estadales y municipales de la Constitución;" de José Ignacio Hernández, "Reflexiones sobre el nuevo régimen para la Gestión Comunitaria de Competencias, Servicios y otras Atribuciones;" de Alfredo Romero Mendoza, "Comentarios sobre el Decreto con rango, valor y fuerza de Ley Orgánica para la Gestión Comunitaria de Competencias, Servicios y otras Atribuciones;," y de Enrique J. Sánchez Falcón, "El Decreto con Rango, Valor y Fuerza de Ley Orgánica para la Gestión Comunitaria de Competencias, Servicios y otras Atribuciones o la negación del federalismo cooperativo y descentralizado," en *Revista de Derecho Público*, Nº 130, Editorial Jurídica Venezolana, Caracas 2012, pp. 127 ss.

2210   Esta misma norma se repite en la Ley Orgánica de las Comunas (art. 64). El 31 de diciembre de 2010, aún estaba pendiente en la Asamblea Nacional la segunda discusión del proyecto de Ley Orgánica del Sistema de Transferencia de Competencias y atribuciones de los Estados y Municipios a las organizaciones del Poder Popular.

2211   Como observó Cecilia Sosa Gómez, para entender esta normativa hay que "aceptar la desaparición de las instancias representativas, estadales y municipales, y su existencia se justicia en la medida que año a año transfiera sus competencias hasta que desaparezcan de hecho, aunque sigan sus nombres (Poderes Públicos Estadal y Municipal) apareciendo en la Constitución. El control de estas empresas, las tiene el Poder Público Nacional, específicamente en el Poder Ejecutivo, en la cabeza de un Ministerio." Véase Cecilia Sosa G., "El carácter orgánico de un Decreto con fuerza de Ley (no habilitado) para la gestión comunitaria que arrasa lentamente con los Poderes estadales y municipales de la Constitución," en *Revista de Derecho Público*, Nº 130, Editorial Jurídica Venezolana, Caracas 2012, p. 152.

2212   Véase en *Gaceta Oficial* Nº 6.015 Extraordinario del 28 de diciembre de 2010.

2213   Véase en *Gaceta Oficial* Nº 6.011 Extra. de 21-12-2010. Véase sobre esta Ley el libro de Allan R. Brewer-Carías, Claudia Nikken, Luis A. Herrera Orellana, Jesús María Alvarado Andrade, José Ignacio Hernández y Adriana Vigilanza, *Leyes Orgánicas sobre el Poder Popular y el Estado Comunal (Los Consejos Comunales, las Comunas, la Sociedad Socialista y el Sistema Económico Comunal)*, Colección Textos Legislativos Nº 50, Editorial Jurídica Venezolana, Caracas 2011. Véase además, Allan R. Brewer-Carías, "La Ley Orgánica del Poder Popular y la desconstitucionalización del Estado de derecho en Venezuela," en *Revista de Derecho Público*, Nº 124, (octubre-diciembre 2010), Editorial Jurídica Venezolana, Caracas 2010, pp. 81-101.

sufragio universal, directo y secreto (arts. 63, 169). Es decir, conforme a la Constitución, no puede haber "entidades locales" con gobiernos que no sean democráticos representativos en los términos mencionados, y menos "gobernadas" por "voceros" designados a mano alzada sin elección universal y directa, siendo en consecuencia inconstitucional su concepción. Las comunas, a pesar de que se las denomine como "entidades locales especiales," no son gobernadas por órganos cuyos integrantes sean electos por votación universal directa y secreta, no tienen autonomía política ni pueden formar parte del esquema de descentralización territorial del Estado. Como se dijo, están bajo el total control por el Poder central, al punto de que de acuerdo con la Ley Orgánica del Poder Popular (art. 32), adquieren personalidad jurídica mediante el registro ante el Ministerio del Poder Popular de las Comunas y Movimientos Sociales, con lo que, en definitiva, se deja en manos del Ejecutivo Nacional la decisión de registrar o no un Consejo Comunal, una Comuna o una Ciudad comunal, y ello debe hacerse, por supuesto, aplicando la letra de la Ley, lo que significa que si está dominada por "voceros" que no sean socialistas, no cabe su registro ni, por tanto, su reconocimiento como persona jurídica, así sea producto genuino de una iniciativa popular.

Con todo ello, ni más ni menos lo que se ha buscado es la destrucción de los Municipios, cuyos representantes electos, conforme se llegó a afirmar en el texto de la Ley Orgánica para la Gestión Comunitaria de Competencias, Servicios y Otras Atribuciones (Decreto Ley N° 9.043), supuestamente habrían "usurpado lo que es del pueblo soberano;" buscándose con el establecimiento del Estado Comunal, supuestamente "restituir al Pueblo Soberano, a través de las comunidades organizadas y las organizaciones de base del poder popular, aquellos servicios, actividades, bienes y recursos que pueden ser asumidas, gestionadas y administradas por el pueblo organizado" (art. 5.3, Ley Orgánica de 2012).

A todo lo anterior, en el proceso de desmantelamiento del Estado Constitucional como Estado federal, se regularon durante los últimos lustros, diversas estructuras en la Administración Pública nacional, dependientes del Vicepresidente Ejecutivo de la República, en forma paralela y superpuesta a la Administración de los Estados, para terminar de ahogarlas, denominadas como "Órganos Desconcentrados de las Regiones Estratégicas de Desarrollo Integral (REDI),"[2214] a cargo de funcionarios denominados "Autoridades Regionales," o "Jefes de Gobierno" según la denominación de la Ley Orgánica de la Administración Pública Nacional de 2014 (art. 34.41), como integrantes de "los órganos superiores de dirección del Nivel Central de la Administración Pública nacional" (art. 44, 71); con "Dependencias" en cada Estado de la República, que están a cargo de Delegaciones Estadales, todos del libre nombramiento del Vicepresidente de la República.

Estos Delegados, que ejercen sus funciones "dentro del territorio del Estado que le ha sido asignado" (art. 19), concebido como supuestos "canales de comunicación" entre los Gobernadores de Estado y el Poder Nacional, montados en paralelo a las autoridades estadales, en realidad lo que tienen a su cargo es asegurar el vaciamiento

---

2214   Véase Resolución N° 031 de la Vicepresidencia de la República, mediante la cual se establece la Estructura y Normas de Funcionamiento de los órganos Desconcentrados de las Regiones Estratégicas de Desarrollo Integral (REDI), en *Gaceta Oficial* N° 40.193 de 20-6-2013.

de sus competencias y la neutralización del poder de los Gobernadores de Estado, siguiendo la pauta del mencionado esquema del gobierno establecido inconstitucionalmente para el de Distrito Capital, totalmente dependiente del Poder Ejecutivo, para vaciar de competencias las autoridades de gobierno del área metropolitana de Caracas (Alcalde y Consejo Metropolitano), mediante la Ley Especial Sobre la Organización y Régimen del Distrito Capital.[2215]

En esta forma, al fraude a la Constitución, que ha sido la técnica constantemente aplicada por el gobierno autoritario en Venezuela desde 1999 para imponer sus decisiones a los venezolanos al margen de la Constitución,[2216] olvidándose de las promesas constitucionales, se ha sumado posteriormente el fraude a la voluntad popular, al imponerle a los venezolanos mediante leyes orgánicas, un modelo de Estado por el cual nadie ha votado y que cambia radical e inconstitucionalmente el texto de la Constitución de 1999, que no ha sido reformado conforme a sus previsiones, en abierta contradicción al rechazo popular mayoritario que se expresó en diciembre de 2007 respecto de la reforma constitucional que se intentó realizar incluso violando la propia Constitución

VI. EL INCUMPLIMIENTO DE LA PROMESA CONSTITUCIONAL DEL ESTABLECIMIENTO DE UN ESTADO SOCIAL MONTADO SOBRE UN SISTEMA ECONÓMICO DE ECONOMÍA MIXTA

La Constitución de 1999, además de prometer la configuración del Estado como un Estado democrático de derecho y de Justicia, prometió estructurar el mismo como un Estado Social, montado sobre una Constitución económica que reguló un sistema de economía mixta, en el cual la iniciativa privada debería tener un rol tan importante como la del propio Estado. En efecto, en los términos de la promesa constitucional (art. 299), la misión fundamental del Estado Social es la de velar por la satisfacción de las necesidades colectivas de la población, en conjunción con las iniciativas privadas, mediante el fortalecimiento de los servicios públicos, para garantizar a todos el goce y efectividad de los derechos sociales, como son los derechos a la salud, a la educación, a la vivienda, al trabajo, a la seguridad social, a la cultura, a la asistencia social y a la protección del ambiente, de manera de asegurar la justicia social.[2217]

El objetivo de este modelo de Estado social prometido en la Constitución, fue asegurar el "desarrollo humano integral y una existencia digna y provechosa para la

---

2215   Véase en *Gaceta Oficial* N° 39.156 de 13 de abril de 2009.

2216   Véase Allan R. Brewer-Carías, *Reforma constitucional y fraude a la Constitución (1999-2009)*, Academia de Ciencias Políticas y Sociales, Caracas 2009; *Dismantling Democracy. The Chávez Authoritarian Experiment*, Cambridge University Press, New York 2010.

2217   En términos de la jurisprudencia de la Sala Constitucional del Tribunal Supremo de Justicia expresada en 2004, "el Estado Social de Derecho es el Estado de la *procura existencial*, su meta es satisfacer las necesidades básicas de los individuos distribuyendo bienes y servicios que permitan el logro de un *standard* de vida elevado, colocando en permanente realización y perfeccionamiento el desenvolvimiento económico y social de sus ciudadanos." Véase sentencia N° 1002 de 26 de mayo de 2004 (caso: Federación Médica Venezolana vs. Ministra de Salud y Desarrollo Social y el Presidente del Instituto Venezolano de los Seguros Sociales), en *Revista de Derecho Público*, N° 97-98, Editorial Jurídica Venezolana, Caracas 2004, pp. 143 ss.

colectividad;" teniendo el Estado, con tal propósito, sin duda, deberes de actuación que debe realizar "conjuntamente con la iniciativa privada," lo que implica garantizar los derechos y libertades económicos de las personas; y todo ello, con el objeto de "promover el desarrollo armónico de la economía nacional con el fin de generar fuentes de trabajo, alto valor agregado nacional, elevar el nivel de vida de la población y fortalecer la soberanía económica del país," para lograr una justa distribución de la riqueza" (art. 299).[2218] Lo anterior, además, mediante un sistema tributario que debe procurar "la justa distribución de las cargas públicas atendiendo al principio de la progresividad, así como la protección de la economía nacional y la elevación del nivel de vida de la población" (art. 316).[2219]

La consecuencia de lo anterior es que la noción de Estado Social está imbricada con las otras nociones que resultan de la configuración del Estado en la Constitución,[2220] como que tiene que ser democrático, de derecho, descentralizado y de justicia y en un marco que necesariamente tiene que ser el de un sistema de economía mixta,[2221] que debe desarrollarse en un ámbito de libertad que debe garantizar la iniciativa privada y la libre empresa y la satisfacción de los derechos sociales, de manera que la interpretación de estos no puede conducir a vaciar totalmente de valor y contenido a los derechos de libertad de los ciudadanos.

Por ello es que el Estado Social en la Constitución, no se puede desligar del sistema de economía mixta que de acuerdo con el artículo 299, se fundamenta en los

---

2218   La Sala Constitucional del Tribunal Supremo en sentencia N° 85 del 24 de enero de 2002 (Caso *Asociación Civil Deudores Hipotecarios de Vivienda Principal (Asodeviprilara)*, precisó en cuanto a "la protección que brinda el Estado Social de Derecho," no sólo que la misma está vinculada al "interés social" que se declara como "un valor que persigue equilibrar en sus relaciones a personas o grupos que son, en alguna forma, reconocidos por la propia ley como débiles jurídicos, o que se encuentran en una situación de inferioridad con otros grupos o personas, que por la naturaleza de sus relaciones, están en una posición dominante con relación a ellas;" sino que dicha protección "varía desde la defensa de intereses económicos de las clases o grupos que la ley considera se encuentran en una situación de desequilibrio que los perjudica, hasta la defensa de valores espirituales de esas personas o grupos, tales como la educación (que es deber social fundamental conforme al artículo 102 constitucional), o la salud (derecho social fundamental según el artículo 83 constitucional), o la protección del trabajo, la seguridad social y el derecho a la vivienda (artículos 82, 86 y 87 constitucionales), por lo que el interés social gravita sobre actividades tanto del Estado como de los particulares, porque con él se trata de evitar un desequilibrio que atente contra el orden público, la dignidad humana y la justicia social.". Véase en http://www.tsj.gov.ve/decisiones/scon/enero/85-240102-01-1274%20.htm.

2219   Véase Leonardo Palacios Márquez, "Medidas fiscales para el desarrollo económico," en *Revista de Derecho Tributario*, N° 97, Asociación Venezolana de Derecho Tributario, Legislec Editores, Caracas 2002, pp. 179-224.

2220   Véase la sentencia N° 1158 de 18 de agosto de 2014 (Caso: amparo en protección de intereses difusos, Rómulo Plata, contra el Ministro del Poder Popular para el Comercio y Superintendente Nacional para la Defensa de los Derechos Socio Económicos), en http://www.tsj.gov.ve/decisiones/scon/agosto/168705-1158-18814-2014-14-0599.HTML,

2221   Véase Allan R. Brewer-Carías, "Reflexiones sobre la Constitución económica" en *Estudios sobre la Constitución Española. Homenaje al Profesor Eduardo García de Enterría*, Editorial Civitas, Madrid, 1991, Tomo V, pp. 3.839-3.853; y lo expuesto en relación con la Constitución de 1999 en Alan R. Brewer-Carías, "Sobre el régimen constitucional del sistema económico," en *Debate Constituyente (Aportes a la Asamblea Nacional Constituyente), Tomo III (18 octubre-30 noviembre 1999)*, Fundación de Derecho Público-Editorial Jurídica Venezolana, Caracas 1999, pp. 15-52.

principios de justicia social, democratización, eficiencia, libre competencia, protección del ambiente, productividad y solidaridad, a los fines de asegurar el desarrollo humano integral y una existencia digna y provechosa para la colectividad; garantizando por una parte la libertad económica, la iniciativa privada y la libre competencia, y por la otra, la posibilidad de participación del Estado como promotor del desarrollo económico, regulador de la actividad económica, y planificador con la participación de la sociedad civil.[2222] Es decir, como lo interpretó la Sala Constitucional,[2223] un Estado que es *"opuesto al autoritarismo"* que promueve "expresamente, la actividad económica conjunta del Estado y de la iniciativa privada en la persecución y concreción de los valores supremos consagrados en la Constitución," persiguiendo "el equilibrio de todas las fuerzas del mercado y la actividad onjunta del Estado e iniciativa privada," lo que impide por supuesto, el sacrificio de ésta última en beneficio del Estado, y menos esgrimiendo la noción de Estado Social. [2224]

2222   Véase en general, sobre el tema del Estado Social y el sistema de economía mixta: José Ignacio Hernández G. "Estado Social y Libertad de Empresa en Venezuela: Consecuencias Prácticas de un Debate Teórico" en *Seminario de Profesores de Derecho Público*, Caracas, 2010, en http://www.uma.edu.ve/admini/ckfinder/userfiles/files/Libertad_economica_seminario.pdf ; y "Estado social y ordenación constitucional del sistema económico venezolano," Biblioteca Jurídica Virtual del Instituto de Investigaciones Jurídicas de la UNAM, en http://www.juridi-cas.unam.mx/publica/librev/rev/dconstla/cont/2006.1/pr/pr14.pdf; José Valentín González P, "Las Tendencias Totalitarias del Estado Social y Democrático de Derecho y el carácter iliberal del Derecho Administrativo", CEDICE-Libertad, 2012. http://cedice.org.ve/wp-content/uploads/2012/12/Tendencias-Totalitarias-del-Edo-Social-y-Democr%C3%A1tico-de-Derecho-Administrativo.pdf; y José Valentín González P, "Nuevo Enfoque sobre la Constitución Económica de 1999," en el libro *Enfoques sobre Derecho y Libertad*, Academia de Ciencias Políticas y Sociales, Serie Eventos, Caracas 2013.

2223   La Sala Constitucional del Tribunal Supremo en sentencia N° 117 de 6 de febrero de 2001, reiterando expresamente un fallo anterior de la antigua Corte Suprema de 15 de diciembre de 1998, expresó: "Los valores aludidos se desarrollan mediante el concepto de libertad de empresa, que encierra, tanto la noción de un derecho subjetivo "a dedicarse libremente a la actividad económica de su preferencia", como un principio de ordenación económica dentro del cual se manifiesta la voluntad de la empresa de decidir sobre sus objetivos. En este contexto, los Poderes Públicos, cumplen un rol de intervención, la cual puede ser directa (a través de empresas) o indirecta (como ente regulador del mercado) [...] A la luz de todos los principios de ordenación económica contenidos en la Constitución de la República Bolivariana de Venezuela, se patentiza el carácter mixto de la economía venezolana, esto es, un sistema socioeconómico intermedio entre la economía de libre mercado (en el que el Estado funge como simple programador de la economía, dependiendo ésta de la oferta y la demanda de bienes y servicios) y la economía interventora (en la que el Estado interviene activamente como el "empresario mayor")."Véase en *Revista de Derecho Público*, N° 85-88, Editorial Jurídica Venezolana, Caracas, 2001. Véase José Ignacio Hernández, "Constitución económica y privatización (Comentarios a la sentencia de la Sala Constitucional del 6 de febrero de 2001)", en *Revista de Derecho Constitucional*, N° 5, julio-diciembre-2001, Editorial Sherwood, Caracas, 2002, pp. 327 a 342.

2224   En ese sistema de economía mixta, la Constitución, en efecto, regula los derechos económicos, en particular, siguiendo la tradición del constitucionalismo venezolano, la libertad económica como el derecho de todos de dedicarse libremente a la actividad económica de su preferencia, sin más limitaciones que las previstas en la Constitución y las que establezcan las leyes, por razones de desarrollo humano, seguridad, sanidad, protección del ambiente u otras de interés social (art. 112), y el derecho de propiedad; y la garantía de la expropiación (art. 115) y prohibición de la confiscación (art. 116). La Constitución, además, regula el derecho de todas las personas a disponer de bienes y servicios de calidad, así como a una información adecuada y no engañosa sobre el contenido y características de los productos y servicios que consumen, a la libertad de elección y a un trato equitativo y digno. (art. 117). Por la otra, en el texto constitucional se regulan las diferentes facetas de la intervención del Estado en la economía, como Estado promotor, es decir, que no sustituye a la iniciativa privada, sino

Esa promesa constitucional de Estructuración de un Estado social montado sobre un sistema de economía mixta, tampoco se cumplió en Venezuela, y durante los últimos tres lustros, al contrario o que se ha estructurado es un Estado totalitario, montado sobre un sistema de economía socialista que ha excluido y perseguido la iniciativa privada y la libertad económica.

1. *La propuesta de reforma constitucional fracasada para sustituir el Estado Social por un Estado Socialista y su implementación a margen de la Constitución*

Ello, incluso después del fracaso de querer incorporar el modelo socialista a la Constitución con la reforma constitucional de 2007, fue implementado legalmente, por supuesto en forma fraudulenta, mediante la Ley Orgánica del Sistema Económico Comunal de 2010,[2225] como la "herramienta fundamental para construcción de la nueva sociedad" pero solo con base en "los principios y valores socialistas," también supuestamente inspirado en la doctrina de Simón Bolívar (art. 5), en la cual como se buscaba en la reforma rechazada, la propiedad privada quedaba reducida a la mínima expresión, sustituyéndosela en la Ley por la "propiedad social" como dominio del Estado, lo que significa que en la práctica, no se trata de ningún derecho que sea "de la sociedad," sino del aparato Estatal, cuyo desarrollo, regido por un sistema de planificación centralizada, elimina toda posibilidad de libertad económica e iniciativa privada, y convierte a las "organizaciones socio-productivas" en meros apéndices del aparato estatal, en el marco de un capitalismo de Estado, alimentado por el Estado petrolero, sin base constitucional alguna.

Una muestra final del proceso de incumplimiento de la promesa constitucional abandonándose el modelo de Estado Social de economía mixta está en la mencionada Ley Orgánica de Precios Justos de 2014,[2226] como resultado de la negación de la iniciativa privada al tener por objeto "la determinación de precios justos de bienes y servicios" por parte de la burocracia estatal, fijando "el porcentaje máximo de ganancia" y fiscalizando "la actividad económica y comercial;" todo ello, supuesta-

---

que fomenta y ordena la economía para asegurar su desarrollo, en materia de promoción del desarrollo económico (art. 299); de promoción de la iniciativa privada (art. 112); de promoción de la agricultura para la seguridad alimentaria (art. 305); de promoción de la industria (art. 302); de promoción del desarrollo rural integrado (art. 306); de promoción de la pequeña y mediana industria (art. 308); de promoción de la artesanía popular (art. 309); y de promoción del turismo (art. 310).Además, se establecen normas sobre el Estado Regulador, por ejemplo en materia de prohibición de los monopolios (art. 113), y de restricción del abuso de las posiciones de dominio en la economía con la finalidad de proteger al público consumidor y los productores y asegurar condiciones efectivas de competencia en la economía. Además, en materia de concesiones estatales (art. 113); protección a los consumidores o usuarios (art. 117); política comercial (art. 301); y persecución de los ilícitos económicos (art. 114).Igualmente la Constitución prevé normas sobre la intervención del Estado en la economía, como Estado empresario, (art. 300); con especial previsión del régimen de la nacionalización petrolera y el régimen de la reserva de actividades económicas al Estado (art. 302 y 303).

2225 Véase Allan R. Brewer-Carías, "La reforma de la Constitución económica para implantar un sistema económico comunista (o de cómo se reforma la Constitución pisoteando el principio de la rigidez constitucional), en Jesús María Casal y María Gabriela Cuevas (Coordinadores), *Homenaje al Dr. José Guillermo Andueza. Desafíos de la República en la Venezuela de hoy. Memoria del XI Congreso Venezolano de Derecho Constitucional*, Universidad Católica Andrés Bello, Caracas 2013, Tomo I, pp. 247-296.

2226 Véase en *Gaceta Oficial* N° 5156 Extra de 19-11-2014.

mente, con el "fin de proteger los ingresos de todos los ciudadanos, y muy especialmente el salario de los trabajadores; el acceso de las personas a los bienes y servicios para la satisfacción de sus necesidades;" y además establecer un marco de criminalización a la iniciativa privada, mediante la previsión de "ilícitos administrativos, sus procedimientos y sanciones, los delitos económicos, su penalización y el
resarcimiento de los daños sufridos;" y todo lo anterior, no para asegurar un Estado
social de economía mixta, sino para lograr la "consolidación de un orden económico
socialista productivo," que el artículo 3 precisa que es el supuestamente consagrado
en el "Plan de la patria," totalmente alejado del Estado Social en el marco de una
economía mixta que fue el que se prometió en la Constitución.

Después de haberse destruido en los últimos quince años la economía mixta como sistema político económico, no se ha logrado "alcanzar la mayor suma de felicidad posible;" no se ha logrado "el desarrollo armónico y estable de la economía" a
los que se refiere la Ley, habiendo la determinación de supuestos "precios justos" de
los bienes y servicios, conspirado contra la protección del salario y demás ingresos
de las personas, y contra la iniciativa privada y la productividad. Destruida la producción privada, no se ha garantizado "el acceso de las personas a los bienes y servicios para la satisfacción de sus necesidades" ni por supuesto, se ha privilegiado "la
producción nacional de bienes y servicios," resultado en que no se ha podido proteger a al pueblo contra las prácticas que puedan afectar el acceso a los bienes o servicios.

La Ley, en realidad, finalmente decretó el fin de la libertad económica y de la
iniciativa privada, haciendo depender toda la actividad económica de la burocracia
estatal, al sujetar a su normativa a absolutamente todas las personas naturales y jurídicas de derecho público o privado, nacionales o extranjeras, que desarrollen actividades económicas en el país, "incluidas las que se realizan a través de medios
electrónicos" (art. 2), imponiéndole a todos la necesidad de "inscribirse y mantener
sus datos actualizados en el Registro Único de Personas que Desarrollan Actividades Económicas," estableciendo que dicha "inscripción es requisito indispensable, a
los fines de poder realizar actividades económicas y comerciales en el país" (art.
22). En el pasado, y en el olvido quedó, por tanto, la promesa constitucional que
garantizaba a todas las personas el derecho a "dedicarse libremente a la actividad
lucrativa de su preferencia" y la obligación del Estado de "promover la iniciativa
privada" (art. 112).

Al contrario lo que ha resultado en la práctica es un esquema de persecución
contra la iniciativa privada, que incluso se aprecia por la atribución a la burocracia
estatal de establecer "el margen máximo de ganancia" "de cada actor de la cadena
de comercialización" estableciendo un límite máximo de "treinta (30) puntos porcentuales de la estructura de costos del bien o servicio" (art. 32); persecución que se
materializa con el conjunto de "medidas preventivas" que se regulan en la Ley y que
la burocracia estatal puede imponer durante las inspecciones o fiscalizaciones que
realicen los funcionarios, cuando detecten "indicios de incumplimiento de las obligaciones" previstas en la Ley, como son el comiso; la ocupación temporal de los
establecimientos o bienes indispensables para el desarrollo de la actividad, o para el
transporte o almacenamiento de los bienes comisados; el cierre temporal del establecimiento; la suspensión temporal de las licencias, permisos o autorizaciones emitidas por la burocracia; el ajuste inmediato de los precios de bienes destinados a co-

mercializar o servicios a prestar; y en general "todas aquellas que sean necesarias para impedir la vulneración de los derechos de las ciudadanas protegidos" por la Ley.

En definitiva, lo que resultó de esta normativa es un régimen de terror económico que pone a las empresas a la merced de la burocracia y lamentablemente, en manos de la corrupción que tal poder genera; siendo ella la negación más paladina de los principios más elementales que configuraron la Constitución sobre libertad económica y derecho de propiedad, y por tanto, del modelo de Estado Social de economía mixta.

La Ley comentada, dijimos es la muestra final del total desprecio y olvido de la promesa constitucional respecto del establecimiento de un Social y de Economía Mixta en Venezuela, que comenzó sin embargo a desmantelarse progresivamente al desarrollarse un desbalance sin precedentes a favor de la participación del Estrado en la economía y del desarrollo de poderes reguladores de todo orden en reacción con las iniciativas privadas, con lo cual se comenzó a frenar la producción, y la subsiguiente implementación de una política desenfrenada de estatización generalizada de toda la economía, que se agudizó después de la reelección del Presidente de la república a finales de 2006.

2.   El establecimiento del Sistema Económico Comunal al margen de la Constitución

Basado en el hecho de que durante su campaña electoral había abogado por la implementación de una política socialista, en la reforma constitucional que propuso en 2007 propuso configurar un modelo de Estado,[2227] diametralmente distinto al Estado social de economía mixta previsto en la misma, [2228] basado en un sistema de economía totalmente estatal, de economía comunista que sin embargo se calificó de "socialista," es decir, de planificación centralizada, de propiedad pública de todos los medios de producción, y de proscripción de la propiedad privada y de libertad económica.[2229]

2227   Véase los comentarios a la reforma constitucional de 2007 aprobada por la Asamblea Nacional en Allan R. Brewer-Carías, *La reforma constitucional de 2007 (Comentarios al proyecto inconstitucionalmente sancionado por la Asamblea Nacional el 2 de noviembre de 2007)*, Colección Textos Legislativos, N° 43, Editorial Jurídica Venezolana, Caracas 2007.

2228   Véase los comentarios al proyecto de reforma constitucional presentado por el Presidente de la república a la Asamblea Nacional en Allan R. Brewer-Carías, *Hacia la consolidación de un Estado socialista, centralizado, policial y militarista. Comentarios sobre el sentido y alcance de las propuestas de reforma constitucional 2007*, Colección Textos Legislativos, N° 42, Editorial Jurídica Venezolana, Caracas 2007.

2229   Véase por ejemplo lo expresado en el Voto Salvado del Magistrado Jesús Eduardo Cabrera a la sentencia N° 2042 de la Sala Constitucional del Tribunal Supremo de 2 de noviembre de 2007, en el cual expresó sobre el proyecto de reforma constitucional de 2007 sobre el régimen de la propiedad, que: "El artículo 113 del Proyecto, plantea un concepto de propiedad, que se adapta a la propiedad socialista, y que es válido, incluso dentro del Estado Social; pero al limitar la propiedad privada solo sobre bienes de uso, es decir aquellos que una persona utiliza (sin especificarse en cual forma); o de consumo, que no es otra cosa que los fungibles, surge un cambio en la estructura de este derecho que dada su importancia, conduce a una transformación de la estructura del Estado. Los alcances del Derecho de propiedad dentro del Estado Social, ya fueron reconocidos en fallo de esta Sala de 20 de noviembre de 2002, con ponencia del Magistrado Antonio García García."

Como hemos señalado, la reforma propuesta fue rechazada por el pueblo en el referendo sobre la reforma constitucional de diciembre de 2007, lo que sin embargo no fue impedimento para que se implementara en los años subsiguientes, en fraude a la Constitución y a la voluntad popular, en aplicación al llamado "socialismo del siglo XIX" obedeciendo a todos los principios que se quisieron incorporar en la Constitución con la rechazada reforma constitucional. El Estado, así, dejó de ser ese Estado Social de economía mixta, trastocándose en un Estado Totalitario,[2230] Comunista, Burocrático y Populista.

Ello, incluso deriva del texto expreso de la Ley Orgánica del Sistema Económico Comunal de 2010,[2231] a la que antes hemos mencionado, que define el "modelo productivo socialista" que se ha dispuesto para el país, como el "modelo de producción basado en la *propiedad social* [de los medios de producción], orientado hacia la *eliminación de la división social del trabajo* propio del modelo capitalista," y "dirigido a la satisfacción de necesidades crecientes de la población, a través de nuevas formas de generación y apropiación así como de la *reinversión social del excedente*" (art. 6.12). Basta destacar de esta definición legal, sus tres componentes fundamentales para entender de qué se trata, y que son: *la propiedad social, la eliminación de la división social del trabajo y la reinversión social del excedente*; que los redactores de la norma, sin duda, se copiaron de algún Manual vetusto de revoluciones comunistas fracasadas, parafraseando en el texto de una Ley, lo que Carlos Marx y

---

2230   Pompeyo Márquez, conocido dirigente de la izquierda venezolana ha expresado lo siguiente al contestar a una pregunta de un periodista sobre si **"¿Existe "el socialismo bolivariano", tal como se define el Partido Socialista Unido de Venezuela (Psuv) en su declaración doctrinaria?" Dijo: "**-No existe. Esto no tiene nada que ver con el socialismo. Después del XX Congreso del Partido Comunista de la Unión Soviética, donde Nikita Jrouschov denunció los crímenes de Stalin, se produjo un gran debate a escala internacional sobre las características del socialismo, y las definiciones, que se han esgrimido: Felipe González, Norberto Bobbio, para mencionar a un español y a un italiano son contestatarias a lo que se está haciendo aquí. // -Esto es una dictadura militar, que desconoce la Constitución, y la que reza en su artículo 6: "Venezuela es y será siempre una República democrática". Además, en el artículo 4 habla de un estado de derecho social. Habla del pluralismo y de una serie de valores, que han sido desconocidos por completo durante este régimen chavomadurista, que no es otra cosa que una dictadura. // -Esto se ve plasmado en la tendencia totalitaria, todos los poderes en manos del Ejecutivo. No hay independencia de poderes. No hay justicia. Aquí no hay donde acudir, porque no hay justicia. Cada vez más se acentúa la hegemonía comunicacional." Véase en *La Razón*, 31 julio, 2014, en http://www.larazon.net/2014/07/31/pompeyo-marquez-no-podemos-esperar-hasta-el-2019/

2231   Véase en *Gaceta Oficial* N° 6.011 Extraordinario del 21 de diciembre de 2010. Véase mis comentarios sobre esta Ley Orgánica, en Allan R. Brewer-Carías, "Sobre la Ley Orgánica del Sistema Económico Comunal o de cómo se implanta en Venezuela un sistema económico comunista sin reformar la Constitución," en *Revista de Derecho Público*, N° 124, (octubre-diciembre 2010), Editorial Jurídica Venezolana, Caracas 2010, pp. 102-109. Véase además el libro Allan R. Brewer-Carías et al., *Leyes Orgánicas sobre el Poder Popular y el Estado Comunal (Los Consejos Comunales, Las Comunas, La Sociedad Socialista y el Sistema Económico Comunal)*, Colección Textos Legislativos N° 50, Editorial Jurídica Venezolana, Caracas 2011. Véase igualmente, Allan R. Brewer-Carías, "La reforma de la Constitución económica para implantar un sistema económico comunista (o de cómo se reforma la Constitución pisoteando el principio de la rigidez constitucional), en Jesús María Casal y María Gabriela Cuevas (Coordinadores), *Homenaje al Dr. José Guillermo Andueza. Desafíos de la República en la Venezuela de hoy. Memoria del XI Congreso Venezolano de Derecho Constitucional*, Universidad Católica Andrés Bello, Caracas 2013, Tomo I, pp. 247-296.

Federico Engels escribieron hace más de 150 años, en 1845 y 1846, en su conocido libro *La Ideología Alemana* al definir la sociedad comunista.[2232]

Ese es el Estado que una Ley Orgánica, por supuesto, en incumplimiento total a la promesa constitucional le ha impuesto a los venezolanos a pesar de que votaron contra el mismo en el referendo de diciembre de 2007, y cuya implementación legal a simplemente eliminado o minimizado a la casi inexistencia al sector privado, mediante ocupaciones y confiscaciones masivas de empresas, fincas y medios de producción, sin garantía de justa indemnización, y que luego han sido abandonadas o desmanteladas, acabando con el aparato productivo del país y eliminando la libertad de empresa y la principal fuente de ingreso que puede tener un país.[2233]

[2232] Por ejemplo, Marx y Engels, después de afirmar que la propiedad es "el derecho de suponer de la fuerza de trabajo de otros" y declarar que la "división del trabajo y la propiedad privada" eran "términos idénticos: uno de ellos, referido a la esclavitud, lo mismo que el otro, referido al producto de ésta," escribieron que: "la división del trabajo nos brinda ya el primer ejemplo de cómo, mientras los hombres viven en una sociedad natural, mientras se da, por tanto, una separación entre el interés particular y el interés común, mientras las actividades, por consiguientes no aparecen divididas voluntariamente, sino por modo natural [que se daba según Marx y Engels "en atención a las dotes físicas, por ejemplo, la fuerza corporal, a las necesidades, las coincidencias fortuitas, etc.] los actos propios del hombres se erigen ante él en un poder hostil y ajeno, que lo sojuzga, en vez de ser él quien los domine. En efecto, a partir del momento en que comienza a dividirse el trabajo, cada cual se mueve en un determinado circulo exclusivo de actividad, que le es impuesto y del cual no puede salirse; el hombre es cazador, pescador, pastor o crítico, y no tiene más remedio que seguirlo siendo, si no quiere verse privado de los medios de vida; al paso que en la sociedad comunista, donde cada individuo no tiene acotado un círculo exclusivo de actividades, sino que puede desarrollar sus aptitudes en la rama que mejor le parezca, la sociedad se encarga de regular la producción general, con lo que hace cabalmente posible que yo pueda por la mañana cazar, por la tarde pescar y por la noche apacentar ganado, y después de comer, si me place, dedicarme a criticar, sin necesidad de ser exclusivamente cazador, pescador, pastor o crítico, según los casos." Véase en Karl Marx and Frederich Engels, "The German Ideology," en *Collective Works*, Vol. 5, International Publishers, New York 1976, p. 47. Véanse además los textos pertinentes en http://www.educa.madrid.org/cmstools/fi-les/0a24636f-764c-4e03-9c1d-6722e2ee60d7/Texto%20Marx%20y%20Engels.pdf. Véase sobre el tema Jesús María Alvarado Andrade, "La 'Constitución económica' y el sistema económico comunal (Reflexiones Críticas a propósito de la Ley Orgánica del Sistema Económico Comunal)," en Allan R. Brewer-Carías (Coordinador), Claudia Nikken, Luis A. Herrera Orellana, Jesús María Alvarado Andrade, José Ignacio Hernández y Adriana Vigilanza, *Leyes Orgánicas sobre el Poder Popular y el Estado Comunal (Los Consejos Comunales, las Comunas, la Sociedad Socialista y el Sistema Económico Comunal)*, Editorial Jurídica Venezolana, Caracas 2011, pp. 377-456.

[2233] El que fue Ministro de Economía del país, Alí Rodríguez Araque, y artífice de la política económica en los últimos lustros ha explicado la situación así: "Hay que hacer ciertas definiciones estratégicas que no están claras. ¿Qué es lo que va a desarrollar el Estado?, porque la revolución venezolana no es la soviética, donde los trabajadores armados en medio de una enorme crisis asaltan el poder, destruyen el viejo Estado y construyen uno nuevo. Ni es la revolución cubana, donde un proceso armado asalta el poder y construye uno nuevo. Aquí se llegó al Gobierno a través del proceso electoral. La estructura del Estado es básicamente la misma. Yo viví la experiencia de la pesadez de la democracia. Una revolución difícilmente puede avanzar exitosamente con un Estado de esas características. Eso va a implicar un proceso tan largo como el desarrollo de las comunas. Un nuevo Estado tiene que basarse en el poder del pueblo. Mientras, durante un muy largo periodo, se van a combinar las acciones del Estado con las del sector privado. Tiene que haber una definición en ese orden, los roles que va a cumplir ese sector privado, estableciendo las regulaciones para evitar la formación de monopolios. Está demostrado que el Estado no puede asumir todas las actividades económicas. ¿Qué vamos a hacer con la siderúrgica? Yo no estoy proponiendo que se privatice, pero ¿vamos a continuar pasando más actividades al Estado cuando su eficacia es muy limitada?. ¿Qué vamos a hacer con un conjunto

3. *El Estado Populista en sustitución del Estado Social*

En todo caso, lejos de haberse desarrollado un Estado Social, lo que ha resultado de la persecución del sector privado y la destrucción del aparato productivo, como política social para solucionar el desempleo, ha sido un descomunal proceso de burocratización mediante el aumento del empleo público a niveles nunca antes vistos, por supuesto bien lejos de la meritocracia que prescribe también como promesa la Constitución, conforme a la cual el ingreso a la función pública debería ser sólo mediante concurso público (art. 146). La consecuencia de esta política ha sido que en Venezuela, después de quince años de estatizaciones, se logró que el número de empleados públicos civiles sea el mismo que por ejemplo existe en la Administración Federal de los Estados Unidos.[2234] Pero en cuanto a calidad de vida, lo que resultó en el país, fue la escases de todos los productos básicos, que afecta a los que tienen menos recursos, pues sus ingresos resultaron cada vez menores por la galopante inflación que ha padecido el país, que es no sólo la mayor de toda América Latina, sino ahora de todo el mundo,[2235] habiéndose llegado a implementar a partir de septiembre de 2014, sistemas de racionamientos para los bienes de consumo, sólo vistos en Cuba,[2236] y en Corea del Norte. [2237]

---

de actividades en las cuales se ha venido metiendo el Estado y que están francamente mal y no lo podemos ocultar? Esto no es problema del proceso revolucionario, su raíz es histórica". Véase "Alí Rodríguez Araque: El Estado no puede asumirlo todo.", en *Reporte Confidencial*, 10 de agosto de 2014, en http://www.reporteconfidencial.info/noticia/3223366/ali-rodriguez-araque-el-estado-no-puede-asumirlo-todo/ Véase igualmente lo expuesto por quien fue el ideólogo del régimen, y a quien se se debe la denominación de "socialismo del siglo XXI", que ha expresado: que "El modelo del socialismo impulsado por Chávez fracasó: siendo "El gran error del gobierno de Maduro es seguir con la idea de Chávez, insostenible, de que el gobierno puede sustituir a la empresa privada. El gobierno usará su monopolio de importaciones y exportaciones para repartir las atribuciones en las empresas," en *El Nacional*, Caracas 19 de abril de 2014, en http://www.el-nacional.com/politica/Heinz-Dieterich-Venezuela-surgimiento-republica_0_394160741.html.

2234 Véase la información de la Office of Personal Management, en http://www.opm.gov/policy-data-oversight/data-analysis-documentation/federal-employment-reports/historical-tables/total-government-employment-since-1962/

2235 Véase la información en http://www.infobae.com/2014/04/24/1559615-en-un-ano-la-inflacion-oficial-venezuela-llego-al-60-ciento

2236 El 23 de agosto de 2014: "El Superintendente de Precios en Venezuela, Andrés Eloy Méndez, informó que todo establecimiento comercial estará controlado por las máquinas captahuellas. El control será extendido más allá de los alimentos y las medicinas. Méndez dijo que antes del 30 de noviembre deberá estar instalado en todo el país el sistema que contempla máquinas captahuellas para registrar el control de las compras que hacen los consumidores. Adelantó cuáles serán algunos de los rubros que serán controlados." Véase el reportaje "Gobierno de Venezuela impone racionamiento de productos," en *Queen's Latino*, 23 de agosto de 2014, en http://www.queenslatino.com/racionamiento-de-todo-en-venezuela/." Información ratificada por el Presidente de la República. Véase la información: "Captahuellas' para hacer mercado en Venezuela comenzaría en 2015," en *El Tiempo*, Bogotá, 23 de agosto de 2014, en http://www.eltiempo.com/mundo/latinoamerica/captahuellas-para-hacer-mercado-en-venezuela-comenzaria-en-2015/14419076. Sobre esto, la Nota de Opinión del diario *Tal Cual* del 22 de agosto de 2014, con el título "Racionamiento," expresa : "Si se entiende bien lo que nos ha avisado el superintendente de precios justos, por ahí viene rodando el establecimiento de cupos para la adquisición de artículos de primera necesidad, alimentos en particular.[...] Es, pues, un sistema de racionamiento, pero en lugar de una cartilla, como en Cuba, los avances tecnológicos (y los dólares) permiten apelar a mecanismos tan sofisticados como el del sistema biométrico." Véase en *Tal Cual*, 22-8-2014, en http://www.talcualdigital.com/Movil/visor.aspx?id=106710. La propuesta ya se había

Con la destrucción del aparato productivo y la material eliminación de las exportaciones, ya que lo poco que se produce no alcanza para el mercado interno, y lo que en buena parte sale del país es mediante contrabando, el único que puede obtener divisas es el propio Estado, para lo cual depende en un 94% de la producción de PDVSA, cada vez más mermada y comprometida.[2238] Por ello, para controlar la adquisición de divisas, el Estado ha montado todo tipo de sistemas de control de cambios, constituyéndose en una de las principales fuentes de corrupción administrativa, y de tráfico de influencias, quedando incluso la posibilidad real de importación de bienes sólo a cargo del propio Estado.[2239]

Todo ello ha originado en el marco interno, una economía social basada en el subsidio directo a las personas, recibiendo beneficios sin enfrentar sacrificios o esfuerzos, con lo que se destruyó además el valor del trabajo productivo como fuente de ingreso, que materialmente se ha eliminado, sustituido por el que encuentra que es preferible recibir sin trabajar. Ello trastocó al Estado social en un Estado Populista, con una organización destinada a darles dadivas a los sectores pobres y garantizar así su adhesión a las políticas autoritarias, [2240] provocado más miseria y control de conciencia sobre una población de menos recursos totalmente dependiente de la burocracia estatal y sus dádivas, en las muchos creyeron encontrar la solución definitiva para su existencia,[2241] pero a costa del deterioro ostensible y trágico de los servicios públicos más elementales como los servicios de salud y atención médica.

---

anunciado desde junio de 2013, "Venezuela instaurará en Venezuela la cartilla de razonamiento al mejor estilo cubano," en ABC.es Internacional, 4 de junio de-2013, en http://www.abc.es/internacional/20130603/abci-maduro-cartilla-racionamiento-201306032115.html.

2237 Por ello, en el *The Wall Street Journal* del 23 de octubre de 2014, se indicaba que "Entre el agravamiento de la escases, Venezuela recientemente recibió una extraordinaria y dudosa distinción, y es que alcanzó el rango de Corea del Norte y de Cuba en el racionamiento de comida para sus ciudadanos," refiriéndose a la imposición del sistema de "capta-huellas" digitales en ciertos establecimientos, para el control de la venta de productos. Véase el reportaje de Sara Schaffer Muñoz, "Despite Riches, Venezuela Starts Food rations," en *The Wall Street Journal*, New York, 23 de octubre de 2014, p. A15.

2238 Véase los datos en "1999 versus 2013: Gestión del Desgobierno en números," en https://twitter.com/sushidavid/status/451006280061046784

2239 El Ministro de Planificación y Economía durante los últimos años, Jorge Gordani, al renunciar a su cargo en 2014 calificó esas entidades como "focos de corrupción," pero sin que durante su gestión se hubiese hecho nada para extirparlo. Véase el texto de la Carta Pública, "Testimonio y responsabilidad ante la historia," 17-8-2014, en http://www.lapatilla.com/site/2014/06/18/gior-dani-da-la-version-de-su-salida-y-arremete-contra-maduro/. Según esas denuncias, "a través de los mecanismos de cambio de divisas "desaparecieron alrededor de 20.000.000.000 de dólares." Véase César Miguel Rondón, "Cada vez menos país," en *Confirmado*, 16-8-2014, en http://confirmado.com.ve/opinan/cada-vez-menos-pais/. Por todo ello, con razón en un editorial del diario *Le Monde* de París, titulado "Los venezolanos en el callejón sin salida del chavismo", se afirmaba que con todo eso "*Se ha creado una economía paralela, un mercado de tráfico interno y externo que beneficia a una pequeña nomenklatura sin escrúpulos.*" Véase Editorial de *Le Monde*, 30- marzo 2014, en http://www.eluniversal.com/nacional-y-politica/140330/le-monde-dedico-un-editorial-a-venezuela.

2240 Véase Heinz Sonntag "¿Cuántas Revoluciones más?" en El *Nacional*, Caracas 7 de octubre de 2014, en http://www.el-nacional.com/heinz_sonntag/Cuantas-Revoluciones_0_496150483.html

2241 Como el mismo Area lo ha descrito en lenguaje común y gráfico, pero tremendamente trágico: "Vivimos pues "boqueando" y de paso corrompiéndonos por las condiciones impuestas por y desde el poder que nos obligan a vivir como "lateros", "balseros", "abasteros" mejor dicho, que al estar "pe-

La consecuencia de todo este esquema de ausencia de Estado Social y de Estado de economía mixta, y el establecimiento en su lugar del Estado comunista, burocratizado, populista y clientelar, ha sido que en nombre del "socialismo," Venezuela hoy tiene el record de ser el país que ocupa el primer lugar en el índice de miseria del mundo,[2242] y la sociedad con el más alto riesgo de América Latina.[2243] Esa es la hazaña o el milagro de la política económica del gobierno durante los pasados quince años, que tanto va a costar superar en el futuro,[2244] lo que se suma el indicado primer lugar en criminalidad, falta de transparencia e inflación. Por eso se ha hablado, con razón, de que la política de Estado en Venezuela ha sido la de una "una fábrica de pobres,"[2245] conducida además, por un "Estado inepto, secuestrado por la élite de la burguesía corrupta gubernamental, que niega todos los derechos sociales y económicos constitucionales, y que manipula la ignorancia y pobreza de las clases sociales menos favorecidas."[2246]

---

lando" por lo que buscamos y no encontramos, tenemos que andar en gerundio, ladrando, mamando, haciendo cola, bajándonos de la mula, haciéndonos los bolsas o locos, llevándonos de caleta algo, caribeando o de chupa medias, pagando peaje, tracaleando, empujándonos los unos contra los otros, en suma, degradándonos, envileciéndonos, para satisfacer nuestras necesidades básicas de consumo. Es asfixia gradual y calculada, material y moral. Desde el papel toilette hasta la honestidad. ¡Pero tenemos Patria! Falta el orgullo, la dignidad, el respeto, el amor a uno mismo." Véase en "El 'Estado Misional' en Venezuela," en *Analítica.com*, 14 de febrero de 2014, en http://analitica.com/opinion/opinion-nacional/el-estado-misional-en-venezuela/

2242   Venezuela tiene el "ignominioso" primer lugar en el Índice de miseria del mundo. Véase el Informe de Steve H. Hanke, "Measury Misery arround the World," publicado en mayo 2104, en *Global Asia*, en http://www.cato.org/publications/commentary/measuring-misery-around-world Véase igualmente *Índice Mundial de Miseria*, 2014, en http://www.razon.com.mx/spip.php?ar-ticle215150; y en http://vallartaopina.net/2014/05/23/en-indice-mundial-de-miseria-venezuela-ocupa-primer-lugar/

2243   Véase en http://www.elmundo.com.ve/noticias/actualidad/noticias/infografia-riesgo-pais-de-venezuela-cerro-el-201.aspx

2244   Pedro Carmona Estanga ha resumido la hazaña económica del régimen explicando que: "Por desgracia para el país, a lo largo de estos 16 años se han dilapidado unos US$ 1,5 billones que no volverán, de los cuales no quedan sino la destrucción del aparato productivo, el deterioro de la calidad de vida, de la infraestructura, de la institucionalidad, y distorsiones macroeconómicas y actitudinales en la población de una profundidad tal, que costará sudor y sangre superar a las generaciones venideras. Esa es la hazaña histórica lograda y cacareada por el régimen." Véase Pedro Carmona Estanga, "La destrucción de Venezuela: hazaña histórica," 19 de octubre de 2014, en http://pcarmonae.blogspot.com/2014/10/la-destruccion-de-venezuela-hazana.html

2245   En tal sentido, Brian Fincheltub, ha destacado que "Las misiones se convirtieron en fábrica de personas dependientes, sin ninguna estabilidad, que confiaban su subsistencia exclusivamente al Estado. Nunca hubo interés de sacar a la gente de la pobreza porque como reconoció el propio ministro Héctor Rodríguez, se "volverían escuálidos". Es decir, se volverían independientes y eso es peligrosísimo para un sistema cuya principal estrategia es el control." Véase Brian Fincheltub, "Fabrica de pobres," en *El Nacional*, Caracas, 5 de junio de 2014, en http://www.el-nacional.com/opinion/Fabrica-pobres_0_421757946.html

2246   Por ello, con razón se ha dicho que "Si Venezuela fuera un Estado Social, no habría neonatos fallecidos por condiciones infecciosas en hospitales públicos. Si Venezuela fuera un Estado Social, toda persona tendría un empleo asegurado o se ejercería plenamente la libertad de empresa y comercio. Si Venezuela fuera un Estado Social no exhibiríamos deshonrosamente las tasas de homicidios más altas del mundo. Si Venezuela fuera un Estado Social no estaría desaparecida la cabilla y el cemento y las cementeras intervenidas estarían produciendo al máximo de su capacidad instalada. Si Venezuela fuera un Estado Social todos los establecimientos de víveres y artículos de primera necesidad estarían abarrotados en sus anaqueles. Si Venezuela fuera un Estado Social las escuelas no tendrían los te-

4. *La manipulación del nombre de Bolívar para justificar el incumplimiento de las promesas constitucionales: el "socialismo bolivariano"*

Entre las innovaciones que se introdujeron en la Constitución de 1999, además de la invocación por el pueblo, para sancionarla, de "la protección de Dios," estuvo la "del ejemplo histórico de nuestro Libertador Simón Bolívar" (Preámbulo), y además, el cambio de la denominación de la República de Venezuela, que de República de Venezuela pasó a ser la "República Bolivariana de Venezuela," con la indicación de que la misma "fundamenta su patrimonio moral y sus valores de libertad, igualdad, justicia y paz internacional en la doctrina de Simón Bolívar, el Libertador" (art. 1).

Por ello, además, en la Constitución se impuso a todas las instituciones públicas y privadas, la obligación de enseñar en todos los niveles "los principios del ideario bolivariano."

Ese ideario, relativamente bien conocido, y tradicionalmente difundido en frases y expresiones aisladas, en todo caso, quedó expresado en los documentos, proclamas y manifiestos del Libertador, quien las expresó hace doscientos años antes, reflejando el ideario cívico y militar de una Nación en proceso de consolidación. La invocación a dicho pensamiento fue sin duda un reconocimiento a la labor del grande hombre, pero doscientos años después, calificar un Estado como "bolivariano" no era en sí mismo más que un anacronismo.

La intención del cambio de nombre, sin embargo, era otra bien alejada del pensamiento de Bolívar, y más bien usar su nombre para calificar una "revolución" que se quiso imponer mediante el proceso constituyente de 1999, a pesar de que Bolívar no comandó revolución alguna, sino que lo que hizo fue a partir de 1813, liberar militarmente un país que había sido ocupado por las fuerzas españolas, después de haber logrado su independencia (1811). Y ello se comenzó a evidenciar del discurso que el mismo Hugo Chávez dio el 5 de agosto de 1999 en la instalación de la Asamblea Nacional Constituyente, en el cual al afirmar que el país en ese momento estaba en el curso de "un indetenible proceso revolucionario que no tiene marcha atrás" y que "nada ni nadie podrá evitarla," situó su origen en el "contexto bolivariano cuando nació o cuando nacieron las primeras repúblicas que se levantaron en esa tierra venezolana." En definitiva, afirmó que era de Bolívar de donde venía la revolución, de "Bolívar que vuelve con su clara visión, con su espada desenvainada, con su verbo y con su doctrina." Se trataba, conforme a la visión de Chávez, precisamente de la "revolución bolivariana," para lo cual hizo referencia a una absolutamente errada apreciación de la división de los períodos históricos venezolanos en cuatro diversas Repúblicas, de las cuales las tres primeras habrían ocurrido en un breve período de

---

chos llenos de filtraciones, estarían dotadas de materiales suficientes para la enseñanza-aprendizaje y los maestros y profesores serían el mejor personal pagado del país. Si Venezuela fuera un Estado Social no habría discriminación por razones políticas e ideológicas para tener acceso a cualquier servicio, beneficios y auxilios públicos y bienes de primera necesidad. Si Venezuela fuera un Estado Social el problema de la basura permanente en las grandes ciudades ya estaría resuelto con los métodos más modernos, actualizados y pertinentes a la protección ambiental." Véase Isaac Villamizar, "Cuál Estado Social?," en *La Nación*, San Cristóbal, 7 de octubre de 2014, en http://www.lanacion.com.ve/columnas/opinion/cual-estado-social/

ocho años, entre 1811 y 1819, denominando como "Cuarta República" al Estado de Venezuela que se reconstituyó como Estado independiente a partir de 1830 por la disolución de la Gran Colombia que históricamente, en realidad fue la única real "República bolivariana."

Dicha división de los períodos históricos republicanos en la existencia de supuestas tres repúblicas iniciales que Venezuela habría tenido en 1811, 1813 y 1819, en realidad es errada. La única República efectiva que existió en Venezuela en esos tiempos fue la de 1811 establecida en la Constitución federal de las Provincias Unidas de Venezuela, que formalmente funcionó, con todas sus vicisitudes, hasta 1830, cuando se reconstituyó la República después de la separación de Venezuela de Colombia. En 1813, como se dijo no hubo ninguna "nueva República" habiéndose solo iniciado ese año la guerra de liberación de Venezuela; y en 1819 sólo hubo un proyecto de Estado centralista que no llegó a cristalizar en Venezuela, pues al mes de aprobarse la Constitución de Angostura, el propio Bolívar sometió al mismo Congreso la Ley de la Unión de los pueblos de Colombia proponiendo la desaparición de Venezuela como Estado (y como República), con su fusión a Colombia, como en efecto ocurrió y logró constitucionalmente algo más de un año después, con la sanción de la Constitución de Cúcuta de 1821. Por eso la verdad es que como antes dije, esa Constitución de 1821, inspirada en la de 1819, fue con la que se puede decir que realmente se estableció la verdadera "República Bolivariana," una donde Venezuela no existía como Estado, y que desapareció como nación conformando, su territorio, solo un departamento más de la República de Colombia.[2247]

En ese contexto, en todo caso, calificar el período que se extiende a partir de 1830, durante todo el siglo XIX y el siglo XX hasta 1999, como una llamada "Cuarta República," no sólo fue un disparate histórico, sino que era una manipulación inaceptable de la historia del país, todo con el propósito de tratar de justificar, en 1999, una "revolución" llamándola como "revolución bolivariana" que daría origen al nacimiento de una nueva República, la "Quinta República," que quince años en 2016 después estamos viendo desmoronarse a pedazos. Por ello Chávez dijo en su discurso el 5 de agosto de 1999 ante la Asamblea Constituyente:

> "Hoy, así como aquella Cuarta República nació sobre la traición a Bolívar y a la revolución de Independencia, así como esa Cuarta República nació al amparo del balazo de Berruecos y a la traición, así como esa Cuarta República nació con los aplausos de la oligarquía conservadora, así como esa Cuarta República nació con el último aliento de Santa Marta, hoy le corresponde ahora morir a la Cuarta República con el aleteo del cóndor que volvió volando de las pasadas edades.

2247   Esa fue la idea de la República Bolivariana que quería Chávez; una donde Venezuela desapareciera. Así, quizás por no haber logrado, tras apoyar abiertamente la guerrilla colombiana, apoderarse subversivamente del gobierno de Bogotá y fundir de nuevo a Venezuela junto a Colombia en una nueva "República Bolivariana," Chávez terminó sus días en 2012, soñado también con la eliminación de Venezuela y lograr su unión con Cuba, en otra nueva "República," como en su propuesta de reforma constitucional de 2007 lo llegó a esbozar. Véase Allan R. Brewer-Carías, *Asamblea Constituyente y proceso constituyente 1999*, Colección Tratado de Derecho Constitucional, Tomo VI, Fundación de Derecho Público, Editorial Jurídica Venezolana, Caracas 2013, pp. 74 ss.

Hoy, con la llegada del pueblo, con ese retorno de Bolívar volando por estas edades de hoy, ahora le toca morir a la que nació traicionando al cóndor y enterrándolo en Santa Marta. Hoy muere la Cuarta República y se levanta la República Bolivariana. De allá viene esta revolución *(aplausos)*, de los siglos que se quedaron atrás desde 1810, desde 1811, desde 1813, desde 1818, 19, desde 1826, desde 1830 *(prolongados aplausos).* "[2248]

Concluyó Chávez proponiendo como su "idea fundamental" el que la república en 1999 debía declararse como "bolivariana", es decir, "que la Constitución Bolivariana declare que la República de Venezuela será una República Bolivariana," producto de su revolución, a la que también llamó "Revolución bolivariana" y que históricamente no había sido no fue otra cosa que una revolución militarista y centralista que fue la que se puede atribuir a Bolívar, con la cual incluso acabó con la Venezuela independiente al integrarla a Colombia.[2249]

Siete años después, en 2007, en todo caso, la doctrina bolivariana se convirtió en una "doctrina socialista" plasmada en la propuesta de reforma constitucional que fue rechazada por el pueblo, y que en 2010 se convirtió en una "revolución comunista," con la adopción oficial del marxismo leninismo como doctrina de Estado, y la sanción de las leyes del Poder Popular y del Estado Comunal. Y todo ello, siempre siendo llamada por Chávez y sus seguidores como "Revolución Bolivariana".

En la discusión del texto de la Constitución de 1999, en todo caso, el tema fue debatido, habiéndose aprobado, sin mayor discusión el cambio de denominación de la República como "República Bolivariana," respecto de lo cual salvé mi voto expresando mi total desacuerdo por estimar que:

"con la invocación que se hacía en el texto aprobado en primera discusión respecto del pensamiento y la acción del Libertador, bastaba para identificar el país cultural e históricamente con el nombre de Bolívar. Pero cambiarle el nombre a la República en la forma aprobada no tiene justificación alguna, pues no se corresponde ni siquiera con la realidad histórica. La única República Bolivariana fue la República de Colombia, producto de la ley de la Unión de los Pueblos de Colombia sancionada por el Congreso de Angostura en 1819, consolidada en la Constitución de Cúcuta de 1821, y que se extinguió con la muerte del Libertador.[2250]

A pesar del voto salvado, en todo caso, se aprobó el cambio de nombre de la República, lo que se consideró por el historiador Elías Pino Iturrieta como un "des-

---

2248   Véase en *Idem.*

2249   Véase Allan R. Brewer-Carías, "Cádiz y los orígenes del constitucionalismo en Venezuela. Después de Caracas (1811): Angostura (1819), Cúcuta (1821) y Valencia (1830),"en Andrea Romano y Francesco Vegara Caffarelli (Coord.) *1812: fra Cadice e Palermo - entre Cádiz y Palermo. Nazione, rivoluzione, constituzione, representanza politica, libertà garantite, autonomie,* Università degli Strudi di Messina, Palermo-Messina), Biblioteca centrale della Regione siciliana "Alberto Bombace", 2012, pp. 167-195.

2250   Véase Allan R. Brewer-Carías, *Debate Constituyente (Aportes a la Asamblea Nacional Constituyente),* Tomo III (18 octubre-30 noviembre 1999), Fundación de Derecho Público-Editorial Jurídica Venezolana, Caracas 1999.

propósito" o una "tropelía", agregando que "identificar oficialmente a la república con el nombre del Libertador significa la creación de una calificación errónea, falaz y perjudicial de los hechos sucedidos dentro de nuestros contornos desde el Descubrimiento, por lo menos."[2251]

Era claro por tanto, que el cambio de nombre, que no tenía basamento histórico alguno, tenía otra explicación y la misma no podía ser otra que una motivación política, partidaria, partisana o partidista, que como lo expresé apenas la Constitución de 1999 fue publicada,

"deriva de la denominación inicial del Movimiento político que estableció el Presidente de la República electo en 1998, Hugo Chávez F., y que como partido político, pretendió funcionar con el nombre de Movimiento Bolivariano, denominación que tuvo que ser cambiada por exigencias de la Ley Orgánica del Sufragio. El partido del Presidente de la República entonces ha sido el "partido bolivariano" y es por ello que se le pretendió imponer como nombre de la República. Ello debe ser rechazado no sólo por ser antibolivariano (no se olvide que el último grito del Libertador, en la víspera de su muerte, fue por que cesaran los partidos) sino porque pretende consolidar, desde el primer artículo de la Constitución, la división del país, entre bolivarianos y los que no lo son; entre patriotas y realistas; entre buenos y malos; entre puros y corruptos; entre revolucionarios y antirrevolucionarios; y todo ello manipulando la historia y los sentimientos populares con el control del Poder." [2252]

Como lo observó el profesor John Lynch, uno de los destacados biógrafos de Bolívar, "en 1999 los venezolanos supieron con asombro que su país había sido renombrado como 'República Bolivariana de Venezuela' por decisión del Presidente Hugo Chávez, quien se llamó a sí mismo como "revolucionario bolivariano." Agregando que:

"Populistas autoritarios, neocaudillos, o militares bolivarianos, sea cual fuere su nombre, invocan a Bolívar en forma tan ardiente como lo hicieron anteriores gobernantes, aún cando es dudoso que él hubiese respondido a sus llamados... Pero los nuevos herederos, lejos de mantener continuidad con las ideas constitucionales de Bolívar, como se ha alegado, le han inventado un nuevo atributo, el de Bolívar populista, y en el caso de Cuba le dieron una nueva identidad, la de Bolívar socialista. Explotando la tendencia autoritaria, la cual ciertamente existió en las ideas y las acciones de Bolívar, los regímenes de Cuba y

2251   Véase Elías Pino Iturrieta, *El divino Bolívar. Ensayo sobre una religión republicana*, Los Libros de la Catarata, Segunda edición, Madrid febrero 2004, pp. 232 y ss.

2252   Véase lo que expusimos en Allan R. Brewer-Carías, *La Constitución de 1999*, Editorial Arte, Caracas 1999, pp. 44 ss. De acuerdo con la Ley de Partidos Políticos, *Gaceta Oficial* N° 27.725, de 30-04-1965, los partidos políticos no pueden usar los nombres de los próceres ni los símbolos de la patria. La organización política que el Presidente había formado antes de la campaña presidencial de 1998, se llamó el Movimiento Bolivariano 2000, nombre que no podía ser usado. Por ello, el partido político que fundó se denominó Movimiento V República.

Venezuela proclaman al Libertador como el patrón de sus políticas, distorsionando sus ideas en el proceso."[2253]

Es decir, concluyó Lynch, "nunca antes la adhesión a Bolívar condujo al cambio de nombre de una república y a la invención de una "doctrina bolivariana" para justificar las políticas de un gobierno como Chávez lo ha hecho en relación con el "socialismo del Siglo XXI."[2254]

Y fue ello, precisamente lo que se evidenció siete años después del cambio de nombre de la República, al trastocar la llamada "doctrina bolivariana" en una "doctrina socialista" para justificar la reforma constitucional que propuso el mismo Chávez. La realidad, sin embargo, es que por supuesto, ello era históricamente insostenible pues no hay forma alguna de poder vincular "la doctrina del Libertador Simón Bolívar" con los principios y valores socialistas. En la obra de Bolívar y en relación con su concepción del Estado nada puede encontrarse al respecto,[2255] no habiendo sido la propuesta sino una pretensión más de continuar manipulando el "culto" a Bolívar para justificar los autoritarismos, como tantas veces ha ocurrido antes en nuestra historia. Así fue el caso de Antonio Guzmán Blanco en el siglo XIX, y de Cipriano Castro, Juan Vicente Gómez, Eleazar López Contreras y Marcos Pérez Jiménez en el siglo XX, y así fue el caso de Hugo Chávez. Por ello, el mismo John Lynch ha señalado sobre esto que: "El tradicional culto a Bolívar ha sido usado como ideología de conveniencia por dictadores militares, culminando con los regímenes de Juan Vicente Gómez y Eleazar López Contreras; quienes al menos respetaron, más o menos, los pensamientos básicos del Libertador, aun cuando tergiversaron su significado." De ello concluyó señalando su apreciación, antes referida, de que en el caso de Venezuela, en el régimen iniciado en 1999, el proclamar al Libertador como fundamento de las políticas del régimen autoritario, constituye una distorsión de sus ideas.[2256]

2253   See John Lynch, *Simón Bolívar: A Life*, Yale University Press, New Haven, CT, 2007, p. 304. See also A.C. Clark, *The Revolutionary Has No Clothes: Hugo Chávez's Bolivarian Farce*, Encounter Books, New York 2009, pp. 5-14.

2254   Otro de los intentos para apropiarse completamente de Simón Bolívar para la "revolución Bolivariana" además de cambiar la imagen oficial iconográfica del Libertador, fue la exhumación televisada de sus restos mortales en el Panteón Nacional en Caracas, el 26 de Julio de 2010, conducida por el propio Chávez y otros altos funcionarios, entre otros propósitos, para determinar si Bolívar había muerto envenenado con arsénico en Santa Marta en 1830, en vez de la causa de la tuberculosis. Véase Simón Romero, "Building a New History By Exhuming Bolívar," *The New York Times*, August 4, 2010, p. A7. A todo ello se suma la desfiguración de la iconografía del Libertador, como parte medular del "culto" chavista al Libertador.

2255   Véase Allan R. Brewer-Carías, "Ideas centrales sobre la organización el Estado en la Obra del Libertador y sus Proyecciones Contemporáneas" en *Boletín de la Academia de Ciencias Políticas y Sociales*, Nº 95-96, enero-junio 1984, pp. 137-151.

2256   Véase John Lynch, *Simón Bolívar: A Life*, Yale University Press, New Haven 2007, p. 304. .Véase también, Germán Carrera Damas, *El culto a Bolívar, esbozo para un estudio de la historia de las ideas en Venezuela*, Universidad Central de Venezuela, Caracas 1969; Luis Castro Leiva, *De la patria boba a la teología bolivariana*, Monteávila, Caracas 1987; Elías Pino Iturrieta, *El divino Bolívar. Ensayo sobre una religión republicana*, Alfail, Caracas 2008; Ana Teresa Torres, *La herencia de la tribu. Del mito de la independencia a la Revolución bolivariana*, Editorial Alfa, Caracas 2009.

Y efectivamente, nada en la doctrina de Bolívar podía servir de fundamento no solo para calificar el Estado como "bolivariano" en 1999, sino tampoco para identificar la "doctrina bolivariana" con la "doctrina socialista" en 2007 buscando que el modelo socialista de sociedad y Estado fuera parte del "bolivarianismo" y pasara a ser la ideología política del país.[2257] Por ello, incluso, en la reforma constitucional de 2007 se propuso denominar a todos los componentes de la Fuerza Armada como "bolivariana" (art. 156,8; 236,6; 328 y 329), a la cual se le asignaba el cumplimiento de su misión de defensa que debía realizar "mediante el estudio, planificación y ejecución de la doctrina militar bolivariana."

La reforma constitucional de 2007, como se dijo, fue rechazada, pero sin embargo, a partir de 2008, mediante decreto ley contentivo de la Ley Orgánica de la Fuerza Armada Bolivariana,[2258] el gobierno comenzó a implementarla sistemáticamente, adoptándose oficialmente la denominación de las Fuerzas Armadas como "Bolivarianas", incluso con la creación de un componente adicional, la "Milicia Bolivariana", y la creación adicional de la Policía Nacional Bolivariana.

Sobre la historiografía en relación con estos libros véase Tomás Straka, *La épica del desencanto*, Editorial Alfa, Caracas 2009.

2257   Vinculado a la "doctrina bolivariana," con la propuesta de reforma constitucional de 2007 se buscó sustituir al Estado democrático y social de derecho y de justicia previsto en el texto de 1999, por un Estado Socialista o del Poder Popular, a cuyo efecto en el artículo 16 de la Constitución de buscó crear las comunas y comunidades como "el núcleo territorial básico e indivisible del Estado Socialista Venezolano"; en el artículo 70, al definirse los medios de participación se pretendió indicar que era solo "para la construcción del socialismo", haciéndose mención a las diversas asociaciones "constituidas para desarrollar los valores de la mutua cooperación y la solidaridad socialista"; en el artículo 112 se propuso establecer sobre el modelo económico del Estado, que era para crear "las mejores condiciones para la construcción colectiva y cooperativa de una economía socialista"; en el artículo 113 se buscó regular la constitución de "empresas mixtas o unidades de producción socialistas"; en el artículo 158, se buscó eliminar toda mención a la descentralización como política nacional, y al contrario definir como política nacional, "la participación protagónica del pueblo, restituyéndole el poder y creando las mejores condiciones para la construcción de una democracia socialista"; en el artículo 168 relativo al Municipio, se buscó precisar la necesidad de incorporar "la participación ciudadana a través de los Consejos del Poder Popular y de los medios de producción socialista"; en el artículo 184 se buscó orientar el vaciamiento de competencias de los Estados y Municipios para permitir "la construcción de la economía socialista"; en el artículo 299, relativo al régimen socioeconómico de la República, se pretendió establecer que el mismo se debía fundamentar "en los principios socialistas"; en el artículo 300 relativo a la creación de empresas públicas, se pretendió precisar que ello era sólo "para la promoción y realización de los fines de la economía socialista"; en el artículo 318, sobre el sistema monetario nacional en el cual se pretendió indicar que el mismo era solo para el "logro de los fines esenciales del Estado Socialista", todo de acuerdo con el Plan de Desarrollo Integral de la Nación cuyo objetivo, se pretendía regular que era "para alcanzar los objetivos superiores del Estado Socialista"; y en el artículo 321 sobre el régimen de las reservas internacionales, respecto de las cuales los fondos de las mismas se pretendió que fueran solo para "el desarrollo integral, endógeno, humanista y socialista de la Nación.

2258   Véase Decreto Ley N° 6.239, de ley Orgánica de la Fuerza Armada Bolivariana, en *Gaceta Oficial* N° 5.933, Extra., de 21 de Octubre de 2009. Véase en general, Alfredo Arismendi A., "Fuerza Armada Nacional: Antecedentes, evolución y régimen actual," in *Revista de Derecho Público*, N° 115 (Estudios sobre los Decretos Leyes), Editorial Jurídica Venezolana, Caracas 2008, pp. 187-206; Jesús María Alvarado Andrade, "La nueva Fuerza Armada Bolivariana (Comentarios a raíz del Decreto N° 6.239, con rango, valor y fuerza de Ley Orgánica de la Fuerza Armada Nacional Bolivariana)," *id.*, pp. 207-14

También, posteriormente, en 2010, mediante la sanción de la Ley Orgánica del Poder Popular,[2259] se estableció que "la organización y participación del pueblo en el ejercicio de su soberanía se inspira en la doctrina del Libertador Simón Bolívar, y se rige por los principios y valores socialistas" (art. 5).[2260] Ello por supuesto, como se ha dicho, era históricamente insostenible sin olvidar que si algo hubiese habido de "socialismo" en las ideas de Bolívar, Karl Marx, quien una década después de haber publicado su obra fundamental sobre el comunismo, en conjunto con Engels, que fue *La ideología alemana*,[2261] escribió la entrada sobre Simón Bolívar en la *Nueva Enciclopedia Americana* editada en Nueva York,[2262] lo habría advertido. Lejos de ello, dicho trabajo de Marx más bien, ha sido uno de los escritos más críticos sobre Bolívar que se conocen en la bibliografía bolivariana.

Todas las reformas constitucionales propuestas en 2007, que fueron todas rechazadas por el pueblo, como se ha dicho, fueron sin embargo sistemáticamente implementadas, evidentemente en forma inconstitucional y en fraude a la voluntad popular, una vez que el gobierno adoptó un definitivo signo marxista, tal como resultó de la declaración del propio Presidente de la República a comienzos de 2010, de asumir el marxismo,[2263] todo lo cual fue incorporado también ese mismo año 2010, en la Declaración de Principios del partido oficial. [2264] Y esa implementación se hizo mediante la sanción de una multitud de leyes y sobre todo, de decretos leyes dictados por el gobierno, en todas las áreas a las que se referían las propuestas, decretándose una transformación radical del Estado, estableciendo un Estado Socialista por el cual nadie había votado, y más bien había sido rechazado. Todo se hizo, como hemos indicado, estableciendo un Estado paralelo al Estado Constitucional, denominado Estado Comunal o del Poder Popular, que ha afectado sensiblemente la organización territorial del Estado.

2259   Véase en *Gaceta Oficial* N° 6.011 Extra. de 21-12-2010. Véase en general sobre estas leyes, Allan R. Brewer-Carías, Claudia Nikken, Luis A. Herrera Orellana, Jesús María Alvarado Andrade, José Ignacio Hernández y Adriana Vigilanza, *Leyes Orgánicas sobre el Poder Popular y el Estado Comunal (Los consejos comunales, las comunas, la sociedad socialista y el sistema económico comunal)* Colección Textos Legislativos N° 50, Editorial Jurídica Venezolana, Caracas 2011.

2260   La misma expresión se utilizó en la Ley Orgánica de las Comunas respecto de la constitución, conformación, organización y funcionamiento de las mismas (art. 2); en la Ley Orgánica de los Consejos Comunales respecto de los mismos (art. 1), y en la Ley Orgánica de Contraloría Social (art. 6).

2261   Véase en Karl Marx and Frederich Engels, "The German Ideology," en *Collective Works*, Vol. 5, International Publishers, New York 1976, p. 47. Véanse además los textos pertinentes en http://www.educa.madrid.org/cms_tools/files/0a24636f-764c-4e03-9c1d-6722e2ee60d7/Texto%20Marx%20y%20Engels.pdf

2262   Véase el trabajo de Karl Marx en *The New American Cyclopaedia*, Vol. III, 1858, sobre "Bolívar y Ponte, Simón," en http://www.marxists.org/archive/marx/works/1858/01/bolivar.htm

2263   En su Mensaje anual ante la Asamblea Nacional, el 15 de enero de 2010, el Presidente Chávez declaró, que "asumía el marxismo" aunque confesó que nunca había leído los trabajos de Marx. Véase María Lilibeth Da Corte, "Por primera vez asumo el marxismo," en *El Universal*, Caracas 16 de enero, 2010, http://www.eluniversal.com/2010/01/16/pol_art_por-primera-vez-asu_1726209.shtml.

2264   Véase la "Declaración de Principios, I Congreso Extraordinario del Partido Socialista Unido de Venezuela," 23 Abril, 2010, en http://psuv.org.ve/files/tcdocumentos/Declaracion-de-principios-PSUV.pdf.

En todas las leyes reguladoras de esas materias, y en tantas otras más relacionadas, se ha venido calificando a absolutamente todas las políticas del Estado solo para
la construcción del socialismo, y para el establecimiento de un Estado socialista,
denominación que además se fue incorporando sistemáticamente en todo tipo de
servicios, dependencias, institutos autónomos o empresas del Estado, de manera que
en la actualidad es difícil encontrar alguna institución o entidad que no tenga la denominación de "socialista;" y todo ello, en el contexto de la construcción del Estado
socialista bajo la "doctrina bolivariana."

VII. EL INCUMPLIMIENTO DE LA PROMESA CONSTITUCIONAL DE RES-
PETAR LA VOLUNTAD POPULAR

Estando concebida la Constitución de 1999 como la norma suprema y fundamento de todo el ordenamiento jurídico (art. 7), la principal promesa constitucional que
de ello deriva es la que se configura en torno al principio de su rigidez, que se materializó con la previsión de procedimientos específicos para la revisión de la Constitución, proscribiendo que puedan realizarse modificaciones a la misma por la
Asamblea Nacional, y menos por el Presidente de la República, mediante el solo
procedimiento de formación de las leyes o de decretos leyes, exigiéndose siempre
para cualquier revisión constitucional, un procedimiento especial con la participación del pueblo como poder constituyente originario.[2265] Si la Constitución es producto de la voluntad popular, solo la voluntad del pueblo expresada mediante una
votación puede modificar su texto.

Esos procedimientos especiales de revisión conforme a las previsiones de la
Constitución son: las Enmiendas Constitucionales, las Reformas Constitucionales y
la Asamblea Nacional Constituyente, según la importancia de las modificaciones a
la Constitución, de manera que para la aprobación de las "enmiendas" se estableció
la sola participación del pueblo como poder constituyente originario manifestado
mediante referendo aprobatorio; para la aprobación de la "reforma constitucional" se
estableció la participación de uno de los poderes constituidos, -la Asamblea Nacio-
nal- y, además, del pueblo como poder constituyente originario manifestado mediante referendo; y para la revisión constitucional mediante una "Asamblea Nacional
Constituyente," se estableció la participación del pueblo como poder constituyente
originario, para primero, decidir mediante referendo su convocatoria, y segundo,
para la elección de los miembros de la Asamblea Constituyente (arts. 340 a
341).[2266]

2265   Véase sobre este tema Allan R. Brewer-Carías, "Reforma Constitucional y Control de Constituciona-
        lidad," en *Reforma de la Constitución y control de constitucionalidad. Congreso Internacional*, Pon-
        tificia Universidad Javeriana, Bogotá Colombia, Bogotá, 2005, pp. 108-159; y en *Libro Homenaje al
        Padre José Del Rey Fajardo S.J.*, Fundación de Derecho Público, Universidad Valle del Momboy,
        Editorial Jurídica Venezolana, Caracas Valera, 2005, Tomo II, pp. 977-1011. Igualmente, Allan R.
        Brewer-Carías, "Modelos de revisión constitucional en América Latina," en *Boletín de la Academia
        de Ciencias Políticas y Sociales*, enero-diciembre 2003, N° 141, Año LXVV, Caracas 2004, pp. 115-
        154.

2266   Sobre el significado de estos procedimientos, véase sentencia N° 1140 de la Sala Constitucional de
        05-19-2000, en *Revista de Derecho Público*, N° 84, Editorial Jurídica Venezolana, Caracas, 2000.

Cada procedimiento de revisión constitucional tiene su motivación y propósito, por lo que no puede utilizarse uno de los procedimientos para fines distintos a los regulados en la propia Constitución. De lo contrario se incurriría en un fraude constitucional,[2267] como fue el caso de la reforma constitucional de 2007, que fue sancionada por la Asamblea el 2 de noviembre de 2007 en fraude a la Constitución,[2268] pues por la importancia de la reforma propuesta tendiente a sustituir al Estado democrático y federal de derecho por un Estado Centralizado, Militarista y Socialista se requería de la convocatoria de una Asamblea Nacional Constituyente. La reforma, sin embargo, fue rechazada por el pueblo mediante voto popular en el referendo del 2 de diciembre de 2007, pero posteriormente y en fraude a la voluntad popular, fue implementada mediante leyes y decretos leyes sin que el Juez Constitucional se hubiese pronunciado, o mediante mutaciones constitucionales impuestas por la Sala Constitucional.

La Constitución, ciertamente, establece la forma cómo el pueblo podría reaccionar cuando se realizan reformas o modificaciones a la Constitución mediante otros mecanismos distintos a los regulados en ella, es decir, en forma ilegítima, estableciendo el derecho del mismo a rebelarse, como lo expresa el propio texto de la Constitución de 1999, al declarar que "el pueblo venezolano, fiel a su tradición republicana, a su lucha por la independencia, la paz y la libertad, desconocerá cualquier régimen, legislación o autoridad que contraríe los valores, principios y garantías democráticas o menoscabe los derechos humanos" (art. 350). Esta norma es el fundamento constitucional contemporáneo del derecho a la desobediencia civil,[2269]

2267   La Sala Constitucional del Tribunal Supremo de Justicia en la sentencia N° 74 de 25-01-2006 señaló que un *fraude a la Constitución* ocurre cuando se destruyen las teorías democráticas "mediante el procedimiento de cambio en las instituciones existentes aparentando respetar las formas y procedimientos constitucionales", o cuando se utiliza "del procedimiento de reforma constitucional para proceder a la creación de un nuevo régimen político, de un nuevo ordenamiento constitucional, sin alterar el sistema de legalidad establecido, como ocurrió con el *uso fraudulento de los poderes* conferidos por la ley marcial en la Alemania de la Constitución de *Weimar*, forzando al Parlamento a conceder a los líderes fascistas, en términos de dudosa legitimidad, la plenitud del poder constituyente, otorgando un poder legislativo ilimitado"; y que un *falseamiento de la Constitución* ocurre cuando se otorga "a las normas constitucionales una interpretación y un sentido distinto del que realmente tienen, que es en realidad una modificación no formal de la Constitución misma", concluyendo con la afirmación de que "*Una reforma constitucional sin ningún tipo de límites, constituiría un fraude constitucional*". Véase en *Revista de Derecho Público*, N° 105, Editorial Jurídica Venezolana, Caracas 2006, pp. 76 ss.

2268   Véase Allan R. Brewer-Carías, *Reforma constitucional y fraude a la Constitución (1999-2009)*, Academia de Ciencias Políticas y Sociales, Caracas 2009.

2269   Sobre la desobediencia civil y el artículo 350 de la Constitución de Venezuela, véase: María L. Álvarez Chamosa y Paola A. A. Yrady, "La desobediencia civil como mecanismo de participación ciudadana", en *Revista de Derecho Constitucional*, N° 7 (Enero-Junio). Editorial Sherwood, Caracas, 2003, pp. 7-21; Andrés A. Mezgravis, "¿Qué es la desobediencia civil?", en *Revista de Derecho Constitucional*, N° 7 (enero-junio), Editorial Sherwood,Caracas, 2003, pp. 189-191; Marie Picard de Orsini, "Consideraciones acerca de la desobediencia civil como instrumento de la democracia", en *El Derecho Público a comienzos del siglo XXI. Estudios homenaje al Profesor Allan R. Brewer-Carías*, Tomo I, Instituto de Derecho Público, UCV, Civitas Ediciones, Madrid, 2003, pp. 535-551; y Eloisa Avellaneda y Luis Salamanca, "El artículo 350 de la Constitución: derecho de rebelión, derecho resistencia o derecho a la desobediencia civil", en *El Derecho Público a comienzos del siglo XXI. Estudios homenaje al Profesor Allan R. Brewer-Carías,* Tomo I, Instituto de Derecho Público, UCV, Civitas Ediciones, Madrid, 2003, pp. 553-583.

cuyo antecedente remoto se podría ubicar en el artículo 35 de la Constitución Francesa de 1793, que era el último de los artículos de la Declaración de los Derechos del Hombre y del Ciudadano que la precedía, en el cual se estableció que "Cuando el gobierno viole los derechos del pueblo, la insurrección es, para el pueblo y para cada porción del pueblo, el más sagrado de los derechos y el más indispensable de los deberes".

Pero por supuesto, ese derecho a la rebelión en el Estado constitucional, no debería tener posibilidad de ejercerse si funcionaran adecuadamente los mecanismos que la Constitución establece para su propia protección, y en particular, la Jurisdicción Constitucional, llamada precisamente a garantizar la supremacía y efectividad de las normas y principios constitucionales con potestad para anular los actos estatales de ejecución directa de la Constitución que la viole (art. 334, 335).

La Jurisdicción Constitucional, y en general, los sistemas de justicia constitucional, por ello, con razón, ante las violaciones de la Constitución por los órganos del Estado, se han considerado, como el sustituto al ejercicio del derecho de rebelión popular. Como lo recordó Sylvia Snowiss en su análisis histórico sobre los orígenes de la justicia constitucional de Norteamérica, los sistemas de control de constitucionalidad efectivamente surgieron como un sustituto a la revolución,[2270] en el sentido de que si los ciudadanos tienen derecho a la supremacía constitucional como pueblo soberano, cualquier violación de la Constitución podría dar lugar a la revocatoria del mandato a los representantes o a su sustitución por otros, en aplicación del derecho a la resistencia o revuelta que defendía John Locke.[2271]

Es decir, si bien antes del surgimiento del Estado de derecho, en caso de opresión de los derechos o de abuso o usurpación del poder, la revolución era la vía de solución a los conflictos entre el pueblo y los gobernantes, con la consolidación de dicho Estado de derecho, como sustituto del ejercicio del derecho de rebelión, precisamente surgió el poder atribuido a los jueces para dirimir los conflictos constitucionales entre los poderes constituidos o entre éstos y el pueblo. Esa es, precisamente, la tarea del juez constitucional, quedando configurada la justicia constitucional como la principal garantía al derecho ciudadano a la supremacía constitucional, de manera que si ésta no funciona o es inoperante para proteger la voluntad popular, surge entonces de nuevo el derecho a la rebelión del pueblo.

Y esa ha sido precisamente la situación trágica en Venezuela, donde en contraste con todos los principios y previsiones constitucionales, ante el desprecio manifestado respecto de la supremacía y rigidez, de la Constitución, la misma en realidad, ha sido convertida en un conjunto normativo maleable por absolutamente todos los poderes públicos, cuyas normas tienen la vigencia y el alcance que los órganos del Estado han dispuesto, sea mediante leyes ordinarias, decretos leyes e incluso mediante sentencias de la Jurisdicción Constitucional, todas hechas a la medida, y con la "garantía" de que dichas actuaciones constitucionales no serán controladas preci-

---

2270   Véase Silvia Snowiss, *Judicial Review and the Law of the Constitution,* Yale University Press 1990, p. 113.

2271   Véase John Locke, *Two Treatises of Government* (ed. Peter Laslett), Cambridge UK, 1967, pp. 211 y 221 ss.

samente por la sujeción política de la Jurisdicción Constitucional al control del Ejecutivo.

Ello ha provocado que en los últimos años, la Sala Constitucional del Tribunal Supremo, lejos de haber actuado como Juez Constitucional en el marco de las atribuciones expresas constitucionales, más bien haya sido el instrumento más artero para la destrucción de la institucionalidad democrática y el apuntalamiento del autoritarismo, particularmente por una parte, al abstenerse de juzgar sobre la inconstitucionalidad de las leyes que han sido impugnadas; y por la otra, al ejercer su facultad de interpretación del contenido y alcance de las normas constitucionales (art. 334).

En este último caso, como máximo intérprete de la Constitución, al margen de la misma y mediante interpretaciones inconstitucionales, la Sala Constitucional al ejercer su facultad de interpretación, lo ha hecho, en cuanto a normas constitucionales incluso legales, que nada tienen de ambiguas, imprecisas, mal redactadas y con errores de lenguaje, con lo cual lamentablemente lo que ha hecho es modificar ilegítimamente el texto constitucional, legitimando y soportando la estructuración progresiva del Estado autoritario. Es decir, ha falseado el contenido de la Constitución, mediante una "mutación"[2272] ilegítima y fraudulenta de la misma,[2273] habiendo resuelto, al contrario de lo establecido en la Constitución, , por ejemplo, que una "competencia exclusiva" de los Estados, no es tal, sino que una competencia concurrente y sujeta a la voluntad del Ejecutivo Nacional, el cual puede intervenirla y reasumirla; que la prohibición de financiar con fondos públicos a las asociaciones con fines políticos, ya no es tal, reduciendo la prohibición de la norma a sólo financiar el "funcionamiento interno" de los partidos, pero estableciendo, en cambio, que las actividades electorales de los mismos si son financiables por el Estado, por lo que la norma que dejó entonces de ser prohibitiva; que los tratados internacionales sobre derechos humanos no tienen prevalencia sobre el derecho interno sino sólo

---

2272   Una mutación constitucional ocurre cuando se modifica el contenido de una norma constitucional de tal forma que aún cuando la misma conserva su contenido, recibe una significación diferente. Véase Salvador O. Nava Gomar, "Interpretación, mutación y reforma de la Constitución. Tres extractos" en Eduardo Ferrer Mac-Gregor (coordinador), Interpretación Constitucional, Tomo II, Ed. Porrúa, Universidad Nacional Autónoma de México, México 2005, pp. 804 ss. Véase en general sobre el tema, Konrad Hesse, "Límites a la mutación constitucional", en *Escritos de derecho constitucional*, Centro de Estudios Constitucionales, Madrid 1992.

2273   La Sala Constitucional del Tribunal Supremo de Justicia en la sentencia Nº 74 de 25-01-2006 señaló que un *fraude a la Constitución* ocurre cuando se destruyen las teorías democráticas "mediante el procedimiento de cambio en las instituciones existentes aparentando respetar las formas y procedimientos constitucionales", o cuando se utiliza "del procedimiento de reforma constitucional para proceder a la creación de un nuevo régimen político, de un nuevo ordenamiento constitucional, sin alterar el sistema de legalidad establecido, como ocurrió con el *uso fraudulento de los poderes* conferidos por la ley marcial en la Alemania de la Constitución de *Weimar*, forzando al Parlamento a conceder a los líderes fascistas, en términos de dudosa legitimidad, la plenitud del poder constituyente, otorgando un poder legislativo ilimitado"; y que un *falseamiento de la Constitución* ocurre cuando se otorga "a las normas constitucionales una interpretación y un sentido distinto del que realmente tienen, que es en realidad una modificación no formal de la Constitución misma", concluyendo con la afirmación de que *"Una reforma constitucional sin ningún tipo de límites, constituiría un fraude constitucional"*. Véase en *Revista de Derecho Público*, Editorial Jurídica Venezolana, Nº 105, Caracas 2006, pp. 76 ss. Véase Néstor Pedro Sagües, *La interpretación judicial de la Constitución*, Buenos Aires 2006, pp. 56-59, 80-81, 165 ss.

ALLAN R. BREWER-CARÍAS

cuando la sala Constitucional lo decida, y que no tienen aplicación inmediata por los jueces; que sólo los tribunales nacionales pueden controlar las violaciones a derechos humanos, siendo las sentencias de la Corte Interamericana de Derechos Humanos inejecutables en Venezuela; y que el referendo revocatorio ha pasado a ser un "referendo ratificatorio" no previsto en la Constitución.[2274]

Para dictar las sentencias mencionadas, la Jurisdicción Constitucional no sólo desconoció el principio de la supremacía constitucional que se impone a todos los órganos del Estado, incluyendo al Juez Constitucional, sino que ejerció ilegítimamente su potestad de interpretación de la Constitución para mutarla, es decir, modificarla sin alterar su texto, conforme a los deseos del régimen.

Contra esas prácticas autoritarias, y contra un Juez Constitucional que dejó de ser el instrumento de control de la inconstitucionalidad, renunciando a ser el sustituto la rebelión del pueblo para proteger su Constitución, fue que entre otras razones, el pueblo venezolano efectivamente se rebeló el 6 de diciembre de 2015, aun cuando por ahora, solo votando en las elecciones parlamentarias mayoritariamente en contra del gobierno autoritario y sus prácticas. La nueva Asamblea Nacional, en consecuencia, tiene ahora la tarea de completar la implementación de la manifestación de la voluntad popular, lo que implicará, por sobre todo, reestructurar el Tribunal Supremo para devolverle al Poder Judicial la autonomía e independencia que se le quitó, y en lugar de ser el instrumento para el cumplimiento de las promesas constitucionales del texto de 1966, sea efectivamente el garante de las mismas.

New York, 13 de enero de 2016.

2274 La Sala Constitucional del Tribunal Supremo de Justicia en la sentencia N° 74 de 25-01-2006 señaló que un *fraude a la Constitución* ocurre cuando se destruyen las teorías democráticas "mediante el procedimiento de cambio en las instituciones existentes aparentando respetar las formas y procedimientos constitucionales", o cuando se utiliza "del procedimiento de reforma constitucional para proceder a la creación de un nuevo régimen político, de un nuevo ordenamiento constitucional, sin alterar el sistema de legalidad establecido, como ocurrió con el *uso fraudulento de los poderes* conferidos por la ley marcial en la Alemania de la Constitución de *Weimar*, forzando al Parlamento a conceder a los líderes fascistas, en términos de dudosa legitimidad, la plenitud del poder constituyente, otorgando un poder legislativo ilimitado"; y que un *falseamiento de la Constitución* ocurre cuando se otorga "a las normas constitucionales una interpretación y un sentido distinto del que realmente tienen, que es en realidad una modificación no formal de la Constitución misma", concluyendo con la afirmación de que "*Una reforma constitucional sin ningún tipo de límites, constituiría un fraude constitucional*". Véase en *Revista de Derecho Público,* Editorial Jurídica Venezolana, N° 105, Caracas 2006, pp. 76 ss. Véase Néstor Pedro Sagües, *La interpretación judicial de la Constitución*, Buenos Aires 2006, pp. 56-59, 80-81, 165 ss.

ÍNDICE GENERAL

CONTENIDO GENERAL.. 7

PRESENTACIÓN 11

PRIMERA PARTE
MODELO POLÍTICO Y DERECHO DEL ESTADO

SEGUNDA PARTE
**EL DESMANTELAMIENTO DE LA DEMOCRACIA.
EL EXPERIMENTO AUTORITARIO DE CHÁVEZ**
*DISMANTLING DEMOCRACY.
THE CHÁVEZ AUTHORITARIAN EXPERIMENT*

INTRODUCTION
*DEFRAUDING DEMOCRACY THROUGH NONCONSENSUAL
CONSTITUENT ASSEMBLIES*.. 47

PART ONE
*THE POLITICAL ASSAULT ON STATE POWERS AND THE FRAMEWORK
FOR AUTHORITARIANISM* 67

Chapter 1:
THE 1999 EXCLUSIONIST CONSTITUTION-MAKING PROCESS 68

I.   THE 1999 NATIONAL CONSTITUENT ASSEMBLY 69

II.   THE 1998 CRISIS OF THE POLITICAL SYSTEM AND THE NEED FOR
      DEMOCRATIC RECONSTRUCTION 73

      1. *Party Domination and Demand for Participation*.......................... 74

      2. *State Centralism and the Crisis of Decentralization* 75

      3. *The Demand for Reform* 77

III. THE CONSTITUTION MAKING PROCESS AND ITS DEFORMATION ... 78

      1. *The Choice of a National Constituent Assembly*............................. 78

2. *The Constitutional Debate Regarding the Election of the Constituent Assembly* 80

3. *The Electoral Rule for the Election of the Assembly*............................... 84

4. *The Seizure of the Constituted Powers* 85

5. *The Drafting Phase: Haste and Exclusion*... 88

IV. THE PARALLEL TRANSITORY REGIME 91

V. THE DEMOCRATIC FAILURE OF THE CONSTITUTION-MAKING PROCESS... 92

Chapter 2:

THE ENDLESS AND ILLEGITIMATE TRANSITORY CONSTITUTIONAL REGIME... 94

I. FAILED EFFORTS TO CREATE A CONSTITUTIONAL FRAME-WORK TO TRANSITION PUBLIC POWERS THROUGH AN APPROBATORY REFERENDUM 95

II. THE ILLEGITIMATE REGIME FOR THE TRANSITION OF PUBLIC POWERS... 96

1. *Elimination of Congress and Creation of the National Legislative Commission*.. 97

2. *Dissolution of State Legislative Assemblies and Creation of State Legislative Commissions*.. 99

3. *Control over Municipalities*... 99

4. *Intervention of the Judiciary*.. 100

5. *Dismissal and Appointment of Officials of the Citizens' Power* 102

6. *Dismissal and Appointment of Members of the National Electoral Council*.. 102

III. JUDICIAL ACCEPTANCE OF A DOUBLE CONSTITUTIONAL TRANSITORY REGIME.. 102

IV. THE KIDNAPPING OF THE CONSTITUTION AND SUBJECTION OF THE JUDICIAL BRANCH TO THE GOVERNMENT 107

Chapter 3:

THE 1999 POLITICAL CONSTITUTION AND THE REINFORCEMENT OF CENTRALIZATION 108

I. THE CONSTITUTION OF 1999: FRUSTRATION OF THE NECESSARY POLITICAL CHANGE 108

II. THE NEW "BOLIVARIAN" REPUBLIC AND ITS PARTISAN CHARACTER 111

III. THE PROBLEM OF A POLITICAL CONSTITUTION DRAFTED FOR CENTRALISM AND AUTHORITARIANISM... 114

IV. THE DEMOCRATIC REGIME AND POLITICAL PARTICIPATION 118

1. *Representative Democracy* 119

2.   *The Mixed Electoral System and Its Distortion*   121

3.   *Principles of Participative Democracy and Their Distortion*   122

4.   *Direct Democracy Institutions, Referenda, and the Distortion of the Recall Referendum*   126

5.   *Plural Political Parties and the Move toward a Single-Party System*   131

6.   *Institutions of Government Accountability and Liability*   135

V.   THE SYSTEM OF GOVERNMENT AND THE SEPARATION OF POWERS   136

1.   *Presidential System and Its Reinforcement*   136

2.   *Unbalanced Powers Due to Concentrated Power in the National Assembly*   137

3.   *The State of Justice and Its Incongruence*   139

4.   *The Constitutional Base for Militarism*   142

Chapter 4:

THE 1999 SOCIAL AND ECONOMIC CONSTITUTION AND ITS PROBLEMS   144

I.   CONSTITUTIONAL VALUES AND DECLARATIVE PRINCIPLES   145

II.   THE GENERAL FRAMEWORK ON MATTERS OF HUMAN RIGHTS   149

1.   *General Declarations*   149

2.   *Social Rights and the Social State*   155

3.   *Limits to the Exercise of Constitutional Rights That Can Only Be Established through Statutes*   157

4.   *Freedom of Expression and Its Limitations*   158

5.   *The New Indigenous People's Collective Rights*   161

III. THE PROBLEM OF AN ECONOMIC CONSTITUTION CONCEIVED FOR STATE APPROPRIATION ("STATIZATION") OF THE ECONOMY .   162

1.   *The Mixed Economic System*   162

2.   *Reduced Property Rights and Economic Freedoms*   163

3.   *The Almost-Unlimited Possibility of State Intervention in the Economy* ...   165

PART TWO

INSTITUTIONAL DEVELOPMENT TOWARD CONSOLIDATING AUTHORITA-RIANISM   168

Chapter 5:

CONSTITUTIONAL FRAUD AND DEFRAUDING DEMOCRACY   170

I.   POPULAR AUTHORITARIANISM AND CONCENTRATED STATE POWERS   170

II.   THE PROCESS OF CONCENTRATING POWER SINCE 1999   173

1.   *The Germ of Concentrated Power: The National Assembly's Authority to Remove State Officials* 174

2.   *The Political Supremacy of the Executive and the Absence of Checks and Balances* 176

3.   *Continuous Interference and Subjection of the Judicial Power* 178

III. CENTRALIZING POWER AND THE ABSENCE OF EFFECTIVE POLITICAL PARTICIPATION 182

1.   *The Meaning of Democracy and the Illusion of Participatory Democracy* 183

2.   *The Reaction against the Federation as a Decentralized State* 187

3.   *The Reaction against Local Governments and the Centralized Communal Councils* 188

IV. THE FORESEEABLE OUTCOME: THE DICTATORSHIP OF DEMOCRACY 191

Chapter 6:
THE REINFORCED CENTRALIZATION OF THE FEDERATION 194

I.   HISTORY AND DEVELOPMENT OF THE VENEZUELAN FEDERATION 195

II. FEDERALIST CONSTITUTIONAL PROVISIONS IN THE 1999 CONSTITUTION 197

III. LIMITING THE CONTENTS OF SUBNATIONAL CONSTITUTIONS 198

IV. CONSTITUTIONAL DISTRIBUTION OF POWERS 200

V.   THE FINANCING RULES OF THE FEDERATION 201

VI. THE RECENTRALIZATION OF THE FEDERATION 202

Chapter 7:
CONCENTRATION OF POWERS AND AUTHORITARIAN GOVERNMENT 204

I.   THE SEPARATION OF POWERS IN MODERN CONSTITU-TIONALISM AND THE VENEZUELAN CONSTITUTIONAL TRADITION 204

II. SEPARATION OF POWERS AND DEMOCRACY 207

III. DEFRAUDING POLITICAL PARTICIPATION IN APPOINTING OFFICIALS 209

IV. THE SUPREMACY OF THE EXECUTIVE AND THE ABSENCE OF CHECKS AND BALANCES 210

V.   THE RUPTURE OF THE RULE OF LAW AND THE REJECTED 2007 CONSTITUTIONAL REFORM 211

Chapter 8:

THE CATASTROPHIC DEPENDENCE AND POLITICAL SUBJECTION
OF THE SUPREME TRIBUNAL OF JUSTICE 215

I.   THE SUBJECTION OF THE SUPREME TRIBUNAL OF JUSTICE 216

    1. *The Confiscation of Civil Society's Right to Participate in the
        Appointment of the Magistrates of the Supreme Tribunal in 2000* 216

    2. *The Appointment of the Magistrates of the Supreme Tribunal of Justice* .. 218

    3. *The Consolidation of the Commission on the Functioning and
        Restructuring of the Judicial System and the Complete Political Control
        of the Judiciary* 220

    4. *The 2004 Reform of the Supreme Tribunal Organic Law and the
        Reinforcement of Executive Control over the Judiciary* 223

II.   THE SUPREME TRIBUNAL AS A TOOL TO DISTORT THE
      CONSTITUTION AND RECOURSE FOR CONSTITUTIONAL
      INTERPRETATION 226

Chapter 9:

STATE APPROPRIATION, NATIONALIZATION, EXPROPRIATION,
AND CONFISCATION OF PRIVATE ASSETS 230

I.   THE COMPULSORY ACQUISITION OF PRIVATE ASSETS 230

II.   THE 2006–2007 STATE APPROPRIATION OF PRIVATE
      ENTERPRISES IN THE NATIONALIZED OIL INDUSTRY 234

III. THE 2008–2009 NATIONALIZATION AND STATE APPROPRIATION 238

    1. *The Nationalization of the Iron and Steel Industry* 238

    2. *The Nationalization of the Cement Industry* 239

    3. *The State Appropriation of Assets and Services Related to Primary
        Hydrocarbon Activities* 240

    4. *The Reservation to the State of Petrochemical Activities* 243

IV.   THE STATE APPROPRIATIONS OF RURAL LAND AND ALIMEN-
      TARY INDUSTRIES 243

PART THREE:

*CONSTITUTIONAL REFORMS DESIGNED TO CONSOLIDATE AUTHO-
RITARIANISM* 244

Chapter 10:

THE FAILED ATTEMPT TO CONSOLIDATE AN AUTHORITARIAN
AND ANTIDEMOCRATIC POLITICAL SYSTEM IN THE CONSTI-
TUTION 245

I.   A NEW FRAUD ON THE CONSTITUTION 245

II.   PROPOSED CHANGES TO THE FUNDAMENTAL PRINCIPLES OF
      THE POLITICAL SYSTEM 250

    1. *Bolivarian Doctrine* 252

2.   *The Substitution of the Social-Democratic State for a Socialist State*   253

3.   *The Elimination of Decentralization as a State Policy*   254

4.   *Fragmentation of Public Administration*   256

5.   *The Abandonment of Budgetary Discipline and the Unity of the Treasury*   257

III. PROPOSED CHANGES IN THE POLITICAL SYSTEM: FROM REPRESENTATIVE DEMOCRACY TO PARTICIPATORY DEMO-CRACY   258

1.   *The Elimination of Representative Democracy at the Local Level*   258

2.   *Elimination of Republican Alternation in Office by Establishing the Possibility of Indefinite Reelection of the President*   260

3.   *The Contradictory Restrictions on Citizens' Right to Political Participation*   261

   A.   *The Elimination of the Civil Society's Participation in Nominating State Officials*   261

   B.   *Limits to Political Participation by Means of Referenda and Restrictions on Direct Democracy*   262

   C.   *Limits on the Right to Political Participation in Constitutional Review Procedures*   263

4.   *Reducing the Right to Political Participation to Implementing Socialist Ideology*   264

5.   *Political Parties, Political Association, and Public Financing of Electoral Activities*   264

Chapter 11:

THE FAILED ATTEMPT TO CONSOLIDATE A CENTRALIZED STATE IN THE CONSTITUTION   265

I.   PROPOSED CHANGES IN THE STATE FORM: FROM CENTRA-LIZED FEDERATION TO CENTRALIZED STATE   266

1.   *The Destruction of the Federation*   266

   A.   *Taking Away Territoriality from the Federation*   266

   B.   *A Territorial Division of the Republic Tied to the Central Power*   267

   C.   *The Capital City: No Political Autonomy or Democratic Government*   268

2.   *Abandoning Vertical Distribution of the Public Powers*   269

3.   *Nationalizing Federated States' Competencies*   269

4.   *Obligating States and Municipalities to Transfer Their Competencies to the Organs of the Popular Power*   271

5.   *Eliminating the Constitutional Guarantee of Municipal Autonomy*   272

II. PROPOSED CHANGES IN THE ORGANIZATION OF THE NATIONAL LEVEL OF GOVERNMENT   272

1.   *Proposed Reforms Regarding the International Activities of the Republic* 272

2.   *Proposed Reforms to the Executive Power and Reinforcing the Presidential System* 273

   A.   *The Extension of the President's Term and Unlimited Reelection* ... 273

   B.   *The New Executive Organs: Vice Presidents* 274

   C.   *Extending the Powers of the President* 274

3.   *Proposed Reforms Regarding the Legislative Power and Political Permeability* 277

4.   *Proposed Reforms Regarding the Appointing and Dismissing of the Head Officers of the Nonelected Branches of Government* 277

III. PROPOSED CHANGES IN THE ARMED FORCES: FROM A CIVIL MANAGED STATE TO A MILITARIST STATE 278

Chapter 12:

THE FAILED ATTEMPT TO CONSOLIDATE A SOCIALIST CENTRA-LIZED ECONOMIC SYSTEM IN THE CONSTITUTION 281

I.   PROPOSED CHANGES ON MATTERS OF ECONOMIC FREEDOM AND PRIVATE PROPERTY 282

1.   *Eliminating Economic Freedom as a Constitutionally Protected Right* 282

2.   *Eliminating Property as a Constitutionally Protected Right* 284

3.   *The Elimination of the Latifundio* 286

II.   PROPOSED CHANGES ON MATTERS OF PUBLIC ECONOMY MANAGEMENT 287

1.   *The Regime Governing State Intervention in the Economy* 287

2.   *Proposed Changes in the State's Fiscal and Economic Regime* 288

   A.   *Eliminating the Autonomy of the Central Bank of Venezuela* 289

   B.   *Macroeconomic Policy at the Mercy of the National Executive* 290

III. PROPOSED CHANGES IN MATTERS OF HUMAN RIGHTS 291

1.   *The Extension of the Principle of Equality* 291

2.   *Proposed Changes in the States of Exception* 292

   A.   *The Expansion of States of Exception* 292

   B.   *The Elimination of the Duration of a State of Emergency* 292

   C.   *The Possibility of Suspending Constitutional Guarantees* 292

   D.   *Changes Regarding the Constitutional Guarantees of Human Rights That Can Be Suspended or Restricted in Situations of Exception* 293

   E.   *The Elimination of the Control Mechanisms of States of Exception.* 293

3.   *Proposed Changes in Education Rights: The Limits to University Autonomy* 294

4.   *Proposed Changes in Labor Rights: A Useless Constitutional "Reform"* 294

Chapter 13:

THE IRREGULAR FRAUDULENT IMPLEMENTATION OF THE
 REJECTED CONSTITUTIONAL REFORM THROUGH LEGISLATION.. 295

Chapter 14:

THE ILLEGITIMATE MUTATION OF THE CONSTITUTION
 THROUGH JUDICIAL CONSTITUTIONAL INTERPRETATION 299

I.   THE ACCEPTANCE OF A TRANSITORY CONSTITUTIONAL REGIME
     NOT APPROVED BY THE PEOPLE 301

II. FROM REVOCATION REFERENDA TO RATIFYING REFERENDA 302

III. THE ELIMINATION OF THE CONSTITUTIONAL PRINCIPLE OF
     ALTERNATE GOVERNMENT AND THE LIMITS TO CONTINUOUS
     REELECTION 304

IV. LIFTING THE PROHIBITION ON REPEATING REFERENDA FOR
     CONSTITUTIONAL REVIEW 306

V.   ILLEGITIMATE TRANSFORMATION OF THE FEDERAL SYSTEM 308

VI. THE LIFTING OF THE PROHIBITION ON GOVERNMENT
     FINANCING OF ELECTORAL ACTIVITIES 310

VII. THE ILLEGITIMATE ELIMINATION OF THE SUPRACONS-
     TITUTIONAL RANK OF INTERNATIONAL HUMAN RIGHTS
     TREATIES 311

VIII. THE ELIMINATION OF JUDGES' POWER TO IMMEDIATELY AND
       DIRECTLY APPLY INTERNATIONAL HUMAN RIGHTS TREATIES .. 314

IX. THE DENIAL OF THE PEOPLE'S RIGHT TO INTERNATIONAL
     HUMAN RIGHTS PROTECTION 315

Chapter 15:

THE ALTERNATE PRINCIPLE OF GOVERNMENT AND THE 2009
 CONSTITUTIONAL AMENDMENT ON CONTINUOUS
 REELECTION 318

I.   THE REPUBLICAN PRINCIPLE OF ALTERNATE GOVERNMENT
     AND THE VENEZUELAN TRADITION OF NO REELECTION 318

II. THE LIMITS IMPOSED BY THE CONSTITUTION ON
     CONSTITUTIONAL REVIEW 320

III. THE BINDING CONSTITUTIONAL INTERPRETATION 321

FINAL REFLECTIONS

*THE RIGHT TO DEMOCRACY AND ITS VIOLATION BY VENEZUELA'S
 AUTHORITARIAN GOVERNMENT: SOME RELEVANT FACTS FROM
 THE PAST DECADE* 322

I.   REPRESENTATIVE DEMOCRACY AND THE VENEZUELAN
     AUTHORITARIAN GOVERNMENT... 322

II. REPRESENTATIVE DEMOCRACY AND ITS DEFORMATIONS 326

III. PARTICIPATORY DEMOCRACY AND THE VIOLATION OF THE
      CITIZENS' RIGHT TO PARTICIPATION 333
IV.   DISRESPECTING HUMAN RIGHTS 338
V.   ACCESS TO POWER AND ITS EXERCISE CONTRARY TO THE RULE
      OF LAW 344
VI.   BROKEN REPRESENTATIVE DEMOCRACY 347
VII. WEAKENED DEMOCRACY DUE TO THE ABSENCE OF PLURALISM . 348
VIII. VANISHING DEMOCRACY AND ABSENT SEPARATION OF
      POWERS 351
IX.   DEMOCRACY AND PROBLEMS OF TRANSPARENCY 354
X.   FEEBLE DEMOCRACY AND RESTRICTIONS ON FREEDOMS OF
      EXPRESSION AND THE PRESS 356
XI.   DEMOCRACY AND SUBMISSION OF THE MILITARY TO CIVIL
      POWER 358

TERCERA PARTE

EL ESTADO TOTALITARIO Y LA DEMOLICIÓN DEL ESTADO DEMOCRÁTICO Y SOCIAL DE DERECHO Y DE JUSTICIA, DE ECONOMÍA MIXTA Y DESCENTRALIZADO

INTRODUCCIÓN:
EL ESTADO Y LA LEY (EL DERECHO ADMINISTRATIVO Y EL ESTADO) .. 364

I.   EL DERECHO ADMINISTRATIVO ENTRE EL DEBER SER Y LA
      REALIDAD QUE RESULTA DE LA PRÁCTICA POLÍTICA 364
II.   EL DERECHO ADMINISTRATIVO Y EL PARADIGMA
      DEMOCRÁTICO EN LAS FORMULACIONES CONSTITUCIONALES 366
III. EL DERECHO ADMINISTRATIVO Y LOS AUTORITARISMOS 368
IV.   EL DERECHO ADMINISTRATIVO Y EL DESEQUILIBRIO ENTRE
      PODERES ESTATALES Y DERECHOS CIUDADANOS 371

SECCIÓN PRIMERA:
LA AUSENCIA DE ESTADO DE DERECHO 375

I.   LA CONSTITUCIÓN VIOLADA 376
II.   LA CONSTITUCIÓN MALEABLE 377
III. LA CONSTITUCIÓN MUTABLE 378
IV.   EL ABANDONO DE LA RIGIDEZ CONSTITUCIONAL 380
V.   LA DESINSTITUCIONALIZACIÓN GENERAL DEL PAÍS 384

SECCIÓN SEGUNDA:

LA AUSENCIA DE ESTADO DEMOCRÁTICO 385

I. LAS FALLAS DE LA REPRESENTATIVIDAD DEMOCRÁTICA 387

II. LAS FALLAS DE LA LLAMADA DEMOCRACIA PARTICIPATIVA 388

III. LA AUSENCIA DE SEPARACIÓN DE PODERES 389

IV. LA AUSENCIA DE AUTONOMÍA E INDEPENDENCIA DEL PODER JUDICIAL 392

V. LA ADMINISTRACIÓN DEJÓ DE ESTAR AL SERVICIO DEL CIUDADANO 396

VI. LA NEGACIÓN DEL DERECHO DE ACCESO A LA INFORMA-CIÓN ADMINISTRATIVA 397

VII. EL MILITARISMO PREVALENTE Y AVASALLANTE AL MAR-GEN DE LA AUTORIDAD CIVIL 398

VIII. LA ELIMINACIÓN DE LA LIBERTAD DE EXPRESIÓN Y COMUNICACIÓN 403

IX. LA VIOLACIÓN Y ELIMINACIÓN DEL PRINCIPIO DEMO-CRÁTICO ... 405

SECCIÓN TERCERA:

LA AUSENCIA DE UN ESTADO SOCIAL Y DE ECONOMÍA MIXTA 407

I. EL ESTADO SOCIAL Y SU IMBRICACIÓN CON EL ESTADO DE ECONOMÍA MIXTA 408

II. LA LEY ORGÁNICA DE PRECIOS JUSTOS Y EL FIN DE LA LIBERTAD ECONÓMICA 413

III. EL INTENTO Y RECHAZADO PROYECTO DE REFORMA CONSTITUCIONAL DE 2007 PARA SUSTITUIR EL ESTADO SOCIAL Y DE ECONOMÍA MIXTA 415

IV. IMPLANTACIÓN DE UN ESTADO COMUNISTA 417

V. DESARROLLO DE UN ESTADO BUROCRÁTICO, ACAPARADOR DE TODA LA ACTIVIDAD ECONÓMICA 420

VI. IMPLANTACIÓN DEL ESTADO POPULISTA 427

VII. ESTRUCTURACIÓN PARALELA DEL ESTADO COMUNAL Y DEL PODER POPULAR 432

VIII DESARROLLO DEL ESTADO CLIENTELAR 435

SECCIÓN CUARTA:

LA AUSENCIA DE ESTADO DE JUSTICIA 439

I. AUSENCIA DE LEYES JUSTAS Y MULTIPLICACIÓN DE LEYES INCONSULTAS 440

II. INFLACIÓN DE LA INSEGURIDAD JURÍDICA 441

III. EL SOMETIMIENTO POLÍTICO DEL PODER JUDICIAL 444

IV. EL ESTADO IRRESPONSABLE, ESCAPADO DE LA JUSTICIA
     INTERNA.. 445
V.   EL ESTADO ESCAPADO DE LA JUSTICIA INTERNACIONAL 448
VI. LA JUSTICIA AL SERVICIO DEL AUTORITARISMO............................ 449
VII. LA AUSENCIA DE JUSTICIA 450
VIII. LA INJUSTICIA DE LA IMPUNIDAD 451

SECCIÓN QUINTA:
LA AUSENCIA DE ESTADO DESCENTRALIZADO 453

I.   LAS FALLAS DE LA DEMOCRÁTICA REPRESENTATIVA 454
II. LAS FALLAS DE LA DEMOCRÁTICA PARTICIPATIVA.......................... 456
III. LA CONCEPCIÓN CENTRALISTA DE LA "FEDERACIÓN
     DESCENTRALIZADA" 458
IV. EL DESBALANCE HACIA EL NIVEL NACIONAL EN LA
     DISTRIBUCIÓN TERRITORIAL DEL PODER 459
V.   EL MUNICIPIO QUE NO SE QUISO REGULAR EFECTIVAMENTE
     COMO LA UNIDAD PRIMARIA EN LA ORGANIZACIÓN NACIONAL ... 461
VI. LAS COMUNAS VERSUS LOS MUNICIPIOS 463
VII. EL AHOGAMIENTO DE LA INSTITUCIÓN MUNICIPAL 465
VIII. EL AHOGAMIENTO Y NEUTRALIZACIÓN DE LAS ENTIDADES
     TERRITORIALES POR PARTE DEL PODER NACIONAL 469
APRECIACIÓN FINAL:
EL ESTADO TOTALITARIO Y LA DESCONSTITUCIONALIZACIÓN DEL
ESTADO CONSTITUCIONAL.. 472

CUARTA PARTE

LA DESCONSTITUCIONALIZACIÓN Y DESJURIDIFICACIÓN DEL ESTADO CONSTITUCIONAL Y LA ESTRUCTURACIÓN PARALELA DEL ESTADO COMUNAL O DEL PODER POPULAR

SECCIÓN PRIMERA:
LA DEMOCRACIA Y LA PARTICIPACIÓN POLÍTICA Y POPULAR, Y EL
AHOGAMIENTO DE LA DEMOCRACIA REPRESENTATIVA EN
NOMBRE DE UNA SUPUESTA "DEMOCRACIA PARTICIPATIVA" 482

SECCIÓN SEGUNDA:
LOS ANTECEDENTES DEL NUEVO RÉGIMEN DEL PODER POPULAR Y
DEL ESTADO COMUNAL EN UNA LEY INCONSTITUCIONAL DE
2006 Y EN EL INTENTO DE REFORMA CONSTITUCIONAL EN 2007 .. 486
I   LA "DESMUNICIPALIZACIÓN" DE LA PARTICIPACIÓN
     CIUDADANA Y LOS CONSEJOS COMUNALES CREADOS EN 2006 487
     1. *Los Municipios y los Consejos Comunales*............................... 487

2.   La "comunidad" como la unidad básica de organización del pueblo   489

3.   Las asambleas de ciudadanos...   490

4.   La organización de los Consejos Comunales   491

5.   La organización centralizada de la participación ciudadana   494

II.   LA RECHAZADA REFORMA CONSTITUCIONAL DE 2007 Y EL PROYECTO PARA LA ESTRUCTURACIÓN DEL ESTADO SOCIALISTA DEL PODER POPULAR O PODER COMUNAL....................   495

SECCIÓN TERCERA:

LA INSTITUCIONALIZACIÓN LEGAL DEL ESTADO COMUNAL O DE CÓMO SE IMPUSO AL PAÍS UN MODELO DE ESTADO COMU-NISTA, DE EJERCICIO DEL PODER POPULAR Y DE SOCIEDAD SOCIALISTA POR LOS CUALES NADIE HA VOTADO   500

I.   EL ESTADO COMUNAL O COMUNISTA Y EL PODER POPULAR..........   500

II.   LOS FINES DEL PODER POPULAR   507

III.   "PROFUNDIZAR LA CORRESPONSABILIDAD, LA AUTOGES-TIÓN Y LA COGESTIÓN."   508

IV.   LAS INSTANCIAS DEL PODER POPULAR...   509

1.   Las diversas instancias del poder popular y su personalidad jurídica   509

2.   Los voceros de las instancias del poder popular y su carácter no representativo   510

3.   Sistemas de agregación comunal...   511

V.   LOS CONSEJOS COMUNALES...   512

1.   Las Comunas   513

2.   Las Ciudades Comunales...   514

VI.   LAS ORGANIZACIONES Y EXPRESIONES ORGANIZATIVAS DEL PODER POPULAR   514

1.   Formas organizativas del Poder Popular...   515

2.   Los fines de las organizaciones y expresiones organizativas del Poder Popular   515

VII. ÁMBITOS DEL PODER POPULAR   516

1.   Planificación de políticas públicas...   516

2.   Economía comunal   517

3.   Contraloría social..   518

4.   Ordenación y gestión del territorio   519

5.   Justicia comunal   519

VIII. LAS RELACIONES ENTRE EL PODER PÚBLICO Y EL PODER POPULAR (O LA TÉCNICA DEL "MATAPALO")....................................   519

IX. LA MARGINALIZACIÓN DEL MUNICIPIO EN RELACIÓN CON LAS ORGANIZACIONES DEL PODER POPULAR...   522

SECCIÓN CUARTA:

EL RÉGIMEN DE LOS CONSEJOS COMUNALES O LA RESURRECCIÓN DE LOS SOVIETS EN EL CARIBE, CASI UN SIGLO DESPUÉS 525

I. LOS CONSEJOS COMUNALES COMO INSTRUMENTOS PARA LA DEL SOCIALISMO 525

II. INTEGRACIÓN DE LOS CONSEJOS COMUNALES 527

   1. *Las Asambleas de Ciudadanos* 528

   2. *La Unidad Ejecutiva y los voceros de la comunidad* 530

   3. *La Unidad Administrativa y Financiera Comunitaria* 531

   4. *La Unidad de Contraloría Social* 533

   5. *La coordinación de las Unidades de los Consejos Comunales* ... 533

   6. *La Comisión Electoral Permanente* 534

III. LA SUPUESTA "ELECCIÓN" DE LOS VOCEROS DE LAS UNIDADES DE LOS CONSEJOS COMUNALES 535

IV. LA CESACIÓN DE LOS VOCEROS COMUNALES 537

   1. *La revocación del mandato de los voceros de las Unidades del Consejo Comunal* 537

   2. *La pérdida de condición de vocero de las Unidades de los Consejos Comunales* 538

V. EL CICLO COMUNAL COMO PROCESO DE PARTICIPACIÓN POPULAR 539

VI. LOS RECURSOS DE LOS CONSEJOS COMUNALES Y SU GESTIÓN Y ADMINISTRACIÓN 540

   1. *Los recursos de los Consejos Comunales* 540

   2. *Los fondos de los Consejos Comunales* 541

VII. EL RÉGIMEN DE ADAPTACIÓN Y CONSTITUCIÓN INICIAL DE LAS ASAMBLEAS DE CIUDADANOS Y DE LOS CONSEJOS COMUNALES . 542

   1. *La adecuación de los Consejos Comunales constituidos conforme a la Ley de 2006 a las previsiones de la Ley Orgánica de 2009* 542

   2. *Régimen para la constitución inicial de los Consejos Comunales* 543

   3. *El registro de los Concejos Comunales* 544

   4. *La nueva adaptación de los Consejos Comunales en 2011* 545

VIII. LA CENTRALIZACIÓN DE LA CONDUCCIÓN DEL PROCESO DE PARTICIPACIÓN CIUDADANA A TRAVÉS DE LOS CONSEJOS COMUNALES 545

SECCIÓN QUINTA:

EL RÉGIMEN DE LAS COMUNAS COMO SOPORTE DEL ESTADO COMUNAL O LA DESMUNICIPALIZACIÓN EL ESTADO CONSTITUCIONAL MEDIANTE UN SISTEMA DE "AUTOGOBIERNO" NO REPRESENTATIVO MANEJADO POR EL PODER CENTRAL 550

I. PROPÓSITO Y FINALIDAD DE LAS COMUNAS 550

II. ÁMBITO TERRITORIAL DE LAS COMUNAS 551

1.   *Ámbito territorial variado* 551

2.   *Inserción en ámbitos territoriales centralizados superiores* 551

III. CONSTITUCIÓN DE LAS COMUNAS 552

1.   *Iniciativa popular y aprobación de la Carta Fundacional mediante referéndum* 552

2.   *Control centralizado del proceso de constitución por el Ministerio para las Comunas* 553

3.   *La comisión promotora* 553

4.   *Redacción y difusión del proyecto de Carta Fundacional* 554

5.   *Referendo aprobatorio* 555

6.   *Registro de la Comuna* 555

7.   *La Gaceta Comunal* 556

IV. LAS CARTAS COMUNALES 556

1.   *Contenido* 556

2.   *Corrección de estilo* 557

3.   *Publicación* 557

V.   LA ORGANIZACIÓN Y FUNCIONAMIENTO DE LAS COMUNAS 558

1.   *El órgano de autogobierno comunal: el Parlamento Comunal* 558

2.   *Atribuciones del Parlamento Comunal* 558

3.   *Integración de los Parlamentos Comunales* 559

4.   *Sesiones del Parlamento Comunal* 560

VI. EL ÓRGANO EJECUTIVO DE LA COMUNA: EL CONSEJO EJECUTIVO 560

1.   *Carácter e integración* 560

2.   *Funciones del Consejo Ejecutivo* 560

3.   *Los Comités de gestión* 561

VII. LA PLANIFICACIÓN COMUNAL 562

1.   *Plan Comunal de Desarrollo* 562

2.   *El Consejo de Planificación Comunal* 562

3.   *Finalidad* 563

4.   *Competencias del Consejo* 563

VIII. EL CONSEJO DE ECONOMÍA COMUNAL 564

1.   *Carácter y composición* 564

2.   *Funciones del Consejo de Economía Comunal* 564

IX. EL BANCO DE LA COMUNA 565

1.   *Objeto* 565

2.   *Propósito* 566

3.   *Funciones* 566

4.   *Organización* 567

X.   EL CONSEJO DE CONTRALORÍA COMUNAL 567
     1.   Integración 568
     2.   Funciones del Consejo de Contraloría Comunal 568
XI. RÉGIMEN DE LOS VOCEROS DE LOS ÓRGANOS DE LA COMUNA 569
     1.   Rendición de cuentas 569
     2.   Revocatoria del mandato 569

SECCIÓN SEXTA:
EL RÉGIMEN DE LA CONTRALORÍA SOCIAL O LA INSTITUCIONA-
LIZACIÓN DE LA TÉCNICA DEL ESPIONAJE SOCIAL Y DE LA
DENUNCIA POLÍTICA INDISCRIMINADA PARA IMPONER LA
IDEOLOGÍA SOCIALISTA 570

I.   OBJETO, PROPÓSITO Y FINALIDAD DE LA CONTRALORÍA SOCIAL. 570
II. EL EJERCICIO Y LOS MEDIOS DE LA CONTRALORÍA SOCIAL 572
     1.   Formas de ejercicio. 572
     2.   Condiciones para el ejercicio de la contraloría social 573
     3.   Deberes de los voceros para la contraloría social 573
III. EL PROCEDIMIENTO PARA EL EJERCICIO DE LA CONTRALORÍA
     SOCIAL 574
IV. LA FORMACIÓN DEL CIUDADANO EN LAS FUNCIONES DE
     CONTRALORÍA SOCIAL 575

SECCIÓN SÉPTIMA:
EL RÉGIMEN DEL SISTEMA ECONÓMICO COMUNAL O DE CÓMO SE
DEFINE E IMPONE LEGALMENTE UN SISTEMA ECONÓMICO
COMUNISTA POR EL CUAL NADIE HA VOTADO 576

I.   FUNDAMENTOS DEL SISTEMA ECONÓMICO COMUNAL
     VINCULADO AL SOCIALISMO Y AL MODELO DE PRODUCCIÓN
     SOCIALISTA 576
II. LAS DIVERSAS ORGANIZACIONES SOCIO-PRODUCTIVAS 581
     1.   Empresas del Estado Comunal (Empresas de propiedad social directa
          comunal) 582
     2.   Empresas públicas (Empresa de propiedad social indirecta comunal) 583
     3.   Unidades productivas familiares 583
     4.   Organizaciones de trueque (Grupos de intercambio solidario) 583
III. EL RÉGIMEN CENTRALIZADO DEL SISTEMA ECONÓMICO
     COMUNAL 584
IV. RÉGIMEN JURÍDICO DE LAS ORGANIZACIONES SOCIO-
     PRODUCTIVAS 586
     1.   Constitución de las organizaciones socio-productivas 586
     2.   Derechos de las organizaciones socio-productivas 588

3. *Obligaciones de las organizaciones socio-productivas* 588

4. *Régimen jurídico de las organizaciones socio-productivas* 590

V.   ESTRUCTURA ORGANIZATIVA Y FUNCIONAL DE LA
     ORGANIZACIÓN SOCIO-PRODUCTIVA 591

1. *Las unidades de las organizaciones socio-productivas* 591

2. *Integrantes de las organizaciones socio-productivas* 591

3. *Los Voceros de las unidades de las organizaciones socio-productivas* 592

4. *Condición para ser productores-integrantes de las organizaciones
   socio-productivas* 592

5. *Normas sobre la gestión productiva y administración de los recursos
   de las organizaciones socio-productivas* 594

VI. EL SISTEMA ALTERNATIVO DE INTERCAMBIO SOLIDARIO 595

1. *Fines y función del sistema alternativo de intercambio (trueque)* 595

2. *Los derechos y deberes de los "prosumidores"* 596

3. *Los espacios del sistema alternativo de intercambio solidario* 596

4. *La moneda comunal* 597

5. *La red de comercio justo y suministro socialista* 598

VII. EL RÉGIMEN SANCIONATORIO DE ORDEN PENAL 598

QUINTA PARTE

EL DESQUICIAMIENTO DE LA ADMINISTRACIÓN PÚBLICA

SECCIÓN PRIMERA:

*LA ADMINISTRACIÓN PÚBLICA Y LA CONCEPCIÓN DEL ESTADO:
EL PASO DEL ESTADO DEMOCRÁTICO Y SOCIAL DE DERECHO Y
DE JUSTICIA, Y DESCENTRALIZADO PREVISTO EN LA CONSTI-
TUCIÓN, AL ESTADO TOTALITARIO DESARROLLADO AL MARGEN
DE LA MISMA* 602

SECCIÓN SEGUNDA:

*EL IMPACTO DEL ESTADO TOTALITARIO SOBRE LA ADMINIS-
TRACIÓN PÚBLICA: LA INFLACIÓN DE LA ORGANIZACIÓN
ADMINISTRATIVA Y LA CREACIÓN DE LAS "MISIONES" NO
SOMETIDAS A LA LEY ORGANICA DE LA ADMINISTRACIÓN
PÚBLICA* 613

I.   LA BUROCRATIZACIÓN DE LA ADMINISTRACIÓN PÚBLICA 613

II. LA INFLACIÓN ORGANIZATIVA EN LA ADMINISTRACIÓN
     PÚBLICA CENTRAL 614

III. LA INFLACIÓN ORGANIZATIVA EN LA ADMINISTRACIÓN
     PÚBLICA DESCENTRALIZADA FUNCIONALMENTE 619

IV. LA CREACIÓN DE UNA ADMINISTRACIÓN PÚBLICA PARALELA:
     LAS "MISIONES" 620
V.   LA REGULACIÓN LEGISLATIVA DE LAS "MISIONES". 625
     1   La Misión como política pública: 626
     2.   Prestaciones de bienes y servicios a cargo de las Misiones 627
     3.   La Administración de las Misiones o el aparataje burocrático de las
          Misiones 627
     4.   Principios para la creación de Misiones 628
     5.   La organización popular en el marco de las Misiones 628
     6.   El Fondo Nacional de Misiones y el financiamiento de las Misiones 629

SECCIÓN TERCERA:
LA FORMA FEDERAL DEL ESTADO, y LA CENTRALIZACIÓN
PROGRESIVA DE LA ADMINISTRACIÓN PÚBLICA 629
I.   EL ESTADO CONSTITUCIONAL EN VENEZUELA, COMO
     FEDERACIÓN CENTRALIZADA, LA CENTRALIZACIÓN DE LA
     ADMINISTRACIÓN PÚBLICA 630
II. EL DESBALANCE HACIA EL NIVEL NACIONAL EN LA
     DISTRIBUCIÓN TERRITORIAL DEL PODER 632
III. EL AHOGAMIENTO Y NEUTRALIZACIÓN DE LAS ENTIDADES
     TERRITORIALES POR PARTE DE LA ADMINISTRACIÓN PÚBLICA
     NACIONAL 634

SECCIÓN CUARTA:
LA CREACIÓN DEL ESTADO COMUNAL O DEL PODER POPULAR, EN
PARALELO AL ESTADO CONSTITUCIONAL Y EL AHOGAMIENTO
PROGRESIVO DE LA ADMINISTRACIÓN MUNICIPAL 636
I.   LA CREACIÓN DEL ESTADO COMUNAL EN PARALELO AL
     ESTADO CONSTITUCIONAL 636
II. LAS COMUNAS VERSUS LA ADMINISTRACIÓN MUNICIPAL 640
III. EL ESTADO COMUNAL Y EL AHOGAMIENTO DE LA
     ADMINISTRACIÓN PÚBLICA MUNICIPAL 642
IV. LAS ORGANIZACIONES Y EXPRESIONES ORGANIZATIVAS DE LA
     ADMINISTRACIÓN PÚBLICA DEL PODER POPULAR 647
V.   LAS DIVERSAS ORGANIZACIONES SOCIOPRODUCTIVAS DE LA
     "ADMINISTRACIÓN PÚBLICA" DEL SISTEMA ECONÓMICO
     COMUNAL 648
APRECIACIÓN GENERAL 653

SEXTA PARTE:

CONSTITUTIONAL LAW. VENEZUELA (2015)
DERECHO CONSTITUCIONAL. VENEZUELA (2015)

GENERAL INTRODUCTION 655

Chapter 1. An Outline of Venezuelan Constitutional History 655

§1. *First Constitutional Period (1811–1864): The Independent, Autonomous, Semi-Decentralized State* 658

§2. *Second Constitutional Period (1864–1901): The Federal State and the United States of Venezuela* 661

§3. Third Constitutional Period (1901–1945): The Centralized Autocratic State 663

§4. *Fourth Constitutional Period (1945–1999): The Democratic Centralized State of parties* 665

§5. *The Beginning of a Fifth Constitutional Period after 1999: The Centralized, Military and Authoritarian State* 668

§6. *The Outgoing Constitutional Process in Defraudation of the Constitution and of Democracy (1999–2015)* 672

Chapter 2. Some Basic Aspect of the Political System of Government According to the 1999 Constitution and Its Distortions 679

§1. *The Democratic Republic* 679

§2. *The 'Bolivarian' Republic of Venezuela* 681

§3. *The Social and Democratic Rule of Law and Justice State* 685

§4. *Separation of Powers* 687

§5. *Presidential System of Government* 689

§6. *Alternating Government* 691

§7. *The Centralized Federation* 692

§8. *Judicial Review System* 693

Chapter 3. Global Values in the Constitution 694

§1 *Constitutional Values and their Prioritisation* 695

§2. *The Incongruences between Declared Values and Political and Judicial Practice* 709

    I. *Superior Values of the Constitution and the 'Political Project'* 709

    II. *Erosion of Public Participation in Political Decision Making* 711

    III. *The Erosion of the Democratic Principle* 713

    IV. *The Contradictory State Intervention in the Internal Life of Civil Society Entities* 714

    V. *The Dangerous Expansion of Security and Defence Values* 716

Chapter 4. State Territory 718
Chapter 5. Population (Demographic Data)... 722
Chapter 6. Constitutional Relationship between Church and State 723
Chapter 7. Constitutional Principles Regarding International Relations 724

SELECTED BIBLIOGRAPHY 726

PART I. SOURCES OF CONSTITUTIONAL LAW 729

Chapter 1. The Constitution 729
§1. Supremacy and Rigidity... 729
§2. Procedure for Constitutional Review... 730
     I.   Constitutional Amendment.. 730
     II. Constitutional Reforms 731
     III. The National Constituent Assembly 733
     IV. Limits to the Constitutional Review Powers 734
§3. The Sub-national Constitutions 734

Chapter 2. The Treaties 735
§1. Incorporation to Internal Law 735
§2. Hierarchy... 736

Chapter 3. The Legislation.. 737
§1. Types of Laws at the National Level 737
     I.   Ordinary Laws 737
     II. Organic Laws.. 738
     III. Other Laws: Enabling and Cadre Laws 739
     IV. Decree-Laws 739
§2. Equivalent Legislative Rules: The States Laws and the Municipal
     Ordinances.. 740
§3. Hierarchy... 741

Chapter 4. The Jurisprudence... 741
§1. The Obligatory Character of the Decisions of the Constitutional Jurisdiction . 741
§2. The General Value of Jurisprudence 742

Chapter 5. The Unwritten Law 742
§1. Constitutional Principles and Values 742
§2. General Principles of Law... 743

Chapter 6. The Executive Regulations and Administrative Acts 744
§1. National, States and Municipal Regulations 744
§2. Limits to the Executive Regulatory Powers 744

Chapter 7. Codification, Interpretation and Publication 745

§1.   *The Codes* 745

§2.   *Interpretation* 745

§3.   *Publication and Derogatory Effects* 746

PART II. BASIC ELEMENTS OF THE REPRESENTATIVE AND PARTICIPATORY DEMOCRATIC POLITICAL SYSTEM 747

Chapter 1. Representative Democracy 748

Chapter 2. Electoral System 750

Chapter 3. Direct Democracy Institutions and the Referenda Voting System 752

§1.   *Referenda* 752

§2.   *Popular consultation of statutes* 754

§3.   *Local participation* 755

Chapter 4. The Plural Political Parties Regime 757

Chapter 5. Institutions for Governmental Accountability 760

PART III. THE FEDERATION AND THE TERRITORIAL DISTRIBUTION OF STATE POWERS 762

Chapter 1. The Centralization Process of the Federation 763

Chapter 2. The Contradictory 'Decentralized Federation' in the 1999 Constitution 764

§1.   *Constitutional Provisions Relating to Federalism in the 1999 Constitution* 764

§2.   *Limits to the Contents of the Sub-national Constitutions* 766

§3.   *The Constitutional System of Distribution of Powers within the National, State and Municipal Levels of Government* 768

Chapter 3. The Organization of Public Power in the Territory 771

§1.   *The States* 771

      I.   *The Limited States Autonomy* 771

      II.   *The States' Executive and Legislative Powers* 771

§2.   *The Municipalities* 772

      I.   *The Municipal Autonomy* 772

      II.   *The Municipal Executive and Legislative Powers* 773

§3.   *The Capital District and the Metropolitan Municipal Government of Caracas* 774

Chapter 4. The Financing System of the Federation 775

PART IV. THE CONSTITUTIONAL SYSTEM OF SEPARATION OF POWERS 777

Chapter 1. The Principle of Separation of Powers 777

§1. *The Venezuelan Constitutional Tradition* 777

§2. *Separation of Powers and Democracy* 778

Chapter 2. Concentration of Powers and Authoritarianism in Defraudation of the Constitution 779

§1. *The Constitutional Supremacy of the National Assembly* 780

§2. *The Defraudation of Political Participation in the Election of High Governmental Officers* 782

§3. *The Catastrophic Dependence and Subjection of the Judiciary* 783

§4. *The Factual Political Supremacy of The Executive and the Absence of Check and Balance* 787

Chapter 3. The Rupture of the Rule of Law, the Rejected 2007 Constitutional Reform and Its Illegitimate Implementation 788

§1. *The Sense and Objectives of the Reform Proposals* 789

§2. *The Irregular and Illegitimate Implementation in 2008 of the Rejected Reform Proposals Through Ordinary Legislation* 796

§3. *The Unconstitutional Implementation in 2010–2011 of the Rejected Reform Proposals Through Organic Laws* 802

§4. *The 'Communal State' conceived in Parallel to the 'Constitutional State'* 805

PART V. THE GOVERNMENT 807

Chapter 1. The National Executive 807

§1. *The President of the Republic* 807

   I. *Head of State and of the Government* 807

   II. *The Absences of the President of the Republic and Its Substitutions* 808

§2. *The Executive Vice President* 809

§3. *The Ministers* 810

§4. *The Council of Ministers* 811

§5. *Other Constitutional Executive Organs* 811

Chapter 2. Constitutional Powers of the National Executive 812

§1. *The Political Functions of Government in the Constitution and the Parliamentary Control* 812

   I. *The Direction of Foreign Relations* 813

   II. *The Executive Initiatives on Matters of Constitutional Review and of Referendum* 813

   III. *The Military Powers of the President of the Republic* 814

   IV. *Executive Powers Regarding the National Assembly* 814

V.   *Executive Powers in Situations of Exception* 814

VI.   *Executive Pardon Powers* 816

VII.   *The Legislation Veto Powers of the President of the Republic* 816

§2.   *The Administrative Functions of Government in the Constitution and the Parliamentary Control* 817

I.   *The President of the Republic as Head of Public Administration* 817

II.   *The Formulation of the National Development Plan* 818

III.   *The Regulatory Powers of the President of the Republic* 818

§3.   *Liabilities* 818

Chapter 3. Public Administration 818

§1.   *The Constitutional Principles Related to Public Administration and Administrative Activities* 818

§2.   *Constitutional Provisions Related to the Organization of Public Administration: Centralized and Decentralized Public Administration* 821

§3.   *Constitutional Principles Regarding Administrative Information* 821

§4.   *Constitutional Principles Regarding Civil Service* 822

§5.   *Constitutional Principles Regarding Public Contracts* 823

I.   *The Public Interest Contracts* 823

II.   *Obligatory Constitutional Clauses in Public Interest Contracts* 825

A.   *The Jurisdiction Immunity Clause* 825

B.   *The 'Calvo' Clause* 826

C.   *The Environmental Protection Clause* 826

III.   *The Parliamentary Approval of Public Interest Contracts* 826

IV.   *Principles Related to the State's Contractual Liabilities* 827

§6.   *Prerogatives of the Administration* 827

Chapter 4. The Military and the National Security System 827

PART VI. THE LEGISLATURE 830

Chapter 1. The National Assembly 830

§1.   *The Unicameral Parliamentary System* 830

§2.   *The Representatives* 831

I.   *Eligibility Conditions* 831

II.   *Tenure, Incompatibilities, Accountability and Revocation of Mandate* 832

III.   *Liability and Immunity* 833

§3.   *Organization and Commissions* 833

§4.   *Sessions of the National Assembly and Its Delegate Commission* 833

§5.   *The Attributions of the National Assembly* 834

Chapter 2. Legislative Procedure 835

Chapter 3. Political and Administrative Legislative Control Procedures 837

PART VII. THE JUDICIARY 838

Chapter 1. General Constitutional Regime Referred to the Judiciary 838

§1. *Justice and the Judicial System* 838

    I.   *Justice and the Components of the Judicial System* 838

    II.   *Independence and Autonomy of the Judicial Branch* 838

    III. *Judicial Process as the Instrument for Justice* 839

    IV. *Judicial Liability* 839

§2. *Judicial Jurisdictions in the Constitution* 840

§3. *Governance and Administration of the Judicial Branch* 841

§4. *Regimen Governing the Judicial Career and the Stability of Judges* 842

Chapter 2. The Supreme Tribunal of Justice 843

§1. *Composition* 843

§2. *Jurisdiction* 844

§3. *Status of the Supreme Tribunal Magistrates* 844

    I.   *Conditions to be Magistrate of the Supreme Tribunal Justice* 844

    II.   *The Nomination and Election Procedure* 845

    III. *The Removal and Dismissal of the Magistrates* 849

**Chapter 3. The dependence of the Judiciary and factual absence of judicial
autonomy and independence** 850

§1. *The Judiciary packed by Temporal and Provisional Judges and the use of
the Judiciary for Political Persecution* 851

§2. *The use of the Judiciary to facilitate the Concentration of Power and the
Dismantling of Democracy* 856

PART VIII. OTHER BRANCHES OF GOVERNMENT 860

Chapter 1. The Citizen Power 860

§1. *The Republican Moral Council* 860

§2. *Election of the Head of the Organs of the Citizen Power* 861

§3. *The Peoples' Defender* 862

§4. *The Prosecutor General of the Republic* 863

§5. *The Comptroller General of the Republic* 864

Chapter 2. The Electoral Power 864

PART IX. THE CONSTITUTIONAL SYSTEM OF HUMAN RIGHTS AND GUARANTEES 866

Chapter 1. General Principles Regarding Human Rights and Constitutional Guaranties 867

§1. *The Basic Principles Regarding Human Rights* 867

    I.   *Principle of Progressive Interpretation of Constitutional Rights* 867

    II.   *The Declarative Nature of the Constitutional Declarations of Rights and Freedoms and the Open Constitutional Clauses* 867

    III. *The Constitutional Rank of International Human Rights Treaties* 868

    IV. *The Principle of Freedom* 870

    V.   *The Principle of Equality and Non-discrimination* 871

§2. *General Principles Regarding Constitutional Guarantees* 871

    I.   *Prohibition of the Retroactive Effects of Law* 871

    II.   *Nullity of Acts Contrary to the Constitution* 871

    III. *Due Process of Law Rules and the Right to Have Access to Justice* 872

    IV. *Guarantee for Rights to Only Be Limited or Restricted by Statutes* 873

    V.   *State Obligations to Investigate* 873

    VI. *The Regime of Restricting Constitutional Guaranties in States of Exception* 874

    VII. *Judicial Guarantees of Human Rights* 874

    VIII. *International Guarantees of Human Rights* 874

Chapter 2. The Status of Persons and Citizens 875

§1. *The Constitutional Rules on the Venezuelan Nationality* 876

    I.   *Venezuelan by Birth* 876

    II.   *Venezuelan by Naturalization* 877

    III. *Dual Nationality* 877

    IV. *Loss and Recuperation of Venezuelan Nationality* 878

§2. *The Constitutional Rules on Citizenship* 878

    I.   *Citizenship and Political Rights* 878

    II.   *Equality between Venezuelans by Birth and by Naturalization* 879

§3. *Constitutional Condition of Foreigners* 879

    I.   *Migrant and Non-migrant Aliens* 879

    II.   *Asylum and Refugee Aliens* 880

Chapter 3. Civil Rights 882

§1. *Right to Life* 882

§2. *Right to own name and to be Identified* 882

§3. *Personal Freedom* 882

§4. *Personal Integrity* 883

§5.   *Inviolability of Person's Home*   883
§6.   *Inviolability of Private Communications*   883
§7.   *Right to Petition Before Public Authorities and to Obtain Due Answer*   884
§8.   *Right of Association*   884
§9.   *Right of Meeting*   884
§10. *Freedom of Movement*   884
§11. *Freedom of Expression and of Information*   884
§12. *Right to be Informed and to Reply and Rectification*   885
§13. *Right to have access to Personal Information*   886
§14. *Right to the Protection of Honour and Private Life*   886
§15. *Freedom of Religion and Cult*   886
§16. *Freedom of Conscience*   887
§17. *Right to Personal Security and to be Protected by the State*   887

Chapter 4. Social and Cultural Rights   887
§1.   *Family Rights and Rights to Social Protection*   887
      I.   *Right to Family Protection*   887
      II.   *Right to Motherhood and Fatherhood Protection*   888
      III. *Right to Marriage Protection*   888
      IV.   *Rights of Children and Adolescents*   888
      V.   *Rights of Elderly Protection*   889
      VI.   *Rights of Disabled Protection*   889
§2.   *Right to Dwelling*   889
§3.   *Right to Health*   890
§4.   *Right to Social Security*   891
§5.   *Labour Rights*   891
      I.   *Right to Work and State's Obligations*   891
      II.   *Rights to Have Work Protected*   892
      III. *Working Hours*   892
      IV.   *Right to Salary and other Benefits*   893
      V.   *Stability Rights*   893
      VI.   *Trade-Unions Rights*   893
      VII. *Right to Collective Bargaining Agreements*   894
      VIII. *Right to Strike*   894
§6.   *Cultural Rights*   894
§7.   *Educational Rights*   895
      I.   *Right to Education*   895
      II.   *Education As a Public Service*   896
      III. *Right to Educate*   897

IV. *Principle of the University Autonomy* 897
V.   *Science and Technology System* 897
VI. *Right to Sport* 898
§8. *Environmental Rights* 898
I.   *Right to the Protection of Environment* 898
II. *The Land Use Planning* 899
§9. *The rights of Indigenous Peoples* 899

Chapter 5. Political Rights 901
§1. *Right to Political Participation* 901
§2. *Right to Vote and Electoral Principles* 901
§3. *Right to Be Elected and to Exercise Public Offices* 902
§4. *Right to Be Associated to Political Parties* 902
§5. *Right to Demonstrate* 902

Chapter 6. Constitutional Duties 903

PART X. THE CONSTITUTIONAL REGIME OF THE ECONOMY 904

Chapter 1. Principles of the Economic System 904
§1. *Private Economic Rights* 906
I.   *Right to Exercise Economic Activities* 906
II. *Property Rights* 907
III. *Quality Services and Good Rights* 908
IV. *Popular Economy Rights* 908
V.   *Limits to Private Economic Activities* 909
§2. *State Participation in the Economy Regime* 909
I.   *State Promotion of Economic Activities* 909
II. *State Economic Planning* 910
III. *State Direct Assumption of Economic Activities* 911

Chapter 2. Taxation Regimen 912

Chapter 3. Budgetary System 913
§1. *Principles of Fiscal Policy* 913
§2. *Principles of Public Debt Policy* 914
§3. *Principles of Budget* 914

Chapter 4. Monetary System and the Macro-economic Policies 915
§1. *Autonomy of the Central Bank of Venezuela Regarding the Monetary Policy* .. 915
§2. *National Currency* 916
§3. *Macro-economic Policies* 916

Chapter 5. Constitutional Provisions on Public Domain 917

Chapter 6. The Progressive Nationalization and State Ownership of the Economy 918

Chapter 7. The Implementation of the Rejected 2007 Constitutional Reform through Legislation in Order to Establish a Communal Economic System 919

PART XI. RULE OF LAW AND JUDICIAL REVIEW 923

Chapter 1. Judicial Review System 924

§1. *A General Overview of the Systems of Judicial Review and the Venezuelan System* 925

§2. *The Diffuse Method of Judicial Review* 927

§3. *The Concentrated Method of Judicial Review: The Popular Action* 929

§4. *Other Concentrated Judicial Review Means* 930

  I. *The Obligatory Judicial Review of 'State of Exception' Decrees* 930

  II. *The Preventive Judicial Review* 931

    A. *Preventive Judicial Review of International Treaties* 931

    B. *The Preventive Judicial Review of the Organic Laws* 932

    C. *Judicial Review of Statutes Sanctioned before Their Promulgation* .. 932

  III. *Judicial Review of Legislative Omissions* 932

  IV. *Judicial Review of the Constitutional Controversies* 933

  V. *Recourse of Constitutional Interpretation* 934

  VI. *The Constitutional Chamber's Power to Assume Any Cause from Lower Courts* 936

§5. *Some General Conclusions* 938

Chapter 2. The distortion of Judicial Review and Constitutional Mutations 939

§1. *The Acceptance of a Transitory Constitutional Regime not Approved by the People* 940

§2. *The transformation of the repeal referenda into a 'ratifying' referenda* 941

§3. *The elimination of the constitutional principle of the alternate government abd the limits to the continuous re-electionas* 943

§4. *The modification of the prohibition to repeat referenda on constitutional reforms on the same matter during the same constitutional term* 945

§5. *Illegitimate transformation federal system, changing "exclusive" attributions into "concurrent" ones* 947

§6. *The illegitimate reform of the constitutional prohibition to finance electoral activities of political parties with government funds* 949

§7. *The illegitimate elimination of the supra-constitutional rank of international treaties in matters human rights* 951

§8. *The elimination of judges' power to immediately and directly apply international treaties on human rights* 954

§9. The denial of the peoples' right for the international protection of the human rights and the non enforceability of the decisions of the inter-american court on human rights 955

§10. The ilegitimate creation of an autonomous recourse for the abstract interpretation of the constitution 958

Chapter 3. Judicial Protection of Constitutional Rights: The Amparo Proceeding 960

§1. The Right of Amparo (to be Protected) 961

§2. The Various Judicial Means for Amparo 963

§3. The Universal Character of the Amparo Proceeding 965

Chapter 4. Judicial Review of Administrative Action Jurisdiction (Administrative Contentious Jurisdiction) 967

SÉPTIMA PARTE

LA CONSTITUCIÓN COMO PROMESA INCUMPLIDA

I. EL SENTIDO DE LA CONSTITUCIÓN: UN PACTO SUPREMO Y RÍGIDO COMO PROMESA DE SER CUMPLIDA 971

II. EL INICIO DEL INCUMPLIMIENTO DE LA PROMESA: UN RÉGIMEN TRANSITORIO NO APROBADO POR EL PUEBLO QUE SUSPENDIÓ LA VIGENCIA DE MUCHAS NORMAS CONSTITUCIONALES 974

III. EL INCUMPLIMIENTO DE LA PROMESA CONSTITUCIONAL DEL ESTABLECIMIENTO DE UN RÉGIMEN POLÍTICO DEMOCRÁTICO Y PARTICIPATIVO 975

1. La promesa de la elección popular de los titulares de los Poderes Públicos y su incumplimiento 976

2. La promesa de la participación popular en el funcionamiento del Estado y su incumplimiento 977

3. La promesa de la participación popular en el proceso de formación de las leyes y su incumplimiento 978

4. La promesa de la democracia participativa y protagónica como ejercicio democrático cotidiano, y su incumplimiento 979

5. La promesa de que el gobierno debía ser siempre alternativo y su incumplimiento 982

IV. EL INCUMPLIMIENTO DE LA PROMESA CONSTITUCIONAL DEL ESTABLECIMIENTO DE UN ESTADO DEMOCRÁTICO DE DERECHO Y DE JUSTICIA 984

1. La ausencia de separación de poderes 985

2. La ausencia de autonomía e independencia del Poder Judicial 987

V.   EL INCUMPLIMIENTO DE LA PROMESA CONSTITUCIONAL
     DEL ESTABLECIMIENTO DE UN ESTADO FEDERAL
     DESCENTRALIZADO 991
     1.   *Los intentos de desmantelar al Estado federal* 991
     2.   *Las propuestas de creación del Estado Comunal o del Poder Popular
          sin representatividad democrática para ahogar al Estado federal* 993
     3.   *La desmunicipalización del país al margen de la Constitución* 996

VI. EL INCUMPLIMIENTO DE LA PROMESA CONSTITUCIONAL
     DEL ESTABLECIMIENTO DE UN ESTADO SOCIAL MONTADO
     SOBRE UN SISTEMA ECONÓMICO DE ECONOMÍA MIXTA 998
     1.   *La propuesta de reforma constitucional fracasada para sustituir el
          Estado Social por un Estado Socialista y su implementación a margen
          de la Constitución* 1001
     2.   *El establecimiento del Sistema Económico Comunal al margen de la
          Constitución* 1003
     3.   *El Estado Populista en sustitución del Estado Social* 1006
     4.   *La manipulación del nombre de Bolívar para justificar el
          incumplimiento de las promesas constitucionales: el "socialismo
          bolivariano"* 1009

VII. EL INCUMPLIMIENTO DE LA PROMESA CONSTITUCIONAL DE
     RESPETAR LA VOLUNTAD POPULAR 1016

ÍNDICE GENERAL 1021